THE DIARY OF RALPH JOSSELIN 1616–1683

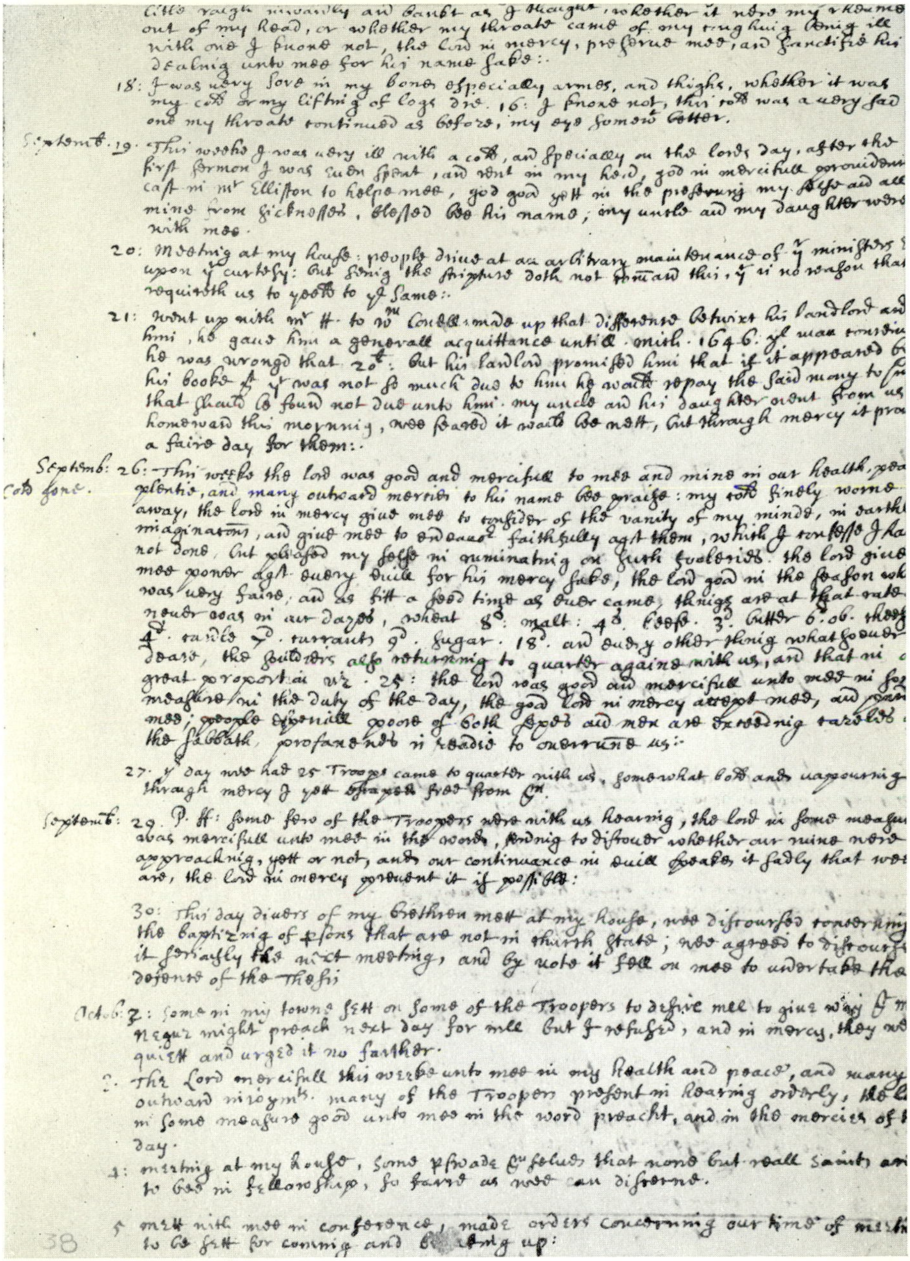
litle rough inwardly and doubt as I thought, whether it were my rheume out of my head, or whether my throate came of my coughing being ill with one I knowe not, the lord in mercy, preserve mee, and sanctifie his dealing unto mee for his name sake:

18: I was very sore in my bones especially armes, and thighs, whether it was my cold or my lifting of logs die. 16: I knowe not, this cold was a very sad one my throate continued as before, my eye somewhat better.

Septemb. 19: This weeke I was very ill with a cold, and specially on the lords day, after the first sermon I was even spent, and wett in my head, god in mercifull providence cast in Mr Ellison to helpe mee, god good yett in the preserving my selfe and all mine from sicknesse, blessed bee his name; my uncle and my daughter were with mee.

20: Meeting at my house: people drive at an arbitrary maintenance of ye ministers upon ye curtesy: but seeing the scripture doth not command this, ye is no reason that requireth us to yeeld to ye same:

21: went up with Mr H. to Wm Cowell: made up that difference betwixt his landlord and him, hee gave him a generall acquittance until mich. 1646. ye man considering he was wronged that 20s. but his landlord promised him that if it appeared by his booke yt ye was not so much due to him he would repay the said mony to him that should bee found not due unto him. my uncle and his daughter went from us homeward this morning, wee feared it would bee wett, but through mercy it proved a faire day for them:

Septemb: 26: This weeke the lord was good and mercifull to mee and mine in our health, peace plentie, and many outward mercies to his name bee praise: my cold finely worne away, the lord in mercy give mee to consider of the vanity of my minde, in earthly imaginations, and give mee to endeavor faithfully agt them, which I confesse I have not done, but pleased my selfe in ruminating on such fooleries. the lord give mee power agt every evill for his mercy sake, the lord good in the season which was very faire; and as fitt a seed time as ever came, things are at that rate never was in our dayes, wheat 8s. malt: 4s. beefe. 3d. butter 6d. ob. cheese 4d. candle 7d. currants 9d. sugar. 18d. and every other thing whatsoever deare, the souldiers also returning to quarter againe with us, and that in a great proportion viz. 25: the lord was good and mercifull unto mee in some measure in the duty of the day, the good lord in mercy accept mee, and pardon mee; people generally poore of both seeds and men are exceeding carelesse of the sabbath, profanenes is readie to overrunne us:

Cold gone.

27. ye day wee had 25 Troops came to quarter with us, somewhat bold and unsavoury through mercy I yet escaped free from em.

Septemb: 29. P. H: some few of the Troopers were with us hearing, the lord in some measure was mercifull unto mee in the word, tending to discover whether our ruine were approaching, yett or not, and our continuance in evill speakes it sadly that wee are, the lord in mercy prevent it if possible:

30: this day divers of my brethren mett at my house, wee discoursed concerning the baptizing of psons that are not in church state; wee agreed to discourse it seriously the next meeting, and by vote it fell on mee to undertake the defence of the thesis

Octob. 2: some in my towne sett on some of the Troopers to desire mee to give way yt m negus might preach next day for mee but I refused, and in mercy, they were quiett and urged it no farther.

3. The Lord mercifull this weeke unto mee in my health and peace, and many outward enjoyments. many of the Troopers present in hearing orderly, the lord in some measure good unto mee in the word preacht, and in the mercies of the day.

4: meeting at my house, some perswade themselves that none but reall saints are to bee in fellowship, so farre as wee can discerne.

5 mett with mee in conference, made orders concerning our time of meeting to be sett for comming and breaking up:

38

An extract from Ralph Josselin's Diary, September–October 1647. Reproduced by kind permission of Colonel G. O. C. Probert

FOR

INGE, ASTRID AND KATIE

RECORDS OF SOCIAL AND ECONOMIC HISTORY
NEW SERIES · III

THE DIARY OF RALPH JOSSELIN

1616–1683

EDITED BY
ALAN MACFARLANE

LONDON · *Published for* THE BRITISH ACADEMY
by THE OXFORD UNIVERSITY PRESS
1976

Oxford University Press, Ely House, London W. 1

GLASGOW NEW YORK TORONTO MELBOURNE WELLINGTON
CAPE TOWN IBADAN NAIROBI DAR ES SALAAM LUSAKA ADDIS ABABA
DELHI BOMBAY CALCUTTA MADRAS KARACHI DACCA
KUALA LUMPUR SINGAPORE HONG KONG TOKYO

ISBN 0 19 725955 3

Printed in Great Britain
at the University Press, Oxford
by Vivian Ridler
Printer to the University

PREFACE

COLONEL G. O. C. PROBERT of Bevills, Bures, Suffolk, the owner of the Diary, gave permission for a complete edition to be prepared. He also helped in a number of practical ways, including depositing the Diary temporarily at Cambridge. I am most grateful to him for these kindnesses. His father, the late Colonel Carwardine Probert, made the editorial task easier by preparing a half-length edition of the Diary, now deposited at the Essex Record Office. Where notes prepared for that edition have been used, there has been a direct acknowledgement (Probert). The Essex Record Office also kindly gave their permission to quote from documents in their custody, and the staff, particularly Arthur Searle, have shown their usual courtesy and helpfulness, thereby making the work more enjoyable than it would otherwise have been. My own work on the edition was made possible by a Research Fellowship at King's College, Cambridge, and I am most grateful to the Provost and Fellows. The material upon which the footnotes and appendices are based, as well as the map, was collected as part of a Social Science Research Council project on the parish of Earls Colne and I am again grateful for its support.

When Professor D. C. Coleman first suggested that a full edition be prepared for the British Academy it was believed that though a very large task, the text would only consist of a maximum of 160,000 words. It was thought that the main work would consist of checking the existing typescript against the original, word for word. Later it emerged that another 130,000 words of completely new text had to be fitted in, and that the full text would be about 290,000 words. There is no doubt that the edition would have had to be abandoned had it not been for the help of a number of people. The result is very much a collaborative work; many of the stages of checking and indexing would have been impossible single-handed. Audrey Eccles, Assistant Archivist at the Westmorland Record Office, helped with specific queries on medical matters, as indicated in the footnotes (Eccles). Malcolm Thomas of Friends' House Library provided information about Quakers in Earls Colne. Cherry Bryant helped with the Latin translations and also with the manorial background to Earls Colne. John Walter of Trinity Hall, Cambridge, helped with footnote references. Brett Harrison, also of the Westmorland Record Office, provided material for the footnotes, especially concerning clerics and theological controversies; he also checked one-quarter of the original Diary against the transcript. Mrs. M. Kirsch, Mrs. M. O'Flynn, and Mrs. Hazel Clark helped to type the text and indexes. Iris Macfarlane checked three-quarters of the original Diary with the transcript and provided a good deal of the information on the local background in Earls Colne. For accuracy, it was essential to have two people for each checking. Since the Diary had to be checked against the original twice, four complete readings by single individuals were needed. The brunt of this task has been borne by Sarah Harrison, who has read through and checked the full text twice. She has also undertaken the very large task of producing the name and place indexes and the larger part of the background information on Earls Colne has been assembled by her, including the material upon which Appendix 2 and the map of residences are based. She also contributed to the footnotes. While my debt to all those who helped is very great, there can be no doubt that without Mrs. Harrison's energy and accuracy this edition could not have been produced.

INTRODUCTORY NOTE TO THE NEW SERIES

ONE of the earliest publishing ventures of the British Academy was the launching, in 1914, of the series entitled 'Records of the Social and Economic History of England and Wales' which reflected the pioneer work then being done in this field of study. The series was continued until the appearance, in 1935, of Volume IX, after which it lapsed. Since then, however, interest in social and economic history, far from abating, has greatly increased; more and more scholars have been drawn to research in the subject, and the teaching of it has so developed that it has become an integral part of the curriculum in most universities, whether in social science faculties or in departments of history. The Academy has therefore thought it appropriate to revive its original project, slightly expanding its scope, and in 1972 it issued the first volume of a new series of 'Records of Social and Economic History'. The title of the series has been thus abbreviated to permit the introduction of material other than that relating only to England and Wales, and in accordance with this policy the first volume—*Charters of the Honour of Mowbray 1107–1191*—covered the whole honour of Mowbray, thus including charters concerning lands in Normandy as well as in ten different counties of England. Similarly the fourth volume is planned to include surveys of both the Norman and the English estates of the Abbey of Caen. The creation in the last half-century of many new local record societies and the increasing activity of many old ones have opened up fresh opportunities for the publication of social and economic records relating to a particular locality.

It is hoped, however, that this new series will prove especially valuable as a means of publishing material which, like that in Volumes I and II does not fall within the scope of any one local record society or which comes from any area not covered by any local record publishing society. It was not until after this volume was accepted by the Academy that the Essex County Council launched its own new series of Essex Edited Texts.

E. M. CARUS-WILSON
Chairman
Records of Social and Economic History Committee

CONTENTS

PREFACE vii

INTRODUCTORY NOTE TO THE NEW SERIES ix

LIST OF ILLUSTRATIONS xii

A NOTE ON ABBREVIATIONS AND CONVENTIONS xiii

INTRODUCTION

I. History and nature of the Diary xix

II. Previous use of the Diary xx

III. Accuracy and coverage of the Diary xxii

IV. The village background and the 'personnel' of the Diary xxiii

V. Major themes in the Diary xxiv

THE DIARY

APPENDIX I. Major families 662

APPENDIX 2. Earls Colne families 673

INDEX OF PLACES 699

INDEX OF PERSONS 707

LIST OF ILLUSTRATIONS

An extract from Ralph Josselin's Diary *frontispiece*

MAPS

I. County of Essex, showing location of places mentioned in Josselin's Diary 695

II. The main street of Earls Colne; residence of people mentioned in Josselin's Diary 696

III. The parish of Earls Colne; also land owned by Josselin 696

A NOTE ON ABBREVIATIONS AND CONVENTIONS

ABBREVIATIONS

BOOK TITLES

(Place of publication is London, unless otherwise specified)

Beaumont	G. F. Beaumont, *A History of Coggeshall, in Essex* (1890).
Besse	Joseph Besse, *A Collection of the Sufferings of the People Called Quakers* (1753), 2 vols.
Calamy	*Calamy Revised* (Oxford, 1934), ed. A. G. Matthews.
Compleat Housewife	E. Smith, *The Compleat Housewife; or, Accomplish'd Gentlewoman's Companion* (15th edn., 1753; facsimile reprint, 1968).
Complete Peerage	*The Complete Peerage* (1932), by G.E.C.
Culpeper, *Herbal*	Nicholas Culpeper, *English Physician and Complete Herbal* (1652; modern edn., 1961, arranged C. F. Leyel).
Davids	T. W. Davids: *Annals of Evangelical Nonconformity in the County of Essex, From the Time of Wycliffe to the Restoration* (1863).
DNB	*Dictionary of National Biography*
Evelyn	E. S. De Beer (ed.), *The Diary of John Evelyn* (Oxford, 1955), 6 vols.
Foster	Joseph Foster (ed.), *Alumni Oxonienses; the members of the University of Oxford, 1500–1714* (1891–2), 4 vols.
Fox	J. L. Nickalls (ed.), *The Journal of George Fox* (revised edn., Cambridge, 1952).
Gardiner	S. R. Gardiner, *History of the Great Civil War 1642–9* (1886), 3 vols.
Gardiner, *Commonwealth*	S. R. Gardiner, *History of the Commonwealth and Protectorate* (1894), 3 vols.
Gerard, *Herbal*	John Gerard, *The herball* (modern edn. by M. Woodward, 1964; from T. Johnson edn., 1636).
Hockliffe	E. Hockliffe (ed.), *The Diary of the Rev. Ralph Josselin, 1616–83*, Camden Soc., 3rd ser., xv (1908).
Jepp	Edward Jepp, *An Essex Dialect Dictionary* (1923; enlarged edn. by J. S. Appleby, Wakefield, 1969).
Kenyon	J. P. Kenyon, *The Stuart Constitution* (Cambridge, 1966).
Kingston	Alfred Kingston, *East Anglia and the Great Civil War* (1902).

Macfarlane	Alan Macfarlane, *The Family Life of Ralph Josselin; A Seventeenth-Century Clergyman* (Cambridge, 1970).
Morant	P. Morant, *History and Antiquities of the County of Essex* (1768), 2 vols.
Newcourt	R. Newcourt, *Repertorium ecclesiasticum parochiale Londinense* (1708–10), 2 vols.
NED	*A New English Dictionary* (Oxford, 1908), ed. Sir J. A. H. Murray.
Nuttall	G. F. Nuttall, *Visible Saints; the Congregational Way, 1640–60* (Oxford, 1957).
Pepys	R. Latham and W. Matthews (eds.), *The Diary of Samuel Pepys* (1970, in progress), 11 vols.
Quintrell	B. W. Quintrell, 'The Divisional Committee for Southern Essex During the Civil War' (Manchester Univ. M.A. thesis, 1962).
Shaw	William A. Shaw, *A History of the English Church, 1640–60* (1900), 2 vols.
SOED	*Shorter Oxford English Dictionary* (3rd edn., Oxford, 1970).
STC	A. W. Pollard and G. R. Redgrave (comp.), *Short-Title Catalogue of Books, 1475–1640* (1963).
Smith	Harold Smith, *The Ecclesiastical History of Essex* (n.d.).
Smith, *Clergy*	Harold Smith, *Sequence of Essex Clergy, 1640–1664*, 2 vols. (A typescript in the ERO, given to the Essex Archaeological Society, 1937).
Thomason	*Catalogue of the Pamphlets, Books, Newspapers, and Manuscripts . . . Collected by George Thomason, 1640–61* (1908), 2 vols.
Venn	J. and J. A. Venn, *Alumni Cantabrigienses: a biographical list of all known students . . . at the University of Cambridge* (1922–7), 4 vols. (to 1751).
Visitation of 1634	W. C. Metcalfe (ed.), *The Visitation of Essex, 1634* (1878), Harleian Soc., xiii, pt. 1.
Visitation of 1664–8	J. J. Howard (ed.), *Visitation of the County of Essex, begun 1664, ended 1668* (1888).
Walker	*Walker Revised* (Oxford, 1948), ed. A. G. Matthews.
Wing	D. Wing, *Short-title Catalogue of Books printed in England . . . 1641–1700* (New York, 1945–51).
Wright	Thomas Wright, *History and Topography of the County of Essex* (1836), 2 vols.

OTHER ABBREVIATIONS

BM	British Museum.
EC	Earls Colne, Essex.
Eccles	Audrey Eccles (see acknowledgements).
ERO	Essex Record Office, County Hall, Chelmsford.

Hearth Tax, 1662	Essex Hearth Tax for 1662 (ERO, Q/RTh 1).
PR	Parish Register for Earls Colne (ERO, D/P 209/1/1–3).
PRO	Public Record Office, Chancery Lane, London.
Probert	Col. Carwardine Probert (see acknowledgements).
RJ	Ralph Josselin.
Ship Money, 1636	Essex Ship Money, 1636–7 (transcript in ERO, T/A 42).

CONVENTIONS

CONVENTIONS CONCERNING PUNCTUATION, SPELLING, CONTRACTIONS

The use of brackets in the text

Throughout the text round brackets are used to indicate that the Editor has altered words or phrases in order to make the text more intelligible. In certain cases punctuation has also been added or deleted to improve the sense and this is always indicated by round brackets (for further notes on punctuation see below).

Square brackets are always used where parts of the Diary have been torn or become frayed and these indicate either a doubtful reading of literals, words, or phrases or a missing portion of the text. Some of these missing sections were legible in the 1930s when the transcript was made under the direction of Col. Probert (see page xx). Portions which were then legible but are no longer so are included in square brackets and the use of italics indicates letters which existed but were unclear at the time when Probert saw the Diary and which have now completely disappeared.

A few words and phrases have been crossed out by Josselin. Such words have been included in round brackets with the letters c.o. at the start of the brackets, e.g. (c.o. father). A subsequent reader of the Diary has also crossed out a few words, but most of these have been indicated by brackets with c.o. (in italics), e.g. (*c.o. later*).

Where Josselin has left a blank this is indicated by (   ), but where Josselin himself employs brackets, sometimes failing to close them, this is indicated by *(   )* in italics.

The condition of the original text improves after the first few years and deteriorates badly again for the last few pages. The use of brackets is intended to make the work more readable without corrupting or restructuring the text.

Expansions and contractions

Mr has been expanded to Master (and Mrs to Mistress) where appropriate. 'Of' and 'off' are used interchangeably by Josselin; this is retained. Josselin often uses initials for names, for example K for King, Q for Queen. Such initials have not been expanded unless they refer to local names where the reference is not obvious. O.C. has been expanded to Oliver Cromwell, and N.E. to New England only on the first occasion it is used.

The following have not been expanded or standardized:

Hinningham: Hedingham (usually Castle Hedingham), Essex.
Coxall: Coggeshall, Essex
Taine: Great Tey, Essex

Mrs Mary: Mary Church
Harl or W. H: Harlakenden

A number of the words which Josselin almost always contracted have been expanded without the use of brackets to indicate such expansions. They are as follows:

agst = against	g^o = glory	s^t = saint	r^d = received
l^d = lord	$coven^t$ = covenant	jun^r = junior	qter = quarter

Three common contractions employed by Josselin which have not been altered are:

100^c = 100 cwt   c = centum (i.e. 100)
m = mille (i.e. 1000)

The letter 'j' has been substituted for the letter 'i' where necessary, and likewise 'th' for 'y', for example 'the' for 'ye' and 'that' for 'yt'. Josselin often used the symbol '&', but this has consistently been changed to 'and'. Since it is easy to read, his use of 'c' instead of 'ti' (as in 'porcons' for 'portions') has been left unaltered.

Punctuation

Josselin's punctuation has on the whole been left unchanged and two special features need to be noted. Firstly, he had the habit of adding a full stop after and sometimes before numerals and sums of money; these have been retained. Secondly, he tended to use the right-hand edge of the Diary as an alternative to punctuation. Since the present edition does not keep exactly to his lines, it has been necessary to use punctuation marks in round brackets at these points. Another problem is that it is often impossible to distinguish between Josselin's comma and full-stop and his capital letters and lower-case letters are often undifferentiated. The dangers of repunctuating the original are made clear in the Essex Records Transcript for the sense has often been completely changed and some of the flavour of the original lost. The present method entails a small sacrifice of ease of reading but was felt to be better than repunctuating and hence endangering the integrity of the original Diary.

Textual marks

There are occasional blank spaces in the Diary between certain months. These were usually left after Josselin's birthday, or at the New Year, March 25th (see below). They appear to be left so that the next entry would start on a new page. They are indicated thus: -----.

Josselin sometimes drew a hand in the margin ☞ presumably to emphasize some observation in the Diary. Where Josselin used an asterisk in the margin this has been indicated by *.

Where Josselin has underlined a passage this has been underlined in the text.

The insertion of a solidus (/) in the text follows Josselin's usage. It is difficult to say exactly what purpose this serves but it probably both replaced punctuation or marked the end of a section of writing.

DATING

All dates are as Josselin wrote them. England then used the Old Style or Julian calendar, which meant that its dates were ten days behind those of the rest of western Europe. Josselin also started the new year on Lady Day, the 25th of March. Where reference is made in the indexes or elsewhere to days within the period 1st January to 24th March, a year-date which includes both styles is given. Thus 24th February 1644/5 would have been written by Josselin as 1644 but would be, according to present dating, 24th February 1645.

WEIGHTS, MEASURES, AND COINAGE

ell: an English ell was 45 inches (1·37 metres)
rod: 5½ yards or 16½ feet (5 metres)

peck: quarter of a bushel or two gallons (9 litres)
bushel: four pecks or eight gallons (36 litres)

score (of flesh): 20 or 21 lb. (9 kg)
jag (of hay): a one-horse cartload

ob = obolus: a halfpenny (*£ s. d.*)

Inflation, both in the seventeenth and twentieth centuries, makes it impossible to give more than a very rough estimate of the comparative value of money now and then. But £1 was probably worth more than eighteen times as much in Josselin's time as it is now (1974).

INTRODUCTION

1. *History and nature of the Diary*

RALPH JOSSELIN was vicar of Earls Colne, Essex, from 1641 until his death in 1683. The Diary which he kept during this period appears to have remained in the family for a few years. At the turn of the century it was probably with his youngest daughter Rebekah, for there is a note in the Diary 'Mr Spicer his book' and Rebekah had married a Steward Spicer. During the eighteenth century it passed into the Lord of the Manor's hands, for in 1765 it is known to have been at Colne Priory.[1] In 1846 it was still in the Colne Priory family, by this time the Carwardines, who were descended from the Harlakendens.[2] There is a note that 'the original diary was bought by the late Mrs Oliphant (the novelist) off a London bookstall for 6d. having been lent or stolen from Colne Priory about the year 1850'.[3] Having survived 170 years, it was nearly lost, so it is not surprising that the 'notes, almanack &c' and account book to which Josselin refers in his Diary should not now be known to exist. Since its recovery it has remained with the Carwardine family and their heirs and it is now in the possession of Colonel G. O. C. Probert of Bevills, Bures, Suffolk.

The Diary itself is bound in leather with the royal coat of arms and the initials 'G' and 'K' on the two respective sides. The pages measure 147 by 200 mm (approximately 5 by 8 inches) and both sides of the paper are used. It is written in a very small but neat hand, with a considerable use of abbreviations (see frontispiece). There are 182 pages plus some endpapers. Although tiring to read because of the size of the handwriting, the difficulties are only considerable in the few places where the paper has worn thin and writing on the two sides has merged. Approximately the last fifth of the Diary is also less easy to read since Josselin's handwriting deteriorates with old age. Over three-quarters of the pages are in good condition, but a number are frayed along the edges and two pages have been badly torn. No pages appear to be missing entirely, though over-tight binding obscures some of the writing at the top of pages. The diary starts with a summary account of Josselin's life from

[1] Hockliffe, p. ix. Full titles of works cited in the footnotes are given above in the list of 'Abbreviations and Conventions'.

[2] *Topographer and Genealogist*, i (1846), p. 257.

[3] The note occurs at the front of a copy of Hockliffe belonging to Colonel G. O. C. Probert at Bevills, Bures, Suffolk.

his birth in January 1617 until August 1644. During the next twenty years of his life there are usually several entries a week, many of them very detailed. The period 1646–53 is especially well covered and includes two-fifths of the total Diary: from the mid 1660s the entries usually occur weekly and are much briefer.

II. *Previous use of the Diary*

In 1908 Hockcliffe edited the Diary for the Camden Society, in which he explained that 'Less than half the original diary is here published'.[1] This remark gives a slightly false impression for approximately three quarters of the original was omitted. Hockliffe described these omissions as 'many entries of no interest whatever—endless thanks to God for his goodness "to mee and mine", prayers, notes about the weather or his sermons, innumerable references to his constant "rheums" and "poses", trivial details of every day life, records of visits to his friends etc. etc.'[2] Such has been the shift in historical interests that many of these topics are precisely those about which we wish to learn. By omitting the apparently repetitious religious exhortations much of the essential flavour was also lost. The other major use of the Diary during this period was by the historian of Essex nonconformity, the Revd. Harold Smith, who wrote an article and a section of a book based on the original.[3] There also seems to have been a tentative project to publish a much longer edition of the Diary during the 1930's;[4] as a preliminary to such an edition a full transcript was made, under the direction of the then owner, Col. Carwardine Probert.[5] Perhaps awed by the length, for there were over 900 pages of typescript, the editor decided to shorten the original to about half its size, which would still have made it twice the length of the Camden Society edition. To this end, he cut out almost all the repeated religious utterances of thanks and supplication; he cut short a number of long descriptions; and he omitted everything that seemed offensive or bizarre. Hence, for example, the long descriptions of worm-infestation of Josselin's family, of Josselin's suppurating navel, and of many other illnesses were left out, as were almost all the very long passages of millenarian reflection. The editor's method was to snip and

[1] 3rd series, xv.
[2] Hockliffe, p. v.
[3] H. Smith, 'The Diary of Ralph Josselin', *Essex Review*, xxxiv (1925), pp. 126–35, Smith, ch. ix.
[4] There are notes to this effect in the *Essex Review*, xxxix (1930), p. 151, and xli (1932), p. 106.
[5] Only a few pages of this complete transcript have so far been located, at Bevills, Bures, Suffolk.

re-stick passages, but sometimes they were stuck in the wrong order and dates were muddled. This edition was never published, but a copy of the shortened typescript was deposited at the Essex Record Office with 'A full transcript' erroneously written on the front.[1]

Although Josselin's Diary was known to specialists on seventeenth-century England, he was generally regarded as of minor importance on the basis of the Camden Society edition. The Diary is occasionally used by general writers on the period,[2] but it was only Smith who exploited this source in any detail. In 1970 a full-scale study of Josselin and his religious, economic, social, and political world was published,[3] based on the transcript in the Essex Record Office, which was then generally believed to be complete.[4] The present edition, however, contains approximately 130,000 words that were not used as a basis for the above book. Thus the Camden edition contained approximately 70,000 words, the amended transcript in the Essex Record Office about 160,000 words, and the complete Diary about 290,000 words. It is hoped that it will now be possible to correct some erroneous impressions derived from using the amended typescript. There are, particularly, two major areas where a new study is needed; the topics of Josselin's millenarian beliefs and his health. Both these subjects were largely expurgated by Colonel Probert and therefore both were under represented in the work on Josselin. There is considerable evidence to show that during the years 1647–57 Josselin was a fully convinced millenarian, even if somewhat sceptical towards the end.[5] There is also a very great deal in the Diary concerning the illnesses of Josselin and his family which makes more

[1] ERO, T/B/9/1.

[2] For example, W. Notestein, *English People on the Eve of Colonization* (Harper, Torchbook edn., 1962), pp. 152, 153 n.; C. Hill, *Economic Problems of the Church* (Oxford, 1956), p. 294.

[3] Alan Macfarlane, *Family Life of Ralph Josselin; A Seventeenth-Century Clergyman* (Cambridge, 1970).

[4] Naturally, all quotations used in the book were checked against a (microfilm) copy of the original Diary. But working from transcript to Diary in this way did not reveal the frequent omissions in the ERO transcript. Furthermore, the first twenty pages of the transcript were checked, page by page, with the original Diary at Bevills. By an unfortunate chance, however, these happened to be pages which were fully transcribed. Even when starting to edit the full Diary, it was believed that this merely meant checking the ERO transcript. It was only after a number of days' checking that it began to emerge that very substantial portions had been omitted.

[5] The evidence for this remark is in the Diary between these dates. Dr. Lamont correctly guessed that the earlier assessment of Josselin's view on millenarianism might be wrong, see W. Lamont, 'Richard Baxter, the Apocalypse and the Mad Major', *Past and Present*, lv (1972), pp. 73–4. An introduction to the extremely complex topic of millenarian beliefs, apart from Lamont's article and his book *Godly Rule* (1969) is provided by N. Cohn, *The Pursuit of the Millenium* (Mercury edn., 1962), esp. pp. 321–78; C. Hill, *Puritanism and Revolution* (Mercury edn., 1962), pp. 323–36 and *Antichrist in Seventeenth-Century England* (Oxford, 1971); B. Capp, *The Fifth Monarchy Men A Study in Seventeenth-century English Millenarianism* (1972).

comprehensible his attitude to sickness and death.[1] Furthermore, there are a number of dreams which somewhat modify the previous analysis of the subject.[2] On the whole, however, it would seem that the full Diary adds further documentation to support many of the arguments sketched in the analytic work, rather than contradicting its conclusions, though the original is a far more rounded and moving document than was hitherto realized.

III. *Accuracy and coverage of the Diary*

Whenever it is possible to check either Josselin's figures or his observations against other sources it appears that he was almost always accurate. Although he mis-dated the attempt on the five members by Charles I by one day, he amended a mistake he had made when copying the figures from a London Bill of Mortality. If we compare his references to baptisms, marriages, and burials in the parish with entries in the parish register, or his description of crimes with entries in the Quarter Sessions records, whenever the event occurs in both sources Josselin's dating and description appears to be correct. Instances of such comparison are given in the notes to the text.

It is more difficult to evaluate the degree to which Josselin noted events which should have been in other local records and yet are missing, and vice versa. Josselin refers to a considerable number of burials, marriages, and baptisms which should have taken place in Earls Colne, but do not appear in the parish register. He also mentions a number of sexual offences, thefts, and other crimes which we might have expected to find recorded in legal records but are not. His Diary provides a warning concerning the inadequacies of local records. The reverse is also true, for it is possible to see to what extent Josselin noted the village events which appear in other records and which we might have expected to appear in the Diary. Apart from two references to people of Earls Colne being gaoled for 'highway trade' and 'robbery', Josselin only mentions three thefts in the township over his forty-two years of residence. Only one of these appears in the surviving court records. On the other hand, from Quarter Sessions and Assize records we find eleven thefts

[1] These attitudes are discussed in Macfarlane, ch. 11.

[2] The earlier analysis of dreams appears in Macfarlane, pp. 183–7. This forms the basis for some remarks in a general study of seventeenth-century dreams by P. Burke, 'L'histoire sociale des rêves', *Annales* (1973), no. 2, pp. 329–42. The newly discovered dreams occur under the following dates: 13/11/1650, 23/1/1652, 21/11/1652, 28/11/1652, 18/5/1653, 10/7/1653, 30/6/1654, 25/12/1654, 24/1/1655, 8/3/1655, 23/11/1655, 3/10/1656, 12/4/1657, 19/2/1671, 4/3/1679. The most interesting is probably a dream not of Josselin but his son Tom, recorded on 8/12/1654.

and robberies involving Earls Colne villagers in some way. One of these is mentioned in the Diary. It should be noted that only one of the cases was a major larceny. Bastardy was another topic that might be expected to receive his attention. He did note this offence in 1645, but thereafter paid little attention to the subject. Thus there is no mention of the three bastards appearing in various records for the township in 1656, or of the Earls Colne woman presented at the Quarter Sessions for having a bastard in 1654, or of three other bastardy cases mentioned in local records. These two instances warn us that though Josselin appears to have been substantially accurate, he was very selective. He only noted a fraction of the events, even of an apparently major kind, that occurred within his own parish during his residence.

IV. *The village background and the 'personnel' of the Diary*

Josselin was also selective about whom he mentioned; he named only a very small fraction of the total parish population. In the Hearth Tax of 1671 there were 239 taxable dwellings in the parish, which would give it an approximate population of 1,100 persons. Allowing for the rapid turn-over of population, both as a result of geographical mobility and a high mortality rate, it would be reasonable to assume that during his forty-two years, between three and five thousand people passed through the parish and lived there for at least several months. Yet Josselin only referred directly or indirectly to between two and three hundred of these. He mentioned by name approximately one-twentieth of his congregation in any context. Since he often omitted christian names, or there were several members of the same family living in the parish, it is frequently difficult to be sure to whom Josselin is referring. Appendix 2 and the map which accompanies it provide, in conjunction with the name index, a means of locating and distinguishing many of the individuals to whom he refers. It also provides biographical details, thereby supplying a context for remarks in the Diary which are otherwise incomprehensible. Josselin frequently refers to members of neighbouring gentry families, especially those connected to the Harlakendens, patrons of the living and Lords of the Manors of Earls Colne and Colne Priory. Again the difficulty of distinguishing his allusions is partly resolved by the name index and the genealogies in Appendix 1. The parish itself lay in an area of mixed arable and livestock husbandry and also on the edge of the cloth-making belt near Colchester. It was dominated by the Harlakenden family at the Priory, a Puritan and parliamentarian family with whom Josselin had a great deal of contact.

v. *Major themes in the Diary*

Only a very brief introduction to the topics with which Josselin deals will be given here, since a book has already been devoted to the analysis of the Diary, the background to Diary-writing, and Ralph Josselin. Furthermore, it is a document that speaks for itself and is immediately enthralling. For those who wonder whether it will yield them specific information it does seem worth briefly listing some of the subjects which are covered and the periods when entries on selected themes are most common.

Perhaps the most striking feature of the Diary is the daily interblending of different topics, from which we obtain a rounded, richly complex, picture of Josselin and his environment. This is largely because the diarist himself combined so many roles. He was a clergyman, a prosperous farmer, a schoolmaster, a member of the village community, a father and husband, an author and book-collector, and a parliamentary chaplain. He was also a frail human being, suffering from all the physical and economic insecurity of seventeenth-century living. These roles and features generated an interest in a broad spectrum of opinions and events.

Josselin was a clergyman throughout the more than forty years covered by the Diary and this, above all, gives it its shape. It is an intimate record of his ministry and his private doubts and triumphs as a Christian. A few specific aspects of this concern are worth singling out. During the years 1650–6 he was particularly interested in the promised Second Coming of Christ and speculated extensively on millenarianism. From 1655 to 1656 he was especially fearful about the Quakers and records their progress in the neighbourhood. Between 1660 and 1669 his Diary illustrates the insecurities of the Restoration for a man on the borderline of nonconformity. Throughout there are descriptions of religious behaviour at the village level. The numbers who attended church and communion are frequently given, particularly after 1661. There are frequent mentions of the godly group, the 'Society', which met under Josselin's leadership, particularly during the period 1647–57, of whom he gives the names of thirty-eight members probably of Earls Colne and twelve definite outsiders. Josselin's own backslidings, fears of death and damnation, attitude to the neighbouring ministers, all these and many other subjects are dealt with.[1]

[1] Harold Smith, both in his article (see p. xx, n. 3), book, and unpublished *Clergy*, shows how important a source Josselin's Diary is for the religious history of mid-century Essex. There is a brief discussion of Josselin's ecclesiastical career in Macfarlane, pp. 21–32.

Josselin gradually built up a large farm in Earls Colne, starting with a land purchase in 1646. The Diary thus provides a detailed description of farming life in the middle of the century. The price of commodities, state of the harvest, debts and loans, yearly accounts of his estate, the weather, manorial transfers, farming methods, all these topics are dealt with, often at considerable length. The second half of the Diary is especially full of these subjects. The descriptions enable us to piece together a unique picture of yeoman farming in this period.[1]

Josselin was married before the Diary proper commenced. His wife had ten livebirths during the period 1642–63, but survived him. There are numerous allusions to the rearing of the children. These range through the agonies of pregnancy and childbearing, weaning and teething, apprenticeship, and final marriage. There is also a very great deal of information concerning relations within the nuclear family, especially between husband and wife. Ties with other kin, both Josselin's own and those of his wife, can also be studied. It is thus possible to build up some estimate of the nature and importance of family and kinship relationships in this particular instance. Josselin's role as father and husband generates a series of observations which also seem unique for this period.[2]

Josselin's role as a villager of Earls Colne has already been alluded to. He was a member of a certain status hierarchy and was tied to his co-villagers by numerous neighbourly bonds. His descriptions of various village events, for example smallpox epidemics, small accidents, crimes, witchcraft beliefs, fires, provide us with a rare chance to see what it was like to live in a seventeenth-century parish.[3] His terms of reference to various neighbours and the frequency of his allusions to specific persons and categories—the Lord of the Manor, the prosperous, the poor, and the wicked—all indicate his notions of rank and status.

Josselin was clearly interested in local, national, and international politics. He served with the parliamentary army as a chaplain on two occasions, though he also disapproved of putting the King to death. His frequent comments on events occurring on the Continent as well as in England indicate how well-informed and absorbed were the lower levels

[1] These topics have been analysed at some length in Macfarlane, chs. 3 and 4. The discussion there includes maps of Josselin's landholdings which are also shown on the map on p. 696 below.

[2] The whole of Macfarlane's part two is concerned with these topics. For a diagram of Josselin's kin, see Appendix 1 below.

[3] The only other two documents which would seem to be comparable to Josselin in this respect are the *Rev. Oliver Heywood's Diary, 1630–1702*, ed. J. Horsfall Turner (4 vols., Brighouse, 1882), and Richard Gough, *Antiquityes and Memoryes of the Parish of Myddle* (Shrewsbury, 1700–1875, various reprints).

of the 'political nation' at this period. The full Diary contains long summaries of political events which have not before been published, though much of this material was selected for the Camden Society edition.

Sickness and disease, as much of a preoccupation as politics, were of less interest to the previous editor. Throughout the Diary, but particularly in the years 1648–50, there are very long and graphic descriptions of the author's reactions to the almost constant series of minor and major afflictions which he and his family suffered. Intimate details of Josselin's own health, moving descriptions of the frequently fatal sickness of his children and numerous comments on epidemics which afflicted the village, all are included. The overriding importance of death and disease in the seventeenth century have seldom, if ever, found such a chronicler.

Josselin was schoolmaster of Earls Colne from 1650 to 1658 and a certain amount may be gleaned concerning this activity, especially the economic aspects. The diarist's interest in reading, which provides a useful sample of educated taste in this period, had preceded this appointment and most of the titles he gives fall in the period 1648–50.[1] It was during his schoolmastership, which also coincided with much of his millenarian speculation, that Josselin recorded most of the dreams that are mentioned in the Diary. These are most numerous in the years 1655–6.

Among many other topics to which he turns our attention are the following: accidents, food, geographical mobility, gifts, gossip, imagery, insanity, the poor, pregnancy, servants, wages. Anyone interested in seventeenth-century thought and society is likely to find information of interest. An ordinary subject index cannot do justice to such a rich and complex document. The Diary is, above all, unique as a total document. With all its redundancy and repetition, it can still be read straight through with great enjoyment. Idiosyncrasies of grammar and style may, at first, provide difficulties, but there are rich rewards for those who persevere and enter Josselin's world, so strange and yet familiar. He himself does not emerge as lovable, or even endearing—his conscientious and suffering figure simply stands before us, to wonder at, pity, and for all its frailty, respect. Posterity will judge his right to stand beside Pepys, Heywood, Woodford, Kilvert—the great English Diarists of all time.

[1] Most of the titles are collected in Macfarlane, p. 23; the reference to Hooker's work should be to Thomas Hooker, *A Survey of the Summe of Church-Discipline* (1648), not Richard Hooker's work. I am grateful to Dr. Geoffrey Nuttall for pointing this out.

A thankfull observacion of divine providence and goodnes towards mee and a summary view of my life: by mee Ralph Josselin:

26

An: D^{ni} Jan: 25: 1616: I was borne to the great joy of Father and mother being
1616: much desired as being their third child and as it pleased god their only sonne, I had this happines in my birth to bee the seed of the righteous both parents being in the Judgment of man, gratious persons: the place of my birth was Chalke-end[1] my Fathers patrimony: I was the eldest sonne in our whole Family and yett possest not a foote of land in which yett I praise god I have not felt inward discontent and grudging, god hath given mee himselfe, and he is [all] and will make up all other things unto mee.

1618: My father selling his inheritance, retired from Roxwell to Bishop Stortford in Hartfordshire, where my Father my mother being received up into heaven(,) gave mee good educacion, by his owne instruction, example and in schooles as I was capeable I having devoted my selfe to the worke of the Lord in the Ministery

In my infancy I had a gratious eye of providency watching over mee, preserving me from dangers by fire, a remembrance I shall carry to my grave on my right thigh, by knives being stabd in the forehead by my second sister, a wild child but now I hope god hath tamed and sanctifyed her spi[rit,] falls from horse, water and many casualtyes:

But that which I have most cause to admire was the goodnes of god to preserve mee from poysonous infections from servants, and bestowing his grace upon me to restrayne mee from lewdnes, though full [of] spirit, and of a nimble head and strong memory, preserved from many untowardnesses that young [boys] fall into, I hope I shall never forgett gods fitting mee for a scholler, and giving mee a spirit for the same from which nothing would divert mee at last god putt it into my fathers heart to listen [to] mee, I confesse my childhood was taken with ministers and I heard with delight and admiracion and desire to imitate them from my youth, and would be acting in corners: 2. I had a singular affection to the

[1] In Roxwell, Hertfordshire.

historyes in the bible being acquainted with all those historyes in very yong dayes, and so with divers historyes prophane and civill, upon which I emulated other languages that I might see what historyes were in those tongues: 3: My father was a widdower, and my corrupt heart feared a mother in law[1] and undoing by her and truly so it proved in respect of estate as will appeare: and therefore I desire to bee a scholler, so should I make the better shift if from hence, and bee able to live of my selfe by gods blessing:

My Father moved by god yielded to my desires and placed mee with Mr Leigh[2] a painfull man to me whom I have cause to love and blesse god for his labours, and praise the Lord for his blessings upon mee, in the schoole I was active and forward to learne which contented my master and father: I thank god for his goodnes to mee insomuch as for not saying my lessons I remember not that I ever was [whipt,] once I was for an exercise when my master was passionate: it might bee I might often des[erve] it, yett I made it my aime to learne and lent my minde continually to reade historyes: and to shew my spirit lett mee remember with griefe that which I yett feele: when I was exceeding yong would I project the conquering of kingdoms and write historyes of such exploits. I was much delighted with Cosmography[3] taking it from my Father. I would project wayes of receiving vaste est[ates] and then lay it out in stately building, castles. libraryes: colledges and such like: and withall which [was] worse oh the strange prodigious uncleane lusts when I was yett a child. how often have [I] walkt with delight to meditate upon such courses being too well acquainted with those sens[ations] by bookes which I had. yett I blesse god who kept mee from all outward uncleanesse. praise bee [to] him, and for this I desire to loath and abhorre my selfe,

1631: In processe of time when I was growne up to 14 or 15 yeares of age my father marryed, upon which he projected to raise an estate for mee as he had sold his patrimony for which my grandfather th[en] gave his other lands from him though the eldest giving him only 10^{li}. which according to his will [was] due to mee, which I had also duly payd to mee after 12 yeares by my two uncles his exe[cutors] but that plott fayled, my father loosing therby above 200^{li}.

[1] Here, as elsewhere, Josselin's terminology differs from modern usage. He is referring to his step-mother.

[2] Thomas Leigh, the distinguished headmaster of Bishop's Stortford school from 1621–66 (?); formed a valuable library. Venn.

[3] The Science which describes and maps the general features of the universe; formerly often meant geography. SOED.

besides against all my intreatyes went to farming wherby he lost most of his estate.

1632. March: My fathers love was such towards mee that when I was neare 16 yeares old I went to C[ambridge] to Jesus Colledge[1] entred pentioner under Mr Tho: Lane. my loving and I hope godly and hones[t tutor] he dealt lovingly with mee, but I was forced to come from Cambridge many times for want [of] meanes and loose my time in the contry yett would I endeavor to gett it up and I thank [god] notwithstanding all hindrances I was not behind many of my time and standing: and now [my fathers love] would budd forth in expressions of [love and tea]res towards mee exceedingly living at Bumpsted in Essex under Mr Symons his landlord and Mr Barradale[2] a godly man his [ ][3] I bless my god to restrayne mee by his grace from lewdness, and in particular though my father [ ] mee exceedingly and my mother in law though I hope an honest woman yett was [of a somewhat] soure spirit yett I remember not that I ever caused any debate or division betwixt them [for any]thing, though I was sensible of her disrespect in somethings towards mee: I can call [to mind] not many things in my life: In reference to my father I blesse god to give mee a spirit c[arefull] to please him so that I had his blessing being a joy and not a griefe of heart unto him[. He was] grieved that he should leave mee no estate and I told him if he had enough for himselfe I hoped god would so blesse mee as that I should if need were bee helpefull to him; tis a [conti]nuall comfort to mee to thinke of my tender love to him, and my care for him in which I was able [to do] his busines, for his creditt, for his estate, much went through my hand and yett I gave him alwayes a just account but only for about 5^{s}. at one time which I spent upon my selfe in [his] imployment and not lavishly. When I came to Bumpsted I heard Mr Borradale with delight; whom god used an instrument to doe [mee] good when I heard him my use was to walke home alone not with other boyes or company. and sta[y] not in the churchyard but immediately away, and meditate upon the sermon and example my selfe by the same. I could not afterwards but relate the same to him, who heard it with much joy [and] comfort, it was my constant course to performe dutyes of prayer betwixt god and my selfe twice and sometimes thrice a day, and to read the scriptures.

1 RJ admitted pensioner at Jesus, 5 March 1632/3. B.A. 1636/7; M.A. 1640. Venn.
2 John Borodale, vicar of Steeple Bumpstead 1622–49. Smith, p. 395.
3 One line torn, and a corner torn shortly after.

Towards my sisters god gave mee a heart to seeke their good in some measure, my father living and dead, and especially my sister Anna in hindring her from marrying a widdow(er), when my father had cast her of, and. in reconciling her unto him agayne and this I did before I was 17 yeares old[.] When my father was dead in my poverty, I blesse god I did not forgett to doe for them:

Besides what I sayd before of my slips twice was I mistaken ignorantly and unadvisedly my god forgive and pardon the same to mee in the bloud of his Christ, which I desire most earnestly and I had too much familiarity with a neare and deare freind of mine, though I praise my god who kept mee from uncleannesse: the lord tooke her away young, yett he gave mee [an] opportunity first to bemoane it with her, and to intreate her to seeke of god pardon and forgiveness for the same: I blesse the Lord for that spirit that having beene a cause with others of erring the Lord gave mee grace to lament it with the partyes and aske them forgivenes, and advising them not to bee misled by my example. I desire to looke upon this branch alwayes in respect of my selfe with trembling, and gods preservacion with thankefulnes: oh the opportunityes that I have had in the affection of y(o)uth, I should not have thought there had been that wantonnes in youth if my experience had not manifested the same:

In Cambridge in my studyes I was close and dilligent: my fault was to omitt too many mornings by reason of my tendernes, either in bed or by the fire: the supersticons of the Church were a perplexity then unto mee: god gave mee mercy in blessing me with love, and prospering in [the] Colledge, few fallings out, but one to speake by or rashnes, which wee lamented as be[ing] upon a Sabbath day when wee should have beene at publique ordinances;[1] there god kept from infection strangely:

For my health god was good unto mee: preserving mee from the small poxe when I have oftentimes beene neare and in danger,

1636: While I was in this way compassed with mercyes: being newly come up to Cambridge on Tuesday night Oct: 25: came up my brother Hodson[2] about 10 a Clocke at night and brought mee word my father was sicke, speechlesse, senseles, and like to dye: I rid home that night, but had not the comfort to have one word from him that he knew mee, so as on Friday: Octob: 28: my Father gave

[1] Public worship as ordained by the state.

[2] Thomas Hodson, RJ's brother-in-law. For this and all other family relationships see the genealogy of the Josselin family.

up the ghost, and is now in rest, in joy and glory: he was about 53. yeares old or very nigh and I wanted one quarter to 20: Now was my condicion sad: young, and friendles and pennylesse: my father making no will[.] Octob. 30: wee buryed him in Bumpsted Churchyard: with greife of heart I layd him in[to] the grave, but my god lives for evermore: My mother in law tooke not as I conceived a course to doe us Justice, wee could not agree I departed from her; tooke my degree at Cambridge: Batchelor of art with money I had from her, and putt my selfe into apparrell, so that of 20^{li}. my (c.o. fathers) share in my fathers estate. I spent 10^{li}. before Feb: 1: 1636:

But now what course should I take, sometimes I thought upon my fathers farme: then upon the Law, but god and the perswasions of Mr Borradale and Mr Thornbecke setled mee againe upon Cambridge, well I tooke my degree and in Feb: ult: Mr Thornbecke had word that one Mr Kempe of Sutton in Bedfordshire want[ed] an usher,[1] I resolved to goe over thither with their letter, but I wanted money for my jorney: oh how ashamed was I to aske: one Edward Bell upon my intre[aty] lent mee 5^{s}. to pay my charges, oh how hardly with teares in [my eyes did I] looke upon my condicion, much a doe I procured a horse and a sadle: my [proud] heart thought this was very meane: in tedious wheather I went my jorney [providence] cast mee upon a carryer that went that way otherwise I could not have performed my jorney, I escaped some danger at Potton of miring sett up my horse their and downe that night to Mr Kempes late, he entertay(n)ed mee, but in conclusion he was provided of an usher and so my jorney was lost, home I came with a sad heart a tyred horse, and empty purse, I rid almost all night because, I neither would nor could pay another dayes horse hire, when I was come home I borrowed 10^{s}. of Mr Thornbecke to carry mee into Norfolke to my unckles: thither I went having payd my former 5^{s}. my uncle Benton entertaynd mee with love and pity and offered mee to stay a while with him, here was providence, aboad I had none, money none, and frends were not so kinde as I expected, oh but my god tooke mee up and had a care of mee, forever blessed bee his name[,] now I was as it were at an anchor, when loe within 2 dayes on Satturday at night comes in a messenger with the offer of a place unto mee, it came about thus. Mr Kempe had a letter sent to him from Mr Neale of Deane in Bedfordshire to helpe him to an usher, he sent over kindly to Mr Thornbecke, and he to mee

[1] Usher: a schoolmaster's assistant; an under-master. SOED.

in Norfolke, my uncle Mr Benton advised mee [to] accept the place, I lookt upon it as a gratious providence, returned to Bumpsted, payd the(e) messenger, and resolved into a Country and among persons that I never heard of before: all my things at Cambridge I sold to my sister Anna and in conclusion I gave her them: I made even with all the world, provided mee my horse, one suite of clothes, and Coate which I borrowed at 1^{li}. 12^{s}. 4^{d}. upon my uncle Miles his creditt, when I had fitted all, disposed my bookes and some linnen in my trunke, I left it with a carryer to bring after mee: I tooke horse and rid towards Huntington, I had in my purse the charges of my jorney deducted: 1^{li}. 5^{s}. 9^{d}.: I was indebted 10^{s}. above that formerly expressed for my Coate: when I came upon the Bridges betwixt Godmanchester and Huntington, I ruminated upon Jacobs speech with my staffe I passed over this Jordan:[1] my condicon was lowe, I went I knew not whither, if I had not sett downe in this place, I had been undone: well I considered what a plentifull returne Jacob had: I considered loe in this condicon thus lowe, a litle money, a few bookes and only 10^{li}. my mother still ought mee of my part in my fathers estate: I stayd and went softly and made this Convenant. with god to serve him, and whatever became of mee, to use no unlawfull and dishonest way for my subsistance or preferment. in this my sad heart was somewhat cheard, at the foote of the bridge the prisoners were begging. my heart pittyed them in their distresse and out of my poverty I gave them 3^{d}. riding on my jorney, I found I could not well reach to the end that night upon which I tooke up my inne at Spalditch their was some charge unexpected: the next morning March 24: 1636: anno aetatis the twentieth and somewhat upwards I came to Deane, alighting from my horse and calling at the Doore the gentlewoman of the House welcomes mee into her parlour and calls her housband: it rejoyced mee to see their faces, they expressed goodnes in their countenance(.) well in conclusion I agreed to stay; the present schoolemaster was
March: 25: not yett gone, but I was to enter upon it as from the next day he
1637: laying it downe as that day the end of the quarter: my entrance was harsh, 10^{li}. per annum was I to pay for my diett: 3 schollers afforded mee: 7^{li}. the first quarter was worth 4^{li}. to mee and I had hopes of increase dayly: now was I in a hopefull way, I applyed my selfe to

[1] 'O God of my father Abraham, and God of my father Isaac, the Lord which saidst unto me, Return unto thy country, and to thy kindred, and I will deal well with thee: / I am not worthy of the least of all the mercies, and of all the truth, which thou hast shewed unto thy servants; for with my staff I passed over this Jordan; and now I am become two bands.' Genesis 32: 9–10.

my schoole and studyes I was much ingaged to Mr Dillingham[1] for his love and respect: I read through all chamier[2] there and abrid[ged] him: I had acquaintance at my Lord Mandevilles[3] of Kimbolton Castle and the use of h[is] library by meanes of Mr Merrill[4] his chaplaine: I rid sometimes into Essex and Norfo[lke] once per annum payd my debts received my money of my mother, had the countenance [of] my freinds having now no need of their
1639: helpe: having stayed their 2 yeares at Spring 1639: at Easter comming out of Norfolke, I was taken sicke with an ague and fever,[5] which brought me lowe, as if it would have by a deepe consumption layd mee in the grave[,] my freinds feared mee, yett I did not, but trusted in god for recovery, who sett mee [on] my leggs againe: in a word at deane I bought mee bookes, clothes, and saved some money: upon Michaelmas day. anno: 1639. I preached my first sermon at Wormington [in] Northamptonshire at the intreaty of Mr Elmes[6] upon Acts. 16.31: some discontents were in my head so that Mr Gifford[7] of [Olny] coming to mee and proffering mee 12^{li}. per annum and my diett, to bee his Curate: I went [over] to Olny in Buckinghamshire and left D[eane] Octob: 4: 1639. being Friday: my stocke was: 20^{li}. 7^{s}. 9^{d}. in money and about 1^{li}. owing mee, so that I putt up in money besides all my expences about
Olny: 10^{li}. in money and paid my debts:

The first quarter at Olny I was only assistant to him in his schoole, the first Lords day being [Octob:] 6: was my eye fixed with love upon a Mayde; and hers upon mee: who afterwards proved my wife: Decemb: 13: my uncle Mr Joslin in Norfolke, sent mee the offer of a place [by] him; but my affection to that mayde that god had layd out to be my wife would not suffer mee to stirre, so I gave the messenger: 5^{s}. and sent him away. in that month of December I was ordayned Deacon by the Bishop of Peterburg.[8] the charges

1 One of the illustrious family Dillingham of Deane, Beds., among whom were Francis, one of the translators of the authorized version of the Bible, and Theophilus, Master of Clare Hall. DNB.

2 Daniel Chamier, minister of the Reformed Church of France, 1570–1621; *De Oecumenico Pontifico* and other works.

3 Edward (Montagu) Earl of Manchester, styled Viscount Mandeville or Lord Kimbolton, parliamentary general. *The Complete Peerage*, vol. viii.

4 John Merrill, vicar of Kimbolton, Hunts., 1637–40. Venn.

5 An ague is an acute fever, especially a malarial fever, with paroxysms, consisting of a cold, a hot, and a sweating stage. SOED.

6 Thomas Elmes of Lilford and Green's Norton; his son William is mentioned in the Diary under 12 July 1654 and is in Venn.

7 Richard Gifford, vicar of Olney, Bucks., 1638–40. Venn.

8 John Towers, a high church supporter of Laud, impeached and put in the Tower in 1641. DNB.

amounted to: 1^{li}. 14^{s}. 9. in my jorn[ey]. in my returne I preached at Deane. December 25^{t}. and coming home from thence, I read prayers at Olny, and that day found Jane Constable the mayde before mentioned in our house. which was the beginning of our acquaintance. the next Lords day I preachd at Olny: on Acts. 16.31. [and] so also on. Jan: 1: Newyears day: at night invited to supper to Goodman Gaynes: I went in to call Goodwife[1] shepheard, and their my Jane being I stayed with her, which was our first proposall of the match one to another, which wrought a mutuall promise one to another Jan: 23: and by all our consents a Contract: Sept. 28. 1640: and our marriage. October. 28. following: Now hencefor-ward I preachd once a fortnight and Mr Gifford gave mee. 10^{s}. per quarter more out of his love for my paynes: here I lived with them very comfortably and contentedly wee used Shovelboard for our recreation of which I grew weary presently: about latter end of Feb: I was ordayned minister at Peterburg by the Bishop and
1640. 6. ministers: I would not bowe towards the Altar[2] as others did and some followed my example charges amounted to: 1^{li}. 6^{s}. 10^{d}. that spring I went up to Cambridge to visitt for my degree of Mr in arts as our custome was: charges their and for my gowne and Cassocke amounted to: 19^{li}. 18^{s}. and somewhat upwards: this was a hard pull, from thence I went to Norfolke, and coming home to preach at Olny fayr flouds were so great as I narrowly escaped drowning in divers places. I hope I shall nev[er] been umindfull of gods goodnes to mee in my preservasion. Likewise at Olny mighty [stone] fell from a chimny into a place where I walked presently as soone as I was passed by. now being Mr of Arts and minister I began to thinke of marrying being sure to my wife: but I could not see any convenience how to live, beginning of July I was at Cranham in Essex and preachd their 2 sermones: 2 Pet: 3: ult: about growing in grace: my uncle and all the Towne desird mee to live with them, and I seemed not much against it: to olny I returne: and having had some offers from my Lord Mandevill which I durst not accept least I should loose my selfe in a loose Family, I repayrd to Kimbolton thence to try providence but neither time fitting mee, I resolved twas not gods pleasure to raise mee that way. I sought him

1 Goodwife (or 'goodee') literally means the mistress of a house; goodman is also used by RJ and means the male head of a household, a man of substance, not of gentle birth. SOED.

2 The act of bowing to the altar symbolized high church or Roman Catholic beliefs and was among the grounds for a loss of ecclesiastical office during the Commonwealth period.

for direction, and about August I was continually perswaded ere 3 months god would lay out a way for my livelyhood: one day in September setting a part in private to seeke unto god for his direction, as I ended prayer god perswaded mee I should have a present answer of my desire, as I stood up at window I heard one inquire for mee. I went downe and it was one sent from Cranham to intreate mee to live with them. his name was Goodman Taverner,[1] at length wee came to this conclusion that the minister[2] allowing: 24li. per annum and my uncle my diett or 10li. and the Towne. 10li. more I would come over to them. home he came made up my proposicons and came over for mee: Friday. Sept: 25: I went my jorney: 26. at London wee mett the joyfull newes of this Parliament that is now sitting. 1644. and god long continue for his glory, and his Churches good. I was first contracted to my Deare wife at Cranham I waited. 3. weekes for their Minister, he comming over, wee concluded: so as I sent a wagon for my stuffe and came to Olny and marryed Wednesday. Octob. 28. 4. yeares after my Fathers death. and Monday Following wee began our jorney and Nov. 4. came safe to Cranham. returning I thought of my thoughts at Huntington Bridge, and god had brought mee backe, increased with wife goods and parts, loe this was the Lords doing twas merveylous towards mee.

Cranham. 1640: Being come to Cranham I taught schoole at Upminster, which was great trouble, but no great advantage unto mee, their I had a loving people, but I could not injoy my health, being continually subject to Rheumes,[3] I wanted the conveniency of a house, and offers began to be made to mee so as to my parishes great greife it was probable I would [remove] from them; the Inhabitants of Hornechurch layd in for mee and made mee [good offers] of 80li. per annum vijs et modis[4] certayne without any trouble on my part: [only] to preach twice on the Lords day. without medling with other dutyes:

Being in this condicon Mr Wharton[5] of Felsted was with a freind of his at Upminster and I having some business with him went over to see him, where I found they had told him I was removing from

[1] John Taverner of Cranham; assessed at 7*s*. in the 1636 Ship Money, whose will was proved in 1643 (ERO, 330 BW 57) as a 'husbandman'.

[2] Ignatius Jordan, sequestered (removed from the living) in 1644 and restored in 1660. Smith, pp. 118, 125, 349, 401.

[3] Rheum: watery matter secreted by the mucous glands or membranes; a cold in the head or lungs, catarrh. SOED.

[4] In kind and cash.

[5] Samuel Wharton, vicar of Felsted. Smith, pp. 47, 50.

them upon which he propounded Earles Colne in Essex a place in a very good ayre the meanes he sayd was about 50li. per annum: the towne was able to make it more; upon this I promised him to goe over upon notice from him, being ill I had word from him that they desired mee on the next Lords day. in the meane tyme one of the Towne came over to mee, March. I came over and my loving uncle Ralph Josselin with mee, wee came that night to Mr Rich: Harlakendens[1] at the priory: I was affected with that family exceedingly and the situation of the Towne, the next day being the Lords day I preachd, upon their approbacion they desired mee I would come and live with them as their Minister, I in a word answered them if they would make the meanes a competency such as I could live on which I conceived was 80li. per annum I would embrace, they gladly entertained it and valewed it thus to mee:

Earles Colne } Comit Essex:

Tithes they would make good at. 40li. 0s. per annum	
Mr Rich: Harlakend: wood and money ----------	20. 0:
His tenants in contribucon: ---------	2: 0:
Mr Tho: Harlakenden: -----------	3: 0:
And the towne contribucon ---------	15: 0

The House, close, churchyard and the dues that accrewed to the Minister they conceived to bee worth. 10li. per annum. thus seing gods providence in it, I accepted their offer, and their was this proposicon more that if I found not the Towne as good as their words, upon 6. months warning wee would part: I should have my free leave to depart from them: They desired mee to keep a Fortnight Lecture,[2] which though I did not engage my selfe by promise to keepe yett I did for sometime: things thus acted wee posted
1640: March: up to London and passed all with the Bishop.[3] so that I tooke peaceable possession, returned to Cranham and after a fortnights stay I brought my wife over, my uncle and Goodman Robjohn[4] accompanying mee but not one man of Earles Colne came to meete us on(e) the way, neither did any come to welcome us to Towne, which seemed to mee an unkind part, and made mee suspect that I was deceived in the disposicon of the people.

[1] For a description and genealogy of the Harlakendens, see Appendix 1.

[2] Begun in 1626 after the endowment by Dr. Wilson, a physician, with the annual sum of £30. Smith, pp. 28–30, describes the lecturership and one of the previous lecturers, the illustrious New England divine Thomas Shepherd.

[3] William Juxon, later Archbishop of Canterbury, a friend of Laud, yet respected by the nonconformists. DNB.

[4] John Robjohn assessed at 2*d*. in the 1636 Ship Money for Cranham.

1641: well I stayed with Mr R: Harlakenden untill Apr: 1641: when wee went to board with Mr Edw: Cressener: wee paid: 6^{li}. per quarter, here wee lived, quietly, and very contentedly. I would not desire better usage, tis but their due commendacion of their love and respect to us. I fell to my worke, in the Ministery, and now I began to prepare my house, money came not in from the Towne as was expected in a word. I layd out my. 20^{li}. and Mr Harlakenden. 20^{li}. The Towne should have raysed 20^{li}. more, but there was none would take any care for it: to this day they have not brought in 5^{li}. that I can give an account of; this was a litle trouble when my quarters came: one or 2 was gatherd not by their care but by my procuring men to doe the same; 2 persons refused at first. my. 3^{li}. 15^{s}. per quarter: fell under. 3^{li}. the first quarter, neither did any take care to make it up: when Tithes came I must doe it my selfe: I compounded(:) with all my toyle I thinke that yeare I could make them amount not above 33^{li}. and since they are come to lesse, and all the losse to this day hath fallen upon my shoulders: I confesse I was stumbled at their dealings, and some abuses offered mee about the Protestasion[1] so that I wonderd at the people, and supposed it would grow bad indeed, that made so bad an entrance, in the Contry I must confesse I had many private guifts, which helpd to make amends for the towne losses:

June I rid to my fathers[2] left my wife their came home by Deane, and June 28. I rid to olny in a day. my father came home with us, who was much affected with Colne and delighted to bee with us untill his death, July. wee rid to my Lady Dennies,[3] and then I began to have some hopes of my(.) wives breeding which proved so indeed to our great joy and comfort, blessed bee thee name of the Lord. returning I applyed my selfe that summer to hasten the compleating the House fitt for our winter dwelling, which being in some measure effected October. 20: with a mayd Sarah Browne to whom wee gave 1^{li}. 18. per annum, wee came up to our owne house in the high streete, no neighbour came to welcome us to our house but Mrs Cousins[4] with 2 from Gaynes

[1] The Protestation of May 1641 was prepared by John Pym as an appeal to the nation, and was approved by the House of Commons. It was interpreted by many as forbidding some of the ceremonies hitherto in use.

[2] Here, as often, 'father' is used for father-in-law.

[3] Probably Lady Margaret Denny, widow of Sir Edward of Bishop's Stortford, and mother of Richard Harlakenden's second wife Mary.

[4] She was wife of the schoolmaster of Earl's Colne, William Cousins. Biographical details concerning EC inhabitants will be found in Appendix 2.

Colne. and Mrs King[1] and her sonne and daughter one night: I esteemed it some disrespect and unkindnes but such expressions I perceive now are not so much used in our towne as in others. This Michaelmas upon an order of the House of Commons to that purpose wee tooke downe all [images] and pictures and such like glasses: thus this winter passed away a time of hopes, and yet sometimes feares, but the King being returned out of Scotland. Jan: 5. 1641: he attempted the house of Commons in case of the 5 members;[2] but being disappointed he packd away from the house and came to them not to this houre: Aug: 8: 1644: and in Feb: following
1642: ing the Q went over beyond seas: thus spinning out my time I began a litle to be troubled with some in matter of separacion:[3] My wife now growing bigge and ill my mother came from Olny to us upon a Tuesday lecture day April: 12: after sermon having waited upon god in his house, my wife called her women and god was mercifull to mee in my house giving her a safe deliverance, and a daughter which on Thursday April: (21st) was baptized by the name of Mary: Mr Rich: Harlakenden: Mr John Litle:[4] Mrs Mary Mildmay[5] and my wives mother being witnesses. I entertayned my neighbors all about it cost me 6^{li}. and 13^{s}. 4^{d}. at least: they shewed much love to mee from all parts: god blessed my wife to bee a nurse. and our child thrived, and was even then a pleasant comfort to us: god wash it from it corruption and sanctify it and make it his owne: but it pleased god my wives breasts were sore which was a grievace and sad cutt to her but with use of meanes in some distance of time they healed up: this Spring times grew fearfull in the rising of the yeare about Midsummer wee began to raise private armes: I found a musquett for my part and the King was beginning to raise an army. The Parliament did the Like: Aug: 1: wee met at Colchester to underwrite, where for my part for my affection to god and his gospell having endeavoured publike promoting it beyond my estate I underwritt and payd in to Mr Crane.[6] 10^{li}. but

[1] Although married to a D.D. impossible to locate; not of EC.

[2] The attempt on the five members was on January the fourth, not fifth; here as elsewhere Josselin gives dates before 25 March under the previous year, he is therefore referring to January 1641/2.

[3] Those who regarded themselves as true believers wished to separate themselves from the less godly.

[4] For the Little family of Halstead and Colne Engaine, see Appendix 1 and Morant, ii, pp. 220, 257.

[5] For the Mildmay family and their connections, see Appendix 1.

[6] Robert Crane, probably of Coggeshall, colonel in the Eastern Association, a member of the (1644) Committee for the sequestration of scandalous ministers in Essex. Smith, pp. 116, 336, 393; Beaumont, pp. 60–1, 73.

my Rings[1] wanted something so it fell short nigh 3s. being at London I provided for my selfe Sword. Halbert. Powder and Match, the drums now also began to beate up for my part I endeavoured to encourage outhers to goe forth, our poore people in Tumults arose and plundered divers Houses[2] papists and others and threatened to goe farther which I endeavoured to suppresse by publique and private meanes: Edgehill battle being fought Wednesday following being the fast day I was told the newes as I was going downe the churchyard to sermon. the time and place hinted the answer of our prayers on the Lords day being the day and the time of battle, when I was earnest with god for mercy upon us against our enemies: Upon this the contry was raised and I for my part sent a man out with a months pay. but he returned presently but spent the most of my money.

1643: In spring now my wife weaned her daughter and began to breed againe: god gave us both our health in a greater measure than I had had before or my wife of late dayes. I should have mentiond our associating[3] in which service I underwritt a whole armes,[4] they went out to our great charge, and did litle or no good. I began now to find my meanes grow scant, that notwithstanding all our industry and good husbandry and many guifts that I could have but litle upon which I gave notice to the Towne to prevent it that I might not bee forced to leave them, June: 10. 1643 my wives father dyed: the Lord prepare us for our latter ends. and gave us mercy with him through Jesus christ: New Townes came to mee to remain Fordham: Thaxted: and. I went and preachd with the last but would not accept the sequestracion.[5] In July upon occasion of a plot to betray the City their was another new covenant[6] propounded and began to bee pressed. I tooke it but the state lett it fall, things were now sad with us Waller routed, and Fairfax and Bristol lost, and Hull like to be betrayed, the City divided: Essex's army also

[1] RJ is selling his jewellery to pay for the underwriting, i.e. to finance troops for the parliamentary army. For examples of such underwriting at the village level, see Kingston, pp. 81–5.

[2] The most famous of such incidents was the sacking of Lady Rivers's house at Melford on the Suffolk border, described in Kingston, p. 66.

[3] On 20 December 1642 an ordinance had been passed for an association of the eastern counties, including Essex, to improve their administration during the war. Gardiner, i, p. 89.

[4] One headpiece, 1 corselet, 1 muskett, or sword. Probert.

[5] Sequestered ministers were not entirely deprived of their freehold, but were prevented from enjoying their income, which was received by sequestrators and paid to a minister appointed by the Committee for Plundered Ministers. Smith, pp. 160–1.

[6] Known as the Vow of 1643, it was ordered on the discovery of Waller's plot, but later abandoned. Smith, p. 95.

came to nothing but god remembred us in our low estate, August: 2: being Wed: I was taken very ill with a quotidian[1] ague I had 3 fits, the phisitian told mee I would have one harsh one more but on Friday night seeking god for my health that if it pleasd him I might still goe on in my calling; I was strangely perswaded I should have no more fitts neither had I: lord lett mee never forgett thy goodnes: but lett mee the Lord because he hath heard my cry answerd my request.

My Towne also rather then I should goe from them, seeing some likely hood of the same, agreed to raise mee for that yeare. 10li. more which was payd in with about perhaps: 10s. lesse But now I layd downe my Lecture which I had kept unto this day.

September. 20: I joyned with Mr Wharton in a day of humiliacon at my Lady Edens[2] and while wee were praying, god was blessing our forces in that great fight neare Newbery, where the E of Essex had the better against the Kings forces.

I went on in my constant course of preaching, since good god was blessed to doe by mee. our divisions were sad about church—Government. the Lord in his due time cause our breaches to praise his name.

Our Freinds at olny were miserably plundered at olny: and I lay in peace without disturbance and my family the Lord make me walke answerable to his mercy.

october. 29: Lords day at night, as light as if the moone had shone I never beheld the like, lett thy truth oh lord shine beyond darke errors.

In November stanway me(n) made mee a proffer of the sequestracion: I yeelded not they gott it for mee, yett I did not accept of the same, oh Lord my desire is to serve thee in Colne if it please thee, I seeke not great things, only blesse me with thy grace and mine, and make mee an instrument to doe good to the soules of others:

December. 29: Or towards Morning december: 30 indeed; 2 houres before day; being Satturday morning my wife was deliverd of her son: which Jan: 14: was baptized by the name of Thomas: Mr Tho: Harlakenden and my Aunt Shepheard were his wittnesses, god gave my deare wife strength to nurse, health, both to her selfe

[1] Quotidian: an intermittent fever or ague (see p. 7, n. 5 above) which occurs daily; tertian ague is characterized by a paroxysm every third (i.e. every alternate) day; quartan agues occur every fourth (in modern reckoning, every third) day. SOED.

[2] Mary, second wife and widow of Sir Thomas Eden of Ballingdon, Essex; one of her sons, John, married Anne, daughter of Richard Harlakenden of EC. Wright, i, pp. 551–2.

and babe, wee were scared with our Chamber chimney Hearth firing but espying it in time it was prevented from any great hurt. this was agreat mercy: so hath god kept mee upon my way. by land and water, prevented falls from Horse, preserved mee in falling, for which oh my soule bee thankefull,

1644: March: 29: keeping a day of Humiliacon[1] at my Lady Honywoods[2] while wee were praying god was making Waller victorious over Hopton, neare Alsford; and turned backe the forces of Rupert that wee feared would have come on after they had routed our forces at Newarke, [oh] the sonnes of Jacob never seeke the Lord in vayne: Going in April. to Cranham I was taken ill with a cold which sadly afflicted mee for about 3 weekes, but god delivered mee, and gave mee more health, and cheerefulnes and content in himselfe, wife, children, his wayes, my people then formerly; so that my earnest desire is still towards them.

July: first weeke I rid forth to Sir Tho: Honywoods Regiment. to Newport Pannell. Northampton to the Randevow of Sir Will: Waller and Major Browne, neare Geton Pastures, visited my freinds and came home safe, my wife family freinds and all in Health, many things I have omitted that may be found in my notes, almanacks: etc. But now henceforwards I shall be more

August: exact and particular, thus much to this present day. Aug: 8: 1644:

5. I have bought a part in a shippe it cost mee 14^{li}. 10^{s}. god send mee good speed with the same I have sent my part in a bagge of hops to Sunderland, my sister Mary is come under my Roofe as a servant, but my respect is and shall be towards her as a sister, god might have made mee a waiter upon others, our former Mayde Lydia Weston having dwelt with mee 1. yeare and almost 3 quarters marryed into our Towne, the first that marryed out of my family. the plague that arrow of death is sadly at Colchester, brought by a woman that came to visitt her freinds, their have already divers dyed; what a mercy of god is it to respite our Towne Lord spare it, and lett not our sins, our covetousnes and pride of the poore in the plenty of their Dutch worke[3] cause thee to bee angry with us, I

[1] A public day of fasting and prayer, prescribed by the State.

[2] Lady Hester Honywood, of Markshall just to the south of EC. RJ had many contacts with this staunchly parliamentary family, whose genealogy is sketched in Appendix 1. Samuel Pepys also knew the Honywoods well, for they used his father's house as their London lodgings (Pepys, i, p. 181 and p. 220 n.).

[3] These were the new draperies, bays, and says, introduced by Dutch immigrants in the 1560s. From at least the 1580s there were problems in EC with fluctuations in the cloth trade upon which many of the villagers were heavily dependent. J. E. Pilgrim, 'The Rise of the "New Draperies" in Essex', *Univ. Birmingham Hist. Jnl.* vii (1958–9), describes this rural industry.

heard from my Mother at Olny of her present health, and also of my sisters, the spotted fever[1] is in towne with them wherof divers have dyed Lord show thy mercy towards them and us in our preservacion make us wise to number our latter ends that wee may apply our selves to true wisedome:

Aug: 12: God good to mee all the weeke last past, in my health, in my estate, comforts, freinds: in my family my deare wife and babes, mercifull in carrying mee on in my calling; enabling mee for his Sabbath, wheron I made my last mocion (in respect of present resolucion) to my parish, to be carefull to gather up my meanes for mee that I might not want; if they did not though I shall not cease to love them, yett I must of necessity then serve providence in another place; Lord stirre up their hearts to embrace this offer if you have a will to use mee here, if not, I am thine, thy will be done, And now Lord I confesse my selfe unworthy of this goodnes in many respects, especially my carriage towards thee, make mee more painfull and dilligent in my place, and profitable, more cheerfull and contented in my famyly. helpe mee and heale mee, I blesse thee for delivering mee from gross wickednes: keepe me by thy power to salvacion

Aug: 19: This weeke I heard from divers of my freinds of their healthfull condicon, a great mercy, the Lord continue it and give a heart to use it to his glory: Aug: 15. god called me to preach at Coggeshall, and enabled mee with strength for the same, kept me going and returning; that day wee buryd two neighbours[2] and afterwards had communion and godly conference with divers of my christian Neighbours and freinds god was good to mee in all my outward injoyments, in wife, children, our health, in peace and plenty in actions and dutyes, good to mee in enabling mee for the Sabbath: And now Lord I blesse thy Holy name in all thy love to mee, harden my great unworthynes, deadnes, drowsynes of spirit, the sins of all my dutyes, neglects, my unevennes in any particular towards thee my family, people, country, sanctify mee, and in christ accept mee.

26: Aug: This weeke my sister Hannah came over to mee, I sent her away in some hopes to helpe her about her house, and with some expressions of love, lord remember mee and mine (and) hers in mercy. Aug: 20: being with my men when they layd the hall

[1] Spotted fever: specifically typhus. NED.

[2] The EC parish register (henceforth PR) gives under this date, 15 August, the burials of John Read, senior, householder, and the wife of Thomas Pryor.

floore and [pulling] downe the walls for the doore, an hand-saw which was used against mee, missed m[y] face very narrowly, Lord make me to prise that mercy, the plague continued and increased at (Col)chester, our towne yett in safety Lord keepe that distroying arrow from among us. / times now ve[ry] sickly Ed. Clarke my Christian freind taken sicke and very neare death, divers in our towne and others sickly. Lord Sanctify thy hand to them, my wife suddenly ill, yett through mercy well agayne, Mr Nettles of Lexden[1] carryed through towne in a coach deprived of his sense, and very mad as they reported. god good to mee and mine yett in our health and senses oh that wee might use them to his glory(,) leaping over the pales[2] I scratched my face, but god bee praisd I had no further hurt though I might if providence had not preservd mee, and also in our fall when my wife and I pulling downe a tree with a rope with our pulling all fell togither, but no hurt god bee praised: such falls my children have many times and yett safe Mary fell out of the Parlour window with her face against the bench and had no hurt, a strange providence all the witt of the world could not have given such a fall and preserved from hurt to god bee the praise. / all this weeke god was good to mee in health, in family and in many mercyes. pardon Lord my great sins, and heale my soule, make mee more content and satisfyed in my condicon, more usefull and profitable in my places, familye, blesse mee and us all with thy feare and favour.

Aug: 21: wee kept a day of humiliacon at Goodman Mayers to beseech god for ourselves and brethren in all mercyes needfull for soules and bodyes: god good to me in opening extempore Ruth: 1: Lord I will waite upon the(e) for all promised mercyes and for an answer of our prayers: I listen oh speake grace and peace to us: divers of our christian freinds then with(in) us within two or three dayes taken sicke in thes feverishe times:

Aug: 27: A dronkard came into my house, lord thy name be blessed in keeping mee from that sin; I chid him he seemed apprehensive of what I sayd the lord amend him and pardon this sin to him and sanctify him was the publike day of humiliacion god good to mee

Aug: 28: in carrying mee on through the same with strength, the Lord make

[1] Stephen Nettles of Lexden and Steeple. He was described by Wood as being 'dispossessed by force of arms', though he was not finally ejected until 1645. He was charged on 16 August 1644 before the County Committee for frequenting taverns, behaving indecently with several women, neglecting fast days, and other offences, though the DNB gives a more complimentary account of him. DNB; Walker; Smith.

[2] Pales: a fence. SOED.

his word effectuall upon me and my people, and grant that wee may worke with god and prevaile with him for the naciu(n) and mercyes for familyes for soule and body. /

September 1: This weeke besides particulars before god was good to mee in my health, and in my familyes. and in preserving our towne from the plague, in keeping our sicke neare the grave from falling into the same, in the hopes of raysing some up againe, lord sanctify thy hand to us all, my Freinds[1] Mr Benton and his wife with us which shortned my time for studdy, yett god inabled mee in some measure for the Sabbath, god good to me in my course towards my family Lord keepe us in perfect peace all the day long, subdue my corruptions, my sister Mary received her things from Walden which wee feard had miscarryed, Lord blesse mee in all my wayes, direct mee by thy spirit, helpe mee agaynst vaine thoughts and imaginacions and preserve mee and mine, god gave us very good newes this weeke, wee h(e)ard of divers hopkills[2] burnt downe at Captain Chipburnes,[3] and Knights of Hinningham, wee preserved from fire, Lord still keepe us. wee heard the lost shippe belonging to Colchester was taken by the Irish rebells richly laden, Lord preserve ours in the waves; —oh bee my god and of my spouse, and our seeds after us, fitt mee for my calling and condicon, and blesse me in the same. / I heard my Cosin Abrahams sonne was dead; my Cousin Benton miscarryed and now through mercy up againe, Lord lett thes things cause mee to (my) love the my god who sparest mine and dealest more gently with mine. and sanctify thy hand to them.

September: 1: On Monday it was related unto mee that Mr Pilgrim[4] Minister of Wormingford fell downe dead in his pulpitt *(*, he was an honest man but very weakly and sickly*)* he dyed not outright but their was expected no great hopes of his life: Lord thou keepest mee, oh keepe mee in a gratious and watchfull frame that you mayst find mee about thy worke when you shall call mee

S. 3: Visited a sicke man one Guy Penhacke who was much troubled in minde upon his life; he had strong temptacions from Sathan. I urged him to a Covenant with god to bee a new man if he recovered the Lord sanctify his hand to him and make me carefull of my

[1] Either his father's sister Mary and her husband John, or their son Jeremy and his wife. See Appendix 1 for the Josselin genealogy. Here, as elsewhere, RJ uses 'friend' as equivalent to kin.

[2] Hopkill: a kiln for drying hops. NED.

[3] Captain Hanameel Chipborne of Messing Hall. Wright, i, pp. 385–6.

[4] Thomas Pilgrim, vicar of Wormingford, Essex, 1608–44; Josselin later bought his library. Venn.

conversacion, oh how sadly is the Soulel(d) afflicted that in death hath its sins a dreadfull load, and apprehends not mercy but justice alone in god. /

Sept: 4: Mr Will: Harlakenden and my brother Jeremy came from the army to us; in good health preserved from so many dangers, by enemies and sicknesses, Lord sanctify that hand of thine unto them.

5: Stung I was with a bee on my nose, I presently pluckt out the sting, and layd on honey, so that my face swelled not, thus divine providence reaches to the lowest things. lett not sin oh Lord that dreadfull sting bee able to poyson mee.

6: Liberty of the sermon at Halstead. Sir Tho: Honywood, gave mee great respect for my love in going forth with him towards the army, payd my ordinary[1] for mee. I heard that a child in the towne was burnt almost to death, and mine safe oh mercy and goodnes to bee adored.

Sept: 8: This weeke the Lord gratious unto mee in my wife and children, in our peace our health providing for us, in keeping us in some measure in his feare, and from the evills my heart is subject unto, our people that were weake and like to dye through mercy are upwards agayne, the Lord keepe them and strengthen them and lett them walke to his glory I heard vile things of one E.C.[2] which I should not have beleived, god in mercy keepe mee and mine from the like, Lord pardon all my sins, Sabbath and weeke day and fitt mee to doe thee more honour in my place, and keepe my heart in a dependance upon thee in all condicons, and lett mee not be lead away with any passions.

Sept: 9: In a breviat of Archbishop. laudes life[3] I find how the strings of his legge brake without any stepping awry. Lord how many sad wrinches have I had in my walking, and yett thou / hast preserved mee, let thy gratious protection be still over me for good.

This day I heard the dolefull newes of the E. of Essex his losse in the West, all his ordnance and ammunicon being a prey to the enemy, it was a sad providence, and speakes our sins aloude and gods continuing his displeasure in lengthening the warre, yett oh my heart be encouraged in the Lord he is the same still, and the time of the enemyes ruine is not one houre the(e) farther of for this

[1] Ordinary: an eating-house or tavern, or meals provided at it. SOED.

[2] Probably Edward Cressener of EC rather than Edward Clarke of the same; see under these names in Appendix 2 for their biographies.

[3] William Prynne, *A Breviate of the Life of William Laud* (1644), a mutilated edition of Laud's 'Diary'.

there successe, nay it may bee their blasphemyes shall hasten their ruine as it did Rabshakehs[1] and his Masters. Lord worke for thy own glorious name sake and lett it not become a reproach to them that feare thee not.

S. 10: Mr Michel[2] with mee, his wife was alive; it was reported shee and hee were both dead of the plag[ue.] he had much trouble about a sequestracion to attayne the same,

11: Gods mercy in using mee at the funerall of a good woman Garrad[3] by name, the Lord good to mee in eaysing up my heart in Christ above the feares of death, Lord keepe my heart their and fixe it upon thee continually. /

Septem: 12: They say dreames declare a mans Temperament, this night I dreamd I was wondrous passion with a man that wrongd mee and my child insomuch as I was ashamed of my selfe, god in mercy keepe mee from that evill, in the day, I did that and that in passion for which I was sorry. but I desire thee oh Lord to keepe mee for my passions are too strong for mee,

September. 14: I rid to Colchester, my horse stumbled god preserved mee from danger, god was pleased to give mee good dispatch in my busynes for the towne to the whole committee;[4] Sir Tho: Honywood payd my ordinary for mee. I had conference with Mr Ellis; he told mee separacion from the true church was lawfull in some cases; as being not rightly constituted; so did Luther from the papists and yett there was a true church among them wee from the Lutherans, whom wee owne as churches. and so the independents from us: in their controversy their are 2 things considerable. the matter of which are church consists, visible Saints and then that the government of the church bee within its owne body and bulke; but grant thes two and I see no reason but by mutuall consent wee may erect classes to assist particular congregacions in poin[t] of government[5] as I came home I heard our shippe was returned safe from Sunderland, the plague is wee hope almost

[1] A servant of the King of Assyria who blasphemed the God of Hezekiah, King of Judah; the angel of the Lord destroyed the Assyrian army. See Isaiah ch. 37 and 2 Kings ch. 18.

[2] William Mitchell, rector of Chickney. The living was sequestered to Thomas Archer in 1645. Smith, pp. 281, 360.

[3] There is no burial recorded in the PR, though Garrad was a common EC name.

[4] The Committee for the sequestration of scandalous ministers in Essex, set up by the Earl of Manchester in February 1644. The members included many of RJ's acquaintances, among them Sir Thomas Honywood, Henry Mildmay, Richard Harlakenden, Thos Cooke, and Robert Crane. Smith, p. 116.

[5] The theological controversy alluded to here is discussed at length in Nuttall and the practical aspects in Smith.

stayd at Colchester, the Lords name bee praised for ever Lord teach me to love thee.

September. 15. This weeke the Lord gratious to mee and mine in our health, (only my wife somewhat ill,) and children much comfort, and plenty in our condicon, inward peace, preservacion from greivous outward sins, assistance to walke in his feare, helpe for Sabbath, Lord whatsoever is evill in mee and mine pardon in this weeke and all others, and keepe me in thy feare continually. Goodman Clarke praised bee god is now up and walking about againe. my brother[1] returned to the army againe this was sad weeke for the affayres of the kingdome, the Lord can give a turne when it pleases him: and on him wee will wayte for the same.

Sept: 17: Rid to Sudbury, god good to mee outwards and homewards, and in the seasonablenes of the ordinance,[2] god accomplishing every thing in its time, I say. 60. ult:[3] I injoyed the sight of divers of my good freinds, when I came home my good Freind Mr Har: had sold one bagge of hops for mee wherin I was advantaged 1^{li}. 15^{s}. this was gods good providence.

19. A *day* of sad tydings, but it pleased god most proved false.

20: Mary in danger by a horse preserved, injoyd the oppurtunity of the lecture at Halsted. when affliction (are upon) us we should more earnestly seeke god. powre out prayers: I injoyd the company of my freinds my brother Smith and peacocke and their wives;

21: A great part of the night my wife was very ill, it pleased god it passed over. shee slept and was very well the next morning.

Septem: 22: This weeke God was good to mee and mine, in our healthe, peace, estate, the Lord kept mee from grosse sins, good in the Society of my freinds, in enabling and carrying me through[?] on which we had a collection for one Hastivile a French Baron that forsooke the popish religion and all his honours for the Protestant religion; I might have beene a beggar whereas I am yett a giver; Lord pardon the sins of this weeke, Sanctify mee and keepe mee in thy feare give mee more love and zeale dayly / for thy name and honour.

September: 23: I heard that Major Cletheroe,[4] September: 21. coming homewards at Redgewell his Horse stumbled and fell downe upon him, and brake his bowells, he was taken up and spake but he dyed

[1] Brother: i.e. brother-in-law.

[2] Ordinance: a practice or usage authoritatively enjoined or prescribed, especially a religious or ceremonial observance. SOED.

[3] Ult: at the latest. Possibly referring to the year 1660.

[4] A member of the Essex Committee for the Eastern Association. Kingston, p. 385.

about 4 or 5 houres after, Lord in how many dangerous falls and stumbles hast thou preserved mee, how often have I gone forth and returned home safe againe, thy name have the praise and glory, Lord still watch over mee and keepe mee and bee my safety and protection. /

Sept: 24: The kitchin boy at priory had a fall upon his brow and broke it, yett was his eye preserved; Mrs Church throwing out a bason of water, threw her selfe out of her doore she had a sad fall, yett god preserved her from any great hurt oh how doe gods angells keepe us in many dangers(.) wee began this day to putt the County into a posture of defence; it will cost mee an armes; Lord blesse us and make us looke up unto thee to be strength to all our meanes and endeavours.

Sept: 25. Was a day of publique humiliacon; it would make a man bleede to see how regardles people are of the same nothing moves them. affect me that others are not affected. god good to me in the same in performance of my place, acceptance in Christ and cover my weaknes; and lett us find that wee prevayle with god; a load of wool was passing upon the road our men stopt the same, oh that men would give an outward reverence to the worship of the Lords. /

26: My wife and I rid to Wethersfeild and from thence to Bumpsted, saw our freinds in health, gods good providence was over us for good: 27: rid to Clare injoyd the lecture, saw my aunt who is going againe into the troubles, Lord keepe her, my uncle shepheard had a fall from his Horse, wee came safe home found our children well, oh that I could be thankefull unto the Lord for this his goodnes. /

Sept: 29. This weeke the Lord good to mee in my health, I had a litle cold but it was not much, and in the health and outward mercyes of and to my family, in preserving mee from grosse sins; in many comforts in my freinds and family, in good newes to his people, in helping mee in the Sabbath, oh Lord what shall I returne the(e)! how shall I bee thankfull! make mee to take warning that I come not with that condicion of them that reject the Lord; accept mee in thy Christ forgive mee all my sins and make me active for thy glory continually.

30: This day I putt of John Layes hops to good advantage if I am dealt well withall, sad newes in our divisions the Kings coming to oxford. god can turne it to good: it proved false.

October. 1: I rid to Wethersfeild injoyd the company of good freinds. saw some manuscripts of things in K James and Charles his time of consequence; I had their a good bargaine of bookes(,) god good to mee in keeping mee safe from stumbling and falling, and from hurt at Gosfeild gate. where my Horse rushd my foote upon the gatepost.

3: God good to mee in my jorney to Colchester homewards and outwards: in Colchester I saw a child beate downe with the packe of an horse and the horse passed by without doing it any hurt, their were 2 brothers mett that had beene at difference divers yeares, and their was no likelyhood of making peace betwixt them, wee for our part could doe nothing in the busines though I did Labour the same, their I payd. 4^s. excise for 2 bagges of hoppes. much love in my freinds the commissioners who payd my ordinary for mee. /

October. 6. This weeke the Lord good to mee and mine in our peace, plenty, health in all outward mercyes and favours, the Lord kept mee in his feare, watchd over mee in divers jorneyes and actions yett was I negligent in dutyes towards him: this day I publishd and exhorted subscriptions for Sir Will: Bretheton[1] that noble Cheshire Gentleman: I cannot blesse god over all my people only indeed a few contributed those that did, did it voluntarily, god good to me in helping mee through the worke of the day, giving mee an heart to cast in my mite Lord pardon my sins and sanctify mee, enable mee to live this weeke better than ever. /

I now gave over to gather my quarters my selfe,[2] I left that worke to the Towne; divers brought up their quarters for their owne particulars, but I would not receive them. I doe not perceive the towne intends to stirre in it; gods will be done I am content. /

Oct: 7: In the morning I went out and god gave mee more than the day before I layd out in the publique(,) I never found I lost any thing by imploying my selfe that way but god sent mee in more by my freinds beside the comfort in my conscience to have done in his cause(,) I went up to Goodman Bridges and bought his hops at an easy rate. I was used there kindly. when I came home Stissted men where with mee about their reference to Mr Boroughs[3] and my selfe, whether Mr Archer or Mr Templer had the clearer call to their Towne:[4] I found god had gratiously kept my daughter

[1] Sir William Bretherton, 1604–61, a parliamentary commander in Chester. DNB.

[2] The quarterly payment of tithe in kind or cash.

[3] Thomas Burrowes of Pebmarsh, later chaplain to Colonel Cooke at the siege of Colchester. Smith, pp. 132, 159, 167, 297.

[4] Thomas Templar was appointed and was at Stisted by September 1645, though Thomas Clark had replaced him by 1648 (Smith, *Clergy*, p. 59). It is not clear whether RJ here, and later, is referring to William Archer, lecturer at Halstead, and minister until 1648 (Smith, *Clergy*, p. 46), or Thomas Archer, rector of Chickney 1646–60 (Calamy; Venn).

Mary who was strucke with a Horse her apron rent of with his nayles. and her handchercheife rent and yett shee had no hurt, many thought shee had been spoyled. the Lord he appoints his angels to keepe his from hurt. Lord keepe her for thine and let us never forgett the same, goodwife Bridge broke her kneepan with a litle fall upon her knee:

9: Att Halsted, Mr Borough and I mett upon Stissted busynes, about a minister for them. the towne was divided, and would not condiscend one to another, oh Wofull, sad divisions, god was good to mee homewards and outwards.

11: Went to my Lady Honywoods, disappoynted in my expectacion to have joyned with them in a day of humiliacon but it was putt of, my Lady had a man that broke his shoulder with a fall from his horse, my loving neighbour goodman Burton escaped a great danger his mare kickt him backwards upon his belly. it begun to swell, oh gods protection and providence to be adored; my wife and sister and sonne finely well, the Lord be praised who the day and night before were very ill, oh my god remember them for good. thou hast been good to my family, continue so still.

October. 13: This weeke the Lord was good to mee and mine, in our peace, plenty. continuance of our health, and in restoring us to it in some measures, in food, rayment, in all outward mercyes, in inward peace, in preservacon from grosse sins; in the light of his countenance, in continuing tendernes of Spirit, in the Sabbath, he was good to mee; exhorted to Contribucions for Sir Will. Brereton obtayned, a litle, whatsoever I have done that is not right in thy eyes lord pardon the same.

14: a frost and snow, very cold. I rid to Stisted to assist in the choyse of their minister, both parts stiffe; divided, a most sad towne, no care almost of any thing, I spoke to them but could not drawe it to a conclusion though I hope to a good forwardnes; Mr Alstone[1] made a serious offer to mee of 10^{li}. out of his owne purse, and great likelyhood to carry it if I would yeeld to them but I would not, I was ingaged in the busynes and therefore would not endeavour any such thing to my selfe: the place hath 140 acres of glebe and the tith are worth about 100^{li}. per annum. god good to mee outwards and homewards; this day Mr Newbold received our money for Sir Will: Brereton, this day invited and promised to assist in a day of humiliacion at Markeshall:

16: Rid to Markeshall joyned in a day of humiliacon injoyd the labours

[1] Probably Lestrange Alstone, landowner in Stisted. Wright, ii, p. 15.

of Mr Carr[1] and Mr Symkins[2] it was so late that I could not exercise, god good to mee outwards and homewards; lord pardon the sins of this day, accept, answer be gratious and lett us find it in thyne and our wayes to the(e).

17: receivd in 3 bags of hops from Goodman Bridge at 40^{s}. the hundred the weight was 7 hundred and 3 quarters goodman Burton run a share with mee.

18: Spent part of the day at Goodman Clarke in settling matters betwixt Mr Harlakenden and him. at night Mr Commissary generall[3] was with us told us my Lord Manchester was advancing towards the King. their is expectacion of a battle god goe along with us and blesse us and wee have enough.

19: This day 3 of my townesmen made an entrance in gathering the towne contribucon it ought to bee at the least 5^{li}., every quarter, and yett I shall not make much above 70^{li}. per annum. wee resolved to try what the Parliament would doe for us, for the augmentacion of our small living.

Oct: 20. This day the Lord was good to mee and mine, in our peace, plenty. estate, freinds health, in food and rayment, in dutyes, in the Sabbath, in some measure enlarging my spirit in the worke, in preserving mee and mine from grosse sins, and dangers, what hath beene amisse in mee Lord pardon and forgive, Mr Faringdon here, he sayd he would endeavour to satisfy Henry Abbat, god grant it may, I love no quarrells, I seeke peace, but I will not offend god to gayne the same.

23: This day I injoyd at dinner the society of Mr Faringdon; I saw a yong rooke that fell out of the nest in the priory yard this day, I have not knowne the like in all my dayes that they should build and breed at this time of the yeare.

24: Heard from my deare freind Mr Harlakenden from Cambridge, this day I begun to practice dayly in Hebrew and greeke. god blesse mee therein that thereby I may come to more perfect knowledge of the sense of the scripture.

Octob: 27: This weeke god was good to mee and mine in our peace, plenty, health, freinds, estate, food and rayment, in dutyes, in the Sabbath, standing by mee in a gratious manner for the same in

[1] Gamaliel Carr, rector of Markshall 1642–6, probably ejected from Lambourne *c.* 1660. Smith, p. 366.

[2] No such minister can be located in any of the standard sources; possibly a mistake for one of the many ministers named Simmonds.

[3] William Harlakenden of EC, Commissionary General to the Earl of Manchester. See Appendix 1 for the Harlakenden genealogy.

preserving mee from grosse sins, I have many unworthinesses I humbly intreate the(e) pardon and forgivenes of the same, enable mee in my calling faithfully to serve thee, my deare litle sonne is now very ill, my god I hope and trust will raise him up to his former health, I hope its nothing but breeding teeth. /

28: A day of our marriage entring our 5[t] yeare, god good to mee in that relacon blessed bee his name forever, my sonne well again, god good to mee in society with my loving freinds. Mr Farringdon made an offer to imploy some moneyes for mee. which I take thankefully: I spoke to goodman Abbutt he seemes more reasonable than formerly god sanctify his hand upon him for good.

29: bought 2 pigges for 9[s]. the first beasts that ever I bought in all my dayes hitherto;

30: Day of Publique himiliacion. god good to mee in the same, the good Lord in mercy accept us and pardon and answer in Jesus Christ his annointed, wee longd to heare of the saving us in the west.

31: I heard the report of our successe against the Kings forces,[1] oh lett god have the glory of our deliverances

Nov: 1: God good to mee in the society of a deare freind, Mr F: in the lecture at Halsted; in hearing from Mr H: my kind freind of his good health, and the victory of our forces in Lincolneshire; Crane home safe who was abroad along time: good to mee in freinds at night:

2: great expressions of kindnes from Mrs H: there is of gods love to mee in all my mercyes.

Nov: 3: This weeke god was good to mee in my health, and in the health of wife, children and sister, in our peace, plenty, for soule and body praised bee his name in many mercyes and comforts, in the Sabbath, Lord pardon all my sins accept mee in thy christ and delight in mee and mine continually.

4: concerning the increase of our living by the Parliament there was no hope from them for the present,[2] all that was to bee done was to be expected from the Impropriator. and that was Mr H: I cannot thinke he will mount higher than he hath already done, gods will bee done, this is my comfort I have endeavord the good of the towne in it I am content with a nay and so I should with a yea:

[1] The second battle of Newbury, 27 October. Gardiner, i, pp. 501–7.

[2] After the dissolution of the monasteries there were many Impropriate Rectories in the possession of laymen, as well as others belonging to Bishops, etc. If the impropriator was hostile, then the rents reserved were at the disposal of Parliament. The Committee for Plundered Ministers made grants for increases in the maintenance of ministers with poor livings out of these. These were called augmentations, and were recognized by an ordinance of both Houses of Parliament, 2 May 1646. Smith, p. 200.

blessed bee my god. one old Turner 84 y. old, dwelling in the house with one Markham a separatist, this day drowned himselfe,[1] Lord thy judgments are secret and righteous keepe thou mee and mine I humbly intreate thee,

5. This day god was good to mee in the publike exercise and in the society of loving freinds, Lord remember our bloudy enemies make us to remember thee, thy mercyes and serve thee with them. /

9: This day I injoyed the society of my deare Freind Mr H: who came home from the committee to spend a Sabbath with us. and then returne, told us of a man in Some, Camb: that is about 150 yeares old who had 6 wives 32 children, and very lately carryed 2 comes[2] of pease: 2 furlongs: 8 bushels a quarter of a mile,

Nov: 10: This weeke the Lord was gratious to mee and mine in our health, plenty, peace inward and outward comfort, Freinds, I and my wife were both ill in our stomaches, many are very ill, yett god he preserved mee and mine blessed be his name, god good to mee in the Sabbath exercises, Lord humble mee and pardon and accept me in thy christ: I heard our ship was come home safe more mercy yett. Mr H. was with us at home; read an order wherby alehouses are in the power of the well affected and the minister of the parish:

11: God good to mee this day in the society of divers loving Freinds.
☞ heard of the wellfare and preservation of my friends about Olny for which god be praysed: Mary my daughter was preserved from hurt by the fall of a waynescott doore at the priory, thy name Lord be praised; my deare Freind Mr F: children tooke their leave of us. the Lord goe along with them and blesse them; this day I counted 50li. to him to improve for mee. The Lord blesse it for the good of my family, he that endeavours not their good is worse than an infidell. /

12: This day Mr F: my loving and deare Freind departed from the towne, and this day I received a bill of his hand for the mony he received last night of mee. the Lord prosper him and his:

13: In the night, my wife awaked by the child, found her sonne had a most sad cold ready even to stoppe him up. So had my daughter, but that wee knew of, but not of his, this putt her into such a feare that shee was even at deaths doore, the morning through mercy was more comfortable to us all.

15. This day gods good providence was towards our towne in generall

[1] No record in PR, but probably Clement Turner of EC, whose wife was buried in 1641 and who was almost 83 years old according to the PR.

[2] Comes: coomb or comb, a measure of corn containing four bushels. SOED.

it being a boysterous high winde and towards James Niccols in particular, whose servant brewing and having much steame in the kitchin being gone out it fired, burnt vehemently, begun to kindle in the boards and woodworke but it being espyed it was timously through gods mercy quenched and stayed.

☞ Three of my parishioners. Rob: Carter, John Read. Rich: Appleton gathered up Michaelmas quarter; instead of 5^{li}. they brought mee 3^{li}. 0^{s}. 1^{d}. divers refuse to pay. divers used them crossely. insomuch as they were much discouraged. I am beholding to them yett for their particular love. /

November: 17: This weeke god exercised mee and my family with some illnes. yett for my part: god was pleased speedily to remove it, and so in great part my wives, only a faintnes continues with her. my left eyelid at one corner workes and twinkles very much, I hope my god will preserve my sight safe unto mee, my children both ill with colds, yett chearly. there is a sweett mixture of mercy and goodnes in all gods wayes to us,

the Lord good in my peace and plenty in the worke of the Sabbath his assistance, Lord blesse my poore endeavors to the people for god. fitt mee for my place and accept of mee in discharge of the same, pardon my sins bee my god in covenant and the god of my seed.

Nov: 20: we kept a day of humiliacon at Mr Cresseners; god good to mee in the duty and day and in discourse upon Psal: 32.12. Lord make mee the blessed man there mentiond, and pardon my sins, and purge me from all guile, lord wee looke up to thee to speake peace to us lord doe it for thy names sake, lett my lusts bee subdued. at night I injoyd the society of my deare Freind Mr H. who returned from the Commitee at Cambridge.

Nov: 24: All this weeke god exercised us with colds. I had a rheume in my eye, and in my necke that did a litle breake out, my wife and son had great colds, my daughter prettyly well recovered, the Lord gave us but a litle affliction, and a multitude of mercy and loving kindnes: lord doe thou sanctify thy hand to us, his mercy we are not consumed, god good to mee and mine in our healths generally, peace, plenty, in his ordinances in the Sabbath, oh that I could love and feare him for he is my god(,) pardon my sins and fitt mee to honour the(e) more every day than other,

27: A day of publike humiliacon, the Lord was good to mee in the same, the good Lord heare accept and answer in mercy, our proposicons for peace are gone to the King. the good Lord in mercy send a good end for his names sake:

28. Mr W: Harlakenden, Comissary generall to the E. of Manch: was with us in good health, I was at Sir J: Jacobs,[1] he went backe in some part from his promise to mee, but I knowe no remedye. /

December: 1: All this weeke the Rheume continued in my eye, sometimes worse than other, yett allwayes very gentle, god was good to us all in our healths, my children well recoverd from their colds only my sonne is somewhat troubled with ringe wormes but they dye, god good to me in Sabbath Lord pardon my sins and accept mee continue thy love to mee.

3: Mr H. went towards London god prosper him, heard sad newes of the E. of Manchester, I hope its false. god good to me in conference, with my people at goodman Clarkes. /

6: god good to me in the society of loving Freinds; heard that Tho: Prentis was almost kild with a kicke by his horse, Lord sanctify this sad hand of thine to him and mee, my sonne Tho: now would walke up and downe the house of his owne accord, he wants above 3 weekes of a yeare old.

Decemb: 8: All this weeke the Rheume continued in both my eyes, yett very gently; god good to us in our health, peace, in estate and comforts, presevacons from dangers; god was good to me in the Sabbath in the dutyes thereof, Lord pardon my sins and accept mee in Jesus Christ: god good to mee in company of my loving uncle Richard and in many other mercyes, Lord what shall I returne thee for all thy love: all that I am Lord is thine, fitt mee to use all to thy glory.

10: My Lady Honywood sent us tokens,[2] shee invited mee to a day of humiliacion there, but I could not for many occasions:

11: Dind at a strange vaine wedding a poore man gave curious ribbands to all, gloves to the women and to the ringers, yett their was very good company.

13: My Uncle Richard went from us, my brother Thomas with mee, I blesse god who inables mee to give to him, my sister not well, god hath visited her with much sicknes, Lord sanctify it, and my health, my eyes better. I pray with a perswasion to be heard. Mr H: returned safe, heard of the wellfare of my brother Jeremy: the strange vote of the house of Commons to call home their members.[3]

Decemb: 15: All this weeke god was good to mee and mine in inward

[1] Sir John Jacob of Stansted Hall, Halstead, and West Wratting in Cambridgeshire had bought an estate of 370 acres in Earls Colne and consequently owed tithes there. Morant, ii, pp. 212, 256.

[2] Tokens: small presents; often given at Christmas and New Year.

[3] The first Self-Denying Ordinance, sent up to the Lords on 19 December. Gardiner, ii, pp. 29–32.

and outward mercyes; in my health in my sight when I began to pray with confidence my eyes mended, oh that I could see the sweet answer of prayer and be thankefull, god good in the Sabbath carrying me on in the same to him bee glory. I gatherd liberally for a poore Ministers widdow who was plunderd and housband slaine Lord I blesse thy name for the mercy, oh tis of goodnes that it was not my condicon before this day. pardon all my sins in Jesus Christ, in whom accept mee for in him I give up myselfe to bee thine in all thy services oh my god accept mee;

Dec: 18: this day my noble freind Mr Harl: was made Major of the Horse by the Country and my good freind Captaine Haynes Major of the foote, the contry did acquitt themselves very well in the choise and worke of the day in my estimacion.

20: This day Mr H. with us and my brother Jeremy, who hath been very sicke but now through mercy well recoverd, I lent him 20^{s}. he and his Master both are gone towards London

December 22: All this weeke god was good to mee and mine, in our health peace, plenty, in inward comforts in the society of divers loving Freinds; in the Sabbath, in enabling mee and helping me in the day. I made a serious exhortacion to lay aside the jollity and vanity of the time that custome hath wedded us unto, and to keepe the Sabbath, better which is the only Lords day wee are commanded to observe Lord pardon the many sins of this weeke, and accept mee in thy Christ my blessed redeemer,

December 25. This day of jollity by providence was a fast day, the Lord was good to mee in the same the Lord my god in mercy pardon my faylings here as for the nacion and accept of us.

28: As I was riving a ledge and forcing in 3 wedges togither, the midle one with the force of the blow flew out and strucke me in the shinne yett so did gratious providence dispose, that it scarce broke the skyn; it might have proved sad to mee; my sonne was held out of the fire by his litle sister, who held and cryed untill I came to him. Heard of the wellfare of my loving freind Mr F. and his family. the Lord be praisd: he sent my wife good remmembrance of his love, a kind letter and 4 sugar loaves.

29: All this weeke god was good to mee and mine in our health, peace plenty. the Lord upheld mee in my ways, resolved my spirit against the vanity and superstition of the times. And by me in the worke of the Sabbath Lord pardon and accept mee.

30: This day god was good to mee in the society of my loving freinds, Mr Sawyer gave mee testimony of his acceptance of my engagement for him at Halsted, a sad accident at Cogshall one shott into the breast with a peice, likely to dye: the Lord good to mee and mine in our preservacions.

Jan: 1: This day god good to mee in conference with divers of my people and others at J: Clarks, the Lord good in divers expressions of love from others to mee, in the society of my freinds at home at board with mee,

3: A most tedious snowy day: the greatest snow in my memory all wayes made even impassable, God good to mee at night in the society of divers loving freinds abroad.

Jan: 4. This weeke the Lord was good to mee and mine in our healths, peace, plenty, in preservacon from dangers: lord pardon all my sins, humble my heart in all my faylings. make mee alwaye(s) mindfull of thee in my wayes, the Lord good to mee in the Sabbath, assisting mee, his name bee praised: at night it frize most bitterly, yett before morning it raind and thawd apace, a good providence; if this had beene on the Lords day, wee could not have satt in the Church.

8: This day Court kept in towne the Jury of Colne Comit chose for constables 2 men very unfitt[1] to order the alehouses and loose people of the towne.

Jan: 10. 1644: The Archbishop that grand enemy of the power of godlynes. that great stickler for all outward pompe in the service of god lost his head at Tower hill London, by ordinance of Parliament. This weeke the great snow melted gently, never were houses in many yeares so filled with snow and padled when it melted away. heard of the wellfare of my freinds from Hadham by my cousin Edward Miles.

Jan: 12. This weeke the Lord was gratious to mee and mine in many outward mercyes, peace plenty, health, oh that I could prize this love, mercifull in preserving from danger my son from the fire, good in keeping us from many iniquityes not having dominion over us, the Lord good to mee in the Sabbath, letting out my spirit to beseech mee to leave their sins Lord command a blessing, the Lord have the glory of all, the good Lord forgive my many sins, accept of mee, and blesse mee in Jesus Christ.

13: Sent my sister Dorothy 3^{s}. for a token(,) god good (to) mee that day in expressions of love from my freinds: I was with Sir John Jacob, and received content from him, he payd me my money

[1] The constables chosen were Henry Aymes and Francis Moule (ERO, D/DPr 79).

17: This day one of the butchers brought mee in a quarter of mutton, told not who sent it but went his way. I shall inquire whose love it was, and be thankfull for the same. He that gives to the(e) poore lends to the Lord. I have often observed my liberality or rather ☞ my poore mite imployed for the publike, or upon others indigent hath returned in with gaine and advantage: I must observe the weeke: on mooneday I sent to my poore sister. 3^{s}. and some other small things to others not worth the mentioning: now this weeke I received 9^{li}. from Sir John Jacob which was in part due long before, and promised but was not payd untill now, divers invitacions of freinds to their houses: one sends me a parcel of plums and sugar, another a quarter of good mutton, another a fatt goose, another a capon and cheese, an unexpected income of a summ of money layd out before, and good to my family and nacion(.)

Jan: 19: This weeke past god was good to mee and mine in our peace, health, strength, for soule and body preserving mee from grosse sins, keeping mee in my wayes towards my family, the lord was good in inward peace and comfort, the Lord was good to mee in Sabbath o sweet Jesu bee the price and ransome of my soule, and lett thy blessing bee upon mee, for from my soule I desire to love and obey thee, this weeke there was divers passages of providence for the good of the church in disappointing the attempts and plotts of the enemy. /

21: Injoyd the society of Mr Harlakenden and his children and others at a plentifull and comfortable dinner through the goodnes of go d unto us in our condicon.

23: God good mee this day in prayer in the ordinance of baptisme, in the society of my freinds, all mine in health, when I heard this day a carryer of Coxall[1] and his horse were killed at Brooke street: the Lords name be blessed for our preservacon, this morning I was kind to a poore woman, I had 2^{s}. given mee by another.

Jan: 26: In the latter part of the weeke god exercised mee with a cold and pose,[2] oh how gentle is this trouble, and how seldome to what I formerly underwent, Lord this is thy doing that shalt have the praise my wife also was ill with cold. oh how gentle is thy hand upon us. my children in very good health, god good to us in many mercyes and injoyments, in the Sabbath in carrying me on in the worke, Lord in Jesus Christ accept mee, sweet Jesu who ever art at the right hand of the Father intercede for mee, bee my and

[1] Coxall: here and frequently used for Coggeshall, just south of EC.

[2] Pose: catarrh, cough, a cold in the head. NED.

mines advocate for we have sinned against the good newes in divers particulars this weeke to the church:

28: The contry mett to choose their officers, they waved their former Collonels and nominated Mr Harlakenden. Col: Mr Haynes Major of Horse: Mr Cooke: Col. Mr Crane. Lieut: Coll. Jermaine, Major of foote, men honest and I hope faithfull, how it will be reconciled with the former election I knowe not, but I feare: det bona deus: One Robert Davy of my towne a butcher cutting out of meate, his sonne in law Kendall stood behind him, was strucken with the cleaver upon the forehead dangerously, beat out his eye etc: Lord thy name be praised for my preservacon, lett this affliction doe them good they have need of it!

29: This day wee kept the monthly fast, the Lord good to mee in the same, prayd for a speciall blessing upon the treaty, Lord accept pardon and be gratious: 30: Mrs C. gave me in kindnes 3s. to buy mee a satten cappe, and my wife. 2s.

30: This day my wife began to weane her sonne Thomas the Lord god in mercy preserve them both in their healths: god good to mee in his ordinance preachd. he doth not suite his as he doth others, no, no, and corrects his to amend them that they should not perish.

Feb: 1. Received advertisement that Mr Montjoy had payd my money to Mr H: I am glad it falls out so well for mee.

2: This weeke the Lord was good to us all in our outward injoyments; good in the Sabbath in the word in the ordinance of baptisme. Lord strengthen my spirit to all thy services and enable mee to subject my selfe to thee in all things.

4: This day god was good to mee in society of my freinds, and also with divers of my people and neighbours in conference and prayer, and in a deliverance from a desperate fall with my daughter in my armes, mercyes are multiplyed Lord make mee thankefull.

6: This day I injoyd the society of divers loving freinds at Taine,[1] coming home I received a letter signifying the wellfare of our freinds at Only for which god bee praised.

7: Injoyd the society of divers loving freinds with mee, sent for to preach at chelmsford: my son Thomas now 13. months old would easily shutt the parlour doore, the first time I observed it

F: 9. This weeke the Lord was good to mee and mine, in our health, peace, plenty, in preserving of us from dangers, my wife weaned her sonne, with much ease to her selfe, and the child also quiett and content: god good in preserving of us from grosse and scandelous

[1] Taine: Great Tey, a parish neighbouring EC.

sins, god good in the Sabbath, in his words, in assisting mee, Lord pardon my sins accept and blesse us in Jesus Christ thy beloved.

11: Rid to chelmsford the wayes very well beaten and dry in the roade, like the latter end of March or Aprill, god good to mee in sight of my freinds, in unexpected love and good society.

12: Preacht at Chelmsford by desire of the standing Committee, on 2 Cron. 25.9., dind with them and received thanks from them: somewhat wett coming home, the weather that day changing: one of Wittam, motioned that place to mee, Lord direct mee, god was very good to mee in my jorny and in assisting mee in his service, to whom be glory for ever Amen.

16: The Lord good to mee and mine, in our health, peace, and plenty, in reviving my litle daughter: preserving us from dangers and grosse sins: good in the Sabbath in assisting me with strength for the same, the good Lord in mercy pardon mee and blesse mee.

17: This day Mr H. rid with his son to Stortford School the Lord blesse him there, heard good newes from Plymouth, but very sad concerning the divisions that are in our armyes, Lord heale them for thy mercies sake, and give us one heart and spiritt.

18: The regiments of the County reduced to 2. a base busines in our parts of the County but its likely to bee ashame to the authors.

20: Overheard a separatists sermon against learning, a most poore peice, men of ignorance and of very great and high conceits; but I injoyd good company and society with divers freinds.

21: Injoyd the lecture, god affects to purge, oh Lord let thy chastisements and teachings drawe mee dayly nearer unto thee,

Feb: 23. God good to mee in my peace, health plenty in my family wife and children, the Lord preserved us from many grosse sins: the Lord good in mildning of my spirit, in giving mee more command of my spirit, the Lord was good in the Sabbath, in some measure enabling mee for the same, the good Lord in much mercy accept of mee pardon and forgive my unworthines, when I came out of the pulpitt I read a letter from Mr H. wherein he writes exsellent newes from Scarborough, taking by storme the sands Church, 120 ships: 32 peice of ordnance, and endangering the Castle, the Lords name bee praised and magnifyed for the same, The Treaty is likely to hold some time longer.

24: God was good to mee this day in his ordinance in publique upon occasion of Goodman Bruce his buriall[1] the good Lord make me

[1] Probably Jeffery Bruce, yeoman, of White Colne, whose will was proved in 1645, though there is no mention of RJ in it (ERO, 76 CW 14).

to love and prize Jesus Christ by whom wee have deliverance from the fear of death, I buryed also one of my towne, Lord make mee mindfull of my latter end worke my heart nearer to thee by all occasions I humbly intreate thee. /

Feb: 26. A day of Pu Humiliacon, the Lord good to mee in the same, oh Lord never was there more need of personall reformacion than now stirre me up to it I humbly intreate thee.

27: Preachd at Maplested. god good to mee going and returning, in the word preachd in the company of good freinds in the mercyes of family, and in my strength notwithstanding my more than ordinary labour, and often exercise in preaching. /

Dry Feb: 1644. This month was dry all the time wayes like summer on the 10 and 11 day: upon the 12 it raynd afterwards dry and a litle frost, but generally very warme, ushering in the spring our streets all over dry, wayes plaine, grounds so hard they could scarce be plowed no old man could ever remember the like: so it continued untill March. 3 then it rayned. violets were commonly blowne, rose bushes fully leaved; apricockes and my malegotoone[1] fully blossomed out:

March: 2: This weeke god was good to mee and mine in outward and inward mercyes, comforts of spirit, preservacon from grosse sins my wife aguish, but pretty chearfull, hott within very much but now using oringes, sugar and rose water cooled, the Lord bee praysed for his blessing therein, god good to mee in the Sabbath, word preachd ordinance of baptisme, I desired my neighbours to bee carefull in their choyce of Coll: on Tuesday and not to neglect it. pray god blesse us in that busynes. /

4: God was good to mee in my jorney to Braintree and home agayne, keeping me safe and prospering the worke wee had in hand, in the free choice and election of officers, without any considerable opposicon, although much was perfected and intended, the division consisted of 10 hundreds; the officers were the same men, and chosen into the same places as formerly Jan: 28. 1644: god give hearts sutable to their places and make them a blessing to the Contry.

6: 7: 8: My Cousin Abraham Josselin came to us from New England, about by the Canaryes after a sad long jorny and one tedious fight with a Kings pyratt: heard by him of the wellfare of the plantacion for which god bee praised, this summer N E had divers losses at sea, and scarce any before: wee rid to my Cousin Bentons, god good

[1] Malegotoone: melocoton, a peach grafted on a quince. NED.

to us outwards and homewards preserving us from water and dangers at night heard newes of the routing of my Lord Fairfax his forces, which was reported as a very great losse, endangering much the North parts of England.

M: 9: God was good to mee this weeke in my health, peace, plenty, in my family, in preserving us from grosse sins, in shining upon my spirit, in leading us in his wayes, good in the Sabbath, in his word, and in assisting mee for the same in some measure, Lord pardon my faylings, accept mee in thy christ. the weeke was a sad rayny windy time.

March 16: This weeke god was good to my wife and little ones in their health and in many other mercyes, and to mee in particular, yett I was exercised with a pose and great cold, yett not so bad as formerly, and as god might justly have exercised mee withal, I have not walked answerable to mercy receive (me) Lord thou knowest my faylings in rich mercy forgive them unto mee; on the Lords day I moved for one Wade to repayre his house: god opened the hearts of diverse wee collected 18 or 19s. some not only gave (not) but spoke against it, oh Lord give mee a spirit never to shutt up my bowells[1] from my brethren in distresse, the Lord was good to mee on the Sabbath, for which his name bee blessed for ever,

17. 18: Rid to Dedham, bought bookes by the way at Colchester. god give me strength and grace to use them and all other helps to his glory and his peoples advantage, at Dedham I found much love when I (as) was ready to have gone towards Church, my notes being layd by, and some thoughts in my head of choyce bookes and matters too high for mee, in comes one and tells mee another was come to preach, I willingly assented, Lord pardon my faylings accept mee and sanctify my spirit and teach mee to keepe my thoughts for thee. coming home and galloping a dog barking my horse fell. I satt him and had no hurt I thanke my god, coming home I saw my brother Jeremy; god was good to mee in my jorny, I was aguish and very ill at night, a violett cake[2] through gods mercy did much to revive mee, I saw at Dedham Harwich point running out into sea, and the ships riding at harbour nigh the open maine sea,

M: 23: God was good to mee this weeke and mine generally in our

[1] Bowels: taken as the seat of the tender emotions, hence pity, feeling, heart. SOED.

[2] Culpeper, *Herbal*, p. 112, states that violet is good for the liver, jaundice, and all hot agues. Gerard, *Herbal*, p. 200, writes that 'There is likewise made of Violets and sugar certaine plates called Sugar violet, Violet tables, or Plate, which is most pleasant and wholesome.'

healths, and many outward mercyes and comforts. only my Litle daughter ill with wormes, I hope that mercy that gave her and hath hitherto preserved her, will continue restore and sanctify her. this weeke I saw the directory,[1] and an Ordnance of Parliament to take away that heavy burthen of the booke of Common prayer in all the parts of the same, this day god was good to mee in the publike exercise the sacrament of baptisme, in gatherings for divers poore the Lord in mercy pardon my faylings sanctify mee: I made a serious mocion to all to joyne with the Magistrate in a civill reformacion. /

25: Our fayre day, through mercy freer from disorder than at some other times.

1645: 26: March. a day of publike humiliacon, the Lord raysd up my spirit with boldnes, and enlarged mee in the worke of the day: the good Lord pardon all my faylings on the same and accept us in Jesus Christ and Command blessings upon all. I was earnest with god for Sir Will: Breretons preservacion and protection I trust god will for his mercy sake give us an answer of peace.

29: A darke day in respect of our intelligence. matters went ill in the west, our forces compelled to retreate and somewhat worse was feared by Waller and Holborne. in the Northwest the enemy preserved and releived their distressed garrisons and by report fell downe towards us: thus wee see tis not in man but in the Lord only to doe us good oh that we could trust and depend upon him only. etc.

March. 30: This weeke the Lord was gratious to mee and mine in our health, peace, plenty, in inward and outward mercyes. in the Sabbath in inabling mee in some measure for the same, Lord pardon my failings and accept mee in thy deare sonne.

April: 3: My wife divers dayes very ill, this day shee beganne to perswade her selfe she was breeding, if it be so god in mercy give her a contented thankefull spirit, preserve her, and her fruite, and make it his owne and provide every way for it. /

4: my wife was now even confident shee was breeding, and supposed it a daughter, the Lord give us thankefull contented spirits, the times, our neglected condicion in the towne, and the ruinous coldnes of our house, and the time of yeare in the depth of winter are some discouragements, but gods mercy is above all thes.

[1] In October 1644 the Westminster Assembly was asked to frame a new Directory of Worship to replace the Prayer Book, and this was published as a schedule to an ordinary on 4 January 1645. It was only in August, however, that an ordinance enforcing its use and penalizing use of the Prayer Book was passed. Kenyon, pp. 255–7.

5. preachd at Gaines Colne on Rom: 14.12. the funerall of old Molins; his sonne and gran(d)children of our towne would not bee present, lord teach mee to number my dayes. heard of the Jewes returne can it bee.

Apr: 6. All this weeke (only my wife weakly). god good to us all in health and outward mercyes, heard of the wellfare of divers of my freinds, god good to mee in Sabbath, Lord pardon, and accept mee in thy Christ.

7: Heard of the sicknesse of my Uncle Miles by his sonne Edw: the Lord sanctify it to him and raise him up againe, received this day. 10^{li}. 10^{s}. of Mr Montjoys money, payd Mr R. Harlakenden the 4^{li}. I ought him, so now I am out of his debt, received 1^{li}. 5^{s}. for the widdow Reeve.[1] 1^{s}. weekely.

N: E: Sent a letter thither contayning the sum of our English newes untill almost the latter end of March: 1645.[2]

8: Rid towards my uncle Miles god good (to) mee in preserving me thither. there and homewards, in setling my sisters busynes, my uncle weake, Lord thou hast power to restore him, oh raise him up for thy names sake, returned April. 10.

10: An anabaptist of our parish being pressd for a souldier I writ and procured his release, lord learne mee to doe them good against their reproaches towards mee.[3]

Apr: 13: This weeke god was pleased to exercise mee with a cold my wife with faintnes, some dayes wondrous hott, but oh how sweet was his mercy our chastisements being very gentle, god good to us in our peace and plenty, in the Sabbath in enabling me in some measure for the same, Lord learne me more knowledge of thy wayes, and prowesse of spirit to honour thee in the practice of them for the Lord Jesus Christs sake. /

April. 15: my pose exercised mee litle or much for 5. dayes; May was now blowne in divers places, very hott, likely to bee a forward yeare, I dreamed my uncle Thomas Miles was prettily well recovered,

18: This day being at Halsted after sermon, my aunts man came to mee and acquainted mee with the death of my deare Uncle Miles of Hadham Berry he dyed die. 17. a litle before sunsett, he had not

[1] Probably Grace Reeve, whose husband John was buried in 1624, and who herself died in April 1658. PR.

[2] His correspondent was probably John Haynes, sometime governor of Connecticut. See the note under 18 March 1650/1.

[3] Anabaptists were opposed to warfare; thus Prynne in 1643 wrote 'Intoxicated with an Anabaptisticall spirit, condemning all kinds of warre'. NED.

very lingring sicknes so arose almost to his death, The good Lord sanctify this losse and make mee and all of us mindfull of our latter ends. given mee a tree by Mr R. Harlake(nden)

20: This weeke the Lord was gratious to us in our peace, health, plenty, in the Sabbath, Lord pardon my many great faylings and accept mee, and renew a right spirit within mee, and mine, this day I intreated the Lord for raine, and he was pleased in the night and the next day sweetly to water the earth from heaven. praise be his name.

21: I was somewhat ill, cold in my bones: yet rested at night well I praise god.

Jone: 22: My sister Mary went downe to the priory, the Lord make her fitt for her place and give her favour in the sight of them shee serveth, Jone my mayd came to us the Lord make mee faithfull to her and blesse her for soule and body under mee, Mr Harl: received his Commiss. to bee Deputy Lieutenent.

25: Mr H: rid to Colchester my wife and I rid with him in his coach, god was gratious to us in our jorney homewards and outwards,

Ap: 27: God was good to us this weeke in our health, peace and outward mercyes; Mary Grant a bold wench whose mother had 6 or 7 bastards. her flesh rotted from her armes, complained shee was gotten with child.[1] oh Lord keepe all thine from this scandalous wickednes. humble us for no such abomination ought to be named among us; the fellow shee accused John Besse run away, this day the Lord was good to mee in the word. in standing by mee and in enabling mee in some measure for the same Lord accept pardon and seale my soule, my Cousin Abraham with mee he is going into New England, the lord blesse him and prosper him:

28. Jone my mayd went to her mothers very sicke, urina nigra.[2] god restore her to her health.

Apr: 30: This day the day of publique fast, god inabled mee in some measure for the same, he accept mee and pardon and forgive mee, a sweet seasonable weather, very forward spring, Lord accept mee and mine and delight in us, looke upon the nacion in mercy, over night my wife in want of fresh butter for our children, late at night a neighbour unexpectedly sent us in two pound, here was a providence suited to our necessitys

[1] Bastard-bearing had run in this family for at least three generations, see the biography in Appendix 2. There is no reference to this event, however, in either PR or other contemporary court records.

[2] Black urine; diagnosis of disease was often made by the colour of urine.

May: 4: This weeke the Lord was good and gratious to us in our peace, plenty, health, in many speciall mercyes and favours; on his owne day he gave mee occasion to praise him in regard of his mercy and goodnes towards the nacion. he was good to mee in the Lords day pardon oh Lord and accept mee for thy deare sonnes sake,

May: 11: The Lord was good to us this weeke in all our healths, in peace, outward mercyes my loving neighbour, goodman Burton was very ill with a cold, and fever, the Lord in mercy rayse him up to the comfort of his family, the Lord was good to mee in strength for the Sabbath, oh lett the word of peace, bee accepted. Lord pardon in mercy all my sins and faylings in all thy services, stablish my heart in obedience to the truth and lett mee growe up in the same,

12: At Pebmarsh, God good in the love and society of freinds. Mr Shepheard of Maplested[1] accused by his mayd for endeavouring to abuse her, his patience was so moved that he stroke her on the mouth whereupon shee bled much, it made much against him, the Lord discover truth, shame us in our selves and preserve us from reproach, it might have beene my condicon if mercy had not prevented itt.

18: The Lord was good to us this weeke in outward mercyes and favours, peace and plenty, my litle daughter only somewhat ill with cold; the Lord good to mee in the worke of his day. dispos[e] my heart more and more to his service, pardon my faylings and accept mee in Jesus Christ.

19: payd 2 yeares tenth[2] to the parliaments messenger, 1^{li}. 14^{s}. 2^{d}. the messenger received from me for his paynes, 3^{s}. his power was harshe: his carriage was yet indifferent curteous, tis a tryall to bee thus dealt withall; I blesse god my spirit was under, and I hope ever shall.

May: 25. This weeke the Lord was good to us in our health and outward mercyes, my litle daughter Mary had a great cold. streynd and spitt much bloud, I hope the Lord will preserve her my wife through gods goodnes held out very well (though weakly in the want of a mayd servant, god in his good time will supply us,

May: 28: This day was a day of publique humiliacion wherin god was

[1] Edward Sheppard, vicar of Maplestead from 1639. Clearly he did not please the majority of the parishioners and was opposed to the Interregnum church settlement. He accused Eliz. Spurgion of stealing various possessions, while she and others accused him of being a common barrator and disturber of the peace, in 1645. Both sides were acquitted. By 1650 he still farmed some of the tithes, but the parishioners had hired another preacher. Smith, p. 296; Walker; ERO, Q/SR 325/32, 34.

[2] Tenths were the parliamentary tax or assessment.

good to mee. oh when shall I learne more and more to love him. my daughter Mary very ill with a cold, exceedingly streyning by fitts and fetching up bloud wee went to my Lady Honywoods who gave us divers things for her. my wife used oyle and found it wrought presently upon her upwards and downwards,

June: 1: This day the Lord was good to mee in his ordinances, oh make me a sonn of gratious and holy peace, and lett his word and ordinances bee advantage to us, Mary continued ill, wee used meanes the Lord blesse them; god stedded[1] us with a young servant the Lord fitt her for us and blesse her under us, shee came May. 29. 1645.

The newes was sad to us ward that the king was coming downe to Newarke, had faced Leicest(er.) god knowes how soone wee may bee alarmd indeed.

2: A comfortable meeting of Ministers at Stanway, at home an alarme, Leicester lost,

7: an alarme to raise our regiment of Horse, the feild officers from home, I was resolved to have sent orders to have raised them, but the Coll. coming home at night I only assisted him in his worke that night,

8: preachd at Cogshall god was good to mee in the day, and worke and in the weeke my wife and daughter somewhat weakely,

10. 11. 12: I was out with our regiment wee marchd to walden, muster(e)d(,) I sung psalmes, prayd and spake to our souldiers on the Common at Walden and also at Halsted, god was good to us in accommodating us, and preserving us, Mr Josselin of Chelmsford brake his legge at Walden his horse threw him, our souldiers resolute some somewhat dissolute, the Collonel was pleased to honor mee to bee his Comrade I shall never forgett his great love and respect, I found my family well I praise god at my returne, aboundance of love made my wife greive, for which I must the more respect and love her, I rid to my sister at Wenden I had not seen her in divers yeares, the Lord hath made a difference in our outward condicions I gave her and her children 6ˢ. Lord thou canst doe more than returne it againe to mee

Ju(n). 14: at my Lady Honywoods wee agreed to meet on Tuesday to seeke god for our armyes and I went to prayer, dum,[2] even while wee were in prayer our armyes were conquering,[3] the Lords name bee praised and receive the glory of all;

[1] Stedded: stead, to supply with something helpful. NED.

[2] Dum: while.

[3] At the battle of Naseby.

15: The Lord was good to us this weeke in many mercyes, we had our weaknesses yett, my eyes troubled with rheume, my daughter with her cough, and my wife ill, the Lord yett gave us our peace, plenty, good to mee on his Sabbath, I was stung and swelld much with one of our bees, yett it hindred mee not from my worke, his name bee praised.

16: A meeting of ministers at my house.

17: Mr Sedgwicke.[1] Mr Grey,[2] and my selfe kept a day of humiliacion at Markshall, the Lord our god be found of us intreated by us, and answer our prayers upon our severall familyes for good;

18: This day was I ordered by the Committee as Constant Chaplyn to attend upon Coll: Harlakenden regiment at musters and to receive 10^{s}. per diem as a salary for the same, this morning if not last night was Leicester taken. oh the Speedy returne of our prayers.

June: 22: This was a weeke of much mercy to my family, to mee my eyes better. my daughter recovered, I was designed to a place of service in the army. Lord inable mee for it and make me faithfull and usefull in the same; to the nation in the great victory and the consequences of it, as also in smaller fights in divers parts of the kingdome; god was good to me in the sabbath his name be praised, in the ordinance of baptisme, I baptized after the order of the directory; I gave notice of a fast. and a day of thanksgiving, Lord fitt and enable mee with ability and strength for the dayes thereof in much mercy I intreate thee. /

25: A day of publike humiliacon the Lord was good to mee in the same, in yeelding me strength for the same, the good Lord in mercy forgive my many sins, accept me and my poore endevours and answer our prayers both for publike and private good. /

27: A day of thanksgiving for the great victory in Naseby fields over the Kings army, by Sir Tho: Fairfax, the lord was pleased in some measure to raise up my heart in the worke, and helpe mee with many expressions and unstudyed meditacions, for which his name bee praised, Lord lett us heare a sound of much mercy and draw out those praises that waite for thee in Zion:

June. 30: This weeke god was good to us in our healths my sonn and daughter, shaking of their colds, my labours this weeke great: preachd. 4. whole dayes in 8. it was an emblem of our times. the Lord carryed mee through, he in mercy accept and pardon.

[1] Obadiah Sedgwick, vicar of Coggeshall, 1639–46, and member of the Westminster Assembly. Smith, pp. 93, 332.

[2] Robert Gray, sometime of Mashbury, but sequestered from that living about 1644. Smith, pp. 119, 127, 163, 281.

July: 1: 3: Rid to Wethersfeild with my wife returned safe to god bee thee praise.

6: the Lord was good to us in all mercyes this weeke I preachd at Markshall and Mr Lorkyn[1] for mee

7. a meeting of ministers at Mr Ludgaters.[2]

9. Saw the sea from great Wicborough hill. 10. returnd home safe from Maj: Haynes, but yett troubled somewhat with a cold.

10: Coll: Harlakenden payd me 50s. for waiting as preacher upon his Regiment. to Walden, this is the first mony that I received of the states, god can this way pay in my layings out in his cause and service.

July. 13: This weeke the Lord was good to us in all our outward mercies and contents and on his owne day in some measure enabling mee for his service his name have the praise and honour.

20: This weeke the Lord was good to mee and mine in our health and all outward mercyes, preserving us from dangers, and from the evils of our wayes in some measure. on his owne day he was pleased in some measure to stand by him, his name be praised.

22: A day of thanksgiving, our notice but short I durst not neglect it god in some measure good to mee in the same, now wee had 2 dayes of thanks in the intervall of the fast(,) oh hav mercyes come in upon us on the suddaine

July: 23: Mr Archer[3] and I mett, about his accusing mee, Lord learne me patience and wisedome by this dealing, and helpe mee to watch my heart that I may bee kept from every evill way, and the good god be praised for his mercy in damping my acusers in some measure,

July: 27: This weeke the Lord was good to mee and mine in our health, and outward mercyes, in his mercy for eternity, in standing by me and framing my spirit in some measure to his will good in the extraordinary successes of his Church and people against the enemy in all parts, on his owne day the good Lord pardon me and take the glory of all that I am.

July 30. A day of P. humiliacion: the Lord was pleased to afford mee strength for the same, never was there more neede of bowing our spirits, to yeeld obedience to the Lord than now, and yett never

[1] John Lorkyn, minister of Markshall; later of Ongar and ejected in 1662. Smith, p. 382; Calamy.

[2] John Ludgater, then holding sequestered living of Great Birch; ejected from Witham in 1660. His son John was a later vicar of EC. Smith, p. 383; Calamy.

[3] Presumably Archer accused Josselin of partiality in the dispute about who should obtain the Stisted living; see p. 23, n. 4 above.

lesse care and regard, oh Lord doe not looke upon us according to our dutyes but according to thy tender mercyes save us for thy names sake.

Aug: 3: this weeke some injuries put upon mee, there are no commodityes but have their discommodities, and wisedome must make crownes of crosses, the lord was good yett therin to mee and mine in our peace health and other mercyes, in the exercises of the day, the(e) good Lord forgive my faylings, renew his compassions dayly towards mee, and accept mee in his beloved.

6: 7: Imployed in composing matters betwixt Mr Harlakenden and the Nevills,[1] which I praise god I effected to their contents, and I hope it was a worke of charity and love.

13. 14. 15. god good to mee in the company of divers of my worthy freinds, received divers expressions of love from them. I hope poore Finch to my power in his building, at Halsted I was a hearer, the Lord make mee wise to discerne betwixt good and evill, Lieut. Col: Tindall[2] payd my ordinary, I should have mett one Potter this day about busynes, and he was sicke of the small poxe, what rich mercy god affords in my preservacion.

Aug: 17: God was good to mee in many mercyes and comforts this weeke, and to mine for which his name bee praised. this day I baptized 3 children. John Read held his owne child; the first that I ever baptized so; god was good to mee in the dispensacion of his words: Mr Harlakenden my deare Freind so ill with a fever, loosenes and vomiting that he was not fitt to come to Church the Lord bee mercifull unto him in his recovery.

19: God good to me in my jorney and returne from Dedham where I preachd the lecture.

20. Day I heard a sermon at Colchester. Coming home Henry Abbott his wife was buryed.

Aug: 24: God was good to mee in many outward mercyes, in inward support and goodnes to mee and mine this day I exchanged with my Cousin Benton and preachd at Upper Yeldham, in the night I heard the drummes beat at Nether Yeldham, it proved an alarme upon the Kings coming downe to Huntington.

27: Fast day, I preachd once after that I rid to my Coll: quarters to great Chesterford, where wee had an alarme of the enemyes advance

[1] Richard and William Nevill were landholders in EC in the 1630s and were related to the Harlakenden family (see Harlakenden genealogy, Appendix 1). RJ later bought some of their lands. For the Nevill family, see Appendix 2.

[2] Deane Tindall, Lt.-Colonel to Sir Thomas Honywood, and later Deputy Lt. of the county. Quintrell, pp. 20, 107.

to Cambridge, and presently of his intentions to fall upon our owne quarters.

Aug: 31: I preachd at Royston one sermon where our quarters were for present, god good to us in our march, in our accomodacions his name for ever bee praised.

September: 4: Returned home safe with our troops: no damage to any man. one horse shott in the legge through a mistake: my horse eye hurt: god good to mee in enabling mee for my jorney. I found my wife indifferently chearfull, only in my absence, shee was wondrous sad and discontented.

Sept: 7: This weeke god good to us in our returnes of peace the enemy fled before us and gone downe to other parts of the kingdome, good in our health and plenty in seasonable harvest weather, in his sabbath, in some measure enabling mee for the worke and service of the same.

9: some fayling that had promised to goe along with mee, I went alone towards Major Haynes, come safe to Cambridge, heard he was at Grantham or Lincolne, upon which I resolved home, and so went to bed in Sydney Colledge.

10: Having the opportunity of a convoy I resolved to find him out, wee came safe to Huntington, there I refreshd my selfe with Mrs Taylor; hearing that divers of their Cabs rold upon the road wee made ready for our defence and marchd on, before wee came at Stangate hole, Captaine Warner and divers in his company overtooke us, at Stilton I mett the welcome newes that Major Haynes at 9 of clocke was at Stamford; much a doe I perswaded them to march that night to Wainsford bridge. 7 miles in the night. our supper was a hard egge, and tough cheese, and pretty course lodging. blessed be god wee had any thing.

11: I and 3 more in the morning rid to Stamford. 5 miles found the Major who was riding unto Grantham, very glad of my company, wee quartered at Mr Wolphs a grand malignant here wee had good lodging and diett.

12: A day of publike humiliacon for Scotland, preached once at Saint Maryes stamford.

13: Continued at stamford heard the good newes of Bristol. Saw the Sad face of Burleigh house,[1] a litle surfetted with eating grapes:

14: Lords day. continued at Stamford preachd 2 sermons. very ill with my cold(,) one hurt with his own pistoll upon the guard,

[1] It had been besieged by Cromwell. Probert.

15. An alarme that the enemy with Horse was entring our quarters, the guard sayd they discryed a great body of them(,) the Major had a fall god preserved him, it proved false and was soone quieted.

16: Wee marchd through Rutlandshire a pleasant litle County to Bilsden in Leicestershire. Coll. Rossiter[1] with 4 troopes of horse came up to us, wee quarterd that night at Houghton at a poore house, beefe to our supper, pittiful blacke bread, I gott a white loafe crust; our lodging was upon straw and a quilt; in our clothes, I slept well I blesse my god. heard that Montrosse was entred England.

17: Marchd out with a short breakfast, randevoud at Leicester. where Coll. Rossiters troopes marchd from us, beheld the ruines of a brave house sometimes the Earle of Devonshire nothing standing but the stone worke; from hence wee marchd towards Ashby: refreshd our selves upon the way. but our meat smelt, I pocketted 2 white loafes against the worst.

quartered at Ibstocke, Lauds living. now Dr Lovedyn a great Cavailier, our diett very good, and lodging indifferent,

18: Marchd in the head of two troopes to Rounston in Derbyshire, thence to Ashby much infected with the plague, wee faced the house: I prayd with the Councell of Warre, wee summond the house. we drew of about night: lost 2 men: one shott in the breeches and yett had no hurt, killed one of the Cavaliers: heard the newes of routing Montros Sept. 13: the next day to the Fast: here I Eate some of my bread. wee had no beere all day long: marchd backe to Ibstocke: rid in a pretty while before our troops; 6 men in towne they sayd, of Leichfeild. it scard our men and made them ready to run. I was in the house and heard nothing. I have cause for ever to praise god for the(e) mercyes of this day. one of the men was slaine on the ground where I had stood closely a litle before not knowing of the pardue[2] in the ditch who shott this man presently after.

19: marchd through Leicester saw the ruines of some part of the towne. So to Roulston quarted there our usage good praised bee a gratious god.

20: randevoud at Shemington. 3 troopes marchd of with Rossiter to Grantham, and the other 5 Came Safe through providence to Stamford.

21: preachd 2 sermons at Stamford. god good to mee in the same. I

[1] Edward Rossiter, M.P. for Grimsby and Lincolnshire 1646–60. Venn.

[2] Pardue: a section of soldiers for desperate services or forlorn hope. Probert.

hope not without good to the people: wee spoyle one of their Church Feasts this day. people are still for their old wayes.

22: left the Major and came safe to Cambridge, suppd with the Comittee: angerd them at Huntington.

23: returned safe to Colne to my deare wife and freinds. my place supplyed in my absence I praise god:

Sept: 24: P. Fast[1] preachd once. suddayne meditacions on. Cron. 36:16. god good in the same to mee:

27: Mr Harlakenden came from Chelmsford, he had (been) and still is ill. god in mercy preserve him.

28: preachd 2 sermons at Colne: god good many wayes and in the Sabbath unto mee baptized 3 twins one of the 4 dead: and another child. 4 in all. /

October. 5. This weeke God good many wayes unto mee, as also in the Sabbath, it was a day of thanksgiving, and the occasions and causes therof very many, praised bee his name the Lord pardon mee and accept mee.

6. rid to Copford returned: 8. strucke through Mr Co. Harlakendens bargaine:. 7. rid to Colchester returnd safe, praisd be god:

10: the County newes about presbytery.[2] and the alarme of the Kings coming with 2000 horse to Newarke;

Octob. 12: This weeke god was good to us in our healths and outward mercyes. my Servant sicke but well by the end of the weeke, god was good to mee in the exercises of the day. wee gathered for poore Taunton, wherin god was good to mee in opening my mouth and opening my peoples hearts wee gathered 8^{li}. 4^{s}. 4^{d}. beyond any presidents about us:

13. Mett with divers ministers at Mr Thompsons.

14. preachd at the buriall of George Potters child; dyed with a sudden illnes. reported the plague is at Kelvedon. Mr Sawyer chose burgesse of Colchester an unworthy act but suitable to the men.

16: A day of thanksgiving, god was good to mee in the same. presently after came the wellcome newes of the taking of Basing. its to be razed, of a truth many habitacions are layd waste.

18: Heard the newes of Major Heynes his routing 300 of the enemies horse and taking an 150 of them, lord prosper that man: my mayde went away. send mee one Lord that feareth thy name.

[1] P. Fast, P.F.; a public fast, or day of general prayer and fasting as ordained by the State.

[2] The discussion concerning the adaptation of the Scottish Presbyterian system to English conditions, which was especially heated during September and October 1645, is described in Gardiner, ii, pp. 367–9.

Octob. 19: This weeke god was good to mee and mine in our health, peace inward contents and peace, good in his word make mee to live according to the power of godlynes and make my life a continuall Sabbath. my wife alone without a mayde, oh my god gratiously provide for her and helpe her.

20: Many times I sought god for a servant a mercy I prize my mayde Sarah promised her mistris to come to her for a quarter of a yeare, this was from thee oh my good god.

21: Rid to Chelmsford motiond my busynes with Mr Archer to Col. Cooke[1] pressed him to nominate place and time to end the same, he answerd he knew not that it was reserved to him. my horse was a stumbler yett I was in no danger by it I praise my good god Came safe to Chelmsford: wee discoursd about our busynes: Mr Grimston[2] so kind as to pay my ordinary being $2^{s}. 0^{d}$. I pressd Mr Sayer. to have a care in his activenes for the publike good to shew him self our freind and so to cleare jealousyes.

22: Mr Newcomen[3] preachd: wee made a fayre progresse in our busynes about the church as in other papers that beare reference to this time appeares, the hand of our god was upon us for good. praisd bee his name.

23: finishd our busynes: E of Warwicke[4] payd my ordinary $2^{s}. 6^{d}$.: in so great a meeting not an oath sworne, came home safe, found my wife babes well, my son had the shingles, Mrs Mary very kind to keepe her company night and day in my absence,

24: L: Coll: Grimes with us, god preserved him hitherto from many dangers, not to loose one drop of bloud, no wounds, but dry ones great blowes and bruises.

October. 26: This weeke the Lord was good to us in our condicons; his workes are worth the noting: my selfe troubled with a cold in my head, my sonne with bleaches[5] in his face, my wife with the illnes of her condicion being bigge, god provided us with a servant my old mayd Sarah, he was a god quietting and satisfying our hearts. good in the mercyes of the Sabbath gratious in continuing the successes of his people, there is no end of his mercyes.

27: This day in the feilds I found a bucke Mr R. H. was with mee,

[1] Colonel Thomas Cooke, of Pebmarsh; parliamentarian and sequestrator. Morant, ii, p. 263.

[2] Later Sir Harbottle Grimston (1603–85), of Bradfield Hall; M.P. and Speaker of the House, deputy-lieutenant of Essex. DNB.

[3] Mathew Newcomen, lecturer at Dedham 1637–62, when ejected; a member of Westminster Assembly and author. Calamy.

[4] Sir Robert Rich, 2nd Earl, leader of the Puritan party in Essex (1587–1658). DNB.

[5] Bleaches: 'a disease of the skin'. SOED.

with his greyhounds, after much sport wee kild her in the river, this was an unexpected providence.

29: This day was the P. Fast, wherin the Lord was good to mee, my heart Lord thou knowest is not easd up in thy wayes with that life and vigour as it ought, oh when will thou lift it up; a meeting at Goodman Mathewes to declare to our christians and others what wee had done in the Church busynes. I hope it will be our healing, the good Lord command it to bee so.

31: Two of Thaxted were with mee early, about accepting their place, I gave them an answer of my unfitnes advised them to consider how to make the place comfortable for a minister, the good god direct mee what to doe,

November: 2: This weeke the Lord was many wayes gratious to us upholding under weaknesses. preserving in colds and distresses that they were a sicknesse to us. good in the Sabbath. made a mocion to the towne, now to settle my meanes, or else to leave mee to my due liberty. my sonne troubled with bleach, but very jocund, praised bee my gratious god.

3: rid to stanway. god good to mee going and returning, missd my company their

5: Preachd upon the occasion, wherin god good to mee; my townesmen made some beginnings to better my meanes.

6: 7: Thaxted men came not, a good providence for my townesmen had not yett settled their busynes.

No: 9: This weeke the Lord was good to mee and mine in our healths, in inward and outward mercyes my cold wearing away, and not much afflicting mee; my wife holding out very well my sonnes face mending, god was good in his word, and in the mercyes of the day coming out of the pulpitt I had another invitacion to Major Haynes; and a great desire I have to comply with it, Lord if thou seest it good for mee, order it in providence that I might doe some good to some poore soules in those parts,

10: My good Freind Mr Harl: perplexed about his shrivaltry: an offer of an under sheriffe unto him Mr Crane with him about it.

14: My wife with mee at Mr H. heard the newes of the taking of Chester, the Lord be praised this is of consequence to the reducing of Wales, and making Ireland useles to the present designe of the king and his company.

No: 16: Chester newes untrue: This weeke god was gratious to us in many outward mercyes. I was somewhat troubled with pose and cold but not much I praise my god: my wife held up and indifferent well, my sons face almost well only very red: god was good in the Sabbath, he goe out with his word and make it effectuall, some subscribed a peticion of my drawing to the parliament for some addicion of meanes to our living from them. it must be god that prospers every designe.

Nov: 23: This weeke the Lord was gratious to us in our health peace and outward contents and injoyments; my wife held up her head well, good in preserving my poore babes in dangerous falls with knives: My deare freind Mr Harl. rode up to London: I preachd at Markshall and Mr Lorkyn for mee, the Lord accept and pardon mee,

24: I had sought to god for my wife (that was oppressed with feares that she should not doe well on this child,) that god would order all providences so as wee might rejoyce in his salvacion, I had prayd with confidence of good successe to her: about midnight on Monday: I rose called up some neighbours: the night was very light: goodman Potter willing to goe for the midwife, and up when I went: the horse out of the pasture, but presently found: the midwife up at Buers, expecting it had beene nearer day; the weather indifferent dry; midwife came, all things even gotten ready towards day. I called in the women by day light, almost all came; and about 11 or 12. of the clocke my wife was with very sharpe paynes deliverd. Nov: 25. of her daughter intended for a Jane, she was then 25. y of age her selfe; wee had made a good pasty for this houre, and that also was kept well, wife and child both well prais bee my good and mercifull father,

Nov: 26: The day of the P. Fast, preachd twice. god was good to mee in the same, and in giving mee sweet rest the night before: wherby my he(a)d ake was allayed, the dayes are common and neglected, and yett sins and judgments continue, and now no sense of neither, Lord whither will this evill tend; oh that mercy might humble us and prepare us for good, accept mee and mine oh Lord intreate thee.

29: Heard of the returne of Mr Harl: sworne high sheriffe for Essex, I had a payne in my right shoulder and that part of my necke, I conceive it was cold; heard that my wives sister Elizabeth was marryed to London: My neighbour Burtons wife miscarryed, others harmes should make our mercyes greater, sanctify thy dealing to us all I entreate thee gratious god, no action from our armyes as I could heare.

No: 30: God good and gratious to us: in my wives and babes health, enabling her to nurse, in many favours both for soule and body, good in his word to him bee the praise

This weeke of december was a sad weeke to mee, to review my wayes and find the continuing strength of my corruptions. the dogging of vaine thoughts, oh where shall I leave thes. I sticke in the mire oh Lord pull mee out. I have covenanted more watchfulnes oh Lord ingage my heart to performe, make mee not a slave to lusts and foolishnes.

Dec: 4: my dearest very ill, as if shee would have even dyed, shee utterd as formerly thes words thou and I must part. but my god continue us togither to praise him.

December: 7. This weeke the Lord was good to mee and my family, in their health and preservacion. the Lord deliver mee from every evill worke, the Lord good in his word on the Sabbath, in the baptising of my daughter, he in mercy accept me.

December. 14: My wife weakely and faint, yett chearly when not troubled with toothake, my babe troubled with a cold, and so my daughter Mary. the good god preserve them, and take of his hand in affliction from them. This weeke acquaynted with the scandall of Edward Potter in solliciting the chastity of the widdow Ward, Lord this ought not to bee named among christians, god gave mee a heart to endeavour the punishing of this sin, he in mercy stirre up the Magistrates against all evill wayes; it was gods goodnes that I and mine are not in the same condicon, god good in our mercyes, as also in the Sabbath, and the dutyes therin, his name be praised.

18: A day of Thankes in the associacion for the preservacion therof, wherin god was good and gratious unto mee in the same.

19: Strange report that Mrs Tiffin was in labour she pretended such a matter, but it proved not so,[1]

December: 21: God gratious this weeke in our mercyes and preservacions: I found my heart more dull in dutyes especially in prayer. the Lord quicken and revive mee; my sonne Thomas was sickly; he forsoke his meat, my daughter Jane a cold: nurse went home from us.

December. 15. my mayde Margarett came to us; the Lord make her ☞ helpefull and serviceable unto us; and lett her gaine for soule and

[1] One line has been crossed out in ink unlike that used by RJ. It reads as follows: 'but thereby shee is discovered herself, yett she sayth it was by her *nere* kins*man*'. Mrs. Tiffin was Elizabeth Harlakenden, sister of Richard, baptized in 1608, and married to William Tiffin, lord of the manor of White Colne. See the Harlakenden genealogy, Appendix 1.

body. god good to mee in the exercises on his owne day. he in mercy pardon my sins and accept my soule.

22: Edward Potter bound to his good behaviour for abusing the widdow Ward, he putt in sureties to dischardge the towne; he challenged one Paflin to have beene naught with her, I suspected the matter and called for a warrant for them, what god will discover, he onely wise best knoweth:

23: went to Sir Tho: Honywood: with the high sheriffe and his sonne. Sir Tho. and I played 4 games at chesse. wee parted upon equall termes. Hereford wonne by stratagem the neatest in all our warres

24: At Coll: Cookes(,) Paflin cleared in the matter of the widdow Ward, he accused Potter about the death of his mayde Alce, and children by her, upon which Edward Potter tooke out a warrant to examine the matter wee satt all 25. day about the business and in conclusion the justices had so much against him as to send him to jayle, the chamber where he had his mittimus was the roome where he was borne at mother Abbotts, the Lords finger was in this businesse; to him bee the praise and glory, whatsoever we doe we desire to seeke and ayme att that, and to remove iniquity from us.

December. 28: God was gratious this weeke in our healths, peace, plenty and mercyes wee wanted nothing that was convenient for us: a great discovery this weeke in our towne it is from the Lords free grace to preserve mee, the Lord watch over mee and keepe mee continually in his feare the Lord was good in his word and in carrying mee on in my place, hee in mercy pardon my faylings and accept mee.

Jan: 4: This weeke the Lord was gratious to mee and mine in our healths. peace provision, all well with us and our litle ones, yett the times sickly and many dyed suddenly, in his name bee praised in our preservacion. the Lord was good to mee in the fast day, and on his owne day, he purge my thoughts and keepe my heart more close every day to himselfe, Jan: 6 the time was cold frost very hard, the thames now frozen: Major Haynes wee heard was coming home with his men:.

6: Heard of Major Haynes his returne into the County

8: 9: Rid to Chelmsford and returned safe, the Lord be praised, who kept us upon the way, I was with Mrs Francis Mildmay found her in good health, The Major my noble Freind very well, returnd with him to chelmsford.

10: Received 6 weekes pay of the Major as his chaplayne: it was a good providence of god towards mee to supply all other wants, I find god shining upon my estate. praised bee his name, I gave two of his servants 10s. /

Jan. 11: God good this weeke in our health, and preservacions, in the Sabbath, the lord purge my soule, and heale my nature, and sanctify mee as a chosen one to himselfe,

Jan: 18: The Lord was good to mee and my family in many wonted mercies and favours, many families under his correcting hand, wee in health, and if sadnes or illnes over night joy cometh in the morning, god was good to us in the Sabbath and in the duties thereof.

25: This weeke the Lord was good to us in our health and peace. providing warme house. wood. firing and our screene extraordinary for us in the cold time beyond any in former yeares, good likewise in mercyes to state. and in his Sabbath in carrying me forth in the same.

Jan: 28: A day of P. Humiliacion wherin god was good to mee. I was over night ill with a paine in my side about my heart. I was at chesse with Mr H. my heart checkt mee for it for I was not fully provided for the worke of the next day. the Lord accept us, and give a blessing upon our endeavour for good. one thing I desire to lament before god the vanity of my thoughts taken up with unprofitablenes. Lord make my meditacion every day sweet of thee, and lett my refreshments and retirements bee in heaven. Amen, Amen.

Long &: Hard Frost. 1645./ December: 8. at night, on Monday, new moone, it began to frize, and so continued exceeding violent, the ice of wonderfull thicknes, after a months time it thawed, a litle, and raynd, but continued to frize untill. Jan: 28. it begun to thawe, and raynd; the frost wonderfully in the ground, and the ice of wonderfull thicknes, nigh half a yard in some places. a quarter of an ell at least in my pond: by reason of thawes it was wonderfull glancy: the thawe was as earnest as the frost: admirable in its kind, the frost and ice was sooner out of the ground then expected:

30: ☞ This day I received a mercifull providence from god in my son who fell most dangerously of a chayre his mother feard his skull had beene broken, also before in freing him and his sister from scalding, of which they were in very great danger.

Jan: 30: 1645 Wheras a supply of bookes is necessary for mee, and my meanes but small to purchase them, I have layd downe a resolucion. to buy but few, and those of choice and speciall concernment, and to allott towards the same a moity of all those moneyes, that providence doth by guift or otherwise unexpectly and freely supply mee withall; and to purchase them at the second hand, out of libraries that are to bee sold.

31: Heard Mrs Cooke, the Coll. wife dyed in chilbed, having lyen in a fortnight, oh how gratious hath god beene in the preservacion of my whole family.

Feb: 1: This weeke god was good to mee and mine in our peace, health, and in other mercyes, in the Sabbath, and in the dutyes therof, the Lord accept mee and guide my heart in his feare and pardon my many sins and heale my soule.

4: This day I resolved upon and entred agayne upon the practice of Hebrew, I find it so usefull that I resolve to spend a good part of my time therin, and the Lord blesse and prosper my endeavours therein.

F: 8: This weeke the Lord was good to us in our health; and all outward mercyes, in giving mee a heart to desire to walke with him: Mr Cookes child came to our towne at night and dyed next morning, god gratious in preserving mine; rid to Coxall and preachd for them, a tedious jorney: god preserved mee safe in the same, assisted me in the Sabbath, gave notice of a day of thankesgiving. Lord prepare me thereunto:

9: A woman buryed in our towne that intended: die. 12. to have marryed a man whose wife was buryed but on the 12 day of Jan:[1] before, I perswaded him to the contrary, to stay a longer time. but god hath prevented it for ever. sett an Apricocke tree, by my buttery window:

12: A.P. day of thankesgiving, the Lord gives us sweet revivings before our full deliverance god good to mee in the day.

13: God good in the sermon, in sight of my freinds, coming home I found the brother of Alse Sewell had beene in towne Potter himselfe having spoken to him about the matter, being still the occasion to stirre this businesse, more and more.

Feb: 15: The Lord was gratious to mee and mine this weeke in our health, peace, providing for us, in preserving us from grosse and scandalous sins, in giving mee a heart to endeavour in uprightnes to walke before him; the Lord was good to mee in the Sabbath, the Lord in mercy accept mee, and owne mee for his owne,

16. rid to Wormingford kindly entertaynd by my Lady Waldgrave.[2]

[1] 9 February 1645/6, buried Margery Kendall widow; 12 January buried, the wife of John Hinkin. PR.

[2] Jemima, daughter of Sir Nicholas Bacon, and second wife of Sir William Waldegrave, lord of the manor of Wormingford-hall, who had this estate in dower in 1635. Morant, ii, p. 232.

17. bought Mr Pilgrims library for 16li. 18: brought it to Colne a very rayny afternoone, the bookes had no hurt, unloaded them. die. 19.

Feb: 22: The Lord gratious in our healths and peace, and providing for us, protecting of us when divers robbed; good in giving mee a heart in endeavouring to walke with him good in the Sabbath and the exercises therof, the Lord in mercy accept and pardon mee.

24: Lent Mr W: Harlakenden. 30li. god hath shined upon mee and increased us somewhat in the midst of all thes difficult times.

25: A day of P. Fast: wherin the Lord was good to mee, in his word, he accept mee and blesse our families people, and nacions, make me, an example of the doctrine of repentance and amendment of life. Since the last fast god hath beene gratious to our forces at Chester, in the west at Torrington; and though many in South Wales especially in Glamorganshire have revolted, the Lord is able to turne it to the best.

28: Heard of my sister Dorythy her great losse by catle, how good hath god beene in preserving my estate, the Lord in tender mercy sanctify thy hand to them, and make them inquire into their wayes and turne unto thee, that thou mayest blesse them.

March 1: God was good to mee and mine this weeke in our peace and plenty and health, and in preserving mee from grosse sins, and in giving mee a heart desirous in uprightnes to serve him the Lord good to mee in the Sabbath in the exercise therof. I preachd on humility the Lord make me truly so.

5: A day of P. thanksgiving for chester, and the victory at Torrington, god good to mee in the same, my wife very ill in the morning; yett came downe to the Pryory to dinner with Mr Harlakenden, Lord accomplish our worke thou hast begun, wee had mention of divers places taken by our forces.

6: Heard god was pleased to trouble one man with the sermon last Fast day; the Lord make his sorrow and trouble end in joy; I had gone to him but for the tediousnes of the weather.

7: The Falling doore in my chamber being carelessly haspt[1] fell downe presently after my mayde and daughter were gone downe, it was gods great mercy to preserve them. Lord lett mee not forgett it etc.

☞ March 6. 1645: carryed 4. quarters, of barly which I bought of Mr Litle at 18s. per quarter to Goodman Potter to malt for mee.

8: March: This weeke god was good to us in our health, and providing

[1] Falling door: folding door. Haspt: fastening for a door. SOED.

for us, my wife somewhat ill, and weakely. yett indifferent cheerfull. good in preserving mee from grosse sins, and in giving a desire of soule to walke humbly and uprightly with him, god was good to mee in the Sabbath the Lord forgive my faylings, accept mee in Christ Jesus, and make me serviceable in my place to the good of my people!

11: Received a letter from Mr Shepheard[1] out of N. England, heard of the wellfare of that plantacon for which the name of the Lord bee praised; god good in the preservacion of my sonne in a very dangerous fall from a horseblocke.

13: Mr Archer preachd as if the Presbyterians were all of them proud conceited persons, upon which I asking him whether he meant so, he sayd he would not answer mee, but gave mee very unkind words, Lord thou callest mee to blessing, helpe me to walke humbly.

M. 15: God good to mee and mine in our peace plenty. in the many mercies wee doe injoy, in preserving mee from grosse sins, in patienting my heart under some trialls, the Lord give mee an humble condescending Spirit, weeken my soule, and cause mee to walke as becomes thee. the Lord good to mee in the Sabbath and exercises therof in the affayres of state, the Lord in mercy blesse his people and accept my soul:

19. God good to mee in preserving my house from fire, the children having made a fire in the roome under my studdy, which might have beene a more than ordinary damage in respect of my bookes, My wife spyed it, and quenchd it, so that it tooke hold of nothing in the roome to god bee the praise.

My eyes were ill, and sore at one corner, and so continued for some ☞ time, it was a rhewme in them, the Lord continue my sight perfect, and give mee grace to use it to his glory that christ Jesus might have some soule brought home by my ministry.

M: 22: God good to us in our peace and preservacon, on the Sabbath, and exercise therof the Lord in mercy accept me and forgive my sins.

24: Heard that Mathew Sir. Tho: Honywoods son dyed suddenly, It was a litle elder than my boy Tho: god good in preserving my babes his name bee praised; my Lady fell in travayle upon the fright my god in mercy preserve her.

25: Day of P. Fast, god good to me therin, he was pleased to give mee

[1] Thomas Shepherd, famous New England divine, and formerly lecturer for a short period at EC. Smith, pp. 28–30. His Autobiography, which includes a description of his EC experience, is published in *Transactions* of *The Colonial Society of Massachusetts*, xxvii (1932), pp. 347–400.

a good helpe of Mr Ludgater that day, my wife very ill at night, but mercy preserved her unto mee, heard of the route of the Lord Ashley. thus gods enemies fall everywhere;

March: 29: 1646: God was gratious to mee and mine in our peace, plenty and preservacion, filling us with every good thing, the Lord good in preserving from grosse scandalls in preserving all ours, good in the Sabbath, and in the exercises therof the Lord in mercy accept of mee and bee reconciled unto mee.

31: Rid to Mr Owens:[1] god preserved mee from a dangerous stumble of my horse; his name bee praised, Mr Owen removes to Coggeshall, he proposed a new project for gathering of churches, nothing but projects, and conceits our devices are best. god give us a good and helpefull(.) neighbour of him.

April: 1: Went to my Lady Honywood found her ill in bed, submissive to providence, Lord give mee a heart rejoycing in thee in all condicions, the Lord raise her up in mercy, my wife went forth, wee mett safe at night, when I heard a man at Halsted with a fall had broken his legge, which might endanger his life; my good god preserved mee the day before; another man is distracted and god gratious in preserving mee and mine, praised bee his name; my daughter Mary was a meanes to save her brother out of the pond, he being on the stayres his sister called out to the maydes this was thy mercy oh lord.

Ap: 5: This weeke the Lord was good in our peace, plenty, health, and in many outward mercies, his name bee praised, good in the Sabbath and in exercises thereof, the Lord god in mercy pardon mee and accept mee for his owne:

this weeke busy about wood, and bringing it home all my workemen preserved from danger to god bee the praise: Mr Guoyon[2] much out of temper. Lord its thy mercy to preserve mee. Injoyd the society of divers good freinds. Mr Wm. Harlakenden come to his house. I hope he will bee a very good neighbour.

Ap: 12: This weeke the Lord was good in many mercies and good providences to us, he in love continue his goodnes to us. I had experience of my owne weaknes, Lord uphold mee I am thine and cause me to delight in the(e): God good to mee in the Sabbath and exercises thereof, given notice of a day of thankesgiving, heard that an Anabaptist, rebaptizing a mayde who dyed presently was

[1] John Owen, eminent Puritan divine and author, later Cromwell's chaplain; at this time at Fordham, and later at Coggeshall. DNB.

[2] Robert Guyon, curate of White Colne 1634–*c.* 1644 when sequestered. Smith, pp. 115, 125; Walker.

committed to prison, the good Lord in mercy accept mee and keepe me from every error and evill worke, heard how I was threatned by Potter, but in my god is my trust, knowing I have not done more than I ought to doe.

Ap: 16. Kept a P. day of thanks. for our Westerne successes and over Sir Jacobb Ashly. wherin the lord was good to mee, as also in breaking up a match of wrestling in the towne, wherat were gathered nigh 500 people; Exeter was now in the catalogue of our mercies.

17: went to my Lady Honywood, a spectator of gods goodnes to her and child. as wee begd the mercy, the lord inable us to be thankefull, now wee have received it. etc.

Apr. 19. This weeke god was good to mee and mine in our health, peace, plenty, in outward mercies, in goodnes to soule and body, he was good to mee praised bee his name in the exercise of the day: my Lady Honywood ill with a fever, god heard mee for her, in respect of her deliverance and child, I hope he will also in this particular, answer prayers I mett their Lieut. Coll. Grimes who received an 100^{li}. guift from the Parliament for the newes of Exeter, which he brought to the houses.

20: I had a great loosenes:[1] which yett I conceive was a mercy, it made me somewhat ill, I was somewhat ready to vomit also at night, no meditacion so sweet as god, neither is it a comfort to bee well in comparison of seing, god in christ, I blesse god, my thoughts were more stayed in seing god mine then in hopes of my health, god answered my expectacion and desires in 21 day, having rest, and being much refresht: god good in the company of divers good freinds, Mr Earle[2] came out of the West unexpectedly to us, die 21. Mr high Sheriffe rod up to London, god in mercy preserve them and returne them safe.

The kindnes of Mrs M. Church to mee, 5^{s}. which was the more considerable as being gods returne to mee, having opened my hand to others, god opened her hand and heart unto mee.

April: 22. Went to my Lady Honywoods, mett good and honourable company. baptized my Ladies daughter Martha, the first person of that quality; god good to mee in the exercise therof, god hath hitherto holpen, lord still uphold them; at night had the company of Mr Wright an unexpected guest, but wellcome, I may find like kindnes from others.

[1] 'Looseness' and 'flux' were the commonest terms for diarrhoea at this time.

[2] Christopher Erle of Toppesfield, Essex, gent; related to the Harlakendens. Venn: Visitation of 1664–8, p. 32.

Rose-buds: wee had damaske rose buds in our garden before the midle of April this yeare 1646.

26. Mrs M: Ch: gave her litle Jane a coate, is it not the Lord who puts this love into her towards us Lord requite it a thousand fold into her bosome.

April 26: This weeke god was gratious to mee and mine in our healths, peace, and plenty, in preserving from grosse sins his name bee blessed and praised, Lord give mee a spirit of uprightnes and integrity, my dearest fayles somewhat in her household dilligence, a wise woman builds her house, Lord thou hast made her so, still continue her so. give me a heart of love and care towards her continually, god good in the Sabbath the dutyes and exercises of the day the Lord in mercy accept mee and forgive mee, heard of the good jorney of my deare freinds towards London, Lord give them a safe and happy returne;

April: 29. Day of Humiliacion Pub: god was gratious and mercifull to mee in the same, for which his name bee praised: Spoke with 2 in troubles of mind, wherof one professes much good gotten by my ministry, oh my god, it is a pretious comfort to heare of any workings upon the spirits, of any in thes backe sliding dayes. I gave them in pitty and act of love to my god the best directions I could, oh Lord in mercy accept their soules and quiett them and doe them good.

May: 2: Good society at the Priory Mr Harlakenden returned safe from London. and his company, newes that the King in a disguise was gone from Oxford: sic transit gloria mundi.[1] a report that their was a chardge drawne up against him about the death of King James: its reported when he was dressing of him, the Duke of Richmond asked him what he meant what he intended to doe, and whither to goe, he told him he must goe, but whither he must not tell him, but I goe sayd he to my freinds and thine, wherupon some supposed he intended the Scots army and Contry, but I imagine he intends either to lye hid somewhere or els for Ireland, which is most ☞ probable. this day on a suddaine sitting by the window in the priory parlour I had such a noise at my eare, which I supposed had been a great night dorre,[2] and lookd about for it, I presently perceived it was an exceeding noyse in my head, it ceasd without payne or hurt I blesse god.

1 Thus passes the glory of the world.

2 Dorre: dor, dorr, an insect that flies with a loud humming noise, spec. the common black dung-beetle, which flies after sunset. SOED.

May: 3: This weeke god was gratious and mercifull to mee and all mine in our health peace and plenty my dearest somewhat ill, yett no continuing distemper on her blessed bee the Lord. god was good to mee on his day, and in the dutye and exercises therof blessed bee his most holy name, oh keepe mee from sin and reconcile mee unto thy selfe in mercy I intreate thee. /

May. 8: At my Lady Honywood: heard of the sad end of one Rust who drowned him selfe, my preservacion is of god, of a monster borne about Colchester, first a child, then a serpent, then a toad which lapped; Mr Seymer[1] of Colchester dyed suddenly Lord make mee to waite all my time till my change come(.) the King found in the Scots army; Lord preserve the kingdomes in union; my Lady gave my daughter stuffe lace and silke for a very good coate.

May: 10: God good to us in our health, I was troubled a litle with a pose. it was very gentle blessed bee the name of god; the Lord preserved us there from grosse sins that others fall into, its of his goodnes, wee stand not in our owne strength, god was good to mee on his owne dayes in the duties and exercises of the same, for which I desire to blesse him, and to waite on him as the god of my salvacion.

11: With Sir Tho: Honywood, he gave mee two trees, their is no love or kindnes in any to mee but it proceeds from god.

12: At priory. trod on Courtiers legge a curst dogge, he whined but bitt mee not. a good providence. /

May. 17: This weeke god was good to mee, and mine in our peace, health, and plenty, the Lord a preserver from many evills, his name bee praised. lord forgive all my faylings in mercy I intreate thee, give mee to watch my heart, and Spiritt narrowly, the lord was good to mee in the dispensacion of the word, and the exercises of the Sabbath he in mercy accept mee and pardon and forgive my iniquity unto mee:.

19: P. Day of thankes. the Lord good to mee in; few of the parish hearing, upon which I desired people to take notice if the kingdome fall in as ours to slight god in his mercies and the word, this place might repent it and bee quickly barren enough, at night I heard of the health of my aunt Shepheard, I had an invitacion from them of olney to come over to them, but yett I shall make tryall of Colne. etc.

21. Stubd[2] my two trees, which Sir Tho: Honywood gave mee. my

[1] Samuel, son of Mr. Samuel Seamer of Colchester, or his father. Venn.

[2] Stubd: stubbed, cut down to a stub or near the ground; also, deprived of branches or pollarded, 1575. SOED.

lady was very well and came downe below stayres to god bee praise for this mercy to her: an exceeding hot day.

☞ 20: This day I had in my garden a full ripe and blowne damaske rose: May: 17. the Lords day before my wife had, a fayre bud: I conceived it argued a very early spring.

May: 24: God was good and mercifull to mee and mine in all outward injoyments, and keeping us in some measure in the way of his feare, Lord give an heart of uprightnes, and helpe mee to arrouse my selfe to watchfulnes against every corruption, that I may neither be burnt nor scorcht by them, god was good to mee in the Sabbath and the exercises therof, almost at night my dearest Jane went out of Church very ill, her lookes manifested it. it had troubled mee more, but that I considered I was in gods service, it was not fitt for me to lay out my passions of feare or love on the creature, when I was serving him that ought to have beene with all my heart. I praise god next morning shee was finely well and cheerfull, our good freind Mrs Mary Church also was in this last weeke very ill on a sudden, but well recovered againe next day, to god bee the praise of all his goodnes

25: My daughter Jane had a tooth cutt, this day shee was just 6 months old:

27. May. Day of Humiliacion publicke for the sins and miseries of the kingdomes.

May: 31: God was good to mee this weeke in our peace plenty in providing for us, my last quarter was now brought in and that fully by Mr Elliston. and Mr high sheriffe: I was somewhat troubled with a cold in my throate; this weeke waved a contest against my fellow ministers, in the case of independency;[1] layd the foundacion of my kitchin chimney May: 29: 1646. that day my wife began to still roses,[2] their was divers had mowne grasse for hay; god was good to mee in the duty and exercise of the day, he in mercy, accept mee and pardon and forgive all my unworthinesses unto mee, prayd for raine, the lord caused it to raine sweetly about 2 houres before sun went downe, and though at night it seemed the heavens promised none, yett I perswaded my selfe the Lord would give it us, it rayned very sweetly in the night, so that the wayes stood with raine. divers of Halsted come now againe on Lords dayes hither to heare;

[1] A public debate on the merits of the Independent or Congregational systems; it is implied that Josselin would argue their cause.

[2] Still roses: to distil or extract the essence of, probably for medicinal uses. SOED.

June. 6: Neyled my oven and made cakes in it for our workemen: this was the first I ever made for such an use in my life.

June. 7. This weeke god was good and gratious to mee and mine in our peace, health, plenty, he in mercy accept mee love mee and delight in mee, he was good to mee in the worke and service of the day.

11. A day to bee remembered with humility in respect of the experience of my owne weaknes and yett with thankefulnes in respect of gods great goodnes. that passage in Isay: 57.17.18 smott my heart.[1] ever Lord give me a tender spirit. I hope it tended to good, to greater care and watchfulnes, I am nothing in my owne eyes, nay Lord worse then nothing,

June: 14: A weeke of favours and goodnes from god to us, in health, peace, and plenty in variety of the creatures. the towardlynes of Mary to learne, give Lord to her the annoynting of thy owne spirit, that may teach her, and intrust her; the lord was good in the worke and duty of the day(.) I went to visitt Mr Tho: Harlakenden who was suddenly ill, my god make mee to waite all my dayes till my change come, after the full satisfying of the earth with raine I earnestly begd of god a season suitable to the time and creatures on the Earth, Lord in mercy answer our desires wee intreate thee.

16: At my Lady Honywoods, shee used us with much love, likely to raine, wee came home, but it held up untill wee came in Mrs Churches orchard and then rayned earnestly; a good providence,

18. At Mr Ellistons, my daughter Mary would staine behind, but at night nothing would content her but home. well bids the scripture wee should long after the word as the child for the breast. oh that no contents might ever keepe my heart from seeking the comfort of my soule in god.

19: Puld downe part of my old house; escaped one danger in espying the timber flying from mee, I had another fall with a fall upon mee but through mercy, I had no hurt, I had provided carts to bring home my trees but the unseasonablenes of the next day hindred.

June. 21. God was good to mee in outward mercies and favours, my wife onely ill with cold a mixture yett of mercy with the sorrow, the lord bee gratious to her for soule and body, god good to mee in giving mee a spirit sensible of my owne weeknes and desiring to live in uprightnes before him, god good to mee in the Sabbath and the exercises therof, enlarging my heart and enabling of mee to

[1] Isaiah 57, vs. 17–18, 'For the iniquity of his covetousness was I wroth, and smote him: I hid me, and was wroth, and he went on frowardly in the way of his heart.' / 'I have seen his ways, and will heal him: I will lead him also, and restore comforts unto him and to his mourners.'

speake home and close to my people gatherd also nigh 40^{s}. for poore Leicester.

24: Day of P. Fast, wherin the Lord was good to mee, my heart was troubled for the day in respect of my many occasions before, the good god accept, and pardon my poore soule.

☞ 25. 26. June. 25. my kitchin wood frame fell downe in the afternoone
27: towards night, and through gods providence no living soule received any hurt, I was at worke in it all the morning my selfe, divers went too and fro in it, it fell into goodman Brewers yard missd his pumpe, which I feard it would hurt if it fell; the next day I gott my pale sett their and left Goodman Brewer the most part of their bay tree, though it was sett under my eves droppe: I was now in taking of cold sensible of it most in my throate, a roughnes and kind of sorenes at the upper part next my mouth and especially on the left side, my former part of my head waxed grey apace,

June. 28. God answered my prayers, and blessed the meanes I used so that my throate was indifferently well, and no wayes hindred mee on the Lords day, wherin the Lord was good to mee as in the word taught, as also the weeke before in our peace and plenty, health and all other outward mercies,

29. This day I held against Oates, the Anabaptist,[1] morning and afternoone, argument that they had no ministry, and that particular christians out of office had no power to send ministers out to preach, he confessd it, and held only to doe what he did as a disciple; I shewed him it was contrary to scripture; our discourse was without passion. the man boldly continued in towne till wednesday, exercising all three dayes.

July: 1: Mr Watson[2] and Goodman Gaunt[3] with us, and heard by them (c.o. of the death) of my deare Aunt Josselins of Cranhams death my uncle Ralphs wife, shee had before her death sweet incomes of gods love, and desiring to joyne in prayer to god in thankefulnes, dyed in the conclusion of prayer: Lord keepe mee alwayes in thy feare and favour.

July. 5. This weeke the Lord was good to mee and mine in our peace, plenty, and preservacion in all outward mercies; in giving mee an heart desirous to bee serviceable unto him and to walke in

[1] Samuel Oates (1610–83), father of Titus, who gained some notoriety as a 'dipper' or anabaptist in East Anglia in 1646. DNB.

[2] Robert Watson, minister of Cranham by sequestration, 1645–*c.* 1652. Smith, pp. 398–9; Calamy.

[3] A John Gaunt of Cranham was assessed at 5*s.* in the 1636 Ship Money.

integrity, and uprightnes before him; god was good to mee in the Sabbath and the exercises therof he in mercy pardon and accept mee.

8: Rid to Colchester with my wife returned safe, praise be given to god for it.

J: 12: This weeke the lord was good in outward mercies; my heart still clogged with old corruptions, how cunningly Sathan endeavours to winde into mee, lord enable mee to trample him under my feete, the lord good in his day to him bee praise.

14: My Lady Honywood writte to mee to joyne with them in a day of humiliacion.

16: Ridde to Coggeshall to preach, but Mr Westly[1] preachd.

17: Joynd in a day of humiliacon with Mr Lowry[2] and others, the Lord good in giving mee a Spirit to eye him and to ingage with him against my corruptions, he in mercy give mee power over them. Mrs Mary went with mee thither.

My wife had taken pills and they wrought very kindly and carryed the winde sensibly out of her side, this night the payne returnd and the toothake, which brought her as it were to deaths doore, before sun, shee tooke some tobacco, it gave her through mercy much ease, Mrs Mary rose so early to come over to her, at night my wife tooke tobacco found much ease in it, and slept very comfortably: my sonne Thomas his eyes very ill:

July: 18: A motion made to buy the widdow Bentals land.

19: This weeke god was good to mee and mine in supporting and delivering my wife from great paynes: in the day, I was very unprepared, but god was pleased to goe along with mee and to helpe mee in the same to him bee praise: Mrs Wilsby dyed of a feaver, being well brought in bed, the greater is gods mercy in preserving my spouse: heard of the illnes of John Clarke, wee may be hid from one another but not from god;

20: Mr Harlakenden and I went up to the widdow Bentals, to view the land, which was hers by inheritance, John Kent her father had an estate in it for life, if redeemed but at present, it was in morgage for an 150^{li}. to two of Coggeshall, her father promised to joyne in the sale, shee asked mee, 220^{li}. as shee had been bidden, and I bid her price within 3^{li}. and parted till next day,

[1] John Westley, incumbent of Stanway in 1650, and perhaps 1645–53. His will proved in 1654, and in 1653 (8 April and 15 August) RJ purchased his books. Venn; Smith, p. 311.

[2] Thomas Lowry, sometime incumbent of Great Braxted, and later of Market Harborough. Smith, p. 405; Calamy.

21: Wee mett againe I gave the widdow her price, her father and shee surrendered it to mee wherupon wee tore a bond of 300^{li}.[1] that Kent had given not to trouble the widdow nor her heyres in the estate, so I came home very well satisfyed: but going up to John Read, he holds the surrender was good for nothing, because the morgagers stands for present possest of the land, this perplexed, especially because of Kents bond that was rent, wherupon I went up againe to them and giving them bond for their money they entred both into 300^{li}. bond to strengthen their act, with any further surrender at the next Court,[2] this wee feard Kent would not have done, but by providence he was willing.

22: I rid to Colchester to advise with my Cosin Josselin the steward, who advised mee to press the morgagers to surrender to mee, our Kent and Bentalls act was good for nothing wherupon I rid to Cogshall, and spoke with them and found them very willing to doe any reasonable demand, wherupon I sent to the steward who came over unto us

23: This day, and kept Court, Coxe(,) Gray surrendered the land to mee, paying them in their money, which I had all of Mr Harlakenden, to whom againe I surrendered the land for his security, in all this busines here was the providence of god and I hope indeed for good, all used mee kindly(,) Lord and stewart, and morgagers, and the sellers of the land, if had knowne thes parties could not have surrendered I had never then ventured on the land, but god kept that from us, which it was strange wee should not observe at first,

24: I lett my farme for 3 yeares to Brewer old Spooners sonne in lawe, without wood to dischardge Lords rent, tith, and pay mee 12^{li}. 5^{s}. per annum: I am to sett it in repayre and he is to keepe the same:

25. I put of the fallow to my tenant for 13^{s}. 4^{d}. rent, and 10^{s}. plowing, the rent I promise him, when he leaves it againe,

July: 26: This weeke the Lord was good to mee and mine in our peace, plenty, and other mercies, in the worke of the Sabbath, the good Lord in mercy pardon my sins and accept of mee.

Aug: 2: This weeke the Lord was good to me in outward mercies and mine, the Lord in mercy spiritualize mee and dispose of mee to

[1] It was customary to 'tear' deeds or indentures so that each side had one part which corresponded to the edge of the other's copy.

[2] At the court held on 21 October 1646 for Colne Priory, Edmund Cox and Ann Gray, widow, surrendered Mallories farm to RJ (John Kent and Anne Bentall, wife of George, acknowledging their release of the premises to RJ). ERO, D/DPr 22.

magnifie his name he was good to mee in the Sabbath, I gathered 8s. for an honest poore man because so.

3. My litle sonn Tho: very ill with a fever very sickly times; busy at priory in entertaining freinds:

4: Rid towards chelmsford with Mr high sheriffe a great trayne of gentlemen, and about 30 liveries.[1] he dined us all at his owne cost, ☞ I procured a chamber and entertainment for the Ministers, I lay well accomodated at my Cosin Rogers to god be praise.

5: Preached the assize sermon before Judge Bacon,[2] and Seargeant Turner[3] Judges of Assize, on Rom: 12:3.4: wherin god was good to mee, for voyce, and memory, and spirit, I dined with the judges who used mee with respect. Heard of my Uncle Joseph Josselins death. made no reckoning that his land would fall to mee.

8: I stayed all the assize time as chaplayne to Mr High Sheriffe, waiting on him at his board to say grace; he used me very lovingly and kindly, this day wee returned home safe to god bee praise: I was very ill at night after my travayle, but god removed the qualme speedily.

Aug: 9: This weeke the Lord was good to mee and mine, only my sonne Thomas continued ill of his ague, the Lord in mercy helpe him and deliver him and rebuke the distemper god was good to mee in the Sabbath, the Lord in mercy accept of mee and forgive mine iniquities

11. payd mony on my purchase, rod to Woodham Waters, returned safe, saw the house and some part of the land my Father bought of Mr Sammes.[4]

13: I grew ill with a cold, and a litle aguish distemper. preachd at the baptizing of Rob: Potters child: dind with divers freinds at the priory. my Cosen Josselins opinion was I had a right to Josephs land.

Aug: 16: This weeke my cold, and my sonnes distemper continued: gods hand is gentle. oh lett our lives and health bee pretious in thy sight, the rest of my family in health god good to mee in the Sabbath to him bee praise: Heard of the peace betwixt the Rebells,

[1] Liveries: retainers or servants in livery. SOED.

[2] Sir Francis Bacon (1587–1657), admitted to King's Bench in 1642. DNB.

[3] Sergeants were members of a superior order of barristers, from whom, until 1873, the Common Law judges were always chosen. NED. This was Arthur Turner of Parndon, Essex, Sergeant at Law, 1636. Venn.

[4] It has been impossible to trace this land, but it is probably connected to the 'Sams land' and 'Langford business' to which RJ frequently alludes, and which is almost certainly in the parish of Langford, Essex. The Sams family were big landholders there, and the court rolls allude to 'Sams Land' (ERO, D/DK M119, 1652 and 1660).

and the Kings party in Ireland. Lord helpe for designes are layd to enthrall us againe, and againe.

Aug: 23: This weeke also my [*cold contin*]ued and a very sad one it was, also my sonnes ague god was good in my wi[*fes health*] and the litle babe, wherby wee injoyed our rest well in the night, and her nu[*rsing*] helpe, the Lord drew in my thoughts. and helpt mee against some temptacions: its good to bear the yoke in our youth, the lord mix mercie with our sadnes, he was good to mee in the Sabbath, in the duties and exercises therof, the Lord in mercy accept and pardon mee and be gratious unto me[*e*]

24: Mett about Guy Penhacke: a fellow servant of his at Mr Litles chargd him to have beene 5 times naught with her and that shee was with child by him, the man denyed, wee pressed both and prayed with them, labourd in all solemnes of spirit that could bee to discover the truth, he denyed, and sayd he was cleare, he stood like an astonyed man that could say nothing, shee continued constant in her tale: shee died within 2 yeares Lord thou keepest mee, preserve from occasions that tend to this sin by thy grace, he said he saw the divel in C(*olne*) E(*ngaine*). but is yet alive.[1] This day my sonne Thomas tooke physicke for his ague, it wrought well on him to god bee praise the blessing upon meanes comes from god.

25: This day was exceeding wett the streets flowed exceedingly, I never saw the like in a shoure(,) I rid up to Sam: Brewer. prayd with him, he dyed presently, a young man left a widdow and 2 children. its good to bee sometimes in the house of mourning, the lord I hope will make me more closely to endeavour a spirituall communion with him, in the sight of the creatures emptynes.

Aug: 26. P. Fast. wherin God was good in enlarging my heart in praying and preaching, affectionat(ly) moving my spirit, he in mercy moved my spirit, pardon my sin, accept my soule and doe mee good.

27. Preacht the funerall sermon of S. Brewer, he had an imposthume[2] in his side, with very exceeding wringing paynes for some time before, the Lord better me by this warning.

28: A commission sat in the co[*ntry for ch*]aritable uses to inquire into lands disposed or moneyes for such end, and had n[*ot beene*]

[1] Guy Pennocke, 'farmer' of EC was ordered to answer for begetting a child on Judith Neale of Stisted on 27 August 1645 (ERO, Q/SR, 330/58). On the same date Sir Thomas Honywood examined Judith Neale who claimed that she had been impregnated by Pennocke and gave details of the times and places of intercourse (Q/SBa, 2/62).

[2] Imposthume: a purulent swelling or cyst. SOED.

performed. Heard of the death of my freind Mr Turner[1] minister of Wormingford, a lusty young man. the minister of Midleton[2] a young man dyed in a very short time of illnes. oh how watchfull, ought wee to bee, and to walke with the Lord all the day long my sonnes ague hath ever since his physicke taking come every day.

Aug: 30. This weeke my cold continued, but through gods goodnes much abated, and so was my sonnes ague onely it came every day; god good in the health of the rest of my family, and to my soule in this chastisement, drawing my spirit to eye him more, & helping mee against corruptions, the Lord was good to mee in the Sabbath in the worke a labour of the day, the Lord in mercy pardon my soule accept of mee and doe mee good:

31: This monday my wife and I rod to Havingfeild: I from thence, Sep: 1: to Cranham. found my uncles well, and fayre respect, in thes busines of my uncle Josephs land; die: 3: returned safe home, praised bee god who kept us, and preserved us in our way, Mrs M. Church having in the meane time tenderly looked to my children I found them all well, and that my sonne Thomas his ague had left him, to god alone bee praise: Lydia my former servant nursd my litle daughter in the meane time.

September: 4: Rod to my Lady Honiwoods where I mett much great company. their I saw one that once for divers yeares was accounted as handsome a man as was in the world, but now he was decayed; onely god is eternall.

Sep: 6. This weeke the Lord was good to mee in many outward mercies, in the visitacions and afflictions upon others. the plague increaseth and devoureth at London, the Lord in mercy aswage the same; the Lord was pleased to drawe my heart hereby to more watchfulnes and industry against corruption but above all to shewe me a righteousnes beyond mine owne, that of Christ to make me lovely. I found him good in the Sabbath, in the exercises of the day, my sonnes ague left him, he began to recover his colour, to god bee the praise of all,

7. Rid to Colchester god good to mee, going and returning, my Cozin Josselin told mee my cause in the busines of Josephs land was good, and he wished mee to proceed therin: a case at Assizes of a tenant that stood suite against his Lord for demanding 1 yeare and a halfe fine upon a descent.

[1] Thomas Turner, on the Classis in 1645, administration granted 1647, thus at Wormingford for only a very short time. Smith, *Clergy*, p. 94.

[2] Francis Gisborough, probably rector of Middleton 1645–7. Venn.

8: Rod to Wormingford, god good in going and returning; the sad change of that place and family, they were breaking up of all, the man dyed full of strong comfort, and peace. sent by Mr Toby Cressener letters to both my Uncles the executors of my grandfathers will to acquaint them with my clayme and intent to stand by my title unto the lands: bought some of Mr Turners litle paper with money Mrs M. Church gave mee, whom god stirres up to bee a faithfull loving and constant freind to us: the plague very much in London, and sicknesses in the contry, oh how great is thy goodnes oh Lord to mee, that the lives of my selfe and my family should be bound up, and pretious in thy sight

☞ 12: Upon an apprehension of the weaknes of my owne spirit, I made serious covenant with a deare freind to be a helpe to mee in the way of god, and to watch over my heart. I hope my god will assist mee and preserve me spotlesse and blamelesse to his owne comming Amen, Amen,

Sept: 13: This weeke the Lord was good to mee and mine in our health, peace and plenty, in many outward mercies, only my cold and stuffing did still continue, but it was gentle with great mixtures of mercy, god was good to mee in the dutye of the Sabbath, he in mercy pardon mee and accept mee.

15: Rid to Chappell with Mr Harlakenden and Mr Nevill to setle businesses betwixt them and the sisters, I blesse god I brought them to a fayre end and gave them all content, Mr Nevill promised to allow to his sister Mrs Mary. l^{li}. quarterly to helpe maintaine his sisters(,) wee came home safe, praise to god. my endeavours acceptable to them all, and above all I knowe tis an acceptable service unto god to continue peace and concord among brethren.

A merveylous wett season winter coming on very early, a great hop yeare, wheat this yeare was exceedingly smitten and dwindled and lanke, especially on strong grounds, all manner of meates excessive deare, beefe at cheapest 2^{d}. per lb. butter and cheese very deere and yett it was a very rich grasse yeare.—

September: 20: This weeke the Lord was gratious to mee and mine in our peace, health, and plenty, in helping us in our race, in preserving and delivering mee to temptacions the praise and the glory thereof be given unto him for the same: yett I was troubled with a pose, and rheumes exceedingly, god in his due time can strengthen mee against them, it is but a light affliction unto what others meet withall, the season was exceeding windy and wett: the Lord was good to mee in the duty of the Sabbath, and in my labour therin he in mercy accept mee, and make the word usefull; I gave notice of a day of thankesgiving on Tuesday following: on Monday September. 14: 1646 the Noble Earle of Essex died. his death is a great weakening to the Peerage of England;

Essexs death.

22: A Publike thankesgiving wherin the lord was mercifull to mee, in some measure enabling mee for the same, a very thin congregacion, oh how backward are people to waite upon god in his ordinances, lord continue thou thes mercies and opportunities to us, I intreate thee, and doe not strippe us of them as we doe deserve.

Septemb: 23: This day was a day of much mercy, some freinds fayling mee, I was supplyed with an horse for my jorney, and Mr Jeffery Little rod with mee; the day was exceeding pleasant the like not in divers weekes before, I had like with a packe horse to have beene beaten into a deepe loome pitt but[1] god preserved mee, I rod safe and returned safe praise to the Lord that kept mee. I found my uncle Simon at home, I made a demand of the land before three witnesses, which is in the box with my writings of Mallories; my uncle seemed perswaded and convinced of my right, and to deliver up the land to mee without any suite or trouble, when I came home I was very ill, I had a great inclinacion to vomitt, which through mercy I did and brought some water off my stomache, upon which I was well, went to bed and rested comfortably to the Lord be praise: whose stepps are goodnes towards mee.

24: drove through a bargaine betwixt goodman Death, and an Orphan of the Nevills for her land more to her advantage then shee expected: etc.

26: Mr Lorkyn with mee for his certificate of his qualificacion for a minister: to whom I gave my hand: the Lord in mercy more and more fitt him, and make him a shining light in the place where god shall sett him: I never gave my hand to any other but only Mr Carre as yett to my best remembrance: and herin I desire of god caution and warynes.

27: My distemper of cold and pose, continued and returned still, but without much present prejudice unto my gratious god be the praise, all the rest of my family in health, only my wife also complaynes of weaknes in her backe, this day the Lord was good to mee in the worke and duty of the day, he in mercy accept mee and pardon and forgive my great faylings, I was troubled with a paine on the right side of my head, yett praise bee god I continued able

[1] Loome pitt: loame-pit or lome-pit, a clay pit. NED.

to doe my worke, I received a letter from my uncles the Lord direct my spirit what to doe(.) I made a motion to my people, that the yeare being out, if they continued their contribucion and made it good 80^{li}. a yeare I would continue with them god willing, if not I must cheerfully serve the providence of god: and so I doe resolve by gods grace; Heard of the tumults at Halsted, (c.o. the doctor pulled out of the pulpitt) great disorders, Lord this ought not to bee thus. its thy mercy it is not so with mee also. etc.

28: Writt to my uncles to meete at Chelmsford Octob: 8. with either of us a freind to make a finall end and conclusion in our busines if possible.

Septemb: 30: This was the day of P. Fast. the Lord was good to mee therin, he in mercy accept of mee, and bee reconciled to mee and the nacion:

Octob: 1: Dind at Mr Braclyes:[1] my wife went with mee, Mr Ludgater brought mee this day my money, I payd the widdow now Penhackes wife all that I ought her, so that now all my debts are come into Mr Harlakendens hands.

Octob: 4: This weeke my cold and sometimes pose returned, and continued, but very gently through the mercy of my god, experience of gods goodnes in preserving our children from danger when neare them, the lord was good to mee in the Sabbath, he in mercy passe by my failings, pardon my sins and be gratious unto mee, and lett no iniquity have dominion over mee,

5: This day I rod to Yeldham, about goodwife Davyes money; I hope shee shall injoy her owne againe, I was wett coming home:

7: Rid to Colchester and preacht there upon: Phil. 2:3: wherin god was good and gratious unto mee, dind with Mr Mayor: I observed their a tame gelt rabbitt, like a litle lambe. it weighd about 7^{lib} the fatt on the kidney about a pound; I returned home safe to god bee praise, and without wett, providence casting mee betweene showres so that I was litle troubled with the raine.

8: Rid to Chelmsford, there by 9 of the clocke and very dry, and so also homewards, though very much raine fell that day, and before us on the road, my uncles mett not only Simon(,) wee resolved to goe over to Josephs executors. Mr Grimston kind in giving mee advice in my case; some hopes to get an augmentacion for our living out of Feering Berry being an impropriacion of the Bishops of Londons whose estate is now sequestrated:

9: Denham removed out of my house I thought I should have beene

[1] Thomas Brackley, incumbent of Colne Engaine from 1628. Venn; Newcourt.

very much troubled with him, my new tenant Brewer setled in the same:

October: 11. This weeke my cold continued, it lay in my head and chest, it was very gentle, god was a mixer of mercy in my condicion, the Lord was good to mee and my family in our peace and in preserving of us, keeping us from scandalous sins: Springats daughter with child againe as reported: god was good to mee in the Sabbath, in the duties and exercise therof, inabling me in some measure for it, the weather continued very wett and sad in respect of the season, litle rye and mislem[1] or wheat sowne, the Lord in mercy, looke upon us in regard of the season, the Lord pardon, and accept mee. / This weeke I drew up a peticion for augmentacion of our meanes it was presented to Mr Grimston, who promiseth all fayre respect, this was October. 9 and 10. god in(,) mercy prosper our desires and give us favour in the eyes of them that have power, and meanes in their hands to doe us good:.

14: 15: Rod to my Uncle Hudsons, god gratious in his providences towards mee, in ,providing me with horse: fayre season, out and home, in finding my way, preserving mee safe in my jorney. my Uncle Simon mett not, my other Uncles are very confident they shall injoy the estate, which if they justly doe I am content, wee agreed that our Counsell should discourse in the businesse:

16: went to Halsted: I was much troubled with a paine on my breast over my heart I conceived it was winde: spoke with Mr Fookes in Goodee Davies busines I find the mans debts so great that their is litle hope for her; went in with Mr Tompson[2] to take view of Mr Litles sisters: went up to the widdow Brewer to speake with her father, who will promise nothing toward the childrens portion though his eldest sons wee left it to his owne conscience, conceiving he cannot dispose the estate from them without some consideracion:

October. 18: This weeke my cold continued, but wearing away, blessed bee god, the Lord was good herin to mee and mine in divers mercies preservacions, good to mee in the duty of the Sabbath the Lord in mercy pardon and accept mee.

19: Went up to Mr Litles and made a motion of Mr Tompson to the eldest daughter(.) a new bridge laying at the stone bridge for the ease of passengers to passe in flouds:

[1] Mislen: maslin, etc., mixed grain, especially rye mixed with wheat. SOED.

[2] Robert Thompson, rector of Copford 1639–62. Smith, pp. 395–6; Davids, p. 378; Calamy.

20. 21: Mr Harlakenden kept his Courts; they were payring Courts[1] men coming in with their wives to take up houses most poore people, one man purchased a house to him and his wife, and their heyres, and for want of such heyres to the (c.o. rig) heyres of the survivor. wee chose two honest men for our constables Edw. Clarke, and Christopher Mathew, one Ames refused to make good a surrender; tenants whose estates are passed away upon morgage may not safely take a surrender.

23: Payd Mr Harlakenden 50li. I borrowed of him.

24: received a letter from Mr Harrington that my money was ready and that I should have it when I sent for it, for which I blesse god, at night I heard by Major Haynes that our shippe wherin my part was about 18li. was cast away, three men drowned, but the merchants saved their goods, this was the first froune upon my estate from my first being of age, it is the Lord lett him doe what pleaseth him; if I can upon the sense hereof be more faithfull in my place, watchfull over my wayes and vaine thoughts, I shall have cause to rejoyce: the Master of the shippe oweth mee above 6li. for hoppes, which I doubt will come in heavily: god hath given mee, if he take away shall I not blesse him. shall wee receive good and not evill, yes and in every condicion be content and blesse his name. This is but a losse of wordly things, to have beene overtaken with sin against my god hath cutt my heart, but this I value not so as to bee troubled.

A wonderfull sad wett season, much corne in many places abroad, rotted and spoyled in the fields, grasse exceedingly trodden under foote and spoyled by cattle through the wett which hath continued almost since the Assizes, worke very dead, woole risen to 16d. in the pound and upwards, butter and cheese, and meate very deare, and corne rising(.) litle corne sowne, and a very sad season still continued, great divisions and feares of our utter ruine in the kingdome. the Lord only is able to helpe, helpe for in vaine is all other helpe and assistance,

25. October. This weeke my cold continued I was seldome troubled but in the wheezing; it was a very gentle rod, and mixed with abundance of mercy, god was good in our preservacions and in our health, and peace, Mrs Mary our deare freind very ill with headake but by gods

[1] An example of husbands and wives joining or 'pairing' in the Colne Priory court for this date was the transfer of a tenement to Edward Somerson and wife Katherine, and to Giles Crowe and his wife Anne (ERO, D/DPr 22). The surrender referred to just below, of 'one Aymes', appears in this court as the surrender of Henry Aymes to Henry Hunt.

mercy now well againe; my wife hath had many brunts, but they blowe over to the Lord bee praise, god was good in keeping us from divers evills, mercifull in enabling mee for the Sabbath, my heart smites mee for my neglect of my studdyes through multitude of occasions; I hope god will blowe them over, gave notice of the Fast:

28. October: This day the P. Fast: sadly neglected by people, and my heart very much out of frame to such dutyes, custome makes us insensible, the Lord enabled mee for my place in speaking and praying he in mercy accept, and bee gratious to me a sinner and reconciled to this nacion: this day 6 yeare viz october. 1640. I marryed my dearly beloved Jane, the Lord continue us togither for his glory and the(e) good of our families many yeares if it bee his will.

29. Made a motion againe in Mr Thompsons suite to Mrs Elizabeth Litle; I conceive he may be welcomd, I acquainted him therewith by letter, and desired him to come over againe to her.
An unexpected breach with my deare freind Mrs Mary Church, but made up againe, to bee forgotten for ever, but the providence of god in it to bee remembred,

31. Mr Sayer writte us word that an augmentacion was conferred upon mee out of the impropriacion of Feering; if it prove effectuall, it will ease mee of much care and enable mee more closely for my studdyes: god can make up my losse at sea when it pleaseth him:

Novemb: 1: This weeke my cold continued, yett very gentle, god good in my health, as also to my family, in our preservacions, it appeareth likely to bee a hard time, the wettnes of the season continued with litle or no intermission and so it hath continued for above two months: god was good to mee in keeping mee from temptacions, and grosse sins, and directing of my pathes before him, and storing mee with comforts in himselfe. God was gratious in the worke and duty of the Sabbath, the Lord in mercy accept mee and forgive my iniquity.

4: My cold continued, I was also a litle troubled with a pose, this day god was good to mee in the publike exercise: a wett day, god in mercy amend the season and shine upon us in mercy,

6: Went to Halsted, heard good things about preparacion to hearing: afterwards heard that Goodwife Davy was likely to loose all her money about Purchas; heard also that my Cousin Benton had buried both his children, reported also himselfe very ill, the good Lord make mee to see and prize my mercies, in continuing his goodnes in our preservacion what am I that thou takest care of mee: Lord lett thy love inlarge my heart towards thee.

Nov: 8: My cold still continuing in stuffing and a litle wheezing in nights: I found a great mixture of mercy with gods dealing, receiving no prejudice thereby; god was good to me in the health, and preservacion of the rest of family, good in the Sabbath and in the dutyes therof, the Lord in mercy accept mee, and pardon my many sins, I have great experience of the treacherousnes of my owne heart, Lord undertake for mee and deliver mee from the power of every evill worke: Heard my 50li. per annum was likely to come to nothing, gods will be done, he is allsufficient to provide for mee.

12: A frost, and pleasant day, at night I was subpenad into the Chancery[1] by my Uncle Hudson, and Ri: Josselin: the lord order things for the best, and give mee a heart of peace and love, and lett not strifes alwayes continue, it was in the businesse of Josephs land. These dayes my deare wife was very ill, a great loosenes tooke her, which was for good.

Nov: 15. The wett season continued, so did my cold, it was long but moderate my wheezing even a litle abated glory be given unto god, the Lord make mee to gaine him my health and strength under all my bodily weaknesses, it is very observable that all this time my colds neither hindred my studdyes nor preaching, nor sleepe nor stomache, as god enabled mee for his worke so my body was serviceable to my owne comfort, the Lord was gratious to mee in the health and preservacion of the rest of my family good in the towardly disposicion of my daughter, giving her an aptnes to her booke the Lord make mee wise to trayne her in his feare: my litle daughter Jane began to goe alone: god was good to mee in the Sabbath, in enabling mee for the dutyes of the day, the Lord accept mee, and forgive my faylings.

18: This day I went to Stansted hall and received 8li. Sir John Jacob ought mee, I account it a good providence of god, I had great need of money, and had beene long putt of, I fear I had 6d. too much which I intend to restore to him injoy much love and good society at Mr Litles.

19: received an old promised guift of 20s. of Mr Wm Harlakenden. This weeke I found god very good in enlarging the hearts of divers unto mee in their acts of love, I observe no kindnes of mine at any

[1] An extract from the Chancery suit (PRO, C. 10. 38/110) is printed in Macfarlane, pp. 219–20. RJ finally gained the land, but soon sold it.

time to any poore distressed ones but god quickly makes it up, but their is not the least love I injoy from my freinds but it was of gods putting into them.

21: Heard of Mr Harlakendens Wellfare; also that he had received my money at London in which I rejoyce in gods providence towards mee for good, as also of his likelyhood to gaine an augmentacion for mee, thy will be done oh my god that providest for mee.

November. 22: This weeke partly fayre, and partly wett, not quite so much as formerly. two or 3 dayes exercised with a pose, which I hope god will turne to purge out my rheumes and abate the continuance of my cold. my wheezings cease: my deare wife exceeding tender and carefull of mee, which love of hers I hope I shall never forgett. the lord was good to mee and the rest of our family in our peace plenty and preservacion in the worke and duty of the Sabbath, he in mercy accept of mee, heale my soule and sanctify mee throughout,

25: This day was the P. Fast, it was wett in the morning so wee went not to Church untill eleven and I continued preaching untill sun was sett. wherin I found god exceeding good to mee, make mee oh Lord to taste of thy gratious loving kindnes more and more, and make mee endeavour to walke worthy of the same, the sad wett season still continued: Some sewe mislaine November: 23. et 24: I shall observe how so late sowne rye prospers it was on lusty lands, my cold through mercy is somewhat better, it lyes not so much in my breast as formerly.

26: Heard from London that Elizabeth my wives onely sister was well delivered of a sonne at Olny to god bee praised, her brother

27. Jeremy sent my litle sonne an Hatt: Mr Harlakenden came from London, he received 56[li]. for me of Mr Harrington, I made it up threescore and twelve pounds towards the payment of the hundred pounds I borrowed of him.

He and Sir Tho: Honywood joyntly obtained an order to receive the bishops rents out of the impropriacion of Feering 10[li]. or 12: out of Wittam 12[li]., out of Wethersfeild 15[li]. out of great Dunmowe 36[li]. and to divide it betwixt the two townes of Earles Colne, and Markshall, for my part, I conceive and trust in god that this may be some addicion to our meanes, the will of the Lord be done.

☞ 28: In point of Temptacions wee many times resolves watchfulnes, and eying of god and it is good, and to pray lord leade us not into temptacion, there are two degrees of watchfulnes, in the temptacion not to be allured, and 2[dly] before the temptacion to avoyde that and the circumstances that lead to it, the latter is the wisest course and the practice of many saints, lord make it my wisedome and my practice.

Nov: 29: This weeke the wett continued, when god once breakes the course of nature, wee and our reason is silenced: wee hoped upon the changes of the moone, fayre starlight, and frosty evenings, this winde, and that, but god in his time can send seasonable dayes, and provide for the seed and corne to thrive, he can provide against next yeare, food and clothing, oh that I could learne to depend on him and live by faith. My cold continued, but very gentle to god bee praised, an exceeding paine in my side. god good to mee and my family in outward mercies, in a heart sensible of my infirmities, there is healing in my god, I see it, nay thou wilt heale mee: the lord gratious in the worke of the day(,) word, duties and exercises therof. in society of divers honest neighbours at Goodman Mathewes. where speaking concerning our intermission of the Lords Supper,[1] I told them that perhaps some feared offending people in point of my maintenance they would deny mee my stipend, I told them for my part loving his ordinance, and to pursue the injoying of it by scripture rules, I would willingly trust god with my meanes and would not have them intermitt for that: and this I may doe and trust god who in his way will provide, the Lord in mercy pardon my faylings and accept(.)

30: Finding the exceeding misse of Hebrew, (*w*herof although I have a litle smattering) yett I begun this day to assume my dayly studdy therof, which I indent[2] god willing to prosecute, and not to give over if the lord give mee life, untill I have obtained some indifferent skill therof, oh my folly to forgett my school entrance, and to neglect this studdy and Cambridge and with no more dilligence to pursue it since, Lord in mercy forgive mee, and this I doe to fitt mee for a dayly exposicion of the scripture, which I intend ere long to sett upon its good to doe that wee doe quickly, for there is no working in the grave, whether wee hasten.

December: 2. 3: My tongue was sore, its easy with god to deprive me of any member, oh that it were my wisdome to improve it as my glory to his praise, as davids awake my glory, my dearest very ill this night, god was pleased to blowe it over speedily, an exceeding

[1] The payment of tithes was regarded with disfavour among Congregational fellowships, where the voluntary principle was stressed. Even a collection taken during a break in the celebration of communion was regarded as offending against this principle.

[2] Indent: to covenant, stipulate, agree about, promise. SOED.

winde in the night but god bee praised I had no hurt done at home, but my vine blowne downe. Mrs Mary promised to buy mee a frame[1] for my studdy, if my heart were but fully set to follow god, surely I should find him very good to mee, I cannot say I have kindl[ed] a fire upon his altar for naught, nor intended my service for him, but he hath beene seene for my comfort in the same,[2] Lord learne mee thy feare that may preserve mee and honour mee:

D: 6: My tongue continued a litle sore, yett praised bee god, it did not unfitt mee for the worke of the Sabbath: my cold continued, but very gentle: I went on in my endeavour in the Hebrew, and made good progresse therin, blessed bee on my god as also my family continued in health, the season still wett, but generally warme, men sewe, and corne did thrive well upon the ground, the Lord gratious in opening my condicion more to mee, in keeping mee from evill, and in ingaging my heart more closely to him, the Lord was good to mee in the exercise of his day, he goe out with the word and blesse the same; Things are duobtfull for the Scots and us, but Ormond in Ireland playd deceitfully.

8: I spoke to the joyner to make the Frame Mrs Mary promised to give mee; and gave him a patterne of what I would have done and how made, wee dined this day at Mrs Churches wee had some words, and discontents (c.o. about Mr Thompson) the lord give mee wisedome how to live inoffensively, and make mee to see his will in every particular, went up to Harry Abbotts, wee agreed indifferently well.

9. Mr High sheriffe with me, I drew up a peticon for him to the Lords to take of his burthen, he was much afrayd it would continue another yeare. I ventured with him, it would bee passed in both Houses a sheriffe for Essex, before Christmas, or I was to give him 5^{s}. for two bookes which if, I was to have them for nothing. Mr Wm Harlakenden went towards London I gave him 5^{s}. to buy me two Hebrew Grammers: his cheife occasion was about the sheriffes businesse.

10: Mett with divers of my freinds and neighbours at my speciall freinds house Mrs Church where wee had sweet and good discourse about the love of god to the creature, and truly wee knowe god

[1] Frame: a supporting or enclosing structure, applied to utensils of which the 'frame' or border is an important part. NED. Hence, probably a book-case.

[2] Passage crossed out in later ink: 'I called in and saw the poore sad case of Mrs. Tiffin *as* its nere cas*t* of by god and man, shame being proved out upon her, tis of the Lords mercy my condicion is not like hers'. See p. 51, n. 1 above.

loves us partim sensu[1] by experience of the same, in the steps of his gratious providence, and not onely by outward good things and partly by faith, in living upon him for love, as the fountaine of it, this spirit witnesseth to us that god loveth us, blessed bee the Lord that hath not shutt up his compassion towards mee, but hath kept mee from sins, temptacions, not suffered me to lye and live in the same(.) wee pitch upon a method and order for our meeting, to discourse of the principles of religion, and beginne, with mans creation, in what estate framed, and to what end framed. appointed our meeting at my house December. 25. following.

11. Mr Wm Harlakenden made a speedy and safe returne from London, our high sheriffe, likely to bee of that being another passed by both Houses, I received my two bookes from him, I am glad he is so neare an end of his troubles, and care in that office; the goldsmith of Chelmsford kild and robd upon the road, as he returnd from Braintree markett by three troopers its gods mercy and goodnes that preserves mee, my house, and that I injoy in safety

December. 13: Some dayes of this weeke windy and fayre, so that men continued to sowe corne but some dayes cold and raynie; my cold or inward stuffing, and in my head continued, but very gentle praised bee the name of god, my family in health, the Lord good to mee in keeping mee from many strong corruptions and temptacions, oh setle mee on Christ my resting place and waite on him to bee all unto mee, the Lord was good unto mee in enabling mee for the Labour and worke of the Sabbath, he in rich mercy accept of mee, and make mee more close in my walkings with him.

14: Went out a coursing. I tooke cold which turned to a very sad pose, which made mee very ill. Margarett went away from us,

15: Elizabeth our new mayde came, our deare Freind Mrs Mary could not bee quiett untill shee had hastened her to us, being tender what a trouble and greife it would bee to us to bee destitute but a few dayes, and indeed it was a good providence for at night wee were both very ill, and not fitt to rise till very late next morning.

16: Our deare Freind Mrs Mary out of her great love bestowed a 20^{s}. peice upon mee; I am never able to answer her love, Lord I will reckon it upon thy score doe thou returne it an hundred fold into her bosome, make mee a soule helpe and comfort to her, at night my cold begun to thicken, and to stuffe and wheeze exceedingly, the Lord in his due time will ease mee, I find it an exceeding hindrance in my studdyes.

[1] Partly through feeling or emotion.

December. 20: This weeke my cold continued and was strong on mee, yett through gods blessing it tooke not away my voyce nor strength nor stomache, and by meanes also I was not much the unfitter for my Sabbath imployment: I had a great payne on my left side; which went and came(.) in due time all sorrowes and troubles shall fly away, the Lord was very mercifull to the rest of my family in their health, my litle Jane was ill two or 3 dayes with teeth, oh our mercies, when others are in their graves and so left empty of their comforts, god good in keeping mee from many temptacions and evills, thou wilt in mercy to my soule restraine the rage of evill, oh continue this thy goodnes, my dearest, and Mrs Mary were exceeding carefull over mee in this my distemper, lett thy love oh father answer it, the lord was gratious and mercifull unto mee in the worke of the Sabbath, in carrying mee through the same, the good Lord in tender love pardon my unworthines, and accept mee, and inable mee in every condicon to live by faith on Christ to bee my all, gave notice of an extraordinary Fast, in regard of the sad raines, which abated this weeke in a great part, now this day it rained againe.

21: Mr Harlakenden received his dischardge from his shrivaltry, one Mr Pyott[1] being sworne in his roome for next yeare, I hope ere long he will act as Justice for the good of towne and contry. Mr Earle removing towards London they used us kindly att their departure, he gave me an 11^{s}. peice, shee my wife some toyes.[2] it was an unexpected kindnes, the Lord requite it againe in mercy to them.

December: 23: This day was a publike fast, on the lords day morning in regard the monthly fast followed the next Wednesday die 30: I was in a duobt what to doe, whether to keepe it or not, seing I had no notice, but considering its my duty to call for a mercy as well as any mans else, and if I neglect I doe my endeavour to continue the evill, I resolved to keepe it, though without publicke notice, but that morning before sermon I received an order, which I published, and on tuesday. 22: I saw an order wherin the rents of 12^{li}. per annum out of Feering: 12^{li}. out of Witham: 15^{li}. out of Wethersfeild and 36^{li}. out of dunmow. in all 75^{li}. was allowed toward the augmentacion of my meanes, and the Ministers of Marskhall equally which is 37^{li}. 10^{s}. yearely, and this the sequestra-

[1] John Pyott of Lowe Leighton, Esq. (Sir R. B. Colvin, *The Lieutenants and Keepers of the Rolls of the County of Essex* (1934), p. 184).

[2] Toyes: small articles of little intrinsic value. SOED.

tors are to pay at the due time, now its possible here may bee some diductions, but I looke upon it as a mercifull providence, and question not but that the order will prove in some measure effectuall, it was and I hope shall bee a further incouragement to waite upon the service of god my experience of his providing for mee; this day wee kept and through mercy I was in some measure able for it, I found my cold a litle in my voyce, and in my head, the day was very pretious and a very fayre drying day, and the season very good and pleasant, to god bee praise, answering our desires as it were before hand; I received a letter from my sister Dorothy to borrow 30^{s}. of me, blessed be god I have to give or lend, though now in great straites for mony, yett I intend either to give or lend, its better to give then to receive,

24: I rid to Stistead and preached and baptized Mr Alstones sonne Daniel, I injoyed very good society their, the day was pleasant: I was very aguish and sore when I came home and afterwards, but through gods goodnes, and my deare wives tendernes over mee and carefull use of meanes for my good. I was well after it:

December: 27. This weeke the weather was very seasonable, dry and cold indifferent, corne did worke very well on the ground, men continued still to sowe wheate, my cold continued very much upon mee, and some aguish humour in my bones, but blessed bee the lord it was wearing away. the lord was good to mee and my family in our health and peace, in tendernes of spirit, good in the duties and exercises of the day, the word and sacrament of baptisme, the Lord in mercy accept of mee, and in mercy delight in mee.

25: This day I had a meeting of divers honest christian freinds and others at conference at my house; the first meeting of that nature in my habitacion(,) wee discoursed of the image of god in man,

28: My Uncle R. Josselin of Cranham with mee, he went away this day, he brought mee my 20^{li}. when he went away he promised to buy mee a colt and fitt him for my sadle, a singular act of love, he related to mee the sad fall of Mr Watson their Minister, who had gotten with child one of Mr Thurgoods daughters, and marryed her against freinds consent, and one that was promised to another man(,) the act was foule especially from a minister, the lord humble him, and drawe him nearer by his fall, oh gods goodnes that keepes mee, Lord I stand altogither by thy mercy and goodnes oh keepe mee that I dishonour the(e) nott. heard of the distracted condicon of Mr Huson of Halsted, oh how great are thy mercies towards mee, received lately divers tokens of love from divers, mercies of my god towards mee.

December: 30: Monthly fast. I preachd but once, my heart is dull, and my body out of tune, the lord my god helpe and pardon and forgive and sanctify my spirit, and heale my soule and the nacion and delight in mee to doe mee good. heard the King was slipt into Holland, but I hope its not true,

31: This day I went downe to the Pryory to Mr Harlakenden and fully dischardged my morgage, and made even with him, I gave him a bill of my hand for tenne pound, and then when his fine is payd, I am in a good forwardnes out of debt to god alone bee praise. Mrs Church gave mee 5^{s}. for a new yeares guift when I was quite destitute, love in season, I was very ill this day and night with a loosenes, and aguish distemper in my bones.

Jan 2: This day Mr Faulkner[1] demanded his writings of Mr Harlakenden, he said he received 10^{li}. in part of 20^{li}. for the tithes sold, but now seing the time was expired, and he was compelled to what he did, he would not performe his bargaine:

Jan: 3: My cold continued, but not in the height, dayly abating, to god bee praise, the season was now dry, and indifferent warme; the lord is glorious in his doings(.) men continued to sowe, Mr Earle sent mee downe Jus divinum[2] putt out by divers London Ministers; this day, I preached and god was good to mee in the word, the lord enable mee to live the life of faith, and to depart from all iniquity for his love and mercy sake.

6: This day mett and discoursed with divers christian freinds at Mr Ri: Harlakendens concerning the end of our creation and remaines of the image of god in man, wee appointed our next meeting at Mr Wm Harlakendens:

7: This day wee begun to digge a well, which I lett to Fossett at 9^{d}. per foote: about 5 foote deepe or therabouts wee found water and so the spring continued for about 6 foote; wee digd about 14 foote, the chardge of them came to about ( ) shillings for digging, and ( ) hundred well bricke. it was a good providence of god wee found water so soone, they hope it will bee a fresh and a quicke

[1] Daniel Falconer of Aldham, instituted in 1624 and sequestered after a long struggle by 1645; died by 1653. Smith, *Clergy*, p. 77; Smith, pp. 115, 125.

[2] *Jus Divinum Regiminis Ecclesiastici: or the Divine Right of Church Government asserted, in which it is apparent that the Presbyteriall Government may lay the truest claime to a Divine Right.* By sundry Ministers within the City of London (2 December 1646). Thomason, E. 364(8).

spring and very serviceable one, its the mercy of god that maketh anything wee take in hand to prosper.

8: Went up with Mrs Mary to Mr Tho: Harlakendens, found him indifferently chearly, he complaind of divers paines. god mixeth many mercies with his trouble: divers very rude children their: the Lord make me wise and the educacion of mine and make them towardly for his names sake; returnd safe and dry,

Jan: 10: This weeke continued dry, and very warme for the time of the yeare, it rained on the 9. corne thrived this open weather, men still sowed, my cold through mercy exceedingly abated, so that I have litle or no mention of the same, god was this weeke mercifull to us in our health, and preservacion and outward mercies, my sonne had two fitts of an ague but no more, the lord good in preserving in and from divers temptacions, oh make mee humble and watchfull, good in his day, and word, and in helping mee in the same, the Lord, accept and bee mercifull to mee.

About Mr
Faulconers businesse:

I distinctly remember that Mr Faulconer sold to Goodman Taller[1] of Aldham a portion of tithes which he had in lease from Sir Robert Quarles which anciently did belong to the priory; he was to receive 10^{li}. presently, and 10^{li}. att the making of the deed, or setting over his right as Councell should advise and that within a short time,

Now wheras Mr Faulconer saith that Mr Harlakenden was to arrest him that so he might receive something from Sir Robert Quarles heire: I remember no such agreement in my presence but this I remember that Mr Faulconer giving in bond to redeliver the deeds to Goodman Taller, was to have the use of them if he could therby make any advantage against the heyre of Quarles:

And wheras Mr Faulconer saith he was to make neither bond or promise. I remember no such condicon agreed unto: only thus much that he was only to sett over his owne right, and to bee at no farther charge.

11. My workemen hewed one of the trees Sir Tho: Honywood gave mee for a pumpe tree, it was likely to make an exceeding good one: I sett up the wood that Tho: Cowell gave mee: Goodman Taller had the writing about Mr Faulconers businesse, Mr Harlakenden

[1] In the ERO (D/DPr 557) there is a loose sheet dated *c.* 1650 which has the name 'George Taller' on the back. It is headed 'The partable tithes of Aldham' and lists some nineteen pieces, including 'Of George Tollers land called Bonnobles 5 parsalles—19*s.* o*d.*'.

and he, both were confident I had it. I searched and it was trouble to mee I could not find it, att last it was in their owne possession in which providence I rejoyce:

Jan: 16: This day, my workemen sett downe the pumpe, they promise to keepe it 7 yeares for nothing.

Jan: 17: This weeke was partly wett and dry, very warme for the season: die 16. the sun shone very hott yett wee have not had scarce any snow I saw none, hardly discernable if any, nor scarce 24 houres continuing frost; Mr Ri: Harlakenden very ill, the Lord in mercy to mee and to the family raise him up, my cold exceedingly abated, I scarce feele it, to god bee praise; the lord was good to mee and mine in our health, peace and plenty; my sister Mary somewhat ill, with an ague, heard from my sister An, I sent them somewhat to refresh them, blessed bee god enables mee to give any thing the lord good in withholding mee from evill that my nature is subject unto, oh keepe mee for my trust is in thee, the Lord was good to mee in the dutie of the Sabbath, in carrying mee through the same, the good Lord in mercy, pardon my sins and accept my soule.

18: Went downe to Gaines Colne, present at giving possessions of land, the manner thus any one cutts up a clod and sticke, and stickes it in the clod, the man that is in possession remaines alone in the ground, he to whom he delivers possession enters to him to whom he delivers the clod and so possession of the whole according to agreement, then he comes forth and leaveth the other in possession who then presently comes out: Memorandum that Robt. Potter is to pay to Mr Nicholson[1] the surplusage of the yeares rent for the fen[2] deducting the Parliaments taxes if he doe not redeeme it and upon that condicon received 4^{d}. of him. when I came home mine and my parents old freind Mr Dixon came to see mee, my young hopes Mr Rich: pretty cheerfull, a wonderfull darke night.

19. Mrs Mary gave me 5^{s}. towards my pumpe, none in all the towne shew so much liberallity towards us, oh that my god would abountantly answer all her love, for its for thy sake oh lord that wee find that love from her.

weather: 20: This day it snew for the space of a quarter of an houre and upwards: 21. it was a frost with the winde and so continued untill. 23.

[1] Probably Francis Nicholson, lord of the manor of Marks Tey from 1625 to *c.* 1656, citizen and mercer of London, whose son Francis held his first court in 1657. Morant, ii, p. 203.

[2] The fen: a part of Mallories farm, called Mills Fenn.

Sometimes it did not frize, but continued dry and did not thawe; thus this weather continued dry and warme and a night or two frost untill the end of the month.

Jan: 24: The Lord this day good to mee, in the worke of the Sabbath, in enabling mee for the same, he in mercy make the word effectuall; Mr Ri: Harlakenden, upwards againe, to the Lord alone bee the praise; my litle daughter aguish, the lord in mercy raise her up, and pardon my many failings, and my distempers this weeke and att all times for his Christs sake:

27: P.F: preachd about payment of debts, and restitucion; some are stirred, the lord make his word throughly effectuall, Mr Tho: Harlakenden and Wm Kendall, at suite, wee drew them both to arbitracion, they entred into bonds to performe it, but providence through the death of Mrs Kings daughter, so crossed us, that wee could not perfect our hopes of peace,

29: Goodwife Potter. in testimony of my many acts of love to her and in testimony of her love to me gave me an 11s. peice. this love is from thee oh god, requite it fully into her bosome againe,

I am now preparing for London to answer the suites of my Uncles about Josephs land my resolucion is this (by gods grace) to repaire to learned Councell, and if they say the right is mine, to endeavour an arbitracion, and make an end of the controversie peaceably if possible, and to stand to the end of the arbitrators whatsoever(.) if I have no right I will no way molest or trouble, but endeavour that those that have right may injoy it; the issue I leave to the providence of god with cheerfull and contented submission bee it for my gaine or not, as knowing his will is best, and had it not beene for waiting on providence, and according to my Counsells opinion that my case was good, I should not have lookd after the estate(.)

Jan: 31: The Lord this weeke was good to mee and mine in many good providences outward mercies, only Mary continued ill of her ague, and my dearest wife was taken ill, and had an ague fitt Jan—30: twice disappointed in our reference about Kendalls businesse; the Lord was good to mee, in the worke and duty of the Sabbath, he in mercy accept mee and pardon mee and keepe my heart humble.

Feb: 1: It snew, but not much, I had fine weather and indifferent good way, it being a litle frost, and came safe at night to Cranham, yett very weary and sore my horse trotting hard,

2: Rid safe to London, well entertaind at Mr Cresseners, but very weary of my jorney, I spoke with both the seargeants in our suites; gave seargeant Turner, a peice for his advice in both my causes: he declared to mee he was of my Cousin Josselins opinion, the issue I leave to providence.

3: Went downe to Westminster spake with both the seargeants concluded a meeting to end our businesse, March. 3. at London, bought a few toyes. payd my tenths to Abbott, returnd safe, to Cranham praised bee god, but very weary and sore, the wind blow hard in my face, Mr Watsons wife brought a bed.

4: Came home safe to god bee praise, and received a penny at my owne doore as a poore man, being unknowne to all mine; found my wife had continued ill of her ague, and Maries come to(o) every day. Mrs Mary had beene a tender nurse to mine in my absence, the day was cold I was weary, and somewhat sore, but my greatest trouble was my swelling in my groyne, on both sides but I hope through mercy it will not long continue,

6: I was very ill on my necke, with the winde, which chapt my necke very much. Newcastle ours, the King with our Commissioners, and the Scots going out of the Kingdome hopes of good agreement the Lord continue it.

Feb: 7. This weeke god was good to us in many mercifull providences, my deare wife and daughter very ill with the ague, the Lord in mercy sanctify it to mee and to mine and drawe mee nearer to him, and make us more mindfull of serving of him, the Lord give mee strength in mercy against my particular faylings; the Lords day was a very snowy day, god was mercifull to mee in giving mee strength for the same, the Lord in mercy give mee a heart alwayes to walke with him, and to serve him acceptably all my dayes; I had sensible experience of the deceitfulnes of sin, the Lord in mercy preserve mee, and give mee wisedome to walke with him,

9: This day, my wife had very litle of her cold fitt, her hott fitt was very bad, the lord in mercy bee praised for every beginning of good to her.

11. This day, to the Lord bee praise and honour, who gave us much the desire of our hearts my wife missing both her fitts, having only a litle aguish gr*in*ding of them about her, oh perfect this mercy for thy names sake.

Feb: 14: This weeke the Lord was very good to us in many outward mercies, my swelling abating, and growing well as also my necke, my wife continued well to god be praise, only my litle daughter Mary, ill, the lord in mercy in his due time restore her, my heart

I hope shall be quickned in seeking unto god for her, the Lord was good in the Sabbath and in the duties therof, he in mercy accept mee, and pardon my unworthinesses.

16: preacht a baptisme sermon for goodman Burton, dined their at a plentifull dinner, with good society and divers of my freinds, my wife abroad with mee, to god bee praise.

Feb: 21: This weeke our healths continued, only Maries ague, my wife and children have colds in mercy sanctify them oh god, and then take them away, heard the King came die 16. to Homeby with our Commissioners: the Lord good and gratious in the Sabbath, as also before in the weeke, in keeping mee in some measure close, unto him, the Lord in mercy pardon accept mee and doe mee good:

22: This day my uncle of Epping sent to mee to meete Thursday at London, but because of the fast I could not, Major Haynes suddenly ill, but well againe through mercy

P: Fast: die: 24: wherin god mercifull in giving mee strength for the labour of the day the good god in mercy accept us, and bee reconciled unto the nacion, very hard times I never knew the like want for money in my life, blessed bee god I have anything, learne mee in every condicion to blesse thy name, and bee content with thy providence.

Weather: The winter was warme, very wett, untill the Publicke Fast for good weather and since kindly: no frost untill February that month, most frost, the latter end very fayre, and comfortably warme, my apricocke and Mallegotoone tree had either of them a blossome or more upon them Feb: 27.

27. received notice by letter to bee at London March 11. to end our suite, all parties willing. I intend god willing to bee their, although it is the day after the fast, the Lord in mercy afford mee some opportunity of helpe for my place,

Feb: 28: This weeke god was gratious and mercifull to mee, and mine, in our outward mercies Maries ague continued, but I trust the violence of the fitt is abated, my wife is somewhat troubled with her goomes,[1] the Lord in mercy Sanctify his dealing to us all, the Lord was good to mee in the Sabbath, and in the duties therof, the good Lord in mercy accept of mee, and pardon mee according to the riches of his grace, I blesse the Lord that in some measure hath kept mee in integrity, give mee a pure and holy heart I humbly intreate thee, to serve the(e) acceptably.

[1] Goomes: gums at base of teeth.

Cromwell called home from the army to attend, the affayres of the house according to the ordinance upon which the new Modell was raised: reported so but not true.

March. 3. God good to mee in freindly and pious conference with divers Christians at Mr Cresseners, the lord affect mee with the vilenes of my nature, and make mee watchfull in thy might, and power against the Same. gathered Something to refresh the loynes of a poore man, although my present need of mony was great, yett I had something to lend to the Lord, which he in his time will repay.

6: God in mercifull providence, when I was at a great straite, had tryed all my freinds and could not provide my selfe an horse, supplyed mee with one from Robert Potters: this day heard that Sir Tho: Fairfax his army was come to quarter in our parts of the kingdome, the Lord in mercy turne it unto good, some of the generalls owne regiment att Halsted.

7: God good to mee and mine this weeke in our health, peace plenty in many outward mercies, the Lord in his due time raise up my litle daughter Mary her ague abates, but her colour is gone, the Lord good in preserving of mee from divers temptacions and keeping and ordering my pathes before him, the lord mercifull in the Sabbath the duties and exercises therof, a horse Captaine and some troops here attending on the word: baptized three children, the Lord be gratious unto mee and accept mee for his names Sake.

9. This day rid to Cranham but my horse was ill of the yellowes,[1] which perceived, I had him lett bloud, and gave him a drinke, I kept the fast at upminster where I sawe divers of my old neighbours and freinds

11: Rid to London safe, mett my uncle Simon, went downe to Sargeant Turners he could not attend to end our businesse, went downe to Westminster, wee delivered two peticons to the Lords and Commons to remove the souldiers out of the County,[2] the lords gave us thankes for our good affection, and promised to take it into consideracion, went to Mr Kequickes, found his sister Mrs Elizabeth King sicke of the small poxe; but in good hopes of her life, god good to mee in keeping mee from feare and distrust, though my head wrought somewhat with feare upo(n) it; as I returned into

[1] Yellows: jaundice, chiefly in horses and cattle. NED.

[2] 'On the 11th the Houses received a petition from Essex warning them against the danger of an approach of the army to the neighbourhood of the City, and imploring them that the petitioners might not "be eaten up, enslaved, and destroyed by an army raised for" their defence.' Gardiner, iii, p. 34.

London, I mett my uncle Ri. and Hudson, wee went togither lay togither, and that night and next morning, wee concluded our businesse. I to injoy the land, and to pay to them an 100^{li}. came safe to Cranham.

13: Came safe praised bee god to Colne, no souldiers with us as yett blessed(,) bee the name of god, found all mine well, and Mary rid of her ague, to god alone bee glory and praise, my charges besides jorneyes came to l^{li}. 10^{s}. and no more(,) the lord bee praised for this comfortable, contentfull end, the lord blesse them and theirs with the mony, and mee and mine with the lands.

March. 14: This weeke god good to me and mine, in our health, and preservacion, adding something to our estates, Keeping mee from many vanities of mind and spirit enabling mee for the duties of the Sabbaths, free from the noyse of souldiers the good Lord in mercy accept of mee, and keepe mee in his feare, and blesse mee continually.

17. A comfortable meeting at Goodman Johnsons, the lord continue our love, and lett the truth make us free, gatherd something for the poore,

18: resolved upon an exposicon of the Scripture, as I was preparing my bookes, I had a comfortable refreshing token sent mee.

19: Blessed bee god for the good newes Mrs King heard of the hopes of her daughters recovery(.)

20: My wife concluded shee was with child now gon 7 weekes with a boy. shee useth not to bee mistaken, lord give her strength, and cheerfulnes, and a heart to trust in thee at all times, and give mee more then ordinary tendernes of spirit over her.

M: 21: God was good to mee and mine this weeke in our health, and outward mercies: good in the Sabbath, the duties therof, good, in the preaching the word. I began to expound the scriptures beginning. Genesis: 1: the Lord in mercy fitt mee for the worke and make mee a blessing.

25: god good to mee outwards and homewards to Wormingford, and in the preaching of the word at the burial of old Mrs Pilgrim whose only will was to desire mee to preach and to give mee a 22^{s}. peice, which was performd, to mee a refreshing providence,

1647: 26: This yeare I begun in a visitt of the generall his Excellency Sir Tho: Fairfax. at my lady Veeres in Hinningham,[1] where I had the honour and favour to discourse with him, and dine with him,

[1] Mary, widow of Horace Vere, 1581–1671, when she died at Kirby Hall, and was buried at Castle Hedingham. *Complete Peerage.*

he is a man thankefull for respects, and yett casts away honour from himself(.) wee rid outwards on his way with him, tooke our leaves, and returnd in safety praise bee unto god:

Our Constant loving Freind Mrs Mary gave my wife a gold ring, and my selfe a silver tooth, and eare picke, as a remembrance of her love, my dearest wife would needs also bee so bounteous as to give mee a silver seale, to use and not loose for her sake. /

27: betwixt 4 and 5 of clocke come up Major Haines, and told mee Mr Owen desird to bee excused in his exchange with mee, I fell to my study, I was wholly unprovided, and my thoughts were disturbed, yett through mercy I went on in my worke:

Mar: 28: This weeke god was good to mee and mine in our health, and plenty. yett free from souldiers(:) the Lord in mercy deliver mee from the power of every corrupcion and keepe mee in integritie, Lord thou knowest the vaine boylings of my spirit, oh throughly mortifie them, and lett them never bee too hard for mee, god was good in the mercie of the Sabbath, in some measure enabling mee for my worke, and in my ordinary course, I had experience of gods goodnes towards mee, as also good, in the exposicion of a part of the scriptures, the Lord blesse all occasions and meanes to mee, mine, and my peoples: this day was a very sweet and cheerfull raine, this weeke wee brought a skippe[1] of bees from Malleries to the Vicaridge(.)

31: P. Fast, the Lord was good and mercifull in the same in some measure helping mee in the day in preaching and opening the word, the lord in mercy heare, and bee reconciled.

Ap: 1: This day rid to Mr Downings,[2] six of us mett, wee agreed to conferre about the lawfulnes of our ministry, to meete next month at Mr Westlyes

4. This weeke god was good to mee, and mine, in our peace, plenty, the lord gratious in shewing mee the weaknes of my spirit in any measure to serve him, or to resist my corruptions my god bee strength unto mee, and make mee dilligent and faithfull in the use of all meanes to serve him, god good in the Sabbath, the duty and exercises therof, sermon and exposicons, Mr Rogers[3] helpt me one part, many make fair for god and misse, some roote of bitternes, I lord have my bitter rootes of minde vanity and pollucion which then knowest, make mee watchfull and jealous that I bee

[1] Skippe: skep or skip, a beehive or hive. SOED.

[2] Joseph Downing, rector of Layer Marney, Essex, *c.* 1628–*c.* 1646. Venn.

[3] Daniel Rogers, author and sometime incumbent of Wethersfield, son of the well-known divine Richard; died in 1652. DNB.

not overcome with them. this weeke seemed blacke and darke in providences as if mutinies and troubles were yett neare at hand, the lord in mercy prevent them, and fitt us for whatsoever he will bring upon us.

5: Above 60 of Major Desboroughs troope quartered with us one night, I was free through providence, by them heard the gentlemen sent up about the peticon, that caused the declaracion of both Houses, were returnd, the matter quiett, that all officers in comission were shortly to meete att Walden, the lord in mercy direct affaires for the best, and prevent our jealousies: the souldiers are civill, divers of them cast out evill words, against presbyterians, and ministers particularly. L.E.[1] the presbyterians are so bitter; he did not desire but to quarter with some honest independent.

6: Captaine Laurence a very faire civil gentleman with some part of his troope came and quartered among us.

11: This weeke the lord was good to mee and mine, in our peace, plenty, and health, I had some remaines of an old cold about mee, but I hope in god, it will weare away, the lord made use of me to make up some differences, I have lost some honest men good neighbours, whose necessities for subsistence forced them to remove, lord I beseech thee in mercy make it up for mee, the lord was good to mee in the Sabbath, and in the opening of some part of his word the lord in mercy sanctify mee, and make mee an instrument of good to others: heard of the fall of Omsted, and of the strange transport of Mr Wm Sedgwicke about the day of judgment,[2] that should have begun on the last Lords day, Lord keepe mee in thy feare, waiting all my dayes on thee unto my change and walking with thee, the lord good in preserving mee in some measure in his feare, the lord make me upright before him.

16: Mrs Church hurt her legge: my wife suckt with leeches. Jane and Thomas a litle ill, and so am I with a litle cold: the Lord sanctifie all providences, and doe us good by them.

M: 18: This weeke the Lord was good to mee and mine in our health, peace, plenty, some bondages more of, my spirit, nothing will give any setled comfort but god, as occasions of feare returne, so will they, but god is a dayly support: the Lord good to mee in keeping me above my temptacions in some measure, the

[1] The sense is not clear, but RJ may be quoting a saying of the recently deceased Lord Essex. Probert.

[2] William Sedgwick, brother of Obadiah who had been vicar of Coggeshall, and rector of Farnham. Known as 'Doomsday' Sedgwick, claiming to have special revelations, visions, etc. DNB; Calamy.

good lord keepe me blamelesse before him for ever, the lord was good to me in expounding of the word, and in preaching of the same he in mercy accept me and owne mee and doe mee good forever.

20: Mett in conference with divers of my christian freinds and neighbours in conference at the widdow Clarkes, a sweet warmth of spirit: the lord keepe us togither in union and fellowship: at night wee had a kind invitacion and plentifull supper at my loving freinds Mrs Church.

April: 25: This weeke the lord was good to mee and mine in our peace, health, plenty, and outward mercies, mercifull in preserving from many evills and temptacions wherunto I am subject, the lord throughly sett my spirit right for himselfe, god was good to mee, in the exposicion of his word, and in preaching therof, the Lord in mercy make it profitable to the hearers, and continue to delight in me, and use me as an instrument to speake his praise: the weather was very wett, the season very sad and had continued so very long, I earnestly entreated god for faire weather, I could beleive it should be granted and so waited an answer:

27: this day and before, very faire, as the gratious answer of prayer, and so I looke upon it and desire to magnifie the Lord, and trust him in greater matters, a great part of Mr Harlakendens wall fell into the streete, by the bridge, no hurt done, only his owne damage, I received this day some mony from my tenant Brewer. this is gods goodnes when anything yields increase.

28: P. Day of humiliacon, the Lord made my spirit earnest and solomm in the word preaching the Lord make it take deepe impression, for the lord he eyeth how wee carry ourselves under his dealing with us.

29: a freindly and comfortable and profitable meeting of ministers at Mr Westlyes.

30: This day rid to Bollinghatch, all my uncles mett, and gave mee free and peaceable possession of those parcels of land given to Joseph, I payd the executors of Joseph 20^{li}. gave them bond for 80^{li}. received 7^{li}. 16^{s}. of the mony of my uncle Simon for rent due: god good in his providences towards us, outwards, and homewards(.) this land part of our ancient inheritance. now I have above 20^{li}. per annum in land, besides my wives land, and my stocke, but I owe in all above one hundred pounds.

May: 2: This weeke the lord good and mercifull to mee and mine in our peace, health, plenty(,) in many outward mercies, jorneyings, and occasions, only my left eye in the outer corner ill with a rheume, what I dresse it withall cometh with a haucke[1] downe into my throate, the lord mercifull in preserving of mee from many evills wherunto incident, good in expounding scripture and preaching the word, the Lord make mee dayly more light, for I am darke and weake the Lord in mercy bee gratious unto mee and mine and continue to use mee and delight in mee and pardon and accept mee for his names sake.

4. Souldiers removed their quarters from us, a busy day with mee in my owne private and in publicke towne businesse, yett toward night steppe in to conclude a day of mourning before the lord, he in mercy accept us and pardon for his names sake

May: 9. This weeke god good to mee and mine in many outward mercies, health, peace, plenty and in keeping mee from many temptacions incident to my nature, the lord gives me dayly to see in my owne slender abilities, and weaknes blessed bee his name for it, and blessed bee the lord for what I am, god good to mee in my studdyes in the whole weeke, mercifull in the Sabbath, preaching and expounding the word, congregacion growes very thinne, oh lord doe not give my flocke over to loosenes and error, people seldome frequent hearing the word, litle care of his worship: this weeke my wife weaned her daughter Jane, shee tooke it very contentedly, god hath given mee much confort in my wife and children, and in their quiettnes, which hath made my bed a rest and a refreshing comfort unto mee, this weeke gave us some hopes of blowing over the discontents of the army, and hopes of accord through the meanes of Skippon entertaining the command of Ireland, and the houses yeelding to the souldiers in divers particulars. heard of the sad condicon of young Mr Ri. Simons being sadly distracted, the lord in mercy pittie him, and raise him up, and show him favour

12: Injoyd the company and society of divers christian freinds at Mr Cosins house, where wee had very good and profitable discourse about divers particulars, especially about the sin against the holy ghost, this day I received in 50^{s}. quarteridge[2] from the towne, a greater summm then I had received in divers weekes before, heard also the good newes of my Lady Honywoods being brought abed well delivered of a sonne:.

this weeke produced two observable remembrances; of a freind Mr T(hompson) and Mrs E(lizabeth) L(itle) towar(ds) home I had

[1] Haucke: hawk, hauk, to make an effort to clear the throat of phlegm, to clear the throat noisily. NED.

[2] He should have received £3. 15*s*., one-fourth of the £15 due to him yearly from the town. Hockliffe.

shewn great love and care, in ripening marriage resolucions: yett though my neighbours married and never acquainted with the same untill past: when invited to come to them, I thought it wisedome to forbeare: the other of my Cosin Benton growne excessively fat and grosse for so short a space, as lesse than a yeare; he is now destitute of a place, an unsettled condicion is much to bee lamented, and pittied:. I received in two good jagges[1] of wood for my fire from my owne grounds:.

May: 16: This weeke god was very good to mee and mine in the continuance of our peace, health and outward mercies, in keeping my feete in his pathes and delivering mee from the power of many temptacions: the lord makes mee to possesse my wants, and surely one end why he shewes them unto mee, is to make me more earnest in begging, asupply for my emtines out of his fulnes, god very good in the mercies of the day, in reading and expounding the scripture, and in preaching the word, oh how sweete is the meditacion and apprehension of god a father, oh how love streames out from thence, god good to mee in my family, my eyes also somewhat bettered, tooke notice of the rudenes of divers about the congregacion, reproved them, and incouraged the officers to punish them, heard Mr Ri: Simons was indifferently recovered out of his distemper, lord sanctifie that dealing and chastisement of thine unto him:

17. Heard high language of the souldiers intencions and resolucions, though I scarce may creditt they should be so bold, yett I shall observe whether a multitude dare not attempt any thing, and learne not to judge hastily of things and persons and waite conclusion of thing(s.) reports of souldiers foote, abusing of women, they are now coming towards us, the lord be our guard and protection from their violence and insolency. I had some rugged wordes from one of them a Lieutenent about quartering, wherby I perceive how unable poore men are to containe their spirits, if ever they are in imployment.

May: 23: This weeke the Lord was very mercifull to mee and mine in many outward mercies, the rheume in my left eye that was some trouble to mee, through mercy wholly stayed(,) my wife is faint, but I hope having weaned her daughter, shee will gather strength: my litle Jane pineth and falleth away, as if inclining to the ricketts, the lord in his mercy to us preserve her, and strengthen her, and sanctify her, a comfort unto mee, a darke time for feares, murmurings, discontents, but in god is my refuge, this spring was forward

[1] Jag: a load (usually a small cartload) of hay, wood, etc. SOED.

yett all things continued excessive deare, if grass had not come on, our wants would have beene very great, wee had plenty of roses stilled some May. 22: heard of Mr Ri: H. welfare at London, busyed some part of this weeke in repaires at my litle farme; the Lord was good to mee in the Sabbath in the duties and exercises therof, expounding and preaching, the Lord in mercy seale mee with his holy spirit of adoption, and pardon all my faylings, and bee my god forever, and ever.

26: This day was the P: Fast. I expounded Gen: 9. and preacht once, people are very negligent in attending on the word, my heart is very unsensible of the sad state of things, Lord my god accept mee, and in thy christ be reconciled unto mee, and lett they love bee upon mee the praise of the riches of thy glorious grace.

☞ May: 27. Rid to Mr Ludgaters where divers ministers mett, and discoursed of divers particulars in reference to church government, but came to no conclusion, the widdow Rugle delivered mee 10^{li}. in mony which Thomas Cowell lent mee for a certaine time, the moneyes I intend from Mr Harlakenden to pay his fine that I owe him

May: 30: This weeke god was good, and mercifull unto mee, in my health, peace, and outward mercies, and towards all mine, my litle Jane takes her weaning patiently and I hope gathers strength, to god bee the praise of the mercy, my towne full of foote souldiers but very quiett and orderly, without any disturbance from them hitherto: the lord was good and gratious unto mee in the duty of the Sabbath and the ordinances therof, in the sweetnes of the word, the Lord in mercy accept mee and forgive all my faylings.

31: Payd Mr H: his fine: 8^{li}. for my land, he used mee reasonably, and lovingly.

June: 1: Mett in conference my cosin Josselin called mee away to desire me to preach at the baptisme of his child, 160. souldiers came to quarter in our towne, they should have marched and disbanded this day, but they refused, fell into distempers, and marcht towards their generall, the Lord in mercy give a good issue unto things: the souldiers marchd from us, June. 2: quietly, but afterwards they were a greater burthen where they became, it was a providence of god towards us, the lord doe us good by the same(,) the reports of the souldiers distempers continued, and their words very high, wee are still in the hands of god, and his purposes shall and must stand:.

3: A hearer at Cogshal lecture, mett Mrs Mildmay and divers good freinds, brought my wife home some cherries, wee had pease before: the Lord in mercy make mee to himselfe as ripe early fruite.

June. 6: This weeke god was good and mercifull to mee and my family in many outward mercies, only my deare wife faint, the Lord in mercy, preserve her, and sanctifie her, as a choice vessel to himselfe, and comfort unto mee; the lord gives mee to lay to heart our confusion, our disorder, and I intent no rest in my spirit untill I can bring in people into communion, and fellowship; lord in this make my heart upright, and give mee wisedome to walke in this worke according unto thy word; This weeke there is a sad turne and change on the face of the kingdome, what god will doe wee knowe not, the counsell of Jehovah shall stand, the poore ministers are in straites on all hands, but the name of the lord is a tower unto his; the lord was good to mee in the worke and duty of the Sabbath, make me more usefull holy god in my place I intreate thee; and continue me in thy love for thy name sake. /

9. Rid to Colchester. heard a very good sermon: promises that require condicons stand with grace 1: because wee having broken covenant tis of grace that god will renew covenant with us on any terms 2: because grace workes the condicon in us: 3. because grace accepts the condicon though imperfect 4: and because it gives a reward: our good workes are gods per modum principii. 2. operandi. per modum excellentie, et debiti[1]

preacht and baptized my Cosin Josselins sonne and heyre, Nathaniel. at Saint Nicholas Church. returned safe that night to god bee the praise.

June: 13. This weeke god was good to mee and mine in many outward mercies, only my wife though indifferently well, yett weakely and fearefull of illnes. the lord in mercy be grace, health and strength to her. my litle daughter Jane was very weakely: our confusions and disorders and want of communion are a trouble to mee, my resolucions are to the utmost to draw into some church order. Lord herein make mee sensible of my corrupcions and faylings and give me an upright heart in the worke and wisedome to manage it for thy glory and lett no discouragments make me give backe, make mee all things to all men that I winne some to glorify thy name, this weeke our distempers continued, but our hopes were the issue would bee good: the Lord was good to mee in the Sabbath in the duties and exercises theof to his name bee praise and glory.

[1] Through the rule of the operation of the foundation, through the rule of perfection and duty.

Spent much time and tooke especiall care to drawe up a faire peticion to the house that they would have speciall respect to our safety and the content of the army.[1] and this wee did as farre as possible without passionate overswaying affection to either part. and this we rather did to prevent the subscribing divers heady peticions that went up and downe the contry tending to disturbance:.

June: 20: This weeke god gratiously continued to mee, and to divers of mine, our wonted mercies of peace, health, plenty, only my deare wife somewhat faint, but when over, as merry as the pleasant roe, my Litle Jane weakely in some danger of the ricketts, Lord thou hast hitherto continually done mee and mine good, lett thy mercy for strength bee on that tender plant for thy goodnes sake; our disturbances in state continue and increase, the issue wee hope will bee for the good of the nacion: amen, amen: our present want of order and discipline is sad, I injoyed a meeting of divers of my people and invited divers others to tast their spirits in reference to discipline, and the hand of god was upon us for good, the lord my god make mee as a hee goate before my flocke in this worke, and continue mee in the worke to manage it with sinceritie, and zeale; wee endeavoured a faire peticion to the house, it was generally resented in the house, I hope it will prevent higher ones in the County from taking place, the lord was good to mee in the word preacht and opened, he in mercy accept mee, purge me, make mee to resemble him in holines to his glory.

21: a meeting of neighbours at my house, where wee made some progresse into our worke; 22. mett in conference at Bar: Clarkes where wee had good discourse. supped and used with good respect at our deare freinds Mrs Maryes: 24: at Cogshall Mr H. paid my ordinary for mee; wee had some discourse against our peticon, but it was very weake and irrational.

June: 27. This weeke the Lord was good to mee and mine, in our peace, plenty, in many inward and outward mercies, the times were sad the reproaches on the ministry, and threats against them very great, and many gaping for evill to come upon us, yett god is our helpe and refuge: and in him is our trust who is our sheild: god was mercifull to mee in the worke and duty of the day, the lord in mercy, accept and pardon.

[1] *Four Petitions to Sir Thomas Fairfax from the Inhabitants of Essex, Norfolk and Suffolk, Buckingham, Hertford* (*against the disbandment of the Army*). 12 to 16 June. Thomason, E. 393(7).

30: publicke Fast, reports sad, and feares great, the hand of god not considered, though sadly lifted up over us. at night contracted Tho. Prentice and Grace Bull.

July: 1: our gentlemen went towards London with our peticon, the Lord prosper and succeed them in the worke and undertaking, and give them favour in the eye of our Magistrate, mett at Mr Owens for conference, the peticion was well accepted, and thankes returned.

4: This weeke the Lord was good to mee and mine in our peace, plenty, and many outward mercies to the glory of his grace, and my comfort: the Lord is pleased to give mee to see into my weaknes and frailty, how unable to walke in the presence of god uprightly as I ought, and how ready to waxe wanton and abuse my mercies, the lord in mercy pardon mee, and accept of my soule, and all this vanitie on my spirit, even in the midst of these troublesome times, lord lett mee have power over all temptacions for thy name sake the lord was good to mee in the duty and worke of the Sabbath, his presence with mee in the word, but oh Lord thou dost not goe out with thy word to convince, and convert as of old, lord make me throughly to search my heart, and see whether tis not for my sin, that the word is so ineffectuall, lord honour thy truth in saving soules for thy owne name sake.

5. Mett at my house, I spent divers houres in discourse to acquaint my people with the misteries about church order, the lord direct us therin, and keepe our feete in his owne pathes.

6. The charge against the 11 members was this day delivered into the House of Commons.

8: Thomas prentice married I preachd and married them in a method that gave great content to honest people, Tho: Frends offerd freely he tooke above 56 pounds.

11: This morning Mr R: H. his kells,[1] were fired with new charcoale layd into them, it was discovered, and prevented, with litle damage, to god bee praise, who watcheth over many preserving them. and sheweth unto others (as here) the danger, and then prevents it:. two scares more with fires in our towne, but no hurt of consequence done through mercy: this weeke the lord was good and mercifull to us in our health, and outward mercies in the duty of the Sabbath, he accept and pardon.

12: Mett at my house, wee discoursed of divers particulars, the worke is weightie; the lord direct us in the same, people are full of their

[1] Kells: kilns, a furnace or oven for burning, baking, or drying. NED.

particular fancies: Mr Cressener at my house he was very bountiful to my children.

13. Mett at Moales in conference, I hope not without some effect.

July: 18. The lord was good to us in our peace and outward mercies. the good lord affect my heart with my faylings, and neglect of my watch, and lett mee never be in bondage to any corrupcion whatsoever. the lord was in some measure good in fitting me for the worke of the day, yett I am exceeding unfitt for the worke, lord inable mee, and helpe mee to performe the same to the glory of thy name.

25: The lord was gratious and mercifull in many outward mercies, in keeping mee from many evills my heart encline towards, in the worke of the Sabbath to his name be the praise.

26: This day the parliament was forced by the Londoners in the matter of their militia(,) the busines was plotted, and brake out on this occasion as some report, its like to (the) the rise of troubles to us, the King endeavourd to make escape from the army and joyne with the Londoners

27. House of Commons adjourned until: 29.

28. P. Fast, some intimacion this day of the busines, it is a sad busines and portends gods displeasure against us.

29. Mett at Mr Tompsons, agreed to keepe a solemne fast at Coggeshall August: 5: to intreat god for this poore nacion

This day the most of the Lords and members being withdrawn the members that continued mett chose a new speaker one Pelham,[1] voted themselves a parliament(,) Massey[2] was chosen to command the City forces, Skippon refusing.

the army marching up towards London to redresse tumults, the City makes great preparacions to defend themselves, and impute the combustions to the army, medling with their militia which they told them would raze the foundacions and cause tumults,

31: 2 Troopes of Dragoones were sent by the Generall to surprise the blocke house at Tilbury in Essex to command the Thames, which was effected:

Aug: 1: This weeke the lord was good to mee and mine, in many outward mercies; and although divers of us have colds, yett they seeme not at present much to impaire our healths blessed be god, the lord letts mee see into my weaknes and inability for the great worke that lyeth on my shoulders, the lord in mercy more inable

[1] Henry Pelham, M.P. for Grimsby and Grantham, Recorder of Lincoln. Venn.

[2] Col. Edward Massey, see Gardiner, iii, pp. 168–9.

mee and pardon my faylings: the lord gives mee to see my vanitie of minde, and pron(en)es unto mistakes, oh lord in mercy, prevent any roote of bitternes from springing up for thy name sake least I should be defiled: the lord arme my heart with a full resolucion against every evill, and possesse my heart with thy feare. the Lord was good to mee, in the word, and duty of the Sabbath, oh make it to take impression togither with thes sad dayes, and pardon my weaknesses for thy most holy names sake:.

5: Sett apart to seeke god in regard of the straites and difficulties by reason of the London tumults, wee mett at Coggeshall, and there the newes mett us of a preparative accord betwixt the City and army and much good newes concerning the same, the Lord answering our prayers while the thought was in our heart, the day was very comfortable. 8 ministers prayed and in the midle one preacht, god was very good to us his name have the praise of all

Aug: 8. This weeke the lord began to blowe over our feares of a new warre, the citye was in division and not as one man for a new warre blessed bee god, and that made way especially by the meanes of South-warkes complying with the army, for an accord which in my apprehension was one of the greatest acts of the army, per-
July: 27. formed on so great a city, a pretended parliament sitting to encourage them what was in their power and that from Tuesday when they had the first notice therof, by Wednesday sennight following, in (9) nine dayes the army entring Southwarke Aug: 4. and the accord made that night with London, the army being scattered the head quarters at Bedford, some souldiers in Suffolke, others 100[d]. mile and more from London. they say in their declaracion some were gone from them 200 miles, this was wonderfull in our eyes: this weeke the lord was good and mercifull to mee and mine for our health peace, plentie and many outward mercies unto his name bee the praise, the lord trieth mee with scornes and reproaches, and in some measure god gave mee patience and wisedome to silence the mouth of such persons, so as their was no just cause of compaint though I was taxed for lording, and domineering and doing R.A.[1] the greatest wrong that ever any did him, the lord by all tune my spirit to lowlynes and to live on god beyond all creatures. the lord was good to mee in some measure in the exercises of Sabbath, he pardon mee for his glorious name sake.

August: 15: This weeke the lord was mercifull to mee and mine in

[1] R. A. is probably Robert Abbott, a later Quaker with whom Josselin had a close and uneasy relationship.

our health, plenty and in aboundance of outward mercies, wanting no necessaries in thes exceeding deare and scarce times; and in times of great sicknes and illnes, agues abounding more then in all my remembrance, last yeare and this also, feavers spotted rise in the contry, whether it arise from a distempered and infected aire I know not, but fruite rottes on the trees as last yeare though more, and many cattle die of the murraine,[1] this portends something: the lord mercifull unto mee in giving mee some aprehension of my vanitie and taking of from those delights that my heart contemplated on, making them many times a burthen unto mee, when my thoughts are bending towards them. the lord was good to mee in the duty of the Sabbath. in the word, the lord make it profitable to mee and those that heare the same for thy name sake:.

August: 22: This weeke the lord was merciful to mee and mine in our peace and many outward mercies, this weeke the lord exercised mee with a rheume and sorenes in the inward corner of my left eye, but in a weeke finely well: my wife quickned this weeke, the lord in mercy carry her safely through, and give grace unto my litle ones oh make them thine, I had great experience of the weaknes of my heart to resist temptacions, oh lord undertake for mee, and sanctifie my soule for thy name sake, the lord in some measure with mee on his owne day his name be blessed and praised for the same,

Aug: 25. P. Fast, expounded, prayed, and preachd, about 5 houres, the word was solemne and my perswasions have many time beene that god would hasten some scourge upon the contemners of his word and ordinances, and his abusers of mercy and patience what the Lord will doe he only knoweth he in mercy spare and be gratious

26. rid to Mr Whitings[2] had conference about baptisme of the infants of scandalous and ignorant persons in the church, and wee resolved in the affirmative as not finding the faith of the immediate parent required as a scriptural qualificacion in ecclesia constituta, though it was in constituenda.[3] and therfore your children holy,

[1] Murrain: an infectious disease in cattle. SOED.

[2] John Whiting, at this time rector of Easthorpe, and from 1650 to 1657 rector of Lexden; he was of Lexden when Josselin noted his death. Venn; Smith, pp. 320, 339, 345.

[3] In the established Church of England (*ecclesia constituta*) it is not regarded as essential that the parents should be believers before the child is baptized, baptism being understood as a sign of regeneration and preceding conversion. But it was essential in the early apostolic or founding church (*constituenda*) that one parent be a believer before the child be baptized.

because the children of one parent beleiving. returned safe home to god bee praise.

28. The lord lett mee see my selfe a poore empty creature, and that I have no strength to stand unless he helpe. yett the lord mingles his mercy with my infirmities

Aug: 29: The times were very sickly and ill, but blessed be god, who was good to mee and mine in our healths, my wife exercised with qualmes and weaknes incident to her condicon, I had a cold and pose my continuall distemper and my litle Jane ill with loosenes and vomiting, but staid in some measure, but our illnesses, are gentle not taking us of from our imployments, god good in the season harvest generally had in, and the most of it, exceeding well, to god bee praise, who could have distroyed that litle crop on the ground: the lord was in some measure mercifull unto mee in the duty of the Sabbath he in mercy accept mee and pardon my faylings:

30: Meeting at my house, but very few, people are wonderfull backward, and opinionative(,) the lord in mercy give them a willing heart.

31: rid to Much Lees to see Mrs Ellin that went from her uncle without his consent and marryed my Cosin Josselin,[1] I hope they may live well, though they made an ill beginning(.) Hops were a very ill crop on the ground likely to bee deare, corne and all things very deare, an hard time for poore people. and all others.

September: 5: This weeke I was somewhat troubled with a pose, but though rheumes and pose haunt mee I praise god, they doe not cast mee downe, my deare wife ill of this child the lord in mercy sanctifie his dealing, and give her strength, and cheerfulnes of spirit and an happy deliverance, gatherd for a poore man of Felsted; I injoyed much mercy to god be praise in the health of my family, the times sickly. old Mr Tho: Harlakenden taken suddenly ill with the num palsy,[2] all on one side, the lord was good to mee in the Sabbath and the duties therof, my heart is not lifted up in the wayes of the lord as becometh mee,

6: Our deare Freind Mrs Mary ill with cold, the lord preserve her, and command health for her I received 10^{s}. given mee by R.P. wife: the lord requite her love into her bosome an 100 fold, acquaint

[1] Mrs. Ellin was the daughter of Jane Harlakenden, sister of Richard, by her husband Henry Clench, gent. Cousin (John) Josselin was the steward of EC manor and is not known, actually, to have been related to RJ. See Harlakenden and Josselin genealogies in Appendix 1.

[2] Num palsy: numb, deprived of feeling, or of the power of movement; palsy, paralysis or a condition of utter powerlessness, an irresistible tremor. SOED.

her savingly with Jesus: went about to gather tith, but I have not yett at twice received one penny: mony is dead, people are bare.

9: poore Bridget brought mee 2^s. 6^d. a great act of love and expression therof, in so poore a mayde, lord make her a gainer by the word an 100 fold. I was with poore Wm Hatch and there is some litle hopes of his recovery. oh Lord lett soule and body live in thy sight.

11: Heard of the ilnes of Mrs Turner, that shee lay at the point of death, who was lately with us but somewhat ill.

Sept: 12. The lord was good and mercifull to mee and mine this weeke in our peace health plenty, in many outward mercies, and in watching over, and in preserving of mee from temptacions and keeping me in some measure from many evills, that my heart is subject unto, the lord good and mercifull in giving me health in thes crazie times, though exercised with rheumes causing mee to wheeze when layd in bed, the good god mercifull in some measure to mee in the labour and duty of the Sabbath, the lord in mercy accept and pardon mee for his owne name sake.

16: a fayre day, land is through mercy in a good case, and the seed time good the lord send us plenty, all provisions are excessive deare and scarce to be gotten for our money, my deare Freind Mr Harlakenden lent me his cart, wee had home 5 jagges of logges, and there are about 4 more behinde; the tree was well nigh 5 loade with offall,[1] this was a great curtesy, and there is gods providence as well as mans kindnes in the same; in the afternoone wee rid to Fordham streete and made an end wee hope in the matter betwixt Mr Faulconer and Taller returned in good time to gods name bee praise; my cold that I have now taken lyeth very much in my (c.o. head) chest, the lord in mercy remove it for his mercy and for his goodnes sake:

Eyes: 17: When I was at the priory; my eye was suddenly a litle ill, it was my left eye on the inward corner; where sore formerly, and also my throate a litle rough inwardly and bankt as I thought, whether it were my rheume out of my head, or whether my throate came of my coughing being ill with one I knowe not, the lord in mercy, preserve mee, and sanctifie his dealing unto mee for his name sake:.

18: I was very sore in my bones especially armes, and thighs, whether it was my cold or my lifting of logs die. 16: I knowe not, this cold was a very sad one my throate continued as before, my eye somewhat better.

[1] Offal: that which falls, or is thrown off, as chips, dross, etc.; refuse, waste. SOED.

September. 19. This weeke I was very ill with a cold, and specially on the lords day, after the first sermon I was even spent, and rent in my head, god in mercifull providence cast in Mr Elliston to helpe mee, god good yett in the preserving my selfe and all mine from sicknesses, blessed bee his name; my uncle and my daughter were with mee.

20: Meeting at my house: people drive at an arbitrary maintenance of their ministers and upon their curtesy: but seing the scripture doth not command this, there is no reason that requireth us to yeeld to the same:.[1]

21: Went up with Mr H. to Wm Cowell: made up that difference betwixt his landlord and him, he gave him a generall acquittance untill. Mich. 1646. the man conceived he was wrongd that 20^{li}.: but his landlord promised him that if it appeared by his booke that there was not so much due to him he would repay the said mony to him that should be found not due unto him. my uncle and his daughter went from us homeward this morning, wee feared it would bee wett, but through mercy it proved a faire day for them.

September: 26: This weeke the lord was good and mercifull to mee and mine in our health, peace plentie, and many outward mercies to his name bee praise: my cold finely worne away, the lord in mercy give mee to consider of the vanity of my minde, in earthly imaginacions and give mee to endeavour faithfully against them, which I confesse I have not done, but pleased my selfe in ruminating on such fooleries. the lord give mee power against every evill for his mercy sake, the lord good in the season which was very faire, and as fitt a seed time as ever came, things are at that rate as never was in our dayes, wheat 8^{s}.: malt: 4^{s}. beefe. 3^{d}. butter 6. ob. cheese 4^{d}. candle 7^{d}. currants 9^{d}. sugar. 18^{d}. and every other thing whatsoever deare, the souldiers also returning to quarter againe with us, and that in a great proportion viz. 25: the lord was good and mercifull unto mee in some measure in the duty of the day, the good lord in mercy accept mee, and pardon mee; people especiall poore of both sexes and men are exceeding careles of the Sabbath, profanenes is readie to overrunne us:.

cold gone

27. This day wee had 25 Troops came to quarter with us, somewhat bold and vapouring(;)[2] through mercy I yett escaped free from them.

[1] The problems of Congregationally inclined ministers with the question of voluntary or enforced maintenance are discussed in Nuttall, pp. 138–9.

[2] Vapouring: vapour, to talk fantastically, grandiloquently, or boastingly; to brag or bluster. SOED.

September: 29. P. F: some few of the Troopers were with us hearing, the lord in some measure was mercifull unto mee in the word, tending to discover whether our ruine were approaching, yett or not, and our continuance in evill speaks it sadly that wee are, the lord in mercy prevent it if possible:

30: This day divers of my brethren mett at my house, wee discoursed concerning the baptizing of persons that are not in church state; wee agreed to discours it seriously the next meeting, and by vote it fell on mee to undertake the defence of the Thesis

Octob: 2: Some in my towne sett on some of the Troopers to desire mee to give way that Mr Neguz[1] might preach next day for mee but I refused, and in mercy, they were quiett and urged it no farther.

3. The Lord mercifull this weeke unto mee in my health and peace, and many outward injoyments. many of the Troopers present in hearing orderly, the lord in some measure good unto mee in the word preacht, and in the mercies of the day.

4: meeting at my house, some perswade themselves that none but reall Saints[2] are to bee in fellowship, so farre as we can discerne.

5 mett with mee in conference, made orders concerning our time of meeting to be sett for coming and breaking up:

7: Troopers removed their quarters, having staid with us 10 dayes. we had 25. of Capt. Tailours troope in Fleetwoods regiment.

Pose: This night I began to be much stuffed in my head, the next day. viz: 8: my nose rann exceedingly, and I sneezed also very much, thus doth the lord exercise mee with thes rheumes the lord in mercy, drawe my heart nearer unto him by his dealing with mee:.

9: my pose (through mercy) was staid, and I did not much feele my cold. my sister Anna was here with mee, I lent Mr Wm Harlakenden 5^{li}. to lend her for my sister Mary, whose mony he had, the bond was made to Mr Harlakenden but the mony is my sister Mary Josselins, my brother Tho: Hodson is to repay the same to my sister Mary, on Feb: 1: next ensuing, I also paid unto him 1^{li}. that was due unto him as a legacy, by our agreement:. I am glad I am in a condicon to bee helpfull unto my freinds:.

Octob: 10: This weeke the lord was mercifull in continuance of mine and my familyes health especially in thes times of sicknes and

[1] Though a well-known name in Essex religion, it is difficult to place this Negus, the most likely candidate being Paul, in 1650 minister of Butsbury. Smith, pp. 253–4.

[2] The word 'saints' was used by Puritans, as by the Apostles, to describe all baptized and converted Christians without distinction. More extreme Calvinists made a further distinction between the elect and mere professing Christians. For a lengthy discussion, see Nuttall, ch. iv.

providing for us in dayes of scarcity. the lords name be praised in the same the lord mercifull in keeping mee from grosse sins, make mee sensible of all my heart vanities, and lett my soule contribute the the praise of thy name; the lord was good to mee in my studies and preparacions for the Sabbath, and affecting my heart with the things under my hand, in strength to deliver his word, my cold through mercy being no hindrance unto mee the lord pardon and accept mee and doe mee good for his names sake.

Cosin Josselins businesse.

14: Mr Harlakenden paid my Cosin Josselin his wifes Mrs Ellens portion, they agreed very well in the businesse, he in my presence and others acquitted him and her from all Lords rents, fines, board etc: he told mee moreover that he had in his hand a legacy of three pound that her grandfather gave her which notwithstanding his generall acquittance, he intended to pay her afterwards.

October: 17. This weeke the lord was mercifull to mee in the continuance of the health of my family; and good in keeping my heart from many evills that I am subject unto, oh blessed bee the Lord that hath not suffered iniquity to prevaile over mee, the lord in mercy give me a spirit endeavouring to walke with him, the lord was good to mee in the word preacht, and expounding, wherein, on the consideracion of Rachels calling her child Ben-oni.[1] and on the contemplacion of this fact, such a passion surprized mee that I could not well speake, the Lord in mercy preserve my dearer then Rachel, the season was very faire and wholesome, the plague abated in London and chester blessed bee god, the kingdome in a strange unsetled frame.

20: My sister Dorothy and her houseband with mee, wee gave them such old things as wee any wayes could spare, I paid her 20^{s}. for her legacy. and I lent her 20^{s}. more, the lord be blessed that enables mee to bee a freind to any of my kindred, its better to give than receive:. / this day our meeting for conference at Mr Wm Harlakendens, where divers christian freinds

Octob: 24: This weeke wee had a continued experience of gods goodnes towards us, in the health, peace, plenty, and outward comfortable enjoyments of mee and mine, the times sad and darke for the state, every weeke full of expectacions but nothing done, the lord in mercy helpe us. the lord was good to mee and mine in the Sabbath for which his name be praised

[1] 'And it came to pass, when she was in hard labour, that the midwife said unto her, Fear not; thou shall have this son also. / And it came to pass, as her soul was in departing (for she died) that she called his name Ben-oni*: but his father called him Benjamin**.' Genesis 35: 17–18. (* son of my sorrow; ** son of the right hand).

Mr Owen very ill of the stone, the lord sanctifie his hand and spare him.

27. P. Fast.

28. Meeting at Mr Burroughes of Pebmersh: Coll. Cooke with us, who lovingly invited us unto his house to meete their one time in course; I positiond and maintayned the question: my brethren and I are none of the nimblest disputants, but exercise will quicken us I hope. Mr Harlakenden subpenad into the Exchequer at Mr Faulconers suite wherin both sides rely on mee as their witnesse, I hope in god, I shall dischardge my conscience uprightly:

30: My litle Jane fell downe the staires, I was going up and so catched her and saved her falling downe halfe of them, the mercy of god was great that shee should fall and have no hurt, and I also their so opportunely to save her; blessed bee the lord for all his goodnes herein

31: The lords day wherin god was mercifull to mee and mine to his name bee praise and to the soule of his servant in the word:

November: 7: The lord was good to mee and mine in our health peace in many injoyments deliverance from temptacions in the Sabbath to him bee praise

10: made an end after many jorneyes and much trouble of a suite between Mr Tho. Harlakenden and (c.o. Sir J. Jacob) Wm Kendall. Sir J. Jacob and Mr Jacob, in my presence and Mr Wm Harlakendens and Elias Savills did promise to see 12^{li}. 10^{s}. paid to Mr Tho: Harlakenden.

11. preacht at Coggeshall god good to mee in the same and in going and returning, I had conference with 2 troubled soules, and one of them god used mee an instrument to stirre blessed bee his name.

13. A day wherin I had experience of my weaknes and infirmity, falling against many promises and covenants. there is no uglines like sin make mee feare nothing nor beware nothing like it.

Nov. 14: The lord was good to mee and mine in our peace and plenty, and in the mercies of the Sabbath to his name bee the praise, The King Nov: 11: about or before supper time escaped from Hampton Court and went downe to the Ile of Wight to Coll: Hammond, who is one of the Coll: of the army (and is to marry Cromwells daughter) and its conceived this businesse was not done without the privitie of many great ones in the army; this is certaine letters dated that evening conjecturing whither the King was gone mention it as most probable to the Ile of Wight. great endeavours to divide the army, but not effected hitherto.

18: payd the last 40^{li}. of the hundred for my land at Roxwell, the lord in mercy who hath thus encreased mee, pardon my sins, and weane my heart from all vanities, and enable mee to serve him acceptably:

Nov: 21: God good in our health, in my freedome from Colds, onely I have a litle stopping in my pipe, which makes me wheeze a litle in the nights: the lord was good to mee in the Sabbath blessed bee his name.

24: P: Fast, generally neglected, for my part I shall endeavour to keepe it, and preach, though other ministers, and my owne people should lay it downe

25: Mett at Mr Brackleyes:

November: 28: The lord good in the continuance of our health, onely my wife very ill many times with this child, the lord in mercy blowe over those fitts god good to us in the Sabbath to his name bee glory:

December: 5: Lords day wherin god good to us, and in continuance of our mercies and also so also the next weeke and lords dayes: troopers among us, very erroneous fellowes, but otherwise indifferent civill The Lord was good in continuing mee free from pose and colds, onely now and then a litle stoppings, my deare wife under great feares she shall not doe well of this child: ill in her head and backe, one night ill as if she should have dyed, the lord in mercy revive her spirits, and give her comforts, and lengthen her dayes
divers sad accidents about us persons suddenly kild, hurt, the lord worthy to bee observd and praised in our preservacion:

December: 12: The lord was mercifull to us in our health, and in providing for us in thes scarce times, so that hitherto we have wanted no outward accomodacions, the lord in mercy remember my deare wife, who lieth under many sad feares by reason of her approaching travaile, teach her to trust in thee and doe thou command deliverance for her. the lord good and mercifull in the Sabbath and in the duties thereof, he in mercy pardon mee, and accept mee for his name sake;

D. 19: This weeke the lord was good and mercifull to mee in continuance of our health, lengthening out our tranquillitie, and in providing for us, so that we wanted no needfull refreshment, and in delivering from the power of sinfull temptacons he was good to mee in the Sabbath and the duty therof, unto his name bee the(e) praise therof

25. People hanker after the sports and pastimes that they were wonted to enjoy, but they are in many families weaned from them.

Dec: 26. This weeke the Lord continued gratious and mercifull unto us, in our peace, plenty, health, in all outward mercies, I was never so free from rheumes, poses, and colds, in all my memory as hitherto in this winter, only troubled now and then with a fulnes in my chest, and a litle wheezing when layd in bed, the lord mercifull in preserving mee from many faylings wherunto subject, he in mercy accept mee and incline his heart to feare him: god was mercifull unto mee in the Sabbath, and in the duties therof to his name bee praise.

29. p. Fast: 30. mett at Sir Tho: Honywoods discourse about infant baptisme:.

— — — — — — — — — — — — — — — — — — —

Jan. 1. my uncle Ralph Josselin was with us, he and his family in health,

2: the lord was mercifull unto us, and mindefull of us in our health, peace and enjoyments good in the Sabbath:

7: Endeavourd all I could the paying in the 6 months rate[1] upon promise to abate 3 more due, and to take of free quarter.

Jan: 9: The lord continued good to us in our health, and in the Sabbath, heard of the Votes of the Commons, which seeme to tend to the laying aside of the King, the lord direct them:

13: Our souldiers removed from us, I have through providence to this day never beene troubled to quarter either horse or foote; nor received any affronts from them:

14: paid in the most part of our 6 months assessment into the hands of the high Collector and received dischardges:

15: Went out a coursing with Mr R. H. and others, returnd home, and was very ill with head ake and sudden fluxe[2] of rheume, at night, 60 of Major Swallowes Troope in Whaley's regiment that were on the guard that night the King removed from Hampton came to quarter with us, though ill I was forced to make the ticketts:[3]

Pose. Jan: 16: My cold and pose continued, otherwise in reasonable health blessed bee the lord, and so were all mine the lord was good and mercifull to us in the Sabbath, and in the duties therof.

17. mett with divers of my people at goodman prentice, his house. I have received of late very many kindnesses and tokens from

[1] Probably the so-called Monthly Assessment, levied between 1645 and 1649 at irregular intervals.

[2] Flux: a flowing out, issue, discharge, an abnormally copious flowing of blood, excrement, etc. Rheum: a mucous discharge caused by taking cold, catarrh. SOED.

[3] Tickets: billeting tickets, to reclaim the cost of quartering troops.

divers of my parrishioners which I desire the lord to requite, and to make up an 100 fold into their bosomes:

18: Heard good newes of Mr Haines hopefull recovery in new England also the tidings of Mr Hurrells[1] death, who hath left a poore shiftlesse widdow, and of the dangerous illness of my Lady Denny, the lord still good to mee and mine.

22: Heard my Lady Denny hopefully recoverd(.) Mr H, come home safe to us to my comfort in his presence blessed be god

Jan: 23. The Lord good and mercifull to mee and all mine in our outward enjoyments the lord gratious and mercifull to my wife, who is more cheerfull and free from headaches then formerly, my cold indifferently over, not very tedious as formerly. heard Mr Burroughes ill and not able to supply his place the lord bee blessed for my strength, the lord make mee sensible of my faylings and breach of covenant and make mee more watchfull over my wayes I intreate thee; the times sad and full of troubles especially at London, the lord gives us peace and freedome in all our quarters, the lord was good to mee in his word and the exercises of the day, oh make mee dayly to redeeme my time I intreate thee

26: P. Fast, preachd and expounded the lord good to mee in the same, mett at Mr Coll: Cookes, few ministers there present, wee discourse concerning baptisme of infants.

Jan: 30. The Lord good and mercifull to mee and all mine in our outward enjoyments my wife still holding up her head, and going to Church with mee, the lord in mercy preserve her and give her a comfortable lying downe; and rising up, the lord mercifull to mee in the Sabbath, and in the duties thereof to his holy name alone, bee praise and glory. This month of January passed without any frost to mention, or much wett but was dry, and open, and warme, and free from winde even to the admiracion of persons: roses leaved out: fruite trees beginning to shoote out and so apricockes more, hedges budding out, gooseberries had litle leaves on them.

Warme January.

Febr: 6: This weeke the Lord was mercifull to mee, and mine in our peace, plenty, and health my deare wife weary and sometimes faint, yett through mercy they passe over, and shee still holds up her head, the lord in mercy bee good to her; this time was a sad deare time for poore people onely their worke beyond expectacion continued plentiful and cheape; money almost out of the contry;

[1] Nicholas Hurrell of Sible Hedingham, yeoman, had his will proved in 1649 (ERO, 100 BW 59).

what I spent now I borrowed and yett I wanted nothing nor mine; But Lord when wilt thou make me watchfull over the vanities and follies of my heart, I pray thee keepe mee that no corruption lead mee aside, the lord was mercifull in giving mee strength to preach and expound his word constantly morning and evening, he in mercy accept mee, and blesse his word to his glory and mine and my peoples good.

1. fit 7: meeting at Mr Wm Harlakendens, wee had good societie and discourse I felt my selfe somewhat aguish

8. Mr Haines tooke his leave of us to goe for New England. the lord in mercy conduct him thither in safety.

2 fitt. 9: Ill with my ague I was not sensible of a cold fitt, but I was very sensible of my hott fitt, my wife also very ill, I hope the lord will command deliverance for mee. I left my studdy window open it was a driving snow, but lay on the other side the house, so that I had no hurt in my bookes

10. Thursday at night I went to bed tooke a carduus possett,[1] slept and swett well my wife ill by me,

3d fit. 11. on Friday morning, one houre and halfe before day my wife was delivered of her second sonne, the midwife not with her, onely foure women and Mrs Mary: her speed was great, and I thinke the easiest and speediest labour that ever shee had, and shee was under great feares, oh how is the lord to be noted and observed in this mercy(.) I was very ill, with a hott fever fitt, my freinds but especially Mrs Mary very carefull of mee, the lord filled my heart and tongue full of himselfe, and made mee to enjoy peace in himselfe not withstanding all my iniquities

12: I was indifferent well and chearfull, the Lord sent Mr Rogers who did supply my place on the Lords day.

4th fitt 13: 2 Houres before day I was taken very ill, a litle chilling cold, and with a pronesse to vomiting; some neighbours came in, I was very sicke for the time, I vomited thrice, phlegme, and Choler, my burning fitt was short, and then I lay in a sweatt untill 3 of the clocke, which sweate spent and wasted the humour. I blesse the lord for a spirit of patience and submission he was pleased to give mee, and for the comfort of his countenance in my spirit, so that his love tooke away the dread of sin and death,

14. I drew up my thoughts, and purposes concerning my estate in

[1] Posset: a drink composed of hot milk curdled with ale, wine, or other liquor, often with sugar, spices; used as a remedy for colds, etc. SOED. A carduus (posset) was a thistle posset, used, for example, by Ashmole in 1647. NED.

writing, and tooke above 2 ounces sirrup roses which wrought very kindly with mee, gave mee 9 stooles brought away much Choler, I went to bed, with a perswasion after seeking of god, that he would rebuke my distemper; and however resolving to submitt with patience to his dealing, blessing him because his rod was hitherto a comfort

15: Missd my fitt, according to my perswasion, through the goodnes of god, my heate much abated; I kept in not having had such a restraint never since I was of age of discrecion; I had a good stomacke, but blessed bee god I moderated my desires for meate and drinke, taking many coole things that were sent unto mee, but especially by Mr Wm Harl. wife, I had the especiall care of Mrs Mary in this sicknes, my wife through mercy growes upward also apace thus god loades mee with mercies, oh that the Lord would give a heart unto mee that this strength and mercy might be layd out for his honour.

17: my child was ill, full of phlegme, wee sent for the physitian, he gave it syrrupe of roses: it wrought well. my wife perswaded her selfe that it would die it was a very sicke child indeed: I tooke my leave of it at night, not much expecting to see it alive, but god continued it to morning and it seemed to mee not hopeless: lord its thine, I leave it to thy disposing onely I pray thee give mee and my wife a submitting heart.

in this weeke dyed in this towne: 1: woman in childbed and 2 children. or before her time shee travaild and dyed: 2 young children more, and one young woman the lord make mee sensible of my mercy. Mrs Mary would not goe home, but staid all night with our babe, hitherto my wife preserved from feavers, and upwards, the lord perfect her recovery, and if thou lord breake in with death into my family, oh make mee more carefull to live unto my god, and waite untill my change cometh.

18: This day was somewhat colder than yesterday: my water was better coloured more like to citron than formerly, but it brake, and so it did not the day before; my former breakings and sediments were red brickish stuffe, and much flegme like putrified stuffe in the bottome: Mr H. came in to mee, wee had some discourse about baptizing my infant, and in that time came in Mr Thompson, who was ready to performe that act for mee, the lord wash my Ralph and sanctifie him and accept him, and give him this life togither with a better if it bee his will, my sonne finely revived, but the night was unto it a very sicke night, but god preserved the life in it.

19: this morning my water mended, the colour was more to citron than ever formerly and clearer as if the humour were indifferently well digested. the lord bee praised, who gives me in some measure to bee content with his dealing, and to submitt to his hand; he knoweth what is best for mee, and therefore his will bee done. presently the child was as if it had fallen asleepe, the sicknes was very strong, and that cannot but move bowells, but thou shalt goe my infant into the land of rest, where there is no sicknes nor childhood but all perfection every one expected its death, but it revived againe, blessed bee my god. and gave us hope of its recovery: this day I went downe below staires, in the afternoone my nose bled about a spoonefull.

the day before and this my sonne was very still and quiet; in the last night very ill: at night I eate some oysters which I desired

20: this night againe my sonne very ill, he did not cry so much as the night before, whether the cause was want of strength I knowe not; he had a litle froth in his mouth continually, in the morning there came some redd mattery stuffe out of his mouth, which made us apprehend his throate might be soare: Lord thy will bee done, he cheerd up very sweetly at night; and in the night was very still, what god will doe I know not, but it becommeth mee to submitt to his will.

Feb: 20: This weeke I was through mercy well, heard no newes of my ague, my wife getting upwards as well if not better than ever. all my familie in health except my litle Ralph(,) he is not so tedious to us, because he doth not shrieke nor cry in his fitts but lieth quietly; we gave him brest milke at last, and litle else:. On the Lords day Jane fell into the fire, and afterwards daggd a paire of scissors in Thom: eyebrowe, but god preserved both from any great hurt blessed bee his name: I ventured abroad and preacht twice, knowing my strength belongd to god that gave it and he could preserve my body from danger while I was in his service, which in mercy he did, and gave me strength for the worke, lord thou knowest my weake heart and temptacions I pray thee give me watchfulnes and power against it, that I may follow the(e) fully, and that this rod may doe mee good, and if thou take away one babe lett mercy stand betwixt the living and dead to spare us.

21: This day my deare babe Ralph, quietly fell a sleepe, and is at rest with the lord, the Lord in mercy sanctifie his hand unto mee, and doe mee good by it and teach mee how to walke more closely with him: I blesse god for any measure of patience, and submission to his will. oh Lord spare the rest of us that are living for thy name sake wee entreate thee; this correction though sad was seasond with present goodnes. for first the lord had given it us untill both my selfe and wife had gotten strength, and so more fitt to beare it, then if in the depth of our sicknes; the lord gave us time to bury it in our thoughts, wee lookt on it as a dying child, 3 or 4 dayes: 3 it dyed quietly without schreekes, or sobs or sad groanes, it breathd out the soule with 9 gaspes and dyed; it was the youngest, and our affections not so wonted unto it: the lord, ever the lord learne mee wisedome and to knowe his mind in this chastisement.

22: Thes 2 dayes were such as I never knewe before; the former for the death, and this for the burial of my deare sonne whom I layed in the chancell on the North side of the great Tombe; their thy bones rest out of my sight, but thy soule liveth in thy and my gods sight, and soule and body shall assuredly arise to injoy god, and thes eyes of mine shall see it: yea and my god shall make mee see this dealing of his to bee for the best.

this litle boy of 10 dayes old, when he dyed was buried with the teares and sorrow not onely of the parents and Mrs Mary Church, but with the teares and sorrowe of many of my neighbours. Mrs King and Mrs Church: 2 doctor of divinities widdowes: the gravest matrons in our towne layde his tombe into the earth: which I esteeme not onely a testimonie of their love to mee, but of their respect to my babe. Mrs King and Mr Harlakenden of the priory, closed up each of them one of his eyes when it dyed: it dyed upwards, first in the feete and then in the head, and yett wonderfull sweetly and quietly:

Feb: 23: As often times before so on this day did I especially desire of god to discover and hint to my soule, what is the aime of the god of heaven more especially in this correction of his upon mee; and when I had seriously considered my heart, and wayes, and compared them with the affliction and sought unto god; my thoughts often fixed on thes particulars:

Wheras I have given my minde to unseasonable playing at chesse, now it run in my thoughts in my illnes as if I had beene at chesse, I shall bee very sparing in the use of that recreacion and that at more convenient seasons

whereas I have walked with much vanitie in my thoughts and resolved against it and had served divers lusts too much in thought, and in actions, wheras both body and soule should bee the lords who hath called mee to holynes, god hath taken away a sonne:

I hope the lord will keepe my feete in uprightnes that I may walke alwayes with him, and I trust it shall bee my endeavour more than ever

and also that I should bee more carefull of my family to instruct them in the theory of god, that they may live in his sight and bee serviceable to his glory. This day was the fast, I was neither provided in meditacions, nor durst not well if I had, have ventured abroad, and so I preacht not this day, the lord in mercy accept mee, and pardon this in mee, and not impute it to mee, when Aarons sons dyed he forbore to offer sacrifice the next time, my strength I promise in thy service by thy grace, I endeavoured to spend the day religiously in my family wherin god was good and mercifull unto mee.

24: Somewhat sensible of my cold and rheume than formerly; my wife weake and faint with the turning of her milke. yett blessed bee god finely upward in the day and at night, shee thought her milke was even gone away, heard old Mrs Harlakenden was likely to die, the good lord fitt her for that change, I was almost quite without money, and this day by good providence Mr Lewis paid mee 11^{s}. a supply to my present need,

25: Somewhat worse with my cold; I sneezed; I had the pose; my nose was full of thicker matter than at some other times; I had a great paine in my right side, but with warme clothes its gone praised bee god, my chest is not very much stopt, neither doe I wheeze very much, I hope through mercy it will cleanse mee and conduce somewhat toward my health, my water had upon it all that illnes like a litle fatt swimming at the top, when cold and sometimes perceivable presently it would hang on the side of the urinall when the water went away from it and this day it broke very white and thicke, like fludde, or pudled water in some clayey wayes: I brought up much rheume with annice seeds and colts foote in a pipe,[1] went to bed, was much troubled, but better through mercy than I could have expected.

26: heard Roger Londons wife of Gaines Colne[2] was dead who was well and at our towne at a meeting Feb. 15. the lord good in sparing my life and my wives: Lord in mercy to our soule thou shalt raise us up, and give us thy grace and we shall serve thee. my cold this day lay much in my chest, it straitned the same and made

[1] Coltsfoot leaves were used for smoking as a cure for asthma, anice-seed to expel flatulence. NED.

[2] The London family were of neighbouring Colne Engaine, where they had a five-hearth house in 1662 and owned the manor of Bromptons. Morant, ii, p. 219.

mee breath with wheezing, and some paine and difficulty: but the light of thy countenance is my banner, oh continue thy love and thy goodnes, and I shall in all condicons praise thee, at night much stopt with phlegme, especially when layd in bed, I tooke butterd beare[1] againe, and then word was brought Mrs Harl: was dying if not dead. I cannot say my minde was moved with any feare, but I grew cold, and quakt and could not hold a joynt, but in short time my heate returnd and shaking ceased, and the night was comfortable to mee, the meditacion of thy love and goodnes was my banner oh god.

27. This weeke the lord who afflicted mee, was very good and gratious to mee in giving mee inward peace and content of minde under his hand, and in the apprehension of his smiles and goodnes upon mee, through christ in the pardon of my sins and accepting of mee, which was a sweete support unto mee; the lord began to perfect his mercie in raising both of us upwards, my cold somewhat abated, I preached twice through mercy, and found no prejudice though the day was bitter cold god is as able to preserve mee in the open Church as in my close chamber when he calleth mee out to performe his service therin.

28. this day our nurse went from us: I was toward night somewhat faint and ill, but one sending us in a sacke posset revived mee, this was a mercifull providence of a gratious god.

29: My water stood all the day and night, and broke not, my cold through mercy did breake away, the lord bee gratious and mercifull to us all and preserve us and lett his grace sanctifie us. some neighbours with us to visitt us.

March: 1: this morning heard old Mrs Harlakenden, after 4 dayes lying senseles and expecting continually death dyed; the small poxe at chappell, our affliction in the feaver in our towne how gentle in comparison of theirs, the lord in mercy doe us good by his chastisements. heard Mr London was sicke of a spotted feaver, and that there was no likelyhood of his recovery; my water broke very much this day.

2. A very tedious snowy sleeting, wett cold day. Mrs Harlakenden[2] was buried with out one teare, neither was their a teare shed for her at home as I can heare. Roger London died last night, he lived not full 5 dayes after his wife, he was at our Colne on Satturday

[1] Buttered beer: buttered ale, a beverage composed of sugar, cinnamon, butter, and beer brewed without hops. NED.

[2] According to the PR this was Sarah, wife of Thomas Harlakenden senior, buried on 2 March.

last. he left 8 children, a sad family: To the lord comes thus suddenly on men, it should renew our care more especially to waite all our appointed time untill our change come; I had a very ill nights rest.

3. My water brake still, white clodded ragges[1] as it were; and a litle reddish I was indifferent well this day to god bee praise. onely sore in my flesh in many places. the night before god gave us a great deliverance, a cap[2] was flaming upon a coverd stoole and neare our screene; how fired I knowe not, its likely through our maides sleepines or carelesnes: but through gods mercy it did no farther hurt: rested through mercy comfortably this night.

4: A very snowy morning, much time wherin I kept in was weather, not very fitt for mee to stirre out in; my water brake very ragged and a litle red sediment it argued as I conceive a remainder of ill humours in mee and that nature was concocting and expelling them: my water almost continually when cold had as it were a cover of fat over it, floting upon the same, my throate was banked and soare, they said the pallate of my mouth was downe, but I rather thinke it was streyned with hauking up the phlegme or with coughing, and sweld partly with rheume fallen into it, I tooke some hot broth with pepper and found it eased presently

March. 5. All this weeke long I and all my family through mercy were upwards, and truly in all our trouble the lord was mercifull to mee in quieting my Feinde, and bestowing sweet and inward peace on mee in the apprehension of his love towards mee through Christ Jesus bloud and merrit: I praise god for it, and the remembrance of it to mee is very sweete that notwithstanding the sense of my wretchednes: my heart was staied in god, so that death and judgement was not feared, because of the love in god through Jesus: this day was a calme and shining day, though sharpe and cold; the lord in mercy was good to mee in the same in strength for the worke of the Sabbath, I preached twice and stood two houres in the afternoone; divers places round about had no sermons this afternoone, its gods goodnes to raise mee up and give mee strength that people that came from divers places might heare the word: through mercy I was onely a litle ill in my head, but at night, I

[1] Ragges: rag, a fragment, scrap, bit, remnant. SOED. Thus, a cloudy appearance of the urine.

[2] Cap: as well as meaning a cover or case, it can mean a closed wooden vessel or cask, and also a wooden bowl or dish, often with two handles, formerly used as a drinking-vessel. NED.

slept indifferently well. my water this day broke as formerly, my cold broake away very tuffe and thicke,

6: This day my water broke as formerly, through mercy in the day-time I found no trouble with my throate or cold, though in the morning my throate was swelled, and my rheume did abound more, and was thinner then the former morning; my night rest is with Continuall dreames: my wife in the night very ill faint and weake and rested not, our maide wonderfull out of quiett with a sore finger, so that shee especially had litle rest, I lay most part of the night in a great sweete untill time to arise.

7: When up, I praise god my selfe and wife indifferently well and cheerly. I was out a litle this day, not having stired out so much since I called the women in to my wife, I never had such a restraint before I thanke god, neither had I ever lesse mind to goe abroad; wee had this day some calves head to dinner which I much desired and Mrs Mary Church procured mee, who in all things hath beene as kinde to, and tender of me and wife, as if shee were our sister Lord doe thou repay it into her bosome:

I find my going abroad, did adde something to my rheume and cold, I was ill in my stomacke at night as if I should have vomited, but yett I did not.

8: This morning was snowy, windy and cold, which made mee keepe in, at night my wife in kindnes came and lay in my bed. heard of more persons dying at Gaines Colne and Halsted. I was never so bare of mony, and in my ilnes I had use for more then was ordinary, and yett I thanke the god of heaven my minde was quiet and content, and some lent, and others paid mee in mony aforehand so as I thanke god I wanted nothing all this time;

9: A pleasing morning but presently clouded and overcast, and blustring, and snowy. my deare wife faint and weake, and under great feares by reason of the same, my maide was ill with the headake. so as wee were in a poore shiftles case, but god gave us a good helpe Mrs Mary Church, who tended us all.

10: This morning was comfortable and cheerly to us all, the lords name bee praised for it; wee removed this morning downe into the hall. the lord in mercy command his blessing in health and all other goodnesses to rest upon mee and my family:.

11: This day I and my family cheerly through mercy, wee found not the hall cold but that wee could well endure the same; my wife only hath gott a cold in her necke which maketh it very stiffe; at night a poore woman fell into Goodman Burtons seller, and hurt her very much, its of gods mercy that my litle busy children have been preserved all this time. at night wee removed, and lay in our old chamber, It was a strong winde and stormy night, I feared my pales had beene blowne downe, but in the morning I found it otherwise.

March. 12. This weeke the lord mercifull in restoring mee to my health, so that on the lords day, I was neither tender nor weake as formerly and was able to expound and preach twice for ever blessed be his name, the lord hath made us forgett my sonne, who is dead and out of minde as to my sorrow, but I hope I shall remember his chastisement so as to bee carefull to walke closely with him: the lord good in giving mee a heart to follow my studdies, oh that it might continue, so that thereby I might bee the more fitted for his service, and many vanities might bee prevented, god kept mee from temptacions so that they have not dominion over mee, I find old vanities ready to looke me in the face, oh lett mee never give them entertainment againe; the lord gave me to heare the newes of the Indians their looking towards Jesus Christ,[1] oh lett them also find mercy, oh lett them be grafted on, and lett them become a people, and obtaine mercy, for thy Christs sake; heard from divers of my freinds, yett there is peace, oh lord send forth thy truth among us and bee thou our righteousness.

16: March: it hayled exceeding great hailestones, as bigge about as my digitus annularis[2] or one inch and halfe; there was no strong winde with it, neither were there many of them and so no hurt done,

March. 19. This weeke after a long restraint; god was pleased to sett mee at liberty againe I went abroad now commonly againe to any of my freinds and neighbours houses in my restraint, I read over Meads Clavis Apocalyptica. and Usser. his successio Eccles: and halfe Crakanthorpes history of the 5^{t} Gen. councell,[3] this day also my wife went to church with mee, the lord bee praised for this mercy in raising her up againe: my litle ones in health: oh Lord I finde my lazines and neglect of my studdies to take mee againe, and my old dregs and drosse returning oh lord I pray thee lett not my temptacions be ever entertaind as formerly. oh give mee a heart to

[1] It was during this time that the Society for the Propagation of the Gospel in New England was being set up, and John Cotton, whose works RJ read, was active. Davids, p. 163.

[2] Ring finger, or third finger on left hand.

[3] Joseph Mede (or Mead), *Clavis Apocalyptica* (1627); James Usher, *Gravissimae quaestionis de christianarum ecclesiarum continua successione historica explicatio* (1613); Richard Crakanthorp, *Vigilius dormitans, Romes seer overseene, or a treatise of the fift Generall Councell* (1631). All are in the STC. Joseph Mead is especially interesting (see DNB), being one of the most important millennial thinkers, and this work being his chief contribution on the subject.

handle them roughly at the doore and not lett them in, but lett my soule bee preserved wholly for thee, for in thee doe I delight, this weeke I received many kindnesses from Mrs Mary Church: who doth all things towards us, with aboundance of love, I might fill my booke with expressions, but they are too litle. oh Lord doe thou requite it into her bosome as thou seest best for her. god was good and mercifull unto mee in giving mee strength for the Sabbath and carrying mee through in the same, the good Lord in mercy accept mee pardon all my sins and bee gratiously reconciled unto mee;

20: a meeting at my house; divers christian people were not there but what was the occasion therof I knowe not, only I desire of god a patient heart to submitt unto him, and waite upon him in what he Library: will doe for us. made a full end about the library, I receiving from Mr Layfeild,[1] the mony and the residue of the bookes:

23: god hath cast us into times of reproach, called us to act in matter ☞ of government; which is loaded with aboundance of evill from many and those in the maine good men, in and under all this with the grace of god helping mee my resolucon is: to take more care to my feete least I offend: watch my words least I speake amisse, and my heart that it bee not impatient; also to be more faithfull in the worke of the ministry, and more carefull to search into truthes, putting on bowells of compassion towards others, and love to winne them, and impatience possessing my soule trust and leave all with my god:. this day the wife of Richard Appleton was taken suddenly ill, so that all accounted her a dead woman, and some said shee was dead, yett upwards againe next morning, oh lord doe it in mercy to her soule.

24: word was brought mee of the death of Mr Tho: Harlakenden. there is a good and a loving man removed from the earth to heaven, the lord make up my losses in this poore towne, good men die and remove and few or none doe stand up in their places

March:26:1648: This weeke the Lord was good and mercifull unto mee in my peace, and plenty, wanting nothing necessary in thes scarce times as also good in giving sweete health, and strength unto mee, the lord mercy in giving me strength for the Sabbath, and enabling 1648: mee in some poore manner to serve him in the same, this weeke seemed to portend new stormes and troubles, but if yett blessed bee our god that liveth for ever and ever; the lord bee magnified who hath kept mee this weeke past from the power and rage of Satan, and not suffered iniquity to have dominion over mee, the

[1] Edward Layfield, rector of Wakes Colne, 1640–66. Smith, Clergy, p. 83.

good lord in mercy keepe mee blamelesse unto the end, and in the end for Jesus sake.

27: This day was buried Mr Tho: Harlakenden the elder: a good old man who went downe to his grave, in a good old age, having lived about 10. yeares more then any of his ancestors, he was buried with creditt by his son, and with the love of his neighbours; who in multitudes accompanied him to the grave; I preached his funerall sermon on Job: 5.26.27. verses. he gave mee in his will a legacie of 20^{s}. and left his will with mee to keepe, which when I had read to the children, I delivered up to his executor Mr Tho: Harlakenden junior:

28: at night I was ill; yett I had a fine sleepe in the morning through

29. mercy, and slept very much in the night. and was loose: the next morning I was very soare especially on the outside of my thighes; my uncle Ralph Josselin, was with mee early on the fast day morning: the day was dry and windie and the sun shone though the morning was tempestuous, the lord was good and mercifull unto mee in enabling me to expound and preach: their was the thinnest audience that ever I had, the lord pardon my sins and accept my soule for his holy and pretious name sake;

31: rid to Colchester, mett Mr Newcomen, and divers other Ministers, wee had much discourse concerning falling into practice; and in the first place, seing that elders are to bee chosen; by when shall it be done, the parliament proposeth by the people that have (c.o. chosen) taken the covenant. others as Mr Owen conceived this too broad, and would have first a separacion to bee made in our parishes; and that by the minister, and those godly that joyne unto him, and then proceed to choosing:.[1] my horse threw mee as I returned home, but through the good providence of god, I had no hurt, at all.

April: 2: This weeke the lord was good to us in our health, and outward mercies, so that wee wanted nothing that was needfull, the lord to my soule also supply every grace, and make mee to abound therein to the glory of his name; I find my old vanities ready to putt up head againe, and sometime quasht at first, sometime I am dallying with them, and therfore I desire to nourish in my minde a daily remembrance as of gods deliverance, so of his chastisement and the engagement of my spirit therin: this Sabbath day I preached thrice; once I holpe a sicke neighbour of mine, expounded but once. the god of heaven good in giving mee strength for the same,

[1] There is a full discussion of this controversy in Nuttall.

he in mercy accept and pardon, and doe my soule good. I was ill in my stomacke, and yett very loth to enter into a course of phisicke(.)
Loosenes. this weeke I had a great looseness and griping of my body, avoyding thereby much choller, whiche I looke upon as a good providence of god towards me.

6: a hearer at Coggeshall, heard that the ministers with earnestnes endeavourd to promote church government.

8: Heard of one that dyed this morning in the feilds as he was coming unto towne(.)subscribed a peticon for government to the parliament, as also an encouragement to those London Ministers[1] that appeare against Errors. the lord heale a sad divided kingdome; Mr Newcomen sent to us to meete on Wedensday at Mr Thompsons about proceeding in the matter of church government, but by reason of occasions it was intended the wednesday following.

9: This weeke the lord was good to us in health and many outward mercies, the lord good in the revivall of the spirits of my deare wife from under sad feares of ilnes and death approaching, good in providing for us in this scarce and necessitous times; the lord in mercy make my lusts and corruptions stoope, and keepe mee that no iniquitie may have dominion over mee; the Lord good to mee in the Sabbath I preaching in the morning at Pebmersh, and in the afternoone at home; its a mercy that god hath early raised mee up to bee helpefull unto my neighbours I rid and returned safe; the good Lord pardon my faylings and in christ accept mee.
on this lords day at night, it rained a fine shower, blessed bee the lord who heard our prayers, it thundered and lightned also; and if I bee not mistaken my deare Jane will remember this night,

10: meeting at my house our discourse was concerning baptisme; mr Harlakenden was afraid of a writt from my lord of Oxford by a stranger from London, but he came about another businesse, by whom I heard of the sad tumult and rising of divers prentises and other rude people at London, wherin 5 or 6 persons were slaine, the lord in mercy quiett mens mindes and prevent new broiles, and troubles for his name sake, on the Tuesday morning it rained most sweetly, praised bee our good god, and the earth craved it.

Ap. 16: This weeke the lord was good to mee and mine in our peace health, and plenty the lord in mercie continue the same; through want of watchfulnes I find my old vanities returning, and sin entising; and ready to conceive, the lord make mee circumspect

[1] The Essex Testimony, in support of one published in December 1647, by fifty-eight London ministers. See Davids, pp. 307–8; Smith, pp. 102–10.

god good to mee, in the Sabbath, and duties therof, the lord in much mercy accept mee, and delight in mee and doe mee good.

17: Meeting at my house, people growe weary, and endeavour to give over thoughts of reformacion

April: 22: Mr Harl. sent for unto Stortford, and the next day he sent for his wife, the Lady Denny being a dying woman, the lord in mercy Sanctifie this providence unto them both. the Lady is exceeding ancient, and life cannot long be expected.

23. This weeke the lord good in continuance of our peace, health and plenty, in thes daies of want and sadnes blessed bee his name, wee wanting no outward needfull accomadacions: our times growe sad, and threaten stormes every day more than other places growe very much disaffected unto the parliament, our County now sett on a very dangerous peticon,[1] but I hope in my towne it is prevented, and not likely to proceed. the lord was mercifull unto mee in the Sabbath, and in the duties and exercises therof, the lord in mercy pardon my sin accept my soule and doe mee good and lett no iniquitie have dominion over mee,

24: rose and went downe to see my loving freind Mrs King take horse, who is going to London the lord in much mercy send her thither a sweete and comfortable journey.

preaching on the lords day concerning the duty of those that professe the faith to unite into mutuall societie, some of my people found their affections stirred up unto the same; others did seeme to oppose rather than to endeavour it:.

26: Fast day wherin the lord was mercifull: to him be the praise

27. 28: I find on observacion a mighty strength of corrupcion in my heart, deading my spirit, taking of my heart from spiritualnes in my life, and filling mee with vanitie in my thoughts; ready to hurry mee into great faylings: oh Lord I am weake. oh lord undertake for mee.

this day wee gardened: wee plant and labour, Jehovah the lord must give us all blessings.

30: Mr W. H. came home, all our freinds now indifferent well at Stortford, Mr H. my deare freind goeth on cheerfully in his businesse and that without any toile of spirit as he feared, and suggested to us by letter. the lord give him patience.

31: This weeke the lord good to us in our peace and health, my deare

[1] 'On May 4 a petition from Essex was brought to Westminster. . . . It was said to represent the wishes of 30,000 of the inhabitants of the county, who prayed that the King might be satisfied and the army disbanded.' Gardiner, iii, p. 372.

wife onely faint and complaining of weaknes as if swownings would seize on her, then presently prettily well and chearefull, the lord for his mercy sake raise her up to, and keepe her in perfect health for my comfort, and mine, and for the serving of his holy name. god hath cast mee into sad times, and yett my heart is as vaine as ever, and exceeding prone to forgett mercies, and promises made unto god, the lord in mercy make mee more zealous for his glory, and carefull to honour him, the lord in mercy was good to mee in giving mee strength for the worke and duty of the Sabbath, but my heart is guilty of not doing duties with all my might, I pray thee holy god therfore in mercy make mee more more carefull to attend to thy service for thy glorious names sake.

May: 1; This day I promised Tho: Cowell the 10^{li}. I borrowed of him, which by gods good providence I gott togither ready for him, that I might carefully performe my promise unto him; but he came not unto mee for his mony, this day wee had a comfortable meeting of divers persons at Goodman Johnsons, where wee had loving and sweete discourse especially concerning this subject; the Almightines of god, a stay in sinking and trouble some times, wee went on visiting divers of our neighbours this day, heard a report of a tumult at London: Norwich: and this day at Colchester, and through mercy all this time wee are in peace:. that at Colchester more in feare and rumour then in any thing else, upon which the Trayne band was raised

2: This day I paid unto Thomas Cowell 10^{li}. that formerly I borrowed of him; now my debts amount to about 50^{li}. I hope through gods goodnes towards mee in some short time to pay them all, if no troubles arise to hinder mee; writt this day divers letters to my freinds in Buckinghamshire, and sent them up to London to my brother Worrall to send thither for mee.

4: Mr Cosins dyed: and 6. buried(.)Mr Brewer preached

May: 7: This weeke the Lord was good and mercifull to mee, and mine, in our health, peace, preservacion, only in this day my wife very ill with a fitt of a feaver, occasioned, by being bound,[1] and so hindered in her rest, and distempered: the lord good in preserving mee from grosse sins, but my heart is subject to unevennes, and vanitie, and haste, and in my haste to speake rashly, lord in mercy pardon mee, and direct mee I intreate thee the lord was good to me in the duty of the Sabbath, enabling mee with strength and making

[1] Bound: confined in the bowels, costive. NED. Can also mean pregnant, but this is unlikely, especially as the next birth was twelve months later.

the word sweete, and savoury, the lord in mercy accept mee, and blesse the word that it may profitt many.

9. This day rid to Castle Hinningham, preached the lecture, on Cant. 1.3. dined at the ordinary with the gentlemen, who paid my ordinary, god was good to mee in my jorney outwards and homewards, to his name be praise. Among all the severall judgments on this nacion: god this spring in the latter end of April when rye was earing and eared, sent such terrible frosts, that the eare was frozen and so dyed, and cometh unto nothing: young ashes also that leavd were nipt, and blackt, and those shootes died, as if the lord would continue our want, and penury, wee continuing our sins.

Rye blasted:

May: 14: This weeke the Lord was good and mercifull to mee, and to mine in our peace preservacion, health of myselfe, and family: the lord good and mercifull unto us in good and comfortable tidings out of Wales, in quelling the power their in armes in such a sad time, when all the Contrie cried out against the parliament, and army and mutinies were in most places, plundering honest men, and continuall threatenings against such. mens minds exceedingly inraged; all the base false reports raised that could be to dishearten good men, and to encourage others, multitudes of base bookes written to stirre up to sedicon, and render the parliament odious unto the kingdom: truly words cannot convey to the understanding of men, the ability to judge what the times were(.)god was good and mercifull to mee in the Sabbath, in giving mee strength and ability for the same, he in mercy accept mee and pardon mee for his holy name sake:.

16: mett in a day of humiliacon at Goodman Mathewes, to lament our divisions, and to seeke god to unite us in one, as to seeke him for the kingdome, the lord in mercy was good to us in the same, wee entred into a mutual engagement men and women present to hold communion togither, and not to breake societie or suffer our selves to be rent from one another without giving account to one another, at night wee heard the good newes that Bury mutiny was appeased. the lords name bee praised for the same, he goe on to accomplish the deliverance of the nacion, and establish us.

May: 21: This weeke the Lord was good and merciful to mee and mine in our peace plenty health, outward enjoyments, in the season, which was exceeding comfortable, dry, warme, and some showers in some places the raine was exceeding violent, but with us temperate, heard from olny of the health of our freinds, onely my aunt

Berrill is dead; the goodnes of god appeareth in the preservacion of my deare wife god good to us in lengthning out our peace, and in quieting tumults abroad, vile men have lifted up themselves exceedingly, and presumed by the people to bring about their old wayes, and that this cause thus farre advanced should fall to the ground and come to nothing but blessed be the lord, they are hitherto disappointed. the lord was good to mee this weeke in preserving mee from grosse sins, especially when strongly tempted unto the same, the lord keepe mee, that no iniquitie may have dominion over mee the lord was gratious and mercifull unto mee in the Sabbath, and in the duties and exercises therof, giving mee strength to performe the same, the lord in mercy give a blessing and make the word comfortable and profitable to mee and my people.

23. my deare freind Mr R. H. with us from Stortford; this day I was in conference with divers christians, and others that were independents and Mr Archer where wee had good sweet and comfortable societie; as also wee had good societie and sweet discourse with christians at Goodwife Wallers,

25. this day I rid to Cranham wett by the way, god good to me in bringing me safe to Cranham: 26. at London rid in a great shoure but I was their before I was wett through, Dr Wright[1] not at home, I came downe and finding not the Dr by the way, came safe to Colne on Satturday 27. about 1 of the clocke, god good to me in my jorney, I was somewhat weary but, I blesse god, I did not take cold.

I had 2 women buried this day one indifferent well when I went up to London, heard that Mr Owen was very ill with a fever,

May: 28: This weeke the Lord was good and merciful to mee in my peace, health, and in comfortable injoyment of aboundance of outward mercies, which are the more considerable in regard other places and persons through the tumults and troubles of the times are deprived of the same, god good in the season warme and moist, the earth is richly laden with the creatur(*e*) the lord mercifull in preserving me from molestacions by divers temptacions, he was good in the Sabbath, the duties therof and enabling me for the same, onely I could not being streitned for time goe on in my ordinary courses of expounding the scripture,

[1] Laurence Wright, son of John of Wrightsbridge, Essex, and physician-in-ordinary to Cromwell, died 1657. Venn. Through his influence RJ obtained the mastership of EC school for a time.

29: the schoolemaster that is nominated for our towne came over unto mee, my Cosin Josselin[1] with us: heard Mr Tho: Harlakenden junior was married privately, suddenly.

30: this day lovingly invited to my neighbour Matthewes to dinner and at supper to Mrs Churches, where wee had loving and plentifull entertainment this is of the lord. I heard and sent a letter to Mr H. Thomas Prentice a new married man of my parish resolves for new England.

31: P Fast, preacht once I spent 3 three houres, the good lord in mercy bee gratious unto us, and pardon and accept us, in Jesus christ our lord Amen

June: 1: our Committee[2] men putt out a declaracion of the sense of the Counties peticon, I was earnestly pressed to appeare in it from them, but I refused

2. our comittee men mett at Chelmsford and were secured by the peticoners the morning was very wett wherby Sr Tho. Honywood and Coll. Cooke who intended to bee their, were reserved at home to doe their country service as they did

3. Captaine Maidstone[3] brought the newes to Sr Tho. Honywood: 2 Deputy Leius. Mr Tindall Mr Sawyer burgesse for Colchester refused to joyne with Sr H. Th. in raising forces to oppose in our owne defence,[4] which yett wee agreed to doe, wherin some few did their best for their poore contry, for my part I went daily to Coggeshall to observe the worke, wherin I was no hindrance I went and returned commonly by my Lady Honywoods whom god used as a pretious instrument in this worke,

June 4: was the lords day which we enjoyed quietly, without any disturbance to his name be the praise(.) I feared our gentlemen would have beene surprized, but if they plotted and were disappointed in the same, wee cannot but admire god in it. all this weeke full of rumours and feares, the enemies increased apace, our towne went in on Tuesday: 6: day to Coggeshall, and were the first of the country that appeared(.) June. 8. Mr H. came in unto us, wee begun to send out parties of horse this way and that, brought

[1] RJ is again using 'cousin' loosely it would seem, since John Josselin, gent., of Feering (where he had a twelve-hearth house in 1662) is not known to be related to him.

[2] There is an account of the meeting of this County Committee, and its seizure, a prelude to the royalist uprising, in Gardiner, iii, p. 395. Gardiner gives the date as 4 June, however.

[3] John Maidstone, one of the standing committee, probably of Pond House, Boxted. Quintrell, p. 78; Morant, ii, p. 241.

[4] There are many accounts of the royalist uprising and the subsequent siege of Colchester, among them Gardiner, iii, pp. 391–418.

of the magazine from Braintree, the way was stopt that wee could have no intelligence, Goring[1] and the Kentish men were come into Essex, wee were all young and raw men, yett god in mercy disposed our spirits to resolvednes and a willing laying out our selves, we had many alarmes but all false, the enemy never attempted on us at Coggeshall.

June: 11: the enemy marcht on to Braintree die: 10: and this day being up and downe plundering and taking away. Mr Nicholson 2 miles beyond us upwards to Colchester, our people assembled in armes, wee were not able to drawe into Church for the keeping the Sabbath, but were deprived of that opportunity: wee sett good guards in the towne, at 8 of the clocke that night the enemy advanced from Braintree to Halsted; wee heard they intended Colchester, but wee knew not for certaine this

12: on Monday morning the enemy came to Colne, were resisted by our townes men. no part of Essex gave them so much opposicion as wee did. they plundered us, and mee in particular, of all that was portable except, brasse, pewter, and bedding.[2] I made away to Coggeshall, and avoyded their scouts through providence, I praise god for this experiment, it is not so much to part with any thing as wee suppose, god can give us a contented heart in any condicion, and when our losses may serve to advance gods glory, wee ought to rejoyce in the spoiling of our goods, this day I borrowed mony for to buy hose, and borrowed a band[3] to wear having none in my power. I was welcome unto, and pittied by my Lady Hon:

13. I returned home mett with danger by our owne men; who by some suddaine accident mistaking mee sought for mee, but I escaped their hands through gods mercy, who in their fury might have done mee wrong; I was called for by my freinds and acquainted that there was no danger, and espying the men still in the streete, my poore babe Mary cryed and pittied mee, but one desired mee to goe out of her house for feare shee should be plundered: it cutt my heart to see my life no more regarded by her, and it was the greatest dampper and trouble to my Spirit for present that ever I mett with; a true freind shewes it in adversity, and such I found Mrs Church and her daughter, I am perswaded it cutt the heart of

[1] George Goring, Baron Goring (1608–57), royalist commander. DNB.

[2] The County Committee book for Essex contains the following note, that Widow Harris of EC 'was a great sufferer by the march of Goring's forces; they plundered to the value of £30. Her two sons did gallantly oppose the army in Earls Colne.' Quoted in Smith, p. 167. Josselin received £12 from this committee, see under 19 January 1650/1.

[3] Band: a pair of straps hanging down in front, as part of clerical dress. SOED.

the Gentlewoman for what shee said, and therfore I willingly in my spirit passed the unkindnes by. my deare wife was with mee, much amazed: I went to my Lady Honywoods that night, and my wife and all the children, where wee have beene kindely entertained, the lord requite her love; I my wife, and children, could not shift us, untill my Lady furnished us with the same; that night the Gen. marcht to Colchester, where was a sad skirmish, wee retreated to Lexden, and resolved to drawe a line about the towne,

I went divers times to the leaguard, but through gods providence, I mett with no danger, yett the musketts divers times, and the Drake bullett[1] flew with divers noises neare mee, my dayes are in gods hands, but I have not returned unto god according unto his great goodnesse, but have found my owne heart more out of frame, and more subject to temptacion and evill in this time than at other times: the lord in mercy pardon mee and accept me and sanctifie me

June: 18: I preacht at Markeshall and Mr Clopton[2] for mee, I preacht in my litle coate as I goe every day; I could not with that confidence venture to Colne at first as afterwards, but being wonted to the troubles, and rationally considering the same, and submitting unto, and resting in gods providence I was daily more, and more emboldened

25: this Lords day I preacht at Earles Colne to my owne people, who were glad to see mee preach to them. the lord mingle instructions with his judgments

28. This was the P: F: I was perswaded not to preach, but I did, and had the greatest audience, I had many dayes before, but truly our hearts are not cleansed nor our wayes reformed: the lord goeth out against us in the season which was wonderfull wett, flouds every weeke, hay rotted abroad, much was carried away with the flouds, much inned but very durty, and dangerous for catle; corne layd, pulled downe with weeds, wee never had the like in my memory, and that for the greatest part of the summer, it continued to August: 14: when it rained that it made a litle floud, and commonly wee had 1 or 2 flouds weekely, or indeed in the meadowes their was as it were a continuall floud.

Wett summer.

July: 2: I preacht at home, and so I did every lords day that month, and on the fast day, wee were not troubled with one alarme, but the carts went continually to the leagurd, and so did persons. that

[1] Drake: a small sort of cannon or field piece invented in the seventeenth century, probably by Mr. Bellingham. NED.

[2] William Clopton, incumbent of Markshall 1646–54 when he went to Rettendon, from whence he was ejected in 1662. Smith, pp. 203–5, 370; Calamy.

there was no distinction made of Sabbath, so that warre truly is ready to make people more vile(,) a rare thing to see men made better.

August: 13. the 2 lords dayes in this month I preacht to my people. my minde cannot be so setled as it ought yett through gods goodnes I was able to supply my place, the good lord in mercy pardon all my sins and accept mee. my lady Honywood continueth to afford entertainment still to mee and to my wife and children:.

15: a sad wett morning, corne is much layd, and some empty, and rotten on the ground hay is much spoyled and some even rotted. this morning I saw an evidence of the worlds vanity and inconstancy, litle did Sr Edward Denny or his stately Dame Edgecombe,[1] thinke at first any of their sonnes should carry briefes[2] about as one Mr Denny their sonne did this day to mee, and as he saith its their employment, the lord make me to serve him, and treine mine up in his feare, who knoweth the want and povertie any may come unto,

16: a very great floud with the great raines last day and night: the season sad and threatning, this day I retired my selfe to seeke to god by reason of his judgments on us, to bewaile not his afflictions which we suffer, but especially the sins wherby he is provoked for he doth not willingly afflict.

the nacions sins are many and sad, Lord lett publike ones be pardoned; the nacions judgments are continual raines to the spoyling of much grasse, and threatning of the harvest: 2: the sad charge by warre to the undoing of contry: the sad decay of trade in reference to our poore, to our undoing except god finde out some other way of subsistence.

the Warre in the nacion, the divisions among our selves; our cryings out after peace on any termes to save our skins, and estates whatsoever become of others, lord remove thes judgments from us for thy name sake.

and in respect of my soule. my heart is full of sinfull and vaine meditacions, not being cleane in the eyes of god, my conversacion is not even in the sight of god. oh give me a cleane heart; and keepe mee in uprightnes: oh make this nacion happy in peace and truth, and make mee righteous and holy in thy eyes for thes things I poure

[1] Dame Edgecombe: another name for Lady Denny (see p. 11, n. 3 above), a descendant of the Edgecumbe family of Cornwall.

[2] It is difficult to decide whether this refers to a lawyer's brief, or, from the context more probably, a church brief, i.e. a 'letter patent issued by the head of the church licensing a collection in the churches throughout England for a specified object' (NED).

out my soule in thy presence, bee gratious oh lord to us wee intreate thee.

16: 17. dayes: fayre and good harvest dayes: at night Mr John Lamott[1] taken with a vomiting, and very ill and disquietted with the same, the lord in mercy spare his life, it is a great affliction to my Lady:

18. My Lady sent home my 3 children gave us 2 paire of sheets, our children and wee were there 9 weekes and 4 dayes, and had continued their still if Mr Honywood had not fell sicke: this 18 day was a very wett day: I was with a company at night seeking unto god for mercy in respect of our troubles:

19: a cheerfull and comfortable morning: my wife at my Lady Honywoods helping her in attending her sicke child, oh lord showe favour unto it, for thy tender mercy sake. I went thither this afternoone, and found it very well, wee returned thanks unto the name of god: it rained a very great shower(,) still the lord refuseth to heare our prayers, and sends us a season, that doth much threaten the creatures on the earth.

August: 20: This weeke the Lord was good unto mee in providing for mee, and mine so that wee wanted nothing god made my Lady Honywoods house a harbor for mee and mine and so had beene longer if an illnes had not taken her sonne which is now recovered: strong are my corruptions and vanities of minde, the lord suffer them not to have dominion over mee, and in due time deliver mee from them: the season continued sad, and wett. the corne in danger on the earth, warre in our doores, and sinful lusts on our spirits. the lord made divers freinds very kind to mee when I came to towne Mr R. H. Mrs H. Mrs Church and her daughter lord requite it. through mercy we have had constantly the libertie of Sabbaths, the lord give us the favour of his word unto life.

22. mett in a day of humiliacion at my lady Honywoods, at night wee heard the newes of the Scots rout,[2] a confirmacion wherof wee expect.

24. dayly raines, but especially this morning, wee found it exceeding wett, it caused a very great floud, aboundance of hay rotten, much corne cutt and not cutt groweth, and yett men repent not to give glory unto god: this day a thanksgiving at the Hith church for the victory in the north, the enemy in Colchester demand very high termes on which to surrender the towne

[1] John La Motte (? 1570–1655), merchant of London, father of Lady Hester Honywood: see Honywood genealogy. DNB.

[2] At the battle of Preston, 17 August.

25. day. very hott but close untill towards 11 of the clocke when the sun did shine and it was a right summers day indeed: 26: it thundered and rained in the morning, but not very much, wee had hopes it would be an harvest day and so through mercy it proved, it being close, and rainy a litle now and then but men followed their worke. great hopes that Colchester would have surrendered presently, but so great a worke, must aske a longer time to effect the same 27. 28. 29: were very seasonable dayes, men followed their harvesting without any interrupcion.

August: 27. This weeke the Lord was good, and mercifull unto us, in respect of our peace and preservacion, providing for mee and mine at my Lady Honywoods, but oh how wretched is my heart, oh how vaine and filthy, lord when wilt thou subdue all my iniquities under mee,

22. we kept a day of humiliacon: that night we heard of the scots route, on friday the season sett in comfortably, and on the Lords day, Colchester agreed to surrender(.) Speedie and sweet answers of prayers.

28: Colchester yielded, infinite numbers of people went thither. our Councell of warre adjudged 3 to be shott to death. Sr Charles Lucas. Sr George Lile who accordingly suffered, and Sr Barnaby Gascoine an Italian who was sparred.[1]

29: a dry day: my wife and Jane came home from my Lady Honywoods and Jane where wee had stayed: 11: weekes. the lord requite all her labour of love to us, coming home Mrs Mary Church visited us, and was kinde to us, but no other person in the towne shewed any respect or kindnesse unto us, yett I praise god I desire in all wants and forsakings of my people to submitt to thee I have deserved the same I pray direct me in my great thoughts about leaving of Colne, that if I must begone I may doe it, so that I may have peace in it.

P: F. Aug: 30: a wett night, and wettish day, as if god would have calld men to his worship: but their was no regard of the same, my thoughts growe strong within mee to give over preaching at Colne at Michaelmas, and to declare the same beforehand, to the cheife inhabitants, Lord direct me what to doe, I have given out speeches of my enforcement unto it, I preacht once this day on Amos 8:11.12: concerning the famine of the word, wherin having occasion to speake of the condicion of this land, I delivered my thoughts to this purpose.

[1] See Gardiner, iii, pp. 459–60; rightly Sir Bernard (Bernardo) Gascoigne.

People, when our armies had conquered all our enemies, my thoughts were sad concerning the displeasure of god remaining towards England, and I told you Essex must not escape, which is come to passe by the marchings of Goring and his army and plundering many places, persons, the sad ruine of Colchester by fire, the decay of trade by their losses; the charge of the Countie in mainteyning their forces at the seidge, and sending in provisions for above 11 weekes for many thousands of Horse and foote, my thoughts were and are sad concerning England still not from the risings of many Counties against the parliament the strong invasion of the Scots upon us, for my thoughts verily were god would breake them: but when I consider the decay of the power of godlynesse among christians: their flightinesse of Spirit towards gods ordinances. the wofull uncontroulable encrease of all manner of wickednes among us: the awe that was on mens hearts towards god, and his wayes being removed, the slighting all the warnings of god in judgments and by his ministers, maketh mee thinke god is yett angry, and he will leave our great Counsell to their wonted partiality in their wayes, and bring more ruine one way or other on the nacion: or give us up to the cursed wayes of our owne hearts, taking away his ministers, and saints apace from England, and few arising in their stead.

August. 30: 1648. after the route of Hamilton, taking of Colchester, discovery of the City plott, when all our feares seemed gone, and our enemies hopes quite dasht.

the raine that fell caused a floud: the Suffolke forces went home yesterday all the residue of the army was drawne up in a body, and allmost all the Essex forces were disbanded: the prisoners were many of them sent unto Kelvedon this night.

31: a fayre day. September: 1: it was very wett and hinderd men in
Sept: their harvesting; wee feared it would cause a floud. Major Haines returned from the north where they have taken about 13000 prisoners, full of admiring gods providence and joy for our preservacion.

3: This weeke the Lord was good and mercifull to mee and mine in our peace and preservacion, in making mee more carefull to walke with him than formerly, in giving mee more care against vaine thoughts, he in mercy accept mee, god was good to mee in the duties of the Sabbath, I was at Markeshall with my Lady Honywood and Mr Clopton here with mee,

5. Mr Litle with mee, who gave mee something towards my losses the Lord requite his love aboundantly.

this afternoone very faire, and so Septemb. 6 a fine day, blessed bee god for it, my thoughts very much troubled within mee concerning my leaving of Colne being necessitated thereunto, by their withholding my maintenance. the lord goe before mee and direct me what to doe.

the prisoners taken at Colchester are dispersing apace, divers gett away. Sr Wm Compton their Sergeant Major Gen 2 Coll. by meanes of our waggon Mr generall made an escape;

Coll: Culpepper: Coll: chester: Sr Abraham Shipman escaped out of Mr warrens house

New England 6. Sent a letter into new England by a maide servant to Tho: Prentice, contayning the newes forreigne, and domesticke unto that time, the lord in mercy give my frend a faire opportunity to come thither

7. A publike day of thankes for the great and notable mercy in the route and dissipating of the Scotch army by the forces under Cromwell and Lambert. this day was faire, somewhat close, but men had in corne dilligently and in very good case, thankes be given unto god for this mercy.

I had not in all this time of trouble any pose or cold much to trouble me, but now I have one not so bad as formerly, but it maketh my chest somewhat sore, the lord sanctify all providences unto me for his goodnes sake.

8: 9: daies faire, god affording us a good season fo(u)r the inning the latter harvest and our hopps blessed be his holy name;

September: 10: This weeke the lord was good and mercifull to mee and mine, in our lives, and liberties peace and plenty, so that hitherto, though somewhat straitned, wee were in no absolute want of any thing: I drunke my beere for 3 or 4 dayes with as much content out of a dish as at sometimes out of a silver bowle; I desire the lord to give me patience and contentacion in any straites and necessities that his providence may (c.o. sug) leade mee into: I blesse god this weeke my minde hath not run out after some foolish vanities as formerly, yett I find Sathan like the lapwing crying before mee with one temptacion or vanitie, to drawe my minde from my god of my salvacion, oh Lord I am weeke undertake for mee, the lord was good and mercifull to mee in the worke and duty of the Sabbaths in the word preacht, being seasonable, the lord make it profitable to mee and my people: my thoughts much working within mee about leaving Colne. seeing they have not regarded to bring in promised maintenance unto mee,

September. 12. 1648: Being as it were forsaken and neglected by the inhabitants of Earles Colne, and destitute of competent maintenance to live upon, I sett this morning apart to seeke unto god for direction in this matter; whether providence called mee away, or whether I should continue with them still, now the good Lord who is the god of prayer answer my desires, and request, and make mee to understand that which is most pleasing in thy sight.

first my case in reference to maintenance is this: first for tithes the generall maintenance, the last yeare I received in from the towne, at severall times, with much calling upon: 25^{li}. 6^{s}. 9^{d}. and perhaps this yeare may afford thus much, then Mr Jacob is to pay 4^{li}. which perhaps he will continue to pay: Mr R. Harlakenden he its likely will performe his 20^{li}. per annum: so their is about 49^{li}. if the tithes bee gotten in: for the other. 31: pound I have not received 4^{li}. but suppose their should 8 or 9^{li}. pound of it bee paid, this amounts not unto 60^{li}. by the yeare, out of which I am to pay taxes, which will amount to 3^{li}. per annum: tent(h)s to the Parliament, and reparacions which will bring it downe to a matter of 50^{li}. a yeare, and for this I have my selfe wife, 3 children: mayde: my wife a childing woman, so that this summe cannot at the great price all things now beare mainteine us in a very lowe manner

but there are 2 things more incumbent on mee, and that is to bee hospitable and mindfull of the poore. Titus: 1:8: and our towne is full of poore, and a roade way, and their are great occasions for a liberall releiving hand, which those that have not cannot performe, this then brings a scandall on the ministry, as if he had much but would not releive them:

fa(r)ther a man is bound to provide for his family, and lay up for them, this Scripture alloweth: commendeth, requireth: Gen: 30: 30: and now when shall I provide for my owne house also: 2 Cor: 2:14: I Timoth: 5:8: and in a probable way when a mans children are young, and he is young is the fittest time to doe this duty, but when the yearely income cannot mainteine, what is their to lay up: againe what a distraction it is for men to be intangled with thoughts of providing for their tables, when wee should be attending our studdyes: under the law tithes were brought in to the preists now wee must run out after them, its a great discomfort when a man is not mainteined freely, and cheerfully though it be sparingly.

ob(jection): but god hath increased your estate here at Colne.

Ans(wer): It is true, the secrett treasures being his, he hath done it, but those dayes are past, how to subsist with any freedome I

knowe not nowe, and if I could I professe I would not remove, I have bought something while I lived at Colne, but halfe I have gained hath not beene from Colne but on other occasions: ob: but it may be Colne doth for your maintenance what they are able: Ans: 1: not, the towne is able to mainteine a minister, and his family with an 100li. per annum, if they were willing: but people are regardles and careles of the worship of god, as if they could well spare it:
2: that litle, promised by contribucion and tithes, is payd very unwillingly: the contribucion not regarded to be gathered of them; a man or 2 is willing, but not any other are willing so much as to gather it up from others.
3. The parliament hath added augmentacions to other livings; our townesmen neglect ours, true an addicon was granted, but it is ineffectuall, neither doe wee take any course to make it effectuall: Upon this and many other consideracions: seing my ministry thus barren, and slighted in Colne, I have cause to be humbled, and search my heart, and see whether it bee rather a punishment on mee for my sin, or a providence of god withall to remove mee from them,
1: I cannot but acknowledge many iniquities in mee, and neglects in my calling, and indeed great unfitnes and inability for this weighty worke, and this lord I lament from the bottome of my heart. and questionles when the lord makes people neglect their ministers, there is a respect to them in it, though perhaps not principally.
2. but in regard the state of things stand thus: I have continued to beare many wants, contented my selfe with small meanes, stirred them up to regard the condicon of the towne and so others have also, and yett nothing done but my condicon is worse and meaner than before, I continued about 11 weekes at my Lady Honywoods, and it was knowne it was for want of meanes to keepe house, yett in all that time, though I was plundered, did my people consider my condicon, gather up any of the moneyes due unto mee, so that it seemeth cleare to mee, providence invites mee away, my heart being also more inclined to lay downe, having no offers of a place, but leaving it to gods providence to provide, then I ever was when I had offerres of good places made unto mee,
and in this condicon it seemes to mee cleare that I may depart. I doe not leave them untill they have forsaken mee, I desire no great meanes to live richly in the world, but convenient food and

rayment, and the lord ordaines that they which preach the gospell should live upon the gospell; and that in many places of Scripture, 1 Corinth: 9:14: and surely then when any place doth not afford him a subsistence he may observe his providence in going unto another, and when the preists had not their tithes brought in whereby they might waite in the Temple but were scattered into their severall cities and feilds for bread: here is the worship of god neglected, the preists leave the Temple: whose sin and fault was it: being they wanted their meanes of livelyhood, it was the peoples, and the princes they are blamed for the same, Nehem. 13.10.11. and he gathers them togither and setts them in their places, and provideth for them: v.13.14:

So then I lay it downe as a conclusion that my towne affords me not a competent maintenance; if they make it appeare they have, then lett the blame of it rest on mee, and this is the reason I will insist on; and I will not be my owne judge lett any understanding men judge whether 80li. bee not as litle as a man can live on in thes times, and this place, and seing they doe not, it is a just and a warrantable reason by scripture, and nature, to provide otherwise according as providence shall direct.

So then after looking into the word to be my counsellor and seeking unto god to direct mee(,) my resolucion, is acquaint Mr Harlakenden with my condicon and what I must of necessity bee inforced to doe, and if by him and the townesmen, I bee provided for in paying in my dues last yeare, and in securing the next yeares, if I live with them, if not, that then, I must though with lothnes lay downe at Michaelmas and leave the townesmen to take care of the same, to provide another minister, and for my perticular to cast my selfe on gods providence to provide for mee, as he seeth best; and this resolucion I intend to prosecute, and to observe god in the same, and whatsoever his providences are to take them with as much patience, and quietnes of Spirit as may bee, and with a thankefulnes unto god, for whatsoever he appoints mee unto;

I shall also alwayes acknowledge that their are some in this towne, that to their power, and beyond their ability have beene loving to mee, and done their parts to continue the Ministry of the word among them, whom it greiveth my soule to part with, but for what they have done they will have god and their owne conscience bearing them witnesse, and affording them peace and comfort in whatsoever condicion cometh upon them;

I went downe to Mr R. Harlakenden acquainted him with my purpose to leave Colne, he is sorry, wisheth it were otherwise; but there is no proposall of remedy and indeed the fault is not particularly in him,

11. 12: dayes, wett, and no harvest weather, except to reape hard corne, the season was very sad, but men repent not to give glory unto god;

13. 14: very faire and comfortable weather, fitt for the harvest and plow. calling upon us to blesse god, who hath a regard unto us.

Septemb. 17. This weeke the Lord was good, and mercifull to mee, and mine in our peace, and in preserving us, and affording aboundance of needfull mercies: god was good to mee in giving me power against some vanities of minde, but against some others, I have neither heart nor care to resist nor power, the good Lord in mercy affect me with my condicon and make mee sensible of the same for the glory of his owne holy name,

this weeke die 20. 22: was very wett the season very sad both in reference to corne and unto fallows, very few lands being fitt to bee sowne upon; some say that divers catle that feed in the meadowes dye, their bowells being eaten out with gravel and durt.

on the 17 of August I intimated that, it was probable I should not very long stay with them, but truly very few in the towne regard it, or that seeme to take any notice of it;

September 24. This weeke god was mercifull to mee and all my family in our health in peace, and preservacion, in the creatures for our use, in looking into my heart, I finde, that vaine thoughts lodge within mee, oh how hard it is to serve god with all the heart, and strength, oh remember mee, with thy grace and thy righteousness oh god of my salvacion, the lord was good and mercifull to me this day in the Sabbath and in the duties and exercises therof, the lord in mercy pardon my sinnes, and make his word a blessing unto me and my people. I thought to have finisht my text this day, and given notice of laying downe preaching, but I could not finish the same. Some of the womenkinde of the parrish desire mee not to goe away, and Mr Elliston, who promiseth his endeavour to the uttermost to better the meanes; but other men stirre not, say nothing.

25. mett in a day of humiliacon at Goodman Johnsons, who is going from us, as also Mrs Cressener to London, thus Colne is thinned of good people: all thes things are especially against mee, oh lord blesse them, and sanctify this rod unto us, and direct my heart what to doe in going or staying in Colne, loth I am to remove if it

were but thy good pleasure to stirre up their hearts to afford a subsistance.

26. The season very faire and pleasant, plowes sowing, especially rye and some lands that were carefully tilled,

27. P.F.: Heard before I arose in the morning that Mr R.H. was very sicke with a vomitte and loosenes even unto death, the Lord in mercy gave him recovery presently continue him to my comfort, this day was the P.F. wheron I preacht, the lord was gratious and mercifull to mee in the same, I have a litle stuffing cold that doth a litle trouble mee, but in gods due time it shall weare away, this day and in sermon time fell downe the bell great chimney, belonging to Sam: Burton,[1] through gods mercy it did no great hurt to the house, neither was any person hurt with the fall of the same, to gods name bee the praise of it: divers dayes before I judged it would fall where it did, and the day before and especially this morning I was confident it would stand, but a very short space,

October. 1: This weeke past was a very comfortable, and cheerefull season, a summer time indeed, there in god was good to mee, and mine in our peace, health, plenty, in my litle ones, who answer their mothers paines and learne comfortably with her, the lord good to mee in delivering mee from the power of many corrupt temptacions oh preserve me spotlesse and blamelesse to the coming of Jesus Christ, the lord was good to mee in the Sabbath in the duties and exercises therof, the lord in mercy pardon my sin and accept mee for his name sake,

2: Mr Harrington came to sojourne with us; our agreement was without two words, the lord blesse him, and make him an instrument of much good to our youth, and make us a comfort to one another. I cannot so great is thy goodnes to mee oh lord but admire it: thou hast called mee to a knowledge of thy selfe when blind and ignorant of my selfe, thou hast many times prevented mee in mercy, when on the brinke of sin through my dallying with temptacions: thou hast quieted my heart and comforted mee with thy love when thy terrors were ready to take hold of mee.

This weeke John Reads mayde went away with child, and accuseth him for father. the man once a great professour, admired for his parts, but his base corrupcions grew too strong, he fell to dronkennes, to neglect god in ordinances, the communion of his people, followed idle company, and when at worst was confident of mercy for Christ had dyed for his sins and all pardoned, god may make

[1] The chimney of the Bell, owned by Samuel Burton (see Appendix 2).

him to awake by this great fall, which as a cracke may amaze him but he keepes out of mans sight in regard of the shame, but thy eye is every where oh god, rebuke him that he may returne and live oh what mercy is this that god, hath not lett my corrupcions loose, and made them too strong for mee.

Octob. 8. This weeke god was good to mee and mine in our peace, and plenty, wee have thy mercies in aboundance, blessed bee thy name; and in mercy to my soule thou hast given me more advantage against my corrupcions, in giving me a loathing of the same, and taken of my heart my musing on evill, for indeed the heart is the sinner, the lord hath beene good and mercifull to me in distempers of cold and sorenes of my navell,[1] on mee they are light, and I trust thou wilt cure the illnes of both in due time: god was pleased to lett some bitter apprehensions fall into my minde, but I desire to make it my worke to dye dayly, and to make it familiar to mee, and prepare for it, that my soule may live with thee, but the Lord hath removed those feares, and giveth me some strength of patience to waite his time, and not to feare worse inconveniences therby. Some time in this weeke I spent in reading Hebrew and I resolve now I am neare 32 yeares old to set myself more closely to the studdy of it, god was good to mee in the Sabbath, in the duties, and exercise therof. in his good word of his unchangeable and immutable love, nothwithstanding our faylings, he in mercy accept mee. the season was dry, and somewhat cold most frosts, which was good for our healths and very comfortable for the housbandman, bringing the earth in season, so that wee must praise god, who remembered us in our low estate: things are yett very deare I gave 8^{s}. 2^{d}. for a bushel of new wheate, the greatest price I ever gave in my time of housekeeping,

11: visited Mrs Cressener, a good woman, shee is ill, a woman of much selfe judging and feares concerning her condicion Lord cleare up thy love to her: I find through mercy god putting a stoppe to my vanities. the lord cause his grace to prevaile in mee, that I may hate every evill imaginacion, and through thy grace, gett dominion over the same;

the day before Mrs Cressener went up to London to dwell there with her housband, the lord thins our towne of christian people much, the lord in mercy make up our losses herein, the 10 day

[1] This is the first reference to the suppurating navel which was to cause RJ so much pain during the next few years. The affliction was almost certainly made worse by the remedies he used.

Mr H. brought home Mrs H from Stortford, after neare half a yeares absence, the lord make our soules prosper.

Octob: 15: This weeke the lord was good and mercifull to me and mine in our peace, health and in providing sufficiently for us, the lord was good and mercifull also in taking of my heart more from vaine earthly thoughts then formerly: now here steps in Sathan and saieth that this is not done by the power of grace, but only by more dilligence in (in) my calling: to this I say. so that sin be stopped, I therin doe, and will rejoyce: again its a great advantage to be dilligently imployed. its of god to be faithfull therein, but my heart disrellisheth those temptacions, as empty and sinfull, for with my minde I am to serve the lawe of god: now Sathan was stepping in with other thoughts, but thou shalt keepe mee oh god:

my navell continueth sore and so hath beene 5 or 6 weekes, the good lord in mercy heale the same, blesse remedies applied. I desire with patience and submission to waite gods leasure, for my hope is in him, but lord just art thou in this correction: the Saturday at night was a wonderfull violent winde, and raine togither, causing a floud. the lord was mercifull to me in giving me strength for the Sabbath in making the word sweete to my meditacion, lord accept my soule and pardon my iniquities, when sermon was done we were amazed with Mrs Tiffin,[1] the lord in mercy heale her of her wickednes, and dissimulacion

19: I and my wife went with Mr Harringtons to his fathers, where wee had very free, and loving entertainment, wee stayed their that night, when in bed and sleeping. 2 of Colne knocked at the gate called for mee, which I heard, my wife was afraid, divers thoughts were in my head, my expectacions were confused, but I gathered up my spirits, and wisht my wife not to give way to passion, and create feares to her selfe, and waite the knowledge of their message, a good rule to be followed in sudden affrights, and it proved onely businesse about the thankesgiving day at my Lady Honiwoods. which in regard it was next day, and I not coming home, thes men were sent with letters to mee, that I might not faile to bee there, and accordingly the next morning I arose, and went to Colne, and from thence to my ladies, where wee mett much good society, Mr Rolls[2] and my selfe preacht: my lady provided a great dinner and stayed all the people poore and rich that were at home, this day wee

[1] 'Tiffin' has been subtly changed by a later hand into Gifford.

[2] Richard Rolle, probably vicar of Witham between 1645 and *c.* 1653. Smith, p. 303; Venn.

vowed in our distresse and lowe condicon, and blessed be god, who made us to keepe our vowes only Lord pardon our sinfulnes, our want of affectionatenes, and vigour of spirit in the same, smell a sweete savour and delight to continue thy goodnes towards us for thy holy names sake,

October: 22: This weeke the lord continued his mercy and goodnes, to mee, and mine, in all our outward injoyments wanting nothing: my navell was very sore, god gave mee a heart to seeke unto him for helpe, and my heart was raised up therby more to trust in him than formerly: it is not yett well, but as an answer of prayer, and an earnest of perfecting this mercy, I find it much better, and I hope god in his due season will recover me perfectly, and make me by thes changes, to lay more sure hold on him that is unchangeable, and more carefull to honour him, att all times, who is in distresse my only rocke, and helpe:. the lord was good, and mercifull to us in the season, all this weeke from Tuesday faire, plowes at worke againe, men committing their seed to the ground: Major Heynes went from us this weeke, his regiment is in Scotland, and thither he must goe, the lord in mercy affoard him a good season, which will take away much of the trouble of the jorney; all things are at excesse rates; and yett our people having plenty of worke, they make a good shift, which is a mercy beyond the expectation of most people, I find my corrupcions of minde in contemplative vanities not so stirring as formerly oh lett them never recover strength againe I intreate thee, god was good to me in the Sabbath, and in the duties therof, the lord make his doctrine of free and unchangeable grace, the continuall stay of my soule, for his glorious name sake;

25: This day was the P. Fast, a cold day, and wee like it in our affections; the lord was good to mee in giving mee strength for the same, he in mercy accept mee, and blesse my labours.

28: This day 8 yeare, my deare wife and I were married; this day shee was very ill and likely to swound away, the lord good in giving her strength and removing her distemper, the lord increase our grace, and make our lives more serviceable to him and one anothers good, but good is god to mee, in wife and children, and my comforts in them, oh sanctifie them thou god of grace, this day I felt my navill sore; I had left the stuffe lye in it, and whether that grated it or not I knowe not, but I found it at night, red, rawe, and moyst, wee applyed unguentum album[1] to it; to which the lord in his mercy give

[1] Unguentum album: made of wax, oil of roses, and ceruse (or hops grease and

a blessing that it may have a perfect recovery, I have reason to trust in god, because of his former goodnes, and I find him a god that answers prayer.

October. 29. This weeke the lord continued his mercy, and goodnes to mee, and mine in our peace, plenty, and health, my wife somewhat ill but only qualmes, and the sorenes of my navel not much, and being it becometh me to trust in god, and stay my soule on him unamazedly on him, in variety of condicons, it becometh mee now not to detrust him, and indeed inward and outward troubles they are much for the triall of our faith; this weeke I bestowed some time in the studdy of Hebrew, vita brevis ars longa,[1] and much time I have and doe misspend, and find it hard to redeeme the time; the lord good to mee in keeping me from sins and sorrowes that my heart is subject to, and are in and upon others, oh keepe my feete in up rightnes; the lord in mercy letts me see the vanity of the creature, and in reference to death that gods time is best, and it is never too soone to be with christ, the lord was good and mercifull to mee in the Sabbath, in the word preached, oh that it might be practised of me and mine, in giving me strength, neither did I much feele the sorenes of my belly, and truly lord I may say it was good it should be thus with me, for by this thou hast lett me see my emptines, and vanity, and made me to ruminate on, and minde my condicon, and earnestly to long for thy grace and mercy, yea sins in particular discovered and stirred up indignacon, and resolucion and watchfulnes against them, so that it was good I was afflicted, and trouble was light gentle, and shall bee but for a time and this as an kind wind to drive me to god my haven, yea thou stirrest up my faith by it oh I will love the(e) my god, for thou dealest mercifully with mee,

Oct: In the latter end of October I begun to reade: Bell: de 15: staires our ladder steps to god,[2] a prettie discourse, it containes 418: pages in 16°. I also read in mornings, Feri Specimen,[3] a learned discourse, it containeth: p. 559: I observed the most materiall things in him, Lord I have lost much of my time, oh enable mee to redeeme it; and give mee oh god not only industriousnes, but to studdy out of

ceruse), 'It is a fine cooling drying ointment, easeth pains, and itching in wounds and ulcers' (N. Culpeper, *A Physical Directory*, 1651, p. 109).

[1] Life is short, art is long.

[2] Roberto Bellarmino, *De ascensione mentis in Deum per scalas rerum creatarum* (Cologne, 1615); an English translation of the following year is noted in the STC, no. 1840.

[3] Paul Ferri, a Protestant divine and preacher (1591–1669), wrote a number of works, but none with this title are to be found in the STC, Thomason or Wing.

love to the(e), and charitie to the soules of my people, and give me strength of body, and of my eyes especially, and blesse my endeavours

November: 3: Heard from our freinds at olny, of their health by my aunt Shepheards letter, who in kindnes sent unto us 12 elles of cloth, for shifts,[1] hearing the enemy had given us an unkind stripping.

4: a very rainy day: heard that Coll: Rainsbrough was stabbed in the North by 2 that pretended to bee sent from the Leiu^t^. Gen: with a letter unto him;

November: 5: This weeke the Lord was good and mercifull to mee, and mine, in our peace, plenty comforts, health, my wife onely weakely, the good Lord bee her strength, and sanctifie her: my navell I hope well againe, I have not had any trouble with it divers dayes oh lord thou hast given mee a heart to seeke thee, and trust in thee, and therby was my heart freed from feare and perplexitie, and hast thou also healed mee; I will praise thee oh my healing god, but lett me not returne to folly. oh Lord, it was good that thou hast chastened mee, for hereby thou hast lett me see my wretchednes of heart, I call to minde my youthfull vanities, contemplative lusts, and the delights of my soule therin, and this sin assaults me to this day, oh lord that I should cast sweetnes, and take delight in sin, the bitterest evill in the world, and that cannot comfort mee, heale mee, oh my soule casteth sweetnes in thee beyond hony, and seeth goodnes in thee, oh lett mee never more returne to my former follies never goe to delight my selfe in sinfull objects. the lord was good to mee in my studdies, giving mee a litle dilligence therin, and to reape some proffit therby, thou art my end and aime oh lord, and the honouring thee among my people, oh make all my endeavour helpes to knowe thee and thy christ, for thou art the perfection of sweetnes and excellency.

this weeke the Lord kept me from falling into grosse sins, and from my old temptacions, I find Sathan tempting, but I am not at leisure for him, through thy grace, oh keepe me for I am weake(,) undertake for mee, oh thou my strength: and make me to find sweetnes in serving of thee, expecially in calling upon thee, lett my heart powre out it selfe, and lett me tast thy goodnes flowing into my bosome, The Lord was good to mee in giving mee strength and ability to preach oh blesse the word to mee, and my people, and lett us not

[1] Shifts: a body-garment of linen, cotton, or the like; usually a woman's 'smock' or chemise. SOED.

bee as those that eate, and are not strengthened by the same, good is god to give mee the libertie of his Sabbaths, he in mercy, accept mee, and pardon mee, my subject was about faith out of 2 Thes 1: v.3.

☞ 6: Wee begun this morning to rise early, and to spend some time by fire and candle, I intend in morning to read over the liberall arts, and began with Vossius Rhet. Tom. 1. in 4°.[1] it containes 433 p. ceptis aspira nostris domine,[2] that hereby being more skild in the tongues and arts I may be more usefull in my generacion,

Vossius institute orat

this day going in at Appletons; doore, where horses stood; one horse kicked either at another or at mee, and strucke me twice, but through gods goodnes, I had no hurt, oh lord if thou hadst not watched over, how neare was I to danger, and not aware of the same;

☞ 7: walkt out to Mr Ellistons where I dined: my deare wife very ill, but at night better, shee rested well in the night blessed be god, oh continue her a comfort to mee and mine, I hope it was only about her quickening, this night I felt my navell ill againe, there was blacke stuffe in it, in the bottome white matter, wee dressed it as formerly, the lord in mercy in due time give a perfect cure and healing to the same, that I may praise thee, and rejoyce in thy great goodnesse.

8: This day Mrs Tiffin[3] being distracted was removed to Mr Lagdens, a sad example, the lord humble us, and restore her, Mr Seamor delivered livery and seisin of Pryors freehold land to Mr Elliston; both layd their hands on the deed and he delivers possession of all the parcels mentiond in the deed to the other according to the true intent of the same, some buy and some waste, and such an one is one Read a great professor, whose goods are sold to divers in the towne

Posses-sion of land

Ferrius: 9: This night I perfected the reading of Ferius Specimen, god was good to mee this day in preserving mee from a dangerous kicke of a bullock, it mist mee through mercy, to his name be the praise ascribed:.

10: Mr Daniel Rogers of Wethers-feild came to us, and promised to helpe me on the lords day: the season began very sharpe, and cold, with frost and snow, portending a cold winter:

Novemb: 12: This weeke the lord was good and mercifull to mee and mine, in our peace and plenty, and health, my navel was sore and

[1] Gerardus Vossius, *Rhetorices contractae, sive partitionum oratoriarum libri v . . .* (1631).

[2] Inspire, oh lord, our ideas.

[3] Again changed by a later hand into 'Gifford'.

moist, but it dried up againe and so continued at present, the lord bee magnified for this goodnes towards mee, oh heal it perfectly for thy goodnes sake I intreate thee; this weeke the lord kept me from being suprized with my old vanities blessed be his name, oh suffer no corrupcion to have dominion over mee, but lett mee proceed in grace, in wisedom, in patience for thou knowest all my weaknesses: this weeke I did somewhat in my studdies, lord increase my knowledge especially of thy selfe; and of thy christ and of my selfe, and lett me be usefull in thy pathes, and make me serviceable for the good of many soules: the lord was good to me in the Sabbath, I had a good providence in the helpe of Mr Rogers; one part of the day.

Hookers and Cottons treatises:

13: begun the reading, and noting the principal things, out of 2 treatises concerning church goverment by Mr Hooker, called a survey of the summ of church discipline; in 4 parts: the first part conteineth: 296 pages in 4to: part 2. p: 90: part. 3. p 46: part. 4. p: 59: in all 491 pages: the second treatise by Mr Cotton, called the way of congregational churches cleared in 2 treatises, one historicall, against Baylie disswasive, the other polemical, art(*icle*) pag: 148:[1] both treatises conteine: 639 pages: their scope is to cleare the scripturalnes of congregational government against presbytery: especiall in those 2 points: the matter of church society saints the extent of church-government authoritative onely to a particular congregation: the time I allotted for this was in the forenoone togither with my Hebrew studdies: viz what time I could picke before dinner, having read Vossius ante solem, and being to learne a part every morning in the Heb: Grammar.

Bellarmini scale etc.

15: My navel was a litle sore againe, lord purge the corrupcion out of my heart, and give me patience, and improvement of thy dealing, and it shall bee my gaine that thou thus dealest with mee: this night I made an end of reading Bellarmines scale ad deum, a booke that containeth divers sweet meditacions in it, and now I intend on nights to reade over the ecclesiastical history:

Cent: 1^{e} lib: 1:

16: My navel was somewhat sore this morning, in thy good time oh lord thou wilt perfectly heale mee, and then I shall praise thee: this night I began by candle light to reade the ecclesiastical history, called the Centuries of Magdeb:[2] pend their by divers learned and

[1] Thomas Hooker, *A Survey of the Summe of Church-Discipline. Wherein the way of the Churches of New-England is warranted out of the Word* (May 1648); John Cotton, *The Way of Congregational Churches cleared from the Historical Aspersions of Mr. Robert Baylie in his Disswasive from the Errors of the Time, and from Mis-constructions of Mr. Rutherford in his Due Right of Presbyteries* (February 1648).

[2] *Ecclesiastical History of the Magdeburgensis* (compilation by Lutheran scholars).

laborious men: the first booke of the 1t Century containes: 372 columns, columne due in una quaque pagina:[1] this I intend if god give mee strength to read on nights, that therby I may understand the state and affayre of that body wherof Christ is the head, and observe from history, the witnesse of the several gratious preservacons of gods truths, and servants in all ages:. give me lord strength for this worke, dilligence, and memory, and make it an advantage to my newe spirituall estate, and a further fitting me for the worke of thy house among thy people for Jesus sake I intreate thee; I read the preface to the worke this night, oh lord I have not parts to serve thee in writings as others, make me somewhat usefull to thy glory, in converting, and confirming soules;

17. My navel continued sore; the corrupcion in it was blackish, I applied nothing to it, hoping in god it will doe well, my tenant was with mee, acquainting mee, that he had hired another farme;

18: I finisht the reading of Vossius his first tome: my navel was full of blackish stuffe, yett not very sore, my trust is in my god for perfect healing of it.

Pose. I found the upper part of my head, cold and full within, and very cloudy, this day it distilled in a wonderfull pose, and then setled in my chest

Novemb. 19: This weeke the lord was good and mercifull to us, in all our outward mercies; onely my navel continued ill, which yett was not very sore, or troublesome at present, but only in apprehension, and in reference to that; I blesse god, that my heart is fixed, and stayed on him, that he will in due time perfectly heale it; and that I might not bee troubled over much with both ills togither, my pose taking mee, I felt not the illnes of my navel, my wife and family in indifferent health, I praise god for the same; my cold was sad on the lords day, yett through mercy I preacht twice on that day, the lord in mercy kept my heart in some measure close to him, and estranged mee from my vaine thoughts to his name be the praise, as also gave me with some dilligence to attend on my studies, he in mercy, use mee, as a blessing to the soules of his people:.

November. 26. This weeke full of variety of providences towards my selfe, and family. the lord reacht out his hand to us all but the children, but very gently and mercifully. my cold was very violent and sharpe, and my rest very unquietly and restles 2 nights, but then I rested better, on Tuesday I searcht my navel, and whether that or a fitt of coughing moved mee, I knowe not, but I was neare

[1] Two columns on each page.

swouning but afterwards I had hope in my navel, keeping lint out of it, and washing it with plantane[1] water and loose sugar, the lords name bee praised for it, and for an insight he giveth me into the vanitie of my heart, and raising up my soule to an opposing of every vanitie, the lord was mercifull to the residue of our family to hold up our heads, and to remove our weaknesses, my navel was now in a hopefull way of healing, and my trust is in god, to perfect the same, the lord with a sad providence overtooke a Trooper slaine by a Cavalier neare us, oh keepe me that the bloudy minded man have not an advantage against mee, the lord was good to me, notwithstanding the aking of my head, and my cold and aguish distemper to give me strength for my studdies, and to preach(.) unto the(e) looketh my soule to blesse the word, oh make it a blessing for thy name sake, I had not that liberty nor ability by reason of my illnes to follow my studdies this weeke; make mee to gett good for my soule, and strengthen my inward man I intreate thee.

29. This day was P.F: my cold continued sad, and the former dayes I was very feaverish and aguish, so that I could not studdy, this whole day, I lay in a great sweate, my place was not supplied.

30. Mr Harlakenden was with me from London, he did nothing about the augmentacion, neither doe any regard to bring mee in any moneyes to live upon,

December. 3. This weeke my cold continued, but my aguish distemper at the latter end was somewhat abated: and my navel was well, and seemed perfectly sound, to god be the praise, the meanes used was washing it with plantane water and loose sugar, and keeping it cleane, thus the lord in laying on one trouble did remove another, answering prayer and shewing himselfe a god hearing even my infirmities, the lord in mercy sanctifie both unto mee, my cold did trouble me with coughing in the night, I hope it will cleare and cleanse mee, my deare wife was also very ill with her cold, hereby my studdies were much hindred, and yett I gott up my sermons, and ventured to preach god giving me strength, and he preserved mee that my going out was not hurtfull to mee, my stomacke was very bad, but god provided meate for mee that I rellished: a siknes is a straite and this difficultie we litle remember when in health, the lord shined on my spirit, gave me inward peace and stayed my

[1] Plantane: plantain, especially the Greater Plantain, 'a low herb with broad flat leaves spread close to the ground' NED. Both Culpeper and Gerard in their herbals mention it as a soothing agent, applied internally and externally.

heart on him, oh fetcht of my heart to a full compliance with and submittance to thy heavenly will oh my god

December: 10: This weeke my cold continued but much better I was than formerly, it cleansed my chest very much so that I did not wheeze in the nights as I did formerly for many weekes, yett by the breaking of my water, and the fulnes therof of white crewde phlegme, I conceive my body is not yett setled, but full of cold waterish humours: my stomacke returned to mee againe; my wife was very ill with a cold, the good lord in his mercy sanctifie his hand to mee, and doe mee good by the same; this ilnes hindred me in my studdies, yett I did something therin daily, the lord gave me strength in some measure for the worke of the Sabbath he in mercy accept mee, and blesse mee and mine,

11: ventured downe to the priory this day where I had not beene in above three weekes time; the lord in mercy give me health that I may serve him with cheerfulnes: I was hard putt to it for money receiving none from my peop(le). thou seest good thus to try mee, provide for mee oh lord, and in due time lett their care of mee ☞ revive, and in the meane time patient thou my spirit. All along this illnes I was very illish in my bones, given to sweeting my water broke very pudled, most commonly all white, sometimes a reddish sediment, and as it were a fatt slimynes upon the top of my water

Bakers Chronicle:— 13: finisht the reading of Vossius Rhetoricke, tomus 2^dus^ conteining 527. pages in 4to. I read Bakers Chronicle of England, now and then for my recreation, and the Archbishops triall,[1]

December. 17. This weeke my cold, and illnes continued, but much abated through mercy I find I doe take a litle cold now and then, but through mercy I and mine are preserved, and gods hand on us is very light and gentle, this weeke Mrs Tiffin a sad woman died, even suddenly, and yett the lord continueth me a place in the land of the living, now is Mr Harl: left alone in England of all his fathers family, my stomacke was very good, but I find my selfe full of waterish and aguish humours and keeping my selfe warme makes me apt to take colds, my navel indifferent well to god bee praise, after above 30 houres illnes in my stomacke I fell into a great loosenes which I conceive did me much good, I wrapt my selfe up warme, and preacht twice on the lords daye, god giving me strength for it, I could doe but litle in my studdies: Sathan is busy in his

[1] Sir Richard Baker, *A Chronicle of the Kings of England* . . . (1643); it is impossible to decide which, if any, of the accounts of Laud's death which appeared in January 1645 (Thomason, i, p. 356) RJ is referring to.

troubles and temptacons to old vanities, and ready I am to neglect my watch, oh how good is god that doth not leave me to his rage, nor give me up to inward troubles of spirit, oh continue thy love unto me that I may praise thee and delight in thee,

December: 21: this day Mr H. and Mr Ell(iston): went about to gather my money that was much in arreare, they brought me in 3[li]. 6[s]. and a good report generally of a willingnes in the people (to) doe something towards my maintenance, which is the goodnes of god to make their care to revive againe, and it shall engage my heart to the Lord, and this people,

De: 24 This weeke the Lord was good and mercifull to mee and mine in our peace plenty and health, which god very comfortably in all particulars restored unto mee, for which I desire to praise him in his christ to recount his goodnes speaking well of his name desirous of his grace in living unto him, the lord good in restraining wonted temptacions, and when they have putt up head in giving me grace and strength to crush them, the lord was good and mercifull in giving me strength and libertie for the same, and in carrying me on in the worke, for which is named be praised: oh prevaile, with mee and mine, that wee may serve thee in uprightnes

Decemb. 25. This day Mr H. and Mr Ell: went to gather up some contribucon for me, and found some persons willing to contribute, which were not yett in the bill, they brought me in, in money 3[li]. which was a good refreshing to mee, my wife had this money, who was very ill this day.

27. This day was the publicke, the last month I kept my bed all day in a great sweat, and troubled with my cold, and aguish distemp(t)er, but god in his mercy and goodnes hath revived his mercy as of old in restoring me to my health and my strength, and now what remaineth unto me, but to serve this god, with all my strength, and to delight my soule in his goodnes; the Lord was good and mercifull to me in my wife, who was better and cheerfullier and free from paines than formerly, as also in preaching his word enabling mee for the same and helping me with strength for the delivery of it; the good Lord pardon mine and the nacions sins and heale us for his names sake,

My wife was very ill now adayes, with a paine in her head and backe, the lord support her, and sanctifie it unto her, and deliver her from the same, and make her to mee dayly a meete helpe,

Mrs Harlakenden very ill divers nights togither, Lord preserve her, and let her live in thy sight and with us, for thy mercy and goodnes sake, wee dined with Mr Harlakenden die 30: where we were bountifully entertained, as a few nights before with Mrs Church.

31: This weeke the Lord was good to mee, and children in health, peace, in providing necessaries for us, so that in straites and times of scarcity, wee are sufficiently provided for, my wife not very well, I hope they are but her childing illnesses, which god in due time will remove; this weeke, I had divers disquietings and I find they disquiett me, lord strengthen me with patience that no outward thing may move mee to any unseemelines, and helpe me to watch my selfe continually: god good to mee in keeping mee from my old temptacions, and my follies theron, they are cutts to my heart and before my eyes, but thou oh lord of thy mercy wilt not only pardon them, but doe them away, and I find them after putting up head but through gods goodnes they lead me not aside as formerly to walke with vanity: the lord good to me in my health my cold only very gentle: my navel whole and sound all this weeke, but I was divers times afraid it had been sore, the lord merciful to me in the Sabbath, in giving me liberty, and strength for it, blesse thy word unto me and my people, and give me a spirit to walke with thee, this weeke also I had some moneys from my people: as if the lord would cause their care of me to revive, if it be thy pleasure doe, and give me with comfort to serve thee with this people all my dayes if it be thy pleasure, for my desires are specially here.

Bakers hronicle read: Reconciler.

January: 4: This day wee were kindly entertained at my neighbour Potters; I finisht the reading of Sr Ri: Bakers chronicle in folio of 614 pages divided into foure parts; also this day I entred upon a great worke, wherin I intend some care and paines to collect the places of scripture, (c.o. and) that seeme different one from another, and the reconciling of them, Lord assist mee with health, strength and wisedome for this great worke;

This day 7 yeares King Charles came to demand the 5 members, and it was thought with an intencion to have offered violence to the house, this day the Commons of themselves, ordered the Tryall of the King, many men cry out of this worke that it will ruine the kingdome, the army religion: etc. for my part I conceive it strange extraordinary, and that it will occasion very much trouble betwixt the prince, and his freinds, and the joyners in the new representative, but if the worke bee of god it will prosper, if not it will come to nothing,

5: this day, I went abroad to Sr Tho: Honywoods, I found him at home, and heard by him good hope that the augmentacion granted by Parliament may prove at last effectuall, if so, I shall blesse god, if not I shall bee content.

Jan: 7: This weeke the lord good and mercifull to me and mine in our health, peace, in providing for us, notwithstanding the great dearnes of everything, beefe at 3^d. ob. per pound; wheate 7^s. 6^d. rye: 6^s. 4^d. cheese 4^d. butter 6^d. ob per pound, and men expect it will bee dearer and dearer, the Lord good to me in my studies, good in keeping mee from many temptacions that though they put up head, yett they prevaile not over mee, Lord keepe mee for my trust is in thee, god was good and mercifull to mee in the Sabbath, in giving me some measure of strength and affection for the exercise and the duties therof, he in mercy accept me and blesse my people. divers people in imitacion, or in abuse sitt with their hatts on when wee are singing psalmes, lord heale all our distempers.

11: heard of the illnes of my Lady Honywoods daughter, I went thither found it was her younger sonne, but I hope it is not unto death, lord heale it, and sanctifie all thy rode unto us, this day wee were very kindly entertaind at my Neighbour Burtons with divers good neighbours.

13: my navel hath continued finely well for 3 weekes onely, one day a litle reddish I found it somewhat worse this night. when thou hast done thy whole worke thou oh lord wilt heale mee, in the meane time give me patience to submitt unto thee, and waite on thee, and withal to gird up the spirit of my minde to eye and walke with thee, so that nothing may dismay mee.

Navell.

my hall chamber was finisht by Mr Harrington, the Masons worke and stuffe one way or other amounted to, about 50^s. the timber I found onely(,) he payd the Carpenters:

Hooker and: Cotton:

This weeke I finisht the reading of Hookers discourse about church government(.) I find it a peice worthy the perusing, I observed the most materiall heads out of it, and blesse god, for the opportunity I had to enjoy it

Jan: 14: This weeke the Lord was good and mercifull to mee, and all my family, in our healths and yett wee had our distempers, all my children but especially Thomas breake out in their heads: my selfe feel an heavynes, coldnes, or moistnes in the crowne of my head, as if it were rheume, and a paine in my sides, with a litle sorenes in my bones sometimes in one place and sometimes in another. my wife faint and paind with her child in her backe, but yett through mercy wee rest, eate drinke, and walke about within and without doores, though the times are very dangerous in reference to the healths of people: god good in providing food and rayment for us in the dayes of want, firing most people having nothing to burne this weeke(,) I find my minde vanities assayling mee, and my deceitfull treacherous heart, hankering after them, and missing on earthly vanities, but not with full swinge as formerly oh helpe me to beware of Sathans slights, and to beware of relapsing backe unto any folly which is discoverd unto me, I having resolved in my strength to keepe thy commandements oh faile mee not I intreate thee, this day the Lord was good to mee in giving me health and strength for the worke of the Sabbath, oh how litle is my heart raised up, and set on god, oh for mercy sake quicken mee, and make mee a blessing to my people, I stird up people to a care of the poore, in incouraging the officers and cheerfull paying their rates, the necessities of the times are very great.

15: I began to read Smalcius the Socinian, against the incarnation of Christ, in latine it containeth 29 pages in a large quarto.[1] heard of the death of young Mr Rogers of Taine: lord its thy goodnes my wife is not a widdow, and my children fatherless: Oh spare mee if it bee thy pleasure to doe the service in thes evill dayes, and keepe me from the evill of them for in thee doe I put my trust: I leant to Mr Lagden at his need 8li. unaskt, neither he nor shee had dealt very neighbourly with us, but I blesse god I can doe good against evill

Smalcius P: 29:

Mrs Church and her daughter gave us a free gift.

Amama: p: 240.

16: Began to read dilligently over Amama's Heb: Grammer[2] it containes about 240 pages in 8°.

17: finisht the reading of Smalcius discourse, a man of a subtle witt. this day (and) the 18th Mr Harlakenden kept his courts,

19: 20: Mr Harlakenden perfected his agreement with Mr Tiffin payd him 300li.: writings sealed and delivered and the mony paid by him in divers of our presence, and of Mr Smith and Mr Stephens his brothers by marriage,[3]

21: This weeke the lord continued good and mercifull to mee in outward mercies, as also to mine my wife onely ill, but I hope it will blowe over, god was good in preserving mee from temptacons and

[1] (Faustus Socino), *Brevis discursus de causa ob quam creditur aut non creditur Evangelio Jesu Christi* . . . (1618); Jacobus Smalcius was a German unitarian writer, fl. 1620.

[2] Sixtinus Amama, *Grammatica Ebraea* . . . (1634).

[3] In Richard Harlakenden's Account Book (ERO, Temp. Acc. 897/8) there is a detailed memorandum of this payment, where Harlakenden notes paying £300 to William Tiffin, 'in the presence of his brother John Smith, gent., and Mr Wm. Stephens his brother'. John Smith was probably of Creping-Hall, Wakes Colne. Morant, ii, p. 223.

sinfull evills, good to mee in the Sabbath in giving mee strength for the same, I preacht in the morning at Markeshall, and in the afternoone at home, the lord in mercy accept me, and pardon mee,
Lessius: I read over Lessius,[1] and the treatises with it, and though I am not
22. satisfied concerning a constant measure of provision, yett I concurre with him, that a full diet is not best, plus necat gula quam gladius,[2] a slender and a hard diett and exercise is very much conducing to our health, and to mine in particular, and therfore my thoughts are to bee more moderate in my diett, then formerly.

23: This day was very cold, the sharpenes of the winde made a very great frost, my navell was a litle sore, but now rawe, Mrs Mary Church had a great fall, and hurt her legge with it, god in mercy make her well againe. my deare wife more cheerfull this day then divers dayes, the small pox are about in divers places, the god of heaven in much mercy preserve mee and mine: this night our mayde was ill, and feared as if shee would have the pox. two things troubled mee. the sicknes in regard of mee and mine, but god upheld me in the consideracion of his providence, that nothing cometh to passe without, he can preserve my family or me when others ill, and he can afflict it when others well, and therefore I was resolved to submitt to his hand cheerfully. another trouble and that was death and judgment. here I cast my soule upon that love of god that hath done great things in me to perfect them and crowne me with his glory. I praise god in the morning she feared only as if it had beene a sore throat.

— — — — — — — — — — — — — — — — — — — —

33: year: 1648:

January: 25: this day I have compleated my 32 yeare, and enter now upon my 33 y. this day I was in conference with divers of my christian freinds and people at the priory coming home I found my wife gone to bed very ill, and full of paine, yett god in mercy refresht her in the night with rest.

Jan: 28: This weeke god was good to us in our health peace, and plenty. the season was cold, all things deare, people pincht with want of food, which we want not to god be praise, my deare wife was very

[1] Leonard Lessius, *Hygiasticon; or, the Right course of preserving life and health unto extream old age . . .* (also: *A Treatise of Temperance and Sobrietie*: written by Lud. Cornarus, translated into English by Mr. George Herbert), 1634.

[2] Gluttony kills more than the sword.

ill some dayes but now cheerfull. god good in preserving us from infectious diseases: his mercy great in giving me a heart in any measure to walke with him, and in keeping mee from my iniquity, the lord was mercifull to me in the Sabbath in giving me strength to preach, and in the fitnes of the word of patience to the times, the lord in mercy make us practicers of it; this day I was troubled with a most eager pose, and with sneezing, I thinke scarce ever more in my life. god in his due time will remove all thes. I felt not my navel sore all this latter part of the weeke. nor the cloud in my head: I followed my Hebrew studdies this weeke, but not so seriously as I intended. I did somewhat also in my reconciler. to the 15th of Genesis:

Pose.

31: Heard K C was executed, but that was uncertaine, he was adjudged to dye Jan. 27. 1648. Bradshaw, the lord president pronounced sentence, this day was a fast a very cold day. I suppose they will now be layd downe, people doe so exceedingly neglect the same

Febr: 2: troubled with a great pose: 3. I had home some wood from my vicarage close worth neare 20s. but I gott a great cold, and was much troubled with it;

4: This weeke I was much troubled with pose, and cold; but through mercy they did not setle in my chest: otherwise I enjoyed many mercies outward and that in perticular in my health: I was much troubled with the blacke providence of putting the King to death, my teares were not restrained at the passages about his death, the lord in mercy lay it not as sinne to the charge of the kingdome, but in mercy doe us good by the same, the lord was good to all mine in their healths, the small poxe on some familyes of the towne but spreadeth not, to god be the glory therof: my vanities of minde returned to my trouble, oh when shall vaine thoughts depart from mee. this weeke I could doe nothing neither in my Hebrew nor in my reconciler: the Lord was good to mee in the Sabbath in enabling me with strength for the worke the lord in mercy accept me therin, and blesse it to my people, and owne soule eternall good:.

the death of the king talked much of, very many men of the weaker sort of christians in divers places passionate concerning it, but so ungroundedly, that it would make any to bleed to observe it, the lord hath some great thing to doe, feare and tremble att it oh England:.

Monday it was debated about Kings and Peeres(,) on Tuesday the house of Commons ordered to null the house of Lords as uselesse, and on the next day to lay aside the Goverment by Kings, and to sett up a councell of state,

Feb: 11: This weeke the Lord was good to me and mine in our peace and plenty. the times are very sad and full of difficulties, and yett god provideth for mee, and mine, god good to us in our health: my cold causeth me to wheeze in the nights but not much, my children preserved in divers dangers, Jane fell into the fire, her hands only a litle hurt, I had more experience of my heart looking backe after old vanities then along time before, I had well nigh slipt, but god upheld mee, this weeke I omitted the studdy of my Heb: but observed 6 chapters in Genesis in my reconciler, wee had a lusty woman dyed this weeke in our towne suddenly, I preacht at her funerall.

God was good to me in the Sabbath, in carrying me on in the worke of it, the good lord in mercy accept me and pardon for the glory of his owne rich name, doe me and my people good. the weather was frost. snow, and windy, which made it very cold and thus it hath continued about three weekes,

13: Went up with my wife to visit Mr Elliston and his family. comming home, I heard that Mr Edw: Cressener was dead, and it was true he dyed even suddenly, and yett he was quite worne out, and dyed in a good old age: and in a good time, before troubles which he very much feared:

14: Visited old Spooner, found him more cheerfull, then wee expected: came home by my Tenants who begins already to abuse my woods; so as I feare him but a slippery fellow.

17: Mr Cressener buried, many people present, I preacht his funerall, he was layd in the sepulcher of his fathers in a good old age, it was reported that old Spooner was dead he swounded indeed, but revived againe,

Feb: 18: This weeke the Lord was good and mercifull to mee, and mine, in our health peace and plenty, providing food and rayment convenient for us in this great dearth and want of all things, I gave 4^{d}. per pound for porke, divers sickly and ill, yett wee in health through gods mercy, the lord was good to me in preserving me from and in(n) temptacions of Sathan, who busily assailes mee, but god keepeth me by the hand so that though I slippe, yett I am not utterly cast downe, my deare wife weakly but yett cheerfull, the lord good to mee in the Sabbath, giving me strength and liberty for the same, the lord in mercy accept of me and blesse me in his worke, great threats to ruine the ministry, for my part my heart is att peace and rest, the will of the Lord bee done, but they that medle with the lord shall smart in due time.

I did but litle this weeke in my Heb, and but 3 chapters in my reconciler; being hindred with other occasions:. but the next weeke through gods mercy I intend to follow my studdies very closely:.

19: I was dealt with to subscribe a manifest of the Minist(ry). against the present proceedings and the agreement of the people, and a dissent in the matter of the King,[1] there are some things are well done, but for Ministers to intermedle thus in all difficulties of state, I question the warrantablenes therof, and therfore I could not concurre, but my advice is that the civill part might be undertaken by some able statesman and the religious part by some able ministers, and then proceed to a subscription

19. 20: David saith it was good for me that I was afflicted; and I trust in god, I shall say so, my navels sorenes god made use of to minde me of my folly, god was good to me, Sathan he came on with old temptacons and I was ready to be overcome, but I trust in the Almighty God, he will preserve me, and sanctifie mee, and then I shall say, it was good that the lord dealt thus with mee;

Navel sore:

before this fell sore, I went abroad up and downe, and might take cold, whatever it bee Lord I accept of thy punishment, and submitt unto thee, and give glory to the lord in and under the same, and I desire thy grace wherby I may bee enabled to improve it to make mee more holy, and heavenly minded.

also I observe that I swett very much too or three nights before it was sorish

22: this day my navel continued sore, I washt it, as formerly, divers christian Freinds women mett at my house in conference this day, about our spirituall estate and condicon, the lord helpe us therein, my freind Mr R. H onely of any men was with us:

24: I felt no paine nor sorenes in my navel praised bee god, but I found my throate full of phlegme, and a litle sore and rough, I gargard and brought up much phlegme, but I was very hoarse, and it troubled my thoughts in reference to the Sabbath

Feb: 25: This weeke the lord was good to me and mine in our peace, plenty and preservacion and in our healths though both my wife and selfe had some distempers, yett so gentle as not much to unfitt us for our employments, some sadly distressed under the small

[1] The Essex Watchmen's Watchword, February 1649, signed by 63 ministers disappointed at the final outcome of the war, and opposed to the Agreement of the People. Smith, pp. 102–4.

pox, the lord made us helpefull to our mayde Lydia and her children: the lord stand betwixt the whole, and the sicke, and suffer his rod to proceed no farther if it bee his will; wee had 6 persons: 3 old men, 1: young woman and 2 infants buried in the space of 14: dayes: I did something though not much in my Hebrew I have finisht the 30 chapter of Exodus in my reconciler, I intended to have enterd upon my course of exposicion but my hoarsenes hindred mee, my daughter this weeke abroad with our loving Freind Mrs Ellistons daughter; that part of the army before Pomfrett hangd a minister a Cavalier they condemned him for holding intelligence with the enemy in the Castle, and that he had a hand in betraying the same, this weeke their seemed to appeare some differences in the Councell of state, and in the army especially, a dangerous peticon as they say being sett a foote, and truly the enemies onely course is to divide them on the peoples interest and their owne, for probably if they continue united it will cost a sea of bloud, and a world of trouble to alter what is now in setling: this day I began my exposicions againe my voice failes me very much. the lord pardon my sins accept mee and make me serviceable to himselfe.

I felt my navel sore againe at night.

28: my navel continued sore, not so bad as in former times. I had a great cold and hoarsenes with it(.)this day I preacht on Ezech. 22.30.[1] make me oh lord as I have therin mentioned the condicon of the nacon, and the helpe therof in standing in the gap to endeavour the same, that my god may witnesse my endeavours for the good of England.

March: 2. went with all my litle ones to my Lady Honywoods, came home that night, the season cold, seed time so backward that litle soft corne is sowen, and hard corne not come up,[2] upon the ground, die 3: it snew exceedingly, the lord thinke upon us in mercy, and doe not in all things fight against us to pine us, and consume us: but though there should bee no foode yett will I through his grace rejoyce in him, and trusting in him waite for him.

[1] 'And I sought for a man among them, that should make up the hedge, and stand in the gap before me for the land, that I should not destroy it: but I found none.'

[2] RJ's use of the terms 'hard' and 'soft' corn do not correspond completely with other contemporary usage. Plot in 1686 described wheat and rye as 'hard' corn; oats and barley have been suggested as 'soft' corn. The former were 'winter' corn, sown in the autumn and harvested the following summer, the latter 'spring' corn, sown and harvested the same year. RJ, however, included barley as 'hard' corn, which suggests that he was differentiating them on the basis of their value for bread-making, or gluten content. For Plot, see W. Ashley, *Bread of our Forefathers* (Oxford, 1928), p. 30. I am grateful to Dr. Joan Thirsk for advice on this matter.

March: 4: This weeke the Lord good and mercifull to mee and mine in our health, peace, and plenty. but oh how unthankefull have I beene to the lord, and unmindefull of his many benefits; oh how prone is my heart to backsliding, lord I sticke fast and my corruptions are too hard for mee, when wilt thou deliver me, lord make me watchfull against vaine thoughts for from thence springeth my misery; I did something in my Heb. this weeke, and in my reconciler I finisht the 36 ch: of Genesis: I had experience of god in not giving me to delight in any of my faylings, oh lett me delight onely in thy selfe, my navel lateward was indifferent well I felt no paine in it, thou dost me good though I rebell, when shall mercy and gentlenes overcome mee, the lord was good to me in the Sabbath and in the severall exercises therof, in restoring my voice, and giving me strength, the lord accept me and blesse all ordinances to the soules of my people, and family.

7. returnd this day from my Lady Honywoods who used my wife and my selfe with aboundance of respect and love, and sent us not away empty, the lord remember and reward her labour of love, to her, and hers, Mr Clopton returned from London, he could effect nothing in the businesse, only he entertained a sollicitor to looke after it:.

March: 11: God was good and mercifull to me and mine in our peace, in our plenty, we wanted nothing in all thes straits of times, in our health, my navel well all this weeke, my cold did much abate, the lord good to us in the season, it being calme, cleare, dry and warme, only in the nights very cold frosts, oh how great is thy goodnes unto us; oh that our soules might love thee for it, the lord mercifull to mee, in not leading mee into some temptacion, which at some times I am continually dogged withall, oh lett no iniquity have dominion over mee, I went on in my reconciler unto Exod cap: 5: and did something in my Hebrew studdies; I intend to prosecute those studdies mostly beside the labour of my calling, the good Lord in mercy assist mee therein, the lord was good and mercifull to mee in the labour and service of his day, in expounding the 14th chapter, for divers passages therin, letting me see that mens opposing him, and troubling his people, hinders not his peoples good but hastens their own ruine upon them,

Navel sore 13: my navel was sore againe, not so bad as formerly, I blesse the(e) for my correction, oh purge out that corrupcion thou doest discover in mee, heard of one that after 2 yeares illnes was killd with a rawnes in his navel, but god shall heale me of this infirmity, and I shall praise him, and being thus fixed in heart upon him I enjoy sweet peace. die 14: I perceived and felt my navel stiffe, but no illnes in it blessed be my god

March: 18: This weeke the lord was good, and mercifull to mee and mine in our peace, our health, our plenty, wanting none of those necessary outward good things that others are deprived, the season was sadly cold, this day a great snow: Mr R. H. much troubled in reference to his office in thes times, wherin I was somewhat serviceable to him: cheese now at 4^{d}. q and ob per pound, butter sold by some at 8^{d}. porke 4^{d}q. or ob. beefe 3^{d}. ob. q. great feare of the decay of trade, yett lord, in all assayes wee will putt our trust in thee, this weeke my navel sore, I blesse god for it: if god will heale me of any corrupcion by his chastisement, is it not good, I see more into the deceit of my heart, my weaknes, heale me also oh god, my heart is fixed on god that he will doe me good by it, and therefore I am now at rest. Mr W. H. likely to be a justice of peace, the lord make him usefull and serviceable for his glory in his place, the lord lett me see my weaknes, and therefore I will presse the more to lay hold on him, and to trust in him, the good lord keepe me from every evill way for his name sake, the lord was good to me in giving me strength to preach, and to expound the word, the lord in mercy pardon my many iniquities and accept of my soule, and continue to lift up the light of his countenance on mee and mine, and then full safe are wee.

20: I find the preists, and altars under the law contracted uncleannes, and they were to be cleansed Levit. 16.6.19: now on this alter were only their sacrifices burnt so that their was sin in them, and indeed

V 20: lord their is sin, corrupcion uncleannes in my duties that I performe before thee their is the iniquitie of my holy things, but that is my comfort, I have a preist an alter that doth sanctifie my services and mee, one that contracts no pollucion from me, though I that am uncleane touch him, yett he is not made uncleane by me, but I am made cleane by him. I find find V.29.30: upon the anniversary when the preist made attonement for the people that the people also efflicted their soules Jesus is make attonement for me every day and I will every day looke up to god to accept of his attonement as Levin I rest: but I will seeke unto my god by him.

22: Mr W: H. came home from the assizes he was sworne the justice of peace, we have 3 justices now within 2 mile of our towne on either hand with him, the lord make him serviceable for our good, there are but few in the countie, its a good providence that wee are so well supplyed: there fell out worke for him as soone as he came home, pretences of slaughter, heard by him that L. Col. Lilburne and his partie did gather about St Albans to goe on with their pretended principle of libertie, and to ease the subject of taxes, tis true there are burthens on us, and divers pretend to amend them, but they are but easy easyers, they rather increase then ease our burthens, Martin, and some others its said joyne with him, and encourage him,

Navel. on the 12 day my navel was sore, it was washed as usually, and so it was on the 13 day as I remember, I had a very great confidence in god to heale me of this infirmity, I found it well on the 13 day at night and so it continued to this day. viz. 24:

March: 25: This weeke the lord was good and mercifull to mee and mine, in our health, peace, plenty and in all other outward enjoyments: the season was dry, windie, indifferently cleare in the nights very cold, and much given to frosts, I should hope the season was good to purge the aire, and to prevent infection, the small poxe is about in the country three houses in our towne visited, god hath spared all their lives hitherto, oh that thy rod were sanctified unto us all, still oh lord watch over mee and mine for in thee doe I put my trust: the Coroner was sent for unto our towne about the death of one Beckwiths wife, by Holden, the Jury acquitted him, This weeke I was very sensible of my iniquity, and the corrupt inclinacions of my heart to evill, oh how prone oh lord am I therunto, but

Meditacons & Vowes. I have sworne that I will keepe thy commandements, oh forsake mee not; I was very neglectfull in my Hebrew studdies this weeke; but I begun a peice of worke which I hope will not be unprofitable to mee in my spirituall estate. viz, as I read over the scripture, some places yeild me much spirituall solace, matter of rejoycing, and some of ingagements, which I take notice of in a booke for that purpose; I went on more speedily then formerly in my reconciler I finisht Number: Cap: 12. this weeke, the lord mercifull unto me in giving me strength and voice for the labour and duty of the day, I preacht twice and expounded almost 2: chapters, oh let it not be as water spilt on the ground, make the words profitable to me and us

1649 all(,) I found no illnes in my navel all this weeke, oh continue thy goodnes to mee, that I may praise thee, and delight in thee;

27: Yesterday I bought mee a new felt, it cost mee, 7^{s}. this morning Mr Nicholsons stable being robbed; Justice Har. came over to mee, I made out two hue, and cry's after the horse on the road; the first that I ever writt, in my life,

(29:) March 29: This day I and my deare wife (with our true freind, Mrs Mary,) sett apart to seeke god; to bewaile our sins, the corrupcion, and deceit of our hearts before the Lord, and to seeke of god strength to preserve us in our uprightnes, and to heale us of every corrupcion: that god would remember my wife and give her a good and safe houre of deliverance, and preserve her and our family from diseases, that the lord would perfect my health, and a mercy runn downe herein to others especially our good Freind Mrs Mary, and Mr R: Har: Mrs Harlakenden in the streete, Goodee Burton, and Goodee Potter, which foure are ill, and I am especially bound to pray for them, for their good in this life, and a better; in a word that god would in the riches of his mercy give us of the fulnesse of Jesus, according to every one of our measures, which he seeth we want and have need to be supplied to us, oh heare us for thy christs sake, oh our god, oh my god;.

we had about two houres conference at Mr Harlakendens.

Aprill: 1: This weeke the lord was good to us in all our outward mercies; and in the season which was dry and healthfull, this morning was a growing warme, moist morning, divers times this weeke I feared my navel, but through mercy it was not sore, the lord I trust will heale mee, I putt my trust in him, and am at rest. I did not much in any of my studdies this weeke, spent much in visiting freinds, etc. the lord was good to me in giving me strength and ability for the Sabbath, but I found my heart assaulted with vile thoughts in the same, oh change mee throughly oh my god for my eyes are upon thee;

2: this day, I payed Mr R: Harlakenden 10^{li}. that I had long since borrowed of him I now owe him nothing, but love, and respect as a christian and Freind which I doe and I trust shall have occasion daily to owe unto him;

3: This morning god sent us a merveylous sweet refreshing raine, as the answer of our prayers, oh lett thy eyes watch over England continually for good, and over my heart that in any straite, I may not sin, or repine against thy providence,

4: mrs King went to her daughters Mrs Clarke, I cannot be against it, but I shall misse her for my deare wife, we cannot be with all our freinds at once, but our god in being present with one is not absent from another, he is able to fill every place, and to answer all persons wants, being the fountaine of all good, and present in all places:.

April: 8: This weeke the lord was good and mercifull to mee and mine in our peace health, plenty, wee wanted no convenient good outward thing in all the time of want and scarcity, some dayes of the weeke were warme, and moist and brave growing weather, others cold, there were great apprehensions of the famine, people feared it, especially at London among the poore, the lord was mercifull to us in preserving us from infectious diseases, the small poxe but in one family, and both of them in good hopes of recovery, the woman was fearfull shee should die of the disease, but our lives are in gods hands, and our surmises cannot hurt us, when he pleaseth, I was sensible of the vanity of my heart, and of neglect of seeking god; I rellish not god in my private duties and prayer as I have sometimes I doe not stirre up myselfe to lay hold on god, the lord was good to mee in preserving me from my iniquitie, oh lett no corrupcion whatsoever have dominion over mee this weeke, I spent some time in my Hebrew studies, I went on in my Reconciler to the 6 of Deuteronymy, and observed something, by way of meditacion and resolucion out of the scripture, all this weeke my navel was well I often supposed it ill, but I blesse god that it was neither moist nor open, it seemes to be a litle loosed, the lord in mercy hath healed me, oh keepe mee that I sin not, least a worse thing happen unto mee; Dr Glissons[1] opinion was that some repelling, strengthening knitting plaister were very good for the same, and it stands with reason, he approved what was used, oh I will praise the lord for he hath dealt bountifully with mee, the lord was mercifull unto mee in the worke and duty of the day, about rest in our trouble, the lord made it a suitable word, oh lord teach mee to live in thee to be such a god to mee oh lett mee never give the(e) over untill thou blesse me herein,

10: This day I joyned in keeping a day of humiliacion at Sr Tho: Honywoods with Mr Owen, Mr Clopton and some others, our jorney was troublesome, but the presence in the ordinance was cheerfull, the lord heare and accept, subdue my corruptions, and hasten whatsoever purposes thou hast to doe,

12 This day wee had a christian meeting at Mrs Cresseners:

April: 15. This weeke the Lord was good and mercifull to mee and mine in all outward mercies, when as their is a great scarcitie of all things, beefe ordinarily 4^{d}. per lib: butter 7 or 8^{d}. cheese 5^{d}. wheate 7^{s}. 6^{d}. rye 6^{s}. 8^{d}. yett we wanted nothing needfull or fitting for us(.) I was somewhat troubled with a rheume, it fared as if my teeth were

[1] Francis Glisson (1597–1677), Regius Professor of Medicine at Cambridge from 1636, one of the most distinguished physicians of the century; lived near Colchester. DNB.

a litle on edge my navel continued well, thus when one trouble is over another succeeds, wherin I observe gods goodnes not to try with all at once, and indeed I ought not so much to desire remove this or that and thinke then all will be well, as submitt to all gods purposes and endeavour to gaine spiritually by all his providences, partly through businesse and partly idlenes I omitted all my studdies this weeke: the lord was good to mee in the Sabbath, in giving me strength for it; and making his word a refreshing unto mee

16: 17. thes dayes were most pleasant weather, giving us great hopes both for a good seed time and for corne that it would flourish on the grounds: I received divers kindnesses from divers lord make me thankfull and carefull to serve thee,

April: 19: This day by act was sett apart for a day of humiliacion but was not kept in most places by reason the act was not divulged abroad, wherby ministers and people might have timely notice to prepare for the same,

April: 22 This weeke the lord was good and mercifull to mee, and mine in our peace, plenty, and health, my navel hath continued well through gods goodnes about 6 weekes, and yett I have travailed, swett, and taken cold, I am exercised with a pose, and wheezing in the night, as if my chest, and head, were full of rheume, god in his due time will putt an end to thes illnesses, but through mercy, they doe not much take me of from my imploiment, this weeke I had experience of gods mercy to mee, not being lead into some temptacions as formerly, Lord I am very apt to sin in many things against thee, oh keepe me for thy name sake. I did not much in any of my studdies this weeke, but only against the lords day, my wife held up her head beyond expectacion, this weeke another family afflicted with the small pox and we hitherto preserved blessed bee his name, this is the fourth family in the towne thus dealt with, and yett not any have dyed. the season was cleare, dry, windie, warme and sometimes coole, a most comfortable seed time, the lord was good to mee in the Sabbath, in the duties and exercises of the same, the preaching and expounding the word, my subject was about the future glory of the church of Jesus Christ here in this world:

☞ 24: This day I went to my Lady Honywoods, who was very ill, and so encumbred with the troubles of the world, that her life was sorrow and bitternes to her, and their lyes hardly any way out of them, I received this chardge from her to love her children, and as I had any opportunity to instruct them in the feare of god: which as I faithfully promised, so I desire grace from god that I may performe it: the lord in mercy raise her up, god hath mingled her cup with many sorrowes, her sonne Mr Tho: hath newly broken his army,[1] which I advised them to conceale from her, god is good in the preservacions of mee and mine.

Cold 26: I had a very great stuffing cold and cough with a great wheezing, this day I tooke a stybium vomitt[2] prepared at Cogshall, it wrought well on me to god bee praise, but I find gods mercies and my corrupcions still meete,

29. This weeke god was good to us in the aboundance of our outward mercies, the lord makes me sensible of my corrupcions, but they are not mortified, heard ill words of L.C. Gr:[3] oh lord make me humble and watchfull in my walke with thee my necke was sore under my throate, I kept it warme, god was good to mee in the dutie of the Sabbath to his name bee praise,

30: my uncle Josselin of Cranham with mee, I paid him the 35li. 5s. which I ought him of 40li. I borrowed of him, 35li. I borrowed of Mr R. Harlakenden at the priory, the Major, my deare freind was now with us, at night I tooke some methridate,[4] it made mee sweate, and so I hope did mee good, at night my wife was ill, and sent for her midwife, but it was for present but a scare, my cold weareth away, and my feaverish distemper, to my god be the praise therof.

May: 5: My deare wife had beene very ill for 3 weekes, now towards night paynes came fast on her and shee was delivered before nine of the clocke of her 5t child, and third sonne god giveing us another sonne instead of my deare Ralph whom he tooke away, the lord command grace for my poore infant, and make it his, and perfect his mercy towards my deare wife, and keepe mee in uprightnes that I may feare his name, my wife was alone a great while with our good freinds Mrs Mary, and her mother, some few women were with her, but the midwife not, but when god commands deliverance there is nothing hinders it

Navel I feared my navel this daye, there was some lint that sticke in it, I thinke it was by reason of my former sweating, I medled not with it, but I looke up to my god perfectly to heale mee.

[1] This is clearly meant to be 'arm', since Thomas was only a child.

[2] Stibium: 'black antimony', trisulphide of antimony, formerly used for metallic antimony or any of its salts, esp. as a poison or an emetic. SOED.

[3] L.C.Gr: Lt.-Col. General, i.e. Cromwell.

[4] Mithridate: a composition of many ingredients in the form of an electuary, regarded as a universal antidote against poison and infectious disease; thus almost synonimous with 'medicine'. NED. (An electuary is a powder or other ingredient mixed with honey, syrup, etc.)

May: 6: This weeke past, god was good and mercifull to mee and mine in our peace, plenty, wee wanting no outward good thing that is needfull or necessary for us, god good in our health for so I called, though my wife were troubled with throwes, yett they were such as shee comfortably endured with gods helpe, and wee could not expect much otherwise from her, I was ill with my cold, yett through mercy, I growe better rid of it then formerly(.) this weeke I had experience of my owne weaknes in sinfull temptacons, following mee, and troubling mee, as if gods goodnes in letting none gett dominion over mee I praise my god for a heart of indignacion against evill; oh yett if I were not dogged with them it would bee more peace to mee, if thou wilt try mee oh lord, oh lett mee not be over come of any corrupcions I humbly intreate thee, I had litle libertie and leisure to doe any thing in my studdies this weeke, but in those that lye ordinary before mee, god was mercifull to mee in giving me strength and freedome for his Sabbath, he in mercy accept mee and doe mee good for the glory of his owne holy and pretious name,

navel: 12: I did not medle with my navel for above a weeke, but the lint stucke in it, I perceive it is not best to lett the lint stick in it, but wash it out, of this day I found it was somewhat sore, wherupon I washed it as formerly, it savoured very much was full of white stuffe; it looked a litle red and open. I thinke yett that it was not rawe it continued well above 8 weekes through gods mercy unto mee and I hope in god he will command his blessing on me therin

May: 13: This weeke god was good and mercifull to mee and mine in our peace, health, and in his free provision for us in thes dayes of scarcitie. oh that thy grace might so keepe mee, that no iniquitie might have dominion over mee, this day I baptised my sonne Ralph, the lord wash him, sanctifie him that he may bee his owne, my babe was troubled with winde, and made water with a great crying fitt, god blessed meane(s) so that he was finely well,

15: this day I was at my Lady Honywoods invited thither to dine with his father Mr Lamott, I motioned the sale of Hall meadow to them. my navel was a litle open and a litle white, but not rawe nor sore, my wheezing is ready to returne on every litle cold, lord keepe me for my trust is in thee, great difficulties by reason of the proceedings of divers souldiers designed for Ireland

17: This day was a day of publike humiliacon, many men in great straites and difficulties in regard of the Levellers attempts to raise troubles, and many of the souldiers discontents; god was mercifull to mee in giving me strength for the duty of the day wherin I spent publickely above 4 houres,

18: This day I payed Mr Harlakenden of the priory: 12^{li}. I now owe unto him 23^{li}. for which I gave him a bill to pay it upon demand, and I intend god willing to pay him well and truly with all speed: my lady sent her daughter Mrs Elizabeth, and kinswoman with her cost to give my wife a visitt; wee testified the utmost of our respect unto her, I gave her the choice of any booke in my library, which shee accepted very kindely and lovingly from mee,

N My navel was indifferent well, I applyed pouder sugar beaten very fine the god of my mercies give a blessing thereunto, heard the newes of quashing the Levellers; a glorious rich providence of god to England:

May: 20: This weeke the lord was good to us, in our peace, in health, and providing for us notwithstanding the great scarcity of all things rye at 6^{s}. 8^{d}. bushel, butter at 7^{d}. pound, cheese 6^{d}. beefe: 5^{d}. lambe 7^{d}. this weeke I had experience of the aptnes of my heart to listen to vaine temptacions and of gods grace to keepe and preserve mee from being overcome with the same, my navel was not well all this weeke neither was it very sore, onely some moisture in it, and the lint apt to stick in the same, this weeke I had no time for any studdies but my sermons and exposicions, the lord was good to mee in the day, he in mercy accept mee and blesse my labours for his mercy sake, our audience was very great this day from Halstead and other neighbour townes:.

22. went to my Lady Honywoods. found her troubled with feare that Mr Tho: her sonne was sicke of the small poxe, but I hope not so: I received this day my money from Mr Tho: Harlakenden and paid Mr Harlakenden 4^{li}. I now owe him but 19^{li}. wherof the greatest part I hope to pay very shortly.

25: the day before god sent us a very pleasant raine, for which his good name bee praised, the lord sent it in the very season, this day I paid for beefe about 4^{d}. ob. quarter a pound, and 6^{d}. the pound for mutton, but beefe was commonly 5^{d}. the pound; 9^{s}. and 10^{s}. the score, the best in the markets,

Sleidans Commentarie 26: begun to read this history, horis successivis: conteyning 26 bookes and 458 leaves:[1] its in a large octavo, but a smal character and close it containes the merveylous dawning and spreading of the reformacion

[1] Almost certainly Joannes Phillipson (Sleidanus), but no such title in STC Thomason, or Wing.

of religion in thes latter dayes under Luther, and the progresse therof for divers yeares

Medes discourses: Begun to reade Mr Medes discourses on several texts,[1] conteyning 527 pages in 4to. and to observe, some of the most materiall things therin.

May: 27. This day and indeed weeke god was good and mercifull to mee, and mine in our peace health, plenty, in all needfull outward mercies, wanting nothing needfull in all thes dayes of scarcity, The lord was good to my deare wife in her uprising, my litle boy was some what unquiett, but I hope it will weare away, god was good to mee in keeping mee from the vanities and sinfulnesses of my heart, the lord in mercy keepe mee from every evill worke and preserve me spotles to the glory of his owne most holy name, the lord was gratious and mercifull (me) to mee in fitting mee for the duty of the Sabbath, and in the preaching and expounding of his words, the good lord in mercy accept me and spare mee for his owne pretious name sake,

31: my loving uncle Mr Nathaniel Josselin came to mee, he stayed with mee that night, I heard much of gods mercy towards him, and he from mee wherin we desire to rejoyce,

June. 3. This weeke the Lord was good and mercifull to mee, and mine, in our peace health plenty, in the season wherby the earth is refreshed with dewes, and this day was very warme and comfortable, I gave 8^{s}. 2^{d}. for a score of indifferent beefe, the lord was good to mee in my health, and the health of my family, my navel through mercy continued well since May: 25: my neighbour Goodwife Burton was very ill, the Lord in mercy restore her unto health for his name sake, the lord was good to mee in keeping from some temptacions, and vanities with which formerly I have beene overtaken oh lett no iniquitie have no dominion over mee for thy most holy name; I spent a litle time in my Hebrew did a litle in my meditacons and reconciler to Deut: 12: and spent some time in Sleidan, were I observe the strange progresse of the gospell in Germany and other places many princes and families renouncing the pope, and of late yeares none have, neither hath the gospell any entertainment in Spaine, Italy. Sicily, and in the territories of the Venetians, I did somewhat in Medes discourses, the good lord forgive my many sins, and sanctifie my heart, and give mee to honour thee in all my wayes for ever

Navel

6: preacht this day at the baptizing of my Cosin Josselins sonne at

[1] Joseph Mede, *Diatribae. Discourses on divers texts of Scripture* (1642).

Fering; went on foot thither and returning, god was good to mee in the same to his name be praise.

9. heard my Cosin R. Josselin of Colchester was dead, and buried, my dayes are in thy hand oh fitt mee for my change I intreate thee.

June. 20: This weeke the lord was good and mercifull to mee in our peace, plenty health, my wife through mercy went abroad to both sermons for which mercy the lord be gratiously praised of me for evermore, god was good to us in the season, through mercy we had hopes of an indifferent crop, beyond our expectacion: my navel continued well all this weeke god gave mee comfort in hearing from, and seing some of our freinds, concerning some I heard that which afflicts me, lord helpe them, and make mee in their afflictions to reade my mercies, the lord was mercifull to mee in keeping me from those snares in which I have beene taken, oh how my heart

Pose doth hanker after folly, oh Lord sanctifie mee, the lord was mercifull in making mee instrumentall to compose divers differences and prevent suites this weeke; oh heale me of that corrupcion is in my vaine heart. I had a great pose and sneezing this day and divers touches of a cold almost perpetually, and apt to wheeze anights, yett I do not as yett. I spent some time in my booke of meditacons and reconciler to Deut: 23: as also in my Hebrew and other studdies, the lord was good to mee in the duty of the Sabbath in strength for the worke, in the word delivered, he in mercy sanctifie mee and accept mee for his most holy names sake,

13. 14. 15. I had a very comfortable and contentfull jorney to visitt some freinds at Maplested, returned safe all in health, god was good to my daughter Jane in preserving her from a very dangerous fall.

Navel: divers dayes this weeke my navel did a litle owze, but it was not rawe nor sore, the good lord in mercy heale mee, that I may praise and glorifie his holy name,

June: 17. This weeke the lord was good and mercifull to mee and mine in our health, peace and plenty, in preserving us and indeed the most of the towne from infectious diseases when as divers families were visited with the small poxe, the goodnes of god great to mee in making me sensible of former corrupcions and keeping mee from being overcome with the same, lord subdue all and keepe my heart in a holy frame for thy name sake, and heale my navell throughly oh my god: I went through Deut in my reconciler and did something in my other studdies: god was good to mee in the worke and the duty of the Sabbath, though I find my heart cold, I hope god will revive mee and perfect his grace in mee.

18: rid with Mr Harlakenden to Stortford, I there saw my old habitacon, Master, was much affected with the thoughts of my deare mother and 2 sisters who were their buried. the day was wonderous hott, and cleare, but in our jorney it was cloudy and much cooler than wee could have expected. 19. wee and Mr. H: son rid to Cambridge where I viewed with delight my old colledge, the Master and fellowes, very good men hope of their good: 20: Mr R.H. admitted fellow commoner of Jesus, wee returned to Stortford, and 21. to Colne: god was good to mee in this jorney, I had not rid for above a yeare 10 miles outright: I was not very weary, a litle sore not at all gauled,[1] my navel was moist and open, but not rawe nor very sore, good lord in thy mercy and goodnes heale mee, I humbly intreate thee, oh my god, that I may praise thy name, and declare thy goodnes continually, I returned and found all my family in health, oh that I could praise the(e) according to thy goodnes towards mee,

22: this day I left of my head cap. and wore a thinner stomacher,[2] I formerly left of my night wascoate, and found no damage thereby, and I hope I shall not now:

23: this day I was busied in bringing loggs from Wakes Colne. goodman Spooner very lovingly helpt mee with his cart.

June 24: This weeke the lord was good and mercifull to mee and mine in our health peace plenty in the midst of scarcity: he gave us a gratious answer of our prayers(.) most part of the day it dewed, and wee hope the earth shall be watered, I looke after my god how thou hearest mee, heale me of my infirmitie oh lord I humbly intreate thee the lord mercifull to mee this weeke in keeping in my wayes and not suffering my headstrong temptacions to prevaile, Sathan is busy bee thou my strong god and keepe mee: this weeke I did litle in my studdies by reason of journeys and other occasions; I was very unprepared for the Sabbath, the good lord in mercy pardon mee and accept mee in thy christ, god was good to me in his assistance oh never leave mee for my eyes are on thee continually, gave notice that June 28. was appointed for a day of publike rejoycing: my navel continued a litle moist, but not rawe nor sore, thanks bee to my good god: finisht Mr Medes discourse, and his altar[3] conteyning 26 pages or therabouts.

Navel

Mede:

27: spent most part of this day in a day of prayer, entreating god for

[1] Gall: to become sore or chafed. NED.

[2] Stomacher: a kind of waistcoat worn by men. SOED.

[3] Joseph Mede, *Of the name Altar . . . anciently given to the Holy Table* (1637).

John Burton who was to be cutt of the stone, for my owne distemper, that god who healeth his would bee an healing god to mee and to others, I desire to looke after our prayers, my heart was acted to a dependance on god that wee should be heard

28. A day of publike Thanksg: I spent the morning in preaching, wee dined at Mr Harlakendens, our entertainment was very free, and kind, Major Heines was with us, he gave me a good paire of gloves: my navel was dry and close this day to god bee the praise, I was somewhat subject to a rheume in my head: heard from my sister Hodson of her povertie, and the sicke condicon of her housband; I cannot doe much for her, being to pay 5^{li}. for her togither with my sister Mary, I sent her 5^{s}. which was in my hands that my uncle Richard Josselin had sent unto her, lord helpe her in her lowe condicon and raise up my heart to be helpefull to her as occasion shall offer it selfe.

29. r(eceive)d in some wood this day wherin I was helpt by the Cart of Goodwife Brewer(.) my navel was somewhat ill, but well in the morning and so continues

July: 1: The weeke past god was good to me in my health, and in the mercies of my family in providing for mee, in all my straites, I was this weeke so taken up with businesses, and partly so indisposed to studdy, that I was wonderfully unprepared for the Sabbath: and I account I had a check for it, the lord in mercy make me more to attend to my studdies for that is mainly my worke the good lord in mercy give me strength against corruptions, and grace to take the right course against them in the practice of the grace that is most opposite to them: the newes from Ireland this weeke was sad that the enemy was come before Dublin, the lord in mercy provide for them if it bee his pleasure, and give us successe against them, the lord was good to mee this weeke in keeping mee from divers temptacions and lusts, oh purge my heart throughly I intreate thee. god was good to mee in the Sabbath notwithstanding my neglect, which I desire to acknowledge and give him the praise of the same,

3: 4: 5: abroad at dinner, visiting some of my freinds, from whom I received besides kind entertainment, reall expressions of their love. and the more to be observed, in regard I was quite destitute of mony: Some ministers who have farre better livings then I complaine how meane their owne estate is, truly its the blessing of god that maketh rich, and it is his blessing whence I have encreased

7: received newes and true that Major Heynes my good freind, had procurred me 15^{li}. for my pay as chaplaine to the regiment for

Colchester service, it was a singular kindnes in him towards mee: my losses were great to mee, my patience I praise god in reference to them was my comfort. god tooke this time, and this way to repay them, in a fitt season to helpe mee out of troubles, and debts oh that I could love the lord for his mercy, and bee more faithfull to serve him: surely god hath something for me to doe at Colne, he provides for mee, when others faile who should: my good freind Mrs Mary brought mee in 20s. from her selfe, and 20s. from Mrs Mabel[1] to buy mee a booke, the lord in mercy requite it into their bosomes:

July: 8: This weeke continued very dry, and hott, onely now and then the winde tempered the heate my son had July: 7: a great swelling suddenly arose under his right eare and this day under his left my wife annointed it, god in his mercy heale it; all this weeke through mercy my navel was well, I continued now and then to wash it though it was well the lord heale me, for he is my trust. I perused some discourses of Medes this weeke, and 2 or 3 bookes in Sleidan: I was often abroad visiting of freinds this weeke, the lord was good to mee in providing for mee, in the dayes of scarcity. so that wee want nothing that is convenient for us, I was much to blame in not providing for the Sabbath, I am sensible of my hearts neglect in my work and in seeking god, oh lord heale mee, when one corrupcion tempts not then another starts up, oh undertake for mee that no iniquitie may have dominion over mee. this weeke reports were heard from Ireland, wee looked when Cromwell should goe, but yett he did not. John Burton for whom wee sought god June 27. was cutt for the stone July 6. and good hopes he will recover, and doe well, god of his mercy say Amen thereunto. made a collection for Lancashire which is much afflicted with famine and pestilance,

Navel.

10: 11: rid to chelmsford, and to my uncle Josselin's saw the sad condicon of a family without a mother, oh that I could blesse god for my wife, and pray for her, that shee might bee more my comfort: received a yeares rent for Boll(inhatch): land from my uncle and sett of 2 yeares taxes, returned safe, my navel not a whitt disturbed in this jorney.

Pose. 12. I found I had a cold, my nose run, and so it did die 13: I have beene free a great while, the lord by my health, and better me by corrections, for I need it. my sonne Thomas went to schoole with Mr Harrington. god in mercy blesse him and fitt him for educacion and make him a comfort;

[1] Mrs. Mabel Elliston of EC.

14: This day there fell very much raine in many places; god sent us two very sweet shoures at Colne for which we blesse god, they are pledges of more mercies in their seasons, the newes from Ireland this weeke is sad, Culmore Castle lost, and so no releiving of Derry by water: Tredagh likely to be lost(,) their magazine being blowne up with powder by the treachery of some aldermen, tis many times gods season to helpe when wee are low, Cromwell marcht out of London in great state, they goe with wonderfull confidence, the issue is in gods glorious armes disposing.

July: 15: This weeke the lord was good to mee and mine in our peace, plenty, health, the lord in mercy forgive my sins and heale my nature, I began formerly and now to bee sensible of a distemper and weaknes in my backe about the reines;[1] I have had the same divers yeares, what it tends to I knowe not, the lord was good to mee in the worke and duty of the Sabbath.

16: received 15^{li}. of Major Haynes which he procured for me, I gave his youth 1^{s}. my cold was somewhat in my chest and made mee wheeze.

18: Kept a day of humiliacon at the priory, for the good successe of Ireland, for raine, for my owne illnesses, when I came to pray for raine, my heart was carried out to blesse god for the sweet showres god gave us, and was full of confidence god would remember us with a full blessing therein, the next day was very hott, but at night, die 19 it clouded, and rayned very sweetly, and so continueth now on the 20th day, so that I hope god will fully satisfie the earth, and heare us in other perticulars as in this of the season. I brought home a bible for my sonne Thomas which cost mee 3^{s}. 2^{d}.: this

Sleidan: booke is now very cheape, finisht the reading his 26 bookes of Commentaries July 20: I begun to reade his discourse on the 4 Empires conteining 50 leaves and finisht it July 29[2]

21: heard from my sister of her housbands illnes, sent them something againe, lord give me a heart to remember them, and to doe what litle I can for them with cheerfullnes.

July. 22. This weeke god was good to mee, and mine in our peace, health, plenty in all outward mercies: my cough continued now and then when phlegme was tough, it was not much trouble to mee through mercy. my navel continued well, though sometimes I am apt to feare it, the lord in his due time shall perfectly heale mee, wee had this weeke very sweet and comfortable raines: I did something in

[1] Reines: the region of the kidneys; the loins. SOED.

[2] Joannes Phillipson (Sleidanus), *De Quatuor summis imperiis* (1559).

my studdies but indeed very litle. I find my heart very dull to doe the worke of my calling oh I doe it not with all my might, my sermon studdies are much neglected by me, lord lett me not be a negligent doer of thy worke I intreate thee, the lord was good to mee in the worke of the day, I was full, and large, my cold was no great hindrance through mercy unto mee; went downe with Mr Harlakenden who was very much perplexed in order to taking his oath, we resolved to goe to Mr owen which he tooke very kindly from mee,

23. rid with Mr H: to Mr owen's, there wee mett with good company, I enjoyed the opportunity of one of the church meetings at Coggeshall, wherein they discoursed, divers of them of one and the same text of scripture.

24. Mrs Cressener died a very good woman, a widdow, one of a duobting spirit, yett very quiett and submissive at her death, as appeared unto mee, Mr Har: would not goe to the assizes the other justice went.

26: This day I bought of John Beereman a parcell of land, now Sarah Haukesbees it containes 3 acres and more rents: 2^{li}. 10^{s}. besides the lords rent, it cost mee 36^{li}. 15^{s}. I am to pay all his mony even downe and to take the rent due at Michaelmas: I payd him 15^{li}. home with him; this is gods providence to blesse mee, and to adde to that litle which I have, he in mercy give mee an heart endeavouring the glorifying of his holy name according to his goodnes made knowne unto mee. this afternoone I did preach at the funerall of Mrs Cressener on psal. 73.26. wherin god was good and gratious unto mee.

July: 29: this weeke the lord was good and mercifull to mee and mine, in our peace, health plenty, my wheezing and cold finely over, my navel continues well, the praise of it bee given to my god; perfect my mercy oh lord therein, I most humbly intreate thee; god hath aboundantly satisfyed the earth with raine, wherein he hath fully answered our prayers, and I thinke wee have had rather more raine than other places about us: I was abroad at Melford on the business of Glensford,[1] did no good therein, I saw a sad divided towne: I saw the ruines of that great plundered out desolate without inhabitant, the lord was good to mee in the hopes of my childrens learning, the Lord perfect every mercy for mee; this weeke our newes was sad for Ireland, no forces gone and Tredah, and Trim,

[1] Glensford and Long Melford were villages on the Suffolk side of the Stour river, where Lady Rivers's house had been sacked in 1642.

and Carickfergus, and Carlingford lost; Dundalke beseidged, and also Dublin close beseidged by the enemy, Cromwell not yett ready to goe over, publisht this day an order for a day of humiliacion to seeke unto god, for a blessing on the forces designed for Ireland, gods providence hath beene very good towards mee I have payd since last yeare I was plundered already full 40^{li}. which I ought and I have payd 15^{li}. on a purchase, and hope through gods goodness to pay of shortly twenty pounds more; the lord good to mee in carrying mee forth in the duties of the Sabbath, the lord in much mercy accept mee, and delight in mee that I may praise his most holy and pretious name, John Burton came home from London cutt of the stone, his life spared, his wound healed, I hope cured, answered very sweetly in our prayers, the lord still helpe us to pray and carry on our spirits to all thy purposes untill they are accomplished.

August: 1: a day of P. Humiliacon for Ireland and a blessing from god upon the forces that are designed thither, the lord in mercy goe along with them, and blesse and prosper them, I expect that Dublin should become a prey to the enemie, the lord alone is able to prevent it; we spent from three of the clocke untill sun downe at the priorie, in continuing the exercise, the lord remember us for good for his owne names sake,

3: this day I went to my Cosin Josselins, and from thence to Mr Wakerings,[1] I came home by my lady Honywoods, who feared shee should miscarry, the almighty god in mercy watch over her and raise her up that shee may praise thee.

August: 5. This weeke the lord was good and mercifull to mee and mine, in our peace plenty, in our health, and outward mercies, oh that I could praise thee lord according to his bounty, my navel continued well all this weeke also, but oh my soule, why dost thou breake covenant with god, and turnest aside unto that which is not good, oh lord humble mee, oh lord forgive mee oh teache mee to feare pose thy name at all times: I was somewhat troubled with sneezing and on the lords day, I had a very great pose, and sneezed very much, learne mee to proffitt by thes gentle dealings of thine; the lord was good and mercifull to mee in the worke of this day, in carrying mee through in the same, in preaching, and expounding, wee had divers from Halsted, the lord in mercy provide for that poore divided scattered people, make mee a blessing to my people, and lett them growe in knowledge and in grace,

[1] Dionisius Wakering, of Church Hall, Kelvedon, M.P. for Essex 1654–6. Venn.

6: my pose was finely gone next day, neither did my cold fall downe into my chest as for mercy blessed bee my god: I found my navell continud well. this weeke I went about to gather up some tithes, I find mony scarce; I was invited to my Cosin Josselins to a
9: dinner die: 9, but wee mett at Goodman Mathewes; christians make promises of better accord, god in mercy grant it, the lord heare our prayers for Ireland, and for a refreshing showre, Lord and give mee grace to serve the(e) acceptably and evenly for thy Christs sake.

10: this day I heard from my sister An that her housband was dead, the lord sanctifie his hand to her, shee is very lowe, and poore, I gave her in, a bond of 5^{li}. which I borrowed for him, the lord in mercy raise her up freinds, I resolve through gods blessing on mee, to be kind to her not onely as the sister of my father,[1] but as the daughter of my gratious god

Aug: 12: this weeke the lord was good and mercifull to mee, and all mine in our health, peace plenty, in all our outward mercies and accomadacion, of the least wherof we are altogether unworthy, my navel continued whole, my cold finely gone, onely a litle troubled with rheume in the morning, the lord was good to mee this weeke in keeping mee from those temptacions which had formerly gott above mee, oh when shall thy grace rule mee, in all things, the lord in mercy keepe mee in his feare continually, I did litle in my studdies this weeke but for my sermons, the lord was good and mercifull unto mee; in the worke of the day in enabling mee thereunto, the lord in mercy accept of mee, and heale mee for his owne names sake, and continue to delight in mee, and doe mee good

14: received of Mr Harrington 7^{li}. there remaines due tenn shillings of midsommer quarter. this day wee had fine refreshing dewes, newes wonderfull uncertaine sometime reported that Dublin was lost, sometime that a part of ormonds army was routed 100^{ds}, and sometimes thousands slaine,

16: This day wee perfected the agreement betweene John Bearman and
Sarah: Hausk: land: my selfe, I payd him all his money, viz. 21^{li}. 10^{s}. he bated me: 5^{s}. in regard the lords rent was more than wee supposed: blessed bee my god, who feedeth mee, provideth for mee and increaseth my litle,

pumpe: 17: My pumpe drew very litle water, the fault was in the buckett, the frame was open which we now nailed, and the leather was too close above,

[1] My sister (by our father).

Aug: 19. The lord was good and mercifull to mee and mine this weeke in our peace and plenty, oh what are wee, that we want not in thes times of scarcitie; the lord good in my health, my navel continued still well to my god bee the praise oh my good god heale mee for thy names sake, the lord made this to us a good weeke in the answer of prayer a weeke of harvest(.) corne abated in price a litle, 2. in seasonable, fresh dewes, which comfortably cheared the earth: 3. in the glorious successe in Ireland: the next day after the publicke fast, August. 2. the first rumour I heard of it was August. 14. in the morning: god was good and mercifull to mee in my publicke worke this day, but in private my heart was sadly eaten out with vaine and earthly meditacions, oh lord forgive them unto mee, and heale mee, I was saluted when I came home with a letter from Ipswich concerning the death of my very good freind Mrs Cosins who dyed this morning at Ipswich.

20: Rid this day with Major Haynes to Mr Eden,[1] where wee were curteously used.

21: wee rid to Hingham, heard of my uncles sicknesse and recovery for which I praise the lord my god.

22: 23: stayd with my uncle at Hardingham, the dayes very hott, my uncle hath a great living, but a bad people, I preferre my condicon to his, the lord make me serviceable to him in my generacion

24. returned from Hardingham to Colne in a day, it was in the morning very coole riding, in the afternoone hott. god was good to me in my jorney in my company, health, I was not weary, my horse carried me very easily.

25. went to see my Lady Honywood who had beene very dangerously ill, shee was wonderfull full of god in a ravisht frame, I prayd with her, the Lord in mercy accept our desires and raise her up.

August. 26. The lord was good and mercifull to mee and mine in our health, peace, plenty. the Lord in mercy pardon our sins and accept us for his glorious name sake, the good god preserved mee from hurt in my jorney made it pleasant and comfortably unto mee, the lord preserved all my family in health, my navel continued well, the lord was good to mee in the Sabbath giving mee strength for it, though indeed I was weake and faint, the lord in mercy sanctifie mee, and preserve mee and make mee a delight unto himselfe.

[1] John Eden, of Ballingdon, Essex, who married Richard Halakenden's sister Anne; he was a member of the Essex Committee for the Eastern Association. Kingston, p. 385.

27. heard my Lady Honywood was upward, oh that my god might have the praise of this his mercy and goodnes

29. This day a P. Th: for the great victory over Ormond; the lord good to mee in the worke of the day, oh that my heart might henceforward bee more lifted up in the wayes of god, and made more carefull to walke with god: wee dined very freely and comfortably with Mr Harlakenden at the priory.

31: This day went to visitt my Lady Honywood, found her hopefully upwards, and carefull and desiring that shee might improve her mercy in her life to the glory of her god, the lord in mercy answer her desires

September. 2. This weeke past the Lord my god was good and mercifull to mee, and mine in our peace, health, in providing for us, the lord did this weeke most mercifully and comfortably refresh the earth with dewes to a satisfying of the same, which gives us hopes of a second spring, and summer. my navell through mercy continued very well, onely I had some feares of it, but no cause as I could perceive, god excercised mee with a stopping in my chest which made mee wheeze in the nights, when the lord seeth best he can ease me of my distemper for the present I desire to see it best for mee that it should be thus with mee, I was this weeke sensible of much vanitie of my minde in fancying thes outward things, freer yett through mercy from some former temptacions, oh that I could cleave to the lord with a full purpose of heart, that I might not bee forsaken, I was this day at Halsted preacht twice and expounded Hosea 14 the lord in mercy blesse the labours, thereof to my people, the lord in much mercy accept mee, my poore flocke were left destitute this day.

7: Came home from my Lady Honywoods, where I was this weeke. Mr Clopton went up to London about our augmentacion, and returned but without any successe, Mrs Crane gave mee a payre of gloves which shee ought mee about a wager when her housband was prisoner with the Cavaliers

Sept. 9. This weeke past the lord was good to us in our health, and plenty of provisions wanting nothing needfull, and quiett in my minde, though I and my wife have not the command of one penny of money. my litle Ralph ill of his cold. my cold and wheeze continues my head is much stuffed my navel continued well, I somewhat feared, but my god hath hitherto preserved mee, who I trust also will keepe mee, I preacht and expounded this day, wherein god was good and mercifull unto mee my heart very much musing on the vaine delights of the world and apt to returne to old follies, lord I looke towards thee, lett mee never be cast downe, Mrs Jacob with us on foote, shee desired to bee prayed for the lord in mercy give her a safe deliverance,

10: I was with Mr Harlakenden, his crop of hops wonderfull small much about 800 weight upon twentie acres, my freinds have given mee enough for my use,

11: This day I went to visitt Mr Jacob, heard of some stirre at Oxford, by the regiment their upon the levelling score, I and all my company supd and were very kindly used at Mr Wm harlakendens, this day Jo: Rushbrooke and I came to agreement, he leaves the land and I promise him some time to eate of his pasture, I am very glad of it, for I feared that I might have had some wrangling with him;

Sept: 16. This weeke god was good and mercifull to mee, and mine in our outward enjoyments. onely I was troubled with a great cold

Cold: which I tooke in going thinn,[1] my navel continued well to the lord bee the praise of it, the disturbances at Oxford over in a good season, and by a very finger of god, the lord kept mee this weeke in my pathes, though my heart is prone to vanitie, god good to mee in the Sabbath, though I cannot but lament my negligence in my employment: Mr owen is going for Ireland, the season is very good and gallant, the rate of things continueth dearer and is likely to encrease,

18: this day at a venison feast at Mr W. Harlakendens, where wee had good entertainment, I had much kindnes from her afterward, my cold begun through mercy to breake away

20: goodman Burton hurt himselfe exceedingly with a bruise by a fall. the lord good in my preservacion: heard my Lady Honywood was well recovered, and that shee dined below in her parlour the lords name be praised in her recovery.

September: 23. This weeke god was undeservedly gratious to mee in many outward mercies, only my cold continued, it was very violent, but not so sad as I have formerly had: tis of his mercy that I am not destroyed, all mine in safety, this weeke our neighbour Mr Nicholson was robbed of about 200^{li}. in money and plate, the theives in all probability lay in our towne, the night before,[2] I imagined they were such manner of men; I had sad experience of

[1] To go thin: to wear thin clothing, to be thinly clad. NED.

[2] There is no reference to this or the previous robbery from Mr. Nicholson in contemporary Assize records.

the inconstancy of heart, and my heedlesnes in the way wherein I should walke, this weeke, oh that my faylings might bee my warnings, and stirre up, indignacion and watching, and purging my selfe, the lord was good to us in sweet dewes, durt is now our daintie that last yeare was our dislike, thus god changes seasons. god was good to mee in the worke and dutie of the Sabbath, the good lord in mercy pardon my sins, accept my soule and delight in mee to doe mee good:

at night I was very ill. full of sorenes about my bones; I was very sicke, and burnt violently, then I vomited, and fell into a sweate, which through mercy did mee good, I am much clogged with phlegme,

27. my cold continued which made mee keepe in, my navel felt round about as if it had beene sore, it was not, I washt it, I conceive it was a humour that formerly had vent there, and still assayes to vent it selfe there: my night wheezings are not as formerly, I praise god

Sept: 30. This weeke I continued ill, and feavourish, yett therein I had much experience of gods providence towards mee, my family continued in health, I was through mercy able a litle to studdy, and to supply my place on the lords day. god good to mee in keeping my heart close unto him: and making me sensible of my vanitie. Mrs Mary church was ill this day, and so continued, god in mercy raise her up, and restore her to her former health againe

October: 3: at night begun to studdy a litle before supper, I begun with the first part of the Ecclesiastical history of the Magdeburgensis which is in folio divided into 2 colummes on every page, and con-containes: colum: 372.

Magd: Cent: 1: lib: 1: Colum: 372.

I begun about the beginning of this month to reade Sennertus in-stitucons[1] in a large 8°. smal print. it containes this part. 3 bookes and 917. pages this I did in the day time,

Sennerti: Inst: vol: 1: p: 917:

This day I finisht Josephus of the antiquities of the Jewes[2] whereof I read a great part, especially where the history of the scripture is silent and I intend to read the residue of his booke.

6: I began to find my former cold being gone, that I had renewed it againe, I sneezed in the day: I had a litle pose, I wheezed a litle at night I cannot conceive how I take it, but through my tendernes and disposition of body thereunto without any notable occasion thereof, make mee submissive to thy will oh god: I humbly intreate thee, and strengthen mee unto all thy services:.

[1] Daniel Sennertus, *Institutionum Medicinae* (many English and Latin editions).

[2] Flavius Josephus, *The Famous Workes of Josephus; translated by T. Lodge* (1598).

Octob: 7. This weeke the lord was good and mercifull to mee and mine in our peace, plenty health, having no want of any outward good thing, yett were all things very deare, wheate. 8^{s}. 6^{d}. rye: 6^{s}. barley. 5^{s}. a bushel, cheese 4^{d}. ob. butter 7^{d}. ob the pound, the good lord in mercy thinke on us, and send us helpe at need as I trust he will, and provide for mee and mine because I trust in him and in his goodnes according as I have found him my refuge; god was good to mee in keeping me in my pathes from divers follies and vanities after which my heart hunted, and wherewith I had beene entangled: I found my selfe backward to my studies, oh the time that I loose, wheras I should redeeme the same, I had experience of gods good to me in the Sabbath, in the duty, and excercise therof, the lord in mercy make me an instrument of good to my people. wherin his name may receive glory.

Sennertus: 9: this day I saw the waters out in the meadowes, which I had not seene before since the last winter, this day I finisht the reading the 1^{t} booke of Sennertus institutions in physicke. containing 153. pages:

Navel 10: feared my navel was ill, it seemed that it issued a litle, dresd it die: 11. and found it a litle ill, I stirred my selfe a litle a day or two, perhaps that might occasion it I must patiently waite on god for his helpe, who will afford it. Mrs Mary very hopefully well this evening, god in his mercy restore her and spare her for all our goods and comfort. this day I lent Mr Wm Haukesbee 25^{li}. on his land for one yeare the surrender was into the hands of Mr Elliston, and Ambros waller, it comes out october. 12. 1650. my debts are now 44^{li}.

13. my sister An with mee her condicon very sad to the world wards, but very hopefull and happy heaven wards; my heart cannot but simpathize with her under her burthens, I sent her not away empty; I promised her during her want and while god enables mee
☞ 20^{s}. yeerly. towards her rent, my deare wife is willing to afford her helping hand to her, I have 3 yeares due to mee on my augmentacion whatsoever I receive on it, the tenth part I will freely bestow upon her, my deare freind Mrs Mary, gave her 1^{s}. so did goodwife Mathewes, the lord requite them.

October: 14: This weeke the lord was good to mee and all mine in our peace, health, provision for us so that in the midst of straites we want nothing necessary for us, the lord good in the health of my wife in particular notwithstanding the stirringnes and unquietnes of her sonne, which yett my good god moderates very much; Mrs

Mary is in a good way of coming abroad againe to god bee praise;
Navel. my navel was a litle illish as if it had issued but dressing it through gods blessing it did appeare perfectly well the next day and I trust shall continue so through gods blessing, god was good to mee this weeke in keeping mee from many temptacons with which I had formerly beene molested oh lett me hate every evill way, and bee kept in uprightnes through thy grace and goodnes: I did somewhat in my studdies this weeke, for the Sabbath, my heart was affected with the word, and I was somewhat enlarged in my spirit through the good hand of god upon mee, I pray thee oh god in mercy pardon all my sinfullnesses and weaknesses, and delight in mee to doe mee good for thy mercy sake.

20: this weeke I moved divers freinds in my sisters businesse, and found the hand of god was upon mee for good towards her, there bowels being opened and enlarged unto her, I this day finished the reading the first part of the 2d. (c.o. part) booke of Sennertus institutucons ending pag: 236. containing 83, pages.
Sennertus

Oct: 21: This weeke the lord was good to mee and mine in all outward mercies, in keeping me in some measure in my uprightnes, I preacht twice at Halsted god was good to mee therin, and in my comfortable walke, homewards

22: a great day of trouble at priory, I made an end of their businesse at last, as well as I could but glad I brought in peace,

23. rid to Haverhill, the season very contentfull, and corne good on the ground, send us a yeare of plenty if it bee thy holy will oh god, found my sister in a poore but in a good condicon, god provides for her, I left her 3li. to trade with as my stocke, and 20s. to buy her wood, and 4s. I gave her children, it was almost all the bounty of some freinds, who I acquainted with her condicon, god opened their bowels to her and it shall I trust bee repayd them from god, it was a comfortable refreshing unto her, and hers

24 preacht at Haverhill on 1 Tim. 1:13. the people attended, many wept, god blesse the seed among them, saw divers of my freinds, who visited mee very lovingly. I came home well, and before it was
Navel. quite darke, the lord was good to mee in my jorney, at night I found my navel was worse then it had been a long time, issuing, and open, thou art my healing god and in thee I trust, blesse the meanes used for thy mercie sake,

25. mett in a day of humiliacon at Mr W: Harlakendens, I was sensible of much deadnes and slouth of spirit upon my selfe, and company, wee sinke downe into formes and tracks which I bewaild before the

lord: the lord in mercy cure it, we releived divers poore persons with what wee gathered that day.

Octob: 28: The lord was good and gratious to mee and mine this weeke

Navel. in all our outward mercies my navel well with one dressing, and so continued from 25. to this day, notwithstanding I stirred my selfe die 26. 27. very much about my wood: I had some experience of the deceit and weaknes of my heart, apt to turne aside from following the lord, and heedlesly, and foolishly doe that which my soule loatheth, lord my salvacion is a worke made up with rich mercy and glorious power:—the season was dry and indifferent warme, onely somewhat cloudy. the country full of reports of Cromwells route in Ireland, but its hoped there is no truth therein, this day I and my deare wife have beene married nine yeares, the lord make our yeares to come many, and our comforts in one another and our posteritie many, if it be his pleasure, and lett us live to serve that god who hath abounded in much goodnes towards us. the lord was good to mee in the worke of the day, in letting out my soule in the doctrine of faithe, give mee the savour and the practice of it: many of poore Halsted were here this day, who were destitute of helpe at home,

27. day I was cutting wood my axe slipt and cutt the leather at the toe of my shoe almost through without any hurt, to god bee praise.

Thomas: Nov: 1: my boy is now lively, somewhat fuller of spirit, of a good memory, a good speller apt to learne, and attaine the hardest words in his bible or accidence[1] in which he reads, he was almost mopt[2] in his disposicion, that he would not by any meanes bee drawne to speake, I feare his Mrs severitie was the cause of it: I blesse god for his goodnes towards him, and his sister mary, and Jane, who are hopefull and promising buds. this day we kept a publicke thanksgiving for the successe against Tredah, and before we heard the great newes of the taking Wexford, and putting the garrison, and some say the inhabitants to the sword, wee were kindly entertained at the priory by Mr Harlakenden.

3. Mrs Mabel Elliston, in great perplexity, about a match proposed to her, wherein her freinds are very willing but shee not, upon a full inquiry, shee finds god disposing her heart altogither to continue a virgin life, lord make her path peace and quietnes and satisfie her freinds for her, and direct her in all her wayes,

[1] Accidence: that part of Grammar which treats of the Accidents or inflexions of words. SOED.

[2] Mopt: moped, stupified or bewildered, affected with ennui, melancholy, low-spirited. NED.

Nov: 4: This weeke the Lord was good to mee and mine in all outward mercies: only my litle Jane had a painfull, troublesome rising in her head, which much disquieted her, and yett gods mercy was not restrained therin, in breaking it speedily and in mitigating the paine therof, I had a litle angry bite on my right cheeke, which was somewhat painfull, I had experience of the aptness of my heart to corruption and vanity, my heart is full of it, lord if thou keepe mee not, I am undone, the season was open, dry, temperate, and warme sometimes foggy, corne thrivd excellently, our peace continued in England, and successe very great in Ireland, blessed bee our god, the lord was good to mee in my strength for the duties of the day, my navel continued well, oh that I could praise the lord who abounds in goodnes towards mee,

11. This weeke the Lord was good to mee in many good providences, in divers kindnesses received from others. But my wayes were not towards good according to his goodnes unto mee, oh that my heart could breake within mee in the apprehension thereof, my navel was a litle ill at the bottome No. 10. with white matter as it were, and so on the lords day morning, and herupon is a sense of gods displeasure therein my heart trembled and turning to proverbs. 3. there the text saith feare god depart from evill, it shall bee health to thy navel and marrow to thy bones, I desired with joy to close with the word of promise, and to give up my selfe in obedience to the name of god, give mee grace to close with thee, and doe not then faile mee nor forsake mee, god was good to mee in the mercies of the day, strength and voice, my face swelled with a cats bite, and the carnel[1] in my necke, but my god will command mercies for mee, oh that then I could praise him

Navel.

25: Both thes weekes god was good to mee and mine in our health, I was free in a great measure from colds, and although I stirred much, yett my navel did continue well, god being health therunto, wee wanting nothing though the times were wonderfull hard, wheate at above 9^{s}. and rye above 7^{s}. a bushell god good to us in our health, only my litle Ralph was ill, but I hope it was onely breeding of teeth, Mary was out at Mrs Ellistons where shee learned to sew: god was good to mee in my sonne Tho: who learned well, and I wish if ever he bee a man he would remember I undertooke the teaching the schoole at this time cheifely for his sake, among the boyes, though my highest aime was to doe good while I live, god was mercifull to mee in giving mee and my deare

[1] Carnel: kernel, an enlarged gland in the neck or groin. SOED.

wife bowells towards the poore, we begun this weeke to fast our selves a meale or 2 in a weeke, and give away a meales provision in meate broth, or money to the poore, god was good in giving mee an heart in some measure to walke closely with him, restraining temptacions, and the strength of corruption in my heart oh that I might be throughly sanctified, and delivered from every evill worke, and preserved spotless to the coming of Jesus Christ the lord was good to mee in the Sabbaths I continued yett to expound a chapter both parts of the day, but I did not write them downe being so much overlayd with businesse. The times were very sad in England so that men durst not travell, and indeed rich men were afrayd to lye in their houses robbers were so many and bold, men knew not how to carry monyes, and many gentlemens houses were sett upon and pilferd: the affayres of Ireland went well, the hand of god was notable that when our interests was lowe their then the natural Irish, and the meere popish party joyned not with ormond but rather assisted us, but seing no hope from us, when ormond was lowe, and our forces begun to prosper then oneale, and his party fell in with ormond. god can divide men to weaken them, and unite them and harden their hearts to destroy them.

December: 1: to 16: This time god was good and gratious to mee and mine, in our peace and in provisions for us, yett all things were wonderfull deare, wheate. 9^{s}. malt. 4^{s}. 8^{d}. rye. 7^{s}. 6^{d}. oatemeale: 8^{s}. per bushel, and cheese 4^{d}. ob. all things deare, yett the season was indifferent warme and drye. beggars many, givers few, lord of thy bounty provide for the poore, I constrayned my selfe to doe more then ordinary for our poore, it is better to give then to receive, and yett poore people were never more regardles of god then now adayes: god good in our health, except my litle Ralph, who pined and grew very tedious thes cold nights to his poore mother, god in mercy preserve them both, gods goodnes was very great to her, god good in the educacion of my children, especially Mary and Tho: for whose sake I tooke care of Colne schoole all this time, I find my selfe somewhat stopped in my pipes making mee in the night apt to wheeze, but I perceive it not in the day time, which is a great mercy that I should rest so free from colds for so long a time, god was good to mee in keeping me from old lusts and temptacions, which yett are ready now and then to put up head in mee, Lord lett thy grace be sufficient for mee, and preserve mee spotles to thy heavenly kingdome, Lord lett me live every day more and more spiritually, in the strength and power of thy rich grace, god was good to mee in the Sabbath, in the duties and exercises therof, Mr Rogers was an helpe this day to mee, god good to mee in my navel which continued still well notwithstanding my walkings, and stirrings, the lord have the glory of all his preservacions; the earth yett gives hope of a good crop for the next yeare, the eyes of god bee on it in mercy all the yeare for good

18: This day I rid to witham, and 19. to chelmsford, where I subscribed the engagement the first in the County of minist. and the 13th man of the County:[1] god was good to mee in my jorney, I could not dispatch some businesse I intended, I must waite gods leisure, and season for everything, I subscribed the engagement as I considered it stood with the Covenant. while the government actually stood establisht, and my faithfulnes, is not to create any troubles, but seeke the good of the Commonwealth.

19: Margaret Potter came to dwell with us god in mercy make her his servant and to gett good with us, and make her faithful and comfortable unto us,

20: 21. my wife went to my Lady Honiwoods with her boy, my Lady feares he is in a consumption, but indeed he is troubled with the ricketts, my Lady adviseth an issue[2] to which my wife hath no minde god in mercy blesse other meanes that are used I sent to the 2 Mr Harlakendens and Mr Elliston some tokens as expressions of my thankfulnes to them for their great love to mee and mine,

Dec: 23. This weeke the lord was good and gratious to mee, and mine in our peace, plenty preservacion, gods providence called me to Halsted, where I endeavourd to speake home to my heart, and the peoples, the lord second the word with a blessing, I went at night to Mr Harringtons at Maplestead, where I was kindly entertained, I found his sonne ill. but in my opinion somewhat better then formerly.

D 30: This weeke wee continued at my Lady Honywoods, my deare babe was hopefull to recover, his poore mother endures much toyle with him, I preacht this day at Colne once,

Jan: 1; preacht at Markeshall, where Sr Tho: entertaind us with a
Navel, bountifull dinner, Jan: 2. my navel was somewhat ill, god in mercy heale it,

[1] 'I do declare and promise that I will be true and faithful to the Commonwealth of England as the same is now established, without a King or House of Lords.' Gardiner, *Commonwealth*, i, p. 196.

[2] Various techniques of giving vent to the 'humours' were employed, including red-hot irons laid on the skin, and drawing a thread through the flesh with a special needle and leaving it there. Eccles.

5. my sister Dor: boy went home I gave him. 2s. 8d., blessed bee god who enables mee to give, I sent my Lady a sugar loafe which cost 7s. 4d., and a goose which was sent mee,

Jan: 6: preacht at Coggeshall, dainty healthfull frosty weather, the lord was good to mee in the worke of the day, Mr Clopton preachd once for mee,

7. this day we came home from my Lady Honywoods, where wee had beene kindly used, Mrs Mary, had the care of our babes in our absence her love, and care was great towards them.

8: dressd my navel, it was somewhat moist but not sore, oh heale it and my heart, that I may praise thy name, thou art my god in thee I trust att all times,

Navel

9: Rid to Colchester, preacht the lecture, kindly entertaind by Mr Mayor, I saw Mrs Cooke whom god hath strangely afflicted with an excressence of flesh in her belly, which hath now encreased for about 9 yeares, to an exceeding greatnes, yett when I looke on the greatest afflictions they seeme as nothing to the smallest sins, oh how sad is my condicion when my heart is dogged with many, and indeed when corruption is entred the heart it is insatiable, pride, lust, vanitie, earthlynes, oh lord thy weapons only can helpe to pull down sathans strong holds and defeate his wiles, oh furnish mee with thy complete armour I intreate thee, god was good to mee in my returne home, Mr Harlakenden troubled at the greatnes of his sons expences at Cambridge, I writt to Mr Richard, to be frugall of his fathers purse, and to improve his time for learning and pietie, god blesse my advice to him

10: this day I began to teach the schollers for Mr Harrington. the good god in mercy blesse my labours and endeavours among them,

Jan: 13. This weeke the Lord was good to us in his bounty and provision for us, my deare wife often very weakly, but the lord in mercy holds her up to our comfort, our litle Ralph merry. Maries eyes are very ill; my navel was a litle open but die. 12 my wife found it at night, close, white, and well, it feared some dayes before as if it would have beene ill, thy chastisements oh Lord are fatherly, and very gentle towards mee, oh that I might cleave close to thee lord, and walke in all uprightnes before the Lord, then should the Lord bee health to my navell, lord I have no strength of myselfe bee thou the same unto mee, the Lord visited mee with a litle pose 2 dayes this weeke, but I was no farther troubled with it, I was never freer from colds, I kept mee warme in nights, but never went thinner in dayes then I have done this winter, my dreames gave me matter

Navell.

of loathing this weeke, my heart is foule, and it vents even then, the lord was good to mee in the worke of the Sabbath, in preaching and expounding the word, gatherd somewhat to encourage a grecian in printing the Confessions of the Churches[1] in their tongue, I desire to make my estate serviceable to the Lord Jesus Christ, this day as also the former, were exceeding rainy, but neither tempestuous, nor cold; Jan: 4: 1649: there was much mischiefe done at London by blowing up divers barrels of powder, which blew up divers houses, and persons it was thought neare an 100^{d}., the fluxe is much in London, and in some parts of this kingdome, it hath cutt downe, many of the army in Ireland

15: This day Mr Wade[2] of Halsted sent mee a dozen of candle, and Mr Hickford a sugar loafe,[3] a liberall and bounteous guift, its an act of thy love and goodnes, towards mee and I desire to give thee oh lord the praise of thy mercy. Mrs Church gave mee 5^{s}. none in the towne sent mee any considerable guift els, but old Spooner.

16: This day I was sensible of a great cold I had taken, I went out to my boyes, I was lowe in moneys and one bowles payd mee 10^{s}. of his owne accord, the which I looke upon as a good providence towards mee, in the night at my lying downe I was followed with a wonderfull fall of rheume out of my head into my throate as I never had to my knowledge before, I slept very well a great part of the night, a candle was sett by, which fell, but one of the children was awake and spyed it, it onely singd the carpett, it might have done much hurt, many times a house fired by such meanes, oh that I could blesse the Lord for all his goodnes towards me.

18: my cold very bad, but not so extreme as formerly, the latter part of the night I rested: heard that some arrears of our augmentacion were procured for us, which if will bee thankefull received by mee, die. 19. heard by Mr Clopton that their were some hopes, that the moneyes in the contry would come to something, in all thes things, the will of god be done: Halsted men came for mee this day but the warning was so short, and my cold troubleous that I durst not promise any thing unto them,

Jan: 20: This weeke the Lord was good and mercifull to mee, and mine in all our outward mercies my cold was finely wearing away, it was

[1] Probably *A Confession of Faith According to the Best Reformed Churches for the satisfaction of tender consciences* (1647). Thomason, E. 370(5).

[2] John Wade of Halsted had a large, nine-hearth, house in 1662.

[3] William Heckford of Halsted had a seven-hearth house in 1662. Sugar loaf: a moulded conical mass of hard refined sugar. SOED.

violent, but it was not lasting through mercy, god was good to mee in the Sabbath his name have the praise of it

24: This is in my account the last day of my 33 yeare: god hath beene good and mercifull to mee and mine and provided for mee in the same, and kept mee that my corruptions have not beene too hard for mee, though I have beene foyled yett I have not beene utterly cast downe and I hope he that hath kept mee will keepe mee, wee mett this day at Moles, spent it in conference for most part, oh tis sad how christians are led astray.

Feares and jealousies of troubles from among our selves by reason of the ingagement and other sad affaires among ourselves ended the yeare

— — — — — — — — — — — — — — — — — — —

Jan: 25: 1649: an: aetatis 34:

Jan: 25: I was sensible it entred mee into a new yeare, and I eyed god in perticular for his presence with mee, to keepe mee close to him, and to blesse mee, and I hope in his mercy he will, I had intimations of heart that god would have a respect to mee, and provide for mee, this day Mr Clopton told mee that 30li. was paid in from the Trustees to my use, an evidence of gods answering my desire, and performing his mercy hinted: this was a merveylous sweet warme season, continued warme divers dayes Feb: 2. was also a merveylous warme hott sun shine, grasse grew thes dayes:

Weather

Jan: 27. God good to mee and mine in providing for us, and in our health, the times are sickly my mercie is the more notable, my Ralph ill, and his mother sickely with toiling with him, yett god strengthens her to beare her toile, this day I was att Halsted, none at my place publickely.

Feb. 2. This day I heard from letter by Mr Clopton that 20li. more was paid in to my use the lord is bounteous in his provision for mee, I hope my heart shall bee, more enlarged in his service. heard as if Mr Harrington were not likely to continue long.

Feb. 3. God good to mee in my health, and in upholding the rest of my family. this weeke as also last month I taught the schoole, my Tho: towardly, the lord blesse them all. god was good in keeping mee from my base lusts oh that every vanity of minde might bee rooted up. this day raynie. I was at home, the Lord good to mee in my labours(,) oh season, and sweeten my heart, with the sense of thy love and favour.

☞ 4: The night past, and the 2[d] at night, I had a litle pose, and sneezed some times, I trust god in mercy will ease mee of it, my right legge on the outside of it is a litle nummed with cold and so hath beene about a fortnight, and was so formerly.

5: dind this day at Mr Littells with divers of our good freinds, he gave mee a young vine which I sett at the jame[1] of the chimney by the pantry, if god see good I may eate of the fruite of my planting therein, through the strength of gods goodnes to mee I observe my heart eyeing god in all my mercies, and owning them as the guifts of god, and eyeing god in services for strength, acceptance: oh lett mee live more out of my selfe, in, and unto my god, and Jesus every day; oh my god I intreate thee, this night my Ralph was very sicke as if he would have dyed, he vomited, and something stirred in the bottome of his stomacke, which he endeavoured to bring up but could not.

6: Mrs Church invited us to supper where wee were kindely entertaind. G(oo)dee Mathew sent us a lovely breast of veale, this love and kindnes is from god, at night my right side aked very much.

Navell. 7: went to visitt Mrs Jacob, I supd at Goodman Mathewes: at night I washd my navel wherin there was a litle white matter, the morning my wonted issue appeared

8: my navell appeared very well, Feb: 9. I received: 2[li]. 19[s]. from Mr Harrington by his brother.

10: This weeke the Lord was good to us in our health, only my litle sonne was ill, and my daughters eyes continued ill, the lord in due time will ease them, I desire to search my heart and turne to god that thes stormes may not bee on them for my sins, and I blesse god that my heart and wayes have not beene so clogged with some corruptions as formerly, I preach this day at home and in the afternoone at Halsted, god in mercy blesse my labours my wife and I went to see Mr Harrington, a picture of death.

17. This weeke our condicion as formerly only my daughters eyes well to god bee praise, my good freind Mrs Mary upwards, lord perfect her recovery.

18. this weeke busied with ditchers, and loggerivers.[2] my navel well. litle Ralphs eyes wonderfull ill as if he should bee blind

21: married Mrs Eliz. King to Mr Potter: heard Mr Harrington was dead, this the second that dyed as it were of my family, in the

[1] Jamb: each of the side posts of a chimney-piece upon which rests the lintel. SOED.

[2] Log river: rive, to split or cleave wood, etc.; thus wood-cutters. SOED.

families wherin I have lived, divers young ones dead, and I preserved god give mee grace to serve him

22 rid to Chelmsford: a tedious jorney god good in my preservacon outwards and homewards I did not my businesse, I intended, but putt it into a hopefull way, saw my uncle Simon Josselin, who promiseth to helpe mee with my rent

Feb: 24: This weeke my sons illnes continues and my daughters, god hath heard our prayers for them and I trust he will, and recover them. god was good to mee in my health, my left side of my face sore, but easie to bee borne through mercy. Mr Potter preacht both times for mee

25: Made an end with my Tenant, he is to plowe no more than what is plowed, he is not to medle with my wood, and to lay 8 load dung on the mowing peice, and to quit the farme at Michaelmas. 1651.

28. concluded this month with a day of publike humiliacon sett apart by the state, I hope god will make it a day of mercy and goodnes unto us, I remember my poore babes for life, sight, and grace, lord I will listen for they answer, which I trust shall be mercy and peace, I preacht twice this day, the lord was good to mee therein, this

Weather month was dry and warme at beginning, dry, windie and cold at latter end as pleasant a Feb. as came in many yeares, my apricocke was blossomd foure or five dayes before the end of the month,

March: 1: Gods hand was towards us for good in our children. maries eyes mended somewhat, and so did litle Ralphs, his glisters[1] did him good, and the best outward meanes were rose oyntment, and plantane water steeped with white sugar candie: this day my sonne Thomas began to learn his accidence by heart as wee say, memoriter, he is now 6 yeares old and about two months, the lord command his blessings on them, and us and goe on to answer all prayers putt up for them. the weather was now frostie s(w)nowy, and windie, but healthfull according to the season of the yeare,

debts: 2. Reviewed what I owe, and I perceive all my debts one, and other, amount to somewhat above 40^{li}. and I have so much and more owing mee this present day.

March: 3. This weeke the lord was good to mee and mine in providing for us under the straites of the times, enabling mee to give, which is better then to receive, my litle sonne was somewhat better in his

[1] Glister: clyster, a medicine injected into the rectum; an injection, enema, occasionally a suppository (a plug of conical shape inserted in order to stimulate the bowels to action). SOED.

eyes, he rested very ill 3 nights, but the 4th night god heard our prayer and refresht his wearied mother, Mary recoverd in her eyes the lord was good to mee in keeping my heart in some measure close to him, and in preserving mee from foolish and vaine thoughts and dreames—god good to us in our deare freind Mrs Mary who groweth upwards againe, I preacht one part of the day at home the other at Halsted, god was good to mee in his word and in my going and returning the lord in mercy accept mee and rejoice over me and doe mee good

Navel 4. at night I found my navel moist, and very red, it was not so bad for many months before, I felt 2 or 3 dayes before an humour as if it were moving thereabouts, and I felt it not so much when it was moist: I rid the day before to Halsted, and stirred my selfe in preaching, my god will command healing for mee, and then I trust give mee a heart to praise him.

5: one with mee about the schoole, another rid about it towards Halsted, I trust gods providence hath layd it out for mee, my navel well through mercy to sight as if never ill my sonne Tho: escaped a great danger from a great mastive bitch, who runne mad, and snapt at him, and a litle grated his flesh, his stocken being downe(.) I was this day at Colchester, Mr Haukesbye and I could not goe through with the bargaine for his lands:.

8. Went this day to Maplested, I found Mr Harrington had made over the schoole to his kinsman Elliston,[1] and so had broken his promise, and ingagement unto mee, this is the world, his sonne was taken up foure dayes after his buriall in the chancell, and buried in the churchyard

M. 10 This weeke the lord good and mercifull in many things to mee and mine, my sonne is somewhat better then formerly, he breakes out in very many angry pimples and the rhewme continues, the lord shewe mee, if there be any particular sin in mee why he afflicts and heale mee of it, and pardon it to mee and mine, my mayde was very ill this day, my deare wife is toyled above measure the lord support her, I desire every day more and more to see all my strength in god, and all good things proceeding from him, and that I may live more in him and to him, and lesse to my selfe and not at all to my corruptions: the lord was good to mee in the dutie of the Sabbath, my heart somewhat of, when out of the ordinance, many of Halsted came downe to us, as not agreeing in the minister

[1] Probably Joseph Aliston (1605–63), son of Mathew, and William Harrington's sister Anne. Probert; Venn.

that should preach, god make our habitacon peace, and blesse mee in it for his names sake, and supply my wants as I trust he will

15: Very ill with the toothake, at night I found my bible in my studdy, which I thought I had lost, I was very glad of the same, this day, I was warned to appeare at Westminster die.[1] 20th

March: 17. This weeke the lord appeared, mercifull in the visiting my daughter Jane, with strange fits as of the collecke,[2] and giving her speedy ease, as also in Mr will Harlakendens: in supporting my wife under all the trouble of her sonne, and in giving mee hopes of his sight and recovery, my mayde also is somewhat better, god gives mee an heart to pray for them, and through mercy he heares mee,: wee had divers expressions of love from Mrs Wm Harlakenden this weeke, I received 6li. of my com(mitte)e money from Chelmsford, and a botle of sacke from London, from Mr Linch, god using mee as an instrument to helpe them in their poore sister Goodwife Markham, thus gods provisions are towards mee, but my heart is unworthy in his sight, and divers abominable vanitees annoy, I sigh and looke up to thee, when will my god subdue them I desire to live on god for all spirituall and outward good, and observe him in all his wayes towards mee, and mine towards him, I blesse god for divers smitings of heart, in the first buddings of temptacons: I desire to familiar my change to mee, and waite for it, and to bee dying by peices and not all at once and see death as my enemy (for Jesus calls it his) in keeping mee from christs immediate presence, rather than its parting me from outward freinds, god was good and mercifull to mee, in the worke and duty of the Sabbath, wherin I desire his blessing may be upon mee continually.

18: rid up towards London, saw my uncle Ralph Josselins children, whom god hath preserved under that troublous disease of the small pox, god was good and mercifull to mee in divers providences, keeping mee safe, seing my freinds, dispatching my business according to my hearts desire, in a great measure; I catched no cold in my jorney, divers discourses about the schooler, I hope god hath alotted it to mee, the subcomittee voted mee 43li. per annum augmentacion, the issue of this businesse I shall waite with patience,

23. gave over teaching the Schoole[3] for present.

[1] For examination by the Committee for Plundered Ministers, in order to assess RJ for an augmentation: see below under 18 March.

[2] Collecke: colic, severe paroxysmal griping pains in the belly. SOED.

[3] EC school was a free school, founded temp. Henry VIII and endowed with lands and houses to the annual value of £64 p.a. at this period, in Ardleigh, Stisted, Messing, Coggeshall; a number of scholars are recorded by Venn (e.g. Mathew Alliston) as entering Cambridge from the school.

March: 24. This weeke god was good, and mercifull to mee, and mine in our healths, only my litle boy very ill, wherupon wee resolved die 22. to weane him, Mary was very well, god giveth mee great hopes in their educations, the lord good in keeping mee from many vanities of heart, and subduing temptacons, good in my hea(l)th my navel a litle moist, but not red, dry againe at night, my issue nothing for divers weeke, neither hath it beene much a long time, the lord was good to mee in the word, and duties of the day, the lord in mercy accept mee. Mr Wm Haukesbee preacht in the morning for mee, divers dislikt it much, god was and is good to mee in giving mee the hearts of most people,

1650. 26: rid to Braintree; Coll: Cooke promised to doe for mee, what he could in the matter of the schoole, returned safe praise to god, heard when I came home that the Schoole was disposed, I goe about this whole businesse with submission to gods providence, which I conceive hath layd it out for mee, I payd a considerable debt this day.

Debts: 27. Cast up my debts this day and they are 45^{li}. o: 1^{d}. including 23^{li}. 12^{s}. which I shall owe to Mr Haukesbee, and now my estate is as followeth.

Value of my estate, which (god) god hath given mee.

Land:	Mallories part Bollinhatch 2 closes in Colne	27^{li}. per annum
Moneyes in Major Haines hand to bee payd to Mr John Littell.—		50^{li}.

My debts are much about 10^{li}. more than my moneyes that are owing unto mee this increase is from gods goodnes, and providence towards mee.

Mr Harrington sent mee word by his sonne that he would pay mee my money as soone as possible,

28: perfected an agreement with Goodman Paine, he is to have the close at the old rent 3^{li}. per annum until Michaelmas in 1651. he is to lay on 80 load of dung, and sowe it with barley this yeare, and with oates the next, and when (c.o. both) either of his crops of corne are taken of, then am I to have the pasture, and the layer of my catle in it for the winters,

M. 31. This weeke god was good to mee and mine in our health, peace, plenty, preservacion, I was sometime this weeke especially on Satturday at night, greivously tormented with the(e) toothake, so that I rested not one winke, untill late in the morning, I rid to Pedmarsh and preacht for (c.o. Coll) Mr Burroughs dined with Coll. Cooke. I returned home, and preacht in my owne place in the afternoone, god was good to mee in giving mee strength for the worke in abating my paine, in hearing prayer in the sweetnes of the season it being warme, and dry.

Ap: 2. Mr Harrington came not before I went to London as I expected, so that I could not treate him in the affaire of the schoole, I rid away to Cranham safe that night, god good to mee in preserving mee upon the way. die. 3°. I came to London could not find Major Haines went and dined with Coll. Cooke. by whom indeed I expected god would bring about the affaire, he rid with mee in his coach to Dr Wrights. he promised mee if Mr Harrington and wee could agree, he would then depute mee. I thought it was but a cold businesse. I could not doe much in the matter of my augmentacion I lay with Major Haines, returned home safe die 4°. and found Mr Harrington had brought his kinsman Mr Alliston to towne; which was a great disturbance to us, but he proffered termes of accomodacion, wee expected his unckle, but he came not till night die 6°. when wee came to an agreement(.) thus farre gods providence hath managed the businesse in a way and method beyond my expectacion. I stayed my selfe on his providence if he had layd it out, he would one way or other effect it, I desire my prayer may bee still answered, and that god would make mee serviceable to his glory, and other persons good herein, which I hope and trust he will doe.

Ap: 7: This weeke the Lord was good and mercifull to mee and mine in our peace, plenty, in our health free from the toothake, onely I feele a kind of stiffenes in my jaw, my navel through mercy continueth dry, and I hope well, god shall perfectly recover mee, and restore mee unto health, my aunt Miles with us, I had experience of base thoughts putting up head in my heart, and my readinesse and aptnes to comply with them, god was good to mee in my health, in the Sabbath in the duties and mercies thereof to whom be glory for evermore,

8: went to Sr Tho: Honywoods, a coach could not there, or at pryory bee procured to convey backe Mr Alliston, as he came he must endeavour to returne,

11: This day I tooke the surrender of Sawyers from Mr Wm Haukesbee to the use of my daughter Mary Josselin, and her heyres for ever, the purchase cost mee 50[li]., which I fully paid to him and received an acquittance from him for it, and bond to make it good, tis of

X gods mercy thus to blesse mee and provide for mee and mine, thes day and 10: and 12: I sew the barly in the yard, the lord give a blessing theronto that it may encrease:

Navel —my navel did moisten, both gold colour, and a litle whitish, it was not sore, it may bee of gods mercy that it doth issue preventing the keeping up of corrupt matter in mee,

Ap. 14: This weeke god was good to mee and mine in our peace, plenty, health, good in making provision for mee and mine in thes dayes of want, my wife faint, my litle Ralph very unquiett in nights. the imployments I have now upon mee are divers, I in some measure have cause to blesse god for it, for my minde is not so subject to its vanities being otherwise impl(o)yed, oh when shall the strength of thy grace make mee more than conquerour over my corruptions. the season merveylous pleasant, gods eye is on the earth for good, oh lord lett it be still upon us, and give us such seasonable and comfortable showres as wee may have occasion to blesse and praise thy name for it, I was this day at Halsted, my place unsupplyed, I doe not purpose to goe another whole day unto them for a long season.

16. sent a letter to Major Haines to send into New England containing three sheets in my small hand, being a relation of affaires forreigne, and domestique, from the rendicion of Colchester untill April. 16. 1650. this present day, the Major is my speciall freind, and I doe not thinke any service too much to doe for him, the good Lord in mercy blesse him, and those that have beene instruments of good to mee either for soule or body. yesterday my Lady Honywoods, and the high-sheriffe's Coaches were both overturned their Ladies and freinds in them, and no hurt done to gods name bee the praise and glory. the season was very warme and comfortable the springe comes on very cheerfully.

17. a sweete refreshing showre. Mr Jo: Littell, putt mee in good hope to lett mee his litle meadowe for 2 yeares which if my occasions require it, I shall esteeme a very great kindnesse, and good providence towards mee, I had for 2 dayes past a litle cold, a pose, and stuffing in my head.

19. This night and the former, I lay at Mr Elliston's, where wee were used with much love and respect. it was a very sweet refreshment unto mee, for-as-much as my eare was taken up with the musicke of the birds, my eye with the pleasantnes of the creature, and my heart was refreshed in contemplacion of gods providence and grace towards mee all along, and cares and troubles that are incident to

my condicon were layd aside, my deare freind Mrs Mary Church was very cheerfull and her mother in good hopes of her wellfare which god for his mercy sake afford to her, god hath made her a freind of freinds to mee, and I shall love her memory, and cannot but endeavour her good, and rejoyce therein.

☞ 20: Bee Cautious of speaking to Mr Harlakenden in the point of his royaltie, for being intent on the proffits of them, he takes it ill, as I found this day. which I hope shall learne mee some prudence in the world. I would willingly bee a gainer by others mens tempers.

April: 21: This weeke the Lord was good to us in our health, peace and plenty. my litle boy continueth ill, and sore, and forward, my pose hath continued now seven dayes litle or much, especially in mornings, with much sneezings, wherby I hope my head will be throughly purged, god seeth what is best for mee, my navel was moist, it was full of lint which stucke therein, very redde it had not beene so bad 10 months before, it was washt and cleansed as usually the lord for his mercy sake, give a blessing thereunto, the Lord was good to mee in keeping my heart in some measure upright with him, divers of those lusts and temptacions which formerly annoyed mee, are silent, yett I have my burthen still, for now my mind is readie to muse too much on those imployments and their maintenance in which I am engaged, and though my heart endeavours to eye god, and admire his providence from whence all the(e) good in my condicon flowes, yett is my heart ready to bee sometimes too much taken up with the musings on thes things, and new for present in forecasts and in endeavours to bee out of debt. tis very hard to bee at rest to outward things when wee have never so many of them, god was good to mee this day in (the) my labour on his day, and in the word, but my heart is very unsutable to the sanctifying of the Sabbath betwixt god and my owne soule, lord pardon mee, and heale mee of this evill I intreate thee, and lett my labours bee blessed by my god to many of mi(ne) and thy people I humbly intreate the(e), and lett it convert and bring home some to the(e).

22: Mrs Mary very ill this day, many perswade themselves shee will not outgrowe this illnes, thou wilt give her a condicon that shall knowe no sorrow, nor infirmity(.) wee made our rate this day, I tooke it kindly from the townesmen, who did not raise my rate upon the close, I hold in my owne hands

23: it rained a most sweete showre, god is opening his hand to fill us, with his bounty. Mr Harlakenden and I had a great discourse about our Lords rent, I find and he acknowledges by comparing

Lords rent.

the copies, and the rentalls, that 10^{s}. for the aldar car part of Oxenfen is sett on my head, and Kents, and 7^{s}. for Mills fenn etc is sett now on osbornes, and Tills—head, he was somewhat moved, I blesse god who gave me a patient command, of my selfe this day Mr Harrington paid mee in 7^{li}. for keeping the schoole, from Jan. to March. 25. 1650. he promiseth to dischardge all to mee, and the moneyes I am out, when he sendeth for his sonnes things, the matter of the schoole in a great uncertainty, now the Dr, desireth to bee secured in the matter of the reparations, by bond, which for my part, I shall never condescend unto, the lords will be done, to him, I committ all my wayes to bring them to passe for mee, and it may bee the Lord aimeth at good to mee therein, and therfore I will quietly waite upon him therein; this night my wife fainted as if dying, but to god for ever bee praise, shee revived againe, my heart was not sadded in order to her death, because I was fully perswaded, god would not then snatch her away,

24. Mrs Mary Church made an issue in her knee, god give a blessing unto it if it be his most holy will and pleasure, my deare wife cheerfull this day.

25. a most goodly day, there was never knowne a more mild, dry, and warme winter so forward and fruitfull a spring, god suited it to our necessities, for how should catle else have subsisted, notwithstanding this, hay was very scarce and deare, at 3^{s}. and 3^{s}. 4^{d}. per hundred weight.

27. Mr Harringtons things, were fetched away this day, our life is but a buble, my weake body is preserved through gods goodnes, when many younger and stronger fall away, I desire even to rejoyce in my infirmities, I have thereby meditacons of god, and Christ, and death, and of his providence, which surmount in sweetnes the dolour of my illnesses. my tenant this day at Mallories paid mee 6^{li}. 10^{s}. for Lady rent, I sett of 10^{s}. for taxes, forgave him 18^{d}. which was his part of them,

Ap: 28. This weeke the Lord continued good to us in our peace, and provision for us, the spring very comfortable, affording great hopes of plenty: for health, Jane and Tom, very well Mary, and my wife, ill but not downe sicke. Ralphs distempers continues, he hath slept
Navel. very quiettly which hath revived us all. my navel issued, but not very sore and so it hath continued this weeke, I have had a stuffing in my head and pose and sneezing ever since April. 15. and it continues still, wherby I have voided a great aboundance of rheume, and moisture, and being somewhat feavourish some dayes, through

mercy, I had no farther trouble, all thes illnesses my god shall remove, and doe mee good by them, my heart was more free from former vanities, and taken up with meditacions of god, and observing him in varietie of providences, our deare freind Mrs Mary continued ill, full of paine, Lord ease her if it by thy good pleasure, the Lord was good to mee in the Sabbath, in expounding and preaching the word, his name have the praise, the lord in rich mercy accept of mee and delight in mee and doe mee good:.

May. 2. This day a hearer of Mr Owen, his discourse was good, about instructions how to endeavour stablishnednes in beleeving, dined at my Lady Honywoods, shee resents Mr Tho: harlakendens dealing with her in the meadowe very ill, my navel was very well this night after my walke, the lords name bee praised therein.

May. 5. This weeke god was good to us in our peace, and in provision for us, the lords hand was towards us in our health, somewhat better, my pose though not gone yett that and my stuffing not so bad, my navel continued to issue, but very litle, and god tooke of any feare from my heart, in the apprehension of his turning it to good, and perhaps as I thinke even, an outward good, and in due time he will heale mee, the lord was good to us in the season, it giveth great hopes of plenty. Mrs Mary Church continueth very ill as formerly, her issue runneth but her paine doth not asswage, the lord in his season send her helpe, my deare wife complaines much of her head, the Lord good to mee in giving mee an heart in some measure to watch against my iniquity, though I humbly acknowledge my unevennes and aptnes to revolt, god good to mee in my lightsomnes of heart in his inward and outward goodnes towards mee, for which I blesse his most holy name, the Lord was good to mee in the worke and exercise of the Sabbath, and this day my Ralph is a full yeare old, he hath grapled divers months with strong distempers, it is of gods mercy and goodnes he is alive

7. joynd in a day of humiliacon at my Lady Honywoods, my heart was very much dull and drowsy in the former part of the day, but in prayer more affected the glory whereof(,) I ascribe unto the name of the lord; god sweetend the earth with pretious showres, I hope the frosts will abate, which begun to bee feirce; when the duty was finisht, I was sent for to Mrs Mary who lay speechlesse, shee made alwayes promises of great things to mee and mine, which she had not yett done, and if shee should bee unable to performe it, it would bee a great losse to mee yett, I stayed my selfe on gods providence, what he appoints he will effect, and tis folly for us to

interpose, this stayed my minde, so that it was no way moved when I came home to her, I found it so indeed, but now shee was cheerfull, and revived for the present: Litle Ralph wee conceive is liver-growne,[1] there is no passage betweene his short ribs, which is a signe thereof.

9. I had this day, an exceeding great pose, the season showery; Die: 10. 11. my right side of my face, and teeth fared as if I should have the toothake, Lord if it bee thy good pleasure remove the paine, and the terror of it. Mr Harlakenden came home from London, he brought mee downe the writing about the schoole, and an ingagement therewithall not to goe on with Mr Harrington in that agreement, mr Rogers came to the pryory this afternoone, which was opportunity for mee to helpe my neighbours at Halsted who were destitute,

May. 12. I preacht at Halsted in the afternoone, my toothake returned, I prickt the hollow tooth and made it bleed very much, I cannot say it did mee either good or hurt, the dealing of god with mee was very gentle, my Litle Ralph I hope better then formerly, as bleach is not so much, yett he is very forward, the lords name be praised, my deare Mary, very ill, she is heavy, and joylesse as it were, god in mercy restore her and spare her life, I had much experience of vanitie taking up my minde in this morning, and so its with mee frequently Lord lett thy grace bee sufficient for mee I intreate thee, and helpe mee against my corruptions that they bee not too strong for mee, my navel continued well to gods holy name bee the praise ascribed. navel

13. morning navel had issued, my face and gummes very sore, my gumms swelled and so continued die. 14: This day Mr Harrington, and I came to an other agreement, I gave him a summ of mony, and so was to part with him, I hope gods providence intends good to mee therby. I have cast my selfe on god, and with rejoycings in him, I professe he hath not failed mee,

17. This day Mrs Mary Church made a disposall of her estate, which amounts to 21^{li}. per annum in land, the trust whereof, shee layed on mee, a burthen heavy but I durst not refuse it, in regard providence lead mee to it, god in mercy raise her up if possible, if otherwise, give mee life and wisdome for the worke that I may performe it faithfully.

May. 19. This weeke the lord was good to mee in my perticular health,

[1] Liver-grown: having an enlarged liver. SOED. 'Livergrown' was one of the 'causes of death' listed in contemporary Bills of Mortality.

and some children but my deare Mary, wonderfull ill, and so is litle Ralph, the lord in mercy sanctifie his hand, and dealing with mee, and showe mee, why he contends with mee(.) this day also my litle Jane was taken ill, the good lord in mercy doe mee good by these rebukes. I freely submitt to thee, oh god, and kisse the rod, there is mercy in thy dealing, and of mercy it is, that I and mine are not consumed the lord in his time heale all this, my heart is quiett in my god, the lord doth not find amazement, and feare along with his corrections, but supports mee in hope that hee will shine upon my tabernacle, the lord was good to mee in abating the
navel swelling of my gummes: my navel issued twice this weeke, I thought I felt the rhewme in it, a day or two before, my sister An came to mee, and continued with mee this day, gods providence is good towards her though her discouragements are very many, the Lord was good to mee in the Sabbath, my heart still hangs downe-wards on the creatures, and occasions, oh that I were raised up above them, spiritualised, and fitted for communion with my god.

21: The last night Mary talked idely, shee began to sweate, god takes the feare of her death much from my heart, her fitts are violent in her head, the lord in his tender mercy raise her up. and purge my dross out by this correction, and rod of his, my sister Ann went from us, I sent her not away empty. Mr Harrington with mee, I made a full end with him, he is to receive his arreares, he now oweth mee in all 1^{li}. 5^{s}. 6^{d}.

22. my litle Mary, very weake, wee feared shee was drawing on, feare came on my heart very much, but shee is not mine, but the Lords, and shee is not too good for her father, shee was tender of her mother, thankefull, mindefull of god, in her extremity, shee would cry out, poore I, poore, I. I went downe to the pryory about a medicine for wormes, as I came up, my heart cheered exceedingly, I was hopefull of her life, feare went of my heart wonderfully through mercy. when I came home, shee had had a stoole, and 3 great dead wormes,[1] Lord in mercy to her, and mee, thou wilt bring her up from the grave, and I shall praise thy most holy name, divers texts in the psalmes I read this day cheered my heart, the lord I hope speaking those things to mee my faith endeavoured to lay hold on them psal. 27.v.1.5.10, both of us even gave her over, and then god gave a reviving, but if I will see this mercy, my duty

[1] 'There be divers kindes of wormes in the belly, as long, short, round, flat, and some small as lice . . .'. Thomas Phaire, *The Boke of Chyldren* (1545; reprinted Edinburgh, 1955), pp. 49–50.

is to waite. v.14. psal. 28.v.1.6.7 psal. 30.v.2.3.10.11.12, wee gave her a glister it wrought very well praised bee my god, shee rested sweetly in the afternoone, Major Haynes from London with us,

23. my wife and I rested comfortably, I have a b(o)ile on my hippe, which paynes mee the lord I knowe ordereth it for good unto mee, my Mary rested very litle the night past, yett shee knew mee in the morning, the Lord was good to mee in the thoughts of the morning, I went to him in his word for something to live on this day and I lay at catch[1] waiting what he would touch my heart with, and in reading thes texts spoke to mee. psal. 31.15. wormes, and weaknesse can do nothing to my babe further than god commissionates them, 22.24. apt I am to feare my babe, but god will give me strength to trust in him, psal. 32.v.1.6. happiness is not in the waies of the vaine creature, but in the mercies of the living god. v.7. psal. 33.18.19.v. gods mercy reacheth to deliver the soule from death.

24: I rested very comfortably with my deare wife this night past, but my Mary very ill, this morning shee sleepes sweetly, soundly(,) to god bee praise, this morning many passages in the 34 psalme refresht mee,[2] my litle Ralph very ill, when the lord seeth good, he will shine againe on my tabernacle, and I shall praise him. Dr Wright hath fully invested mee in the schoole for his time, and for his right, the lord make mee serviceable to his glory therein, and lett it turne to my good and advantage, my deare Mary voyded sixe wormes more this day(.) I went to bed at night, but was raised up, with the dolour of my wife, that Mary was dying, she was very neare death, but the lord preserved her this night also, oh lord suite my heart unto all thy dealings, shewe mee why thou dost contend with mee, oh mother saith shee if you could but pull out something hansomely here, (and layes her hand on her stomacke) I should bee well, lord doe it beyond all meanes, thou alone art more then all,

25: hopes of Maries life especially towards night, but it was onely hopes, god is her life, shee shall enjoy it in heaven not here, Ralph ill, Lord sanctifie thy dealings to mee, god hath taken the feare of it, much from my heart, and helpes mee in bearing it for which I blesse and praise his holy name,

[1] To lie at catch: to be on the watch for an opportunity of catching or seizing something, especially of catching a person's words. NED.

[2] Vs. 17, for example, reads: 'The righteous cry, and the Lord heareth, and delivereth them out of all their troubles.' Vs. 22: 'The Lord redeemeth the soul of his servants: and none of them that trust in him shall be desolate.'

May. 26. This morning all our hopes of Maries life was gone, to the Lord I have resigned her and with him I leave her, to receive her into his everlasting armes, when he seeth best, shee rests free from much paine wee hope in regard shee maketh no dolour the lord makes us willing shee should bee out of her paine, and why are wee at any times unwilling, when god is about such a worke, that he should take them up into his glory, this day the word was made merveylous comfortable to mee, my heart could not but mourne over and for my babe, but I left it with the lord, and was quiett in my spirit, in gods taking it, to whom, I did freely resigne it, my litle sonne in all peoples eyes is a dying child, lord thy will bee done, thou art better to mee then sonnes and daughters, though I value them above gold and jewells. my navel continued well this weeke for which I blesse god, my bile grew sorer, and my carnels in my flanke, which god I trust will ordaine for an aboundance of good unto mee,

27. This day a quarter past two in the afternoone my Mary fell asleepe in the Lord, her soule past into that rest where the body of Jesus, and the soules of the saints are, shee was: 8 yeares and 45 dayes old when shee dyed, my soule had aboundant cause to blesse god for her, who was our first fruites, and those god would have offered to him, and this I freely resigned up to him(,) it was a pretious child, a bundle of myrrhe, a bundle of sweetnes, shee was a child of ten thousand, full of wisedome, woman-like gravity, knowledge, sweet expre[*ssions of god, apt in her learning*,] tender hearted and loving, an [*obed*]ient child [*to us*.] it was free from [*the rudenesse of*] litle children, it was to us as a boxe of sweet ointment, which now its broken smells more deliciously then it did before, Lord I rejoyce I had such a present for thee, it was patient in the sicknesse, thankefull to admiracion; it lived desired and dyed lamented, thy memory is and will bee sweete unto mee,

28. This day my deare Mary was buried in Earles Colne church by the 2 uppermost seats, shee was accompanyed thither with most of the towne; Mrs Margarett Harlakenden, and Mrs Mabel Elliston layd her in grave, those two and Mrs Jane Clench and my sister carryed her in their hands to the grave, I kist her lips last, and carefully laid up that body the soule being with Jesus it rests there till the resurrection. god gave mee a submitting heart to his will, and even a heart rejoycing in him for what he hath done for her; I rest confident of her glory, not only because the Covenant of god is with mee, and so also with my seeds and from the riches of his

free grace; saving whom he pleaseth, but the sobernes, towardlines in obedience spiritualnes of her conversacon for a child, argued the reall impression of the image of god upon her; the lord was wonderfull good to mee and my deare wife in this correction; the lord gave us time in our thoughts, to bury it, wee expected nothing but death two or 3 dayes before, he bore witnesse to my spirit that it was not in anger towards mee or my babe, but in love to both that he did what he did, and perswades mee he will doe mee good, and point to some corrupcions, which he will assist mee in the further mortifying of them; I eyed her glory and gaine and set that against her life and my losse, and her balance infinitely outweighed, the lord gave mee strength of heart to eye him, and quiettnes of heart to submitt to him, for which I blesse his name,

These 2 dayes I had 14^{li}. 6^{s}. 6^{d}. paid mee in unexpectedly, which was an ease to my minde, in my outward condicon which was much straitned, Mrs Mary groweth wonderfully weake and ill every day, my neighbour Potter sicke of the small poxe, a mercy my Maries disease was not infectious, the lord spare her life and preserve mee and my family for his mercy sake

29. This day I had a litle pose, and roughnes of rheume in my throate, my god will ordaine all for my good and make up by the enjoying of himselfe all my losses, troubles and sorrowes and cause them to passe away as the waters, my desires are with David that god would purge and wash mee throughly from my sins, oh lett the humour have no setling stay behinde if it bee thy pleasure,

June: 1: Mrs Mary Church setled her estate, taking up her reversions, and surrendred them to the use of her will,[1] the surrender in Mr Ellistons hands, and also acknowledged her will before Mr Harlakenden Mr Josselin steward Mr Elliston, Rob. Crowe and Robert Johnson the affaire will bee to mee, exceeding chargeable, Lord I trust thou wilt free mee from troubles, and give me life, and an heart to perform the trust reposed in mee with all faithfulnes and honesty.

June. 2. Called up this morning to see my deare freind Mrs Mary Church who departed to an eternall rest, and Sabbath about 9 of the clocke, shee is free from paine and free from sin which is the greatest happinesse of all(.) There is another good freind in heaven

[1] A copy of the original will, in RJ's hand, is in the ERO (280 CW 15) and is reprinted in Macfarlane, p. 216. Josselin was left all her property, after the death of Rose, Mary's mother, on the condition that he paid out various bequests, including £100 to his daughter Jane.

against my going thither, for which I desire the lord to fitt mee every day more and more, my deare Ralph very ill wee cannot long enjoy him, the lord wash his nature from his filth, and defilement, and doe him good, the love sanctifie thes sad strokes to us, for the lord Christs sake(.) god was good to mee, my wife and other two children in our health, I had a litle pose and stuffing in my head, taking cold on my feete, the lord was good to mee in the duties worke and exercise of the Sabbath, the lord in mercy heale my
N heart, nature, and doe mee good for Christs sake. my navel issued on Friday god in his due time will heale it. when he seeth it best for mee, and unto him, I doe committ my selfe, and all my wayes, my deare Ralph before midnight fell asleepe whose body Jesus shall awaken, his life was continuall sorrow and trouble, happy he who is at rest in the lord, my deare wife, ill as if she would have dyed, the Lord revived her againe for which his holy name bee praised, it was one of the most lovely corpses that ever was seene,

4: This day my deare freind Mrs Mary Church and my sweete Ralph were buried togither in the church, I preached her funerall on Mathew. 25.34[1] verse god hath taken from mee a choyce speciall freind, the good Lord in mercy sanctifie that his dealing unto mee, and truly my heart lookes wholly to god herein, who is my life, my grace, my all, I am poore and empty. in some respect I see great mercy therein, for Satan lieth in waite to corrupt our affections and that mine were not, was gods aboundant grace, who keepes mee that though I fall yett I am not utterly cast downe. when Mrs Mary dyed, my heart trembled, and was perplexed in the dealings of the lord so sadly with us, and desiring god not to proceed on against us with his darts and arrowes, looking backe into my wayes, and observing why god had thus dealt with mee, the lord followed mee with that sin no more lest a worse thing happen unto thee, and the intimacion of god was he would proceed no farther against mee or mine, and he would assist mee with his grace if I clave to him with a full purpose of heart, which I resolve, oh my god helpe mee, oh my god faile mee not, for in thee doe I putt my trust.

6: Mrs Church this day delivered unto mee the will of Mrs Mary deceasd, many suppose shee hath given mee all her land, others shee hath given mee nothing but what is done is gods providence

[1] 'Then shall the King say unto them on his right hand, Come, ye blessed of my Father, inherit the kingdom prepared for you from the foundation of the world.'

and therein I delight, I trust he will bee uprightnes to mee in the worke, and blesse mee therein because of them that lye in waite for my hurt: lett Harris the house at Coggeshall[1] till Michaelmas, the first tenant that I agreed withall.

June. 9: God was good to mee and mine this weeke, in our health, in peace, and outward mercies, stopping the infection in the towne, that it proceeds no farther, my navel very well through mercy. lord provide mercy and truth for mee which may preserve mee: The Lord good to mee in bearing up my heart under my trialls, I seeth emptines of thes things more, and gods worth, and my soule desireth to follow hard after him to enjoy him, all things: and all things in and through him, in the affaire of Mrs Mary their are divers discourses, but the uprightnes of my heart therein affords through god peace to mee, and I trust will more, and more, others esteeme I shall loose very much by it; what gods providence casts out I desire to bee satisfyed with as best for mee, my deare wife hoped shee did somewhat recover strength, the Lord watch over mee and mine for good, for his mercy sake, and because of them that desire my hurt, lord pardon it, unto them, and take their evill minde from them for christs sake; what ever my condicon bee, to thee oh lord I come because of thy goodnes, lead mee, sett mee, stay mee on that rocke that is higher then mee, god was good to mee in the worke, and duty of the day the good Lord in mercy owne mee, and accept mee, I was offered helpe this afternoone, but I thought best to refuse it, received a very kind, consolatory letter [from my Lady Honywood, of] whose illnes I heare by her selfe,

[10: Began to teach the schoole. 8 children came, but none of their parents, the lord is pleased to] give me [some m]ixtures and rubs in my con[dicons t]hat my *heart* may upon every thing [look] up to him,

11. received in 2 loads and half of wood which Sir Tho: honywood gave mee, gods providence leading mee thither when it was even all gone, 2 of my neighbours brought it home for mee.

June: 13: A day of P: humiliacon, there were a great many people, and strangers there, which doth occasion mee to thinke that it was neglected in divers places, the lord in some measure gave mee a heart sensible of filth of state, and sinfulnes, the lord in due time

[1] The first mention of school property being let by RJ. Henceforth all references to tenants at Ardleigh, Stisted, Messing, and Coggeshall allude to school lands from which RJ drew the profits during his mastership. A survey of these lands, with description and maps, made by an earlier schoolmaster, William Cousins, in 1623, is in the ERO (D/Q 6/35).

comand all mercies needfull for mee, the lord in mercy thinke upon us in respect of the season, and delight in us to blesse us, and doe us good: I had the opportunity this day to see Collonell Cooke, and to returne him thankes for his respects unto mee, and my thankes by him unto the Doctor,

June: 16: God was in many outward mercies exceeding good to mee and mine, my deare wife somewhat faint and weakely but cheerfull, god helpes us under our great losses I am sometimes ready to bee overwhelmed in remembrance of my deare Mary, but when I eye my god, and thinke on his wisedome in all providences my heart is cheered, and in her gaine I rejoyce, and indeed I would not have it otherwise, because its my fathers will that it should bee so, onely the lord cleanse mee from my drosse throughly, and doe mee good which I trust hee will, my heart seeth more into him, he is sweeter to mee. and my converse is more with him than formerly, my lusts and temptacions are not so violent, god in mercy not only chaine Satan, and restraine my corrupcons but subdue them also, my debts are great and they are too much in my minde, yett not with much disquietment, the lord free mee from the caring after or about the things of this world, so that I may use it, as if I used it not, god strengthened mee for my weekely worke in schooling, and I hope will carry mee on in the same with moderacion of spirit, and ease mee of care and trouble for my subsistance thereby, god was good to mee in the duties of the Sabbath in strength for it, in my affaires and occasions the weeke past(,) he sweetned his word to mee, and doth brase up my heart to eye, and rely on him

19. Had some discourse with Mr Harlakenden about Mrs Maries businesse wee agreed very lovingly in the value of the land, Mrs Marys part. 6^{li}. per annum. the other at 10^{li}. per annum: the free at 5^{li}. per annum: he sett both the fines at 20^{li}. he acknowledged they were too hard and I hope in god wee shall doe all our businesses with quietnes god leads mee into it lovingly.

June: 23: This weeke the lord was good to mee and all mine in aboundance of outward mercies: on Monday. 17. our two children tooke physicke, and were sicke even to death, so that our hearts trembled, fearing the issue, but the lord in mercy to us quickly blew it over, **navel** and they revived and are now well, I praise him: die: 21: my navel issued, I did not wash it this time, it did well presently: the lord good in drawing both our hearts nearer to him, so that wee do endeavour more to enjoy communion with him, and he affords it to my soule for which I praise him: I find I goe through the matter of the schoole without any extraordinary burthen, the times of schoole I make my times of studdy, so that at other times I have occasions attended, the lord was good to us in the towne in steying the infection of the small pox wherin he answered our prayers, so that it spread not to any persons farther, the lord teach us to proffit by his dealings: the lord was good to mee in the Sabbath, in the word preacht and opened, the unreverent carriage of divers in sitting with their hatts on when the psalme is singing is strange to mee, the good Lord in mercy keepe mee spotlesse, and pardon all my sins, and purge mee throughly and sanctifie mee, I intreate thee.

24: This morning I bought Smiths cowe, he saith shee tooke bull, last ☞ Satturday 3 weekes, viz June: 1: her price was 6^{li}. 10^{s}. 0^{d}. I also bought of him, the pasture of Dagnall till Michaelmas for. 3^{li}. 10^{s}. he is to pay me the tith which I told him of, and to pay all towne taxes untill michaelmas: I am to enter on them on Wednesday. I borrowed the mony of Goodwife Mathew: 40^{s}. I now paid him: in hand: if I buy cowes I am to putt them now on the ground: the lord my god give a blessing unto mee herein:

25: went to Messing, received. 10^{s}. of Atthayes: 7^{s}. 6^{d}. of Medcalfe: 11^{s}. 8^{d}. of Bridge(,) Shawe promiseth his.[1] August: 1: there is some improvement to bee made towards our repayres, which will cost, nigh: 10^{li}. this night wee begun to milke our cowe bought of Smith: god good in my jorney I went. 18 miles. spent 6^{d}.

27. This [day I fetcht] a cow from Westney's[2] of Halsted it cost 6^{li}. 5^{s}. I had great trouble in the cowes unquietnes, god enters mee into many of my affaires with trouble that I might eye him still in them, and see he is my only content, and thes are all vexations without him, I paid Smith 8^{li}. the residue of his bargaine, I lent Polly 20^{s}. I receivd in 30^{s}. from my schoolerents. gods providence bee over mee in all things for good for in him I put my trust, and on his grace in christ, I stay my soule.

28: Heard Huggins was undone, care taken about my rent in seizing the crop. Hedge bad mee 18^{li}. per annum. and Dawkin: 19^{li}. receivd from Overell. 4^{li}. 17^{s}. 6^{d}. rent,[3] and the survey booke from Mr Harrington.

June: 30: This weeke past god was good to us in our peace, health, in providing for us, some afflicted with the small pox, the lord for his name sake preserve my habitacion, and bee health and safety for

[1] Rents for school lands in Messing.
[2] Edward Wasney of Halsted had a four-hearth house in 1662.
[3] RJ's school tenants at Ardleigh and Stisted.

us, heard this weeke of the consuming plague in Ireland thy hand oh lord is lifted up, lett thy poore saints, be hidden under thy wings. Cromwell is made Gen:(,) Fairfax hath layd downe his
N commission, the good lord order things for good: my navel issued sometime this weeke but not much: the lord good to mee in helping mee to forgett my sorrow, sweetening my heart in the meditacions of him selfe, stilling my minde from running after foolish vanities keeping it in my thoughts much, to doe Jesus Christ some service in my place(.) the lord was good to mee in the Sabbath, for which I blesse his holy name

July. 5: Layd in, 3 load of hay out of Hall meadow, excellent hay, and in good case it was well washt but being well cockt[1] it saved it selfe, I was troubled with my hogs breaking away on the lords day morning, and having looked for him and not finding him. I observed still a vexacon and trouble in all thes things and thinking gods providence might bring him backe to mee, I was just then told that he was driven home from of the greene.

July: 7. This weeke the Lord was good to us all in our peace, health, in providing for us in doing many of my occasions comfortably. I desire to give god the glory thereof the lords name be praised in making mee much to forgett my sorrowes, in keeping my heart from divers temptacions with which I was formerly annoyed, the lords most holy name bee praised for the same, I find my heart more sweetned with apprehensions of his goodnes to mee, and taste him above all creatures and condicons as my choice, and speciall good, I find him helping mee in my imployment, so that my businesses though much and many are easy and delightsome unto mee. the day was very wett, god afflicts Ireland with the plague most sadly, and now Scotland and wee are likely to engage into bloud, arise and save us for in thee wee trust, and doe us good for thy most holy name sake wee entreate thee. god was good to us in the mercies and goodnesse of the Sabbath for which I blesse his name,

9. proved Mrs Maries will at Kelveden, and returned safe, —10. ind 3 jaggs of hay from my vicaridge close, I had about 45^{c} of very good hay, I blesse god for it: I had at night a great pose, and so die. 11. which day I lett my farme at Ardleigh to Hedge for 19^{li}. per annum for 3 yeare(,) one Heckford undertakes the rent for the 3. yeares

13. Rid to Colchester dined with the Commissioners[2] that were there

[1] Cock: a conical heap of produce; especially of hay in the field. SOED.

[2] Probably the Parochial Inquisition of 1650 to secure a 'preaching ministry and better maintenance of the ministry' (Smith, pp. 233–5); the Inquisition was held in September in Essex.

about the livings of the ministers, returned well praise bee to my gratious god.

July. 14 This weeke the Lord was good to mee and mine in our lives: health, peace plenty my deare wife was very ill, and would be lett bloud, and was so, but is(,) god bee blessed finely well. god was good to mee in the duties of the Sabbath, in his word, which was sweete and comfortable unto mee, god good in restraining my corruptions, the lord chaine up Sathan, and also putt him under my feete(.) many times I find the memory of my deare babes bitter as death, and no rest till my meditacions rest on god, who is my present peace, oh how happy are they, that have a god in their difficulties to goe unto, I will rejoyce under the shaddowe of thy wings; the Lord bee gratious to mee and all mine in all mercies he seeth needfull and give mee an heart to delight in him.

16. This day kept at priory for gods presence in our hearts to sanctifie them to heale our breaches, prevent the warre with Scotland, the day was very wett, god was good to us in the worke thereof, the lord give the answer of prayer into our bosomes

18: This day Tom coming downe the schoole stayre fell from the top to the bottome he hurt his cheeke; gods providence was very good over him that he was not spoiled, lord when you dost strangely preserve any, I hope thou hast some speciall service for them to doe for thee,

July: 21: This weeke the lord was good to mee, and mine in our peace, plenty, health in all outward mercies, preventing the infections of the small pox that it doth not spread in our towne(.) corne at a great rate. 11^{s}. and 11^{s}. 6^{d}. a bushel at Colchester, the crop very good on the ground, but the season oftentimes dangerous, the good lord giveth us hopes of a fine season by this and divers dayes formerly(.) The Lord good to mee in letting mee see the evill of some former temptacions, his goodnesse in preserving mee from them, and in carrying my poore soule more and more forth towards him; I have some experience of sorrowes, and trials in the world, and they make mee the more to prize my god knowing nothing in sweete or good without him, the lord was good to mee in his word, and in the dutie of the day, but my heart was full of wandrings, lord pardon mee, heale my backeslidings, I humbly intreate thee.

23. 24. The Publike Courts for our Mannors were kept, in which I was admitted in reversion[1] to all the land of Mrs Mary Church, and my sonne Tho: to the land of Mr W: Haukesbee.

[1] In reversion: conditional upon the expiry of a grant or the death of a grantee. SOED. In this case, upon the death of Rose Church, Mary's mother.

25. Mr Bearman came, and I was admitted to both the parcells of his wives land being now tenant of both mannors, this is not of my selfe, but it is the Lords blessing upon mee, the good Lord in mercy sanctifie my heart, that I may love him the more, and minde the world lesse. as a pricke in the flesh I am troubled with rheumes,
n. cold. my goomes swelling: my navel issueth a litle now and then. and die. 26. there was some bloud in my easement, the Lord is my all and in all and I will delight in him. my colds and stuffings in my head have continued about a fortnight, god is my health and my strength

26: Pub: day of Thanksg. for the route and slaughter of the popish irish army under Cloghers command, which I kept with rejoycing in god, who hath given them bloud to drinke, who had shed themselves so much. kindly entertained at Mr Ri: Harlakenden's.

27. This day I payd Mrs Church her 20^{li}. so I have now paid her 50^{li}. and 5^{li}. to the poore, and other charges layd out in money. 1^{li}. 19^{s}. 6^{d}. so in all I have layd out. 56^{li}. 19^{s}. 6^{d}. this day on Mrs Maries estate, the good lord in the riches of his grace blesse mee and mine, there are that waite for my hurt.

July: 28: This weeke the lord was with mee, and mine in supplying us with all outward needful mercies, the lord make mee thankfull and to walke worthy of them(.) the lord makes mee sensible how vaine and worldly thoughts throng in upon mee, and hinder mee in the service of god, make mee watchfull against them, for I acknowledge I have not, gods mercy was and is great in preserving us from infection of the small pox, lord thy name bee praised that watcheth over us(.) my cold caused wheezings in nights: my navell was a litle moist the Lord in his due time will cause all these to cease, he knoweth what is best for mee, unto him I submitt, whose promise is all things shall worke togither for good, the Lord was good and mercifull to mee and mine in this his day, his word sweete, and pretious, oh that my soule might bee established in obedience
pose before him, all my days, I had a great pose this afternoon

[29: 31: My] pose continued very much. on Tuesday 30. my cold began to setle in my chest and my wheezings were very great die. 31: and
pose my rheume a litle thickned. at night I rested very litle: I was not
Cold so straitned in my chest as sometimes I have beene. yett my wheezings were much. I was inwardly a litle pent and listles. but not so bad through mercy as I expected I went to bed without any supper.

this day reports common all lost in Ireland. Cromwell beaten, tumults at London but their was no truth therein.

August. 1. This cold was breeding two or 3 weekes. my phlegme now began to thicken and to breake away, my wheezings were very much. at night I was chillish I went to bed early, tooke only a posset, god gave mee some rest. my thoughts were not very troublesome, my cold thickend and brake away, much to my ease, for which I desire to give praise to my god: yea my soule rejoyce in him.

2: This night my navel was washt it was corrupt and saverd much: at night on the left side of my belly it felt inwardly sore, and so I apprehended. and my minde began to be disquieted, but at what time I am so, I resolve to goe to god. I left my selfe to his providence. I submitted, I was quiett. he gave mee intimacion of healing mee and pardoning mee, I expected it from him and rejoyced: the next day. die. 3. it was finely well. I rid to Colchester, gods providence good to mee in my occasions, I returned safe praise to my god, heard that the Scots were routed and thousands slaine.

August. 4. This weeke the lords favour was towards us in outward mercies: my deare wife very faint and ill, especially on Satturday night. wee sent for neighbours. I apprehend shee disquiets her selfe in greife for Mary as the occasion of it the lord revived her speedily. for which I blesse his most holy name, the lord good to mee in keeping mee from being overcome with temptacions he in much mercy fill my soule with his grace. the lord good to mee in abating my cold, it weareth away blessed bee his name, and I take some rest comfortably in the nights, the lord was good and mercifull to mee in the Sabbath, in the word preacht, the good Lord in mercy accept my soule and pardon my sins for his deare sonnes sake, my poore wife was very ill at night.

9: A very sad wett day, it begun to overflowe into the meadowes.

August: 11: This weeke the Lord was bountifull in his provisions for us and outward mercies towards us, my wife better then formerly. my sonne Tho: was as if he had strained his insteppe, and was very lame, but went indifferently well the next morning, navel for which and all other mercies the lord bee praised, my navel through mercy continued well all this last weeke, my cold did weare away by litle and litle, I thinke I sometimes renew it by my sneezing and wheezing a litle in nights, it spends by sweating, and otherwise, my phlegme is white, tough, and frothy: I heard from divers of my freinds this weeke of their health: thus god continueth his favour to mee. god left mee not this weeke to my lusts and temptacions to have dominion over mee, but kept my heart close to him wherein I doe rejoyce, nay my soule desires to see him, my quickening and my strength in all acts whatsoever without whom I can doe nothing; the lord was good and mercifull to mee this day in the worke thereof, oh command a blessing on mee, and mine for Jesus Christ his sake. I intreate thee, my sonne Tho: went to church with me this afternoone for which I blesse my god.

16. Kept a day of humiliacion at my Lady Honywoods, my heart was dead, and drowsy, and wonderfully tost with corrupt imaginacions, the good Lord heale mee and pardon the same to mee,

17. Heard Mr H. had received my money at chelmsford a good providence of my god towards mee, my wife returned home, very faint, and weakely my lady used her very curteously. and sent mee as an expression of her good will to mee a silver boate the lords name bee praised in my love and kindnesses, I receive from any. tis of my god who puts it into their hearts:.

August: 18. This weeke god was good to mee and mine in outward mercies, onely my deare wife faint and weakely, the lord strengthen her body, and quiet her spirit(.) my navel well. my cold wearing away, the season very comfortable, Mr Woodcocke[1] preacht for mee, and thereby I had an opportunity to helpe my freinds of Halsted: my heart very vile and annoyd with divers corrupcions, Lord cure mee of them for thy name sake.

21: heard reports of great successe in Scotland, my goomes this day did swell very suddenly, and at night were very sore on the right side. 22. my cheeke on the right side swelled much and was very sore and painfull, it went upwards out of my goome. shall I receive good at gods hand and not evill. tis my part to receive all at gods hand humbly, and thankefully.

face swelled.

23. face swelled more than formerly, but I thinke not so painfull, my wife shee thinkes shee breeds: I gargarishd:[2] I leave my selfe in all condicons to bee at the lords disposing, who knoweth what is best for mee, heard of the death of Mary Peacocke my fathers second wives daughter by a former housband, shee dyed in childbed not delivered; the good lord bee praised in all his mercies towards mee, the lord pitty, and helpe us under any part of his rod, and make it a staffe to us.

Resolved henceforward whatsoever money comes in on guifts, or

[1] Probably Thomas Woodcock, Fellow of Jesus, rector of Gravely, Cambs., in 1655, nonconformist. Calamy.

[2] Gargarize; replaced by gargle, to wash or cleanse the mouth or throat with a gargle. SOED.

curtesies, all incomes, and receipts on the schoole besides the rents, and whatsoever is saved by preaching at any places, shall bee layd out in bookes:.

24. The night past I annointed my face with oile of roses, that night I rested very litle, in the morning my face was more swelled up into my eye, and more above my gumme, in my cheeke, it is the lords worke, I am his lett him doe as he pleaseth for he doth what is best.

Aug: 25: My face was very much(.) swelled, and gummes very sore, my rest was very troublesome last night, but through mercy I tooke some rest. otherwise gods hand was good to the rest of my family in their health, and truly his hand was gentle on mee, tis a new triall, and so I want experience, but I desire to act my faith in his love towards mee and care of mee and exercise my patience in bearing his hand, and submitting unto him(.) I was resolved to preach this day though ill, at noone my gummes brake which gave mee much ease for which I blesse my god who remembred mee in my illnesse. I blesse my god for strength which he gave mee for the Sabbath, carrying mee on comfortably in the same, so as I feele my selfe better for my labour, the good lord accept mee and doe mee good for his christs sake.

26: my rest was comfortable the night past, and my swelling abated,
n. this day I found my navel sore, my god in his season will heale it, it was well the next morning blessed bee god

29: paid: 11^{s}. 3^{d}. for driving[1] my fetherbeds and bolsters, wee made us a very excellent downe bed: I payd Mr Harrington 1^{li}. 5^{s}. I owe him now 2^{li}. 10^{s}.

30: This morning I found my head cold. I wheeze in the night, I sneezed in the morning and fetcht up aboundance of rhewme, my nose posed a litle.

September: 1: This weeke past god was good to mee and mine, in our peace, plenty, health my face abated, the paine left mee, and my
Cold: face well. onely I was troubled with a cold: stuffing in my head, it ticles in my throate, and maketh mee to cough and wheeze on nights, thy hand is light, I have need of corrections oh my god. sanctifie them to mee, and doe mee good by them, my Jane was very ill last night the lord I trust will preserve her. god gave us great hopes of plenty. my minde not so perplexed with foolish, sinfull imaginacions as formerly, the lord good therein, the lord make mee walke closely, and uprightly before him, the Lord was good

[1] Driven: of feathers or down, separated from the heavier by a current of air. SOED.

to mee in the duty of the day, and in strength for it, my voyce failed mee, when I had almost done, the Lord watch over mee for good, upon whom I roule and stay my selfe.

2 rid to Colchester at their feast and banquetts, when I returned home I found the small pox at Goodman Abbotts and Burtons, the Lord stayed my heart on him to preserve mee though 100^{ds} and 1000^{ds} fell on each hand.

3. This day heard of the taking redhouse in Scotland: the Lord give a good issue to that dangerous affaire, receivd a bushel of good new wheate at 5^{s}. 4^{d}. tollfree a comfortable abatement, from 10^{s}. and 11^{s}., the lord make us thankefull.

4: my deare wife very ill, as if she should miscarry, I somewhat question whether she were with child or not, but shee concludes she was, oh lord humble mee, and drawe mee nearer unto thee by these providences.

6. This day my cowes were driven away from Smiths, from of his ground with his for rent by his Landlady. I apprehended it might have beene some trouble to mee, I followed after them, overtooke them, and had my cowes delivered quietly to mee,

Sept: 8: This weeke the Lord was good and mercifull to us in our outward mercies in being our health in these dayes for which I blesse his name, my wife ill, and yett mercy raisd her up. die. 7°. to bee a speciall instrument to save a womans life in travaile, my navel ill one day, but well after a dressing to god bee ascribed the praise, this weeke I suppt very litle; god hath kept us this weeke past in some measure of uprightness free from some former vanities of minde, oh that I might receive strength and grace to serve the(e) perfectly fully. the Scottish affaire very difficult, give a good issue unto it for thy glory and peoples good wee entreate the(e), its not so much layd to heart as formerly. heard of the route of the Scotch army[1] that 4000 weare slaine 10000 prisoners: 22 peices of ordnance taken, and this done September. 3. newes London die. 7°. this was reported to mee just when I came downe out of pulpitt.

Sept. 15. This weeke past the Lord was good and gratious to mee, and mine in many outward mercies, in our health, peace and plenty, the small pox proceeded no farther this weeke, blessed bee the name of my good god. my navel was a litle moist one day, but not sore, I did not dresse it, The weeke was wett the waye wonderfull bad, much corne still abroad, the lord for his mercy sake give a good seed time, this weeke wee returned thankes to god for our

[1] Battle of Dunbar, 3 September.

Irish victories, the Scots victory true, wee heard of the wellfare of Major Haynes after our victory, for which the lord bee praised, this weeke the Lady Elizabeth second daughter of the King dyed in the Ile of Wight whither shee and her brother were sent, this is the first of them that fell by the hand of god in all thes trouble, there are 5 more of them still living. 3 sons and 2 daughters; This weeke I had much experience of corruption of spirit, easily yeilding to corrupt meditacions the good Lord in his mercy heale mee, Lord to thee I look doe not thou leave mee in or under the power of my lust of heart whatsoever. god good to mee in the Sabbath for which I blesse him

17. sold my pasture in litle Bridgmans to Hatch, he is to leave it November. 1: next he is to pay mee. 6^s. 8^d. I received 1^s. in hand, this I sold because he trespassed mee very much in it, and so I shall not bee troubled in these wett seasons to looke after it.

Sept: 22: The Lord mercifull to mee and mine in our health, peace and plenty, he hath preserved the towne this weeke also from the infection of the small pox that it hath proceeded no farther, for which the lord bee praised: The season is very sad in wett hinders seed time, raiseth corne already, rotteth our muttons how sensible wee are when god is against us in the creatures, but not sensible of our sins which are the occasion of this. my navel continued well this weeke I did not dresse it when it was last moist, in time my god will perfectly heale mee, he knoweth what is best for mee, and on him I will waite for the same my heart very apt to some of its former vanities, lord bee thou my strength for of my selfe I have no power to keepe close unto thee, The lord was good to mee in the day which was a comfortable day, he in mercy pardon my sins accept my soule, and make mee serviceable to the glory of his name in the good of my people. my sonne Tho: goeth on very well in the learning of his booke blessed bee my god, sanctifie his heart also oh my god that hee may bee thy servant, and a comfort unto us

26. a messenger with mee from Cambridge to acquainte mee with the sicknesse of Mr Richard Harlakenden, I went downe to his father, he was very much composed in spirit, for which I rejoyce, he sent to Cambridge, I had offers of an usher I demurred therupon untill the spring. my schoole lands ordered to pay taxes which will bee 7^{li}. a yeare to my hindrance,

Sep: 29. This weeke the Lord was good to us all in outward mercies, the latter part of the weeke very comfortable and fair, which abated the price of corn which was encreasing: Jane very ill one night but comfort returned in the morning(.) my deare wife complaines of a weaknesse in her knees the good lord heale her of it for his pretious names sake, my stuffing continues so as I wheeze I doe not find my breath short, the lord in his due time will helpe there, my navel and issue through mercy no trouble nor perplexity to mee of many dayes, the good lord command mercy for mee therein I intreate him, my heart full of its old pranks lord take them into thy hand and subdue them utterly I intreate thee and doe mee good, the lord good to mee in the Sabbath good hopes of Mr Ri: Harlakenden at Cambridge the lord spare him for his goodnesse sake.

Oct: 2: a very comfortable day. wee heard also good newes from Mr Richard from Cambridge, of his recovery the lords name bee praised for it, the engagement is prest in Cambridge to out many honest men,[1] and to admitt divers young and rude blades because engagers, Tho: Humfry came to keepe with mee October. 1: 1650: god blesse him with mee for soule and body.

Oct: 6: This weeke the Lord was good and mercifull to mee, and to all mine, in all outward mercies, my cold continues which occasions mee to wheeze and to cough now, and then a litle, god will command mercy for mee therein, in his due time; This weeke through mercy I was not so annoyed with vanity in my minde, tis a mercy when sin is diverted and prevented by imployment. but when it is mortified that is as life from death, lett not my heart bee only purged, but healed I intreate thee, the lord gave us divers good dayes for seed time, corne fell wee are beholding to god, and not to one another for what wee have, wee are apt to make a prey of one another, the lord was good to mee in the worke of the day, in the seasonablenes of the word; the lord in mercy, make it to prosper on my heart.

7. Paid Mr Harrington his money due by bond

Oct: 8: A day of thanks for the great victory in Scotland, wee rejoyce not oh Lord in their calamities but in our preservacon, wee preferre not ourselves to them because of our successe, but acknowledge wee stand in the greater and stronger ingagements unto god, wee continued the day at the pryory untill night, the lord rejoyce over us to doe us good

9: went about the paire of staires out of the hall into the chambers, sett up my skreene in the hall the weeke before, which wee find

[1] The Engagement was finally passed on 2 January 1650; it was made obligatory on a long list of officials, including graduates in the universities and ministers to be admitted or receiving augmentations; it was cancelled in January 1654. Shaw, ii, p. 76 (note).

very warme and convenient for us: tis of god wee enjoy any refreshments that others want(.) the small pox at Pilgrims, lord preserve mee and mine, and as thy affliction hath beene very gentle in due time remove it from us.

10: 11. 12: busy about my house; which was effected with indifferent good content to mee the lord make mee to enjoy it free from violence with the love of my people amongst whom I am that they may not bee of a forward heart, and then give mee in his time a tabernacle made without hands

October. 13. This weeke past the lord was very good to mee, and my company in many outward mercies, my wheezing continues, but my cold is not so bad my chest was not very much stuffd, the continuance of it was the trouble or rather the feare, my wife made mee a sirrup of steeped hissope in hissope water,[1] which through mercy did mee good,

The lord good to mee this weeke so that my worke was done without hurt or discontent, the lord kept mee more free from divers annoyances of heart then formerly, the lord in his due time putt all corrupcions under mee, the lord gave mee mercy in respect of my navel, which though it fared as if it were ill, yett I did not find it so, neither did my issue though it appeared not at stated times as formerly cause any sorenes, the Lord was good to mee in the worke and duty of the Sabbath, he ingaged my heart in love unto him

Oct: 20: This weeke the Lord was good to us in many outward mercies, my litle ones a great greife to mee in their sudden cryings out in the forepart of the night, my heart out of frame because of my unquietnes, when in frame it troubles mee not what is amisse, Lord what a mercy it is to have a wife to cover infirmities, to remove occasions,[2] so that a man hath no outward helpe, but what he hath from thy grace, my navel was moist this past weeke, not dressed this weeke the weather variable, my head troubled with a great pose this day(,) I cannot positively imagine how taken except with cold at a night, or going abroad till I was hott, god was good to mee on the Sabbath

23. dined and lay at my lady Honywoods. Mr Harlakenden was very wett in his coming home, it was a good providence to mee that I escaped the raine, Mr R. Harlakenden and his tutor came to Colne, the engagement outs many deserving men from their fellowships,

[1] 'A decoction of Hyssope made with figges, water, honey, and rue, and drunken helpeth the old cough', Gerard, *Herbal*, p. 131.

[2] A line crossed out in RJ's ink as follows: 'but what another trouble when out of frame, all *provocacion* to set *on mee* farther'.

its thought there will fall a sad blowe upon the ministry, the universities, and their meanes, the report is that one moved whether there should bee any standing ministry in England, but that is somewhat too much yett for this early day.

Oct: 27. God was good to mee and mine this weeke in our outward mercies, my litle ones, now and then shreeke out in their sleepe perhaps by reason of wormes the lord bee their helpe to whom I commit them, this day I was at Halsted and Mr Collins for mee, the season is wonderfull wett

28. received my tith from Goodman Abbott, very lovingly and quietly for which I blesse my god, was with Mr Jacob, and kindly entertaind by him he promiseth mee my money speedily.

31: this[1]

No: 10: The dayes past, god good to mee and mine in outward mercies health to us, while others sicke, god good therin, to my good freinds at Priory. the lord good to mee in my navel which I dressed not many a day, its now and then moist but not sore, blessed bee my good and mercifull god, the lord was good to mee in keeping my heart in some measure close to him, he in mercy pardon my sins and accept mee for his name sake

11: writt and sent by Mr Harlakenden a lattin letter to Dr Wright, in humble thanks for conferring the schoole upon mee, die 8. 9. 10.

Pose. I had a pose some litle stuffings in my head and chest, and on the 13th my gummes swelled as usually: I am advised to take 5 pils sine quibus esse nolo.[2]

☞ 13. at night, my thoughts having beene much on the kingdome of christ that shal bee sett up in the world, and desirous of god my eyes might see his salvacon, I dreamd that wee of our nation were instrumentally imployed about that worke in France, and that the court thereof was pure, I was making joyned[3] worke to use there and that I should receive a letter from the grandees of the army in Scotland the latter part thus as for that academicall opinion what wee shall doe in that wee knowe not. Erit aliquando nu(ov)o nunc est[4] viz a kingdome of christ in the world—implying that worke is begun already in England.

when I was awake and musing on it, and of my thoughts: my

[1] One line blank.

[2] Without which I do not wish to be.

[3] Joined: put together as a whole, specifically of furniture made by a joiner (a joiner, a craftsman who constructs things by joining pieces of wood). NED. The sense of the passage is not clear.

[4] It is now I declare it will be at some time.

thoughts were filled with the expressions to Simeon,[1] wherein my heart rejoyced; Lord I desire to helpe on this worke, for thy glory, my saviours glory. oh hasten it the power to effect it that must come from thee,

our actings in France in my apprehension were not above 2 or 3 yeares hence in a short time,

16: This night Mrs Church invited mee and my company to supper, where wee were used very curteously, my wife apprehends shee breedeth, lord if so, give it life and grace to serve thee and comfort our grey haires.

Nov: 17. This weeke the Lord was good to mee and mine in our health and in providing for us, when others are in great wants, and the smal pox in two families yett my god hath kept mee and mine for which I praise his most holy name the lord good in keeping mee freer than formerly from divers annoying lusts, oh that they might rott, and rise no more, my thoughts much that god was beginning to ruine the kingdome of the earth, and bringing christs kingdome in, and wee English should bee very instrumentall therein; god taketh away our enemies abroad viz the Prince of Orange, which is

Navel

a great worke as things stood there and here, my navel was moist and so had continued about 2 dayes: the lord was good to mee and to mine in the Sabbath, and in the exercises thereof he accept mee in mercy, and doe mee good for his names sake.

21: my wife concluded shee was with child, with a sonne, the lord sanctifie it for his owne, recieved of late divers kindnesses from divers of my freinds, the lord in mercy, requite them,

No. 24. This weeke the Lord was good to mee and mine in our peace, plenty, health, a great mercy considering the times and sicknesses of others, onely my deare wife droopes in her apprehension and I sometimes feare it, which shall make mee more tender over her, oh that wee could feare sin, as wee doe outward troubles, the lord was good to us in outward mercies, and inward, peace of conscience, a freedome from many vaine imaginacions, lord bring my heart in tune for thee, the season continued open, and wett, yett indifferent winter weather, heard of the health of Major Haynes, Mr Owen, Mr Harlakenden ill, lord restore his health to him, and to his family for Christ Jesus his sake, god was good to mee in the worke of the Sabbath, and in the word, the Lord in mercy accept mee and doe mee good: my deare wife complaines much of her head; shee is

[1] 'And it was revealed unto him by the Holy Ghost, that he should not see death, before he had seen the Lord's Christ', Luke 2: 26.

now certaine shee breedeth not, Lord lett her health and dayes bee pretious in thy sight.

26: I was now without mony, and so had beene for divers dayes, and having 2 threepenny peices, I seing the wants of others great resolved to give them both, and one I did, I could not see the other woman I intended to releive, see gods mercy when wee eye him in what wee doe, I received in divers moneyes presently for my want, there is no losse in giving where god gives opportunity.

30: This latter part of the month good and seasonable weather, and this morning it was a very fine sharpe morning, and snowy. This day Mrs Harlakenden shewed mee Mrs Bettee's water, I conceived it portended the stone, and shee two or 3 dayes after, concluded that it was no other, heard of the death of young Robert Crowe, the lord taketh where he pleaseth, oh lett mercy and goodnes follow mee all my dayes,

December. 1: The weeke past the Lord was good to mee and mine in our health, peace, plenty. when sicknesse, death, and scarcity is in the houses of so many, it is matter of rejoycing to mee, that god give mee an upright bent of heart to perfect holynes in his feare, notwithstanding my weaknesse and corruption, the lord sett my heart much after the kingdome of christ that shalbe in the world, not for any advantage to my selfe, but nakedly that I might bee instrumentall to honour him in the same, the lord is good to mee in making my studdies and employments easie unto mee, as also in contenting my heart under various providences, he was good to mee in the Sabbath, he accept mee and mine and people and blesse mee for his names sake,

3. warrants out to raise the Horse and foote in our County, because of the troubles in Norfolke, this matter is in the darke to us as yett though talkt of divers dayes god I trust will give a good issue hereunto, gave in a particular of my schoole rents as they were September. 29. 1650. viz. 62^{li}. 3^{s}. 4^{d}. yearly, its pretended to ease us of our assessments which if so I shall bee glad, but I duobt not.

☞ 4: Sett this day a part for a day of fasting and prayer, to seeke god for his blessings and grace in and through christ for mee, and all mine, to make mee instrumentall for his glory in all my relacions and imployments, and that he would bee my hiding place in all troubles, especially to discover to mee, what he is about to doe in these dayes, and that not for my sake, nor for any honour or advantage to my selfe, but that I might serve him, and his christ therein,

The Revelacon containeth a prophesy concerning the church, and the state thereof not only meete to bee knowne, but wherein lieth a great happines, Revel. 1.3.[1] lord how shall I keepe it except I knowe it, and how shall I knowe it except thou shewe thy minde to thy servant. for this end I read, and meditate of these things and compare them with the rest of thy word, and use the labour of thy servants, and joyne supplications and fastings. Hosea. 14.9. wisedome and prudence is required to knowe thy wayes, and righteousnes to walke in them, lord I would knowe them for this end I might walke in them to thy honour. Lord thou art the god of wisedome, give it mee (c.o. up) for thy mercy sake in christ;

what is in thy pleasure to doe, ought to bee in our hearts to desire, and that with confidence, Psal. 25.14 The secret of the Lord is with them that feare him, Pro. 3.32. his secret is with the righteous, and so thou didst to Abraham, tell him what thou wert about to doe and so for Daniel, John. Lord the things of our age and generacion discover to thy servant, or other of thy servants for thy christs sake.

Thou blamest thy people, that th(e)y knowe not thy judgement, Jerem. 8.7. when the storke and crane knowe theirs. Isay. 1.3. alas lord, what is my minding and considering without thy helpe. Lord unto thee, I lift up my heart, direct mee, leade mee not into any error, suffer mee not to be ledde into any for thy name sake oh my god—make a covenant of life with my sisters in the flesh my deare wife, children, servants

I found no present answer, but in one particular, hopes of one Layer, awakened by the word who was with mee, and in the morning called up and acquainted by Mr Harl. who was sent for to (c.o. Cambridge) Chelmsford; that the Norfolke businesse was somewhat allayed, it being only an attempt of a few mad blades to proclaim the King. and this proved true, god shewing us the rod, and telling us, what might have beene done, but not letting mans rage prevaile to doe us the least hurt,

December: 8. This weeke past, the Lord was good and mercifull to mee and mine in our peace, health, plenteous provision, the small pox spreadeth no farther yett blessed bee god, the Lord stay it for his mercy sake, The lord was good in not letting any sin full lust have dominion over mee, oh that my soule could admire him, and walke worthy of him, and obey him: the Lord was sweete to my spirit in the word shewing mee the realnes of his fullnes and of that

[1] 'Blessed is he that readeth, and they that hear the words of the prophecy, and keep the things which are written therein: for the time is at hand.'

supply that is in him suitable to all my straites and wants whatsoever(.) the lord maketh mee still inquisitive after the times and seasons and what he is doing, lord lead mee not into any error or mistake thereabout I humbly intreate thee, but preserve me spotlesse to the coming of christ, that I may give up my account with joy: tasted of gods goodnes in the bounty of some freinds towards mee

Revelacon & Brightman. 9. Begun to peruse the Revelacion, and Brightman upon it,[1] a great encouragment thereunto is what is written. Rev. 1:3. of the blessednes of them that knowe, and keepe the words of this prophecy.

12. at night I dreamed that Major Haynes writt mee word, that all the Scots feild forces were broken, and driven to the Orkney ilands, and that they had taken foure shipps with rich accomodacions, and that now there remained nothing but to reduce a few scattered castles and strengthes. heard this morning as if Carr and his Scotch forces were routed by our horse.

14. Being at my Lady Honywoods this night and viewing the passages of the 7 vials. I conceive they are all powred on the beast, and his accomplices. Rev. 16.1: all on the earth: the 4th vial on the sun. is on Kingly gover(n)ment, and rulers under them the angels that powre them out Revel. 15:6. are great Magistrates that feare God and raised to their power by joynt endeavour of people with them. this hath taken effect already in England, though not compleated.

December. 15: This weeke past, the Lord good and mercifull to mee, and mine in our health, peace plenteous provision for us, I was this Lords day a helpe to them at Coggeshall in Mr Owens absence in Scotland, I had a good jorney outwards, and homewards for which I desire to blesse the name of my god.

17. Heard farther good newes out of Scotland our army getting health, the enemies now sickening, their divisions, still confirming me god is casting downe princes, and that family in particular, that he shall not be crowned, nor reigne long their, but die an untimely death to himselfe, but in good time for his kingdomes.

18: was with Mr Harlakenden discoursed of our meeting, the lord was much with him, and somewhat with mee, wee intended to bee at it early,

December. 19. My deare wife and I wakt and rose in due time, my morning frame very comfortable, my heart with wife and family,

[1] Thomas Brightman, *A Revelation of the Apocalyps* (1611); the most famous commentary and source of much millenarian speculation.

and by my selfe bent to the worke, and a restraint of vaine thoughts, the lord bee with mee, and poure out affection and grace upon us all in the worke for his owne holy names sake. the Lord was very good to mee and the company in the day, our number was very great more then ever I saw at such a meeting, and the lord gave to us more affection then ordinary, wee had a very large contribucon, and my wife had provided plenty of cake.

at night my heart settled much expecting within a short space of 3. 4 or 5 yeares to see christs worke against the beast much advanced, and that on these grounds. from 395. when the Beast and Kings arose to 1656. are just. 1260 dayes or apocalipticke yeares: to 1653. are 6 times Adams age who dyed at 930: which is annus mundi. 1580: —1656. in the same yeare after christ in which the world was drowned after the (c.o. floud) creation that being anno mundi. 1656.

Decemb: 22: This weeke past the Lord was good and mercifull to mee and mine in our peace, health, plenty in outward mercies, watching over mee and mine and in preserving us from the sound of violence, when two of my neighbours houses have beene broken up whereof one lost much, for which I am heartily aggreived(.) the lord good to my deare wife who doth not so much complaine of illnesses as formerly, oh that mercy might throughly sanctifie us, I have not had much trouble in my navel or issue many a Day, for which I desire to blesse the name of my good god, many annoyances of heart I have not much heard of, the lord in mercy to my soule preserve mee from every evill way, the lord was good to mee in the worke and duty of the Sabbath for which I blesse his holy name; Margaret Potter went from us, and Mathye Bull came to us at night December 20. 1650. god blesse her with us and doe her good for soule and body;

This day I quoted that place. Revel. 21.9.10. whence my heart noted; from one of the 7 angels pouring out the vials shewing the bride: that some of the angels that poure out the vials should live to see the new Jerusalem; this shortnes of time a great depth of comfort: and this sight is on a mountaine which is an allusion to the passage of the divel towards christ, noting out a kingdome a great distance from Jerusalem, and what should that bee but our deare England in the farthest corner of the world.

Ezech. 40.2.

23. Mrs Barrham went from us towards Ireland, this day sealed a lease of Pickstones to the widdow overal for 22^{li}. per annum the first lease I sealed of the schoole lands. 24. paid Mr Harlakenden my

fine for Mrs Maries land viz. 12li(.) The times are hard tis a great mercy that in these declining dayes I am able to pay any of my debts.

☞ 27. The slaying of the witnesses is either general or particular, if particular as it seemes to bee, tis where there is a tenth of the City. and that is England a separate part from the rest, and in the Popes opinion alter orbis. if so their slaughter was before this parliament, and there rising by them who called them up to heaven anno. 640. who slew 7000 of clergy men and their dependants and courtiers deprived them of their revennewes about that time that is shortly after, for they attempted that yeare and effected afterwards, the remnant affrighted and gave glory to god, the nation generally honoured good men complyed with them who lead them in their peticons and actings and landings: now Ezechiel saith the visions of restoring was like the vision of destruction: chap: 43: 3: now he tells us chapt. 40. 1: in the 25 yeare of their captivity in the begining of the year (of) the 10th day of the month, in the 14. yeare after the City was smitten. he saw the vision: so then. 11. years from his captivity the City was smitten. so that anno 1651. will complete the smiting worke of the 10th part of the City. where the ruine of anti christ begins, and 14 yeares after that bring forth the new Jerusalem viz Anno Domini 1665;. the glory of god went from the temple; at the north doore. Ezech. 8.3. rested on a mountaine on the east of the City Ezech: 11.23. and goeth out at the east gate. Ezech. 10.19. in those gates the wickednes committed, and the way the lord reenters the way sin disposed him Ezech. 43.1.2.4, Ezech. 44.4. so at the north gate;—Lord shew mee the patterne of thy house the goings and entrings in of the same, and though thou stealest in upon us as a theife in the night, yett lett thy servant see his owne abominacions, and bee upon his watch for christs sake to discerne the entrance of thy glory.

[Margin: 1651 or 53 annus gratius sanctis in anglia 1665. in universo gentio-(rum)]

This great worke the Kings of the East, helpe on mostly, but the North England and other parts also and the worke in England was eastern worke, the armie were in the Easterne association when they refused to disband, seize on the King, and Cromwell is of the East, and there are many more in the East than in any parts of England that attend this worke, and now they are gone into the North for the like attempt on Scotland and then declared king. Lord for thy christs sake lett thy secret bee with thy poore servant. Psal. 27.4.5. in my ordinary course of reading were a refreshing to mee, and sett home upon my spirit, according to former apprehensions, that god would marke mee and preserve in these desolacions to see him in his temple in glory.

Dec: 29. This weeke the lord was good and gratious to mee and mine in our peace, health plenty and all outward mercies for which I blesse the name of god, still the lord keepes us from the small pox, which continueth still in some families, my deare wif(e) somewhat more healthfull than formerly, both my lambes somewhat troubled with settings in their chests, the Lord in his due time will ease them of that also, my navel a litle issueth but not sore I blesse god, my backe part of my head itcheth and paineth me, as former yeares it did, I conceive its a rhewme(.) my heart is exceedingly troubled with vanities and turned this way and that so that I cannot with quietnes of spirit attend to gods worship. good lord cure mee of it, the lord gave me helpe this lords day Dr Youngs sonne.[1]

☞ The great things in the Revelacon are held out by 7.7 seales, trumpets vials, thunders that utter their voices when the sixt seale is opened then is the breast bustle against the empire heathen. Revel. 6.12. the 7 seale as a seale is a rest, and nothing done untill the trumpets that then sound, act their parts. Revel. 8:1:2:
at the 6 trumpet stirres to purpose. Revel. 9:13. when the seventh sounde then time no more, the rest is at hand: so the 6t vial is the acting one Revel. 16.12. when the 7 poured out then rest v.17. now it come into my minde the creation distinct by 7 dayes is pointed too. the 6 day is created the least and in the latter part man. the 7th day is a day of rest god ceaseth from his worke of creation.—the 6 dayes are the 6000 yeares of this worlds continuance but that they are shortned by the wonderfull numberer: this day at the 9th houre was Adam created at the 9th hour of that day christ suffered, here is 250 yeares abated, and perhaps if wee deduct christs age. 33 yeares and a halfe. the bringing in of the second Adam to reigne in the restitucon of all things should bee perfected anno 5726: 1/2: the shortning for the elect sake answerable to Adams shorting of his day. may bring the beginning of these things very neare our times. however wee are come into the afternoone of the 6 day of the worlds age, the world now being 558 yeares old, yett a litle while and he that will come, will come and will not tarry. Cant: 8: a history of the church arising and a wildernesse, a desolate condicon, wherein the profession of religion scorn and neglect of ordinances abound, so that scarce any face of religion, and unsetled condicon, all as it were pluckt up by the rootes, and all to bee now planted:

[1] The son of Edward Young, D.D., Dean of Exeter, 1660. Venn.

national church dissolved, and particular churches taking place, which being a new plantacon, the national church and principles lye desolate, but shee leaneth on her beloved to uphold her, and to enable her to effect her worke against anti christ.
the litle sister the Jewes to be converted: the vinyard the church Sol: 1000. the 1000 yeares of christs reigne on his saints. the 200 y(ear) of particular saints living and continuing on earth by the peices: the conclusion is the churches prayer, which is mine, come my love, oh my deare saviour, lett thy salvacion drawe neare, oh how thou skippest over the hils, leape in at the morning windowe of my spirit I humbly intreate thee; two things my soule pants after. viz. The great worke and alteracions god is making and doing in the world, the advancement of his saints. the giving the nations to his christ, the particulars of this worke, and the season of these, for they have their sett time. oh bee with mee an unworthy creature, for mercie sake to discover thy minde to mee though an unworthy sinner my heart is sett on that on this worke for thy sake oh my saviour.

December. 31: Before the final ruine of the Romane Empire (which is ☞ the horse man of Austria, and the Kings of the west which are part of that fourth beast, and all of them are the whole beast) there shall bee a spirituall kingdome of christ, which towards the end shall have instruments quite fallen of from the Imperiall and popish interest, which god will make use of towards setting up his king- * dome and ruining the other worldly kingdome. Dan. 2.44. Revel. 17.12.13. 14.16.17. now out of this tract of the Earth where these hornes reigne, shall arise the persons that destroy the whore, v.16. so that it seemeth still as some arise in every home or kingdome to carry on Christs kingdome and sett it up. some shall arise to oppose, but the side of christ prevailes, now in the doing this worke, and when he is doing it, the lord he calls his people out of her. Revel. 18. 4. how doe the reformed Churches or any persons of them still remaine in Rome. for they have renounced her doctrines as hers. her worship her discipline. as its beyond, beside, against the word: ay but not her interest, which is royaltie, and abetting that power that tends to keepe the Saints lowe: God calls them out from this, and calls it her, come out of her. (her other things are her marke, name or number of her name. thus god calls his servants in England and Ireland and Scotland, and those of his servants that stucke to her interest what havocke is made of them in Scotland, and how putt out of employment in England: lord save thine who are now like a firebrand in the fire, now wee heare many of the most godly Scots doe fall of from the King and his party, bring us of more and more. the Parliament. all along and the now acting party declare against popery. anti-christianity in all things, and Kings whom they call tyrants, and for libertie

This day heard that Edinburgh Castle was surrendered December. 24. past to General Cromwell, nothing can withstand gods purpose, nor hinder that which he intendeth, to accomplish, this castle was counted invincible, it endured about. 15 weekes seidge.

Jan: 1: This day I went to Messing, and dispatched my businesse with my Tenants, finding them at home, and receiving from them some moneyes I went thence to Toleshunt bushe to speake with one I desired to live with mee, in all gods providence was very good, over mee, I returned that night, it was exceeding snowy all my return this jorney was 18 miles by account, I was not gone 8 houres.

2: Peleg(ius) was borne anno. 1757: from the creation, abate 24 yeares for the odde dayes in our yeare more than the 360 in the solar yeare being 13 months 130 dayes to a month or at lunar yeares. 350 dayes. then there is abate. 73, which falls in anno Domini 1685, for Christ to finish his worke—nimrod rose in pelegs time, the first beast, the original of the golden head, in such a time from the 2d Adams shall christ ruine the Nimrod of the world.—or take current yeares. 1757. there is a promise of shorting these dayes for the Elect sake, which shorting what length of yeares it is time will discover: the word used for halfe time is uphala*g*, closely alluding to pelegs age the ground to mee of the noting Dan: 12. his 1290 dayes reckend (from Julians setting up the heathnish oracles, and from the Jewes endeavour to sett up their temple, which god overthrowing from heaven, they were thereupon dispersed and never since by any publike edict or attempt of their owne returned to Canaan, being in the 3d of Julian anno christian 363. as Baronius[1] computes, I end anno 1654. entring when wee may expect a preparation to the Jewes conversion, and that worke before completed in the Turkes ruine will require. 45 yeares the 1335. yeares ending 1699. entring.

so that the 1260 dayes in the Revelacon and the 1290 dayes in Daniel did not appertain to our people, or to one date for their entrance though perhaps they may end neare about one time.

[1] Cesare Baronio (1538–1607), cardinal; his *Annales Ecclesiastici* were first published in 1588–1607, and went into many volumes. The following allusions by RJ are to the years A.D. under which Baronius records events.

8^{li}. 10^{s}. This day sett of to Mr Richard Harlakenden. his quarter: 3^{li}. 15^{s}. and paid in money. 4^{li}. 15^{s}. in all 8^{li}. 10^{s}. towards the bond of 25^{li}. due to him Jan: 27 or 28. next. now my roll of debts is 77^{li}. 18^{s} 0^{d}.

4: The history of the world and the affaires thereof, from Julian. 360 or to the fall of the Romane Empire in Augustulus, is to be carefull observed by him that intends to understand the Revel.

383. A great decay of Gentilisme. Baronius.

389 Edicto Imperatoris inchohata hoc anno Templorum et confractio simulachrorum per *univer sum* orbem Romanum per plures annos ducavit: Baronius.[1] Gentisme a litle reviveth anno. 392. and afterwards. Baronius.

394. Theodosius wonderfully conquers Eugenius and gentilisme, and dieth. 395. annis natus 50. nō. *60* in which yeare Ruffinus exceedingly ruines especially the Easterne Empire in the keepe of barbarous nations. Baronius.

400. Gainas acts against the Empire: a comet that even toucheth the earth, and a sword barbarians ever hanging over the heads of the constant citizens. Ba.

404. Gentilisme acted. Bar.—A fire out of Chrisestome seate that burnt the Senate house: Baron: that note the rise of Antichrist on the ruine of the Empire, his fall and the fall of princes from such spirits as chrisostome was. ad annum: 1664: vel 66.

R.F. Innocent was then pope, and Innocent now is pope.

406 Rhadagalssius the Goth and all his army ruind in Italy. Bar.

407. The miserable destruction of Gallia by the barbarons. Bar. thy day of ruine is at hand oh France. R.E.

409. Rome beseiged by. Alaricus: the Temples of the Gods spoiled to redeeme the City Bar. the City beseidged againe and Spaine

410. divided by the conquering barbarians

Rome taken that yeare. by Alaricus and spoyled. Innocent the pope absent.

411. Millenariorum heresis per hoc tempus multos habebat sectatores[2] etc. Bar. this opinion now arose and was condemned not being rightly stated or understood, tells us the opinion in a due revolucion of time shall flourish and see Rome ruind. R.J. An Innocent now sitts at Rome, *(* the former in Alaricus time satt 16. yeares, *)* to whom it was moved this present yeare of Jubilee to make a universal

[1] From the emperor's unfinished decree in this year, the destruction of the temples and idols throughout the whole Roman world lasted for many years.

[2] Millenarian heresies during this time had many followers.

league of all his party against the English. I hope this passage being so like those passages of the ruine of Antichrist that in his dayes or

R.J. in this century of yeares it will bee fulfilled. Amen.

I conceive this was the last of the Jubilees. 25. yeare more shall doe much

Three famous ruines are of the Romane Empire, the 1st 365: the 2d 45 yeares after that: 410: the 3d. 45. yeares after that viz: 455: in the two last the City was taken and in part burnt. if wee adde Daniels 1290. yeares to 365: yeares: it is 1656: for my part from all numbers I expect before that time the darkening of the seate of the beast and his kingdome, or the Scotizing his kingdome, which is desolating it as Scotland in that part that is attempted, or else leaving them to a blind nonapprehension of gods judgments on them, as the Scots in 1650 were, so as to comply with Charles 2. to their ruine and so with these men not avoide it: adde 45 yeares more to this period and it will complete the dayes of our trouble and bring in our blessednes. Heard for certaine of the spoiling P. Ruperts fleete upon the Coast of Spaine Nov: last, the Spanish shew great affection to our Commonwealth: the French since gave the Spaniard a great overthrow at Rhetel neare Mouron. Philip one of the Q. of Bohemias sons slaine there.

Jan: 5. The Lord was good to us in our health and outward mercies this weeke past, in his presence with mee, and refreshing my heart with his love, tis he onely enables to beleeve, all the world cannot quiett the conscience. but god alone, my sinfull heart trembles if he suport mee not, the small pox now in divers families. god still preserveth mine for which I blesse and praise his most holy name, this day Mr Woodcocke preacht both times for mee

9. mett at Goodman Mathewes to endeavour to unite so as to receive the sacrament of the lords supper. divers willing. Goodman Mole, he fell of, because none were officers in his account,[1] and in respect of the publike place, my sonne Tho: ill with an ague I was apt to thinke more, the lord preserve us in mercy from diseases, if it bee his good pleasure towards mee,

10: This day my sonne was well, blessed be my god, it was a fit of the ague the lord prevent more of them, this day it rayned apace for divers houres, and freize as it fell and continued so divers houres, afternoone it thawed

frizing raine

11. This day my litle Tho: ague tooke him againe earlyer, the lord in mercy restore him,

[1] He believed that one did not need special officers to administer communion.

Jan: 12. This weeke past the Lord was good to mee and mine for soule and body in outward mercies, good in giving mee an insight into my estate and condicon and in an heart to eye him as my cheife joy, the lord good in my deare wife, who is somewhat better than formerly apprehends she breedeth, oh that my heart could delight in thee, lett it not be shutt up nor my heart straitned towards thee I intreate thee oh my god, the Lord was good and mercifull to mee in the Sabbath, and in the worke of the day for which I blesse his most, holy name,

preachd on phil. 4.19. and on Rom: 8.21: liberty from sin and freedome in holynes heard of the death of Mrs Elizabeth King who married Mr Potter, and dyed in childbed, thy goodnesses to mee in mine are great and many teach me to value them.

☞ 13. The reports from Ireland as if they intended a generall rising of all the Irish to destroy the English, and also from Scotland their King crowned they would all rise, and many in England to destroy this interest, my deare sonne had a very sad day of it, the good Lord in mercy revive him;

Rev: 16: I apprehend now the seate and throne of the beast al(l) one viz Rome, which is now darkened not destroyed til the 7 vial when the Cities of the nations as London Paris, Lisbon; naples etc fall also.

Jan: 15: bargained with old Taylor to sett up leantoo's to my barne for cowes and strawe and horse, I bad Appleton 20^{s}. at first and so I reckond it at utmost, I afterwards agreed to give him 6^{s}. 8^{d}. more, but he advised mee to Taylor who doth it for 20^{s}.

my sonne Tho: fitt much gentler than his former. blessed bee the god of his health.

16: The 3 great lights by history into the Revelacon are the Ruine of the Romane Empire which is the thing that letteth.—the rising of the 10 Kings with the beast. and these are past. and Seeme all to bee in the 4th Century wherefore I intend throughly to peruse the history from Dioclesian and downewards to find the period of these things: for the fall of antichrist I marke the passages of these times: afternoone mett at Goodman Mathewes, found persons in a great strangenes and lothnes to the worke, rubs. yett we cast our selves on god and proceeded.

17. my deare wife very ill, shee breedeth with difficultie, all our enjoyments are vanity and vexation, the lord uphold her, and blesse her fruite: my sonne through mercy missed his fitt. blessed bee the lord. my deare freind Mr W. Harlakenden had an invitacon from

Cromwell to take an imployment with him in the army. the lord direct him, and prosper him, I hope I have some freinds that shall helpe ruine antichrist.

Jan: 19. This weeke the Lord Good to mee and mine in our health, my sonne recoverd from his ague(.) my wife this day better than former blessed bee my good god. the Lord good especially in giving me a spirit more free from annoyances of Sathan, I having beene a through-fare for many vile uncleane, worldly thoughts, oh deliver mee for thy goodnes sake, I find a heart annoyed with vanitie in praying and dutie, the lord shall subdue that also: my heart many times quakes in the apprehension of my sinfulnes former and present, and the everlastingnes of wrath; which the lord seeth good to cast into mee, Lord thou shalt bee my righteousnes and my peace, the lord inclineth mee to search my heart, and helpeth mee not to cast away my confidence, but my soule closely followes him and he is my peace and sweetnes blessed bee thy name, neither doe I question my condicon to godward, though I tremble the Lord was in some measure comfortably with mee in the worke of the Sabbath I preached twice on Philip. 4.19.

Now I come to review this last yeare of my dayes past viz 34: and I find the lord hath made good the intimation that he sett upon my heart to provide for mee for my livelyhood: he hath in mercy given mee an indifferent proportion of meanes from my people: a large supply from the Committee for plundered Ministers, and also somewhat from the Committee of the County towards my losses by Goring,[1] and the death of my deare Freind Mrs Mary occasioned her to entrust mee with her estate, which I question will be no hindrance to mee, who also gave my daughter Jane one hundred pounds, and this yeare also god gave mee Earles Colne schoole(.) the Lord hath beene good to mee in my health, not so much subject to rhewmes and colds, my navel though sometimes moist, yett not sore, it dryeth of itselfe so as I have not dressed it for about 4 months, neither have I beene much troubled with my issue in the summer as formerly, nor seene it as yett this winter but in these mercies I have found chastisement, the death of my Deare Mary and Ralph, but they were not mine but the Lords. and Mrs Mary Church all togither in the space of 7 dayes, and yett this mingled with mercy, in the preserving my two that yett live, and giving mee hopes of another seed by my deare wife, but above all gods presence with mee to keepe

[1] Josselin received £12, according to the records of the County Committee. Smith, p. 167. For the events referred to, see 30 August 1648.

my heart upright with him, sensible of my failings, weaknesse, learning mee to cleave to christ at times of difficulty—speaking peace to my soule although sinfull and sometimes perplexed oh who can value this mercy.

Jan. 24. Concluded this yeare with my neighbour Mathew, in godly conference, and prayer with rejoycing and love, and cheerfulnes. our publicke affaires ended with peace at home. the nations abroad fearing us. only the Scots having crowned their King prepare great armies to invade us.

☞ The Summer past there was a great Earthquake in Archipelago. Candia, and reported by Mrs King an earthquake for a short time at Geddington in Northamptonshire where shee was. great innundacions in (c.o. Brussel) Flanders, and of the Seyne by Paris doing great hurt, these signes portend something.

35. Yeare of my age. 1650.

Jan: 25. Sensible it entred mee into my 35 yeare, lord bee with mee in the same, my heart lookt up to god in some more speciall measure than at other times for his presence and blessed(ness) and I trust in him for the same. Mrs King returned to us from her daughters buriall Mrs Elizabeth. Heard of Major Heynes health, the Scots intend a great army, and great matters, god will cull his owne out of them that shall bee a seed for after dayes and worke and many of the rest shall bee dung upon the face of the Earth, even so, when difficulties are on us, hold mee up oh thou my god.

26. This day preacht in order to the sacrament. the lord was good to mee and mine the weeke past in the word preacht. he in mercy accept of mee and owne mee for good, this day I sayd freely clearly ☞ as seing it, that one of the bitterest pangs of Englands travaile was yett to come, in this latter push of the Scots troubles, and stirrings within our selves,

29. Heard from Mr Clopton as if my 40^{li}. per annum were ordered by the Committee and that he had an order to receive 30^{li}. upon which mony is expected very shortly.

30. A day of publike thanks for divers successes in Scotland and at sea, I apprehend a great noise of trouble over England, and a great sound of praises of the saints who shall bee delivered from it, mett at Mr Harlakendens, I shewed them out of the scriptures what manner of persons were admitted to fellowship, upon their profession

of faith, not upon any reall worke of true sanctifying grace on their hearts

Tooth. 29. at night my tooth began to ake on the left side. 30. in the morning I bled them much with a branch of rosemary, which made them sore, at night it aked very much but 31. towards morning, my face swelled and was sore, and the paine for present out of my tooth, face.

Feb. 2. This weeke past the lord good to us in our health. my wife breedeth with difficulty(,) my face swelled and pained, I looked up to god on Satturday at night, for rest strength, and mitigation of it that I might goe on in my Sabbath worke and he gave it not as I expected, but abating the swelling and almost removing of prayer a sweet mercy, but sweete is his goodwill to mee in answering my calling unto him: the season was very faire and comfortably all last weeke, god he was good to mee in the word and worke of the day, went on indeavouring to (c.o. up) drawe up to a communion wherin lett thy presence oh god bee with us, the lord mercifull to mee in letting mee see the filthynes, and weaknes of my heart so that if I keepe not close to him, I cannot stand of myselfe, the lord was peace to mee in my Spirit, and uprightnes in some measure, blessed bee his name

5. Sett apart this day to seeke unto god for my wife, the continuance of her life and loines: 2. god would bestow upon mee a frame of her heart and on her, that suites the ordinance of his Supper, and helpe mee in trying my owne heart 3. that god would in mercy stand by mee in this worke with wisdome and uprightnes, and lay an awe upon the spirits of carnal persons not to bee a trouble unto us.

☞ 8: Lewis now reigning is the 65. King of France. its probable he may loose his crown and some other atteine it or the command of the kingdome, and he that is the 66. will doe feates to some purpose.

Feb. 9. My god was good to us this weeke in our health onely my sonne Tho. had fits of his ague, the lord sanctifie it to mee and remove it from him, my former illnes well, no paine or trouble almost with my face, the weather very good this weeke also, dry and sunshine much, the wind cold, Mr Owen returnd from Scotland, heard by him of Major Haines health, and successe in his employment, there are expectacions of some bustles in Ireland and Scotland, France is tampering about Mazarine, the lord was good to mee the dayes past, in helping mee against divers lusts that assaile mee, the good lord subdue all under his grace in mee, and make mee wholly and nakedly thine, the lord was good to mee in the word and worke of the day. the next weeke I appointed two meetings to receive the names of persons that intend to receive the sacrament togither, and to receive informacon concerning their fitnesse to joyne in that ordinance, the lords presence bee with us therein for good.

Feb: 11: 13. mett at my house as appointed, gods providence good to us in it, which I desire never to forgett.

14. Mr Harlakenden returned from London safe, to god alone bee given the praise of it

Feb: 16. This weeke the Lord was good to us all in our health. my sonne Tho. I hope is free from his ague, I find Satan now and then putting up old lusts into my minde and meditacion and god helping mee in some measure by his grace to crush them in the shell, I desire to give the lord praise and glory for standing by mee in my worke and calling(,) the lord owne mee and accept of mee therein for the glory of his owne name;

The weather very fine and gallant this weeke also, to god bee praise

Feb: 23. This weeke past the Lord was good to us in our peace plenty, health, in all our outward mercies for which I blesse his most holy name, his providence was sweete in the season, the weather dry and healthfull, my family and schollers preserved from the small-pox which yett is in the towne, the lords name bee praised, and for being health to my navel, and freeing mee from coughs and colds, but his sweetest mercy is his presence in my bosome sometimes to shake mee, and sweeten my heart with his consolacion and cause troubles to vanish, and to fly away,

he was good to mee in the word, and in the meeting of both sacraments this day(,) which had not been celebrated for neare 9 yeares.

Lords Supper,

The day after the humiliacion at my house wherein gods presence was much, Mr Harlakenden propounded if christians would, wee might proceed to administer the lords supper which I entertained with joye, and so did divers, twas propounded to divers christians about us, but wee had no helpe nor joyning from them but from Wm Cowell, but meeting privately about it, wee were still letted, but god gave us a resolucion to goe on wherfore wee desired Mole that hindred if he would not helpe to stand of and not hinder, who dissented, and reckoned no pastors now are in the earth as wee could gather, disowned baptisme; I declared if men did not in some measure owne all ordinances, I could not owne them in this: so now wee resolved on the worke, how few so ever would joyne and to trust god with the same, and to give publike notice to prevent offence, and yett to admitt none but such as in charity wee reckon to be disciples. Jan: 30. wee mett at Priory, divers presd that persons must make out a worke of true grace on their hearts in order to fellowship and this ordinance, I was ill with the toothake, yett I could not but speake, and turned them to all places in the Acts and shewed that beleeving admitted into Communion, and none rejected that professed faith, and then if their lives were not scandalous that wee could not turne away from them in this ordinance; this gave good satisfaction to our company, wee went on(,) appointed two meetings at my house to take names and admitt by joynt consent. Feb: 11. was the first, when divers came that wee could not comfortably joyne with, my heart quakt and our company feard before I did any thing, I sought god in private, and he sweetly answerd mee who art thou that art afraid of a man, and fearest not mee, which came with life, and brought of my heart upon it, I spake as god enabled mee, that wee should search peoples knowledge and admonish them in point of scandall, and Mr Harlakenden seconded mee, then praying I dismissed the company, and gave a liberty to go forth, and bade our company give in their names, most went, a few gave in their names: Thursday came Feb: 13. went stranger faces appeard. I sought god, he answerd not, I was resolved to rest on his former answer, I sought againe, and he answerd, I will never faile thee nor forsake thee, which word came with power, and commanded my heart. I admonisht divers, admitted others with consent, divers christians hung backe. wee mett. Feb. 20: in a day of humiliacion at priory, and there god was on our hearts and our company there gave up themselves to this worke about 34. after the ordinance was done, and the collection for the poore the rest withdrew wee stayed, and proposed whether any had any thing against another that wee might joyne as one bread, wee gatherd for bread and wine, and proceeded, Feb. 23. to celebrate the ordinance.

wee all sat round and neare the table, the bread was broken not cutt in blessing it, the lord pourd out a spirit of mourning over christ crucified on me and most of the company, and my soule eyed him more than ever, and god was sweete to mee in the worke, no vaine thoughts but wholly intent on the worke, no difficulty among ourselves, a savour on my spirit, but not that healing to my soule at present I desired, but I will waite on god in the way of his ordinances and blesse his name and leave his manifestacions to his owne time, praising him that it was not empty to mee

received an account from many of our society of the sweete and comfortable presence of god with them, the livelynesse of the actions in breaking the bread, and in powring out the wine, the lords name have the glory of all.

March: 1: the season cold and very sad, worke scarce, the poore in a sad condicon, and its feared it will bee farre worse with the spinner,[1] a great snow this day. Mr R.H. had a cowe died suddenly, the lord blesse my litle stocke, the small poxe are spread in the towne, about Holdens very much into foure families as said, the lord hath sweetly kept my family hitherto for which my soule admireth him, the lord in goodnes still protect us, and bee our health.

M. 2. The Lord was gratious to mee, and mine in our health, and outward mercies my deare wife apt to qualmes, but pretty cheerfull. my heart in some measure in a good frame, and my annoyances of heart which formerly troubled and swayed either appeare not or kept under by the grace of god, the season cold, and things hard, price of corne and commodities rise, and litle or no worke, the worke at a present stand in Scotland, all things for present quiett in England blessed bee his name, last Monday morning Jane a litle above 5 yeares old, dreamd that Jesus christ was in our church, and went up into my pulpitt, and there he stayed a while, and then he came downe, and came into bed to her. shee sayd to him, why dost thou come to mee; and he answered her to sleepe a litle with thee, and he layd downe and slept, and againe shee dreamd that Jesus christ told her that he should come and rayne upon the earth 10000 yeares

the lord was good to mee in the Sabbath and in the worke and service of the day for which I desire to admire the holy name of god, Browne on the greene very sicke with the small poxe, my god preserve mine, I putt them under thy protection, say so it shall bee, ever amen sweet Lord.

5. I bought two cowes of Day at Halsted, and brought them home this day. they with their calves cost mee 10^{li}. 15^{s}. the lord prosper them with mee.

March: 9. This weeke the Lord was good and gratious to mee and mine in our peace, plenty and health, the small pox is in 6 families, lord still preserve mine. I gatt a great cold it continued two or 3 dayes. not so bad in my chest as formerly I blesse god at the first of it my nose bledd a pretty quantity. the season was very cold, and snowy. not very windy. a lions entrance and continuance untill now.[2] I

Cold pose.

[1] Spinner: a manufacturer engaged in spinning. SOED. Thus, those engaged in spinning wool for the making of the new draperies, widespread in this part of Essex.

[2] 'March comes in like a lion and goes out like a lamb', a proverb from at least 1620. *Oxford Dict. of Eng. Proverbs*, comp. W. G. Smith (3rd edn., Oxford, 1970), p. 511.

heard from sister Ann I sent her 10^{s}. and some other refreshings, blessed bee god that gives mee an heart, and hand to helpe her, the Lord was good to mee in this weeke in my spirit kept comfortably towards god, and my deare wife(,) my annoyance of heart not stirring, blessed bee god, oh cleanse (them out throughly) heard of the health of divers of my freinds, the lord was good to mee in the Sabbath for which my soule blesseth him, yett our tranquillity and peace is continued.

13. Mett at Mrs Churchs. our discourse was of the practice of love mutually one to another, wee resolved to meete Ap. 2 at priory, and to continue the day of prayer there. heard of the hopefull progresse of the gospell among the Indians in N. England the lord water it every moment. Rab: ben. Israel[1] is of opinion that the Jewes are scatterd from the North of Asia and Europe into America.

John Eliot[2] advanceth the worke. Eli is my god. John gracious. the instrument doth speake the gratiousnes of god unto them, in his name is the number of 52. perhaps by that time wee shall see a progresse to purpose.

His opinion is to rule them in civill and church matters by the word alone, and then god reigneth as king, which saith he is the kingdome of christ, and then the Saints take the government.

March. 16. The Lord was good to mee and mine in our peace, health, preservacon. three married women died out of one house of the small poxe, blessed bee god that hath kept mee and mine. T. Humfry was sickish one morning, my heart lookt up to my god and he was my trust, but the feare was blowne over presently, the weather was dry and indifferently warme, the lord in mercy stayed my heart on him, and made mee to keepe more close to him, for which I blesse him, and I find not my heart such a through-fare of vanitie as formerly. cleanse me lord throughly. god was good to mee in the word and worke of the Sabbath: the state seeme to act towards banking meanes for ministers and schooles which what it may prove towards mee I knowe not, but to my god I commit my selfe and wayes who hath and will provide for mee.

17. Ardleigh taxes at 32^{s}. 7^{d}. ob. repayres cost mee. 1^{li}. 10^{s}. 0^{d}. which

[1] Manasseh Ben Israel (1604–57), Jewish theologian and chief advocate of the readmission of the Jews to England. DNB. He was convinced of the imminent fulfilment of the Messianic prophecies of the Bible, and confirmed in this by the story of the discovery of the lost ten tribes amongst the American Indians. Hence the conversion of the Indians was necessary before the Second Coming.

[2] John Eliot, styled the 'Indian Apostle'. He learnt the Indian language, translated works including the Bible, and set up settlements, a College, etc. DNB.

I allowed: this day I payd Mr Har: 16^{s}. for use of his bond on which I owe 10^{li}. I payd. R. Johnson: 3^{li}. I owe him 8^{li}.

18: Brownebacke calved, the first of creatures that brought us young, god blesse our stocke(.) rid to Feering, baptized Elizabeth Josselin, the lord make her his, god good to mee in my jorney. received a letter from Mr Jo: Haynes of N. England.[1]

22. reported that Cromwell was dead, the Lord liveth, and reigneth, and dependeth not on any instruments for his worke, and this was my meditacion, and gods appointing Joshua to succeed Moses to lead them into Canaan wheras Israel was making them a captaine to returne into Egipt, when as Moses was in the mount, but a few dayes, and the promise of god was to mee he would not faile mee nor forsake mee, and my intimacion to my heart continued, god would preserve mee amidst all these stormes. at night our newes came, and Major Haynes letter of 8. of March, which said the Gen. was sicke and could not bee spoken with.

Mar: 23. This day the two chapters I read in course very comfortable, especially the latter Rev. 18 and .v.1: and that passage Babylon falls when shee sits as a queene, the newes of Cromwells death if true will extremely lift up the enemy, but god can ruine them when he pleaseth(,) after sermon I perceived by Mr Cressener that his death if so was kept close, he said the Scots army was come on this side Sterlin, the lord arise and awake for our good: the small pox hath spread no farther in the towne since, the lord bee praised in the preservacon of my family, those visited are upwards againe through mercy. Mr owen hath a place of great proffit given him vz. Deane of christ-church; the god of heaven was good to us in many outward mercies for which I desire to give him glory, lord cleanse my heart, and in mercy keepe it so, that I may live in thy sight, the lord was good to mee in the word preacht for which I blesse him. in the chapter that was read being. 1 Cr. 18: Commissioners are gone downe to order the affaires of the army in the unfitnes of the generall to doe it.

Spring was very backward this yeare. my apricocke tree had one white fayre bud on it, and my malegotoone another, never a blossome to this day.

24. bought two peices of timber of Mr Jacobs bayly at 6^{s}. 6^{d}.

1651. 25. Sett Day of Halsted a price of my farm called Mallories viz 245^{li}. I am very indifferent to sell or not, lord direct mee in all my outward

[1] John Haynes, governor of Connecticut, also of Copford Hall, Essex. His second wife was Mabel Harlakenden (see Harlakenden genealogy). DNB.

affaires for the best(.) the small pox appeared a new in 4 families more two neare us, the lord in his rich mercy preserve my family, in thy protection and goodnes I rest and am at peace, heard as if Cromwell alive, wee lost in attempts on a castle in Scotland 180 men as its said,
the small pox in two families more, the lord in mercy watch over us

Mar: 29. 1651: the value of my outward estate which god hath given mee.

Imprimis land as formerly Malleries Bollinhatch. 2 closes Colne	27^{li}. per annum.
In Mr John Litles hand money as was formerly mentiond—	50^{li}. 0.
this yeare I have paid the fines for my closes at 4^{li}. built, and layd out for the schoole about. 26^{li}.	
I have in money on Mrs Maries land and the improvement of it March. 25. 1651. past.	81^{li}. 0. 0
stocke. 5 cowes at 5^{li}. round. my nagge. 3^{li}. my hogges and hay. 4^{li}.	32.

I was then in debt 45^{li}. now I am about 70^{li}. which is 25^{li}. more than last yeare which taken out of my stocke there remayneth 7^{li}. which added to 81, is 88^{li}. and so much my estate is betterd blessed bee my god; but I hope my soule hath gained infinitely from god, whom I praise for all.

heard this day Mr Barnardistons[1] house at Colchester was burnt; the lord was good in his preservation, and my god hath hitherto kept me from fire and water and disease and I trust he will doe it:
Mar. 30: Preacht at Markeshall, my heart was very dull gods worke cometh of very heavily with mee, oh my god arrise and quicken mee. my heart very much anoyed with lust, yet the lord made them a loathing to mee, I did not yeild to the thoughts of them through mercy, oh that the lord would cleanse mee throughly, god good hitherto in the preservacion of my family, for which I blesse him and I trust he will still, the lord taketh of the bondage of feare much from my heart.

[1] Probably Arthur Barnardiston, recorder of Colchester, son of Sir Nathaniel, leading Suffolk puritan (for whom see DNB).

☞ read a paper sent from Poland, which on my grounds ends the Apocaliptique numbers in 1655. and accounts the slaughter of the witnesses to bee at hand in Silesia as the last tragedy, and then Romes ruine hastens by some Evangelical potentate, that shall unexpectedly be raisd up for that worke

☞ Lewis now reigning in France is 65th. king of that nation: he will loose his crowne, and the next that taketh it, or at least hath the power but perhaps not either the title of king or formality of a crowne ruineth Rome,

Ap: 1: mett to choose officers, wee agreed not, most scurrilously abused by old Wm Adam for dawbing with untempered mortar,[1] for Kendalls bond, for going to Halsted for 20^{s}. per day: lord I apprehend tis for thy sake I am thus dealt with, my soule desireth to submitt to thee and blesse thee,

2: This day sett apart for a publicke fast, the congregacion very full; my heart not broken though somewhat enlarged in prayer, the word very pretious, sweete, and comfortable, the lord was good to us in prayer at the priory, for which I blesse his name, heard of the relapse of Cromwell, the lord raise him up. there are 2 dead now in the towne of the small pox the lord in mercy keepe mee and mine in safety under his wings. this day wett and cold.

3. mett cast up the overseers accounts, it amounts unto 14 quarters within a litle, wee choose our officers without any trouble, and did our businesse with as much peace and ease as might bee,

Ap: 6. god good to mee and all mine in our outward mercies; I went to Kelvedon kindely entertained by Mr Wakering, the lord good to mee in the word preacht, I returned againe die 7°. a very comfortable day, the lord was good in the preserving mine. Cromwell well recoverd, the boates come to the Firth upon which wee expect actions,

Navel. this 7: day of April my navel was moist at bottome, the lord my god will keepe mee and preserve mee.

9. This day was goodwife Day with mee, I perceive shee is resolved to give mee my price for my farme of Mallories, and I intend to lett it goe, the lord was good to mee in my possession of it, and I hope will direct mee, and blesse mee in laying out my money in an other place,

Ap: 13. The lord renewed his mercies towards mee and mine in providing for us, and protecting of us(,) his hand is abated in the

[1] To temper: to bring (clay, mortar, etc.) to a proper consistence for use by mixing and working it up with water. SOED.

distempers of the small pox in the towne, they are up, and well in all families except two. the sense of his goodnes towards mee is
na. renewed in mee for which I admire and blesse him: my navel continueth a litle moist, but not very sore, I apprehend I feele it, the intimacions of god on my spirit are goodnes towards mee, but my wretched unbeleiving heart is apt to distrust god, I blesse him, that my heart is more tender towards him, sweetned with his presences ready to submit to his wise providence. for he knoweth what is good, and best for mee, and according to this word he doth, and will act; the season was very comfortable and cheerfull the weeke past; the lord when he seeth good will refresh the face of the earth with his dewes, that it may yeild increase, to the sons of men, the lord was good to mee this day in the word that was preach, I began this day to expound againe at Judges. 9. wee gave over our jangling chiming as they call it, the lord in mercy helpe mee in his worke, and watch over mee for good unto whom onely I resigne my selfe,

14. the small pox in a family upland, feared the wid. Rugles will have it, the good lord in mercy and goodnes pardon all my sins, preserve my family, sanctifie thy hand to them that are afflicted under the same,

15: In the 15 Chapter of that booke written by Bishop Usher entituled de primordiis ecclesianum britannicarum;[1] I find the Scots and Irish are one nation, and so the Irish owned them in the first of this rebellion. Fergusius 1us Scotorum rex, assists Alaricus in sacking Rome, they were terrible to the Britannes anno 360. and so on for many yeares, it may bee their fate is like the Irish to smart now by the Britans

Ap: 17. mett at Goodman Mathewes, I and Mr R.H. went from thence to Thomasin[2] to admonish her in respect of her peevishnes(,) the worke was solemne, and the lord I blesse him was with mee in the same. shee seemed to have a very slighting spirit in order unto communion and ordinance, the lord in mercy perswade her heart throughly, with whom wee leave her, praying for a blessing on this his ordinance.

19. This day I and divers others were witnesseth to Goodman Deaths tender of his 186^{li}. to Robert Reeve. heard goodman clarke was likely to returne into towne

[1] James Usher, *Britannicarum ecclesiarum antiquitates* (1639) is the nearest title in the STC.

[2] Thomasin is almost certainly Thomasin Harding (see her biography, Appendix 2).

April: 20: This weeke also the god of my mercies renewed his protection towards mee and mine, some others downe of the small poxe, my yett preserved for which my soule desireth to bee thankefull: my
na. navel continued somewhat moist, and foule but not sore, I did not yett dresse it: I leave my selfe to my god who knoweth what is best for mee: and I trust he will direct mee for the best, and will bee health to my navel and marrow to my bones. the season dry and now somewhat cold inviting unto action; many suppose our Commonwealth lost. Spaine and France and Holland against us. Ireland and Scotland heavy worke, and not to bee effected, the English divided, and worne out with taxes and burthens, the merchants trade ev(en) ruined, and so all tending to poverty. but if the worke be gods, there is enough in his arme to effect the same, and up to him his people looke to bee their salvation, the lord was good to mee in the weeke past in the frame of my spirit in giving mee a submitting heart to him in order to afflictions, and in leaving my selfe to god with quietnes of spirit for as much as he seeth what is best for mee and mine; the lord was good to mee in the Sabbath, and in the exercises thereof the lord in much mercy pardon my sin and accept my sinfull soule,

Bridge 21: given to Mr Har workemen who were in building the bridge. 6^{d}. the 22. I proceeded almost to finish my bargaine with Day for Malleries: die. 23°. I had 2 sow pigs gelded price 6^{d}. the first wee so had, great hopes of raine this morning. the lord refresh the earth with it: paid William Brand 5^{li}. I now owe him more. 5^{li}.

Ap: 27. This weeke also the lord renewed his goodnes to mee and mine in our peace, preservation and health, when divers are still found out by the small poxe, I trust god will marke ours for preservacion and hides us that evill shall not knowe of us, nor come neare us, the lord he knoweth what is best for us, and there I leave my poore sinfull soule; this weeke continued dry all the time and very cold, the lord in mercy refresh the earth, and not change the seasons, a sweet dew fell last night, and there are some hopes of raine, the
n lord for his mercy sake send it: my navel was well this weeke, I praise my god for I felt it neither sore nor found it moist: I did not dresse it at all, nor disturbe the same; this weeke was quiett no occurrences of moment, but wee beginne to expect action now every day: This weeke I found sluggishnes on my spirit, and a want of reason in my employment. my heart meditations of god are frequent and sweet, but many time in private and family my heart is much shutt up. the lord helpe mee. I found some old vanities

apt to returne againe, lord destroy them root and branch I humbly intreate thee; the lord was good to mee in the worke and duty of the Sabbath, the lord in mercy accept mee and pardon mee, I expounded twice, but writt but litle of it

great buzzines as if the D. of Lorraine would undertake the protection of the Irish, great feares and jealousies are abroad and among men.

April. 30. This day I surrendered Mallories and the appurtenances to Day of Halsted and his daughter. I received 193^{li}. downe and bond for 50^{li}. more, they are to pay mee 3^{li}. more very shortly. the surrender in Mr Littells hand. they are to abate the 14^{s}. for the wood to my Tenant.

May: 1: This afternoone wee spent at Mr Cresseners house in conference, about the Saints mutually praying for one another, with much sweetnes, unity, and unanimity for which I blesse our god, the lord daily build us up.

3. my noble freinds the Mr Harlakends. and one of their wives with mee eating a tansy,[1] and a messe of creame, wee being in preparing for London.—Seaver tooke of mee all the bushes in Dagnal to stubbe up by the rootes and to pull all the broome, he is to cleare the grounds for this I am to give him 10^{s}. and the broome, which I doe account to bee. 13^{s}. 0. 0

May. 4. The lord continued his goodnes to mee and mine in all our outward mercies, the lord spared the towne this weeke so as the small pox spread not, the lord kept all mine as under his wings and feathers for which I blesse him, the State of England beganne to bustle this spring, lord goe along with them and prosper them, this spring was very winterly cold, and dry so that [ ]eth bee exceeding cheape, and commodities grew very reasonable, [*and gods name*] be praised in it, this weeke past god was good to mee in my pathes in sweet[*ning*] my heart with the feare and love of himselfe, and in the apprehensions of his bowels and gratious bosome towards mee in all providences whatsoever. I found my navel well for which I blesse my god: the Lord was good to mee in the word preacht, the doctrine of contentacion[2] I intended sooner, but god would have Mr Potter who buried his wife heare some part of it, he preacht one part of the day for mee, the Lord bee with mee in my intencions for London and returne mee safe againe, I expounded

[1] Tansy: a pudding, omelet, or the like, flavoured with juice of tansy (a bitter herb). SOED.

[2] Contentation: the action of satisfying; the fact of being satisfied. SOED.

the story of Jepthahs daughter, whom I apprehend he did not sacrifice,[1]

5. this morning I sett forth for London, my Scotch hobbie[2] carried mee thither neatly that night, I dispatcht my businesse with Dr Wright, and came to Cranham next day, and home the next, god was in my absence good to all mine, and his hand over mee for safety in my going and returning for which I desire to adore him in the through Jesus christ, my freinds well att Cranham,

8. before I came home it rained and so continued neare 36 houres an excellent ground raine, this morning being 9. the sun shineth very sweetely

10. Jone Rayner buried of the small pox taken with conceit, in that place where often I have smelt a smell, my line and my health hath yett beene pretious in gods sight for which I praise him.

May. 11. This weeke past the lord made mee not only partaker of outward mercies for mee and mine but also made mee sensible of his goodnes to mee therein. the small pox continued in some families in this towne, god yett spareth mee and all mine; the lord was good to mee in the worke of the Sabbath, my heart was very much out of frame, yett the word was lively unto mee, the lord was good to mee in restraining many former follies though I find a core of evill in my heart, the mercy of god was good in the season in aboundant raines yett cold. in the lives of our freinds continued, my deare
n wife very ill, yett chearfull. my navel was moist this weeke, I had a litle red pimple thereabouts, I expounded the 13. and 14 chapter of Judges; its reported that the Irish and the Duke of Lorraine are agreed, he is expected in June next to bee with them.

12. Mrs Wm Harlakenden sicke of the smallpox tooke them with a conceit of a keepers touching her hand. I was with her when come out, but knew not of it, the lord can preserve mee in the fire and water, and in him I put my trust for mee and mine, and I hope he will doe it.

14: made up the reckonings betweene Mr Nevill, and the widdow Browne; and quieted their mindes in their dealings with one another.

17. The small pox at Sextins, still the lord is gratious in our preservacion for which my soule blesseth him, wee were accomodated for our jorny to olny the lord blesse us in the same.

May. 18: This weeke past the lord was good to us in the season, which

[1] Judges 11: 30–40.

[2] Hobby: a small or middle-sized horse; a pony. SOED.

was warme and dry all things very still and quiett in the nacon, the lord yett lengthens out our peace, wee heard of no great matters beyond the seas, nor of our forces in any place, but there are great expectacions that a shorte time will produce very great actions. The lord was good to mee and all mine in all our outward mercies, he alone is worthy of great praise, god good in sparing the lives of divers that are under the afflicting hand of god, the lord preserve them for his mercies sake, my poore spirit through mercy was not cloyed with folly as sometime it hath beene, neither indeed so full of sweetnes as the mournings of others, and my mercies through gods grace might have raised up unto, yett I blesse him, that he was in my bosome as an healing delight, god was good to mee in the word preacht, expounded Judges. 14.15. chap(.) this night I tooke my leave of Goodee Potter, never to see her more in this life, this is a seale of my ministry, whom Christ hath begotten by mee, in this my soule desireth to blesse the lord Jesus. Mrs Harlakenden finely cheerfull, shee sat up this day

May: 19: set forward towards Olny. my wife sonne, and John Crowe. my sonnes horse was broken pasture, and on his way towards Cambridge. at Haverill wee had company almost to our jorneys end. whither wee came safe and well that night for which mercy I blesse my god, 20: wee sett out towards olny. my wife had a fall. but no hurt, the onely hazard in all our jorney. the child held out well. this night goodwife Potter died. wee found our freinds at Olney well. that weeke I continued there, and preacht on the lords day on. 1 Tim. 1.13. there was in the towne a great difference about their Minister, another being presented by the Patron, and come downe, but the lords day was quiet, wherein I tooke some paines: 27. my wife was very ill, so as on 28. I rid alone to Benyfeild Lawne to see my mother and brother Jeremy and sister Betty. who live in Rokingham Forest I found them in health blessed bee my god. 29. Jeremy and his wife came backe with me to olny. 30: wee parted from olny and came well to Cambridge and 31. wee came safe home, the lord(s) mercy was very good to mee in all my jorney. I found all well and Mrs Harlakenden alive for which mercy I blesse my gratious god,

June: 1: This weeke past the lord was good to all mine in my absence, good to mee in the worke of the Sabbath, oh that my soule might bee made sensible of his love and goodwill to mee day by day, the lord was an helpe to mee, but I am neglectful of thee oh my god, oh pardon it unto me for thy name sake.

Norden. The litle blacke northerne cowe tooke bull. May. 31. Smallbigs buld. June. 2. both by brindle bulls; June. 10. morning wessney buld by Mr Littells bull. June. 12. Redbacke buld: June. 15. Brownbacke: July. 2. morning wesney.

3. Spent this day in prayer at Goodman Mathewes, my heart was very dull, and drowsy, the lord in mercy pardon it to mee, yett at latter and the lord gave mee some meltings and stirrings especially for the Navel. interest of christ in the world. my navel hath beene moist divers times but drieth againe of it selfe, the lord watch over mee for good for unto him I resigne my selfe.

6. a hearer at Halsted, the sermon very spirituall and profitable, lord blesse the towne and contry in the labours of that man, heard as if the Scots were neare Carlisle, the lord our god stand up for our helpe in whom I putt my trust: the great rumours of this weeke came to nothing, Cromwell recovers apace for which gods name

June. 8: bee praised. Mr R.H. gave to mee and my deare wife each of us one of his bookes which he printed, which was viewed and corrected by mee, and the postscript I penned,[1] the printer did full ill in the printing of it

This weeke past the Lord was good to mee and mine in all most needfull mercies. he kept mee and mine in health when its sad with others, the lords goodnes is towards the towne, the towne is now free from any that are actually sicke, the good lord still cover mine under his feathers; and teach us to proffit by all his dealings: my heart very apt to frowardnes, and to vanity, the good lord in mercy make mee more than a conqurour over all my many corrupcions, my navel through mercy continued ill, I had one lords day after minding god, god would give us a good issue to the Scotch businesse as a signe of it the small poxe should not proceed much in the towne, I could not then comply with it, as questioning whether it were of god, the lord in some measure begins to doe, and I trust he will doe it, and helpe mee to trust in him for this and all good. the lord was good and mercifull to mee in the duty of the Sabbath, the lord in mercy owne mee, and stand by mee in the same for his name sake,

9. The state of England although worne with civill warres, and scarcity and ill trading for many yeares, being but in bad terms with

[1] *The English Presbyterian and Independent Reconciled. Setting forth the small ground of Difference between them Both* . . . (1651), written by an English Gentleman, a Well-willer to the Peace of his Country. 140 pp. (B.M. E. 635(3)1651). The short 'postscript' says little except to recommend the work and stress the difficulty of treading a middle course.

Holland, and not altogither sure of Spain, proclaimed open warre with Portugall, and is in open warre with France, our fleets being in the midland sea: wee at the same time are endeavouring to conquer Scotland, and Ireland, attempt Silly with a fleet, and yett send a fleete also to reduce the ilands of Barbados in America: and yett the nacion is much discontent and divided, yett feard to name not the attempts of any forreigner against them

10: Lent Mr Litle this day 20^{li}. received of Goodwife Day. 3^{li}. this day my wife went to my Lady Honywood, where unexpectedly wee had a messe of pease for which my wife longed very much, this was a good providence of god, a mercy layd out that wee were not aware of.

12: Heard Goodwife Mole had the small poxe, the lord in mercy spare mee and mine, lent goodman Mathew 4^{li}. for 3 weekes.

June. 15. This weeke past the lord was good and mercifull to mee and mine in many outward mercies the lord knoweth my heart was in a very dead cold frame, for the Sabbath and I was very unprepared for it, carelesnes eates up my spirit, and I doe not stirre up my heart within to gods service, and yett my god (did not) faile mee, my navel moist and my belly in a part on my left side as it were sore, my wife ill, my daughter Jane this day ill, oh my lord quicken mee and doe mee good by all, I preacht twice, the day very hott, grasse burneth away, the lord in mercy heare prayer for a comfortable raine,

16. Dayes daughter came to sojourne with us. this day great hopes of raine, which passed away in the aire but not in my spirit. I expect god will heare prayer: mett this 17 day at Goodman Dowes, great hopes of raine, yett it went over, it shall come in its best season.

19. Heard of a great route given the Irish, a very seasonable mercy. die. 20. I went to Halsted returned well the day very hott, two families in towne more visited with small poxe, and through mercy, I and mine are yett preserved

June. 22. This weeke past the lord was good to mee and mine, and his goodnes was sweet in our preservacion. what am I. and mine, that wee are yett preserved from that hand of his that is abroad. this weeke my navel was moist. I had a litle wheezing cold. I sawe my issue and that with some sorenes to mee that I have not felt for a long time, but tis my gods doing, and I am in his hand, who promiseth all shall worke for good, and so I conceive these may and doe and I am quiet, a base backward heart in gods service is greater trouble to mee and not without cause then these straites.

the drought continued and is very sad to divers things the lord heare prayer and send raine, which I question not but he will in his appointed season, the lord was good to mee in the word preacht twice in Philip. 4.13.v:

23. about 3 a clocke this morning god answered prayer, magnified his goodnes to us in sending a sweete and comfortable raine whereof wee had some hopes the last night. Mrs Wm Harlakenden very ill small hopes of her life. the small pox is at Ed: Pott(er) god still good in our preservacion. this night also it rained so that I hope its at the rootes of all things, and yett their continue likelyhoods of more raine yett.

24: This day I paid Mr Harlakenden 4^{li}. 7^{s}. for his rent for Dagnal. the roll of my debts now is about. 57^{li}. 13^{s}.

☞ The Pope Clement 8: projected about 1530: the league to ruine the protestants, and destroy them in all countries reducing all to the obedience of the sea of Rome; Charles. 5 he projects a universall monarchy: the pope to entertaine the Emp: breakes downe the remaines of the temple of peace: and perhaps peace shall not be given to the world untill he is ruined though he intended the ruine elsewhere.

26: deare Mrs Harlakenden fell a sleepe in Jesus between 4 and 5 a clocke, shee said two or 3 dayes before shee should die on Thursday.

28: Deare Mrs Smythee Harlakenden was buried, I preacht on 1 Thess. 4.13.18.[1] 4 Justices of peace which had buried each of them his wife carried her to the grave where shee is layd up in her owne earth.

June. 29. This weeke the lord renewed his goodnes to mee in many particulars, the lord spared the towne this weeke, so that I heare of no spreading of the small pox. the lord was pleased to keepe my heart more free from any annoyances of spirit then formerly for which I blesse and praise his holy name. but sudden forwardnes in the apprehension of others failing seizeth mee. wheras tis my duty then to bee silent, this I preach, but tis the grace and strength of Christ must helpe mee or I cannot attaine it, god was good to mee in the Sabbath for which I was unprepared I preacht twice on Phil. 14.13.

July: 1. mett in conference at Goodwife Brownes. appointed next

[1] The sermon was published as *The State of Saints departed, Gods Cordial to Comfort the Saints remaining alive* (1652) (Wing, 1095). Extracts are reprinted in Macfarlane, pp. 220–2.

meeting at priory. July. 15 this day I received in 2 jagges of Hall meadow hay.

3. Rid to Redgewell, preachd the lecture on Phil. 4.11. about content, which the lord in mercy learne mee, I have more than ordinary need, having not so much quiet, as I have had, and now I misse my deare and neare freinds, whither I could presently steppe out and injoy their society, but they are gone and their place must knowe them no more

4. preacht the lecture at Halsted on Gal. 4.5. about adoption, the lord in mercy cleare it up to my soule that he is my father, thou dost it for which I praise thee, oh doe it more and more I humbly intreate thee.

July. 6. This weeke past the Lord was good to us in our outward mercies preserved through mercy from those distempers that are abroad: my deare wife hath now and then sad sicke fits: the lord in mercy support her under them, not onely with strength of life, but with the life of comfort, my sonne Tho: very ill one night, a good sleepe through mercy refresht and strengthened him, my selfe had a great pose die. 4° and 5° a litle, but its gone and falls not downe into my chest I blesse my god. even my outward troubles the lord may make use of, for outward good which I desire, and therefore in and under them I desire to waite to(o) upon him: the goodnes of god was upon my spirit more to quiett and still my heart, to enable against attempts of Sathan to keepe my heart from many annoying lusts for which I blesse his name: the successe of our forces in Connaught in Ireland is very great none being able to stand before them, from Scotland wee expect action in as much as the armies are on the march the lord bee with our forces to prosper them. Our ambassadors are returned from Holland, it is apprehended without doing the businesse for which they were sent. the lord was good to mee in the worke and duty of the Sabbath, the lord in mercy owne mee and stand by mee in his worke to that end. H. Hatch wife very ill, lord if it may bee still this infection amongst us.

8. sold my two cowes to Mr Littell I lost about 3^{li}. 10^{s}. by them. lent to Mr Harlakenden of the priory 8^{li}. upon an urgent occasion of his to use a summe of money.

9: drave my 3 wennells[1] to Mr Littells, who is to keepe them a month for mee, this day wee kept a day of prayer at Wm Cowells, and most of the women at Goodman Mathewes, in this day my heart was very much out of frame, caried away with foolish and vaine

[1] Weanel: an animal newly weaned, a weanling (can be any kind of animal). NED.

thoughts, it was a day of heate, prayer was answered ere next morning in one particular for raine, god giving us a very sweet showre, and there are continuing hopes of more which that wee might admire the god of our mercy, and knowe he hath an eare, and learne to trust him, in other straites and difficulties came accordingly. the water run downe the streates in a great shott[1] by 12 a clocke this 10th of July.

July. 13. The good Lord shewed still his graciousnes to mee and mine in the lengthing out our peace and health, one or two more in former families being sicke of the small pox, the good Lord in the riches of his mercy raise them up, and bee the safety of mee and mine in whom alone my soule trusteth, heard that Mr Love[2] was condemned to be beheaded July. 15. he and divers peticon for life, others call for impartiall justice, one Joyce that commanded the guard that surprized the King at Holmeby reports that the Scots commissioners and divers English engaged to rule the King by force and to put divers factious persons of the Comons house, and in the Country to death, my thoughts within mee were many times very vaine and troublesome to mee, oh lord my health and strength unto thee I looke, to frame my heart unto thine owne heart, the Lord was good and gratious to mee in the worke of the Sabbath, the lord owne and blesse mee in the same, and ingage my heart more and more unto him,

15. This day I payde to Wm Brand 5^{li}. I now am out of his debt, but I owe him love for his great kindnesse to mee, my roll of debts is
2^{li}. 13^{s}. now 52^{li}. 13^{s}. wee mett for conference at Mr Harlakendens, some of our company were somewhat from a due temper, the lord was good to us to beare it, wee appointed 24. to meete in day of prayer to prepare for the Lords table on the following day of the lord, the Lord in his mercy bee with us for good: it was apprehended Mr Love a godly presbyterian minister, would loose his head at London this day, the lord shatters us, and layes us lowe, I trust his presence is not farre of when thes shakings are among us. but upon his peticon his wives, and the Ministers of London he was repreived unto Aug: 15. next, blessed bee the name of god for this act of compassion extended towards them,

July: 20: This weeke past the lord extended compassions to mee and mine in our health, and outward mercies, I had an illnes in my

[1] Shot: a rapid movement or motion or discharge. SOED.

[2] Christopher Love (1618–51), an uncompromising Presbyterian, who was accused of corresponding with Charles Stuart; finally executed on 22 August 1651. DNB.

head taken through cold, and sweating in these hott nights. but now I find my head farre better than formerly, for which my soule heartily desireth to blesse my god, the weather hott and dry, no newes this weeke of certainty. though there were very great reports of things, the lord was good to mee in keeping my heart in some closenes to him and eying him in my wayes, he in mercy accept of mee, delight in mee and doe mee good, the lord was good to me in the worke of the day, I preachd in order to the lords supper, the lord in mercy accept of mee, and delight in mee for good. my navel continueth well through mercy for which the lord bee praised.

22: This day Mr Harlakenden went about casting his ponds, my 8^{li}. I lent him, he repaid mee, whereof 4^{li}. I paid to Johnson, I am now cleare with him but 13^{s}. for a loade of wood, my roll of debts now.

$48^{li}. 13^{s}.$ $48^{li}. 13^{s}. 0^{d}.$ Rob: Crow sett forward towards Derby I hope to heare from (c.o him by) my brother Jeremy by him.

23. Heard of the health of our freinds at olny, and that the Minister Mr Walwyn doth continue their still, I lent my neighbour Ri: Appleton 5^{li}. for a fortnights time,

24. This day our society kept a day of prayer at Mr Cresseners. god was with us blessed bee his holy name, two were admitted into our society this day, the lord make us to edefice and build up one another in our most holy faith

25. I lent to Mr Jo: Littell this day 50^{li}. I shall make this up an 100^{li}. he had 20^{li}. before in all. 70^{li}. he offers mee his meadowe at 5^{li}. per annum, which I conceive is very deare,

26: Heard of action in Scotland, the Scots tooke from us Newarke house in the west wherein wee lost 140 men, wee tooke from them Callendar house in the view of their campe, Major Gen Lambert Harrison with his Brigade in Fife routed a brigade of the Scots slew a 2000 on the place tooke many prisoners, the armies on both sides are marcht, action is expected the lord in mercy remember us

2500 slaine 1537. prisoners most deadly wounds.

July. 27. This weeke past the Lord renewed his goodnes to our family in our health, the small pox entred another family. one Isersons prentice(.) still god preserves mee and mine for whose mercy his name bee praised: my cold weareth away, my navell indifferent well, my wife better then formerly her houre draweth neare, the lord in mercy remember her(.) this weeke past the lord was an helpe to mee, keeping mee in his feare, and savouring my heart in the sense of his love, and keeping divers of my old corrupcions under, oh slay them before thy face for mercy and goodnes sake, and make my heart watchfull in mee to keepe close to my gratious god. this day wee comfortably received the communion of the body and bloud of christ, wherein gods presence was with us, wee had two members with us for those two that are now triumphing in heaven, the Lord was good to mee in the preaching of the word for which mercy my soule desireth to blesse the holy name of my god, the weather, was hott and dry, harvest neare, but not yett begunn with us.

28. I had a comfortably jorney to Mr Denhams, kind entertainment. and excellent eeles for my wife home with mee, returned safe at night. Sawe Cromwells letter to Mr Speaker of this Scotch action, he writes not so like a servant in my minde as when he was in Ireland

30: compleated Mr Ellistons and Smiths difference, lent him 3^{li}. 10^{s}. downe to pay Mrs Clench.

Aug: 2: Cast the water out of the pond on the greene, and. 2: cast out the mudde, this day Robert Crowe came home, he brought mee word of the health of our freinds and that next weeke, they intend to bee with us. heard Aug: 1: that Sligo was taken by storme and 3000 put to the sword: on the affaire of Scotland. I heare that divers suppose a weeke or two will putt an end to that businesse. I say stay till December next and then judge.

Aug: 3. This weeke past the Lord was good to mee and mine in our health, peace, outward mercies, mine still preserved from the smallpox, and god will still preserve them(.) one other family in the towne more is afflicted, it is very sore and heavy at Halsted, and a sad feavour also at Coxall as they reporte, harvest is now begunne, the season is very dry the lord in mercy, remember us therein as he seeth good: my heart was the weeke past much disquieted with the heedlesnes of my servant, lord make mee carefull not to doe that myselfe, which I blame in another, the lord was good to mee in the worke and duty of the Sabbath, I moved for poore Mighill whose house was burnt downe, wee gathered neare 3^{li}. for him, the lord bee blessed for this mercy in my people who gave them an heart to give. the lord sanctifie it to him, and requite their loves into their bosomes.

Aug: 10. This weeke past, the lord continued mindfull, of, and mercifull to mee and mine, my navel was a litle but not much ill, it hath not beene dressed neare a yeare, our family yett in health, blessed bee god, and yett one family more in our towne is visited with the small pox, and Hatches children, it is also much at Halsted, the lord still continue his goodnes to mee and mine in our preservacion. the season was very hott and dry, all harvest entred upon by men up and downe, never was their such a poore crop of hops their being none in all the contry as I could either see or heare of. matters went very well in Scotland, great expectacions of crushing, and ruining that Scotch army some suppose they will for England. wee lost about 90 men at Limbricke in Ireland, that army very sensible of gods stroke, and humbled for the same, Lord arise and helpe us(.) the Lord was gratious to mee in keeping my heart, in some measure close to him, in helping mee against old corrupcions, sometimes they shewe their hornes, but gods carpenters are ready to cut them of, the mercy of god to my wife was good, who held up her head with comfort, though with weaknesse, various rumours of great matters in Scotland but nothing of certainty, Mr Elliston preached for mee this afternoone, wee heard as if the Polanders had routed the Cossacks, and their complices slaine and wounded on the place 48000: of them. 14000 slaine. about 80000 slaine and wounded on both sides if so it is the most memorable battaile hath beene in Europe for an 100 yeares.

11. Reported for certaine at Colne, that the Scots were at Dumfreeze, entring England, and that Cromwell and his army was then before Saint Johnstons, the Committees in the severall counties ordered to take care of the kingdomes peace, the forces in the North ordered to March up towards Alnewicke to resist them,

13. Heard the Scots were in Lancashire, and that they had not mett with any opposicon, their emissaries are gone into all the kingdome

16: Heard the Scots entred England with their King and 11 or 12000 men. August. 5. about Carlile on August. 6. and were August. 10: at Lancaster. the 9 at Kendal, that day viz the 10th. Harrison was at Rippon.

Aug: 17. This weeke the Lord was good to mee and mine in our outward peace, plenty, preservacion health, the lord of his grace, and goodnes, keeping my family, when as some are still afflicted, and Ant. Garrads visited this weeke. my navel oyzed a litle, and itched as it were, but was not sore, my god is very gratious and mercifull to mee therein, the lord good to mee in my wife, who held up her head, and cheerful though farre bigger then ever in my opinion; the lord was good to mee in the duties of the Sabbath he in mercy accept and pardon mee,

21: spent part of this day in prayer at my house in seeking god in behalfe of my wife and the kingdome, the enemy wee heard was in Cheshire, all our foote ordered to march to Dunstable.

22. rid to Colchester, heard the enemy intended that night for Lichfield, but that day he entered Worcester, our horse ordered all to march the County left emptie of all force whatsoever.

23. a most dreadful day for thunder, lightning raine, and haile as reported in Dorsetshire, my thoughts were god fulfilled that text. Joel. 3:16. he roared out of Zion and uttered his voice out of Jerusalem. and that Revel. 11. ult. the judgments on the 10 part of the city in their destruction thereon hath such attendance. the general rising, I account gods calling for a sword against them throughout his holy mountaine:

the Scots coming in at first was a great dampe to gods people and all men, but they presently recoverd and beare up very comfortably.

Aug: 24: God good to us this weeke in our health. I had a stopping in my chest which made mee wheeze, the lord helpe mee to beare up my heart more and more as he doth. my soule aloft in this businesse through mercy, the enemy for London as reported, I feare not but god hastens him to his fall.

26: Spent in prayer at Mr Littells where was much company, our hearts very much borne up upon our good god, went to Ed: clarkes spoken as if dying, I am very confident of his recovery.

27. at Mrs Cookes. putt up a request for our successe. heard the enemy had beene at Woster, still said they intended London.

28: at Lady Honywoods, heard nothing, putt up one request more to god in behalfe of his remnant with confidence. sought god. also this day in the behalfe of Mr H. wee received an answer of prayer next day. but done while wee were praying

29. orders to disarme and secure Malignants in the County, and to raise Voluntiers for the security and defence of the same. heard the action likely to bee at Worcester.

I apprehend this Charles is Rex albus for his youth, that he will fall in Worcester or therabouts, and all his attempts come to nothing.

30: Heard Derby routed in Lancashire, divers of quality slaine, many prisoners the levies intended in the West of Scotland, broken. Sterling Castle taken, and our army gone towards Dundee. Cromwell at Warwicke, all marching towards Worcest where they are before this time. spent some part of the day in prayer at my Lady Honywoods. spoke. Amicah. 5.v.8. I listen that god will very much shorten the worke.

Aug: 31: This weeke past the lord good to us in our health, all places and persons recoverd from under the small pox. I stand in as much need of thy mercy oh lord to keepe mee as ever, blessed bee my god who hath hitherto kept mee and preserved mee, the lord exercised mee with a wonderfull pose and sneezing, I hope he will order it for good unto mee, which he can easily doe, and will, I do not question, the lord was good to mee in the Sabbath in the duties and mercies thereof, for which I blesse his most holy name,

pose.

Sep: 1: rid to Colchester god good in my jorney and returne, the night was cold, and I was very ill slept very unquietly, malincholly troubles perplexed my head on my bed very much.

2 at Mrs Cookes in a day of prayer, at night heard by many hands our freinds abroad were well, and that Cromwell was before Worcester and the Scots in it. and their horse in the Contry round about.

3. spent this day in prayer at my Lady Honywoods, much company there, and gods presence with us, our expectacions god will advance his glory in our salvacion. I apprehend that the designe will burst their, and perhaps the cheife designer also:

5. about noone heard at Colne, that the Scots were routed, their horse gone, towards night confirmed that they fell out of towne that they were beate in againe 4000 slaine. 300 prisoners our forces did gallantly, done while wee were praying at Markeshall.

September. 7. This weeke past, the Lord was good to mee, and mine in all our outward mercies, but my heart frame is not accordingly. old thoughts, and vaine, sinfull imaginacions put up their head, and that in such a time as this, when the judgments of god should awe, and his mercies melt my spirit into love and tendernes, lord helpe mee for unto thee doth my soule betake it selfe. heard after sermon of the taking of Worcester. 6000 prisoners. 2000 more slaine, even in the place of prayer I heard it god good to mee this day, though I sinfull and unworthy.

13. received a letter from London signifying the Lords Mayors pleasure unto mee to come up and preach before him, and his brethren the aldermen at Pauls which I intended to doe, and serve providence in it. Mr Wm Harlakenden returned home well, blessed bee god.

Sept. 14. This weeke past, god was good and mercifull to mee, and mine in many outward mercies, in our health, when others are afflicted for which goodnes my soule desires to rejoyce.

the weeke past die 10. wee kept a day of praise unto our good and gracious god at Cornelius Brownsons in Earles Colne,

the lord was good to mee in my poore wife, who held up head. my Cosin Johnson with us, this day our soldiuers returned, the lord good to mee in the Sabbath for which I praise him

15. went to see Sir Tho: Honywood who was very well, for which I blesse the lord, the lady intended a day of thanks to god, on friday, I promised her my helpe according to her desire.

19. This Friday morning my wife was very well delivered of her fourth sonne, and sixt child, much about seven of the clocke, I intend to name him John, the lord bee gratious and mercifull to him, he was borne on a day, that wee had sett apart for a day of thanks, and god begunne with mee in my family, I preacht at Markshall, where was a vast company, and a large dinner, gods hand was toward us for good, exceedingly:

☞ A great Rabbi's saying. If the Messiahs coming bee not before 1656. of the christians account then expect no other Messiah but the christians Messiah

I am perswaded the present dispensacon is the breaking in peices the kingdomes of the earth which god is entring on, and some time when this worke is advanced, will the Jewes appeare; and then comes in the happy season of the flocke.

7 Churches: 20. q(uery). if not meant of churches reformed after the gospel patterne. so (c.o. Smyrna) Ephesus is England and Smyrna Ireland. and in these 2 nations only are particular gathered churches as yett.

Rev: 5.12. worthy is the lambe to receive power. and he afterwards takes to himselfe his great power q(uery) whether then all this prophesy bee not then eminently fulfilled, which was but darkely before. r(eceive)d this day a letter from London that my Lord Mayor expects mee at my day, I shall not faile with gods leave

Sept: 21. This weeke past the lord was very good, and mercifull to mee, and mine in all our outward mercies, my wife nurseth her sonne very hopefully. god preserved us all from the small pox, which hath beene and still is in towne, but when I eye his goodnes to mee in my everlasting estate, oh what shall I say to this way of god, the lord good to mee in keeping my heart from many annoying vanities, the lord is to bee feared for his judgments which he executeth, when the Hollander rejoyced in the false newes of our fall, the enemy fell at Worcester, god hath beene very terrible to Scotland, many of their nobility, slaine, imprisond, and fled into strange lands and that in a very short season, their breake began. Aug. 28. at Ellett. then somewhat more, a litle after at Dumfreeze, then Sep: 1: at Dundee and then Sep. 3. at Worcester, and in their pursuit they are even almost all taken, oh feare, England, and honour god, least he turne the wheele upon thee also. the lord was good to mee in the word, pressed upon gods people to search their hearts and walke answerable to his great salvacion.

☞ 24. Kept a day of holy rejoycing to the conquering Lambe, at the priory, our company was great, our entertainment plentifull, wee thought of the poore Jew, the lord remember that oppressed people, god was very good to us in the worke, and duty of the day and in the sweetnes of it, yett to humble mee, my heart had its annoyance, lord in mercy heale it, thou onely canst doe it.

Sept. 28. This weeke the lord was good and mercifull to mee and all mine, wife and litle John very well, all in health, and yet the smal pox continueth still in 2 or 3 families in the towne, the lord very good to us in the season, which was through mercy, very abundant and comfortable, the lord holpe mee in some measure against the evils and vanities of mine heart, good to mee in the Sabbath worke, and mercy, my sonne John was baptized this day. this was my owne fathers name, the lord make him a gratious and holy John, and an instrument to doe Jesus Christ much service in his generation.

Lords rent (45^{li}. 12^{s}. 6^{d}.)

30. paid Mr Harlakenden all lords rent due until Michaelmas past viz. 3^{li}. 8^{s}. 8^{d}. ob. I received also his quarter. I now owe unto him still 10^{li}. my rol of debts I now esteeme to bee about 45^{li}. 12^{s}. 6^{d}. this day Mr John Littel of Halsted received of mee so much mony as made up that in his hands an 100^{li}. now he oweth mee an 150^{li}. and his brother Jeffery. an 100^{li}.

this day I heard that the smal pox was very much spread in the towne in many families they named. 3 or 4. new. the lord bee mercifull and gratious to mee and mine, and preserve us of his goodnes and mercy for in him I put my trust.

Oct: 3. rid this day to Stamford rivers and so to Cranham. I was very empty, and full of winde and sicke ready to swoune, I had two fits, cold my pulse did not beate at all as I could perceive, I vomited, god was my life and reviving.

5. I preached this day at Pauls in London by order from the Lord Mayor. the audience was great, my text was Luke. 21.v.28. I dined with the Lord Mayor, and by his intreaty preached before him, at his owne church, the lord was good to mee in the worke and service of the day, this was the first time that I preached in the city of London.

7. returned home, well, and found all well at home, blessed bee my good god,

Major Haynes with us from Scotland, for which I blesse the name of my god

Oct: 12: This weeke past the lord was every way good to mee, and mine, the lord was good to mee in Sabbath worke, he in mercy stand by mee in the same, the afternoone I holpe them at Coggeshall

Reported that Cardinal Mazarine of France, abiding at Colen in Germany, had tampered with the Electors and wrought with the Major part of them, and wonne them to transferre the Empire from the house of Austria, and to elect the eldest sonne of the Duke of Bavaria King of Romans

the Prince of Conde and French King in armes one against another, divers forces in England ordered to bee disbanded, Major General Deane one of the Admirals chosen to command in cheife in Scotland

16: Heard Dr Drake[1] had discoverd the whole plott, and actors to bring in the Scots King. and this weeke came the good newes of their pardon of the Ministers and the other their companions in that businesse.

October 19. This weeke god renewed his love and goodnes to mee, and all mine in our peace and health, which was the more to mee in regard the smal pox still did spread and continue in the towne, my deare onely daughter was suddenly ill, and through mercy revived againe, the lord made me sensible of my weaknes, corruption, and neglect in my imployment, lord doe not enter into judgment with mee, but deale gratiously with mee, and mine for mercy sake, god was good to mee in the worke of his owne day, but my neglect was great in preparacion thereunto, Lord pardon mee, and accept mee in the christ.

39^{li}. 2^{s}. 6^{d}. paid unto Wm Hickford what I owe him viz 12^{li}. 8^{s}. so that my roll of debts is now but 39^{li}. 2^{s}. 6^{d}.

22. this day I received 8^{li}. 19^{s}. of Nathan Perry, and made even with him until the last michaelmas, and now all the (c.o. lords) rent for that part is payd unto mee, and I am cleare also with my uncle, and all about the same, this day also I received 47^{li}. 10^{s}. from Goodman Day, of mony for my purchase of Mallories, heard also as if the prince were escaped into Holland, which if then its likely to continue our troubles and bring on forreigne ingagements, god will have it so, and I am perswaded god will make them fall under us: its said he was in London in the habit of a footeman and escaped over in that of a seaman,

[1] Roger Drake (1608–69), medical doctor and Presbyterian, involved in Love's plot (see p. 251, n. 2 above). DNB.

it was said by many he was slaine, but what is man unto god, his life shall contribute to gods worke more then his death could.

Oct. 24. A day of publicke rejoycing for the eminent victory at Worcester. this night I lent Mr Caplyn 5^{li}. until to morrow 3 weekes viz November. 15. 1651,

Octob: 26: This day, and the weeke past, the lord was good to mee in the mercies of my family in our preservation when the small pox still continueth to looke into divers families, but oh my heart is wretched, in my calling very negligent, it hath often troubled mee, and I am not reformed, I am neither spiritual in my worke, carried out nakedly to doe god service, but am apt to eye myselfe in outward conveniences and necessaries. Lord I am resolved in my strength to looke better to my heart, and wayes, lord thou art my all, and my helpe alone is in thee, I pray the(e), stand up for mee, and frame my heart to thy will, and preserve mee and mine for mercy sake I intreate thee,

28: this day Susan Burton had the smal-pox, the lord in mercy watch over that family and mine, and preserve mee and mine for his mercy sake, and oh lett mee understand the loving kindnes of god.

29. this day lent to Mr Pelham[1] and his sonne on their bond. 50^{li}
This day I observed expositors judging haile in the Revelation to
Haile. signifie, the nations invaders and overturners of things in other nations than their own; and meditating of it. I judged it probable, for as much as the haile is produced in an other element, and so falls on the earth, and many note our forreigners warres in a nation: as earthquake being proper to the earth noteth out the commotions of homeborne men, which wee call civill warre, and all alterations of governments done by a contry among themselves:

30. so I went this day to apply this notion. Rev: 11.13. the 10th part of the city fals by an earthquake (and no haile) the 10 part I have conceived to bee these 3 kingdomes: which as they have not had a forreigne enemy so perhaps shall not, though often intended. now I heare the King is in France, I said by October wee should heare where he was if alive, on this ground that a King is too great a person to conceale long. some said he was kild, some said he was here and there and they say Lorraine intends to waft over forces into Ireland, but I feare them not, if this notion hold.

v. 19. when the kingdomes become christs. there is haile. other kingdomes shall bee invaded. Rev. 16.18.21: their ruine shall bee

[1] Herbert Pelham of Bures, J.P. and M.P. during the Protectorate: the DNB gives his death as 1667, but Morant, ii, p. 267 gives it as 1674.

occasioned by civil commotions, and then accomplisht by the haile of forreigners swords: heard Jersey iland was taken.

31: Heard of Mr Cresseners ill minde towards mee. lord forgive him, and give me grace to be more active for thee, in doing service unto

5^{li}. 12^{s}. 6^{d}.

thy most holy name, No: 1: paid Nicholas his 3^{li}. 10^{s}. I borrowed of him. my roll of debts is now. 35^{li}. 12^{s}. 6^{d}. these debts I pay by litle and litle, Jesus christ payd all my debts to the father at once but its lightsome if wee gett the assurance of it, after many steps, and waitings.

Nov: 2. The Lord was good to us in our health, and preservation(.) at night Tho: was ill, wee are ready to have thoughts of the visitacon to surprise us. through mercy my heart is stayed on god that he will preserve mee and mine and that he will watch over us for good but these providences renew the sense of gods goodnes to mee in my preservations I blesse god many former vaine foolish thoughts doe not passe through my heart as they have formerly. but this weeke also I was not so aforehand provided for the sabbath as my desire was. yett god was good to mee in the word for which I blesse his most pretious name,

☞ this night I apprehended all the vials to belong not to the end of the 6th trumpet but to the beginning of the seventh vial, as I intend at large to search into.

thoughts much of babylons fall, and that the passages in old Babylons fall are propheticke of the fall of Romish babylon.

one with mee in trouble of minde, lord thou art acquainted with her estate, make her to see her vilenes to loath her selfe, and to see thee her alone salvation

The King escaping and appearing in France, matters growing very high in that nation, the state of England in this latter end of October, wonne Jersey iland in the lap of France and the castle, as also Man island, and Limbricke in Ireland, which giveth us hope of good successe in our affaires at home, that wee may more vigorously attend forreigne designes, the Scots also are much divided, and divers tender compliances with England.

No: 9. This weeke the lord was good to mee and mine in our outward mercies, still wee are kept when others are under this afflicting hand of god. my sonne Tho: sprained his necke this weeke, I thanke god for his mercy towards us therein hoping that it will bee very well, my heart more annoyed with vaine worldly thoughts then formerly. my debts also runne in my minde and disquiet mee, I finde when any vanity is not handled roughly at the first it gets the more advantage against us; the season was very comfortable wee have not had very much wett as yett. the lord was good to mee in some measure in the many outward and inward mercies, I enjoy in his sabbath for which I praise him

14: This day I sett apart in fasting and prayer as I could on these occasions

1. in regard of the illnesse of my sonne John, that god would shine on him for health, and on us all in outward good, as he seeth best, and bee my god and the god of all mine, to renew and sanctifie them.

2. to seeke god to make mee more profitable in the ministry of the word, and that the word might prosper to begett and strengthen soules, and to blesse our fellowship.

3. that god would discover to mee as he seeth best, his operations that he is acting in the world, that so I may serve him therein, and not stumble at fall against any of them.

oh my deare sonne was ill as if he would have dyed, I cried to my god with teares for him and he heard presently he sweetly revived, the lord sett home to my heart my neglect of worshipping god in my family, delaying it till late, lord helpe mee herein for mercy sake I humbly intreate thee.

Nov: 16: This weeke past the lord dasht water into our wine, in my Johns illnes, he shewed us mercy in Tho: necke which was well, lord I am thine, and at thy dispos(al) and I desire to submit to thee, and leave my selfe with thee, the lord was good to mee in my spirit keeping of it in some measure in temper

this weeke I heard that November. 14: it was noted their should bee a new representative it was carryed but by 2 voices as said

received from Mr Harlakenden my sermon at his wives funerall which he printed, I had a litle peice of my drawing printed in Mr Harlakendens booke, but this was my first at the presse.

god was good to mee in the Sabbath, I have cause to bemone a slothful heart my sonne sweetly revived from under his cold this evening, an answer of prayer.

☞ Luke. 2.34: fal that is the Jewes rejection: rising againe that is their call; and the happines of christ to the Jewes is at their conversion to the faith, which Zach: prophesied Luke. 1.71.74. is then to bee fullfilled for indeed christs coming brought in the Jewes destruction, and their bondage continueth on them to this day.

18: writt up to London for our augmentacion businesse. I am now in arreare 1 yeare 3 quarters at 40^{li}. per annum it is 70^{li}. if I receive in all 60^{li}. I will make the lord a sharer with it for his worke in new England to the summ of 5^{li}. when they gather for the advancement of the gospell in new England.

19. Lent Young of Halsted 3^{li}. who was in great straites to make his rent up to his landlord, I bought of him. 4 bushels wheate at 4^{s}. 6^{d}. the bushel;

☞ The state of England hath in a manner reduced Scotland and Ireland, what probability is their of continuing their command over them, for surely the seed of liberty will remaine in those nations, if not of revenge also, and if ever our troubles and discords, or their happines and valour of some particular person appeare, they may give a turne, to destroy the nations were barbarous, to plant them with English colonies is very hard and unlikely, and Scotland will not invite our men, and yett this must be done besides good garrisons. god who hath done what is done, will effect his owne purpose, and therefore I leave it.

20. This day and the dayes past I have had divers meditacions on some passages of the Revelacion. which are noted in my booke thereon, for which I praise my god

22. Heard of the scandall about Mr Watson of Cranham, lord in mercy watch over mee that no corruption of mine bee too hard for mee. Mr Harlakenden returned from London in good health, where he dispatched Mr R: H. businesse at Mr Merediths[1] the portion is great, the gentlewoman hopefull, the lord in mercy make them helpes to one another, and to this place, if the lord bring them togither, and unto Colne.

No. 23. The Lord was good to mee and all mine in our healths, preservation, recovery from illnes in my sonne John, the lord have the praise and honour of all, which I desired to returne him in the great congregation, the Lord was good to mee this weeke past for soule and body, standing by mee in divers straites, and perplexities of spirit, helping mee in some measure against my corruptions, that they prevail not over mee. the small pox continueth still in towne in many places. this weeke wee heard the house voted November. 18. they would sitt but 3 yeares more, the Cava⟨lier⟩s give out the King of Denmarke is dead, and Charles Stuart called to that kingdome that he should marry the daughter of Spaine. strange things: Its said the P. of Conde hath sent over unto us for souldiers but our state demurse, gods time is not yett fully come

[1] Richard Harlakenden's son Richard married Mary, daughter of Christopher Meredith of London, gent. Morant, ii, p. 212.

see what is done in France 1653. the Lord was good to mee in the Sabbath and in the word on Rev. 1:3. lord make it a blessing to mee and to mine I pray thee.

25. a day of conference at Goodman Mathewes. at night Mrs Cressener had sent us a sugar loafe: I desire to blesse god for it, and bee thankfull to them for their love.

☞ 26. Wm Webb and his brother tooke my ditching, to throw the marle into the feild(,) to cutt the hedge, sett on one againe, and to goe three spitt[1] where need is, to throw of a spitt where I intend to quicke[2] and to raise it up with new earth, I am to give them 3^{d}. ob. per rod, and where worth it. 4^{d}.

29: This day I received of Caplin. 3^{li}. 10^{s}. I lent him more. 1^{li}. 10^{s}. I payd to Wm Brand 4^{li}. that I owe to him, and I still owe him 4^{li}.

☞ mention in the newes of a book that saith 52. will be a yeare of wonders to the ruine of Monarchy in Europe especially in France and Portugal:[3] Heard as if some of my money were likely to bee paid into my freinds hands at London, which if would rejoyce mee: my Jane very ill, but the lord very good to us in her cheering, and my perswasion is he will preserve us from that noisome arrow that is abroad.

No: 30: This weeke past the lord shooke his hand over my Jane, but gently blessed bee his name(.) the lord was good to the residue of my family in the continuance of my health. but oh who can value gods love in giving christ, and the meanes of grace unto us, and unto this nation, oh that my poore soule could love him, and delight in him, the lord was good to mee in the Sabbath he in mercy watch over mee and mine and accept of us that wee may live in his sight.

December: 1: This day we kild a good hogge, through mercy the price of things, and catle abateth very much, this afternoone, my litle Scotch Hobby that I bought my sonne Tho. died(,) the first of such creatures that ever dyed from mee, lord its mercy that it was not a greater and a nearer losse.

6. Mr R.H. returned from London. I received a kind letter from Mr Meredith and my wife a booke for a token: also a dozen pound

[1] Spit: such a space of earth as is pierced by the full length of a spade-blade. SOED.

[2] Quick: quickset, to plant, enclose, etc. with a quickset (especially white hawthorne) hedge. NED.

[3] A number of books appeared during November 1651 prophesying great events; *The Black Dutch Almanack, or, Predictions and Astronimocall* (*sic*) *Observations foreshewing what will further happen to the King of Scots and other Kings and Commonwealths in the year 1652* which appeared on 4 December (Thomason, E. 1372(1)) is perhaps the work of which RJ had news.

candle from goodwife Burton, thus the lord is good to mee in many particulars.

December. 7. This weeke past the lord renewed his goodnes to mee and mine in our lives and peace and health, he is worthy of praise in what he doth for us, the lord helpeth mee with a serious heart to looke into the things of his booke, and he helpeth mee against my roaring running vanities oh bring them under oh my god more and more I most humbly intreate thee(,) the lord was good to mee in the Sabbath, and in the worke lord give mee a discerning of the things written in the Revelation as thou seest it fitt for mee, that my heart may bee knitt to thee to seeke thy glory in discovering thy will to others and framing their hearts after it. heard as if some of Lorraines men were come over into Ireland; I will waite on the Lord and see what he doth.

9: This day I beganne to plow in Dagnal, god in mercy give a blessing for it proceeds from him. I received 25^{li}. of my augmentacion arreares, which my good freind Major Haines procured from Mr Stanbridge.[1] I was at Mr H. where our company mett, wee had lively and sweete discourse on trials of a christians growth, make mee such an one I most humbly intreate thee,

12. 13. received the 3^{li}. I lent Young I paid him. 17^{s}. 4^{d}. for foure bushels of wheate; I paid Nich Hurrell. 4^{li}. I borrowed of his mony from my sister I am cleare with him: Caplin paid me the last of my 5^{li}. and this day I lent Jo. Smith oatemeale man 4^{li}. until Dec. 26: Coxal Destitute sent for me to preach profferd me 20^{s}. but I refused: this day wee heard that Ireton Deputy generall of Ireland dyed at Limbricke in Ireland No: 26: the lord liveth and reigneth, and perhaps hereby will father hearten the enemies to their utter ruine: Ludlow who was L. gen: commands the forces in cheife for the present.

December 14: The lord was good and gratious in the weeke past to mee and all mine, in our peace and health for which I blesse his most holy name, the smal pox continueth still in the towne oh how good is god to us that wee should be preserved, why have I this favour oh lord in thy sight, oh rejoyce over mee to doe mee good, my heart now and then sett on with old temptacions, praised bee my god, that keepeth mee from giving any way thereunto, the lord was good and mercifull to us in the Sabbath in

[1] Among the Accounts of Sales of Bishop's Lands reprinted in Shaw, ii, p. 563 is the following item: 'William Stanbridge, to the use of William Clopton, minister of Markishall, and Ralph Jocelen, minister of Earl's Colne, Essex—£199-0-0.'

the day and the exercises thereof for which I blesse and praise his name.

Pose: 13. at night I perceived I had taken cold in the feild. 14. my nose posed very much but not as sometimes formerly. it fell not into my chest.

18. viewed a paper of a deare freind, wherein I find so much judiciousnes, and understanding of the worke of god on the heart, as maketh mee admire gods goodnes therein and freely brings out this acknowledgement, those that sitt by, may speake, and wee that are accounted teachers sitt by in silence.—

20: releasd from going to Halsted, saw Manasseh Ben Israel, or the hope of Israel. lord my heart questions not the calling home the nation of the Jewes thou wilt hasten in its season, oh my god, oh thou god of the ends of the whole earth: hasten it Amen. saw the good newes of taking of the private excise on beere, the several oppressions of men will spew them out in due time so that their places shall knowe them no more,

Dec: 21. This weeke the lord was good to us in all our outward mercies, the small pox doth continue very breife in the towne, yet god good in my preservation, our mayde was very ill with feare of them, but gods truth was my sheild, his faithfulnes to preserve mee, which I desire to hold out on all occasions. heard ill words of M C. of our society, I shall eye god for him, and call upon him to putt on after god, the lord was good to mee in preserving mee from those evills my heart is prone unto, for which I blesse him, I trust he will preserve mee from every evill worke and present mee without spott to his father and mine; this day was snowy my heart was very dead in preaching the word, shutt up in prayer, the lord make mee sensible of my daily deadnes and straitnes of spirit in calling upon him.

22: menasseh Ben Israel conceiveth a great stocke of the Jewes are beyond the mountaines Cordellery about Quiti.[1] I lent Young of Halsted 10^{li}. for 3 months.

23. mett at my house in conference. and 25. at William Cowels in a day of prayer, the lord was good to us therein, our weaknes is very great, but gods mercy is exceeding large.

27. paid Goodwife Mathew. 9^{li}. of her 15^{li} and I gave her 5^{s}. for her kindnes to mee therein, I received 3^{li}. of Smith and he oweth me 2^{li}. tithes and all which he is to pay mee Jan. 1: next my rol of debt
26^{li}. 12^{s}. 6^{d}. is now, 26^{li}. 12^{s}. 6^{d}. I confesse I owe some more moneys but that also I shall through mercy easily pay, this is my old roll.

[1] Cordilleras mountains which spread over Colombia, Ecuador, and other countries in South America.

Dec: 28: The Holland Ambassadours had their audience Dec: 19. no actions this weeke, our worke willbee to setle our conquests, and to order things at home with justice to content, heard that 12. men. 4 lawyers and 8. gentlemen are chosen to frame a moddell of regulating the Law: its said the Gen. in the house offered them his commission. now Ireton is dead, its questioned whether the power of Lieutenantship shall bee continued to Cromwell, or which way his place, and that government shalbee managed(.) in the weeke past the lord was very good to mee and mine in our health, and outward mercies, not feeling those difficulties that are upon others, the lords helpes mee against old temptacions, oh a constant following our calling and walking with god therein is very comfortable. god good to mee this day in the word and the worke therof.

31: perfected my businesse with goodwife Day, Mrs Church this morning gave mee 20^{s}. this love and kindnesse is of the lord for which I blesse the lord and desire him in mercy to returne it backe againe into her.

Jan: 1: received of Mr Littell all moneyes due to this day, and payd to Mr Harlakenden 4^{li}. 7^{s}. due for his rent of Dagnal at Michaelmas last. paid my sister 12^{s}. 6^{d}. all other reckonings and Mr Harlakenden 10^{li}. so I am cleare with Mr Richard Harlakenden for

16^{li}. 0^{s}. all debts, and my roll of debts is but. 16^{li}.

☞ 3. Heard this day of the reducement of the two Ilands of Jersey and Guernsey to the obedience of parliament. Elizabeth Castle yeilded Decem: 12. the 15. our men tooke possession according to agreement: Cornet Castle was the last of the kingdome of England that held out against the parliament for the King: that was yeilded up. so now here is a 10th part of the city fallen from the interest and worship of Rome. Except wee say its not compleate untill all the appendices of this crowne in Ireland and Scotland are reduced which wee expect shortly. and then speedily the second woe passeth. which is his not troubling the part of the Roman world with his stupendous conquests. but some enemy is raised up to exercise his power, and in due time to abate his greatnes and bring in his ruine in time, even so Lord Jesus come quickly.

Jan: 4: The Lord was good to us this weeke, in our health, and outward mercies, in spiritual refreshments, and in his owne ordinances for which I blesse his most holy name, wee had some unhansome tempers of B. Clarke. and Thomasin. Harding, the Lord heale them and doe us all good by the same.

5. This day I went to Messing and returned(.) my jorney was bad

homeward: my navel felt as if some humours were in it, whereupon at night I found it was moist the lord my god will heale it. paid James day for his wheate. 1^{li}. 12^{s}. and 10^{d}. to his rate, paid. Good-
13^{li}. wife Mathew. 3^{li}. my roll is now. 13^{li}. I owe her. still. 3^{li}.

6: Bat: Clarke with mee, I hope god hath wonne on upon his heart,
☞ it so appeared to mee wherein I rejoyce with thankfulnes: my eye is on the troubles of France, god is disquieting them. in 48 the Germaine. peace was concluded. who would have thought that had not beene a step to reconcile France and Spaine: or afforded liberty to forreine princes to ingage against England: but the troubles of the world shall come on them suddenly as paines of a travailing woman.

9. This day I payd to Wm Brand 4^{li}. I borrowed of him, wee mett the 7 day in prayer at Mr W. Har. god good to us therein. Mrs Mabel and G. Mathew very ill the lord watch over them for good in the glorious riches of his grace. I feard a clash at our breaking of bread on admission of Mr Ell. or divers others. tempers of spirit. but god put of his businesse as I secretly desired, expecting by our next joyning providences on foote would ingage our hearts more togither.

Jan: 11: The Lord was good to mee this day in giving mee strength for the worke and service of the day, notwithstanding my great illnesse upon mee, the Lord was very good to all mine in our preservations wherein I rejoyce, wee had this day a comfortable presence of god in word and in breaking bread, the Major Haynes joyned with us in breaking bread being a member of a church in New-England

15. goodwife Mathewe tooke phisicke it wrought very kindly the lord
☞ restore her. I apprehend in the new Destruction of the nations in Ezechiel. by Tyrus is meant Holland, and by Egipt France,

Rev: 18. those called out of Babylon—especially there intended Italy, are the Jewes who shall apprehend Romes ruine, and there drawing from Italy, an encouragement to the rest of the Jewes in other places.

perused that booke called the great day at the doore for which I blesse god

Jan: 18: God good to mee and mine in our outward mercies, this is a still time for present in England. the french troubles come on, no body knoweth why. and so in England no body can state the cause of the quarrel, I preach at Halsted on Luke. 21.28. god heard prayer for some of our company. the lord giveth mee longings for his coming, I know tis terrible, he only must enable mee to abide it, and he will(.) wickednes reigneth and rageth, it shall end, lord hasten it, I pray thee in mee

23. I was quite out of moneys, and went where some was owing mee, received it not, I knew god would provide for mee against my needs, and therefore I desire not to care for these things, when I came home I found a tenant there with rent, and presently two more paid me some mony so as I paid my sister. 40ˢ. I now have paid her all, and I paid goodwife Mathew 3ˡⁱ. I have also paid her all, and my wife had about 40ˢ. for her stocke. I procured 10ˡⁱ. for goodman Sparrow. my roll of debts is now brought downe to 8ˡⁱ. blessed bee my god, and I owe not 40ˢ. more in all the world.

. debts.

☞ In the thoughts of my head this night one said to me that the Q(ueen) of E(ngland). now in France by wayes of hers should strengthen her sonne to be a rod to the reigning party in England I replyed not to restore him nor ruine them, and that this decad of yeares would accomplish promises and threats

24: This day was the last of my 35. yeare. in which the lord was good to mee in keeping my family when the small pox was so much in the towne in blessing my estate. but especially in bringing us that desire to feare his name into fellowship, and communion and a comfortable enjoyment of him in his ordinances: keeping my heart in his feare and nourishing up his grace in mee keeping downe corruptions, giving mee a continued apprehencion of him my portion, and setting my heart very much to looke after those great things he is about to doe both against antichrist and all the enemies of his church, and for his people both Jewes and Gentiles, I trust he will never faile mee nor forsake mee as he hath promised; my soule admireth the lord in his love, and ascribeth the Lord in his love, and ascribeth all praise to the Lambe who hath redeemed mee by his owne bloud, and my desire is to love him and doe him service all my dayes.

all the threats of our enemies ended in the ruine of the Scotch designe at Worcester, and the flight of their King into France, all Scotland even reduced, by force, and disbanded on treaty, our forces also prospered in Ireland, where the sword, famine and pestilence hath made a great waste. wee are not in good terms with Holland, the new hopes of the enemies are that these 2 states will fall out to eithers ruine and make way for the Spaniard and Stuard to recover their owne againe in both.

France is likely to fall into flames by her owne divisions, this summer shee hath done nothing abroad. The Spaniard hath almost reduced Barcelona the cheife city of Catalonia and so that kingdome the issue of that affaire wee waite. Poland is free from warre with the Cossacks but feareth them. Dane and Suede are both in quiet, and so is Germany, yett the peace at Munster is not fully executed: the turke hath done no great matter on the Venetian, nor beene so fortunate and martial as formerly, as if that people were at their height and declining rather.

the Iles of Silly. Jersey. and Guernsey. Man. and all the proper possessions of England now reduced, and no great feare of any power within, god prevent breaches among our selves(,) our fleets are strong at sea;

there have been great inundations in Spaine at Bilboa, and in Italy. letters from Silly mention an earthquake their on December. 25. past.

Arise oh Lord. Come Lord Jesus. oh thou saviour and hope of Israel. bee not farre from us, judge all thy enemies.

Jan. 25: 1651. y. 36. of my age.

This was the lords day, and I was sensible, that it ended my 35. and begun my 36: yeare: I was joyfull to bee employed in gods worke, I hope the whole yeare my heart shall more savour of god than formerly, and he will rejoyce to use mee in his workes and services. god was very good to mee in his word, and in my utterance, he in mercy blesse mee in his owne service to his owne people.

27. mett at my house, wee gave a sharpe reproofe to some of our company in their weake carriages. I was with Thomasin, poore troubled heart, helpe her oh Lord, heard that Jo: Lilburne when he received his sentence Jan. 20. 1651 and refused to kneele wherupon they ordered him to be banisht within 20. dayes which end I apprehend(.) Feb: 8: he said I shall outlive this sentence of yours, as I have all the rest of them,

☞ at the 5[t] vial the beasts kingdome is darkened, which I apprehend shews their blindnes and ignorance of gods designes not to bee warned by the former plagues, but to beate an alarme to gather all togither against the day of god wherein there is a reference to darkenes the plague of Egipt.

bought 12 bushels white oates at 22[s]. 6[d]. only 1/2 bushell branke[1] given in.

[1] Brank: buckwheat .SOED.

31: A report out of Scotland as is whispered from the West, thereof, that the Rebels had burnt Dublin, this lookt on as a tale, and perhaps is so, but when such a thing doth come, its a signe to the English nation of dismal dayes coming on them,

Feb: 1: This weeke past the lord was very good to mee and all mine in all our outward mercies, the season for divers dayes very calme, cleare and warme, wee appointed a day of prayer for the christians of Halsted to meete with us at Mr Litles Feb. 18 I was with him he willing, I apprehend a storme over our head ready to come in upon us, but whence wee doe not dreame, some people whom wee scorne god may arme to scourge our wickednes, for surely all flesh have corrupted their wayes(.) the lord holpe mee against many corruptions of my heart, now and then I feel them stirring, but the lord alone keepeth them downe, my minde runneth wonderfully on the troubles of the last time; which breaking worke, I am much satisfied in, but what the restitucon shall bee, I cannot yett attaine(.) the lord was good to mee in the worke and services of the day, he in mercy owne mee, and doe mee much good continually.

Pose 7. This day I found I had taken cold with standing still in the winde as I conceive, I did not sneeze so much as formerly, my nose run all this day very much, but not much at night.

Feb: 8: This weeke past the lord renewed his goodnes to us all in our health, and preservation and yett some families still afflicted with small pox, and others taken a new, the lord hath given mine the spice of the itch, which I hope he will sanctifie and turne for their good. the lord was good to me in his presence with mee in my worke and imployment, lord stand by mee therein, and lett mee bee accepted of thee therein(.) the Lord good to mee in helping mee against old motions of my vaine heart, I still daily see my strength is to waite on Jesus, and I hope hee will bee my strength.

9. went to Rob. Nic:[1] kindly entertaind, the man hath a catechisme and peice about baptisme (which its said he will print) wee had discourse thereon and on Acts. 2.39: with much sobernes and kindnes: he is against infant baptisme. for water baptisme. yett not baptizd. for several reasons, one was because baptizers give not the holy ghost R: 1. then also you have no faith, for miracles are the following tokens of faith: Mark. 16.2. baptize(r)d did not

[1] Robert Nichols of Colne Engaine. He had a seven-hearth house in 1662, and during the years 1656–9 had goods worth £50 taken from him as a Quaker, refusing to pay tithes (Besse, i, p. 193). He may have been the co-author (with J. Cotton) of *Some Treasures Fetched Out of Rubbish: or, three treatises concerning the imposition and use of significant ceremonies in the worship of God* (1660. Thomason, E. 1046(2)).

receive the H(oly) G(host) when baptized, some before, and so the baptizers did not conferre it, and many not at all as S(imon) Magus. and others. viz Acts. 8.10: I answerd to his other reasons, which are two weake to beare water in any indifferent mans eye wee all know but in part. and I much lesse than other men, if I have but a weake light, helpe mee with a sincere heart, and strength of love to, and faith in my god that I may through thee run my race with comfort

10: lett Bowles my ditch at Bridgmans for 6^{d}. per rod: Mett this day at Priory in conference our discourse pertinent, spirituall, and profitable, most spoke then I objected against it to shew the weaknes of some answers, and to render the knot discernable, and easily to untie it: discourse how is sin mortified in us, when it so strongly acts

14. Payd the mony I owed unto Bridgett Aylward which was 40^{s}. I am quite out of her debt, and even with all men except about 37^{s}. to Wm Hickford, and also what I intend to bestow on a peice of plate for Dr Wright,

Debts. 6^{li}.

Feb. 15. This weeke past the Lord was very good to mee and all mine in our health, peace outward enjoyments, preservation, when other families are under a continuing affliction of the small pox. the season fitt, wett, cold, sometimes dry and cheerfull, the Lord good to mee in my spirituall state, yett with sense of the strength of my dead earth which renders the taste of goodnes comfortable that I am not left under the power of it(.) the lord was good to mee in many good providences, he accept of mee in the worke of the Sabbath whereunto he enableth mee,

Feb: 6 was Iretons funerall.

17. [1]her heart may be a meanes to doe us all a great outward (c.o. mischief) god in mercy prevent it, and fitt mee for any trial he will call upon mee, this morning Wm Cowell brought mee in 2 bushels of wheate, gods love in freinds kindnesse and in their duty, is both an encouragement, and engagement unto mee to stirre mee up for gods glory, and peoples good

18. Mett in a day of prayer at Mr Littells, there was much company of that towne,[2] and ours, the lord was with us; give us a gracious answer of our requests wee entreate thee, my deare John very ill. its occasiond wee thinke by teeth, the lord our god restore his health and quiett.

[1] A few words crossed out in RJ's ink: probably as follows '*Mrs Rose Church is* (   )'.

[2] Namely Halsted.

☞ 20. Heard that 20^{m} Danes were landed in Scotland: perhaps some not so many. perhaps none but surely(,) there is much trouble yett coming on England, and wee shall not enjoy that constant victorious successe that wee did formerly, yett god will crowne the issue with much good to his remnant: Heard the Q(ueen) and K(ing) were banisht out of France they sending ambassadors to us. q(uery) by what party. perhaps not true. both these proved reports as farre as wee could discerne, the French troubles advance.

Feb: 22. This weeke past, the lord appeared gratious to mee and mine in all our outward mercies, my litle John very ill, but now againe through mercy cheerfull he was full of red spots in his face which surmised might bee the small pox, god was a sweet stay to my heart, as not apprehending they were, and its how easily he could remove feare when he calls in trouble, and command deliverance, when he calls in trouble. my heart much troubled with old vanities not constantly but by fits and starts, lord bee thou my daily strength for my only hope is in thee(.) god was good to mee this day in the word preacht.

26. went to Halsted in my way mett with Captaine Maidstone, who prevailed with mee to preach the assize sermon at Colchester on March. 2. next.

Feb: 29. This weeke past the lord was very good to mee and mine in our healths, preservations and outward mercies, the season was very sweete and comfortable, god good to us in the towne the disease of the small pox doth not spread. I heare not above two familyes, that are now under that affliction, lord lett my selfe and all mine be hidden under thy wings perpetually: the lord with mee in the worke and service of the day for which my soule desireth to rejoyce in him.

March. 2. Rid to Colchester, where I preacht the assize sermon, the Lord was good to mee in my comfortably jorny outwards and homewards, I bought Mr Dells[1] booke cost mee 3^{s} I hope I might doe good, and receive good from the occasions of that day.

4. mett this day in conference at Mr Cresseners, the lord was good to us in our society(.) wee appointed March. 16: next meeting, wee gave Mr R:H. our advice in a case he proposed, and promised silence.

6: sew some white oates on Dagnal hill, I brought home some wood, and paid of my workemen to this day. viz 5 bushels halfe.

[1] William Dell, an independent and author of a number of books, as well as master of Gonville and Caius College, Cambridge. DNB.

March: 7. The season very comfortable the like not in yeares, Mr Sparrow being ill, I went and holpe him. I preacht on psal. 9:10. 11.12. the lord was good to mee in my going and returning hee in mercy accept mee and doe mee good.

8: This day, a sweet warme raine. I sold to Mr Wm Harlakenden. 20^{Q} hay at 2^{s}. per Q. I hope to spare somewhat more, I am loth to venture much least I should want my selfe, though the price bee great.

Mr Nevill received of Widdow Browne this day in taxes: allowed for wood and horse pasture and in mony. in all. 18^{li}. towards last Michaelmas rent.

13. Norden calved a bull calfe shee tooke bull May. 31. 1651. past, which is 40 weekes and 5 dayes.

March: 14: This weeke past the lord in all outward mercies renewed his goodnes towards mee and mine, onely my litle John very ill with an hoarsenes, my god will command mercies for him, my dead heart hath need of stirring, and quickening, oh that my poore soule might attaine unto it, I am sensible of my wandering heart, and of the foolishnes of my thoughts in divine worship, lord when shall my heart attaine unto stablishment, the lord was good to mee in the worke of the day, the Lord my god accept mee for he alone is worthy to bee praised and exalted.

18. at Coxall Mr Owen preacht Mr Sames[1] sett a part that day with fasting and prayer to be an teaching elder to the church at Coxall. he made a confession of faith, that was no open consent of the church, nor no acceptance of it with any words, nor promise to doe any thing. the messengers viz pastors of 3 churches gave their approbation of the act and were witnesses of the churches act one gave an exhortation. 2 prayed for a blessing.

19. at my Lady Honywoods with Mr Owen gave him an account of our proceedings, who seemed to receive satisfaction and rejoyce therein.

March. 21: My god was good to us and all ours my sonne John hath 2 teeth cutt when just halfe a yeare old. my children ill with scab,[2] but I question not but god saw it best for them and mee and sent it, and I hope in order to their health, and preservation from the

[1] John Sams, vicar of Kelvedon and later of Coggeshall; as Smith points out (p. 416), this is the first reference to Sams' succession to John Owen. Smith, pp. 212, 305, 337, 391, 416.

[2] Scab: a disease of the skin in which pustules or scales are formed; a general term for skin diseases, but sometimes specifically scabies, ringworm, tinea, or syphilis. SOED.

threatning illnesses of the time, god preserved all my family in our townes sicknes for which I blesse and praise his holy name. the lord lets mee daily into my owne sinfulnes, unfitnes for his worke, as not meete so much as to make a pin of, and I finde also in people a coldnes towards mee, and litle of love and affection, which shall not dampe but quicken mee, knowing my worke shall not bee in vaine in the lord whatsoever recompense or entertainment it meete withall from men. Major Haines with us, it was said there was some likelyhood of agreement with the Hollander, gods wayes are best I will not prescribe him what he shall doe, but desire to follow him in what he doth and is a doing, Stowen calved a bull calfe, still went 40 weekes 1 day.

March.24.1651: a review of my outward estate which god hath given mee.

Bollinhatch part and 2 closes in Colne, as formerly.

Mallories sold in lieu of that I have in Mr J.L. and Mr J.L. hands- - - - - - - - } 250^{li}

in Mr P. hands that which was in Mr J.L. formerly. } 050.

25. March: 1652. now at hand in mony and improvement of Mrs Maries land- - - - - - - - - - } 85

My stock in all much as last yeare - - - - - - - - - - - - - - - - 32

I was then in debt. 70^{li}. I am now in debt about 12^{li}. so I have paid 58^{li}. and have added 4. to Mrs Maries land. this yeare through mercy gives mee an improvement of my estate to about 70^{li}. for which I desire to give praise and thanks to my good God. I have moreover in. G.Y. hands. - - - - - - - - - - - - - - 10.

24: This day I sew on the lower stetch on dagnal farther hil, and the hither downe right stetch next the brooke, and on the hither hill, 5 bushels oates. Lord give a blessing unto these I intreate thee.

1652. 25. at Mr Thompsons, wee went to the lecture at Birch, the lord was good to mee in my jorney and returne, and in my sweet societie there,

Mar. 28: God gratious to mee and mine in outward mercies my sonne Tho. very raw and sore with his itch, which maketh mee thinke he would have had the small pox very much, which is not now in our upper streete but is in some families below, the lord in mercy in his due time remove his hand from us, my heart much annoyed with old sinfull vanitie lord in mercy make mee sensible of them and in thy due time lett christ heale mee and give me strength against them for unto thee doe I fly: I was very hoarse with my cold

☞ 29. This day I renewed the resolucion of Aug. 23. 1647 about bookes to put it in execution, and to sett out the 10th of all receipts in mony that are paid unto as rents, or profits towards charitable uses. thus. viz in 10s. because of giving many things in kinde at the doore every 4s. towards bookes and necessary things for my study. and the other 6s. to dispose towards such charitable uses, as god shall give mee a fit opportunity for, and this I desire to doe out of obedience unto god, and in love to the service and commands of god, and christ.

This day a great eclipse. see memorials of this day.

30. This day was very hot, like midsummer, went and returned safe from Stanway, the lord was good to mee in the businesse. I had an extraordinary cold and hoarsenes which I tooke I could not tell how, this day and 31: I sew. 7 pecks more of white oates, and 2 bushels 1/2 of blacke and about 5 bushels and pecke of barley in Dagnal, the seed is committed to the ground I waite on the lord for his blessing. I desire to be faithfull in thy house, oh bee thou mercifull to mine as thou alwayes hast, and make me not a reproach oh lord.

Ap: 1. mett in conference at Mrs Churches. wee had great discourse to compose differences and end them all in peace, the lord effect it, who is the prince of peace.

2. preacht this day at Halsted, many souldiers there, god good in voice and strength beyond expectation, I and my freinds were very freely and fully entertaind at Mr Wade. the day very hott, it argueth as if a drought.

3. Wesseny calved. shee tooke but twice; last time was. July. 2. she went not 40. weekes full(.) a blacke bull calfe.

Ap: 4: This weeke past the lord was good and mercifull to mee and mine in our peace and outward mercies(.) my son Tho: is somewhat better I praise god, this weeke past was for many dayes dry. cleare and hott, now cold and windy, but very healthfull weather blessed be god: all my cowes calved well through mercy, god was very good to mee and that in my inward state, giving mee a sight and sensiblenes of my deadnes and emptynes of spirit, oh that I were wise to continue upon my resting place, the Lord was good to mee in his worke on his day. he in mercy owne mee and doe mee good

5. towards night god answered prayer in raine, which continued the next morning in a plentifull ground raine. 6. sent my sister 5s. 2 cheese, and 1s. among the boyes.

7. began Dagnal ditch, I lett it unto my workemen. by the great[1] at 5d. per rod.

paid Margaret 10s. for a quarters wages.

8: Writt a letter to my Freind Mr Haines in N(ew) E(ngland) of passages til about the end of March.

April: 11: This weeke the lord was good to mee and mine in our healths. only I and my 2 children have the scab, they to purpose, the lord intends it, I trust for good to us, I desire therfore to say nothing against his will and pleasure therein, my workings of mind and vaine thoughts returne much upon mee Lord for mercy sake, doe thou lay a restraint upon them, I find my heart much shutt up in prayer, litle of spiritualnes in my thoughts, and wayes, the lord bee my quickning, and my strength(.) the lord was good to mee in the worke of the Sabbath, the lord in mercy owne mee accept mee and doe mee good: heard of a rout given by Conde to part of the French army.

April: 18: The lord was good to mee and mine in many outward mercies: my children grow better from under the scab I praise God. but I find that I for my owne part rather grow worse its thy will oh god, and therefore I am silent in the same, my sonne John ill, the lord in mercy take care of him, the season very good wherin wee owned god with thankfulnes(.) the lord was very good to mee in his worke for which my soule blesseth him, I finde my heart very dead, and vaine, lord cure it, shutt mee not up under straitnes. I pray thee, the lord was good to mee and mine, for which I desire to blesse his name and in which I desire to rejoyce. about this time my navell issued often, and much, it looked very red. but through mercy it was not sore, it also dried up againe of it selfe;

Ap: 25. The lords goodnes to us in our mercies and season, my John ill; I conceive its teeth. all these outward things, how they have their sorrowes and troubles attending them, in the lord alone is pure joy, and pure comfort: god was good to mee in the day, the lord maketh mee sensible of my deadnes of spirit in his service, the lord

[1] By the great, by great: of work done, at a fixed price for the whole amount; by task; by the piece. NED.

bee my hope and my quickning, I see it in him, it is not in mee, lord be my portion I pray thee.

29. This day I made an end of a difference betweene Catt, and Pease, I lent 21^{s}. out of my purse to doe it, Catt, and Wm Adams were by: he and his wife promise mee payment very carefull: before Michaelmas next, the lord was good to us in our day of seeking him, oh my hearts evill frame, and corruption caused mee to flee to thy mercy lett my soule find helpe with thee oh Lord, our sister Hunt of Taine[1] was admitted to our fellowship.

30. at Halsted lecture, concluded this month in visiting our sicke sister Finch, lord in mercy pitty her, and raise her up. thou givest her contentednes, give her deliverance if thou please

May: 2. This day wee brake bread. Sister Hunt with us. their were 2 absent on dissatisfaction as to the place of worship. brother clarke once and sister Thomasin the 2^{d} time Mrs Church away by reason of illnes, the lord in mercy restore her if it bee his will and pleasure, the lord instruct mee about the dissenters. the lord knoweth my heart was darke this day, yett some lively affections were in the worke, the lord maketh my obedience cheerfull, though I have not his witnesse and evidence in my bosome, lord remember us with raine, and answer prayer. god was good to mee and mine in our health and outward mercies, the children well recoverd from their scab, the lord in mercy rejoyce over mee to doe mee good.

6. This day Mrs church setled her estate, twas god brought of her heart to doe it, in disposing thereof, shee dealt very well with mee, wherein I see gods care of mee, who faileth mee not when men doe, oh that my heart might be drawn forth more after him.

May. 9. This morning my wife sent for to Mrs Mabel, shee was very ill, but god gave her a present revivall, Mrs Church satt up, and looked cheerfully, it may bee the lord may restore her, lord doe it for thy name sake, the lord was good to mee and mine this weeke past in our health, and outward mercies, the lord accept us, my itch continueth, and my navel issueth, but not sore, I dresse it not, the lord shall command health, and salvation for mee, this weeke past my heart very dead, litle quickning in mee, the lord revive my spirit, the lord my god minde mee and remember mee in much mercy to doe him service,

May. 16: God was good to mee and mine this weeke in all our outward mercies for which I blesse and praise his most holy name, Mrs

[1] Among the Great Tey landowners in 1660 were Ann, Elizabeth, Mary, and Joseph Hunt. Joseph was a five-hearth man in 1662 (ERO, D/DU 304/40).

Church continueth to recover strength: yett she continueth very ill, the lord restore her in due time. the lord letteth mee see all my strength is in him, there being nothing in mee but deadnes and sloth, but yett I doe not stirre up my selfe to lay hold on my god, the lord was good to mee in the Sabbath, his word sweete and pretious he in mercy accept of mee and doe mee good:

20. rid to Kelvedon. and dispatched. the businesse of publique faith for our poorer sort of people. god good to mee in the worke, he in mercy accept mee, and pardon any unadvisednes in mee,

21. I put my bullocks into Dagnal, they were not 3 weekes with her by 2 or 3 dayes counting the lost time.

Mr W: H. returned from London, the dutch are on our coasts with their fleete, the lord direct us. Major Haines and all our freinds well, wherein I rejoyce

May. 23. This weeke past the Lord was very gratious and mercifull to mee and mine in all outward enjoyments he is worthy to inheritt praises from mee, my heart felt some of its old encombrances, but I trust as dying things that may trouble, but shall not hurt, I desire in the sense of my sinfulnes to make out after the Lord Jesus christ with more earnestnes then ever, thou hast beene a god taking care of mee, I pray doe it for thy name sake, the season is very hot and dry, Lord send raine in thy owne due season wee entreate thee. the Lord was good to mee in the worke of the day and in the word of peace preacht, which I intreate the lord throughly to affect my heart with and give mee more and more the experience of.

24: rid to Mr Jo: Gurdons[1] at Ason in Suffolke, kindly entertained by him, the lord was very good to mee in my jorney. great hopes of raine, some fell in divers places

25. my spirit much perswaded of raine, when it seemed gone, it rained towards morning, and fine shoures die. 26. and so. 27. pastures were much gone before(,) this gave much hope to recover them againe. and so: day. 28. god is mindfull of us, even then when wee are unmindfull of him.

May: 30: This weeke past, god was good to mee and mine in all our outward enjoyments, he is most worthy of admiration and praise, the lord refresht the earth with daily showres which caused the withered creature to revive, but when shall my heart bee freshed to serve my god, deadnes, and sloth, and unspiritualnes, I find

[1] John Gurdon, M.P. for Suffolk in the Short and Long Parliaments, Member of the Council of State 1650–3; buried at Assington, Suffolk, in 1679. Venn.

and feele, but why doth it abide, is there no balme, yes, yes, enough in Jesus. but my deaded heart doth not make out unto him, doth not live on him, then I should finde him my strength I trust he will frame my heart for it more than formerly; god was good to mee in the Sabbath for which I blesse his most holy name,

June. 1: lett Thompson all the corne and grasse that groweth on my ground and an acre of grasse where I buy it, to carry for mee, he is to receive for it 17s. and his man and boy. 1s.

2: Mr H. returned home in good health, god gave us this day a very sweet showre for which wee desire to bee thankefull, hopes of more raine

June: 6: The Lord was good and kind to mee and mine in outward mercies, my deare Jane yett ill, the lord quicken up my dead heart more and more zealously to inquire after him, deadnes and neglect, I find wonderfully growing upon mee, oh when shall I once have power from above against it, the season of the yeare is very dry the creature wasteth upon the ground the lord remember us in mercy. the times are full of trouble god was good to mee in the Sabbath and in the word, he in mercy quicken mee to more livelynes

7. received of Mr W: Harlakenden: 40s. that his wife gave mee for a legacy: kept part of this day to seeke god for a blessing on Mr R.H. and W.H. in their proceedings and raine, which god gave next day, went up to London and returnd safe.

9. a fast day in London. Mrs King dead, the lord sanctifie all his dispensacons to us, and doe us good by them: Kindly used by Mr Meredith

10. presented Dr Wright with a peice of plate cost 5s. 6d. per ounce it cost mee 5li. 19s. 6d. as a token of my love to him in giving mee the schoole.

11. returnd safe home god good to mee in my jorney and all mine in my absence

June: 13. This weeke the god of heaven was good to mee and all mine in our outwards mercies, the small pox much in London god good in my preservation and mine, the lord seeth my heart was much disturbed with sinfull thoughts, which did captivate and carry mee prisoner, blessed be the lord that at last rescued mee(.) the lord with me in the Sabbath. I had helpe, I went to see a poore distressed woman, and prayed for her, the lord helpe her

14. my uncle Nath: Josselin and his wife with mee all their family well praised bee the lord, in the night I rid towards Cranham, the heate was extreame,

16. kept a day of prayer at Mrs Kitely's[1] in Ilford to seeke god in Mr H. businesse

17. returnd safe home blessed bee my god.

June. 20. This weeke past the lord was good to mee and mine in our outward mercies only my daughter Jane not well the lord restore her, the season is most vehement hott, and dry, pastures and many cornes waste very much, the lord still letts mee see my deadnes of spirit, but when shall life and strength flow in upon my spirit, many eyes are on our breach with Holland, and how Lorraine hath lurcht the princes, which speakes the Kings present successe god is shaking the earth, and he will doe it

June: 27. This weeke past the lord was good to us in many outward mercies, my litle Jane very ill, insomuch that wee even feared death, but for present shee is much revived for which I blesse my god: wee apprehended it was the spleene, wee applied an oyntment to it, and a plaister of halfe an ounce of oyntment of
** melilot[2] for the spleene, and also 3 spooneful of juyce of red fennell clarified with 6 spoonfulls of beare and swetned, the lord restore her to her health, the season very dry and hot, great raines in many places, wee had great shewes, but litle raine, the lord will owne in with his blessing herein, it is surely at hand(.) I preacht in order to catechising of the youth, the lord assist mee therein, and learne my people instruction thereby. great reports of hurt to the dutch, but nothing of action this weeke, the lord maketh mee sensible of my deadnes, but I find not strength, and indeed not stirring up my selfe against it, the lord helpe and recover mee this very time before I went out my studdy it began to raine, and ceased and cleared though the heavens promised nothing, I thought of Abraham's not eying the deadnes of Sarah's wombe,[3] and indeed before I had supped it rained a merveilous sweet shoure blessed be god, and more also is coming. and so it did in the night, and very moderately.

June. 30. Concluded this month in a solemne day of prayer, continued it at priory, the lord good to mee in the same, and dispose my heart to waite on the lord to behold his go(od) salvation which he is working, their is a sound of raine for us

[1] Probably Isabell, wife of Edward Kighley of Grayes, Essex. Visitation of 1664–8, p. 56.

[2] Melilot: a sweet kind of clover, the dried flowers of which were formerly much used in making plasters, poultices, etc. SOED.

[3] 'Sarah conceived, and bare Abraham a son in his old age, at the set time of which God had spoken to him. / And Abraham was an hundred years old, when his son Isaac was born unto him.' Genesis 21: 1, 5.

July. 1: in the morning it rained sweetly wherein I was sensible of gods goodnes, and his impression on my heart, the lord begins to give me a praying frame for Mr H. the lord seale mee for his owne. and lett mee walke as his owne before him.

July. 4. The Lord was very good to mee and mine the dayes past, my litle Jane much better then formerly, the lord affect my heart with his goodnes therein to mee, my heart I find often very unspiritual, I desire to bring it to Jesus for quickning, oh when shall I perceive his vertue enliven mee, the Major procured 15^{li}. for mee at London, which is gods goodnes who provideth mee competently, plentifully, but indeed I serve him coldly and negligently. this day I began to unfold the assembly catechisme,[1] the lord in mercy blesse me therein whose honour in the instruction of my people I mainly desire. my Tho: answered first the lord accept mee and doe mee good.

10: I made an end of having in all my hay this yeare. it was good and very well ind I praise god: Wessney buld this day. the great bullocke. called Nan. this weeke

July. 11. The lord good to mee and mine in many outward mercies, my children thrive againe but my wife very ill, the lord in mercy complete her raising up and health, my heart still under deadnes, the lord some helpe, and quickening to mee I praise him, his presence was with mee in praying and preaching but my heart dead, and shutt up, the lord heale mee by his Jesus, and perfect all his mercie and goodnes to mee.

13. preacht at Witham:

15. at Redgewell. god good to mee in my going, and returning(.) these dayes were glum, and some small raine fell.

16: Mr Cressener sent mee 4 bushels malt, it was gods goodnes to mee who heartned him to it, and I desire to eye him with praise: I paid to John Bowles for mowing my grasse 13^{s}. 4^{d}.

Bowles

July. 18: The lord very good to us all in our outward mercies, wherein he hath abounded towards mee, very much in our healths and recovery from under crasinesse and illnes. and my wife, for which I blesse and praise his most holy and pretious name, through the goodnes of god I find somewhat more enlargement on my spirit, and sense of god and my owne condicon, the outward affaires of this life I find a wonderfull comber,[2] and burthen to mee, and inward sinfull

[1] The Catechism prepared by the Westminster Assembly, prepared in the 1640s, but never officially authorized. Shaw, i, pp. 357–76.

[2] Cumber: to incommode, bother, confound, trouble, burden, load. SOED.

annoyance, but when wilt thou ease mee of my groaning, the lord was good to mee in the worke and duty of this day, the gracious god in much mercy accept mee and doe mee good, the children answer well, the lord give them a gracious seasoning.

22: kept a day of thanks at our sister Mathewes to praise god for her recovery to which wee added our occasion of seeking god in order to our breaking of bread, the day was very sweete and comfortable. My son Tho: ill, the lord revive him, its a very sickly time abroad with feavers and measils. 24: god gave us a very com-

24: fortable raine I received of the Major. 15li. which he received of Mr Stanbridge in part of my arreares of augmentacion due unto mee.

July. 25. The lord was good to mee in outward mercies blessed bee god for our healths in these very sickly times, the lord bee praised. I trust he will preserve my deare son and restore him to his health I waite on him for that sweete mercy: the lord was good to mee in spiritual refreshing, and affecting my heart in his word, but at his table, I have but litle incomes from god, yett though I catch nothing, at his command I will lett downe my nett. my brother Bat. Clarke was with us, who was away before on dissatisfaction of spirit, the lord helpe us to walke with him, and answer mee for good I most humbly intreate thee,

30. made an end of wheate harvest, my son Tho: was very ill, the lord in mercy restore him and raise him up, that he may praise his holy name, Mrs Merediths second daughter dead, the lord giveth and the lord taketh, blessed bee his most holy name, the lord learne mee this lesson from the heart.

Aug: 1: The Lord was good to mee and mine in many outward mercies: my son Tho: ill, he had the measles, it might have been sadder. and I apprehend tooke cold, from whence I conceive it proceeded, the lord bear up my heart to delight in him under every state and condicion, the lord shew mee my vaine, and sinfull heart, and how evill thoughts act in mee, the lord in mercy make mee sensible of it, my heart is very much shutt up and straittned in prayer, both at home and abroad, the lord enliven mee and act my spirit, the lord rejoyce over mee for good, the lord was good to mee in the Sabbath for which I blesse and praise his most holy name,

Aug: 8: god very gratious to mee in outward mercies, in the recovery of my son out of a very dangerous illnes, the lord accept my thankfulnes, and give us an heart answerable to mercy, many die abroad, and some suddenly. many sicke in our towne, but none dead blessed bee the name of god. my god, oh what are wee that wee are preserved, all my litle ones have been looking into the grave this summer, and yett all preserved; the lord hath aboundantly refresht the earth with raine, which maketh the grasse to spring upon the hils, the season groweth also very coole, beyond what formerly: my thoughts I find still vaine, oh lord when shall thy strength and grace free mee from them that all my meditacions may be sweete of god:

a wonderfull sickly time, and dry and hot, many died very suddenly, the lord in mercy fitt us for what he will doe with us(.) at night 21: it rayned a very gallant showre blessed be god, before this grasse burnt away very much.

Aug. 22: god very good to mee and mine in our healths, the lord continue it and sanctifie it to me, that I may see him the strength of my dayes and my life, my heart very unsuitable to the lords dispensacions, yet through mercy the lord a litle helpes mee, oh when shall the glorious spirit and presence of christ, make every imaginacion stoope unto his owne will,

25. I was at the burial of Mr Burroughes of Pebmarsh, he was carryed to the grave by my selfe and 5 others and layd into the ground, and so wee came away(.) the time is wonderfull sickly, and very many good people die in many places, which is a sad signe towards us

Aug: 29. The Lord very good to mee and mine in our healths, when very many are suddenly snacht away, and I trust he will reserve mee from the remaynder of these evills that mine eyes may see the good of his Jerusalem, through mercy my minde is more free from former annoyances which were and the remembrance of them is very bitter to mee, but I find much sloth in my imployment, and deadnes of heart not so much eyeing how I doe my worke and how god prospereth it in my hand, I looke up to thee oh Lord I pray thee undertake for mee, the lord gave us a very sweet refreshing showre so that the water run downe many houses, the lord was good to mee in the worke of the day, but my spirit groaneth under much negligence, the good lord revive mee, wee had 3 dyed in our towne this weeke. a man, woman, and child.

Sept: 5. The lord was very good and gratious to mee, and all mine in all our outward mercies for which I desire to acknowledge his goodnes and blesse his most holy name, the season continued very dry, but through mercy cold unto what it was formerly. my heart much stayed on gods goodnes in his Christ towards mee a sinner,

☞ yett I find it yeilding under the assaults of Sathan, though often bearing up against them. my hart full of expectations of great troubles likely to come on England, the lord bee our protection, god was good to mee in the worke of the day for which I blesse his most holy name,

8: Mr Meredith and his daughter came to Colne with his wife, the lord make the young one a blessing unto us all. I paid him

10s. 18s. 10s. and 18s. to Mr Heckford of Halsted for a suite of clothes die. 10th

Sept: 12: The Lord was good to mee and all mine in our health, and outward injoyments, in the society of our christian freinds, Mr Meredith, and his company being with us, the lord was good in discovering the emptines and the corruption of my spirit unto mee, the lord in mercy enliven mee against the exercise of corruption every day more and more, the lord was good to mee in the Sabbath,

☞ and the worke of it for which I blesse his name, I dreamed formerly of our being in France with our armies and the time by November next or the yeare following in 53. now Sept. 4. 1652. our fleet did the spaniards a great curtesy in destroying the French fleete that attempted to releive Dunkirke and for my part I apprehend wee shall warre with France.

15. preacht the Funerall sermon of Mr Burroughs of Pebmarsh, the lord goeth out against many good men and ministers to cutt them of, the lord warne us by his dealings(,) old Mr Rogers of Wethersfeild dead. also Mr Pindar: Mr Smythee.[1] and Mr Buckley[2] Mr Hawker all not farre of in Essex.

18. Mr Meredith and his company went from us, the lord in mercy prosper them, and returne their daughter into the family of the Harlakendens

Sept. 19. This weeke the lord good to mee and mine in all outward mercies, the season dry and cold as if it would bee an early winter, and then very hard for catle, great feare as if wee should no way imploy our poore by reason of decay of trade through our breach with Holland, but surely in all condicons the lord is able sufficiently to provide(.) our towne stood to health, I was with one Polly who much complaineth of him selfe lord make him sensible of sin more than of wrath, and make mee oh lord to keepe close to thee in every condicon, and bee thou my hiding place I humbly intreate thee,

[1] Probably William Smithies, incumbent of Rayne and Gosfield. Smith, pp. 110, 156, 167, 295.

[2] Probably William Buckley, incumbent of Mayland. Smith, pp. 110, 209, 213, 264.

the lord good to mee in the worke of the Sabbath, the lord accept mee and make mee a blessing unto him.

22. Major Haynes acquaints mee that he hath received of Mr Stanbridge 25^{li}. to my use, and that Mr Stanbridge instead of 15^{li} saith he hath received 25^{li}. wherin he wrongeth the Major

Sept: 26: The lord continueth sadly to afflict us, many die of apoplexies,[1] the lord good in my preservation and my families, my sonne John very ill with cold and rheume, the lord spare him, and lett his life be precious in his sight, the good lord accept me and rejoyce over mee for good, oh keepe mee under thy wings and feathers from sin and evill: the season very dry, litler raine hath yet fallen, last night god in mercy gave us a very great shoure, that moistens many grounds, the lord was good to mee in making me sensible of his goodnes, my own emptines, nothinges, lett mee dwell upon it oh lord every day more and more(.) the lord was good to mee in the Sabbath he in mercy accept of mee and doe mee good

28: Heard Mr Tho: Harlakenden was dead at Cambridge, the lord sanctifie all providences unto mee. This day I received of Major
14^{li}. Haines 14^{li}. part of 25^{li}. he hath received of Mr Stanbridge for mee, which I then lent to Mr William Harlakenden(,) the Major hath in hand still 11^{li}.

29: Goodman Bridge with mee about setting up a lecture at Wakes Colne, I advised and encouraged him, and promised my assistance, oh that I could doe my master any service, lord delight in mee for good

30. Kept a day of Prayer at my house with our company, the lords presence was sweete and comfortable unto us, and I trust he will graciously answer us

October. 1: received of my sister Ann the 40^{s}. I lent her, I paid her 5^{s}. and gave Tho. 10^{s}. which I promised him which 15^{s}. I borrowed of mine to bee repayd: went up to visitt Mrs Harlakenden a sad thing, an estate by reason of an entaile[2] passeth away from the wife and daughters to a younger brother, its easy with god to doe what he pleaseth,

2: received certaine bookes from London from Mr Meredith, they amount unto 4^{li}. 9^{s}. he sent a litle booke to my wife

[1] Apoplexy: a malady, sudden in its attack, which arrests the powers of sense and motion: usually caused by an effusion of blood or serum in the brain, and preceded by giddiness, etc. SOED. Probably included strokes and cerebral haemorrhage at this period.

[2] Entail: to settle an estate, land, etc., on a number of persons in succession, so that it cannot be dealt with by any one possessor as absolute owner. SOED.

October: 3. This weeke past the lord was gratious to mee and mine in very many outward mercies, the lord continueth unto us, a very comfortable season, the lord was good to mee in keeping my heart in some measure free from former annoying vaine lusts, the lord good to mee in the Sabbath, in breaking of bread, our company togither cheerfully, the lord in mercy owne us, and accept us continually.

4. my sister went away, and this day my sister Dorothy came to mee, I was kind to Ann, and the lord was good to mee in my businesse that day shee went.

11^{li}. 5: received of Major Haines. 11^{li}. residue of the 25^{li}. which he last received for mee of Mr Stanbridge I have received in all. 65^{li}. in part of 2 yeares and halfe augmentacon due to me on June: 24: 1652. past. I gave to my sister. 20^{s}. and my wife a good coate and some other things. blessed be god that giveth mee any thing, and more a heart to serve him with my estate in the wants of others. I sent 1^{s}. to an old maide of my fathers.

7: This day I began a Lecture at Wakes Colne, the lord in much mercy command a blessing on it to doe good to many soules. our sister Webb was buried this night. the lord in mercy sanctifie this providence unto us all.

October. 10. The Lord was very good and gratious to mee, and all mine in our peace, health and outward mercies, the lord cutts downe very many, oh that I might learne how to number my dayes, and doe righteousnes before the lord, my frame of heart through mercy more free from many annoying corruptions, oh that they might wither, and rise no more, the lord appeare gratious to mee, and mine in evill and sinfull dayes to preserve us from seducing, the lord was good to mee in the word preacht this day, the lord appeare more and more gratious unto mee every day.

13. This day was set apart for a publike fast to seeke gods face in regard of the breach of England and Holland, and that the Lord would direct them, in the things of his worship which I humbly beg the Lord to assist our state in. I expounded Isay. 24: and preacht on Dan: 4:37. the Lord heare and bee gratious in and through his christ.

15. This day I preacht the lecture at Halsted. on Psalme 102.v.16. a sweet heart refreshing truth, the lord was good to mee going
2^{li}. and returning. received from my tenant Shawe 40^{s}. by T. Humfry.

Oct: 17. God continued good to mee and mine, the lord continueth the season dry and cold, the like for drought never knowne, it was so also in other parts.

18. at my Lady Honywoods, the poore people that lent freely, are very likely to have their money returned unto them againe 7s. 9d. ob. in the pound

22. preacht the lecture this day at Halsted, god good therein unto mee, for which I blesse his name, I paid Wm Hickford. 1li. heard the Danish Ambassador was clapt up, till wee heare something concerning our ships

October. 24. The Lord was good to mee and mine in our outward mercies, the season continued cold, but wonderfull dry, oh that the lord would dew in his grace more, and more on my spirit(.) I finde the lord making mee more diligent in his worke, and longing for his coming yet my heart is in a great measure shutt up, and narrowed in seeking to my god(.) oh when shall my spirit bee lift up in the wayes of god

28: this day 12 yeare I married my deare wife Jane, I was called by god to preach at Wakes, wee had a meeting also, and god was good in the word blessed bee his most holy name, at night some of my neighbours supped with mee, the lord make his face to shine on us, and wee shall doe well.

25li. 29: Made up to Mr Harlakenden the Justice 25li. viz. 14li. at the priory and 11li. of the Tickett mony. which wee began to repay this day. 30: much taken up in making an accord with Carter and his tenant. heard this day my son last night was mercifully preserved when the bellrope fetched him up. the lord good to mee when I am not aware of it, a horse killed by a mad bullock, that run downe by mee, the lord good to mee a sinner oh my soule delight then in him.

31: Octob: This weeke past the lord was very good to mee and all mine in our outward mercies, the lord rideth circuite in other places with feavers and agues, the season yett dry. it began to raine die 30. at night, and seemed as if it had been sett to raine, but it was not much, waters are lower than ever I knew them and so very scarce in many places, the lord who much imployed in many workes furnished mee with strength for the same I blesse his holy name, he was good to mee in putting my former evill workings of spirit
No: 5: under, hee in much mercy delight in mee to doe mee good: goodman Burton gave mee 1 dozen candle, the lord in much mercy accept it, and returne it(.) received from Mr William Harlakenden 1li. 10s. for to buy a booke for preaching and printing his wives funerall sermon.

No: 7. The Lord was good to mee in many outward mercies, the times very still, the weather begins to moisten, but as yett not very much, I find my heart apt to unquietnes in my relation and it troubles mee, and yett it returneth on mee, I thinke I have cause, but I am sure I should bee more patient, and counsellable then I am, oh that I could looke on my wife not as under weaknes but as an heire of the same grace of life, and live with her as such, the lord helpe mee, I looke up unto thee. the lord was good to mee in the word preacht(.) the lord in much mercy accept mee and owne mee and doe mee good.

10: our freinds went towards London, the lord prosper them in their jorney, he in mercy owne them, heard. 12. of their wellfare. sent up
3^{li}. 8^{s}. by Nicholas to Mr Meredith. 3^{li}. 8^{s}. towards paiment for his bookes.

No: 14. The Lord was mercifull to mee and mine in outward things, the season warme, and dry the feilds not yet wett, the lord followeth mee on with expectation of trouble, and I am perswaded in 53. either we shall invade France or some will invade us, the lord is breaking
☞ France, they were high but they must fall, and then the Spaniard after them, and Rome also. the lord was good to mee in my health, only I am stuffed in my chest, and so wheeze much every night, the lord beareth up my heart against my old corruptions, and sweetens my spirit, with his mercy and goodnes for which I blesse and praise his name.

17. kept a day of prayer at brother Cowels sought god that he would bee pleased to fitt us to improve his goodnes to prepare for approaching adversity.

20: rid to Colchester god was good to mee going and returning(.) laid out in paper bookes and paper 7^{s}. 9^{d}. when I came home I received a letter from Mr Meredith of London to come up. Decem. 7. to London to marry his daughter.

November. 21: This weeke past the Lord renewed his goodnes to mee and mine in the sense whereof I desire to rejoyce before him, my John groweth up comfortably blessed bee god, my heart is appre-
☞ hensive of great troubles entring on England, then often I thinke on our landing men in France according to my dreame which worketh strongly in my head(,) the lord in mercy giveth mee to see the weaknes of my heart. and helpeth mee much against my old corruptions. I find my spirit much straite and dead in prayer, oh when will the lord enlarge mee. god good to mee in the Sabbath wherin I rejoyce. the weather very warme and hitherto dry very litle raine hath yett fallen.

$1^{li}.7^{s}.6^{d}$. 23. paid Mary Peake. 20^{s}. of the mony due to her from the state remaineth due still: 34^{s}. 11^{d}.

25. received this day the act for propagation of the gospel in new England among the heathen(.) I resolve to give 5^{li} my selfe and wife and children. and to promote it unto the utmost, in love to Jesus christ, and in reall desire of the salvation and fulnesse of the gentiles which I hope and expect as at hand according to the promise

Nov: 28: This weeke past the lord was good to mee and mine in many outward mercies, the lord humble my heart in the sense of my unworthines of them. the lord in mercy give mee that strength of spirit to beare whatsoever I meete with from any calmely. and not to expect any other from the creature but vanity and vexation, and when I carefully waite for good, and behold evill not to be troubled, onely lord heale my heart, and ruine if thou please, the lord shew them their failings if it bee his gracious pleasure, the lord was good and gratious to mee in the worke and duty of the Sabbath for which I blesse his holy name,

☞ This night I dreamed as formerly that the witnesses were slaine in my sight, with greife to mee, I preserved, I thought it was in England at London Criplegate Mr Sp. there and that he knew I was one of that partie

Dec: 2. Heard as if it were the states intention next yeare to send an army into Holland, and if not the Hollanders intended the like against us.

Dec. 5: God good to mee and mine with comfort in our relations and lives blessed bee his name, the good lord continue it, the good lord rejoyce over mee in his love for good, the weather very warme and dry, waters in most ponds lower than any time this yeare, the lord was good to mee in strengthen mee with health notwithstanding my great cold. good in the worke of the Sabbath for which I blesse his name, heard of a fight in the Downes with the Dutch.

6. rid up to London, our jorney comfortable, when at Mr Merediths, I was very ill, even overcome with winde they were very kinde to mee: 7. I privately in Austins church London married Mr R.H. and Mrs M(ary): M(eredith)—9: I came out of London old Mr R.H. paid for my horse and gave mee gloves and my wife, and 2^{li}. towards my jorney. his son promised to send mee downe the Synods annotations etc.[1] but the brides freinds as yet shewed mee no

[1] The only reference to this work in Thomason is *Additional Annotations, or a collection of all the additions to the third impression of that most excellent work intituled, Annotations upon all the Books of the Old and New Testament* (1658) (E. 1777).

respect. I dined at Colne die. 10: found all well blessed bee god it neither was wett, nor windy. but calme frizing weather. a good jorney at such a time of the yeare. I also perfected my businesse with Mr Stanbridge.

$1^{li}. 7^{s}.$ 12. paid Mary Peake. $1^{li}. 7^{s}.$ more, all but $5^{d}.$ due to her, which I will give her with the first opportunity.

Dec: 12. The lord was good and gratious to mee, and all mine in all our outward mercies in my jorney and returning againe, and yet my heart was under many great annoying lusts, my spirit I finde much shutt up in prayer both publicke, and private, and truly I knowe not what to doe, my eyes are towards the lord, oh when wilt thou quicken mee.

15. reckoned with Mr Clopton and paid him his part of moneyes received on the augmentations unto September 29. 1651. past, he oweth mee. $2^{li}. 11^{s}. 0^{d}.$ for bookes.

Wm Clopton.

18: given mee an acceptable guift by Mr R.H. for marrying him the large annotations on the bible.

Dec: 19: The lord continued good to mee and mine in all our outward mercies for which I blesse and praise his most holy and pretious name, the season continueth dry to wonder waters never so low in any memory: the lord good to us in our friends and children my brother Jo: Humphry came to bee with mee a while, the lord was good to mee in the sabbath. I declard I intended to give $5^{li}.$ towards N. England businesse as a loane to the lord, nay tis a debt.

Dec: 26: This weeke god good to mee and all mine in our outward mercies, I made a gathring for the Indians. I gave $5^{li}.$ and my family. gathered in mony more. $4^{li}. 8^{s}. 6^{d}.$ and there was underwritt, more $32^{li}.$ the lord accept what I have endeavoured to doe for him in it both by word and example, and the lord in his christ pardon all unto mee. this weeke two of our brethren are departed from us to the Lord, the Lord in much mercy looke on us to make up our losses, the good lord more and more empower mee against every evill and enlarge my heart in his service.

28. this day wee buried our brother Browne I preacht on Pro: 14.32, the weather continueth still very dry and warme.

30. invited to my Lady H. kindly entertained, heard there that the Londonders bought up bayes[1] fuel and ivy wonderfully in London,

[1] Bay: short for bay-tree or bay-laurel; usually in plural, leaves of sprigs of this tree. NED.

being eagerly sett on their feasts, oh that my heart were as zealous for god

31: I reckoned with Mr Meredith and paid him all I owed to him. viz. 3^{li}. 8^{s}. by nicholas and. l^{li}. 5^{s}. my selfe, he abated mee 1^{s}. 6^{d}. in Burroughs, and in Bridges but had his bill to the full in the rest.

Jan: 1: This wee call new yeares day. it was a cleare lightsome day, the lord give mee a new holy heart, for I expect it a searching troublesome yeare, the lords holy will bee done in all things. heard that the army kept solemne dayes of fasting and prayer. on Jan: 28. and 29. a signe of some great resolucions on foote among them, the lord our god direct and turne all for good, and bottome my heart on him, who is the alone and onely good: I paid Nicholas 1^{s}.

2: the Lord was good to mee and mine in outward mercies, my Jane onely gently visited with an ague, the lord good to mee in helping mee against my many lusts and temptacons, so that they have not that commission to trouble mee as at other times, the lord setts my minde more on himselfe and the worke he is about more than formerly, and I desire more closely to walke with him then formerly, oh lett thy selfe and thy christ bee my portion for I desire nothing else in heaven and earth: the lord was good to mee in the sabbath, I renewed the motion for new England, some poore came in, most of the richer sorte came in(.) I received in money. 4^{li}. 17^{s}. 10^{d}. and Mr Cressener subscribed 40^{s}. wee have somewhat above 50^{li}. blessed bee our god in what wee shall doe in this worke, the lord accept it, and advance his owne glory thereby

10^{li}. 3. This day I lent to Mr William Harlakenden. 10^{li}. heard againe that some great designe is upon the anvill, the lord take care of his owne interest and glory, for all men seeke themselves

4: Mr Fuller[1] preached here at Colne: 5° it rained a very sweete shoure. 6°. Mr Sparrow[2] preacht the lecture at Wakes Colne, this latter part of the day it began to raine, and giveth hope of aboundance, the ground was never so long dry in the memory of man the earth not wett to the shares point since beginning of March; many springs dry ponds almost dry and so continued to this day: my daughter Janes fitt of the ague through mercy much abated, my

[1] John Fuller, at this time incumbent of Stebbing, later ejected. Calamy; Smith, pp. 26, 41, 407.

[2] William Sparrow, vicar of Halsted, but ejected as a nonconformist in 1662. Smith, p. 394; Calamy.

wife somewhat, this points to the creatures vanitie the lord sheweth mee more into the basenes of my heart, and the sense of it filleth mee with trembling and astonishment, so that I am at a(t) losse many times, the good lord stablish mee through beleeving, and fill my heart with joy thereby.

7. Mr Clopton was with mee, he was satisfied in my busines, he promised to give mee an account of my matters at Chelmsford at soone as may bee,

Jan. 9. This weeke past the lord good to mee in many outward mercies, he looked from heaven on us with some showres, and now frost, which is seasonable, into my family god hath looked and gently afflicted my daughter and maide(,) looke into their hearts, lord and mine and therby doe us good: the times darke nothing stirring, though great expectations; the state only issued a proclamation against Jesuites to be gone by March. 1. next. this day it snew very much, I trust the lord will command convenient and seasonable weather for his poore people, the lord was good to mee in the Sabbath, in the worke of it, but I find litle working on my heart or others. gathered. 3^{li}. more for New England designe.

13. preacht this day at Wakes Colne god good to mee therin. heard Mr Meredith was well on the way. Mr W. Harlakenden received 18^{li}. to my use at Chelmsford.

Jan: 16. This weeke the lord was good to mee in many mercies, my Janes ague continueth but gently, the lord in due time will remove it, as going to preach heard Mr Brackly was dead, I promised to preach his funeral, its of mercy my children are not fatherles and my wife a widdow he was taken suddenly with an apoplexy or num palsy. he lay not above 3 dayes, lord stirre mee up by all unto more watchfulnes and close walking I pray thee. the lord was good to mee in the word this day, and yet I was very backward in preparing my selfe thereunto, the good lord make mee more intent on his worke, the lord good to mee in keeping my heart close to him in his wayes, and in helping mee to looke up unto him for strength, and to eye him in his pathes and wayes towards mee.

17. preacht the funeral sermon of Mr Brackley of Gaines Colne. the lord bee good and gratious to mee in my spirituall condicon as thou art in my outward

18: Nan came to us.

22. lent Mr William Harlakenden 30^{li}. he now oweth mee an 100^{li}. he promiseth to give mee 1^{li}. 15^{s}. in the spring for a booke. I hope

it will bee. 40^s. my god is good to mee oh that I could bee mindfull of his service: this day I found the ground was not wett one spitt into the ground.

Januar: 23. This weeke past my heavenly father very gracious unto mee in soule and body. the ague god tooke from my deare Jane. the lord blessed us all with health, divers of our neare freinds recovering, the lords eye is on my outward man to provide for mee its hee that feedeth, and clotheth mee, and indeed the lesse I see of man taking care for mee, the more I see continually of god. I will love thee oh my god! but for thy christ I will not bee silent, oh that the wale for thy name and thy glory might even eate mee up. the lord good to us and our nation. newes as if a strange starre were seen in Denmarke. and a comett over the popes pallace. the lord hasten his worke his strange and his glorious worke.

24: my Janes ague returned, lord in mercy, remember thy wonted goodnes to her and mee. Mr Littell begun to breake up the farther Dagnal for mee, the lord give a blessing to my labour their.

Mr Stebbin[1] with mee to propose a businesse unto mee, wherein he desired my helpe I promised it as far as I might

Mr Clopton with mee about Gaines Colne,[2] men tumble up and downe in the world. I promised to propound him, Mr Meredith and Mr Harlakenden earnest for Mr Fuller of Stebbing who is a good man

This day was very chearfull and pleasant, the yeare riseth apace, the lord raise up our hearts to watchfulnes and care.

and now I am sensible this day ends my 36. yeare. in which the lord hath beene very good to mee and all my family. his provision for mee bountifull, though I have been unworthy, yett I desire in the uprightnes of my heart to owne and serve my god and follow him through any condicon

the great actions this yeare are the troubles of France, where the Princes rather loose then gaine. Orleans fallen of from Conde, Spaine hath gotten much of France, this yeare(,) filled his kingdome with troubles assisting the Princes. winning Gravelin and afterwards Dunkirke.—Barcellona in Catalonia, and thereby even reducing that kingdome,—Casal in Montferrat and reducing that under Mantua to the great prejudice of the French interest.

The Germans quiet, great noise of their diet but nothing done

[1] Probably Solomon Stebbing or William Stebbing, both big landowners in Great Tey in the 1660s. The latter was an elder of the Lexden Classis. Shaw, ii, p. 388.

[2] John Clark began his ministry at Colne Engaine on 25 May 1653, though he was not approved by the Triers until 15 June 1654. He was ejected in 1662. Smith, p. 368.

as yett. the Turkes and the Venetians calmed, and its said now treating a peace,

The English quiet at home and also in all their dominions, favoured by the spaniard, courted by the Portugal with whom wee have almost perfected a peace he buying it(.) the French treate us. the Swedes and wee gaze but each are sending their agents(.) the Dutch fought us all along this summer at our owne doores, the Dane seizeth our shipping and stops us in the Sound

The Dutch and wee are now making great naval preparations, and so is the Spaniard thus the world is togither by the eares, overturning one another, not minding the heires interest and that he viz Christ is not only ready to claime but to take his right in the ☞ world, arise oh Lord and judge among the nations for the right is thine, and I thy poore servant preach and pray for the lifting up of thy kingdome and waite for it, and because I beleeve I make not hast I knowe shakings, deceivers apostacies are at hand, keepe mee as thine, for I trust my selfe under the shadow of thy wings. and when thou comest to take thy kingdome remember mee thy servant and forgett not my family I intreate thee. even so Lord Jesus come quickly.

☞ This yeare great hopes of the Heathens conversion in the West at N.E. and discourse of something in the East, one saith

— — — — — — — — — — — — — — — — — — —

37. yeare of my age. 1652. Jan. 25.

Jan: 25. sensible this day entred me into my 37 yeare. the lord bee with mee therein to keepe mee from sin and temptacion. and preserve mee spotlesse to his owne kingdome with thee I leave all my waies. I am thine I pray thee take care of mee for under thy wings oh god doe I putt my trust.

27. preacht the lecture at Wakes that it might not fall, though on a suddain desire. the lord give mee to tast of that mercy of god of which god gave mee to speake(.) goodman Death, dead, the lord fitt mee for my worke and service.

28: preacht at the buriall of William Death, on psal. 25.14.18: he died almost suddenly the lord make mee mindfull of my latter end, and fitt mee to walke with my god.

29. kept a day of prayer at priory, it was very spiritual(,) my heart vile and base therin the good lord fitt mee for his table—presence

I waite on thee lett mee not bee ashamed. the lord entered my yeare 37. with his worke, the lord continue mee in his employment.

Jan. 30: The lord was good to mee and mine in outward mercies, my Jane only ill with her ague but through mercy it abateth, shee never came into my thoughts this day to disquiet mee(.) the lord was with us at his table in many teares, and heart brokennes, but poore sinfull wretch as I am the lord doth not particularly signally speake to mee but I will waite on him for one day in his courts is better than a 1000^{d} dayes else—where, gods service is a rich recompence and reward. Mr Fuller preacht in the morning for mee, in the afternoone at Gaines Colne, the lord send mee a good neighbour there, and the lord make my heart more spirituall and holy in thy worship every day then other.

31. Mrs Brackly sent for mee, I went unto her, and did her business shee desired, the lord give mee a heart to pitty and to bee helpeful to the widdow and fatherles, whom in this matter I did desire to eye. I promised Gains Colne men to helpe them the next Lords day. Mr R.H. gave mee a token of his love.

Feb: 3. preacht the Lecture at Wakes, a stirring cutting sermon the lord make it so to mee and others, at home I had a letter from my uncle N(athaniel) J(osselin) wherin he and Mr C. desire mee to goe on with my apocaliptiqu(e) studdies.

Feb: 6: The lord continued good in outward mercies to us, Janes ague through mercy is not so strong as formerly, blessed bee the lord, the season dry, and now cold with an east winde(.) I preacht at Gaines Colne afternoone on psal. 128.5. the lord awaken that people to endeavour the good of that place in a minister. the lord good to mee in soule and body wherein I desire to rejoyce

9. this morning Capt. Stebben sent us 2 bushels wheat. it was the lords act, who saith, such neglect my poore servant doe you shew love to him, engage my heart lord by all unto thee. spent part of this day in pryer at Mr Littells, the residue at Gaines Colne in hearing Mr Glover,[1] I drew up the towne peticon for him,

Feb: 13. the lord continueth good to mee and mine in our outward mercies, my litle Jane reviving from under her ague. the season dry and warme, litle or no snow and lesse raine all this winter not

[1] Hugh Glover, rector of Debden 1644–52, then to Stanway and, in July 1653, to Finchingfield; ejected in 1662. Smith, pp. 375–6; Calamy.

one ground raine. I am glad the lord maketh mee to take notice of what he doth in my house and abroad, raise up my heart to more holynes and spiritualnes(.) the lord sending mee helpe, I preacht this day at Gaines Colne, the lord I trust will afford mee a good neighbour in that place.

Feb: 20: This weeke past the lord good to mee in all our healths, the season very dry, and cold shewes of raine, but passing away, and persons are even dead and not consider the work of the lord: the earth was not wett to the share point all this winter, my minde is taken up with expecting what god is doing, and I desire to blesse him, that he hints to my spirit its my wisedome to make peace with him, and to continue therein and walke daily with him, but oh my leanes(,) oh how heavy is my heart in such waies the lord in mercy arouse mee and awaken mee, and let me not be secure or intent on the outward things only. I thought the yeare might bring in want upon the kingdome(.) I provided some bread with Joseph, the lord lay into my soule faith and patience that I may persevere with him; I am waiting for the dawnings of gods salvation in Eng-
☞ land and behold trouble, indeed the next act I expect is the witnesses slaughter, judgement in the house of god, lord fitt mee for what thou art about to doe. the lord was good to mee this day in the word preacht. but I find my deadnes and backwardnes of heart to gods worship to abide still on mee, oh when will the lord arise on mee with healings.

8s. paid Nicholas Hurrell 8s. I now owe him, but, 3li. which was presently paid.

24: a hearer at Wakes, great reports yesterday of our victory over the Dutch, this day it was cold, windy frost, snew and so continued die. 25°

26: Janes ague tooke her againe my wife thinketh with feare and greife to see her mother so tormented as shee was with a felon[1] on her finger.

Feb. 27. The Lord good to mee and mine in all our outward mercies, the season cold, and winterly some frost, and snow, and therein seasonable, water very scarce, most of our ponds and wells even dry. oh lord affect our dead hearts, and awaken us from under our drowsines, and sleepines of spirit, through mercy the lord maketh mee sensible of great things doing, but my heart is not easily raised up to converse with god, my heart is dead in my

[1] Felon: a small abscess or boil, an inflamed sore; especially a whitlow under or near the nail of a finger or toe. SOED.

ministeriall worke. it runs much in my minde that Mar. 3. next may bee a great and strange day with Englands parliament. Lord thou alone art my trust lett mee never bee ashamed I pray unto thee,

28. month ended with a merveilous snow, which melting at night, March: 1. it snew and continued to frize at night and so march entred, haile, and wholesome weather

this day I brought divers businesse for my estate into order, clearing up divers accounts and evening those reckonings that were on my hand, for which I praise my god, oh that the lord alone would cleare the account of my soule.

3. Publique fast, few in the contry had notice to keepe it. Mr Sparrow came of his owne accord to mee to joyne with mee in the worke of the day, but there is somewhat more on my spirit, I shall long to heare what is done at Westminster this day, I hope all is well and quiet there, the enemie begins to appeare both in Ireland and Scotland its but weakely yett, the issue of thes things god only knoweth.

4 and 5. dayes, it was windy, and now and then shoures, so that the wayes and pathes were dirty

March: 6: This weeke past the lord good to mee and mine in all outward mercies, my wife ill in head and teeth but beareth up through mercy and so doe my babes, the weeke past a litle raine, I hope god will give us springing weather, I was afraid of some trouble at London before this: blessed bee god for lengthning out our tranquillity, my heart I find much running out after gods appearing in the last day. but I am very dead in my present worke, lord when wilt thou quicken mee(.) Mrs Mabel Elliston returned safe home after a long absence from her freinds. the lord good to mee in the word preacht, but oh how deadly, and drowsily doe people heare, oh Lord god arise

8: this was a warme showring day. which coming after snow, and some former dewes hath comfortably moistned the face of the earth.

10: a hearer at Wakes lord fitt mee for thy crowne I pray thee. 2. Kings. 8.11.13.[1] that passage I apprehend over this generation, oh the evill

[1] 'And he settled his countenance stedfastly, until he was ashamed: and the man of God wept. / And Hazael said, Why weepeth my lord? And he answered, Because I know the evil thou wilt do unto the children of Israel: their strong holds wilt thou set on fire, and their young men wilt thou slay with the sword, and wilt dash their children, and rip up their women with child. / And Hazael said, But what, is thy servant a dog, that he should do this great thing? And Elisha answered, The Lord hath shewed me that thou shalt be king over Syria.' 2 Kings 8: 11–13.

☞ this generation will doe to the lord in his worship and servants, what not, I desire to weepe over the false hearts of brethren, oh how apt is brother to betray brother, wee are spirited fitt for the evill of the last times

11. a hearer at Halsted, dined with Mr Sparrow, and baptized his son William for him the lord give us comfort in our posterities

March. 13. This weeke past the lord was good to mee and mine in our outward mercies, wherein he hath abounded towards mee, and mine, my wife and John ill with their teeth, which I hope the lord intends for good to him, but oh how ill is my heart, very undigested in preaching and in making mention of god and his truthes, oh lord raise up my heart unto more life and quickning I most humbly intreate thee, come in with thy power from above upon mee for the lords sake I intreate thou. oh enlarge my heart in supplication and seeking of thee, lett mee not bee dead and senseles as it were in thy pathes and wayes. the lord in mercy pardon all my sins and accept mee in his christ.

Oates sown: 15. 16. 17. sew my oates in Dagnal they cost mee. l^{li}. 17^{s}. the lord give a blessing to the seed that is committed to the ground that it may prosper,

19. paid in unto Mr Crane for the use of N.E. towards the propagating the gospell to the Indians, as a freewill offering from divers inhabitants of Earles Colne 54^{li}. 11^{s}. 10^{d}.

March: 20. The lord good to us in outward mercies, my wife farre better in health then formerly(.) the season dry warme, the lord remember us, my heart not stirring for god, the lord in mercy humble mee and pardon all against him.

22. this was a very cleare, dry, and sunshining day, scarce the like at this time, my deare wife had a smart ague fitt, her first was terrible on the lords day at night.

24: I begun to sow barly on the hither hill of Dagnal, my wife was very ill at the coming on of her fitt, the lord was with her to support her and to abate the fitt

March: 25: went this day to Messing, 3 of my Tenants there are lately dead, blessed bee the lord in the preservacion of mee and mine,

1653. I lett Medcalfes land unto one Smith untill Michaelmas he is to pay for it 22^{s}. at Mids: and Michaelmas

March: 26. 1653. a review of that estate god hath mercifully given mee.

Lands as formerly.
Mr J.L: as formerly. 150^{li}.
Mr Jeff. L. paid in 100 that is Mr W.H. hands— } 100
Mr P. as formerly - - - - - - - 50.
25. March past improvement of Mrs Maries land. 4^{li}. 5^{s}. now in total - - - - - - - - - - - - - } 89. 5.—increase 4^{li}. 5^{s}. 0^{d}.
Stocke as formerly about. - - - 32. 0.

in Young's hands 10^{li}. paid in W.Br.	15. 0.	5. 0. 0.
in Mr. W:H. hands - - - - - - - - - - -	100. 0.	100. 0. 0.
in E.J: hands of W. - - - - - - - - - - -	25. 0.	25. 0. 0.

my debts were 12^{li}. now 32^{li}. so that abates the 20^{li}. out of this - 134. 5. 0

their remaineth this yeare a great addicon to my estate, viz - - - - - - - - - - - - - - - - - - - 114. 5. 0.

the lord hath been also good to my family in their healths, the lord in mercy raise up my poore wife who is sicke with an ague, the lord good to mee I trust more in my spirituall estate making mee sensible of my emptines, desirous to live wholly in himselfe, yett I find my heart very dead and unspiritual in my daily, particular waies, at night it rained very sweetly, as if god would satisfie the parched earth: it was a sweetning shoure,

March: 27. This weeke past the lord was good to mee and mine, in many outward mercies only my deare wife sicke with a violent ague, which the lord in due time remove, and sanctifie that hand of his unto us all, the lord make mee more sensible of my sinfulnes so as to endeavour nothing more than to gett power in and through christ, over my unbeleiving and dead and barren spirit, the season dry, and somewhat cold, but how secure, am I and the rest of the nation not minding the hand on the wall in the season, the plague not in London which is very much considering the mortality in the other places and the strange seasons wee have had, heard of B. cowels sad trial, lord helpe him under it, and looke on my posterity in mercy to sanctifie their hearts,

28. sew about 2 acres and 1/2 of barly in Dagnal, my mind much returned to our attempts against France, how unlike so ever it is,

☞ yett I beleeve assuredly it will come about and that will glad good men to see our power bent against Romes power, thy day o France is coming, thou art weighed and found too light, thou art numbered and thy time is even expired, god will avenge the bloud thou hast shed, thou must fall and rise no more, and Frances fall though it rejoyce thee oh Spaine, yet it is but as a lightning unto thee before death.

France

32^{li}. this was the roll of my debts, besides divers engagements in those moneyes which I had appointed unto another use. 29. day the god of my mercies sent us sweet warme showres, this day I made an end of sowing my barly, except a few roddes that I digge

30. this day kept as a preparation to receiving the sacrament, at my brother Brownsons the lord was good in the same to us, the lord was good to my deare wife, who this day in a manner missed her ague fit. oh what shall I render unto the lord?

April: 1. and. 2. entred with very sweet shoures as to us, for which I desire to blesse the lord

April. 3. The Lord was good to mee and mine in our outward mercies my John weaning(,) oh that I and mine were weaned from sin, and our meate were the will and the worke of god, the lord was good in the Sabbath, and at his table my heart much affected with his love, rejoyced to see a stumbling brother there. oh that my heart could melt before the lord, so that I could feare him and his great goodnes, this day the winde was very high, the day cleare.

9^{li}. 10^{s}. 4: paid goodman Mathew 21^{li}. 10^{s}. my rol of debt is now 29^{li}. 10^{s}. very sweete warme growing weather, god hath given us much more raine then in many other places. this sixt day the lord blessed our parts with a very comfortable raine,

7. heard a profitable sermon, the lord ingage my heart against every evill, heard the spaniards had seized our merchants, because of our stop of the hamburg-plate, this day warme and very comfortable after the raine

8. went abroad and returned die. 14. found all in health blessed bee my god, the lords most holy name is worthy of all praise, bought some of Mr Westlyes bookes as many as amounted to 3^{li}. 14^{s}. Mr Tomson had one of mee at 4^{s}. 6^{d}. I owe unto him the rest viz. 3^{li}. 9^{s}. 6^{d}. I preacht at great Birch, god gave mee much comfort and content in my jorney and freinds, for which I praise his most holy name,

5^{li}. 15: I now owe to Nicholas Hurrell 5^{li}. which I have borrowed of him. this is repaid.

April. 17. This weeke past the lord good in many mercies, the season dry yett sweet showres but cold. corne very good on the ground never better. my wife ill with an ague, I was not well, the lord mercifull to mee in my worke, the lord sanctifie my heart owne mee and doe mee good.

N.E. 18: I sent up to Major Haines a large relation of our affaires for 52. to that day, to send into N.E. to his father, I sent up also by Mr R.H. a bill to his father untill this day, the mony I sent was 2^{li}. 5^{s}. I sent for 2 or 3 bookes(.)

☞ 20. This day I was much musing on future events, and I heard somewhat confirming mee, that great mutations are at hand, the lord take care of his owne, and turne all unto good for his own glorious name, this day the army men turned the Parliament out.

23: In my course I read. Isay. 55. a chapter full of refreshing, lord I knowe thy counsell shall stand, and the thoughts of thy heart take place to succeeding generations beare up my faith on thee, thou god of my salvation.

Ap. 24: This weeke the lord was good to mee and mine in many outward mercies for which I blesse his holy name, the lord is worthy to bee loved for he is gracious and of great mercy and compassion, a tender god there is none like him, my heart not much disquieted in thes overtures as seing god breaking one after another, untill he cometh whose right it is which he will hasten in due time, and in the meane time I will pray and waite, the lord was good to mee in the Sabbath and the worke of it, for which I blesse his most holy name.

m: 4: a botle[1] of hay. more: another.

☞ 26: this day I lent Mr John Littell a very great load of my hay,
J.L. he is to give mee the next yeare a load of better hay, and bigger. he had also 4 fannes[2] of chaffe(.) wee mett 4 houres to seeke god, the lord heare and helpe, I reckoned with him, and his account amounts unto. 9^{li}. or therabouts, he now oweth mee 4^{li}. towards this

May: 1: The weeke past god good to mee and mine, the weather very dry, speaking a drought, yet the feild doth not much raine, water exceeding scarce, all quiett every where notwithstanding this great change at hand, most serious men are silent under it, as being an evill time, many rejoyce; the lord stayeth up my heart to rely on him, and leave the issue of all things to him, who taketh care for us,

[1] A botle of hay: a bundle of hay. SOED.

[2] Fan: an instrument for winnowing grain; also as a verb, to winnow. SOED.

it was general discourse now downe goe the Ministers, but why should wee feare to suffer if god please to have it so. I find my base inward vaine thoughts, deadnes, and straitnes of spirit on mee, with a very slothfull common heart. lord how long! I cry, and yet, how long! this day it dewed a litle the former heate abated, and the earth refreshed, the lord was good to mee this day in the worke of the Sabbath for which I blesse and praise his holy name,

☞ 4. In regard of the troubles of the times I resolve to buy no more bookes for present then absolutely needfull untill with the mony set apart for bookes and givings, I have paid the 3^{li}. 9^{s}. 6^{d}. I owe Mr Tompson. and 5^{li}. 10^{s}. to my sister moneys that I owe for bookes and that I borrowed to give away.

5: Lord I blesse thee for inward esteemes of thee, and that I can undervalue all thes things in comparison of thou. heard but not true Cromwell was made Lord High Protector of England, all apprehend a storme on the ministry. lord arme mee with faith and patience

May: 8: This weeke past the lord was good to mee, and mine in our outward mercies, which the lord our god continue, the 3 last dayes the season was very hott, which causeth much corne already to fade at the roote, much talke in these times and very false, men striving how to putt others in feare, the lord uphold my heart in uprightness for in him alone doe I trust, my heart is very much shutt up in prayer, lord when wilt thou enlarge it, oh that my spirit were fixed, thro(u)ghly threwn on thee at all times. this day was coole, heard of the hopefull recovery of my uncle Josselin, the lord was good to mee in the worke of the Sabbath for which I praise him.

9. joyned in a day of humiliacon at my Lady Honywoods, spake from 46. psalme, the lord give us to be still and silent, and waite on him and see what he will doe, evill is determined against this generation. heard againe of very great pressing at London, both for sea and land, the lords will bee done.

11: a fine cooling dew for a quarter of an houre in the morning. the raine afterwards passing away 13. in the morning I found it had rained a sweete shoure, heard of strange carriages in England.

May: 15. The Lord was many wayes good unto mee and mine, my wife ill, but it was as shee desired(.) the lord gave us a litle wett some great showres fell in some places, my heart very dull and shutt up in gods wayes, and yett I cannot encourage myselfe to lay hold on god, but doe my worke very coldly the lord in mercy pitty mee, and heale mee for his name sake,

17. mett in prayer at Mr Cresseners the lord gave mee some brokennes of heart, in seeking his face for which I blesse his most holy name.

☞ 18: Perhaps my dreame and vision of the ruined chappell on one side (there being 2 sides and one end written on) wherof was in capital letters domus Lancastrie ruina:[1] note out the 3 kings that must bee rooted out, and why should not I when I see many of the thoughts of my head fulfilled trust in god for the accomplishment of the rest, apprehending there is something of god in those thoughts and visions, agreeing with the scripture,

20: heard of the death of Mr Meredith, who died the day before, may. 19. 53. the lord intends something. by hastning many of his saints more then ordinary into the grave, the lord fitt mee, and his for what is coming on us.

May: 22: This day lowring hott, the grasse begins to wither, and some corne to fade, yett many places more wanting raine then with us, many springs stopt so that they run not others quite dried up, the lord hasten raine in his due season, the lord good to mee and mine in our health, saw a bill whereby it appeareth 2 have died of the plague, lord stay thy hand. if it bee thy pleasure oh lord, my heart was warme in preaching the word. I blesse the lord for it, but I find such undiscerningnes in my spirit of fellowship with god, and am so unacquainted with the life and power of christ with mee, that my heart is amazed at the same, lord when wilt thou heale my soule.

25. one sett up Cromwells picture at the exchange and over it 3. Crownes, and written tis I, under it divers verses, beginning.

Ascend three thrones, brave Captaine, and Divine
by the will of god, o Lyon, for they are thine.[2]

heard as if endeavours were to bring the cheife goverment to one person. divers pretend the visions of god for it, the title of King probably will bee waved, and some other pitched on.

27. a hearer at Halsted. Mrs Clench somewhat more composed, blessed bee god, the lord raise her up, and bee her refreshment, I dined with them at the ordinary at Halsted: oh that my heart new sett

[1] The fall of the house of Lancaster.

[2] This differs slightly from the version in the Tanner MSS., quoted in the DNB article on Cromwell:

Ascend three thrones, great Captain and divine,
I' th' will of God, old Lion, they are thine,

on god for many looke all for good in their generation, and sett on plenty, fearing no changes

May: 29. The Lord good to mee and mine in outward mercies, my wife ill, and feareth her selfe, the lord I trust will bee her strength, and her support, and spare her as my comfort, this day excessive hot, great signes of raine, it dewed a litle, and so past away, the lord good to mee in the word preacht, my heart is drowsy; lord arouse mee. gods hand very sad in the distraction of Mrs Jane Clench:

30: god answered prayer in a wonderfull, shoure, especially at Colne and so to Halsted and into the North, the lord bee praised for this mercy.

June: 1: rid to London, die. 3°: returned safe, to god bee praise, the lord good to mee in my busines I went about, only my owne heart very carnal, and full of vaine thoughts in my returne, I went and bought no one booke: Camdens Britannia is buyable for. 25^{s}. and Mercators Maps. for. 3^{li}. 5^{s}.

3. newes of a dreadful fight at sea, brought up by the fishermen of our coasts

June: 5. God good to mee in many mercies and also to mine, our cowes put out into the streete by a neighbour put us to very much trouble all this day, my heart hath often runn riott from god, and justly may make everything a trouble, it might have been a sadder providence, my base unworthy heart calleth for disquietments indeed, my heart much on trouble, harping, that successe or losse will hasten it on the lords, yet I alwayes thought our fleet would prevaile, and I had such an intimation against Danes and Hollanders not yett without some losse on our part, the lords will be done in all things

11: rid to Colchester returned exceeding weary, my body very unfitt for travel, at night it dewed very comfortably.

June: 12: our newes of the fight proved not as reported(,) our victory very great and losse litle to speake of(,) the Dutch cowed before us, and stucke not to their worke like men; this weeke came out the summons for the councell to meete at Whitehall July. 4: next, my expectations are very sad and strange over this generacion, the lord fitt mee for what he will doe, oh lett mee not bee carryed away with any temptacion, I intreate thee, I find my spirit very negligent as to my worke, I doe not pen down my stragling spirit to my worke, lord I pray thee helpe mee and make my heart more spirituall and holy, day by day I intreate thee,

13. told that the Anabaptists as called suppose(,) the army against the protestant religion, and that they will downe with it as now established; lord thy will bee done. I know great things must bee done, only take the care of the glory of thy great name.

14: reports that wee had landed men at the Texell; the lord at night untill the next morning gave us a very comfortable refreshing raine. oh that wee could feare the lord and his goodnes, I perswade my selfe, god will give to thes men successe, and prosperity, which will encourage them in their worke, and cause men to account themselves in a very excellent state.

17. a new refreshing shoure for some houres causing the water to run downe the streets. neither moone, nor wind, could promise it, which many persons more looke unto then god him selfe.

18: a great raine, drought, and smiting the earth with a curse, is much in my minde(,) lord performe thy owne counsell. only lett Zions mount be glorious

June: 19. The Lord good and gratious to mee and mine in all our outward mercies for which I praise him, the lord hath given us much raine, and I apprehend, it may bee the purpose of god to smite the crop by raine, not giving this sinfull nation to injoy, their thoughts in the creature, it dewed this day also: my heart a litle and but a litle more quickned and lett out in prayer, this day, wherein formerly I have found much straitnes, I was very drowsy in my body and very dull in my mind unto heavenly things the lord helpe mee, yett very sensible that the lord give mee inward desires and also some endeavours to keep close to him in integrity and uprightnes.

20: the morning was a smiling answer of prayer, it being dry, and cleare, and coole, as if the lord intended a comfortable refreshing of the earth, and then refreshing unto us the appointed weekes of the harvest. sold my black bullocke for 2^{li}. 11^{s}.

23. faire weather: this day wee kept a day of humiliacon at Wakes Colne, Mr Sparrow and I preach and Mr Layfeild. Mr Buckly, and Mr Chandler[1] prayed, I was very sensible of gods going from England called on people to bee found mourners for the abominacions among us, and to sticke close to god in his ordinances, the good lord accept us and doe us good in his christ.

[1] Francis Chandler, incumbent of Woodham Ferrers until *c.* 1653, then of Kelvedon, and later Theydon Garnon; ejected in 1660, but remained curate until 1662. Smith, pp. 367–8; Calamy.

25. hops wasted, and blacked, and made farre worse by the raine, that men thought there would be scarcely any in the kingdome, this god can doe,

June: 26: The Lord was good to mee, and mine in our health, my steps in some measure upheld by him yett I doe not find that sweet refreshing from god in his word that I have done, my family occasions doe rather hinder mee in the way of the lord, I roule my soule on thee for in thee onely doe I putt my whole trust, and confidence, my heart is sensible that the last dayes draw neare, and that sad things are determined against the things of god, helpe mee oh lord in the discerning of thy minde and will to keepe close to mee, and use mee in the worke of my mistery, as an instrument to doe soules good I intreate thee.

29. A day of prayer in order to our breaking of bread, the lord good to divers in the same, helping them with affections and supplications. Mr H. spoke very confidently of the approaching troubles, it made mee glad to see any warned, at night it rained and perhaps it will bee so much raine as will indeed disquiet men.

30: a hearer at Wakes my Cosin John Hudson with mee by whom I heard of the welfare of my freinds

July. 1. and 2: drisling raines that men could not doe any thing in their hay, and made them to feare in order unto the harvest, least weeds and raine should damage it.

July. 3. The Lord was good in many respects to mee and mine, my heart I hope is touched from himselfe, resolving to abide by him, and his wayes, and never depart from following of him, though he strip mee naked, I am resolved to abide by his worship though he give mee the bread, and the water of affliction not to turne aside from him, god good to us this day in his word at his table, oh when shall my wretched heart being above thes things delight it selfe only in the lord.

7. preacht at Wakes Colne god good unto mee therin. sent to my uncle. Josselin into Norfolke. the season now very hot and seasonable.

July: 10: in this morning I dreamed, that divers were in a pulpitt in a church, and that divers heavd it this way, and that but could not make it fall, I dreamed that the Mayor, and great men of the place satt at the upper end, but did nothing one way or other, I thought I came in with a rod in my hand and laid it by the wall, divers looked on mee; I trust god will take care of mee in those church-troubles that are coming on us.

The lord continueth his shade on my tabernacle, blessed bee his name. I want no outward good thing. I find a filthy, wretched heart, shall I never find christ empowring mee to putt every imagination under, oh lord lett thy goodnes doe this for me, for I am weake, and nothing, this day very hot, god good to mee in the worke and duty thereof, the lord was a good god in the season, which suites to the fruites of the earth; some of the separation called Anabaptists hearing this day. doe they hope to injoy our meeting places and therfore will disown their old opinion of abominating the place, come they as spyes to catch, or to make way for others to come: lord I am not sollicitous, I desire onely to serve thee singly.

12. had in all my hay out of Dagnal, about 3. good loads, it cost mee 5. goings thither, it was inned in very good case, the season is very dry, and hott, fitt for the feild worke(.) through mercy I thinke my crop in Dagnal this yeare is a saving croppe.

4^{li}. 15. a very coole day. I layd by towards the Majors. 20^{li}. 4^{li}. resolving to pay him, in his twenty pound, as soone as possibly, I can. heard the N. Councell[1] that call themselves a Par of the commonwealth of England, have as their first businesse taken into consideration the matter of tithes: they speake nothing, but god, and godlines, the issue wee will waite

July. 17. The weeke past divers dayes very hot, and dry, pastures burne away exceedingly, the lord in mercy remember us in the seasons, reserve to us the harvest. my son John very ill this night, the lord in mercy be his health, and lett him live in thy sight, a servant of thine, and a great comfort to my gray haires, and doe so for my poore posterity also. I humbly intreate thee, I find my heart not attending with that dilligence, and zeale to the worke of god as it ought, oh when shall I recover from under this sloth, and unspiritualnes and serve god with more freedome of spirit.

July. 24: The lord my god good to mee and mine in many outward refreshing mercies, which I cannot but wonder at, and say, oh how great is his goodnes towards the sons of men, yea mee a sinfull man: the season wonderfull scorching hott, and dry pastures like a wildernes people preparing on all hands for harvest, oh that my flowers, might bloome and eare and ripen to the exalting of the name of god; the lord was good to mee in the Sabbath I find my heart smiting mee in my deadnes, and coldnes in gods worke, and resolving to bee otherwise, and some strength I feele, and beleeve

[1] The New Council, popularly known as the Barebones Parliament.

I shall find more, and that my bread shalbee sure, and my waters not faile

3^{li}. 10^{s}. 25. Sweet raines and great in some places; god good to mee in my journey, I layd by 3^{li}. 10^{s}. more for the Major in all 7^{li}. 10^{s}. I also made up Mr Thompsons money which I borrowed of him for bookes.

26: delivered to James Linnet[1] for Sir Tho: Honywood. 4 quarters and
2^{li}. 10^{s}. six bushels oates at 20^{d}. the bushell. which is. 3^{li}. 3^{s}. 4^{d}. I determine to lay by of this mony. 50^{s}. for Major

27. in the morning it rained a great shower, I have thought long of a wett harvest, I shall silently waite and see what the lord will doe.

30: received a letter from my uncle Josselin heard of their wellfare

July: 31: wherin I rejoyce, cald up this morning to heare the thumping, thundering Cannon, which filled into country houses, and our beds with the dreadfull noise, I have not ever heard the like shooting in my life, its no question a terrible sea fight neare our doores between the Hollander and us, the lord is our hope in all our straites, This weeke my Jane, and John very ill, god soone revived them, wherin I bless his most holy name, unto all the rest of us god afforded refreshing health, these latter dayes goodly harvest weather, and men follow their worke very closely. I blesse the lord who disposed my heart with more dilligence to attend unto and prepare for the Sabbath, the lord spiritualize mee more, and more, and lett his spirit and presence bee more and more in mee, the roaring Cannon sounded till night, the wind high hindred our hearing of them very much, god give a good issue to England in this ingagement.

7. Aug: very unconstant harvest weather, the weeke past, more showres, in other place then wee had, good is the lord in all his wayes and most worthy to bee praised. wee shall observe the effects of this victory by the estate, and whether they attempt any thing at land against Holland, the lord good to mee in my inward frame, I find the divel ready to disturbe mee, lord doe thou undertake for mee, dreamd of great church troubles, among the rest I thought Iserson an anabaptist threw a stone at mee, lord I submitt to thy pleasure in all things.

13: This weeke continued a most curious harvest weeke throughout, at night musing on the afflictions on the ministry and church of god, I dreamed that one sent mee a bushel of wheate, and in the mouth
☞ of the sacke was a bundle of mony, which I conceived was 10^{s}. it

[1] Probably a member of the Linnett family of Colne Engaine.

proved 13. at first telling, thinking I was mistaken I told it over againe and still it increased more halfe crownes and more 1^s. so that I could not reckon it, but thinking it was not so much I told it againe, and yett it proved more: awaking I thought presently of gods providing for us unexpectedly and by way of wonder. and that his should not want though the young lyons famish.

Aug. 14: This morning it dewed very comfortably. the earth needeth the same. the lord I trust will continue to reserve unto us the appointed weekes of harvest. my heart prone one day to vanity. I find any temptation better kept out then thrust out, oh that I could handle every evill thought roughly and inquire whence it is, before I give admission to the same. god good to all mine in our inward injoyments and outward in which I desire to rejoyce and to blesse his most holy name. the lord was good to mee in the word and worke of the Sabbath, he in mercy frame up my heart, more and more to himselfe.

Mr Thompson pd. 1^{li}. 15: Sent 3^{li}. 9^s. by Mr Jeffery Littell unto Mr Thompson. which I borrowed of him to buy Mr Westleyes bookes I begun to provide for my sister Maries mony, laying by 1^{li}. for her of her. 7^{li}. 10^s. 9^d which I owe unto her.

17. a day of aboundance of raine: so the night, also 18. morning: its looked on as certain that Van-Trump is dead of his wounds: Call: Sillito paid mee. 25^s. for Rog: Turner layd by 1^{li}. for Maj.
20^s. 2^{li}. Haines; receivd also Wm Webbs mony. and layd by 40^s. for him, he oweth mee half a bushell of malt

Aug: 21: weeke past, inconstant weather, last day, dry and windie and so is this, god will remember us in mercy although wee forgett him, and live much out of his sight, litle faith stirring, but much sense and fleshlynes, the lord arme all his people to roule themselves on, and to trust upon him at all times. I found vaine imaginacons troubling mee, and I find thereby an endles roule of evill that is never unraveld. the more vaine the heart is the more vaine its ready to bee, and foolish thoughts in one kind, do not spend and consume that folly that is in the heart, but indeed make it more ready to call in sins of other kinds, oh helpe mee against evill thoughts I pray thee oh my gratious, and almighty father: and I desire thee to keepe my heart in looking up unto thee, because of of this things.—saw in the prints[1] a letter from 2 pretending them-

[1] Prints: the weekly and monthly newsletters from which RJ clearly drew much of his political information.

selves Christs witnesses, false prophets are one signe of the last dayes, god good to mee in the Sab: its a great joy to mee that I carry my worke before mee, and am fully provided the day before for my worke

22. very wett, but gods giving indifferent faire weather. 23. and 24. I sett on helpe and had in 8 litle loads of corne, I have in about 12. jags in all. and ended my harvest very well for which mercy I desire to blesse the name of my god: my boy Humphry very ill, the lord blesse meanes for his recovery.

23. my wife received 10^{li}. by Goodman Newman of Clare, which my aunt Shepheard sent unto mee, promised mee at marriage, I have

25. layd by: 6^{li}. for Major Haines to make up his mony 20^{li}. I also paid one 4^{li}. of whom I borrowed it, so that I praise god I owe but very litle except to my sister.

Aug. 28: this weeke Tho: Humfry was very ill, as unto death, god revived him; my wife very ill, the good lord spare her, and make her a comfort, and joy of heart unto mee, the lord was good to mee in the worke of the Sabbath. I was somewhat ill this day, the lord keepe my mind in frame and doe mee good for his name sake. wee gathered for Marlborough. 3^{li}. and more

Sept: 2. preacht at Clare on Hab: 2.20: god was good to mee outwards and homewards

4: This weeke past, god was good to mee and mine in divers mercies for soule and body, my family in indifferent health, the latter part of harvest very uncertain, the lord was very good to mee in my particular, when very many were under eminent afflictions and many dyed suddenly, oh that I had a heart to doe accordingly: god was good to mee in the worke of the Sabbath for which I desire to blesse his name,

6: This day kept a day of prayer at pryory to intreat god in behalfe of his people and the nation, and that god would own us with hearts to owne him in every condicon

☞ 7. This day it rained so much that the meadowes were overflown, the first floud in our river since. Feb: 1651. not one in: 19. months or therabouts till now, perhaps god will give an ill seed time for the next yeares crop to punish our tithers etc.,

Sept: 11. This weeke past god was good to mee, and mine in many outward mercies. the season is very wett, the lord prepare the earth for a seed time, the lord good to mee in my quietnes of spirit and resolucion to keepe faith and a good conscience, under all the great threats that are cast out against our profession, the lord hasten the deliverance of his people, arise lord, in thy time to our helpe.

Sept. 18: This weeke the weather windy, and dry. Thos Humphry through mercy groweth better and better, and doeth up and downe about my businesse, in which mercy, I rejoyce, my deare wife very ill with her teeth, god in mercy give her ease and continue her health, my heart I find meditative of worldly vanities, and not living on god, and taken up with god, wherby Sathan gets advantage against mee, lord bee my helpe and strength I pray

19. wife went to my Lady Honywoods, where curteously used. 21: Mr R.H. went for London the lord blesse him and his hopes of a child. my boy Hump. not well again, its in many places a sickly time, the lord in mercy doe us good by it. my wife came home well.

Sept. 25. The weather very seasonable, cold, cleare and dry. my family and indeed towne in health blessed bee god, my heart very apt to wander on outward things, and not fasten its meditation on god so as to maintaine communion with him, the lord gave me strength for the sabbath and holpe mee in the same, who am altogither worthlesse and empty.

29: a faire day, preacht this day at Wakes, oh that the word mingled with faith might proffit

Oct: 2: A wett day, after a faire weeke: oh that Sabbaths might dew downe grace and mercies on my soule(.) god was good to mee and family, wee heare of gods drawing towards us in stripping the ministry of their maintenance, doe not strip us of thy protection. heard of the health of my good freind Major Haynes, the lord doe good unto him and us daily in his christ.

7. very ill with my cold.

Oct: 9: This weeke a faire weeke, god good to us in our healths, only I very ill, and feavourish with a cold. I trust god will raise mee up again to his worke as he did this day for which I desire alwayes to blesse his name.

Oct: 16. god good to mee and mine in my health, but my heart dead and listles towards god, so shutt up in prayer publicke and private that I cannot utter my condicon with any feeling before the lord, oh that god would quicken mee that I might recover strength from the god of my strength. oh lett mee feele thy helpe neare at hand, and lett my dilligence be duobled as my god is multiplying his mercy on mee in my health.

☞ 18: I had an answer of prayer and faith in receipts from Hedge this day, and an evidence of gods love and carefull providing for mee.

☞ Mr Clopton

21: received of Mr Clopton: 14^{li}. 3^{s}. 9^{d}. and 18^{li}. before, my part of 55^{li}. 5^{s}. paid in by Mr Man the due for 3 yeares out of Dunmow: which is. 108^{li}. the rest lost: a day wherin god in many particulars shewed great favour unto mee:

Oct: 23: this day 12. y(ear): the Irish rebellion: 11. y: the fight at Edgehill, the lord good to us all in our outward mercies, a weeke wherin god mindfull of mee in outward things, oh continue thy love and thy favour unto mee, my wife persuaded herselfe shee was breeding a girle, the lord beare up her heart under the difficulties of her condicon, god was good to mee this day in praying and preaching, make mee more and more empty in my owne eyes and bee thou my all and in all.

25: a day of prayer a good day at Mr Cresseners in order to breaking bread. James Dayes wife joyned with us. wee supd at Mr Cressener who paid mee my tith more than ordinary freely.

27 preacht at Wakes, god good to mee therein(.) lent Caplin 5^{li}. til. November: 26: next.

Oct: 30: Brother Cooper of Sible-Hedingham admitted a member with us, my poore wife very ill, shee breedeth with difficulty, lord uphold and support for mercy sake I intreate thee; my heart was plodding for its duty, and hope therein, in preaching and at table and all very comfortable unto mee, but not ravisht, I will waite gods time and leisure for every mercy he intendeth mee, very windy, and haile and rain much.

No: 1: lent Hunwicke. 6^{d}. to compound for 1^{s}. and receivd it, lent him 10^{s}. to compound for 20^{s}. he promiseth before Jan. 1. to pay mee: 4: heard Dods wife was dead troublesome people that ended their estate and lives togither, in want: 5: did my businesse kindly with Mr Pelham

6: This weeke past the lord was good to mee and mine in many outward mercies, in my spouse health though weake, the word good and sweet to mee in the Sabbath oh that my heart could mourne after the lord, and delight more in him. my heart expects trouble. and is even straitned until it bee over, most men secure: my heart seldome lett out in private prayer: the things of the world frequently overrunning my minde. heard Mr H and wife at London not well, the good lord take care of them.

10. John Cressener baptized. Jo. Humphreyes 2 bullocks brought mee: snow and raine. No: 13: This weeke past the lord mindfull of mee and mine in outward mercies, on the latter dayes my wife farre better, I find my heart still much musing on worldly objects, and

so my meditations of god are shutt out, I find my heart not so open in prayer as wont, lord I looke up to thee with expectation of helpe, none but you alone can doe it, oh bee neare unto mee, the lord good to mee in the Sabbath: I receivd a kind letter from Mr H at London, god opens his heart towards mee again for which I blesse him

19. heard of Mr H. wellfare at London.

No: 20: This weeke very dry for the season, colds much abroad, and my wife more troubled with one, then ever. I and the children indifferently well through mercy, the lord my god in all accept of mee and doe mee good. worldly, vanities and musings much take up my heart, oh lord when shall I find power from above against them.

M.P. 24: This day in the afternoone Mary Potter came unto us: I paid my sister. 4li. the weather dry and warme.

26: Heard of the birth and baptisme of Mary Harlakenden at London, with the good state of the mother for which I blesse god. received from Mr R. a Ravanella. an usefull booke, and precious guift, the lord remember his love and requite us into his bosome and make mee an improver of thy goodnes in any perticulars.

No: 27. God was many wayes good to mee. my deare John had a fall about the street threshold which made him limpe and made us afraid of hurt, the lord in mercy keepe my heart from creature dotings if it bee thy will, and spare him in his strength unto mee(.) god was good to mee in the Sabbath, but I was carelesse in providing against it, the good Lord in mercy pardon it unto mee.

29. Johns shut-bone in his instep set by Spooners wife, the lord restore his limbe and preserve them, and all mine and give mee to know his minde in this providence.

Dec: 4: This weeke past god good to mee my son John recovering, but ☞ my heart vain. I find time for vain meditations but not for spiritual, and this justles out the worke of god that I doe it coldly, and lamely. lord in thy strength I resolve to finish my notes for the lords day on Satturday, and leave no studdy but meditacion for the lords day and to keepe my mind more intire to god, the lord beare down my corruptions before him by the power of his own spirit in mee, and keepe up this heart in mee alwayes(.) god was good to mee this day, and it was a very healthfull day.

7. and. 8. in the morning, my wife apprehended shee quickned, a daughter the lord own it

9. received a bounteous guift in provision from Mrs Har: why lord

is my heart narrowed towards thee when you art enlarged towards mee. Mr H. returned safe from London.

10: an encouragement from Mr Cress: sister Hunt, gods finger in their love oh that it might enter my heart

December 11: The Lord was good to mee and mine in outward mercies, only my wife very ill, and weakely in her childing, I trust the lord will reserve her a blessing unto mee, I was not so exactly carefull of fitting myselfe for the Sabbath, the lord I trust will perfect his mercy concerning mee, and perfect my heart in his feare. My old vanities came and knockt, but found no roome my heart ready to goe out to them. but I hope god will not only helpe my heart against them, but will restrain them also; this day very lightsome and cheerfull, god good to mee in the Sabbath's worke, he in mercy accept mee and blesse in my Johns foote, for on him I depend.

11. this night my meditacions were, whether, and what farther warnings from the word I should give of the approach of the evill dayes, unto my people, on the dissolucion of this parl. and government which I apprehended would bee though not when, and die. 12°. it was done. 13°. I heard it

Dec: 19. received 2 faire sugar loaves from Mr Eldred,[1] the lord returne his love to him: kild my hogge he proved very cleane and most excellent meate.

23. rid to Ardleigh, and returned, I hope god will prosper my busines there, and give mee a comfortable issue in the same, he was in my jorneying meditacions which was a refreshment unto my spirit.

December 25: this weeke past the lord was good to mee, and mine in many outward mercies(.) the season very unconstant like the times and mens mindes, the lord good to mee in my preparacion to the Sabbath, but my heart is very dead and unspirituall.

30: god in mercy gave mee a good end with Hedge(.) I received this day as many catle as came unto 13^{li}. 10^{s}. but no mony, he oweth mee. 2^{li}. 19^{s}. of Michaelmas rent, its a great mercy of god that I am not forced to sue him at law. the lord in mercy blesse the catle I have received of him.

Jan: 1: The weeke past the lord was good, to mee in many mercies, oh that I had a heart to love and feare him and walke worthy of his goodnes, my spirit somewhat bent after the lord, and more dilligent in my preparation for his day (though too too deficient) the day winterly and wett.

[1] For the Eldred family of Olivers in Stanway, and EC, see Appendix 1.

3. God gave us a good day at the priory, the word usefull, yett not much heart brokennes within

5: I preacht at Wakes, I trust the lord was with mee in the word, and will doe mee, and many good by it, wee were bountifully and kindly entertained there, the lord requite their labour of love

Jan: 8: this weeke past, god good to mee and mine in many outward mercies, many die in many places. 4 here this weeke, the lord prepare my heart for death by a constant watchfull, holy life, the weather as it were growing, the lord make my heart more active for him than ever, I see the dayes growing cloudy, the lord in mercy prepare my heart by his grace and love for my part therein

9. Mr Nevill buried: 10. day another. 5 already this yeare, the lord make mee wise to provide for eternity and spirit my heart with strength, and peace from himselfe: at the funeral I first heard the Dutch peace was made. and 10 assured of it from Lady Honywood, the messenger found mee praying, and so fitting for death, the fittest duties for the peace, though carnal hearts are jocund at it, for this will bee the hornes rise, and the ruine of the protestant interest as one 7. yeares will lett us know, and now have at thy skirts France.

Jan: 15: This weeke the lord in many wayes good to mee and mine, only my wife breedeth with very much illnes, I find the lord weaning my heart from outward things, and making them nothing and base in my eyes, oh lett them never bee a snare to mee. my straitnes of heart in prayer continueth, lord awaken and arouse mee, the weeke was warme, and dry, the lord make us sensible of his doings.

19. dry, warme weather, but very close and darke, lord give mee uprightnes in the inward man

Jan: 22. A dull weeke for newes, yett not without its remarkes, as may bee seen therein, especially relating unto the army: night rainy, my family through mercy in good health, only my deare wife, weakly and fainting in her condicon, the lord in mercy strengthen her: my heart is free from old annoyances in a great measure, but very unactive and sluggish in my converse and walking with god. this yeare the lord was many wayes good unto mee. and mine, continuing us in our health and preserving us in thes backsliding dayes, and I know he that hath kept me will also continue to doe it, this yeare brought forth notable revolucons at home, in dissolving parliaments and declaring Cromwell protector who is to rule by a councell, its said after divers bloudy fights now wee have made peace with the Dutch, the French have had a good yeare of it, as the Sp: last. tooke much from Conde. reduced Bourdeaux. quieted the protestants, mainteined themselves in Italy, and done some feats in Catalonia, Brest their port was like another Dunkirk against us, and I conceive wee shall remember it in due time: the German diet still continueth they have crowned Ferdinand the 4th King of Romans, the Cossacks and Polish are in armes, the Turke also against the Venetian, things are somewhat calmer then formerly, and discourses are of a generall peace: Lord my soule waiteth for thy salvation. hasten thy coming wee intreate thee.

38: yeare: now enters. Jan. 25. 1653.

sensible this was a new yeare to mee, and a yeare of strange transactions at home and preparacions for the like abroad, the lord keepe mee, in soule and body without spott and without blemish, for in thy grace and strength is my strength and tower, oh lett mee not bee ashamed for in thee I put my trust.

Jan. 28: weather dry faire, beyond what ever was in a January, scarce any frost, the lord good to mee in many outward mercies wherin I rejoyce; the lord good to my spirit in making mee sensible of the evills of the times, and watchful over my heart in some measure, the lord watch over mee by his grace in the word and prayer, enlarging my heart and affectiones for which I desire to blesse my god who doth remember mee in my condicon

Mr Eldred with us, he used mee with much respect, and kindnes, and shewed much love to all my children, the good lord returne it, into his bosome.

31: Heard 2 strange passages of O(liver) C(romwell) in his youth, and a strang passage or 2 of other mens thoughts of him, lord make mee wise, and teach mee and fitt mee for thy worke

Feb: 1: This day, our company mett, at my house, there was some presence of god with us, both in heart expressions, and teares, the lord cause his truths to abide with us, and win in our hearts to the acknowledgement of the same.

Feb: 5: The weather was for divers dayes winterly, cold winds with frost, and snow; god good to mee in the health of my relations, in creating mee a heart willing to bee nothing, and to choose my portion with an afflicted suffering christ in his truths, and ordinances, my heart very dead and wretched under ordinances, the lord even said to mee I shall desire to see one of the dayes of the sons of men which I now see and shall not, arme for trials and I have enough.

Feb: 12. God good to mee and mine in outward things, I meet with trials in my condicon, and find it hard to see it good and beare them patiently, and to pray for good in them, beleevingly, some former mind vanities appeared again, oh how apt my heart is to hanker after them, when shall I loath every appearance of evill, and find out Sathan in all his wiles; the weather very dry, and frostie, and cold. sometimes cleare and sunshine(.) the lord merciful to mee in the word. my heart lett out to discover the people whither their corruptions in gods worship tend to prepare them to persecute god in his most dearest, and most precious things, the lord fitt mee to suffer.

☞ 13. R. Harla: in N.E. dying ano. 37. or thereabouts,[1] lay in a trance and recovering told them god shewed him most hideous desolations coming on the churchs of god, in the whole world and afterwards such glorious daies as never were the like unto the Saints.

☞ 15: at night dreamd I was sent for up to the Councell by a messenger to appeare die 6°. and he came on 7°. my heart I thought was not resolved nor yett over dejected. the weather dirty. it was as if it were about some engagement.

16. a good day, heard a good sermon: divers bookes profferd mee of use to mee, but especially, especially psal. 119.98.99.100. sung. oh that I could fix my thoughts intra, and not goe ultra scripturas in what I expect.

Feb: 19. This weeke dry and cold, water scarce with the millers already: god good in the health of mee and mine, heard Mr R.H. had the small pox at London, the lord in mercy restore him, and let him live in thy sight. the lord in mercy was more in my thoughts, and Satans annoyances lesse than sometimes, lord rebuke him, and bid him get hence, give mee discerning in what thou art doing, and let thy grace suffice mee, heard of tumults at London, lord in thee is my peace.

22. Sought the lord this day to enlighten mee in the worke of my dayes from the word, he will. I had his helpe that day. heard of Mr R.H. hopefull doing well.

Feb: 26: My John ill with a tertian ague, I want a fellowfeeling spirit, bearing a part of that burthen under which others lie, I know

[1] Roger Harlakenden, who died of smallpox in November 1638. Probert.

not how to bee at one end of a persons trouble to ease him while he is under it, teach mee this art I humbly pray thee, god good in the health of my family otherwise, the season dry and cold, so is my heart in a great measure(.) lord lett thy selfe into my spirit, I am as one that hath no communion with thee, but am as in the darke and alone, my spirit is straitned, and my heart is troubled, when will thou enlarge thy spirit and bring mee up out of the pitt and snare, wherein I am held(.) god very sweet to mee in the word this day.

27. found a Comedie called Lingua,[1] at Mrs C. I never noted it there, though often viewd the books.

March. 5: This weeke the Lord good to mee and mine in our outward mercies. I hope my sons ague somewhat abateth. the weather very dry. cold and frosty: the lord letts mee see into the vanity of my heart, but I cannot live on god, with that sweet injoyment and tast of him, which his saints have found, and I have tasted, my spirit is very dead and drowsy, and much without god, the lord thinke upon mee with quickening grace,

7. 8: sew my oates in Dagnal by Finch about 7 acres in all. 26: bushels, the dayes dry and cold, the land on the hils very dry. some of the golls[2] wett, the lord command a blessing on the seed committed unto the earth,

10: sent my poor sister Ann. 10s. promised to helpe them in their lecture at Haverill, although the jorney bee very long, the lord make mee usefull in my generation, and it shalbee well. rumoured that peace was with Holland, and France included, and that wee were breaking with Spain, who had cousoned us of much prize gold, challenging as his, when it was not.

March: 12. The Lord good in outward mercies, the season was very dry: my Jo: very ill with his ague, insomuch that one morning I even received his sentence of death into my selfe; I called unto thee lord, but oh my heart is darke, god answered in the event his ague next day abated, but I find not the savour and sweetnes of god upon my spirit, the lord gave us his word, and it was a discovering, peircing word, the lord make it a direction unto mee.

13. dewed, so also in night, and 14 morning sweet raines, answers of prayers with a note of gods respect unto us.

March: 19: The Lord good to mee and all mine in many outward mercies, my John well againe, and my wife chearly; one Webs wife

[1] Thomas Tomkis, *Lingua: or the combat of the tongue* (1607).

[2] Gole: a stream, channel, ditch. NED.

had sad labour and the child dead.[1] god mercifull in mine(.) our two cowes calved well, all is the lords mercy; my heart in some measure made empty and vile and nothing, but findeth no filling, oh when shall I see thee, as thy saints have seene thee(.) my spirit very inquisitive after the providences of god on foote, wherin for my part I desire no worldly advantage, only might I see an upright heart given mee alwayes to keepe close to the lord; I am not without gods encouragements herein: the sermons this day and the former I hope I shall remember. I knowe gods councell it will
☞ stand and take its due effect.

23. rid to Colchester and paid my tenths, god good to mee going, and returning, the day was very cold,

24: rid towards London. 25. with my Cosen Benton, heard my uncle Si. Josselin was dying and he died. 26. preacht at Cranham, their were but 5. men householders in the towne that were there in my time,[2] 27. rid to London: 30. returned home, my heart was in a very vile frame most part of this jorney the lord pitty and pardon mee,

Lands as formerly. and mony as formerly: viz.	440^{li}.
improvement of Mrs Maries lands: 4^{li}. 9^{s}. now in the whole	93^{li}. 14^{s}.
I have paid of all my debts viz 32^{li}. and some odde debts more, and through mercy I doe not owe any person any sum of mony.	
my stocke is worth much about what formerly: and I have in mony more. viz with Mr Elliston	20: 0. 0.
Lent to Robt. Potter. 10^{li}. to Wm Webb. 5^{li}. to Harrington of White Colne.[3] 2^{li}. 10^{s}.	17. 10. 0.
so that my estate is advanced this yeare about 69^{li}. one way and other, which is much in thes broken daies	

for which I desire to blesse and praise, the lord. but oh lett not this bee my portion, but give mee thy holy, holy spirit I humbly intreate thee.

1654

Ap: 2. The weeke past god good to mee, and yett my heart wonderfully out of frame, oh that I could feare him for his patience and goodnes

[1] The daughter of William Webb is recorded as buried on 20 March in the PR.

[2] From Ship Money and Hearth Taxes, Cranham would appear to have had at least fifty households; thus only one-tenth or less had survived fourteen years.

[3] Probably Daniel Harrington, yeoman, whose will is dated 1671 (ERO, 77 CR 9).

to the sons of men, the lord gave sweete raines as if he promised us plenty, oh that our spirits were moisture in the sense of his dealing, heard there would bee an assembly, and that there is speech of an high title for the protector viz Emperour of the South. the lord give mee low and humble heart, and doe mee good in my generacion; I am come to a yeare which is like to bring forth notable counsells, I will mind them, its said Cromwell was borne in. 1600. the same yeare in which K(ing) Charles was borne,

6: reckond with Wm Webb, and paid him all I owed him, he now oweth mee 5^{li}. and also. 10^{li}. and: 1^{s}. 6^{d}. he is presently to pay mee, the residue of the mony I intend to forbeare as his occasions require.

sold 3 bullocks to Mr Elliston at. 3^{li}. 15^{s}. he is to pay mee before Christmas next

7. God was good to mee in some measure for the day, I was 4 houres at the church. the word seasonable. Jer. 5.24. the lord imprint it on all our hearts, the spring is very lively, now its said the Dutch peace is concluded, the lord prepare us for the saddest dayes and bee our god, and all shall bee well.

Ap. 9. God good to mee and mine in many mercies, many very sweet raines, I finde my heart in a very dead and unspirituall frame, the lord helpe mee and heale mee, my heart is not active within mee for good, nor sensible of the evill of the times, but as it were willing destruction and desolation should come upon us, the lord was good to mee this day, but I find not my heart bettered nor enlarged towards him.

13. preacht at Wakes, there appeared I praise god, some affections stirring in divers, oh that I had a heart to sew precious seed, it might come up to my comfort, and redound to my account in the great day; when I not aware of it.

Ap: 16: God good in many wayes to us, for which I blesse him, the season dry and hot, the grasse springeth wonderfully, oh that I could take notice of gods goodnes in every particular, and had a heart loving and delighting in him: heard my freinds well. my Lady Honywood ill, the lord doe mee good by all his dealings with mee: god followes my spirit much with the times I live in, and sometimes I feare: Satan gets advantage thereby to the neglect of my inward and spiritual estate, oh lett Satan never bee too hard for mee, because thou wilt helpe mee when, yea before I call.

Ap. 23. God very good to mee and mine in many mercies, the season, moist, warme and so very fruitfull, the lord maketh my heart sensible of its deadnes, and vanity, but I doe not find my heart watchfull, oh that I called(,) resist Sathan then he would fly from mee. I was very apprehensive of my suddain going up unto London, but through mercy, this night I had word to the contrary.

25. rid to Messing, god good to mee in my jorney, especially in delivering mee from minde vanity

Ap: 30: The lord was good to mee in many outward mercies, of the least whereof I and mine altogither unworthy. the lord is pleased to lett mee see my unspiritualnes, and its my greife, but it is not healed, and god is not communicative, nor free with mee, as sometimes, oh no bosome to thine, thou art my lot, and portion, oh lett mee never bee forsaken by thee, god good to mee in the word, I apprehended a trouble on mee from my Tenant at Ardleigh, but this day god prevented it, I looked on god to doe it for mee, and to give mee a good issue therin, and I trust he will that I may praise his most holy name.

May. 3. rid to Haverill, preached, and returned that night, well but weary. god was good to mee in my jorney, for which I blesse his name,—6 Mr R.H. returned safe from his long jorney unto Worcester,[1] crosse the country, to our joy, the lords name bee blessed for his goodnes therein unto him and us.

May. 7. This day warme after very much cold windie dayes, the yeare promiseth much plenty, which is in gods hand to dispose of as he pleaseth, the mercies of god towards mee in my family, still continued to mee, most unworthy of them, my heart panteth after god as my all, in my continued injoyment of him, and yett, oh how litle of him doth my heart attaine unto, I had some heart warmth, and breathings after him this day, kindled in mee by himselfe, but oh how long, ere the lord please to give mee his strength and his powerfull presence.

9. My neighbours at Halsted, entred into fellowship with the neighbour Independent church(,) lord direct their hearts therein unto thee only, and lett them beautifie the gospell, and bring honour to thy name thereby.

10: Kept a day of prayer, at priory, our company all there, except Bat. Clarke, the lord truly was good to us therein, my troubles in reference to our disorders in communion fell of my heart very much. 11. hearer at Wakes, some good men would faine increase

[1] The Harlakendens obtained the lordship of Kempsey manor in Worcestershire as part of the marriage portion of Mary Meredith, who married Richard Harlakenden in 1652.

a partie, and make hay wile the sun shineth, 12. hearer at Halsted, said the Turke had taken Candia from the Venetian, will god call them into Italy.

May. 14: The lord was good and mercifull to mee, and mine in many outward good things, wherin my soule rejoyceth, this day the lord gave us the libertie of his table, and was good to us therin, my heart mourneth over dissatisfyed spirits but my soule rejoyceth in the lord, my heart is dead, and much prepared unto every good worke, oh lord make ready my heart for thy selfe, that I may bee thine in all my pathes, the lord was good unto mee in his word, in his ordinance at the table, the lord gave us not the company of some, the lord doe us good in all his owne wayes day by day.

15: offered my townesmen my tithes at 4li. quarter to dischardge mee of all rates and dues whatsoever. 16. this day I went to Coll. cookes kindly entertaind by her(.) I gave poore Mrs Burroughs 10s. and bought some books of her at. 9s. the lord provide for her, and remember mee in mercy.

May: 21. The weeke past, god was good to mee, and mine in many outward mercies, whose bounty and goodnes compasseth mee about continually, my wife beareth up very comfortably, the season very hott at present, the plague is begun at one end of the land viz chester(,) the lord prevent the spreading of it, if it bee his good pleasure, I feare he that hath saved us will destroy us, as once he did unto Israel. so. Judd. v.5. our iniquities increase and call for the great M(aster) to take his rod, and walke round his house, oh bee a hiding place to mee and them that feare thy name, the lord good to mee in the word this day yett I cannot but bemoane my unactivenes for god in my place.

May. 28. weeke paste, dry but not excessive hot, signes of raine, but past away. the lord was good in many things to mee, and to mine, wherin I desire to blesse his holy name(.) my wife growes heavy, and wearisome, the lord give her a comfortable lying downe, my spirit very much partaking of the deadnes, and drowsy unactivenes of the dayes wherin I live, oh lord revive, and engage my heart more unto thy selfe, my people and selfe I apprehend very dead under the ministry in all places, and here, the lord recover us, and make us lively and fervent in the worke of the lord.

29. shoures went divers wayes, my desires in heaven were god would not deny them to us, the winde turned, and brought 2 on us, whereof one a very fine one. Mrs Church this day made a surrender of her land.

June: 1. a good rain in our streete and so. Halsted ward.—3. the greatest haile shoure I ever saw it made our brookes run, litle or nothing of it beyond our parish towards Cogshall.

☞ this day reckoned with Mr Ed: Elliston, he oweth mee on tiths and contribucon. 10^{li}. 15^{s}. he is henceforward to pay mee 1^{li}. 10^{s}. tith yearely.

June. 4: a hot day. yet the haile appeared in some places, the lord good in outward mercies to mee, oh that my heart were thereby ingaged unto him, the lord remember mee in mercy for unto thee I desire to committ my cause, the lord owne mee and doe mee good in every condicon, that I may bee in the love and feare of his most holy name, my heart somewhat raised up in preaching, and god doth melt some spirits, blessed bee god oh that I might serve the seed of christ and bee usefull to them.

☞ 8: at night dreamed being in a low lane, the bank over against mee, high steepy and bushy Mr Sams was preaching, and being to quote great and precious promises he went backe to inquire of his clarke for a concordance, I called to him and told him the place he meant was 2 pet. 2.2. a smart place(.)[1]

9: the haile lay in the priory causy[2] this day, divers persons carried it away as a raritie

June: 11. The lord good to mee and mine in many outward mercies. Tho. in danger in the water, but the lord preserved him, oh that I had a heart to love and feare his most holy name, the lord good to mee in the Sabbath, I find my heart a litle more open and enlarged then at sometimes, and yett sufficiently straitned, great noise that the King of Scots is in the land, the season hott, and dry. great signes of plenty on the ground, poore people very briske, god sanctifie this plenty.

16. this day I begun to cutt downe my grasse in sawyers close.

June: 18. The Lord was good to mee, and mine in many outward mercies, my wife holds up her head very cheerfully through mercy, with which I trust god will more and more remember her that wee may yett more and more praise him; my heart very dead and listles in respect of what I would enjoy, though I cannot but owne god in much goodnes unto mee wherof, I am altogither unworthy, the lord accept mee in the beloved.

20: on Tuesday morning, my wife sent for midwife, in the afternoone

[1] 'And many shall follow their pernicious ways; by reason of whom the way of truth shall be evil spoken of.'

[2] Causy: causeway, or highway, especially a paved way. SOED.

between two and three of the clocke shee was well delivered of her. 3d daughter, and seventh child. her labour quicke, the lords name bee therefore, and alwayes praised: my heart was sensible in some measure how great a losse it would bee if god tooke her from mee, and yett my spirit was borne up in expectacon of the mercy, and I am persuaded my particular earnest prayers were moving for her in the very moment of her delivery.

☞ a litle before, and after my wives delivery of this child, I was much musing on this text Jer: 46.27.28: et. 47: god will not make an end of mee nor cutt mee off, in my posteritie, although he will shorten mee, oh that my seed might have an interest in the new Jerusalem, yea it shall, and that most certainly.

22. layd in from Sawyers: 4 jags of hay, perhaps 50C the dayes hot, much mutter there is in the country that the Electors must seale indentures at the choice, the cheife Mag. begins to find a burthen on him(.) our freinds came safe from London. this day I preacht at Colne Wake, the lord helpe mee and others to sitt still, while many persons fingers itch to bee doing in thes dayes.

June. 25. This weeke god was good to mee and mine in the continuance of outward mercies unto us staying my heart also in and under all the difficulties of the times, and the expectacons of evill coming upon us, now busy in choice of p. men, wherin I desire not to medle: the lord was good to mee in the Sabbath, drawing out my heart affectionately in the duties thereof, my deare wife blessed bee god verily well, and gets up exceeding comfortably.

☞ 30: I had a sad dreame in 48. of the death of wife and children none left but Jane afterwards in 49. I buried Mary and Ralph: in 51: I dreamed 3. branches of a hedge growing in my house cutt downe sprouted again, which I feared as a continuance of the trouble of my first dreame, but I hope god intends by this wife, and so I am persuaded that intended, that the 3 children god had taken from mee, he would make up again out of this stocke and now god hath graciously bestowed 2 upon mee and hopes of their life

July. 2. The Lord was good to mee and mine in our outward mercies, my heart made dead to some corruptions, and yett I find how I endeavour to putt life into them, and to follow after them(.) the lord continues yett in some measure to keepe them down; the weather was inconstant yett promises plenty. my good freind Major Haines with us, the lord good to mee in the word, he in mercy accept of mee, and doe mee good.

4: preachd at Gaines Colne lecture, the word sweet, many affections moved, and many teares the lord command his blessing and his favour to attend this word.

7. sett even all my accounts with all particular moneyes once more, and I resolve to keepe my accounts even if it please god, and for that end I will not straiten my daily spending purse: I am clearely out of debt with all men, not owing 20^{s}. that I know of, unto all men whatsoever.

July. 9. god good to mee and mine in many outward mercies, in which I rejoyce, and for which I desire to admire god, my wife, and litle one never better, in any time, my heart more turmoiled then formerly, oh how busy is Satan, and how careles am I apt to bee(.) the lord in mercy strengthen mee against, and preserve mee from every evill worke, the lord was very good to mee in the word I was this day preaching, god doe mee and many of mine good by the same.

10. heard of the death of Mr Strong[1] at Westminster, a good, plain, down right preacher it is likely god hath taken him from the evill to come, his death violent and almost sudden

July. 12. This day sett a part for the choice of parliament men through the kingdome, and I sett it a part to seeke god, in behalfe of my family, god would bee our god, and my litle Ann's god would baptize it with the spirit, and give it his grace and a new name and take it into his family who hath given it into ours, Lord I desire thee to show mee the worke of my generation, more and more clearly and guide mee by thy eye that I may not fall therin,—and my desire is god would take care of his owne, and seing evill is coming on the earth, and then bee thou there refuge(.) The morning was thicke, darke, and misling; walking out at noone, I heard of the untimely death of Wm Elmes,[2] only son of his parents, (c.o. and indeed I thinke onely child,) he fell from his horse, and broke his necke, he was my scholler at Deane and very well disposed: my heart melteth, and mourneth in such a providence, oh lord thy wayes are a great deepe.

this day knights chosen in our county. 13. a very small number of choosers appeared not 500 although it was the sessions time, the choice as to the outsides of men indifferent good, the lord make them carefull and mindfull of him, its said there were a great number of ministers present an 100. or more.

[1] William Strong, minister of St. Dunstan-in-the-West, and pastor of an independent congregation; a famous preacher and theologian, originally buried in Westminster Abbey. Venn.

[2] William Elmes, second son of Thomas (see p. 7, n. 6 above), born 1625, pensioner at Emmanuel, 1646. Venn.

July. 16. This weeke god many wayes good to mee in sparing my deare wife, who much feared herselfe, I find my heart as much annoyed by vain thoughts, as ever, in other persons actings of them, lord thou seest how busy Satan is with mee, I pray helpe mee against him, by thy strength and grace for through my corruption he is too hard for mee, this day thunder in many places, and sweet rains with us.

18: rid to Bumpsted, preacht the Lecture, and returned at night, god was good to mee in my jorney, the first time I preacht among those freinds, the day very cheerfull,

19. My daughter Ann baptized in my hall chamber, the Lord in mercy accept her, make her his owne, I gave my litle ones a solemne chardge to feare god, the lord in mercy lay his feare into their hearts, and it shall doe well.

July. 23. This weeke the Lord was very good in outward things to mee and mine, I have a pose from which free a very long time, but when free from that deadnes and sloth of spirit that I see on all occasions comes upon mee, lord thou continuest very good to mee, when my heart within mee is regardles of thee, oh that god would make mee more meet and fitt to doe his will at all times and on all occasions.

24. This day I saw a license under the hands of the Irish Com^{d} for a souldier to marry, and without such license they may not marry, so that in England there forbidding ministers to solemnize marriage, and the souldiers to marry without their license, may in part fullfill that character which purled mee to apply to this last timed generation. viz. 1. Tim. 4.3.

27. ended a great busines between Rob: Potter and his kinsman, much to my content, with much justice and moderation. I layd downe. 20^{li}. 50^{s}. whereof I borrowed of G. Burton.

28: preacht for Mr Sparrow at Halsted, who was sent for to preach before the protector.

Fatalis necessitas[2] 29. heard the K(ing) of Romans dead. is this Grebners prophesy.[1] will this kindle such flames as will bring in the Turke on the Germans. —observe whether this true and then the effect.

July. 30. This weeke the lord was very good to mee, in many outward

[1] Ezekiel Grebner, *Visions and Prophecies, concerning England, Scotland and Ireland* (1660) (Thomason, E. 1936 (3)). There is a brief account of the history and popularity of Grebner's prophecies in K. Thomas, *Religion and the Decline of Magic* (1971), p. 468. The whole of ch. 13 of Keith Thomas's work deals with the function of prophecies during Josselin's period.

[2] The inevitability of fate.

mercies, divers dayes very hott, harvest entring apace on us, divers good freinds with us, my heart in better frame as to vain annoyances, but sufficiently dead and shutt up, and prone to bee mindles and regardles of god: the lord good to mee in the word speaking, but I doe not find it returning backe into my heart, with that life and power I desire, to disengage my heart from every way of vanitie, and to ingage my heart to serve god with more inward freedome from vanitie of spirit; July ended with thunder and shoures, and harvests begining(.)

Aug: 2. the sun eclipsed not so great as that in March: 52: talke of our fleets going forth.

3. this day kept a day of prayer at widdow Deaths. sensible of much deadnes of spirit, the lord for his goodnes sake accept of us.

Aug. 6: This weeke the lord good to mee in many outward mercies, Wee brake bread togither this day, some melting in my spirit and others, but the world, and deadnes so take up our spirits, that wee stirre not up ourselves to lay hold on the Lord, I preacht on 1. Pet. 2.5. the lord our god accept us in the beloved, in whom my soule trusts(.) harvest common, great plenty, great raines in many places, the lords eye bee on us for good, though wee unworthy of any favour. my litle An so ill that my wife feared present death, I

8: praise god my heart more calme, the child in the night rested and in the morning very hopefull to doe well. my heart sensible of its eternal state, oh that god would lay it out for a precious instrument for his name, and then I shall rejoyce. wee watcht with it this night now the third: 10: John was very ill it fared with him as if he had an ague, Jane complaineth, thus troubles come not alone, they are gentle, and proportioned to assistance from god: this day Coll. Cooke mentiond to mee, a desire to helpe them in a day before he goeth up to the house, which if it goe forward, the lord give me light to speake in season and courage to speake home, An, cheerly in respect of former dayes, for which I praise the lord.

11. thunder, and very much raine, to the cooling, and satisfying of the earth.

Aug: 13. God was beyond expression good to mee in the life of An, receiving it as an answer of prayer, and a token of love, and favour towards mee, oh lay not only life into her body, but the life of grace into her heart, John, and Jane ill with colds but the lord good to them, in bearing up my heart, in a submission to mee whatsoever he doe with mee, only I will trust in him for mercy to my soule, and theirs, the lord good to mee in the word preacht, the day wett, the lord I trust will reserve to us the weeks of harvest, and extend his bounty and goodnes towards us,

15: mett in a day of prayer at Coll. Cookes to seeke god in his behalfe, now he is going up to the parliament. I desired and pressed home to him that he might, not bee, a vessel of dishonour, Mr Wakering desired mee to helpe him on the like occasion. die. 29.

17: I desire now to minde gods goodnes to mee on the occasion of my An's sicknesse. I was sensible of that strangenes fallen in between god and mee, not having had any signal evidence of his taking notice of mee in prayer, and desired my An's life yett with submission, which I received, and desire to weare it as a pledge of his kindnes to mee, over and above I was sensible what a mercy it was my child was not snacht away on a suddain without any warning unto mee, and farther god made my heart very submissive to him in what he should doe with mine, John ill on a suddain, but it was only a qualme, oh that my heart were raised up to close walking with my god.

Aug: 20. This weeke god continued good to us in our outward mercies, my litle Ann, recovering from her illnes dayly(,) Jane is not throughly well, the lord I trust will restore her perfectly(.) heard of Brother Jeremy, and sent unto him, the weather uncertain, yett much corne was gathered in, and I some for my part, the lord looke into my spirit, I find many vanities ready to sett on mee, the lord reserve mee on a peculiar possession for himselfe into whom I may dayly grow.

22. desired by my Lady to assist in a day of humiliacon at her house, heard of the rout of the Spanish army at Arras by the French under Turenne.

24: This day I made an end of harvest, my crop all oats, indifferent. good, and well had in for the most part, I praise god, the lord was good to mee in preserving us by day and night from danger and trouble for which I blesse his name,

26: desired of god he would provide for mee from the hearts of other, seing I was by him taken of, from scrambling in the world, and all my mony gone, going downe a tenant was there with some, I observed in the chapter reading it, god imprints on the heart afore what he is just doing Mark. 9.32.34.

Aug: 27. The Lord good to mee in many outward mercies, yett I find my heart very dead unto the things of god, so much sloth, and backwardnes, to the service of god that I am even weary of my selfe, oh lord helpe mee for my eyes are towards thee, undertake for mee.

28. preacht Bridges funerall at White Colne.—joynd in a day of prayer. die 29. at Mr Wakerings, where I desired to serve my Master in warning men of evill, and giving them good counsel to stand up for the name and gospell of christ.

31. kept a day of prayer at Sir Tho: where I endeavoured to speake plain and home unto men. I heard that the protector was proclaimed Emperour, but for my part I beleve it not, thinking the time and season is not yett come for the doing of it.

Sep: 1: One cald, and told mee, that this Friday. the Pro: was to bee proclaimed Emp: god good in preserving An in a milke bowle, and Jane from swouning who let her fall in. 2. John in falling from the top of the schoole staires. god gives his angels charge over us. it was a wett day

3. god good to mee and mine in outward mercies; the lord good to mee in the Sabbath, Lord succour mee against the temptacons I meet with all for unto the(e) my soule hath recourse(,) oh helpe mee, I pray thee; there was a great and darke storme of rain at noone South west, with a clap or 2 of thunder, this day the Parl. was to sitt, the lord in mercy preserve them from acting any dishonourable thing.

Sept: 10. This weeke much rain fell, the latter end dry, god good to mee in the health, and outward mercies of my relations, oh that they were all sanctified unto mee, the lord was good to mee in the day, opening, and enlarging my heart, oh that I had a heart as becometh the word, and the providences of god that are abroad in the world, this day in course I read Dan: 7: oh is the litle horne, now bustling for roome in the world, our parliament is now sitting, and great strivings are on foote;

13. this day the Parl: appointed a fast at Westminst. and London. I was sensible of their condicon and begd god would shew them the things to our peace, if the decre of ruine were not gone forth; if they had not stumbled in preferring their own things to the lords. which I feared, at night Mr R.H. told this that, tuesday morning. 12. they were shutt out of the house, and a guard of soldiers sett on the house; this amazed many men; I see gods worke going on.

15: Mr. Sp: said on the Parl. newes, ingagement etc. Josselin should write almanacks, it proved so right, lord remember mee. when men scoffe and scorne. and pardon them I intreate thee.

Sept: 17. This weeke past, god was good to mee, and mine, in all our outward mercies and enjoyments. the weather faire, the face of affaires strange, the lord in mercy make mee sensible, that no evill come upon mee unawares, the lord good to mee in the Sabbath. yett I find a want of zeale, and inward fervour of spirit, the lord doe mee good, for his own name sake.

Sept: 24: this weeke a good weeke for seed, some raine fell, yett waters low and dead, the lord good to mee and mine in our health and peace and plenty, oh how doe I find my heart dead and empty, and so apt to receive in base and unworthy thoughts and walke with them, that I cannot but sigh and looke upwards, oh lord when wilt thou undertake for mee. this day cheerfull, coole, and dry. the lord in some measure present in my heart therein.

29. preacht at Halsted, god good to mee therein.

Oct: 1: This weeke past, god was very good to mee, and mine in many mercies, the season very comfortable, a gallant seed time, grasse growing, a great plenty even of all things, wheat wonderfull cheape, the lord by thes mercies draw our hearts neare unto him, and make mee active in my generation for his name, I find my heart very dead, and backward in the things of god, oh Lord quicken thou mee.

3. preacht G(aines) C(olne) lecture, dind with the London gent. one of them rellisht not my apprehension of troublous times coming, judging otherwise of the dayes etc.

October 8. god good to mee in many mercies, injoyment of my freinds, heard of the wellfare of others(.) An this morning wee spied had a toothe cut in her 16. weeke, the season very hopefull and comfortable, the lord good in the word, but still oh my leanesse and deadnes of spirit, and with shaking feares, oh that I could live more in christ, and more above the daily corruptions of my heart.

11: This day kept a publique fast. I expounded. Hos: 14. preacht on Math. 5.8. god good to mee therein, not only in strength, and matter, but in some measure with affections(.) I spent nigh 6. houres in all exercises, the lord make it a good day to mee and to many, he is a good god to mee in his care and provision for mee, and in my health and I would willingly, lay out myselfe for him.

13. at night I was very ill and afraid to die, its gods presence must actuate and strengthen my heart, or I can attain nothing of my selfe, I will make it my busines to live too and with my god, and still desire his strength to bee perfected in my weaknes

Oct: 15. God good to mee and mine in many particulars, I have had painful gripings in my body which I apprehend to bee choller, and it workes away, and I trust god intends to doe mee good by the same, the lord good in the season very comfortable; our house of parl as called doe nothing yett, and perhaps will droll away their time, and give advantage to slurre them, and future assemblies of this nature, god was good to mee in some strength for his worke, though my body griped and troubled,

19. a sad sight of a brother. S.B. whose sister fell to the towne chardge,[1] he said all in his hands was spent. 50li and all her clothes etc. he said he would turne out the 4 children, he would not undoe himselfe for them. nor shew them no more favour than another(,) he seemed to mee void of brotherly and naturall affection; the lord made some of us strangers sensible of her condicon, and resolved to provide for her, and who knowes but god may remember their unnaturalnes, and thinke on their pride

October 22. The lord good to mee and mine in many outward blessings, the season dry and cold, the plenty great, oh that god would ingage our hearts by all to feare his holy name, I had a great pose. 21. at night, but through mercy not much trouble to mee, the lord my god delight in mee for good.

24 kept a day of prayer in order unto publique affaires at Mr Littells, god was good in the word, their was not much affection stirring, the lord recover us

26. my Uncle Nath: and his son and divers freinds of the Josselins dined with mee.

28: This day my wife and I married 14 y. this begins our 15. god bee with us all our dayes with his grace, and consolation, and blesse our posterities; wee eate a messe[2] of green selfe sown pease, sent mee by Goodman Bridge, a raritie that I never saw before, but mentioned in the newes as if comon in the West.

October 29. The Lord good to mee and mine in many mercies, oh lett thy love draw over my heart, and for ever ingage mee with delight in thy worship(.) I blesse god I find not old corruptions so stirring

[1] S.B. was Samuel Burton whose sister Grace was widow of Thomas Waite. The four children mentioned were Sarah, Grace, Sam, and Ann. Widow Grace was living with her mother Ann and in the latter's will Samuel Burton was to buy his sister Grace a house with £20 out of £50 interest which he received as executor. At the Quarter Sessions (ERO, Q/SO/1) on 3 October 1654 it was ordered that 'Grace Waite a prisoner in the house of Correction be moved to Earls Colne the place of her birth' where the church-wardens and overseer of the poor were to relieve her. Samuel did eventually pay her fine for the tenement 'Goulds' in 1657, 'the woman being not well in her mind' (ERO, D/DPr. 100).

[2] Mess: portion of food, a prepared dish, especially liquid or pulpy food. SOED.

in my heart as formerly, make mee dead to all things but to those of thy kingdome, god good to mee in the Sabbath

No: 1: joynd togither in a day of prayer to seeke god in behalfe of the nation, and for the life and presence of god to bee with us in his worship and in our families a good day. the night before I had been very ill with a fitt of an ague.

4: this day and former the Wid: Brown, carried 22. load of dung for mee into Sawyer's,

No: 5: This weeke past god very good to mee in many outward mercies, I had one fit of an ague somewhat sharpe, and no more, I was glad it tooke mee, and I had that evening declined chesse, which would have taken of Mr H. from his meditations against the day of prayer on the morning, the weather wonderfull cheerfull and comfortably. the lord was good to mee in the mercies of the day, his word and sacrament, the times have a sad face, strange reports going abroad, of nothing but divisions the lord our god take care for his, he reigneth, that is our confidence,

11: rid to Colchester, god good in my going, and returning, it was a cold wett day the weather having untill then continued very dry.

No: 12. god good to us, but my heart not lively in the worke of my place. god deade to mee former teptacons, but thes unspiritual natures have their continuing deadnes on them(.) in the preaching my heart was raised, and Christ very precious, but I cannot shake of my sluggishnes, and keepe my heart up on god day by day.

No: 19: The lord good to mee and mine in outward mercies. this weeke was cold and snowy and wett, and now cleare and frosty, and so very seasonable, this weeke a sad hand of god on John Church dying in a very nastie condicon, the lice running by 100^{ds} on his face, and crawling into his mouth, oh that I could tremble before the lord. this day my heart lett out on behalfe of my sister, the lord revive her in mercy, god was good to mee in the word, my heart in some measure plain towards the interest of christ, but its but strait, and I find much unactivenes therein.

21: Kept a day of prayer with Justice H. to seeke god in his behalfe, who hath been visited above 14 months with a quartan ague(.) it was a bitter cold day, god gave mee a heart to speake plainly unto him, the lord in mercy heare for him(.) at night a sad fire at Lexden filling the sky with light it was from 2 corn barns

☞ 22. dreamd I was familiar with the pope. wife dreamd wee were so with the protector lord lead mee not into temptacon.—23. dreamd I saw ships and boats loaden in the heavens a great man on a feirce horse pransing—another with his backe to mee I thought he went not with the fleet. neither of both.

Nov. 26: The Lord good to us in outward mercies, the time very winterly, few such Novembers for quantities of snow, which fatt the Earth, and helpeth the pooles(.) many said there would bee no distinction of winter and summer in the end, for the fine winters, but this came in very sharpe: the lord good to mee in letting mee see how unapt my heart is to bee quiet and still, and waite until he brings things to passe but apt to run in my thoughts before his worke, yett I would bound my selfe with in his word: god good to mee in the word and worke of this day.

☞ This night my wife dreamed, that towards a night. shee saw 3 lights in the skie over Abbots feilds which are North by West, and South a body as the Sun or Moone, the lights blazed and filled the skie with light often, and then the body in the South answered it with flames exceeding terrible; when the lights ceased there arose 3 smokes like pillars out of the earth and ascended. shee thought of Rev: 19.3:[1] afterwards the lights with a whirlewind and noise filled the whole heaven with sparkes, as if it would have burnt all. the body was then of a darke red. afterwards it was more light and in that body as it were flowers, from a roote(,) shee thought of the roote of Jesse, but there were two of them. only twisted into one, and in the circumference inwards many strings like roots, the ayre darke, morning came, and the day darke; shee feared and trembled but bore up her heart on Christs mercy.—I, and Mrs Mabel, and our new mayde Mary were there to see it, and no other.—a floud this morning. die. 27°.—shee thought shee was busy in going to oven but could not doe it, and so thought wee would bee when Christs coming would indeed bee.

29. called in to see H. Hutton where I had not been many yeares. found him in great trouble of spirit, the lord order it for good to him, I bought Wharton's Almanacke[2] wherin are amazing particulars.

Dec: 3: God good to us in our mercies, oh that I had a heart inwardly to feare him(,) I find him good in provision for mee; but my heart is not lett out for god, with zeale for his name, oh I am not restles to have gods salvation discovered to sinners, use mee therein.

☞ 18^{li}. Mr Haines bill for 30^{li}. to mee and Mr Clopton part of Augmenta-

[1] 'And again they said, Alleluia. And her smoke rose up for ever and ever.'

[2] Sir George Wharton (1617–81), astrologer and royalist, published annual almanacks between 1641 and 1666. DNB.

con, in my booke mony(.) this is go(o)ds goodnes to increase mee one 1d.

8. I thought by this day, England might heare of the intent of Blakes fleet, I heard. 7. it was before Naples, but this morning my son Tom. told mee his wonderful dreame. Jesus Christ in a white robe, came into my pulpit while preaching and hugd mee, and I him. then he came to him and put his inkhorn in his pocket, and carried him into the churchyard, and askt him, what hee would have, Tom. said. a blessing: Jesus Christ bad him follow him, and mounted up to heaven, and he after them, next Jesus Christ, they ascended in schoules, none could goe so fast as he, divers would have gone and Jesus Christ bad them goe backe and not follow him; when in heaven they were singing melodiously and praying all in white, Jesus Christ and the company passed through over a mountain and over the sea, and then on the land wee fell a praying and could not see Jesus Christ. the divel came and made a burring, but presently Jesus Christ came, and drave him away and bid him gett him behind his backe Satan, then Christ returned the same way with his into heaven(,) all returning to earth but he, and his sister Mary would not lett him come away; then Jesus Christ told him he must, and he saw him sit at the fathers right hand, which was wonderfull then while in heaven, he thought their was terrible thunder, but he was not afraid, and there was he knew an earthquake below: I turned him to some texts like thes passages, the lord doe my child good by such things

Dec. 10. The Lord good to us in outward mercies, in preserving my house from fire by Johns boldnes to endeavour a fire in the schoole, and my peoples carelesnes; the ground and wayes again very wett, the earth replenished with moisture, my heart yett dull in the lords worke, I find great a sloth on my spirit in my particular worke of preaching, in some other things my heart is lett out—oh I blesse god that weaneth my heart from the world, and maketh mee to choose christ my portion, and value him a goodly heritage

☞ I had an apprehension I might bee reserved to see the world turned into a wildernes, and christs coming and this I eyed as a mercy, but apprehending the excellency of the state of those that come with christ, my heart was in a straite whether I should not rather long to bee dissolved, but this day I was satisfied as to the former, and desire to magnifie the lord if he please so to order concerning mee, Luke. 21.v.36:[1]

[1] 'Watch ye therefore, and pray always, that ye may be accounted worthy to escape all these things that shall come to pass, and to stand before the Son of man.'

where this condicon is held out as a signal mercy, and wee are highly to strive to attaine unto it.

The Litle Horne, shall conquer Canaan out of the Turkes hand, and surely ruine the Turke for Christ takes his kingdome, and no question but Canaan a part. this is much that O.C. in a few yeares should atcheive such things, and doe not thes Italian designes tend therunto.—this was in my thought, and written and presently I viewed with wonder, how Campanella reads that text. of Balaam. p. 10.

13. joynd in priory in prayer. I spoke of living by faith, the lord helpe mee to picke a living out of h[*im*]

16: god opened my heart and hand to divers in want, this night I received a very great guift from Mr Eldred, the lord bee blessed, and returne his love to him.

Dec: 17. This weeke wett, and warme to this day, which was cold and dry. my Tho. ill, the lord in mercy pitty and pardon him, the lord shew him the light of his saving countenance, the lord tooke him with an increase of illnes in the time of hearing the word when my heart was lett out to pray for all and him, the lord good to mee in the word which was delivered with some affection, the lord grant to proffit, prepare my heart for what thou intendest to doe with mee.

☞ 20: meditating in the feild how hard it is to trust god and live on him by faith, I saw enough in god to maintein life, but wee cannot trust him, I resolve in his strength to bee his and to stand up for his truth, and declare his mind, and not bee dismayed, and he will bee with mee

Dec: 24 god good to mee and mine, the time cold, and frostie, healthfull weather, blessed bee god; noisd wee had beat a French fleet, but it was not seconded; the lord god good in quicking my heart towards him, fearing my heart in the times, in giving mee to choose his wayes with crosses, awakeing mee in the dayes I live to warn men, the lord deliver mee from evey evill worke, and make mee alive to himselfe.

☞ 25. after thoughts of the close of the parl: I dreamd I saw one person. as his backe to mee, calling out the lords people to christ (as once Moses) to behold the enamouring name of the lord (with an emphasis) there was then and there as an appearance of the suns glory. but no body seen, I said. lord people will not beleeve nor bee persuaded: it was answered the lord was able and would.

Dec: 31: God good to mee and mine, I much feared some ill would befall the parliament. this weeke was wonderfull dull and malincholly weather, the sun shone not, but on monday morning, and 30 a litle glimmering one glance or two; this day very darke, this day I pressed holines, and without it, no seing of god, the lord pressed it affectionately on my heart, oh lett mee never forget the same, my heart is not lively for god, I had a very great cold, and pose all this weeke, I praise god it fell not much into my chest, the lord remember mee for good in all things. Mr Clopton paid mee. 2^{li}. 11^{s}. for books, and I him. 5^{s}. I owed unto him, and so wee cast our accounts even.

Jan: 4: preacht at Wakes, some affections stirring, at night dreamed one came to mee and told me that Thurloe[1] was turned Jew; I answered perhaps it was a mistake, he might declare he was a Jew ☞ born, the Jewes having lived here, and he pretend by old writings his pedigree from them, to ingratiate with the Jewes, or some compliance with them.

Jan: 7. god good to mee and mine in outward mercies, I am much afraid some evill is on coming to London, and the Parl. the lord hide his own, on that account I mention them before the lord; my heart dead in prayer, oh lord when wilt thou quicken mee.

Jan: 14: My children ill with colds, and my wife also, god a support, and stay of heart to us under our affliction, and a sweet revivall unto us therein, oh that my heart could bee weand from the world thereby, and more, and more sett on Jesus Christ, the lord good to mee in the worke of the day, opening my heart in prayer more than ordinary, the lord make mee mindfull of him, and to remember he reigneth, when the waves roar, and are tumultuous.

I had sought the god of my mercies, on whom I leave my selfe to make provision for mee to facilitate my matters for mee; where I was apprehensive of hard dealing, I had no present answer, my spirit went on in seeking him, then I met with a temptacon, that I must use meanes, I had done that in my power, loth I was to goe to law, my jorneys in vain; while this was a trouble. die. 15. the worst busines was ended to my content beyond my expectation, by the persons coming unto mee, and. die. 16. another busines was dispatcht that was in my mind, this is thy goodnes oh that I could weare this favour and hereby trust thee as my father, and most fast freind.

Jan: 21: God good to mee and mine in outward mercies, sad colds abroad, and wee have had our share in them, but god hath supported

[1] John Thurloe (1616–68), Secretary of State under Cromwell. DNB.

us under them. Jacke full of wormes they come yett away, the lord will heale him in due time, my heart very cold in preparation to the lords worke(.) the lord in mercy remember mee for good, the season, cold, close, and commonly flabby(.) the lord good to mee in the Sabbath worke, no newes of publique affaires only the 5 months are expired, and wee can heare of nothing brought to a head by them.

☞ 24. darke cloudy weather, but not very cold, and a litle drying, no rumours almost in the contry, some talke of granting subsidies which is not very pleasing to rich men, at night I had in my dreames a sense of that dreame, wherin I saw a ship under saile towing a long Boate loaden with pouder, this was the white kings action which was volans, and that fleet, would goe from hence with their long boates:—the horse and man, noted his actions equitans, he would bee in the head of great land armies; a man on a horse mufled up in his cloake his backe towards mee, his action descendens, going far West in forinne countries he would bee ruind. the pullus aquile.[1]—a son of his coming from him when
Psal. 103. 28. beyond sea to us here, the person O.C. I could not much heed this in regard the prophesie is not authenticke.

25. rose this morning, and I found my birth day was. 26. not this day as I thought hitherto(.) going down to a fast, my neighbour Burton cald and told mee the parliament was dissolved on monday. 22. at one of the clocke by the Protector, which proved true, in my night vision that night, I thought it was so, and I mett 4 of the parliament in blacke habits, and gownes walking in London street, or in a great towne, the lord take care of us. I am glad I was about such a worke when I heard it.

Jan: 26: 1654: 39. yeare enters

Jan: 26: My dayes passe, thine oh Lord abide for ever, I shall enjoy thee where I shall dwell for ever with thee, sensible it entred mee a new yeare, in which my heart desired gods presence with mee, as I desire to praise him, for his abiding presence with mee the last past.

[1] Volans: moving swiftly. Equitans: riding. Descendans: going away or descending. Pullus aquile: uncertain, probably either 'the young man of the eagle' or 'the dark youth'. Psalm 103: 5 describes how 'thy youth is renewed like the eagle's'.

Jan: 28. god good to mee and mine, the season frost, this day, the lord gave us his word and the freedom of his table, my sister Mary loth to receive the elements as shee sat with us. I spoke as god directed mee, shee complied, and I trust gods mind was so shee should(.) the lord perswade my heart more to love in his sight, all whist in the nation on the dissolucon of the parliament. the lord remember mee for good under all thes distractions

☞ Feb: 3: I came up to give some poore men 2d. my wife told mee, shee saw, a curious building in the heavens towards North, out of it came men and presently an innumerable company of horsemen marching in ranke towards the South, leaving a path,—presently 3. marcht in ranke wonderfull swift and low, (c.o. as if) they were shee thought marking[1] angels; in the North a smoake and fire great way of, and drums very loud, and presently all whist[2] and quiet; they marcht over my house, and shee thought they were red.—or els destroyed angels. he in the midle was girt, (the other attended in plain habits) garment reddish, so all horses, and building[3] on the earth, and togither.

is this. the 2d woe. Rev: 9.—or the Jewes issuing out of the earth.—or the army in *d.* oh lord so blind are wee, that wee can make nothing of prophesies, visions, nor providences so as to find out directly what god is doing—yet I blesse thee for what thou lettest mee see and heare and read. through mercy I escaped the danger of a horse kicking at mee.

Tom dreamed he saw a wonderfull house in the aer, very fine and shining like the inside of oister shells a great man as big as a house came out, with a great fire on his head, he came to the ground, the house was vanisht to a snaile, and he and sister crept on the ground like frogs.

Feb. 4. The Lord good to mee and mine in many mercies, oh blessed be god that will know and consider such a worm as I am, the lord keepes my heart inquiring after the worke he is doing, and endearing my heart unto him, and helping mee to prefer him to all other things, the word this day very comfortable for which I blesse the lord. Smal pox, observations thereabouts, in several proceedings, Jan: 25:54. Num: 279. p. 4416.[4]

[1] Marking: observing, observant. NED.

[2] Whist: silent, quiet, hushed, free from noise or disturbance. SOED.

[3] There is an asterisk in the text, probably to fill in a blank inadvertently left at the start of a line.

[4] This refers to the bill of mortality of 25 January 1654.

5: This day the persons that have interest in Langford lands,[1] were with mee, this is of the lord to move them to inquire after mee, I promised them a meeting, the lord helpe mee with a wise and christian spirit to seeke his honour, and the lord prosper that affaire, the lord casts one providence to another. Mr W.H. hath offered mee my mony.

6. preacht at Gains Coln god made my heart lively therin, gave Mullins children. 5ˢ. I blesse god for a heart to bee mindfull of, and that I can doe good to any poore worms.

8. met with a notable peice about AntiChrist. almost my notion, deliverd mine to Mr. B. the lord doe good, warn and awaken men thereby.

Feb: 11. god good to us in many outward mercies, the season wett, and glum, I could observe the sun setting but once since Decemb. 20. my heart is very much sett on the worke of the generacon, patiently to suffer, and not to mind the world, oh that I were dead to every evill, my heart a litle warm in the word and worke of the day, lord lett mee feele that love of Christ my mouth from my heart mentions, yea shed it abroad on my soule more and more.

13. rose more early than formerly; heard just as I rose, a fire on Coln green, quencht and no hurt to mention, blessed bee god: one cald mee down gave mee a hint of some trouble at London, presently sent for to priory, saw a letter from Major Haines to call divers to Markshall, to communicate a letter from the protector unto them, to acquaint them, with the present state of affaires which threaten trouble, I was not desired. the Lord shew mee his way, and guide mee therin, I was writing, when I heard thes, against those thoughts that expect Christs kingdom suddenly to appeare, and to bee managed by their armes and weapons. its expected the Cavaliers will rise, and Charls Stuart come and head them. the Levellors are up 300 in the west, its though(t) Grey. and Eyres and wildman head them, also the 5ᵗ monarchy men in London under Harrison and Rich; and what if all this bee but in designe,

Feb: 18. Through mercy the great noise of plots vanish, but whether some mens evill intentions will not take place god knowes, these things and dayes are very misterious, the lord bee good to mee therein(.) the weather is wonderfull uncertain, and moist, god good in the state and condicon of my familie, the lord in mercy delight in mee, and rejoyce in mee to doe mee good, I know great things are at hand, oh that I had a heart to make the state of my soule to

[1] See p. 66, n. 4 above.

godward sure then should I not feare in the day of evill, my heart a litle warmed with Christs love to mee oh that I find strength to live up to his mind, tis in my desires to die to all things, that I might live to him, and god that puts it into my heart I trust will putt it into my life; I wonder when the plot is noised to bee so much in the North, why all forces march to the city, especially from the north, I feare something is to be done in London.

Feb: 25. The lord good to mee, and mine in outward mercies: the season very wett, cloudie, mistie I never knew the like, the lord make us sensible of his dealing therein with us, my heart is still held close to look after the worke of god in the generation, I find that many men great formerly are now in durance. Harrison by name, their is a lex talionis[1] in our sufferings and surely the cup will goe round, let not man trust in man, for he is but a lie, the Levellers and 5^{t}. monarchy men are for present most shot at, the Independents in favour. the presb(yterians) not much medling or medled with, a higher strain of power, and perhaps some execution on some person: is aimed at, and perhaps feak.[2] lord keepe mee from sin, and I shall have enough, I pitty from my heart those that suffer praying god to sanctifie it, and prepare mee for my trial, and give mee bowels to all.

March: 2: Sadly sensible of the old pranks of my spirit, oh how easy a matter it is to fall into sin and to bee overcome for the present thereby. lord wash mee throughly.

4: God good to mee and mine, our cow calved well, which though common is a mercy, and all worthy to be minded and god to bee praised; god good to mee in the word, my heart had some lively affections in it over my hearers and desirous to preach in Jesus Christ into their soules, lord lett not the word bee without its efficacy, Heard of Mrs Haines delivery of a daughter, the name of the lord bee blessed, the season good, and above all Jesus Christ is good to mee, in my inward frame, though I find much daily weaknes, yett he will pitty, and cover all.

6: Wett day rid to Colchester. I find some earnestly oppose Pro(tector) others close with him on grounds that carry a faire face, the lord keepe my heart closely and wisely to retain the doves innocency. said that Rich is committed,

7. this day Major Haynes came to Colch(ester) the day was dry, yett I

[1] A law of retaliation in kind.

[2] Christopher Feake, Fifth-monarchist, sometime Independent minister; imprisoned, though not severely treated, by Cromwell. DNB.

prefer my wett, and this misse in regard of the good meeting wee had, which I feared I should misse if I went this day

8: This day was a day I had thought of as the bound within which some great action would bee, the throning the protector really done; he will come up higher in the season of it, I saw a letter from Major Haines, intimating reall apprehensions of the Cavalier ☞ attempts; said the prince on the seas. Mr Barnardiston dined with mee, at night I dreamed Christ born in a stable as being the redeemer of man, and beast out of their bondage by the fall. I listen what is done in the world past, and henceforward.—

10: a wonderful storme of rain, haile, snow in our parts, the like not known with us, the litle brooks, flowed beyond all measure wee had but the skirts. at Cogshall and chappel tedious it came from the South, and a litle west,

March. 11. The lord good to mee and mine in many mercies, I have my colds, and my thorns in condicons which is to gather up my spirit more unto god, but when shall it bee, the weather wonderfull wett, the divel I find laying his old baits for mee, and I am ready to bee taken oh what a weake thing is man if god uphold not, the lord good to mee in my quiet rest, when the feare of theives is continually with others, the lord in mercy make mee not feare so as to slight him, but indeed and really to give up myselfe unto him, god was good to mee in the word, and worke of the day, the lord in mercy blesse it, and accept mee

☞ 13. heard the Caval(iers) in arms in Wales. Nottingh(am): Shropsh(ire) Wiltsh(ire) where they seized the Judges(.) dreamd at night, one told mee up in Lincolnshire, and I perswaded they would be crusht and come to nothing: I saw the horse march down a long street.

14: H. Abbot. junior. came to mee for 26^{s}. for collection; I desired him to pay mee my tith, he refused and desired that wee might be civil in the law, I told him I would not put him to that trouble but would pay him, neither would I trouble him, I would leave it to that Master whom I served to wright mee, he presently kindly crossed my rate, and there was an end, I blesse god that gave mee that temper to honour him, and gave him such a spirit towards mee, that hand was here for good blessed bee thy name:

16. 17. 18. 19. 20. to 21. I was very ill with cold, and ague in my tooth and face, the lord was good to mee, and my heart bore up on him, though I had not those present answers I did verily hope to have received from him; I was learning thereby, who would sin against

god, for his life, when a litle ilnes that may come next houre, will make it a burthen unto a man.

22. at night, a cow that troubles us much, being ill with the gargett,[1] calvd. for which god bee praised.—23 at night towards the next morning, in my sleepe. I thought something appeard, I saw nothing ☞ distinctly, but thought it was Cromwell, who told mee he had taken the prince, would have had me disposed him. I told him, I would not, but he had enough that would.

March: 25. This weeke I have been very strangely ill, that I cannot 1655. bee any way quiet(.) my gums ill swelled, the lord in mercy remove it in due time, this day I warned Colne to keepe a sober faire, lord aw them if it be thy good pleasure(.) god gave mee some strength, and cheerfulness in my worke for which I desire to blesse him, he in mercy own mee. I writ to Mrs Mabel.

30: a very cold time, dry, wind in the East, healthfull for our bodies(,) my illnes a litle continued, but very much abated so that I know not how sufficiently to blesse god, and my mind was also very peaceable to godward which is a duobling of mercies on mee.

I again review my estate. Lands as formerly, and the same personal estate good that was last. there is added this yeare.

Mrs Maries land. 98^{li}. 8^{s}. 0^{d}.

W: Web:—	5^{li}.		
Mr Elliston—	16:	10.	my stocke which I last yeare valued at. 30.
Mr W: Harl.—	25.	0.	I count worth about 20^{li}: and I am in debt to 2
Edw: Brown.—	20.	0.	persons. 5^{li}. which abated there remains cleared 96^{li}. 10^{s}
Major Hayns—	30.	0.	
in cash:	15.	0.	
thus though I am unprofitable god is mindfull of mee	111.	10.	

my heart is to love and serve him. Mr Sams business was also moved unto mee, I waite on the lord to doe his pleasure therein desirous rather to honour him, than to gain mony, and with my hearty praises of god, I desire to bee made more serviceable to him in my generation, being perswaded he intends mee good in the yeare that is now entring—

[1] Gargett: an inflamed condition of the head or throat in cattle and pigs. SOED.

April. 1: The weeke past very cold and dry with eastern winds but I trust in god, it is good and healthful weather. I was very tender, as being aguish from a great cold, and the pain and swelling of my gums, the lord was good to mee in giving mee strength for the Sabbath, oh that he would bee with mee therein continually blessing of mee.

5: received a sad letter of my sister Anna's povertie(,) lord its thy mercy its not my condicion, lett thy wisdom wayes, and thy direct mee in thy blessing bee continued unto mee, I lent her. 4li.

7. heard of Mrs Stebbings sad affliction in her onely child, who was with child by a base fellow, 7 months gon, and not discovered by them, but all that time shee and they treating with an other; a person I judged sober, and proposed her to a good match, but wee had done long before

Ap: 8: The season, cold and dry to excesse. my aguish listles distemper with the illnes of my face and gums continued, yett god in mercy gave mee to goe through with my imploiment, oh that my heart were tender and zealous towards him and that which is deare, as I find him mindfull of mee and that which is mine

12: rid to Messing, advised with Cousin Josselin in the Sams businesse. he wishes mee to make the best end with them, that I can, I had through mercy a comfortable jorney.

Ap: 15: The weather cold, windy and dry. my ilnes much removed blessed be god, but some dregs of it remaine, the lord restore mee to my perfect health, god good to mee in mine, litle An very ill one day, the next revived, oh that I knew how to praise god, some brokennes in my heart, longings for that inward sweet communion with god which I want, and the drawings out of my heart, in a holy confidence to rely on him; god good to mee in the word, the lord accept of mee for good

16: in the morning my jaw beneath was very much sweld, my gums were better, I hope in god my ilnes will remove by degrees, heard that divers professors turne aside here to deny Christ come really in the flesh, his body only phantastical.[1]

17. rid to Langford god good in my jorney, my busines I commit to god, and I trust he will effect it, I found no great discouragement. I returned. 19. having been kindly treated by Mr Thompson.

Ap: 22. God good to mee and mine in outward mercies, my gums and

[1] Professor: one who makes open declaration of his sentiments, beliefs, etc. (sometimes as opposed to one who merely practises). The theological argument probably concerns the Resurrection or Second Coming of Christ.

face swelled but the pain through mercy abateth, and my distemper much amended for which I blesse the Lord: the season warm some sweet showres both observed as the answer of prayer and gods taking notice of us, god was good to mee in the word, which I prest plainly and nakedly on the behalfe of Christ. the lord take care of mee for to him I resigne up my selfe to take care of mee.

A. 29. god good in many mercies to mee, my face illnes continued, god in due time will remove it, the pain was gon, though the swelling continued, corn especially wheat thrive much(.) persons spake as if scarce any harvest(,) god good in the season which is warm, and I trust in his due time he will give shoures, lord blesse this dayes word

30: this morning I ended a great difference between, landlord and Tenant, which could not any wayes agree formerly, before I came home. Nat: Perry, a tenant from whom I had not heard in 2 y. and halfe, came to mee with a good sum of mony, though not with all, it was a special providence to mee;

May. 3. I observed in the North, light leavings or beamings up of the skie such as I never saw before(.) busy this day in composing young Butchers busines between his father and Mr Harlakenden

May. 6: This weeke continued very hot and dry, the lords will bee done in all things, it is the lord, lett him doe what he pleaseth, my illnes in face continueth, but I hope it abateth, though I cannot remove vanity out of my spirit, he keepeth troubles out of my spirit, but he is god, and I am man, the people calme and quiet nothing troubles them(.) the body of professors so rent divided, ensnared and tangd, that cunning men may doe any thing, and they not say why doe you thus, god good to mee in the word and worke of this day, my face a trouble to mee, but not hinder my worke through mercy.

8: I drew a tooth, very well, I was much satisfied in spirit, in seeking and eying god to doe it, and it was corrupted, and the flesh within it, most loathsome, it bled very much my swelling asswaged presently, the issue I wait on god, to accomplish,

10. the night before I felt something in my tooth place jaggy: my wife looked; and found something in it, as a bladder, this morning early in bed, I pulled out a peice of (c.o. my) bone by the place where my tooth stood; it drew outwardly of itselfe, and fell of from the other part of my upper jaw of it selfe, it was firm, but I conceive begun to rott, it was putrified round about, it must needs have been dangerous if god had not directed mee to draw my

tooth but no such matter was feared as this, the lord make mee thankful and mindfull to honour him in my calling, and quicken my heart thereunto I pray thee, I have no helpe herein, but from thy selfe oh my god,

this day, the Justice, and I married Peg. Nevil to Butcher, the first I intermedled with since the late act,[1] the report is of great officers made at London, oh that goodnes might bee in mee

May. 13. god good to mee in many mercies, the lord very good in the matter of my face, my Lady honywood feared a cancrish[2] humour, and prescribed mee direction, I trust in god all will end comfortably, yett I am sometimes apt to bee afraid, my sinful life may very justly cause it should bee so, but god commonly hides feare from mee, I doe not find any mention in a manner of the humour in my mouth, god good to mee in the word and worke of the Sabbath for which I blesse his name,

18. preacht at Halsted on Jeremy. 3.14. god good to mee, no great incouragment in the audience, oh how deadly and drowsily men heare the word.

May. 20 god good to mee in my face, I did not find any hurt or pain in it, god good in litle Nans reviving who was very ill, wee had formerly and this day comforting showres the lord moisten, and spiritualize our hearts; god was good to mee in the word, I find old foolish imaginacions taking hold on my spirit, and hindring mee in my busines, the lord in mercy deliver mee from vain thoughts, and lett my heart bee reserved for him and for that which is his service,

24. preacht at Buers on psal. 4.6.7. I hope some poore soules were toucht and affected(.) the lord bring persons of throughly to himselfe, I had a comfortable walke thither, I found my selfe not weary, as lately I was in walking

25. kept a day of prayer at priory god with us in some measure(.) Mr H. returnd safe after a long jorney(,) unto god bee the praise, the lord is weaking poore brother Brownson I feare and calling him away, lord fit him, and make up our losse,

May. 27. god good to us in health, I hope my face doth well, yett I feare some dregs and remains of ill humour there, the good lord

[1] The Barebones Parliament on 24 August 1653 passed an Act declaring that only marriages solemnised before a J.P. would be recognized by the State, though people could subsequently undergo a religious ceremony if they so desired. Gardiner, *Commonwealth*, ii, p. 242.

[2] Cancrish: cankerous, cancrous, of the nature of a canker, or eating sore, cancerous, gangrenous. NED.

lett mee enjoy the limbs of my body for his and my service if it bee his pleasure until I goe down to the grave, god gave us very sweet dewes to refresh the earth, times troublous and discontentfull men angry, my desire is to bosome myselfe in the almighty, this day wee broke bread after a somewhat long intermission(,) wee were prettily round togither, the lord was good to mee, who was very unprepared for the service, the lord keepe my heart intire and plain to him, god good in the word

28. This day wee went a great part of the bounds of Earles Colne, and towards Taine especially, the season promises hopes of plentie.

30: Heard, what formerly I apprehended that Cromwell would bee stiled Emperour:

31: rid towards Norfolke, and returned safe. June. 10: having experience of gods goodnes to mee and mine in great deliverances, under the wretchednes of my heart, which might justly have laid mee open to danger.

June: 2. preacht at Hingham lecture.—3. there. and at Hardingham: —6: at Runhall 10: when come home Stevens with mee, who had the divell appearing to him, the greedines of mony, made him desire it, and god sufferd it, he appeared in a blacke gown and then in red, he tooke his bloud on white paper.

June. 10: god good to mee in his word preacht, in lightsomnes after my jorney, wee yett meet with no opposicon, nor disturbance in our worke, lord deliver mee from the vanity of my mind, and reserve mee as a peculiar possession for thy selfe,

14. a fast on the occasion of the Savoyard, at the same time imprisonings of men at home on feare of plots, horse raising in all counties of England. the lord was good to mee in the word and worke of the day, and his presence with mee for which I blesse him, I was with stephens and Mr R.H: he was afraid the divel was coming in upon us, I perceived him troubled, I thought he might, but trusted that Christ would secure us in whose worke wee were

June. 17. god good to us in many outward mercies, the season healthy, and fruitfull, I blesse god for some affection stirring in mee, towards his truth, his people, the poore afflicted Savoyards(.) I find my heart very dead in private prayer, I find my spirit not disquieted often though(,) so lord lett nothing croud any thing of thee out of my spirit, I intreate thee; wee gathered this day for Savoy in publique. 8^{li}. 12^{s}. 2^{d}. the hand of god on mee for good, Lord, thy love to mee ingageth my heart to thine, and what I can doe is thine, made this collection. 9^{li}. 11^{s}. 8^{d}. the 3. reddish cowes tooke bull June. beginning: but 4.5—Westney. June 19. and the Blacke Hedge cowe 20.

23. a sad fire in a poore cottage, the wind pretty high, lay well to save other houses through mercy so that onely that poore house was utterly burnt downe, a small peice of bone came out at that place, where my tooth was drawn, this was not corrupted; the lord be blessed who delivers mee, from such hidden evills, the lord watch over this place and deliver us from infectious diseases.

June. 24. Heard of the wellfare of my freinds in Norfolke, the lord good to mee in very many outward mercies oh bee good in reall and beleiving heart, god provides for mee, but I find my heart sluggish, and not fervent in preparation for my businesse, prosper thy worke, thy hande worke on my spirit, I intreate thee, moved in Mary Peakes busines to consider what was best to bee done on her behalfe, it was a great mercy it was not in the night, the lord was good to mee in the word, and in some cheerlines of spirit in preaching it. its said the last weeke divers good ministers died in London, 3 named the lord prepare mee for whatsoever he shall bee pleased to doe with mee, and the generation,

July: 1: God good to mee and mine in the weeke past, good in my quiet on the lords day, when it was likely I should have had a disturbance as some of my neighbours had, I blesse god for this sweet calme, the lord prepare mee for trouble and lett not any evill come upon mee unawares as a snare I most humbly intreate thee,

3. preacht at Gaines Coln the quakers nest, but no disturbance, god hath raised up my heart not to feare, but willing to beare, and to make opposicon to their wayes in defence of truth, it is an evill that runs much in all places, some think it will bee dangerous to Cromwells interest, and is so, god knows I doe not, yett I thinke he feares them not, and perhaps the clause in his declaration not to disturbe the minister in exercise, was to hint to them, they might doe it after if they would, securely, for that is their practice.

7. Major Haines expected at Coln he came not, the Protector staid him above, some eminent occasion surely interveneth, the noise of his crowning is not as formerly, though neerer it may bee than when most talked of.

July. 8: God was good to us in many outward mercies, gave us peace, quiet, but I find my heart exceeding vain, full of foolish wanderings after things that cannot profit(,) I desire to loath my selfe, but yett I attain not to an inward spirituall frame, and to adorn the gospell in my conversation, I find my heart not so carefull to provide for death, as I desire, but my precious time glideth away. I gathered this day for Mary Peake whose house was burnt down. 31^{li}. 15^{s}. 8^{d}.

July 15. God good to mee and mine in many outward mercies, Major Haynes and his wife with us in very good health, the season is most exceeding hot, and dry, the lord in his tender mercy minde us, under it; those called Quakers whose worke is to revile the ministry, made a disturbance at Cogshall,[1] and were sent to goale, the good Lord direct us what to doe, and keepe down violence in all spirits, a sad story at Markshall, a servant delivered of a child, which shee made away; and could not suppose she could conceale it, persons with her immediately before,[2] the lord keepe mee and mine from any such wickednes, I most humbly intreate thee, and without any spot and blemish to thy kingdom. said Mr Lamot was even dead, and not likely to live til this day, my Lady found him alive and sensible, blessed bee god(.) god gave us another calme, and quiet Sabbath, oh many feare the Quakers to ruine, Cromwell(,) tis not words that alter governments, and rout armies, it must forme it selfe into a military posture first, and when that appears, then enemies of the state, disturbers of the peace seiseth on them

16: gods answer of prayer in so sweet a shoure of rain that I scarce knew the like for a ground rain at such a time as this, oh blesse god and trust in him oh my soule.

17. Tom Humfry went from mee to live at Allens a butcher as a prentice, I promised him. 30^{s}. towards it, lord thou hast been bountiful unto mee, lett mee never bee straitned to thine

☞ on the 16th at night I came from Mr Littels; within an houre or lesse Guy Penhacke, at Stonebridge was heaved into the water by one in the shape of a bull and sett down therein, and could not gett out again the same way. but was carried backe again, he felt nothing touche him in the darke place above(,) it passed by him and as a wind with a rustle it beat him down into the road, then he was afraid; the man is bad, lord in mercy keepe mee, sanctifie him

July. 22. The Lord good to mee in many mercies, but my heart is not mortified to bear contradictions and opposicons in relations,[3] it makes mee meet with some trouble, the lord helpe mee this day in

[1] James Parnell interrupted a service on 4 July at Coggeshall, which resulted in his being taken before the local magistrates and being gaoled. Beaumont, p. 418.

[2] At the Trinity Assizes the following indictment appears: Martha Wade of Markshall, spinster, on 14 July 1655, there gave birth of a female bastard whose jaw she broke, of which the child died instantly. Pleads not guilty; judged not guilty; five (named) women witnesses (ERO, transcript of ASSIZES 35/96/T/12).

[3] RJ usually means his wife when speaking of 'relations'.

the word, with much calmenes to speake to the evill of the times, the lordspeake to the hearts of this people, and preserve them from every evill word and worke in a very sinfull generation, the day close, and cooler than some former dayes.

27. this day Mrs M.E. acquainted mee with the passages of those that have comunion with angels; and said. Mr Sadler. Master of requests[1] to the protector, was gon of unto them and that he had had a vision and trance for 3 dayes togither,

28. The Quakers set up a paper on the church door at E. Coln. lord I and people and truths. are thine, I pray the(e) take care of them, and give mee wisedom to behave my selfe wisely, in thy worke, and among thy people,

July 29. god good to mee and mine in many outward mercies, my deare wife, and Jack, ill, but I hope its but a distemper no rooted illnes, god gave us sweet shoures, and some winde but he holds it at present in, this corner begins to feel the quakers(,) some of their heads its said are among us,[2] the lord bee our refuge; an infallible spirit once granted them what lies may they not utter, and what delusions may not poor man bee given up unto, lord I see trials, let me be fitted for them, and saved through them. thy poore ministry, but precious truths are struck at, arise into the lot of thy inheritance, and maintain it against the strong man, and all his adherents. god was good to mee in his word, and I desire to give praise and glory unto him;—

August. 1: wee mett to seeke god, lord lett mee find thee in all thy ordinances and in my heart to make it pure and keepe it so, wee had some refreshing togither, and I hope our hearts were ingaged to god, and made somewhat more seing into the evill, that is abroad to try the sons of men, but is to bee followed with stupendous trials indeed.

3. Heard my augmentation was taken from mee, on a mistake, but was in good part resetled by Major Haines care. our mouths ful of a great losse at Hispaniola. perhaps it will make the good news that is coming more acceptable, and must rouse us up as Joshua at Ai.[3]

4. followed all day with an exceeding great pose, very thin, not so in months before,

[1] John Sadler (1615–74), a Master of Chancery, as well as Master of Requests, M.P. for Cambridge. In 1662 he accurately prophesied the Plague and Fire of London. DNB.

[2] George Fox described how, in 1655, he 'came to Cogshall, and there was a meeting of about 2,000 people, as it was judged, which lasted several hours . . .'. Fox, p. 213.

[3] Joshua, ch. 8: where Joshua destroyed the kingdom of Ai.

August: 5: God good to mee in many mercies, for soule and body, the health, and reviving of my litle ones, some dayes very cold, a hopeful entrance of harvest, wee this day broke bread, and Brother Har. pressed us to remember Christ in heaven, the lord in mercy grant that wee prove not antichristian indeed in turning aside from that principle, my heart was very dull and formal in this dayes worke, lord bee mercifull to mee, the worke of a service takes mee of much—from comfort in it, especially being so unfitt for it, as I commonly am. I was very hoarse with my cold this day, yett through mercy I continued to preach and performe my worke,

7. rid to Bumpsted, and. 8. preacht at Haveril endeavouring to advance the gospel in the hearts of people, my freinds well, my sisters children I schooled for their disobedience(.) god good to mee in my return my heart much out of frame, the lord purge it, and sanctifie it. when I came home heard old. H. Abbott was dead, who regarded not the lord in his illnes, and was not much capeable to looke after him, just is god when persons doe not mind god in their lives, god should some way or other take them of, from calling on him in the time of death,—received kindnes from Mr Jeff. Littell and his wife, heard as if our successe great in the West Indies and yett our losse of Haines true; perhaps that was to ingage us the more earnestly against Spain, and now if wee can but frame up a religious war of Protestants against papists, wee shall hinder, ☞ the nacions from looking to their ballancings each other, and ruining the papists, by the helpe of protestants, who by their shipps only can in reason hinder it, wee shall doe our busines, and afterwards make them smart.

11: Goodwife Abbott rid to Colchester in a waggon, her housbands freinds not sending her home on horsebacke, nor lending her an horse, it was a stormy day, more thunder then I have heard in this or former summer, followed with very much rain and violent.

Aug: 12: god good to mee and mine in many mercies, and my heart somewhat more in frame, the lord wholly subdue mee that there might not bee a thought, but in subjection to the Lord Jesus Christ, a thin audience, but god good to me in the word.

17. dined at Mr Littels, his sister married, the season very sad, almost daily rains, which is sad for the harvest, but doth increase the hops.

Aug: 19. The weeke past god good to mee and mine in many outward mercies, god left a young hog of mine to be bitten by Burtons dog, it might have been worse, they cut his eare and taile and threw him into the water, lord preserve the poore creature if it bee thy good pleasure. let no trouble thence befall my family I humbly beg of thee, the weather, sad, lord reserve unto us the appointed weeks of harvest, showres this day, my heart is daily taken with the great things coming on the world, the lord in mercy suffer mee not to be led into temptacon, my cold goeth away well through mercy

20. wett especially towards night, lord thou wilt give us the weekes of harvest, my deare wife very ill at night, it ariseth from her nature, the lord in mercy bee her strength

21. a very sad wett day, yet no floud, wee had some eels in the water: —22. a fine day with us, a shoure at night. 23. good only shoure at night. 24. very wett: 25. very faire men inning much corne; Mrs Church gave my wife a faire tablecloth and 6. napkins all dieper[1] which shee gave her formerly by will, and now shee would bee her own executor and deliver them unto her,

Aug: 26. The Lord good to mee and mine in many outward mercies, for which I blesse him, the lord sanctifie all unto mee, and give mee a heart to serve him with all, lord send us refreshing, dry and warm weather for the harvest; my heart is sett to inquire into the daye and seasons, the French, and the Swedes prosper wonderfully, god plucks up the bounds of the nations, and men regard it not, the Lord good to mee in the Sabbath

27. a good harvest day. I was with Mr Crane, they kept their day of thanks for their delivery from Colchester. 3. of the nine dead, and 6. alive Mr Crane. Smith. Ayloffe. Eden. Barnardiston. god gave mee a good day there the lord fitt mee, for what he will doe—this 28. prayer sweetly answered in the season.

Sept: 2: God good to mee in many outward mercies, but my heart is not lively, and intent on doing for god in my place, and to enjoy god. I sometimes lift up my heart for witnesses of the spirit, and divine presences, but my heart is staid in common enjoyments. the season sad with rain, and men worse in being setled on their lees, they doe what they will and will not bee restrained: great revolucons ☞ are at hand, and our great securitie evidenceth it: 1656. from Christ. by the account of this nativity with the creation, begin now in some mens account(,) the lord fitt mee, for trials, are at hand, Lord pitty poore Poland: harrased by Swede and the Moscovite worst of all, god was good to mee in the word it was seasonable let it be effected all but that is thy worke to make it so. a sweet afternoon,

4: a hog I had died, bit with Burtons mad dog, blessed bee god it

[1] Diaper: name of a textile fabric, woven with patterns. SOED.

was not a child; the lord keepe mee from every evill, shall wee receive good at the hand of god and not evill,

5: sunn not a quarter high at night were seen as it were sparkes like starres coming from the sun and ascending upwards very many, it continued about halfe a quarter of an houre; they were scintille volantes prenuncie tempestatu et ventorum,[1] seen in nights but this then, a faire day. the sun was big. shone very bright, with strange beames downward

6.7: *drye* coole cleare so the *8*

Sept: 9. God good to mee and mine in many outward mercies, my wife somewhat ill, with inward feares and tooth ake, and myselfe with inward stoppings, the lord remember mee in mercy to doe mee good, the times very sad, with warres and troubles abroad, yet men wholly glued to the world, and the outward advantages thereof, this day faire but somewhat close(.) the lord good to mee in the word and worke of the day to him alone bee the praise

14. preacht at Halsted, to presse christians to establishednes in the truth.

Sept. 16. God good in many mercies, the season in the seed time generally good, my heart not under former annoyances but lord my desire is, I were delivered from the root of sin and body of death, god good to mee in the word, it was very cheerfull and sweet to mee oh let mee find my heart thereby ingaged unto god, and to his wayes.

17. god gave Mr Harlakenden a good crop of hops, when he expected not much, he gave mee 40^{s}. the lord look on his labour of love and let it bee returned to him

20: preacht at Wakes, prest persons to be firm to Jesus, the lord good to mee in the jorney received kindnes from sister Brown, blessed bee god for it, the W. Indie busines very dismall.

21. rid to Messing and returned safe, heard of divers deaths, god the more gratious in our healths(,) returned well, rid to speake comfortably to some, the horse I rid on even blind, blesse god

Sept: 23. seed time very good, dry, and coole, I was very ill with cold, it made mee heart sicke when I cought. the lord good to mee in his provision for mee, oh that I had a heart to rejoyce in him, my heart quiet, no such hurryings as formerly, the lord ingage mee to him by his goodnes, the lord good in the word of the Sabbath, lord give it a hiding place in my heart and mine

[1] Sparks, prophesying birds from the storm and of the winds.

26: Mrs Caval[1] with mee to acquaint mee with a meeting at Maldon, about Langford, it was a good providence I was within, the lords finger is I hope and trust in it for good to mee and mine(.) I was at Messing Sept: 21: and had thoughts thither, but desire to speake to Mr Tompsons man on the account of Christs interest in them which was very sensible in my heart, led mee home I spared my long jorney, and god sent them unto mee.

27. at Pannels ash in a good day, with divers honest faces, the lord did them good by our labour.

Sept: 30: God good in many outward mercies, my wife ill with an ague, the lord sanctifie it to us, and remove it, my vain thoughts too hard, lord I resolve not to give such thoughts a minding, helpe mee, dead them in my heart, let meditacons of god bee precious, the lord good in the season, latter harvest, and seed time, corn fals, and now wee feare the war with Spain(.) will hinder trade, make(,) mony dead, and commodities to sell worse, thus wee feare so many feares, that wee neglect the feare of god, the lord was good to mee in the worke wherein my soule doth rejoyce.

Oct: 1. Rid to Maldon, in the selfishnes of men I observe the more love of god to mee, if he had not been good to mee and mindful of mee, where would I have found favour

2. Mrs Harlakenden and her daughters rid towards London, god give them a good jorny, home and blesse them in meanes for health, and keepe them from sin and danger.

5: met at Chelmsford about Sams busines I thanke god who framed my heart, waiting to end my business comfortably and for them as for my selfe; I found no such matter in them, no way desiring to end it, hoping the law would bee their advantage, lord pardon them.

Oct. 7. This weeke full of busines, the lord was good to my spirit therein; I wait on him to give the best end to it. he hath mens hearts tutor them to thy mind I pray thee, for unto thee doe I commend all my affaires, god was good to mee in the word, it was seasonable and suitable to my inward frame, the lord dead my working corrupcon for mercy sake(.) my wife not well, the lord revive her, and give her health.

8: my litle An very ill my heart wrought in heaven for her, in the morning finely well, oh blesse the lord oh my soule, who remembers thee, and will for his names sake.

[1] A widow Cavell had a one-hearth house in 1662; and a widow Susannah Cavel of Langford or Ulting had her will proved on 21 October 1668 (ERO, 80 CR 8).

Leaper begun his yeare die. 10: god make him a good servant. and blesse him to gett good here.

13. Mrs H. came home safe from London it was very late.

October. 14. season very good, my wife somewhat ill, wee resolved to wean An. the lord blesse our way therein it is his. heard of my mother in laws death, god is good to mee and mine in many outward mercies, oh that wee had a heart to feare him and honour him with, and under all, the lord good to us in the season it was very sweet and comfortable, make my spirit cheerfull in injoying thy selfe I pray thee, oh my lord and god, most good. Mrs H. brought in bed of a boy very speedily while in morning sermons.

18: went down to Wakes, to heare, but I was called to preach. from psal. 32.6: wherein god was very good unto mee, make the word oh my god a blessing.

Oct: 21: God good to us in many outward mercies; my litle An tooke her weaning very well I blesse god, a curious fine season for the time; the seed time gives hope of plenty, country provision for the belly wonderfull plentifull, and cheaper, god good to mee in the word of the tendernes of Christ to sinners and this to ingage us to abide by him and his truths, oh that it might mee, and poor Coln among others with mee.

23: Sought unto god to give a blessing to mee in Mr Sams busines, and that it might bee ended peaceably, the lord remember mee in this also according to the greatnes of his me[ ]

24. Mr W.H. sent my wife a paire of cobirons;[1] the lord recompence his love, good is my god, who draweth forth the kindnes of any towards us.

25: Mr R.H. his son and heire was baptized at home, the entertainment a banquet, he was bountifull unto mee, the lord reward him, I was straitned in time, but endeavourd to speake well of god in his mercies, and to ingage out hearts to walke suitable thereunto.

27. Mr R.H. junior, a declaration sent down against him, by one who challengeth 2 houses(.) I blesse god I was not now ingaged in law, the lord end my business peaceably, and for his own glory fiet. fiet.[2] seriously eying god in this it rested in my spirit, god would heare mee in this, and accept mee, Lord I trust in thee, I doe not tempt thee,

Oct. 28: God good to mee and mine in outward mercies, my wife gets strength, and An doth well in her weaning, heard of the wellfare

[1] Cobirons: the irons which supported a spit. SOED.

[2] It will be, it will be.

of my Norfolke freinds; this day was the Lords, he was good to mee therein, oh that I could thankfully delight my heart in him, this day I entred my 16. yeare of living with my wife: I looke backe with joy, and forward with faith, and confidence that the lord will continue his loving kindnes therein towards mee; the season moist, and close,

2^{li}. 30: This day I paid Bridgett Aylward 40^{s}. I ought her, I intend by the next to pay my sister Mary, and then I am out of mans debt, any summ.

No: 1: my good freind Major Haynes, and Mrs H. with us, a sad messenger followed him with the newes of the death of his only child, he was afraid of his wife who was bigge, wee broke the matter to her by degrees, and god was good to us therin, shee tooke it with very much quietnes, and submission of spirit,

No: 4: God good to us, in many outward mercies, though he answered not prayer in Sams, and Shaws busines, yet I trust he will, my mind is very quiet, and runs more to god, the lesse it finds of man, in other payments, I was well provided for; An fell of the bed without any hurt blessed bee god, a neighbours infants arm broken with a fall(.) oh how the lords eye is on mee; the lord good to mee in the word preacht, and expounded; an arbitration between sisters was submitted to mee, the lord in mercy helpe mee to walke in wisedome uprightly. I desire to deliver a poore shiftles one from the hand of another that would oppresse, and yet to releive the oppressed.

6. notice given mee of Hedg his unworthines, I will if god blesse mee, rid my hands of so ill a neighbour.

10. rid to Ardleigh and returned safe, blessed bee god. the lord direct mee in that busines make him lord better and more serviceable to thee, or find wayes to remove him,

Nov. 11. god good to mee in many outward mercies, oh that I had a heart to feare and serve him accordingly, but that I want my heart is very unactive, the lord in mercy take care to fitt mee for the troubles of the dayes over coming wherein god will not parcel out judgment by retail as on Israel in the wildernes, but consume his enemies at once, god was good to mee in the word, which had sweetnes of Christ in it.

17. received of Mrs Haynes. 15^{li}.–10^{li} was part of augmentacion that Major Haines procured for mee, blessed bee god that anyway provides for so unworthy a person.

No: 18: God good in outward mercies to mee and mine, the season fresh and dry good weather for all things, Mr R.H. the litle boy was heartily prayed for this day the lord heare prayer on his behalfe. I find a wantones in my heart, and private converse with my wife, the lord make mee more savoury in my spirit and towards her, and attend more attentively to the word and worke of god in my generacon(.) god was in some measure good to mee in the worke of the day for which I blesse him.

19: the litle boy at the priory, died this morning, Mr R.H. senior. very ill, the lord in mercy watch over him for good: 21: spent at Chappel, where I was sole arbitrator in the Nevils busines with hope to end it; 22. married Tibball and his wife, towards morning

23. I dreamed I was intimate and secretary to the Protector, who appeared to mee young, I advised him to heed the interest, and the kingdom of Christ. solus inter nos,[1] at the first entrance to this advice he interrupted mee, told mee I must mention not a word of any such thing for it was an unpardonable fault with the Council; it seemed as if not so to him, it would countenance the Anabaptists and other sects, but I might advise to make good lawes against dronkennes and other vices.

Nov: 25. God good to us in our outward mercies, the season, cold frost, and a great snow, said Mr Marshal[2] is dead, no meanes can preserve life, nor hold the spirit, when god bids it return to him, and its well it can, for others, yee wee ourselves are loth to goe home(.) god good to mee in inward workings to raise up my spirit to a confidence in his mercy unto all eternity. said H. Cromwell trounces the anabaptists in Ireland.

28. kept a day of prayer at Mr W. Harlakenden, where wee blest god for answering prayer in removing his ague, while I was praying brother Cooper an old man had word brought him that his old wife, went to a neighbours house and fell down dead suddenly(.) Lord sanctifie such an amazing providence to us all, I gave him 5^{s}. to refresh him

Dec. 2. a cold day, god somewhat warmed mee in the ordinance of breaking bread, and more might if my heart could presse after him, the lord good in outward mercies to mee and mine, my heart affected with that sad evill that is acted by men towards others the lord affect my heart, and bee mercifull to mee and mine

6. a fast publique a cold day and thin audience, wee are tender of our

[1] Alone amongst us.

[2] The well-known Stephen Marshall, vicar of Finchingfield and chaplain to the Earl of Essex; buried in Westminster Abbey in 1655. Smith, numerous references.

flesh, lovers of our selves, and ease, but what will bee the issue of this frame, surely god will bee careles of those that are so careles carriaged towards him.

Dec: 9. a bitter cold, windie snowy day. the lord good in warm mercies to mee, the word solemn not to bee rebellious against god, oh that it might bee, find in my heart that I might not sin against him.

13 Mr R.H. returned safe through from London blessed bee god therefore.

Dec: 16. The lord good to mee and mine my wife troubled with rheume but in due time will I trust cure it. the day cold, my heart is justly taxed with unpreparednes to the worke and services of god, make mee sensible of my sin, great rumours of the Jewes being admitted into England,[1] hopes thereby to convert them(.) the lord hasten their conversion, and keepe us from turning aside from Christ to Moses of which I am very heartily afraid

20. Heard a good sermon of the savour of Christ from Mr Sparrow. at night I was very ill, and the feare of death, and miscarrying there tooke hold on, and I found no help but a christ, and I trust he will bee my helpe, and deliver mee from the bondage of it. I lookt on it, as a heart teaching of god to own Christ in this his day. heard a good sermon at Halsted of god taking away branches.

Dec: 23. God good in many outward mercies, my wife ill, but somewhat better. the heart out of frame is a sad case, especially when wee will not see it. but thinke our evill is well, and its then evill to awaken us to our duty. and this lord is that some see, I desire to spread this frame before thee to cure it. their is such a heart to thee and man that is like a deceitful bow, it will promise faire, but there is no faithfulnes to performe,—and one misery of such a spirit is that it never quickens up others not the child to its duty not the wife, not the housband, yea is best when all partake of their sloth, it is full of excuses, to put of its own fault to others its a frame that their is litle hope of mending; Lord, my soul groweth to thee if thou please to doe anything for mee herein, doe it speedily, thy will bee done,

26: preacht at Buers god good to mee in all my jorney, blessed bee his name,

December 30: God good to mee, and mine in outward mercies, my two youngest children not well it fareth with them as if not long to live,

[1] A conference took place during December concerning their readmission, and though no formal decision was taken they were *de facto* henceforth allowed in; Evelyn noted their readmission on 14 December. Evelyn, iii, p. 163.

the lord bee their god, and prepare their hearts in their young dayes for thy selfe, the lord good to mee in the Sabbath, and in the worke and mercy thereof, the lord make my heart right unto him:

Jan: 2. the Lady Honywood sent mee 2 sermons preacht at Mr Lamotts death, 3: preacht at Wakes Colne, a discovery of gods goodnes to sinners, and thereby to ingage us to Christ Jesus

Jan: 6: God good to mee in outward mercies, awaken mee to mind the eternal state of my soule, and family. if it may bee lett them live in thy sight, the lord uphold mee in his truth, and let no shaking pul mee from thy selfe, and thy christ, god good to mee in the word and work of the Sabbath and blessed bee god that lengthens out those dayes to mee in peace, oh bee our hedge, and wall of defence I pray thee

12. this weeke god many wayes made bountiful provision in outward things, called out to doe divers acts of love for divers, and god hearted mee thereto. his name bee praised.

Jan: 13. God good many wayes to mee, very much in my deare wife, in our mutual bowels, the lords holy name, have the glory in all I doe injoy, prest stedfastnes to god the presence of god somewhat with mee, oh blesse the word to my soule and people

16: Humphry Cressener baptized, prest to continue in the faith and ordinances of Christ

Jan. 20. God good to mee in my relations, the lord make my heart steady and upright with him, dayes are sad; the onely comfort of soules is in god through christ, oh that my heart were fixed and stayed on god at all times, oh that my heart were reall to god at all times and kept up in my integritie. god was good to mee in the word and worke of the Sabbath, and in the quiet of it for which I blesse his name

25: this was the last day of my. 39. yeare, god very good therein unto mee. This yeare memorable in the world in the attempt of the English on the West Indies, and their strange defeat before Domingo, which yet god intends not as a disappointment of that attempt.—the papists massacred the Savoy Waldenses among them, which action was resented and will occasion troubles.—Alexander 7. the new Pope doth his devoir to make peace between France and Spain, and then general among all the popish partie, which the Venetian promotes hoping succours thereby against the Turke and the whole partie project thereby against the protestants, he is encouraged by the Q of Swedes turning papist: France made peace with England which is a great trouble to them—The Swede invaded Poland, and drove the King out and reduced all under him, no prince hindring, the Moscovite and Cossacke comply. the Tartar nor Turke resist not, nor Emperor nor any other, this action is of wonder in the world, the lord preserve to my soule to keepe mee in his feare better to mee than the glory of all their conquests.

— — — — — — — — — — — — — — — — — —

Jan: 26: my 40: yeare enters. 1655.

I desire to consider how my dayes passe, some thinke the very world would end in 56. others the beginning of good dayes to the church, but I expect troubles on the earth and thereby persons making themselves great, who in themselves or successors, will and shall deepely afflict the lord. I set this day apart to seeke gods presence with mee in all my wayes, that my hope may be sett on him, and this was much on my spirit, that (c.o. man) I have nothing that god will accept like myselfe. this is the sacrifice, not my estate, or parts but soule and body firstly. Psal. 51.17; a selfe empty nothing soule I tender. Rom 12.2.3.—this soule and body for this life and to all eternity. I freely unfainedly dedicate to the lord, even all the remainder of my dayes. 1: Sam: 1:27.28: this I beg from thee, this heart to doe it, and I doe it advising what I doe, as my duty, as my happines, 12.602.8:5. to the Lord and his Jesus bee my soul and body and dayes, and all that I am, I desire thee this day to boare my eare, yea my heart for one that desires never to bee exempt from thee Exod. 21:5.6. and this I doe expecting sufferings for thy sake, this I doe that I may have to answer the Tempters. I am the Lords. I am not my own. 1 Cor: 6.19.20: take possession of my soule and bodie, and all as thine own, by thy holy sanctifying, strengthening, wise spirit. I intreate thee.—oh how willing my soule is to this, one Chron: 29.18. and helpe mee often to consider the vows of god are upon mee, its in the strength of thy gracious spirit, and the sufficiency of the grace of Jesus, I vow, and hope to performe, not in my selfe is there any confidence only accept mee, for I am thy servant, devoted to feare, and love thee, oh my father

And now Lord what wait I for? is not my hope in thee, and my whole dependance upon thee: take care of mee, as thy son, and servant, and of mine, and because thou thy selfe art beyond all other enjoyments, bee thou my porcon and my tower(,) bee thou my dwelling place. yea as my sweet, saviour saith so doe,

John. 14.23. and let my spirit alwayes bee in the hand of thy spirit, and under the teaching, and upholding thereof; furnish mee to all thy services with that strength: phil. 4.13. and to all trials for I looke for sad ones in the world, and to try thine throughly that they may bee approved. Col: 1.11. but in all outward and inward. trials. thou wilt keepe: 1. Corinth: 10.13. and because my heart is not able to beleeve but is often flagging, put thy strength there also into my spirit. Eph: 1:19. and bee thou the helper of my faith, and joy. this is my aime to walke eying thee, and injoying thee. in thy feare, and in thy love.

And oh that wouldst blesse the soule of those I call mine, wife, children, sisters(,) freinds, kindred, people: my worke of ministry, and educacon of youth, that I might bee fruitfull unto thy glorie; and for outward things, I leave my selfe to thy dispose in thy love and wisedom, giving thee this day a testimony of thy mercy and faithfulnes; and this is not in that I am weary of thy bounty, or that I slightly esteeme it, for I confesse I stand in need of thes outward things and I am unworthy of the least. Gen: 32.10.; and doe desire to bee under thy blessing for it is good, but I thus resolve in testimony of my submission to thee, and because I would evidence that my all, is in the enjoyment of thy selfe in thy Christ: in whom I hope to bee accepted and made faithfull, and through his mediacon this sweet day may bee made good on both parts. I thine and thou mine. and thus I leave my selfe with thee as Nehemiah. 9.38: et. 10.39. and in testimony that I am none but thine. I heartily signe

Ralph Josselin.

1. Chron: 29.10 19. in my heart then with joy, that god would thus imploy *mee*

often read this, as well as remember it, and lett my heart, abide stedfast. and seal on thy part, oh lord even then when thou pleasest, and seest best. this day best, beyond the day of my espousals, which was is a good day still

Jan: 27. god good to mee and mine in many outward mercies; the season warm, its said our men left in Jamaica are dead. the lord in mercy doe us good by all his rebukes, and make my heart seing in my duty, and in the practice of it, stedfast and faithfull, god good to mee in the day for which I blesse him

28. imployed with others in making peace between father Appleton, and his son, which was done, contentedly through mercy from god on us.

30: at night my litle dog, came in with a wyer snare about his necke. it imprinted the next morning, the snare is broken and wee are escaped, by this time 62. wee shall see very strange revolucions.

31. heard of sad sins, judgments, one made away himselfe for fear of want: oh this not living to god, and by a word is sad, that temptacon might have been yeilded too, when the want was on men. love of life, make us destroy life.

Feb: 10: God good to us in our family mercies, my old inward troubles in great measure removed(,) oh flay them in the bloud of thy christ, and quicken my spirit to all thy services, the season faire, great noise of people called quakers, divers have fits about us, and thereby come to bee able to speake, the lord helpe us to stand fast against every evil and error(.) I had a great cold this day and hoarsenes, yet god enabled mee cheerfully to goe on with my worke, or rather his, the lord blesse it, and water it for his mercy and goodnes sake.

16. a dreame of mine in Mr R.H. law suit accomplished, wee were in great trouble for his busines, he came home, it ended very well, deo laus et gloria,[1] heard for certain that one Wade a quaker as called comes to our towne, god is able to doe all for mee in him, I doe put my trust that I shall not bee ashamed.

Feb. 17. Weeke past good was god in outward mercies, my hand ill as if spranted, the lord remember mee in my limbs, god good in making my wife an instrument in the life of a poore woman, oh what a mercy it is to doe good with our parts and estates to other(.) wee had a good Sabbath, and quiet, oh how unworthy are wee of the same, the lord blesse mee in all his wayes, and keepe mee therein continually

☞ 20 The Protector and his councill having. Aug: 19.54. passed an ordinance to eject, Ministers and schoolemasters. the Maj. gen. and his deputy required to put it in execucon, on this foote the Commissioners therein named proceeded and began to act:[2] calling on this day, all the ministers(,) Lecturers, Curates, and Schoolmasters through the whole county to attend them at chelmsford to give in under their hands, and churchwardens, how they hold their livings, and how long which I thought was rigour. Exod. 1.14.[3]

[1] Praise and glory to god.

[2] The Commissioners for ejecting 'scandalous ignorant and insufficient ministers and schoolmasters' included many of RJ's acquaintances; it was not until late 1655 that they were active. RJ was later invited to become one of their Assistants (8 January 1658). Smith, pp. 336–8.

[3] 'And they made their lives bitter with hard bondage, in morter, and in brick, and in all manner of service in the field: all their service, wherein they made them serve, was with rigour.'

I was there. the wayes wonderful dirty. close, but it raind not, god good to mee, but my mind was vain, Mr Sparrow preacht, he commended and encouraged the Commissioners(.) for my part I saw no beauty in the day, neither doe I joy to see ministers put under the lay power, and thus on their own head. such is the affection of some that would bee counted the first freinds of god. and religion. hoped wee should have been sent from thence to the Barbados(,) lord remember us for we are become a reproach.

Feb: 24. god good to mee and mine in many outward mercies, my heart vanities returne within the few dayes, I pray thee, slay the rebellion of mind, and let all bee in subjection to thy selfe, god gave mee a peaceable Sabbath, blessed be his name, persons in this corner, much withdraw from the word, mens minds unsound(.) there is feare of Portugal, that he will breake with us, and thereby our fleets miscarry for want of his ports, said Cromwell, tooke his leave of Montague in the morning and then spent the day alone in prayer.

29: preacht at Halsted, gods presence with mee, my wife ill with a cold, so my Jane and maid, lord better us by all thy dealings with us, heard they tooke up many loose wenches at London, to send over to Jamaica.

March: 2. God good in many outward mercies, my family not well, the lord sanctifie their hearts and minds throughly. the lord lett mee find old corrupcons, again annoying mee, I blesse thee, that when they doe not content, that I find not pleasure in them, though sometimes its in readie to doe so, the people about us by wholesale turne away from god, (oh lord keepe Colne, the lord enabled mee with some spirit, and words against the evils of the times in honour of christ, lord accept mee: and pardon all my evils I intreate thee

4: a comfortable refreshment at Goodman Mathews for soule and body, god good to mee therein I hope the kindnes of god shall engage mee unto him

6: Heard gods hand heavy on Dr Owen his 2 eldest sons dead(,) himself neare death, heard Major Haines, lord spare their lives for thy service, I humbly beg.

7. said that the notion of the 5[t] Monarchy spreads very much in some parts of Norfolke,

March. 9. God good to me in many outward mercies(,) my Jane ill with a cold, god in his time will recover her, god good to mee in my cattel, the lord good in keeping my heart free from some old vanities, our Sabbath quiet, and the word useful, for which I blesse god, lord in mercy raise up the Major to his health,

13. a day of prayer at priory, wherein god was good to us, in his word, the lord for his meere mercy in christ accept us. John Crow challenging another to wrestle put his shoulder out of joynt: its not good, either to boast of our strength or skill, or provoke others. said tiths will bee bankt.[1] god sits on the waves. this many states have done.

March: 16: The Lord good to mee, and mine in many mercies, Jane, and An. ill with colds nigh chincolds, I find it most in the nights, litle in the dayes, the good lord for mercy sake pardon their sins, and heale their infermities, the season calme, not much stirring about with us, but wee expect notable contrivances this yeare at hand, wee broke bread this day all our company roundly and comfortably togither, I did not not find much income from god. but I found my heart inwardly warmed, and raised up to make mention of the kindnes: and mercy of god in his covenant and Christ.

18. almost ended a busines between Mr Cress. and Mr Harlakenden, which he feared might have bred a quarrel, but I hope and trust will not, though the man is heady

21: rid to Colchester. and returned safe, god good to mee in the weather. god make provision for Janes educacon at Mrs Pigot. in giving mee a heart to the worke and chardge. and I trust god orders and will as a mercy to future days: saw Mr Bacon Master of requests,[2] he saith our fleet is gone with courage from Plimouth. 43. men of warre. 7. fireships (I thought some vessels ful of gunpowder) and victualers, Gives the Court a good report, that wee may hope all good things from them, but he and they are men, and I will trust in Jehova and waite

March. 23. God good to mee, my litle ones very ill with a feirce and troublesome cough that is too hard for meanes that wee can use, the cure is in god, and their seeking I will wait, this morning I dreamed I was in our church, broake bread, went not home to dinner, (my wife I thought minded mee not), standing up in my deske for afternoone service, I was without a band, and ashamed. I put on a surplice, still ashamed. I stoopt down and put a handkercheife about my necke (to conceale my wives neglect) I begun to sing, but could not read the psalms, nor sing, nor none sing with mee, the booke was a strangers(,) I laboured for my own bible but could not come by it, god was good to mee in the words and peace of this day, gave notice of the fast next Friday.

[1] There were various unsuccessful attempts to abolish tithes during this period. Shaw, ii, 254–9 summarizes these.

[2] Nathaniel Bacon (1593–60), M.P. for Cambridge, one of the most active members of the Suffolk Committee, author, and half-brother of Francis. DNB.

24. went to Mr Tompsons, returned. 26. my jorney very comfortable blessed bee god, my John rather worse with his cough, lord shew us mercy and affect my bowels towards them—27. went down to Wakes Coln and preacht on a suddain, god good to mee therin, there were a good company attending on the word, the lord blesse that duty of hope, and cause my heart to put my trust in him.

1656 and now god hath entred mee on that stupendous yeare of 1656. of which men have had strang thoughts and though I am not of their minds yet I expect notable effects, and the desire of my soule is towards the lord to take an especiall care of mee.

March. 28: Set a part for a fast, by a very solemn call in a declaration in my judgment(,) and for my part I endeavoured to spend the time about 5 houres profitably from Jerem: 29.7. god forgive my ignorant acting in the troubles against the King, and his family, even what I did though the lord is my witnes my desire was his good, and not his destruction, their are some that know the puritans haunts that will take a course with them, unles they walke wisely and circumspectly, and looke to it London that thou hasten not thy fall by standing too much on thy priviledges.

View of Estate. when I come to view my estate this yeare I find my receipts lesse by 10li. than last yeare, and my expenses about 5li. more, and yett god increaseth my lot, above 70li. this yeare, I have paid my debts, my stocke is not worth above 10li(.) I count I am now out upon Mrs Maries land 103li. 6s. 0d. her mother yet living(,) and its not I that will repine at it, god bee my porcon, and dayes to her(.) I find my personal estate to amount unto 670li. this god hath given mee, and when he pleaseth he may call for it again, and in the mean time, tis my duty not to sett my heart on it, but looke upon it, as that which is not, sometimes I have thought god lays this by mee, when outward springs will dry, my joy is a god reconciled, christ having paid my debts, and in outward things to find that I am thus under his blessing, that its no unrighteous dealing of mine, but his grace hath given mee what I have, and spares my wife, and foure children to mee

March. 30. my god good to mee in outward things, my children somewhat better to his name bee the praise of it, Major Haynes with us, recovered, but not throughly, sett him up oh lord as a comfort to us, wee humbly beg of thee oh god, the lord good in the season moist and a litle growing calle forward the springs wee humbly intreat thee, god was good to mee in the worke and word of the day as suitable, make it a word of hope to us I pray.

31. reckoned with Major Haynes about my augmentacon, it fals short, but god bee blessed for any thing that cometh in therby unto mee,

Ap: 1: married one of the priory maids,[1] god give mee to take the counsel I gave, mett in conference(,) oh that I were wise to bound my selfe within the word in my expectacons, season growing

3. kept a day of prayer at Mrs Cresseners in behalfe of Ed: and of my children, the lord in mercy restore their healths, blesse their Educacon and sanctifie their hearts throughout.

5. Rid to speake with Hedge, mett him beyond Colchester, and returned safe blessed bee god, and speedily. I dreamed I was at Colch: and it was so rainy wee could not come home I made the more haste. it raind much in the night, not evening.

Ap: 6. God good to mee in many outward mercies, my children I hope somewhat better than formerly(,) the day cold, spring very backward, quakers increase, but profanes doth not decrease(,) strange for persons to bee silent, not speake when saluted or spoken unto, the lord good to mee in the word this day, oh that my heart could bee affected with it, and stirred up to zeale against the vain evills of my own minde.

7. made a Churchwardens rate, young Henry Abbot, there, he said he would pay it(,) but he had rather give mony to pull the church down and lay it in the high wayes

9. went to Messing a good day to mee, I went about 20, miles on foot that day, heard and true that Turners daughter was distract in this quaking busines, sad are the fits at Coxall(,) like the pow wowing among the Indies, the lord in mercy remember us for good. when Christ came., the nation of the Jewes full of possesd with divels, he is *semia* [c.o.] dei,[2] and then said he casts out divels by the prince of divels why may not the antichrist, or rather the false

10. prophet. Rev. 13. being the divels confident throw out by the divels power, those really possest with the divell. but who thes possest people shall bee; and when deus noverit,[3] certainly he is brooding over some monster.

11. heard this morning that James Parnel the father of the Quakers in these parts, having undertaken to fast 40. dayes and nights, was

[1] The PR under this day records the marriage of William Prentis of Colne Engaine and Mary Prentis of EC, singlewoman.

[2] The caricature of God.

[3] God will renew.

die. 10. in the morning found dead,[1] he was by Jury found guilty of his own death, and buried in the Castle yard, the lord awaken those thereby, that give heed to the light of their own spirits, and will not put themselves under direction of word and spirit; thus god chooseth the delusions of sinners, and wherin men deale proudly god is above them(,) I tremble at his folly, the lord recover poore worms out of the snare. my children much recovered from under their colds, Ann is worst handled, who is youngest.

Ap: 13. God good to mee and mine in outward mercies, children recovering from under their colds. Mr R.H. the younger returned safe, blessed bee god, which quieted the feares of father, and joyed his wife, the season wett, and unchearfull the lord better us by all providences wee meet with, the lord was good to mee in the word preacht, the good lord truly affect my heart with it, and in the living on Christ as my fore-runner. gathered for a pooreman of Coxall 18s. 1d. the lord blesse our charitie, and worke.

14. Mr H. told mee the Spanish fleet was come home, for certain, it would bee much if in their ports it should come into our hands, Mr Layfeild told mee that one Mr Carlton told him he met. R.A. in street and asked him if their were a Minist in the town, he told him no, he said the Mr had an augmentacon, which he intended to bestow on Colne.

15. Mr. R.H. told mee as seing the letter sent by Fleetwood to release Parnel, but he was dead first, had he been delivered the triumph his partie would have made, its said in the country that his partie went to Colchester to see his resurrection again.

17. preacht at Wakes the wayes wonderfull dirty, beyond what commonly known. god was good to mee in sermon, and prayer, lord make the word useful to mee and all.

Ap: 20. This weeke god good to us in continuance of outward mercies unto us the lord affect my heart therewith, and inable mee to walke suitable, god good to mee in the word preacht, the lord prepare for himselfe, who is preparing heaven for mee,

☞ 21: This day one came unexpectedly from Ardleigh, who was a helpe to mee in the carrying Jane to Mrs Piggots, the lord in mercy bestow his blessing on her there his providence was very visible in her going thither.

[1] He was imprisoned for causing a riot at Colchester in 1655 and spent eight months in gaol before his death; the first Quaker martyr. For a detailed account see W. C. Braithwaite, *Beginnings of Quakerism* (1912), pp. 188–93.

23. a day of prayer, god opened my heart therein from psal. 51.7. concerning sin the greatest evil, and that my affliction lord to bee chosen before the least sin

Ap: 27: God good to us in our outward mercies, the season warme and moist, that now the spring cometh on, and promiseth plenty, which god afford to us if it please him, and give us a holy and thankefull heart under all enjoyments, my mind readye to bee pestered with vanities, I find it true resist the divell and he will fly from you, he doth most hurt, where he is parlied with, and the evill suggestions of the heart, are dandled up and down. I was preaching of, and for Christ, he in mercy accept mee, and take care of, some warmth and bite was in my heart from thee, communicate the same to the residue of the people, I pray thee oh lord my hope and strength.

May. 1: Daniel went away, and I refused to take him again, and so I was freed from a very lazie, and stout boy, the lord sanctifie mine they may bee alwayes comforts.

May. 4: The Lord good in the season, I and divers more observed it, that grasse did never grow more in a few dayes then it did lately. things looke with a sad face in the world mens hearts, much out of frame, lord compose mine to thy minde(.) the lord good in some measure unto mee in my spirit more composed, and in frame then sometimes, let my heart alwayes bee right with thee I intreate thee. the presence of god was (with) mee comfortably, and encouragingly oh when I am preaching of Christ, and for him my heart is raised, my feares wither and die, I am another man oh my god accept mee, and beare mee up as on the wings of Eagles.

6. invited to Colchester lecture, I could not answer their first day, which was a matter of trouble to mee, but I ingaged with gods leave to helpe them, wee had a comfortable conference, about the use of Gods word, lord keepe the souls of mine and this people sound and intire, about 100 dipt at Colchester to Tillam[1] a papist convert as he saith, if not still a Jesuite, oh how giddy and unconstant people are, to condemn us as Romish antichristian, and embrace such as are, and mingle themselves with them for evill ends.

8. preacht the monthly meeting at Kelvedon, I had gods presence, with great boldnes to stand up for truth and christ in a great meeting of the contry from all parts the lord pardon my weaknes, and accept mee and blesse mee in his Jesus

[1] Thomas Tillam was apparently born a Jew, trained as a Roman Catholic, and then founded a Baptist centre at Hexham in 1652; his pupils there included Edmond Hickeringill (DNB). Thomason, E. 726 (8) and E. 850 (9) are two of his publications.

9. preacht at Halsted for Mr Sparrow, who was sent for up to London, the lord in mercy accept of mee, and doe mee good, his presence was with mee.

10. rid to Colchester, returned safe, found Jane well for which I blesse God, the lord blesse her in her educacon, and make her his faithfull one.

May: 11: god good to mee and mine, some goodnes of god in mee yett I have my disquietments, but lett them oh lord never draw my heart from thee, or any command or dutie, the lord helpe us in the opposicon is risen against his christs truth and worship. Their are endeavours to remove our neighbour Mr Sparrow to Norwich. the lord good to mee in the word he make it a blessing to mee, and keepe mee from mens mistakes, and delusions I pray thee:

15. Mr Clarke[1] failing, I supplied his place at Wakes, god was good to mee in the word, the lord bee my hiding place in thes sad and sinfull dayes, and bee my peace, in him I desire to hide my selfe and with him

17: Mr Littel of Halsted with mee to desire my assistance in the matter of Mr Sparrows remove, I wondered to heare from them then, the time so short, god direct mee and them in our affaires whatsoever.

May 18: The lord good to mee, and mine in outward mercies, only my An labours under a sad trouble, and is very froward,[2] the good lord sanctifie his hand and remove it, the lord good to mee in the word, he dwell in mee.

May: 21: preacht at Buers about stedfastnes; went to my good freinds Mr Littels at the ries in litle Heney: I preacht. 22. in the fast of the ministers at Bulmere the lord give a blessing to that word of stedfastnes, returned home die. 24. found all well god have all the praise. I was very ill. with gripings in my bowels towards night.

May. 25. I awoke in the morning, my loosenes continuing, but my pain in the bowels very clearely removed through mercy, the lord good to mee in the word preacht this day, the lord in mercy accept of mee and blesse mee, the season was very hot. and wee began very much to need rain, the lord in mercy accept of mee therein

26. rid to Rottenden, viewed the desolate condicon of my uncle Simons children, god hath provided for mee, when I had nothing, they miscarry with aboundance, I observed Fambridge creek. 28: my

[1] John Clarke, minister of Gaines Colne 1653–62. Smith, p. 368; Calamy, p. 117.

[2] Froward: perverse, difficult to deal with, ill humoured. NED.

heart in a very vile frame as it hath been commonly, lord pardon and heale, my busines of Sams, looks very untowardly the lord in mercy thinke on mee vile wretch therin,

30. returned safe home, found my family in health, the lord have the praise and glory of all.

June. 1. god good to mee in many outward mercies, in the morning exercise at home. Mr Simpson[1] preaching for mee in the morning, I went to Gaines colne, and preacht there of stedfastnes, the lord establish mee, and all his in his truth, and ordinances that wee may continue therein to the end.

2: hopes of rain, lord comfort the creature and our spirits in giving us rain; received in 2 loads of logs from Tibbals by way of exchange for small wood, a good providence to mee

3. a Court was kept about the Nevils businesse, I agreed with Mr Butcher for his part and bid faire for Mr Weales;[2] my backe turned, Mr Butcher endeavoured to buy Mr Weals and did, Mr Harlakenden helping it on very earnestly, I was troubled to see mens spirits but not disquieted in my selfe, discerning Gods hand in it, for my good, or some hidden providence to them they are not aware of, I did them the best service in all their affaires that I possibly could.

6: none can imagine the distempered workings of our spirits, but those that have experience.

June. 8: god good to mee in many outward mercies, sensible of great trouble in my family the lord heale all in my soule, and helpe mee to walke holily and humbly with my god, the lord gave us hopes of raine, and some, lord remember us with a mercy herein we heartily intreate thee, the lord good to mee in the word, oh how sometimes my heart is above feare, I could even bee anything for christ make mee so really from inward strength; oh that my heart were above passions, and such inward corrupt workings, heard a millers child drowned at Cogshall, blessed bee the lord who watcheth over mee and mine in our pathes

12. gave my sister Anna. 10^{s}. and lent her 5^{li}. shee doth well in her busines for which I blesse god the lord keepe mee, and mine under his blessing continually. said for certain the tax out as formerly, much the thoughts of persons were they, would have duobled it, said also that its concluded above to call a parliament, and that its

[1] John Simpson, incumbent of Mount Bures. Smith, pp. 115, 121, 125, 309.

[2] Grisella Nevill, one of the five sisters and co-heirs of Richard Nevill deceased, had married Henry Weale. A note at the foot of the full transaction in the Colne Priory manor court roll (ERO, D/DPr 23) states that 'Henry Weals and wife Grisel surrender their 5th part to Mathew Butcher junior'.

thought one cheife end is to raise more money by them upon the subject.

June. 15. God good to mee in many outward mercies, yet not without some mixture of affliction, my wife very ill, shee had thought she had bred, but did not shee thought but was ill in her body, god shine on her in mercy, as I trust he will, An was very ill with the coming down of her fundament,[1] my eyes are towards thee for helpe sanctifie thy hand oh lord unto mee and mine I humbly intreate thee, the season was exceeding hott, and dry, lord in mercy refresh the earth with thy dewes, heard my uncle Josselin in Norfolke was well, and that he will bee with mee shortly, the lord send him well to mee, the lord was good to mee, this day in the word, my heart is not under the vanities I have formerly mett with(.) the lord sanctifie his hand unto mee, and doe mee good by all.

16. Heard more fully that my daughter Jane, doth very well at Colchester, for which I desire to blesse the name of my good god, extend thy soule compassions and graces to my sons, and daughters, I humbly intreate thee.

17. Mr Sparrow called at my gate, and ingaged mee to helpe him 20. at Halsted, I am through mercy free for that worke, he moved mee in Higham busines who pay 550^{li}. to buy in an impropriacon, the worke was evidently for god, and the good of soules, my heart came of to it, and I intended 20^{s}. afterwards other thoughts arose not to draw backe but to ponder it, I thought on 2. Cor. 8.11.12. with Cap: 6.7. and truly it arose from bountie, in my heart found respect to christ my all, towards sun setting, I met Justice Harlakenden who told mee Sir Tho. Honywood would give mee 2 loads of wood which is worth in the woods 26^{s}. oh that I could learn to put my trust in god obeying and beleiving.

18: This morning my wife thought shee miscarried, lord a miscarrying womb is a sad affliction, keepe us from a miscarrying heart, that throweth out wholesom counsell, and the suggestions of gods spirit, which lord wee are sadly subject unto, lord what the matter is thou knowest, only this I know, it is not with my house as it should bee, I am oppressed, and shattered in my spirit, lord undertake for mee, one wave rowleth in upon another, lord bee thou above the waters, make mee wise under my burthens, and if it may bee a healing of that family distemper, which I find, but feare there is some hidden roote of evill, lord pardon my evill therin I begge of thee. this day Mr R. Harlakenden the younger, sent mee down from London.

[1] Fundament; the buttocks, or anus. SOED. Thus, probably, uterine prolapse.

3 peices of Hoornbeeck[1] of his guift worth about 15^{s}. or 16^{s}. and a peice of chewneys.[2]

20: preacht at Halsted god good to mee in the word for which I blesse his holy name

21. Heard of the death of Mrs Meredith, who died: 19. and was buried the 20th. shee was not ill very long, did not lie by it at all, yet had some apprehensions of dying, and made some dispose of legacies, her son, and daughter in town, they feared some trouble with their mother in the matter of her thirds, that busines at an end, the lord fitt us for our changes.

June. 22. god good in many outward mercies, he still denieth us rain, he waters some other places, but passeth by us as yet, he is just, and righteous wee unworthy of any mercy(.) my wife hopefully upwards, lord let us both not only finde a ransom for a few dayes but for our souls unto all eternity, the lord put some life, and weight into my spirit in pressing the word on my people, awaken them, oh arme of the lord, awaken them that they perish not, the soules are thine, oh lord awaken them, god good to mee in the word, it was sweet and solemne on christs part for us. the lord in much mercy accept mee. my Lady Honywood was here this day, in hearing, the Lord in much mercy (c.o. accept) doe her and many good by the word:

23. my uncle, Ralph married children came to mee, who were very heartily welcome unto mee, rejoycing to see them in health, my

24. wife was somewhat worse this day then formerly; 24: I went on foote to Messing, and returned, Shawe dealeth ill with mee, my heart quiet in this untowardnes of men, could it bee spiritual and holy in temptacons how should I rejoyce, I went down to see my old schoolefellow Mr Luckin,[3] to whom I seemed very welcome, he knew mee after 25. yeares distance, the Lord in mercy accept of mee, I hope he is a very honest hearted man. My wife somewhat better this day, blessed bee God for it.

26: Heard strange things of our state affaires: Mr H. returned safe from London, but I could perceive nothing by him, the lord arise for his owne.

[1] Probably works by John Hoornbeeck, who wrote against Independency. Among those who commended Beverley's reply (Thomason, ii, p. 246) to Hoornbeeck were RJ's fellow ministers and friends John Sams of Coggeshall, John Bulkley of Fordham, and William Sparrow of Halstead (Nuttall, p. 39).

[2] Probably works by one of the great Independent writers, Charles Chauncy (1592–1672), President of Harvard College. DNB.

[3] Capell Luckin, like RJ, went to school at Bishop's Stortford under Mr. Leigh, though some five years younger than RJ. Later knighted and baronet; of Messing Hall, Essex. Venn.

28: received in Sr T. Honywoods 2 loads of wood. he was kind therein, but the makers or others unkind for it was nothing comparable to his other sale wood, god bee blessed for his love to mee. Wm Web. told mee one of Gains coln intended never to heare ministers, but turn Quakers, on this her freinds even forced her to church that day I preacht ther about stedfastnes, and there shee resolved never to heare them more, Amen.

June. 29. God good to mee and mine in many outward mercies, my wife at church with mee indifferent[1] well, for which I desire to blesse the name of my good god, the lord good in a most comfortable rain on the 28 at night at. 29 day, oh thy mercy is sweet lett all in us tend unto thy praise, the word this day good to my soule, wee enjoy some measure of peace and quietnes, and not disturbed, the lord watch over us still for good, the affaires of England thrive not, will god leade them into straits, and will ill rise out of it, the lord lead mee not into temptacon, but in mercy delight in mee to doe mee good.

30. Mrs Church made an offer unto mee of her farme on the green, and I accepted thereof, and wee came to termes of agreement, which I judge a mercy to mee, and a quiet to my mind, its the lords worke to make it so, and I trust he will doe so; I dreamed about ditching ten acres the night before and my being there as having to doe therwith, the lord blesse mee, in this undertaking.

July: 3. rid to Colchester; Hedge promiseth but that is all; I preacht the lecture from 2. pet. 1.12. the lord give a blessing to the word, god good to mee in my jorney for which I blesse him, and in my childs health, and educacion.

4: Mr R.H. moved mee from Mr Butcher to buy Mr Weals part when I went down to him, speaking of the freehold, and the lords rent, and there being a mistake in his rentall, he desired mee, I would not medle to buy it, I readily answered I would not, here god puts a bar which stays mee, if it bee a trial he will remove it, if not I will obey him, and not leape over it, I referre my affaire to him as my counsellour, and I am willing to submitt to him

5: within one quarter of an houre, after this was writt die 5°. Giles Crow came to mee from Mr H. who was troubled, promised to rectifie mistakes, prayed mee to goe on if I had any desire thereunto; lent mee his horse to Colchester, and to helpe mee, with the mony, I should want. while speaking in came Mr Butcher, wee agreed for

[1] Indifferent: of medium quality or character, tolerable, neither good nor bad. SOED. RJ frequently uses of health to mean that a person was not sickly.

Mr Weals part, and his daughters, rid to Colchester, Mr Weals was very rough in the matter, and would doe great matter against Mr Butcher; my Cosin Josselin was not at Colchester, and indeed not come from London. which I hope is a good providence to my busines, there I mett with one Mr Hauks of London who is buying Sams land, I hope god is mercifully remembring mee in that busines, my eye is towards him(,) newes of another parliament to be called togither, Sept. next.

July. 6. God good to mee, and mine in many mercies, the lord continue his loving kindnes to us, and to all that feare him, god was good to mee in the word this day oh how sweet the tast, and knowledge of christ is unto the soule. enable mee with grace and strength to live more unto thy glory.

7. Mr Weals at Priory, I did some curtesies again for him, he was somewhat more treatable than formerly. Mr R.H. endeavoured to persuade him to understand his own good, heard my deare freinds Mr and Mrs Harlakendens, the younger were come safe home the lord be blessed for that mercy unto them.

8: my mony cometh in as for my busines very well, heard of Major Haines health(.) received Mr Noels busines from him and I trust he hath done more in other mens. my An ill, and so also is my wife with the falling down of the mother[1] its hard to find out the particular cause of our troubles, but what good wee omitt, or ill wee doe that is hinted to us, its safe to reforme, to thee oh (c.o. how) lord wee come in christ for thy healing in body and spirit, oh doe it for thy loving kindnes sake.

Heard how Dr owen endeavoured to lay down all the badges of schollers distinction in the universities: Hoods, caps, gowns, degrees, lay by all studdie of philosophy he is become a great scorne, the Lord keepe him from Temptacons, least his great heart turne up into the wind of error, and endeavour some great matter against the truth, I feare about him

12. kept a day of prayer at brother Cowels, my body and mind drowsy, lord pardon mee, I gathered 8^{s}. for Mrs Ive to buy her halfe load loggs. which I gave her

July: 13. God was good to mee in many outward mercies, my wife very faint, the lord restore, and comfort her and doe her good, wee brake bread this day(,) god was good to us in the same, in which my soule desireth to blesse and praise his name, great shews and some hopes of raine, but all past from us, the lord make us sensible of his hand

[1] Mother: womb. SOED. Hence, a uterine prolapse.

14: my Cosin Josselin, Mr Harlakenden, and divers of the Nevils mett
☞ at my house 2. parts of five of the farme at Colne were setled on mee, the price is 297^{li}. to both, 145^{li}. down, 2^{li}. in a short time, and 150^{li}. next Decemb 24. 1656. the lord prosper mee in this busines, and give mee good successe, and make my heart more earnest for the kingdom of heaven, and the righteousnes thereof.

16. this day I layed into the ground old Reyner, who fell dead from the cart loading pease on last Monday, there were present, his wife and nine children, the lord sanctifie his hand unto us, and give us wisely daily to provide against our latter end.

17. heard the spaniards routed the French at Valenchienne. see the issue of this event.

18: Mrs Haines, and her son (c.o. retu) came safe to Colne priory, glad I was to see her son living, Mr R. Harlakenden junior ill with gripings.

July. 20. god good to mee in many outward mercies for which I blesse his name, this day wee had a comfortable rain with thunder, the lord good to mee in the word, I was under a wonderfull rheume, yet god carried mee on in my worke, but indeed its his

24 joynd in a day of prayer at Hinningham, god good to us therein, yett for my part deadnes and drowsines tooke up my heart, lord when wilt thou heale mee, god kept mee in my jorney:

25. Much good company and entertainment at the priory. Major Gen: Haines came well to us, heard by him the French had recovered and routed the Spaniard.

July. 27. This weeke god was good to mee and mine in outward mercies, An ill with a feavourish ague which left her at the 3^{d}. fit, my wife somewhat better, some refreshing shoures, god let mee see some old temptacons against, oh that god would helpe mee with daily grace to resist daily temptacons, Sathan gets most advantage against us by our compliance, god good to mee in the word preacht oh how sweete a christ is to an hungry thirsty soule, make mine such and then fill it. heard Jane had the measels, and well again, blessed bee the name of god who taketh care of mine.

* 28. I was with Sr J. Jacob and demanded 6: yeares tith at 4^{li}. which amounts to 24. and this is the due until Sept: 29: 1656. at hand.

30. kept a day of praise to god with Cornel: Brownson for his recovery, the lord good to us therein, oh what is man lord that thou blessest him, and givest him a heart againe to blesse thee with praises.

31: Mrs church sealed to mee a lease of that land which should bee mine after her decease at 18li. per annum, the lord make the businesse comfortable to us both,

Aug. 2: Major generall Haines, and his company, went from us to Bury, the lord goe with him and blesse him, and make good to him the promise of Abraham.[1] Tompson, likely to doe well, I hope its an answer of prayer to mee, doe the like oh lord in my wife

Aug: 3: The Lord good to mee in many outward mercies, my wife was very ill, and more dejected and surprized with feares because of the same. but blessed bee god in the use of meanes much better, than formerly, and I trust god will perfect his mercy to her, my Jane at home with mee, I hope her educacion will bee her good, lord lay in thy grace through Christ into her heart, the season is very hot, and burning, lord in mercy water the earth, god was good to mee in the word, it was most solemne the lord make it to abide in my and mens hearts

5. made an end with Shawe he is to cutt no more wood nor damage the fence, he is to returne the timber to my dispose. Roydon Bridge was witnes to this

7. a very sweet and comfortable raine for which I blesse the name of god

Aug: 10: God good to mee in my wives health, for which my soule blesseth him, shee was not ill with the fall of the mother as shee feared, but an other distemper of the piles, her feare removed: god begun very much to revive her spirits, and to move about, shee gathers strength; reports of a wonderful snake seen in Taine, at Tallers barn as big as the calfe of a mans leg, and halfe a (c.o. yard) rod long; on Thursday, at Feering berry, a brand with which the reapers lighted tobacco by boys being thrown into stubble fired, the wind drave it on the reapers they fled, and so avoided danger, in a trice it burnt before the wind to the lands end about an acre the wind saved the rest of the feild, much more hurt was done neare London so as the grasse, god was with mee in the word, my sleepy hearers are a trouble to mee, lord quicken them therin, and mee also by thy grace,

14: Mr Harlakenden sold his hops for 720li. to Mr Montjoy and run a halfe in them(.) sweet showers, and dewing weather through mercy. paid Mr Harlakenden 40li. that I owed him, he lent it unto mee freely, and he said he should doe so by the 60li. more that I had

[1] 'And I will make of thee a great nation, and I will bless thee, and make thy name great; and thou shalt be a blessing.' Genesis 12:2.

of his in my hand, the lord looke on this love, and requite it. I gave him my dung in the yard for his hop ground.

Aug: 17. God good to mee, and mine in many outward mercies, the lord in mercy accept of mee for good, constant rumours, as if divers old grandees that were commonwealths men were secured, mens ways are full of danger, the great ones tumbling down one by another, the sure standing standing, and safe onely in gods pathes. this day. Sam Burton, and lame Byat. while I was reading the chapter, were sitting in the maids seate, and made a disturbance, the justice, commanded the Constable to take them forth to the cage,[1] the mother went out of the church and tooke her son from the Constable, and said her housband paid scott, and lott[2] in the towne, and her son should sitt any where. lord pitty us, and heale us and destroy us not, the lord bee mercifull to us, under all dispensacons: the lord good to mee in the words, yett I find my heart very careles, and regardles in setting my selfe on his worke, lord humble mee and pardon mee. said that on Tuesday night Aug: 12. two armies were seen in the aire fighting, the watch saw it and heard the noise of their musketts, I shall enquire the truth of it

Aug: 13. at night I found a wonderfull strange skie, or els it was Tuesday I know not indeed certainly which. dartings up of a light cloud.

19. Our women mett in prayer, I with them, spoke from Pro: 31.30. that the feare of god it is the best ornament, and the greatest mercy, the lord make mee to walke accordingly. sister Brown at night gave mee 10^{s}. lord remember them that shew love to us for wee are greatly dispised.

20: This day was appointed a day for the choise of Parliament men in all Counties of England, I sett it apart by prayer and meditacon to seeke god. Job. 22. latter part much moved mee in perusing it in the feild. lord my desires are christs time for his kingdom might be hastned, thou wouldst lengthen out our peace in holynes and gospel ordinances: this day might have a mercy, and not a curse in it for poore England, god would make mee serviceable to his name in soules, shew mee his way in this day in this government and apostacy. and every way blesse my family. in thy christs name I call, oh heare mee for thy mercy sake.

The Sectaries did not very much appeare at chelmsford, not a Quaker in the feild noted to bee so, one Loddington, was in the

[1] The cage: a prison for petty malefactors, a lock-up. NED.
[2] In other words, had paid all taxes and reckonings.

head of that partie, which hindred the choice, that it could not be effected that night, but was adjourned to the next day: between 3 and 4. a remarkeable crosse seen in the skie, vide in my historical notes. our choise was.

Sr Harbotle Grimston.	Mr Wakering.	Mr H. Mildmay	The Independants plotted much in the choise but
Sr Thomas Honywood	Mr Gob: Barrington.[2]	Mr Carey Mildmay	
Sr Rich: Evered.[1]	Mr Ol: Raymond[3]	Mr Archer.	
Sr Tho: Bowes.	Mr Templer.[4]	Maj: Haines.	
	Mr Turner.[5]		

missed two men of their company, the choice to view, is not very good nor very bad, a strange mixture of spirits, lord I cannot trust them with our gospel concernments but I will thee, and I trust thou wilt looke after them, and not suffer the nacon to bee wrapt up by thes men into any evill whatsoever.

Aug: 24: god was good to me and mine in many outward mercies, my wife better, and so my An. god perfect their healths, and heale all infirmities in them, the season very hot and dry, an excellent season for their hops: my heart very dull and unaffected every where in prayer, lord in christ pardon it in mee, I intreat thee, heard togither That the Venetians have given the Turks a mighty overthrow at sea.—the Swedes have routed the Polanders and retaken Warsow. the spaniards taken Conde town.—the Emp. army on their March for Italy. the English attempt and burning the Spanish ships at Malaga. the choise of members for parliament thes newes arrived to us in one weeke. with a report that at Breme a voice was heard in the aire. Woe. Woe. Woe. in the afternoon my heart and affections were up for the glory of god in my people, that they might not slight christ and bee rejected by him from it.

26: went down to Mrs Layfeilds burial, who died of a raging feavour, shee was an useful woman, and much bemoaned by her neighbours, I thinke it may bee in mercy to remove her from the troubles to come, blessed bee God for yett sparing mine

[1] Sir Richard Everard, parliamentarian, sheriff of Essex 1644–5, died *c.* 1680. Venn.

[2] Gobart Barrington, later Sir Gobart of Little Baddow, third son of Sir Thomas of Hatfield Broad-oak. Venn; Morant, ii, p. 22.

[3] Oliver Raymond, elder for Essex classis 1647, M.P. for Essex 1654–5 and 1656–8, of Belchamp Walter, died 1679. Venn.

[4] Dudley Templer or Templar, of Huntingdonshire, one of the Commissioners for ejecting scandalous or insufficient ministers in 1655. Smith, p. 336; Venn.

[5] Edward Turnor, son of Arthur (see p. 66, n. 3 above), M.P. for Essex 1654–60, Speaker of the House of Commons 1661–71. Venn.

28: rid to Wethersfeild, I am promised faire in my busines by Mr Plumbe[1] I returned safe, with good company, kindely entreated by Mr Templer. I endeavoured to give him the best counsel I could as a parliament man.

30: gave Sr T. Honywood, the best, and most solemn advice I could, one J Biford was clamoured on as a witch, and Mr C(ressener) thought his child ill by it, I could no way apprehend it, I tooke the fellow alone into the feild, and dealt with him solemnely, and I conceive the poore wretch is innocent as to that evill.

Aug: 31. god good to mee in manifold mercies, the season very dry, no mists nor dewes, the face of the earth is wonderfully burnt up, the lord helpe us to lay it unto heart, I had this morning a very large worme that came from mee; Robt: Abbot sen: in the street told Tho. Harvy, there cometh your deluder. lord wee are a contempt and scorne(,) looke upon it, oh lord, and heale it, he sat on the horse blocke as people came to church(,) Mr H. spoke to him, the lord helpe us against thes growing evills, god was good to mee in the worke of the day for which I blesse his most holy name,

Sept: 4: I begun the lecture at Wakes Colne, god good to mee therein, heard of a great plott discovered against the protector, said on the K. of Scots interest whom Spain assists.

5. preacht the funeral of George Bull, from phil. 1.23. and buried him at White Colne. I had not above 5 houres warning, I hoped I might doe good and some service to god, which drew out my heart unto the workes, and I trust not in vaine

6: receivd a letter from Sr. J. Jacob, assigning mee 10^{li}. from his tenants, it was writt Sep: 3. when I was taking care to erect Wakes Lecture, lord thou mindst mee, when I forgett thee, its a joy when gods mercies come to mee when I am serving him

Sept: 7. god good to mee, and mine in many outward mercies, the season wonderfull dry. Mr H. hopping that held 16. days to a litle, not disturbed one moment with rain, nor any winde, the lord accept of us, and shew favour to us in the season if it bee his pleasure: wee ☞ had many strangers hearing this day, the lord was good to mee in the word, for whose presence my soule blesseth him, the night before the Sabbath, I much dreamed it being reiterated, that divers ministers carriage gave the Prot. Court advantage to bee curst unto them, I thought at a stile I called to one who was talking with another, in a path the rie neare ripe to aske him, whether Mordechai might not

[1] Samuel Plumbe or Plume, of Great Yeldham and Maldon, gent. Visitation of 1664–8, p. 72.

bee too stiffe in his carriage to Haman[1] though god providenced it unto good. I remember they were fift monarchy men.

8: imployed at Mr Pelhams in peg: Harlakendens and Mr Niccols businesse. Quakers there who pitifully scorne the Ministers. one said as I and Mr Niccols went in, woe to the false prophet, I thanke god their bitternes puts no provocation on my spirit against them. it dewed sweetly this day. said much grasse in the west of England.

11: preacht Wakes Lecture on Heb. 2.3. god good to mee therein, I have not been imployd this time in the parliament mens houses, but in publique preaching I note it. but I knew not the intent of god in it. heard S. H. Vane was sent to the Ile of Wight to Carisbrooke Castle, the Kings prison against whom he was a great agent.

Sept: 14: God good to us in our outward mercies, this morning I awakned comfortably, who lay down very ill, the weather made a great change it raining in the morning a very comfortable showre and so continueth; in reading the chapters being the. 4 and 5. of Judges, I had a thought there was something therein concerned the parliament and protector(.) I saw them hold out the churches deliverance.—Acts. 12. which in course I read did the same we sung in course. psal. 89 part the third; lett the oppressors bee who and what he will bee and purpose what he will; as to the issue the lord will deliver his from his and his parties expectacon. acts. 12.v.11: when I came down from pulpit I heard Mrs Mabel was likely to die, shee hath received the sentence of death in her selfe from dreams. and there visional interpretacions in 56: I hope shee may live, god good to mee in the word preacht:

15. a through ground rain for grasse and for the fallow, except the great clods: gave 26^{s}. to buying in an impropriacon for a preaching minist at Higham in Suffolke(.) Mrs Mabel under hopes and apprehensions of life to us, and her: god bee blessed for it.

16: preacht at White Colne the lords with my (c.o. word) mouth and spirit, one Brett[2] after prayer fell on mee as no minister, accused mee of pride for my cuffes, my heart untroubled, I called to him to chardge any thing I had delivered of errour. but he could not, lord its a glory to bee reproached for thee. heard Hedge has some mony for mee

☞ 17 This day appointed for parliament. the morning lowring, and wett, which is a mercy, I set it apart to seeke god on their behalfe, that

[1] Haman was the favourite of King Ahasuerus, to whom Mordecai refused to bow or do reverence. Haman vowed to destroy all Mordecai's fellow Jews as revenge. Esther, ch. 3.

[2] John Brett of White Colne had a five-hearth house in 1662.

they might be instruments for good if possible, and not circumvented into evill. heard Mr Mede a good man lately died. Mr H. gave mee 3li. towards the 5li. he promised mee for his hops, from tenn a clocke it was a pleasant cleare bright day, my heart most dead so that I could not pray, onely at night at priory, where the Major was, who is going up to the parliament.

18: 600 foot soldiers that came out of Scotland marcht through our town to Colchester great talke of Cavalier attempts again:

19: Heard on die. 17. Dr owen preacht, on Isay. 14.32; the Protector made a long speech before the Parl: men in painted chamber, orders were in Westminster hall that none should goe into house till after sermon. they say. above 160. were not allowed by the Councill to sitt, and none might enter without a ticket of allowance

20. rid to Colchester, Jane well, god very good to mee in my jorney for which I blesse him(.) in the night John was very ill with vomiting, and loosenes, but in the morning cheerfull(,) the lords name bee praised therefore. heard our freinds at Olny were living, but very old and crazie.

Sept: 21: God good to mee in many mercies, the season dry and warme, the lord in mercy affect my heart with his goodnes unto mee, and doe mee good by the same, the lord good to us in our health, it being sickly with many, god was good to mee in the word. Mr. Cress. had running thoughts again, his child in ill handling,[1] not his so much as others because of returns of fits at such a time of the yeare, that (c.o. he is in ill handlin) his legs fall of

23. god gave us a good day at Mr W.H. in a day of praise unto god for delivering him from his ague, I spoke to him from. psal. 103.v.1: to 5. wee had there very many,

☞ 24: let Tibbal the farme for one yeare at 50li. wee lay in 5 load wood at stub, he is to carry it, he is to fallow. Swannels, and Brockhole. Mr Morly joyned with mee,

27. I went on foot to the Heath, and up and down those grounds very much, I did my busines I intended blessed bee god; I had a heart not to value my mony so I might shew my selfe a christian and mercifull, god will make mee amends, I was not overweary at home, I went down to the priory, I went near 20. miles.

Sept: 28: season dry, warm, yet with shoures, and mists, the face of the earth greens, the plow at worke, god give a good crop the next yeare, god good to mee and mine in our healths, in this aguish, and feavourish time, the lord good in some measure to mee in the word,

[1] 'Ill handling' was sometimes used colloquially to mean bewitched.

and worke of the Sabbath; our sister Dow was buried this day, thus god decreaseth our number the lord increase our graces.

30: sold Giles Crow my pasture for. 13^{s}. 4^{d}. this day he enters thereupon. made an end of all differences between Mole, and Iserson, oh how I rejoyce to doe good to a person that gives mee no respect, lord for thy sake, I shall deny my selfe through grace:

Octob. 3. at night coming home I saw a fireball, it gave light to the ground as lightning but soone vanisht, that night in my dreame, I thought I saw a blacke cloud directly in the fashion of a stagge, and ☞ a man sitting on him, his face to the west, and it noted the speed of a great person in his conquests. in the morning die 4°. I was told our fleet at sea had taken much gold and silver from the Spaniard. the newes confirmed it.

Oct: 5. God good in many mercies to mee and mine, I dreamed in the night towards the lords day morning of many things, at length of the unrulines of souldiers in quartering, and on a suddain at a distance towards the Northwest, a mightie fire, and burning rising ☞ up out of the earth, and the fire runing in the face of the earth towards mee as if the face of the earth, were dried turfe, persons a litle before I dreamed as busy in worldly businesse as ever, lord thus it will bee, thy judgements on us before aware of it, I was not afraid, I cannot tel the issue, I went back from it, I saw none when my face was turned up to great Taine from Spooners whither the fire reached in the face of the earth. Sacrament of baptisme administred this day, in publique which was not of a long time before in Colne, god was good to mee this day in the word, which was a heart refreshing word, from Heb. 7.25. lord deliver mee from shines and bring mee to a steady confidence in thy mercy and truth.

7: Yesterday Grace Josselin came to us, and my sister Dorothie, and this morning Mr Cox about Langfords lands, I had dreamed about it, die. 3°. at night. god in due time will bring good out of that busines: a comfortable meeting at my house, about obedience the evidence of our knowing god

8. This morning much overseen[1] in my carriage to my deere wife, the lord pardon it to mee my heart truly sorrowful. spent the day in prayer at mr Cresseners, where my heart was opened, god in mercy blesse our worke.

9. gave my sister Dorothy, good old things, and 20^{s}. blessed be god that giveth mee any thing more than mine, and a heart to doe any thing for them,

[1] Overseen: deceived, deluded, in error; acting imprudently, rash in action. SOED.

11. Dol. went homeward, gods peculiar love and blessing bee upon her.

Oct. 12. God good to mee and mine in many mercies, yet some dashings in our healths(.) god followes mee with dreams portending trouble prosecucons god fitt my heart for all that he will call mee unto, the lord good to mee in his worship this day(,) the lord throughly awaken my heart and doe mee good, this night the lord gave us, a very sweet and comfortable rain, oh let mee find thy grace every day more my strength against corruption indwelling

15. spoke at the priory from Ezech: 33.10.11. of god and Christs willingness to embrace sinners(.) lord give a being to that word to mee and all, and to my poore sister.

Oct: 19. a very seasonable wett day, I hope it will begin to refresh the pooles and ponds(.) the lord good to mee and mine in many outward mercies, the lord delight in us, for the sake of his annointed one, I observe god in some measure looks after my spirit, to keepe my mind in frame to himselfe, and to observe he is my root and spring, and I well discerne he provideth for mee and looketh after his presence with mee in the word for which I blesse his name,

22. A few Souldiers quartered in our town, in the night I dreamed that
☞ being in the churchyard, their were signes in the sun, it was as in a cloud, and some part red, and somepart blacke, it shone very litle, and afterwards looking, but in some other place neare my house, I thought there was a huge tree or oak that even reached to the height of the heavens and covered the face of the skie from East to West in a manner; but it was like a tree in winter, blacke, no leaves on it, but withered in the root and dead, and in all the boughes aboundance of great fowles of all sorts, but I thought in a strange, dejected posture as if neare dying, I called out to my
was it Rev. 19. 17. 18: family to see it, I thought it portended the ruine of a great brit—oake, a government, thence growing, afterwards I thought I was likely to bee put to death and Paul Raynham[1] was the great enemy, I spake to him boldly, he seemed to wave it, but told mee how my preaching tended to disparage his estate, and professing condition, I envied it, I was delivered but I cannot distinctly tell how

24: preacht the Lecture at Halstead from Heb. 12.25 about slighting of christ, the lord in mercy keepe mee and mine from the guilt of that sad sin: a wett day(.) Ned Cressener died this morning after a most strang languishing.

[1] Paul Raynham, whose funeral sermon RJ preached at Chapel (20 February 1668) had a two-hearth house there in 1662. He was an elder of the Lexden classis in 1648 (Shaw, ii, p. 388) for Chapel.

Oct: 26. A very cheerful day after the wett, god very good to mee in many mercies for which I blesse his holy name, my wife somewhat inwardly ill, the lord bee health to her, and fit her for her condicon. gave notice of the fast read the Declaration, the lord good to mee in the word, oh that I have a heart to bee brought over to trade with christs stocke, and to see christ to become an interest in all my soule concernments.

27. preacht Ned Cresseners funerall. Mr R. Harl: and I laid him into his grave,

30. a P. fast, I expounded and preacht from Isay. 5.25. I find my heart very dead and unaffected for and under such a solemne duty. I found litle of god to my heart therein, the lord affect and breake my heart in the sense thereof

31: In the lane sett upon by one called a quaker, the lord was with my heart that I was not dismayed, I had some discourse with him, the lord bee my helpe, I see my own emptines daily on all occasions.

No: 1: at night walking in my study, a fireball fell into the North East, it cast a light into my window as lightning I saw the light over the house in the ayre, but saw not the ball.

Nov: 2. The season very comfortable, god very good to mee in many mercies, my wife better than formerly, the lords presence with mee in the words, oh that my soule could love, and delight in him, gods wrath is dreadful and terrible, oh let my soule never lie sweating under it.

4. feld in Bridgmans and brought into my yard, neare a load of logs

5. kept a thanksgiving day for the Spanish victory, it was a most tedious day for rain, but winde especially that discouraged mee in preaching

Nov: 9. God good in many particulars unto mee, the day cheerful, the word this day of wrath yet continuing against England, which oh that god would turne away(.) I find my heart very much shutt up in prayer, I straiten my selfe in time, I doe not watch unto duties as I ought, I find litle presence of god with mee, but my heart annoyd with temptacons feares. I have a strang numnes in my left arme, I had the like in my right legge, oh that such providence might awaken my heart to close walking with god.

10. A very tempestuous night causing a floud. Mr Honywood went away: 11. towards Cambridge, wee sent him away with prayer, the lord goe with him,

15. Kept a day of prayer at Priory god was good to us in the same for which I desire humbly to blesse his most holy name,

No: 16. god good to mee and mine in manifold mercies, in the word, and worke of the sabbath in his table ordinance, wherein much of gods love in a crucified christ lay before mee my desire is mine, and others hearts should bee engaged unto god by all, I find my heart hath much dust in it, lord helpe mee to a frame in all things glorifying thee(.) I had comfort in my uncle R. Josselins company, I writt his will for him, he was kind therin to mee, the lord lengthen out his days in much mercy.

No: 23. god continueth his mercy to mee though unworthy, he that cals for judgements. in so many nations, and families dealeth out love and favour unto mee and mine, oh that my soule might continually delight it selfe in him, the lord helpe mee against my daily weaknesses. I finde my desires slay mee, the active endeavours of my soule not running out into the things desired, my heart sensible that I doe not lay out my selfe in preaching to my utmost, the lord quicken, and helpe mee.

24: at night. R. Hatch his house robbed, blessed bee god for my continual preservation(.) heard Mr Wakering was sicke of the small poxe. who am I to be preserved

28: heard of the death of Justice Wakering, a great man in our County and freind to the ministers right, he died of the small pox. his name extinct in him onely a daughter left.

Nov: 30. God good to mee in many mercies, the lord draw my heart by his goodnes nearer to him that I may live in his sight, how great a mercy is it to have a quiet and peaceable sabbath, the lord daily continue it unto us, my heart I find ful of deadnes in the wayes of god, much straitned in prayer, lord helpe mee to a more useful converse with thee in my private walkings I pray thee and quicken mee up therunto.

Dec: 1: I began to bee in some strait for mony, and loth to lay out that which I had laid by for my debt. and this morning one of my parish brought mee in a litle tith, and a schoole tenant, a good sum. blessed bee my god who taketh care of mee

4: preacht at Wakes from Micah. 1.12. to awaken men from their expectations of good successe while men continue in their evill courses:

D. 5. a strange darkenes at London like midnight at noone day: it was a strange fogge

Dec. 7. The lord good to mee in many mercies, which addeth to his mercy but to my sin if he is so to mee who am so unthankefull, and unmindfull of him in his service that is on my shoulder, the lord humble mee, and bend my mind throughly to him, oh lord recover mee from under my deadnes of spirit, and straitnes of spirit in prayer, I finde no life in my heart, but a vain frothy heart, I am much a stranger to god in my closet, praying with a meere forme, the heart of man is desirous to receive in from god but is not active to, lay out it selfe for god againe in his wayes. lord helpe mee. I am poore and wretched, lord undertake for mee,

11. preacht at Wakes from. Micah. 1.12. the lord awaken a secure generation. I joyned with Justice Pelham in marrying Bridges daughter.

Decemb. 14: God good to mee, and mine the week past in many outward mercies, my minde in some better inward frame. I have frequent thoughts and feares of death: With if I should miscarry, and be eternally miserable how sad would bee my condition the mercy of god in christ Jesus is alone that which upholds my heart, god good in some measure unto mee in the word, the lord accept of mee in mercy.

Dec: 21: some hard weather, and snow but this day, a mist and thaw, god good to mee in many mercies for which my soule blesseth him, especially his presence in and through Christ to mee, good in helping mee in his word and worship this day in standing up for the honour of gods christ.

23. paid Mr Butcher an 150^{li}. towards his purchase, wee had very good accord in all particulars for which I blesse god. I desired it of god, and he gave it unto mee I saw him much in the businesse, for which my soule praiseth him; I forgot to call unto him for my bond, wherin I observe my weaknes

24: preacht at Buers on Isay. 5.22; oh how dead our hearts are under ordinances

25. let. M. Peartree my close his yeare to end Nov: 1: 1657. at 2^{li}. 13^{s}. 4^{d}. and the value of a Warp[1] of fish. he is to pay to mee the lords rent more. 4^{s}. 5^{d}. and tith

Dec: 28. God good to mee in many particulars good in raising up my heart to open the great mistery of christ unto my people, the lord make mee to be found faithfull to and with him, my uncle Josselin with mee, this day was dry, cold, and cheerfull. the lord make mee truly sensible of his goodnes unto mee for soule and body for mee and my family, that I am not under the power of error in thes dayes.

31: Robt: Abbot came to town, neither Uncle, nor aunt, nor own

[1] Warp of fish: four fish (occasionally three or a couple). NED.

brother, would entertain him, nor his wife, god gave mee a heart, and I did although I never had any kindnes from him, the lord remember mee, whom I desired to serve herein.

Jan: 2. saw the Justice, I did all my businesse comfortably with him. I advised him in the offer of a wife, but could not doe any thing therin wherupon I returned answer as directed—3. Rob: Abbot and his wife went from us, god good to him in his businesse, the brother Henry paid him his mony, they seemed much affected with and sensible of our love to them, in the evening and night afore one Rogers wife delivered of a girle, and two boys alive,[1] very lustie children, oh lord shew compassion to her in soule and bodie.

Jan: 4: This weeke god very good to mee in outward mercies taking a special care of my affaire, I was composed in my mind to more sweet meditations of him, I have my inward feares, and amazements as to an eternal condicon, which put mee onto christ in a way of beleiving, and I find him a resting place, and trust I alwayes shall. god was good to mee in the word, there was something in it unto my heart, lord lett it have an abiding there I intreate thee.

5: sent Jane to Colchester, god gave her a good and safe jorney, wee feared rain.

6. a sweet meeting at James Days. Mr R.H. opened the cause of our unthankfulnes in our lift up heart. mercies should lift up god not us, to make us swell, wee should lay gods good nearer our heart then our comforts, the more mercies, the more need of god with them wee should esteem them as these, gods worship in our families is common worke which should bee most speciall. blessed bee god for this counsel. My An very ill, and my throat sweld.

7. present at Mrs H. setlement of her estate, necessary that the parties bee 21. yeares old.

9. this day speaking with Mr R.H. about his mony, he told mee, he would not take any thing for it, and I might keep it so long as I pleased, and pay it, what and when I would, onely, if he wanted I should lend him some another time, god bee blessed for this providence, it spared mee 30^{s}. that I should have paid die 16°. did Mr Ellistons busines, and provided for Mrs Jane, and pleasured young Mr H. with an 100^{li}. whereby I did many kindnesses in one, and hope Mr Ell. will pleasure mee in my stantie hedges.[2]

Jan: 11. god good to mee this weeke past in many mercies, my An

[1] The PR gives the birth of Benjamin (buried 14 January 1657), Elizabeth (buried 4 January 1657), and John (buried 2 April 1660), all on 2 January. Thus only one of them survived over a fortnight.

[2] Stanty hedge: a stake-and-rice fence. NED.

though very froward yet in good hopes of doing well, my swelling much abateth under my eare, my wife better our hearts more in frame and wayes more comfortable, heard Major Haines had procured some moneys from mee from Dunmow which was in my thoughts somewhat hazardous, thus my god taketh care of mee, and looketh after mee for good(.) god was good to mee in the word, my heart was up for our crucified christ, against the imaginary christ of the Quakers, or their mistery, the same measure coming and appearing in the flesh of any person to judge the world.

14. Met upon an order from the Com. of approbation for Ministers at London: about Mr Rogers[1] in which busines I desired to bee faithful to god and my heart, with tendernes to my brother

15. Mr Layfeild my neighbour a minister about. 60 yeares old, his wife not dead 4 months was reported to bee marrying a maid about 21. I asked him of it, advised him against it with divers reasons(,) I perceive he is set upon. he hath had 2 wives and many children, oh what a poor peice is man if the lord leave him to direct himselfe,

17. heard that Dr Wright was sicke unto death, lord his life hath been a litle livelihood unto mee, and still may if thou please to continue it, I am at thy dispose(.) it was told mee this Saturday afternoon, which I resolve to improve better then I have done if god spare my life and his. how ever I live not as man or by him, but on god that hath, doth, and will take care of mee,

Jan: 18. god good to mee in many outward mercies, for which I blesse him, I find my heart very unfixt in the worship of god, that my heart doth not continue with god therin but runs out into every worldly occasion, which I desire to bemoan before god. I was pressing men earnestly unto setlenes in their faith to hold fast their profession I tasted god in the word, lord bee in it, unto my people.

22. this day in the morning I baptized Davies daughter, rid to chappell bought 25 trees of John Morly[2] for 9^{li}. I preacht at Wakes from Micah. 1.12. I returned and baptized H. Hatchs son, god good to mee in divers peices of the day, having fresh tasts of his love in christ, and to my soule, finding my heart wrought up to price the lord. he accept mee and teach mee to walke worthy of him.

23. Heard Tillam, an anabaptist pastor had set up the practice of the Satturday Sabbath and indulgeth those of his church that will to

[1] Nehemiah Rogers, who had petitioned the government for a dispensation to preach and teach which was granted in October 1656. In 1656 he gained the living of Doddinghurst. DNB; Smith, p. 346.

[2] John Morley of Chapel paid tax on a six-hearth house in 1662, and probably owned an estate in Colne Engaine. Morant, ii, p. 220.

use their trades it being their Colchester market and observeth the lords day, this done in regard of the present temper of the state. the lord helpe us. I expect the Jewes finger in the apostacy before perfected.

Jan: 25. the Lord was good to mee, and mine in many mercies, the lord sanctifie all unto mee, that I may enjoy him in them, and have my heart raised up, and ingaged in all and by all faithfully to serve him; I heard nothing certain of Dr Wright, by whose death the schoole goeth from mee, lord how ever thou deale with mee therein, thou shalt bee my god, my heart I hope shall bee more labourious in thy worke, for thou art my life, and my hope, and my crowne, I am in hope his life is preserved, he is on my heart to pray for him, and I shall praise thee oh god if his life bee continued yet a while, thy time is best, and in thy will I will rest. good was god to mee in the word pressing people to hold fast our profession, lord helpe and inable mee to doe it.

26. received halfe a firkin[1] of good sope, and halfe dozen of brown sugar a guift from Robt Abbot and his wife in sense of that kindnes I shewed him and her at Colne, and this was the ending and begining day of a yeare with mee.

When I review this yeare past in reference to the affaires of the world, I find things much at a stand, no new affaire breaking out but the attempt of the Moscovite against the Swede, which was no great affaire to view, no eminent turne of affaires in the world, except it were the going backe of the affaires of Swede in Poland, the English tooke a prize from Spain: in matters of religion the apostacy proceeds, the pretence of being specially directed by the spirit is drunke in by persons if almost any pretend therunto, and one Nailor in England, was esteemed by some for the christ, the King of Israel, for which a Parliament then sitting sentenced him, but no great discountenance put as the part by the Court, they rather winke then frown, yea release them, god in mercy thinke on us, some sett up the satturday Sabbath, in reference to my outward affaires god good to us, and I find I am blessed by him, my heart is open to god and charitable deeds as my estate is enlarged, I find my inward estate mixt of troubles, temptacons feares and hopes, finding a refuge under christ wings whither I desire continually to resort; a resolution in my heart to abide by the worship of god and his people through grace whatsoever cometh theron, the Venetian gave the

[1] Firkin: small cask for liquids, fish, butter, etc., originally holding a quarter of a barrel. SOED.

Turke a great route at sea, and god sadly afflicts Italy with the plague, the protestant troubles in Savoy, and Switzerland make no noise, they are under some troubles in France, the issue the lord knoweth.

— — — — — — — — — — — — — — — — — — —

Jan: 26: 1656: my 41: yeare enters

The lords presence bee with mee therin for good, my eye is on him for the same(,) I viewed with joy, the passages of. Jan: 26. 1655. blessing god for it, often read it.

30: I expected to heare of Dr Wright this day. I was not afraid of evil tidings, my heart being fixed, trusting in god as to his provision for mee; in the morning I gave a certificate to the army, that a Trooper was alive whom they expected dead but was only sick this was a providential lift. Mr Harlakenden coming from Halsted lecture, caled at my gate, I expected he had newes, about it, he heard nothing, and received a letter from Major Haynes of his wives deliverance, which made him conclude all was well, oh lord, his life is to mee a mercy, but there must bee a sanctifying my heart to make it indeed so; hints as if things wrought towards an extremity between the Protect(or) and Parliament; at night our people thought they saw a great fire towards Suffolk(.) I expected a letter from London it came not, my heart was quiet all the day as to this dispensation, on gods care of mee and mine bee days what they will

31: Heard certainly of Dr Wrights hopeful recovery, spare his days and mine for thy glory, the good of Colne, and my poore sinfull family, which I trust thou ownest as thine

Feb: 1: God good to mee this weeke in taking care of my livelihood, in Dr Wrights life by whose death the schoole had gon from mee worth neare 70li. yearly to mee, and besides the comfort to teach my children, the feare also of a bad neighbour. but lord the mercy will bee the ingaging thereby of my spirit to close walking and activenes for god, which my soul resolveth, oh let mee find a love cord therein pulling my heart closer to god(.) my heart was open and zealous for god and his christs honour in the good of soules and god was with mee therein, oh let mee bee accepted and pardoned according to the greatnes of thy mercies in christ.

5. a wet day, I was in pulpit at Wakes to have preacht for Mr Tompson, he then coming I went down, heard a good word of christ the

desire of nations, my maid went from us having been with us, above 3 yeares. examples of mortality this day,

7. at night I had a great mercy in my studdy, a candle that was the last of a pound, and had the cotton of the rest on the string, was
* laid on the table by my wife on the carpet bookes neare, and inwardly kindled, I coming out saw a sparke and wondering how it should bee there, and so escaped a great danger blessed bee my god.

Feb. 8. Heard a neighbours child at Gaines Colne had the small pox, the lord preserve mine for his mercy sake, god good to mee in many outward mercies for which I blesse his holy name, god good to mee in my spirit in the worke of the day, with life and activity oh lord let it bee blest. my desires are before the(e) use mee as an instrument in thy hand to glorifie thy name, stablish, strengthen, setle mee:

10: was with one Mole in our town who pricking his thumb with a thistle, and picking it out with a pin, it sweld, feared it would gangrene to the danger of his life, this day their was more hope in him, but he is very sicke with it

12 preacht this day at Wakes for Mr Sp: christ gods consolation in troubles to saints(.) god in a gracious presence with mee in the word, shall bless it to us all.

Feb: 15. God good to mee in many mercies, divers old vanities yet in my mind, and yet god left mee not. I find my heart not alwayes rising against temptacons and handle them roughly, and goe to Jesus for helpe to crucify them. but even readie by musing on them, to nurse and beare them up, the good lord in mercy, helpe mee throughly to tread Satan under. god in good measure good to mee endeavouring to ingage my heart, and of my people to a close adhering to christ and the truths

17. I was straitned for moneys, and this day, god ordered it so that two schooleten(an)ts brought mee in neare seven pounds, blessed bee god, who hath not dried that spring.

☞ 20. A day of thanks for the deliverance of the protector from Sundercombs treason who poisoned himselfe, I preacht from Job. 7.20.—received divers kindnesses from Mr Harlakenden the younger.

21: Received divers kind respects and tokens from young Mr Harl. spoke to Mr Jo. Cressener of my sonne being an apprentice, god in mercy looke after my child.

Feb: 22. Good was god in divers mercies, our town escaped but one quarter of an houre a travelling womans liing in with us, the lord in mercy looke on us in publique affaires, and preserve us for himselfe, the lord good to mee in my health(,) my neighbour Mr Clarke ill not able to preach(.) god good in the word, lord preserve my heart from its own folly and peculiar vanity.

26: Going down to Wakes. Mr Sams not there, I preacht from Job. 7.20. I went with Mr H. to Munt, who is troubled about his daughters folly(.) it was windy, wherby I gat a great cold, and rested very unquietly. Judeorum Messias venturus et apostatarum Christus, seu Antichristus est persona eadem.[1] is not the time of his visible working at hand.

wee and others had damaske rose buds in February

27. confident reports that Cromwell was proclaimed King, said also wee shall have an house of lords, some great alteration is in hand, but what it will bee time will discover(,) onely he hath outwitted his coactors in former designes, and no duobt his purpose is the like, but none can outwitt the almighty.

March 1. god good to us, yet dasht us in our healths, but helped mee in the Sabbath, the day was wonderfully blustering, the windows broken the wind lay vehemently cold in them and upon mee, I am persuaded god put forth an act of preservation towards mee, or the day would have produced some ill, on so crazie a body as mine was

2. one mother Davy a butchers wife aged about 67 yeares, a town born child, buried. who was so miserable shee grutcht[2] any thing to her selfe, and one instance, shee would have no fire in her house in her ilnes, shee sent for a poore woman the lords day before. to goe for her to the phisician, and told her shee would send her then because that(,) being shee could not worke shee would goe the cheaper and so shee gave her 2^d. and 2^d. more for the phisitian, whose judgment of her shee was willing to have, but not to receive any thing from him—and thus said shee mony runs away and spread her hands(.) she had hid by her in the ground a vast sum of mony.

4. a meeting at my house to seeke god in preparation to the sacrament of the lords supper(,) our freinds pretty well togither, all that could; in the morning I had a very violent yirke of the crampe in my left calfe. the first I perceived, a warning of old age.

6. Heard Mr Guyon death. death hath been in all the Coln ministers ☞ families since I came hither, and I thinke first with mee in 3. childrens death. then Mr Brackly. then Mrs Layfeild and now Mr Guyon: god prepare mee for the next round.

[1] The coming Messiah of Judah and the Christ of the apostates, or the Antichrist, is the same person.

[2] Grutch: grudge. SOED.

7. Preacht Mr Guyons funeral sermon. the 3d. minister for whom I did that office(,) it was a solemne occasion and worke to mee, the lord better my heart by it

March: 8: My poore sister Mary, whose heart is broken with greife, and trouble with mee from the priory before I was up. I advised her to submitt to god in his providence to her, and to wait on him in his way, and worship in the sense of her emptines, and that fulnes of mercy and grace god hath laid up in christ. the Lord our god in a Christ accept us. this day wee brake bread, my poore sister came not out of the seat(.) I went unto her with the bread, shee came forth and joyned with us, oh lord joyne thou thy selfe unto her I most humbly begge of thee and lett her heart abide faithfull by thee. The Lord was good to mee in many outward mercies, the lord accept of mee in his christ, and delight in mee to doe mee good.

10. Heard of Justice Harlakendens dangerous ilnes, the lord take care of mee. I trust god will spare his life, or give him to setle his estate, his death otherwise would bee a blemish, and a sad providence to mee and many, god pricks thornes into all thes enjoyments, the lord hath cared for mee, and I will hold my peace.

Blacke-thorne own out n divers places.

March 12. I preacht this day at Wakes god good to mee in the word, it was lively on my spirit

13. heard Mr Harlakenden had setled his estate, for which I blesse gods name, and this morning having slept he somewhat amended, blessed bee god for this answer of prayer

March. 15. my heart was refresht in the good newes of the Justice(,) my heart was earnest for him with god, and I know not in vain, the lord was good to mee in the word and worke of the Sabbath, god accept mee therin, the lord good to us in many mercies, feared the small pox in our towne, the lord in mercy prevent it that it spread not. Tho. Garrad[1] with mee tempted to make away his child, the lord helpe him, that by sin he doe not utterly undoe himselfe.

16: heard of the Death of 2 women[2] at my going into street, lord make mee mindful of death, and careful to walke with thee in order to it, and witnes thy love to mee.

17. One John Chrismas[3] a miller in our town, whose parents were godly, and one in a way of doing well, but his heart leading him to tiple and game, and his wife being sharp to him, he gott what he

[1] The child was probably Annis, born on 14 December 1656, daughter of Thomas and Grace, and hence three months old.

[2] The only recorded burial on this date in the PR was of Grace Champney, widow.

[3] John Chrismas is recorded in the PR as buried on 18 March.

could togither, and left her, his brother brought him home, but about a weeke after he was sicke of the pox and died, a warning not to goe out of gods way.

18. spent in prayer at Priory on behalfe of Mrs H. preacht Corn. Brownsons funeral(.)[1] heard more comfortably of Mr W.H. recovery for which my heart blesseth god.

19. preacht at Wakes about Christ the consolation, the word was very sweet to my heart the lord in mercy doe mee good by the same. heard that the alteration intended will not bee to the prejudice of honest people, the protector will provide for their interest. but who will put confidence in princes. there were 13. ministers at this sermon.

21: no hopes of Mr W.H. life, he is sadly distracted by his feaver the lord helpe, report that wee list and raise men apace under pretence for Flanders.

March: 22. god good to mee in many outward mercies, the lord make mee wise to consider my latter end, and redeem the time, careful in my outward estate that what god gives mee in his bounty, I may not wast, by easines to trust men, my heart was enlarged for Mr H. in prayer this day, oh Lord heare. lord I believe thou wilt helpe my

1657 unbeleife, god good to mee in the word this day. 1657

25. I went to Messing and did some busines well, comfortable society with Mr Tomson, coming home.

26: my busines done my heart vain, when our turne is served god is soone out of mind, grace strugld and god holpe mee, I received 15^s^. that I expected not to have received.

when I come to view my estate this yeare, I find my expenses far deeper then divers yeares formerly, and my receipts more then ever, god bee blessed. last year my estate was about 670^li^. I find I have about 590^li^. and I have paid for land to Mr Butcher. 150^li^. and to Mr Weale. 85^li^. which is in whole. 235. so that I have had a great increase this yeare of. 145^li^. or thereabouts. with the life and health of my family, no trouble in my estate, the lords love in christ is my life and joy. I have received into my hand Mrs Maries land on which I am out. 108. 9^s^. this yeare 1657. is like to bee a boisterous yeare in the world, the lord bee my hope, and my shelter, my wisedom, and strength. and let thy blessing rest upon my tabernacle for the lords sake,

27. I rid to Ardleigh god good in my preservacon, riding on a dangerous horse, who fell under mee, my child well at Colchester, the lords

[1] Cornelius Brownson is recorded as buried on 18 March.

love bee to her, heard more hopefully of Justice Har: recovery, lord doe it for thy mercy, mercy sake.

28. heard of the death of my deare Uncle Ralph Josselin, who died at London die 21. and was buried die. 24: by his children. the lord make mee to minde my change and prepare for it.

March: 29. God good to mee in many particular mercies, thes few dayes past I have dwelt with sorrows, but I see out of them, sins sorrows are those indeed that trouble, and amaze men, the season is now coole, hopes of dews, the drought began to grow on us, talke now of a King, the lord bee our King and lawgiver, I was very much down in my own thoughts in the worke of the Sabbath the Lord pardon all to mee. this day I heard of the sicknes of Tho. Humfry by small pox. while I am preaching of christ our preserver, what things doe I see, lord bee the preserver of mee and mine, as thou hast been, Mrs Mabel Elliston so ill, that there are great feares, shee will not continue, lord revive her spirit, as in former dayes, and bee thou her life, and strength in the midst of us.

Ap. 1. Spent in a day of prayer for Mr W.H. Mrs Mabel. Ell. children, god good to mee in the word from psal. 5.3. in prayer, and in the day, the lord my god accept mee; a litle after midnight I was called up to Mrs Mabel, who earnestly desired mee to bee with her at her death, and now sent for mee; I endeavoured to gett to her, but before I came shee was dead, she died full of faith in god, seing Jesus with her eyes as shee said with out any pain or trouble, which shee much feared, god put it under her feet and made her dispise it, shee was her parents onely one, and was my deare freind, one of ten thousand

2. rid to Mr Butcher spent a day in prayer and counsell for the young couple and old, who remove, my subject was psal. 127.1.2. the lord blesse it, I received my bond from them, which was a pleasing providence, I returned that night by Mr Ellistons who ingagd mee to preach his daughters funeral although a member of Coxall, her affections to mee were very intire.

3. at Halsted, promised with gods helpe to assist in my uncle Ralphs executorship visited Mr Elliston, they seemed to beare that great losse of their daughter beyond what could have been expected, lord helpe and teach them to proffit by it. blown may this day.

Blown may.

4. On Satturday Mrs Mabel was buried at the upper end of the North side of our chancel, her father bestowed a beautiful funeral on her, many of her freinds carried her to the ground Mr R.H. and I laid her unto grave at the head and 2 uncles at the feet, the sermon

continued till sun down, a great number of freinds, her disease judged malignant(,) I trust god will preserve us from its danger(,) I preacht from Phil. 1.23. and left my greife and trouble much in the pulpitt(,) my heart lightned and refresht by the word

April. 5. The Lord good to mee, or my greifes, and busines would have bowed mee down, his mercy, and goodnes upheld mee, in the sense whereof my heart desireth to rejoyce. Tho. Humfry sicke of the small pox. I sought the lord for his life and pardon of sin, oh lord shew mercy, I heard he had learned to curse by the pox, if so the lord hath mett with him, oh turne again in mercy, and heale soule and body if it please thee(.) I had great experience of gods mercy in bringing my matter to hand for the Sabbath, in an houre or two, helping mee therein, so that I found the word sweete and lively, the lord in mercy make it so unto many others; god answered prayer in Mrs Harlakenden who was (c.o. about) before 11. a clocke at night delivered of a daughter, the lord inherit all our praises. and the next morning was very cheerfull.

6: saw part of Mrs Mabel Ellistons diurnal of her life,[1] full of spiritual observation and sweetnes, lord thy presence sweetens my cup, for other things are bitter to mee(,) Mr Elliston told mee that April the 1. being a fast (but publique) at night he had such a vision of comfort as he counted it his joyfullest houre, this was Wednesday
1651. in Easter weeke.—this Wednesday in East. weeke 1657. wee kept a private fast at priorie wherin he was with us, and about the same time at night just six yeares, his onely daughter died very much ravisht with joy; in her losse he counts that his most sad houre: the only difference is one day. then April 1. was Tuesday. and the fast was on the 2d.

8: heard Tom Humfry was dead, mine and my two sisters first sons were named Thomas, the eldest sisters is dead, lord preserve ours. he was a boy that did not much mind god, our hearts let out to pray for him, his affliction a sad pox I hope the lord spake to his heart. prayer is my duty. forgivenes belongs to god and judgment final of a person. the lord awaken mee more to keepe up my peace with god, and to a greater serviceablenes to the name of god in my generation, I sent down 6 dozen of cakes for his buriall; oh my soule rejoyce that christ ever liveth, and no stormes can make him to wither, but is able to fil up with his love, all the empty places that death maketh, yea the empty soule

[1] Diurnal: a day-book, diary; especially a journal. SOED. The rediscovery of this missing journal might be most illuminating.

9. By Mr Harl: view of the Justices letter to Capt: Harl. I find the tang of quakerisme on his spirit, which thus setled, a high feaver even distracted him and laid him at deaths doore, he recovered a litle out, and told of his strange raptures into the 3^{d} heaven, none had the like since Paul. god had assured him of his love, given him the white stone new name, revealed unto him he should live, and that he had a worke on him to witnesse against ministers gathering of churches, preaching for hire, receiving tithes, he hath the word written in him, and so hath the true meaning herof. In the mean time the Quakers that heard of his affliction lookd on it as a judgment of god on him for Parnels imprisonment.[1] my thoughts were pensive about him, and his condicon what to doe in it, desiring to eye the rule. 2 texts came into my mind. 2. Tim. 2.24.26. Jude. v.22.23. he is one deceived in his weaknes, and not one that choose the delusion by rejecting the truth, and the text presents hope, in the manner and meanes lord helpe mee, thy glory is concerned herein

April. 12. I awakned this morning dreaming that Mr Sparrow preaching at Wakes I saw Mr Tompson and his wife and told them, the strange newes, that the man under pretence of acting against ☞ blasphemy, had at a meeting of the rulers, given in to arise and act against the ministry, the lord good to mee in many mercies, my heart very calme, lord keepe mee from sullying vile thoughts, the word this day was an awakening word lord make it so and make it a blessing, many lately afflicted hearers a sermon for them, let it take place on their hearts I pray thee,

16: god heard prayer in respect of the season and after many dews this morning gave us a growing rain, the lords name bee blessed for it; this day Mrs Eliz. Harlakenden was baptized, god good to mee in the duty, my heart raised up to hope that god would blesse mee, even mee also in my poore posterity, I was ill used in words by R.A. the elder, my heart was calme, lord pitty us under our affliction and scorne and helpe mee with patience, Jo. Humfry with mee, hoping to have seen his son Tho: who was dead and buried the Wednesday before. lord looke after mine in all their goings out and comings in I pray thee.

[Margin: This ...ht the ...ghting ...s sung ...weetly in all closes ...ut the ...town I never ...rd the like.]

17. preacht at Halsted about prayer there is need of it, divers men

[1] 'The Judgments of God yt overtook ye persecutors of James Parnell were very Remarkable. . . . Wm Harlakinden, one of the Justices, dwelling at Earls Coln, became distracted, so that he would go Into fields without stockins or shoes, and over hedg and ditch, and continued in that Condition, and dyed.' Norman Penney (ed.), *The First Publishers of Truth* (1907), p. 97.

bustle to make Christ king(,) truly Cromwell will carry it from him at present, but surely there is a time when Christ shall reigne more then inwardly, lord my soules desire is to have light herein(,) my meditacons pestringly vile, the lord helpe mee for his mercy sake,

April 18. received a letter from Justice Harlakenden, he declares against tithes

19. This weeke god gave us very dewy weather, the earth yeilds grasse in aboundance for which my soule blesseth god, the lord contineth his wonted goodnes to mee, heard this weeke the men that are to make christ King, were plotting against the Protector, and that he seized on divers of them; in course I read this day. 1. Kings. 11. and 12. chapters, my heart was not lively this day, oh my deadnes in gods service, I find yet my heart picking up hope in gods covenant and promise, and I desire to bee prepared for those difficulties of condition that are coming on us.

21: * Many times my heart feareth as to eternity, because I find temptacons returning and my heart often ensnared with them, my corrupt part taking in with them. so its in the vanity of my mind.
* I find my selfe a burden to my selfe in it, I loath my selfe but what I would not that I doe, and yet I even would doe it also, its pauls case Rom. 7. I find christ more deare and precious to mee, I find often his helpe, but my constant repose is by faith in the promise, and that my faith is not presumption, I find a true worke of grace witnessing it, though not a perfect sanctification in mee, I can trust god, when all sense failes. I know he doth intend mee good, and this arowses my heart against evil, though it often prevaile lord I am oppressed undertake for mee, you that wingest faith, slay corruption

25. Justice Harlakenden returned to see us at Colne, blessed bee god for him, the lord make him a living blessing, his life was given to mee through prayer in the name of Christ, its to mee oh lord a pledge of thy love, oh teach mee to serve the(e) most unfeignedly. he told me how he thought when he saw the glory of heaven, the confusion that Cromwell was in and his Court being forsaken of the people.—this day god watched over my An in the street, who very narrowly escaped the wheele of the priorie cart.

Ap: 26. God good to mee in many good things, but lord I want thy presence in mortifying my heart, and bringing mee in subjection in my inward man to thee, oh when wilt thou helpe mee, I am oppressed oh undertake for mee I pray thee, this day the lord gave mee in a great mercy in Justice Harlakendens being with us at church and very staied and mindfull of god, by his desire I gave publique thanks to god, for him, my faith was up wrestling for his life. and god gave it, the Lord teach mee the use of this and to trust, and love him more, the lord have the honour of all.

30: preacht at Cogshall, at their lecture newly erected, dined and lodged at Markshall. vanity much heads my mind, and often my heart complies, lord helpe mee for I am weake, but worse unwatchfull, oh undertake for mee, the lord bee blessed who hath sett Justice Harlakenden, in his spirit very much of, from the Quakers.

May. 3. The Lord good in another peaceable Sabbath, his mercies with mee and familie(,) his keeping grace in my heart, that I am not overrun with evil that sets on mee, lord if I were to bee perfect out of thee, I should bee most imperfect, wee had an occasion of charitie in a poore mans losse by fire, in doing for him I desired to serve gods command of love and helpefulnes to others in their wants(.) Justice Harlakenden with us, which is an heart refreshing unto mee,

4: received a Theophilact on Pauls epistles given by Mr Thrale,[1] god giveth some encouragements in the midst of the trouble wee meet with, my wife an instrument to save the life of a quaker in childbirth at a pinch

5. mett in conference. Justice Harlakenden with us, which was a great joy of heart to mee. my heart tasted much of gods goodnes to mee, and us in his recovery, the word spoken was precious to mee, and a solace, I would not part with the comfort of it for very great treasures, escaped a danger from Colemans dog flying upon mee.

7. preacht this day at Buers, the lord touch hearts, I was with Mrs Keam[2] who is under feares, and endeavoured to persuade her to rowle her soule on god in christ, heard as if Blake desired land men to attempt the Canaries

May. 10: The Season very promising, god is good to the sinfull: my An not well, lord sanctifie thy dealings to us, and engage our hearts unto thee, and revive my babe, I leave my selfe on thee as my rocke, trusting under thy wings, oh let mee never bee ashamed.

15. Mr. Thrale his wife and freinds went from us to London, god gave them a very prosperous journey, 16°. in the morning on Satturday my wife guessed that shee was with child and about 3 weeks gone, the lord show us mercy therin; at night Mr Hubbard[3] of London.

[1] Probably Thos. Thraell of Essex, gent., rector of St. Mary Mounthaw, London, 1630. Foster.

[2] The eldest daughter of Herbert Pelham, J.P., of Bures, Suffolk. Probert.

[3] Probably one of the Hubbard family of Stansted Hall, Essex, related to the Harlakendens; most likely to be Francis or Edward. Morant, ii, p. 578.

with mee to teach two boys at 3[li]. per annum if they come, if god adde to our chardge one way, he can helpe another way, when he pleaseth,

May. 17. a fruitful season; for all things, but the heart of the nacon never lesse regardful of god, they mind themselves, their lusts, their opinions their own designes no time nor heart to minde or regard the things of christ, our professors that are not apostatized, are under much indifferency, and coldnes of spirit, zeale for truth is gone, though men are valiant for their lies and follies; god was good to mee this day in holding out the mercy of god through christ to sensible sinners, I have need of thy comfort, oh when wilt thou quicken mee, thy word bee life and health unto my soule, oh blessed bee god for another comfortable and quiet Sabbath, god shall yet adde more, oh that my heart were provided for trials before they come, and in that day god would bee my helpe.

19. I baptized 2 boys of 3 yeare old and another infant, one boy wisemans broke my heart to see his desire to bee baptized,[1] freinds promised to see him brought up in the faith of Jesus Christ, lord the love of thy name was on my heart in this doing. I had a good journey to Pedmarsh, visited Mrs Borough, I find god very merciful in his provision for her, a great encouragement to faith, I gave her 5[s]. and I served Christ in it.

22. heard of the death of my old freinds Mr and Mrs Gifford, who died long since, the lord prepare mee for all publique and particular trials, and changes.

May. 24: God good in many mercies to us, my wife onely very ill, but concludes it is childing, and a girle, the lord bee our portion and its in mercy, the Major, and his wife with us hearing, god hath taken his eldest son, my heart very vain yesterday, Satan making a step into temptacon intending mee hurt, the lord helpe mee, I am not sensible of my weaknes, and thereupon stand on my watch, and call in the helpe, and assistance of Jesus Christ, this day the lord put some stop on my heart, oh crucifie every evill in mee I intreate thee, news this weeke that the Swede had routed the Pole, and the Portugal forced Spaine to retreate from Olivenca

27. kept a day of praise at Mr Ellistons on behalfe of Justice Harlakenden, it was a good day, in the occasion and worke at night found a

[1] In the PR is the following note beside the baptism of Mary Wiseman on 19 May: she 'was baptised with another sister and brother which were born divers years before at 2 severall births'.

woman of yeoman quality[1] dead in our town who the former day was taken sicke, and lighted of her horse in the streete,

May. 29. fisht the ponds at Priory. Mrs. H. kept company in the preparing them, which eased my toile,

31: The lord good to us in outward mercies, my poore wife concludes her selfe with child and of a sonne; shee is very sicke in her stomache but I trust in a short time shee shall doe well, the lord for christ sake bee good to her and carry her on comfortably in the worke, god gave us a very sweet and comfortable rain, when it begun to bee desirable to many grounds, he remembers us in our wants, the Lord was good to mee in the word, christs grace our supply, the way of our deriving it from him, the lord helpe mee to doe it in all particulars for mercy sake, I humbly intreate thee,

June. 2. Major Haynes and his wife went from the Priory very early before sun, the lord give them a good journey and blesse them both in soule and body.

5: A day wherin god was good to mee in silencing a temptacon wherin my heart was troubled, and with which annoyed, and in which I found some of the tricks of corruption to blow up and heighten it selfe.

June. 7: The lord good to us in the season very promisingly fruitfull, the lord good in the health of my family, my wife though ill satisfied as to the cause of it, and somewhat better than formerly, the lord good to us in the word, and worke of the Sabbath, wherin I greatly desire acceptans.

9. received by Letter from my Lady Honywood that her son John had the smal pox the lord in much mercy remember him, and command deliverance and sanctify it

10: spent some time in Mr H: new buildings, to blesse god for Mrs H. deliverance in her birth of Betty. for gods presence in their journey, gods favour in their habitacon(.) wee remembered my Lady Honywood and her son, the lord remember us for good.

12. This morning early I tooke my leave of Mr and Mrs Harlakenden, who set forward for London, and shee for Wales, god preserve them safe and returne them so, and watch over all they have here in mercy as I trust he will,

June 14. The Lord good in outward mercies, a very comfortable season, the lord continue it to the end of the yeare, my deare wife not so sicke inwardly which is an ease of mind to us, the lord lets mee see

[1] The PR records the burial on 28 May of Elizabeth Anger a 'stranger that came from Thorpe'.

the difficulties that others have in their condicon that I may not thinke much of what I have in my own, every one having his own sorrow, the lord in some measure abates temptacons, I fall but lord my heart liketh not to fall into any sin and evill against thee, the lord was good to mee in the word, and worke of the Sabbath, make mee to receive that grace I hold out is in christ to communicate to poore humble sinners.

15. Though I know gods wayes have a depth in them beyond my reach, ☞ and that after dayes will discover that I yet know not, yet pondering in my mind why god laid out my lot at Colne, and not neer Peterborough, or about Olny where I married, I find god called mee from those places of trouble, warre and tumult to this where I have had peace but one day by Goring, and why from Cranham(,) my life was pretious to him, their was a great mortality of that people, and if I had been neare London, I might have been in more danger from the men of the times, oh I will love the lord who taketh care of mee in my wayes.

17. Mr Harlakenden went towards London, his familie alone, god give mee a heart to serve him, in the good of that familie.

☞ Payne in my arme and body made mee more sensible of state then at some other time, opening my eyes to looke backe and see my faults, though none can understand his errors at the same time, the follies of my young children awakened mee to see the sad effects of our fall in Adam, how operative corruption is tainting of us, which I hope shall putt mee to exercise faith in the bloud of christ, and to receive daily grace to live and walke more exactly

18: Heard of Mr Whitings death minister of Lexden, who putting his finger into a mans mouth whose throat was ill with a squinsey,[1] and non compos mentis, he bitt it vehemently on which it gangrened, and kild him about 8 days after(.) lord how good you art in my preservation, its not good for men to medle out of their callings, Mrs El. Harl. elder and younger very ill, lord preserve them.

June. 21: This weeke, the Lord good to mee in outward mercies, but I find not my heart serious, solemne with god, and become one with the command of god, but very childish, and slighty: the lord good to mee in the word and worke of the day my heart somewhat warmed towards god and men, oh lord accept of mee, and doe mee good for thy holy name sake.

23. This morning my wife quickned she concludeth a son. god blesse

[1] Squinsy: quinsy, inflammation of the throat or part of the throat; suppuration of the tonsils; tonsilitis. SOED.

her and it the women mett with her in prayer, John Eldred a scholler that brought mee in 40s. yearly went from mee, the lord will provide.

25: preacht at Wakes, my desire was to serve Jesus, lord helpe mee against my corruption(.) Mr R.H. returned safe from London.

June: 28: This weeke as formerly gallant weather for corne, and hay, the crop so great that a litle wett would have been very prejudicial, gods eye is on us therein I trust for good, my heart trembleth to think on the issue of the actings of these dayes, the oaths that in haste, are imposing, the lord watch over us all in much mercy for good, and preserve mee from every abomination, and let mee see the daily evil of my heart and dayes. god good to mee in the word, heard of Mrs Sparrows relapse lord fetch her up from the grave,

29. This day my Cosin Betty Josselin came to mee, intending for the priory, Lord blesse her in her service I intreate thee, and doe her soule good, I desire that love was between her parents and selfe, may continue and descend on her.

July: 4: heard of the safe returne of Mr R.H. to London, god was good to him in his jorney god bring him well to Colne, and command his blessing for him, heard Mr Clarke overthrew R.N. in tithes by meanes of a quaker, who would not for a defect, give away Mr Clarkes right, god can worke out a mans good by his enemie, when he pleaseth, and surely wee may appeale to their consciences for our right to our tith.

July. 5. God removed a meeting of quakers from our towne to Gaines Colne, unknown to mee, I blesse god for the quietnes of the Sabbath(.) my god is good but my heart is very vile, lord change it, and better mee by all I pray thee, the season very hott

July. 12. This weeke continued very hott, and dry bringing on harvest, the lord good in our healths, but our hearts not carefull to honour him, in patient, humble thankefull, delighting in him, and in his goodnes, the lord the last weeke bountifull in his provision for mee, which I looke on as the efect of his mercy and care towards them, lett my eye bee so fixed, and my heart bound up in thy allsufficiency, that my heart may not sinke, whatsoever lieth before mee(.) the lord gave mee a peaceable and comfortable Sabbath, oh that I had a heart to love and delight in him, according to his daily goodnes.

13. heard of Mr Fearfuls dallying with his mayds many years, yett no act of uncleanesse followed, the divel will play at any game, lord uphold thine.

16. god gave us a comfortable raine.

17. Protector proclaimed at Halsted by the Sheriffe(.) Lord Jesus (seing he is come) come thou quickly. quickly.

July. 19. The Lord gave us the weeke of harvest. and some very sweet shoures to coole the aier, and earth, and refresh them, oh that his goodnes might warme our hearts and solace, and delight our soule, my heart very dull and negligent in the worship and service of god, my spirit doth not stirre up, and provoke it selfe in gods wayes.

23. wee mett at W. Webs at Gaines Colne to seeke god, the lord good to us in the word and prayer. when all was done Mr Clarke the minister of the place told us that coming to us he saw one An Crow[1] (counted a witch) take something out of a pott and lay by a grave, he wonders what was to doe, when he drew near he espied some baked pears, and a litle thing in shape like a ratt, only reddish and without a taile run from them, and vanisht away, that he could not tell what become of it, the partie said shee laid them there to coole, shee was under the window where wee exercised. I pressd her what I could(,) shee protests her inocency, lord bee our keeper.

heard as if Dr Wright were very ill, making much bloudy urine, lord I leave my selfe on thee to provide for him, yet let him live in thy sight.

25. young Mr Harlakenden, and his wife came home safe after a long jorney and a tedious absence, god good unto them in their jorney for which my soule praiseth him, let us live together to keepe thy commandements oh Lord

July. 26. God good to mee in many outward mercies, in all which my heart delights in him(.) this day wee broke bread, the lord maketh my heart desirous to cleave to him, in a way of duty, oh my soule is glad to tread in his paths and courts(.) my wife weake and fearfull, god is her strong god and I trust will carry her through all her difficulty and trouble, to her comfort and mine, I doe not find my body nor heart as true, and lively in gods worship, the lord in mercy helpe mee,

Aug. 2. God good to mee in many mercies, I conceive the face of the earth was never more burnt with drought in any time then now, and yett which is wonderfull Mr R.H. hops, heles went on, and upper Chiffin[1] being backward, is likely to prove a great crop, by rains, which wee are likely to have, I was very carelesse in preparing for the Sabbath, the lord pardon it to mee, my heart, is not lift up

[1] There were several women of this name in EC, among them Ann, widow of Giles, buried on 28 April 1661. There was also a Giles Crow in the 1671 Hearth Tax for Golne Engaine. The suspicions do not seem to have reached the courts.

[2] Upper Chiffin is a field name, and 'heles' is likely to be the same.

within mee in the wayes of god, the lord in mercy raise up my heart to spiritualnes, and activenes in my walking with him. it now deweth very sweetly, god in mercy refresh the earth, and renew the face of it.

4: a good meeting at Wallers, oh that I had a heart daily to ponder the way and means then opened in the subject of presumptuous sins, whereby god keepe us backe from living against him, people very neglectful of opportunities.

6: one Mr Stebbing a member of the church at Coxall, being somewhat tied up in his marriage by the church desired mee to goe to them. I did, I found they waved the considerations of age, and insisted on that of godlines, from. 1. Cor. 7.39. et. 2. Cor. 6.14. which prove onely that beleevers professors of the same faith marry. they left him to his libertie, to seeke god, and to observe the impressions of god on his spirit, I desired him to beware of temptacon he was bitt before, thus wee very freindly parted. this day wee had a very great shoure in our parts

Aug: 9. God good in many particulars unto mee, and in the word, lord lett mee never contemne thee, god gave us many comfortable shoures. Dr Wrights son receiving a putt of from Mrs Honywood[1] sent to mee to understand that busines, the lord make mee wise in that affaire. lord help mee against daily temptacions, I am followed with a chest cold, the lord bee my helpe in thes sickly times.

15. received another letter from Dr Wright on the same subject.

Aug: 16: God good to mee, then when my heart is evill, and negligent in my wayes towards him, oh pardon mee for thy name sake, my cold very tedious, but who knoweth but their may bee mercy in it, the season shoury and god reneweth the face of the earth, the lord good to mee in strength for the sabbath, but I was not carefull to watch for it, lord I loath my selfe, pardon thou mee in thy christ I pray thee,

21: at night Rob: Haines[2] ws buried at Coptford, it was reported in June he was dead now he is indeed, the good Lord in mercy prepare mee and all for our change some times such reports are forerunners, wee should take occasion from every thing, as a forewarning, and prepare for it, moriendum est mihi semel.[3] sit bene, lord lett mee never know what a second death is.

[1] Elizabeth, only daughter of Lady Honywood; see Honywood genealogy in Appendix 1.

[2] Robert Haines, elder brother of Major General Hezekiah; see genealogy in Appendix 1.

[3] There is death for me once; may it be good.

Aug. 23. Sickly times, god wonderfull gratious in the health of all my family, Major Haynes sicke at Markshall, desired us to remember him in prayer, the lord in mercy doe it, for his own name sake, and restore him for the good of his people in thes parts(.) by report their never was a more sickly time generally in England then now, the lord good to mee in the Sabbath for which I blesse his name.

28. sent for to Markshall to Major Haynes who was ill, I mett Justice Harlakenden who came from him, who questioned not but he would bee dead before I came to him, my bowels were moved within for my deare freind, I overcame my selfe and concernments in him through mercy, but as useful to poore England my heart could not part with him, I overcame my feares, and had hopes of his life before I came thither, and found it so accordingly, for which I blesse god, the Lord helpe mee never to forgett those walking meditations.

Aug: 30: A good weeke with shoures, and yett faire weather for worke, this day I publisht the act about the Sabbath, the lord doe good by it, for it is high time(.) the lord in mercy accept my praise for mine and my families preservation in thes sickly and aguish feavourish times, prayed heartily for Mrs King by desire, the lord heare prayer, and in much mercy accept us for his christ, god good to us in the word this day, it was tart, and searching from Isay. 57.20

31: Preacht Mrs Kings funeral from Heb. 2.14.15. the lord make the word an abiding word on thes spirits of mee, and the severall hearers. lord preserve the rest of the family, we spent some time to seeke god by prayer for Major Hayns

Sept: 6: The season wett, feavors very common, two persons died of them with us, the lord sanctifie his hand to us, our youth very disorderly in the Sabbath, the lord in mercy amend the severall evills in the midst of us, god good to us in daily mercies, he accept of mee for his own name sake.

9. after hopes of a dry sturbridge faire it rained very much, so that the wayes were exceeding heavy and dirtie, Mr H. had some hope to make 500^{li}. of his hops. the last yeare he made 790^{li}.

11. called to a day of prayer at my Ladie Honywoods to seeke god on her behalfe and familie, and Major Haynes and wife, the lord helpt mee in speaking(.) the good lord helpe mee to live out the councels of god to others, the lord is good in the hopes he giveth us of mercy and goodnes unto them, for which my soule desireth unfainedly to bless him.

Sept: 13: God good to us in our health, yet god hath spared us, my wife very ill last day but I hope its something incident to her childing, the lord sanctifie us, and all providences unto us for good, god good to mee in the word, its dismal to bee in a peaceles state, which is wicked mens, oh lord lett it never bee mine, times very sickly, with feavours that fill many places with pale faces, and very moist, and hott, which giveth us plenty of grasse, oh Lord watch over us for good

19. At night I was so troubled with my cold, as if it would have stifled mee, the lord was my helpe staying of it, for which I praise him, and the light of his countenance is my life, in which my soule rejoyceth,

Sept. 20. God good to mee, and mine in our peace, health, and in many outward mercies, comfortable under my cold, the season dry, but cold, pastures flourish, the lord provide for us of his grace and bounty, it was no smal mercy in my eyes that when agues and feavours as formerly the smal pox stept in at many doores god preserved mee and mine, oh lord helpe mee to keep thy law, and lett me live to it, god is putting on my thoughts to making sure my interest in god, and to prepare against the worst, lord lett them not be thoughts and nothing else, but such as may ripen to actions.

26: my Brother Constable came to us with the welcome sight of home, I heard of the wellfare of his familie and sisters but of the low decaying estate of my old aunt, even worne out, lord renew, and increase her faith, to more and more livelynes

Sept. 27. God good to mee and mine in many outward mercies in which my soul desireth to blesse the name of god. Major Haynes a hearer with us, the lord in mercy shew favour to him and his, god good to mee in the word preacht, it was amazing no peace to the wicked, god casts firebrands in earnest the lord helpe mee to prepare for my everlasting rest in close walking with him.

30: A publique fast in regard of the general visitacon by sicknes, which ☞ was a feavour and ague very mortal in some places, my thoughts run out on Job. 14.14. a meditacon for death, which I desire may bee often, and much in my thoughts, god give mee a heart to practice, and make constant use of it.

Oct: 1. This day my brother Constable returned home, god send him well thither, and blesse him, god hath been good to him in providing for him, the lord make him a faithfull and upright one in his service, he was very kinde to our children.

3. John put in breeches, I never saw two sons so clad before. lord lett thy christ hide their and all our nakedness I intreat thee. one

Perry who was much behind with mee, came and paid mee a good sum and reckond with mee, in which providence I saw much of god, and desire to blesse his name,

October 4. God good to us, the season dry, and cold, oh let our hearts bee warmed in thy love, and feare. god good in the word no peace to the wicked it was to mee an awakening word, it let in notable animosities against sin that would take away my peace with god, oh lord free my heart and heale it of sin.

8: Being up. and riving logs. Mr Elliston came and told mee Dr Wright was most certainly dead, I had no warning of his sicknes, I was troubled that such a providence found mee not better imployed, and disposed, but I blesse god though I am like to loose 60[li]. per annum. yet that is not much trouble. god liveth who is able to provide for mee, and in him I trust he will, that its in love to mee, what he doth, though I confesse I am unworthy of his bounty, it was mercy to mee he lived untill the quarter day was past.

9. rid to Mr Eldreds with Mrs Marg. Harlakenden, where wee were very bountifully entertaind, god good to my spirit, in hinting to mee how he loveth man should trust in him, and I hope my heart will learne that lesson.

Oct: 11: God good to us in the season, a seed time never better, the dayes, warm, and dry(.) the lord good in my families health, I found my heart in and under the providence of Dr Wrights death, calm. submissive to god, trusting in him, that he will of his mercy provide for mee, that my bread shall be sure and my waters not faile, oh lett mee not want an heart to love and serve this god, and to obey him with a perfect and an upright heart.

14: mett at my Ladie Honywoods to blesse god for M. Haynes recovery, and his goodnes to her family, where I endeavoured to speake closely and practically from Jacobs vow at Bethel,[1] I and my wife treated lovingly at my Ladies.

16: Maj: Haynes went from Markshall after nigh 8 weeks stay, god gave them a very good day for their jorney, it raining at night.

Oct: 18: God good to mee and mine in many outward mercies, for which I blesse him, my heart is stayed on him, oh that it might bee immoveable in his wayes, deliver mee lord from the rebellion and vanity of mind meditacon against thee, and practice that truth

[1] 'And Jacob vowed a vow, saying, If God will be with me, and will keep me . . . then shall the Lord be my God . . . and of all that thou shalt give me I will surely give the tenth unto thee.' Genesis 28: 20–2.

herein I preach to others. god was good to mee in the Sabbath, the lord in christ accept of mee and doe mee good.

Oct: 28: I ended Crows and Days difference, a son suing the mother of his wife for a promise of the father in marriage, I found a strange spirit in persons, but the widdow treated us very freindly and freely.

29. preacht at Cogshal from Job. 14.14. saw osburne as I came home a poore sicke man loth to bestow any comfort on himselfe in his sicknes

31: Heard of Mr Cresseners endeavours to gett a schoolemaster into ☞ towne, lord I have been cast upon thee from my youth, I pray thee in much mercy take the care of mee, for as a poor minister none regardeth my subsistance, and by thy grace and helpe I will spend thes Satturdayes more carefully.

Nov: 1: The Lord was good to mee and mine in outward mercies, my heart readie to meditate discontent in some unkind passages of neighbours, lord doe thou heale and pardon all I pray thee, I committ my selfe with confidence to thy provision for mee, doe not thou faile mee nor forsake mee I intreat thee, god was good to mee in the Sabbath and word for which I blesse his holy name.

2. ended a difference between poore Layer and a souldier who wounded him, the souldier gave him 18^{s}. a warning to take heed of quarrelling, Robert Abbott came to us from London, not daring to see his freinds they are so unnatural to him

3. 4: I dispatched mine, and all the businesses intrusted on my hands at Courts. for which I blesse god, Mr Cressener acquainted mee that my Lord of Oxfords Chaplain[1] was come to town and he thought about the schoole. Mr R.H. made some proffers in it, and I desired to observe god therein, but my owne inclinations rather tend to lay it wholly by, desirous god would open some helpe to mee in carrying on the worke of the ministry.

7. Tom Hodson, came to borrow of mee 20^{li}. I wondred at my Cosins boldnes, who had for his mother and selfe borrowed 5^{li}. and never yet paid it. it greiveth mee that relations are so unworthy not to bee trusted, god delivered mee from a dangerous blow on my eye by reason of a chip flying on it, blessed bee my preserver, I had such a meditation before on my heart in my sermon studdies, and presently had the experience. at night I heard Tibbalds house whereof two parts are mine was on fire only spied presently

[1] Dr. Samuel Pullein (1598–1667); first master of Leeds Grammar School, 1624, collated to a prebend in St. Patrick's Cathedral, Dublin, 1642, and Bishop of Tuam in 1661. DNB.

and quencht. lord what cause have I to remember thee in thy wayes.

No: 8: A very cheerfull day, god continued his goodnes to us in familie, oh that our hearts were firmely knit to him, that wee might not swerve from the way of his statutes. the lord giveth mee experience of the lurking evil in my heart, and the vanitie therof, oh the treachery of my heart, and its prones to steale out to evil, no boy so readie to slip out to his sport, oh when lord wilt thou save helpe and deliver mee.

9. sent Mr W: Hauksbee his books to his brother Richard by Nicholas
☞ Hurrell, received in good store of moneys which enabled mee to pay all my debts. Dr Pullein sent mee an offer to procure mee the schoole, if I would helpe him to his living, I had no desire therto, my tenant Fisher was paying mee 15^{li}. I feare its rather a temptacon then a providence, yet Mr R.H. jun: will consult about it.

mee a good day in prayer at the priory. oh what a mercy it is to have a god to have recourse to in all states, such a freind is a comfort indeed

13. In Searching my heart before the sacrament I find I am too neglectfull of private and very dead in family prayer. as also in reading the word in my family, and personal and particular instructing of my litle ones, leaving it to my catechising them and to my wife, and some constant questions; I find I doe not digest my sermons into. my head as formerly, I desire to see and bemoan thes among other evils, and resolve by grace more diligently to watch over my heart and wayes herein lord Jesus remember me with grace and mercy

15. God good to us in many outward mercies, my son Tho: very full of pimples and spotts all over, lord take care of him for thy name sake I pray thee, this day wee broke bread, god good therin unto mee ingaging my heart to him, lord I desire to bee more active, up and doing for thee in my place, and I roule my soule on thee to take care of mee, for unto thee doe I committ my soule. I hope to bee more serious, and not frothy and light in discourse, more intent on my studdies, more diving into thy truths, more carefull of family, more active in my imployment, and sedulous therein.

17. Mrs Marg: Harlakenden having laid out 120^{li}. at London, about wedding clothes, her father being exceeding angry, I appeased him, so that though he chid her by letter for her vanitie, yett he paid the scores.

No: 22. God good to mee, and mine in our healths free from agues that raine generally, the lords name bee blessed for it, he is the god of all my mercies and I will praise him(.) I was very ill with a cold, yett I found no hurt by preaching in a bitter day, the lord remember mee in mercy. Mr Har: writt nothing of my busines from London I leave my selfe on the love of my heavenly father, he knoweth what is best.

25. received my copies of my two fift parts of the farme on Colne Green from my Cosin Josselin(.) that purchase cost mee about 310li. god blesse it to mee and mine

26. word was sent mee Dr Pullein would bee with mee next morning, I knew not his busines, neither what to say. psal. 32.8. was my ending exercise and meditation(.) I am very duobtful what to doe, say. lord I know not but to thee I looke, thou hast been my freind and councellor, cutt out a right way, and lead mee to that which is most aggreable to thy minde; thou keepest my eye waking, thy providence doth not anyway determine itselfe, or my heart, but in thy issue will I bee silent if thou call mee of from this imployment and proffit

27. Dr Pullein was with mee, shewed mee his grant from my Lord, he lost the living, for which I am sorry, and I the schoole, gods will be done, I doe not find any trouble on my spirit in it, he desired mee to teach the schoole till spring for halfe the proffits, I consented, lord I blesse thee for that kindnes and mercy, I have more from thee therein, then I can have from many of mine this is an answer of thy love, and respect unto mee;—I received from London my augmentacon order from Major Haynes, and nothing done in it, I also received Dr Pulleins certificate, and perceive they have done nothing therein. Mr Sparrow signed it, but I cannot apprehend they are able to reverse any thing done,

Nov. 29. God good to mee, under my tedious cold, I sleep well in the night, my voice holds, the lord is good in our peace, a trouble this morning in the march of the souldiers, which I conceive were for Sweden, my heart more calm and quiet then formerly, oh that I might find more of his grace and spirit every day, god was good to mee in the word and worke this Sabbath, though such was my illnes and my heart so unspirited therewith, that I was even meet and fitt for nothing.

30. dispatcht Edward Mr R.H. man to London, with divers letters, the lord shew mee kindnes in the busines above, if he see it bee for my good, and in his will I sitt downe,

Dec. 2. lent W. Reyner to pay Mr Jacob his rent 10li. it was a hard venture, but I hoped god would shew mee kindness and I could not withold my bowels from a widdow

3. Spent some time in prayer at Mr Cresseners, the lord good to mee therein, about that time at London, Dr Pullein's busines, was put to that issue, that if the E. Oxford would stand by his presentacon of Dr Pullein, he might come into his living(,) the lords name bee praised for this kindnes, the issue is in thy hand oh father

5. Riding over to the E of Oxfords to Bently hall, and speaking with Dr Pullein a full issue was put to that treaty about the schoole: I not having it, in which disposall of god I desire to bee satisfied, and sitt down contentedly knowing that he will order and direct every thing for good to mee, I was very sicke at night and vomited which I judged a mercy to mee,

Dec: 6: god good to mee in strength for the Sabbath, as also in other mercies, good to mee in the word, the lord (– – – se) his goodnes to mee to dwell in my spirit and abide with mee ingaging my heart unto him, the lord remember mee in supporting mee in the worke of the ministry in Earles Colne if it been his good pleasure,

8. Talke as if some uprore in the kingdom, the militia horse suddenly called togither and the army foot called of again towards the sea:

9: Heard how my brother John Humfreys left hand had a sore bred on it, wherby he lost 2 joynts of one finger, and feared worse, it being a festering thisteloe,[1] my son Tom: hath had a dangerous cut and sore on each leg, and cured by his mother, but the blessing came from above, others miseries should make my mercies rellish more sweet, I shall not only pitty and pray for them, but open my hand to him, lord doe thou heale him for thy mercy sake.

12. Saw a booke esp: of Welsh prophecies, which asserts that Cromwell is the great Conqueror that shall conquer Turke and Pope. I have many years on scripture grounds, and revolutions judged him or his government and successors. but esp. my heart fixt on him, to bee most great. but sad will bee things to Saints and him, this booke of prophecies giveth mee no satisfaction, but perhaps may sett men a gadding to greaten him

December 13. God was good to us in outward mercies, only my deare wife ill with toothake shee draweth neare her time. the lord keepe her therin, heard of the sad providence of god to Mr Cressener his wives brother Coll: White being cast away at sea, shee fell in travel miscarried and is very ill, the lord shew mercy to them(,) this renders gods providence more sweet to mee, the word was comfortable to mee this day,

[1] Thesteloe: probably a variant on thistolow, an altered form of fistolow or fistula, a long sinuous pipe-like ulcer with a narrow orifice. NED.

15. Mrs Margarett Harlakenden married to Mr John Eldred, her father kept the wedding three dayes, with much bounty. it was an action mixt with pietie, and mirth, die. 18. the company departed the priory. god gave an eminent answer of prayer to him and mee in providing her so good an housband beyond expectation. oh great desire is, god would fitt her for her relation and bestow his blessing on them therein(.) Mr Bridegroom gave mee 1^{li}. and Mr H. 1^{li}. god in mercy requite their love and bounty.

19. Rid to Dunmow returned safe, spake with all persons conveniently, wherby I was fully informed of the state of my busines in my augmentacon rent from Dunmow(.) when I came home I found my wife had gotten sprats, which though a smal thing was a great mercy shee much longing to eat of them before shee lay down,[1] and that shee daily looked for, Mr R. Harlakenden the younger lovingly accomodated mee with his horses, the lord recompense that and all the love he hath shewn to mee.

Decemb. 20: God good to mee in outward mercies, I find through sloth, and neglect I am very dead in praying and preaching, the lord awaken and quicken mee, my desire was to speake a word in season to our young bride, from Pro. 14.1. the wise woman building her house god grant it, and that shee may not plucke hers down which is her good fathers feare.

21. writt to Mr Heynes about Dunmow busines, lord in mercy looke after mee therein(,) I sent up my order to him with 2 acquittances in my letter.

23: preacht at Buers on Cant: 1.4. it was my desire to doe christ some service, some hearts were affected, lord worke them over to feare thy name truly. returned backe 6^{d}. overplus mony that I received in a sume.

December 27. a very sweet winter day, cold, but dry and calme, god good to mee and to my relacions, in outward mercies, and I trust in inward in drawing out our hearts to walke in his pathes, and to delight our soules in him, it was in my desire to dismisse our young bride Mrs Eldred, (both having been bountifull to mee and mine) with counsell and prayer, lord lett it bee blessed of thee unto them. if it bee worth writing this tels that raisins of the sun were sold at 12. 14. 16. 18^{d}. per pound.

29. rid to Stanaway with Mr Harl: company, carrying home the young

[1] Lay down: to bring to bed of a child. NED. Thus, during late pregnancy. It was orthodox medical doctrine that if a pregnant woman was denied a food she longed for, she would miscarry, or the child might be birth-marked. Eccles.

bride, who hath a mercy in a mother in law, if shee know how to value it, god spirit her for her relation. wee had a safe jorney, bounteous entertainment.

30. I returned to my bigge wife whom god kept in my absence, and indeed is the keeper who ever is present,

31. went down to Wakes and preacht Mr Tomson failing, whose wife was that morning delivered of her 7 daughter and 9 child in about 10 yeares, which I blesse god for, hoping this providence will make the midwife more ready for my wife.

Jan: 3. God good to us in the mercies of this life for mee and mine. young Mr H. not well god restore him and continue his health, heard of the sad condicon of my uncle Simon Josselins children, all going ill with them, lord its mercy our blessings were not theirs, and their miseries ours. god good in the word this day, my heart mindfull of my wife, lord remember her in mercy.

5. A savoury meeting about death; that is the robbing the creature of its excellency, and rendring it base, the wages of sin. lord lett words spoken dwell with mee I pray thee. this day my good freinds Mr Harlakenden the younger and his wife gave mee 25^{s}. as an [entrance into a way of bounty] which was alwayes great to mee. Lord it is for my sake, and my works [for mercy] doe it. I pray remember them in mercy and returne their labour of love to them and theirs, this is a new spring thou hast opened thy name bee blessed, their bounty is duobly welcome, because its from hartie freinds and I love to bee indebted to such.

7: God gave mee a very savoury word from Rom. 6.23. at Wakes Lecture, where I ventured to preach a sermon from the discourse I made theron almost ex tempore at our private meeting, I hope it was an useful word. the minister failed in his course.

8: a Hearer at Halsted lecture, received an Order to bee an Assistant in Ejecting of Ministers and schoolemasters for insufficiency, had the offer of two schollers, which I undertake to teach, the lord helpe mee in all my callings.

9. Received two letters from unknown persons at London relating the sad condicon of Robert Abbott once of our town, a great enemy to the ministry, and gods worship, and afterward reclaimed, a person of a family manisfesting much ill will unto mee, to whom I did shew kindnes, he seemed reclaimed, but crosses in his marriage and losse in his estate and some hand of god hath brought him to a sad state, if not distracted and enthusiast then farre worse, I feared ill would bee the porcon of those persons, lord open

their eyes and shew them their evill and pardon and heale I pray thee.

Jan: 10: God good to us in many outward mercies, the lord enable mee to walke suitable to his goodnes, my wife holds up her head still, let thy providence appeare in timing things for her, the lord good in the Sabbath, oh lett thy grace appear in upholding mee that nothing may thrust out of thy pathes.

12. Baptized my neighbour Burtons son, at night the midwife with us, my wife thinking shee might use her, but being sent for my wife let her goe, that another that was in present need might bee holpen, and it was a mercy to us so to dispose my wives heart, her going tending to save a poore womans life, but within halfe an houre, as soon as I had done family prayer, my wife had so sure a signe of her labour and speedie that put us all to a plunge, I sent 2 messengers after her and it was at least 4 houres before shee came. Mr R.H. man fetcht her, but shee came time enough for us god bee praised, my wife was wonderfully afraid and amazed but helpe was speedily with her and in particular young Mrs Harlakenden, who put forth her selfe to the utmost to helpe her, and her presence was much to my wife.

13. her pains ceased, the labour very strange to her, which sett her heart, but her eye was towards him who is the helper(,) my faith was up for her, shee judged at the labour it would bee a daughter. contrary to all her former experience and thought; prayer was for her; wee comended her to god and her warm bed early and all to their rests, none watching this night as formerly. her sleep was a comfort to her mixed with pain, feare, which made her quake and tremble

14. and so increased on her by two of the clocke in this morning that I called up the midwife, and nurse, gott fires and all redie, and then her labour came on so strongly and speedily that the child was borne only 2 or 3 women more gott in to her but god supplied all, young Mrs Harlakenden gott up to us very speedily, and some others; my wives labour was different from all former exceeding sharpe, shee judged her midwife did not doe her part, but god did all, and hath given us new experience of his goodnes, the child was dead when borne, I blesse god who recovered it to life, wee baptized it this day by the name of Mary, young Mrs Harlakenden holding it in my wives place god hath evened my number and made up the three which he tooke from mee my heart was very lightsom and joyful in the god of my mercies

15. 16. my wife very well, a tedious cold time our child was borne with a sore my wife thinketh done with lying neare one of her short ribs

Jan: 17. God good to us in all outward mercies, in the Sabbath, the word was very lively and pretious to mee, the lord in mercy own mee and doe mee and mine good all our dayes.

20: My wife upwards blessed bee god this day(,) the weather changed, the frost and snow going away with an unexpected raine, last night being very cleare and frizing very earnestly, this day on such a change the Parliament was to sitt, god keepe them from doing evill, my prayers earnest to god this morning

21: this day again was an hard blacke frost, with snow die 22. wednesday only being a wett day between(.) my wife upward. R.A. with mee, he told mee how his wife kept him bound in bed to force him to sell his lands, well its a mercy to bee kept upright in our wayes, and delivered from unreasonable persons. I suspend my thoughts in such matters.

23. having made many searches for my copies of clarks, and cats croft, this day on the view of the rolls I concluded they were in Mrs Churches hands.

Jan. 24. The Lord good to mee and mine outward mercies, my wife upwards, as shee rests in the night so comonly shee is in the day, so hee giveth his beloved sleep doe it lord for her, my god accept my praise for his mercy. I never had so much care of the family on mee, having litle helpe in those about mee, indeed our cousin, a cosener rather than a helpe no trust being in her, which made my wife more deare to mee, it was a good Sabbath to mee, the lord uphold mee in his wayes, litle is our encouragement, but what wee have from him, and he is our freind, the season was very cold, the lord bee blessed who provideth for us against the difficulties therof

25. This day was the last of my 41. yeare, in which god hath been with mee and blessed mee, and though Dr Wrights death cutt mee short in the schoole, yett I find my heart quiett, rowling it selfe on god, and no way questioning his providence to take care of mee. Gen. 28.15. god hath been with mee in all places, and I trust he will in all times, he will keepe mee and he will heepe with mee, my boast is of him, he is my sheild, in him I will rejoyce, god hath given mee three children instead of 3 more which I had buried, and thus my ☞ dreame of 3 shoots in my parlor cutt down and growing up againe is made good, the lord spare their lives, and throughly sanctifie them.

When I view my inward state godward, my heart witnesseth its integritie to the lord and his christ, and his worship desiring in all things to keepe a good conscience, yet many are my failings, the pardon wherof my soule beleiveth through christ, my eye is on eternitie, and my hopes are to find favour with god, lord I blesse thee for what you hast wrought in mee, faile not the worke, the new worke of thy hands: Abroad in the world matters are likely to bee sad, yet I find not the apostacy to increase, this yeare the Emp. of Germany died, and no other yet chosen in his stead, his son the K of Hungary assisted Poland wherby the Swedes are driven into prussia. The P of Transilvania forced to retreate home, and was deposed for his attempt to please the Turke. Brandenburg made peace with the Pole and left Swede. the Moscovite was in a manner quiet this summer yet the Swede brusht him a litle in Livonia. Denmarke invaded the Swede in Bremeland, to his losse in Juitland, the Hollander proclaimed warre against Portugal and tooke part of the Brasile fleete: The English assisted France against Spain and gott footing in Flanders, the Venetians beate the Turke, but in the winter he regaind some Iles as Tenedos, the Turke hath issue male. the Q of Spain delivered of a sonne the King 53 yeares old and no son til now, the affaires in Italy and Catalonia not very boisterous. the Spaniards invaded Portugal by land and tooke some places, thus warre breaks out, but no eminent matter was done in the world, the English protector setled by Parliament and a house of Lords in title erected January 20th.

— — — — — — — — — — — — — — — — — — —

Jan: 26. 1657. my 42. yeare enters

26: Sensible this day ended my 41 yeare and begun my 42. the eye of the lord bee on mee for good through the same, I was invited to dinner, and 3 persons paid mee in moneys a comfort to my outward estate. schoole rents, own estate, and as minister, I had the comfort of my loving freinds Mr and Mrs H. the younger, by whom I heard of Capt. Garrads proud carriage, its hard to bee humble in advancement.

28. old Robert Abbott[1] of our town being arrested by Mr H. for his tithes which come to 3^{li}. and which he might have received within

[1] Among those noted as prisoners for tithes in Colchester gaol in the period 1656–9 was Robert Abbott of Colne (Besse, i, p. 194), though he does not appear in contemporary Assize indictments or gaol calendars.

20s. went to prison, refusing to appear by an attorney, poore person he accounts to pay or take tith is to deny Christ come in the flesh, and is as outwardly bold, and confident in his suffering, as if some great service for Christ. lord leave me not under the power of a delusion.

Jan: 31: God good to mee and my family in our outward mercies, my wife and babe well only the child froward, this was one of the bitterest dayes for cold I ever felt the wind being in the East, and coming over the snow, but this frost is a mercy purifying the ayre from the former malignity in the summer, oh that my heart could meditate of gods goodnes, the lord good to mee in the word and worke of the Sabbath wherein I desire acceptance and for which I blesse the name of my god

Feb: 1: Our nurse an honest harmeles quiet women went from us on the 20th day, my wife and child very well, and my trust is god will bee a nurse, and helpe unto them; shee was sent for unto another Dame whom shee had promised. Mr R.H. went toward London

3. Heard R. Abbot was quite distracted, lord keepe and helpe mee my trust is in thee. Reported and afterwards confirmed by letter that the Protector had on Thursday before dissolved the Parliament which was true, wee shall see what he intends, and what successe his affaires have abroad, is this synodus per ipsum convocata et minis dissoluta.[1]

Feb. 7. My wife very ill, I hope the occasion good for her body and spirit, putting her in minde of gods mercy, and making it new and fresh, god blew over the qualme, the lord in mercy ingage us to close walking with him, the season wonderfull cold, much snow god provided for us against such a day, stocke my heart against death and changes(.) the lord good to mee in the Sabbath, and the word and duty thereof, the lord own and accept mee in his beloved.

12. after a long and sharpe frost, and great aboundance of snow, the weather broke very gently, giving some 2 dayes before, but now it thawed indeed, this frost brought up wonderfull plenty of wildefoule on the coast, sold cheap and plenty: A knowne person to mee Taller and his wife dieth within a weeke of one another, blessed bee god who preserved my wife who was in very great danger.

Feb. 14. God good to us in many outward mercies, comfortable rest the last night which is as new life to my wife, my hoaresenes such that one would have judgd I should not have preacht, yet in the night my throat not so hoarse, but I spake pretty intelligibly, the season

[1] 'Is this a synod assembled by itself and destroyed by trifles.'

frosty but yet cleare, sunshine and chearefull; Times are sad in regard of the rupture of Parliament. some great thing likely to bee acted in the government, yet wee are secure, said the protector demands great sums of mony of the City, 1300000^{li}. the lord was good to mee in the Sabbath, I find my heart trembling at his word, in the sense of my own evill, oh lord heale and helpe.

15. I dreamed at night I was condemned to die for religion, another ☞ minister with mee and some women also, I was somewhat afraid at first in my spirit afterwards very comfortable, I was in wonderfull large roome matted, but I awaked before execution, I remember not the points on which done.

16. Heard Grove Hall Major Haines house was burnt downe, lord my preservations from fire are thy mercies still continue them,

Feb. 21: God good to mee and mine in many outward mercies, my deare wife groweth upwards very comfortably, is up and downe in the house, gods name bee praised, my two sons well in respect of their sores which might have been very dangerous, my heart is full of vain musings, oh lord when shall they bee healed, the word this day very comfortable unto mee, oh lett it abide, let experimented goodnes draw up my heart to a fixed setled confidence in god at all times:

22. I bestowed on my daughter Jane a silver tankard cost. 4^{li}. 16^{s}. on John a porringer[1] cost 36^{s}. whereof Mrs Eldred gave him 32^{s}. and on An a spoone of 10^{s}. which Mrs Abbott gave her, the first plate of value that ever I bought(.) this day Dr Pullein here, he hired the Justices house, and intends to come over very speedily, though the schoole bee a great losse unto mee, yet god will provide for mee, and perhaps it may tend very much to my good and my childrens and many others, in and for which I should very heartily rejoyce.

22. rid to Wethersfeild god good to mee in my jorney, and in the dispatch of my busines, my Cosin Ab. Josselin with mee from New-England, hear of Mr Tompsons feavour the lord raise him up

Feb: 28. God good in the season to us, my wife went abroad to church with mee for the which mercy I gave him heartie thanks; god is good in his word, lord cause it to dwell and abide on my spirit bringing forth fruite to perfection, lord teach us to live togither honouring thy name before our litle ones

March. 2: This day mett in conference at my house, wee buried An

[1] Porringer: a small basin or the like, from which soup, porridge, etc., is eaten. SOED.

Willows at our chardge it cost us 16s. lord thou thinest our number, multiply our grace wee pray thee.

March. 7. God good to mee in outward things for which my soule blesseth him, my heart is fully sensible of my carelesnes in the great worke of the ministry for which god may justly have a controversie with mee, lord helpe mee against it to bend my mind more seriously to this worke then ever, oh lett my soule find favour with thee I pray thee.

13. kept a day of prayer at Mr H. at the Priory who was sicke of the ague.

March: 14: I was in a very dead frame, without sense and life in my spirit, there was no sense or weight of sin on my spirit, no longings on my soule after Christ. I was much troubled to find my heart in this frame, I could not pray, nor meditate, nor bee solemne nor serious, but under great distractions of spirit, yea so on the lords day morning, but in morning prayer my heart was somewhat opened, and in the ordinance of the lords table affected, for which mercy my soule blesseth god. Major Haynes joyned with us in breaking bread but good Mr H. was sicke at home, lord thou remembrest mee with thy presence and favour and I will praise thee: I administred the sacrament to Mr H. at his house at priory. the lord raise him up and restore him to perfect health.

15. newes of dangers at home by risings, and from spain by landing men out of Flanders(.) Mr R.H. went towards Worcester, god direct his jorney and returne. I have parted with all the books out of my studdy that were borrowed of my freinds, and am now left to my own stocke.

18: A cold time beyond former yeares, and a very backward spring, I preacht suddenly for Mr Tompson, where I prest sinners from the willingnes of god to save them to return(.) oh lord how glad I am to deliver the glad tidings of the gospel to sinners, oh lord let them bee gladly embraced. Mr H. ague very gentle, god restore him perfectly, his son hath a sad jorney to Worcester, the lord bee his guide and safeguard.

19. John escaped a fall into the fire, god eminently helping his mother to catch him by the backe and hold him up til another helpt him, his sister Jane lookt on amazed and stirred not, gods goodnes bee exalted.

March. 21: God good to us in many particular outward mercies in and for which my soule truly blesseth him, his providences towards mine ought to bee remembred and had in thankfull observation, god was good to mee in the word and worke of the Sabbath, I was aforehand for it, I blesse god, I am sure thou art not behind with mee in mercies, god good to mee in the mercies of some freinds(.) heard of Good Mr Pecks death, the lord fitt mee for that change, an interest in Christ is the onely fitting for it.

1658: 25. My Cosin Abraham Josselin went from mee towards his wife in New England. I gave him 10^{s}. in mony. Reyners works[1] a booke of great use for his soule and family gloves, and divers things testimonies of my love, I sent a relation of the affaires in Europe until this time to my Cosin Henry Josselin at blackepoint in New England in the province of Ligonia, Grace Josselin also went backe to her brother god may make mee to find favour with others in their plenty and my straits,

26: When I come to review my estate. this yeare I find the schoole going from me by Dr Wrights death, wherof I am not so much sad to part with it, as thankfull god lett mee enjoy it so long; yet I begge pardon from god that I attended no better to it while I had it, nor my ministry, which might bee greivous to my god, I am resolved through grace to attend my studdies and preaching more then ever, lord lett mee bee blessed therin. God hath given mee a daughter the lord enter into Covenant with her, my mind here of late more distraught with worldly fond musings then some yeares formerly, lord my helpe is in the assistance of thy grace and spirit through christ, helpe, helpe, and quicken my endeavours and watch for my hope is sett in thee and my expectation is from thee, my soule liveth by faith on god my righteousnes and strength, assailed with feares but not shaken, faith in christ being thereof my victory, god giveth witnesse to the truth and integritie of my heart with him,

For my outward estate. I am out on Mrs. Maries land: 114^{li}. at least

Lands as last yeare only I have paid for the land on the Green fine, and all charges it amounted in whole unto. -	309. 7. 4.

I have paid all my debts, and owe not 5^{s}. any where that I know of, for which particular moneys are not assigned, and laid by, my stocke ☞ is about. 600 that I desire to preserve as an estate for my children which is more then I had in all last yeare.—I have gathered 36^{li}.

[1] Edward Reyner (1600–68), a congregationalist minister, ejected in 1662, among whose works was *Precepts for Christian Practice* (8th edn., 1655). Thomason, E. 1451.

towards Tom's prentiship, and assigned the arrears of my augmentation due Sept. 29. past, all rents, and moneyes due on bond until this time which I hope will make that sum up an 100(.) this yeare was deepe in expences costing mee about 110^{li}. and yet I blesse god I received in above an 100^{li}. more unto my estate, this is gods blessing alone his good will with what I have is better then lands and treasure: god hath added a child to my number I intend henceforward to bring into one receipt all my arreares of tith, quarters augmentation, and what ariseth from my ministerial imploiment towards my housekeeping, which if it effect and adde but 10^{li}. yearely to my estate I shall have no thoughts of any thing but blessing god in reference to my estate. however I shall endeavour to bee thankfull and contented.

what ariseth out of my own private estate the tenth deducted as formerly I desire to lay by intire for the good of my family. I have about 3^{li}. in cash for my expence, and good round summes in arreares. I comitt my wayes unto thee, I pray thee smile upon mee. For thy christ my Jesus sake.

27. Heard Mr Harlakenden came safe to his jorneys end, after a very tedious, wett and dangerous jorney.

March 28. God good to mee and mine in many outward mercies, the time very full of feares and troubles, god was good to mee in the word, it was sweet and pleasing to my case, lord make mee lively, and readie in thy pathes I intreate thee. I finde my heart much cumbred with bootles musings and foolish, lord wilt thou not helpe

29. rid to my Cosin Johnsons.—30. preacht Wittam Lecture psal. 78.8. pressing to stedfastnes, saw my freinds, who were well, god good to mee in my jorney and in divers of my affaires, lord I see many things in other families, that I blesse thy name are not in mine.

April. 3. Mr R.H. by gods blessing returned safe from his tedious jorney unto Worcester(,) god is able to protect and keepe safe; Mrs Jane gave mee the first mony this yeare another neighbour sent us in a pig, blessed bee god for any love.

April. 4: A cold wett day, wee trust and hope god will in mercy rebuke the winde, and call for the spring, but lord call for flowings forth, and aboundings in my soule towards god, the lord was a helpe to mee in the Sabbath. Bat. Clarke that had quite laid by the publique worship and was hankering after Quakers and any thing returned to hearing the word preacht this day and last, I knowe not his roote Lord, thou dost, keepe him in it if thou delight to have it so.

5. The weather was moist which gave hope to breake the wind and

cold, grasse sprang it is the backwardest spring I thinke I ever knew
Martha: 6: Gibson towards night came to us, lord make her a blessing to us, I hope shee will be a good example to our children, lord I blesse thee for the hopes I have of mercy in a servant.
9. preacht at Halsted from I Tim: 6:6. of the gain of godlines, lord I believe it and I trust I shall find it, for I professe godlines is my great portion and its great.
April: 11. A very sweete day. I blesse god for his mercy and goodnes unto mee in my affaire with my Cosin Blondell my heart is often under amazement. but yet I finde vanity returning on mee and taking hold on my minde oh when wilt thou heale mee oh Lord: wee read this day the lamentable relation of the usage of the poles churches by the papists, the relation pend to gain, there is craft in thes things as well as truth, our state by pittying them endeavour to gain favour and estate among forreine churches, but out of bowels to christ and to them as my brethren I shall by word and act helpe to succour them. lord doe thou pitty them. God was good to mee in the word, and worke of the Sabbath for which I blesse him
13. Returnd well from Mr Tompsons whose life god hath spared, lord lett him live to keepe thy word. Jane went again to Mrs Piggots, lord blesse her
14: preacht at Buers on Ezech. 33.11. the lord bee a blessing unto mee and the word
16. Mr H[s]. and I had a comfortable jorney, and fishing with Mr Eldred at Cornards mill in Suffolke. observed the minister a good man and frugall with 4 children and worth nothing, having onely a bare present subsistance. lord thou hast richly provided for mee and mine,
17. rid to Colchester, about union of churches and livings, Lady Honywood paid my ordinary. Jane well, god gave us a safe returne.
Ap: 18: God good to us in many outward mercies, I gathered this day for the Poles, and Bohemians that were massacred and turned out of all for religion sake and the hand of god was with mee for good, wee gathered. 6^{li}. 9^{s}. 10^{d}. ob. The lord accept it in Christ, our goodnes cannot reach thee, oh Lord, I heartily desire it may thine and that it may. god was good in the word, my heart is cumbred with much busines, and not so fitted for the Sabbath, the lord pardon and accept.
19. My litle Ann went abroad to learne her booke, the lord give a blessing to her therin. Mrs Eliz: Harlakenden began to bee ill, and

died 21. in the morning, the lord sanctifie, this stroke to us all, wee may live in order unto death, preparing for it, that when it cometh wee may welcome it.

22. Eliz: Harlakenden buried heard of the death of Young Game suddain, the lord helpe us to consider our latter end and prepare for it, in a holy life, and in getting sure evidences for heaven, the exhortacion I prest on all.

24: Wee heard and it was true, That a Keamer[1] of Cogshall one of the gathered[2] church there, a man orderly in his life, hanged himselfe ☞ on a beam in the chamber where he was at worke, he did it with his working straps. lord what is man if you leave him, temptacions easily swallow him up. lord keepe mee mine, and all thine, oh thou preserver of men.

April. 25: God good to mee in outward mercies, my heart in amazement at the apprehension of eternity. but thy goodnes oh lord it upholdeth mee, the lord is my stay as he is in christ, else I should bee like them that goe downe into the pitt: god was good to mee in the day, duty, enjoyment. my heart had divers sweet refreshings from god, the lord satisfie mee with his kindnes, I gathered this day for Poland, my gleanings a litle vintage. 15^{s}. 2^{d}.

27. alarmd as if Goodman Mathew were dying suddenly. I hasted and found it a fainting fit, he was troubled his estate was not disposed so that his wife should enjoy it, but that wee did the next day to his content he was very cheerfull,[3] I judge it is an ague. god make us rise so to setled our hopes in god that death may not hurt us. Mrs Pullein in towne in a vapouring way, lord keepe my heart low and humble

May. 1: received an account of the families that seldome heare publiquely giving onely 5^{d}. to Poland the residue refusing, and using ill language of them as Heathens(,) lord if thou shew not mercy to them sinners, where are they. I shall a litle note the way of gods providence towards them.

May. 2. God good to mee, and mine, in many outward mercies, in which the lord accept mee, my voice held this day beyond expectation, my sermons this day about worldly mindednes were close, and nipping, god make them profitable(.) god good to mee in my mind, it reposeth on him, yet unkindnesses boile in mee but I finde faith

[1] Keamer: kember or comber, one who combs (wool). SOED.

[2] Gathered church: i.e. Congregationalists.

[3] Christopher Mathew, householder, was not, in fact, buried until 28 August 1670, by which time he had made a will (on 22 October 1669) in which his 'loving wife' was his residuary legatee (ERO, 34 CR 9).

and prayer excellent leeches for my spirit. a great mortality at London about 580. in this weeks bill.[1]

6: preacht at Wakes the lord make the word a blessing, at night my sister Anna was with mee from Haverill, who hath utterly undone her selfe and her children by a second marriage, lord bee the guide of mee and mine in all wayes, lord from thee I pitty her, thou of thy selfe canst helpe her lord I pray thee doe it.

8: This Evening Mr Harlakenden was alaramed that the E. of oxford had taken out a writt of Formedon[2] against him about his Estate. lord take care of them I pray

May. 9. God good to mee in outward mercies, in our health, when many sicke and some die suddenly, the season tending to fruitfulnes, my heart through mercy not so encombred with vanities and perplexities, I desire to roule my soule on god as on one, who taketh care of mee

10. Mr Cresseners daughter Sibilla baptized(,) I spake from psal. 128: the word was good to mee and the ordinance, I had else litle comfort in my being there.

13: Bought some books and an old gowne of Mrs Laney, thus others will have dominion over the worke of my hands, but my soule is oh lord in thy hand and for thee oh Lord onely: Lord order my outward affaires in my estate comfortable I intreate thee.

May. 16. God good to mee and mine in outward mercies, lord I pray the(e) continue it in kindnes to my posterity, and keepe them for thy names sake, my heart is not so sett on my ministeriall imployment as it ought, oh raise mee up to spiritualnes, and cheerfulnes in thy worship and service I pray thee, god was good to mee in the Sabbath, I gave notice of the fast for next Wednesday having order to keepe it.

19. A Day of fasting in regard of a sicknes very general in London and many places in the contry, the lord in mercy accept of mee in my desire to serve him, I expounded. Gen. 19. Abrahams suite from Sodom, I treated of repentance. the lord give mee grace and heart to returne to him, the lord shew mercy to my litle ones, and accept them and give them health and preserve them.

May. 23. God good to mee in many outward mercies, I was very busy

[1] These were the weekly Bills of Mortality for London, published from 1603 onwards; a facsimile of a weekly bill is published in W. G. Bell, *The Great Plague in London in 1665* (revised edn., 1951), opp. p. 20. This facsimile gives the totals for the week 15 to 22 August 1665 as plague 4,237, in all 5,568; RJ under the date 27 August 1665 gives identical figures.

[2] Writ of formedon: a writ of right used for claiming entailed property. SOED.

this weeke in the feild about my wood, wherin god was good and mercifull unto mee, the weather begins to bee warme having been cold which was a great mercy in respect of health a hott may would have been more dangerous in this sickly time, the lord good to mee in keeping in my minde from running out after vanitie, the lord in mercy fixe my heart on himselfe, as my all in all my wayes. imployment is better for bodye and minde then idle withdrawing from action.

27. preacht at Wakes, and went to Copford, thence 28. to Mr Eldreds where I was welcome. saw how well god hath provided for Mrs Margarett. the fruit of prayer(.) the good lord in every condicon and strait helpe mee beleivingly to roule my soule upon him.

June. 3. I returned home god bee praised. the season very wett, meadowes under in some places(.) lord remember mee in much mercy.

June. 6. God good to us in outward mercies as also in the season, which was drying and this evening very cleare. I blest god for the great abatement of the sicknes in London bills being about the ordinary number, I prayed heartily for a good season, the lord was good to mee in the word of repentance this day preacht, the lord in much mercy accept mee, and doe mee and mine good.

Henceforward lord helpe mee not to forgett the condicon of my son Thomas in my daily prayers, that thou wouldst choose his Mr trade, and blesse him in his way.

12. old Spooner buried. one Creake[1] of Cogshal there. I was used very hardly in words by him. lord, pardon any evil fell from mee this day. I am sensible that I spake unadvisedly, lord I bemoan it, heale mee I pray thee.

June: 13. God good to mee in many outward mercies the lord good to us in the season which is very hopefully fruitfull, wee broke bread this day. the lord good to mee in drawing in my heart to ingage in all faithfulnes to abide by the commands and ordinances of christ, and not depart from him, lord keepe it for ever in my heart and spirit I pray thee. god was good to mee in the sermon this afternoon about not delaying repentance, which as it was with affection on my part, so was with affection heard. lord worke out something by it in us all I pray thee.

16: mett in a day of praise at Mr Cressener, the lord holpe mee to

[1] Almost certainly Thomas Creek, a five-hearth householder of Little Coggeshall in 1662, who is mentioned as a Quaker sufferer in the years 1656–9 (Besse, i, p. 194), and who left a will in 1667 (ERO, 161 AW 1).

presse a truth very home the lord doe good by it surely to those persons(,) I am a very unacceptable person(,) I doe not thinke either so much as thanked mee. Lord my recompense is with thee. the day before I gave a great stroke to a purpose of parting families at the priory, and I hope I shall compose that busines quietly.

June. 20: God good to mee and mine in many outward mercies, in fruitful times and seasons in that comfortable measure of health, he affords, the lord affect my heart with all his bounty and goodnes continually. the lord a helpe to mee in the worke and businesse of the Sabbath, the lord in christ accept mee.

June. 27: Still god is gratious to us, the season very fruitfull and divers very good hay dayes last weeke, I received in this weeke part of a debt, which I never expected to have received viz. 7^{s}. 6^{d}. this was from gods providence that watcheth over mee to provide for mee. my heart is dead and heavy in dutie private and publique(,) I find my lively activenes for god abated, lord revive mee and renew mee as thou dost the face of the earth I pray thee.

July. 4, a good time for the season, plenty of hay, and faire warme weather, god good to us in our health, and in his provision for us, oh that I had an heart to honour him suitable to his great goodnes to mee. god was good to mee this day in the word preacht, it was close and home, the lord blesse it to mee and all others.

9. This day Dr Pullein came to towne, he is our schoolemaster(.) god make him a blessing to my children, and mee to him, the lord who hath shutt up this spring will provide for mee, that I shall want no good thing. and in him will I trust.

July. 11. God was good to us in outward mercies, John fared as if he would bee ill, and might have the measles. I submitt, thy will lord bee done, lett mee not bee senseles under thy hand, but lett my soule worke out its daily drosse and corrupcion; Dr Pullein a hearer with us, I trust the lord will bend my heart more to my studdies, and searching into the scriptures in this libertie I shall have, the schoole being to bee taught by an other. god was good to mee in the word preacht this day, the lord affect mee with all my deadnes, and sloth in the things of god, and awaken my heart for his glory.

12. dismist my schollers to Dr Pullein.

13. I preacht at the sessions on Isay. 53.10. the lord good to mee therin, his presence and assistance encouraging, I returned home die. 14. god mercifull to mee in all my jorney, I finde my body unfitt for travell, the mercy of god sweet to mee in preserving my litle ones, who are very weakly.

15. This day was the first day I was at home since my schollers were dismist and I sett it apart to humble my soule before god for all my sins in my relations, to seeke to god to pardon in christ. to beg his presence in my studdies, ministry, his blessing on my litle ones in their education and course of life, and that the lord would provide for mee, and mine upon whose love, and care I rowle my selfe, trusting I shall yett praise him.

16. My son John was entred with Dr Pullein our schoolmaster my sonne ☞ went thither the day before, the lord in much mercy blesse them

July. 17. I rid safe to Hatfeild Peverel, where I preacht, a very chearfull audience as also at Wittam(,) god use mee for his glory, I was helpeful to end my Cosin Blundels, and Johnsons businesse, as also to enlarge Betties present portion(,) god good to mee in my returne, but my mind vain, neither doth my heart rise up in christs power and strength against the same

21. a day of praise for many successes, kept by us at Colne. I preacht from Hosea. 2.7.8. my sister Humphry with mee, poore and sorely afflicted god open hearts to pitty and helpe her.

24: my sister Humfry went from us, and not empty, wee gave her such things as shee wanted and good, my litle Ann sicke of the measles, the lord in mercy sanctifie that providence and awaken my heart to uprightnes in doing his most holy will.

July. 25. God good to us in many mercies, my litle Ann very full of the measles, the lord doe mee good by this rod, use it as an advantage to my spirit, against the evill and vanity of my minde, the lord good to mee in the word it was an awakening word, lord looke after mee, and dwell in my soule to fixe and stablish it with thyselfe in thy pathes I pray thee.

31: My John very ill, as if he would have the measles, lord looke after him and nurse him for to the(e) I committ him, and sanctifie my heart, thou hast restored my daughter, and I trust thou wilt my sonne. heard this day of a certainty of the election of the Emperor on the 8. past wee heard it on the 24:—this man may ruine that house, although this election cause such joy unto them.

Aug: 1: God good to mee in many mercies, bee gratious in all the gentle strokes thou layest upon mine, ingage my heart more with thy selfe, against corruption, I intreate thee; I find my heart not disquieted in parting with the schoole revennew, the lord is all supplies, neither did I find much advantage therby to my studdies; but I trust and hope I shall, god was good to mee in the word, searching into the heart, the lord purge and pardon mee.

4: My daughter Jane came home from Colchester, John up and down againe my maide went home ill of the measles. Mary also had them, god good to us under thes in several wakenings of my spirit

Aug. 8: This day giving the blessing I abruptly gave over in the midle, thinking I was doing it a second time so weake and fraile is my memory from my heedlesnes, doing things with no strength, not drawing out in speech things I have throughly disgested and concocted, the lord make mee sensible of my evill therin and pardon it to mee in Christ Jesus. god good to mee in many outward mercies, my 2 litle ones abroad with mee this day, the lord bee in all things a blessing unto us.

9. My wife wonderfull ill with her teeth, and in the morning I hurt my eye very dangerously; god good to us both that wee found favour with him, not to bee destroyed, awaken my heart by thes providences I pray thee

12. Preacht Sister Wallers funeral sermon, god good to mee in the word the good laid up for mee in christ is my soules life, I was with Sir. J. Jacob, lord shew mee mercy in that affaire I humbly begge of thee, thou only art my close freind and helpest mee in my affaires.

Aug: 15. God good to us in the health of my family, men of opinion that corne will bee cheape notwithstanding the feare otherwise from the mildew, which if it bee but in some places will not raise the price, many great persons said to bee sicke, nothing can exempt from death, oh that I might not draw backe from constant duty, and service, god good to mee in the word and day, but my heart carelesse in providing for it. my eye very well again the lord have the praise of it, and lett mee use it to thy glory I pray.

21: Mr Elliston of Cogshall Grange, and Mr Brewer[1] of Hedingham Castle buried this day, two good men, the lord make mee sensible of such stroaks and prepare mee for my change, by daily close walking, and by faith on the covenant of promises.

Aug: 22. A dewing day, good was god to us in many mercies, the lord accept mee and humble my soule, for my outward subsistence, I find I am cast wholly on the Lord, oh take the care of mee I intreate thee, Mrs Elizabeth Harlakenden ill of the measles the lord watch over her for good.

23. I holpe carrie and lay Mr Brewer into the grave, buried with many teares: he rests from the strivings of people, the lord make mee

[1] Edmund Brewer, incumbent of Hedingham Castle; according to the Parochial Inquisition of 1650 'an able godly preaching minister'. Smith, pp. 297, 378.

careful to serve him in my place, that I may bee blessed of him. heard some thing of my sister An, which is a greife to mee. god preserved mee in a fall of the litle blacke nagge.

26: Helped to make up the Wid: Clarkes marriage with Mr Wheely,[1] which was agreed on all particulars by my interposing.

Aug: 29. A wett season, much corne yett abroad, lord give the remaining dayes of the harvest for thy names sake, god good to us in many mercies the lord awakeneth my heart to consider of my latter end, I find my heart afraid, yet recovering on the covenant in christ. lord stablish and assure my heart in thy love I pray thee.

31: Married Mr Sarjant minister of Chappell,[2] and Mrs Bridgitt Nevill, the lord make them, and mee mindfull of union and communion with christ by our present relation.

Sept: 1: rid to Major Haynes at Hisson to whom I was kindly welcome. god good to mee in all my jorney, preserving my health, bones in a fall of my horse my family well when I returned: our maide Susan Wallis came to us

Susan Wallis

3. Cromwell died. people not much minding it.

Sept: 5. I preacht twice at Hysson, god blesse the word, it was not without some hopes of doing good. my place well supplied in my absence.

8: I was at Sturbridge faire Mrs Haynes sent my wife 4 paire of gloves for a fayringe[3].—9. I returned in a good day, the next night and day being exceeding wett. my owne spirit much out of frame with my sinfull musings.

One Dorothy Layer.[4] being gott with child by a weaver, afterwards was married to him, was delivered before her time, and died. god make such things to bee warnings to us.

Sept: 12. Very wett weather, newes scattered of the new Prot(ectors) sicknes, which proved not true, god good to us in our health, and of my children for which I blesse his holy name, the frame of my heart not pure, yett my aime is at cleannesse, trusting in god, and serviceablenes unto him, oh that I were accepted of god in all.

[1] 'Published a contract of marriage between John Wheelye, widower of Chelmsford and Marie Clarke, of Maldon, widow, 27 August and 3, 20 September 1658.' W. P. W. Phillimore (ed.), *Essex Parish Registers Marriages*, ii: Chelmsford pt. i (1912).

[2] Ordained 24 September 1656, and for some time incumbent of Chapel; subscribed on 21 May 1663 and probably still present in 1683. Smith, p. 329 and *Clergy*, pp. 80–1.

[3] Fairing: a complimentary gift, originally one given at or brought from a fair. SOED.

[4] On 3 September Dorothy Carter, wife of Thomas, was buried; there is no record of a marriage, but she was probably aged just under 30, a Dorothy Layer having been baptized in December 1628. PR.

16: Mr Clerkes dog flew on mee and rent my coate very much, it was gods mercy so much was not done to my selfe, god good to us in our daily and hourely preservations.

Sept. 19. God good to mee and mine in our outward mercies, prayed heartily for rain, and a good seed time, lord answer prayer in mercy I intreate thee, I will waite on thee for a mercifull returne herein, the lord good to mee in the word, oh make mee one of thy freinds oh lord and deale with mee as such, yett their is peace among our-ourselves: said Baxter is dead, a great pillar to Cromwell and his way. but not so.

21: my loving Uncle Mr Nathaniel Josselin and his sonne with mee one night, the lord made him a refreshment to my spirit, oh the savour of christ in a freind is sweet oh but much more, when it cometh of, from his own soule and lips.

22. spent in a day of prayer at priory with young Mr Harlakenden and his wife, the lord answer prayer in much mercy, and give them comfort in their seed.

25. heard wheat was in Bedfordshire. 11^{s}. bushel, with us it is 7^{s}. this ☞ scarcity on a suddain, when there never was a more hopeful crop on the ground: but by laying and mildewing the strong corns a wind that beare out aboundance, and wett in the harvest that spoiled much, this dearth came unexpected

Sept: 26. God heard prayer in the season of the weeke, and yett mixt with rain, the lord in mercy good to us in our health, when many are very sicke in other places, lord I blesse thee for it, continue it, as a mercy to mee and unto mine, our servant went away, as indeed very unfitt for us, the lord blesse us with a servant for his name sake, heard of Mrs Eldreds sicknes the lord open her eyes, and sanctifie her heart, god was good to mee in the word, oh how Christ glorifieth himselfe in his saints, oh that I could heartily sett my heart to glorifie him in his word, and worship and saints that are deare to him.

29. Kept a day of prayer at Goodman Mathews god good to us therin, young Mr Harlakenden prayed pressingly men should serve god with their estates, I proposed to our company to pray to god to direct mee in something that was on my spirit to mention to them in order to myselfe and them, and yett I was not minded to doe it of my selfe, but on their accounts, lest they should in a straite blame mee that I did not, My mind was on my necessity to alter the course of my living, and turne farmour; some of them apprehended my words tended to a remove, and spake as if they would

doe somewhat in the businesse, but what it will bee god knoweth, the lord can open and enlarge my condition somewhat, and if he please to doe it my heart shall blesse his name, A report that Henry Cromwell coming over from Ireland was cast away at sea. but it proved false.

October 3. God good to us in the season which was very comfortable, and suitable to the season of the yeare, the lord was mercifull to mee in the health of my family, destitute I was of a servant, the lord in mercy provide one for me that may bee a helpe and comfort to mee, the lord good to mee this day in the word, intreating sinners to leave their sins, lord lett them receive grace and strength from thee to doe it, I humbly intreate thee. this day wee brake bread togither, all our company togither in this sickly time for which I blesse god

9. returnd well from my Ladie Honywoods where I lay 4 nights. to performe dutie and carry on instruction in the family, while the Ladie Brooks[1] there. I on the hope the 2 young ones may be helpe meet for each other especially in soule worke did my helpe between parties to joynt their businesse. in that time I rode out to preach Buers and Wakes lecture, give mee a large heart for and in thy service oh Lord I begge of thee.

Oct: 10: God good to our family in our health, and businesse in the want of a maide and the sicklines of the time, oh that my heart could bee made sensible of gods goodnes and affected therewith, the season very good for seed time the lords name bee blessed for the same: the Lord helped mee to press upon my people that great duty of forsaking sin, lord arise to and helpe therin(.) I preacht about knowledge and ignorance to stir up people to attend to the means thereof, the lord blesse my labours therein and accept mee according to thy goodnes.

12. Mrs Pelham dead lord make up that losse, the lord good to mee in the fast die 13°. after I went to visit. nurse Crow and Goodman Brand, oh the deadnes that is in mans heart godward; this night I had a servant offered, Lord lett it bee a good one, or made so, I humbly intreate thee.

14. I married Mary Potter late my maid to Jo: Penhacke, and it greived mee not to deale bountifully with her, my heart sad to see her match to a person that minds not god, nor likely to bee good housband. from thence my wife went down to Mrs H, who was safely, quickly and easily delivered of a son, and baptized the next day the lord

[1] Lady Elizabeth Brooke (1601–83), religious writer and 'an indefatigable reader of the Scriptures', whose husband, Sir Robert, had died in 1646. DNB.

good to her notwithstanding her feares, and this was an encouragement unto her to trust in god in farther feares. this son is their heire, lord lett it bee thine.

Oct: 17. God good to us in our many mercies, oh that my heart could indeed praise him(.) the lord good in the Sabbath, our officers punisht some travellers, a new worke with us, the lord helpe mee to serve him sincerely. god gave us a very sweet and comfortable seedtime.

19. rid to Hinningham and returned safe, preacht of gods freindship to Saints. some hearts affected, and mine own with gods goodnes in Christ. oh lett my soule truly love and serve thee. Dr Pullein told mee he would allow mee. 22^{li}. 10^{s}. 0^{d}. for my pains in teaching the schoole.

21. preacht of gods freindship, I tooke in a maid that offered her selfe to us on the account of gods providence, lord bee in it for good, I receivd of Mr Dow something for his sons schooling, which I expected not, god turned mee in to see poore Tomasin and helpe her, shee is thine lord, I trust

Oct: 24: God good to mee in the way of his mercies, my soule desireth to trust in him, and indeed my life and comfort lieth only there, all springs are failing but that of grace in the mediator. god good to mee in the Sabbath my affections to the soules of people, on thy account oh lord, accept, blesse and prosper mee I pray thee.

27. This day I had an evident experience of gods mercy in preserving Ann falling carelesly into a great fire, without any hurt, her mother by and suddenly pulling her up: that child preserved in a fall down the entry staires. I have boile or pile in my fundament, the like I never had formerly. on the lord I roule my selfe to shew mee mercy therin, it is blacke, but nothing issueth.

Oct: 31: God good to us in many mercies, my deare wife very ill, I apprehend it to bee much cold setled in her joynts, the lord in mercy restore her, if a wife so needfull no house without her, what is christ Jesus to the heart of a sinner nothing indeed without him, the season was very pleasant only sharpe with cold frost. I am entring into treatie, about my sonne for London, the good lord shew mercie to mee and my child therin, god was good to us in the Sabbath for which my soule blesseth him.

No: 2. returned safe, god good to mee in my busines especially in my mind, wherin I obtained mercy to bee faithful, I preacht at Wittam on James. 2.23. observed the troubles attended some persons in their affaires, which allayes mine, and sweetens my mercies and enjoyments.

3. sent our squirrel to the Countesse of Oxford, who sent for it, and sent us a silver tankard worth about 3^{li}. 10^{s}. I esteemed it a mercifull providence to us.

Nov: 7. God good to mee, and mine in outward mercies, my heart sensible of my eternal state, for which I am amazed, but the love of god in christ lifteth mee up, Mrs Thrale with Mr H. from London informed of the death of her eldest sonne in Portugal, the lord helpe her to beare that stroke. a troubled busines at Markshall, in disposing my Lady Honywoods daughter, shee recoils in affection from Mr Brooks,[1] but whither it bee her act or others is uncertaine, god good to mee in his word this day, the lord affect mee with his love.

12. returned home, where I found our maide gone, a sad wench, the lord bee mercifull to us in a servant. my body was better where I feared the pile, or some such thing, I joynd in keeping a fast at Cogshall, heard sad newes of my poore sister Anna, the lord bee mercifull unto her, shew her her sins, and heale all(.) Mr Brooke went sadly from the Lady Honywoods, cast of by the daughter, but kindly dismist by the mother,

13. Received a letter from Mr Cressener;[2] wherin he seemeth inclinable to take Tom, but his demands are very high. god almighty shew favour to him therin, his letter was writt that day wee spent at Coggeshall.

Nov: 14: God good to mee, and mine in our outward mercies; My humble earnest desire is that soules and bodies of mee, and mine might prosper, and it is the lord only that maketh us doe so. the root of my crope lieth in his own mercy, and in that covenant of grace, wherof Jesus is Mediator and surety. my endeavour through grace shall bee to avouch this god for mine, to honour Jesus in beleiving in him, to submitt to the spirits motions, to walke in subjection to all their commands, oh that thou wouldst blesse mee indeed, and continue thy sanctifying, prospering presence with us, ☞ god was good to mee in the word I began to catechise this day, I came home nimbler then some old persons, and they thinke that

[1] One of the children (probably Sir Robert, died 1669) of Lady Brooke; see p. 432, n. 1.

[2] For the Cressenor family, see the kinship diagram in Appendix 2. Defoe gave as an example of rich London merchants buying properties in the country 'Mr Cresnor, a wholesale grocer, who was, a little before he died, named for sheriff at Earls Colne'. D. Defoe, *A Tour through the Whole Island of Great Britain* (Penguin abridged edn., 1971), p. 57.

is my advantage, and I apprehend they are nearer heaven and cannot bee long out of it, and I reckon that a good advantage indeed.

18: Mr R.H. with his uncle and company went safe towards London, I writt up again to Mr Cressener by him, wherin I manifest my hope he will bee a good servant and my assurance to bee willing to doe considerably for my child.

Nov: 28: Tedious winter weather, formerly frost, now rain, snow, cold, hard time for poore, who pine exceedingly nipt with want and penury, the lord yett good to mee and mine in our outward mercies for which my soule desireth to blesse and exalt his name, I prest on the families of Colne family instruction, masters to practice it, and inferiours to submitt therunto, but lord if thou presse it not upon them, they will throw this duty behind their backe.

30. Spent in a day of prayer at Mr Sparrows of Halsted with Mr Jo Littel to seeke direction from the lord for him in the change of the course of his life(,) my advice was to marry, and could not but advice him therto as clearly gods mind in his case.

Decemb. 3. Mr R.H. returned from London in my sons busines with Mr Cressener, he brought mee no account, but this he would thinke of it, seemed to value a child of a good disposition more then mony.

5: A very sad cold winter, god good to us in our health, and outward mercies, good in the word, for which my soule blesseth him.

8 Susan Hadley begun her yeare, wee are to give her 40^s., and I ☞ promise her. 4 paire of shoes, if shee give mee and her Mrs content. I went 6. miles to see a freind, and returned, god give Tom his health. 9. this day the season opened after a tedious three weekes frost, and very hard some nights.

11: Mrs Harlakenden the younger bestowed a silver candlestand, and porringer cover on my daughter Mary, whom shee named, the lord returne all their love into their bosome; received some kindnes from some persons this day.

December 12. a sad wett day Mrs Church lieth most sadly, (c.o. *and not yet dying*), lord send out help wee pray thee, the lord good to mee in my protection in the Sabbath, much pargett[1] falling down over the pulpit this day. god good to mee in the word, and in his worship for which I blesse him, wee had news this weeke of a Parliament in the next month.

[1] Parget: to cover or daub with parget or plaster, to plaster (a wall, etc.), to adorn with pargetting. SOED.

17. put an other difference in the family of the Nevil sisters into a faire way of composing the same, lord remember mee for good

December 19: The former frost not yet out of the ground, another came on very sharp(,) Mrs Church heartily comended unto god, as formerly, very often, shee seemes to draw apace to the grave. Lord pardon all my sins in the bloud of christ, and all my evills blot out and accept my soule.

20: this morning about 6 of the clocke Mrs Church died, the lord tooke ☞ her from a sad estate wherin shee lay. lord lett not mee be such a child.

21: buried Mrs Church, and preacht, inventoried her goods, and delivered her legacies out to the maide, and the poore woman to whom given, for which faithfulnes I blesse god, and then delivered up the residue to the person to whom they were given, lord lett thy blessing bee in my habitacon I pray thee

23. ended the bargain between Mr Butcher and Morly and made peace, oh blessed bee god that cuts away out unto persons in their difficult affaires. he will doe so for mee and I shall praise him, heard Mr Honywood sicke of the small pox, lord sanctifie that providence and remember him for good

24: Mrs Churchs busines I suppose may bee 50^{li}. advantage unto mee, besides it leadeth mee into her daughters estate; lord lett mee receive a thankful heart to honour thee with all, for thou art he alone, who carest for mee.

Dec: 26. God was good to mee in the word this day, faiths influence into the pardon of sin, which was sweet to my soule. my life, comfort the lord make it a good word to mee day by day. god good to mee in manifold mercies, he accept of mee, and delight in mee for good

28: A very windy night, but goodly summers day, cleare, shunshine, warme, the ground paving: Knights chosen at chelmsford Mr Charles Rich, and Mr Turnor, a choice not well rellisht by many honest men, but god knowes what is best
210. voices carried an election, Turnor that had most had not 240. divers elections were on this day called Innocents day. will the Parl: bee harmelesse, or suffer themselves, or make others doe so, secreta tibi deus mi.[1]

29. A publique Fast, god gave mee a spirit of prayer. heard somewhat more hopefully of Mr Honywood, lord restore him I pray thee. in the end of this day one offered to joyne with us, and two to returne,

[1] Secrets for you, God for me.

I seriously desire to consult god and my heart upon it, and desire to blesse god for that testimony.

31: exceeding great feares of the death of young R. Harlakenden, and great hopes of M[r] Honywoods life, the lord heare prayer, and heale the sicke. a sweet day.

Jan: 1: This morning young R. Harlakenden. 11. weeks old died, a sad morning to a sad father, and mother, the lord sanctifie the stroake, and doe us good by it.

2: This day wee brake bread, there were divers absent, but I trust Jesus Christ was with us, my heart up to god in service, but so carried away to the matters of my estate that is perplexed, that I knew not what to doe but up to the lord I looke for a blessing, and to cutt my way through in all the passages thereof, and on him alone I rely

3. This day wee buried the litle Richard, god sett that word on my desire and somewhat on my faith, Christ will bee deaths death, and spare their after issue. Hos. 13.14.

4: 5: These dayes by a very strange and wonderfull providence of god I agreed for the farme on the Greene with the Nevils, and had an estate in all the coppie hold, very lovingly and quietly. it was a mercy god wrought out for mee, it was his doing, I was lost in my endeavours and could doe nothing. then he undertooke it, in mercy I hope.—he is my own god, and through him I will seeke his honour in loving and serving him

Jan: 9: God good to us in manifold mercies, in sweet accomplishing my affaires, lord helpe mee to improve all to thy honour and glory. thes outward businessess crowd often into my thoughts, and disturbe lord helpe and inable mee, that I may cheerfully serve thee, I find I want thee oh my god to inable mee rightly to use, and christianly to behave my selfe under any thing I enjoy, as well as to bestow it upon mee, the lord a helpe to mee in the word, and to my spirit to make it calme and quiet under divers unkind dealings.

12. A fine cleare frosty day, wherin I tooke a view with content of my pur[chase] on the greene and found therein, certain small trees beyond what I did expect but a very small quantity of log trees.

15: This day spent with Mr Harlakenden in his chamber to inquire of the Lord, why he contendeth with them, my subject was Job. 10.2. the lord affect their hearts, and pardon their sin, and shine on their tabernacles and doe them good.

Jan: 16: I awaked unto this Sabbath early, but find my mind running to my occasions, and not to bee commanded in, lord tis thy command thy day should bee sanctified, and it is my duty, and desire, and endeavour, lord strengthen mee by grace therto, I hope for an eternall Sabbath, oh lett mee bee with thee in these here. god was good to mee in the word, though I was much afraid because of my unpreparednes, the lord in mercy draw out my heart, more and more unto his service.

19: our deare freinds Mr Harlakenden the younger wife and child went up to London under some likelyhoods to retire from Colne priory, the lord looke after them in all places, and doe them good. and make them prosper in soule and body.

21: Rid to Hinningham to advise poore Cooper to keepe in, and remove to his son, wherin I promised to endeavour it with his sonne.

Pose. very much with sneezing, and so continued all the 22th att night, but not much the next morning I blesse god, I feared a great cold. but thanks to god it setled not in my chest.

Jan: 23. God good to us in our outward mercies, his kindnes and care, glads my soule the more the lesse I meet with and find from others, my heart much meditates on Labans dealing with Jacob,[1] whom god the more increased and blessed, my litle ones about mee hearing, oh they might sitt togither with christ in heavenly places, lord make mine and people sensible of a soules worth, which I spoke of this day, remembered the Parliament that most forgett, and very few so much as speake of them, a spirit of slumber and remissenes is wonderfully upon the nation, awake for thy own things oh lord, my eye is prying, whither this flattery, and smoothnes of nation and prot(ector) will carry things.

25: I had a tedious jorney to Hinningham, where I preacht from Eccles. 9.18, it was discourse in the towne, that this was my liking sermon to bee their minister, and such discourse was offered unto mee, lord I am thine to dispose of as thou pleasest, yett if it please thee make my lott comfortable at Colne, yett not my will but thy will be done.

— — — — — — — — — — — — — — — — — —

Jan: 26: 1658: my 42. yeare ended and 43. entred.

26. This day was pleasant, I was working abroad, and visiting freinds, I am ful of busines about my farme, the lord plant, worke with mee, or all is in vain. lord bee with mee as in the yeare past. and lett

[1] Genesis 29 and 30. Laban deceived Jacob, and thereby benefited from his services, but later realized 'that the Lord hath blessed me for thy sake', and pleaded with Jacob to stay with him.

Jesus Christ dwell in my heart as in his own temple, through the sanctifying, comforting spirit. Amen.

29. Heard from Mr H. from London which joyed my heart. Mr Manwood[1] with mee Mrs Churchs kinsman to whom I gave respect for his freinds sake.

Jan: 30. God good to us in many outward enjoyments, in some sweet soule refreshings in his word, soule concernments are the cheife, lord lett them bee most lookt after(.) I earnestly sought god to direct mee in my going or staying at Colne, things seeme to worke out my remove, and my heart is much loosned from the place lord if soules require mee here, and thy glory lie most in it, lett mee not goe but lett mee not bee barren or unfruitfull in thy worke.

31: Mr Butcher came from Hinningham with an offer of that place unto mee, Mr Harlakenden of the Priory entertaind it very heavily, and when I told him I would not leave it for means, he offered mee an 100^{li}. to spend in 5 years as a further addition, but Feb: 1: he came up and left against my will 50^{li}. with my wife, as mine if he or I died but if wee lived as an engagement for 2 years and halfe until Sept: 29. 61. and then if he did not purchase 20^{li}. yearly and adde to my means if living he would raise and pay out of his estate 20^{li}. yearly.[2]—an act of love not easily matcht evidencing his zeale to god and love to my ministry, oh lord might but Colne proffit by my ministry, I should exceedingly rejoyce. wee mett this day, but no body did mention any thing unto mee, I shall patiently observe what Colne will say to mee.

Feb: 6. God good to mee in divers affaires, I was in great danger of hurt by bushes[3] but I hope god preserveth, a limbe is precious, oh how useful then is grace(,) god good to mee in the Sabbath for which I blesse and praise his most holy name

7. I received 3 fines and this day they were all to bee levied, but mine only was done which I valued as a great mercy, I gave Mr Sarjant bond to pay 150^{li}. at his house July. 5. next, god helpe mee in my worke, and to praise him, when done,

10. preacht Mrs Gladdin's[4] funerall at Cogshall. Heb. 2.14.15. I was

[1] Probably one of the Manwood family of Broomfield, Essex. Morant, ii, p. 77.

[2] The details of the bequest are given in Morant, ii, p. 214. Against the burial entry in the PR on 17 September 1677 is written 'Rich Harlakenden sen. Esq. the good Harlakenden who by deed gave the great Tithes of most of the parish to the church forever'.

[3] Bush: a thorn (in the flesh). Jepp.

[4] The Gladwins were a big cloth-making family in Coggeshall; for example Nicholas, probably Mrs. Gladwin's husband, had a three-hearth house in 1662 and left a will in 1679 (ERO, 54 MR 7).

☞ used very bountifully by them, the lord deliver mee from sin the cause of feares.

Heard much of the strange noise in the ayer Feb. 6.

Feb: 13. God good to us the weeke past in our busines, the lord prosper mee, and doe all with mee, for all is in vaine without him, god good to mee in the Sabbath, but my heart is very neglectfull in my studdies, and preparations, the lord pardon and heale it, lord helpe mee to carry on my worke and thine cheerfully, and vigorously.

Feb: 20: God good to mee in outward mercies in my busines, for which I praise him, oh prosper soule and body. the season cheerfull, god is good to my seed in their health when under rebukes, I gathered this day to rebuild a church. 11[s]. 1[d]. oh how lowe[*ly*] charity goeth on such errands, though I prest the worke and exampled it, the lord good to mee in my spirit more free from roving vanities, not sett on the world, not taken of from my studdies, the lord make mee a blessing, and in any thing may bee on my hand I pray thee prosper it unto mee for Christs sake

23. This day I put faire to end John Church's businesse, and I hope for his good as well as unto my owne content, the lord bee my portion

25. Preacht at Halsted, when I returned found a kinswoman of Mrs Cresseners whom shee sent for to London to teach her children and had been with her about a quarter of a yeare was dead, an awakening providence, god doe them, mee and all of us good by the same, teach us to serve him in our day and prepare for our visitation

Feb: 27. God good to us in many outward mercies our peace, and health, especially in my soule concernments keeping our hearts from many evils, and drawing out our spirits to walke with him in the path of his commandments. wee buried this day a person. god bury our sins before wee die, the season cheerful, but when shall our hearts find that in god that may fill us with joy and make the nation glad even love to commandments.

March. 3. preacht at Wakes about christs being admired in and by his Saints, the word very sweet, and christ very beauteous in my beleiving soule in preaching it, coming home Mr R: Harlakenden, acquainted with the wonderfull enmity he found in his heart against christ, and the way of salvation by him, lord helpe him and slay that enmity by the bloud of the crosse. a very cold dry windie season.

March: 6. God good to us in many outward mercies, yett my wife, and Jane have a litle touch in their health, Jane with a swelling in her necke, lord in mercy doe thou heale them both perfectly, the season cold and searching. the lord was good to mee in the inward frame of my heart, not annoyed with former vanities of my mind, lord lett no worldly busines eate up my heart, helpe mee to make a good improvement of Sabbaths, I find Colne men not minding my slender maintenance, when mentioned they word it better, but they doe not helpe mee. but my lord will and I shall praise him.

orchard 11: made an end of inclosing my new orchard on the green, and planted one crabstrocke[1] in the farther corner. 12. planted a 2d by it, and some plum trees, and filberds,[2] god give a blessing, its he that must prosper our worke.

12. A sad day at my house with my selfe, Morly, and Butcher, our passions were up and hott, the good lord pitty and pardon us in christ Jesus, and doe all our busines well. I blesse god who purgd it out of my heart and made it very greivous to mee.

March. 13. The season vehement cold and dry the east winde notable, god good to us in our health, its his mercy to command it, heard of the taking Coppenhagen and the sad slaughter made there. blessed bee god for Englands peace. god good to mee in the Sabbath.

18: visited, and prayed with sicke Mrs Littell our good old neighbour. god strengthen her heart in him selfe, and beare up her hope on the rocke of ages.

March: 20. God good to us in outward mercies, the season even a drought. god hath changed the aire that it is warme, lord make it moist. Coppenhaguen news not true, the lord send peace among the inhabitants of the earth, my busines weareth of my hand, through mercy, god blesse our labours, god good to mee in the Sabbath, the word of grace pleasant to the tast of my soule; helpe mee to live up to thy glory in all conditions I intreate thee.

24: rid to Wethersfeild, did some part of my businesse, returned very weary

25. A litle past nine a messenger from London brought mee letters acquainting mee with my deare freind Harlakendens dangerous sicknes at Worcester, my heart feared the worst, and indeed then he was new dead. I went down to the priory, and acquainted Mr H. with it, who was striking at a mole. he was troubled, but hoped. my heart utterly under feares, I resolved for London and Worcester, knowing it my duty to my freinds and Christs servant and comitted

[1] Crabstocke: a young crab-tree used as a stock to graft upon. SOED.

[2] Filberds: filbert, the fruit or nut of the cultivated hazel; the tree bearing the nut. SOED.

my selfe to god with a sicke servant and 2 poore horses and rid from one a clocke til past 8. to Burntwood[1] where I received a letter that
1659. poore Mrs Harlakenden was that day gone from London towards her housband.

26. Nic. the man with mee being very ill and providence thus turning, I returnd toward Colne and mett Mr Eldred and Elliston from Mr Harl. desirous some one should goe on I went and came that night weary, and sicke with winde to Beaconsfeild, and mist Mrs H. who hearing on the road the death of her housband returnd to Uxbridge

27. Being Lords day I rid to Aynstone in Oxfordshire, the lord pardon it to mee. it was a worke of mercy, I hoped though I brake the Sabbath in that I was as the preists killing sacrifices blamelesse. men and horses grew better:

28. Monday toward 5. of the clocke heard at Stowton just by Woodhall of Mr H. death which was a sad cutt to my heart. but his gain was death, though my losse.

29. I did what I could in his busines to prepare for a return, visited Worcester, and stood by the Severne not much weary(,) god wonderfully strengthened mee for the jorney and provided for mee, to his praise I make mention of it.

30: Ned Mr H. man returned from London with an Herse to convey Mr H. body which was embalmed, and his bowels buried in Kemsey unto Earles Colne.

31: wee sett out our jorney about 30 horse accompanying our herse wee arrived that night late at Aynstone. April: 1: at Beaconsfeild. 2. I turned in to see sad Mrs Harlakenden whose only daughter Mary had newly had the small pox. and came in a dismal tempest wherin god safely preserved mee, and comforted my heart to Rom-
Ap: ford where wee rested Ap: 3. the lords day.

4: wee came to Colne. not one freind meeting us on the way. 5: I buried my deare freind with teares and sorrow and laid his bones in his bed, for which mercy I desire to praise the name of the Lord most high, who carried mee through so sad a service.

8.(6?) rid and accompanied the funeral herse of Mr John Cooke[2] to Pedmarsh an other losse

9. Heard of Joan Richmonds death. Mrs H. servant who was sent from the priory by Mr Harlakenden, when the small pox was coming out. a sad stroke. god in mercy sanctifie all unto mee, and rid my heart of

[1] Burntwood: Brentwood, a variation in spelling repeated several times.

[2] The son of Col. Thos. Cooke of Pebmarsh (see p. 48, n. 1 above), pensioner of St. John's 1652, and admitted Lincoln's Inn, 1654. Venn.

hardnes and unmercifulnes; accept my praise, my hearty thanks for thy preservation oh my god. lett thy good spirit, lead mee through in all thy pathes, to thy glory I pray thee.

\+ When I come to view outward things I find divers deare freinds dead especiall my deare and never to bee forgotten Harlakenden, an estate of lands coming into my hands so that I may estimate my lands. viz.

John Crows worth - - - -	21li.	8s.	0.
Toms and my close - - - -	5.	10.	0.
Sprigs Marsh - - - - - - -	3.	0.	0.
Bollinhatch - - - - - - - -	7.	16.	0.
Tibbalds. - - - - - - - - - - -	47.	0.	0.
	84.	14.	0.

I am much in debt, but I have mony enough owing unto mee to cleare all my debts, and an 100li. in my purse this is the lords bounty, teach mee to serve thee with a glad and thankfull heart according to thy great goodnes, I found this yeare I saved some mony, and I hope hath gaind acquaintance with and experience of god.

April 10. God good to mee in bringing mee backe Worcester tedious and sorrowful jorney to preach at Colne to my people. the lord helpe them, to proffit, god good to us in our mercies Joane Richmond dead at London put out at the priory when the small pox on her. the agents. Mathews wife. Justice Harlakenden and old Mr Harl: lord lay it not unto their chardge. lord preserve mee from that distemper and replenish my heart with thy grace. pitty that poore widdow, and doe mee good for thy name sake, make mee wise for her soules and estates good. this day my wife puld out a dangerous thorne that had stucke about 6. weeks in my finger as long as a barly corne, and as big as an awle[1] point, without any danger for which god bee praisd

Ap: 17. The weeke past, was dry, and cold, yett now and then a litle moisture so that the ground did not much harden, in it god was very good and mercifull to mee and mine, affaires worke very comfortably for poore Mrs Harlakenden, her fathers heart much coming over unto her, and I trust god will make her a blessing unto us, the

[1] Awl: a small tool, having a slender, tapering, sharp-pointed blade, with which holes may be pierced; especially that used by shoemakers. SOED.

lord was very good to mee in the word, and worke of the day(,) give the fruite of it lord unto my people, that wee may praise thy most holy name

21: This day, and former being to write about my son my heart rowsed it selfe on god who knoweth all things and persons and events, for the good of my sonne, and being in his path, I verily beleive he will doe all for the best.

22: Mr Harlakendens daughters went to Mr Eldred. I was busy in preparing timber for my building. Mrs B. Harlakenden gave An: 20^s. the first kindnes, god returne it to them make my heart faithfull, and lett no guifts blind my eyes, nor sway my judgments.

23. Heard the army had dissolved the Parl: against the consent of the Protector, seized Thirloe, and some others. it looks sadly god in mercy awake for mee and his, I had a very comfortable returne from Mrs Harlakenden, which joyed my heart, god good in my affaire with Mr Cressener, there is life in it, god shew favour to mee therin for on thy blessing, and wisedom I roule my selfe.

April. 24: God many wayes good to mee and mine in our health, plenty, peace, comforts in mutual relations for which my soule blesseth god. the word this day precious, the god of it beautifull, and lovely indeed, there is none like him, on him I rowle my selfe, he is my shelter and trust. the spring backward, wee hope raine, god in mercy send it, to refresh, and comfort the earth.

27. Began to fell and barke my trees bought of Mr W: Harlakenden, assured that the protector had consented to the army to dissolve both houses of Parliament.

30: Heard a sad account of things at London, Prot: deserted; army divided. this selfe seeking, deceitfull crew, are likely to receive the recompence of their deceits wherin they have sported themselves.

May. 1: God good to us in many outward mercies, the weather very dry and winds cold as if drought and famine would come in upon us, a very sad shatterd face of things in the nacion, yet few lay it too heart. the lord awake for our good(.) my wife apprehends shee is breeding. if so, the lord blesse her fruite, shee is seldom or I thinke never mistaken on that point, god was good to mee in the word and the worke of this day for which I blesse his name.

2. a gratious answer of prayer in a most sweet dew. I sent Mr R.H. Burroughs on Math:[1] which he tooke very kindly.

[1] Jeremiah Burroughs (1599–1646), congregational minister and author of *Four books on the Eleventh of Matthew* (1659). DNB.

5. preacht at Wakes. the decimated men confined to their houses and 5 mile for 31 days.[1] lord its mercy I am not an ingaged man in thes hurries. disappointed in my expectacions of seing Mrs H. Lord let her come safe to us, I pray thee.

6: This morning early Mrs Harlakenden and her litle daughter came safe to Colne. for which I blesse god, who hath preserved her, and returned her safe unto us, my god give her comfort here, and make her a blessing unto us, and us to her.

May. 8: God good to us in our outward mercies, the lord accept us, the season somewhat Cold, yet the grasse grew by reason of the dews, the lord good to mee in the word, lord make it my endeavour to walke before thee in all pleasing, matters very quiet in England, Cromwells family under much odium for tiranny etc.

12: Made an end of Mr Harlakendens businesse with his daughter to ☞ my good content, shee oweth him. 2400^{li}. he upon my serious proposall forgave her about 60^{li}. for which I was very glad. promised her, her board and man and maides and one horse for 45^{li}. yearly, a great kindnes, and to give her the diett of a freind

14. Mrs H. having a desire to receive a farther kindnes from her father, writt her mind and sent it by her daughter, he doth it, the good lord make a sweet compliance between them in the family, ended a great and difficult busines between persons because they were crosse, and untoward.

May. 15. God good in outward mercies, and the season, my deare wife, and Jane not well, lord revive them, and comfort them for thy name sake, god was good to mee in the word and worke of the Sabbath, but I find much deadnes on my heart I have not that inward life, nor zeale for acts of worship which formerly I was wont to have and find, lord recover mee to light and life in thy selfe.

16. Mr Cressener brought mee a letter from his brother to send up my sonne to him, the lord make him a blessing, and blesse him, oh my god.

17. rid to Hedingham, and putt an end to Mr Butchers and Morleys troublesom busines(.) gods hand was towards mee for good therein.

19. Heard of the death of Robert Hains only son, and that thereby his estate falleth after the widdows death to my freind Major Haynes, god blesse and preserve his seed long to inheritt.

May. 22: God good to us in our outward mercies, men gaze on this

[1] The 'decimated' were those who, while not being continued active Royalists, had 10 per cent of their property, either land or personal estate, taxed from them for previous sympathy and activity in the Royalist cause. Gardiner, *Commonwealth*, iii, pp. 176–7.

change, sectaries rejoyce others gaze, even all are secure, the lord who knoweth whither things tend take care of his owne, and bee a reviving in the midst of us. our society roundly togither at the lords table, the lord accept of us, and doe us good. the lord is calling up my son Tom. to London, lord goe thou with him, and make him a blessing, and lett him bee a prosperous man for soule and body, lord this I hope and trust, say Amen, wee pray thee. My deare Freind Mrs Harlakenden to whom god draweth out the residue of my affection was at church with us, it was an addicion to my comfort though it might bee at present an increase of her sorrow and trouble.

24: preparing to send my Tom to London, my spirit cheerly in doing it. I am in gods way and that is my comfort, I pray and trust god will bee his god, and shelter him under his wings.

Tom: ☞ apprentice.

25: I and my sonne being Wednesday in Whitsonweeke sett forward for London(.) wee had sweet shoures before and so coole but dry riding all the way wee came safe to London 26. on Thursday that afternoone Tom at Mr Jo. Cresseners putt on his blew apron. I did all Mrs Harlakendens busines. my son is to serve 8. yeares his time will expire. May. 1: 1667. in a good time I hope the lord sparing his life, lord make him like Joseph a blessing to his Master and bee thou his blessing and portion

May. 29. God good to mee in divers mercies, I trust in the comfortable disposure of my sonne. god give him grace and a wise heart. the lord good to mee in the word. there was a great meeting of Quakers in towne. I knew nothing of it, until, I came homeward(.) bee a sanctuary to the remnant of thy inheritance I pray thee.

31: Ended Mr R: H. his great busines with Mrs Eliz: Harlakenden with whose estate he was intrusted, very quietly and comfortably, god keepe all hearts in calmenes and in holy uprightnes

June. 2. rid forth and returnd having preacht Redgwell and Clare lectures, god good to mee in my jorny. heard of my aunt shepheards death, god in mercy prepare mee and make mee mindfull of my change:

4: my carting was not prosperous this day, though no hurt done, blessed bee god, the lord doe mee good by and under all his dealings. Mr R.H. made a bequest of the great tithes to mee and the ministers of Colne. I rejoyce when I draw on any publique good. my wife was so that shee thought shee might not bee with child, shee was not as yett so confident as formerly, nor with her as formerly

June: 5. God good to mee in divers outward mercies, mine healthfully revive again, my soule praise the lord for all, inward peace, silence of inward temptacons, my heart findeth no pleasure in them. lord continue thy sabbaths unto us

10: gott home all my wood and timber, amazed in spirit about Thomas not liking at London. I leave events to god, lord I trust thou wilt shew favour unto mee.

11: This day Tom. returned from London, it was a sad amazing providence to mee but more to my deare wife, god sanctifie all. I hope there is good in it, I must learne in patience to possesse my soule.

June 12. The small pox came out on Tom, the lord bee mercifull to him, and spare him for his name sake, god good to mee in quieting and supporting my heart on himselfe. when I view the worst of things, oh hold up my heart in beleiving for that is my helpe, oh let mee live by faith in this my day

14: I trust Toms illnes goeth on kindly, lord spare his life and pitty his soule, my heart much stayed on god, and quiet, blesse the lord oh my soule.

15. Toms pox came out after a treacle possett. at night they began to run, oh that the inward filth and corruption of our heart might bee drawn out

16: Heard so much of Toms foolishnes at London, that cutt my heart, Lord for, through Christ lay in principles into his spirit, let his life bee a mercy not a crosse to us

June. 19. God good to mee in this day of affliction, my spirit quiett, not hurried about with distrust feares, full of stillnes, peace. oh I blesse god for it, its from thee, for my heart naturally is otherwise, god good to mee in the word. Tom began to sitt up this day, he was weake not able to stand, the lord strengthen his heart against evill, and bend it unto good, and then his life shall bee a mercy indeed. I made an offer to my parish to come to their houses, and there instruct their families, or sett apart some time to doe it at my owne.

21. returned safe from Wittam where I preacht, with hopes of good, the lord use mee for his glory, and spare my family. I have some qualms of illnes now and then upon mee the lord is my trust for all eternity. thes things are empty. his service and doing his will is my creame, and floure in the world.

June. 26. God good to mee in the preservacion of my family. Tom: came down into the hall this day, Lord sanctifie his heart, that he may live to keepe thy word, heard Mr Cressener had buried his litle boy, thus god commands mercy, and deliverance where he pleaseth, god good to mee in the Sabbath, oh ingage my heart for ever to serve thee.

27. Mrs Harlakenden this day gave mee her housbands watch in memory of him, the lord returne her kindnes, greived about Tom this day, lord youth is vanity, thou dost sanctifie, lord overcome all the folly of his heart by the power of thy grace(,) my expectation is thou shouldst doe it, thou hast taken of my uncle Josselins only son, lord lett a duoble blessing bee upon mine.

28: made an end of haying from Sprigs Marsh, whence I had about 20^{c}. hay this yeare, its mercy to have of my own and to depend on god and not on every man, this hay and land was a guift of love. lord make mee faithfull in thy service.

30. I dreamd I had much a doe to keepe a feirce mastive of mee, I was sorely sett on by Mr S. and charged by him in his passion for that which he could not in the least instance it, but the fault evidently in him. he did not turne and say I repent of the wrong. but lord I then thought oh how much doth, must god forgive mee, and this made my heart run over with kindnes to him. lord I am such a poore peice if thou leave mee. but lord I trust thou never wilt, that I should dishonour thee.

July. 2. god this day gave us very sweet shoures with thunder which maketh us hope god hath more in store for us,

July. 3. God good to mee and mine in many outward mercies, my wife upwards from under a dangerous fainting distemper, my family preserved still in their healths, for which my soule blesseth the lord, and desireth the continuance of his goodnes on my poore tabernacle. god continued sweet dews to refresh the earth, god good to mee in his word, lord make mee carefull to advance thee in my family, for thou hast sett me up on high, and maintainest my lott.

9. bought and brought home 3 cowes one pigge and one wennel from Scots they cost me 13^{li}. 13^{s}. 4^{d}. god blesse them unto mee.

July. 10 God good to mee in many outward mercies: Tom hearing at the church window(,) god in mercy sanctifie his heart having spared his life, god pardon my neglect of him in my family, the lord in mercy command his blessing upon mee and mine and doe us good.

14: This night Potters windmill burnt down. I blesse thy name oh god, without any hurt unto the town, and to farmes in particular which were not farre of, the wind lay from them, and from the towne, the woman often wisht it were on a light fire. god sometimes gives in persons their curses(.) the lord keepe me and mine from all every evill.

July. 17. In some perplexitie about my son, his Master not being willing to take him(.) I read in course. 1 Sam. 9. Saul seeking lost asses found the kingdom, and this was some stay, god can order good out of our evill, lord I roule my soule on thee, I committ my selfe unto thee, I pray bring things about for thy glory and our good. my heart made out unto god beleeving in him, that he would not faile nor forsake mee herein. The season is dripping, grasse growing but wheat is mildewed againe and likely to bee deare. the lord make us sensible of his afflicting hand, and prepare our hearts to submitt to, and turn unto him, that he may shew us favour. Tom up and down in the family among us, the lord sanctifie him and us all, and still preserve us for his christs sake.

21. (c.o. This day) I began to raise my litle house in the orchard, I intend it (if god please for a retiring, meditating place to contemplate and view my god with delight in his word and works and doings in the world, other uses will fall in,

July. 24. The weather wett, god in mercy reserve to us the weeks of harvest. god very good to mee in the words, it was lively, his worship precious comfortable, the glory of my life, god shew mee favour in my family. and order my spirit and my wives jointly to buckle[1] in seeking their good, lord give us no rebukes, for we deserve them at thy hand, yea wee even provoke thee

28: A meeting at widdow Deaths in which much of gods gracious presence with us.

John Newton. and Adam Brewer, were both readmitted into comunion with us again on promise to walke closely with us, in gods ordinances.

Major Haynes with us at Priory. 30. This day at the burial of Mrs Wilson a young woman, sicke and dead in 3 dayes, the lord in mercy prepare mee for every change, and spare mine for his mercy sake. alarmed with the Cavaliers intention to make a rising, the Councill of State gave it, god in mercy secure our peace, this was some disturbance to mee on the lords day.

July. 31: God good to mee in composing my minde notwithstanding the hurry of the morning that I attended to the worke and worship of god this Sabbath without distraction our company roundly togither. I thinke onely W. Death, and Hunts wife absent, this day wett, god dew in his grace plentifully into my soule for christs sake

Aug: 3. By when Tibbalds wife was very strangely delivered from hurt by a cart, I did my endeavour to preserve her and god blest it. 4.

[1] To buckle in: to grapple with, engage, adhere resolutely to. NED.

and 5. dayes I preacht at Hatfeild and Topsfeild, some affections stirred, it was a sweet time to my spirit, and comfort in my freinds. god shew mee mercy in my seed, I trust he will, it is on my heart to bee wholly his, I know he will awake for my good.

Aug: 7. God good to us in the continuance of our health, (c.o. the) although litle Mary, and An sometimes ill, yet it setled not yett in any distemper; nor brought forth any small pox. lord continue thy kindnes for soule and body unto us, wee intreate thee(.) the lord good to us in the word, heard of some actuall stirres and troubles in the nacon god quiett us, and turne all for good if it bee his pleasure.

10: Sometime before and this day my litle Ann exercised with an each day ague, very feirce, yett shee vomits, and sweats which makes us hope. lord spare her for thy name sake, our county gentlemen are putting the county into a posture of defence.

Aug: 14: The Lord good to us in many mercies, my litle Ann under his rod, doe us all good by it, for thy name sake, god good in the quiet of the day, gods name bee blessed for it(,) my heart not much dismayed in thes troubles, my bowels pitty men, and I am afraid for the arke of god his worship(,) fearing the ministry will bee made offenders. oh lord awake for thy glory for in thee is my hope oh Lord

16: spent this day in prayer at Mr Littells on behalfe of the nation that god would restore our peace prevent the effusion of bloud, I spake from 1 Sam. 30.6. at night wee were alarmd, the enemy up in Norfolke, and the prince landed or upon landing

20. The season wett. our parts quiett. lord lett thy christ, thy worship and the things of thy glory bee much sett by in their hearts, and lett ours bee sett by in thy eyes, and doe us good. the country filled with very strange amazing reports which were invented to disturbe people, and putt on others to action.

Aug: 21: God good to us in many outward mercies, my An continueth ill, oh god of health restore her, and sanctifie this affliction unto us, god good to us in our peace and in the word, a Quaker wench came boisterously into the church up almost to the deske, I perceived persons expected some disturbance, but shee staid the end and then went out quietly, blessed bee god.

23. Rid out to our freinds and returned 25. god good to all our family in our absence and unto us in our jorney making it very comfortable unto us, but it was a sad time in Cheshire, and indeed the kingdom full of distractions,

Aug: 28: The land again quiet, the souldiers ordered to their old quarters in our parts, my eye much on what it is that renders any part of my life uncomfortable because I find and feare I am not usefull in my generation to others and to my family, something my heart points unto in my relation of vanities and folly in mee which through mercy I desire to bewaile, and beware, and keepe my heart through grace in an holy posture godward, the word this day, a discovering helpe, lett thy grace and truth uphold mee I pray thee.

31: This day a publique fast, I preacht from psal. 119.175. and begg heartily of the lord his judgments may helpe our state, earnestly prayed to god to pardon my sins and families, that he would sanctifie us, and so fitt us for whatsoever wee meet with.

Sept: 2. I observed a word from an ignorant man whose eye was formerly put out in cutting a bush:—god laid for mee, and he would have mee one time or other.

Sept: 4: God good to us in many mercies, my litle An something better than formerly, god perfect her health, and sanctifie it unto us all in mercy, the season very wett much corne abroad, wee neglect god, and the lord rejecteth us, god good to mee in his word, Lord lett thy judgments helpe mee.

10: early my wife apprehends shee miscarried again, lord in mercy blesse us with thy love and favour, I hired this day a youth(,) I give him mans wages, because I trust he will bee an orderly servant, I lookt upon it, as a great mercy to mee lord make it so I pray thee.

Sept: 11. God good to mee in many mercies, the season very wett and sad, lord thou canst change it, when it seemeth good unto thee. god good to mee in the word this day which was pressing on my heart to make gods word my counsellours and my guide, lord helpe mee daily in the doing of it.

12. Mr Eldred calling mee I rid to Major Haynes, god good to mee in my jorney, but my heart very vile as the world is vain, I preacht the die. 18. they in the place remember my sermon the yeare before, lord doe them good by this word(,) returned 20th. to god bee praise

21: I was much rejoyed in Mrs Harlakenden, who is much complying with my mind which argueth her great love to mee, and ingageth my heart in faithfulnes to seeke her good and content, lord remember her who is a desolate one, and is not pittied by many freinds who should pitty her.

22. An. continueth ill, good lord in mercy revive and heale her, and provide for my family for in thee doe I trust.

Sept: 25: God good to us in many mercies, hopes of a good seed time, the lord giveth mee great experience of the evill of my heart, but my helpe is in him, and to him I run and trust I shall not bee ashamed, remember mee in mercy and quicken mee in thy pathes I pray thee.

29: John Crow left his farm sufficiently unworthily, god pitty and helpe mee.

Oct: 2: God good to us in the season it was a very sweet seed time for which gods name bee blessed, my heart annoyed with much evill and vanity, which I begg of god to pardon and forgive unto mee, I loath my selfe but when lord wilt thou cure, or rather when shall I watch, and arise against the corrupcion of my heart in the might of god

6: preacht at Hatfeild, where I had a very comfortable audience god good to mee in my jorney, businesses being well dispatcht, and my returne,

October 9. A very cheerfull seed time, accept my thankfulnes oh god, the lord good to mee in my families health, I hope he will looke out for my sonnes good, and provide for him, my hearts desire is towards the lord that he should doe it, and my soule waiteth on him to doe mee good. the lord good to mee in the word, my soule looketh up to the lord for helpe in temptacons he afford it unto mee,

10: I planted 12. pears. and 24 apples in the orchard, god prosper them(.) the morning lowry, but very fitt for our worke, wherein god answered my prayer and hope. 11. preacht at Wittam, offered a place for my son at London the good lord direct mee therin for his tender mercy sake.

14: heard by Mr R.H. that the army had on Wednesday. 12. interrupted the Parliament. our sins threaten our ruine, but in all shakings god is the same, and he will doe for his name sake: it was done Thursday. 13. and Lambert the cheife agent in it. some treaty for accomodation was, but it ended in a dissolucon: die. 15°.

October 16: God good to mee and mine in many outward mercies, some inward quiet of my heart in the view of god, beholding him in christ, and so made able to hope in him, the season comfortable; mens minds feare, no providences awaken men to search their wayes and turn unto gods. god good to mee in the word, lord let it rule in my heart, and save my soule, some providences of god to mee and mine, I heartily recommend to god, to direct and blesse in the same.

Bat: Hatch begun his yeare October 14: and is to continue until october 13. at night 1660. he is to have 10^{d}. per diem every working day. and 2 meales meate in the weeke.

Oct: 23. Divers dayes past, my deare wife very stomacke sicke and disheartned. this morning shee apprehends shee is with child of a daughter, the lord bee health inward and outward unto her, carry us through all wee are to doe in the house of our pilgrimage to the glory of his own name, my busines much on mee, but I thinke my spirit is better kept therein then when lesse cumbred, lord lett Sathan no way, gett his advantage against mee. god good to mee in the Sabbath, the good lord strengthen me in beleiving for his own sake.

25: Rid in the wett to Hinningham, preacht from psal. 119.175. god returnd mee safe to his name bee praise, the country discontent, but very still, and secure, yett serious men profess to expect, sad and strang actings. but the feare is overly.

27. preacht at Wakes from psal. 119.175. a pretty audience, this the first certain lecture I resolved and engaged them to uphold it, this winter weekly. the lord accept my love, and blesse mee and shew mee favour in my family.

Oct: 30. God good to mee and mine in outward mercies, my wife ill, but they are I hope onely breeding qualmes, the dayes sad, but my god is the same. fresh, sweet, so his word is and duty. and I blesse him that he is so, the lord looke on mine and doe him good, provide for my son of thy speciall grace.

Nov: 3: a speech as if a baily intended to arrest my son Tom. an action I tooke ill, I cannot say it was so, lord help mee to forgive persons but wisely not to trust

5: I preacht this day, a few hearers. by letter I find a place provided for my son at London, god command his blessing therein for him

No. 6. My wife very weakly, in other particulars god good to mee, and lord thou canst sanctifie that hand to mee, prest men to read the scripture, in their families lord overcome their hearts into obedience I pray thee.

8: This day, my deare son Thomas rid towards London, to bee an apprentice, the god of heaven bee with him, and mercifull to him, and give him an heart to feare him, and make him industrious, I sent him away as privately as might bee in regard of his former returne, and Kendals attempt to arrest him(,) lord let mans naughtines turne unto my good.

10: Heard the wagon by which my sons Tronk and he were to goe to London went not and so perhaps Tom is staid, and other inconveniences might fall in, this morning I read 1. Kings. 2. and observed gods kindnes to David, and Davids to Barrillas[1] gods promise to his. is to mee, I claime it, and here I quietly staid, god will turne all to good, and I shall see it, and blesse him. I know god hath kindnes in store for mee and mine for his own names sake, for his love is everlasting. this day spent in prayer at priory, wherein god drew out my heart and was very good and mercifull unto mee.

Nov: 13. After wett, a frostie season. god good to mee in the day, my wife at his table with mee, my heart up delighting in him, and joying in his salvation, oh blessed bee god for a crucified christ, a succourer in temptacons, and a supplier of all grace, god good in the Sabbath the word and busines of the day.

Nov: 20. Frost continued but no violence, a very sweet season, a quiet time in the nacion, yet mens minds exceedingly discontent, the souldiers at present give law unto us, god give a law to us all, my son Tom arrived safe at London god bee mercifull to him, and mee in that affaire, the lord good in his word, he in mercy doe mee good by the same, and gett himselfe a glorious name in my eye

24: I laid in to my yard on the green a load of logs against I goe thither to dwell if god permitt, made even with Dr Pullein all accounts and gave generall releases it was to my disadvantage.

Pullein

26: Heard of my son, he liketh well at London, god grant he be liked and doe well, I blesse god for his providence thus far towards mee for good.

Nov: 27. God was good to mee in many mercies, my head and body fully imployed in my busines, god bee blessed that my heart is not ingaged in evill, yet I find I am very slothful in gods service, and much shutt up in prayer, the lord in mercy bee a sweet reviving unto my soule, god good to mee in the Sabbath, a day most wofully slighted especially by youth.

29. Rid with Mr Harlakenden to Stortford, where I managed his busines, the lord holpe mee, that an account of about 12000^{li}. wherin there was about 2900^{li}. remainder, was given up, and the mony divided, with much love and peace, the lord was very good to mee therein, and the Dennies gave mee 4 peices for my pains and care for them(,) wee returnd December 3.

[1] David at his death instructed Solomon to 'shew kindness unto the sons of Barzillai [*sic*] the Gileadite, and let them be of those that eat at thy table: for so they came to me when I fled because of Absalom thy brother'. 1 Kings 2: 7.

December 4: Good was god to us in outward mercies heard of Tom's health, he is liked and liketh, god continue both, and doe us all good, god in some measure good to mee in the Sabbath though I was much shortned in time. the season very cold.

7. Finisht the Dennies busines, paid their moneys, and they returned I hope safe(.) Mr Harlakenden gave mee 5li. for my paines in that difficult affaire.

December 11. a frostie weeke, but not excessive tedious the snow covering the ground, the lord good to mee in my relacions, Tom doth very well at London, lord in mercy watch over that great city for good

12. Rid towards London, about busines of great import for Mrs Harlakenden wherin god prospered mee, I bound also Tom to Mr Tooky his time expireth if god lengthen his life, and he doe well June. 24. 1667, the day the new Parliament was proclaimed. oh lord give him grace, wisedom, and make him industrious the city very full of tumults, the weather frostie, wayes glancy, yett god brought mee safe for which I returne him thanks, I was welcomed to my freinds and my love greatly accepted which increased my joy: die. 17.

15. being Thursday

Dec: 18: God good to me in the Sabbath, the lord my god accept mee and blesse mee in all his wayes, that I may serve him, and delight my heart in him(.) poore Bridgett hastning into heaven, from trouble to eternall rest.

22. my wife had a blacke ram lambe fell, god blesse all her stocke.

December 25. God good to mee and mine in our publique distractions, enjoying peace and not wrapt up in the actings therof, our country much troubled by Dudley Templars boisterousnes, good was god in the season, dry and cold, the lord good in the word, my heart too prone to sinfull foolish vanities lord when wilt thou heale mee.

26. Heard the officers who entred into so high an agreement. Dec: 22. on the next day being 23. came and gave up their commissions to the Speaker. I hope it is for good, and that the care of the army was by him left at present unto Okey and Allured. and London very quiett.

27. Rid to the burial of Captain Harlakenden, that family fadeth apace, it was sad a person of a family noted for religion should bee laid into ground without a sermon, he died without a will, the lord helpe persons to order their hearts and houses that they come not into snares by surprizes

29. Rid to Wethersfeild did my busines blessed bee god, and returnd safe it was a very sad jorney. dealt faithfully with Mr Templar for his actings, and gave him the best counsell I could for the future. god pitty and him direct him

31: Mr R.H. and I had close discourse of his private affaires, wherin I thinke wee agree, and fixe. I see his great confidence in mee, god stablish my heart that I may never faile or abuse a trust.

January: 1: This weeke past god good to mee and mine in many outward mercies the season frostie and so hath continued now nigh 7 weekes. but the hardnes of our hearts insensiblenes of sin, and regardlesnes of god are Englands miseries(,) this day god was good to mee in the word, his love in his sons bloud was very sweete to mee

4. preacht at Wakes. Mr H. told mee a sad story—the use I make of it, seing people will lie when there is none or litle cause to take heed of giving occasion by doing evil, and not to report a report, men are so vile in slanders

6. Contry ful of Reports. that the secluded members arm to enforce their admission, the city for a full and free Parliament. Lambert marching in hast to London, lord we are thine, save us

Jan: 8. God good in his mercies to mee and mine for which my soule blesseth him. things in the nacion quiet, the souldiers submitting to the Parliament. oh that my heart in a submitting frame to god, a very great general snow, god good to mee in the word, warme my heart by it, I humbly intreat thee.

Jan: 15. God good to us in our outward mercies, his answer of prayer in the welfare of my son is a providence greatly affects my heart, the season very vehement cold, this hard weather hath continued from Novemb: 11. til now which is above 9 weekes, and god knoweth how much longer, snow lying on the ground all this time, and sometimes very deepe, god good to mee this day in the word, my heart very sensible of gods goodnes in the present moderation of men in publique place. General Monck is coming up to London, wee shall see to what intent, god remember his in mercy and all shall bee well.

16. This morning I had in a very deare freind, a sad verbal experiment of our weaknes and rashnes, god in mercy pitty mee, and helpe mee more to depend on thee who art immutably the same, thinking and doing good to thine

18: Rid to Dedham with Mrs H. a very sad tedious jorney, yet god returned us safe againe, and preserved all to his great praise I mention it. 19 I preacht at Wakes Colne, god good therein, I prayed heartily for a young sicke man(,) lord answer prayer in much mercy, some confusednes in state affaires, nothing alwayes the same but our god.

20: Made an end of divers quarrels between Robert Crow and other persons to my good content, lord end thou my wrongs by pleading them and blesse mee who desire peace with thee, and love it, and for thy sake with all others, remember the peacemakers for the sake of the prince of peace

21: turnd in to see Toby Harris wife, a poore soule that yett looketh godward my heart open heartily to pray for her, lord heare in heaven and restore her for thy holy names sake, I have had a very great pose and cold now for a fortnight, it breaketh away, it is not much in my chest, nor any great prejudice unto mee in my rest, blessed bee god who watcheth over mee for good.

Jan: 22th The Lord good to us in many outward mercies, health of my litle ones restoring unto them, a hope prayer shall bee answered for Harris wife, god gave her rest in the day, and a sore appeareth, the season cold, the frost is going away, and yett checkt with cold and snow, the lord was good to mee in his word, the lord make it an abiding savour upon my heart, that I may live to glorifie and praise his holy name.

23: began to plow Sprigs marsh, busy in my housbandry, god in mercy prosper my worke, and command his blessing on the labour of my hand. heard sister Anna was returned home again. god in mercy make her wise for her own good, and the good of her freinds. god gave a mercifull answer of prayer in my Jane whose ague I hope hath thes two dayes left her.

24: This night I feasted my two tenants, and I hope god had no dishonour by us(,) lord bee reconciled to mee and mine, and doe us good all our dayes

25. This day I spent at Priory in a day of praise to my god at Mr H. desire to whom I spake something from psal. 50.v.15. and heartily prayed to my god in Christ for him, lord heare and bee gratious. When I looke backe into the world I find nothing but confusions, hopes of a peace between Spain and France, but sad warres in the North, the Swedes bustling as a rod tearing the flesh of the nacions, but not advantaging them selves and our poore England unsetled, and her physitians hitherto leading her into deepe waters. Cromwells family cast down with scorne to the ground, none of them in command or imployment, the nacion looking more to Charles Stuart,

out of love to themselves not him, the end of thes things god only knoweth, wee have had sad confusions in England, the issue god only knoweth

— — — — — — — — — — — — — — — — — —

Jan: 26: 59: my 43. yeare complete, and 44: entring.

26: This day I reckon my birth day, I preacht at Wakes, church snowy, the way bad, twice I slumpt in[1] and was wett, yet I blesse god for the sermon a birthday sermon from psal: 119.73, and so doe some others, thats a great honour to doe good, lord bee with mee, and blesse mee in christ Jesus, and command thy favour for my seed. I am thine, I looke thou shouldst save mee

28: Mr W. H. told mee that Kendall went on in his suite against Tom. lord in mercy remember mee, and lett not mans ill will hurt mee. Mr Haynes with us, who is put out of his command, which was Coll: Markhams act, I am sorry at this private spleen in our actings.

Jan: 29. Frost continueth and snow, god good to mee and mine in our outward mercies(,) the lord good to mee in the word, yett I find not livelynes in my heart for the services of god. heard of Mrs H. health and cheerfulnes, god continue it and increase, the ague continueth on her litle one, which I hope god in due time will remove,

Feb: 2. God good to mee in my deare freind young Mrs Harlakendens busines with her father, wherin god hath helped mee to steere them both, I hope to a final loving freindly end.

3. Tibbalds and I had discourse about the farme for 6. or 9. yeares. ☞ Tibbalds agreement he is to have Crows: Sawyers. Bridgmans. 2. sonnels. Hobstevens and the meadow: only I am to have the pightell by Mr Littels. and 2 acres in Hobstevens, and passage, the rent 60li. per annum about 3li. lords rent. pay tithes. ditch. 30. rod every yeare allow 2 load logs. 1: of small wood.

Feb: 5. God good to us in outward mercies, lord sanctifie my heart, and of my seed(.) I find Mrs H: busines crowding much into my thoughts lord provide for her helpe, this day it eate much into my heart troubling mee, tis hard to lay by our molesting thoughts, prest catechising family instruction on my people, lord doe thou presse it on them for they will not else heare, the thaw is considerable,

[1] Slump: to fall or sink into a bog, swamp, muddy place. SOED

but yet the frost continueth in the ground, ice and snow also in many places, a very darke time, sun, seldom appearing

6: On Moonday I rid to Dedham, where I found my best of freinds Mrs H. very well, and somewhat cheerfull, glad of the newes I carried her from her father in giving her the 100li. and abating her. 15li. in the interest, 7. I preacht at Dedham, and returned safe die 8o. gods mercy great to mee in all this jorney, lord affect my heart with thy care and tendernes over mee and lett goodnes lead mee to repentance, the season opening the frost almost gone, dry, the pathes pave.

10: Towards night our bullocke calved a brown bull calfe well, thus god entreth us into the world by degrees this. 11th day cheerfull beyond what man can almost suppose.

Feb: 12. God good to mee and mine in many mercies, yett our healths in Tom, Jane, and An. a litle crazed,[1] god sanctifie the providence to us all, and remove the stroake that with heart, and life wee may praise him. a sweet day, the word very good in mercy to mee, the lord affect mee with his goddnes, a sad and troublesome time at London, the Parliament much displeased with the city, and shewing it, the spring riseth, god prevent new troubles if it bee his pleasure.

14: Wm Brand in great misery not able to make water, lord helpe, heard that Monke had declared for and with the city for a free parliament:

18: sew sprigs marsh with white oats, god in mercy give a blessing to my labour and increase mee for his glory in my continuall good that I may praise him

18: A very sweet and comfortable day, accompanied with good newes in all my busines from London, for all which mercies and to my son in health, my soule praiseth god

Feb: 19. God good to mee and all mine in outward mercies, the lord in mercy accept us delight in us, and doe us good, the spring cheerfull, my busines much, god holds my head and heart I praise him, that I am not oversett,[2] god was good to mee in the Sabbath, the rest of it a great mercy to my weary body, oh lett the word bee so to my soule, my heart suckt much comfort out of it for which I blesse and praise my god,

I observe a providence. a Man I was hiring one Peakes son, declined mee to goe to a Quaker I know not his motives, there he fell

[1] Craze: to break down in health; to render infirm, also to render insane, distract. SOED.

[2] Overset: to capsize, to be upset, to fall into disorder. SOED.

sicke of the small pox, and his mother keep[ing] him came home and died, the lord watch over mee and mine for good.

21: Heard Yorkshire were up and headed by the Lord Fairfax, declaring for a free parliament, and until then pay no taxes, expecting the like through the nacon. secluded members admitted into the house.

22. Rid to Dedham to see Mrs Harlakenden, and returned safe, blessed bee that god that keepeth mee upon the way, the season kindly for its time

25. This day I observed one of my planted pears to bud forth, blessed bee god for prospering any of my labours.

Feb: 26. God good to mee and mine in manifold mercies, the lord shine on mine in the health of soule and body, and binde us up in the covenant of life, that wee may continually rejoyce in his goodnes, and say the name of the lord bee praised. the lord good to mee in the word and worke of the day, my bowels moved over the people, that because there is hope of mercy and pardon with god, therefore wee should encourage our hearts to turne from every evill, and neglect of god, and sett up his worship in our families.

March: 1: rid to Dedham to returne Mrs Harl: to Colne, left Jane at Colchester with Mrs Piggott, our returne well and safe blessed bee god, my wife very ill next day, but about the 3^{d}(.) god keepe up my heart in all thes hurries to a calme dependance on him.

March. 4: a calme cheerfull day, my family small only my litle ones with mee the good lord season and instruct mine betimes, and frame their hearts unto thee. I prest family instruction on all to practice and submitt too, lord let thy word take place in the midst of us, lord make my businesse easy to mee, and prosper it for christs sake I most humbly intreate thee.

5 preacht wid. Hatch's funeral sermon on Job. 11.13.18. god good to mee in that word, I tasted my hopes in god, a secure holdfast of my soule.

6: their is a worme in the tailes of cowes that faints them, and loosens ☞ their teeth, and maketh them not eate well, the cure is to cutt that worme in the taile in a soft place where it is, I did so to mine this day, and began to sowe my pease in the orchard, the lord prosper my crop for mercy sake.

7. made an end of sowing my oats 25. bushels in all, god blesse the seed.

8: Mett at Mr Cresseners, my wife ill and not with us, god in mercy to mee and her setle her body and giveth mee hope all will bee well, shee feared a miscarrying

March: 11. God good to mee and mine in our peace, health, and outward mercies my wife sad at the thoughts of my jorney, god was good to mee in the Sabbath words, sacrament. ingage my heart I pray thee, that I may for ever love and feare thy name, received a letter of my daughter Janes writing, god in mercy make her his own epistle, god bee good to mee in my family and jorney, he is my staffe to leane upon and in him my heart quietly trusteth.

12. before 7 a clocke it began to raine very cold. but 13. a warm springing raine

14: This day Mrs Harlakenden and my wife parted, for such deare freinds very composedly. but oh how loath shee is I should bee absent, lord in our love let us taste Christs love, and love him as sensibly as each other, when thou hast returned mee safe as I trust thou wilt, and I almost know it, for I have Abrahams sheild and Jacobs promise,[1] and the god of them both to bee with mee, when I returne it shalbee to her comfort in the increase of my love and tendernes, and in the mean time thou wilt blesse mee and all mine, with thee I leave all as with a faithfull god, I know thou wilt looke after them.

Worcester jorney.

15. Mrs Harlakenden and I. with her kinswoman and manservant, sett out in her fathers coach for Wittam whither wee came safe, yett our wayes excessive dirty. and our coach from London came into our inn before the returne of the other, two mercies god afforded us, safety and protection on the road, conveniences and quiett at our inns, whither wee came alwayes in good time, no raine to trouble us but one day which I desire to acknowledge as gods great goodnes: 16. wee dined at Burntwood, that day afforded a providence not to bee forgotten of mee but esp. of Mrs H. wee came early to London, and then to businesse, all which I dispatcht at London not only to our content, but to our delight, but the weather was so stormy, that it was thought our jorny was not to bee performed. 18: I preacht twice dined with the Lord Mayor.[2] lord give a blessing to the word. 20th. a day that lighted my heart in its providence, though I apprehended hazard to mee by cold. and I was in great

[1] Abraham's shield was the Lord (Genesis 15: 1), and to Jacob's promise RJ had earlier alluded (p. 408, n. 1).

[2] Thomas Allen, son of William Aleyn of London, druggist, created a Baronet in 1660, and head of the commission for trying the Regicides. *Complete Baronetage*, (ed.) G.E.C. vol. iii.

danger at Stow to have been spoiled by the coach, yett god preserved mee, and none of us tooke any considerable cold in the jorny: our law triall putt of, 21th. wee sett out for our jorny our coachman encour(a)g(e)d by the stage coach for Worcester, wee arrived at our jorneys end March. 24th and found all well.—25. I
1660. preacht twice, the minister desirous to leave all his worke on mee, and I very readie. god moved and startled people. they said those sermons would not bee forgotten, god grant they bee practiced; 26:27. wee had but one Tenant with us, riding out into the meadow by Severn(,) Mrs H. resolved to returne on Friday seing there was no busines. I prayed her patience and submission to gods will, at night one came to us with whom wee could never agree, yett afterwards divers did to our very great satisfaction 29. I preacht the Lecture I hope with some successe as also April 1. twice. on Monday wee kept the Court, very quietly, and 3 dispatcht our busines and returnd to London April. 7th. and so home to Colne April. 10th. praise to the name of my gratious god where I found all well and safe, for which my soule blesseth him.

Ap: 14: When I come to view my outward estate I find my lands as formerly, I have paid of divers great debts, putt out my son Tom prentice which cost mee in mony and clothes about an 100li. I have done very much in repaire and cost on my farmes, and begun to stocke one; I am now in debt as in my blew booke 150li. 4s. 6d. I guesse not 20s. more that I know of in the world, and there is owing unto mee. 314li. 15s. 0d. my stocke is worth about 25li. in cowes, hogs corne on the ground. so god enlargeth my tedder[1] daily, yearly. lord enlarge my heart for thee and thy service, and continue to blesse mee and mine indeed, and my soule shall praise thee.

April: 15: God was good to mee in bringing mee safe to my home, relacions, and worke to which I was called this day, god good to us in the seasons speaking fruitfulnes the lord awake for my good and make mee his, and lett his name be glorified(,) I preacht on Ezra. 10.2. god give us hope in himselfe.

17. our choise of Knights at chelmsford, where I saw an evidence of gods providence in ruling the world in the disorders and confusions of publique meetings, the honest partie lost their choice, but god will not loose his right.

19. preacht at Wakes from Ezra. 10. moved to meet and keepe a day of prayer at Mr Littells in this sad juncture, wherein yett my heart trusts in god

[1] Ted: to spread out, scatter, or strew abroad (new-mown grass) for drying. SOED.

April. 22. The Lord good to mee in manifold mercies, and unto mine, my wife though weary yett indifferent cheerfull, and presents through mercy gods former goodnes in the like condicon with her to mee. heard of Mrs Har. and that which pleased mee, because I hope its good for her, lord bee her freind for shee is desolate. god good to mee in the Sabbath, for which my soule blesseth him, the season very sweet

23. heard Lambert made head in opposicon to the present power, and really appeard in Northamptonshire. 24. heard at dinner that he was taken and it proved true quicke and short worke. /

Ap: 25: Parliament began, if wee judge of the temper of the houses (the Lords house satt) by the ministers they choose to preach unto them, it presents hopes being Calany, Garden, Baxter[1]

April: 29. God good to mee and mine in our many outward mercies, for which my soule heartily blesseth him, heard from Mrs H. with whom I hope its well lord heare her prayers, and satisfie her soule in thy favour. god good to mee in the word, its easie with him to render all mens devices useles and give being to the counsels of his own heart; my heart wrecks mee in the troubles of my corrupt thoughts, lord when shall they bee in subjection to thee.

May. 2. Divers Christian people mett togither to seeke god in this difficult houre for wisedom and grace, the lord heare and accept.

May. 6: God good to mee and mine in outward mercies, the spring very excellent, the nacion runneth into the King as Israel to bring backe david, lord make him the like blessing to our England, and lett gods counsell bee in the worke. the word and will of god is good, lett it take place; my heart under this change very calme feares on mee for the arke of god, but that is under his love and care,

jorney: May. 11. set forwards for London whither I came safe and thence to Greenwich 12. at night to my deare Harlakenden.—13. I preacht at Greenwich and prayed by name for K. Charles. 14. I was at Eltham in Kent.—15. god gave us a verdict in trial against our adversary at Guildhall barre. 16. I was with deare Harl. again and returnd from her. 17. god counsell and keepe her safe and make her a prosperous person: 18. returned to my dearest wife and found her and all well for which and all mercies I bow my soule in thankfulnes to my most gracious god.

May. 20. God good to us in many outwards mercies, the season affords

[1] The *Commons Journals*, vol. viii, under 25 April 1660 records that it was resolved that Mr. Calamy, Dr. Gauden, and Mr. Baxter should preach. These were the well-known ministers and writers Edmund Calamy, John Gauden, and Richard Baxter. DNB.

shoures with haile(,) the earth began to require raine, and god gave it, the lord good to us in his word, worship. my heart much out of frame, profanesse appeareth much in persons, god in mercy rebuke it, that wee may praise his holy name.

26: Heard from Mrs Harlakenden, shee sent my wife pease, a rare present to her, god requite her remembrance and tender love.

May. 27. God good to mee and mine in many outward mercies for which my soule praiseth him, yett I have my rebukes in some illnes in my face my knubs on my legs as spices of the scurvy,[1] my wife and children weake(.) god sanctifie all providences unto mee and ingage my heart to him that I may love him, and delight in him, god good to mee in the Sabbath(,) the word a mercy to mee, god maketh good men prosper*ance*, lord make mee so, and I shall praise thee.

June. 1. preacht for Mr Sparrow at Halsted from Pro. 29.21, the season very moist, I looke on it as a mercy, lett there bee no damage in it, to the fruit of my feild, that is now cutt down. nor to my meadow. for oh lord I depend on thee to blesse mee and all that I have

June. 3. God good to mee in outward mercies, my soule desireth to feare the lord and serve him therewith, the lord good to us in the shoures, now give us faire weather wee pray thee, the King returned in safety, and with hopes of being a blessing to the nacion, god good to mee in the Sabbath, the word preacht, thy word is my life. an offer made, concerning Mrs Harlakenden lord of thy mercy provide comfortably for her, shee is a widdow indeed yett thine trusting in thee.

6. Rid to lay claime to the King's pardon before the Maior of Colchester

9. This day deare Mrs Harlakenden came suddenly but acceptably to Colne, I was almost overjoyed to see her, hoping my wife will have great satisfaction in her company, lord lett her jorney and affaires bee prosperous I humbly, heartily pray

June. 10th. God good to mee in divers mercies and also to mine, the season very comfortable, a great calme in the contry, the Kings proclamacion against debaucht courses a cutt to the gentry of England, oh lord make him a nursing Father to thy people., god good to mee in some spirit, keeping it in sweet peace, dependance on him, oh that my heart were more lively and active in the service of god.

[1] Knub: knob, a small rounded lump or mass; a bump, hump, wart, pimple, etc. Scurvy: a disease characterized by general debility of the body, foul breath, subcutaneous eruptions, and pains in the limbs; covered with scurf, scabby. SOED.

13: A time wherin great armies are on foot, and yett an actuall cessacon of fighting in all Europe. except some thing between the Moscovite ☞ and Pole. the Turke and the Transilvanian, after this calme perhaps some very sudden storme.

June: 17. God good in many mercies, my wife sent for her midwife, god in mercy carry her through her condicon comfortably, that shee may blesse thy name(.) the season good, warme dewes, the lord good in the worke, awake my heart to intentnes in thy service I pray thee. this day wee had the liberty of the lords table, god bee mercifull to mee and doe mee good.

18: escaped a great danger in a sad fall, lord my preserver I blesse thy name

June. 20th. This day about a quarter before 3. my wife was delivered of her ninth child, and 5t daughter Elizabeth, god enter into covenant with it, and make it his own, my poore wife was fearfull and had sad long labour but at length very quicke and kindly for which gods name bee glorified in and by mee and all mine, young Mrs Harlakenden with us, very pittiful, tender and helpefull to my wife.

June. 24. God good to us in many outward mercies in the sense wherof my soule heartily blesseth his name, the season dewing, but god will command seasonable weather for us, the lord command his loving kindnes for us, this day my Elizabeth was baptized in the publique congregacion, god in mercy baptize it with his holy spirit, and owne it for his owne.

28: A day of praise for the Kings returne, I preacht on 2 Chron. 17.6. putting on people to pray that mercies may lift up our hearts in the ways of god, my spirit in a very wretched temper, lord without thee I can doe nothing, and it must bee great helpe my corrupcion doth not much.

29. Great stroaks of thunder, my litle Mary even feld down with amazement [in one], and my wife ill, but god preserved all, much rain.

July. 1. A sad season, but god will take care of the fruits of the earth, and preserve them unto us. god good to mee in family mercies, my heart in a dependance on him with hope in the midst of my sins and feares, this evening the sun shineth cheerfully, god in mercy heare prayer.

2. discovered and I hope prevented a wickednes between an old fellow and a youth lord helpe mee to improve it for thy glory, and their good in rescuing them out of the bonds of iniquitie

3. My deare freind sent away part of her goods, a presage of her final remove from Colne. god Almightie who hath thy housband bee a shadow to his Harlakenden and babe, and cast there lott for them.

July. 8. This weeke god good to mee in many mercies, a meanes I trust to prevent an eminent wickednes in two persons; the season mercifull in the midst of our feares, my imployment taketh of my heart from many vanities but when shall conquering grace doe it. my wife faint but upwards, the lord helpe mee to trust in him.

12. This day my deare Freind Mrs Harlakenden and her litle daughter went from Colne, not intending a returne, the providence is sad, all of my deare Harlakenden gone from his habitacion. good lord how uncertain all thes things are. I went part of the way with her, none else doing such an office. this day wee parted with great testimonies of mutuall love. I emptied my meadow, at night it rained, gods providence was good to mee, for which I praise him. my deare wife about in the house her throat sore, but god will command healing.

13. Mr H. and I togither, perhaps I might bee in fault, but I thought I found unkindnes, which god forgive, and help mee to forgett.

July 15. God good to mee in many outward mercies in my family, my losse of the priory family a deepe blow, troubles for some and unkindnes from others cutts deepe into my spirit. god helpe and heale all, god was good to mee in his word, the lord setle mee on his promise, accept mee and doe mee good continually.

July: 20th. Thomas Daniel came beginning his yeare being Friday, god make him a blessing to us for such I value a carefull youth to bee.

July. 22th. My wife abroad this day for which I blesse god, the lord good to mee and mine in many mercies. ministers pittifully put out of their livings while others advanced. our schoolemaster Dr Pullein said to bee made Bishop of London-Derry. Lord helpe mee to serve and trust in the(e) for thou art my hope, heard of threatnings against mee, but the lord is a sheild to mee who never sought the wrong of others.

24: heard divers of my freinds and neighbours in trouble, Lord helpe them out by spirit, freinds, providences, and doe them good.
this day Mr R. H. shewed mee his will, wherin he hath dealt well with his grand-daughter, and used mee in divers trusts. the lord spare him and give mee an heart to bee faithfull unto him and them, in all the things of the lord, and matters of estate.

July. 29. A very mercifull season for harvest, although men feared the contrary, god good to mee and my family in many mercies. I hope he hath given mee a sober youth in my family. god good to me in the

Sabbath(,) gods promise very sweet to mee and my claim to heaven thereby and no other way precious(.) our Dr Pullein said to bee Arch Bishop of Tuam. a place in Conaught, May wee thinke their was nothing in all the Saints expectacons in England, may not one arise and wo to him that is the person to bee the man of sin. horresco.[1] when I thinke. and who it is.

Aug: 3. I preacht at Topesfeild. affections stirring for which god bee praised, the lord heale my heart, which is very vain, I feele it, but help is of thee, the season very uncertain for harvest. god yett will command his mercies for us

4: a very sad tempest especially for lightning, blessed bee our preserver, man is a weake thing in the hand of any creature were it not for a strong god.

Aug: 5. God good to mee and mine in the continuance of outward mercies, I begin to bee straitned in my estate, lord open hearts to deale justly and righteously with mee, and lett it not lodge in their hearts to wrong him that is peaceable and quiet, god gave us a good day after the tempest. the lord helpe mee to keepe my mind in a due and even frame to all the wayes of god which is in the desire of my soule.

6: Had home my timber out of Chalkney wood, the last load overthrown behind, god good in preservation of all, for which my soule praiseth him

10. almost finisht my haying, I had much and good, heard as if the act of oblivion would be moderate. Lord if thy acts of oblivion bee not famous and large what will become of us.

Aug: 12. God good to us in outward mercies, divers sad untimely deaths by us and wee preserved. Mrs Jane highly out of frame, others in sorrow, and wee in peace and rest of spirit. my soule and all within mee blesseth thee, oh frame my heart to faith and obedience continually. a very sweet harvest weeke which many improve; the Arch Bishop of Tuam with us, people wonderfully neglect the Sabbath, and yett god holds his hand. oh that patience might amend us. god good in the word to mee.

17. rumourd as if some stirs in Ireland against Bishops and service booke. the King moulds the English army to his absolute command, but gods hand is over and above all.

18. a thistle in my eye. but through mercy after a while it wiped out. a woman in our town in the harvest feild lost the sight of one eye on a suddain. a filme overspreading it.

[1] I grow fearful.

Aug: 19. God good to mee and mine in outward mercies. my wives throat well. our litle froward child very thriving, a very sweet harvest time(.) the lord bee praised for the covenant. with Noah. and that of christ shall bee made good. my heart very unsatisfied in my selfe, preaching, all I doe poore, empty(,) nothing. lord doe not cast mee out of thine eyes but let mee live in thy sight.

20. Heard of the death of my wifes Uncle Shepheard, whereby a close fell to my wife worth about 50li. the lord helpe me to serve him under any mercy and goodnes of his unto mee.

22. Mr R. H. went to London(,) lord give him a safe returne, at night Mary by a snatch of our maide Alice, had her arme puld out of joynt, the child very unquiet next day. Mrs Withers came and sett it, for which mercy I praise god, my wives instep splinted. lord keepe all our bones safe and sound I pray thee

Aug: 26. God good to mee in outward mercies. Dr Pullein now an Arch Bishop being to remove from us, occasioned great feastings, which are vain tainting things to our minds, god in some measure abased my heart(,) god hath given good harvest weather which yett continueth, god good to mee in the Sabbath for which I blesse his holy name.

Monke Duke of Albemarle made Lieutenant of Ireland.

29. preacht at Colchester for Mr Stockdale,[1] god good to mee going, and returning(,) dined with Mr Mayor. said the act of indempnity past.[2] Mr Harlakenden returned safe from London, gods name bee glorified for thes mercies. talke as if the honest partie were in hazard of a massacre, I feare mens jealous hearts are foolishly at worke, I cannot thinke such a wickednes psal. 4. ult. but if god hath made such great plottes in their vile resolucons fools, and none shall bee establisht by their wickednesse. Paris will witnes.

this day the King passed the act of pardon, I was glad I was so well imployed on a day when so memorable an act was past.

Sept: 1: A sad account in the affaires of my deare Freind Mrs H: Lord bee thou her portion, and bee thou all and in all unto her.

Sept: 2. God good to us in outward mercies, Mary well of her arm. blessed bee god, lord bring my family in frame, and in subjection unto thee, and rejoyce in mee to doe mee and mine good, a quiet Sabbath, lord lett my heart keepe a rest in thee, and so unto thy

[1] Owen Stockton, lecturer at Colchester from 1658 on the nomination of mayor and corporation, died 1680; writer of a diary. Calamy.

[2] 'An Act of free and general pardon, indemnity and oblivion' (1660), which forgave most of those involved in the Civil War, except those responsible for the Irish Rebellion of 1641, and a few regicides. Kenyon, pp. 365–71.

glory. oh the deadnes and wonderfull backwardnes in my heart to a livelynes in doing gods service oh lord, I sigh and looke up unto thee, when wilt thou heale mee.

5. preacht old Dranes funerall, great affections up in mee to doe poore soules good, lord doe it, and accept mee and blesse all thine.

8. begun my well, water came freely at 6. foote. the old fathers rejoycd in a well of water, and so doe I for my habitacon, blessing god who giveth springs on the uppermost hill, my yard being the pitch of the hill of our town, oh give mee of the water of life freely. yea thou wilt and that is my joy and life and my soule shall live and blesse thee

Sept. 9. God good in many mercies to mee and mine, a very sweet and seasonable time, busines going of hand well, the lord good to mee in the Sabbath but my heart dead and listles, lord recover mee, and awaken mine to livelines in thy wayes.

13. made an end of digging and bricking my well. its about 9 foot or a litle more deepe, it hath very fresh springs, if they hold which I hope at that depth in the earth they will doe.

15. heard of the death of the Duke of Glocester second brother to the King, who died of the smal pox. Sept. 13. and lately before Esme Stuart the Duke of Lennox, and this day sister Bridge. lord teach us to number our days and apply our selves to true wisedom.

Sept: 16. Cool drie weather, after hot, and then moist, fit for seed time, blessed bee god, that giveth us our seasons, oh that wee knew the seasons of grace(,) this was the Sabbath my heart up to declare against mans sin, in the evill and danger of it, lord doe thou convince us all of the same, my heart very much disquieted for that evill that is abroad in the world, oh that and the plague of my heart would bee an insupportable burthen were not gods goodnes an ease and support to my heart.

18. preacht sister Bridges funeral from psal. 34.19. a text of her appointment, god make the word seasonable and profitable

19. This day a stocke of planke at the perke[1] fell down, which may bee a warning, and matter of thankfulnes it doing no hurt and my children being wont in the sumer to play and worke under them.

22: Saturday. I begun to sow mislain in Brockhole, the first hard corn that I ever sew, god command his blessing. I wait on thee for it, and verily I expect thou shouldst, yea thou wilt, and I shall praise thee.

Sept: 23: God good to mee and mine in outward mercy, a very sweet

[1] Presumably at Colne Park.

comfortable seed time. I meet with trouble in my servants, lord I am a worse servant unto thee, if thou punisht my failings in my relacons unto mee, how very sad and greivous would they bee. I pray thee, pardon mee, and blesse mee, rejoyce over mee to doe mee good continually. my deare Freind Mrs H. writes of returning unto Colne, the lord make her a cleare way, and quiet her heart with us

25. a good seed time, my land sown over thicke, on foure acres and a rood nine bushels and halfe of mislain, this was in Brockhole by Tom Daniel, and on an acre of wheate land seven pecks and halfe god command his blessing, I made an end. Sept. 27th.

29: Mich. day. Tibbald severed my sheepe and his, put them upon the ground he held, and I now enter upon, and he put on the other ground(,) the lord command his blessing and favour upon us both, and all that appertaineth unto us. etc.

Sept: 30: Very shourie weather, which is an hindrance for present to seed time(,) the lord good to mee in many outward blessings for which my soule blesseth his holy name; god good to mee in the Sabbath, but my soule is inwardly afflicted at the profane conversacon of many, oh that god would in mercy bring in a change upon persons. Sept. 27. in the morning the bullock gave bloud, her bag swelled and so continued bloud on that bigge[1] till. oct. 17. wee found the hedge hog in the feild oct. 4. and kild it. hedge hogge

Oct: 5. This day I preacht at Halsted psal. 46.1.2.3. lord keep up my heart upon thee I begg of thee, for thou art my refuge, this day Grace Newton begun her yeare, shee is to have 50^{s}. god make her a good servant,

Oct: 7. a very cheerfull day, wherin my heart remembreth creator, and redeemer with admiracion and thankfulnes, oh how good and bountifull is god in his goodnes to mee, but in the covenant of promises oh how unspeakably rich, let not my heart distrust I pray thee; god good to mee in the Sabbath, a day of rest a mercy, but calling up my heart more closely to mind god, a mercy of mercies

11. This day I paid 1^{li}. 12^{s}. 6^{d}. for my pole tax.[2] I paid it once formerly in 41. as I remember, this rate unusuall twice in an age. its ground is to disband the army, god in mercy send us peace.

Oct: 14. God good to mee, and mine in many outward mercies, for which my soul praiseth him the season very quiet, and the time of the yeare comfortable, the lord compose my spirit, in submission unto

[1] Big: a teat. NED. It was believed that hedgehogs caused udders to bleed by sucking the milk. The 'bullock' is clearly a female cow.

[2] The two graduated Poll Taxes of 1641 and 1660 are noted in William Kennedy, *English Taxation 1640–1799* (1913), p. 39.

him(,) god was good to mee in the word, oh that I might bee inabled to walke with god, as my soul seeth beauty and lovelynes in it, our schoolemaster in town at Mr Cresseners, and well, but not at church, morning nor evening.

17. Spent this day in prayer at priory, put up divers very earnest peticons publique and private, which the lord in mercy answer(.) heard then that Harrison, and Carew, two of the Kings Judges were executed but to that day 8 in all were executed, Jo: Cooke. Hugh Peters. Tho. Scot. Gregory Clement. Jo. Jones. Adrian Scroope.

Oct: 21. A very sweet season, somewhat cold, wee brake bread this day. Mr Eldred joyning with us. god good to us. god mercifull to mee, in many outward blessings, yett all of us crazie with colds, my litle Bettie very tedious to her mother. lord carry mee patiently, and quietly through all the troubles that wee meete with in a dependance on thee as from my soule I heartily desire

23. my good neighbour Mr Jo. Littell brought home his wife it was a very cheerfull day, god good to us in our jorney, the priory women overturnd, no hurt but to their clothes

27. This day I ended all the outward worke of my building, but onely the oven the lords eye bee on that habitacon for good, and dwell there I pray thee and with mine for good
Said the busines of Hides daughter and the Duke of Yorke, was looked on by the King as one of his greatest afflictions. its said a contract, and marriage is pretended, Hides ruine is apprehended. the Q was sent for to France said to be come. god preserve the King; all ended faire among them.

Oct. 28. God good to us in many outward mercies, this day 20. yeare my Jane and I were married. I am sensible of the mercy, and thankful to god for the same, god good to mee in the word, the lord make mee upright with him, when evills are broad, sheild mee lord by thy grace.

Nov: 1. My sister Dorothy came to see mee. lord my lot is comfortable to hers, its thy mercy not any thing in mee hath made the difference(,) continue thy kindnes oh god

No: 4: the lords day, and a good day.

10: the weather that was pleasant being dry and cold, changed to wett.

No: 11. god good to us in many outward mercies, health, peace. bringing my tedious worke this summer near a conclusion, no hurt nor mischeife being done to any in the same, for which my soule blesseth god. this day god was pressing on my heart to walke with him while I was speaking to others

Sr J. Jacob. in 56. in arrear 6 yeare. being. 24 received since 10^{li}. there is due of that 14 and to Sept. 29. 1660. foure yeares more being in all. 16. besides. 14.

13. rid up to London and returned safe die. 17. by gods mercy towards mee and mine and all well at home for which gods name bee praised. found Mrs Harlakenden very much broken with sorrows and troubles, I did some affaires for her the lord bee her porcon, peace, and provide for her as I trust he will

Nov: 18: God good to mee, and mine in manifold outward mercies, but I find such a vanitie in my spirit that boweth down my soule, yett this trouble is my hope for surely there is the spirit stirring against the flesh, but when shall christ so strengthen mee that I shall in his grace bee more than a conqueror

19: we kild a good hogge, which proved neat and cleane, a mercy to bee observed(,) at night a violent wind and snow which covered the earth die 20. so that wee gave our catle meat twice in the day, having begun to give once a day ever since octob. 29.

21. received in a litle wood from Sprigs marsh, its a mercy when god is our own to have any thing to call our owne,

Nov: 25. The season somewhat more winterly then formerly. I observe how apt wee are to account a harsh time the hardest wee ever felt and a mild the best, letting slip out of our mind what was formerly, and very commonly not eying god that giveth both, god good to mee in many mercies, a zeale in mee in preaching the word, lord warm their soules in the love, and embracement of the truth as it is in Jesus.

27. How busy was I to send up apples to our freind Harlakenden, oh how may I read gods love to us, in ours to our deare relacons.

Decemb. 2. God good to us in many mercies, gospell liberties and freedom yet continued(,) feares on many, said lists are taken of the fanatique and all honest men that are not as formal as others are so accounted, but gods purpose that shall stand(.) god was good to mee in the word this day, helpe mee and mine to walke humbly with thee, and it shall bee well with us.

6. Mr Pelham giving mee leave I went and gathered. elms. ashes. crab stocks, and about halfe hundred wood sett. the moon at full this day.[1] but its god must prosper all our endeavours, he was good to mee in the jorney, but my heart is not sweetned alwayes with him

[1] It was believed that agricultural operations should be geared to the phases of the moon. RJ shows a growing interest in the moon from about this date. For a general introduction to the observance of days and seasons in this period see Keith Thomas, *Religion and the Decline o Magic* (1971), ch. 20.

but turneth aside to empty vanities. lord pardon mee in mercy. this 7. day I sett 32 crab stocks in the new orchard: 11. in my own. 27. trees in Brockhole and 20 in the feild behind my barn.

Decemb: 9. Gods mercy much to us in our children. Ann. had a bush in her knee very dangerous gott out, and healed by the care of a tender mother. my litle Mary fell dangerously into the fire, whom her mother snatcht out and is almost joyd in healing her hands, gods name bee praised for all(,) lord lett my present love, childrens duty, and all of us for future in tendernes bee a comfort to this deare wife and mother that is so usefull to us all, the winter hitherto very mild, and dry, a great helpe to mee that am to goe up to the green so often. god was good to mee in the word awaken my heart to feare thee, and walke stedfastly with thee that it may bee well with mee.

11. This day by gods good providence towards mee, I paid in to Eliz. Web. the 50^{li}. that was given to her by Mrs Marie Churchs will, I borrowed onely 13^{li}. of it, the rest I procured of my own mony. blessed bee god who brings mee out of any difficultie and encombrances which I account debts and building to bee.

15. A winterly day indeed, a rime frost, then *sniuzling* cold thawing, afterwards a windie rain cold, then blustering high winds.

December 16. God good to mee and mine in manifold mercies, I reckon our peace, and libertie in the gospell a glorious mercy, continue it, and help us to walke worthy of it in all things, this is in the depth of winter and yet a comfort. the sun is arising, oh when our state is going on to good its comfortable though the increase bee small and not perceptible, as I hope its in my heart, my root is with and for god, though I beare not such lovely fruite as I desire.

20: very winterly cold, wett weather. I thresht some barly, it was no bad crop for which I blesse god, that giveth any indifferent increase.

Dec: 23. Reports of strange tempests up and down in the world, great violencies likely to bee practiced, thus in Italy, Denmarke, England. Guernsey. oh lord when thou shakest thes things, make mee wise to provide for that which cannot bee shaken(.) this day wett and winterly, god good in his word, my hearts desire is thou wilt not leave mee under deceit, but make mee plain and upright with thee.

25. This day I preacht a sermon of Christ from. Jo: 3.16. divers not there and some in there antique postures, lord I desire to advance thy name, no profanes nor formality, accept mee and pardon mee in thy christ.

Dec: 30: a comfortable day, god very good to us in our health, and all outward mercies god accept mee in christ and rejoyce over mee for good.

Lambe. towards the morning of 31. I found a lambe in my feild our first this yeare, Toms sheep lambd. Jan: 4th.

Jan: 6: God good to mee and mine in manifold outward mercies for which my soule praiseth him, this lords day morning a troop of horse marcht by. gods worship is nothing with them I feare, lord setle truth and peace in this nacon. god was good to mee in the word, though my heart very dead and unprepared to meete with and follow him, the lord accept mee and doe mee good. my deare wife ill with a pain in her side, which putt mee in feare, but I hope in god its only a winde that troubles her to quicken us in the sense of our weaknes.

7. our Tenant Tibbald and his family with us, its a mercy to have any depend on us, but much more to bee dependent Tenants upon god.

8: I gathered about 500c sets of all sorts divers perries[1] and planted them, the lord command his blessing, thence is our increase: my Tenant said he lost a sheep great with lambe, stoln as he apprehends, thou lord art my shepheard I pray thee secure mee and mine and all thine from all evill.

12. poor John Warren of Olny came to see mee, I pittied him as a poore member of christ, and inhabitant of that place whence I had so good a wife, and therefore entertaind and releived him, and procured some releife of others

Jan: 13. God good to us in manifold mercies, the season is very open, no cold, only divers winds, some stirs at London, lord doe not give us up to error it makes men mad. how furious were the fift monarchy men at London a few dayes past, running greedily into ruine, lord lett not particular mens folly bring a generall trouble on them that desire to feare thy name and bee quiet. this day god was good to mee in the word, deliver mee from my own heart, and lett mee be thine to preserve continually.

19. called up to London by Mrs Harlakenden. I resolved readily to goe up.

Jan: 20. God good to us in many mercies, the season very windy, but dry and warm, its a litle spring alreadie, a restraint put on publique private meetings all forbidden but in some church or parochiall chappell.

21. Rid to London returnd. 28. god preserved mee and mine, my

[1] Perry: a pear-tree. SOED.

heart very much out of frame, lord pardon and heale mee, I was a Sabbath at London and my place destitute, which was a trouble Weather very dry and warme, things spring already, a time beyond ordinary pleasant. but now a litle frost in the nights.
(c.o. 30. A Fast to lament the Kings death, preacht from Jerem. 17.9.)

— — — — — — — — — — — — — — — — — —

Jan: 26: 1660. my 45. yeare entreth.

Lord bee with mee according to thy wonted mercy and goodnes.

30. A Fast to lament the Kings death. preacht from. Jerem: 17.v.9.

Feb: 2. I found I had but a bad crop of pease about 12. bushels of an acre it paid not chardges, if weeds hurt corne, what doe they in my heart, its the best housbandry to keep the heart clean and pure.

Feb: 3. This weeke god good to mee in many outward mercies, yett my condicon mingled with rebukes in my Betties ague, and wives illnes by reason thereof(.) god in mercy by his visitacion preserve my spirit, the lord good to mee in the word preacht about the wickednes of the heart, very peircing, the lord affect all therewith and doe us much good therby wee pray thee.

Feb. 10: from the 6. to this night most misling, but darke weather, god good to us. yett my Betties ague continueth. god sanctify his dealing to the parents, and then remove the stroke from the child. god good in the word, awakening to mee(,) the lord sanctifie my heart to feare his name, my catle were lousy, it proceeds from the bloud, lord keepe putrifying corruption out of my heart.

15. a winters day. for cold winds snow, sleett. hail. rain, bad weather(.) formerly heard of the wellfare of our freinds. lord prosper thou our soules I pray thee.

Feb: 17. snow, cold winterly weather, a nip for our pleasant warme winter before. god good to us in many outward mercies, my litle ones ague abated, yett some fits it hath, lord stay my heart on thee in every condicon. this day god helpd mee in the worke of the Sabbath, for which I blesse him

20: A very wett season, great flouds, my crop of corn very indifferent, and no sale for it, but god giveth mee content.

Feb. 24. God good to us, yet our litle Bett's ague continueth, sanctify lord the stroke and remove it, this day wee brake bread togither without any disturbance(.) poore Mr R. H. very sad, and backward to receive, lord heale his malincholly temper, said on this match profferd by Portugall that the King is married to the Princesse de Ligne. oh lord what is doing in the world.

25. Mr R. H. in great agonie of heart sent down for mee, weeping, apprehending himselfe lost for ever. I feard his head most. gott a phisitian who lett him bloud, advised him to alter his course of diet(,) he promised it, I lay with him that night. god gave him rest, and I hope in time perfect health.

28: My wife straind a sinnew formerly(,) this day shee rid for helpe. the day and providence good. and so for a sad brakie feild I cleansd, the next morning very wett. lord sett and keep all right in our hearts

March: 2. two cowes and a lambe calved well. Blesse god my soule in christ, for everything, lord lett thy blessing bee on our hearts and store. a neighbours sonn the stay of his old dayes was strangely drownd

March: 3. God good to us, my familie somewhat better, lord perfectly restore us, in the mean time thy name bee praisd for this, the lord accept of mee, a great floud this day. god good in the word, my heart panting to bee good. yea blessed bee god who helpeth mee to say. I am not wicked.

5. A meeting at my house, I had a lambe, lambd lame on the foore feet, lord lett my feet bee lively and active always for thee. this died soon the first that miscarried.

8: My wife and I went to returne our deare Harlakenden to Colne. gods providence good in the jorny, god give her peace in her habitacon, a wise heart to pursue it. wee had both sweet rest at night. praises to god

March. 10: God good to us in many outward mercies. this day I heard and then saw the youth openly playing at catt on the green, I went up rowted them, their fathers sleeping in the chimny corner, lord heale through grace these disorders. my boys sheepe lambd her lambe dead, lord how good wast thou to mine. lord open his heart by this providence, that minds nothing that good is. god good to mee in the word where our Deare Freind H. was an hearer. a change of weather drying a litle up the excessive moisture in the earth.

12. poore Mr H. in excessive agonies of spirit, I went down to him, lord you art his phisitian helpe and heale. 13. prosper us lord in the worke and busines wee goe about. viz. a match for Mrs Eliz. Harlakenden.

March. 17. God good to mee and mine, in many outward mercies, for which my soule doth heartily blesse his name, my litle Bettie yet continueth ill, god good to mee in his word and worship, lord make my heart good for I am thine, this day faire, few gray pease sown,

and very few oats, yet god will remember his covenant to and with
Wett Noah, and will doe us good in his due time. children very profane
March. their parents sitt at home, and they play in the streets openly at catt and other sports.

21: a wonderfull wett day, being the next to the change of the moon, which is sad. all the last moon very wett. few lands can bee fallowed, nor a plow stird for any occasion, few oats sown. the earth excessive full of water, very few pease or oats sown: praid earnestly with submission for Noahs promise

22. Esther. 4: death stands in the way of our mercies, the soule must venture on god that will obtain good, and those that doe trustingly doe speed

March. 24: A sad season for wett, yett some sow their oats. god good to mee and mine in mercies, Bettie more quiet in nights then formerly. Mr. H. very ill which is a great trouble to mee. lord beare up my heart to thee, that nothing may oversett my soule; god good to mee in the word, awakening my heart unto him, the lord stablish mee in his feare, prayed earnestly for faire weather, this
1661 evening was the most hopefull and cleare I have seen of many for which mercy I praise the lord, but the next morning wett as formerly lord bee not angry with the prayers of thy people.

27. rid to choose Knights of the shire, wee lost it, and my heart quiet, the lord liveth and reigneth and if he putt his own servants and things on suffering his will bee done. Went on to London. returned safe. 30. with a vain heart, lord bee my helpe, and stirre up my soule to endeavour it.

March. 31. My deare freind Mr R. H. under a visible distraction, the lord in infinite mercy raise him up againe.

When I come to view my expences I find I have laid out	233^{li}. 9^{s}. 6^{d}. ob.
I have received in all receipts whatsoever only.	146. 16. o.
but my stocke which I valued last yeare at. 25^{li}. is worth now about. 55^{li}. so though I have laid out. 87. 6. 5. ob more then received yett on the whole matter I am not abated in my stocke above. 50^{li}. and in lieu of that I am sure I have laid out. above 80^{li}. on the house on the green.	
My roll of debts as in the blew booke are about.	80^{li}.
owing unto mee. - - - - - - - - - - - - - - - - - - -	167. 10. o

I have in cash towards my building about 50li. and my uncle Shepheard being dead, I have a meadow befalls my wife worth about. 50li. more, which when it cometh into my hand I shall value.

Yett god even in outward things is good to mee, lord make mee upright before thee in all my wayes, I humbly intreate thee and continue thy kindnes to mee, and all that feare thy name.

April. 1. 2. 3. I sew oats on lay,[1] and other land. lord command a blessing for my hope is in thee. went towards London on Mr H. account, a sad providence, oh lord melt my bowels, accept my praises for my families health, reason, return to them in favour: die. 6. I came home, god with mee in the jorny.

Ap: 7. the season very good, springing. god mercifull to mee in many outward mercies, but sensible I am my heart is out of frame, the lord sanctifie my thoughts, help mee to watch over them, the lord command mercy for mee and mine in christ Jesus(,) I had but litle time for my sermons this day, lord help mee to trust thee but not for any thing to neglect any opportunities

god gave an answer to prayer in the season from March 27. yett, so that men are at worke on all hands for their imployment.

11. This day I sent out a trained armes its gods mercy to estate me for such a service, though its hard to presse a minister to the uttermost.

13. Heard comfortable newes from Mr H. the lord return to him, and restore him unto us, and to his former injoyments for his names sake

Ap. 14: A sweet shourie, growing day for which and all mercies my soule blesseth him, the lord good to mee in his word, awaken my heart for thee, my litle babe Betty very ill, times grow gloomy, the lord prepare mee for the worst

Ap: 21: A very wett day, god good to us in many outward mercies, heard well of Mr H. which was a great reviving unto mee, sad discourse in the nacion, the lord prevent our troublesom feares, my heart up on the Sabbath, the lord pardon and accept mee in his beloved.

22. 23. dry. to serve the pompous shew, and coronacion at London. on which day. 23 I baptized Elizabeth Eldred, the aire ecchoed with cannon shot. towards night it lightned and thundered and raind a very great tempest. it begun London wards. god shott of his warring peices die 24. a considerable floud.

26: received a very large and comfortable letter from Mr Harlakenden,

[1] Lay: lea, ley, fallow unploughed. SOED.

mett also my freinds from London and came safe home, for all which my soule blesseth god

Ap: 28: A very wett season almost continuall flouds since about midle of Feb: men cannot seed their ground but very hopelessly, nor fallow their grounds that are heavy(.) God good to mee and mine, my heart stayeth and liveth on him, who is my peace and my joy. god awakeneth my heart to watchfulnes against some present temptacions that they bee no snares unto mee etc.

May. 3. rid into London and saw the triumphall arches. stately. vanity, no rich cost in the front of one besides Heathnisme. there is this troubled mee,

a statue of K. James	in the midle above prominent, a death	of K. Charles
Divo Jacobo	statue of Charles	Divo Carolo
	Imperium sine fine dedi.[1]	

divers sad particulars on the face of the arch. the High motto being En quo discordia cives.[2] etc. on the side of Charles. there was an effigie of stakes and fagotts to burne people of the Heads of the regicides on poles. and warrelike Instruments broken.

I had sad reflections on the vain flattery, the lord prevent villanous wickednes, but if surely it will not be sine fine.

reported the Portugal princesse will become protestant and goe to Chappell with the King: a Spaniard protestant.

May. 5. God good to mee in many outward mercies, in a joyful sight of Mr Harlakenden at London, and safe return my soule praise god for that answer of prayer, the lord good in the season, lord now and then a shoure to wash the rustie, muddie meadowes, god good this day to mee in his word, the lord affect mee with his bounty and delight in mee for good continually

May: 7. rid to London on which day the citie forces mustred in Hide parke where a remonstrance was gott of the souldiers for restoring Bishops. found Mr Harlakenden pretty well.—8. the King in great state rode to parliament. between the coronacion and this day. viz. May. 5. the Duke of Yorkes onely son died and was privately buried. 6°: some were hurt in the view by a scaffold breaking and one kild if not more: in the throng at the Commons doore to goe out to the King in the upper house Alderman Fowk was said to loose

[1] To the divine James; to the divine Charles. I give power without limitation.

[2] To what end the rebellion of the community?

50. links of his gold chain. I apprehend this Parliament. The convocation mett in Pauls I saw 12 bishops there etc. We returnd to Colne with Mr H. die. 10°. and fetcht his wife to him. 11°. and now lord blesse them togither:—12. a great fire in Scotland yard, part of Whitehall

May. 12. God good to mee in many outward mercies. Mr Harlakenden with us at church well recovered, blessed bee god, god good to mee in the worke of this Sabbath, for which I was exceedingly unprepared, yett I may say god was my helper

14: I began to pull down at Tibbalds in order to building, the lord in mercy build up soule and outward man, and lett mee visitt my ☞ habitacion and not sin

May. 19. God good in many outward mercies, the wett and cold abated, weather kind(,) the King and Chancellor moderate in their speeches, speaking much of good nature the lord divert a storm, it was feard the act of indemnity would bee unraveld etc. god mercifull to us in the peace of the Sabbath. my soule blesse him

May. 26: A busy weeke in my busines, god good in the preservacon of things and persons, though divers dangers at hand. the weather moist and cold, weeds abound in our crop, meadows flown, yett the nacon frolicke as if no displeasure of heaven towards us in all; god good to mee in the word, my babe ill, god awaken my heart to wrestle with him for it, which I hope he will accept, and command deliverance for it

29. A thanksgiving day for K Charles return to the crown. I preacht, very few hearers a sad wett season. etc.

June: 2. And so it continueth, and persons profanely secure and mindles of god, who yett is good, and especially to mee and mine, in remembrance of all mercies my soule shall and will praise his holy name

June. 5. laid the foundacon of our backhouse chimney with much care and pains tis the lords blessing to make it a sure habitacon to mee and mine.

June. 9. God good to mee and mine in many outward mercies, the lord affect my heart with all. Betty weaneth well, the season very cheerfull. god looketh into my spirit with mercy and kindnes, god good to mee in the Sabbath, my heart calme in all thes bustles and leaveth it selfe on god who careth for mee.

June. 16. Gods hand good towards mee, my body and spirit bearing up in the cumber and trouble of my busines. gods day of rest very comfortable to mee for which I praise him

17. our lower meadows overflown, the floud was considerably great. kitchin chimny beg[un]

June. 23. The measles much about, god very good in my preservacon, the lord in mercy accept mee and rejoyce over mee for good, the weather good. said Bishops and their courts are coming in again, lord help us to walke humbly and wisely.

29: A very lovely weeke for mens business, I followed my housbandry close the lord helpt it of hand, he command his blessing on my labours and spirit

June. 30: God good to us in many outward mercies, the Quakers after a stop and silence, seeme to bee swarming and increased, and why lord thou onely knowest(.) my heart very calm at the expectation of trouble, waiting only on the lord to carry mee through the same, who will doe it, and I shall praise his name(.) this day good was god in the word, learn mee to stay on thee in all the afflictions I meet with all.

6: A very good hay season and in great plenty, the meadows not much worse for the flouds in many places the damage not as expected.

July. 7. The Lord good to us in many outward mercies, for which my soule praiseth him(,) my soule mourneth to see how Quakers and profanesse increaseth, gods holy day is most mens vain day. my heart up in preaching the word, and though my busines bee great, yett I sinke not under it.

13. My son Thomas came down from London to see us, so I saw my six children togither on earth, blessed bee god, and lett us all bee togither in heaven

July. 14. The Lord was good to us in many outward mercies(,) a blessed shoure of rain fell this week to refresh our inheritances, all my children with mee in gods worship. I sung the 128. psalm with faith. god good (to) mee in the tast and relish of his favour in outward and inward mercies.

18. Finisht my kitchin chimny and tooke down the scaffolds all in safety that wrought theron, for which mercy I blesse god, the continuance in the like I pray for

July. 21. God good to us in many outward mercies, the harvest ripening(.) said a stop put to the eagernes of Episcopall men, lord send and continue peace and quietnes in our habitacion, men are slippery in their ways, the lord bee good to us in his and fix our hearts upon him.

23. I was raising my backe building at my house on the green,

which was done this weeke, with safety to all persons imployed therein.

July. 28. God good to us in many outward mercies, the season somewhat moist, the lord reserve to us the appointed weeks of the harvest(,) the lord good in his word my heart trusteth and waiteth on him, on whom alone I depend.

Aug: 1: I begun to tile my house.

2. I (c.o. began to) finishd my second backe chimny and heard of my sons safe arrivall at London.

Aug: 4: God was good to mee in many mercies, the season wett, yett god will command the weeks of harvest for us. this day a dry glum day. god good to mee in his word, lord lay thy awe on mee continually

10. had in all my wheat, mislain, and some of all grains, god gave mee a good crop in all corne as the yeare goeth and a good season, praise to him.

Aug: 11. God good to us in manifold mercies, yett my litle Betty. waywardly ill, the lord revive her, that shee may live in his sight. god good in the Sabbath. yet I find a dead heart in my selfe and much deadnes in persons

Aug: 18: God good to us in our health and outward mercies, so many frendes abroad, harvest almost in about us, this a worke for it, to god bee praise. this day a sabbath the lord good to mee in it, for which the lord bee glorified.

24. gathered in all corn, my harvest good to god bee praise

Aug: 25. God good to us in manifold mercies, my wife not well, I see shee apprehends a breeding again with fear, the blessing of a fruitfull wombe is by weaknes of nature her feare. Saw a booke of prodigies,[1] the drift seems to encourage the down cast part of men, they shall up, and the episcopall way come to utter ruine, lord thy word is my counsellour, I pray the(e) help mee thereby(,) god good to mee in the word this day, teach mee thy feare.

Sept. 1. A wett day. god good to mee in outward mercies; in inward stayes on him, in thes reviling dayes, by evill men that turn aside from the truth, whereof divers in our town with ill minds to mee, without any just cause, lord thou knowest(.) god good to mee in the word which was quicke and awakening lett not sinners sleep death sleeps under it. I pray thee.

[1] Prodigy: something extraordinary from which omens are drawn; an omen, portent. SOED.

Sept. 8. God good in many mercies, the price of corne riseth much, much sicknes in many places, the quakers busy about us, good lord awake for thy own things, and lett not man prevaile. etc.

Sept. 15. God good to mee and mine in many outward mercies, my wife and babe very cheerfull beyond what formerly, the season very good for seed time, my heart very negligent as to Sabbath worke, lord quicken mee, and carry mee comfortably through all my businesse for thy name sake.

Sept: 22. God good to us in our preservacon in all our worke and busines, wee find the corne empty beyond expression. rie not a bushel a shocke,[1] and wheat halfe, our leane hearts to godward call for this. god good in the word to mee make my heart calme and still oh lord for in thee doe I putt my trust.

28: a peice of crust stucke in my throat supping at priory, an alarme to mee, my mind still presently. god good to mee, yett I find somewhat amisse in my throat after 20 houres time.

Sept. 29. God good in manifold mercies to us, my son well at London this sickly time(.) god awakens my heart to attend more to my preaching, lord thou are carefull in all my worke and, oh why is my heart neglectfull of any of thine, a very wett time. lord command mercy in the season for on thee doe wee waite.

Oct: 6. God good to mee in manifold outward mercies, the season very good, and so for my building, I was refresht by the labours, and company of my Cosin Benton(.) the lord good to mee in the Sabbath, for which his name bee praised.

Oct: 13. God was good to mee in manifold outward mercies, a very comfortable season my heart through grace not left as sometimes to vanitie, evill is as my death, but when lord wilt thou slay it in the actings therof, all my sisters by my father and mother here at Colne with mee supping this night togither and not togither again though my sister Ann went not til october 16. about noon, my sister Mary in town never coming up to see us in all that time.

This night my daughter Jane was taken sicke very strangely, not able to goe or helpe her selfe and so continued three or foure dayes, and then somewhat better, like the gout or joynt ague.

Oct. 20. God good to us in outward mercies, awakening also my soule against drawing backe, god setle and confirme some, recover others, god giveth hopes of mercy on my child, the season now wett, which is a mercy after so much drought.

[1] Shock: sixty sheaves. SOED.

Oct: 27. God good in outward mercies, Jane and Betty finely upwards, lord lett them live to keepe thy word, my mind much out of frame to gods worship it was so when my purchase could not bee effected, now my occasions shorten my time, with attendances at priory at night, lord give mee a heart and freedom for thee in thy things I pray

Nov: 3. God good to us in manifold mercies, yett his afflicting hand is upon us, but I trust love holds it, and ordereth it, and will turne it unto good, god remembreth his *few low*, and afflicted soever they are, and its their duty to trust in him. etc.

Nov: 10: God good to us in many outward mercies, my Jane upwards and Mr Harlakenden in a very hopefull way for which god bee praised, our Sabbaths yett quiet, and our liberties continued, the lord accept us, his word this day a comfort to my soule, the sound of his mercy to his afflicted saints is wellcome, and precious

No: 17. A very cold day, yett something cheerly; god good to us in the mercies of my family, my child Jane up and down with us again, lord let us live to keepe thy word, a deare time for corne. rye 7^{s}. and wheat 8^{s}. 6^{d}. per bushel, but few consider the famine of the word, and yett men loath the ordinances of god.

Nov: 23. God good to us in outward mercies, a very good season, not cold but that the poore may earne there deare bread, heard of Major Haynes release, lord make mee wise to avoid sin and danger in thes dayes, god good to mee in the Sabbath, though my heart dead and careles, lord pardon and heale, my deare wife and Mary at my L. Honywoods to rest her wrist, god keepe all her and our limbs.

Dec: 8: God good to mee and mine in outward mercies, winter not yet come in a manner, and yett the time worn finely away, god awaken my heart to watchfulnes against corrupcon, my wife very apprehensive shee breeds again, lett our seed bee the blessed of the lord.

Dec: 15. God good to us in manifold mercies, my daughter Jane abroad again hereing the word, the winter yett open. persons wonderfull profane and neglective of gods worship. the lord in much mercy recover the spirits of men to a due regard of his own things.

Dec: 22. God good to us in outward mercies, my wife if breeding feareth miscarrying(,) the lord looke after her. Sam: Burton whose wife a great professor but now both quakers, only he not through paced as shee. died, taken on Moonday past with an apoplexy, the lord awaken that senseles generacon to see his hand and pity and helpe us all for thy name sake.

23. at night my wife miscarried, of a false conception, a mercy to bee free of it, and I trust god will preserve my deare ones life. the conception was reall, god raiseth her up again.

Dec: 29. very open and moist weather to this day, the lord good to mee in the season my health and mines continued unto us, god good in the Sabbath, which is very sadly neglected, profanes wonderfully abounding.

Jan: 5. yett no frost, but this day wind, and drying like March, many feare a pestilentiall rotting aire, the lord bee a sheild to mine for I shelter my selfe in him(,) men regardles of god and profane beyond thought. oh lord what will become of us

8. received a good sober letter from my son Tho: the lord keep it in his heart to love and feare him. heard my freind Mrs Harlakenden was married,[1] all wondered I should not know it, god make it a mercy to her.

11. received a letter from Tho: that he had been very sicke since the 7th. past. lord bee thou his nurse and keeper for my soule trusteth him with thee.

Jan: 12. God good to us in outward mercies. this day dry and cold, a frost in the night, the weather good to set backe rie, that in many places, spindles, and eares, which is a sad providence. this day I baptized a child in publique not done in 12 months before. the lord good to mee in the word, the lord awaken our hearts thereby to love and feare his name.

18: Heard my son Tho: was in the shop again die. 15°. blessed bee god for it, his ilnes a cold. heard from Mrs H. that shee is married to one Colier who desireth my freindship: freinds are not hastily to bee chosen. heard as if Spain. France. and Holland were combining against England. god can make use of adversaries to doe his good.

Jan: 19. god good in outward mercies. this day cleare and cold a frost, corne is eared(,) rie in divers places. and corn mounts in the price,
ux.— my Mary ill of an ague (.) lord sanctifie every rebuke to our soules and seed. god good to mee in the word, his patience much,

[1] Abel Collier of St. Mary Bothaw, London, batchelor, aged 30 and Mary Harlakenden of St. Anne's, Blackfriars, widow, aged 25, were licensed to be married on 3 January 1662, at St. Martin's Outwich, or St. Leonard's, Shoreditch. *Allegations for Marriage Licenses . . . of the Archbishop of Canterbury, 1543–1869*, (ed.) G. J. Armytage, Harleian Soc. xxiv (1886), p. 57.

under my great unpreparednes in his worke, lord quicken thou mee for thy great mercies sake.

22. A publick fast to seeke god in respect of the warm moist unkindly winter threatning a greater famine and pestilentiall diseases. oh how few lay any of gods judgments to heart.

— — — — — — — — — — — — — — — — — — —

Jan: 26: 1661. my 46. yeare entreth.

Jan: 26: God good to mee in many mercies, my litle Mary very ill with an ague my soule waiteth on god for her health, and recovery out of it. this day entred my 46. yeare, god hath been good to mee in the dayes past and will in those are to come, and my saved soule shall praise him(.) good was god to mee in the word, it was a very winterly day, and a litle fluttering snow lay on the ground, I lookt on it as a mercifull answer of prayer, god give us more such dayes if it bee thy will.

28: this day Mrs Harl: now Coliers things were removed from Colne priory, and the things shee gave us worth about 10[li]. and so those rooms are left empty for Mr Eldred and his wife, god make them a blessing to us, though I am afraid of her, but god can prevent it.

30. a publique fast for the Kings death not above 70 persons or thereabouts hearing, surely not an 100. preacht on Jer. 3.22.

Feb. 2. no winter yėtt, and so wee heard until the end of December it was in Denmarke Sweden, and from Vienna in Germany, corne riseth in price. god good to us in outward mercies, my heart not intent on my labours spiritual, lord in mercy quicken mee thereto and accept mee.

8: wee had 5 lambs fell of 3 sheepe, god blesse our stocke and increase

Feb: 9. Cold dry wholesom weather some days; such a dearth of corne that flesh is to bee allowed this Lent, god good in manifold mercies, my Marys ague abateth(,) god purge from mee all my drosse and make mee a new lampe. two fires seen in our town from abroad, blessed bee god that preserveth mee and mine

Feb: 16. God good to us in manifold mercies for all which my soule blesseth him. yett this morning I could not preach, lying in a great sweat after a long ague fit(,) god helpd mee to goe out in the afternoone, I trust he will order it in much mercy for my good

17. my fit very gentle blessed bee god, in the night it raind the wind rose and was 18: violent beyond measure. overturning a windmill at Colchester wherin a youth kild, divers barnes, stables, outhouses, trees, rending divers dwellings few escapd, my losse much, but not like some others, god sanctifie all to us. throwing down stackes of chimneys, chimneys, part of houses. the Lady Saltonstall[1] kild in her bed her house falling—Whitehall twice on fire that day, some orchards almost ruind. 27 trees blown down within priory wall, timber trees rent up in high standing woods. the winde was generall in England and (c.o. Scotland) Holland sea coast, but not in Scotland.

— — — — — — — — — — — — — — — — — —

Feb: 23. In a very open church, and cold wind, god gave us a dry Sabbath, for which I praise him. my ague hath left mee, and as an answer of prayer, and I trust a token of gods mercy and goodnes to mee, I endeavoured from that head of afflictions Heb. 12.5 to improve the stroke in the violent winds for good.

26. began to imploy the carpenters in my worke, the lord in mercy build up my dwelling, and keepe house with mee, and mine

March. 2. A good Sabbath, a dry comfortable weeke, god good to us in many outward mercies, the lord accept mee, and delight in mee for good,

March: 9. A dry and comfortable Sabbath after a sad rainy Satturday in an open church, for which mercy and his word, my soule blesseth him, heard of my son Toms. harsh condicon. good lord bee attoned, lett him live quietly, better us by this stroke, lett no sin of mine, draw on his trouble. oh shew favour my god

14: preacht Goodwife Spooners funerall, from Luke. 14.14. asserting the resurrection of the flesh the truth of god.

15. Heard from my freinds and son at London, no complaints for which my soule blesseth god

March: 16. A hopefull morning for drines, the lord bee blessed for every act of mercy and bounty. god good to us in our many outward mercies, god gave mee a comfortable Sabbath, my heart sensible of its nothing, god good in giving us bowels to releive one in want by fire. my son very cheerfull and looketh well, his fellow

[1] The widow of Sir Richard Salstonstall who died in 1658. Venn. The great wind was also noted by Evelyn, iii, p. 316.

apprentice is going away, the lord doe him good by all. this day. Corbet, Okey, and Barkstead formerly Lt. of the Tower, who were taken in Holland by Sir George Downing formerly scoutmaster of Cromwells army, were committed to the tower, what changes god maketh in the world. who also was Okeys chaplain.

March. 23. An other dry sabbath in an open church, the lord good to mee in many outward mercies, oh lord comfortable carry on my busines, that I may be seated quietly in my habitacon to follow my studdies and serve thee. for my heart reproacheth mee for my neglect herein, my deare freinds at priory very ill, the lord in much mercy restore them, that they may praise thee.

1662.

1662 25. A Quiet day in a great measure so farr as I observed for which the lords name bee blessed for ever and ever.—
a wett season again, very difficult to the housbandman

March. 30. God good to us in many outward mercies, a dry Sabbath in an open church and wett season for which mercy the lords name bee praised. god good to mee in many outward mercies for all my soule rejoyceth in him. my heart up in the word to arouse sinners./

Estate. When I come to view my outward estate. I find my layings out are 192^{li}. 19^{s}. 11^{d}. my whole receipts.—117^{li}. 15. 9. my debts were 80^{li}. now at least. 86^{li}. 5^{s}. my debts owing mee were more by 27^{li}. then now. my charge is 199^{li}. 4^{s}. 11^{d}. which exceeds my receipts 81^{li}. 10^{s}. but through mercy my stocke is better then last yeare by some pounds and my building hath cost mee at least an 100^{li}. so that my estate is not impaired blessed bee my good god.

April. 2. began to pull down my old barn. which was done by 2 carpenters in 2 dayes. the wals and splints gathered up togither in 2 days more, and timber laid by for the working place to frame it again.

April. 6. God good to us in many outward mercies for all which my soule blesseth him(,) good to us in the Sabbath a dry, and a good day. the lord good in the word awakening my spirit, lord sanctifie thy rod to mee and mine, and doe us all good by thy corrections I intreate thee. etc.

9. Evened all my reckonings with Mr Harlakenden to my great content for all which I blesse my god, and am thankfull to him.

11: preacht Wm Brands funerall.

Ap: 13. God good to us, the season comfortable very dry, and often warm. a good seed time for barly, the lord good to mee in the Sabbath, helping mee therin.

Ap. 20: God good to mee and mine in many outward mercies, heard well of son Tom. this day dewing, and shewed much rain, but no publique disturbance though in an open church, a litle abatement of the price of corne, this day wee brake bread, onely my selfe and wife of all the company came up into the street in view, an affecting mercy, that wee were left, and had not left god and his worship. remember mee oh lord for good, and accept my hearty praises oh my god.

Ap: 27. God good to mee and mine in many outward businesses, for which I blesse his name, the season indifferent good for grasse, but there are wonderfull shoures about, on 19. Feb. when Corbett. Barkstead and Okey were executed at Tiburne, Okey said that prophanes was at such an height that if true as said England could not stand 3 yeares. the Court lookt on this with a jear. indeed man knows not to morrow. its not for us to prophesy. but when our sins deserve a curse. its wisedom to heare, feare and repent. the Lords day is most sadly prophaned in all places, lord looke on and helpe.

May. 4. A very comfortable season, god was good to mee and mine in outward mercies, although in particular I was deepely griped in my gutts, but I trust god will turne it to good(.) a cheerfull audience this day. god good to mee in the word, awaken my heart oh lord to more watchfulnes

May. 11. A very comfortable season, good to mee in many outward businesses and in many outward mercies. divers freinds with mee, god hath emptied some of them of all their children and left mee full, god give mee more grace with my mercies to honour and exalt him. heard many strange passages visional and prophetical of alteracions in England, the event god onely knoweth.

May. 18. 25. God good to us in manifold mercies the lord accept mee.

May. 19. on Monday the act of uniformity was past. the King hastened away

20.—to his Queen who landed before at Portesmouth, with litle joy to the nacon, the nacon pressed cannot smile(,) god amend all and keep us upright.

29. A day of thanks for the Kings restauration in 60. I preacht. from 1. Tim. 2.1.2.3. the lord make his reigne a blessing, and lett not the lusts of men bee satisfied on them

June: 1: A very hot dry season, yett god good in many mercies to mee and mine, I had the act of uniformity sent mee,[1] the lord good in the word, he in mercy accept mee

Pigg. Mathews brother at London

June. 8. God good to mee and mine in many outward mercies, the health of my family. heard of a brother of my neighbours shott and kild by another, blessed bee god in my preservacon, the lord accept mee all my dayes, and helpe mee to serve him with delight.

15. God good to us in manifold outward mercies, the season good, somewhat dry and yett the fruits on the earth indifferent. the lord good in the word, awakening my soule especially to gett grace to fitt mee for his worship.

June. 22. God good to mee and mine in many outward mercies, the season very dry, and yett a competency of fruits on the earth, god good to mee in the Sabbath his word very comfortable, lord fill my heart with love and faith, and accept mee in thy beloved I humbly pray thee.

June. 29. God good to us in many mercies, a wonderfull droughty time, god good in the word, lord encourage my heart still to depend on thee

July. 6. God good to us in many outward mercies, sweet rains last weeke and moderate(,) god good in the word, lord helpe mee to eye thy grace, and seeke thy glory continually(.) our church inclosed, and I observe it with thankfulnes, that though in June at the end, wee had two cold windie Sabbaths that peirced, yett wee had not one wett day to disturb or interrupt us.

July. 13. A good day, hopes of a kindly season for harvest, the good lord command it(.) reports as if the King would respitt the penalties on the act of uniformity as to himselfe for a time(,) god in mercy command it(,) god good to mee in the word(.) harvest cometh on.

15. This night with us being called St Swithins day, at night it raind, the old saying is it raines 40 days after, this 20th its wett, and hath bin since.

sun) Satturday and Lords day. July. 12. 13. the sun shone wonderfull redde. I thought it presaged drought. on the Lords day 2 houres before it satt. wee could see the body round and red, giving no light, clouds blew playing over it, it was suddenly not to bee seen the sky not altering.

[1] The Act of Uniformity of 1662 ordered that all ministers were to read Morning and Evening Prayer according to the Book of Common Prayer, and to take an oath of assent to the same book and forswear publicly the Solemn League and Covenant. Kenyon, pp. 378–82.

July 20. a very wett day. god good to mee in manifold outward mercies, for which my soule praiseth his holy name, the lord good to mee in his word, a sad providence in our townsman one Edward Stevens, who formerly spoke of his familiarity with the divel, was accused for buggery a mare, another with him in the stable at Cogshall who intended the like, but was called unto, and so prevented. lord what beastly savagenes is in mans heart.

26. A good harvest day, on which I began to reap. it raind at night, lord reserve the harvest weeks unto us.

July. 27. God good to us in many mercies, in the word, which was sweet to mee, and ingaging of my heart unto god, lord lett my deare wife live in my sight, and all among thy sanctified ones in Christ Jesus

Aug: 3. God good to us in manifold mercies, he hath given us bread, new and good, and gave us an harvest weeke, and will reserve more. good to us in his word;

Aug. 10: God good to mee and mine in manifold mercies, harvest very much over, this day wett towards night. god good in the word, my heart very dead and flatt, a quaker at Church, who spake somewhat but I cannot tell what(.) I looke on it as a call to watchfulnes in all my worke.

16. The apparitor[1] at towne with service books, he asked 8s. for them. so our Churchwarden bought none, and I saw him not. its a sad case that men are likely to bee put in by this act of uniformity.

Aug: 17. The last Sabbath of our liberty by the act. god good to mee therein

18: Mrs Sparrow buried(,) a sad stroke to a good man, when living, and preaching worke is taken away, and the joy of his eyes also.

19. preacht last lecture at Castle-Hedingham.

20. a wett season, much corne abroad, I rid to Wittam. god blest my busines

23. A good day in which I ended harvest, some barly began to grow in the feilds

Aug. 24. God good to mee, my heart cheerfull in his worke, hoping god will make way for my liberty, and many others, my soule trusts in him. sad to see how the shepheards are scattered, the lord bee a blessing to mee, gods hand it toucheth mee in some of my substance, lord even therein doe not contend with mee, but blesse mee I humbly pray thee; some hope given as if there would bee

[1] Apparitor: the servant or attendant of a civil or ecclesiastical officer. SOED.

indulgence given to ministers for the present until the return of the parliament.

The London Ministers nigh 80. generally declined preaching, the Bishop tooke care to supply every place, and the like in the country, some of them petitioned this weeke for liberty as reported.

Aug: 31: all hopes of suspension of the act of uniformity taken away. god good to mee in my freedome to preach(,) three ministers and multitudes of our christian neighbours hearing, oh lord provide for our security, I trust in thee, keepe mee from evill and deliver mee from evill.

Sept: 7. A quiet Sabbath, great droves of people flocke to heare, lord use mee for the good of soules I praise thee, and lett that bee my honour.

11. a wett morning which giveth hopes of a very good seed time corn fallen much. a good wheat for 5^{s}. 6^{d}. mislain. 4^{s}. 8^{d}. god make us thankfull.

Sept. 14: God good to us in outward mercies, our peace, and undisturbed freedom in his worship. lord helpe mee against the polluting vanitie of my mind, deading mee to thy holy things, keep my heart pure, and intire to thee, a very cheerfull day.

15. Buried my tenant Tibbald, a good housbandly man, the lord maintain my lot in every respect, I account it a great losse to mee.

Sept: 21. God good in the season and outward mercies to mee, in his word very sweete to my fast, for which goodnes my soule praiseth him. oh help mee to live on thy righteousnes oh lord

Sept. 28. A good seed time. god good to us in many mercies, the continued liberty of his word and worship no interrupcion or disturbance,

30. began to sow my wheat God command his blessing.

Oct: 5. The weeke past busy about my house, the lords favour towards mee therein, lord make it a quiet habitacon to mee. and lord give my son peace at London in his Masters house I pray thee. god good to us in the word for which my soule blesseth him.

10. Cited this day to the Archdeacons visitacon;[1]—our professors had rather I should lay down than conforme as J Day told mee, but I had it onely from him the lord direct mee. I appeared not.

Oct: 12. God good to mee in manifold mercies, the booke of common prayer laid in the deske for mee.—19: laid again and used in part in the morning, but in the afternoon taken away.—26. brought again, but pitcht and abused. the season hitherto very good, I did

[1] See p. 508, n. 2 below.

much busines about my house, where I have lodged now more then a weeke.

Nov: 2. A cheerly time, and a quiet Sabbath. Mr Crosman[1] preaching actually sent to prison and some others in danger thereof, yett through mercy I am quiet. this day a wonderfull deliverance to Mary and Betty falling down staires with knives in their hands. lord accept my thankfulnes. searching in London for meeters in private with feare that they will send such out of the nacion.

No: 9. A warm winter hitherto, but wett one great floud, god good to mee and mine in outward mercies, new Ministers this day at Colne Engain.—Mr Symonds[2] and at Cogshall Mr Jessop.[3] both of good report, and now I am left alone of the nonconformists, what god will doe with mee I know not. I trust he will bee a hiding place, and help mee that I may worke, and not wound my spirit.

12. A snowy bitter rainy windy morning in which I went to the Court at Colchester cited for procuracons.[4] mine are as large as livings of 120li. per yeare. I paid and returned well blessed bee god. none of the nonconformists being cited appeared but onely my selfe, I reckon that day a good day to mee

No: 16. A dry cleare day after high driving windy shoures, god good to us in the liberty of the Sabbath, oh spare mee for my ministeriall worke. speech of a plot but no presbiter in it. lord keep us, them from every evill. and dishonour to the gospel.

Nov. 23. God good to mee and mine in manifold mercies, liberty of his Sabbath, I baptized with the common prayer publiquely Wm Fossets child, the whole congregacon in a manner staying, god make us quiet and peaceable. the season very wett(.) I am even alone, but lord bee thou with mee that I may not bee alone

25. A fine frost after much wett, wee begun to remove our things from the vicaridge to my own house on the green in earnest. lord thou that knowest the names, dwelling occupacions of thine. Know mee and mine and dwell with us I pray thee, and let our habitacon, bee a dwelling of peace and righteousnes

[1] Samuel Crossman, ejected from All Saints, Sudbury, and Little Henny, Essex, 1662, but afterwards conformed and later Dean of Bristol; best known as author of hymn 'Jerusalem on high'. Smith, pp. 370–1; Calamy.

[2] Samuel Symonds, probably ejected from Ashen in 1660, rector of Colne Engaine from November 1662. Smith, p. 395.

[3] Thomas Jessop, vicar of Coggeshall 1661 to *c.* 1678; he appears to have started as sympathetic to nonconformity and is included (on no evidence) in Calamy, but later Josselin found him intolerant and persecuting. Smith, p. 411; Calamy.

[4] Procurations: a money payment by the incumbent to the bishop or archdeacon. SOED.

27. This day all my family came up to my house on Coln green blessed bee god that giveth us an habitacon, lett it bee for mee and mine: my old dogge died in the yard suddenly, when ready to come up. and a young colt that night(,) thus wee removed between death, the dogs sudden, the colts expected

No. 30. A calme, hard, frizing weather, the first Sabbath here above, the lord good to mee in my liberty, and peace, the lord accept of mee in mercy and doe mee good

Dec: 7. God good to us in manifold mercies, the Sabbath very cold and snowy, I came not home(.) a very deep snow. god good in the word, the lord rejoyce over mee for good

D. 14. God good to mee and mine in manifold outward mercies, my wife onely much troubled with a cold especially in her head, the lord doe us good by every thing, make us humble and holy, a cleare frizing morning after it began to thaw, and carry away the ice, god good to mee in the word, baptized 3 children one 7. yeares old

18: Colchester corporation sent to mee to preach there Dec. 25. I declined it. they discourse to choose mee their weekly Lecturer pro tempore. lord I am willing to doe thee any service though allways afraid of that towne as not fitt to deale with their wrangling spirits.

Dec. 21. God good to mee and mine in outward mercies, the lord accept mee and rejoyce in mee for good, my wife blessed bee god much better. god good to mee in the Sabbath, yett a help to our neighbours about us.

25. preacht on Isay. 53.11. and dined some freinds in our new hall for which I blesse god. a feirce frost with an east wind after a greater floud on a very great floud.

28: God good to us in manifold mercies in the sabbath. also. Jan. 4. the lord rejoyce in mee to doe mee good.

Jan. 8: I planted 15: trees. elmes and ashes before the pales of my house on the green(,) cost. 2^{s}. god in mercy prosper them

Jan. 11. A very cold winterly time. the small pox. in 5 families all taken from Hatch prentice who died. all persons upward, lord bee good to us in sparing our place, our poore sinfull town. god good to mee in the freedom of the Sabbath. Mr Calany comitted to Newgate for preaching at the place where he had been minister.

14. spent in making peace, giving good advice, a good imployment of time. remember mee and mine oh lord, as thou hast, and dost.

Jan. 18: 25. God good to us in outward mercies in our spirituall liberties, in the midst of others troubles, lord keep up my heart to feare thy name

— — — — — — — — — — — — — — — — — —

Jan: 26. 1662. my 47. yeare entreth. 46. ended

Jan. 26. When I looke backe I find I may set up my Eben—ezer[1] hitherto god, hath holpen mee, and when I looke forward, this promise is mine. I will never faile thee nor forsake thee. I am now setled in a habitacon of my own on Colne green which god hath given mee.

30. Fast, and sad frost preacht. Rom. 6.23. not an 100. people hearing the word

Feb: 1. 8: God good to us in manifold mercies a most bitter violent frost yet continueth and increaseth, somewhat calm, a snow covering the ground. gods worship is most sadly neglected, and now I feare the use of common prayer will cause a rent and separacon of divers asserters of ordinances. god setle and stablish mee.

Feb. 15. cleare but frost, snow and cold, god good to us in manifold mercies, another house visited with the small pox, mine preserved, lord lett all thy dealings bee sanctified, god good to mee in the word preacht, the lord make it an efectuall blessing to us all.

Hard Winter. This winter was the hardest I ever remembred, very wett and cold in octob. November on the 24 day whereof it began to frize and so continued frost and snow very hard, until Feb. 18th. it began to thaw much but the frost scarce full out of the earth,

and this 23. Feb. a litle frost again: 27. to this day frost; so. 28: March. 1. snow lying in my guttar. hence goodly weather

Feb: 22. God good to us in manifold mercies. the liberty of his worship. for which I blesse his holy name.

24. a cold frost with a north wind and snow. Mr Harl. set forth for London, the god of mercy, restore him with a quiet mind and sound body to us for the lord Jesus sake. doe, defer not oh lord

28. our freinds well at London blessed bee god, lord restore them sound.

[1] Ebenezer: the name of the memorial stone set up by Samuel after the victory of Mizpeh ('the stone of help'). SOED.

March. 1: God good to us in manifold outward mercies, said some in our town were digging this sabbath morning, lord whither will this profanes tend. to flat atheism. lord arise help for thy mercy sake. lord make mee faithfull and constant in thy truths.

6: went to Mr Butchers at Pannels ash in Castle Hedingham, whiles with him I spied fire in the lane, occasioned by a boy carrying a brand to kindle fire at his Masters house, (but whither wilfull or occasional god knoweth.) this fired hamme[1] in the lane, and that the corner of a barne, and the whole barn worth above 40^{li}. burnt in halfe an houre. I coming in saw the danger of his great barn, and praying to god the wind a litle wheeled which much tended to secure it, blessed bee god, a wonderfull answer of prayer, and by use of due means, all else preserved: Isay. 65.24. god answered while speaking.

March. 8. a goodly season. god good in many mercies. people negligent in gods worship. awaken us lord in mercy and accept of us and doe us good.

March. 15. wonderfull warme, dry calme weather a sweet seed time. I was busy. god command his blessing, this day a windy shoure, god good to us in manifold mercies, lord awaken my spirit to bless thy name.

March. 22. A healthful, dry season, somewhat cold with eastern winds. god good to mee and mine in manifold mercies, only my wife illish, but perhaps breeding, the lord bee our portion. the parliament viz. commons zealous against papists

1663 23. my wife went this morning towards London, the lord keep her every way safe.

March. 29. A very cold east wind dry, and sometimes a shoure. a lovely seed time. god good in many mercies. my wife not with mee, and my mind very foolish, lord pardon and help. gods providence bee towards his for good, said the newes sad in Ireland, the rebells regaining their estates from the English

Estate— When I review my estate, I find my receipts rather more then my layings out and yett my building and stocke have cost mee more above 70^{li}(.) I have sold my wifes land at. 57^{li}. 10^{s}. and paid debts with the mony(,) the lords name bee praisd, that provides bountifully for mee, oh that my soule, and mine might prosper in thy sight.

Ap: 1: begun to pull down the old parlor end, the weather very cold.

Ap: 5. God good in manifold mercies, sweet showres. god good in the

[1] Hamm: a pasture or meadow enclosed with a ditch. NED.

sabbath and his word, make it a blessing to all that heare it I pray thee.

Ap: 12. God good to us in our health, the season cold(.) oh how sadly is the Sabbath prophaned god spare and pardon for his great mercy. visited sicke Mr Elliston. God in mercy restore him.

13. god holpe mee out of a snare in a forfeited surrender, gave directions in Mr Ellistons businesse, I hope with effect about his debts

14. Rid through to London with my son John, found all pretty well, lovingly treated by my old Freind Mrs Colier, returned safe. 17. day. commended Mr Elliston to god who died the 18°. a wett day, god gave us a timely returne.

Ap: 19. God good in manifold mercies, a sweet warm growing rain after cold east winds, the lord hasten the spring, god good to mee in the word buried this weeke two old disciples.[1]

20. preacht Mr Ed. Ellistons funerall a good neighbour, god good to mee in the word and in prayer. 24. present at the view of his just debts, for the payment wherof he made mee one of his Trustees, and I found they are about 500li. the lord helpe mee in my businesse, he left no issue. a good estate to his brothers.

Ap: 26. God good in manifold mercies, dry after much wett. we prayed for a fitt season, the lord in mercy command it, god good in the sabbath, his word sweet and cheering.

May. 3. God good to us, but mans folly, dasheth water often into his wine and imbitters his mercies. the season vehement drying, god good to mee in the word, my freedom and liberty yett continued; my neighbour Mathew very ill. god in mercy restore him

5: sew an acre of barly on the peice by the orchard god prosper my crop.

8. Mr Ed. Ellistons estate made over to mee and Mr Harlakenden for payment of his debts(.) its one of the best peices of morral wisedom to our estates, to live within our bounds and so pay our debts because wee contract none, he that once overshoots on hope of a good crop, to repay and cleare, in my mind runs into the dirt to better his shoes by thoughts of wiping them, If god raise my expense at one time beyond my income, I will shorten it, if I can, to come even.

May. 10. God good in many mercies, my cup is mingled, and blessed bee god, learn mee to prosper by all trials I pray thee(.) a calme time as to newes, the lord good to mee in the Sabbath freedom of

[1] Thomasin Harding and Bridget Aylward, both single; buried on 15 and 19 April. PR.

his worship. a late mercifull answer of prayers in the recovery of C. Mathew whose life I esteem, a speciall mercy of god to mee.

11. This day I paid Mr Morly the last of his mony, and so have paid for all my lands in Colne, and in particular those bought of the Nevils. the acquittance dated before.

Colt. 16. My grey mare foald an horse colt, which I desire god may blesse that I may ride and ease my weary feet upon him; a wonderfull wett and cold season, giving many barlys a surfett, and breeding many weeds in corne. this yeare I sold in hay and straw as much as came to above 8li. my hay was 3. yeares old.

Hay sold 8li

May. 17. God good to us in our outward mercies, the liberty of gods worship is yett afforded mee, and mine in particular, although Mr Layfeild tells mee (who was judge at the visitacon) that I am suspended, gods will bee done, I am a poore useles creature, and if god will have mee laid by his will bee done. I submitt with patient quietnes, but my freedom I rather desire.

May. 24. God good in outward mercies, the yett liberty I have, my great unworthines may cause god to shorten *my time here* if it please thee, awaken my spirit to more fruitfulnes for thy name sake. weather warmeth and dry.

May. 30. God good to us in manifold mercies, this day our Church wardens brought in the booke of common prayer, which I used. the lord good to mee in the Sabbath, his word, the lord make it an effectuall blessing to mee and mine

June. 7. A very wett season, the lord shew us mercy therein. god good to mee and mine in outward mercies, and in the word. heard of ArchBishop Juxons death, a quiet man, an advantage to that hot partie, as they thinke, but who knoweth how god may shackle them, or use them, he can dispose instruments as he pleaseth; one of the greatest shoures I ever knew putting the meadows much under water, lord remember us in mercy.

June. 14: After much rain and great flouds, continuall wett from April to this time, viz. 19. April(.) good store of grasse on most grounds. god good to mee in the Sabbath, preacht of love, god warme my heart with it, unto himselfe. I heard nothing from the Court this weeke of any trouble for which I blesse god.

19. Buried an excise man that died suddenly[1] before Justice Eldred while in their businesse of an imposthume[2] in his stomacke.—oh

[1] The PR records the burial on 20 June of 'John Richards of Colchester dying suddenly'.

[2] Imposthume: a purulent swelling or cyst in any part of the body; an abscess. SOED.

how many people censured him. but I should learn repentance and watchfulnes thereby and doe not conclude him a greater sinner than those of us that were spared.

June 21. A sad wett season, lord heare prayer for mercy to us therin, cause not the fruits of the earth to perish from our mouths. god good to mee in the word his favour be extended unto mee continually for in him doe I trust.

26. rid two miles to Stanly hall, the ways wonderfull deepe, daily rains, and no hopes but in gods covenant. I saw there the biggest whitethorn that ever I saw, and high as a good tree and bigge, my habitacion pleaseth mee better then those I see abroad(,) god raise my heart to thankfulnes.

June. 28. A sad wett afternoon. lord in mercy remember us for good, the lord good to mee in the word, company of freinds, although much griped in my bowels. news as if the Portugal neare Lisbon had utterly routed the Spanish army which was confirmed to bee done neare Evora. on May. 29. in which all the English did like themselves valiantly

July. 5. God good to us in outward mercies; some seasonable weather last weeke for which I blest gods name, the lord good to mee in his word, doe mee good inwardly by it.

July. 12. The wett yet continues, and so almost continually from April 18th. past. now a great floud, meadows drownd again and again, very litle hay had in, lord remember us in mercy and afflict us not continually, spare for thy name sake. god good in the word, this weeke my Cousin Hurril. delivered of another dead son, god spared her.

July. 19. God merciful in the change of the season, the rains with us, much abating(.) a good answer of prayer, this day misling but not much wett, the lord good in the word, his soule rejoyce in mee, a sad letter from Tom lord bee good to him

25. joyd in the comfortable sight of my deare uncle Mr Nath: Josselin, by him I heard from Tom, that he is well, I trust the god of my mercies

July 26 will command good for him. god good to mee in the Sabbath, raise up my heart oh lord

Aug: 2. God good to us in manifold mercies, yet the season thes two dayes somewhat ill, lord remember us in mercy. god good in the word, had a sober letter from Toms master in the main, wherin he offers parting, lord in mercy direct mee.

Aug. 7. God good in the season, wee hope harvest weather, men are now readie to begin to putt in their sicles god command the season, the day cheerly(,) god good to mee in the word

10. Rid to the Lady Veers with my wife a good Lady. 86. old. fresh and lively in her senses, a gracious person, shee kindly gave mee a faire paire of gloves my wife a hood, wee returnd safe. ways at Halsted scarce passable, harvest beginning in many places

Aug. 16. God good [to me] in my harvest season [ ] by breaking away, god good in the word this day, lord engage mee [ ] holy name, heard of the death of one that I [*mention*] lately for a *Saint* a merciful providence to mee

Aug 23. God good in manifold outward mercies, in the season, a dry cool harvest, and I preacht two harvest sermons, god delight in mee and mine for good.

Aug. 30: God good [ ] harvest god good in the word a very thin audience, as if *daring* Magistracy, that begins to punish absentees from publique worship, the lord give mee an heart to serve him faithfully.

Sept: 6. God good to us in manifold mercies, in the season, sabbath, my heart warmd in the sense of gods mercy wherin my soule delights. feares of famine ride in plenty(,) corn falling much again.
☞ being Munday I plowed my selfe Sprigs marsh, god in mercy blesse the plow.

Sept: 20. God good in many mercies, sad newes of the Turks, spoils in Germany. gave thanks to god for gods mercy to Mr Richard Harlakenden the Justices brother. who lately came from Ireland, and, mounted on a young horse, he fell backe upon and broke his bones in his chest. shoulder. neck. ribs, very much, and yett he walks about. I was strucke with a cow on my face, and onely a litle hurt on the lip through mercy, this day divers of the ruder sort of people hearing, the statute of paying 1^{s}. when absent from divine service is more then the feare of gods command.

Sept. 27. God good in manifold mercies freinds health at London, the prints mention as if the Turks were stopt at Ne*w*sol. god grant. old prophesies mention their taking Colen. though Brightman prophecy their destruction. by. 1696. and their begin(in)g to fall 40 yeares sooner. which is begun already, wee may feare Hiltenius prophecy[1] of them to scourge Christians. but then he saith for good.

[1] Johann Hilten, a fifteenth-century prophet popular among protestants, who predicted, among other things, the end of the world in 1651. Christopher Hill, *Antichrist in Seventeenth-Century England* (Oxford, 1971), p. 111.

31. Mr Eldred with mee, his deske twice robbed, the lord watch over mee.

Oct. 4. God good in our outward mercies, the morning very wett. one with mee to tell mee of the apparitors intencion. I invited him to dinner he promiseth fairnes, the lord good in the word, lord doing mee good by others visitacions.

5.	Sr Jo. Jacobs account. 56.6. yeares. 24li. received of Mole and Reyner.		10li. 0.
Jacob	Octob. 18. 1663. 63.7. yeares. 28. of Mr Wolhouse.		10. 0.
	by Mr Woolhouse. ---------- of Mr Woolhouse.		10. 0.
			-----
	52. due still.	22li.	30l. 0.

God good to mee in my jorney to London.

9. where I found all freinds well, and welcome most hearty. the Turkes prevaile(.) the Hungarian protestants incline a submission to him, and so doe the protestants much hope deliverance by him as a means to ruine the Austrian and pope(,) yea said the German princes incline to French protection, and at home newes of a triennial parliament.

Oct. 11: some Freinds here. a wett sabbath, but good day in the word

16. a very wett weeke, a great floud a sad season to sow in, the lord seemeth to bee very angry with us. he justly may. said strang libels cast about in London against the King, who is forced to give up house(,) his table served by a cooke. his Cavaliers very sadly deboist[1] and unruly. a good natured prince but sadly yoked with followers.

Oct. 18. God good to mee in manifold mercies, the lord accept mee in his christ and continue his kindnes unto mee, this sabbath a day of mercy.

23. Heard of the Q. death: 19. at the marriage of Sir Jo. Cotton[2] and Mrs Elizabeth Honywood. god prosper their union with his blessing.

24: This day I had a sheepe died of the rott, an effect of the wett summer, and Mich. time lord make us sensible. how thy hand is against us

Oct. 25. God good in the season, a very good seed time. some dayes. said die 23. the Q. died(.) the lord good to mee in the sabbath, in

[1] Deboist: debauched. SOED.

[2] Sir John Cotton, knight and Bart. of Connington in Hunts, son of the well-known Sir Robert Cotton, founder of the Cottonian Library. Morant, ii, p. 169.

his word for which I blesse him. lord perswade soules to beleive and practice.

Nov. 1. God good in manifold mercies, in the season, a comfortable audience, the word good. newes of the Q. reviving, a mercy I hope to the nacion, now discourse of the phanatique plott, lord hide us from the snares of men.

5. preacht from Joel 2.32. to a smal audience of the churches troubles before her deliverance, by which it seemeth not to bee so near at hand as some apprehend. lord helpe mee to waite with patience for thee. a wett winter day

No. 8: A wonderfull stormy night. a good day. I pleaded hard for the truths of god, and that persons would hold them fast, remember mee oh Lord for good, my wife heavy(,) my bowels towards her, but Lord how much are thine

12. talks of a Northern plot, yea general of the phanatique(,) divers imprisond, and some nonconformist ministers clapt up. god watch over us for good

Nov. 15. A sad day, god good to mee, my wife abroad, and cheerfull, the lord good in outward mercies unto us, many secured as plotters, god good in our publique peace, in the word, the lord accept mee for good

19. 20. 21. Sew great wheat in my orchard by plow and howe. god prosper both

Nov. 22. God good in many mercies a very glum time, the sun not appearing in many dayes, very little sunshine since mid april, my wife cheerly under very lingering pains, god good in the word, a good Sabbath. many over desirous the Turks should overrun christendom, to gain their liberty in former. my soule abhorrd that principle. I looke on them as a sad scourge, but god may doe good by them, and convert them that I should glory in, but not their successe to gain any outward liberty by them.

26: On Thursday morning about seven of the clocke or before, my deare wife after many sad pains, and sadder feares, in respect of the unkindlines of her labour. was yett through gods mercy, delivered of her 10th child, sixt daughter. and our now seventh child, and 5^{t} daughter living, for which mercy my soule blesseth him, and my heart desireth farther to trust in him at all times, to ordain things for mee and mine for the best: when this 7th was borne, I remembered the use, and blessing on 7. in the scripture, and my prayers were god would use, and blesse them all, as I trust he will.

No. 29. God good in the season, and many outward mercies, my wife and babe well, a silence in this part of the nacion, under the talke of the Northern plott. the Turkish pirats, breake with Holland and us also. lord awake against that cruel one(,) god good in the sabbath

D. 1. received the epitome of the German prophesies, oh lord give mee understanding in thy works hold me close to thy words. however I resolve in all my prayers to presse certain publique particulars which I shall here enter.—said our english merchants would fain breake with the Dutch;—the whole earth is quiet.

Dec. 6. Great winds, frosty, very much snow, god good in mercies, in the word, the lord awaken mine to fear his name. divisions among the Germans, while the Turke prospers, and withdraws not yett to winter quarters beyond former presidents

Dec. 13. God good to mee and mine in many outward mercies, the lord accept mee and mine and delight in mee to doe mee good. offered up in faith my litle Rebekah to the lord in baptism. god in mercy bring it under the bond of the everlasting covenant. the lord good to mee in his word, good in my freinds society, with whom I returned most hearty thanks to god for his goodnes unto mee. and mine, and begged his presence and blessing with us to the end, and to see the god of Jerusalem, my freinds here togither(,) wee had a cheerly banquett and away.

19: Had home 2 smal loads of wood from Morleys land with safety god bee praised: and dry

Dec: 20: Close, moist weather to admiracon, rare to have a sunshine, or cleare day, but mistie. fog. close, thicke aire. god good to mee in the word, lord awaken my heart to eye thee and thy doings in the world. dreamd the church were I preacht full, multitudes standing without at windows.

☞ 25: Preacht from. Jo. 3.16. A very close aire. rare to see sun, moon or starres togither one q(uar)ter of a day, or night, weather open, not wett. my wife busy through mercy in the family, few hearing, divers freinds comfortably with mee for which I blesse god.

Dec. 27. Close weather still. the sun in weeks not shining out two houres togither. nor stars by night. god good to mee in my wives recovery. in the Sabbath and word lord make mee a blessing and make my heart lively—I am expecting the churches redemption at hand in the fall of oppressing powers. Austria and pope, in the conversion of nations, restauration of exiles for religion. come Lord Jesus come quickly

Jan: 3. After two brown daies, wherin the sun shone somewhat this day very calme cleere sunshine, and frost, my deare wife abroad with mee for which mercy my heart rejoyceth in god, Lord continue thy kindnes to us, god good in the word, his presence with mee therein, the quakers meetings are in great place disturbed driven from thence, and other meetings of the nonconformists much omitted. god good to mee in my liberty. read the German prophecies in a booke stiled Lux in tenebris.[1]—

Jan. 10. God good in manifold mercies. the season dry and dull no frost(,) god good in the word and his worship.

14. weather continues close and dul, yet open after great winds this day some rain(.) this day Rebekah was coated,[2] lord clothe us with the garments of thy righteounes in Christ Jesus.

Jan. 17. weather somewhat clearer, yet very dry and warm. when others in trouble, I goe about my busines quietly. lord bee Englands and my security in much mercy and spare us. god good in the word, cheerly, awakening, let it bee so to us all in thy goodnes to us

23. received home 8 score and 10 puppets from Mrs Elliston tith. weather calm dry and 21. warm like April

Jan. 24. continual snow. god good to mee in outward mercies. my Cosin Hurril under a distraction, lord remember her in mercy and restore her. God good in my relations, in the liberty of his word and worship give mee an heart for thy glory.

When I looke abroad thus in England publique quiet, and yet nothing but discontents(,) the state brooks no publique religious meetings, but legall. Denmarke, Swede. Holland, in peace, the Turkish pirats harsh to our traders in the midland seas(,) the great princes young. Turke about 21. or 22. France. 25. Emp. 23. Swede a boy. Savoy very young. the Emp. at Ratisbone diet engaging the Emp. to assist against the Turke the popish party joyn. France would have the auxiliaries commanded by a freind of his and then he would assist, but

— — — — — — — — — — — — — — — — — — —

The great difference between the pope and France, which accused the world that the french designes run high, likely to bee agreed by condescension on the popes part

[1] Thomas Fauntleroy, *Lux in tenebris, or, a clavis to the treasury* (1654).

[2] Coat: a garment worn suspended from the waist by women or young children. NED. Hence, probably taken from swaddling clothes.

The polish king carrieth warre to the Moscovites doore with hope of peace, but that not likely, great endeavours to declare Duke d Enguyen. successor in poland(.) The Turkes make great preparacons against christendom. Apaffi; gets many places from the Emp: submitting to him all Germany and Italy in an amaze, the northern kingdomes quiet. Spain warring to reduce Portugall

Jan: 26: 1663. my. 48. enterd.

Sensible of this day, ending my former yeare with remembrance of gods goodnes to mee and mine, hitherto god hath holpen mee, and seeking god my heart filled with hopes, he will never faile nor forsake mee: very cold weather since Jan: 23 in the morning, snow after the nights frost.

30. My Cosin Hurrill sadly distracted, the lord restore her. about 80 or 90 hearing the sermon this day. a freind robd his freind at London and hangd for it, called Col. Turner.[1] Lord deliver us from unreasonable men.

Jan. 31. God good to us in outward mercies, and inward. helping mee with quiet submission to god in all condicons. carrying out my heart to trust, yea to rejoyce in him as my porcon, when man would rob mee of his grace and favour. but wee stand and fall to our master and not to one another. my heart more than ordinary desirous to doe good by preaching this day. Amen. and these desires checkt some vanities. divers honest christians from Halsted with us.

Feb. 7. God good to us, yett my heart very dead, and listlesse to his service, oh lord recover mee and the nacion to a spirituall, steddy walking with god

Feb. 14. winterly weather. god good in outward mercies to us, my heart yett very dead and awkward to gods worship. negligent, heartles. lord doe not only shew but cure those evils in mee for thy name sake

two goodly days, my wife in danger by a cow, preserved by god. my praises to the god of my mercy.

Feb. 21. Sad close weather. god good in manifold mercies. my soule resolves more to depend calmly on god, and mind to his worke, his acceptance with mee. my sonne John sadly ill with an ague but god giveth hopes of his recovery.

[1] For a description of the gallows scene on 21 January 1664, see Pepys, v, p. 23.

24. buried the daughter of Wm Peartree. who would not in a long sicknes, and needing the very help of the towne, once see or releive her. lord thou art not such a father. the child was proud and stubborn by report.

Feb. 28. The weather. dry. and cleare, fallows already stiffing, yet no springing season, a very clearly time many days. promising a drout. the lord good to mee in the day and in his word, yett oh my leanesse. I heartily bemoan my neglect of god.

March: 5. planted 4 walnuts before the house. 3. quodlings:[1] 5. quince trees. the lord in mercy prosper them

Mar. 6. God good to us in manifold outward mercies, the season cheerful, heard from dear Colier at London her intencion toward midsummer to visit us, god good to mee in the word, my heart awaking to my duty more than formerly. lord incourage mee in thy pathes

9. Grafted. 20. heads of pears and apples moon toward last quarter.—10: about 12. more.

12. Heard from my son of a losse of cash of 20li. I praise god not by his unfaithfulnes. but its a trouble to mee, oh lord watch over us for good.

Mar. 13. Cold, dry weather. god good to us in manifold outward mercies, lord remove and sanctify thy hand on my litle ones ague and teach mee to profit by all dealings(.) god good to mee in the day. yet I find my heart dead, as partaking of that evil of profanes so much abounding in our town and all places, lord awake for thy honour in the world and let thy holy spirit prevail in the hearts of men

19. Heard Tom had recovered the mony lost. blessed bee god for this mercifull providence(.) grafted neare upon 70 heads of pears and apples, wind bitterly cold after it. lord prosper them if it bee thy good pleasure.

March 20. God good to us in manifold outward mercies for which I blesse his name, very sensible of my own neglect in his worship, busines. cumbrances, lord give mee the art so to doe things, they may be no hindrance to my spiritual imployment I resolve to endeavour. I pray thee oh lord helpe mee. pardon mee. and accept mee for thy great mercy sake.

22. 24. Imployd in getting Cosin Hurrill and Mr Harl. to London whom I accompanied to Ingerstone; lord shew them favour in their recovery for thy name sake,

[1] Quodling: codling (whose forms include quodling) is a variety of apple. NED.

25. grafted. 9 heads. 6. excellent pippins. pomewaters.[1] 2. 1. junity. lord prosper.

1664.

March. 27: Cold but good weather, god be praised, the lord aboundant in his goodnes towards us, a cheerful Sabbath, god good in the word, his goodnes, christ, pardon(,) presence sweet to my soule, lord quicken my heart to walke with thee

When I come to review the wayes of god toward mee in the yeare past, I find it mercy and truth, he still smiles on us, he hath added a litle Rebekah to our number and the rest grow up. my publique libertie strangely continued unto mee, and people, I have purchased this yeare a close cost 28^{li}. for my son Thomas, my receipts more then expences by 8^{li}. receivd. 168^{li}. 18^{s}. 4^{d}. laid out. 160^{li}. 13^{s}. 2^{d}. my stocke as good as last spring. my debts were then due to mee 20^{li}. more then now. so that I have saved clearly about 8^{li}. and my building which was at least 40^{li}. now I have about 15^{li}. in mony and my tenants owe mee. 70^{li}. blessed been god

April. 3. dry. cold. cleare weather. god good to us in manifold mercies, many, strangers with us, lord make us to profit, make mee dilligent and faithful.

Squire Bowes[2] freinds with us this weeke. a jovial troope. Mr R. H. returned from London very discontent but Mrs H. well.

Ap: 10: Growing misty weather, yett somewhat cold, the lord good to us in manifold mercies, the lord accept mee and doe mee good, god good in our sabbath liberty, and in thes awakenings of his word to feare his name.

Ap. 17. God good in manifold mercies, good in the sabbath, and his word, the dry weather continues. 24.

May. 1. God good in our peace, reports of smart penal laws lord bee our helpe.

7. All this weeke imployed in getting home wood wherin god was very good to mee in my busines. the 6. a very comfortable rain in our parts

May. 8. God good in his manifold mercies towards us in the liberty of the sabbath the preserver of his people. and lett *mee bee* in thy sight as thine.

[1] Both pippins and pomewaters are types of apple. SOED.

[2] Thomas Bowes, of Great Bromley, Essex, husband of Eliz. Harlakenden; see Harlakenden genealogy, Appendix 1.

May. 15. The season very dry, the drought great. god hath yet visited our feilds with rain beyond the portion of others blessed bee his name, our daily dependance must bee on him, and in all my straits, I trust him and leane myself upon him, and he will provide: god good to mee in the liberty of his holy day, he in mercy accept mee and doe mee good(.) heard hopefully of the recovery of my Cosin Hurrill for which mercy I returned god thanks.

16. Parliament adjourned until Nov. 20. passing a sharpe act against conventicles(.)[1] my litle Rebekah very full of boils lord heale her and help us.

21. my uncle. N. Josselins daughter and her housband came to us, a mercy to bee in a capacity to welcome our freinds.

May. 22. God good in manifold mercies, yet the season very dry, some litle dews lord satisfie the earth in mercy, god good to mee in his holy day and the word, a reviving joy to mee

23. it seemed to cloud over my head from god, in many particulars. my wife very ill, with our Rebekahs illnes, who was sadly afflicted with boils. I apprehended it fading, my colt lost, things ill in family, the court lookt on by mee as if my liberty might bee restraind, my heart was awd, and humbly desirous of gods favour, he would not meditate unkindnes, or lie in waite to bruise a poor reed. I sought him humbly, and hope in all particulars before mee(.) my colt came home. the court (,)[2] except a litle, not meddling with mee, my childs boils breake and I have more hope. lord sanctify all unto mee for good.

May. 29. This day. as a caution to forelooke our ways, and to doe things advisedly, I fell into a great error. bidding to morrow for restauration day of the king which was this day. season very dry and cold. god good to mee in my family their boils breaking with greater hopes of doing well, god good to mee in his word pressing obedience with lively sense on my people.

[1] Any person aged 16 or over present at a conventicle (i.e. meeting or assembly concerning religion not authorized by the Church of England) with more than five other persons would suffer three months' imprisonment for the first offence (or £5 fine), and double this for the second offence. Kenyon, pp. 383–6.

[2] There are no Archdeaconry visitation books or act books between 1660 and October 1663, hence it is not possible to see the court's reaction to his non-appearance in October 1662 and to find evidence concerning his supposed suspension to which he refers on 18 May 1663. It is possible to check his comments on 23 May 1664 for, in the record of the court held for the Archdeaconry of Colchester on 18 May, Mr. Ralph Joscelyne was presented for 'That he hath not Administered the Sacrament of the Supper the whole yeare and the parishioners want [i.e. lack] it' (ERO, D/ACA/55 fol. 118v). He was presented in the same wording on 17 June (fol. 151), but does not seem to have conformed.

June. 4: This weeke god good to mee in my businesse, very comfortable showres again and again giving great hope of plenty for which my soule blesseth god

June. 5, God good to us in outward mercies, my family recovering more health(.) the war with Holland proceeds. the King abused by infamous pictures. for which lewd courses give occasion, the lord remember afflicted christendom(,) but men are troubled to see their evill represented to them, though they glory and boast among their likes in the doing of it.

9. a very sweet rain, discourses aloud of our breache with the Dutch. called on again to Court for not administring the sacrament.

June. 12. God good to mee. and mine in manifold outward mercies, this day a day of holy rest, is now the sport, and pleasure day of the generall rout of people, oh lord awaken persons from their sensuall walking(.) a very hot day. god good in his word in a very great assembly of people.

18: 19. very sweet, refreshing showres, not lesse in our apprehension than ground raines

June. 19. God good to mee and mine in outward mercies, the lord my god accept us, and rejoyce in and over us for good, the lord good in the word, and the opportunitie to waite on him, and in the continuance of my libertie and peace, the Turke prospers, is their conversion at hand, lord hasten it for thy names sake. god good to mee in his word this day, command oh lord thy blessing.

June. 26. A good season for our busines blessed be god A sad affliction of the smal pox at the priory the lord sanctifie to stop it and preserve town and my family, god good in the sabbath his word of judgment had awakening unto my soule

July. 3. God good in manifold mercies in a *morning*. ended my haying. two *hanke* end that business good and a good quantity, the lord good to mee in the word of the day. blessed bee his name

8: My best of freinds Mrs Colier, and her deare daughter Mrs Harlakenden, the onely branch of my never to bee forgotten Harlakenden, gave us a visitt from London, my heart leaped for joy to see them. god almighty prosper them.

July. 10. God good to mee in the word and worke of the day, at night called to Major Haynes to baptize his son James, which I willingly did and returned. the King narroely escaped drowning, July. 5. god can deliver and smite when he pleaseth.

13. Mr Harl, kept his courts, very close in his busines, wee had some unkind passages there, but all ended well I hope. blessed bee god, he gave mee my sons fine.

16. Heard my son Thomas could not come down this summer, a hard master not to give a litle respitt in 4 yeares, when also promised, lord be thou his freind I pray

July. 17. season sett in wett, lord reserve the harvest weekes to us. small pox much in the country, such aboundance of cherries, brought by carts one in Colne July. 15 sold 3 pound for 2^{d}. uttering[1] a load in our street, a sickly fruite, and great sicknes feared, but where is the preparation for it. Coxal sermon bell sounded very light for morning sermon into my studdy, which is accounted a signe of raine. god was good to mee in his word and worship this day for which my soule blesseth him.

July. 24. A very wett season the complexion of the skie sad, no harvest is entring(,) lord in mercy remember us I pray and looke up, the lord good in his word, and the comfort of deare freinds.

26. Mr H. family of the priory returnd 25 backe from the street, and this day afraid a maid servant is visited with the small pox(,) lord preserve them and it was not so at present

July. 31. Wonderfull wett day and season, rie, especially wheat growing commonly in the feilds as it stands, thus god contends with England. in Holland the plague rageth, famine and sword in Spain, Poland; but the sword sadly in Hungary and those parts but profane man minds nothing, lord make us to turne at thy reproofes oh pitty and spare for thy name sake.

Aug: 1: 2. In the midst of divers shoures that fell in other very neare places within 40. 80. rod. and some drops in my feilds. I gott in my mislain. Dr Colier gave us a visitt from London. this. 3. a very promising day; yet great shoures goe about. so it was. 4. and 5^{t}. days. the 6. I scarce saw a shoure. yett through mercy it was to us, an indifferent harvest weeke.

Aug. 7. God good to mee in manifold mercies the season hopefull, the lord good in the word to mee, make it a word of grace oh lord, likely that wee quarrel the Dutch.

8: Johns illnes that appeard a litle aguish die 6°. was very violent in a feaver as if it would have puld him into the grave, oh the rowlings of my bowels over him knowing something of god, this morning gods answer sweet in our hopes of him, it was a great mercy Dr Colier was with us

[1] Utter: to sell. SOED.

10: heard the Turks were routed: 12. confirmed to bee done. July. 31. if they are the persons god designes to ruine Austria. if they were dead and wounded men they should all rise up in their places to doe it. as said of the Caldeans. Jer. 37.1.10.

Aug. 14: a good harvest weeke without any considerable shoures in our parts, though wee had pretty dewings severall days, and this morning a pretty quantity of raine, the lord good to us in many mercies. Johns illness turnd to an ague(,) Jane limps, god very good in the word. thou hast put mee to it, to choose and thou art my choice, and thee will I own and serve continually.

19. Friday morning early my dearest Freind Mrs Colier, with her deare housband the Dr and daughter parted from mee for London, which parting was to my spirit troublesom. minding mee of the comfort of gods eternal presence and how happy wee are to enjoy him in *abiding* good. weather wett.

18. dined with Sr J. Jacob visiting his house at Halsted where he was 7 or 8 yeares agone very low, pincht for many yeares with the Kings debts, not knowing scarce how to provide for his family, ☞ which he born to my view with prudence. patience and submission to god, now he is in a very old age, full disposing his children high in the world, paying debts, clearing all. and cheerfull(.) I minded him of this change, and that the filling up his dayes with goodnes that he might die truly blessed. was to serve god faithfully and holily, which he tooke kindly from mee. [ ] god [ ] returne the captivities of his.

20. This day I made an end of harvest, and ind my corne very well blessed bee god although the weather was very unseasonable. the lord inherit my praise

Aug. 21. God good to mee in manifold mercies, in the word, my soule warming in love to Christ and to advance his name and glory in the *worke* oh lord lift up thy selfe. heard of the Turks successe against the Imperialists. which did not hold true.

Aug. 28. God good in outward mercies. cited to an episcopall visitacion. the lord give mee a resigning spirit. I leave my selfe to his dispose, not knowing what to desire. yett my libertie with no other lords(,) god good in the word heart war(m)ing

Sept. 1: a wonderfull wett day, the wayes for dirt and water like the depth of winter

Sept: 4. God good to mee and mine in many mercies, yett my family very crasie, but our affliction is gentil. the lord sanctifie and doe mee good in the same. god good in the word this day, the lord give mee his spirit and comfort mee, my heart calm in the expectacion of the issue of this visitacion, wherin my liberty at stake.

11. God good in the word, I had some apprehension it might bee my last sermon.

Sept. 14. was the Bishops of Londons primary visitacion 1664 where I having committed my selfe to god appeared, and through mercy mett with no rubbs, but my path clear so that I hope I may serve my Master with freedom a while longer, till I see those wonderfull revolucions. Mr Smith[1] a nonsubscriber was threatned by the Bishop to bee made an example: blesse my god oh soule

Sept. 18: God good in manifold mercies to mee, and in my sabbath liberty, divers faces hearing I used not to see. lord continue my liberty(,) help mee to [ur] it and use it thankfully.

23. began to sow my rie field: ended. 27. wett sown.

Sept. 25. A wetting day, a mercy after much dry weather, the lord good in outward mercies unto mee, the lord accept and own and doe mee good.

29. preacht Mrs Bulkleys funerall at Stanway chapell. oh the sad breakings in a family by a good wifes losse; blessed bee god for my preservation and mine

Oct: 2. A faire morning to a good day the lord meet my soule with favour and my labour with a blessing in his word, many hearing(.) my spirit sensible of gods goodnes to mee in the word of affliction, said wee have great successe against the Hollanders in Guinee

5. Heard the Sextin that buried Mrs Bulkley. died at Stanway Hall that night of an Apoplexie, lord helpe mee to watch untill my change come,

Oct. 9. God good in outward mercies, yet our sores continue, lord heale for thy name sake(.) wett, cold weather, god good to mee in the word for which his name be praisd, his weeke. talk our fleet gone against the Dutch under Rupert. and peace with Turks.

Oct. 16. God good in manifold mercies, yett my family crasie, lord my soule mourns after thee seeking thy glory and thy favour, shew it more and more to mee. god good in the word, endeavoured a sacrament of the lords supper for my lords honour and remembrance

20. at night, my Jane very ill, her mother tired out without a servant, but then Ann pain came to live with us. god make her a blessing and helpe, lord smile on my tabernacle and revive all my litle ones I pray thee.

[1] Probably John Smith, curate of Castle Hedingham, Essex, in 1662, or his son. Calamy; Smith, p. 392; Davids, p. 384.

Oct: 23. The lord good in many outward mercies, accept mee oh lord, prest for coming to the lords supper, lord in obedience to thee I manage this worke accept oh lord

Oct. 30: A sad windie day, after rain, causing a very wonderfull floud. this day I gave the sacrament of the lords supper. 12. present. some with great devotion and brokenes of heart, the lord accept mee who desire to bee his, ingaging my heart to him, in his wayes. my poore deare wife with mee, lord smile on us for thy names sake. god very good in the sacramental sermons

31: Saw Mr Eldreds will, wee had good discourse, my soule pittieth him, he is apprehensive of an ulcer, but very gratious in his temper. kind to mee, lord return

No: 5. preached from Joel, lord arise and save thy afflicted people. hopes in Mr Eldreds case(.) the Dr much on my mind, lord help us, in the(e) I hope. Sermon suitable to him.

No. 6. Wett windie day. god good to mee and mine in manifold outward mercies, lord embrace mee as thine own and sanctifie all to mee.

7. made an end of sowing wheat with plow: 8. 9. sew in the orchards. the times very wett, for all my wheat and late, a great blessing to give a crop and for that I hope in my god.

Nov. 13. God good in manifold mercies, yett our family illnes continueth (but moderat[*es*] lord Sanctifie thy rod, that wee may all proffitt by it and helpe lord and heale us, the word of god good tending to better us by affliction, good lord doe it

Nov. 20. God good to us in manifold mercies, A poore man at Gaynes Colne, yet worth. 16^{li}. lands yeerly, fearing want, hangd himselfe, but cut down revived and lived. lord what is man left to himselfe. a cheerfull day, and a good day in the word of affliction(,) better mee lord by thy rebukes.

24: Ingaged at the priory in a good day to seeke god for Mr Eldred, and all our afflicted ones, there was that exercised Mr Stockdale. Mr Buckley. Mr Sparrow silenced Ministers. and my selfe, wee continued untill neare nine at night, lord accept us and returne a gratious answer.

No. 27. God good to us in manifold mercies, the lord good in the word how afflictions tend to sanctification, lord let mine worke to that end, and doe mee good and mine.

Dec: 4: God good in our afflictions, lighting his hand on us, and I trust sanctifying it to us(.) wee are upward blessed bee his name, the weather wonderfull inconstant and uncheerfull. last weeke Sr

Sam: Tryon.[1] Col. Sparrow:[2] Rich Guoyon[3] the greatest webster in England. Mr Savil. considerable persons died by us. the lord awaken us, the plague begun in Yarmouth. the report contradicted.

An 5. Lohd *d* this morning a blazing starre[4] seen in Earles Colne as several said, I endeavoured much to see it til the 11. but could not.

Dec. 11. God good to us in manifold mercies, he sent us a servant, lord let her bee a mercy to us, and restore my family to perfect health, the lord good in his word let there bee sweetnes in it. to all thy afflicted ones, great flouds, a wonderfull wett, raw, winter.

Dec: 18. very ill with a feavor fitt all night, I feared I should not be fitt to preach. cald up to see litle Eldred that lay dying in their thoughts, whom I earnestly commended to god for life and glory, god help mee in the sabbath worke. lord accept mee. its my great joy, I have a heart and liberty to preach.

Dec. 24. a starre appeared in the South with a stream, for about an houre

Dec. 25. God good to us in manifold mercies, lightning his hand from of us, when heavy on Mr Eldred(,) the lord in mercy sanctifie it to them

Jan: 1: Begun the new yeare in the Sabbath worke, wherin god good to mee, the season good winterly, I had my company at church and praises to god for our liberty to walke abroad.

Jan. 8. A very cold time; god good to mee and mine in many mercies—our family abroad again, to god bee glory; news stronger of a dutch warre.

19. buried old Hutton, that went out to worke and fell down dead in the feild by his house. said his father died 2 feilds farther, there were living at once in the parish, workemen to Mr Harlakenden. Henry Hutton his first wife. Guy Hutton son, his first wife. Henry grandchild his first wife. and Henry sons to 3 children, but now the string is twice broken[5]

[1] Sir Samuel Tryon, Bart., of Boys Hall, Halstead, Sheriff of Essex 1649–50. Venn.

[2] John Sparrow of Havering Park, Deputy Lt. of the County in 1643, and a Colonel at the siege of Colchester, in 1657 High Sheriff of Essex; John Sparrow the mystic was his son (DNB). Quintrell, p. 179.

[3] Probably in fact Thomas Guyon of Coggeshall, whose funeral sermon by Thomas Jessop was noted by the diarist Bufton: 'the fourth (sermon) was at the buriall of Old Mr Thomas Guyon, the great clothier, upon Satterday, in the evening by candlelight, Nov. ye 26th.' Quoted in Beaumont, p. 220. A webster was a weaver (NED).

[4] Evelyn noted this comet on the 14, 25, 26 December: Evelyn, iii, pp. 392–3.

[5] The passage from 'his first wife . . .' is out of order in the Diary, having been written in at the bottom of the page.

Jan. 15. 22. God good in outward mercies, the season cold, gods word reviving, likely hood of warre. all persons say cometa malum omen, and now all nations promise themselves good. in particular England and the Imperial family.

Jan: 26: 1664: my 48 y. ended and 49. entred.

Sensible that this day begun a new yeare with mee, with thankfulnes to god for his continued goodnes to mee and mine, with hopes that the lord will never faile mee nor forsake mee, oh quicken my flagging heart, that I may not goe lower in any holy dutie I intreate thee oh my god, and saviour.

29. God good in manifold outward mercies, in the word of the day, lord lay thy life into my soule to comfort mee, for others decay, and troubles multiply.

Feb. 5. A very cold season, god good to us in our outward mercies, exercised with reproofs which I beare with patience for thy name sake oh lord, god good to me in the sabbath and in the duties thereof.

9. Mett at priory to seeke god on behalf of church, state, family. ☞ Especially Mr Eldred who is throwing himself on god to be cutt for the stone. Mr Sparrow. Mr Stockden, my selfe, spoke and prayed. Mr Shirly[1] prayed. god good in the day, wee had a large collection for poore freinds, god in mercy heare and savour our spirits with his truths.

Feb. 12. God good in outward mercies, the season warme, the times yett wonderfull hard, no trade by reason of the Dutch troubles. this frost was not very long viz from Wednesday. Dec. 21. to Feb. 9: eight weekes, but it was wonderfull sharpe beyond what known for so long, in my memory, neither is it gone though it abates

14. it freeze hard again. 15. very hard and tis likely to continue; gave. 19.

Feb. 19. God good to mee in manifold mercies, the scab a very great trouble to mee, lord heale and helpe mee, god good in his word, he essays to bring my heart to more inward seriousnes with him, lord effect it, and lett me live unto thee.

Feb. 26. The frost continues, though so moderate the plowes stirre. god

[1] James Shirley, vicar of Dunton, Bucks., from before 1650 to 1662; in 1665 living 'on his temporal estate' at Braintree; will, as of EC, July 1676 (PRO, PROB 11/351/95). Calamy.

good in manifold mercies for which my soule blesseth him, the lord good in the word full of warmth and life, quicken mee to thy service, and accept mee I pray thee.

27. a great frost in the morning.

March: 5. frost continued. this is a most bitter day with north wind and snow, at night my inkhorn frosne. god good to mee in the sabbath word and worke, a sad time for worke, trade, and yet people setle on their lees, lay nothing to heart.

7. my pump frozen. most persons feare ries are even kild with cold.

☞ made a good end in Cosin Hurrils busines blest bee god 8. a pretty snow.

March: 12. a cold wett day. god good in the word, tooke my leave of Mr Eldred. the lord returne him safe to us, frost at night.

Frost. 14. the last I saw of the frost, the ice generally melted, and the frost gone out of the ground, it continued, from Wednesday Decemb. 21.

☞ to this day being 12. weeks very violent. this an effect of the blazing starre, and now it tends unto drought

March. 19. God good in manifold mercies, in the word, my selfe and family ill, the lord remove his hand and sanctifie it, doing us good by all rebukes

1665 26. March: 1665. Easter day. 12 of us received the sacrament of the lords supper publiquely for which I blesse god, I beleive its 22. or 23. yeares since received on that day and occasion, the lord good to us in the season, and in the word, he accept and blesse us, my daughter Jane a communicant with us

27. kept a day of prayer at priory for Mr Eldred who this morning at London intended to bee cutt of the stone.[1] wee pray and looke up, lord bee thou gratious to him, our newes of him very, very good

Ap. 2. Weeke past, dry and windie and cold. god good in outward mercies and yett his hand on us especially my self in a scab, and my spirit much ill, for which I humble myselfe before god and beg his pardon and grace. god good in day and word a cheerfull audience

4 This morning I saw the third blazing starre northeast. it arose about 3 in morne, and ascending was taken from our sight by light. the stream direct upwards, the star ruddier and brighter then

[1] The very great danger of the operation is not only shown by the fact that a commemorative feast was still being held eight years later (see under 27 March 1673), but by a reference to the event by John Eldred himself. In a list of the major events in his life, which otherwise only contains births, marriages, and deaths of kin, is a note under 27 March 1665 that 'A Stone was taken out of my Bladder by Cutting and in 14 Days the Wound was healed' (ERO, D/DPr 454).

that of December 24 at night and the stream more luminous. this day I fetched all my wood from chadwells safely, yett neare dangers, god caution mee against sin.

5. A fast kept for good successe in our naval forces, god in mercy grant it.

Ap: 9. God good in outward mercies, a gallant seed time. lord remember us with rain in season(,) the skie threats a drought. the lord can command plenty.

Estate: When I come to view my estate expenses are 141^{li}. 4^{s}. 9^{d}. receipts. 139^{li}. 4^{s}. 8^{d}. losse. 2^{li}. 1^{d}. and some debts lesse then last yeare. I cannot say I either loose or gain directly. yett my thoughts are my outward estate will this yeare appeare to better. god prosper my soule.

14. Heard yesterday of a strange light northwest(,) saw it this morning very red as big as the sun, not directly round.

Ap. 16. God good to mee in his word. freinds family, I preacht at Markshall god prosper his word. season dry, night almost continually cold frosts

21. preacht my good freind Mr Tompsons funeral on his own text. phil. 3.9. at little Horsely. lord pitty us in our losses

Ap. 23. God good in manifold mercies, some shoures with haile, others onely rain, the lord water the earth in mercy, god good in the word, and this providence prayers answer.

24. at Cogshal, where I did my busines about armes to content

28. Mr Eldred returned safe to us from London being cutt of the stone, and healed to admiracon, praise god, oh my soule—.

Ap. 30. God good in manifold outward mercies, the season windy and dry, yett shoures in some places, lord in due time command them. god good in the word and worke of the day the lord in mercy accept mee for good

May. 3. This day imployed in returning thanks to god for Mr Eldreds deliverance, wherin my soule was hearty, god accept. season cold windy dry: strange a wife never pittied him ill, nor once said pray for him. nor spoke a good word of god in his recovery.

May. 7. God good in manifold mercies, the lord continueth his kindnes unto mee for which my soul blesseth him, I began to expound things out of the church catechism for the informacion of youth, god good to mee in the word, the season dry

8. at the visitacon, with respect, heard of successe against Smyrna fleet, the countenances of many ministers sad to eye, lord heale our manners, sermon was pressing to labour and holynes.

10. rid to Mrs Tompsons who in 19 yeares litle increased their estate being in a great living and a good estate of his own worth above 1600li.—11. kept a day of praise for Mr Eldred(.) sensible of returne of old corruptions and my long affliction, lord melt down my drosse and make mee a new lumpe.

May 14. God good in manifold outward mercies the plague certainly in London.[1] 9. dyed last weeke, the drought doth not only continue, but the heat groweth very much(.) 9 died of the plague at London, lord helpe us to gett into the gap to turn away thy wrath, god bee gracious to mee and accept mee in the beloved

May. 21. god good in various mercies, dews and after sweet rain. 22. one Mr Talbot, kild in our town by a fall down his staires at new-house in Coln. on Sunday morning(,) he had never been at church since in town. Caplins son almost kild in the gravel pitt(.) god good to mee in the word, and at Cogshall where I preacht to a great and attentive audience. god uphold my heart in his truth.

26. one Brocke a maid died suddenly in our towne—one Brownson buried that died within 24 houres of her sicking(,) god awaken us by all providences to watchfulnes

May. 28. God good in manifold mercies, my personal illnes abateth blessed bee god, the plague gott into our land at Yarmouth, and London. 14. dying this weeke. god good to mee in the word preacht, at which our concourse was this day great, its good fishing where many are(,) catch some oh lord I pray thee.

June. 4. God good in manifold mercies, my son Thomas with mee, and all my children in health blessed bee god, cast the skirt of grace over them. the season hot and dry to wonder. pastures burn and the land sins. the guns mention a great fight yesterday. this day god good in the word lett it bee a word of grace

June. 11. God good in our health and peace, the plague increaseth to 43. this weeke, the lord good in our wonderfull successe against the Dutch, good in his word, the season dry, profanes common, piety very rare.

June. 18. plague increasd to 112. god good in a sweet raine this day and a comfortable word, the lord extend his mercy and kindnes to mee and mine that wee may live in his sight, judgments increase and sins continue, lord brake our hearts and then stepp in(,) save and deliver us for thy mercy sake.

June. 25. plage increasd to 168. [by my sons Master. god shelter him.

[1] This is the first reference to the Great Plague of London; RJ's statistics were clearly derived from weekly bills of mortality (see p. 425, n. 1 above).

the season somewhat] shouring. 2063. prisoners dutch at Colchester: god good in the season to mee for which I blesse his holy name. good in his word and worship. all my 7 children hearing the word on whom bee the devine blessing.

July: 2. plague increased to 267. bill. 684: my son have leave to continue in the country, god in mercy preserve us, and heale the city. medicaments used. but no publique call to repentance(,) the king goeth to Wilton by Salisberry. the old Queen gone for France. Lawson our brave seaman dead of his wound, the season very moist, lord sent not all in anger. god good to mee in the word the lord accept mee and bee gratious unto mee

4. the earth about us fully satisfied with raine, this day a day of praise for our victory over the Dutch June. 3. my soule praise the lord in holynes.

July. 9. God good in our preservacon, the plague feares the London they flie before it and the country feares all trade with London. died. 1006. of the plague. 470 the Lord stay his heavy hand. heard from my wives sister Worrall out of Ireland which joyed us(,) returnd her letters, the season ticle[1] for hay time, the lord good in his word, god in mercy render it a blessing to my people and soule.

July. 16. God good in our mercies. London sad days increase. 1268 buried. 725 plague, lord hold thy hand. god good in the season, and in his word, the lord quicken my faith.

July. 23. The weather somewhat uncertain, I am even overclogd with busines and few hands(,) god carry mee through this trouble, my farm turnd into my hands, the plague hott. 1089. burials. 1761. lord hold thy hand, proceed not in wrath.

28: my Tenant Tiball turning my farm into my hand, I bought some
32^{li} of her corn and begun harvest this day. god prosper us. it looks like
9. an unkindly time. god in mercy prevent it, plague grows hott. persons fall down in London streets. 1843. of plague total. 2785. lord spare thy people

July. 30: God good in his word and manifold mercies to my soule.

Aug. 2. First publique monthly fast, wee gathered for distressed London

Aug: 6. God good in the season, harvest comes in well, a great rain which the earth needed to Aug: 1: a small increase of the plague beyond what feared. viz. 2010. burials. 3014: god good in the word, great multitudes even of Coln goe from hence to heare strangers at white Coln. lord make them to proffit and I shall gain.

[1] Tickle: not to be depended on, uncertain, unreliable. NED.

Aug: 13. A sad windy, stormy violent morning. to Aug: 9. a great increase of plague. 2817 total 4030. Giles criplegate 690. lord bee not angry with our prayers, and now Colchester is infected, and when will Coln lay it to heart, the lord good to mee in the word and manifold mercies.

16: kept a day of prayer at Mr Cresseners great resort. god in mercy, heare our prayers(.) Colchesters infection looketh sadly, by a joyner. Dedham clapt him into a pest house[1] presently. god spare that place.

Aug. 20. God good to us in manifold mercies, Londons visitacon sad. 3880. plague 5319. all diseases, spread almost over the whole city, and much in the country(,) lord arise and helpe. Colchester seeke into the country for dwellings, lord wee refuge our soules with thee, god good in the word.

Aug: 27. God good in our preservacion, yet much endangered by Colchester. a lad of our parish coming then died in White Colne, feared of the infection, another among us of his company(,) lord preserve us. the weather sad, but this day cooling, died at London plague 4237. all. 5568. god in mercy stop infection. the increase was small in comparison of what feared. god good in the word, make it lord a soule blessing.

Sept: 3. God good in our preservacon. Halsted in danger. god spare the place. god good in the word a very full audience, yett some stragle. the plague rageth 6102. total 7496. and twenty some days at Colchester. lord doe us good by our afflictions and spare for mercy sake

Sept. 10: God good in manifold mercies, the season cooled and yet the bill. Sept. 5. increased 6978. plague—8252. died, they ordered continuall fires in London for 3 days and nights at every doore. Lord cease thy hand, god good in his word to us, the weather wett and stormy.

Sept. 16. God good in Colnes preservation, yet Colchester increaseth in illnes being spread over the whole town, after frequent reports of a most wonderfull increase this weeke it abated through mercy. from Sept. 5. to 12. 562. there dying in all. 7690. of plague 6544. and towards the full of the moon; lord secure mee from care and evill.

Sept. 23. God good in our publique preservation. a poore woman Wades wife drownd her selfe this night. thought there died at Colchester

[1] Pest house: a hospital for persons suffering from any infectious diseases, especially the plague. SOED.

this weeke 184. from Sept. 12. to 19. the moon at full on the 14. though the weather cold, and winds stirring yet their was an increase again and especially within the wals where there died. 1493. of the plague 1189. this bill was 8297. of the plague 7165. and yet Coln preserved.

Oct: 1. A good seed time, blessed be god, deaths at Colnehill,[1] and hazards at Coln, and yet preserved god inheritt our praise the small pox with Coln at potters. a great abatement of the plague at London: 5533. totall. 6460. and so at Colchester. 59. abated there dying 126. or thereabouts. god good to mee in his word and worship, oh lett us live out thy truths.

4: The publique fast, and our calamities great, yet oh how few mind this hand of god that is lifted up, but goe on in their vain wayes, wee remembred poore Colchester in our collection neare 30^{s}. and sent them formerly. 4^{li}. god accept us and spare us for his mercy sake.

Oct: 8: To thy goodnes wee own it with praises that wee are preserved from the smal pox in our town and plague in the country. which is hott at Ipswich. Harwich an 100 dying in 3 weeks. their graves fill the churchyard alreadie, and have called for a new burying place; at Colchester it spreads exceedingly this weake buried. 188. feares of Cogshall.—Halsted. Feering. certainly at Kelvedon up land, Braintree, and yett Colne, sinful Colne spared, my soule re-
720. cords thy kindnes with meltings for thy mercy; in the midst of this
929. sadnes London begins to cleare up, an abatement of above 700 this weeke also and Spains King dieth that gives our merchants a wonderfull bay[2] market so that god finds out ways for our subsistance. god good to mee in the word(.)

ibbald/ Widdow Tibbald and I evened all our reckonings, and shee still ☞ oweth mee 10^{li}. for which shee is to give bond and on payment of it before April next I promise to give her 20^{c}. of hay.

Oct: 15. God good to us in manifold mercies(,) the season cold dry and frostie considerable ice after wett beginning. Wednesday. 11: the plague lookt on certainly at Coln - ford hill, and yett Coln preserved, it abates blessed bee god at Colchester above 50. and 652 at London. god good in his word for which my soule prays(.) at

[1] Colne Hill (or Colneford Hill) was at the slightly detached, poorer, eastern end of the village. This is the first among many references to the plague in the parish. The parish register only notes five deaths as specifically caused by plague, all in April and May 1666.

[2] Bay: one of the lighter cloths, the manufacture of which was introduced into England in the sixteenth century. NED.

Colchester died. 145. their charge above 500^{li}. per month, wherupon the country within 5 miles round, were charged towards there releife.

Oct. 22. A wonderfull sweet season. dry, cold and frosts, god gave a great abatement to the plague. 3219. in all. plague. 2665. decrease. 1849. London praise god, the lord good to us in his word, our tax at the parl. at oxford encreasd to $140,000^{li}$. per month for 18 months to begin. Jan: next, likelyhoods of the French warre also, we assist Bishop of Munster with mony. without a trade it will bee very heavy to the nacion; god good in Colnes preservacion, although at Colnford hill. 7 have died and 3 have plague sores as wee apprehend. at Colchester only. 22. abated died 106. of the plague. 121 all. [c.o. about 123 or 30]

27. saw the London bill. gods name bee praised for the great abatement of the plague 1413. decrease. total, 1806, of the plague 1421. lord remove the plague of our hearts and heale the whole land; Cambridge. Royston and many places much visited, scattered much in the south—

Oct: 29. God good in manifold mercies for which my soule praiseth him over (c.o. neare) 101. died at Colchester. lord remove thy rod, blessed bee god Coln is preserved(.) the plague at (c.o. Colchester) Oxford. the visitacon Court suspended one, and I am free. blesse god oh my soule, a great audience. Halsted in hazard.

Nov: 5: God good in his manifold mercies our preservacon to this present, abated at London again (c.o. above) 408. burials. 1388. 1031 of the plague, yet at Colchester it increased above 20 new houses infected, buried there about 147. oh lord remove thy hand for thy name sake.—god good to mee in my liberty in the word, my soule sensible of its evill, and yet god heard prayers(.) Mr Eldreds litle daughter very ill for whom wee prayed, few leaves left on the trees, except those witherd on the oaks.

8: Fast and a good day. lord blesse mee with thy favour.

Nov: 12. A good season and god good in his mercie to us, said the plague mortal to many masters of families at London it increased 399: in all dying 1787 of the plague. 1414. abated at Harwich yet
frost not cleare. at Colchester their died 110. lord cleare the nacon—

Nov: the Dutch snapt some of our Tangier fleet, provision ships2 . and 18. 1 fregate, and the French tooke 3 of our Levant merchant men, there is a fleet going to the straits.

Nov: 19: Good cleare frostie weather blessed bee god, sharper penalties in the act against non-conformity, yett I hope. one suspended is

restored on promise once a yeare to weare the surplice. the plague
1050 abated a litle at Colchester. viz. to. 106: at London abated 428. more then the last increase the total. 1358: lord make us thankfull, a still time abroad in the world only here, and in poland embroilments. god good to mee in manifold mercies, his presence in the word, and beauty of his assembly

Nov: 26: Frostie weather with wind clearing the aire, the plague abates at London 905 dying in all of plague 652. at Colchester also much abated, blessed bee our preserver. 70 dying this weeke, wee heare the like from all parts. oh lord continue thy favour and goodnes to mee and mine, my heart dies if thou bee not gracious. thy favour supports when all are unkinde.

Dec: 3. open weather, god good to us in manifold mercies, plague abates
544. at Colchester to 48: at London. 544. plague 333. and wee still pre-
333. served blessed bee god, god good to mee in the word of mistificacon by faith, lord acquitt my soule

6: publique fast, a very thin audience, yett god good to us in withdrawing his pestilence and our preservation, sent Colchester. 7^{li}. 10^{s}. collected at our severall fasts, lord accept and bee gracious unto us.

Dec: 9. Weather open and warm, the plague decreasing litle at Colchester there dying. 45. but blessed bee god abated at London. 116. bill being. 428. and Colne still preserved. plague. 210. god very good and gracious to mee in his word, for which my soule blesseth him.

Dec: 17. Heard of the wellfare of my old freind Mrs Colier and hers. a wonderfull inundacon the end of Nov: which did much hurt to the English coast. but incredible to the Netherlands. the plague increasd this bill: burials. 442. plague. 243. increase. 14. so said at Colchester. 67. of plague. all. 71. the weather frosty begun Dec: 14. god purge our aire and heale the nacon: Halsted much strucke with the small pox and a fever at Colne in divers poore families. lord watch over us for good

Dec: 24: frost continues Londons increase. 83. plague. 280. bur. 525. said increasd at Colchester, but not. 60. god good in mercies and word for which I blesse his name

Dec: 31. Frost continues, likelyhood of ill times and trade, yet through mercy there was a great abate of the plague at London, when reports contrary. plague 152. total. 330 so at Colchester. total. 24.

Jan: 3. Fast, an indifferent audience, gathered well for Colchester god accept us and crown our endeavours(,) weather open and warme.

Jan. 7. God good in manifold mercies though weather open and warme, plague increasing at Colchester to. 29. yet at London it comes low. plague. 70. total. 253. blessed bee god, lord cleare us that it gett not into the spring. the Dutch and wee are preparing to out fleets. to sea early. they under Ruyter and wee Monke.

Jan: 14: Weather open: damp. no raine or litle and so ever since Nov: 64. no water in ponds they drive their catle to water in the hundreds(.) the plague increasd at London to 89. bur. 265: at Colchester died. 54. pl: 46. lord remove thy hand in much mercy(.) god good to us in his word, a comfortable audience. lord increase our faith.

Jan. 21. weather cold and wettish for which god bee blessed our ponds empty and almost without water. plague increasd at London to 158. burials. 375.—110 increase lord pitty and pardon. Jan. 10. the Q. mother of France died of a cancer in her breast, that King intends great matters, shee did not long overlive her brother philip of Spain, Colchester (c.o. about 48) 46. god good to mee in preaching his word, lord make it a blessing to us all. heard of my sons masters health, he writes for him, wee intend him up, god in mercy preserve him

These particulars I observed in the generall bill. ending Decemb: 19. 65.

97.	parishes. buried.	15209.	pl. 9887.	Males	48569	97306.
14.	parishes b.	41351.	----- 28888.	Females	48737.	
12.	p. -------	28554.	----- 21420.	plague	68596.	
5.	p. -------	12194.	----- 8403.			

Christnings 9967.—increase in burials this yeare. 79009. The greatest plague in England since that in Edward the thirds time, and yet it continues, as very feirce in many places of England, this Jan. 26. what god may doe, the weather being now cold frostie, I know not, but hope well.

Jan: 26: 65. my 50. entred.

I was not aware this begun the yeare, the lord remember mee for
good, when my eye is not distinctly on him, I was employed in
Jan. ending a difference between one Bull and Sr Tho: Honywood,
28. rescuing that poore man from the bailes, we have had rain that fils
the river, and maketh the wayes washy. an abatement of plague at

Colchester to 36. London 272. plague. 79(.) god good in preaching the word,

30: Fast preacht from psal. 111.10. its our wisedom to bee religious. commonly said the French have proclaimed open warre against England.

31. My son Thomas went up to London having been with us since beginning of June, the lord return with him and preserve him to bee a continual comfort to mee and mine

Feb: 4. This month, cold winds, frost snow, purging the aire, plague abates. 56. total. 227. a low bill. Colchester holds ill still. increasing to 43. god good to mee in the word, my Jane ill of fits of the mother, oh lord lett not thy favour and blessing in any kind bee withdrawn from the tabernacle of thy servant.

Feb: 11. London reviveth, blessed bee god. plague abated 4 to 52. the burials increased to 231. god good to us in the season, the lord in mercy doe our soules good, hopes of an abatement at Colchester. died, 28. god good in the word calling to faith, helpe lord

Feb: 18. a cleare weeke. yet plague increaseth, London. 59. total. 249 Colchester 30. lord help and heale, a wonderfull dry season with cold and fogs, wee had plenty of sprats this Feb: 16.—god good to us in his word, my Jane gets heart again

Feb: 25: A very dry season, cold not much windy, the plague yet increaseth. 69 London. burials. 252; so said at Colchester. 39. Queen miscarreid. the lord make us to lay to heart our sins against him, oh let not ruine come in upon us for wee hope in thee; corruption busy in my heart lord rescue mee by thy spirit, stirring up thy grace, and making mee watchful against it(.) god good to mee in the word, my thoughts much about giving over preaching

March. 4. Weather cold, with some snow and haile stormes, the grounds excessive dry(,) plague through mercy abates at London. 42. pl. total 237. but a great increase at Colchester to 55. Yarmouth cleare, lord heale our land, and open our trade in mercy. god good and gracious to mee in the word, but oh the evill of my heart, lord helpe and heale it I pray thee.

7. Fast. people at worke, oh I find cores of corruption in my heart, oh lord cause it to run out and give mee thy saving health. hopes of London still.

March. 11. God good in outward mercies, the season excessive dry, cold frizing in the house(.) plague decreaseth at London. 28. total
7. died increase one 238(.) some say it abates at Colchester. a still time in the affaires of the world abroad

March: 18: a cold, dry time. at London plague. 29. burials. 207. very low blessed bee god(,) Colchester 43. I was very ill in my head, yet the lord helped mee, blessed bee his holy name and therefore soule take up thy rest in god

21: great experience of the evill of my heart, oh the snares Satan lays for mee(.) the plague increaseth; lord deeply humble my heart, this morning wett and windy. the lord shews mee my particular sin, calls of from it, with hopes of pardon my soule detests it, which my folly betrays mee.

March. 25: plague somewhat increaseth at London. dying: 33. in all
666 233. more at Colchester. 53. some places cleare. The lord good to mee in leading mee up unto Christ as my soules releif under the experience of the working of corruption, god good to mee in the word, accept mee in Christ, my heart went along with the notes of faith, as true in my soule blessed bee god

1666

Ap: 1: Wonderfull dry. plague abates at London. viz. to. 17. total 224. but it sadly increaseth at Colchester to 70: lord heare and bee gracious, god good to mee in the word. the lord watch over mee for good,

3. some small shoures. but very refreshing to our dusty lands, cool and close die. 4°. which was the fast day. still cool shoures, a cheerfull audience(,) god did good by his *good* word: 6. fine shoures.

Ap: 8: [God] good in manifold mercies. plague gentle but increaseth at London. viz. 26. tot. [211]. feare worse at Colchester,73 its at Dedham and severall villages, lord in mercy remove thy hand.
73 wett and cold, the lord in mercy own my soule and looke after mee for good. rie in my feild coming out of the hose.[1]

Ap. 15: God good in manifold mercies, very full shoures but cold. great expecting wonderfull plenty. plague increasd at London to. 28. total 195. sore at Colchester dying 90 of plague. total. 92. administered the sacraments. 16. present. god good in the word

Ap: 22. After long shouring weather moistening the outward face of the earth, warm springing weather(,) god make the yeare fruitfull.
72 plague increased at London: to 40. total. 215. at Colchester very ill yet abated. 72. it spreads in several places of the country, lord arise and helpe. the heat sucks up the raine, god good to mee in his word

[1] Hose: the sheath enclosing the ear of straw or corn. SOED.

26 visited several freinds. the ground clothed wonderfull richly, weather dry and warm(.) heard Bishop of Munster had made peace. and Sabbatai the Jewes prophet killed.[1]

28. apprehensions of one Wades wife a quaker dying of the plague. god take care of us. I procured her speedie buriall.

Ap. 29. God good in manifold mercies aire warm and dry. plague blessed bee god decreasing at London. viz to 24. bur. 215. feares of a great increase at Colchester. 94 died(.) a large audience, god preserve us, and prosper his word

May. 2. Fast. many strangers with us, notwithstanding the rumour of our towne, we prayd heartily for Colne and Colchester, and the land, the lord heare and heale

May. 6. God good in our preservacon, yet sadly called on for the plague one dying of spots at night, it increasd at Colchester sadly to 177. at London to. 40 total 213. many people resort to the word; lord doe them good by it.

10: at night much lightning with some thunder; very hott, gods mercy therin I hope to purge the aire.

May. 13: plague increasd at London. to 53. total. 234: sad at Colchester dying. 174: the lord in mercy remove his hand no more dying at Coln this weeke. this day one family viz Alstons left to their libertie to worke in feilds, at the other the nurse sicke. many attending on the word, the lord blesse it unto them.

from the 10th to this day. viz. 19. the aire very cold, and very much rain as if god testified against us, and likely to turn our thoughts of unspeakable plenty into scarcitie

May. 20: god wonderfull gracious in our preservacon. nothing of infection appearing farther(.) lord hold thy hand I intreate thee.— London increased to 58. total. 236: its thinly peopled whatsoever persons speake, most by places empty and thought the deaths were beyond our counts by far, lord spare. feares of Spains quarrelling
161. us(,) lord humble us, and owne us. sad still with poor Colchester. 161 dying. the lord good to mee in the word, a troublesom coming up street, where wee found another child stricken; and old lea not well. lord pardon for thy name sake.

May. 27. cold month, but indifferent dry, god good to us in our preservacon, under a strang carelesnes of people, London abates to

[1] Sabbetai Levi or Sevi (1626–76), who led a crusade to liberate Palestine from the Turks in 1666 by peaceful means: under pressure, however, he adopted Islam and was banished. His attempt was eagerly watched since it could well be taken as a prelude to the Second Coming. For a full biography see G. Scholem, *Sabbati Sevi—the Mystical Messiah* (Princeton, 1973), trans. R. J. Werblowsky.

31. total. 203. Colchester abates also to 110: and not so mortal at Bocking, god in his rich grace preserve poore Coln, god good in the word, lord make it a mercy day, the affliction day

June: 1. did my last duty to Sr Tho: Honywoods dust, laying him up in his earth. and long home at Marshal. who died at London.

June: 3. God good in a cheerfull season and good word, the lord gentle in our affliction, but yet it continues, one buried this morning. god mercifull in abating the plague send lord deliverance. London:
99. pl: 20. tot. 201: Colchester. 101. rumours of a great fight, wee prayd heartily for successe, and hope it, though some cry a losse.

6. the publique fast, divers from severall places attending on the word

June. 10. God good in season, yet moist, matters at sea hard, yet god good in our deliverance yett losse great, god good in the word. plague increasd at London to 27. total. 191. increasd at Colchester
120: at least 20. god good in our health, yett wee had a fright at Henry Hatches, lord lett mercy bee to us therin

June. 17. God good in the season very hot and dry, good in our peace preservacon. word god good in London yet increasd. total. 196. pl.
150. 31. increasd at Colchester. to 150 lord in much mercy remove thy hand from us.

23. On a suddain, by reason of shoures upwards, a great floud, to the great harm of our meadows. god sanctifie all to us.

June. 24. God good in manifold mercies, the lord accept mee and doe
112 mee good, the sicknes decreasd at Colchester. 32. being. 112. at London to 23. total. *119*. god good in the word, the lord in mercy to my soule, delight in mee to doe mee good

July: 1: God good to admiracon in our towns preservation, when so sad in all other places, Cambridge. Oundle. Needham. Braintree. but above all at Colchester increasing to 180. London. 33. tot. 223. after much rain which threats the crop. this day was cheerfull god remember us in all for good. god good in the word my heart evill and treacherous. helpe Lord Jesus with thy spirit

4. Fast. prayd heartily for our fleet, and land, and harvest. god gives some hopes of better weather. the land at a low ebbe, our enemies brave it on our coast(,) god in mercy, helpe and deliver.

July. 8. god good in the season. I was blamed to neglect a hay day on the fast, in sad skies my hope was god would make it up and he did. London plague. 35. tot. 222. Colch. 175. the plague in many places in the country hott(,) the enemy braves us at sea, our fleet unreadie, threatning invasion, our counsels divided, and very low in the esteem of the nacon, god good in the word, a very cheerfull audience.

14: Begun harvest, the greatest hailestones fell I ever saw as big as hens eggs, and some round and flatt, with strange pictures as some say. the Dutch continue to brave it on our coast, all our forces upon the shore east

July. 15. a very hot season, plague rageth at Braintree. Colchester. 169. at London abated to 33. total increased to 247. god good to us in manifold mercies, the lord accept for his name sake.

July. 22. A hot season, good weather for mee as my busines was(,) blessed bee my god, the plague sad in many places of England, lord remove thy hand, our town well, praisd bee god, London increasd to 51. tot. 294 Colchester to 178; I had a sad providence though yet mingled with mercy in my servant Barrets hurt with the rake, god for christs sake continue thy favour on my tabernacle.

23. dismal tempest with rain, much hurt done by light(n)ing, barns burnt creatures and men kild wounded. one Finchs[1] a quakers barn burnt at Halsted at noone day. 24.—the guns roared. 26. said a fight began die. 25. god shew us favour, good harvest dayes

July. 29: God good in the season, signs of shoures, plague sad at Braintree 40. 50 or more dying in a weeke. at London bill increasd to 326. plague decreasd to 48. Colchester abated to. 113. god good in his word the lord preserve mee for in him I trust.

Aug: 1. Fast,

Aug: 5. God good in our harvest season, plague abates through mercy in country wherin its much spread. London. 341. plague 38: Colchester. 111. god good in the word, lord doe good and my soule shall praise thy name(.) Braintree abated from 57. to 23. this weeke.

Aug. 12. god good in outward mercies, sensible of the evill of my heart. learing evill. god good in our preservacon when the plague spreads in country. London increasd total. 336. pl. 42. Colchester decreasd to 95. god cease it at his will(,) lord lett thy presence bee with mee in thy word and worship. harvest almost in.

Aug: 19. Season wett, but I hope for good. winds cold and boisterous, our fleet wee have of Holland coast, where they were very successful.
Colch. plague much in our country London. 332. plag: 48: lord direct
71. mee in my sons businesse. lett there be mercy and truth in it for mee. its darke but I can trust thee for thou art mine.

[I] sett my selfe to seeke god in my houshold affaires that god would direct [a] right course for mee and mine, and prosper us in

[1] John Finch paid tax for a four-hearth house in Halstead in 1662.

our ways: my first way to [pu]tt iniquity from my heart and tabernacle.

23. day of praise for our victory over the Dutch.

Aug: 26. God good to us in manifold mercies(,) a good season for our grounds(,) the plague abates London. 290: p: 42. Colch: 51. gott into Cogshall. the lord sanctify his hand to us for good, god good in his word, under experience of the evill of my heart, lord pardon and heale mee; feared again in Colne on our green.

Sept: 2. A wonderfull dry season, the Dutch again on our coasts, forces raisd, god in mercy send us peace, our land full of sins lord leave us not, my heart full of evil and vanity, lord succour by grace, London abates: 266. pl. 30. Colchester feard to increase. 57.

this day. begun Londons dismal fire, laying the city. the goodliest of the world in ashes. quis legens hoc temperet a lachrimis[1]

Sept: 9. This weeke dolefull, a fire began in London in pudding lane at a French bakers about one of the clocke Sept: 2. being lords day, and on the 3. and 4 burnt down almost the whole city but a litle quarter from the tower to Moregate, and as low as Leadenhall Street, it burnt up all to Temple barre, few perishing in the flames, it ceasd the 5 at night, on which day being the fast wee prayed heartily, with teares and faith, that henceforward god would blesse us, wee are not too low for god to raise us up, and provide for us; a cheerfull audience, a good day, but dry season.

Colchester abated to. 37. god command his mercy on our low estate.

12. Tom. went towards London. god in mercy prosper his jorney. and give him a good foundacon for trading I pray thee. returned again empty.

Sept: 16. God good to us in outward mercies, the season very dry. plague abated at Colchester to 25. sad at Cogshall, and other places, god in mercy preserve us, god good in the word, a cheerfull audience(,) give mee oh lord, that forgivenes of sin, my soule holds out to others.

Sept. 23. The aire moist. plague at Colch: 18. god cleare that place, restore our peace and trade, god good in the word. saw the sad state of Braintree die. 21. my heart dies as to leaving coln, lord direct mee, and provide for mee for I relie on thee for mee and mine.

London bill was. 104. of the plague in 3 weeks. 16: parishs. within walls. 14 without by that compute: 81. wholly burnt within wals and 2. without besides peices of others

[1] Anyone reading this should refrain from tears.

Sept: 30. season wet, threat(n)ing our seedetime; the lord good in outward mercies, oh that my heart, went wholly subdued to him, plague abates at Colchester about. 10. or. 11. dying. god in mercy spare the country. god gracious in the word, forgivenes is my mercy, lord lett mee obtain it at thy hand I pray thee

Oct. 6: A good weeke for seedtime, the lord good in outward mercies, at Colchester died. 9. Cogshall under hope. the lord remove his hand fully.

10: a publique fast in regard of Londons burning with a collection. gathered. 6^{li}.

14 7

Oct: 14: A wettish time, plague abates at London and Colchester, litle mention of it, the lord remove his hand that is heavy upon us, god good to mee in the word, the sacrament of baptism publiquely, administred

Oct. 21. A very wett season. hindring seedtime. in the low estate of the nacon 1800000. more voted for the Kings supplies, god awake for Englands prosperitie in this low day. god good in his word, engage mine to feare thee and it shalbee well with them

22. a night of deepe sorrow to mee, lord help that my evill heart overset mee not(,) lord I am wanting to thee and my selfe. not
☞ thou to mee thou art good but I am vile.

27. My son sett out towards London with above 80^{li}. in his pocket to buy goods the lord blesse him, heard of great robbing. die. 26. but god shall preserve him

Oct: 28: God good to mee in my outward mercies, a cheerfull season, men sow late; a very cheerfull audience. lord doe in all good. plague Colchester bill: 5. Lond: 210: p. 16.

29. preacht Mrs Reeds[1] funeral sermon at much Tay.

Nov: 4: Good weather, a good day in gods house, my son was returnd safe from London. the lord my god blesse him. Col: 4: London. 220. p. 14; many hearing, but few practicing.

5. paid my son 1^{s}. for plums the first he sold.

7. fast. a good day. lord turn it to joy and answer us with rich mercy in the supplication of the day. god did in Mrs Eldred

10: preacht funeral god bury sin, the lord good to us in our particular wayes

Nov. 11. wett dirty weather, London: 213. pl. 10. Colc. 2. plague abates blessed bee god(.) but the war, damps all trade, the lord drive his spiritual trade. feares still in London. a Frenchman

[1] Henry Read held a five-hearth house in Great Tey in 1662.

suffered for firing the house in Pudding lane first, by throwing fire into the barns. god good this day in the word to us.

No: 18: kings stables fired. feares fill us, and yet careles. plague abated. London. *3*. and Colch: 3. lord sanctifie thy hand to us. god good in his hand. the lord turn us to him

19: son sett out for London. god enters his trade with difficulties, but he will command his lovingkindnes, and prosper him, and our soules shall blesse his name.

Estate ☞ I have neglected by reason of wants to lay by of my estate for good uses as I once engaged(,) the nature of my estate is very much altered. but I resolve hence forward. to lay by the 10. shilling that comes in clearly of mony for all ministerial dues. and the 20: shilling of rent. and for every quarter of corn I sell. 1^{s}. and to divide this thus. 12^{s}. of 20. for good uses to freinds. and the 8^{s}. to dispose to ease mee in my own particulars for 10th visittacons: books: etc. having first out of the whole cleard my debts to town. br etc. which are about. 40^{s}.—and the 10. shilling profitt of fatting catle

Nov. 25: A very wett morning. the country cleare of the plague. London.

Col. 1. 235 p. 8 increase after the appointment of thanksgiving for decrease. my son safe from London. lord blesse him for thy mercy sake and prosper soule and outward man(,) god good in the word the lord prosper my labours to his glory.

Dec: 2. A cheerfull day, after much wett, troubles in Scotland, god continue our peace(.) plag: L: 7. bur. 147. god good to mee in the word.

5. Fast a very wett day. I intend to keep it if I may til god perfectly restore us(.) heard great hopes of a dutch peace. Amen good lord

Dec: 9: Various troubles in my house, god sanctifie all unto mee; sad afflictive rainy weather, Scots routed, lord bring not mans wrath on thy people, god good to mee in the word, let mee see a blessing in all my afflictions.

Dec: 16. God good in his word, and many mercies, god is removing the plague from us for which his name bee praisd. oh that my soule could delight in him at all times

D. 23. weather frost and snow.—fears of an invasion from France one wave after another is this lives procon. rest my soule seeth only in god and there seekes it

Dec. 30. Frost and litle snow continue. god good to mee in his word, the lord make my afflictions a blessing, for my family affords mee disquiet—helpe mee to releive my selfe in patience and silence.

some fears continue of the plague at Cogshall. god in mercy remove that scourge fully.

Jan: 3. my daughter Elizabeth preserved in a fall at Burtons staires into his sellar going into Court to take up her house.[1]

Jan. 6. Frost continued, gods goodnes abideth with us, for which I blesse him. lord bring mine near thee, and lett the word worke for their eternal welfare.

9: John my son went towards London, the lord Jesus bee with him for soule and body. received a letter from him of his safe arrival there for which god be praised.

Jan. 13. god good in his word, and providence, a sad day, the lord deliver us from our feares of a French invasion, and preserve us for his name sake.

Jan. 20. Cold wholesom weather continues. god take of my heart from vanity and set it on himselfe and service. as my text prompted, that I may live out his word

Jan: 26: 1666. my 51. entred.

sensible this day entred my 51. yeare. lord bee with mee therin for good. and to the end of my days. and blesse mee and mine, and let a covenant bee between us. I was early on my studdies this morning.

Jan. 27. a dry windie day. god good in outward mercies, and in the word, yett my heart dead and cold in prayer, the lord in mercy, quicken. heard uncomfortably of my son John. lord yett in mercy shew mee favour in him, making him a comfort

28. writt up about John. lord blesse my letters and counsell.

30. fast. received a letter from John and all well in it. the boy kindly sent tokens to us all.

Feb. 3. God good in manifold mercies, the weather close, my heart very much troubled in my hard usage from all mine in these necessitous times, lord our porcion cals for thanks, and I will give it thee, and thou wilt favour mee and revive mee from under all thes publique sorrowes, god good in the word. lord I am and wilbee ☞ with thee owing thy things, and thou shalt own mee and mine

Feb. 10: God good to us in our outward mercies, the season wett. things sad in the nacion. the lord good in the word accept mee oh lord and blesse mee and mine

[1] Elizabeth Josselin appears in the court roll as taking a cottage with yard and pond at Colne Green from Thomas Wade in January 1667 (ERO, D/DPr 23). The manor court was obviously held at the Bell, owned by Samuel Burton.

Feb: 17. Sadnes in my family, John returnd. lord my eye is on thee for good. oh compose our troubles and blesse us, and give mee grace and peace.

Feb: 24: God good, my condicon troublesom. lord remedie it let thy grace bee sufficient, help mee out of all my briars for I seeke thee with hope

28: a wonderfull deepe calme snow, one of the deepest I ever saw. the lord gives me some hopes in John. lord answer prayer

March: 3. A cold season. the lords hand on my deare wife in illnes god in mercy remove it, and sanctify all to us, god good to mee in the word, the tast of it sweet. I hope god will providence all things well for mee.

March. 10. The frost continueth beyond measure vehement. with bitter northeast winds, and a wonderfull deep snow with mighty drifts, and so hath been for this month. god good in the word, few hearing. the snow hindred some places from meeting to preach as Gains Colne. god good in my poore wives recovery.

cold snowy March.

March: 17. The snow yet lieth. but the frost is broken, which continued very violent this march, much endangering corne. yet it went away not as feared with a cold easterly raine. but gently though in part cold. all people said it was the bitterest march in their remembrance; the seedtime was bad at Michaelmas.—the winter wett. and then frost. few pease and horsecorn yet sown. 18: frost morning, but after warm and clear: 19. clear and warm: so. 20. 21. 23. wett. 24: cheerfully warm. 25. cold stormy. 26. 27. 28 cold wind, and some storms: 29. 30. frostie mornings, but calm warm days: 31. so but not frost—dry and warm to Ap: 7. 13. barly land wrought well though not laid up by reason of the frost. persons sow pease and bullemarg.[1] such weather till. Ap: 22. then smal shoures but cold. corn yellow. May 3. drisling shoures but very cold. scarce a shoure in Aprill. cold and dry to the 19. May. some few shoures in most places, great in some. May. 24 turnd hot and dry. so til. June. 16. and then a ground rain blessed bee god a great drought July.—grasse scarce. corn thin on all dry grounds, but good on many cold and heavy lands, so that it was a good yeare. confirming that a drought breeds no famine in England.

M. 24: God good in outward mercies my soul presseth after him as my excellency and alone good. lord strengthen mee to delight in thee. prest to own god in his ordinances and beare our testimony unto them.

[1] Bullimong: a mixture of grain (as oats, pease, and vetches) sown together, for feeding cattle. SOED.

Mar. 31. God good in his word, and in his providences hope of peace, and hopes in Poland and Crete that the Turke shall not carry all before him; the season cheerfull.

Estate. When I come to review my estate, I observe my stocke is fuller then it was last yeare. my debts rather more, but the visible advantage is in Wades house which I have purchased worth 20^{li}. but 8^{li}. was paid before. and in setting up my sonne Thomas to whom I gave. 50^{li}. but 22^{li}. or thereabouts was gold gathered formerly, I have built nothing this yeare. I have no moneys by mee not above 4^{li}. besides what is in my debt booke and that is in my sons hands neither had I any summ last yeare. my expenses were: 95^{li}. 15^{s}. 4^{d}. yet I reckon it a saving yeare, my family all about mee. and gods mercy on mee which is my crown, and I trust his holy blessing shall continue on mee and mine through christ all our dayes

April. 7. God good in manifold mercies(,) this day brake bread only. 13. present. the lord good in his word, accept mee in tender mercie and blesse mine. hopes of peace. but threats of war, and said the Dutch will presently blocke up the Thames mouth.

Ap: 14: sensible of great difficulties on my affaires, and my heart tells mee of my neglect of gods things, and no wonder god neglects mee; lord I humble my selfe as is my duty. and beg thy blessing, and promise a carefull respect to all thy wayes

Ap: 21. preacht at Markshall, my wife there 5 or 6. days. god blesse that family.

Ap: 28: Going to preach. H. Morly of my parish delivered mee a note of receipt of my procurations. and therein notice I was suspended. I forbore to preach in the afternoone

May. 12. weather cold and dry to May: 12. god good to mee in his word, worship. jorney when I saw Londons ruins, and first raisd up a good report of building. saw my good freind Mrs Colier, the lord *was* [   ] found all well his name bee praised

May. 19. Cold dry season some put not to grasse till now. god good to mee in the word the lord in mercy accept mee and crown mee with his favour. many strangers again with us, lord give us hearing eares, and beleiving hearts.

May. 26. the season turnd. 24. very hot and dry, god good in many outward mercies preacht at Coln engain, lord make mee a blessing and thy word to beare fruite.

June. 2. season cold and dry, my deare Uncle Nath. Josselin with mee. the word very encouraging he accounted it worth his 60. miles jorney, god good to mee in it, lord thou givest mee thoughts of thy kindnes to mee continue them. I made mocons in a match for Tho. and a farme buying, I shall observe the issue of those providential disappointments, both came to nothing.

June. 9. Season hot and dry. god good in his word, the hand of god on the land in the season and by our enemies who ride on our coast, the lord remember us for good; god good in the word, yet deadnes and unspiritualnes is on my heart.

June. 6 the Dutch on Harwich coast. Thursday—June. 12. Wednesday. they attempt Chatham river to destroy our great ships with successe and continued their pleasure. June. 27. they came up near Gravesend, they put a stop to all trade, and forced us to defend the whole shore. to our charge and amazement.

June. 16. god good to us in manifold mercies, hopes of comfortable raines, the word encouraging from psal. 35.3. save us lord for thy name sake.

June. 23. hot and dry extreame. a sad face of our nacon(,) the French said in the downs(,) lord thou art in heaven. helpe. preacht a sermon of repentance affectionately

June. 30. God good in sweet dews, his hand heavy on our land and trade, our hearts hardned under judgments. god remove them. my family toucht with affliction; god yett good to mee and in his word for which my soule blesseth him.

July. 2. The Dutch landed on the Suffolke shore, attempting Langer fort. but beat of(.) Raspigliosi Pope by the name of Clement. 9.71. old.

July. 7. A good hay time and very hot. god good to mee in his word, remember the nacon in its low estate, yea I trust god will, this is my hope, my faith. one day wee feard the French invasion. then the papists rising, the farther burning of the city. the stop of all trade. then hope good men come in place. delinquents called to account then hopes of peace.

July. 14. 21. God good in manifold mercies, a very sad droughtie season. fears of papists, and of the Courts army at home(.) god good to mee in the word the lord in mercy prepare us for the worst, and give us to see good dayes.

July. 28: it raind on the 27. I having reapd the 26. a sweet shoure it was. the dutch busy on our coasts, the peace said concluded. the parliament high against a standing army. god good in his word. hopes of England reviving out of troubles: said the plague in London to 80. increasing from. 2. last weeke. not so

Aug: 4: The parliament sent home til oct. 10. by reason of the peace concluded July. 21. at Bredali betwixt all the nacons and us at warre. France prospers in Flanders, now our fears are of a standing army, papists and persecution. but my hope is in god, I ended my sermons on Jer. 4.3.4. breaking hearts the way to save a nacion from breaking, and god sends us hopes of peace, saving us on the account of his soveraignty and goodnes

Dendermond: The attempt on this place put a stop to the French progresse, giving them much losse in their baggage by innundacon, and losse of men by storme and sally. the Spaniards also had a good bout upon 500 of their horse. and on an inrode by their garrisons into Picardie, yett they attempt Lisle.

Aug: 11. God good to mee in manifold mercies, in his word, deliver from profanes(,) my heart trembles in regard of my children. lord pardon my sin.

Aug. 18: Weather cold and some shoures, god good in manifold mercies, yett my returns unkind to god. I loth my selfe. lord love mee and doe mee good

Aug: 25. Severall of my kindred with mee, to behold gods goodnes towards mee but my crown is his grace. and my covenant. interest. god good in the word the lord make it a seasoning teaching word to all.

Sept: 1: God good to mee in manifold mercies, in his word and worship. very ill I was with gripings, oh how willing I was to die, and bee with Christ which is best

5. rid about a busines for Jane. the providence suited not my desires, but my heart is very lightsome in the promise of god for good to mee and mine and will trust him

15: god good to mee in manifold mercies, my soules desire is after him and my heart trusts in him, his word good, and his mercy sweet to mee.

16: This day I fetcht in my own wagon a load of goods for my son from Colchester. the first load the wagon carried, lord prosper us in mercy.

Sept: 20. my wife rid towards Haveril god prosper her in our intents, I hope in his mercy. 21. I preacht at Braintree. 22. at Haverill. so. 23. 25. I returnd home. 27. sad. wett season, god good in my preaching, in the other busines I still continue to waite for his mercy, which I moved earnestly this day.

Sept: 29. God good to mee in manifold mercies. this seedtime at first dry and good. but to this day, wett, and latward with us, a sad driving wett cold day. god good in his word to mee, but my heart bad towards him for which my soule is abased before him.

Oct. 2. preacht Mr Richardsons funerall sermon in the darke. god assisted mee

Jane. 5. My daughter Jane went to waite on old Mrs Harlakenden, her mother wept for it.—6. the weather good to sow, god give a good seede for his blessed word. prayed for a blessing on this session of parliament. litle hope and faith, lord I looke up; answer mee in thy mercy and truth.

Isaac Hodson 7. Oct. began his yeare, he is to have 3li. per annum.

10: I[1] Parliament began. my morning prayers for gods blessing on their meeting. the weather cold but clear and dry, blessed bee god: the Keepers speech by order of the King. good. leaving accountants for their own innocency, and wishing them to reckon the Kings and peoples interest the same: Tompkins with the Commons moved to give the King Thanks for disbanding the armie. putting out papists: daming patentees, and laying aside the E. of Claringdon the late chancellor. agreed to. a handsome beginning even as I desired.

Oct: 13. God good to us, a calme, and dry day. god good in the word, awakeing my heart from under all sorrowes and trouble to trust in him. my son Thomas aguish

14: John and I had a hard bout, the next days better. he promiseth duty. oh that the lord from hence would incline his heart to duty and dilligence.

Oct: 20: A sad wett day. god good in the word, lord incline my childrens heart to feare thy name continually: oh bow their soules to thee.

Oct: 27. Dry weeke for most part(,) I ended my sowing. Oct. 22. god blesse our crop(.) the. 23. day. the King laid the first stone of the exchange on which day. 26. years before the flames began to burn in Ireland. god good to mee in his word. a very cheerfull audience.

No: 3. a cold day. god good in his word, a means of peace at Lady Honywood. my poore wife ill of her backe. this life is a bundle of sorrows. god our only comfort.

No. 5. preacht from psal. 137.7. sermon books. P(*salms*) presents that subject with observacion how god opens the doore of hope though there bee many adversaries.

Nov: 10. A cleare day. dry, the lord good in his word, awaken my soule after thee.

24: A wett day. corn falls. a sad hard time, in the midst of plenty, mony scarce god good in his word. my litle Beck. very ill. god revive her.

[1] This line is unfinished, there being a gap of a few words' length.

Dec: 1. christ sweet to me in his providence, my daughters hopefully well oh blesse my sons inwardly; god good in the word, sett my selfe to depart from drunkeness. a wett day and few hearing.

D. 8. A cleare morning, god gives health in my habitacon. and I will praise him. but told John was ill, god revive him. Jonathan Clerke dead of a wound his brother drownd a litle before and scalded to death,[1] the sad effect of dronkennes(.) god good to mee in the word, many from severall places hearing.

13. a private sacrament at night. I will love thee saith god. god an everlasting love. and I will serve thee for ever saith my heart. this and the 12. two winter days for snow and raine. the ground is very wet:

Dec. 15. my family in health, blessed bee god, god good in the word, my heart is setting it selfe against my busines in its irksomnes lord let thy inspiracon help

Dec: 22. winter kept of, our servant ill, god sanctifie all strokes to us, god good in the word. deliver mee from covetousnes oh lord

25. Preacht and *feasted.* my Tenants and all my children with joy. lord sanctify

Dec. 29. an [ ] time god good in manifold mercies, good in the word. Lord provide for mee and deliver mee from covetousnes. lord heare prayer for mercy sanctifying their hearts to feare thee, and make them industrious in their imployments(.) lord I looke up answer mee in thy faithfulnes and mercy.

Jan: 1. I began this new yeare in my studdies, god prosper them for the good of soules. one of my sons customers broke. another Cook drownd himselfe. lord prosper us, one Davy formerly of our town worth near 1000^{li}. questioned on his childs death, starving it. lord how brutish is man:

Jan: 5. God good in manifold mercies, in the word, dead my heart to the world(.) the day dry and windie like march weather;

9. Lady Honywood sett forward for her daughters with a litle grandchild. shee was scarce from her grounds but it snew. 10. windy and

[1] There is an Assize indictment that Bartholomew Huske of EC labourer on 7 December 1667 'there assaulted the said Jonathan (Clarke) with an iron spade worth 12*d.* on the left side of his head above his left ear, giving him a mortall bruise of which he instantly died', he was found guilty of homicide and was ordered to be transported. P.R.O. Assizes 35/108/4, no. 15 (transcript by ERO). The 'brother' drowned and scalded to death was John Warren, aged 17, who on 19 July was thrown into a tub of scalding malt, and died on 21 July. The Assize indictment (35/108/4, no. 1) named Wm. Busbye as his assailant; Busbye was branded. Warren was, in fact Jonathan Clarke's wife's sister's son; Warren was Busby's stepson, Warren's mother having remarried Busby only two months before the incident.

cold to a great height god in mercy preserve her safe: 11. frost—thawing.

Jan. 12. a cleer thawing cold day. god good in the word, outward mercies. my family, my greife in their unwise, uncounsellable carriage.

Jan: 19. Dry warm weather; god good in his word lord awaken my heart, and mine to attend to the things of thy glory

Jan: 26. 67. 52. yeare enters:

sensible this day entred my 52. and completed my 51. yeare. thus my dayes flee away, and good see I not the world, Lord my eyes are towards thee, thou art my porcon. blesse mee and mine, this day was gods holy sabbath, in reading that verse affected mee say to Archippus Col; 4.17.[1] deadnes, and neglect getts into my old yeares

Feb: 2. A very dry, calm, warm Jan. but the night wett. but sun shone, the lord good to mee in his word and worship: Mary at White Colne with Mr Shirly who preacht there. lord lett the word prosper. Johns hand very ill(,) lord sanctify this affliction to him.

Feb. 9. The weeke past cheerfull. discourst the Dutch chose our King their Protector. wee have great plenty of corne, but scarcity of mony to admiracon. god good to mee in the word, the lord accept mee and delight in mee and mine for good.

Feb: 16. a cheerful season. but 10. the sitting down of parl. and actings was with great distast. no moderacion heard of, taxes propounded. Court careles, god good to mee in the word, his blessing in it, and prosper it unto godlines

My fathers second wife died surviving him 31. yeares shee was nigh 80 old.

20. preacht paul Raynhams funeral at Chappel. a great audience. one Mrs Martin[2] said I being in my coat. if shee should see one preach a sermon in coat or cloake shee would run out of the church: thus ordinances left naked.

Feb. 23. Cheerfull weather, after many shoures. many sheep kild about, mine preserved. lord still watch over them; a good Sabbath; lord make my heart lively with thee

March: 1. Wett weather. god good to mee in his word, the lord accept and blesse m[ee.] thefts, murders and adulteries very common.

[1] Colossians 4: 17: 'And say to Archippus, Take heed to the ministry which thou has received in the Lord, that thou fulfil it.'

[2] Probably the wife of William Martin, rector of Wakes Colne from 1667 to 1678. Newcourt.

March. 8. a wett day god good to mee in the word, for which my soule blesseth him

March. 15. Cold dry weather. plenty and yet no comfort in it, in aboundance wee are in very great straits, prest to receive the sacrament, lord helpe;

March: 22. Easter day. cold and dry season. administred sacrament. 14. present. some come in, lord compell all, and make them worthy of thee. the lord in mercy shew himselfe gracious to us and our land

When I come to view my estate. I find through mercy all my children about mee, my eldest sonne trading in the world, and I hope with gods blessing, some others able to doe something, I find no great gain, and its of mercy I doe not goe behind hand, my stocke I thinke is rather better then last yeare, I have purchased and paid for an house on the green cost mee. 16li. and I have laid out at least 6li. on it, and I am not in debt, but have 20li. owing mee since last yeare, the lord adds to my graces and comforts, for I find a decay in nature I observe since the three comets though wee had droughts and scarcity of hay yett plenty and so a great cheapnes of corne

1668:

March: 29. God enter and end this yeare to his glory, and my families good. lord good in the season, a sweet dew after dry and cold. god good in the word. the lord own, and accept us

Ap: 5. a sweet raine and warme; god good in his word, my soule loveth him. a wett weeke, 11. day a considerable flood

Ap. 12. a close cold day, god good to mee in hopes of joynting my families, the lord in mercy own mee for good, all my dayes, remove Englands sins

Ap: 19. Cold and dry. the 17. was the hottest day I ever knew at this time of yeare(.) god good to mee in our publique mercies, in the word. [? and] in soules mine mine lord I pray thee

Ap: 26. weather good, spring better then last yeare, after a very gentle winter(.) god good to mee in manifold mercies, god good in the word, preacht and praid at Gains Colne with life and affection, my god blesse it to us all. noise of the peace with France and Spain, and their invading England.

30: a cold morning with ice, on the water.

May. 3. This month entred most cold and windie and wett, god good to mee in many mercies, yet my sons a very bitter affliction, lord give mee wisedom to win them. thy word doth not.

May. 10: rains, but cold. strange newes of attempts to fire London, of feares of French ruine by their great comings over. I committ my selfe to god and am quiet from the feare of evill as pro. 1.33. god good in that word

16. my sister departed home. I sent her not away empty. Lord blesse mee I was glad I had to helpe her, but more that I had an heart to doe it

May. 17. A sad sight of 8. motherles children.[1] tears are fruitles its god must helpe. lord give mee thy helpe in all my straits. god good in the word. much raine.

May 19. 22. 23. Wonderfull wett, flouding the meadows. corn weeds
23. exceedingly; the rie light. and strong corne laid; the lord good to mee in the word, in hopes of the recovery of Sarah Hatch out of the jawes of death; god intreated for her. faire weather followed.

June. 4. my people overthrew a load of timber. but to the praise of god without any hurt to man or beast and but litle to the cart.

June. 7. shoures and thunder threating rain. god can command the harvest dayes(.) Mr Cresseners son died and supplication not made for him his death so suddain(.) the lord good in the word. strange suspicions in mens spirits the lord bee our hope and help, man buzzeth nothing but amazing feares.

June. 14: An indifferent good hay weeke. I preacht H. C. funerall.[2] 13. gave thanks for M. H. deliverance from drowning. this day my bodies sorenes fully visible on mee(.) a servant went sicke out of my family.—a place proposed for Ann. lord direct. for thou art my hope and help. god good in the word.

16. wett. an old fellow buried dying about 80. that was thought a bloudy and adulterous villain and went to his grave without any remarke of god but a stupid spirit;[3] his estate was miserably setled, the issue god knoweth.

June. 21: god good to mee in manifold mercies, had in some hay though rainie weather. a place at London for An. lord direct us. god good in his word. it thundred. the rains great. 23.

Ann went this 24 towards London, lord goe with her, bee the guide

[1] The PR records the burial on the 21st of Elizabeth Clarke, wife of John; for her marriage in 1657 and numerous children since then, see Appendix 2.

[2] Humprey Cressener, son of Mr. George, was buried on 9 June. PR.

[3] Edward Potter, householder, was buried on the 16 June; he was baptized on 5 September 1585 the son of Edmund, and was hence nearly 83 years old. RJ described the suspected adultery on 22 December 1645.

of her youth—25. left her by agrement with Mr Gresham in the exchange at London. returned weary and sore. but thankfull to god. 27. lord prosper thes shoures die 28. god good to mee in the word, my son a great greife lord reclaim him from disorderlines.

July. 1. sought god for faire weather, shoures with us and about the weather far better. die. 5. a good Sabbath faire day. my brother Worrall with us

July. 12. shourie weather, this day faire and hot, god good in his word, and outward mercies to mee, my daughter Ann very well at London blessed bee god [ ]

July. 19. god good in manifold mercies. the season good, my improvidence of [heart] not over much, the ground is clothed with store of grasse. god good to mee in the word, the lord accept us, and house us, though our sins are very many.

July. 26: the 25 a very wett day. beating us out all worke, the skie threatens us. lord doe thou smile; god good in the word, make it effectuall I pray.

Aug: 2. on the first much rain, hindred my ending hay. god can further our business when he pleaseth—the morning cool, but cheerfull, but proved wett. hay time was wett at first after good, harvest enters ill. god good in the word, the lord heale mee and mine.

Aug. 9. a very wett harvest weeke past. yett wee were doing. god good to us in various preserving providences; good in his word, though my heart dead and in great part of the day liveles. the clouds return but gods the same.

16: very wett in most dayes, yet doing. this evening cold and dry. god good to us in the word, the lord in mercy accept and own mee and mine and prosper us in what wee goe about.

17. Haveril faire being on the 15. and Satturday. I went this day and bought 7 heifers. 6. runts. at 32^s^. only 2^s^. abated. god prosper them. charge. 5^s^.

Haverill:

Aug. 23. after wett. a good harvest weeke, blessed bee god, wherin I finisht my hard corne. this day a rest; which I sanctifie to the name of my good god. An bound on Aug. 20. her time out. June. 24. 1674. lord remember her for good

Aug. 30. A good harvest weeke. I gott in some rowen hay from Kimbold[1] very well. god good in manifold mercies, I preacht of kindnes, I find it in god to mee, my heart desirous to expresse it, for bowels I blesse my god

[1] Rowen hay: second growth or crop of grass or hay in a season. SOED. 'Kimbold' is the name of a meadow.

Sept. 6. A good weeke, yet harvest and hay time continueth, god good in the word, while I preach of deadnes I feel my own. god revive mee.

8. Fetcht home my timber from Mr Pelhams. gods goodnes much to mee therin I was sensible of it and much joyd therewith

Sept: 13. Finisht my hay. after tedious labour. god wonderfull good in the drines of the season; gods word very sweet to my tast, oh let my soule live that I may praise thee.

Sept: 20. on the 18 I begun to sow, god good to us in a dry season, good in his word, the lord deliver my soule that I die not a death in sin.

24. going out in the morning (to end a tedious difference between the Ladie Tryons housband and Mr Woolhouse, which I effected blessed bee god) I mett the news of my uncle Nathaniel Josselins death, the last of that family line, when I came home my maid dead,[1] and no supposicon of danger the lord sanctifie this providence to mee and all mine;

26. heard An ill at London, lord sanctifie all—lost a bullock. went to Colchester with waggon, came home empty. a weeke of disappointments. lord in all remember mee for good

Sept. 27. from the 16. of Aug. to this day. scarce a shoure the driest seed time(,) many sow not. god good in his word, I shall waite the issue.

Oct: 4: on Friday wee had a sweet shoure. Oct. 2. misled the 3. but it only touches the surface of the earth, heard An hopefully upwards of the small pox.—8. spent with earnestnes to seeke god for Mr Cresseners sons and mine, that god would bee their guide and they serve him spake from Pro. 3.6:

Oct. 11. no rain yet, forced to hold my plow into ground, some furrows. some thoughts of sending John to London, lord bee with him

14. John went towards London. under a sentence of death, having no hopes in him as formerly, the lord trieth my faith, and the hopes for mercy from god for him, lord answer prayer in him.

17. ended my sowing. the yeare continued wonderfull dry. a seed time without a shoure wetting one quarter into the earth, god good in Becks preservacion, lord blesse mine for good. let them live in thy sight.

Oct: 18. cold, and hopes of rain, the lord good to mee in his word, my wife hath a quartan ague. god in mercy sanctifie all these strokes to us, and better us by the same for his mercy sake.

Oct: 25: The day past very afflictive in my wives illnes, and in fears

[1] Probably Elizabeth Willowes, buried on 25 September according to the PR.

for my children at London.—a reviving in all blessed bee god. I will hope in thee to doe mee good, dewes but no rain to wett: the lord good to mee in his word.

28. a rain like a ground rain. my sister came before the wett. daily shoures so that the wayes are dirtie.

No. 1: god good to mee under our affliction: 5. preacht. my sister went from us. glad to see one another. and joying in gods goodness, the day was cheerfull

No. 8. god good to mee. my daughter Jane at home to tend her mother the lord restore and blesse thes.

10. went to London on Johns account. came thither by 4. wett and wett through: found Mrs Colier well, but old kindnes is dying 11. saw An after the small box (pox). 13. bound John to Mr Buggin at the Globe in Barbican. he is to receive. 45^{li}. got not home til. Nov. 17. being sicke by the way. god blesse this jorny it was sad to my body. my wifes ague continueth.

Nov. 22. dry after rain. a prisoner this day. god giveth mee hope and strength, and I shall see hope in John for lord bee thou his root and then he shall prosper.

Baptized publickly a child of John Cobs.

/ after illnes Dec: 4. from 3 of the clocke till about 5 I apprehended by the pains in both my sides, that those small ribbs were full of phlegme, and began to close upon mee and would end mee within 48 houres. I had been indifferent to die and in this illnes had not heartily begd my life of god, this appeard to mee a great crueltie to my babes(,) I sett my selfe to prayer. use of meanes at hand. rubbing stirring tossing a great booke, I perceived it wind, I was very well till I went to bed, and then that wind came as if it would have choakd mee, rubbing and warmth gave mee ease and since I have sensibly recovery: yett I am bound. I snez not, my nose runs not, I have great hopes of perfect recovery, and that I shall serve god in bringing up my litle ones.

Dec. 13. I preacht this day twice. baptized 2 children but was faint(.) my wives ague continueth, lord pardon our sins and heale our diseases.

Dec. 20. god good in his word his hand strikes but his right hand strokes(.) waters filling the dry heart of the earth.

Jan: my wives ague continues and comes to every day. Maries neck-cloth fired with a candle and shee blew it, which increased the
53 flame, my man dampt it. and I with both hands over it quencht it the lords name bee praised. Jan. 13. at night.

Febs: 7. God good in his manifold mercies to mee, he in Christ accepts us(.) heard of my childs health at London. god good in the word accept his

Feb. 14. God good in many providences(,) I was entred my 53 yeare before I was aware. a good dry weather. my wives ague continues, a still time to all publique affai[res]

March ?: God good in mercy, [most *fully*] recovering season backward, the lord spirit mee for him selfe;

March. 14. God good in manifold mercies. heard of my childrens welfare, my wife after a sicke vomiting fit, grows better. god good in his word to my soule make mee a son of peace

☞ For some time mony very scarce, yett my experience how god hath enabled to pay Johns 50[li]. when considerable summs failed oblidges mee to thankfulnes for that mercy. and a patient waiting on god to provide and carry mee through in all the difficulties I doe or shall meete with; yea and I desire to presse my own heart, and children to goe about all their affaires in a holy confidence, god willbee with them and prosper them in the accomplishment of them.

21. God good in the word; the day coldly shouring: dreamd of the K. deposing or worse, a view of govern(ment) names in paper. M. Hey with mee and the K: D. Y. B. M. overturnd in a coach in Holborn going to the race at Newmarket: March. 8: the K. lost his race: 10: the D. of Yorks closset searcht. March. 19. said robd

M. 28. God good in his word, I had two fits of the ague, and was between hope and feare in reference to the Sabbath my fit day. god carried mee through sweetly, and his loving mee as Christ is precious to mee.

Ap: 3. ended the carriage of one bargain of logs. I shall gain by them, if I am well paid. the weather is droughty. god good in the Sabbath

4. many hearing, lord angle up some soules to ordinances, two gave notice of their receiving the sacrament. lord prepare mee, and bee thou one howsoever.

Ap. 11. God good in his word. the sacrament administred. 20. present, my heart very dead in duty. yet upheld in my obedience to gods command.

Ap: 18: God good in his word, the sense of his love perfume my heart. shew it lord to my son John sicke of the small pox. he is the seed of my covenant. servant(.) lord own him as thine for good: my chimny at Bunners on fire, yet god preservd

Ap: 25. Heard hopefully of Johns recovery, an answer of prayer wherin

I tast love and sweetnes, as my subject this day w[hen] difficulties encompasse my outward conciens, but god loves mee, I [*know he*] will provide for mee, and this is my life.

May. 2. God good in manifold mercies, the season cold and dry; god good to mee in his word, my heart stayeth it selfe on him, and he provides for me

6. my wife went towards London, god returne her safe.

May. 9. Drought continues. hot after much cold, lord favour my poore inheritance with a particular merciful shoure, thou god of my praises, my heart very vain, lord cleanse, god good to mee in the word preacht; make it effectuall

May. 16. God good in his word, his love my heart reviveth. heard from my wife at London, gods goodnes in Johns life, lord restore him and let him live to thee

May. 23. dry, burning weather, heard not from London, my mind very full of roving thoughts, in my wives absence, Lord return her safe, god good in his word, began to expound the catechism

27. my wife returnd safe, blessed bee god, dews but no full rain, all freinds well at London where my wife received extraordinary kindnes. said the Q with child.

May. 30. God good to mee in the word, society of freinds, troubles grow out of our mercie, that I may learne to sett all my hope in my god alone.

June: 6: Weather continues excessive dry, soft corne thins, and grasse, god good in the word to mee, oh how the Sabbath is profaned and persons hate to bee reformed, though officers endeavour the doing of it.

13. Drought continues, god good in manifold mercies, blesse lord thy word, my stocke. my all. heard ill of Ans eyes. lord heale them in much mercy

June. 20. heard better of Anns eyes. gods providence is *given* to his for good, and I wil trust him, drought great, the heate lesse, god good in his word.

June. 27: drought continues, good hay weather, god good in providing for mee in the straits of my occasions. heard cheerfully of An, and wisely in her busines, for all my soule blesseth him, as also rebukes in others, god good in his word, my soule liveth on his mercy for salvacion.

July. 4: shoures in the days past. hurt with thunder. I feare thy power oh god[1]

[1] One line is illegible here because of over-tight binding of the Diary.

[9. rid to Court whither summoned for not wearing the surplice, dismissed] without fee. wife and I both preserved in a dangerous fall. god be blessed for all.

10: made an end of haying for this yeare, and my hay very good god bee praised for this mercy. it cost mee the least of any yeare, mowing and making and inning not above 40^{s}. besides my own helpe.

July. 11. dry season. god good to mee in his word, lord let it be salvation word, to us. provide for my relacions of thy grace, for on thee I hope.

July. 18: A good rain, in season for corne. on the 16 I had in about 5 acres of oats, heard of An that which troubled mee, an unkind quarrell betwixt her Mrs and her. paid Anns. 50^{li}. at London and almost paid it in the country, for all mercies my god bee blessed; god good in his word, make mee to walke with thee

July: 24 preacht old Bridges funerall. 25. at Markshall. god good in his word. sad about my children at London; but sad to Mr Elliston who lost his daughter and all her children. almost togither. lord save mee in mine

30. Rebekahs house by Layers candle fired, espied by one rising early. and so that and all preserved. Lord thou afflictest, but I am not destitute of thy kindnes; ind all my hard corn. July. 29.

Aug: 1: Weeke past a good harvest weeke. though often *samie* mislings, god good in his word, my heart drawn out to perswade people to follow god. Writt up to London lord prosper my letters for good and peace.

8. God good in his word, my heart dull and heavy.

10. Rob: went away Tuesday morning without my good will.

Aug. 15. God good in his word; comfort to walke with god who is my choice. my soule waits on him for favour in Ans busines.

Aug: 22. A good weeke, harvest even finisht, Ans eyes better; now the visitacon trouble is at hand, one wave follows another. but my god will deliver mee out of all. others have their troubles(,) Mr Eldred about his father, god good to mee in the word. great company present. god ingage some to walke with him.

Aug. 29. God. good in manifold mercies, the Lord accept mee in his beloved one. god I hope mercifull to my children at London. hear nothing but well god good in his word; lord I cast my burthen on thee, be my helper.

Sept: 5. drought and heat continues, sickly at London nigh 700 in this bill near 300 of the plague in the guts, god good to mee in his word.

the lord own mee and keepe mee a shepheard to my sheepe(.) heard of the Q mothers death, that St Albans hath her joynture of 50000^{li}. 2 yeare

7. began to committ our seed to the ground, with prayers and expectacion. god should blesse my tillage, according to promise

Sept. 8: Bishops visitacon of London at Kelvedon, where committing my selfe to god without sollicitousnes, I appeared with quiet, for which I blesse the Lord and desire to serve him with more faithfullnes and care, my remaining dayes: visit: fee. 2^s. 4^d.

Sept. 12. God good in his word. drought continues. 707. died at London. mine well

Sept. 19: god good in his word, my heart drawn out towards him, the drought continues, god will provide; signes of rain, stand in church *giving*

20. preacht Ed. Johnsons[1] funerall at Wittam. my desire was to honour god in it

26: drought continueth(.) finisht sowing misl. on 25: god good in the word, lord lett mine bee blessed: I rid to Ladie Veres 88. old. her senses continue(,) her great grandchild a man. E. of Lincolne.—three homely ladies there. the lords beauty is best. but bloud gives nothing good—Mr Meriton. his man and a Smith. hurt with his waggon going over them, both wheeles(,) yet spared

Oct: 5: rid to litle Badew. preacht there, lord blesse the word. opposed by Sir Mundeford Bramston,[2] I waved the surplice. he seemed very well satisfied after all done: saw mens fine things. a view of mens temper. returnd this day safe: on the 4th. a shoure god bee blessed for it. found our maide here Sarah Penhacke. god make her a blessing to us; shee came late on the 4th at night.

10. cold, the day before shoures, god good in my health. his word a comfort to my soule.

11. Peter hired for another yeare, which is to end the day after Halsted faire. and to have 4^{li}. 10^s. and paire of shoes, With Col. Cooke. no place or condicon graspeth all mercies, litle hopes of children.

12. sew 3 bushels of white wheat on the peice at Hobstevens gate. bought of Niccols cost. 10^s. lord prosper it in mercy to mee. thou carest for mee.

14. found my best hog dead in the cott. lord let all doe mee good.

[1] Edward Johnson of Witham's will (ERO, 140 CR 8) is unfortunately incomplete, and any bequest he may have made RJ is missing.

[2] The second surviving son of Sir John Bramston, judge (for whom see DNB), and Master of Chancery from 1660; of Little Baddow, Essex, died 1679. Venn.

Oct: 17: after a litle shoure, the weather cold and frostie. god good to mee in his word. witnes I am thine.

24: drought with cold winds. pastures seared up, god yet the same; god good to mee in the word, I intend London, the lord in mercy returne mee safe(,) heard of my children there. Jane rid thither, october. 21. past.

Oct: 25. rid through to London, and returned No. 3, that day mett my wife coming to seeke mee fearing I had been sicke, but god was my health, the wett detaind mee. all well at London. preacht at St Mary Overies. my heart vain. I engage to more care of it, and family worship. lord helpe. help lord, for all my good depends on thee; some shoures in the contry.

No. 7. dry *cold* weather, the Lord good to mee in his word on the 5^t^. and this day my heart is set to seeke the lord for mee and mine, rowling my soule on him, and my expectacions are to receive good from him.

11. went to preach a funeral with longings of heart to doe good.[1] Lord hast thou no children there that I may feed, comfort. bring them thither. helpe me to doe it(.) a great audience, and cheerful. I received 20^s^. paire of gloves and blesse god

No. 14: dry, warm weather continues. lord. meet us in thy worship. and let my words feed soules. the soules of thine. I thirst to doe good, the lord was good to mee in the word and I hope to others. I eyd one mourner

No: 21: after frost, a smal shoure slabbing the ground only; god good to mee in the word, awakeing my heart with desires to live to please him, death about us, god fit us for changes. heard of my childrens health. and advised with in Mrs Harlakendens proposall for marriage.

No: 28: Good weather and shoures. but litle dirt: state disturbances. fears of insurrection, charges of treason against Orrery. and Ormond. etc. god good in my desires to serve him, preacht against dronkennes.

Dec: 11. in the morning my sons shop broke open, and nigh 50^li^. of goods stollen(.)[2] I providentially heard of them and pursued, but returnd, troubled, yet hoping well.

[1] Notes on this sermon for 'Old Mistriss Porter' were made by one of the audience, John Bufton, and are partly reprinted in Macfarlane, pp. 222–3.

[2] The Assize indictment states that Gilbert Tingle, labourer, Elizabeth his wife, and Anne Seamor, widow, all of EC., on 11 December stole various goods to the value of about £20 from Thomas Josselin. The defendants were found guilty and ordered to be hanged. The full indictment is reprinted in Macfarlane, p. 219.

12. God good in the word, the lord prosper it against dronkennes. blessing mine this day, those that robbed us were first found by the man I imployd to pursue. one escaped with a good part of the goods, the other three committed to Cambridge jayle. Dec. 13. my son returnd the 14. and most of our goods fetcht home. 16; god alone have the glory

Dec: 18. God good in outward mercies, in his word, the season dry, waters low beyond whatever I knew, god can fill them when he pleaseth; I was forced to water all my catle at Pitchers pond.

Jan. 2. God good in his word, John well with mee. the frost violent and yet is

4. a very sweet thaw. preacht Mrs Cooks funeral. 5. John went up a trouble to mee, lord help by ordering his heart aright.

Jan. 9. God good in his word, the lord in mercy accept mee. deaths many(.) Monke died. I thinke it was on Wednes. Jan. 5. it thundered 3 straks one very violent with lighting. god preserve us

Jan. 16. A dry season to wonder: preaching on god my help. I had light god would helpe in portioning, placing, providing for and sanctifying my children. even my John. a child of trouble. I believe lord. lett it bee so. had a letter from John pleasd. lord let his heart bee so.

Jan: 21. Jonathan Woodthorp of our town, a Tanner askt my consent to come to my daughter Jane and had it, on this ground especially that he was a sober, hopefull man his estate about 500[li]

22. read but sad letters from An of her condicon, worse of her brother, lord helpe mee for thy name sake.

Jan. 23. God good in prayer and in the word, lord my heart trusts in thee for my posteritie, and my litle ones, help for thy name sake, the weather cold and drie, no water in road or ditches

Jan. 26. 69. 54. y. enters

sensible of my birth a sinner, recommended my selfe to gods care to blesse mee, in all my ways. fears for my children but I leave them on gods care.

Jan. 30: Frost and snow forced to water my cattel on green. god good in his word to mee. heard of the Emp. death the last of the male Austrian line. none but the boy in Spain living(,) a matter likely to make a great change in the world.

Feb. 2. Monks dutches died. Jan. 23. 20 dayes after housband. persons that by bringing in the King came to a vast estate. but base and sordid

Feb: 6. frost and snow continued, driving my catle to water. god good in his word, my servants very untoward. lord bring us into a due order.

Feb. 13. After a close candlemas day, when persons said litle winter to come great frost. wonderfull snows. Feb. 10. 12. then thawing with but a few drops of rain, at night frost. god good in his word, my heart hopes god wilbee a help to mee and mine in all condicons

Feb. 20. The Frost went away without rain: heard well of John. but a sad letter of An(,) the lord is my help. and mines, and therefore I feare not man. god good in his word, the lord plant his fear in us and wee shall doe well.

Feb: 27. Heard nothing from London, which makes mee hope god hears and helps(.) the weather dry, waters low, my god yett will send forth his mercy and helpe: god good in his word of blessing, that I claim(,) for I feare god.

March: 3. 4: Sew. 8 acres oats, weather dry. my children I hope well at London. prayer hath gon for them, and I hope god answers it.

6: god good in his word this day, lord lett my soule have ease in thee

11. returnd my subpena to Mole. an end of his suite. Lord my heart endeavours peace with thee and all.

March: 13. drought continues, ill with a cold. lord its mercy I have a being(.) threats of severity against nonconformists. god can stop all if pleasd(.) god good in his word, oh lord let my soule dwell at ease in thee. son returnd, the theives remitted to (c.o. Cambridge) Chelmsford to bee tried there. burgla[ry.]

16. a very sweet raine for neare 20. houres. this day my sons 3 theives condemned at Chelmsford to bee hangd. afterwards they confessed the fact: 18: Jonathan Woodthorp. and my daughter Jane testified their agreement to marry, god in mercy blesse them(.) a malt kilne burnt at Mr Wrights in our town, much mercy in the affliction

March: 20: dews. the Lords moderate the act against meetings, opposing magna charta. trade; god good to us, yet my wives ague hath returns, the word cheering, give me soule ease, and keepe thy hedge strong about us

1670.

25. a sweet day for Colne faire. 26. wett in the afternoon. 27. a glorious

M. 27 morning after rain. lord my soules desire is after thee, prest to sacramental order in receiving. went to Mary Car at Markshal. ill in her head, but very heavenly in her words. cutt my small wood off my own ground for this year as also the last.

Ap. 3. cow calved; administred the sacrament, only 14 present, god good in his word to mee, saw my good freind Major Haines with joy.

Ap. 14: divers shoures this weeke, and warm like an April: gods word is my comfort(.) pressed with earnestness all(,) but young ones esp. with a respect to mine to feare the lord. lord blesse thy word. many very ill, and light headed in their feavours.

Ap: 16: divers shoures, but cold. my barn feild pond had not a barrel of water in it, but now this 17. it was a full river, heard very comfortably of my children at London, according to my prayers, the lord good in the word; 18. a floud some of my ponds pretty full, blessed bee god.

20. Warmish weather. baptized the daughter, buried Wid. Death who outlived her housband 3 quarters of a yeare to bring forth, and died.[1]

Ap. 24. showrie and warme, god very good in the word, shew thy freindlines in my heart, and in doing good to mine.

29. I paid Holden his 100li. which he paid by Mr Brown and Hovener to Dr Colier for mee, I borrowed 40li. towards it; I am now to gather for Jane.

May. 1. Cold, yet grassie weather:

5. broke bread. Mrs Eldred there. god good to us.

May. 8: Heard of my childrens wellfare at London, god bee blessed; god good to mee in his word, the lord in mercy own mee his freind.

May. 15. warm weather, a calme in the world and affaires therof; the day good, Sabbaths the best days. I choose the lord for the best freind to mee and mine: many attending on the word. the last Lord day I began to expound the Lords prayer.

21. an afflicting account of John, but home carriage as greivous

May. 22. hot, dry weather(.) my *mind* stais it selfe on god, and my expectation is from him. god good in the word ingaging my heart to obey him.

May. 29. rid towards London. returnd June. 5. Johns busines greivous to mee yet the lord mixt mercies to support, and I hope in his name. servants out of order at home, lord recover us into an holy frame; the lord turns in my heart to looke for him my gain. lord

[1] The husband, William Death of Great Tey, householder, was buried on 25 July 1669; Susanna Death, widow, was buried on 20 April 1670, nine months later, as RJ remarked. Susannah Death, daughter of William and Susannah, 'both dead', was baptized on the 20th. PR.

bee so, experience of the kindnes of god in Mrs Colier, and some strangers.

June. 12. Summer weather, god good in his word, heard of John, lord I pray and I looke up to thee in christ for good: 14. my good freind Mrs Colier came safe to Colne, oh what glad welcom shall we have with our heavenly father; 18. had in 3 load good meadow hay.

June. 19. A good day, Johns letter a litle pleasd. lord answer prayer in the soule good of all mine. the word good in all damping providences, god is my trust and hope, and he will doe mee good.

June. 26. a wett weeke past, my heart in much busines not so out of frame as when litle on my hands, the Kings only sister died suddenly in France, within a few days of her return from Dover where the king entertaind her with all pleasures might bee, lord sanctifie this. the ArchBishop of Canterbury ill, the poore nonconformist harried. one Hunwicke a disturber in our parts,[1] lord doe thy worke

July. 3. Good weather. John writt of a proposall to a partner, the lord direct, god good in his word, lord give mee wisedom that I value

July. 10. Good hay weather. god good in his word, my heart at sins brinke, lord recover mee to mind my soules good closely. heard as if Nan intended to come down, god send her well.

15. Dr to London. my wives sister to our joy came to us, a wetting day so was this after Swithins, heard more hopefully of John

July. 17. A cold wind, god good in his providences, in the word, discovering the hurt sin doth, lord keepe mee from it,

July. 24. Oats carrying, days hot. god good to mee and mine. an ill lamb kild and eating by my dogge, a trouble to mee.

25. begun a jorney into Sussex, returnd Aug. 2: having seen much of Englands glory, Hampton Court, Thames(,) returnd safe

Aug: 5. sister went from us. my daughter with us. the lord good in his providence to us, when by storme divers places by us had their feilds threst with haile. Cogshall 50^{li}. of hurt done in the glasse. this was July. 28. a continuall thunder in the aire for 3 quarter of houre the lord good to mee in the word(,) my 5 daughters at church.

Aug. 14: Good weather, yet dismal shoures in some places. god good to mee in his word. my eye decays I rub them, but its an inward weaknes not recoverable I feare.

[1] Probably John Hunwick, 'an Informer of Braintree, had been a Shopkeeper of good Reputation there, but seeking to enrich himself by the Spoil of his Neighbours, he proceeded with much Uneasiness'; Quakers were his main target, and it may well be that RJ now sympathized with Quakers, as with other 'poore nonconformist' groups. Besse, i, p. 204.

Aug. 28. dry, scorching weather. water scarce, yett it proved a very good harvest though Swithins a wetting day. a sickly time about(.) the Lord bee mercifull to us(.) god good in his word. all my children with mee. god winge them under his gracious covenant.

30: My daughter Jane married to Jonathan Woodthorp. our first ☞ marriage, the lord blesse them with his grace and favour; for porcon I am to give her. 200^{li}. her clothes and wedding cost mee 10^{li}. shee hath a prettie thing in joynture. blessed bee god who hath thus provided for mee and mine: her plate and worke is worth 40^{li}. and shee hath in mony. 20^{li}.——

Sept: 4: rainie. god good in manifold mercies, good in the word. lord sett my heart against evill. 5. I had home Jane. god give her rest in the house of an housband. sett out for Sussex. where I arrived and did my busines to content, the lord returnd mee safe(,) found all well for which I blesse my god. An well at London. preacht. 11. Sept. at Warnham in Sussex with hope of good to some soules. saw in Essex severall effects of the storm in the barly *e*aches[1]

20. at Markshall, dispatcht divers affaires for my Lady, shee shewed much kindnes to mee and my children

Sept: 25. God good in the season. I sew about 3 acres misl. god in mercy prosper it. our town in good health, my spirit in a better temper

Oct: 2. God good in the season [ ] a good seed time(.) good in his word, the lord blesse it to all [*mine*] and provide lord for them as thine to thee I give them(.) Tho: is going for London. John would trade in the country,

4: In the midst of all provisions I am to make for my children. I was forced to helpe her with 4^{li}. to pay Tho: which shee had in her prudence scored up by 1^{d}. and ob. my son had an 100^{li}. in my hand. and that in her wise anger he must pay mee in rather than allow mee some small matter for it, untill I have paid 60^{li}. I ow of it. I blesse god for my patience and kindnes, under all I meet with. [*I trust thee oh Lord to blesse mee*]

6. Thomas sett forward, for London with intent to continue there(.) my god shall goe with him and prosper him for soule and body. its my faith on Thom[as] and prayer and through trust for my other sonnes. 11 bullocks [stray]ing my son sent them backe, a good providence

8. made an end of sowing about 7 acres wheat, began to rain god prosper it. it proved a great rain on the last jorney next Smiths

[1] Etch: an after crop. SOED.

Oct: 9. A sad morning with John, his stout heart outwardly submitted(,) I forgave him and god I hope mee. god good in his word [ ] tried what the counsell of Mr Eldred. and Cressener would doe. god blesse it

10. Rid to the visitacion, and found no trouble. god bee praised. preached at Halsted.

16. God good in his word my soule desire is to him and his feare, my heart longs for thy grace as the glory of mee and mine, god good in the word.

Oct. 23. Saw Thomas and heard of An with comfort, received two tables(,)[1] presents(.) gods goodnes in any love: god good in the word. lord heare this morning and evening prayer put up in much faith, for our posteritie that they may not bee sett to doe evill, but sanctified throughout

Oct: 27: Peters yeare is to come out Octob. 31. 1671. he is to have 5^{li}. wages and his mare going untill. candlemas day.

Oct: 30: God good in his word, many hearing, lord angle them into thy poole.

Snow: Nov. 4. and very considerable; went this day to move a match for my son. I rest in gods providence [ ] 5. the Sabbath wett, I was at Halsted, and at my own place in the afternoone. god with mee.

No: 13: A dry Sabbath, god good in his word, my soule earnest with god in prayer to [*turn*] the soules to himselfe, lord heare prayer.

N. 20. a dry Sabbath [ ] earnestly for soule good, lord enlarge thy *tents* in the world, and prevaile for mine of thy grace.

24. came home from preaching Cosin Johnsons funeral. maried another(.) thes vicissitudes are here, the condicon above hath no changes

Nov. 27. Frost and cleare.—29. John tooke his clothes and mony and in the morning unknown to any of us. or without a line to tell ☞ what he aimed at went away. Lord let him not outrun thy mercy. I will daily seeke to god to keepe him. to breake his heart and deliver him from his own evill mind, and save his soule. lord heare prayer. hasten an houre of love for him for Christs sake.

Dec. 4: faire and dry. John returned, but lord change his heart, make us wise to win him to thee, god good in his word, lord owne us for thine

Dec: 11: Moist weather: god good in his word, but our hearts so out

[1] Table: a board or other flat surface on which a picture is painted; hence the picture itself. SOED.

of order, that it causeth a most wearisom life; a considerable floud, yet our ponds fill slowly.

Dec: 18: God good in his providences, my son Woodthorps mother dead(.) the lord prepare us for our change. god good in the word, make mee wisely to redeeme my time which I loose in vain thought,

20. preacht Mrs Woodthorp. fun. at Lamersh: lord blesse that word to us.

Dec. 25. Heard of Tho. feavour at London; god good in his word lord make mee wise to order my steps to win my son to thee

Jan. 1. God give us himself and new hearts, and his blessing this new yeare and for ever. heard the feavour left my son. [god good] in the word, oh how sweet it is to bee perswaded as I am of gods mercy in the merits of christ for my salvacion.

3. present with joy at a kinswomans marriage. god blesse them(.) at good Lady Mildmays funeral, kind to mee. but I unkind to god(.) Mrs Mildmay sent Becke a good guift, ponds fill apace.

Jan. 8. god good in his word, oh how unquiet my life is, lord helpe mee to find an absolute composure in my selfe. and keep such a watch that nothing may move mee. for I looke for no help from any other. Mr Humphry:[1] dined with us. Jan. 10. Tuesday. lodged with us. Jan. 11. god in mercy blesse him under my roofe, and make us solely blessings to one another, he is to pay 27^{li}. per annum.

Jan. 19. purchased a tan office for my son. setled it on Jane for her life. god blesse them. for outward things shee is provided well(.) John came home. all well at London bless god oh my soule, this purchase was with her portion.

Jan: 22. God good in his word, I learn Christ must mediate for all through him I hope to reclaim John to feare the lord.

Jan: 26: 1670 my. 55. enters.

Lord thou hast been my god, my hope is in thy mercy. looke after mee and mine for soule and body for on thee I trust.

Jan. 29. preacht with affection to doe good to afflicted soules in holding out christ to them. Smith of our town drownd in his dronkennes and found this morning, god in mercy sanctifie all meanes

Feb: 4: Satturday. Peter reported he was that day married. weather

[1] William Humphry, the new schoolmaster. He did not last long, for the PR on 27 September 1673 records the burial of 'Mr William Humphrys a Scot and schoolmaster of the Free School of EC'.

now cold and frostie. Johns debauchery in swearing sad(,) lord helpe mee(.) so bad. 6.—7. that I resolve to put him to his shifts, for the lords sake. lett it tend to his good.

Feb. 12. A good day in my affectionate strivings to recover sinners out of Satans and their hearts snare, my soule yearnd over John. oh Lord overcome his heart in obedience to thee. another cow slunk[1]

Feb: 19. A sad weeke with John, his carriage intolerable. uncertain what to resolve. Lord direct mee. a day of comfort in the word, though troubles in my house. 26. came home opportunely to save a cow cast.[2] found John within, but as I dreamed high and proud so he was(,) cast him lord down as that cow that he may rise up again.

Feb. 26. God good in his word many hearing, god make his word to proffit, the season dry and cold, 28. paid 50^{li}. on my daughter Wood-thorps purchase. god in mercy blesse their soules and habitacons I hope its the dwelling thou hast looked them out:

March. 5. God good in his word, lord bee good in my family, and servant mee as may bee pleasing to thee and good for mee, turne to mee oh lord and bee gracious, and turne our hearts to thee and one another.

M. 12. Sad with my sons as to their trades, and sadder nearer mee. the lord helpe mee, for I stand alone as to all helpe and comfort, but from thee. god carries on my outward affaires beyond expectations(.) a sweet raine

Mar: 19. Good weather after raine, the lord afflicts and this is my affliction my heart is shut up both in prayer and much in hope; and litle gain by troubles which are such that I had mee gett much good by, or I shalbee a great looser(.) god good in his word to mee for which I blesse him.

John rid away, carried some things with him. without taking his leave of mee. on Wednesday. March. 22. god in mercy looke after him

March. 25. 1671.

March: 26. day warm and calme. death hauseld[3] us at Colne this yeare. god in mercy prepare mee and mine for it, that it come not unaware(.) many hearing(,) god blesse the word. the wickednes and in*sobriety* of England increase. Lord Lucas likely to be sent to

[1] Slunk: of calves, cast prematurely. SOED.

[2] Cast: to bring forth young, give birth. NED.

[3] Hauseld: probably hustle or hussel, to knock about, disturb, etc. Gepp.

tower by Lords for speaking somewhat freely against the taxes. which are heavy beyond measure the 20th part of our yearly state.

Ap: 2. my busines goeth on very dully. my wife afflicted to see John again(.) god good in his word, my heart hopes in god, and in his word I trust.

6. set out for London returnd. 15. found Tho. ill, and dismayed. lord thou art displeased and afflicts, accept an atonement and bee reconciled in Christ Jesus

Ap: 16. dry cold weather. backward spring, but all good awkward indeed.

23. still the same weather, and evils in our hearts and lands, god in mercy turn our hearts into his paths, administred the sacrament only. 15 there

28. preacht. Minister Josselins funerall(,)[1] I am spared. god gave us a sweet rain

May 1. sett forth and returnd. 17. found much losse in my absence, my heart reflected on the providences of god, and my heart learn instruction resolving in the strength of god to turn foolish vanities out of mind, and anything that hath the semblance of evill out of my practice. 21: god good in his words, hopes of shoures.

May. 24. 25: god shoured on my inheritance, and neare about us especially(,) I lookt on it as a pledge of mercy, for my sons and selfe in order to my ministry at Coln and Elsewhere, I will pray and looke up.

June. 4. God good in his word, the lord gives hopes in my sons life, god hath heard for the dewes plentifully wett my inheritance, which I lookt as a pledge that he would reclaim John, and direct mee in my affaires of Colne; bee my porcon continually

5. rid towards Sussex. returnd 21. god good to mee and mine at home only John robd his mother and sister of neare 30s. and away. god in mercy breake his heart for good.

July. 2. A great raine with thunder after a fortnight good hay weather. I did not improve my season for want of helpe(.) god help mee that I loose not my time to eternity.

Estate. Through gods blessing I have accomplisht in my estate the utmost that I desired by June. 24. viz. an 120li. but my stocke is low(.) I have all this of gods graciousness to his servant.

[1] Hezekiah Jocelin, schoolmaster of Harlow in 1640, rector of Copford, Essex, 1662–71. Venn. There is no mention of RJ in his will (ERO, 499 BR 9), nor are they known to be related.

July. 9. God good in the word and season. god in mercy awaken soules and ingage them against sin. my dayes weare away, and my soule desires thee(.) my son Tho. with mee. lord revive him. heard John was in a service having spent all his mony. lord in faithfulnes call him

July. 16: Swithins day very wett in many places, a shouring time that our haying goeth not on. gods busines neglected, and hee regard, not ours. god good to us in the word, baptizd two children

July. 23. A good weeke, much abroad, preserved and prospered in my affairs(.) ind much hay, blessed bee god. the Sabbath cheerful in my great wearines, god good in his word. And Aaron held his peace and so.[1] I

July. 30. God good in his word, the weather very uncertain; looks foule

31. god good in dispatch of son Woodthorps affaire with the Lord Lucas(,) compounded two fines at 14^{li}. saw a sad object of Mrs Caplin. in her mouth. Lord in mercy spare her soule, and helpe us to honour god with every member.

Aug. 2. begun to reape. god blesse us, rain put mee by ending die 6°

Aug. 7. God good in his word and manifold mercies, oh lord doe mee and direct my way in obedience unto thee

Aug. 21. God good in his word, his providence good to mee in my straits

27. God good to mee in the season, a good after harvest, blessed bee my god, and yet the greatnes of the bulke made our worke very heavy.

Sept. 10: a good day after many shoures, made my hay worke tedious, yet overcame it, never cutt that ground late, my sister Rebekah with mee her husband also. 12. the most stormy day I knew.

17. God good to mee in his word, my heart drawn out for the good of soules. heard much of the prodigiousnes of the floud. in many parts

Sept: 24. being the last Sabbath of the yeare, I publiquely declared my submission to their putting mee away, having for 15 yeares with held their contribucon which was 25^{li}. per annum, as also most of there tithes. and now that which others allowed, which I tooke

[1] One commentator writes of this passage (Leviticus 10: 3); Aaron 'patiently submitted to the holy will of God in this sad providence, was *dumb, and opened not his mouth*, because *God did it*. Something he was ready to say by way of complaint . . . but he wisely suppressed it, *laid his hand upon his mouth*, and said nothing, for fear lest *he should offend with his tongue*, now that his *heart was hot within him*.' Mathew Henry, *An Exposition of the Old and New Testament* (1828), i, p. 281.

from god with the greatest patience. but from them with great unkindnes, but I trust god will turne it unto good.—I am thine Lord, though not theirs—

Oct: 1: I rid to Coptford and preacht there. god good in my jorney.

5. I baptized Henry son of Coll. Henry Mildmay,

Oct: 8. wett again. this day I went down to preach, and found Mr Serjeant there: he read. Ezech: 2. lord lett it bee known I have been thy servant and thou acceptest mee. the 12. ps. was sung. not one person spake to mee, coming out of the church. Lord I am dispised, but my confidence is in thee. and with quietnes I roule my selfe on thee, for in thee is my helpe.

15. rid to Coptford 7 mile preacht. returnd to Colne and preacht, that no occasion should bee taken against mee. god blesse the word(.) I had a very comfortable day of it, without much wearines. things seem to tend to union. lord bring it about

22. cleare shining after rain and floud, god good in his word, the season threats, clouds gather as if troubles with our neighbours yett wee repent not, my heart resolved to preach and doe for my god.

29. God good his word, sensible of the evill of my heart, oh lord lett thy grace bee sufficient; shew mercy in my relacions(.) a letter delivered from John as I came from church. lord in mercy direct mee what to doe.

No. 5. Good weather, Freinds and children with mee, John only as an outcast, lord reclaim him. god good in the kindnes of divers persons, lord own mee and thy word and bless us

No. 12. Frost with cold winds as it hath been about 10 days. god good to mee in the word, my heart very desirous to bee usefull.

17. visited persons whose child was kild by an other with a shot: also a sad timpany[1] woman. releived her. god spare mine and blesse us(.) paid to my son Woodthorpe, all Janes portion and her mony, for which I praise my most gracious god. its mony I thought well bestowed. the bond I received in.

No: 19. preacht at Coptford. where I mist a young Gentlewoman, that was well when I was last there and now dead of a gangreen in the whole flesh; god good in his word. lord preserve mee and mine. sensible of gods hand on Mr Eldreds family. his brother Barfoot buried. Nov. 21. and his brother Wm Eldreds wife the same day: his Cosin Thurston died that day. breaking his skull with a fall dronken some said the brothers to blame therin, Lord amend us.

[1] Timpany: tympanites, distention of abdomen by gas or air in the intestine or uterus; also sometimes used for a tumour or morbid swelling of any kind. SOED.

No. 26. open good weather, god good to my family in health. Lord reclaim John. god good in the word, my heart enlarged in desiring publique good

Dec. 3. Calme open weather, men degenerate in their manners beyond measure, lord awe my heart into holy obedience(.) said the Dutch and Montery will attempt the French. that nacion possibly may fall: god good in his word, my heart mindfull of eternity.

Dec. 10. Calme dry weather but turnd to a floud. 11. and 12. god good in the word, my heart out of frame. lord helpe and compose all.

15. Lay at my son Woodthorps. god blesse him and his all 17. went to see Mary Eldred. I found her upwards. blessed bee god. I was afraid of a blow. god good in his word, lord I am slighted by men doe thou value mee

Jan: 2. at John Josselins burial of Kelvedon. father and 2 sons being all of that branch dead in lesse than 16. months. lord lett mee and mine live in thy sight. its my desire. my faith. answer so in Christ.

Jan: 7. a good faire season: 10. at the Funeral of the good Lady Vere who lived beloved and blessed of god. 90 yeares. died lamented of all.

12. Preacht Sarah Londons funeral,[1] endeavoured to stir up young persons to bee good. 14: god good in his word, my soule encourages it selfe in god, under all neglects from my people.

Jan. 21. open weather, god good in his word. my house is sett to keepe up gods ordinances here, expecting my reward with Abram from my god. though my people bee unkind.

March. 3. wee had some sharp weather, but to this day a good winter(.) god good in the health of mine, but I find a dead heart, and no wonder at any troubles I meete with, my heart sett to ingage mine and people to bee the lords people.

13. Wednesday rid to London(.) that day Sir Robert Holmes that fired the Fly attempted the Smirna fleet. 16. a declaracon came out for liberty of conscience: 19. the Dutch warre proclaimd and fast appointed both ordered by the King and Councill on the Lords day. March. 17. returned well but very weary. March. 21;

March. 25. 1672.

The season calme, and cold but good, the times lowring the hearts and lives of men bad, judgments strange and sins worse(,) a child of 8 yeares a dronkard: Moles wife sought to split a woman at the

[1] Sarah London of Colne Engaine, spinster, left a will in 1672 (ERO, 57 CR 9).

secrets whom her housband raped. Smiths daughter by a forke forced her body inter anum et vulnam,[1] Lord in mercy keepe mee from evill.

Ap: 1. 3. imployed in ending differences among neighbours. lord lett there bee none between thee mee or mine, but let us have peace in christ

11. In a great difficultie of my affaires as to person and estate(,) I this day received 2 ginneys of Mr Eldreds guift, which thogh it bee small to former love, yett I looke on it as love, and hope his heart may returne to a care of my affaires

Ap. 14. God good in his word, my affaires behind hand and spirit ill.

17. A fast on occasion of the Dutch warre, which all are against

28. or thereabouts a monster born in our town;[2] the grandfather, esteemed religious, but the children wretched.

Ap. 29. Monday neare 3 a clocke afternoon my daughter Woodthorpe delivered of a son. the first grandchild. god blesse him with his christ

May. 1. received a tith lambe of R. Bridge. junior. the first I received. when I came home I found my dog kild a kosset[3] lambe in the house to my great greife.

8. went to London. 14. sealed the marriage writings. may. 14. between Mr Andrews. and Mrs Colier.[4] married the couple. 16. came home. 18. god good in all his providences, but my heart out of due frame.

May. 19. God good in the word, ill with a cold, the season dry: heart bad.

May. 26: A dry droughtie season, The Dutch beare up gallantly. the Lord send shoures. god good in his word. oh Lord heale mee and mine

28. The Dutch set on our fleet in Solebay fight continued (c.o. June 1)

June. 2. dry and windy, prayed for rain, god in mercy send it. god good in his word, the lord heale my family of sin. my son Thomas very well for which god bee praised. my onely grandchild. John Woodthorp. buried. June. 4.

[1] Between the anus and vulva. There is no reference to this curious attack, or the previous rape in the court records.

[2] The nearest baptism was that of Ann Cob, daughter of Edward and Ann on 21 May.

[3] Cosset: a lamb brought up by hand; a pet lamb. NED.

[4] A licence for the marriage exists as follows: 15 May 1672, Daniel Androse, bachelor, aged 25, son of Daniel Androse of St. Stephen's Wallbrook, London, Esq., and Mary Harlakenden, aged 19, daughter of Mary Collier, of St. Foster's, London, widow, were licensed to marry at St. Giles, Cripplegate, or at two other (named) churches. Harleian Soc. xxiv (1886), p. 123.

June. 9. rain passeth away. lord helpe in our need. god afflicts the Dutch by French; the rain passeth away. Lord remember our feilds our

June necessities great. let not sin hinder: sad with Holland the French
16. prevaile at land. god good in his word. he lives and he reigneth and he will turne all to good. either raising them up a Savior, or by turning frances armes against Italy.

June. 23. Drought continues, Holland drowns it selfe. oh the evil of sin(,) Lord drown it in Christs blood. god good, though affaires unquiet to mee. oh let my house live in thy sight.

June. 30. drought continueth when rain round about us, god good in his word. sad with Holland, some speake of peace between us

July. 7. The earth fully satisfied. I cleard my meadow. July. 5. by a good providence. god good in his word, doe good Lord to the many hearers

July. 21. A good season. litle thoughts of a Dutch peace. our councel so for the French, its likely the Dutch come wholly under them. god is good howsoever it bee.

28. preacht twice at Newport, W. Mathews funeral who gave mee a good legacy.[1] I had a great desire to doe good in that jorney(.) people flockt to the word with attencion and affection. saw my sisters with delight: returnd. 30. through much rain. Aug. 1. a floud in chelmsford river. busy. in harvest and tithes.

Aug. 4. A good season. for which god bee praised. god good to mee in the word, the lord blesse it, my sister ill and Jane. god helpe

Aug. 11. My harvest went in well blessed bee god, sometimes rain. my Jane and John ill. lord raise them up. that they and I may praise thy name. lord thou givest mee bread out of the feilds. make mee serviceable to many soules.

Aug. 16. A wett day. god good in his word, he sets my heart against sin. some hopes in Jane. but John is John. but I will hope in god

25. A good day. god good in the word, striving to beate men of from their lusts, blesse lord our labour.

Sept. 1: God gave an indifferent good harvest. a good heart is best. let mine bee so. my desire is to serve thee. who blessest mee(.) god good in the word my heart stirred up to take men of from lusts.

3. presented our supplications to god at L. H. for our families and nacon. with faith god will heare and doe our seed good: praised

[1] Widow Bridget Matthew, not buried at EC, but stated herself to be of that town when she made a will on 9 October 1671 in which she left RJ a legacy of £5 (ERO, 210 BR 9).

god for the answer of prayer in the families preservacon and in Janes life from death(,) I will remember and make mention of thy love my deare father.

Sept. 8. Jane went away well. Tho. came down well. but John sicke indeed. lord he is thine lord save him. prest to feare god as blessednes(.) began to sow, but the time wett and bad.

Sept. 15. Some litle hopes of Johns recovery and affectednes with his state(,) my god answer mee fully, a good day. Lord sow thy feare in all our hearts and lett it grow up in us to perfection.

Sept. 22. Both my sons at dinner hopes in both, god bee praised(.) the season bad: but gods day and word good, sin abounds but gods mercy more yet in sparing us.

27. My litle Beck fired a bed matt with a candle. my wife run up into chamber and quincht it. the circumstance rendred it a mervellous mercy of god, my soule praiseth him. my care for my child, who gott aside. as a father so god pittieth his.

Sept. 29. Very wett weather, and a bad seed time, god every way frowns on a poore nacon, yet wee consider it not, I find the last yeare god was better then in any former yeare in providing for mee

Oct: 6. The season wondrous wett. god good in his word. lord awaken our hearts after thee. my son John abroad lord sanctifie his heart, that he may practice that seasonable sermon in absteining from fleshly lusts.

10: ill Coat, hose and wett bootes brought on a feavourish cold(,) scarce able to preach.

Oct. 20. heard of my Cosin Birds death and wee all alive this day. a goodly season.

Oct. 27. A wett day. I gatt out and preacht. but with no satisfaction to my selfe. I gett strength blesst bee god, but slowly. Tho. went for London

No. 3. A good morning, wherin I am cheerfull(.) with a heart very desirous to doe good in the worke of my master, as a due thankfulnes for his care of mee in my sicknes(.) the souldiers went from us, god keepe us quiet in our selves.

9. A dry day after shoure, wherin I emptied my meadow of wood, and so free of the feare of weather for that. buried Capt. Stebbin at Tain. god enabling mee to goe and preach,—Nov. 10. a goodly day. and god assisted mee in my worke beyond expectacon, so that I repeated at home.

14: Thomas Honywood Esq. eldest of this branch buried, meanly enough(,) his memory seems to fall, no course taken to creditt him. 15. preacht G. Potter funerall a young mans, with great desire to doe good. a floud

No. 17. God good in the worke of the day, preaching on the mustard seed, I heard the report of the French endeavour to reforme in religion, if of god it will prosper. god grant it true. it came to nothing at present

No. 27. being at my daughter Janes at Lexden I was taken in my bed. or coming out of it with the sciatica pain in my hipbone so that I could not step. and when I came home not turne my selfe in my bed, wholy deprived of strength on that side but through mercy, god gave mee in the use of meanes some helpe(.) there was a surfett with oysters, which though they did not nauseat my stomacke, mett with so much phlegme in my stomacke, and being bound. they lay corrupting in my stomacke(.) I eate at first litle but dranke wine. strong beere[1] pretty freely, and that carried them of, and my vomits had a tincture of them to Tuesday. December. 3. I sweat;
D. 24 eate well but gather strength slowly this being 24. but I am under great hopes of a perfect recovery and I hope quickly: I had a servant died(,) this a mortal time in our towne(,) about. 15 buried in 7 weeks; to the praise of my good god I record that on the 25. 26. I began to take many steps without sticke or stay

Jan. 5: This day afternoon I went down to church and preacht. Eccl. 9.5. a great audience. I was not overweary, I had a good day, and I hope catcht no cold. for all I bow my soule in thankfulnes to god in christ.

27. went to Markshall. my L. Honywood sent her coach for mee. there I stayd to March 10. in which time my Lady was my nurse and phisitian and I hope for much good. on Thursday. Feb. 27 or sooner some red spots appeard on my lame thigh, which they conceived the scurvy. I tooke purge and other things for it, they increased some to a penny breadth, my thigh and leg swelled. but not on the other side, and so they did before I went from home, and continue so still; god was good to mee in the temper of my heart though I am sensible I beare my infirmities about mee, but my wife taxes mee for great impatience. when I feare there is a provoking cairelesnes in her etc. and impatience too much, that beares nothing but expects I must beare all. god inable mee therto. for I have need of patience when I have done my duty.

March 10 returned home. a wonderful spirit of zeale against the papists. 15. heard my L. H. successe in a Fulmer busines, wherin I had

[1] A recipe for making 'strong beer' is given in the *Compleat Housewife*, p. 254.

been their grand contriver of defence. 16. preacht twice at home after six weeks absence. the scurvy in red spots much on thigh and leg and both feet. god in mercy bring mee of this trouble.

22. my son Tho. came home ill. but with hopes as also for my selfe, gathering strength against my distemper.

March. 27. Mr Eldreds cutting day, feasted. gave mee 2 ginneys I prayed heartily for him; 30. Easter sacrament. 16. there god good in the administracion and in the word preached.

wett Easter and Snow. April. 6. From Easter day. and so this day, in a manner continuall snow, rain and cold, with flouds, the ground never more wett; hay scarce, god good to mee in my health and sonne the lord perfect his mercy towards us

13. whether it proceeded from the change of weather or otherwise, it being a wett day after a dry weeke, I know not but I was very lame on my hippe, scarce able to goe(.) god good in his word to mee, but all out of frame.

May. 11. weather dry and cold, litle grasse: a very hard spring to the farmer(.) god good to mee in my health. I walkt twice to Markshall and returnd once the same day, report the Dutch fleet on our coast, and wee unreadie. god fitt mee for my worke. things hard in my family(,) I desire to submitt and to improve all to spiritual advantage.

omas selin June 15. about one a clocke in the morning my eldest sonne Thomas and my most deare child ascended early hence to keepe his everlasting Sabbath with his heavenly father, and Saviour with the church above(,) his end was comfortable, and his death calme, not much of pain til the Satturday afore. in my course this morning I read Josh; 1: which had words of comfort, god making his word my counsellour and comfort(.) He was my hope. but some yeares I have feared his life, god hath taken all my first brood but Jane. lett all live in thy sight sanctified(.) a wett morning, the heavens for some time have mourned over us.

17. Son buried. June. 23. rid to Braintry. by coach to London and returnd safe with An very ill home July. 3. a wett flouding yeare like that in 48. god in mercy looke down upon us.

July. 20: God afflicts mee, my An ill and deafe and therby unchearfull, and so I scarce can comfort her soule: Lord marre not my inheritance, a blacke cow died suddenly of the blacke gargett. my heart pants after god as my hope, and my trust is in him for good, lord leave mee not(.) some good days in answer of prayer the lord will adde more, oh lett my labours doe much good to soules, god good this day in his word, and my soule hopes in his mercy, and that his blessing shall abide with mee.

23. rid to my daughter Woodthorps, brought her with mee to see sicke An(.) saw her new building with delight, returnd home with comfort

July. 27. Wettish hindring weather, after some hopes this day An worse. Mr Humfry ill, god sanctifie afflictions to mee and mine, god good in the word which is a reviving unto mee, to heare god useth affliction to fitt us for heaven and so I hope mine, my son John writes sermons. I am glad of a litle hope Lord write them in his heart, I humbly pray thee. and bring him home to thee.

Ann Jos -selin July 31. This morning after 2 of the clocke my deare Ann in her twentieth year died with mee at Colne. a good child, following her brother to London. and from thence hither, to lie in his grave, loving in their lives and in their deaths they were not divided. lying in the same grave(.) twenty three yeares before god opened the grave and Mary first the eldest of that brood and Ralph the youngest after, lay in the same grave(.) god hath taken 5 of 10. lord lett it bee enough. and spare that we may recover strength; bee reconciled in the blood of thy son my saviour and make all mine thine as I hope thou wilt and shine upon mee for the Lords sake in mercy.

Aug. 3. a misling morning, a Sabbath wherin my heart awakens for god to doe good to soules that he may bee glorified. my soule humbles it selfe before the Lord with hopes in his mercy. from whom I encourage my heart, to trust in him for all good, he wilbee my salvacion Lord bee so to poore John and my daughters; a very wett day and sad time(,) god good in his word to mee giving mee a view of some fitnes for a better state.

6. This day I had a load of Chalkney wood brought in. blessed bee god for anything

8. This morning a man brought mee a rope. it was the first harvest day for mee in town, I lookt on it as a good signe, I prayd god would open the hearts of my people to deale well with mee. I agreed with one that I was jealous of as being no publique ordinance man.

9. Begun harvest god blesse mee therin. found in my grounds my 5 sheep which wee feared lost. god is good to mee in my affliction all praises to his name

Aug. 10. God hath stood by mee in many straits, and carried mee through them. I trust he will carry mee through all the difficulties of my outward condicon and inward. I will stir up my heart from this promise, and god shall command his blessing: A fine morning, my heart presseth after god with delight in him as my porcion and my hope. god was good to mee in the sabbath word and affections, my heart working warmely after him.

Aug. 17. The weeke past a good harvest weeke. ind all my hard corn, and forwarded my hay(,) much gott in(,) a good share of my tiths. rid to Perry. god shew mee favour in that affaire. my man ill, which amazed mee, but all praises to god who holds up his head. a good morning, praises to my god who plants my heart with hopes and faith in his goodness, I will love thee oh lord for thou hast dealt graciously with mee, god good to mee in his word the lord accept mee and mine in Christ Jesus. news of a Dutch fight.

Aug. 24. A good harvest weeke, I have received in almost all my hard corn tith for which I blesse god, who I trust will put life and comfort into spiritual and outward blessings to recover body and soule to a further strength for his service, for which I hope with a holy confidence, and that he will recover mee out of staleness as my heart is recovered(,) blessed bee his name, a cheerfull morning. god good to mee in his word for which my soule blesseth him.

26. received in 25^{s}. of the Wid. Laurence. the first person that sett a day of pay, and performed it

Aug. 31. A bad harvest weeke, this day very wett. god good to mee in many mercies, the lord good in his word, my spirit full of hope in him, that he will order all things for my good,

Sept. 7. A very bad harvest weeke. yett wee gott in some corn now and then: god good to mee in some temper of spirit, which bands itselfe to trust in god as my helper, and that he will helpe mee out of my troubles. god good to mee in his word, a good day unto mee for which I praise him.

Sept. 14. A bad harvest weeke. this day dry, the lord good in all his ways, and to mee his servant. my sister Hodson with mee, entertaind with joy.

Sept. 21. Last night it thundered, and the night very wett, and so is this morning, the weeke sad for harvest and seedtime; gods providence good to mee, when many faild mee yett I have as much mony as I aimed at for the faire, and I trust god will blesse mee in laying it out, and prosper it to mee, my heart trusts in him for all. my daughter Woodthorp with us, and I trust god will shew us mercy in her: my hearts desire is to bee with god in this sabbath worke. and through grace I find my soule cleaving to and trusting more in my god.

23. Received in my 20 load of wood, all praises to my god, who looketh on mee for good

25. Mr Humfreys died in my family, by whom I shall have a great losse(.) ended my harvest, praises to my god, who stands by mee when all faile. my sister Ann departed from us, loaded with her freinds bounty. esp. ours.

Sept. 28. God good to mee in the word, this day dry for*merl*y wett, my *soule is called* out to trust in god in all condicons which is a life to my soule.

Oct: 5. A good seed weeke. a cold frosty morning cheerfull day, very lightsome to my soule was my god, providences cloudy in my son, but out of all god will bring mee and I shall praise him

Oct. 12. A wett season and great floud, my life very unquiet, lord bring persons into a due order towards one another. lost an heifer this day. yett my god is good too mee, and in his word, drawing and fixing my heart in my dependance on him at all times, my health seems in hazard this weather, gods blessing is my refuge, more then my own care. my daughter Woodthorp holds up, god send her a good delivery. my grounds are full stocke, and my barnes pretty full. I hope god will sett mee free from state intanglements, my hope is onely on him. who careth for mee, and still will, and so I put my trust in him.

17. My daughter Elizabeth admitted to Maries and Tho: land. the 3[d]. fine on that land. lord spare this child to enjoy it. the lord was curst in his fine but the steward Mr Eldred kind in his fees. I eye my god in all.

Oct. 19. A fine day after bad weather, god sanctifie all providences and doe us good by them, my heart desirous to spend and bee spent for god, god good in his word. baptized a child publiquely.

21. About 5. of the clocke my daughter Jane delivered of a daughter which wee baptized that day. god almighty blesse it. us. and the parents of it. her name Jane.

Oct. 26. A dry brown day. go(o)d good to mee in his word, oh the comforts in Luke. 15. for poore sinners on there repentance

28. this day my wife and I have been married 33. yeares. this day my son sold Bollinhatch land for 123[li]. for which I have been bid. 150[li]. god blesse mee in the dispose of the mony. I was the last Josselin that sold a part in that inheritance, but a heavenly

inheritance I will never part with by the goodnes of god, which he hath laid up for mee above.

Nov. 2. Good weather god good in his word, 3. I ended sowing wheat. was at White Colne, where I did some kindnes for poore Bull; god grant no snare to mee.

5. preacht from ps. 107.2. gods deliverances a hope to us he will deliver against the feares of popery at present in England. the Duke marrying Modena's daughter.

No: 9. Frost and snow, the Parl. prorogued, god looke after his own things(.) the lord maketh mee sensible of my relative sins. even men whose hearts are upright with god, have there neverthelesse in something remisse

16. Frost continues. upwards through mercy. the lord good and I will praise him

23. A good day for soule and body: with joys in my god, who is my ease in all outward troubles; all my family in health etc.

No: 30. All in health. praises to my good god, a comfortable sabbath. my soule dedicates itselfe to my god in christ fill mee with grace and comfort with thy H. spirit. that I may live on thee in every condicion which is my desire

Dec: 2. My daughter Woodthorp and her daughter my grandchild. went home. wel for which my soule praiseth my good god, who opened not the mouth of the grave on us. Lord thou hast heard prayer for her. heare it for John my onely son to sanctifie his heart, and also my other childrens. my wife and daughter Mary went home with her. Mr Martin robd. god preserve mee and all that I have from violence. no good friend to mee.

7. God good in his word, my hearts desire are soules might bee deare to all. my heart thoughts are vain: Lord helpe. but where are thy endeavours. lord looke after all mine for good I pray thee.

Dec. 14. God good in his word; lord make us all to mind our soules and thy glory

21. Warm as if gods providence lookt on the want of coals, and helpd the want of fire, with the warm drines of the aire. the lord in his mercy turn all unto good, god good in his providences this weeke. I roule my soule on him, and he will not faile mee. god good to mee in his word.

25. Preacht at Colne. my wife selfe and children rid by coach to the Lady Honywoods where I also preacht. god [good in the word] the lord had his hand then on my sister Anna. who was taken suddenly ill. dropsicall when with us, and went away cheerfull. a good woman

and now happy. shee died Friday 26. god hath broken the brood there are now but three of us. shee was next above mee in age. lord fit mee for my change. returnd home Jan. 9. from the L. Honywoods.

Jan. 11. A wett day. god good in his word. prayd heartily for the agreement of King and Parliament. god heare. Reb. not well this night god in mercy spare her.

Jan. 18. A sad snow after a great raine. high floud. no frost. god good in his mercies to mee oh that mine might live in thy sight. all in health. but how are our soules out of frame. the lord shine on us in all outward and inward blessings.

Jan. 25. God good in his word as a good and gracious god make mee and mine partakers of it. I had glimmering hopes here for my stubborne John the lord can change his heart, when he pleaseth, and my strength shalbee to sitt still and waite

Jan. 26. 1673. 58. enters.

Joseph Slie. Jan. 23.

Sensible this day begins my 58. yeare, in which I desire gods presence and blessing with mee, but above all his grace in mee and mine and gracious presence with us, oh that John might live to thee, this morning I had two lambs fell, well for which I praise god(,) I hope a token of a good yeare.

28. Supt with my sister with all mine. god returns love. coming home alarmd that Wm Partree of our toune a butcher was drownd.[1] lord keep mee and mine in thy protection, and let us walke in thy wayes. told of a light like a candle or fire in the guttur of my house.

Feb. 1. A wondrous wett day. my leg occasions thoughts of the dropsie, the Lord I looke unto to bee my phisitian. I prest gods love as the banner over his people, the word good to mee(,) hopes of peace god in mercy continue it and perfect it.

8. For some dayes frost. god good to mee in his word. ever I hope I am under grace and mercy in all the afflictive providences I meet with in son and wife, which are greivous only mercy doth in some measure lighten them.

10. This morning found my lost sheep with 2 lambs. 3. sheep lambd well this morning(,) oh that my stray sheep might return to thee oh god. say thou Amen when I pray

Fast. 11. set a part for a fast. god in mercy heare us in christ, and let all our sins bee forgiven. and let the lord have respect in him to mee and

[1] William Peartree senior (drowned) was buried on 30 January 1674. PR.

some in Colne that wee may contribute something to the account of publique and private mercies: on this day the K. in the house of Lords declared to them and Commons that the peace was made with the Dutch. safe, honourable, and he hoped lasting, the D. of Yorks marriage by the French interest with Modena. his inclinacon to the R. religion. the great offers of the French to the English to continue the war. hastned the peace. god adde truth and his blessing: with a heart to England to improve this mercy.

Feb. 15. God good in publique mercies(,) I have had a good weeke with John, minding busines, and keeping home, lord adde thy grace and all shalbee well. my heart will hope in thee(.) god good in the word, with inward tast and perswasion that he is gracious to mee.

Feb: 21. A bullocke died almost suddenly. Lord there is nothing sure but thy selfe, helpe mee to live on thee my constant stay. weather wett. God good in his word and I will trust in his mercy. 23. a sheep lost 2 lambs; yett god is good for he is mine.

22. Parliament prorogued to Nov. 10. K. speech smooth. a disappointment to the country. no notice of it in the Thursday gazet: they toucht Arlington succession not in a papist. Ireland where the papists are mighty. and popery here and would give no mony. god waited to bee gracious by them to make peace with the Dutch. he wilbee exalted to doe great things in his own time.

March. 1. a snowy Sabbath. a good day to mee all in health, I pray and hope for grace for all mine

3. A snowy, shrovetuesday, of a great depth; one of the greatest snows I knew

6. The priory estate setled to all their contents; the tithes setled on the ministry.

M. 8. The greatest snow and longest for this time, with extreme cold. yett god warmd my heart to love him, and from his goodnes stirred me up to serve him. much snow fell this night. 9.

March. 15. This day cleare. and a great floud. snow lying in many places. it snew almost continually, every day from Monday Feb. 23. to March. 12. when fell a great snow then it thawed with a wonderfull flood. lost a sheep and lambe. a great rott. lord I am sensible of thy afflicting hand and I turn to thee kissing thy rod. not murmuring at loses but praising thee for injoyments. god good in his word affaires calme, all things deare

16. 17. rain. 18. a great snow in the morning, melted by night. 19. cold wind. snow. litle frost: 20. snow covering the ground: 21. continuing still: 22. small snow.

March. 22. dull weather: mortality at London: sad with John. but I will hope in good. the promise is to mee and mine if thou art faithfulnes. God good in his word and outward mercies(,) reports of a new Parliament, all change(,) only god abides the same.

23. began to plow. brake one. they say an ill beginning makes a good ending. a cow slunke: others untoward, which put mee to a more carefulnes of my heart. to delight it in god for all thes are vain and empty.

25. March. 1674.

25. A cheerfull morning god make it in all things a good day to mee. received an 100li. of the purchase mony for the land at Roxwell and two ginneys for my wife. god blesse it to them, and mee in the dispose of my mony.

March. 29. A glorious day after a good weeke. hopes of a faire spring. god good in his word(,) I magnify gods good word and will learn to live on his truth therein and faithfulnes theretoo

30. wind came North East. cold: so. on April. 3. signe of shoures. returnd from seing my children at Lexden. my outward affaires goe heavily. lett my inward be bettered therby.

Ap: 9. Warm, dewing morning, god good to mee in the providences of this weeke: my heart to please him in my life, lord accept mee in christ Jesus.

Ap. 12. A dry weeke mixt of cold and warm and wind. some shews of rain passing away yett. though smaller droppings fell for which god bee praised. recovered from a listles, restles illnes in my left kidney(,) spleen with stomacke illnes. by natural vomitt. gentle sweating. so that next day. 11. I went abroad. and this day preacht. lord prosper all my soule works I pray thee: oh reclaim mine to thy feare, esp. disobedient John. oh shutt him not out.

16. made an end of sowing my barly. god blesse my crop. on that blessing my all depends

Ap: 19. Easter day: sowing almost over. the season dry and cold. close, corn works but grasse stirs litle, god good in my morning meditacons, of the rich veins of grace and mercy that are in christ for sinners. In a heart to come to his sons feast, when others turn of, if not make light of it. accept mee oh lord: Christs number at this sacrament. 6. men and 6 women and my selfe. Lord accept mee.

22. sought god by prayer to blesse my daughters, going forth to schoole: 23. they rid towards Berry. lord blesse them: came well thither praised bee god.

25. sent Mr Bowes an 100^{li}. my desire was if I bought not Morleys land to make up my mony. 270^{li}. I shall I thinke want. 10^{li}. of that summ. and I question whether I shall pay all my debts. by reason of my daughters going out. thy will bee done for it is best.

Ap. 26. Dry cold windie weeke. grasse stirs litle; lord blesse my childrens educacon. god good in the word prayed heartily for all and their relacions, god answer it to all and mine in particular.

May. 1. some days past, rain some warm. some cold. gentle shoures. a cloud brake at Ratlesden in Suffolke and did much mischeife. ours a sweet answer of prayer, heard my children well. Lord bring mee out of all mires that I may praise thy holy name; 2. a litle floud, in my meadow.

May. 3: wett, very afflictive season. all out of course. our hearts not right with god, and no wonder that his eye is no more with us for good. god good in his word, my condicon very much afflicted in a relacon wherin I desire and may say deserve love. but thy will oh lord is best but tis not good for any to doe evill.

5. A day of outward mercy wherin god open springs to refresh mee when dry. I had nigh $3^{li.}$ 10^{s}. given mee. but gods love and care was more than a 1000 times so much to mee, in whom I will trust while I live.

May. 10. Warm, growing weather. god good to mee in the word, my private very afflictive. yet god smiles in some outward things, and sweetens my heart(.) preacht on callings, to my greife my son hath none. lord give him a call(.) baptized a person this day about 20. yeares old god blesse her[1]

13. This day Mrs Colier gave me 5^{li}. having been a great means to setle her estate at the priory. I blesse god for this kindnes, the lord requite her love and doe me good. and mine

14. received a letter from my daughter Mary from Berry. the first letter I received(.) shee and her sister well, god continue it, with his blessing on them and all

May. 17. Good and warm weather. my daughter and her litle one here with us in health, god good in his worship. and word, lord doe mee good by all providence

May. 24. Good weather, many shoures. god good in the health of my relacions, lord lett their soules prosper. some litle peace within us. a favour yett on our outward concernes. gods blessing on ordinances, a heart to serve him under all discouragements.

[1] According to the EC parish register, Sarah Reyner, daughter of John and Mary, was baptized on 10 May, born on 3 March 1654/5.

27. wife returnd safe from Berry(,) children well. praises to my good [god]

May. 31. A good season. god smile on my outward affaires for which I blesse his name oh Lord leave not my children destitute of thy grace. Oh that John might live in thy sight. weather good, my heart desirous to honour god in preaching and to advance him in the refuge and sanctuary of mine and others soules in all troubles by the practice of David at Ziklag.[1]

June. 7. A good weeke to mee in the providences of god, but afflictive in Johns carriage, lord reclaime him if it may bee, the season dry. a good time for the farmer blessed bee my god. the lord was good to mee in his words, sensible how hard it is with many of gods dearest ones.

12. gave Ned Harris. 1[s]. on condicon to be sober, quarter of a yeare and spend only 2[d]. at a sitting, with a great intent and praye to god and counsell for his good. lord second it(,) hee tooke it kindly. said never 1[s]. given to any person with so good an intention.

hay. 13. ind 3 loads hay from Fordmead. lent H. Abbott my bull for his cowes to his ground, who for many years pays mee nothing. I went and offerd it to shew my masters spirit.

June. 14. dry. soft corn wants rain. John followd the haying some dayes well the lord reclaim him(.) god good to mee in his words, lord bee my life in all straits.

15. sent away John Outing my kinsman and with good counsell(.) gave him a coat to keep him warm, mony for his worke to his content, a man came whom I hired this day. god accept and blesse, ind 4 loads hay.

20: a good hay weeke, ind my 2 meadows woundrous well, 14. jaggs in both. blessed bee my god. John followed his worke, oh that grace might enter into his soule.

June. 21. God good to us in our preservacon, many have the measels all spared. god good in his word, affectionate and natural that parents

Mark 25. greatest concern are in their children. 25. Thursday night. M. Grimes came.[2]

June. 28. God good in manifold mercies, he accept mee. season dry. lord refresh the earth(.) wore a new gown and cassocke, my old

[1] 'And when David came to Ziklag, he sent of the spoil unto the elders of Judah, even to his friends, saying, Behold a present for you of the spoil of the enemies of the Lord', 1 Samuel 30: 26.

[2] Probably not a normal servant, since he seems to be of the wealthy Grimes family of Great Tey and may, indeed, be the Mark Grimes gent. of Great Tey who left a will in 1720 (ERO, 102 CR 13).

one still being in use after 35. y. of age. an old freind and a new heart are good.

29. Went to see Mr Pelham. he knew mee(,) died the next day. a choice Saint but faultie in his children. he minded them not to counsell them in sicknes. he was as noteles to good yett minded some litle other things. I commended him to god. lord what is man

July. 2. A choice day of civil concourse mixt with religious at the L. Honywoods whither came the Countesse Dowager of Warwicke.[1] and her sister the L. Renula:[2] goodnes and greatnes sweetly mett in them, I writt to the Countesse who invited mee to Leez

July. 5. A weeke affording some sweete dewes. Jane my daughter came to see mee. god good to us in the words, my god is my life and the strength of my soule; received a letter from the Countess of Warwicke writt with her own hand inviting mee to Leez and promising mee a kind welcome as long as shee liveth.

July. 12. A goodly morning after a somewhat ill season for hay. my wife heard of her lost brood of Turkies, received in my 10 load of wood this weeke god will keepe open his springs for mee, gott most of my hay on cockes. blessed bee god for all(.) my Cosen Rogers with mee, a man of an uneasie spirit but good. lord heale us all. god good to mee in his word, he is the life of my soule.

13. Gave him. 5^{s}. the son of that good man, out of love to thee oh my god

July. 19. stormy weather, corn riseth yett god is where he was to provide for his own(,) god good in the morning, the lord remember mee and mine in mercy. a thunder shoure; a god good in the word, oh how clearly doe I see god able to provide in all condicons of his people, he hath been my helpe and my faith liveth on him.

20. great rains, threating the stronger corn. this morning I went down to H. Abbot who will pay no tithes, but in regard of kindnesses he gave mee 5 ginneys. god be blessed who opened this spring in a rocke. doe it farther for I committ my concernes unto thee

July. 26. Good weather good day. administred the sacrament of the Lords supper. the lord good to mee in his word he is my all, and I will trust in him.

Aug. 2. God good in manifold mercies the season keeps harvest backe. god good in his word lord to thee I give up my selfe, I am thine

[1] Mary Rich, Countess of Warwick (1625–78), diarist; her biography by Charlotte Fell Smith (1901) gives some indication of her influence on the Puritan movement in Essex.

[2] Katherine, married to Arthur Jones, later Viscount Ranelagh, the favourite sister of Mary Rich, Countess of Warwick.

and thou wilt save mee, I have some hopes that my dropsical[1] humour or what it is abateth. lord bee my health

7. almost continual shoures, and now a most louring skie. yett some have got in corn but hazardously. lord my hope is in thee.

Aug. 9. A good day after prayer my heart fixed on gods promise and believe for a harvest season and god gives us hopes, he was good in the word, my soule owne god for mine, encouraged by word and example to liberality

Aug. 16. A good harvest weeke wherin I had in much good and weighty corn and very well with some tithes for which I blesse my good god, the lord good in our healths(,) god good in the day and season, but my heart dull and slothfull in the word.

Aug. 23. A good day. hard corn harvest well over, mine all ind seasonably, blessed bee god, the lord good in his word for which my soule praises him

27. a wondrous wett day causing a small floud, wheat abroad now groweth very much, a carelesnes to neglect our seasons for any thing, all my old corn sold.

Aug. 30: Sad reports of much corn abroad and growing in the feilds; this day a great fog. god in mercy remember us in the season; but blessings to my god who is my soules porcon and subject to no miscarryings ever the same. I will live on thee as such to my soule in christ Jesus. god good to mee in his word, day faire praise to god.

Sept. 4: Mrs Colier and my wife went for London. gods blessing bee always with them. Lord returne her safe. the weather a litle better blessed bee god.

Sept. 6. A lowring skie. lord continue the harvest dayes to us, god good in his word, warning my heart with desires to g(lorify) him, that others also Especially mine might doe so.

9. bled my Haverill steers, god blesse them. Sent to Stanaway for seed rie. this day I gott into my barnes all the corne of my own breeding very well. for which I blesse my good god and bounteaous father. who sprinkles the bloud of christ on my mercies and savours my heart with his love.

sowing: 10. This day I began to sow my rie in Hobstevens. lord give a seed time according to thy covenant. and a blessing promised to him that is thy servant. made an end of sowing that feild rie and wheate die. 18. on which day I received 11^{li}. 8^{s}. 9^{d}. of Mr Cressener for tithes,

[1] Dropsy: a morbid condition characterized by the accumulation of watery fluid in the cavities or connective tissue of the body. NED. It may indicate a number of ailments, kidney failure, cardiac failure, etc.

the greatest sum I ever received at once. he paid grumblingly. yett lord blesse him. and blesse it to mee thy unworthy servant.

19. my wife returnd safe from London. heard of frinds welfare blessed be god

Sept. 20. a good day: praying for Newtons daughter. mine well. make them good(.) the lord good in the season. in the word, make mee rich in good. gathered for a church which I prest, and by example endeavoured in love to god and his worship

22. made an end of harvest very well for which I blesse god.

23. preacht Newtons daughters funeral in the darke. my memory held. I was ill. yet desired to presse young men to bee religious early. god blesse his word.

Sept. 27. A good day, my wife returnd from Bury. our children growing, and indifferent well, but wonderfully dissatisfied with Johns carelessnes and lewdnes. her eye bruised with a fall. blessed bee god for her preservacon, the Parl. prorogued. and Arlingtons house burnt by fire. Sept. 22 at night, to his great losse. lord order all for good.

30. This day afflictive to us in John, who sets himselfe on evill. Lord sett thy selfe to overcome him with thy goodnes, all our endeavours have the sentence of death on them; god good this day in the kindnes of Mrs Harl. and received 10^{li}. 12^{s}. arrears from the priory. a spring opened in a dry place. I will love and serve the lord with a glad heart all my days with all the powers of soule. and outward things, and trust in him at all times, for he never faileth his; Lord give them a bountifull heart and blesse

Oct. 4: Wett. flouding low grounds, skie lowring, god good in all mercies to mee, heard of the health of my children, oh let not an only son bee an outcast, god good in his word, make mee a bountifull lender to thee, in an humble thankfulnes to thee for thy great mercy and goodnes to mee.

Oct. 11. moist weather. wee observe that daily when it answers not our occasions, but how hard we note the failings of our spirits especially to correct them. passions overtooke mee. yet lord they lodge not. let mee bee more watchfull. but let thy grace helpe mee. god good in his word to mee. I will love and secur thee all my dayes

16. ended sowing my home field with wheat, with a good season. with blessing god, and feasting my servants. that my labourers might partake of gods bounty and goodnes to mee.

23. rid towards London, returnd. 29. did the busines I went for well. that day a tenant of one of my parish. Tho Bowes Esq. being Lord

Mayor Viner had his show. the K. and Court dining at Guildhall, my jorny comfortable, all well at home for which I praise the lord.

offer to John before his mother and foure sisters.

John set your selfe to feare god, and bee industrious in my busines. refrain your evill courses, and I will passe by all past offences. setle all my estate on you after your mothers death, and leave you some stocke on the ground and within doores to the value of an 100^{li}. and desire of you, out of your marriage portion but 400^{li}. to provide for my daughters or otherwise to charge my land with so much for their porcions(,) but if you continue your ill courses I shall dispose my land otherwise, and make only a provision for you for your life to put bread in your head.

No: 1: stormy weather. a good sabbath, my soule stired in mee for the advancing my Lord and saviour Jesus Christ. oh lord lett him bee gracious to mee and mine how light soever others make of him

5. kept it a day of praise, my grandchild went homewards well weaned

No. 8: God good in his mercies to mee for which I praise him, oh lord overcome mine in obedience to thee, that they may bee comforts to mee, the weather calme, I preacht up Christ with earnestnes. lord blesse my endeavours.

11. rid to Wittam in coach and returnd. brought Mrs Mary Androws to town to nurse. who is left to my care and wives to looke after it.[1] god blesse it and its nursing. gave 5^{s}. per weeke.

27. brake bread at priory, weather very wintry god good in that houres service. it was to my soule. a sweet lifting up and as a gate in heaven. oh a day in thy courts how sweet

28. Heard our only grandchild. Jane Woodthorp. burnt so as they feared the life thereof(,) Lord if thou watch not(,) all watch in vain. or indeed who is not careles, but our keeper. lord restore her. two buried this night, before thou open the grave for mee, open heaven gate.

No. 29. A good day in the word in pressing after christ. he is mine lord give him to all mine, heard that my grandchild was not dangerously hurt, for which I praise my god, my wife rid thither in a sad wett, thawing day. I and my children comfortably togither.

Dec: 6. God good in the day oh make christ my porcion, sensible of affliction in my relacions

8. rid to L. Honywood, about one Harvy formerly my servant. his case was diabolicall. injections against god and christ, I spake seriously to him, god must better and comfort him

[1] There is no further reference to this infant daughter of Mary Andrews (*née* Harlakenden), thus RJ probably arranged for the child to be wet-nursed in the village.

Dec: 13. God good in his word, a call to pray for two sicke persons which I did heartily, as if in their dying condicon, lord heare, the lord opened my heart to preach christ earnestly. lord accept(.) a very calm winter hitherto.

15. John this day ownd his debauchery, god give him a true sight of it and heale him(.) this day at Mr Eldreds wedding dinner, company civill blessed bee god.

Dec: 20. preacht for Mr Perkins.[1] god good in his providence to mee, and in an earnest desire of soules to doe good. my sermon was my thoughts on Col. 1.12. lord make mee and mine fitt for that glory which thou preparest to my owne.

25. This day I preacht and feasted my tenants plentifully without disorder(.)

Quakers increasd(,) John Garrad their head in our town, building them a meeting place appointing to meet once a (c.o. week) month. I am not over sollicitous of the effect. having seen Abbotts meeting house left, expecting god will appear for his truth, and I hope in perticular for mee in this place who truly desire to feare his name. I doe not determine why; but this morning viz 26. that Garrads wife died, within 6 weeks of the use of that house, I onely desire to feare and tremble, but doe not question the downfall of that sect under the feet of christ and his servants.

Dec: 27. God good in his word. calm. dry chrismas like summer. this 30 it raineth; S. Burton said to have the small pox in our town. god in mercy spare him, and all in this sinfull place of his mercy

Jan. 1. A new yeare, wherin I lookt up to god for his grace and blessing. he sent me mony paid a guift. an old debt. he gave mee a heart to shew love to poore and brother. god own mee and mine, for on thy blessing I depend.

Jan. 3. a good and cleare day for which I blesse god, and for his good word, lord lett thy grace abide with mee continually.

Warme. dry. calme chrismas, grasse springing, herbes budding, birds singing plowes going; a litle rain only in two dayes, viz. Dec. 29. 30: fogge. Jan. 5. 6. no mention of frost. though some dayes cleare sun shining. moon and starrs appearing by night. most persons said never such a Chrismas known in the memory of man yet I suppose. 37: yeares before the like and one said 46 or 47 was such an one.

Jan. 10. The same weather still. heard with joy of our freinds wellfare at London. Mr Ed. Thurston. a swearing dronkard. died at Sr Will.

[1] Thomas Perkins, rector of Colne Engaine 1671–86, when he died. Venn.

Wisemans.[1] occasiond if not in a drunken fitt. whersoever he dances they dance their rounds and hold on their frolicks. lord open mens eyes. the lord good in the word of faith, which I find and believe all things shall worke for good as losse of fathers estate so I know the miscarriage of children I hope John. and I yett hope for him

Jan. 17. preacht morning at Gains Coln. afternoon at home not weary. I praise god for my legs. season dry and cold, a spitt of snow. god good in his word to mee, lord doe mine good by it and all that heare it

Jan. 24 This weeke past. some small frost and rain, but no hindrance to worke(,) this morning cheerful, much troubld with toothake. my heart desirous to doe good this day. praised by god this day wee had our first calfe. and yesterday 2 sheep lambd 3 lambs. all at present well.

John declared for his disobedience no son; I should allow him nothing except he tooke himselfe to bee a servant, yet if he would depart and live in service orderly I would allow him 10li. yearly: if he so walkt as to become gods son. I should yett own him for mine.

Jan. 26. 74.—59.

Sensible this day ended my 58. and begun my 59 yeare. lord bee good to mee in this and all that are to come. sweet thought of christ this daye(.) my wife in a great pett, and my heart in great tendernes for her.

Jan. 31. Weather very calme though with some litle frost and raine.

Feb. 4. entertaind divers freinds. Mr W. H. mad conceit of marrying, lord make me serious and blesse mee and mine

Feb. 7. weather cold windy and drie. god good in our health, when the smal pox is in many families and towns about. god still preserve us. arowsed my heart to doe good to soules this day. blesse lord thy word. sensible my dayes steale away as a post; news of putting the laws in execucion against papists and nonconformists. lord command thy laws into our heart against sin. I count the English of *Christ*(.) the parl. shall sit in April, and bee cajold to give a great taxe. observe.

Feb. 9. It began to snow very much; weather, calm. Cold frostie to Feb. 24. then misling. god good to mee in his bounteous provisions. Jo. Finchs wife died of a dropsie strangely. suddenly in a manner. lord

[1] Probably son of Sir Thomas Wiseman of Rivenhall; M.P. for Maldon 1677–9, and died 1688. Venn.

bee the god of my health; and preserve mee from all evill for I am thy dedicated one.

Feb. 28. A moderate time. dry frostie. yet this day rain. god good to mee in many mercies. yet heard my children ill at Lexden lord preserve them. sett my selfe on the subject of heart ingagement. bring mine owne to mee. very sensible of the workings of my inward corruptions.

March. 7. weeke past cold, wett. god good in his word, all mine well, my heart desirous to doe god service and helpe the poore which are in great wants. made Mr W. Harlakendens will who is very sensible. but scarce likely to live.

18. Mr W. Harlakenden died. a good man. an illnes in his feet from his running abroad brought the madnes out of his head, but he recovered no great use of his reason spirituall or natural, only on discourse, he savoured of both. heard hopefully of my daughter Woodthorp. for which I blesse my god.

19. a most bitter snowing, driving morning. wee buried W. H. I observd my spirit hopeles in prayer for him but ful of hope for my daughter

27. buried W. Hatchs son in law. who taking horse by the grave rid to Colchester and found his own daughter on the beir for the grave. lord sanctifie all to us.

March. 28. God good in his word. prest to the Lords supper one of White Colne offered to receive next day; lord convince all of duty(.) a lovely season(.) my daughter Jane hopefully upward. lord blesse mee and all mine

31. April. 1. wett weather hindring seed time, I am involved in troubles for other mens businesse. if the lord please to bring mee cleare of thes, as I trust he will. I will not engage while I live but in my own and childrens concernes. Mrs Colier came safe to Colne for which I praise god.

Ap. 4. A cheerful morning. Lord my heart looks up to thee in christ with delight. my hourly joy is fixed in thee, and thou art my joy in my many troubles, my soule glories in a crucified christ, whose dying love I remember with greatest thankfulnes. gave the sacrament. only 15 present wherof 3 strangers. lord I prest duty with all earnestnes, accept mee Lord, though thy word, and servant bee not accepted

Ap: 11: A cold time with the wind, which keeps the spring backe though the winter was mild and dry. I sew some white pease die. 10: and 9. ended sowing Brockhole and ten acres next the road with barly.

lord god prosper thy servants labour. who trusts in thee for all and desires to lay out himself for thee. our family temper unlovely(.) lord heale all for thy mercy sake

Ap. 18. great appearances of a dry summer. god good in his word, in his mercies to mee. oh remember us in soule blessings, wee serve god in peace when others are hurried about by informers.

Ap. 25. My sweld leg brake, which at first occasiond thoughts as to sorenes, gangrening by the blacknes of it, and following of the humour. but I blesse god I know it is my father, and he will not doe only what he pleaseth but what is best for mee(.) many hearing this day, whom I prest to particular covenanting with god, the lord accept mee and mine in that bond through the beloved one. my ill leg sweld very much, with some pain, stiffnes and a kind of numnes in the former part of both my feet as I have had formerly; it had great influence on my thoughts, god in mercy stood between mee and the thoughts of death and the feares of it, my leg issued a litle, I applied a searcloth,[1] it run but not much. it broke at a blacke spott. the like is lower, on my inward knocle(,) my wife applied a large roule to my leg of bole arnimake[2][ ] to dry and abate the humour. I praise god my mind is composed on his good will.

May. 2. A dewing morning. cold yet somewhat warmer than formerly. god good to mee in his word, pressing persons to gett wisedom, above all things give it to mee

May. 9. wee have had some small shoures for which god bee praised(.) this day god good to mee in his word, my leg ill, but I dare not say worse.

May. 16. my leg continues, sweld, broken and gently issuing. the lord bee health to mee, my spirit submissive and quiet under gods good pleasure. desirous to honour god and leaving all to him

17. applied a poultis of red rose leaves and milke. 18. used Tabors pills[3] they purgd but twice, I almost apprehend its not a setled humour. (c.o. *lost*) the scurvy. but humour which I hope will weare away.

[1] Cerecloth or serecloth: a cloth smeared or impregnated with wax or other matter; a poultice. As the *Compleat Housewife* put it (p. 333), it 'is good for any pain, swelling, or bruise'.

[2] Bole armoniac or Armenian bole: a pale red-coloured earth from Armenia, used medicinally. NED.

[3] Pills prescribed by Dr. Talbor, who treated RJ on 7 June. Probably Sir Robert Talbor, author of *Pyretologia, a rational account of the cure of agues* (1672) and *The English Remedy: or, Talbor's wonderful secret for cureing of agues and feavers* (1682). Talbor was the first Englishman to work out the method of using quinine to cure agues, and thus RJ's 'pills' may well have contained this drug.

May. 23. Summer weather, the blacknes and swelling of my legg abates, but lord when shall corruption be mortified in our hearts. how sensible of outward pains, lord evill inwards afflicts also. help in all estates. for on thee I stay my selfe; god good in his word lord stocke mee and mine with true wisedom.

25. 26. Very instrumentall to bring on the match between Mr Marryon son of Braintree and Rose Abutt of Colne, their fathers seemd satisfied with mee on both sides. god prosper it. I reflect on the providence of god to him in his children. with my afflictions. I cannot say thou never bearest rule over them. he is an untoward Quaker. but Lord I am thine and subscribe with my hand I am thine in Christ Jesus. I grudge not. I am not worthy what I enjoy—oh why is my son a shame of youth. my soules greife. and thy trouble, oh turn to mee and bee gracious, and stir up my heart and help mee to win them

May. 30. A fine day after many sweet dews, the lord good to mee in his word, yett his hand against mee in John and in my leg. I own thy rod oh lord and kisse it, intreating thee to shew mee favour in all things, tis to thee I committ my soule. Many freinds with us. 8. of us at night broke bread at the priory. god bee with us in all for good.

June. 2. My wife with our 2 daughters Mary and Elizabeth went for London to Hackney school,[1] god blesse them in their educacion both for soule and body. my wife returnd well. 5. that day Capt. Brag and Mrs Colier agreed their match as to the main.

June. 6. a comfortable season after the dewes, god in mercy remember mee in my health(.) afflicted in John, who abounds in his evill. yett I will hope in my god; god good in his word, the lord make me carefull to gett and improve true wisedom.

sue. 7. on Monday Dr Talbor made an issue on mee in order to the cure of my leg, lord blesse it and restore mee to my perfect health. read Dr Owen of Mortif.[2] I blesse god for some passages therin

June. 13. Lowring weather, god give us an hay season, god good in his word, lord direct mee in my affliction state what to doe and rescue mee out of it, for thy name sake; the parliament prorogued. June. 9. to Oct. 13. it prevented the Test. it was said by the King the fewd between the houses was from the enemies of the King and Church of England the commons voted they knew not of any such thing, it

[1] Possibly the same school as that to which Sir John Bramston had sent his two eldest daughters in February 1648, when it was run by Mrs. Salmon. *Autobiography of Sir John Bramston*, (ed.) T. W. Bramston, Camden Soc., xxxii (1845), p. 108.

[2] John Owen, *Of the Mortification of Sinne in Believers* (1656).

arose about an appeale to the Lords in the case of Sir. J. Fagge a member of the commons

16. contracted Captain Bragg and Mrs Colier. lord blesse them.

June. 20. A wett season. god good in his word, my leg ill, but I have light in my spirit that god will not only recover mee to my health, but also doe my soule good by it, and I shall praise him.

June. 27: very stormy cold weather, god in mercy blesse his word to mee and mine. prayed heartily for seasonable weather. Mrs Colier gone from Colne.

July. 1. The weather gave hopes. for rain and cold a sad time, yett it made no floud god bee praised. corn rose again, rie being gappie. and feard wheat setts ill. yett there is no feare of gods failing his creatures, much more his children, if they faile not him; god heard prayer in the season. lord heare it for John and the rest of mine.

July. 4. A hott day. married a servant, god good to mee in his word, many hearing lord catch some and deliver them from the power of evill.

July. 11. a curious hay weeke after wett, cutt and ind my fordmead, god good to mee in his word, intend for Tunbridge(,) god in mercy bee my phisitian(,) the waters are his prepared phisicke. the small pox next doore to my house, god preserve mee

July. 12. sett out for Tunbridge wells. whither I came. 13. begun to drinke. 9. 8 ounce glasses. the. 14. I drunke. 15 glasses and so continued from. 17. to Aug. 1. inclusive(.) wee came thence Aug: 4. and so home. Aug: 12. god merciful to mee in my jorney. the waters passing well with mee, and good to mine in my absence for which his name bee praised; and yett my minde was very unduely imployed to my great greife; the 10. Mrs Colier married Mr Brage. he gave mee 10 peices of old gold.

Aug. 15. A very wett day, corn laid(,) the threating was great. all against us. but the mercy and faithfulnes of god in his promise, which I heartily publique pleaded. and god gave a wonderfull good season(.) I ind my corn well and some tith. before it raind. 20. at night. the. 21. 22. faire. for which I intend to praise god and for his mercies to this place. in the small poxe wherof only a woman by neglect and her child died.

Sept. 5. A harvest beyond expectation I beleive I lost not above one houres worke in 3 weeks. praise the lord for this answer of prayer, bee good to all mine oh my god

Sept. 12. A bad hop yeare. god good in his word. wetting weather. harvest not in for as much as corn not yet ripe. god good in our towns health. smal pox not

16. Thursday begun to sow mislain in my feild Pitchers god prosper it. the lord sow his grace in my heart and of my children. etc. and make it grow increse more

17. A dangerous fire, mercifully prevented, god used mee an instrument, a hazard on my face from a bush. lord in mercy preserve mee for my care is nothing.

18. Made an end of my own harvest only 3 small parcels of tiths abroad ind them well, quietly. for which I praise my good god.

Sept. 19. Dry after shews of raine. a blessing in the sabbath, not only for rest but the sweet call in to delight in god.

25. Sew part of Pitchers with misl. 1. day in Readings. 1. in Sawyers and both those feilds in. 9 days about. 11. acres. the short land in readings wett. it raining gently this afternoon

Sept. 26. God good in his preservations. a neighbours cow die suddenly as soon as milkt. lord I daily put all I have under thy care and blessing watch over mee for in thee is my hope. esp. lord let my soule and the soules of mine live in thy sight(.) a good morning after a good rain, the lord good to mee in his word, awaking mee more against evill, lord make mee a conquerour in thy strength(,) coruption will not let mee. but oh my strong redeemer destroy it. Heard Northampton was burnt down to the ground about 800 houses; sad fire but not so

28. rid to Lexden. 29. to oister pits. 30 returnd not well. Oct. 2. I tooke pills which wrought but a litle. my shooting pains in my leg are abated. tis mercy all troubles are not continued yea multiplied.

Oct: 7. rid to visitacon(.) heard of our Bishops[1] sicknes and death. at 84. a quiet man to mee. god in mercy send us one that may bee a comfort to us. 8. at Royden.[2] 10. preacht a(t) Layham a great audience. 12. came home all safe praisd bee god. others have their troubles teach mee content(.) a wonderfull dry time.

Oct. 17. drought continues. great fears of our poor rising up and down our contry. esp. those that belong to the wool trade: just at the Parl. meeting. said no troubles any where else god allay them. one Rugles of this parish. a quaker. a rude fellow. disobedient to his mother sent to the house of correction. Lord watch over our publique peace. sett myselfe to sanctify this sabbath, lord accept mee, and doe me and mine good and doe good by mee.

at Nayland etc. stormes, wind. two wenels of mine died of the

[1] Humphrey Henchman, Bishop of London 1663–75, dying on 7 October of that year, aged 83. In both Venn and Foster.

[2] Captain Brag, married into the Harlakendens, owned some property at Royden, now called Rayden in Suffolk. Probert.

murrain. lord spare the rest(.) my leg somewhat painful. the two Abbuts how hot and high against one another, this day. 30. very cheerly.

Oct. 31. Heathful, dry calm weather. god good in his word and our publique peace.

No: 5. dry after shoures, preacht from Mic. 6.5. now. after 700 yeares remember a mercy. gave a narrative of the plot. at night a sad fire in the street two houses of Pain my workman and having fellow burnt. a great wind, yet no farther hurt. blessed bee god.

No. 7. preacht at Markshall. 8. rid to London. 9. did my Ladies busines with satisfaction returnd home the 11. god be praised well except a cold, which is general at London and on our coasts. Sells sealed a bond for a 100^{li}. to pay my Ladie. 12. came to Colne safe. 13.

No. 14. A lovely day. dry as summer. god good in his word my heart desirous to doe good to all

25. dry frostie and cleare. god sadly afflicts us with the smal pox in one family. the lord spare us. good in his word, make it good to all mine esp. John.

No. 28. a summers day after sweet rain. 27. god good in his word. give mee a gospel spirit. god good in our place. coughs common(.) parliament prorogued to Feb. 76.

Dec: 5. warm. calm. dry. god good in his word. the lord make mee sensible of my emptines as his dear Saints doe. news of a parliament. the smal pox in another house at the mill. lord spare for mercy sake.

Dec: 12. dry weather with onely now and then a small shoure. god good in his word, his mercie for sence and body. the smal pox stops at present. god stop it in much mercy.

Dec: 19. shoures but open warm weather. god good to us in our health. Hatch's family abroad againe the lord preserve all. god good in his word that it may bee a blessing to us all and mine in special.

25. The sun rose gloriously. discernd it at my wash place window, at the side of the end of Amies house. the dayes visibly lengthned. god give mee and mine an interest in that Christ whose incarnation wee remember with thankfulness open. dry. though windie. no frost hitherto(.) preacht with affection, a smal company present. all shops open. trade goeth. religion sad

December. 26. A good day. god good in his word, my condicon unquiet at home. but peace within.

28. reported the King dead among mean people. I know such passages in some histories were designed forerunnings of the same.

Jan: 16. winterly weather about 10 dayes. my leg runs waterish. god in mercy preserve my health, well in my body. lord bee good in thy holy day.

18. report again of the Kings death. lord preserve his life for good.

23. open moist weather. my leg runs. sadly. painful. healing is thy blessing thou hast and wilt doe it. god good in his word to mee my soule trusteth in thee

Jan. 26. sensible this entred my. 60. yeare. I grow an old man. my leg swels hard on the calfe and so continueth in mornings. god fitt mee for all providences(.) the weather is cheerfull this Feb. 1. god good to mee. oh bee good to mine.

Feb: 5. In the morning a litle rubbing my leg, it bled exceedingly above the sore place. my leg asswaged thereupon. it bled a quart as my wife thought, blackish and cloddered,[1]

F. 6. Very well. leg much asswaged. wett. god good in the morning providence. my soules desire being to awake to and live with him: god good in the worke of the day, my soule much with god in it, some say my leg will swell after bleeding very much

Feb. 13. A warm day. open weather, springing, my leg painfull in the instep. god good to mee in his word, help me to live on thy truth in the promise for my children. oh lord my soul wrestles with thee give strength to prevaile.

Feb. 20. weather dry and cold. leg not so much sweld as formerly. it heals not. sometimes painfull. drest but seldome. my heart full of troubles from my family, and somewhat from my debts, and cumbers. god is my joy, and he I hope will order all for good(.) this day my heart alarmes itselfe to delight in god and his wayes my only comfort(.) a wonderfull decay of trade and so of traders, corn cheape. hard with poore for want of worke and rich for want of mony: a fire upland burning down a small cottage of Henry Abbott.

Feb. 27: Summer weather, dry and cleare only colder. saw blowne blackethorne, god good to mee in his word, he in mercy accept mee and mine: likely to find an hard time against the nonconformists upon a trouble at Ipswich where was the first stirre at the Scotch troubles. dry cleare, calme. but coole weather

March. 5. Weather good. my pain is a litle in hip, and instepp. but not so much in my leg god bee blessed for all goodnes, my heart is desirous to please god this day, and doe good to soules, own my desires and endeavours.

[1] Cloddered: clotted, run together into clots, coagulate. SOED.

March. 12. cold, wind and dry to admiracon, god good to mee in his word, my heart sensible of its backwardnes to good, heale all in mee.

March. 19. a gentle dewing day: god was good to mee in his word, citizens broake(,) a sad ruinous day in England. the lord good in our health, my instep painfull.

23. John in danger of a killing mischeife by Toller, his dronken comrade(.) lord I feare for him. doe thou restrain him. oh lord renew him.

March. 1676.

26. Fine dewes some dayes. god awakened my heart to bee with him this day in all the duties therof. the sacrament of remembrance especially. 15 of us received. Mr Harlakenden offering to stay, and yet goe I told him in the sincerity of my heart, that before his illnes he was a meet receiver and though now troubled I judgd his estate as thine and would not reject him. his wife stayd with him. I blesse god for their presence: god good in the word, lord own mee and mine.

Ap. 2. Dry and coole. god good in his word, freinds with mee at a good Turky. I delighted to eate the good creature with them, blessing my good god.

3. At night a child was left in my barne. gods providence I hope will find us out the mother that left it. on the 10th. following the father came and fetcht it away, my wife hastening it hence. our townsmen seemed angry(,) as minding to punish the father

7. at visitacon, our mony paid(,) all peace, yet some contrary thoughts were(.) I rid to Roydon. preacht at Layham. at Dedham. ap. 11. baptized Dol Androws. returnd safe. 13. 14. sweet showre. god good in my jorney.

Ap: 16. Good shourie weather. giving hopes to the crop. the King past from Newmarket by Hiningham to Newhal. and so London. it was thought all our county forces should have mett. but did not. god good to mee in the day and in his worke.

Ap. 23 God good to mee in manifold outward mercies, my affliction in Johns debauchednes is a thorne in my side. lord thou canst pull it out. the weather drie and cold, corn forward but not grasse. god good in his word. my legge very painfull.

Ap. 30. afore day Jonathan called my wife to her daughter. after I dreamd shee told mee her husband was dead. I awakened with wonder. weather dry and hot god good in his word, lett mercy oh lord watch over mee for good.

May. 3. did my busines at Tain. fires and dangers in several places. god preserve mee. on 1. of May. Mr Ludgater[1] had a dangerous fall. his brother that day drownd. lord let mercy and truth preserve mee.

May. 7. Weather dry, hot sometime windy. grasse burns away on hot grounds. god good in his word, oh how mindles is England of her sins or miseries. said the Emperor is dead. he is sonles and the last of that branch. if so it wilbee hard to choose an Austrian. and if not, it will occasion a great change in Europe.

May. 14. God good in his word, several small shoures. 16. a boy dischardging a pistol in the street at a dog, shott a man in his wrist to great hazard: 18. a muster of our County forces, lovely shoures; the Emperor sicke but not dead as reported.

May. 21. God good in his mercies(.) heard of the death of some relacons. blessed bee god spare mine. discourst a father of an undutiful son, experience maketh him pitty. lord there is I praise an inwardnes therein; toucht, and grasps to pitty others evil(.) god good in the word, dries but cold. lord make mee holy and fruitfull.

26. a dismal fire in Southwarke lord thou cuttest England short, many hundred houses burnt, in the cheife street. there was treachery and firing. god thinke on us.

May. 28. God gave us sweet shoures even satisfying the earth. god good in his word(,) heare prayers lord for my relacions and lett them live in thy sight.

June. 4. Heard our litle grandchild Mary not well lord spare and sanctifie, trouble in my relacons. but lord I have peace in the(e), calme in my heart, and let my soule lie at rest. windie and drying. 3 buried in our town in 24 houres. god good in his word. my desire to call persons to use their time for repentance and fruite, least god cutt down for cumbergrounds.[2]

June. 18. for many dayes past. weather very hot. my leg in that heat swealt on the shin about the calf. read fiery as if it would have come to an head. it abated over 24 houres, with a white bread poultis. it indangered a feavour(,) god in mercy teach mee to prosper by his dealings, troubles in the carelesnes of my children. god in mercy sanctifie them and make them his.

[1] John Ludgater, schoolmaster at Kelvedon, Essex, in 1664, ordained priest in 1690 and from then to 1710, when he died, vicar of EC. Venn. Schoolmaster of EC from at least 3 December 1677, at which point RJ comments on the mastership.

[2] Cumber-ground: a thing or (especially) a person that uselessly cumbers the ground; a useless or unprofitable occupant of a position. NED.

June. 25: Hot. harms by thunder in several places and by fire, I am preserved to god bee all the praise, the french prosper. god in mercy blesse the word to mee and mine.

July. 2. good shoures, god good to mee in outward mercies. yett I have my afflictions but they learn mee meeknes. submission, and I hope all shall turn to good. god good in his word, mens minds discomposed in the times with fears of french papists

July. 9. Very wett weather. yet god is the same to preserve our crop. heard of Mr Shirleys death at London hastned by a son of disobedience. lord I thanke thee for thy support under all the trouble and carlesnes of my family. god good in his word

15. Swithins wett, especially at night. but tis god rules the shoures

July. 16. God good in manifold mercies harvest ripens. lord lett thy word bring forth truthe in my soules perfection.

18. began harvest. 22. some freinds and harvest men with mee at a [plentifull dinner. drisling weather.]

[July. 23. a lovely morning after raine.] god good in his manifold mercies my old Tutor preacht for mee, god good in his word. thunder and shoures.

July. 30. a lovely harvest weeke. I ind most of my hard corn tithes. and some of my white oats: my leg very painful hindring my rest. god good in his word to mee. a sweet comfort to my soule.

Aug. 2. through gods goodnes my 2 horses and wagon escaped a great danger in Coes pond. hired a servant god blesse him to us.

Aug: 5. Satturday night ind all my own harvest, and most of my tith in 17. dayes not a jagge ill. a good and plentiful harvest. I was able to direct and looke after my busines. John in some order, my heart in frame. not troubled nor vain nor having but thankful contented, this is gods goodnes and for all I praise him and dedicate myselfe and my all to his service.

Aug: 6. God good in the morning up early to seeke and serve him; prest fruitfulnes lord make mee and mine so, glorifying of thee.

Aug. 13: The drought continues. cooler. god good in his wayes. which yett are afflictive on my daughter Jane. my leg. yet good as letting mee experimentally find all things are empty but himselfe. there is an infinitenes of good and perfection(.) god good to mee in the day, lord bring and keepe my heart in a due frame.

Aug. 20: Drought continues. the disorders of my family doleful. lord helpe mee with patience to weare out my dayes: some harvest still abroad. god good in the mercies of the dayes to my soule: saw some strange tempers in men.

23. finisht my tith harvest. not one jagge of corn wett(,) god bee praised
24. likely to raine. but not. rid to Janes. better then shee was. returnd safe god bee praised for my mercies and spirit in my observacon on others.

Sept. 2. a young man Mr Smith from London proffered his love to my daughter Mary shee refused him, as shee had formerly done another of good estate. he went away. Sept. 5. very sorrowfull. most of our affections much to him.

4. with the Countess of Warwicke at Markshall, god gave mee favour and wisedome there. most noted Mr Jessops absurd carriage.

5. at night, and in morning til neare noone, gentle comfortable shoures

Sept: 10. Weather dry and coole. my eldest sister Dorothy with us(.) George Cressener died. lord awaken his young companions. god good in his word. the lord make mee and mine watchful against sin.

13. brother Worral went from us. I sent him not away empty. god
Sew: prosper him(.) on the. 12. I began to sow in Bridgmans: dry, but wett much at night 13. sew. 14. 15. in morning much wett fell. that was the farther side of litle pitchers, ended all that. Sept. 30. in 15. dayes, sew. oct: 12. 13. 14. 16. 17. 18 and then ended my own dry and well.

Mr Cressener buried his eldest son. lord doe young men good by it

Sept. 17. a good after rain, god good to mee in the word, my earnest desire to win soules to god, and withhold them from reproaching god.

19. This day wee had a parochial visitacon,[1] somethings complaind of. as the want of a surplice, in other things it was well. god will secure mee against troubles, I trust. my old club horse drownd this day.

Sept. 24: Goodly weather. oh for a good seed time in hearts, that evill may not abound in us, my family still administers cause of sorrow, but god shall turne all to good.

25. a day of busines, which I dispatcht with content. and comfort. god I may say was in the quiet of it. Abbutt gave mee his part in the pied steere; god prosper all. at night Mr Shirley.[2] made an offer of his service and love to Mary, god direct that affaire.

Oct. 1. God good in his word, my soule longed to see conversion worke. said the French tooke a ship of ours, worth. 100 ^{mli}. in the mouth of the river(.) the season good, the season of grace is my comfort that I have taken it, lord give it to mine.

[1] There is no archdeaconry visitation for this date. There is one, however, on 27 April 1677 which RJ does not mention in the Diary: 'send out a monition for Mr Josselin to appear at the next courte to certifie that he does read all the divine services and to make a declaration that he is willing to weare the surplice if there be any' (ERO, D/ACV/7).

[2] James Shirley, eldest son of the Revd. James Shirley (for whom, see p. 515, n. 1 above).

3. my sister Dorothy went from mee, wee parted in much kindnes. I sent them not empty away. I was much in my thoughts to buy the Newhouse lands in Colne, but I found Mr Eldred was backward. at night Mr Shirly came to Mary, which seemd a speaking providence to the contrary. my wife was ill pleasd with it. I submitt to god.

Oct. 8. 7. received a kind present from London from Mr Smith. awakt with a great desire to doe god some special service in my Sabbath worke. lord prosper mee(.) ground satisfying raines. oh but the dew of grace bee on mine for good. some places preacht not it was so wett, I intermitted not.

Oct: 15. God good in raising mee with prayers to doe him service and soules good(.) sew some dayes last weeke. lord blesse all, my son the seat of drunkennes(,) oh lord can thy spirit ever come to delight in him. oh lord doe. a great deliverance of the priory from firing by Mr Bowes boy with a candle at the racke firing the hay, the boy in beere, oh lord watch over us for good.

18. made an end of sowing my wheat in Mrs Brages ground by her house. seed time good lord send a good crop. I have sown about 25. acres.

Oct. 22. good dry weather. god good to mee oh bee good in the soule concernes of mee(,) oh lord direct mine to live with thee in thy feare.

Oct. 29. weather good. my soule praiseth god for the continuance of his goodnes over all I have. lord direct the path of mine into thy feare and favour. desirous to serve god in this his holy day, and doe good. Move us lord with thy blessing and presence. advised with a surgeon for my leg, but my hope is in god I use him lord as thy means, and looke up to the(e) alone for a blessing, which thy spirit prompts my heart to expect, from thy mercies in my saviour

30. tooke pills for my legge. the lord blesse them to mee.
ended a busines between Hatch and Newton, being a wilfull unkindly suite

Nov. 4: preserved in my jorneys, and in a dangerous fall on the priory planks. blessed be god. there was one with mee had no hurt. I was bruisd. I had a thought, lord why fell this arrow not on him. lord twas thy pleasure. perhaps I had more sense of the mercy. perhaps to abate pride. I was not better than he. why should god looke on mee(,) mercy his own he may bestow it where he pleaseth.

No. 5. a desire to speake something against popery. a wett Sabbath morning, the weather likely to bee winter, but its a mercy for water is wanting.

No. 12. A cheerfull day. my leg very ill, the sore increaseth, yet my heart hopeth in my god, that he will be health to my bones, and restore mee to perfect soundnes that I may praise him with joy, lord I humble my soule and kisse thy rod, oh lett mee see thy goodnes to mee in the land of the living. god good in the word. Edward Abbott a quaker for many yeares, last day, and this was attending on the word publiquely.

13. The L. Honywood sent for mee. the businesses shee intended came not to mee, but I ended matters between her and Mr Livermore[1] and her Tenant Balls about tiths to all contents. blessed bee god. wherin I observe the headie mistakes of persons

16. Heard one Mills about Bewers drinking and going home fell into a ditch and found dead. lord awaken sinners by such providences; at night my wife on some discontent which I know not. would not assist mee in dressing my poore leg, Mary did, my heart taxd in with david, the lord hath bid her: it may bee he will the more helpe. John out and so all night. I feare a ruine on his body as well as soule lord preserve thes afflictions from thee oh god. Ile be quiet lord doe thou helpe.

Nov: 19. A cold frostie day. god good to mee in outward mercies. I hope in him for my legg and good by it, he is my god, and I will trust in him. his word was good.

20. rid again to my surgeon. Jane ill. god in mercy raise up her heart to trust him

No. 26. frost continueth, god good in his word(.) received from Mr Bowes Pierson on the Creed[2] a booke worth 10^{s}. I accept his love. god return it 27. Paying John 8^{s}. and chardging him not to be an ill housband, that night he lay out,

Dec: 3. God good in his word, my spirit and affaires. this weeke John wholly out in his filthy courses, I am resolved to leave him to thee oh god, only I will pray for him. the weather frostie after some thawing fogs.

Dec. 10. After a tedious cold frostie season, a wonderfull snow out of the North, I gott down to church, never so few there on any lords day. it was the generally deepest that I ever saw to my best memory. I preacht twice. and so will by gods helpe while I can; god good to mee in his word. received my wole home, the last part,

12. snew again at night. it was the deepest snow I ever remembred

[1] John Livermore, rector of Markshall 1674–1718, when he died. Venn.

[2] John Pearson (1613–86), Bishop of Chester, *An Exposition of the Creed* (1659). DNB.

lying about knee high of a man every where without any great drifts.

Dec: 17. Tedious cold and snow, lord warm our hearts in the sense of thy love and with kindnes to one another, I have some hope of my leg healing, but *went.* I looke up to my god I am perswaded of it, lord looke after thy glory in the world,

19. Set a part this day with my familie to humble my soule before god for our sins to seeke his direction for and blessing on us and ours: the speciall occasion Johns ill housbandry: and Eliz. offer of a young man from London who is coming down, and shee s[ee]ms very averse it. lord in the Christ of god, thy beloved one I expect [ ] and blessings. I read in course in morning Mic: 4. passages therein comfort [passages in] altering things from bad to good, lord make them so among mine. I first pro[posd] a duty to looke up to direction from god. Ezra: 8.21. who hath the casting our lott. Is. 34.17 then I commended all to god in prayer: if god cast your lot rest in it. and to know it. observe. Pro. 3.6. own god and he wil dwell therein Psal. 32.8. now gods direction is by our parents for children. Eph. 6.1.2.3. its right. answer that in Ezra rest in a housbands house: Ruth. 1.9. thats done when both bring gods feare. mutual love and industrious prudence, the way is by parents provision and children following their counsell as Ab. tooke a wife for Isaac. whom he tooke and loved. Gen. 24. and thus god comforts in losses in one another; Ruth shee followes Naomis counsel and all well. though the counsel at the barnfloure seemd strange. let mee shew you an instance of a headie marriage in Sampson. it turnd to his death(,) against his parents advice he would marry etc. god casts your lot in parents choice Exod. 2.19.21. Numbers. 30. vows to god alloud or disalloud by parents other wise sad(,) therefore my children receive this counsel as gods not mine. tis mine because gods and so its gods being mine, to father that is to counsel which wilbee your crown as theirs. 1. Thes. 2.13. it will effectually worke obedience and therefore hear him. pro. 23.22. pro. 8.9. I am perswaded a blessing will follow this counsel even read Is. 55.3. your soules shall live; and I hope god will give an answer of peace(,) I wilbe his and looke up. and my god shall speake peace, I praid thrice with them. their mother gave them the same advice. god in mercy give them his blessing.

23. Mr Smith[1] came safe: 24. it thawd and presently frost again. god

[1] Gilbert Smith of St. Martin's in the Fields, 'colourman' (one who deals in paints, NED), who subsequently married RJ's daughter Elizabeth.

good in the word my desires to advance the name of christ in the worke. so 25. Mrs Harlakenden sicke in the 89. yeare. gives us hope of recovery a gracious answer of prayer. 27. a greivous loosenes, lord bee my helpe for I am thine. invited our poore tenants this day.

29. Mr Smith returnd towards London satisfied in his jorney with hopes of my Elizabeths love. god seen in inclining her heart, which was very awkward at first. my affections drawn from the hopes his sobrietie and good nature gave(,) that grace and industry might meet to make him a good housband(,) for his estate was small. I had two lambs lived. lost my two first. god provide for mee. the winter very hard.

Dec: 30. cold and snow continueth. god good in his word of salvacon by ☞ christ, invited a poore widow to dine with mee, and so shall some that I find hearing the word.

Jan. 3. 4. 5. a very pleasant day. shining but windie yet warm. the snow and frost which had continued of and on not wholly out of the ground since about October. 24; passing very gently and mildly; the ice and waters not so tedious as some persons apprehended. oh lord inherite our praises. sent some presents to friends

Jan. 7. warm and windie, ponds filling, ice almost melt. in all thes changes the hearts and vices of men the same. oh lord new hearts for new years. I was very ill die. 6. and at night. lord bee my porcon. heard of the illnes of Mr W. Eldreds eyes, lord in mercy sanctifie all providences to us.

9. ill my selfe. called up with newes of a 2^{d} bullocks death, I read in course Hab. 3. god is my trust. I will serve him, and he shall and will provide for me(.) This. 10. day about 1 of clocke I had of my ☞ selfe a small stoole; not having had that benefit of nature since the fift in the morning. god bee blessed for the hope of my better ease and quiet

Jan. 14. after stormes of rain and winde. this morning faire and cleare, serenity is above and in a heavenly heart. storms and troubles attend earth. and earthy low spirits.

Jan. 21. a lovely day, though cold(,) the earth satisfied with rain. god good to mee in his word, my health in body seems impaired, lord let my soule be lively

1676. Jan. 26. 60. 61. enters

Sensible this day ends my 60. and enters my 61. wherin I begun with thoughts of god who bespeake might to seeke his grace and my inward thought was with long life he would satisfie mee and shew mee his salvacon, oh lett mee see peace in Israel. I renewe all my ingagements to *love* the Lord, and to serve him and this day so seeke his grace in Christ Jesus, to strengthen me therto.

Feb. 5. I was at Markshall and preacht there die. 4. god good in several particulars to mee, the lord own mee as his and blesse mine in Christ Jesus.

Feb. 10. The snow covered the ground, and although the weather was often open that wee stird our plowes yet the frost never fully out of the ground(.) my heart desireth to do god some service in the worke of this day. god was present with mee with life and sweetnes to my soule in the delivery of the word. the Chancellor Finch was robd of mace and purse.

Feb: 18. A very wett season. a troublesome life with my relacons, whose spirit is too high for their estates and condicon, the lord make my heart as low as the dust, and lett thy blessing and grace bee sufficient.

Feb: 26. A wonderfull wett season, in which Mr Smith came down to us. this morning is very cheerfull, god remember us for good; god good to mee in the word this day, perswading me am not sinles. nor I hope saviourlesse:

28. A lovely day, wherin I made all good offers possible to John, god in mercy bend his heart to good. all my children with me(.) Mr Smith parted with good comfort and content.

March. 4: Bitter winde frost, while in vain musings and troubled, one brought mee a sheepe dead. god sanctifie all providences, doe mee good and make mee cleane and spiritual. god good to mee in his word, the Court partie prevaile in Parliament. god bee our defence, my dreams were as I now find it,

6: The night before I found I had a cold, sneezing much which continues this day, with a great pose(,) the like I had not since my sicknes nor of any yeares before

March: 11: Wett weather. my minde out of frame bring it lord to thy minde in all things; 12. present to adjust the Potters busines whose daughters housbands married them without porcons, and yet were willing to stay till after his death six and twelvemonths, I never saw such kindnes to father in law. and his second wife: 13. a considerable snow, rain. 14 rain and floud

March: 18. gloomy weather, yett god will command his loving kindnes for us, even in the season and I will trust and hope in his mercy. I reach of a new heart lord lett mee not live an old one, helpe mee to strive for newnes of spirit. great numbers of hearers from all places round about us. god blesse his word.

24: a great floud this day, one before this weeke, hindring sowing barly.
1677 the moon changed 6. in the morning. about 3 hours after it began to fogge and about 4 raind so hard that this morning the floud high and rain continueth.

March: 25. dry and cold with winde. god good to mee in his word. Lord renew my heart

Ap: 1. a smiling morning, but in mee a vain heart, lord it wearies mee and yett I follow it, stop up my path lord, this morning a calfe dead. afflictions slay not sin, its grace must mortifie them.

Ap: 8. a faire weeke. but a foule heart. god helpe mee. if grace assist not all my counsells come to nothing. give that holy spirit oh lord that may effect all. heard as if the French had given a great route to the dutch and spaniards. is he likely to bee the great conqueror.

Ap: 15. some old receivers away, some new there in all 20. god in mercy accept mee and mine whereof 3 daughters my selfe and wife receiving. a dewing day.

21. rid to Royden. preacht two lectures at Dedham. returnd May. 2. a bad jorny god good to us. in the mean time at Colne. owers the dronken servant of Mr Bowes died with drinking within 16. houres of his drinking.[1] god awaken persons by it, he was in greater horror before his death. a great floud in the meadowes. May entring wonderfull wett.

May. 6. a lowring skie. lord bee merciful in a threating season, my vain mind knows not how to compose. lord sett all things straite; prayd for faire weather and lookt up. lord helpe mee in all condicons to
Legg. doe so for thou onely art my helpe. my leg as if it would breake out about its sore place. I preacht of a new heart, but with litle successe to my own experience, tasting its old vanitie.

May. 13. a good weeke, god remembred us in the season, the lord good in his word, my Bettie flieth of from Mr Smith. lord bee thou my comfort.

May. 17. God good in my jorny to London and returne(.) left Becke at Hackney and Mary in Southwarke(,) god looke after them for good. sweet shoures(,) god good in the Sabbath.

May. 27. hopes of rain. god send it on wearied lands(,) god good in his word. but my heart old and vain.

June. 3. god sent rain, and now the skie is very moist. god command seasonable wheather, that our soules may rejoyce in his goodnes, as

[1] John Owers, householder, was buried on 26 April. PR.

wee doe in him in all condicons(.) heard our children well(,) give inward soule soundnes

June. 5. After some difficulties to mee on both hands. Mr Gilbert Smith and my daughter Elizabeth married by my hand in Lexden privately. 8. shee rod towards London(,) lord for Jesus Christs sake blesse them and prosper them in soule and body, and let them live happily in thy sight, and give mee comfort in their loves and lives. the ground and bottom of the match among us was not estate. but good qualities lett them shine lord in them both. let her bee as Elizabeth in scripture: 9. a wonderfull wett time threating the meadows, lord bee not angry with the field, wee have sind(.) I own thy chastisment(,) spare lord and blesse mee and mine.

June. 10. a glum day, god good in his word, the lord remember us in the season and breake my heart and the hearts of mine that wee may feare and serve him

16. got some course hay into house: cockt all my clover(,) at night a great raine. heard of the welfare of my children at London for which I returne my praises to god. sent some houshold towards London for my daughter Smith:

June. 17. A lowring skie, lord looke mercifully on us in the season. god good in the word affecting my heart, take away the stonines therof from thine and mine

19. Received in an 100^{li}. from Mrs Brag. I was so run behind hand and layings out so great that I was forced to sinke 30^{li}. and pay only a bond of 70^{li}. lord I hope thou wilt recover mee again from this losse.

June. 24. a glorious skie, a good hay season and I will endeavour to use it, and the season for my soule mercies, lord deliver us from hardnes of heart of allsorts.

28. preacht at the funeral of Mrs Sibley from a text of her choice. Is. 57.1.2. many hearing.[1] god good to mee therin, lord doe us all good; good hay weather.

July. 1. A glorious day, wee had another death with us. my Tenant Mrs Benyon by an imposthume. I have not followed my busines as I ought. god continue the season which I will endeavour to improve. preacht twice at home and then rid to Markshall and preacht Mrs Benyons[2] funerall, where were many people(,) god inabled mee for

[1] Mary Syblye wife of Mr. Nathaniel, citizen of London, was buried on 28 June 1677. PR.

[2] Probably the widow of Henry Benyon, gent., of Markshall (will dated 1674: ERO, 147 CR 9); the Markshall PR gives her burial on 1 July 1677.

that hard service, lord doe all good therby, and accept and blesse mee and mine.

4: Mr Cressener died I was much affected with his sicknes. I prepared to preach on that text ps. 71.18. his death impressed on mee to live more to god, who spake to mee of dayes and my heart speaks that my age may bee lord a good old age. in hopes whereof I praise thee

7. Wee buried Mr George Cressener. a good man, lord fill up his roome. my daughter Jane with mee affected with the providence, and careful of mee in providing sirrup of pellitory. god give a blessing(.) I preacht from 2. Sam. 1.2. greife, seizing on him weake kild him.

July. 8. I arose early my desire is to doe god some service in my place, enable therto and blesse mee. oh my god. heard mine well at London(.) begun to take sirrup of pellitory[1] god almighty doe mee good by it for on him I trust.

13. My deare wife rid towards London carrying nigh 20^{li}. to lay out on her selfe and children and to visitt them, it was a dry morning(,) god in mercy send her well up and home againe, the best day in the weeke.

July. 15. after a very bad, wett weeke for our busines, a wett Swithin. god shall command his mercies for those that trust in him, wherof I am one, knowing the seasons are in his hand: I was alone, yett cheerfull. did not Johns ill course of life afflict mee; heard all well at London for which my praises are to god through christ Jesus, I prayd for faire weather. the skie cleare. sett my selfe to seeke god for old age. ps. 71.18. lord bee my stay therein.

July. 22. Mary came safe home, all well at London for which all praises to my god, the weather good, dry. wee followed our busines. a cheerfull morning. my leg not so much sweld as formerly, but my heart evill is a continuall burthen and greife, this morning I preacht at Gains Colne and in the afternoon at home, god good to mee in the day. saw white oats cutt. god send a good harvest.

July. 29. my wife returnd from London safe, and left all well for which I praise my good god. wee are yett but on the skirts of harvest some few begin. god good to mee in many mercies. and they are the greater my heart being vile

[1] Pellitory: either a composite plant, a native of Barbary, the root of which has a pungent flavour, and is used as a local irritant and salivant (and other plants resembling it, especially masterwort, sneezewort) *or* a low bushy plant with small leaves and greenish flowers, growing upon or at the foot of walls (generally called 'Pellitory of the Wall' and widely used). SOED; Eccles.

Aug: 1. ended haying, after a long season, begun harvest god prosper our labours and blesse our crop

4. an exceeding rainy day hazarding a floud in low grounds. lord spare us.

Aug: 5. cold with shoures, god will send mee harvest weather(.) observed Mr Harlakenden much decaying. god give him a quiet end, god good in his word lord make my age good, my heart so

Aug: 12. a very uncertain harvest weeke, I thanke god I gott in some corn well but my tith very ill; a lowring skie. all threatens rain but lord however thou deale with mee I will sett my love and trust on thee and serve thee for thou art worthy. but lord how mercifull art thou. others as Flanders and Schonen have bloud, and wee only raine.

18. Some days my leg full and swelled in the instep. num and sleepie,
Legg hindring my going.

Aug 19. After bad cometh good weather, and some hopes of its continuance, my busines goeth on but not so as it was wont when I could bustle. god bee praised for our health, oh give grace and to my only son.

25. In a trouble Bullocke put mee too in tithes, he suffered. I blesse god for his mercy.

Aug. 26. A lovely day. god good to mee in his word, his mercy great to mee and I will praise him.

31. preacht at Stisted the funerall of Mrs Aylett. I was kindly used and I trust god had some honor by my endeavours, came home with comfort

Sept. 2. A dull morning after a good weeke. I lost some time, but could not helpe it, received with joy letters from my children at London, lord continue health give grace to them, and withhold it not from my onely son oh thou god of my salvacon. our booke of common prayer was taken out of the deske.

Sept. 4. about eight of the clocke old Mr Harlakenden died, none assisting at his death(.) I was glad the day before I was praying with him and commending him to god, he was very quiet, Mr Bowes gon that day on a jorny of pleasure. Mr Eldred on busines

5. At visitacon, where I receivd admonicon to use all the prayers alwayes, I went to him after dinner, I found all deboist persons generally find the most favour. but with my god is time(.) I found at home a gentleman from London to proffer his love to Mary. etc.

8. ended harvest blessed bee god, and received my deare Rebekah,

well home. Mr Tims who proffered his love to Mary returnd to London. satisfied in us. but not in her. it wrought much as Betties busines god knoweth the issue. direct lord(.) Betties doth wonderfull well. lovingly. for which I blesse my good god.

Sept. 9. Lovely weather. My desires to doe god some service in the word preacht: the Priory women keepe home in state, david after his childs death went up to the Temple(.) some freinds here which were a comfort to mee.

Sept. 16. dry hot weather. a wonderfull hornets nest in Maries garret. god will keep us from every evill, my desires were to honour god in his church services accept and blesse oh holy father.

17. old Mr R. Harlakenden was buried with the concourse of a vast multitude of people of all sorts. god blest mee in the sermon with his presence: it seems to make way for his sons wife and daughter to return to Coln which I have desired and expected.

19 read Mr Harlakendens will, wherin he shewed much love to mee. and gave testimony of my love to the family. I was ingaged by all to assist in their busines, H. Abbut gave mee 5. ginneys. lord thy name bee praised for all mercies, accept mee in thy beloved for to thee I dedicate my strength and service.—

Sept. 30. returnd safe from Bromly where kindly used by Mr Bowes the minister.[1] god hath cast my lott in a better place. for which my praises with him. harvest scarce ended there: this day dews. god good in his word, heard of a great fire at London, lord blesse and preserve mine there and the whole city.

Oct: 7. fire arose by a dronken man, burnt in his bed. sin brings forth death. this weeke showrie, arose this morning with desires to serve my god in my office. lord assist me therin; and warn my son by such examples. but helpe him by grace

Oct. 14. dry with great winde. god good in his word, saw the sad effects of debauchery at Markshall. god in mercy heale our land,

Oct. 21. I was taken with a great pose and cold in the chest. occasiond by cold in my legs by thin stockens, I apprehended it might have had a bad influence on my illnes. but I found it not so. my leg heales slowly. god bee praised for all his mercies.

Oct. 28. dewing. the news of the Ladie Maries marrying the prince of Orange pleasd the kingdome, god good to us in many mercies heard my children well at London. god good in his word, the lord awaken mine to obedience to his will.

31. ended the great busines at the priory, to all contents, I am an

[1] Richard Bowes, rector of Great Bromley, 1661–1700. Newcourt.

ingager there, the lord in mercy blesse mee, and prosper my endeavours.

Nov. 2. I hope I putt the marriage at Pateswicke into a hopeful conclusion. there was no pain, nor faithfulnes wanting on my part. the terms are all agreed but one and I hope that shall never breake; but for my own children to some I am even useles, my counsell nowayes regarded.

No: 4. Hastned my wife to a neighbours labour, weather foggie. my dreame very strange this night, tending as I apprehended much to my good, but I am sure the doctrine of obedience to god would if practised by *men*, as I hope it shall(.) my leg heales in the old sore, there being an issuing sore below it. god blesse all.

No. 11. frost after wett. god gives mee comfort in himselfe. in other things I experience vexacon; tis a mercy when we can have quiet by patience. it seems hard. that relacons should turn all to their wills and know nothing of duty and kindnes, heaven will sweeten all. a cheerly morning.

Mr Tims came again. returnd on the 14. unkindly used by Mary, though kindly by us(.) heard, to my joy how lovingly Mr Smith and his wife live, which marriage I urged gods blessing goe with him. I shall observe gods providence herein. oh let kindnes *be to me*

16. Heard that the city was alarmd that the papists plotted a massacre there, was the marriage a pillow to lull us asleepe. my preaching was on Isaac deliverance; there was

Nov: 18. A cleare shining day. god increase my faith, that cleaving to god may remove all incumbrance and see gods provid*ence* all Yea and Amen. oh that it might [ ] John a convert. thou art all

No: 23. Heard of the death of James the eldest son of Mr [Shirley.] who made great love to my daughter and then fell of. a mercy shee is not a widdow. shee never shewd respect to any young man but to him. god warn my son and doe her good by it.

Frost: begun. 19: a litle misling in morning, sharpe with winde the 21. and so continueth this 25: gods holy day. warm my heart oh god with a holy zeale for thy service and heare my prayers on all occasions for Christs sake I pray thee. a snow. thawd at full moon.

December. 1. I thought matters were not only uncomfortable, but also unprosperous. I cast up my account and I estimate that my mony ☞ stocke my debts paid was about 300li. I thinke I have been to blame in my charitie moneys. straits make us forgett ourselves. Lord I am now old and I have no worke like serving thee, and

assuring my salvation through Christ. I will by grace attend to it more than ever, in all holy duties and in the life of faith. relying on the(e) in Christ for life eternal and for the accomplishment of all promises, and for that to bee the god of my seed and let my son be thine; for outward things I relie on thy blessing without carefulnes, thou hast led mee into farther dealings, lord prosper mee therin, and bee my health that I may serve thee in this place, I shall endeavour by thy grace to stir up my heart after thee: and keepe my vain mind seriously with thee: a Sabbath day (2) wett season, but any weather is good to serve god in and goe to heaven and in the best seasons without care the heart wilbee vile, my right legg somewhat cold and num. the care of god for his an encouraging word to mee, in worship god good found a hopefull effect of the
3. advice I gave Mr Ludgater preventing his losse of the schoole

Dec: 9. a wonderfull wett season, hindring all busines, this morning the skie cleare but very waterish. my hearts desire to doe good in the word, lord helpe for man is nothing of himselfe

11: our new Lords kept their Courts very quietly. 14. in the morning my wife had a very strang fitt, poore heart her passions master her. but my love and tendernes by gods blessing shall master them, lord preserve her to thy glory. and my comfort.

Dec. 16. Sensible of the discord in some families. parents neglected by children their deaths gapd for to enjoy that they have. I shall observe gods returns. lord lett it not bee so with us. open season: sheep decaying. my heartie thoughts to doe god some service in his
☞ holy day. read in my family the judgment of god on John Duncalf of old Swinford in Staffordshire, who running from his trade. to idlenes and intemperance came to want a morsel of bread, to theft and of a bible and being charged with it denyed it with this imprecacion would his hands might rott of if he stole it. within a fortnight a simptome of rotting appeared and so both did and his legs. god set this home to mee and mine to make us more careful of our wayes.

Dec. 23. frostie weather. god good to mee in outward mercies, lord accept mee in Christ Jesus

25. warm open weather(.) preacht from Jo. 3.16. I will oppose(,) god so loved(,) to my(.) I have so *said*(,) and trust in him seeing his mercy in the roote that beareth all my comforts.

Dec. 30. after a summer day, a sharpe rime frost. toward morning old Robin Abbutt the great profaner of the Sabbath, and scoffer at gods worship. tooke dumbe and seemed dying; I suppose it a palsy. god good to mee in his holy day, and in the word, lord *try* and accept mee in christ

Jan. 1. Robin Abbutt died. lord helpe mee to live to thee. I find god good to mee in the providences of the day. I gave above 20s. to my tenants and poore in meat, I received in by guifts several moneys, etc. lord blesse my store. but above all my grace(.) Jane with us full of her discontents, lord help and heale her.

Jan. 6. a wett dampish season, lord how unlovely discontent is, helpe mee to thankfulnes to thee in every condicon, and let others troubles and unhansome frames make mee more carefull of my wayes(.) it appeard to mee Mr Cressener died in an ill time for his family. and things unsetled.

Jan. 13. after open wett weather. frost and snow. I am amazed to consider the selvish temper that appears in men. their mischeivousnes to others if handsomly it can be done lord give mee a just. merciful, helpfull. spirit to all, this morning my bed was uncomfortable, its best to bee up early and with god. lord make my day good

Jan. 20: wett. god good to mee in endeavouring to command my heart in all providences, when men interprett ill that which is openly good. gain how it blinds men, lord keepe mee from it, I am on my watch observing gods dealings with persons, learne mee heedfulnes, and care to walke close to god(.) my family, are sett on their wayes, lord I am not of counsell to them, bee thou their counsellor

25. I was often thinking of the providence of god that was putting an end to that familie of Harlakenden, being good men, and thoughtfull of the females, my heart trembled, and though I were getting up moneys for corn more than ordinary and paying debts, yet this day I reflected on gods providence in my estate. Having of my Welsh heifers three dead calves and but one living, lord teach mee humility, and submission. I am the greater sinner.

Jan: 26. 1677.

Sensible it entred my 63 yeare, read in course. Acts. 14. of the impotent man in his feete with faith god would keepe my distemper from hurt, would heale it and doe mee good. v. 27. I could rehearse much god hath done for mee and mine and setting up my store of helpe, I looke forward and know he wilbee with mee to old age. lord I wilbee with thee by the help of thy grace; but oh how litle have I hitherto done for god. our life eating, sleeping, caring, sinning. litle of holines. [*Grat*]ified John in his desires, so that he in

a prospect of 11. in hand 5^{li}. but at [*present he is*] in his old sottish humour. what must kindnes rise in judgment against him. lord [ ] give mee a holy heart suiting that day.
[ ] out with two plows to forward our work. lord blesse and prosper mee therin for [ ] and hindred. 30. at night heard sad shrickings it proved a child about a mi[le] prentices was drownd under the ice. they within at cards. tis comfortable [when *tro*]uble comes finding us well imployd. preacht to a small audience, bapt. 2 children. [H]eard of the eagerness of our king for warre with France: the Parl. voting 70^{m}. to bury the [*la*]te King after (after) 29 years being in grave. strang things. why is not mony voted to buy [ ] and harlots petticoats: god wilbee seen in the mount as I preacht. I have no opinion [*of*] our medling with France. of our conduct or sincerity. but thou lord reignest, and Ile bee quie[t.] this weeke faire. god good in my calling, lett thy blessing bee on my substance bu[*t e*]specially blesse my labours towards soules. the mound on my leg sweld painful and blacke. I much scratched it. my desires are this morning with my god. Mr Harlakenden being dead. and Mr Cressener, and the 2 gent. at the priory going away, I thinke my selfe much concerned for the town, lord I will put forth my selfe even beyond my strength for publique good. lord blesse my endeavours.

Feb. 17. That day the Parliament sat down the French King began his jorny towards Germany [*and*] the King receiving an addresse from them schoold them(,) they voted 20. regiments foot[*e*] 4 horse. 2 of dragoons. 90 ships to support the Dutch alliance. Sp. Netherlands and abate the French(,) weekely charge per month at 28 days $157^{li}000$ and upwards. [Mr] Eldred returnd. his ant Parker dying gave her estate from her family to her housban[d] a great trouble and disappointment. possibly god may call over young Harlakenden[s] wrongs. Mrs Androws mother in law to my freind dead, which easeth them of a great charge and trouble. god good to mee in the labours of the day which were great.

20. My brother in law Finch died, I had the comfort to shew him much love, 21. my daughter Smith to my great joy on a sudden came to mee. it was an amaze at first, some raine. the sad troubles and miserablenes in a great family an afflicti[on](,) lord help mee to value my own mercies. I preacht his funerall sermon Feb. 23. [he] was a young man to mee, and unlikely to have gone before mee, my leg swel[ls] and pitts very much(,) lord heale mee for thy mercies sake.

Feb. 24. Lovely growing weather, a million granted the King to begin the war with France(,) wee are a people peeled and polled, help lord, see the issue of things.

March: 1. winde northerly. extream cold; my leg swelld. much. with some pain especially on outside it being very red. I suppose it would have had some cats bites or bigger on it. sore places ceasd ☞ running. 3.5. I dressed it once a day, I was feavourish my wat[*er*] high and breaking presently, I am in the hand of my father in whom I trust to [*do*] for my good and who will doe it; I lett Mrs Bragges house to my great content. [*and*] good, and they are my strength in the lord my god: the French K. passing on for [*Germ*]any to Nancy in Lorraine on a suddain came backe to Flanders. his forces see[*m likely*] to attempt Namur the Dutch forces marcht to Hasselt, the French in the [ ] ring all arming many places approach Gaunt.

March. 10. heats over. yet said Gaunt was taken after defence of severall dayes. After very windy weather. this day coole but a litle growing with a night dew. gave notice of S[*acrament*]

15. Mrs Androws the only daughter of my deare and good Harlakenden who was the only [*son of the*] good old Harlakenden came to live at the ruined priory: I trusted to see that [*day where*] in that estate shalbee on her and hers, and I pray for it, and wee will live [ ].

17. more moisting raines, a good sabbath, but my body out of frame with [ ]abate through mercy, and I hope even all my troubles thence god will ov[er] oh lord my strength.

20: strucke a good stroke in Mr Androws busines to setle it with [*all goods*] therin, and I observd how hardly Mr Eldred and Bowes yeilded [*to my contentions who knew what*] those wrongs were. but god will doe the oppressed right.

March. 24: it raind this morning at my lands were. I judgd it mercy. I ca[ ]er it so I pray thee: I administred the sacrament. present. 12 women [*and . . . . . with*] us. my two deare freinds Mrs Brag, and Androws with us. owning gods [*presence*;] use of it my heart very pathetical in pressing to the ordinance.

28. the family at the priory broke up. old Mrs Harlakenden put in [*to Olivers*][1] the gentlemen did what they pleased with persons and things not [*settled*] in the morning Mr Eldred cald up with the news. by the waggon came [*to tell mee*] his mother was very ill, he said to mee he questioned whether he sh[*ould find her alive*] but

[1] 'Olivers' was the house of Mrs. Harlakenden's daughter Margaret (married to John Eldred) at Stanway.

did not desire our prayers. Mr Bowes intended for London in his [*coach . heard that the*] coach man gott drunke by nine a clocke. so that but like and his wife. with . . . .[1]

lord make it a blessing to the hearer [. . . . .] parl: adjourned until April. 11. the King intends [ ]

April. 1. God good to mee in our town affaires for which I blesse his name [*Rec^d^. from M^r^*] Eldred his letter of his mothers death and intents to bury her here. lord sa[ ] I feard: 4: farther discourse with Mr Eldred about the burial, th[*en of the*] progresse in the affaire of Mr Androws and his grandmother Har[*lakenden Blessed be*] god I ended the law suits between Ravens. Newton and Appleton [*remember mee*] my god for good.

Ap: 7. God good to mee, my heart dull and heavy, at night cold shou[*res*] [ ]

10. buried Mrs Eldred the elder at Colne, with some plain state, [*and many freinds to*] helpe out the ceremony, wee fetcht her from Olivers. the grea[*t preparation for*] 14 and for the people in Colne. who all went thither, few of [*other parishes.*] I preacht. god good to mee, and with satisfaction to them. [*I made it*] my excuse to bee away at the visitacion, a mercy to [*be absent*] when perhaps some did expect he should have continued the [*suspension*]

Ap. 14: after a sweet Satturday shoure that closed my sowing with the pl[*ows, a very*] close morning the rain moisting the ground, lord blesse my [ ] desire to honour my god, and serve my generacion in doing g[*ood*]

19. made an end of sowing my howed barly. weather growing. god in merc[*y*] us in full employment about our busines(.) Mr Pindar came to setle n[*ear us. lord in*] mercy make him a good neighbour.

April 21: A lovely growing morning, the seasons are, lord let thy gracious seasons bee in [ ] of us, that ours may live in thy sight, a strange calm in England though dr[ ] my desires to honour god in his holy daies worke, accept mee oh my god.

24. a publique fast, which I endeavoured to keepe with all solemnes, Fast ☞ and I had a consi[*derable*] audience of my people and some strangers. it was called by the King. no mention of his Co[*unsell*] our parliament advising though in sitting. the proclamation past March. 30. no mention of it in th[e *Ga*]zet of Monday. Ap. 8 til the Thursday Gazett: no mention of war or peace nor bles[*sings*] desired on the Counsells on foote. the King and city kept it Ap. 10. while the Parl.

[1] Three lines torn and missing.

was ad[*journed*] so that neither house kept it by themselves and called preachers to them. I thought it shewd [*that the*] King had no great esteem for his good and blessed parliament. a sweet dewing day. lord [ ] thy grace into our hearts. and heare supplication wee begge of thee. I doe expect ab[ ] from the prayers of this day. I will hearken for god for Christs sake will speake peace to hi[ ] no notice in the gazets of the keeping this fast.

Ap. 28: Wett, cold weather. god in mercy awaken my heart to his service, my desires doe good in the great worke of this holy day, the lord my god accept mee.

May. 5. Things in a cloud at London, the King saith the Dutch bafle and ruind a sepa[*rate*] peace with the French. the Dutch jealous of the English least they have some[*e*] designe to greaten Orange. Lord secure England in religion from popery and in libe[rty] from an army. weather growing(.) god good in the worke of the day. lord accept [ ]

May. 12. used a new water to my legge, god blesse it. a good Sabbath, and a growing day.

14: went not to Court I came of well for present as to surplice.[1] gods name bee praised

May. 19. a cheerfull morning, my thoughts somewhat troubled in reference to my children but I will goe to god for peace; The King asking his Parl: Counsell, and they denying to raise a million of mony and reflecting too plainly on the evill counsellors. the King pa[*ssed by*] some private acts. signifying his displeasure. prorogued them from 13. to 23: news of a pe[*ace*] beyond the seas.—23. the Kings speech imports displeasure against the Parliament demand[*ing*] mony. etc.

May 26. wett, growing weather, god keepe down weeds, my leg swels and is painfull in the inside beneath the sore and aside my instep. god good in his word. the King seems to chide the Parl. to a doing what he would have: I was very ill at night, my head light and dreams troublesome. god watch over all for good

2. after raine that flouded our meadows, and a lowring skie. yet of gods goodnes the earth drieth, and in our troubles god remembers mercy and give ease in himselfe to our wearied minds and in our publique affaires(.) hopes that that crisis wee apprehended to our rel[*ig*]ion and liberty may admitt a longer putting of, god is unsearchable in

[1] On 9 April 1678 the archdeacon's court sought 'to know why he [i.e. RJ] officiates without a surplice or that he does not present there is none' and exactly the same wording was used at the court on 14 May. (ERO, DACV/7).

his ways [ ] therefore I will waite on the god of salvacion. god good in the word and worke of [*the*] day. my legge much swelled in instep and full of pain, broke in 4 places

[*The*] Parl. voted to disband the army presently.

A moist weeke, a wett night, god in mercy remember us in the season, for which [*my he*]art trusts in him and pleads the covenant with Noah and mankind: prayed hear[ ] [f]aire weather, hoping it from god against all signes of fowle. god good in [ ] was to direct to plead the covenant

[16. *the*] sun had shone very red some dayes and especially on the 15. this morning the skie [was] unbright. god give us good weather which I pray for with lo[ ]eth my spirit, peace and good in him, other things vanity and [ ]

heard of the health of my children at London: god good to mee in the day, and in my spirit and in his service, for which I blesse his name(,)

17. his answer of prayer in another bullocke calved.

June: 23. Shoures with thunder that hindred our worke about us, in some places more in some none. lord thy wilbee done. I kisse thy rod, how ever thou deale with mee lord remember thy covenant. never greater signes of raine. I doe not find my leg worse or pain-

leg. fuller, but rather healing for which I praise god, the word was lively and useful to mee lord make it so to my hearers, news that Spain France and Holland have made peace. England is to bee the securitie for it(.) the King demanded theron 300 m^{li}. yearly for his life therupon, but the house voted negative

June. 30. God gave us a good hay weeke(.) I did not use my time as I might yet I was not wholly negligent. it thunders and shews rain but I pray and urge the covenant for weather to gather in our fruits. he that hath holpe will helpe. god good in the word, lord may desire and endeavour shalbee to doe well.

July. 1. rid with Mrs Harl. to see olivers. 3. returnd ill from Janes and so continued til 7th(,) in morning my pain in side abating, it was a dry weeke god good in our businesse(.) heard Jane in bed of a daughter die. 6°. this day a good sabbath to mee.

July. 14: Goodly weather: which is the more thankfully owned by mee, being sensible of the bad season at first. god gave mee a great heart of prayer for dry weather. and he hath given a great answer of prayer: I was very ill divers dayes but god hath shewn mee mercy in my health and ease, and I will enlarge my heart in duty and service to him and his, I have been hindred from taking my season. my leg not so sweld as at some times, nor sore, nor painfull.

July. 21: sweet shoures die. 19. 20. which hindred my hay. being partly careles but cheifely my mowers failing mee. but I was recompenced in corn. hops, turneps. my praises are with god in Christ. my hopes that the holy spirit will assist mee in gods holy day. my legge better, my health better. lord make my heart better and better.

24. with some difficultie I bought a parcell of Fletchers land. viz. Loveland and the feild that lieth to the river, setled it on my wife. and Rebecca at present(,) it cost mee an 150^{li}. god blesse us in the injoying of it.

25. I almost ended my hay, and began harvest with a jagge of white pease, our crop is good god give a good season yet the weather seems to loure on us.

July. 28. god good in manifold mercies. heard from my daughter Smith that shee is about 5 months gone. god blesse her and her seed, a good season(,) I was busy in my worke, god in mercy send a good season. my heart desirous to doe some service for god against sin in my brother. lord blesse my endeavour.

Aug. 4. a goodly harvest weeke I was doing and had in much corne. heard my litle grandchildren ill. my wife rid to see them, I praid for them with earnestnes but humble submission. I am feavourish, yet able through mercy to doe the worke of my ministry. lord blesse us and let thy grace bee sufficient for us.

Wood: 9. cleared Chalkeney wood of my share. poles. tits.[1] longwood, without any considerable hurt to beast, waggon, and none to man, for which my praises are to god. I turne again blessing that peice of land from the lord, that made the heaven to shine over it, and the earth to bee fruitfull under it. god send mee good pay, that I may ble[ss] the traders as I have payd well to a 1^{d}. and performed with my men to a fagott. This day I had in all my own hard corn, very well for which I blesse god, my busines at home and abroad goeth on well. god give mee patience and thankfulnes and I shalbee a greater gainer in every condicon. god good in may health, the fourth feaver fitt last. I could up about my busines. H. Abbutt is very ill, and keepeth in.

Aug: 11. A lovely morning. some shoures causing some litle hindrance but litle or no damage. good to my turneps and our hops. my heart pittieth sinners. bee thou my helpe against every evill.

13. had in my last load of hay for which I blesse god in the midst of

[1] Tit: Essex dialect for a small faggot of wood for heating an oven. Jepp.

corn harvest. visiting Henry Abbut in his sicknes telling him I hoped to see him live that wee might pray togither and joyn in gods publique worship. he told mee that would never bee, I replied he knew not what thoughts god would give him. he replied he knew or was certain that would never bee. lord hath he puld his heart absolutely out of thy hands. lord I will cleave to thee in thy worship though others will not and I will eye thy providence to that man.

Aug: 18: A goodly harvest weeke: which I in some measure improved, god good in our health and outward mercies he accept mee in his beloved, my heart quiet as to former vaine thoughts for which I blesse my good god. desirous to doe god some extraordinary service(.) peace between France and Holland, but before known in the Holland camp. in order to releiving mons they fell on the French with great fury and slaughter, the French retired. so the honour of the field was to the Dutch and English who fought valiantly

19. a drisling morning, I yett chose to gather a jag of raking oats, and ended oat harvest which was very plentiful. god blesse mee with an heart to serve him with his bount[*ies*]

Aug: 25: This morning looks very loury. my stacke lieth open. and 2 jags of barly stand abroad. lord as thou pleasest. the last weeke a goodly harvest weeke and I endeavoured to follow. loading almost all my barly. a lovely crop. and mine in health for which my praises to my good god, whom I desire to serve this day and all my days with all my talents and his bounty; it gathered up and rained very sweetly about 7 of the clocke, it cometh excellently for my grasse, especially. a great feild of turneps.

26: coole and dewing, hindring harvest, yet pickers went into the hop ground. god blesse us in all

29. Made an end of harvest to the praise of my good god, I ind 206 jags of one corne and other. blessed bee the lord for his earth his seasons. his goodnes on our labour our health and preservacon. lord give us a heart to serve thee with thy great goodnes(.) I hope I used my labourers well and gave them all content. excellent weather for my crop of turneps.

Sept: 1. God good in our health and manifold mercies for which my soule praises him. for he is the roote that mainteines all my good. ended all harvest, and begun to prepare for another crop. a goodly hop season. lord enlarge my heart and lift it up in thy wayes, and let mee not place any whit of my heart on anything but thee but use all to thy glory, and in the good of others.

Sept 8: Weather wonderfull hot day. pasture burns away much, god good to us in the season his day a good day. lord gather mee and mine under thy wings I pray thee.

12. mett the Bishop at Wittam. I was much complaind of to him by Mr Lampkin[1] preist of Hatfeild and Mr Paul[2] preist of Easthorp and but coursely used by the Bishop. I thanke god for my patience and his goodnes to mee going and returning.

Sept. 15. Weather dry. I urged for pauls, wee gathered 3^{li}. god good to mee in the word the lord accept mee and continue my libertie day by day.

17. rid to Olivers found the family had been sicke, but upwards(,) Mrs Harlakenden sett a day to return, assisted our collection for pauls, came home safe. tried another surgeon for my legge one Mrs Doughtie. god blesse all endeavours for good.

19. the weather turnd cooler, closer, seemed rainlike. but the shoures kept of.

Sept: 22. Coole, and yet dry. rain still passing away. my leg very painfull, running, bleeding(,) god in mercy heale and order all for the best. many hearing, god good in the word preacht for which my soule blesseth him, lord gather many soules my family home to thee.

Sept. 29. still dry and cold. my leg deeply sore and bleeds much(,) god I trust will heale it. this day a good day. my soule lord desireth after thee.

30. Heard Mr Eldred by letter forbid the payment of my 20^{li}. my wood. gave no reason for it(.) lord I have given him no cause. he sent mee word I had busines of my own I should not trouble my selfe with his mother. shee had children of her own to looke after her. I know lord them and their care. love to my deare freind and her put mee to it. the letter was brought on the lords day morning on which a pay was due. lord lett not man have their will on mee, I looke unto thee to save mee: my thoughts bad mee stand still and see the salvacion of god: I will stand still. next morning in course read. Heb. 10. lord I desire thy mercy to breake his heart and preserve mee.

Oct. 3. wee came of well at Cogshall. the Bishop not there. Mr Eldred at priory. said his letter writt in his anger, my desire to have his

[1] William Lamplugh, vicar of Hatfield Peverel 1672–82, later prebend of Ripon, and died 1705. Newcourt; Venn.

[2] Obadiah Paul, rector of Easthorpe, Essex, 1670–1703. Venn.

mother at Colne the occasion. lord in mercy looke after mee for good for on thee I depend.

Sowing 5. began to sow first mislain in farther Readings. god prosper the seed for his blessing is my repose, it raind at night.

Oct: 6. after a through ground rain, a clear morning. nothing from London. heard Jane ill. sent my daughter Mary to bee with her. my legge in a hopeful way. though rain and new moon, lord lett mee live to thy honour. enlarge my heart in thy services

Oct. 13. like an after summer. I preacht though very ill with winde in my side binding up my body, and hindring sleepe, eating nutmeg I slept towards morning.

Oct. 20. My people are all well from Ely faire. a dry cold day. god good to mee in his word. blesse us lord for in thee is my trust, heard of Mr Humphrys sad death. lord preserve mee and mine

21. Giles Crow and I came to an agreement about his sons tithes, I used him kindly.

22. rid to Cogshall. Mr Croxon preacht about catechising. 12. ministers dined togither(,) it greived mee to heare, the janglings, reproach of preaching. taking notes of sermons and other things, especially by Mr Jesop. and Rogers.[1] they tooke notice of my calmen(e)s but with reflections. god forgive all.

23. my deare wife rid towards London to bee with my daughter Smith, god bee with them

25: My daughter Jane went home with all her children indifferent well, god blesse them

Oct. 27. Good weather. god good in his providences(,) my daughter Smith delivered well of a daughter the 19. day. before her mother came to her; god in mercy send her well up again, god good to mee in his word(.) a lowring providence on England, god send all to end well for his

No: 3. When up saluted with a sad letter from my wife, Bettie having the small pox, it found mee in an ill frame and entred deepe into mee, but my heart returnd into god with hope that he will bee gracious, a cheerfull summer day.

5. a lovely day. my desires to keep it a day of holy rejoycing. if the plot now discovered had taken wee had not been owners of that mercy this day.

Nov. 9. god answered prayer in Bettie, who is well upward, god prosper the mercy. god good in his word, a very lovely season

[1] Zecheriah Rogers, son of Nehemiah (see p. 388, n. 1 above), vicar of Great Tey from 1660 to at least 1700. Smith, *Clergy*, p. 92.

12 my wife and daughter came safe from London. Bettie upward, a miracle of mercy [ ] and a very gracious answer of prayer.

No. 13. a good day, my heart up to hope in god, a great congregacon and quiet streete in many yeares not so many poore there. god turne it unto good.

Nov. 17. A good day: the plotters seem to make opposicon in our councels. god good in my Bettie at London. lord assist mee thy grace and thy people with power to quell thes enemies

No. 24: Good news from Bettie, coming down into the house, the family well. my wife feavourish; continuall matter to depend on god. heard of Mrs Harlakendens sicknes at Olivers. god good in his word. the house committed Secretary Williamson to the tower, the Q (c.o. King) released him, a passage that looks not well, god amend all

25. some thoughts that my wife had the small pox, god in mercy preserve her, as I trust in him he will and myself and family. it proved so

29. Certain Mrs Harlakenden my good old friend was dead, I always said shee would not endure the winter at Olivers: losses in my catle. while god is mine all is well he is my porcon and I trust in him for good and patiently kisse his rod.

Dec: 1. Frost with a litle snow. my deare wife sore. god will heale and preserve us for I expect through Christ this mercie from him, and I shall live to his praise. my desires up to doe him some special service on his holy day. heard good news from London, said the Queen is accused in this plott.

Dec. 8. A dry chearfull day. god good in his word, lord putt no interution to this worke, the King and house of Commons are a litle off, one another, god prevent a breach to sever the parliament. the army is to bee disbanded, god in mercy watch over us, some threat as the greatest revolucion wee ever saw, were at the doore, the lord order all for good(.) my deare wife in a hopefull way of recovery and all my family continue well, to god bee the praise of all. I will waite, for god will speake peace to his people and let not mee nor mine oh lord returne to folly.

10: Good Mrs Harlakenden buried, dying at Olivers in Stanaway. Mr Eldred his wife and children would not lett her come to Coln. I told them shee could not live a winter there. I preacht her funeral, I had a scarfe, gloves, hatband. no mourning nor legacy. no one of them gave mee thanks for my sermon. neither Mrs Eldred nor her daughters would vouchsafe to speake to mee. lord thou art my glorious porcon. and thou lookest after mee and I will praise thee and live to thy glory.

Dec: 15. a good day. alarmed that John Pain was ill, god held up my heart, he well.

Dec: 22. Early my maide rise and groand, I was alarmd, and so have I lord on thy day. is it that I neglect thy Sabbath, surely I might and should spend them better, I trust in god it will blow over. the moon shall not hurt us by night, or the sun by day. I trust in god for preservacon(,) still I see what a dependant creature man is. Jesuits tried and condemned. lord all my desires are before thee and to the remembrance of thy name

25. preacht from Rom. 3.25. not many hearing.

Dec. 29. My wife hopefully upwards. god good in his word, the season warm and drie: the treasurer impeacht by the Commons. the Jesuites. Groves. Pickering and Ireland that were condemned repreived by the King, during his pleasure, the houses addrest to know the reasons. god amend all.

Jan. 1. New yeare entred with the news of the prorogacion of the Parliament till Feb. 4th. people lookt on it as much troubled, so am I, but god is where he was and that is my soules hope. my wife tooke a purge, which wrought wonderfully it amazed us. but god was our helpe.

4: read Job. 5. though I know not which way. not whether god will honour the Parl. to doe any service for him or the nacon. yet deliverance shall arise to his remnant and in their confidences I waite, pray, and looke up. my wife came down into the parlour. very well.

Jan:5. my heart affected with things, I went to bed and wisht I might even foreseingly dreame: being on the road in my thoughts. I thought there was a great concourse, and I overheard a commissioner say. as for our ecclesiasticks I know not what they are, whether the ministers of Jesus Christ or not we must give them the test.[1] waking. the secret of the lord is with them that feare him. I will doe so. and I interpreted this for good. a calme frostie morning, god raiseth up my heart to waite on him(,) all still and calme, god good in the word, yett few minde it.

Jan. 12. Cold, snow: my family in health, but Mary hath an ague. god will soone remove it, my wife begins to come among us, god preserve her and us, matters calme as yett abroad. the souldiers under the best officers disbanding, my hope is in god, his word good.

[1] The first Test Act (1672) and its successors required all officials to make a declaration against transubstantiation and to take the sacrament.

17. Spent the day at priory in praying to god for a blessing on the nacon. the advancement of Christs name and religion in the world. for particular blessings on our family. with our praises to god for his goodnes to my wife and family in our preservacon

Jan. 19. A horie frost, calm. a good day. christ is the true discovery of gods love to us. Titus 3.4: his giving manifests love indeed. thats the day spring visiting us, a peaceable day, its said the French make great preparacion, notwithstanding their peace with Spain, and as said likely with the Emperor and others. I cast my care on my god in christ.

21. heard that the Parliament was prorogued for 3. weeks longer until Feb. 25. the King declared in Councill on Satturday he would doe it. lord publish then thy decree.

1678

Jan. 26. I awaked toward morning and was sensible this day ended my 62. and begun my 63. yeare glad a Sabbath, I had a comfortable review of gods mercies and goodnes to mee from my cradle and a foresight god would bee with mee for good. that I should see the good of his chosen ones with a hope as Jacob(,) to see John a Joseph(,) a comfort to mee. I in thankfulnes devote my selfe unto the lord and to his service, and in all my relacons to seeke his glory with praise

27. In the morning before I rose, about 6. of the clocke I awakned and had just dreamed, that one told mee that the parliament was to meet but for a morning and that there were 11. men intended to make speechs. about 10. of the clocke I heard it was to bee dissolved and a new one chosen. god is still where he was. it cannot bee chosen till March. this was according to the Counsell in Colemans letter. god is where he was. honest men formerly desired the dissolucon thereof but now its continuance was desired in reference to the discovery of the plott. I supposed the cabal doth it to gaine time and to bring on the French assistance, many thought this parliament had so corrupted themselves and done so ill in the matters of the nacion and were formerly so odious that god would doe his worke by some other and never honour them; on the 26. at night a great fire at London, which amazed us in the country(,) pittying the city under the treachery against them. my legge sore with cat bites.

Jan. 30. Fast. a sharpe glancy morning; divers hearing. god doe them all good.

Feb: 2. Cold, thawing(.) god good in his word, my legge very ill, he in mercy accept mee for good

4: after reproachs, backbitings abroad, home chidings reading in Leighs fall of AntiChrist,[1] with an horror I thought the K. of France was likely the litle horne and that England was one kingdom he should, or that horn pul up by the roote; lord who liveth when thou doth this 5. dreamd. of a sermon god will give salvacion. waiting but loving answer he will doe it. he can appoint command it and wee believe it. pray for it. yea he bids us command it

Feb: 9. A cold snowy day, news of the kings illnes continues. busy in chosing parliament. the first choice I heard of was at Harwich two royall officers to the fleet. god good to Israel.

Feb. 16. Calm good working weather, my family in health(.) the nacon busy about the choice of parliament. god direct them, that they bee not outwitted, as the former were to raise an army(.) said good choices in many places and that the K. saith the contry would choose a dog if he stood against a courtier: the peace goeth on (the) beyond the seas, and the fears of france are on this side. wett and windy and cold god good in his word for which I praise him, my family hopefull.

21: Heard the Duke of Yorke had taken the Test and oaths and that he was made Admiral and Generall(,) things worke, but god is awake and there I rest my selfe. the lords must bee saved also.

Feb: 23. after cleare warm dayes. this was darke and cloudie, my deare wife pretty well after her frights god preserve her. said good choice made of Parl. men; god good in his word for which I blesse him and I will endeavour to shew that a true Christian is the best man in the world.

25. This day all our town in a manner went with Mr Androws and my son for the choice of Knights of the shire. I endeavoured for my contreys good, wee choose Mildmay. and Harvy, without the opposicon of any one person in the feild appearing against them.

March. 2. God good in our hitherto preservacon, he abideth, when all faile or are undone and I will trust in him for salvacon. the weather dry, calme, and not very cold. god good to mee in his word, his christ and spirit is precious to my soule.

3. a vehement. cold east winde: 4. a calme deepe snow. I hope god will fill our pits: 5. snow.

[1] Edward Leigh (1602–71), writer of numerous books including *A Treatise of Religion and Learning* (1656) in which he explained that the Pope was Anti-Christ. DNB. No title resembling that given by RJ has been found.

March: 6. a bitter cold morning. I desired to send our choise men into the Parl. house with a blessing; the country shewd themselves in the choice though much divided in sects. lord shew thy selfe with a blessing, let it bee a day of thy creating. and remember not our sins against us. I read ps. 19. 20. 21. in course encouraging mee. I pray lord and looke up(.) the day proved very cleare and sunshine.

7. 8: the old Scotch regiment of Douglas marcht for Harwich. and so for Ireland, or sea to have an eye on the French. said the Duke of Yorke gon out of the kingdom to Holland.

March. 9. Dry. calm and cold. god good in manifold mercies, good in his word, for which I praise him

16. Calme and dry. my wife at church praises to my god, heard of the health of mine at London and Lexden. god good to mee in bearing up my heart to hope in him in all calamities(,) who feare who have god our hope, what doe they that trust only an arme of flesh and carnel policy. god end all well.

March. 23. God good in his word, the weather very wett, not to fill our ponds, but even continue all droppings. quiet times, still wee hope god will blast the plotters. sensible a very afflicting time with mee in the untowardnes of relacons, losse of sheepe by dogges(.) wennell, catle ill, things goe heavily, lord bee mercifull to mee. with patience.

March. 30. very dry. god good in his word. I buried two by one another. the parl. seemeth wonderfull couragious not fearing prorogacions or dissolucons. Court are surely plotters or knowing of it.

Aprill. 6. wett and such the weeke hath been hindring seedtime, holding backe the spring. god good in his word to mee. my deare wife came into my chamber to mee last night god preserve her, a blessing and comfort unto us all. gave notice of the publique fast, lord accept us. this day most excessive cold winde. a sheep drownd.

11. cold wett uncomfortable season. a day of fast, my heart much shutt up and dampt, yett I hope god will save for his name sake. and gods mercy shall have all the honour of it,

April. 18. This weeke very wett and cold. this day cold and gloomy, keeps the spring wonderfully backe. my heart in some measure up desirous to serve my god in the worke of the day, the lord fitt us for his table worship. reports of troubles tumults, wee shall see whether the K. will comply with Parl. advice or the cabal. god incline his heart to his glory and publique good.

14: I hope god heard my prayer for seed time. a lovely morning we went out, god prosper us. it dewed before night and drove us home.

19. heard the treasurer Danby yeilded himselfe, the lords sent him to the tower, and the King prorogued the parliament. said he was going to Windsor: not true

Ap: 20. Cold and dry. god very good in his word, in my desires to raise his worship, wee had 4 men. 12. women at sacrament. lord I mett thee and I trust thou wilt alwayes meet mee. Rose Cressener hath the small pox(,) prayed heartily for the family, heare lord.

24: perfected the purchase of Robert Carters land and setled it on my daughter Mary(,) the lord blesse my provision for her, for christ Jesus sake.

Ap. 27. warm and calm. god can change the face of the skie, a great change in the face of affaires. god in mercy preserve the King, and our nobles from French fraude.

May. 1. It continued dry. hot and calm. the contry quiet without noises, I went to plow at my daughter Maries litle farme, god blesse her and mee in it.

May. 4. dry, hot and calm. affaires darke, yett the K. and Parl. seeme to bee on good termes. god good to mee in his word the lord my god accept mee.

5. a sweet growing shoure. an answer of prayer, incouragement to faith in after straits(.) My inheritance was very thirsty. a great mist this 6. in the morning.

8. abundant shoure in our street, but litle further from us. gods name bee praised. wee had newly drawn up about 3 bushels of floote fish at one draught by Collier

May. 11. a cold day. but dry. god good in his mercifull peaceable healthful providences to us(.) my spirit exceedingly provoked lord keepe mee humble and quiet. my desires to advance gods glorious name and to encourage soules to trust in him.

May. 18. Weather continueth very dry and sometimes hott. my son as sett in his disorder as formerly. and the old man as prevalent under new mercies, god compose my heart to evennes, which is not easily kept, though through grace recovered, my full desire is to serve god cheerfully in spirit this day.

May. 25. great shews of raine, yett it passeth away. the weather very dry, but not very hot, god good to mee in his Sabbath worke, my hearts desire to serve him, Lord accept mee: I prayed for raine Lord I trust thou wilt command it.

28. heard of the prorogacion of the Parl. not amazed, I thanke god not senseles. I know whom I trust. in course I read Pro. 10 I hearkned what god spake. who is my counsellour in his word. many places

sweet. v. 25. thes shall passe as a whirlwind they may mischeife. but not destroy, nor last long.

June. 1. A warm day after an earth satisfying raine. lord remember England in this day of calamities. a sad morning for my spirit. I have no help, I will beare the indignacon of god for I have sind against him. its hard lord to dwell in the fire. stop the lyons mouth, and bring meate out of the eater.

June. 8. God good to mee in my preservacon and our publique peace. heard of my Cosin Bentons death found dead in the road. god in mercy preserve mee and mine, fruitful seasons

16: I rid to London, saw my child at her house in Longacre, I was very ill there but returned safe die. 21. for which I praise god, had a mercifull providence of Bettie Goodman on Halsted (c.o. preacht) bridge, preacht twice die 22. was with Robin Harris who was found in his feild after 20 houres in a wett season, dangerously ill of the palsie. god in mercy spare him, and preserve mee and mine to his service.

27. all my children and grandchildren with mee at my sisters at dinner. a hot season.

June. 29. dry and hott, I drunke two glasses water. lord help and heale, for in thee alone is my repose. heard of the Scots route, lord thou wilt maintein thy interest.

July. 6. brave hay weather, my children and grandchildren all with mee and in health(.) god good to mee in the word and in our preservacon, when very much mischeife was done by haile at the Waltam and other places to thousands of pound, in the corn

9. Mrs Hester Cressener buried in good state, that which was most observable, was that her 2 married sisters going to London just before her death though they had part of 4 dayes time. yet neither came down. our thoughts possesse us. litle are wee affected with the condicons of others.

leg. 10: 11. 12. the weather being very hot, and after the day I preacht(,) I found a great humour in my legge. hot, pimpling, sore as catbites, running, hard as tending to an inflamacon, I was as quiet and litle urging of it. god in mercy preserve my health. and remove the troublesome pains

July. 13: Ill news of affaires, but while god is good, all shall doe well. I found some indifferent strength for publique service(,) the lord my god in mercy accept mee.

15. after I had fetched in my last hay at home, it rained presently most

Swithin sweetly praised bee my good god, it came more then ordinary well for mee, the raine continues 16. when I heard the P. was dissolved.

July. 20. news amasing. said Sr. G. Wakeman and divers Jesuites all cleard by a vast shout of the papists. lord I understand not the secret strings of this busines. bring things to light, and let wickednesse punish the wicked whence it comes. a coole pleasant raine(.) god good to mee in manifold mercies, in the goodnes and drines of the day.

22. Gods ordinances afford sweetnes and strength to soules. this morning I read in course Isay. 25. and tasted it as speaking of the deliverances god in the end of dayes will afford his people and w[ee] shall see much of it in my day.

July. 27. alarmd with much ill news, as if the wheele were coming on the good interest(,) lords its thine and it shall not miscarry; they doe but dreame of successe(,) when awake they shall see their losse. wee may bee scourged, but they destroyed. I read in course. Isay 30. my strength is to waite on god. after much heate drisling weather this morning. god good to mee in the word, I could say, it was good to draw near to god my god

Aug. 1. My daughter Smith went towards London, my desire was to send her away as they sent Rebekah(,)[1] the lord blesse her in all, her babe staid with us.

Aug: 3. Col. Mildmay with us, about his choice. a great rain. my leg much better I praise god. make my heart better. death can scatter the churches enemies. Nel Guins mother died by one sudden and violent, drunke with Brandie as said.

9. preacht at the burial of Mr Perkins only son, he had twice preacht for mine, the lord blesse the word, some affections stirring

Aug: 10: I had in some corne finisht my own hard corn harvest, the choice of Parliament men at hand, I publiquely stird up people to choose; ind all my corn very well.

Aug: 24. God good in manifold mercies, the skie loured, my hope in god to stop the clouds. god good in the word, my dependance is on my god, to doe all for mee and in mee.

26: begun to picke hops. Rebekah very sicke in a sickly time. shee spake of nothing but dying(,) my wife and her sister Mary halfe down with feare. I was sensible that man is a dependant creature, I had answers of prayers and I lookt for one in her case and I praise god this morning shee slept well. I will glory in my troubles that the power

[1] 'And they blessed Rebekah, and said unto her, Thou art our sister, be thou the mother of thousands of millions and let thy seed possess the gate of those which hate them.' Genesis 24: 60.

of christ may rest upon mee, and his goodns. 27. wett closed our harvest with strange lightning and thunder. 28. exceeding wett, fetcht a jagge of oats from old lodge

30. sun shone but very waterish. proved a good day. loaded my raking barly.

Aug: 31. I have thoughts its easie for god to take things into his hand. great reports of the Kings dangerous illnes, lord spare him if thy pleasure. a dry morning, god good to mee in the word my heart beareth up in trusting him. Rebek: somewhat better god perfect it.

Sept: 7. a very wett time: Rebekah up in the house praisd bee god, a bullocke like to die. often the Sabbath morning afflictive; lord it was mercy this death fell not on wife or child. the lord good to mee in my peace with him, although very afflictive on mine at home and Jane at Lexden, lord smile upon my tabernacle and soule for thy christs sake.

9. my waggon went up to Sturbridge faire with hops. very wett time. god preserve us and all safe. a great crop of hops, but a low price. returnd safe. 11. praised bee god.

Sept. 14. Some London freinds came to see us. said Monmouth. banisht. lord stand by us with thy favour and it shalbee well, god good in his word in manifold mercies he accept mee.

15.16. a wett season. god testifieth against us, and wee testifie not against our sins. helpe lord.

Sowing: 17. wee ended our hoppicking. this 18. day I begun to sow mislain. god blesse our labour and prosper our seed. our family ill. god in mercy sanctifie all providences to us.

Sept. 21. wett. my heart very much out of tune and negligent in my service to god. lord recover mee to more lively vigour and industry, and blesse my labours I pray thee

Sept. 28. A dull day. but something drying, the lord good in his word, but my heart out of frame. things seem to goe heavily with mee. Lord purge out my drosse and accept mee in thy beloved one. a thin family of us. Mary and babe at London. and Reb: abroad.

Oct: 5. A wett day, and season. bad seed time. god in mercy remember us, whom I much forgott in this day, oh negligence creeps on mee help mee lord against it by thy grace in Christ. I desire to stir up my spirit against it.

10. cast up all my accounts with Mr Androws for all owing mee, that I also owed to him(,) it was for two years, til Mich: 1679. past. I was in their debt. which I paid.

Oct. 12. After a wett weeke continual flouds. raining if not day and night, yet every night towards the day breaking. that I could not stir a plow. this night it rained not, yett the skie looketh lowring, god in his due time will give us our seed time. god good to mee in the word, times looke lowring, I cannot but thinke the Courts designe is to make parliaments useles, or rid the crowne of them.

Oct: 19. a wonderfull wett season, I could not stirre a plow the whole weeke; the parliament is prorogued to Jan: 26. next, god bee merci-full to us for in him is our trust, tis my birthday as I reckon and I hope a good day. lord in mercy preserve us, he was good in his word, my hearts desire to serve him all my dayes.

Oct: 26. plows went almost this whole weeke. I plowed 4 days and halfe. god remembred his promise. god good in our health, in manifold mercies(.) Kings towre. but god is good

29. received a letter from my freind Mr Dillingham of Dean.[1] returned him a kind answer. received his.

No: 2. A good weeke, I followed my busines what I could. god good in his word to mee, lord teach mee

Nov. 9. A snowy cold morning, god good in his word, followed my sowing, god prosper the seed.

12. Heard certainly of the death of Mrs Dorothy Dillingham, one I thought loved mee intirely, before my wife. I heard shee never married, but now I find shee died a wife. which was content to mee, shee left no children. perhaps in mercy god disposed thus of us both. Ended Clare hall busines wherin I was a commissioner with Mr Potter to all contents. etc.

Nov. 23. a lovely day, warm and dry. sensible of my coldnes in gods service. lord lett mee not fall into the general spiritual lethargy. but help mee to stir up thy grace. heard Mary had a kind of pox at London(,) blessed bee god for her preservacon. John hampd with the ague lord sanctifie it

Dec: 14: Good winter weather, god good in our health. a strange fog formerly at London which caused colds that the bills were above 700 in beginning Decemb. it decreased 307, god preserve us.

21. The tempestuous snow in church time I ever saw. times sad. wee must not peticon.

25. after feirce frost, thawd: a sad time for affaires but worse in mens carelesse spirits.

Dec: 28. a wett day. my Cosin Gatton brought Mr Williams to mee on Maries account, whom I entertaind kindly and dismist well satisfied. god blesse them. god good in his word.

[1] See p. 7, n. 1 above.

Jan: 4. not a child at home, sensible of the comfort of my wife, my love. seing every thing more pleasant because I have her, god good in his word. there shalbee deliverance

Jan: 11. A glorious day. god good in his words. sin I am sensible the greatest evill.

Jan. 18. A dry day wayes pave. god good in his word, he is the quieter of my heart under all the baitings I meete with, things have a troublesome face yet I hope

Jan: 25. A goodly warme dry season; Allen the quakers speake(r) buried,[1] the men and women following severally in some order: god good to mee in his word. my family afflictive. I will strive by patience and kindnes to win them, how ever to make my life peaceable.

Jan. 26: 79. my. 64 enters

I was sensible of it and affected with gods goodnes, not troubled in 63. as a critical and dangerous year though I often thought of it.[2] I find the danger in my body of death, and indwelling corrupcion which worries. night and day, but it sweetens christ to mee, when right is bitternes. read Ezech. 26.2. I feare Holland and France thinke England is broken, and our glory and trade will fall into their hands while wee groan under misery. but god will a[ri]se and help. the Parl. should have satt this day. its petitiond for. but if they may not sitt for gods interest he will stand up for it. parl. broke Monarchy. perhaps god will have Parl. broken by Monarchicall. time was no addresses to the King by subjects. now the K. will admitt no addresses to him, we will to god who will heare.

29. at Colchester I endeavoured to compose the difference between Mr Wheeler and Mr Harrison, I heard Mr Jessop Minist. of Coxal. a great Parl. formerly now feirce against all dissenters and very intemperate in his speeches died of a cancer in his mouth. thy judgments a great depth.

Feb: 1. A frost with a great wind. god good in his word. my heart negligent. paid for it, with unkindnes, there seems a disappointment in Mary. lord direct mee. wett die 2°.

[1] William Allen, a noted Quaker, co-author of *The Glory of Christ's Light within expelling darkness* (1669), died aged 63, having been a Quaker since 1655. There is a four-page account of his ministry and death in John Tomkins, *Piety Promoted, in a collection of dying sayings* . . . (new edn., 1812), pp. 231–4. These references were kindly provided by Malcolm Thomas of the Friends House Library, London. For his occupation, will, etc., see Appendix 2.

[2] 'The great Climacterical which few escape is seven times nine, which makes sixty three' (Mrs. Jane Sharp, *The Midwives Book* (1671), p. 174).

Feb: 8. dry and windie. great apprehensions of danger to the city and kingdom from the papists on the Dukes return from Scotland. god send peace. a sheep had 3 lambs. god good in his word.

Feb. 22. A goodly season, with some shoures. times gloomy yett quiet. Maries busines at an end. god I hope did it in mercy to us all; god good in his word, and my soule praiseth him

Feb. 29. dry and cold winde. news of a bullocke, ill tidings often on Sabbath morning, I feare I neglect my god in them, but in love warne mee thus to recover my selfe, which by grace I shall doe(.) god good in his word, I find him my only good and joy therefore my heart trusteth in him.

March: 6. great winds with often wett. things quiet. god good in his word. my leg much sweld, yet my heart quiet

13. faire morning and calm after storm and wind. passions trouble things, god good in his quieting word

March 21: A most glorious day, calm in our publique affaires. god good in his word, in whom I will rejoyce

28. A glorious morning, dry. backward in my busines, god good in his word. things looke ill.

Ap. 4. wett cold windie. after much soft corn of all sorts sown. god good in his word, my heart to advance the practice of the lords supper. advance thy name on the whole earth oh my god

Ap: 11: 4 men and 13 women received the sacrament. god good in his word, the weather stormie

Ap. 18. A wett and cold weeke. buried Pain my old workeman, who would boast of his strength, goe almost naked worke in rain, as if nothing could hurt him, colds strucke him into a dropsie, swellied and died. lord thou art my onely hope(.) Mary came home(,) god bee praised for our peace and the gospell

Ap. 25. dry and warmer corn recovering(,) god good in his word, my spirit vain in thought, help lord

May. 2. A goodly day, god good in his word, the lord accept mee and mine of his mercy and doe us good.

May. 9. God was praised for the sweet raines he gave us, things looke ill. god amend all. god good in his word, I will cast my care on him for he hath, doth and will care for mee

May. 16. my wife and daughter returnd safe. god bee praised. an offer to Mary god direct, a wett good morning: I wore the surplice. Jane buried her youngest daughter. gods word good I will roll all my care on him for he careth for mee and I will to the end.

17. rid to court, I avoided receiving articles, through gods goodnes, I cast my care on him, he cared. the matter is the surplice, which I see no sin to use, and shall endeavour to live as quietly as may bee to the end of my race. said the King much better.

May. 23. A great floud and very foule in the meadows: god can make up our losse and I will trust in him, good in his word for under all troubles he taketh care of mee.

27. Rebekah sicke of the small pox: this care also I cast on my god and father. shee hath a mother to nurse her, whose endeavours god blesse; it proved only measles.

May. 30. preacht on the Kings day not 30 there. 2 great flouds in one weeke, a wonderfull lowring skie. all our meadows lost, but gods providence abideth to preserve us. god good in his word, he taketh care of mee, and my care is to please him I prayed for faire weather *z*elously

June. 6. God good in his word, the season cold and shourie my care is cast on god to doe for mee

10. rid to Colchester, ended the difference between Mr Newton and Mrs Seymour about dilapidacons. saw mercy in sparing my son Woodthorp his kill fired. returned safe.

June. 13. A dribbling weeke, that scarce any could farther their haying. god will provide for his and so I cast my care on him. gods word was good, and he will performe his promise of harvest which is a season of ingathering the fruits of the earth.

15. many at R. Hatch funeral. god doe some of their soules good: sweet weather.

June. 20. Good weeke in main though lowering. I pray and hope. god good to mee in the word I hope I shall be enabled to cast all my cares on god for I find he hath card for me

June. 27. wonderful hot. scarce workemen to bee had. I trust god will helpe mee on him I trust. my legg much swelled. we laid burdock[1] leaves to leg and foot. god preserve mee

legg:

Sr Jo. Jaco

I wrot to L. Allington[2] about tithes in Colne parke, old Sr J. J. died 65. and young Sr J. Apr. 4. 1673. my demands are above 30^{li}. my bill to Thacker[3] above 22^{li}. god send mee good speed and pay.

July. 4: a weeke unfitt for work. great raines; lord awaken my heart to

[1] 'Burdock leaves are cooling, moderately drying . . . whereby it is good for old ulcers and sores' (Culpeper, *Herbal*, p. 24).

[2] Sir John Jacob of Stansted Hall, Halstead, who owed tithes on land in EC had married Catherine, sister to Hildebrand, Lord Allington of Horseheath, Cambridgeshire, and died in 1675. Morant, ii, p. 256.

[3] Probably Godfrey Thacker, barrister at law at Gray's Inn from 1675. Foster.

livelynes in holy duties, that the peace of god may make up all outward losses. gods word very sweet

July: 11: a cheerfull morning. god give the light of his countenance for man giveth troubles

18: dull heavy weather. worse times. but worst hearts. god is not minded and no wonder he minds not us, wett Swithins. this day shoures. god good in his word of peace.

July. 25. dullish morning yett I hope well. let it bee a good day wherin Christ may bee preacht and welcomd into hearts, legge something
leg. aswaged by the use of clote leaves(.)[1] god good in his word. my Lord Jesus through his blessed spirit the root and rocke of peace to mee

Aug: 1. A very wett morning, dry hay and corn, in great hazard, but my hope in god to turne all about for good. 6. made a beginning of harvest like to bee long and chargeable.

Aug: 8: A lowring morning, yet I hope in gods covenant. mercies. god good in the word, my desire was to exalt the name of Christ. this day found a lamb dead(,) my man sicke, that which is my best day, often the day of ill tidings, I feare I neglect the Sabbath

Aug: 15. the change die. 14. raind all day. very wett this, yett though in the midst of harvest I am at rest in my mind for weather. oh that my heart could find the influences of grace as sweet and powerfull in my soule. my desires are to honour Christ Jesus

Aug: 22. A good weeke. I made a good progresse in my harvest blessed bee god; this morning my dogs kild a lambe. and a sheep dead: often on Sabbath mornings I have thes losses lord lett me see why. lord I will endeavour more to serve thee in it, and doe thou bee a speciall protection in the same.

28. A great shoure with thunder, caught in it with my raking barly out of Loveland. I was cutting my clover, god in mercy give mee a good time for making it.

Aug. 29. a drisling day. god sweetens all the bitternesses of my life, and in him I trust for it to the end. I had the comfort of it this day(.) god good in his word, I will love thy blessed Jesus.

Sept: 5. A good weeke for businesse. god good in many particulars to mee; god good in his word, my heart in a great calme, my god will take care of mee.

6. the visitacon god good to mee therin. a sad, careles, debaucht, clergy. minding worldly pleasures but slighting if not scoffing at powerfull goodnes. lord awake for thine

[1] Clote: another name for burdock (see p. 628, n. 1 above).

Sept. 12. Very dry and hot. god good in his word, make it good and effectuall to others.

17. returnd from Bromly safe, saw my good freind Harlakendens daughter and her family in health, and my daughters also good be praised. weather hot calm

Sept: 19. dry and hot. Rebekah hopefull. leg runs much(,) use green

leg. Tobacco leaves much asswaged:[1] god cure, god good in his word, visited some sicke. god watch over us for good

Sept: 26. my wife cheerfull after a very weaking fitt. rains and looketh. lowring, my seed time backward. I have sown but 3 dayes.

Oct: 3. Hobstevens sown but one peice. wee are ill and weakely but I hope recovering(,) my leg drieth and healeth and asswageth; I found god good in his word.

Oct. 10. my wife very ill. litle hopes of life. my faith held god would spare her and I hope it shalbee so. my body emptied by vomitt and purge that my leg is very small. I hope this sicknes recovered will even make us young againe.

Oct. 17: Weather very sweet. god gives hopes of great mercy to us, my heart plise him for grace to honour him. I preacht with some life, working for god helps mee

Oct. 24: Good weather, god addes to my hopes in my wife(.) Parl. satt. and Kings speech good the lord blesse the assembly: Mr Androws father died. troubles to them. wherin I am desirous to helpe them. shee and her mother 25. went towards London. god gave mee strength for the day

Oct. 31: a lovely. dry. brown day. good news of our Parliament. god good in his word to mee

No. 1. a constant wett day. John gott two places ended sowing in farther Readings. I feare bad.

No: 14. a cheerful day no frost as yett, god good in his word. my wives cold holds still

Dec: 5. Frostie weather, began (c.o. Tuesday) Monday. Nov: 20. god good in his word(.) received 20s. to distribute to our poore at my discretion, given I beleive above 30. yeares agone.

Dec. 12. frost began Tuesday night. Nov: 30. yett continueth, saw such a taile of a blazing star never saw the like for length.[2] god good to mee in his word.

[1] Culpeper, *Herbal*, pp. 89, 94, gives recipes in which the green leaves of both English tobacco (yellow henbane) and tobacco (henbane of Peru) are made into salves for sores.

[2] Evelyn noted this meteor on the same day, and gives a detailed description of it. Evelyn, iv, p. 235.

Dec. 26. windie and dirty, god good in himself and word. things sufficiently troublsom.

28. I buried Major Bowes at Bromly. neither wife nor child at grave shee gone to Olivers and the son in the house. a tedious jorny returnd by Olivers and gave them the best counsel I could: 30: safe at home.

Jan. 2. Frost continues: 6. the blazing star almost vanisht: 10. Parliament prorogued to Jan: 20. City petitioned. 13. they might sitt again: 16. frost continues in the ground.

16. 16. god good to us in our health, in the word. lett my soule live.

1680

26. sensible this day entred my 65. yeare, I morning it with god that he would bee with mee. subduing my corruptions; and keeping my heart close to him through the grace of Christ, and blesse mee and mine, and I hoped in his mercy.

Feb. 1. frost continues

Feb: 6. a cold day, god good in his word all peace about us for which god bee praised(.) wee were gathering for the captives of Algiers, god blesse our worke.

Feb: 13. open. wett. yet ice in ponds. god good in our publique peace. my families health. yet my heart full of vain thoughts and on my bed. god good in his word.

Feb. 27. our choice without opposicon, wettish weather. god good in his word on him I lay hold.

March. 6: cold winterly weather. all quiet in the nacon. god good in his word, praise to him

March. 20. My wife very ill again god restore her, weather dry yet cold; my heart is vain, oh lord fire all on thy selfe his word good, one of our town in jayle for the highway trade to my great losse I feare.

27. A wonderfull cold time and wettish, the spring backward. Mary is gone to London(.) parliament sits god was in our healths and in his word, which is comfortable to mee

Ap: 3. dry. 12 of us received the sacrament. son Smith with us. 28 Parl. dissolved. god liveth for ever and that is my hope, he is good and will doe good. Duke expected at London

Ap. 10. dry. windie, times quiet. god good in his word in manifold mercies(.) my wives ague returns often. lord restore her and give her a thankfull and quiet minde.

Ap: 17. drie. and windie, I prayed for raine with hopes in god, when all signes against it. god will command it in his due time, god good in his word. trials call for patience

Ap: 19. a sweet raine and though no signes of any. this 24. yet god will give us a plentiful raine and I hope in its season, times looke louringly god give mee a submitting heart to him.

May. 1: Rain holds of, it will come in its season and I look up for it, grasse backward(,) hearts naught, my wife afflicts mee and her self, god learns mee patient submission(.) god good in his word.—2. observed the grasse in severall grounds burnt

May. 8. the ground a litle moistned. god giveth a view of rain, my need is more then my means, I doe pray and looke up and god will heare, preacht of affliction. I hope god will arme mee with patience, for I have need of it.

May. 15. drought and heats the earth drieth away, shews of rain. god good in his word

May. 22. rain past away, god afflicts mee in my deare wife. god kind in my inward quiet

29. A very severe drought continues an effect of gods displeasure. caused by the comett god remove his hand in mercy. yea he will or support mee, who feel as much of it as any in our parts.

June. 2. hopes of rain but past away so. 4. on June. 3. Mary quitted Mr Rhea.[1] her exceptions were his age being 14 yeares older, shee might bee left a wid. with children. shee checkt at his estate being not suitable to her porcon. which estate of his I suppose not above 350 at most besides his living of an 100[li]. considering his debts, he seemed to her not loving, it was no small greif to mee, but I could not desire it, when shee said it would make both their lives miserable. I shall observe the issue on both parts, Mr Rhea's estate was not as I thought

June. 5. a great drought no hopes of rain, the earth faints, god will heare(,) his word was good.

June: 11. 12. My good daughter Smith came to mee safe, very late, my people feared hurt by my horse. but the coach came late, I will praise the lord for his mercy, none can thinke the trouble I had with my catle by reason of drought, yet our god shall blesse us. god good in his word, help mee patiently to waite on god, praying and looking up.

June. 19. Great drought prayed with hope for rain in our particular if god

[1] Ambrose Rhea, rector of Wakes Colne 1678–92; from the date of his admission at Cambridge it appears he was born in 1644, which would indeed make him fourteen years older than Mary Josselin, born in 1658. Venn.

will not give to all places(,) there was a shoure at night past over us, leg: dashing us and giveth assurance of more. my legge swels, painful god will heale, his word good and I will patiently waite on him; June. 23 it raind in the night, and all day, very fast, but without wind, it thundred. it continues to raine. 24: I suppose it will bee a satisfying raine. I take it as a token for good.

June. 26: god good in his word, my heart pants after him as my cheife joy and setts up its rest in him, and this rendors my troubles gentle. my desires are to bee sweeter to those that trouble mee. setting up all my comfort in god, who will make up all to mee

July. 3. growing weather, and peaceable dayes, god continue his kindnes, leg. my leg indifferent, I take the golden spirit scurvy grasse;[1] god was good to mee in the word of affliction. I hope he will helpe mee to beare them christianly.

9. sew above 5 acres turneps farther side (c.o. Tiballs) Pitchers, with lesse than 3 quarts seed.

July. 10. A good season. god good in his word, all quiet in city and country, under noise of imprisonments.

11. a goodly rain for my turneps pastures and corn. I had no grasse down.

July. 17. A rainy day. ill hay weather. god good to mee in his word, my old neighbour Burton died

July. 24. uncertain weather, yet wee gett in hay, turneps come up. our leg: quiet continues, my leg is as painfull and angry with heat, my heart is to doe god some service in my place. Bettie my good child went for London god prosper her. god good in his word, its a comfort in my afflictions

July. 31. A gloomy day. bad haying not yet done. god give a good harvest, by my troubles here I hope a better porcon. I will serve and trust in god who was good to mee in his word and providence

Aug. 7. A goodly harvest weeke, god good to mee, in inning all my hay down about 6. load and in most of my hard corn, and some tithes. John a severe trouble, lord change him if it may bee. all things quiett in the country. god good in the word help mee to consider my ways.

Aug. 14: An uncertain weeke. thunder and rain interrupted our harvest, my troubles continue and I hope god will encrease patience. I am almost beat out of familie duties

Aug. 21. Indifferent good harvest weather, praise to god, yett wee gott in

[1] Scurvy grass: a herb (cochlearia officinalis) believed to possess anti-scorbutic properties, i.e. to prevent scurvy. NED.

but litle, it being a strange scattering harvest. hard corn done and scarce any soft corn ripe but oats. a great fog. god good to us in our publique peace and in his word, the lord in mercy accept mee in his christ.

Aug. 28: god good in his word and in outward mercies, my wife was at London god preserve her.

Sept: 4: a very wett season, much soft corn abroad: wife was ill and lett bloud, god send her well home. 13. day. very sensible of my great
13. neglect of prayer and stirring up my heart after god so that thence vanity, gets great strength in my mind, lord helpe in christ Jesus

Sept: 18: Heard not from my wife and children from London 2 weeks togither, I hope the best(.) a sad season for hay, worse in my heart. god was good in his word when shall I find my heart in a due frame.

[*25*] Heard all well at London. god blesse my seed time. my heart vain, lord helpe mee with the grace in that to overcome all evils, gods word very good and precious.

[*Oct*: 2.] [*M*]oist. it was with regret Mary rid to Lexden with the child. god preserve them. I neglect prayer and my heart contrac. the word good with intimacons I deale not well with Christ and suffering so many vaine thoughts to lodge within mee. lord helpe mee.

made an end of sowing dry. Oct: 8: Oct. 1. my daughter Elizabeth
Oct. 9 safe delivered of her first son: This morning begun to raine, all calm in the nacon. god good to mee in his word, blesse mee lord and mine and make us blessings to all ours

Oct: 16 Saw ice in a skillet,[1] a curious coole day. John married unknown to mee,[2] god pardon his errors. pray god blesse him. his word very good to mee, make it so to all

19. The good Lady Honywood died early.[3] I went to see her and found shee was dead, I prayed with her the 17. shee was in a good frame, shee was my good freind, and I hers(,) wee lived in love about 40. y. acquaintance, I was serviceable every way to her for soule and body, and in her estate more then ordinary, shee left mee no legacy in her will, shee said shee would adde a codicile to remember mee and some others, but not done. Mr Honywood desired mee on 17. however god dealt with his mother, I would continue my respect to him and the family.

[1] Skillet: a cooking utensil of brass, copper, or other metal. SOED.

[2] To Martha Bentall of Halstead, see Josselin genealogy in Appendix 1.

[3] She died aged 75: Morant, ii, p. 169, writes that 'She is said to have been one of the most remarkable persons of her time for Wisdom, Piety, and Charity'. Notes of the sermon preached by Mr. Livermore at her death were taken by Bufton (Beaumont, p. 229 quotes extracts).

Oct. 23. Some rain, heard all well at London my praises to god for the same, god good in his word. I have great experience of mind vanity, lord help mee against the same, it imbitters my life

26. The good old Lady Honywood buried. not a glove, ribband, scutcheon, wine, beare. bisquett given at her burial but a litle mourning to servants, the servants carried her, six persons with scarfs and gloves bare up the pall.

Oct. 30. A very wett season, yet no floud, the ditches and ponds not fild. sensible of the vilenes of my heart, christ is precious, but oh when when shall his grace be victorious. my soule hopeth it

Nov: 6. Very wett causing great flouds, yet I brought in some wood I wanted, all quiet, comforted in the news of my wives designed returne, sensible of the vanity of my mind, yett god was good in his word, my soul thirsteth to be constant to god, oh when when.

11. One Creffeild came a servant, lord lett him gett good and doe mee good; my wife came not down from London. I stopt rising troublous thoughts, and heard all was well, a speciall occasion detained her, which shee did to content mee, and so I accept it. the confidence of god my fathers providence quiets mee against causeles feares in disappointments

No: 13 A calme dry morning, my heart wrought to doe god some special service in soules that they might live as those that have received from god in christ.

17. my wife came safe from London, very plumpe and fatt, god blesse us with peace.

No: 20: Yet no winter weather, my wife at Markshall, to see the family at their breaking up, god good to mee in his word, lord blesse it to all that heare it

No. 27. dry and windie, nothing yet of winter, heard of E. of Shaftesbury acquitall, by the grand jury, the country and city wrung of it with joy. god good to mee in his word. my legg. swelled much in the
leg: calf and upwards, lord bee my salvacon

Dec: 4. Cold, dry. pleasant. this morning the first meat given catle abroad, gods providence good to his interest in the world. possesse my heart and rule it for ever. god good in his word(.) gathered for the French protestants.

Dec. 11. Some rain in the night. windy and cleare, yet the skie is rain-like. god good in his word(.) my wife and I lovingly entertaind abroad. at home an undutiful son troubles us.

Dec: 18: Cold. windie, a great floud. god good to mee in my health, in his word, good in publique and private providences, lord accept mee in thy welbeloved, who is my life

D. 25. A stormy wett day, a peaceable calm in the land, when wee expected troubles on the meeters[1] against home occasion was sought, god good in his word, he in mercy acept mee

Jan. 1. God good in his word, things very quiet in the land notwithstanding threats against dissenters(.) a stormy night, litle Jane not well, god bee the porcon of mee and mine.

Jan. 8. Various weather, now wett, no snow scarce frost quietnes in our borders and in the city. on which by a quo waranto they endeavour to gain mercy, god good in his word my heart to him

Jan. 15. Various weather, yet no frost, a calm in affaires at present, my god exerciseth mee with troubles, and there is cause. I see him my onely good, his word my comfort I repine not.

Jan. 26. 1681

Sensible this day entred mee into my 66 yeare, read this day in course Deut. 30.20 god is my life and obedience the way of life. there is nothing more pleasant than cleaving to god and to him I devote my soule, to love him and trust in him, and to take more heed to please him(.) hitherto a moist windie, open winter, tree springing and budding: Mr Androws ill. and this day died which will occasion much trouble to mee, but as my dayes and so I hope my strength shalbee.

Frostie Jan. 29. some cleare days and this frostie, god was good to us in outward mercies, the lord make providences sweet and comfortable to mee, god good to mee in his word, and he causeth my heart to hope in him according to it. Ps. 119.49.

The east wind brought a great frost very vehement. Feb. 2.

Feb: 12. My son Smith came very welcome to see us, and his thriving child, a glorious shining day. god good in his word, he will not leave us comfortles, but comforts in our afflictions

Feb. 19. Some days very moist aire all said much wett, this morning very cleare, day dry but gloomy, god good in his word, that is the great comfort in afflictions

Feb: 26. Wett. heard of my daughter Smiths illnes. god send her well. god good in his word.

March: 5. frost and cleare so two days before, god good in his word. this

[1] Meeter: one who attends or takes part in a meeting, esp. nonconformists. SOED. Dissenters still called 'meetingers' in some Essex villages. Probert.

weeke alarmd by an hastie letter and messenger as if my daughter Smith were dying: her mother arose and away presently for a coach to London, and found her better of which I was certified speedily(.) Mrs Androws whom I brought into the priory, would not lett it to my son and mee, but to one that married into the family of Abbutt, that bearded her housband, and hated Mr Harlakenden, and unconcerned her self with mee. god bee my porcon and that is enough.

March. 12. My wife and Beck safe from London indifferent well there(,) god bee praised(,) this weeke, cold, frost some snow rain hindring
1682 the plow all quiet(.) said D Y. come to yarmouth to meete the King at Newmarkett god send all well. god good in his word.

March: 26. A cold weeke and windie, yett our plowes went. heard all well at London, for which I blesse god; Jane Woodthorp had a dangerous fitt, god good in his word, perform thy promises oh lord.

Apr. 2. Cold, dry and windie, our plowes goe, the ground hardens apace. god good in his word. the spring much like last years

9. Cold, dry yett cheerfull begun to sow barly. 8. in Pitchars; things calm, most *secure* but surely the papists have some great thing in doing.

barly. Sew part of Pitchards dry, but 13. a wonderfull rain on it. so continues 14: 15. a wonderfull shoure of haile. Foster a robber of our town taken here supposed he intended to have robd Mrs Ellistons.[1] 14 of us at sacrament. the lord accept us, whom wee praise for an heart to own him, his word was very good give mee a bottom sincerity.

Ap: 23. Said Foster dead. nothing affects some(.) I found a wett weeke not sown my oats yett, god good in many mercies, yett my life very unquiet esp: from my wife; 26. the greatest floud that hath been for many yeares, a very cold season hindring both sowing, and fallowing.

Ap: 30. faire, but a lowring skie, much land even drownd and mired, publique quiet to god bee the praise; health among us in this wett season. god good in his word for which I blesse him.

May. 7. wett. flouds this weeke, I could not stirre a plow, much soft corn spoild. I had a bad markett for corn, my family troubles continue,

[1] Joseph Bufton of Coggeshall noted in his 'Diary' (ERO, T/A, 156) that 'About Lammas 1682 there was one Foster a baker of Colne hanged at Chelmsford for robbing'. This was John Foster, said to be of Ingatestone when indicted at the Assizes for robbing John Richardson on the highway, yet clearly of Earls Colne, as the biographical details in Appendix 2 show (PRO, Assizes 35/123/2, no. 16).

esp. a froward wife. god give me patience for its with him I have to doe, to whom I humble my self. it proved a drying day. god is good

May. 14. a dry day. meadows dirty, god good to mee, John went to his house. god blesse him send peace.

16: rid up to London. found my children well, returnd safe. May. 26. for which my god bee praised, the citie much hated by the Court, the Judges much pervert justice(,) looke on oh god, for matters work down to thee alone, thou art the helper of the poore

May. 28. dry, warm, ill with cold and jorny, all things indifferent well at home. fruitful yeare for grasse. god good in his word. lord doe mee and mine good in all our wayes.

June. 3. Some shoures this weeke with great haile, weather coole, god good in the season and good in his word, the lord preserve mee to his holy kingdom.

June. 11. bad hay weather. yet publique peace. a cool morning: god good in his word, lord keep up the spirit of supplicacon among us in mee, and save our land.

Ju: 18. my daughter Smith and her son came safe to mee. no good hay weather, our publique peace a great mercy. god good to mee in his word, the lord blesse mee and mine

June. 25. a bad hay weather, lately wett. this night raind, and now lowring the change some hours past. yet gods word for a season shall stand. yet publique quiet. prayed for faire weather with hopes. god good in his word, make it a blessing lord to all of us. and thine. well at Lexden.

July. 2. cold. windy ill weather the like not known in my memory raind every day last weeke and some say about 7 weeks past, and I cannot say the contrary. god was good to mee in his word, yet quiet, though things sone to goe high

July. 9. hitherto some rain daily, in some places flouds, wee cleard our washt feilds. yet publique peace through mercy. Jane went home, gods blessings in Christ bee on all mine: my leg swels much and is painful, lord help and heale. prayed for faire weather. god good in his word

July. 16. A good weeke for busines. hot, I did not loose my time but could not improve it as I would wanting mowers, yet publique peace; god good in his word for which I blesse his name.

23. A bad weeke for busines in our parts, god help us out in our busines, yet peace. daily shoures, god good in his word, his pleasure taketh place in all things

July. 30. an indifferent good hay weeke blessed bee god, I gott *inish* and cocks and some into houses. this day cheerful. they harvest about us. god good in our publique peace. god good yett my heart very dead, lord quicken mee that I may provoke others, faire after fears of wett.

Aug: 6. I was wonderfully cast in my businesse, I gett forward slowly yett a good weeke past(.) I trust god will help mee out of all thes straits, oh if a gathering time for hay and corn bee good what is it to gather in Christ and his pearles and soule mercies; a very great shoure in our parts with thunder. god trieth us. yet good in his word and in our publique peace

Aug. 13. A good harvest weeke. god helpt mee in it. got all my hay on cocks, many loads in(,) got in all my hard corn. and tith. most of my oats down, and neare 5 acres in. blessed bee god(.) the popish partie seem to overdrive and flag. yet publique peace. lord give mee a publique heart to doe for thy glorious name, in my place. it deweth but god will helpe mee. god in his word was good to mee, oh that my heart were more drawn out to him

15. My deare child Mrs Elizabeth Smith and her young boy, went from mee towards London, healthful and thriving, shee was with mee with sweetnes and content, that made her company pleasant to mee, I parted with her in all love. gods blessings with her

Aug. 20. comets seen.[1] yet publique peace. I preacht without a cap, god preserve mee, wee strucke a great stroke in harvest. god good in his word and season.

22. I made an end of mowing all my corn.

[Au]g: 27: more grasse, bad weather, god will send good and I will trust him he lengthens out our publique peace. bapt. Cobs child publikely many of the congregacon present.

Sept: 3. Mary at home all well at London. yet publique quiet, an ill day for hay, but I trust god for better, the word of mercy, this day was good and sweet to mee,

Sept. 10: yet peace, Box refuses to bee sheriff. a dry time. I got forward much in my businesse. blest bee my good god that helpd mee. This day great shews of rain, but I hope well(.) god good in a doctrine of mercy.

Sept. 19: yet publique peace, the drought continued. finisht my tedious haying, god good and merciful to mee in his word, oh my soule blesse him. Beck gon for London god preserve her

Sept. 24: A dry weeke, yet publique peace. heard all well at London, rid

[1] Halley's comet, which Evelyn also saw (Evelyn, iv, p. 291).

to Lexden found all well. god good to mee in his word, Johns wife likely to bee a trouble to us.

Oct. 1. drought continues, things dishonour themselves in arbitrarines. god is the same and he will continue his goodnes to his. the word of mercy was sweet to mee.

Oct. 8. drought. a good weeke(.) heard well and comfortably of all my daughters, my busines went of well. god good to mee in his word, yet peace, poore London findes trouble

Oc: 15. drought. though shews of and some litle dewes, peace continues, god good in his word of mercy, I trust and hope in the mercy of god for ever

Oct. 22. ground wett to the shares point, peace continued, news forbidden, god was good to mee in his word, the lord my god accept mee.

Oct. 29. Dry. Cool weather; finisht sowing 24. still publique peace, god good in the season, smal pox with us, god stop it. Mr Day[1] writt about Mary and his son. god shew us mercy therin. a painfull day, that weaknd strength, but god good to mee in his word.

Nov. 5. much troubled with my leg, and backe with pains. it may bee god doth it to better my soul. thats my hope. and it may bee, yet revive my old age, however I will hope in his mercy, who remembers his in their low estate.

No. 12. frost with cold east winde, yet quiet though alarmd with a great tumult, 6. about the bonfires, god good in his word, he remembers mee, lord lett mee never forgett thee and thy christ

Coal. 14. began to burn coal: 15. it began to raine

No. 19 shining morning after much wett(,) quiet in our streets, persons forcd to church about us, the lord good in his word who doth and will remember his in their low estate.

24. Jo. Burton buried(.) he had wife and 3 sons, shee and one son rich and would not bury him, nor accompany him to the grave, but left him to the town to bury.

No. 26. dry, cleare day. a great fire at Wapping by the towne, a 1000 houses said to bee burnt. yet publique peace, god good in his word and his mercy shalbee with mee all my dayes.

30 Reading Job: 33.14.15.[2] dream: I called to mine my dreams often this summer and last night how I had some way put my self voluntarily out of the ministry, and afterwards was always greived and

[1] The father of Edward Day who, on 10 April 1683, married RJ's daughter Mary.

[2] 'For God speaketh once, yea twice, yet man perceiveth it not. / In a dream, in a vision of the night, when deep sleep falleth upon men, in slumberings upon the bed;'.

troubled for it. and that by heeding others I was hindred from preaching. my not that an instruction of god to doe what lieth in mee to keep up my ministrial care and imployment.

Dec. 3: cloudie but dry. our plowe went. god good in his word of mercy, lord glad my soule with it.

10: Cloudie and dry. much foggie weather our plowes went, all corn riseth bad, and price cheape. troubles to goodmen at London, yet publique peace. god good in his word, lord bee gracious

Dec. 17 cloudie, open and dry weather, all well at London, god good in his word of mercy. heard of my son Woodthorps being at markett, god good in providing for mee this bad yeare for tenants.

B. Gatton Dec. 24. on the 25 at one of the clocke my freinds came from London. the greatest chrismas I kept there being 2 young men Mr Day and Mr Spicer.[1] wellwillers to my virgin daughters. wee had good society. 3 of them went away. the 29th. well satisfied.

Dec. 31. Strange various weather, god good in his word: all in publique peace.

Jan. cold wind, very various weather, heard our freinds gott well to London, received good presents from them, god direct our affaires, god good in his word of mercy.

leg 8. at night ill: 10. my knee on the sore side red and sweld, god will help and heale. 11. it began to bee wett weather.

21. a winter day, snow. wett and cold. my knee indifferent praisd be god, I sleep better(.) god good in his word, all our freinds well at London. troubles about meetings

Jan: 26: 67. y. begun

sensible this entred my 67. y. I blest god for his presence thus far with mee. I heartily repent me of my sins and hope in his mercy. Pro. 28.13. I read in course. Ps. 31. which was a comfort to mee, I committ my soule. and all concerns to god and hope to see Israels sons.

Jan. 28. A bitter morning from my wife, twice I mett with it already: god give mee patience and to see all my springs are in him, god good in his word. poore dissenters hatterd,[2] yet wee are in publique peace praisd bee god.

30. kept the Kings day. Mr Day with us, poor dissenters hatterd at London.

[1] Both subsequently married RJ's daughters, see Josselin genealogy.

[2] Hatter: to harass, to wear out. SOED.

Feb: 4. A brown day and dry. god good in his word, I find my breath short, and much of my strength, god fitt mee for what he pleaseth to doe with mee, mercy and truth shall follow mee all my dayes.

Feb: 11. dry, and yet a backward spring, yet our publique peace continues, freinds well at London. god good to mee in his word, I will trust in his mercy for mee and mine and praise his name.

Feb: 18. This weeke my breath was much stopt, which in such a body of humours was very dangerous, but my hope is in god to turn all to the best, my leg sweld much: the season dry. god good in his word(,) all ours well at London. but freinds hattered.

Feb: 25. This morning being cold windy and wett I preacht not, god pardon mee(,) it was not out of neglect, it was a force on mee. some days past my breath so short as if I should have died if I stird but a litle. my leg sweld wonderfully. and issue run out litle. when I sat still I felt no pain nor trouble, the thoughts of the dropsie returnd on mee [*but I felt*] no water in my body. wee used opening things. this morning my urine was a blacke [*settement*]. god [*took*] the feare of death from mee, my two daughters on their marriage which I was desirous to perfect.

26. at night wonderfull ill, I took pils. I had two stooles in the night and some after [ ] which did much open and lighten my body. 27. I slept ill. and find pains in my right side. god [*be*] praised for all wee meet with.

March: 3. I walkt before the house, my children. alarmd at London Mr Day ca[*me*] hastily down and found mee at the gate. god gave mee liberty for his holy word(,) my breath returns, the season very good: 6. my children came down. 7. Jon[athan] came with his bullocks: 12. Mr Day, Mary Bettie and my litle Jane rid up to London. 15. 16. [*I took*] of Daffy Elixir,[1] it wrought much with mee. 17. I was taken ill at the priory. sneezing(,) all things present[*ed them*]selves duoble to mee. I was lead home; none preacht. 20. my children came from London, Gilber[*t Smith*] with them, my great and dangerous cough ceasd. 27. 28. sweld down to my fundament. with a very [*great pain*] and so I am this 31: god bee mercifull til all his good towards mee bee accomplished.

April. 1. This day I had an indifferent good day. Mr Ludgater supplied my place. god teach us al[ ]

[1] A recipe to make 'the true Daffy's Elixer' is given in the *Compleat Housewife* (p. 274) and includes fennel-seed and two gallons of brandy; another recipe in the same work (p. 350) states that 'This elixir is excellent good for the cholic, the gravel in the kidneys, the dropsy, griping of the guts, or any obstruction in the bowels; it purgeth two or three times a day'.

April. 8: my freinds being here from London, Mr Spicer and son Smith came in before 8 of the c[*lock. I*] went down and read prayers and preacht a litle more than an houre from ps. 8.6. I will dwell in [*the house*] of god for ever, goodnes should stirre up to more obedience *once* in gods outward worship.

10. Mary Josselin my 3^d daughter being somewhat above 25. y. old married to Mr Edw[*ard Day by*] license under Bets hand. he was a tallow chandler of St Martins, he saith he cl[*early receive*] *weekely*, he is his fathers only child, a man of a good estate, and godly conversacon. I [*gave*] her for porcon, my house I dwell in and land belonging thereto worth 400^li. and an 10[0^li.]

11. Mr Smith. and Mr Spicer rid towards London. so did old Mr Day and his son Mr [*Edward.*]

Ap: 15. I was very short winded and with much difficulty went and up and down to church w[*here preacht*] I was very ill, and concluded by the swelling of my thighs and belly it was the dropsy [*I sent to*] London to Dr Cox[1] about it, god blesse the means I shall use.

May. 2. my children went to London. their sister Jane tooke on at mee and them for their great porcons [*My wife set*] upon mee also die. 4°. god give mee patience for I have more than ordinary need of it.

4: heard of the health of my children: Cox sent mee his old receits: the Apothecary made [*mee*] pay deare. god in his mercy doe mee good by them. Mr Livermore preacht twice for mee.

8. Mr Spicer married my youngest daughter Mrs Rebekah: I rid down in her coach and [*held*] it for them, my son Smith came down with them; they returnd die the 12: my wife [*at*] first much troubled, I was joyd god had so well provided for her. I gave her 500^li. down and with my blessing sent her away. I tooke my phisicke from Dr Cox in the meane t[*ime.*] my wife apprehends it doth mee no good, but I cannot bee fully of that minde. Mr Rhea p[*reacht*] not himselfe but procured Mr Perkins to preach for mee in the afternoon. I slept about an [*hour*] in the hall, I was refreshed by it I praise my good god for it.

May: 14: taking the harts horne drops[2] I found my phelgm gathered much and thicke in my chest still my hope is in god to bring mee out of all thes troubles though I am much sweld in my [*legs so*]

[1] Probably Thomas Coxe, physician in the Parliamentary Army, one of the original Fellows of the Royal Society, physician to the King, 1665, died 1685. Venn.

[2] Harts horn drops: substance obtained by rasping and slicing the horns of stags, formerly the chief sources of ammonia and used as smelling salts in the liquid form. NED.

that I can scarce goe, and much straitned in the nights in my chest. my stomacke was indiffer[*ently well*] this 19 day and I rellisht my beare, and my bakt meate.

May. 20. Mr Livermore preacht. I began Mrs Spicers ale, I thought it did mee go[od.] more than ordinary stools away. lord I desire to live and serve thee in my relacons, and I[ ] received nothing from London last weeke. yett this I sent to them all. my drinke works well with mee, yett I am [*in pain*] sharp more than ordinary. god will raise mee up in due time that I may praise him. yett its lesse than [ ]

25. drunk my broome beere in my bed I endeavourd to sleepe after it, I sweat indif[*ferently*]

31. a wonderfull wett May, I was as sweld, and short breathd as if I should not have [*lasted the*] night, but god had mercy on mee.

June. 1: I saw my countenance much changed, it was 3 days that my left leg ran much; 3. I did no[*t think*] I gathered strength nor lost any, but in the use of means continued in the same way. however I stay [*myself*] on my good god, that this sicknes doth not issue in death, but in a trial to doe mee much good. Mr Perkins p[*reached*]

9. In April and May my eyes recovered their perfect sight. and my wen[1] went of my ey[*lid. I*] doe not know how this dropsy will cure, but I am perswaded god will remove it, [*and I will*] praise him for it

June: 10: God helpt mee by Mr Livermore. wee begun haying Tuesday.
12. on the 14. I sent up 2 [ ] pigs to my children and spent 3 at
17. home. Mr Rhea preacht for mee, my dropsie surely abat[*ing*.] I am very unfitt to goe up and down. heard from all at London never could pigs [*come so timely*] they having freinds at dinner with them. Sparrow faild mee to my great greife.

22. My wife on a suddain went up to London, to see the children. god send her well. 24. [Mr] Perkins preacht for mee, I slept very well the night passd which much refresht mee.

July. 1: The weeke past, I slept well. my hands dry, my swelling much in my thighs, and cods, above I seem pretty we[*ll*.] I find not my breath so troublesom as some nights formerly, Mr Livermore preacht for mee[, *heard*] of a new plot. said L. Russel and Grey sent to the tower. wee shall heare more afterwards [*heard*] my wife and all the children well at London.

July. 7. my wife returnd safe from London, my six sons and daughters came to the coach with [*her*] in health. Mr Sarjant preacht for mee, god blesse his labours, about the 10th day I [*took*] my scurvy grasse

[1] Wen: a lump or protuberance on the body, a wart. SOED.

drops, 12 at a time. I thought once it purgd mee, I found [*relief from*] the sciatica, laying a plaister to my backe. it was better

July. 15. God good in my preservacon. Jonathan went to Colchester, I rid [*to church in the*] afternoone, where I had not been to preach about 3 months.

July. 22: saw a breif account of my Ld Russels trial and others, who were all condemned b[*the trial*] was at Hicks hall. god good to mee in my support, in my condicon

July. 29. wee begun harvest. July. 27. reaping and mowing. god send us [*a good season.*] heard all well at London, the German nearly [ ] by was the [ ]

Miscellaneous notes by Ralph Josselin, written in the front and back of the Diary manuscript

Jottings in Ralph Josselin's hand at front of diary

4.1.— Sept–Oct. 6. menses fatales. attende sis
5.0.0. quibus in rebus. Sept. 15. 57. videbimus per
Decembris decimum sequentem[1]

yett p in gd 9 on the first day 17th week 1–0–10

Pemble to Constable D*ept*d

Ap; 26; 80 bold mare horse by colt 8 4–11
9 2 6 half that—Cotton on *communion* to Mr Clarke

li	li	s
169458426	7	10
6.16.6.	3.	0.
3:17.6		19.
1.3.10	1.	5.

(c.o. li	s	d)
3.	10.	0.
1.	4.	6.

17984563251 li

10: M.G.	Lambert. laid by. Bridge Butler Berry Fleetwood Barksted Skippon as good as Kelsy is one Goffe Desborough Whalley

Ralph Josselin

3–17–6 possibly I may and yet may not

d.–0. 4. 0.
books–2. 0. 0
seats 0 from Ch. 8. 0

puritans

Lorde owne my soule

[1] 'fateful months. pay attention, you may be in some matters. Sept. 15. 57. We shall see during the following tenth of December.'

the lord is onely Briscoe } Lord keep
yesterday

500
50
50 Lord keepe mee from those evills that
50 1656 layeth the foundacon of
50
50 He that preacheth Christs words is Christs minister. John. 3.34.1.
50 horesco Tim. 4. 6
50 the lord is onely my support
350
850 850li

Jottings in Ralph Josselin's hand at back of diary

7: 16:
14: 0.
2: 10:
24: 6:
2: 6: 8
26: 12. 8.
27. 5. 4.
54. 10. 8.
109. 1. 4.
218. 2. 8.

Ralph Josselin

Toms 8 yeares begin. June. 24. 1659.

1. past. June. 24. 1660.
2. past. June. 24. 1661.
3. past. June. 24: 1662
4. past. June. 24. 1663
5. past. June. 24. 1664.

Mr Cosin's receipt for inke

take galls: / .v:copparas. / .iii:Gumme. / .ii. beate your galls and put all togither into a quarte of raine water, or rather strong worte and stirre it once a day at least. lett it stand. 14. or 21. dayes but not come at ye fire.

Oct. 26: 64: sun shone into the childrens window a litle. but gone out from my chamber at rising

Jan: 4. 67. Saw the sun sett in the kitchin next pane to our dining place.

Dec. 15. Saw the rising sun in the washing place.

Aug: 9th. 1679. I setle the moity of Stonebridge Meadow on my son John for life and I pay him 50s. yearly out of it, and this till I revoke this act. witnesse my hand Ralph Josselin.

Certaine remarkeable things that fell out in my remembrance:

1: The marriage of P. Charles K of England etc: to a papist, with so many indulgences to her religion, and treating with none but papists, as formerly with the Infanta of Spaine.

2: The strange carriage of things in England a protestant state, wheeling in points of doctrine, in ceremonyes towards popery, and in prosecuting orthodoxe men of the ministry and otherwise. this lasted untill. 1638: then abated.

3: The strange carriage of K. James in the Palatinate matters and of K.C. there and also towards Rochell in betraying the same;

4: Gustavus (c.o. Horn) Adolphus the Noble Swedes descent into Germany for releife of the distressed prostestant Princes and for the liberty of Germany where he dyed the warres yett continue by that crowne;

5: The Revolt of Portugal from the King of Spayne, and advancing the Duke of Braganza un[to] that kingdome,

6: The continuall warres betwixt the House of France, and Austria, which could by no meanes bee reconciled.

7: The taking up defensive armes by the Scots: 1638. which was occasiond by urging a popish Liturgy and Canons upon them it ended in the rooting out Episcopacy, and settling Presbytery.

8: The calling of a parliament, and settling it by a standing act. 1640 and marrying the Lady Mary by K C to the prince of orange, when that the plott was to enslave us to popery by the sword

9: The sad bloody warre in Ireland the popish Rebells by the just judgment of god prevayling almost over the whole kingdome excepting a few particular sea townes and some parts of Ulster possessd by the Scots and English. 1641: October 23:

10: The bloudy warre in England, the originall betwixt the King and state was about deliquents it first begun to smoke Jan: 4. 1641:

when the King demanded the 5 Members and Kimbolton: so it smokt untill it flamed and burnt almost in all parts of the kingdome:

11: Death of thes memorable persons: Q Mother of France, who had 3 Kings her sonnes and yett had not a place to live in, in either of their dominions: Lewis. 13. of France: Emperour of Germany: James King of England: King of Poland: Fredericke King of Bohemia the drowning his eldest son: Urbane the Pope. 1644: Death of the Empresse of Germany. 1646.

12: 1643 (c.o. 4): The invasion of Denmarke by the Swedes in revenge of a plott, intended by him and the Polander to fall upon their kingdome on a suddaine and surprise them

13: 1645: The two memorable routs in Scotland, Montros routing the Scots forces where the kingdome was lost, the parliament and most of the Nobles fled out of the kingdome to Barwicke; the routing of Montros. Septemb. 13. by Lesly, wherby he lost all. and was beaten up into the mountaynes againe, a kingdome as it were twice conquered.

14: 1645. The warres of the turkes against the Venetian in Candia. taking Canea; his attempts against Friuli. 1646. and to continue his conquests in Candia. his attempts against Dalmatia, and Istria.

15. Dunkirke that Q of the sea. that famous pyrate towne, taken by the French, how are her so[*rrows*] come upon her in one moment. Octob. 10: or 11. 1646. by Duke de Anguyen.

16. The miraculous and victories proceedings and conquests of the Parliaments forces under command of Sr. Tho: Fairfax and other forces from June. 14. 1645. to Septemb. 1646. and before conquering all out of their hands and routing all their armies except a few small castles,

17. Bavaria breakes his cessacion with Swede holds with France: joyne with the Emperour and forceth the Swedes to retreate and exceedingly hinders their prosperity, and plunders Hassia exceedingly. 1647.

18. A (c.o. totall) defection of Naples from the Spaniard. July. 1647. laying the foundacion of a popular government the French assisting them therin:

19: The parliament of Englands resolucion Jan. 15: 1647. to treate no more with the King nor to receive any messages from him: but to setle the kingdome without him, and securing him in the Ile of Wight.

20: April: 1648. Strong endeavours in all parts, and kingdomes to sett up the Kings interest againe: Inchiqueene revolted from the parliament of England againe; but all [*the*] insurrections were quelled by the army.

21: Scotlands parliament engaged against England in the Kings quarrell Hamilton lead that army, be[fore] he was routed by Cromwell, and Scotland reduced:

22: The army dissolved the indended accomodacion betweene the King and Parliament; and revi[*ved*] the matters of non addresse and by the house accused the King of high treason who was arraigned, condemned and beheaded January. 30. 1648. neare the banquetting house at whitehall.

23: The House of Commons voted the people the supreme power, and voted against Kings and Lords and all power de facto devolved into their hands, their was a Councell of state appointed to rule the kingdome, which began to sitt first at Derby house: Feb. 17. 1648.

24: 1648: A peace concluded in Germany great endeavours to make it take place, 1649.

25. The risings of the parliament and City of Paris with divers of the nobility, and other place[s] about taxes etc. but they came to a peace speadily,

26: The great victory of the Venetians against the Turkes fleet 1649

27. The great successe of Ormand in Ireland; 1649. in composing the differences there and dra[w]ing all under his banner except Owen Roe oneale; and thereupon our great losses in Ulster Conaught and Leinster, provinces

28: Aug: 2: 1649. Ormond beseidging Dublin with about 19000. men: Jones by a sally routed his arm[y] slew: 4000, and tooke his whole campe, Cromwell wafted over into Ireland

26 June. 1650: Fairfax laid downe his commission and Cromwell was made Captaine Gener[al] being returned from Ireland which he had almost subdued.

1650: July. Cromwell with 15000 entred Scotland, after much distresse necessitated to returne at Dunbar. Sept. 3. routed the Scots; Dec: 24. Edinburgh castle surrendred.

Octob. 30. dieth the P. of Orange suddenly almost his wife Mary. K. Charles. 1: eldest daughter not then delivered of a child. this an helpe to Englands affaires. shee was delivered of a sonne. The states would not admitt him into his fathers command but tooke the government into their owne hands in a generall diett of the provinces. Ja[*n*] 1650:

Jan: 1650: Mazarine forced to leave Paris. he released the 3 imprisond princes. he is banisht france; they rule all for present in france: great men stand in slippery places:

[*1651*:] Aug. 51. The Scots and the King entred England, routed and ruind Sep. 3. at Worcester

51: France matters were high. Conde retreated to Bourdeaux raisd armes against the King, the King marcht into feild against him, recalled Mazarine, wherupon Orleans declared on Condes part and divers, and many on the Kings party. so that kingdome is in flames, which the Spaniard endeavours to improve to his regaining Catalonia

Feb: 1651: all powers and judacatories in church and state in Scotland dissolved but such as is derived from the Parliament of England. the Scots were offered to be incorporated into England and made one people with us, and have the same priviledges. they were not ready to embrace it

1652: May. the Dutch and wee began to fight at sea.

Sept. a fight neare Kent. Dutch worsted. under De Witt

November, a fight neare Kent by Tromp. Dutch worsted us, wee lost 3 ships

Feb: another fight in Tromps returne he was terribly beaten

1653. The Dutch and wee fought. June. 2. 3. they were terribly beaten some into their own harbours

July. 31. one of the greatest sea-fights that ever was in the world.

12. December. a new called P. dissolved themselves and resigned their powers to Cromwell, who was. die. 16. sworne protector.

1654: Ap: 26. Dutch peace, wherin Denmarke was included was publiquely, proclaimed.

June. 29. Ferdinand King of the Romans died at Vienna; -Moscovites invaded Poland

Sept. 3. the protectors parliament sat at Westminster. die. 12. kept out of the house until they subscribed a recognition to acknowledge him in the government.

Aug. 15. the memorable seidge of Arras raisd by the French.

Decemb. 20. 25: our fleete under Pen sailed towards Barbados. arrived there. Jan. 28.

28. Pope Innocent 10th. died. Jan: 8 the Cardinals went into the conclave.

Jan. 22. Protector dissolved the Parliament in painted chamber, they having not made one act

March. Alexander 7. chosen said was called Cardinal Ghisi, his countrie Siena in Italy.

1655. April. 6. 7. the massacre of the Waldenses in Savoy.
our forces and fleet disappointed in Hispaniola, saile over to Jamaica and tooke [*it*]
July: the Swedes invade Poland, which the poles Muscovites continue to infest.
Sept. The Spanish seized our merchants goods, and in oct: the Flemings.
Oct. 24. the peace between, France and England signed by our consul and their Ambassadors
Christian late Q of Swede, renounced the protestant, and embraced openly the popish religion at Inspruch in Germany.
December. a warre between the Canton of Zurich, and the protestants switzers, and the canton of Switz, the popish, it had ill procedure on the protestant side. the Bernois being defeated, and the other Switz tired in a winter seidge at Rapperschwill, a peace made in March following

1656. March. 27. a gallant fleet sailed from Torbay toward the Spanish coast.
June: 21: the Swede lost Warsow, and goe down the wind much in Poland
July. 6. a great rout of the French before Valenchienne.
Aug: 20. a general choise of men for the Parl. that is to sit downe. next. Sept. 17.
June. Muscovite. invaded the Swedes in Liefland. could not win Riga
July. 20. Swedes worsted the poles and retooke Warsow.
Feb. Ragotzi Prince of Transilvania invaded Poland, endeavouring to gett that crown
Sept. 9. wee tooke part of the Spanish silver fleet.
March. 23. Ferdinand. 3. the Emp. died, before his son was chosen King of Romans

1657. May. 6000. English effective. marched over into France to assist in their warres
Protector, received new powers and large on a thing called a Parliamentary account
April. Spaniard invaded Portugal, and beseidged Olivenca, he prepared also at Galliciasu*d*.
20. Blake burnt the Spanish fleete at Tenariffe.
May. 25. Danes invaded the Swedes in Breme
June. 26. The Protector setled and sworne by Parliament in Westminster hall.

July. The Swedes invaded the Danes in Holstein. cleared Bremeland only one fort

Aug: The Poles and Austrians tooke Cracow from the Swede, the Transilvanian retiring to his own borders-

Sept: The diet for choise of an Emp: put of longer: The English possesse Mardike and Borborg in Flanders by the helpe of the French.

1658. Dunkirke in the hands of the English June. 15. after a considerable route given the Spanish who endeavoured to releive it.

The Swedish and Danish peace fully agreed. the Danes yeilding all that pertains to Denmarke in Scandia, and some part of Norway. thus he payeth for his folly.

July. 8: Leopoldus Ignatius Joseph 19°. yeare newly entred chosen Emp: crowned at Frankford by the Elector of Colen. July. 22. our stile.

The Swede invaded the Dane in Sealand and tooke Cronenburgh castle Sept.

1659. The Poles. Imperialists, and Brandenburgers, invade Pomerania where the Swede King: Sept: goeth down the wind as also in Prussia. C*u*rland, neither doth he prosper *as* wee yett see in Danemarke; Mazarine and Haro the 2 favourites, parlying on the frontires to make a peace between. Sp. and France as also a marriage which they conclude; King of Sweden died of a feaver. at Gottenburgh.

May. 7. the army restored the last part of the long parliament. and outed them october 13. they overreacht the army and sat again perforce Dec. 27. and new modeld the army, Monk and the City brought in the secluded members. Feb. 20th.

1660: May. 29. King Charles, peaceable and happy arrival at London.

June. A. Generall peace in Europe.

June. Ragotzi prince of Transilvania slain in a battail against the Turkes observe if that bee not initium magnam mutationum in our christian affaires

8: June. Cronenburg yeilded by the Swede to the Dane. oh how loathly did they part with that bridle.

May. 29. the peaceable and pompous return of Charles the second to London and to the government of the 3. kingdome. his 2 brothers with him, of which. Gloucester died of the small pox; Sept. 13.—

Dec: 29. 60. the Parl: dissolved which the King called the healing and blessed Parl

Nov: 62. Charles 2. sold Dunkirke to the King of France for 500000. pistols a pistol is 16. 4^{d}. as I thinke. 400000^{li}. sterling. wherof 100^{m} was paid for the portion of his sister Henrietta. married to Anjou. brother of France the other brought into the tower.

Aug: 63. The Grand vizier came on Hungary with great successe. Some expert [ ]

1663. Towards winter [ ]

turned out of their habitacons to perish in their mountains.

Sept. 64: Turke and Emp. made peace the war not overfurious. the peace was secrett to the worlds wonder.

1664: Dec: 29. The Hollander having taken Gynnee from us by de Ruyter the English under Allen fought the Dutch Smirna fleet neare Cadiz to their damage, though not much to our gain. a rich ship sinking when our men plundering it. 18. men drowned

1665. France in Jan: England in Feb. proclaimed open ware against one another

1666: Dutch burnt part of our fleet in Chatham-enterd the Thames almost to Gravesend.-landed in Suffolke and attempted Langer fort.

peace concluded between Dutch and us

67. French invaded Flanders with great successe. 68. a peace

68: The prodigious fire at Etna in Sicily, the Sulphur making rivers molten burning all before them. extinct: about may. 69.

69. A polish noble chosin K: of poland. all foreign pretenders excluded. June: 5. n:S.—a brave (c.o. Dutch) French fleet sailed from Thoulon with a prosperous wind, arriving in Candia rode. 19: they found the town in great distresse wherupon they resolved a present sally. which they did 24 under the conduct of Duke Navailes, but were beaten in with great losse: the remainder reimbarkd in August. and returnd scarce a 4th part. beg. of October. on their retiring the Venetian surrendred Candia to the Turks, which they entred: Sept. 17. of our account, all the Venetian force and people were retired before not: 20 persons left in it on the 4th Oct. X.S. the visier entred with his army. being their Sabbath day Michael. (on. St Mich: day crownd at Cracow) Wiesniewiski. thes Ukrania which is podolia. where his fathers estate lay, hath submitted to the Turks. this and Candia. successe will raise the Turks.

69. Feb. 14. Valentines day. Parl. mett. the king called earnestly for mony. called them to banq. house, pressing them earnestly to unite. they were had into the wine cellar drinking themselves freinds. and voted the K.

70 800000li. on wines and forreign commodities-brave. made a severe act against dissenters in religion

May. Henrietta Maria. the Dutches of Orleans. entertaind at (c.o. London) Dover by her brother K. Charls, with all plays and jollity. the French abusd by the English players. returnd shee died suddenly of a bilious cholliche. her gusts twisting with hideous

June. 21: pain the lord awaken the two brothers. since restauration: there died D. Glocester. Prs. Orange. Q. Bohemia. Q. Mother. this Dutches

The Pole. married the Emp. sister. the grand diet of Poland brake up doing nothing(,) but a paper discovred a partie endeavouring to depose the King and alter the government. In a diet of Poland at Schodraw. the dieters fell foule on one whom they suspected of that partie and wounded him. to death presently. this act of this litle diet revived the K. freinds. and all cry out for an armed diet.

Aug: The Emperour supprest a great insurrection intended in Hungary against him. Serim the head-The French quasht an insurrection in V*i*varets, and in Sept. seized on Lorrain. The famous Rebel Radzin in Mosco, threats that Empire. but he fell

Oct. 29. Parl. voted to pay the K. debts reckoned at 1300000. and sett out a navy at 800000. it ended in a subsidy of 12d. pound on land and goods

[*The order has been changed in rebinding: 'Josselin's sayings' etc. coming next*]

Sept. 11. Monday. 4 clocke. it raind much: 12. the most stormy driving rain with raging winds that I never knew the like. the wrecks on the north sea and hurt at land, by high floods unexpressible. some match the hurt to Londons fire, continual floods in a manner for 3 weeks. and though some few days dry. yet after that oct. 15. a litle floud: 20. 21. a great floud. a sad seed time to most grounds:

Ap: 4: an earthquake in Italy. war between Holland:-and France England. a toleracion in England.-reformists beare noe places in Hungary.

May. 72. The French invaded Holland. blockt up Maestricht. tooke the towns on the Rhine. so fell down to Utrech, Holland drownd it selfe and stopt them, the Holl. towns declare the P. of Orange stateholder the 28. May. the fleets of E. and H. fought at sea. July. 4. the P. of Orange had his Comiss. as stateholder and tooke his oath. the Spaniards gut garrisons into several towns of the Holl.

that are in Brabant and Flanders: thes tumults laid the states low: The French presse not on Holland as formerly. our fleet doe
Aug. nothing. the Holland East Indie fleete come in. the 2. De Wits are furiously murthered at the Hague.newes of the Imp. coming down and that divers princes will declare for the French.

Oct. 10. 73. At Paris a declaracion of Warre against Spain.poore England.

No. 73. After the House of Commons declared by vote their dislike of the Dukes match with Modena. and refused to give mony. adjournd the chancellour. Shaftsbury was displaced and Finch make Keeper. the Dutchesse landed, and came by water to whitehall and to st.James

Oct 31. 73. The K. of Poland died in 33 y. of his age at Leopol. No. 1. the Polish army attackt the Turks in their camp to an utter route. this may encourage Sobienski. the cheife general to endeavour the crown. gods providence to conjoyn that successe with the Kings death.

He was chosen King accordingly in the June following, I opinion this Sob. aimed at the crown and missing it by Wisnewniski's choice, he hindred him what he could, who quickly went to his grave and some thought by poison. I expect his reigne wilbee troublesom

Aug. 74. The French beare up against Germany. Sp. and Holland. defending their own coast against the Holland fleet and at land giving severall shrewd blows to their enemies

75. Octob. South Holland esp. wonderfully deluged by the sea breaking upon them. Nov: our old prophesies speake great things of a Carolus e Carolo. erit Magno Major. there are now two one in England. he of Swede. like to loose his German interest.

78: begun with a great Zeale from the commands to war with France in releife of the Spanish Netherlands voting to raise about 40000 men and 80 ships in conjunction with Holland. some suspicion fell in England might advance Orange. and France offering them and the allies termes of peace. and Lorrain coming down on Alsace the French having taken Gaunt Ipres gave the Dutch a cessacon. desiring that they would bee newters in the war if the peace succeded not(,) the cessacon begins June 20. of our account.

Great stirrs on the discovery of the plott.79.Jan. began to quash and say no plot of the papists but of the presbiterians. Feb. 22. 79. great preparacons for the D.y. coming to London by sea, orders to entertain him with shootings, and great joy.

May. beg:Duke of York went for Scotland by sea. in great danger of casting away he returnd to London May. 27. the King was taken ill at dinner. he was made presently High admiral at sea and Lieuten[t]. Gen. of all forces by land.the truth of that *quearied*

[*up to six lines destroyed*]

Josselins Sayings.

On good and bad of London: they must bee good that miscarry not, there are so many temptacons. and very bad that miscarry. so many opportunities for good

Our hearts doe us more hurt than our worst condicons: for its our cares. murmurings(,) distrust of god undoe us.—Nothing can keepe good from us but our sins(,) good breaks through all outward obstacles as in Jobs recovery. but sin maketh our blessings curses

If gods heart be towards us.though his hand be against us.it hurts not, sin doth us the greatest mischeife.yett no sin sensibly felt and truly bemoaned shall doe us hurt, but rather good in making us cleave closer to Christ for grace. and watch our hearts more that sin may not gett advantage. against us

Sanctified providences are the best. bee they adversitie or prosperitie

God joyns sin and death. wee sin and mercy. tis true god pardons sin but its where repentance severs them.

when our sins are our hearty sorrow. god pardons us with his own joy in doing it.

if mans age bee 70: then I now being in my 58.am almost at my (c.o. friday) friday midnight, lord fitt mee for a blessed sabbath at hand.

Isay. 39.7.8. Good words of Hezekiah. ah Lord so my son might live in thy sight, all other providences good, but how can I beare to see him a slave to sin his redemption is with thee, bring him to Zion, be it by what way thou please.

Hag. 2: 4.5. bee strong. worke. feare not. where gods promise leads the Van. a christians faithful endeavours may bring up the rear with confidence of successe. though there are never so many difficulties that say our doing is nothing 8. 9. silver. gold.the glory greater. god seems to mee not to looke that way.he intends to make his promises good in.wee thinke in christ it was more glorious but possibly in the present the princes of the earth sent to this 2. temple. beyond the first. gods word shall not faile him ever.

V. 17. I am sensible. of a blast on my corne.losse on my estate. all goeth on very heavily. lord I turne to thee, renewing all my ingagements and stirre up my heart to lay hold on thee and serve thee. turn to mee oh lord. Jan. 20. 1976.

Jan. 24: 76.in night heard Holden dead who fould away his life. gone in an houre or 2. in a sweate not able to beare it. morning. Zach. *03* .9. man is removed in a moment. god can remove a lands iniquitie in a day.I repent lord of all sin this day.and lay hold on Christ for salvacon this moment. lord I question not thy pardon of one mans sin. that pardonest a land in a day.

Oct: 2. 77. In the World trouble. thou fillest our beds sons. daughters with offences against woes to us, our soules with affliction.and yet thou givest thy selfe and christ to us and in him peace and what can man. I desire more.lord but that enjoyment by faith of what thou givest. and I will encourage my heart. at a Ziklag that thou art my porcon. this is my faith. and so my life.

Oct: 4: Tis noble when the love of christ blots all worldly consideracons out of the mind. I can forsake all. die for him. but how base is that person that the love of lust or world blots christ, and all that is noble and vertuous out of the soule. and man seeks to regain honour by heaps of riches / and lavish boules.and this love of sin is so invetorate and deepe rooted that nothing will pull it up but the end of our lives death; so that to satisfie lust wee will trample under foot all consideracons whatsoever.yea the feare of god.year provoke his wrath and put ourselves knowingly in the dint of it—thou that knowest thes things. Rom.

Ap: 30: 82. 2. Sam: 7. Davids case.Lord I find thy love thy christ is the bottom of all hope and good:its for thy words sake, and that reference thou setst him into mee, that thou hast brought mee thus far.but lord all blessings end in thy selfe, and therefore my heart seeing this poures out it selfe, thy christ may stand neare my house as the roote and for his sake as they belong to him thou wouldst blesse them, and give mee the joy to see them blessed with him for this is all my salvacon, that my soule presseth after for mee and them.

Aug. 6: 82. a good weeke in great haying and bad weather formerly *vo*iding. I could not but say.if a few days to gather our hay into cocks, and our sheaves into barns. bee so sweet, oh what are those seasons god gives us to gather up his pearls, his graces. his Christ to bee ours and to prepare ourselves as wheate, ripening us to bee gathered into his granary.

The times of the births of my children by Jane my loving wife, whom god hath gratiously given his servants:wee married october 28. 1640: I being then almost 24 and my wife 20 yeares old.

[*d*] 1: Mary Josselin my first. borne April. 12: and baptized April: 21. 1642. Colne in [ ] buried May 28. [1650]

d 2. Thomas Josselin my second.borne.December 30.and baptized Jan. 14: 1643. buried June [17] 1673

3. Jane Josselin my third borne.November 25 and baptized.December 7. 1645.

d 4 Ralph Josselin my fourth borne: Feb: 11:and baptized Feb: 18: 1647. buried Feb [22]

d 5. Ralph Josselin my fift borne May: 5: and baptized May: 13. 1649. buried June 4. 1650 (3)

6. John Josselin my sixt borne Sept. 19. about 7 of the clocke in the morning, and baptized September. 28: 1651: (4)

d 7. Ann Josselin my third daughter, and seventh child borne June. 20. 1654. on Tuesday about 2 of the clocke after noone, and baptized. Wednesday. July. 19. 1654 buried Aug. 1. 1673

o. June. 1656.my wife miscarried about 2 months gone with child.

8: Mary Josselin my eight child and fourth daughter borne January 14. being Thursday about 3 a clocke in the morning, and baptized the same day in the afternoone. 1657. } 1657

o. May. 59. my wife miscarried about 2 months gon with child

9. June.20th about 3 of the clocke afternoone, my fift daughter and ninth child was borne, and baptized June 24. 1660 by the name of Elizabeth. ooo:miscarried thrice by. December 24: 1661. } 1660

10. Novemb. 26. 1663. about 7. of the clocke morning my wife was delivered of her 6. daughter and 10 child. and baptized Dec. 13. following by the name of Rebekah. } 1663

- - - - - - - - - - - - - - - - - - -

July. 19. 74: The 20th part of all my sheep and wool that I sell, and lambs of my own breeding: I find an enlargment of charity as a comfort so a blessing, the 10th part of all I receive for my labour in any kinde

Nov. 4: 1671.

Lord pardon all my neglect or breach of any vowes in the bloud of christ Jesus, and accept my free offering of my selfe and all mine to bee thine, hoping the same from thee who art my porcion.and in token of my submission to thee and faith in thy promises, I sett a part the tenth of all my incomes in mony as minister.the 10.of my rents in mony, and the 10th of my proffit by any bargains.the 20th. part of the mony I take for all corn I sell. to pay my tenths and to serve in gods worship and for charitable bounty to gods poore as neare as I can, allowing out 20^{s}. yearly for books; and because I have 30^{li}. rents and more due, and corn in my barne full, I charge this gift with charity pay which I esteem about 50^{s}. Christ Jesus accept mee.

PREFATORY NOTES TO APPENDICES 1 AND 2

These two appendices set out relevant genealogical and biographical data on the gentry and village families mentioned by Josselin. Appendix 1 consists of kinship diagrams for all the major Essex gentry families mentioned on several occasions by Josselin, and includes Josselin's own family. Since these families are well documented in Morant's *History of Essex* and heraldic Visitations, only a skeleton genealogy has been provided. These genealogies are based on the Visitations for Essex, Morant, and Wright, Holman's Essex manuscripts, parish registers, and private papers, particularly the D/DPr collection in the Essex Record Office. Smaller families living in Earls Colne or single individuals are much less easily studied and therefore fuller biographical details for these individuals are given in Appendix 2.

The following conventions have been used in the kinship diagrams in the two appendices.

♀	female, name unknown
♂	male, name unknown
=	married
Thos. COOKE	persons mentioned by Josselin are italicized
C	Christened
B	Buried
bn.	born
?	name unknown
d/	daughter of
c.	circa
┬	birth order unknown
1st, 2nd, 3rd above name	order of males at birth and order of females at birth independently known, but over-all order unknown
1, 2, 3, above name	first and subsequent marriages
1658	indicates 25 March 1658 to 31 December 1658 (our dating)
1657/8	indicates 1 January 1658 to 24 March 1658 (our dating)
(^{H})	beside a name indicates that the individual appears in the Harlakenden kinship diagram
(^{J})	beside a name indicates that the individual appears in the Josselin kinship diagram

APPENDIX 1

KINSHIP DIAGRAMS OF MAJOR FAMILIES

CONSTABLE
COOKE
ELDRED
HAINES
HARLAKENDEN
HONYWOOD
JOSSELIN (John)
JOSSELIN (Ralph)
LITTLE/LITTELL
MILDMAY

[J] Jane CONSTABLE

(Later Mrs JOSSELIN)

?

Thomas CONSTABLE = *Anne SHEPHERD* B 1655 — Lawrence = ♀ SHEPHERD B 1660 — B 1659

B 1643

Jeremy = *Betty*?
C 1620

Jane = [J] *Ralph JOSSELIN* (1640)
C 1621
B 1693

Mary
C 1623

Eliz. = ? *WORRALL*
1645

♂

Col Thos. COOKE

Thos. COOKE = Grace UPCHER
of Pebmarsh & Yeldham, Essex — of Fordham, Essex

1 *Eliz. DUKE* = *Thos. COOKE* = 2 Judith St. JOHN

Eliz. DUKE: d. & coheir/John of Colchester, Doctor of Phisick

Thos. COOKE: of Pebmarsh, B *c.* 1684

Judith St. JOHN: d/Oliver, Esq. of Bedfordshire

Joseph

George

Grace

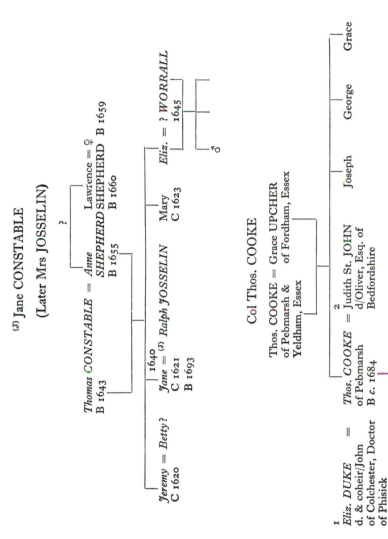

7 sons and 4 daughters

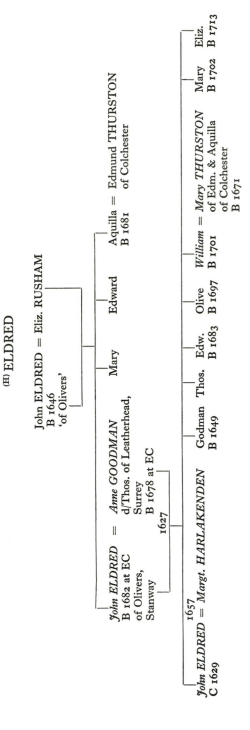

(H) ELDRED

John ELDRED = Eliz. RUSHAM
B 1646
'of Olivers'

John ELDRED = *Anne GOODMAN*
B 1682 at EC; of Olivers, Stanway
d/Thos. of Leatherhead, Surrey; B 1678 at EC
1627

Mary

Edward

Aquilla = Edmund THURSTON
B 1681; of Colchester

John ELDRED = 1657 *Margt. HARLAKENDEN*
C 1629

Godman
B 1649

Thos.

Edw.
B 1683

Olive
B 1697

William = *Mary THURSTON*
B 1701; of Edm. & Aquilla of Colchester; B 1671

Mary
B 1702

Eliz.
B 1713

(H) Major HAINES

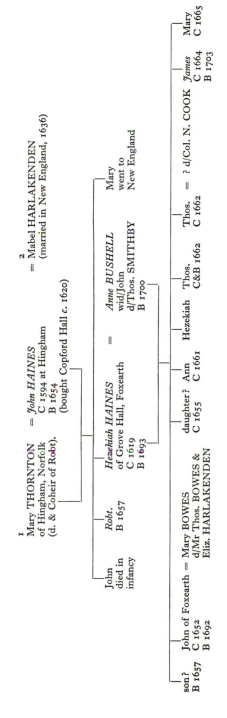

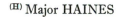

1 Mary THORNTON of Hingham, Norfolk (d. & Coheir of Robt). = *John HAINES* C 1594 at Hingham B 1654 (bought Copford Hall *c.* 1620) = 2 Mabel HARLAKENDEN (married in New England, 1636)

Issue of John HAINES and Mary THORNTON:

- John, died in infancy
- *Robt.* B 1657
- *Hezekiah HAINES* of Grove Hall, Foxearth C 1619 B 1693 = *Anne BUSHELL* wid/John d/Thos. SMITHBY B 1700
- Mary went to New England

Issue of Hezekiah HAINES and Anne BUSHELL:

- son? B 1657
- John of Foxearth C 1652 B 1692 = Mary BOWES d/Mr Thos. BOWES & Eliz. HARLAKENDEN
- daughter? C 1655
- Ann C 1661
- Hezekiah
- Thos. C&B 1662
- Thos. C 1662 = ? d/Col. N. COOK
- *James* C 1664 B 1703
- Mary C 1665

HONYWOOD

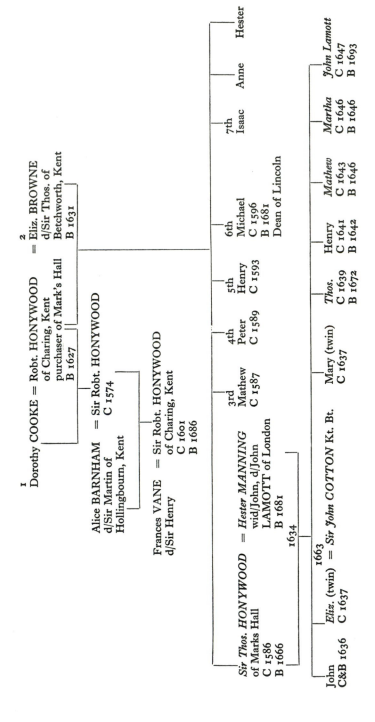

[1] Dorothy COOKE = Robt. HONYWOOD of Charing, Kent, purchaser of Mark's Hall, B 1627 = [2] Eliz. BROWNE d/Sir Thos. of Betchworth, Kent, B 1631

(issue of 1st marriage)
Alice BARNHAM d/Sir Martin of Hollingbourn, Kent = Sir Robt. HONYWOOD C 1574

(their son)
Frances VANE d/Sir Henry = Sir Robt. HONYWOOD of Charing, Kent, C 1601, B 1686

(issue of 2nd marriage)
Sir Thos. HONYWOOD of Marks Hall, C 1586, B 1666 = (1634) *Hester MANNING* wid/John, d/John LAMOTT of London, B 1681
3rd Mathew, C 1587
4th Peter, C 1589
5th Henry, C 1593
6th Michael, C 1596, B 1681, Dean of Lincoln
7th Isaac
Anne
Hester

(issue of Sir Thos. Honywood and Hester Manning)
John, C&B 1636
Eliz. (twin), C 1637 = (1663) *Sir John COTTON* Kt. Bt.
Mary (twin), C 1637
Thos., C 1639, B 1672
Henry, C 1641, B 1642
Mathew, C 1643, B 1646
Martha, C 1646, B 1646
John Lamott, C 1647, B 1693

HARLAKENDEN

* Starred entries: see separate genealogy also.

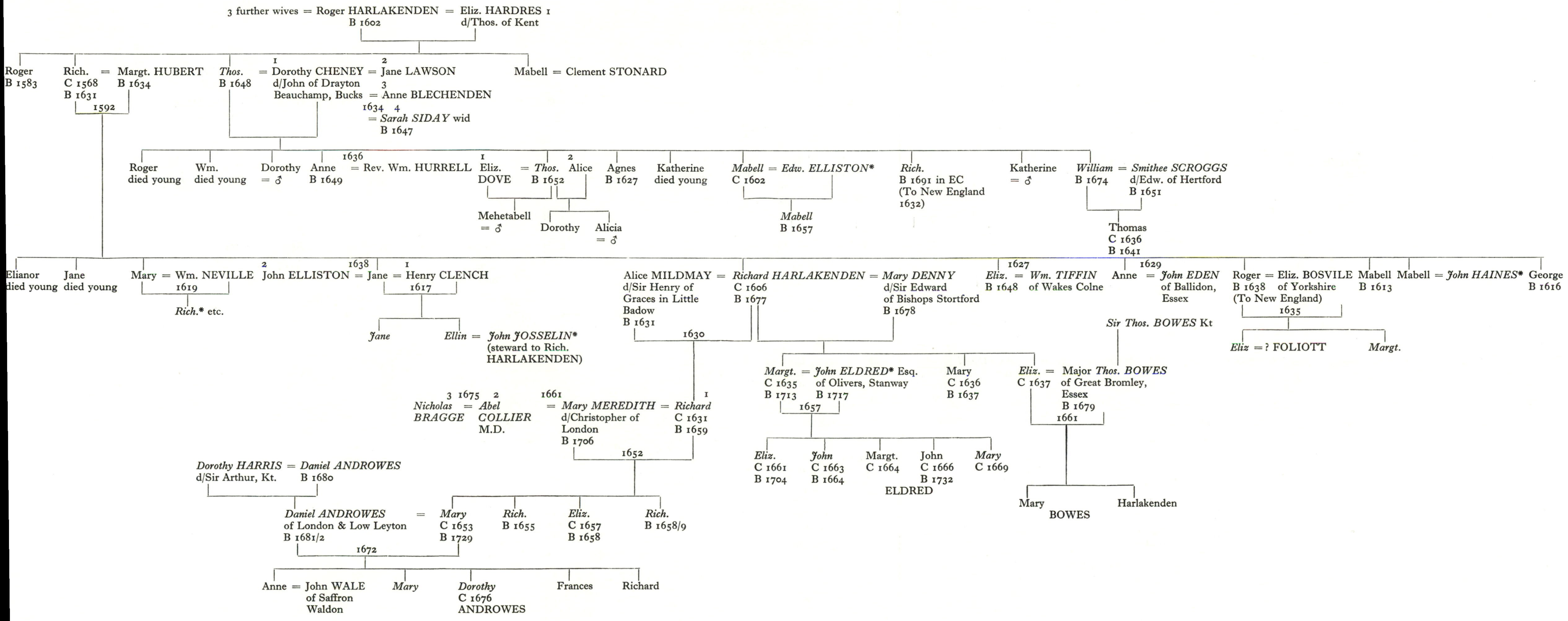

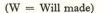

[J] Ralph JOSSELIN

For Jane CONSTABLE see separate diagram

(W = Will made)

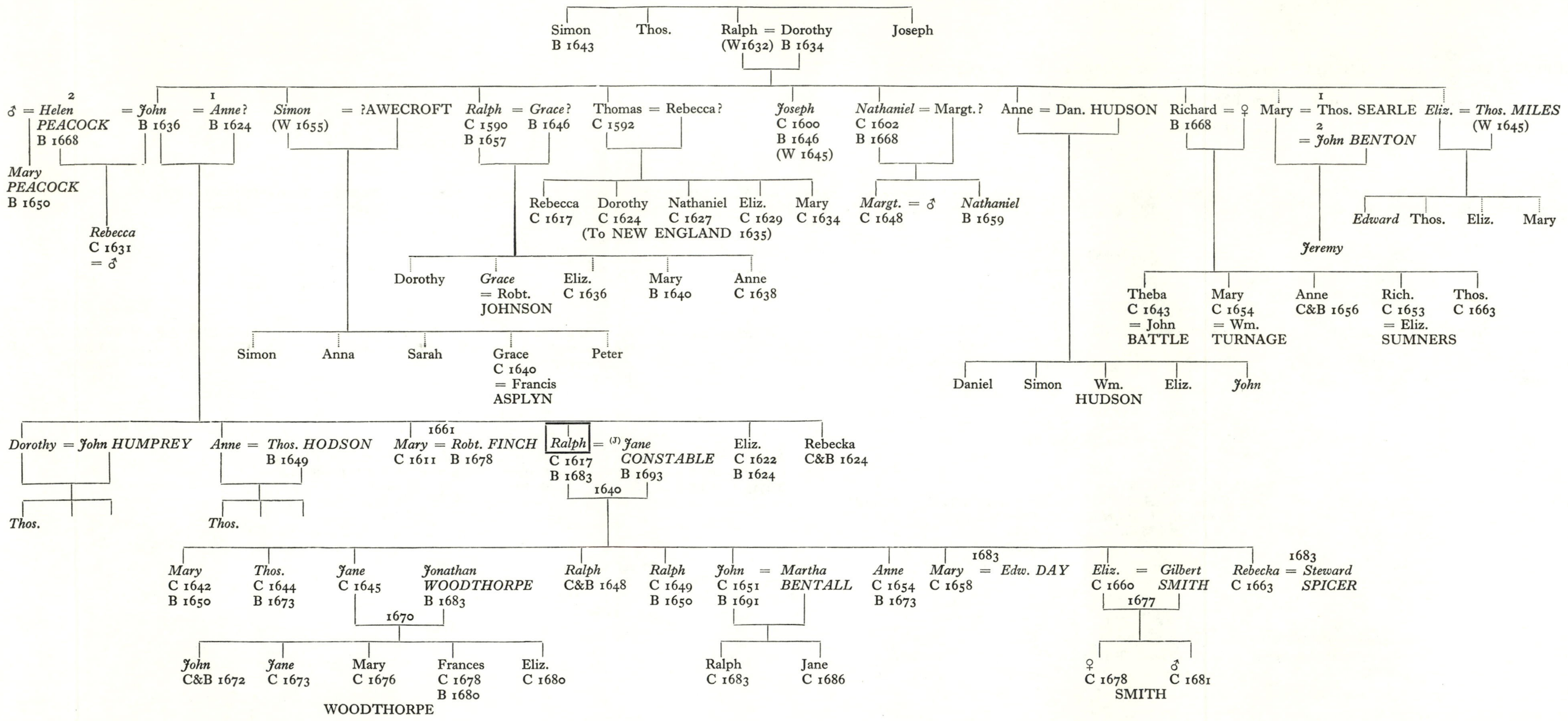

(H) John JOSSELIN

Steward to Rich. HARLAKENDEN

John JOSSELIN = Eliz. WISEMAN
of Hyde Hall, Herts, esq. — d/William of Mayland, Essex

1 *Ellin CLENCH* = *John JOSSELIN* = 2 Mary ALEIN
d/Henry & Jane HARLAKENDEN — of Feering, Essex esq. B 1670 — d. & heir of Nathaniel of Sturmer, Essex, gent.

Nathaniel = Amy BAKER
C 1647
B 1671

John
C 1649
B 1671/2

Eliz.
C 1650/1

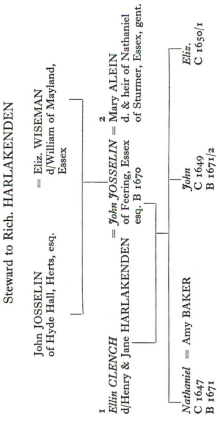

John & Jeffrey LITTLE/LITTELL

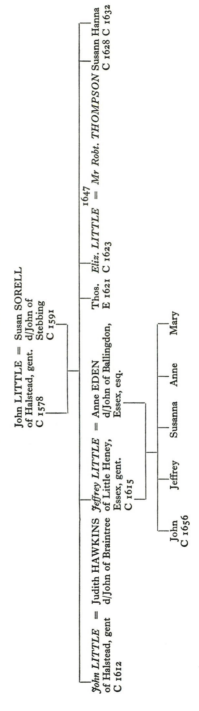

John LITTLE = Susan SORELL
of Halstead, gent. d/John of
C 1578 Stebbing
C 1591

Children:

- *John LITTLE* of Halstead, gent C 1612 = Judith HAWKINS d/John of Braintree
- *Jeffrey LITTLE* of Little Heney, Essex, gent. C 1615 = Anne EDEN d/John of Ballingdon, Essex, esq.
  - John C 1656
  - Jeffrey
  - Susanna
  - Anne
  - Mary
- Thos. E 1621
- *Eliz. LITTLE* C 1623 = (1647) *Mr Robt. THOMPSON*
- Susann C 1628
- Hanna C 1632

(H) MILDMAY

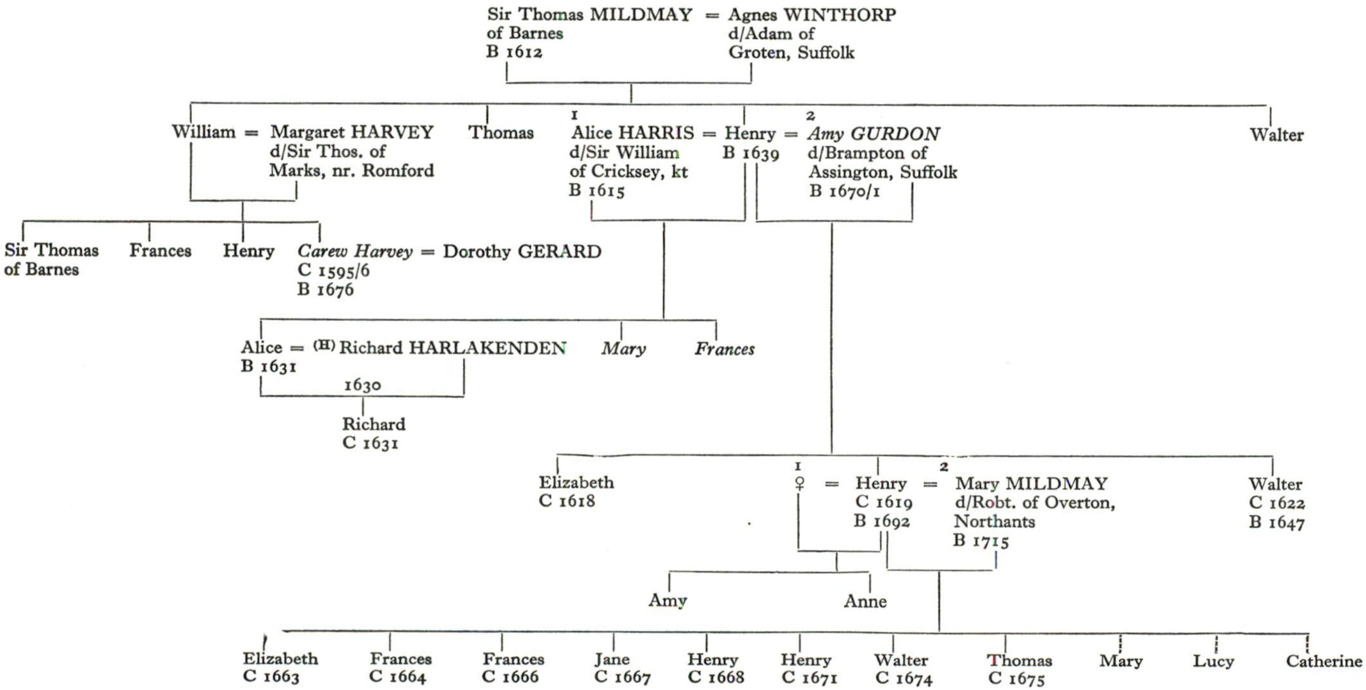
Sir Thomas MILDMAY = Agnes WINTHORP
of Barnes
B 1612
d/Adam of
Groten, Suffolk
William = Margaret HARVEY
d/Sir Thos. of
Marks, nr. Romford
Thomas
1
Alice HARRIS = Henry = Amy GURDON
2
d/Sir William
of Cricksey, kt
B 1615
B 1639
d/Brampton of
Assington, Suffolk
B 1670/1
Walter
Sir Thomas
of Barnes
Frances
Henry
Carew Harvey = Dorothy GERARD
C 1595/6
B 1676
Alice = (H) Richard HARLAKENDEN
B 1631
1630
Mary
Frances
Richard
C 1631
Elizabeth
C 1618
1
♀ = Henry = Mary MILDMAY
2
C 1619
B 1692
d/Robt. of Overton,
Northants
B 1715
Walter
C 1622
B 1647
Amy
Anne
Elizabeth
C 1663
Frances
C 1664
Frances
C 1666
Jane
C 1667
Henry
C 1668
Henry
C 1671
Walter
C 1674
Thomas
C 1675
Mary
Lucy
Catherine

PREFATORY NOTES TO APPENDIX 2

Abbreviations are as outlined in the list of abbreviations at the front of the volume; for example, EC=Earls Colne, RJ=Ralph Josselin, ERO=Essex Record Office. The symbols used in the kinship diagrams are explained at the front of Appendix 1 above.

Josselin mentioned about 250 people by name who seem to have lived in Earls Colne for at least a short period. These people are indicated in the index of persons by italics. Fourteen of those he mentioned cannot be precisely identified because no forename is given or because it is impossible to distinguish which of the several people with the forename and surname living in the parish corresponds to the individual mentioned by Josselin. Another five people, four of them Josselin's servants, do not appear in any other village records. Almost all the remainder have been identified and are described briefly in the following biographies, or in Appendix 1.

Each biography attempts to fill in the following details in the order given here: surname; forename; residence number; birth date and death date; parents' names; occupation and status; marriage date(s) and partner(s); house ownership and number of hearths; whether a will was made; whether an inventory was made with its value; any other information relevant to Josselin's comments on the individual concerned. The details have been assembled from the intensive analysis of the following sources, at the ERO unless otherwise stated.

Surname, forename, date of baptism and burial, parents' names, marriage date and partner, whether a person was a householder at death, can all be derived from the Earls Colne Parish Register (D/P 209/1/1–3) and from the examination of neighbouring parish registers.

House number, which refers to the residence marked on the map (Figure 2) gives the location of the individual when mentioned by Josselin in his Diary. Thus no house number has been given when a person was a servant living with Josselin, or any other kind of boarder with him, or when, at the time of the reference, the individual was dead or living outside the parish. Such instances are, however, indicated by 'servant', 'London', and so on. The placing of individuals was made possible by the discovery of an extremely detailed survey and map of Earls Colne for 1598 made by Israel Amyce (Temp. Acc. 898; D/DSm/Pl). This was incorporated with the manor court rolls for Earls Colne (D/DPr 78–81) and Colne Priory (D/DPr 22–24) manors. The rentals covering both manors in the years 1614, 1629, 1638, and 1677/8 (D/DPr 111, 112, 113; D/DU 292/7) were also used. The task was made much easier by numerous abstracts and workings on the manorial documents, made during the sixteenth to nineteenth centuries (D/DPr 41, 42, 109, 619) as well as a Fine Book for the period 1610–1759 (D/DPr 100) and the Harlakenden Account Book (Temp. Acc. 897). Numerous deeds were also consulted, especially important were D/DHt T73/1–42; D/DU 256/1–24; D/DPr 446–456. The manorial records also gave considerable information concerning marriage partners, death dates, and occupation.

Occupation and status, family relationships, residence, and literacy could in a number of cases be derived from wills, especially in the cases of the thirty-four people mentioned by Josselin who themselves left wills. Most of the wills referred to in the biographies are listed alphabetically in *Wills at Chelmsford*, vol. ii, ed. F. G. Emmison (Index Library, vol. 79, 1959–60), where full references are given. When a will is in *Wills at Chelmsford*, but the testator has moved to a place other than Earls Colne, the location of the place of residence is given in the biography. Likewise, when a will is among the P.C.C. wills at the Public Record Office, the full reference (commencing PROB) has been given in the biographies. If no reference is given, the testator can be assumed to have left a will as 'of Earls Colne' which will be found in *Wills at Chelmsford*. All Archdeaconry, Consistory, Commissary and P.C.C. wills for Earls Colne for the period 1550–1700 were used.

The number of hearths was derived from the following hearth taxes:

Year	*Number of names for EC*	*Reference*
1662	84	Q/RTh 1
1666	58	E179/246/20 (Public Record Office)
1671	195	Q/RTh 5 (+additions in Q/RTh 9)
1673	187	Q/RTh 8
1675	194	E179/246/22 (Public Record Office)

It will be seen that the final three are much more comprehensive. They give names and hearths for those discharged from paying on account of their poverty; such persons have been indicated in the biographies as 'discharged'. Where a 'vacant' or 'new' hearth has been mentioned, this is also indicated in the biographies.

Further information on occupation and status, as well as material on minor offences against the peace, has been derived from the Quarter Sessions (Q/S) records for Essex. The calendar of Quarter Sessions for the period 1558–1714 at the ERO was searched for Earls Colne inhabitants, as were the original bundles of presentments and depositions for 1621–89 (Q/SBa 2) and the first and second Order Books (Q/SO 1, 2).

Nearly all the probate inventories for Essex have disappeared, but inventory totals are preserved in the Archdeaconry Probate Act Books from 1663 (D/ACAc 1–3). Other biographical information, particularly concerning religious deviation and sexual offences, as well as some information concerning dates of death, has been extracted from the other records of the Archdeaconry of Colchester. The most important classes of these records are the Act Books (D/ACA *passim*, especially vol. 55) and Visitation Books (D/ACV *passim*, especially vols. 6–10).

The above were the major categories of sources used in this biographical appendix in order to disentangle the often very allusive references to persons made by Josselin. A number of other records were also of value in estimating occupation, literacy, family relationships, and crime. Among these were the Assize records for Essex (transcribed in a calendar at the ERO); William Holman's 'History of Earls Colne', 1722/3 (T/P 195/11); the Association Roll for Earls Colne in 1696 (Q/RRO 2/1), which is termed '1696 Roll' in the biographies and gives the mark or signature of over 180 inhabitants; Quaker Records at the ERO and Friends House, including Quarterly Meeting Digests, Books of Sufferings, and Deeds of the Quaker Meeting House (T/A 425/1/1).

Where possible, the records of neighbouring townships within five miles of Earls Colne have also been examined, particularly parish registers, hearth taxes, and the Quarter Sessions and Assize records (the last three of these through the ERO name indexes).

APPENDIX 2

BIOGRAPHIES AND KINSHIP DIAGRAMS OF EARLS COLNE FAMILIES AND INDIVIDUALS

ABBOTT	CRESSENER	HARRINGTON
BURTON	ELLISTON	HUTTON
CHURCH	GARRAD	NEVILL

For Abbott kinship diagram: see p. 674.

ABBOTT, Dorothy. (60); (?–?1661); second wife of *Henry I*; had no children by him; probably died at Colchester and, according to her will, had children by a previous marriage. She mentions no members of the Abbott family in her will, which fits RJ's remark implying friction between her and the EC family.

ABBOTT, Edward. (16); (1638–*c.* 1712); son of *Henry I* and Joan; gent, draper; married Mary; sometime of Copford where he gave land for a Quaker burial ground; returned to EC before his uncle *Robert I's* death in 1678; signed the 1696 Roll.

ABBOTT, Henry I. (60); (1595–1655); son of Henry and Thomasine; yeoman, (farmer); married Joan and *Dorothy*; sometime constable of EC.

ABBOTT, Henry II. (60); (1623–1700); son of *Henry I* and Joan; clothier, yeoman, saymaker, (farmer); married Rose; six hearths 1662–75; cited for non-attendance at church with known Quakers in 1663; signed the 1696 Roll.

ABBOTT, Robert I. (16); (1601–*c.* 1678); son of Henry and Thomasine; never married; six hearths from 1666 to 1675; left estate to nephew *Edward*; a Quaker and imprisoned for two years at Colchester castle at the suit of Richard Harlakenden, impropriator of tithes of EC; some years earlier, in 1652 (Assizes 235/93/1), a conversation about tithes between Harlakenden and Abbott is recorded in detail.

ABBOTT, Robert II. (London); (1625–?); son of *Henry I* and Joan; married; inherited a large part of the land that had come to the family by his grandmother, on the death of his father; a few years later he sold the same to his brother *Henry II*; probably died in London.

ABBOTT, Rose. (60); (1654–*c.* 1676); daughter of *Henry II* and Rose; married John Marryon of Braintree.

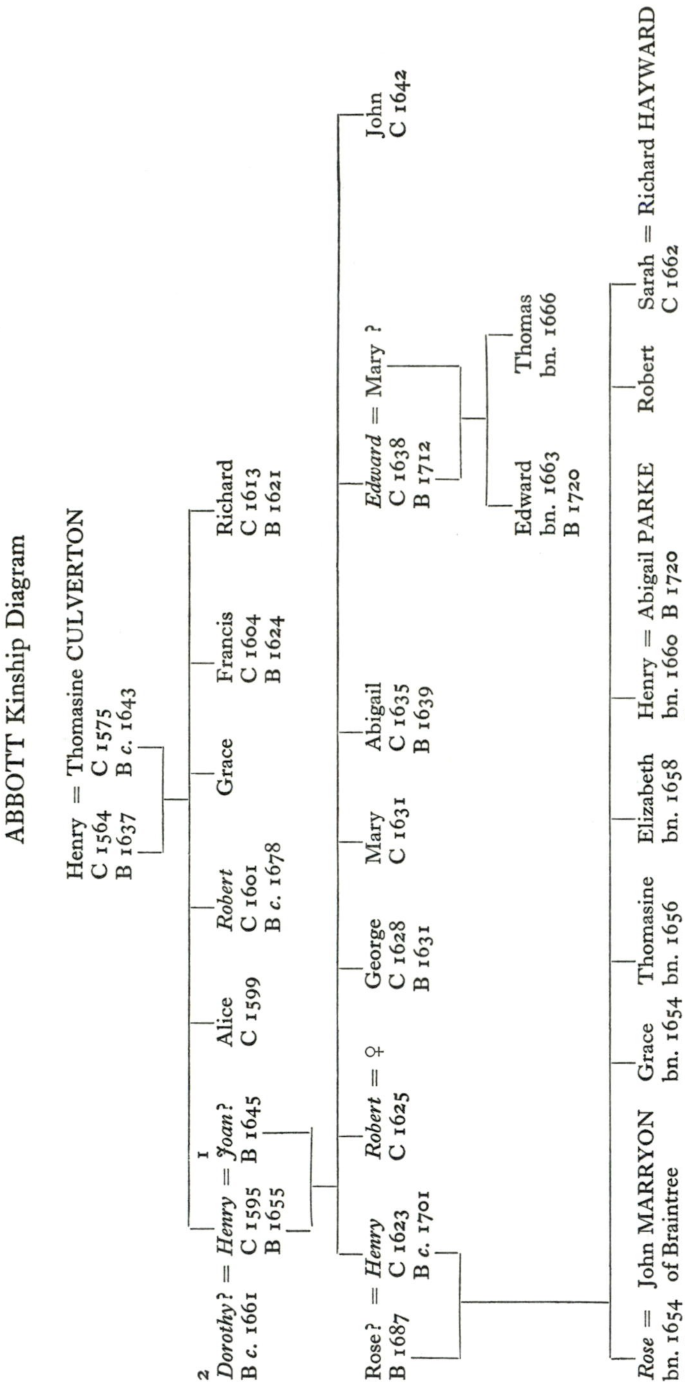
ABBOTT Kinship Diagram
Henry = Thomasine CULVERTON
C 1564 C 1575
B 1637 B c. 1643
2 Dorothy? = Henry = Joan? 1
B c. 1661 C 1595 B 1645
B 1655
Alice C 1599
Robert C 1601 B c. 1678
Grace
Francis C 1604 B 1624
Richard C 1613 B 1621
Rose? = Henry C 1623 B c. 1701
B 1687
Robert = ♀ C 1625
George C 1628 B 1631
Mary C 1631
Abigail C 1635 B 1639
Edward = Mary ? C 1638 B 1712
John C 1642
Edward bn. 1663 B 1720
Thomas bn. 1666
Rose = John MARRYON of Braintree
bn. 1654 B 1676
Grace bn. 1654
Thomasine bn. 1656
Elizabeth bn. 1658
Henry = Abigail PARKE bn. 1660 B 1710 B 1720
Robert
Sarah = Richard HAYWARD C 1662

ADAM, William. (44); (1595–1666); son of William and Joan; mercer, linen draper, sexton, son of the former vicar of EC; married Elizabeth Towers in 1616; scribe in a number of wills; his family accused of assaulting *Abraham Markham* and his wife and stealing rose bushes from them, at the Q/S in 1658.

ALLEN, William. (28); (1617–80); son of James and Clemence; grocer, shopkeeper; married Anne Stallon of Cambridge in 1667 and *Martha Gibson* of Colchester in 1673; well-known Quaker, author of *The Glory of Christ's Light* . . . (1669); cited as of EC for obscene behaviour in church in 1637, but later travelled much and said variously to be of Sampford, Halstead, and Cambridge; for further details see p. 626, n. 1 above.

ALSTON, John. (48); (?–?); married to Joan Clarke daughter of *Bartholomew Clarke*.

AMES, Henry. (of Markshall when mentioned); (?–1669); son of Daniel and Margaret of Markshall; married Ellin Prentis; householder with one hearth in 1662 and 1666; moved from Markshall *c*. 1645 his wife having inherited land there from her brother John; the land mentioned by RJ was seven acres called Little Broadfield, which he sold in 1646 to Hannah Hunt.

AMIES, John. (51); (?–1680); husbandman; son of Daniel and Margaret of Markshall; married Joan Andrews in 1637; one hearth in 1671; at burial noted as 'the blind'; his wife inherited the property in EC in which they lived.

AYLWARD, Bridget. (46); (1596–1663); daughter of John and Grace; never married.

BARRET, John. (servant); (?–?); married Susanna Smith in 1670; possibly moved from EC although children christened there 1671–3; not in Hearth Tax.

BECKWITH, Robert. (?); (?–?); his wife was Mary; in 1636 they were cited to the ecclesiastical court for not-attendance at church and a year later, for the same offence, Robert pleaded his wife's ill health in mitigation; the parish register is missing from February to July so that the burial alluded to by RJ is absent.

BENTAL, Ann. (69); (?–*c*. 1701); daughter of *John Kent* and Ann; married George Bental in 1637 and Henry Penhacke in 1646; in her will she was termed Widow Pennock of Great Coggeshall; she inherited Mallories from her mother.

BIFORD, John. (?); (?–1659); his widow Mary was buried on 10 January 1680 when she was noted in the Register as 'drowned', but RJ does not mention this; possibly her drowning was connected to her husband's earlier reputation as a witch.

BOWLES, John. (57); (?–?); married Bridget in *c*. 1630 and Katherine Hecklington in 1640; cottager.

BRAND, William. (74); (1576–1662); son of Richard; married *Mary* the widow of *Sam Brewer*; bailiff to Richard Harlakenden's father; a five-hearth house in 1662; left a will.

BREWER, Adam. (31); (1613–?); son of John; married Rose *c*. 1632; a one-hearth house 1671–5.

BREWER, Mary. (69); (?–?); daughter of *Edward Spooner* and Ann; wife of *Sam* and later *William Brand*; she had two children, Mary and Ann; her husband Sam leased Mallories from RJ for three years and she continued the lease after his death in 1646.

BREWER, Sam. (69); (?–1646); son of William and Mary of Great Tey; married *Mary*; householder; buried a month after leasing Mallories farm from RJ.

BROCKE, Frances. (?); (?–1665); 'singlewoman'.

BROWNE, Edward. (53); (?–1663) dishturner, husbandman; married Alice Wade in 1612 and then Lettice, they died respectively in 1614 and 1661;

BROWNE, Mary. (?); (?–1660); daughter of *Edward Cressener*; married *Robert Browne* in 1641 who died in 1652 and Richard Bridge of Wakes Colne in 1657; she was referred to as 'Sister Bridge' by RJ at her burial.

BROWNE, Robert. (?); (?–1652); yeoman; married *Mary*; sometime of Sible Hedingham, where he held land according to his will (PROB. 11/246/109).

BROWNE, Sarah. (servant); (?–1678); daughter of Nathan; servant to RJ when he moved to EC and returned as same in 1645; in 1663 named as servant to Edward Elliston, gent; married Thomas Cowell, husbandman, of Great Tey after 1663 in whose will she is mentioned; in 1650 bought a cottage in EC which she left to a kinswoman at her death.

BROWNE, Widow. (?); (?–?); widow of Thomas who was buried in 1635.

BROWNSON, Cornelius. (70); (1610–57); son of Roger and Mary; husbandman, farm servant to Richard Harlakenden, labourer; married *Martha* another of Harlakenden's servants in 1636; left a will; his goods were valued at £17. 16*s*. at death.

BROWNSON, Martha. (70); (?–1665); married *Cornelius*; left a will in which she left a 'fire screen' to RJ; after her death her house and lands were sold by trustees, including RJ, for £41 and the profits went to relatives in New England; her inventory was £24. 1*s*.

BULL, Mathye. (servant); (1629–?); daughter of George Bull of White Colne (*see name index*) and servant to RJ.

BULLOCKE, John. (64); (1617–93); son of John and Anne; married Elizabeth in *c*. 1657 who was buried in 1671 and Mary Brownson in *c*. 1672.

BUNNER, Richard. (?); (?–1682); married three times to Anne Pamphlin, Mary, and Elizabeth Relton; householder.

For Burton kinship diagram: see p. 677.

BURTON, Anne. (12, 14); (1616–81); daughter of John and Anne Read; married *c*. 1633 to *Sam Burton I*; made a will and her inventory was worth £79. 12*s*. 2*d*.; a Quaker who, in 1663, was cited to the ecclesiastical court for detaining money from the church rate and for being an unlicensed midwife.

BURTON, John. (72); (1604–82); son of Francis; miller; married Sarah who was buried in 1679 and appears to have remarried; a three-hearth house in 1662–75.

BURTON, Sam I. (12, 14); (1609–61); son of Sam and Anne; a chandler at the 'Bell'; married *Anne* in *c*. 1633; left a will and signed another will as a witness; later a Quaker; for his relations with his sister, see p. 332, n. 1 above.

BURTON Kinship Diagram

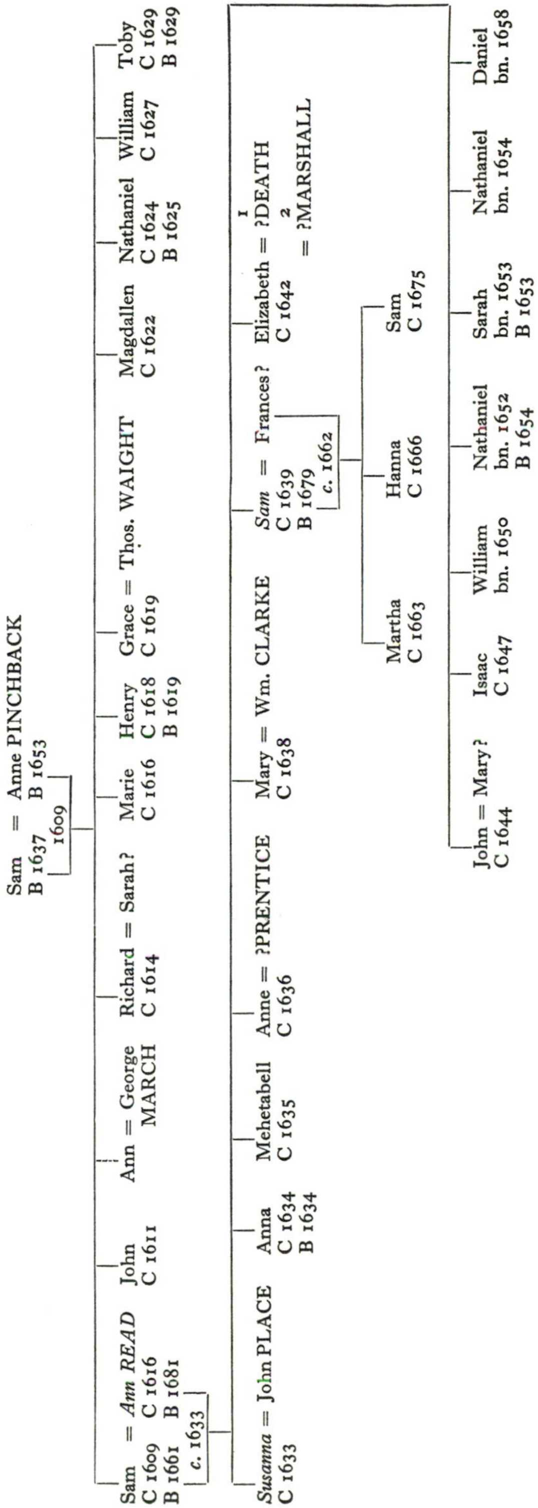

BURTON, Sam II. (12); (1640–1708); son of *Sam I* and *Anne*; churchwarden; married Frances in *c.* 1662; in 1662 a three-hearth house and 1671–5 six hearths.

BURTON, Susan. (12); (1633–?); daughter of *Sam I* and *Anne*; married John Place of Sudbury in 1656.

BYAT, Francis. (?); (?–?); draper in 1661; two-hearth house in 1662.

CAPLIN, James. (29); (1648–65); son of *Richard* and *Mary*; buried on 19 June, less than a month after he was injured.

CAPLIN, Mary. (29); (?–1671); daughter of ? Hunwicke; married *Richard*; she was buried four days after RJ noted her illness.

CAPLIN, Richard. (29); (?–1696); innholder and petty constable; married *Mary c.* 1641; a six-hearth house in 1662–75.

CARTER, Robert I. (67); (?–1671); baker; married Anne; householder with three hearths in 1662–6; alive by 1609 when mentioned in a will; made a will; his inventory worth £38. 13*s.* 1*d.*; churchwarden in 1664.

CARTER, Robert II. (62); (1640–80); son of *Robert I* and Anne; yeoman; married to Sarah; a three-hearth house in 1673–5.

CATT, Paul. (?); (?–?); married Susan Allen in 1630; cited several times at the ecclesiastical courts in the 1630s for incontinency and disorderly behaviour.

CHRISMAS, John. (72); (1628–57); son of Thomas and Agnes; miller; married Anne in *c.* 1654; buried on 18 March 1657; his widow remarried in 1666 to John Bond of EC; the brother referred to by RJ was probably Abraham.

For Church kinship diagram: see p. 679.

CHURCH, John I. (4a); (?–1654); son of John and Rose; gentleman; married Mary Cressener and later Frances Fletcher.

CHURCH, John II. (4a); (1636–?); son of *John I* and Frances; he was left a legacy of £100 by Rose Church his 'kinswoman'.

CHURCH, Mary. (42); (1610–50); daughter of Robert and Rose; gentlewoman; never married; left a will which she signed and RJ wrote.

CHURCH, Rose. (42); (?–1658); daughter of George Cowper of Norfolk; gentlewoman; married Robert, D.D.

CLARKE, Bartholomew. (48); (?–?); tailor; married Jane Ellis in 1609 and Elizabeth Prentis the daughter of *Clement Turner* after 1623; marked, as a witness, various wills.

CLARKE, Edward. (63); (?–?); bailiff to Richard Harlakenden; married Mary Lenton in 1636.

CLARKE, Elizabeth. (43); (1596–?); daughter of John and Elizabeth Brewer; married *John Clarke* in 1628.

CLARKE, John. (43); (?–1646); tailor, husbandman; married *Elizabeth*; householder; marked, as witness, various wills.

COB, Daniel. (?); (1654–1703); son of John and Frances; married Elizabeth Hales in 1673; mark on 1696 Roll.

CHURCH Kinship Diagram

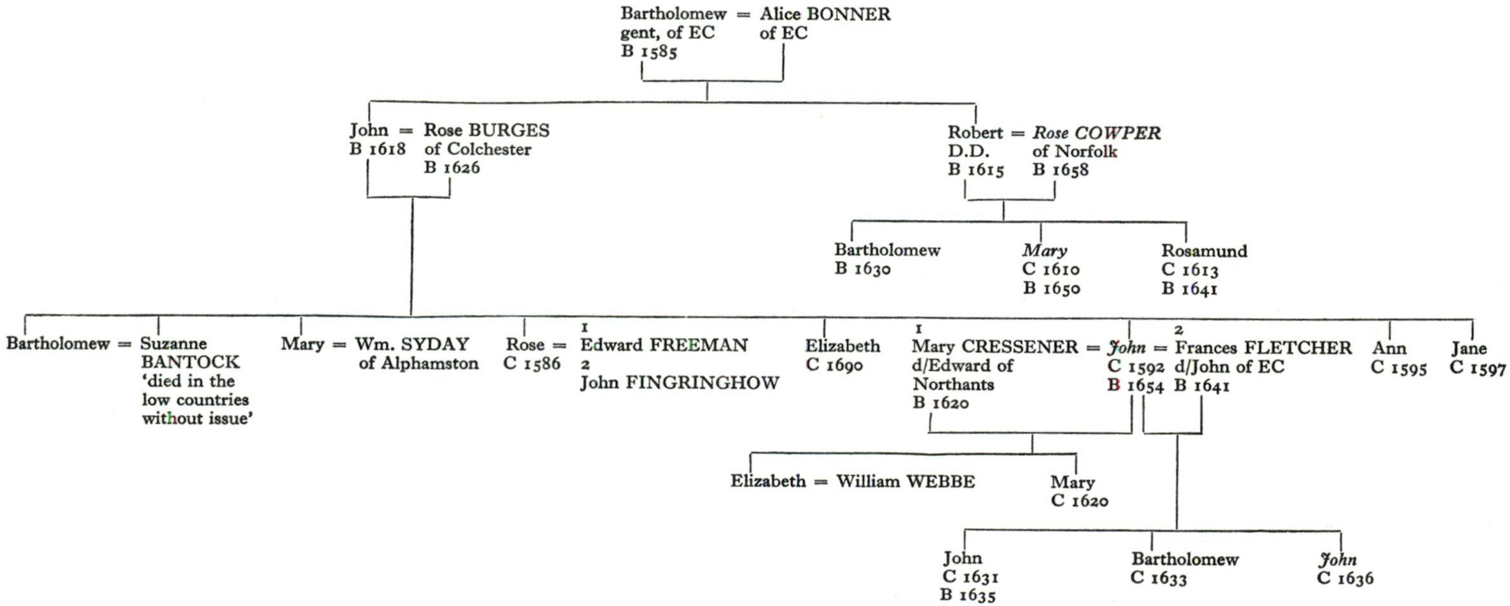

COBBS, John. (?); (1634–1703); son of John and Margaret; labourer; re-married in 1699 to Anne South; one hearth (discharged) in 1673; mark on 1696 Roll.

COLEMAN, John. (63); (?–?); married Mary and then Elizabeth Bunner, widow, in 1683; four-hearth house in 1662 and 1673.

COSIN, William. (17); (?–1648); schoolmaster of EC; signature as witness to wills; Thomas Shepard who later founded Harvard described how, as a Lecturer at EC in the late 1620s, he 'boarded in Mr Cosins his house an aged but godly and chearfull Christian and Schoolmaster in the town; and by whose society I was much refreshed' (*Publications of the Colonial Society of Massachusetts, Transactions for 1927–30*, vol. xxvii (1932), p. 367).

For Cressener kinship diagram: see p. 681.

CRESSENER, Edward. (35); (?–1649); son of George; gentleman; married Elizabeth Halsall; signature, as witness, to wills.

CRESSENER, George. (35); (1618–77); son of *Edward* and Elizabeth; gentleman; married in 1644 to Mary Haling of London; an eleven-hearth house in 1662–75; signed his will (PROB. 11/354/83).

CRESSENER, John. (London); (1620–97); son of Edward and Elizabeth; grocer; married Anne Welde of Herts.; buried at EC though previously of Watling street, London.

CROWE, John. (?); (1631–98); son of Giles and Ann of Colne Engaine; married Ann Day in *c.* 1656; six hearths in 1662, two in 1671, four in 1673; buried in the Quaker burial ground; cited for not paying his church rates in 1686 and 1689; signed the 1696 Roll.

CROWE, Robert. (32); (1598–1671); son of Robert, innkeeper, and Fayth; yeoman, servant of Richard Harlakenden; unmarried; signature as a witness to a will; an inventory worth £181. 1*s.* 8*d.*

DANIEL, Thomas. (servant); (?–?); later styled 'Mr.'; married in 1677 to Mrs. Susan Lawson; a one-hearth house in 1671.

DAVY, Katharine. (19); (1588–1657); daughter of Edmund and Margaret Potter married *Robert I* in 1610.

DAVY, Robert I. (19); (?–1661); butcher; married *Katharine* in 1610; left a will with his mark on it; ordered to appear at the Q/S in 1613, 1623, 1624, 1625, 1628, mainly to undertake to keep the peace.

DAVY, Robert II. (26); (?–1680); son of *Robert I* and *Katharine*; butcher; married Hellena Burton; one-hearth house in 1671, one in 1673 (discharged), two in 1675; ordered to keep the peace, at the Q/S in 1637, 1645, 1658; the child's christening alluded to by RJ on 2/3/1656/7 is not in the parish register.

DAY, Anne. (?); (?–1683); married *Edmund*; one hearth in 1662, two hearths in 1666; left a will; her inventory was worth £122. 16*s.* 9*d.*

DAY, Edmund. (?); (?–1657); yeoman; married *Anne*; left a will with his mark on.

DAY, James. (27); (?–before 1682); miller, yeoman; married Grace; two hearths in 1662 and 1666; signature as witness to a will.

CRESSENER Kinship Diagram

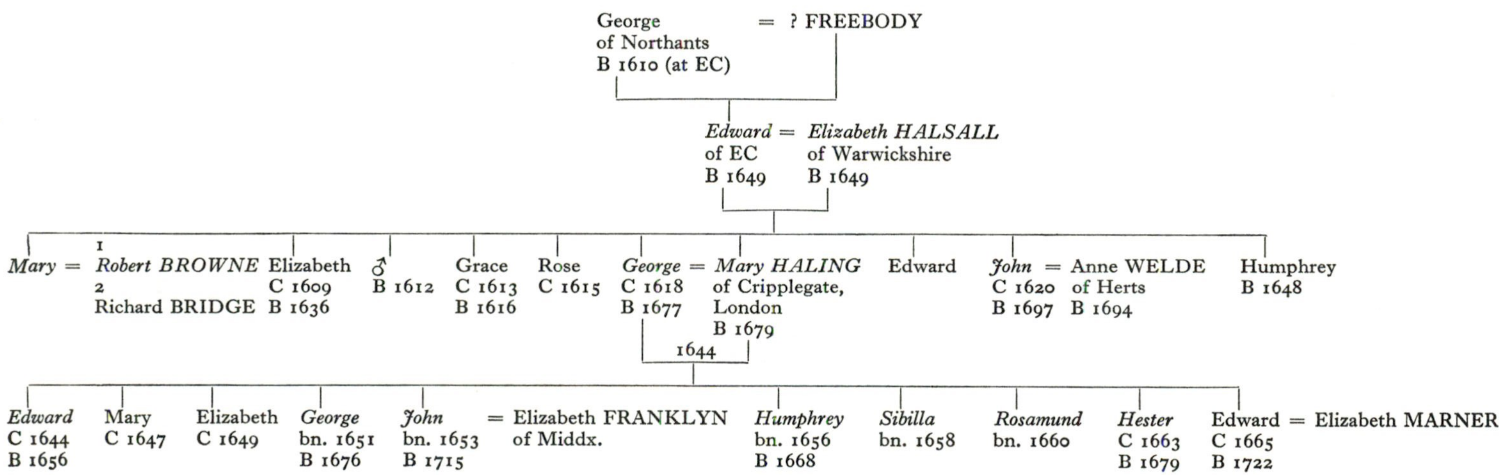

DEATH, Elizabeth. (66); (?–*c.* 1667); married *William*; died intestate with goods worth below £10.

DEATH, William. (66); (?–1653); married *Elizabeth*; householder; left a will (PROB. 11/268/361) which he marked and which included lands in Rivenhall and Great Tey; his son, and possibly his wife, moved to Great Tey.

DENHAM, Henry. (69); (?–?); had a daughter christened in EC in 1645 and then appears to have left.

DOW, Elizabeth. (47); (1596–1656); daughter of John and Elizabeth Brewer; married in 1628 to John Clerke who was buried in 1646, and remarried *Henry*.

DOW, Henry. (47); (?–1652); married in 1621 to Anne Ashfield and then married *Elizabeth*.

For Elliston kinship diagram: see p. 683.

ELLISTON, Edward. (61); (?–1663); son of John of Black Notley and Alice; gentleman; married *Mabel* Harlakenden (see Appendix 1); six hearths in 1662; in 1634 of Halsted and arrived in EC in *c.* 1636.

ELLISTON, Mabel I. (61); (1603–79); daughter of Thomas Harlakenden and Dorothy; married *Edward*; six hearths 1666–73.

ELLISTON, Mabel II. (61); (1627–57); daughter of *Edward* and *Mabel*.

FINCH, Hannah. (42a); (?–*c.* 1675); daughter of ? Fuller; married in 1664 to *John*.

FINCH, John. (42a); (1636–81); son of Robert and Anne; blacksmith; married *Hannah*; householder with one hearth (discharged) in 1671–5; left a will with his mark on, and marked, as witness, another will.

FINCH, Robert. (22); (1630–78); son of Robert and Anne; blacksmith; married in 1656 to Rachel Johnson who was buried in 1657 and then in 1661 to Mary Josselin the sister of RJ; a five-hearth house in 1671–5; left a will and signed as witness, a number of others; inventory worth £51. 12*s*.

FLETCHER, John. (8); (?–*c.* 1679); grocer; married Mary; four hearths in 1671–5; said to be of Great Yeldham in 1667 when he started buying land in EC where he finally moved and where his son was later an innkeeper.

FOSSETT, William I. (56); (?–1657); son of William; mason; married in 1623 to Mary Ashfield.

FOSSETT, William II. (5); (1624–1702); son of *William I* and Mary; carpenter, bricklayer; married in 1650 to Katharine Summerson, widow, and then in 1661 to Susannah; one hearth in 1671 and 1673, discharged on latter occasion.

FOSTER, John. (50); (?–*c.* 1682); baker; married Mary; no children were christened after 1681, though earlier christenings occur in 1676 and 1678; for further information on the highway robbery and execution see p. 637, n. 1 above.

GAME, James. (not in EC when referred to); (1635–*c.* 1658); son of Sam and Jane.

ELLISTON Kinship Diagram

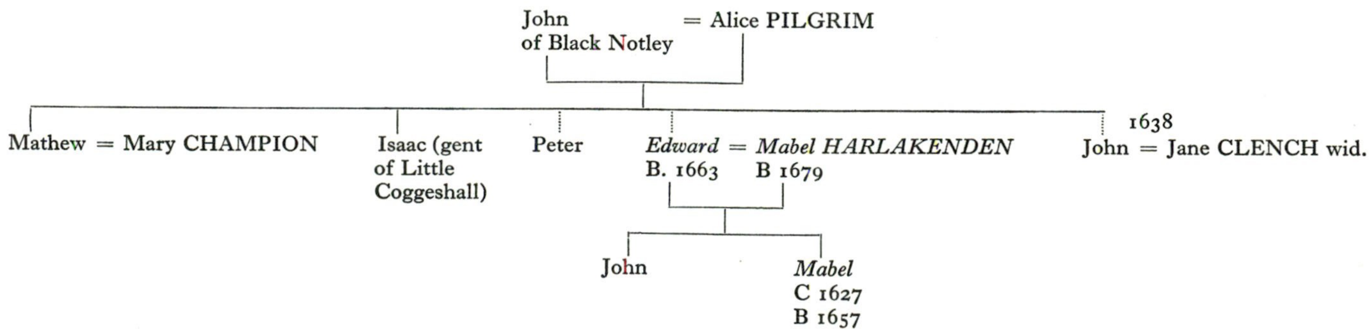

For Garrad kinship diagram: see p. 685.

GARRAD, Anthony. (42a); (1602–59); son of Adam and Judith; married in 1628 to Anne Sillito.

GARRAD, John. (9); (1622–88); son of John and Elizabeth; maltster, gentleman, army captain; married to Anne in *c.* 1665 and Katherine in 1676; four-hearth house in 1662 and five hearths in 1673; a Quaker who, in 1678, gave part of his land for a Quaker meeting-house; the deed of gift has his signature.

GARRAD, Thomas. (?); (1605–87); son of Adam and Judith; married in 1637 to Susan Smyth and in 1648 to Grace Carter; one hearth (discharged) 1671–5; marked, as witness, a will.

GIBSON, Martha. (servant); (*c.* 1638–*c.* 1720); daughter of James and Grace and grand-daughter of *Ambrose Waller*; married *William Allen* at Colchester and in 1681 married Abraham Vangover, both Quakers; left a will as 'of Colchester' where she owned property; her brother was a linen draper in EC.

GRANT, Mary. (?); (1604–61); illegitimate daughter of Thomas Allen and Mary Grant, a couple who had a number of illegitimate children together but never married; there is no record of any child being born to Mary the younger and she died unmarried.

HARDING, Thomasine. (?); (?–1663); never married.

For Harrington kinship diagram: see p. 686.

HARRINGTON, James. (living with RJ); (1628–50); son of William and Elizabeth; schoolmaster at EC; educated at St. John's, Cambridge (Venn).

HARRIS, Edward. (?); (1614–88); son of Edward and Edith; never married.

HARRIS, Robert. (45); (1627–94); son of Edward and Edith; married Mary; householder with one hearth 1662–75, vacant in 1671; churchwarden in 1670; signed 1696 Roll.

HARRIS, Theodosia. (6); (?–1678); married Robert Stamer and later *Toby Harris* in 1656; three-hearth house in 1671 and 1673; inventory worth £37. 19*s*. 8*d*.; RJ's remarks on her health were made ten days after the birth of her daughter Rosamund on 9 January 1659/60.

HARRIS, Toby. (6); (1617–70); son of Edward and Edith; innkeeper; married *Theodosia*; householder with two hearths in 1662 and 1666; left a will with mark; inventory worth £29. 15*s*.

HATCH, Bartholomew. (servant); (1621–1700); son of Robert and Joan; married Elizabeth; one hearth (discharged) in 1671 and 1673.

HATCH, Dorothy. (36); (?–*c.* 1698); daughter of John Wenden of Colne Engaine, yeoman, and Joan; married *Henry* in 1645; left a will with mark; inventory of £27. 15*s*. 2*d*.

HATCH, Henry. (36); (1621–90); son of John and Anne; butcher; married *Dorothy* in 1645; five hearths in 1662–73 and three in 1675: left a will with mark and marked other wills; inventory of £98. 19*s*. 2*d*.; an overseer of the poor in 1676; the son mentioned by RJ as christened on 22 January 1656/7 was Richard, born on 12 January and buried on 6 February, for whom there is no recorded baptism in the parish register.

GARRAD Kinship Diagram

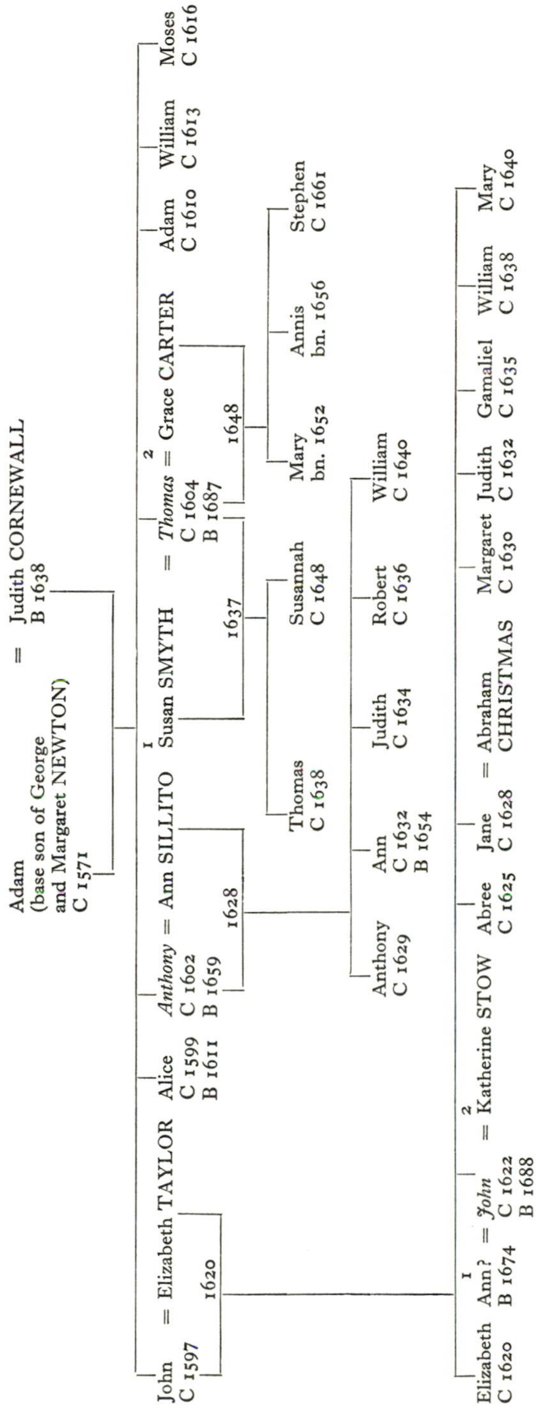

HARRINGTON Kinship Diagram

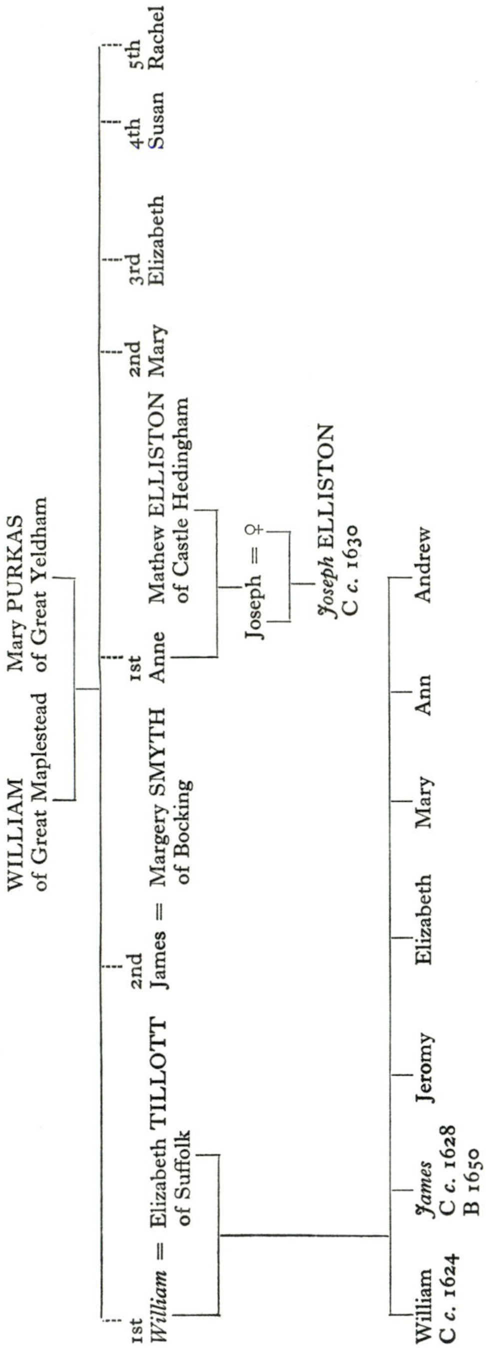

HATCH, Richard. (24); (1615–80); son of John and Anne; butcher; married in 1636 to Susan Rookes and then in 1643 to Mary Day; four hearths in 1662 to 1675, householder; left a will with mark; inventory of £71. 16*s*. 4*d*.

HATCH, Sarah. (36); (1654–?); daughter of *Henry* and *Dorothy*; married John Wenden in 1673; John Wenden had been committed to the care of her father Henry, his 'uncle', in 1669, after a time in the House of Correction as a disorderly person (Q/SR).

HATCH, William I. (?); (1592–1647); son of John; married Anne Newton in 1633; buried on 24 November 1647, two months after RJ mentions his sickness.

HATCH, William II. (18); (1617–91); son of Robert and Joan; fisherman; married Elizabeth Harvie in 1641; householder with one hearth in 1675; the son-in-law mentioned by RJ on 27 March 1675 was Richard Ellis, householder.

HAUKESBEE, Richard. (of Colchester); (1621– ?); son of John, vicar of EC, and Dyonis; by the date RJ mentions him, he was of Colchester.

HAUKESBEE, Sarah. (not of EC); (1629–*c*. 1681); daughter of John and Dyonis; married John Beereman and later ? Bundock; left a will in 1681, as of Ramsden Bellhouse, widow.

HAUKESBEE, William. (at Bulphan); (1625–*c*. 1681); son of John and Dyonis; vicar of Bulphan when he made and signed his will.

HOLDEN, John. (52); (?–1677); weaver, saymaker, unlicensed baker; married Anne Game in 1643 and later Margaret; householder with two hearths in 1672–5; his inventory was worth £304. 16*s*.; there is no evidence concerning 'Beckwith's wife' mentioned by RJ.

HUMPHRY, Thomas. (lived with RJ); (?–1657); son of John and Dorothy and nephew to RJ; servant to RJ.

HUMPHRY, William. (lived with RJ); (?–1673); a 'scot' and schoolmaster of EC.

HURRELL, Nicholas. (?); (?–?); groom to Richard Harlakenden and possibly related to the Harlakenden family.

For Hutton kinship diagram: see p. 688.

HUTTON, Guy. (?); (1618–62); son of *Henry I* and Anne; workman to Richard Harlakenden; married Alice Brown who was buried 1690.

HUTTON, Henry I. (23); (1591–1665); son of Thomas and Joan; servant to Richard Harlakenden, husbandman; married Anne Garrad in 1610; marked his own will; inventory of £7. 3*s*.

HUTTON, Henry II. (33); (1636–1700); son of *Guy* and Alice; workman to Richard Harlakenden; married Alice; one hearth (discharged) house in 1671–5.

ISERSON, John. (10); (?–1682); married Sarah Wall; two hearths in 1662, one hearth (vacant) and four hearths in 1671, four hearths in 1675; at burial he was 'laid in a hole in his own ground' but no other evidence of Quakerism except for accusation of non-attendance at church at the 1679 Assizes.

HUTTON Kinship Diagram

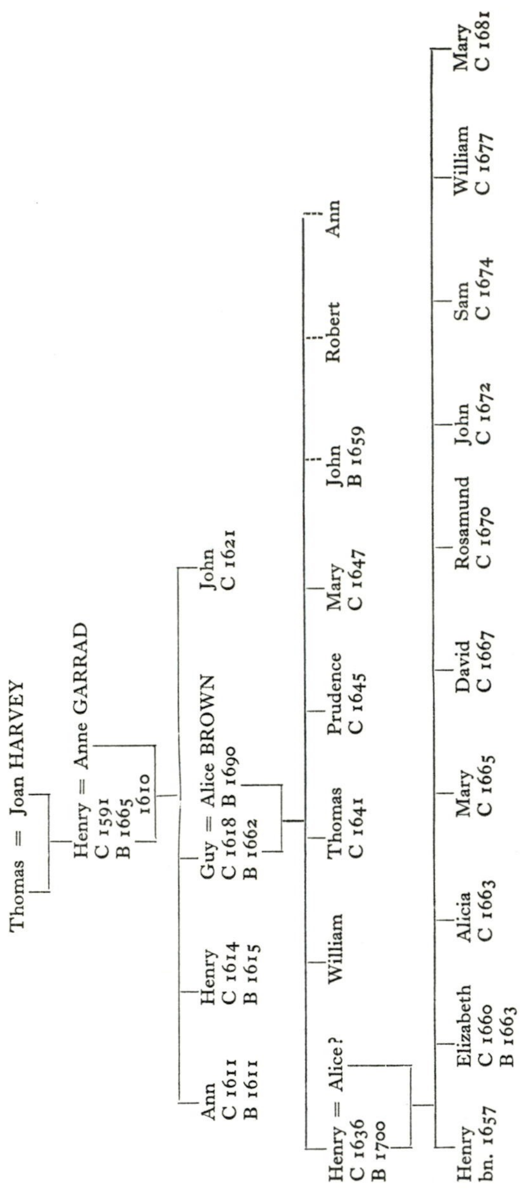

JOHNSON, Robert. (?); (?–?); formerly a servant of Richard Harlakenden.

KENT, John. (69); (?–1662); married Anne Parker and in 1625 to Helen Finch and in 1640 to Margery Smith who was buried 1659; signature, as a witness to a will.

LAYER, Dorothy. (?); (1630–58); daughter of Edmund and Elizabeth; married ? Carter in *c.* 1658.

LEA, Robert. (34); (1605–60); son of Daniel and Elizabeth; married in 1625 to Margaret Sheldrick; both he and his wife died of the plague; he was buried on 24 May, four days after RJ wrote of his illness, and his wife on 3 June.

LEAPER, Daniel. (servant); (1640–1717); son of Daniel and Elizabeth; yeoman; married; marked 1696 Roll.

LUDGATER, John. (18); (?–1711); son of John and Margaret; schoolmaster and later vicar of EC from 1690; married Anne.

MARKHAM, Abraham. (4); (?–1660); married Alice Turner, daughter of *Clement*, in 1633; in 1658 *William Adams* and his family were accused at the Q/S of breaking into his garden and assaulting his wife.

MATHEWS, Bridget. (22); (?–1672); daughter of John Pigge of Newport Pond and Margaret; married *Christopher*; her funeral was noted by RJ on 28 July 1672 but is not in the parish register; she left a will.

MATHEWS, Christopher. (22); (?–1670); cordwainer, yeoman; married *Bridget*; householder, in 1662 a five-hearth house and two hearths in 1666; marked his own will and those of others; inventory of £25. 0*s.* 8*d.*

MIGHILL, Robert. (65); (?–1668); married in 1621 to Ruth Grant, and in 1653 to Grace Hodson at Markshall, and in 1661 to Elinor Harris; householder.

MOLE, Francis. (?); (?–?); married in 1641 to Rose Alcocke; probably moved to Colne Engaine.

MOLE, Philip. (11); (?–1671); married Grace Pease in 1661, when he was given as of Rallesdon, Suffolk.

MOLINS, John. (73); (?–1664); son of Henry of Colne Engaine; yeoman; married Elizabeth; died intestate with inventory of £30. 10*s.*; no children were christened in EC; on several occasions during 1653–4 he was accused at the Q/S of forcible entry and riot in Colne Engaine.

MORLEY, Henry. (?); (1610–93); son of Henry and Grace; bricklayer; married Elizabeth Dobson in 1631; had a one-hearth house from 1662 to 1673, discharged in 1673; left a will; churchwarden 1670–85.

For Nevill kinship diagram: see p. 690.

NEVILL, Richard. (2); (1622–54); son of William and Mary; gentleman; left a will (PROB. 11/257/306) in which he described lands in Chapel parish, where he was born.

NEWTON, Elizabeth. (74); (?–1674); daughter of Samuel and Margaret possibly of White Colne; never married.

NEWTON, Grace. (servant); (1632–?); daughter of John and Alice.

NEVILL Kinship Diagram

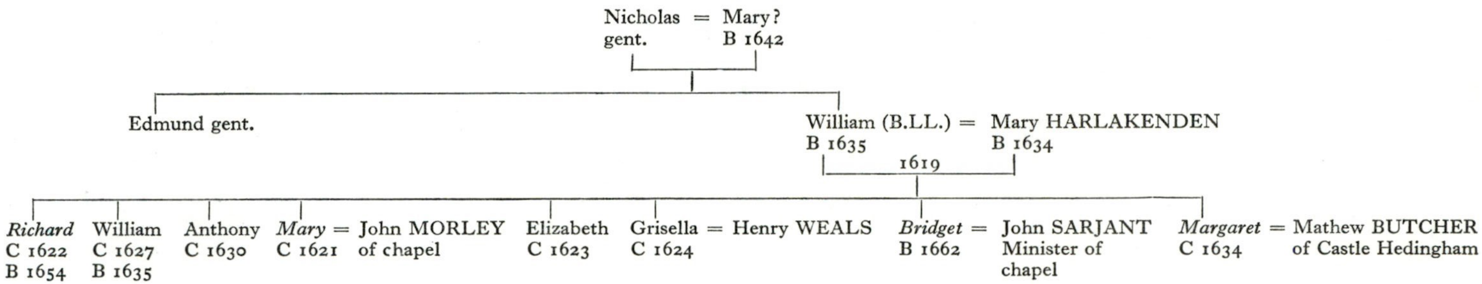

NEWTON, Samuel. (74); (1614–*c.* 1689); son of John and Elizabeth; yeoman; married Margaret Davy in 1636; a five-hearth house in 1666–75; left a will in which he was 'of EC', though it is possible that he lived in White Colne where he owned freehold property.

NICCOLS, James. (30); (?–*c.* 1645); yeoman; married Edith.

OSBORNE, Thomas. (68); (?–*c.* 1657); married Alice Finch in 1638.

OWERS, John. (21); (?–1677); servant to Mr. Bowes; married to Elizabeth and later to Sarah; householder with one hearth (discharged) from 1671 to 1675, during which time he occupied part of Colneford Mill; witness to two wills, which he probably signed.

PAIN, John. (?); (1655–95); son of *Robert Pain* alias Allen and Rose.

PAIN alias ALLEN, Robert. (54); (1625–*c.* 1680); illegitimate son of Thomas Allen and Lidia Paine; labourer, husbandman; married Rose and later Grace; one hearth (discharged) in 1671–5; left a will with mark; an inventory of £3. 14*s.*, though holding four copyhold houses in the 1677/8 Rental.

PEAKE, Mary. (37); (1594–1679); daughter of John and Rebecca; never married.

PEARTREE, Anne. (?); (1638–64); daughter of *William* and Elizabeth.

PEARTREE, William. (49); (1616–74); son of Esdras and Mary; butcher; married on 25 April 1638 to Elizabeth Hatch and remarried Susan Stevens on 5 December 1639; one hearth in 1662–71; he was cited to the ecclesiastical court on 14 May 1639 for incontinency before marriage with Elizabeth Hatch, though she had been buried on 23 December 1638; his daughter *Anne* was baptized on 25 November 1638 and had thus been pre-nuptially conceived; he was noted as 'drowned' in the parish register on 30 January 1674.

PEASE, Walter. (10); (?–1673); married Frances Hewit in 1631; tailor; his daughter Grace married *Philip Mole.*

PENHACKE, Guy. (at Halstead); (1618–84); son of James and Rose; farmer; never married; for further details see p. 67, n. 1 above.

PENHACKE, John. (20); (1631–86); son of William and Anne; married *Mary Potter* RJ's servant in 1658; two hearths in 1666 and then one hearth to 1675.

PENHACKE, Sarah. (servant); (1647–?); daughter of Anne, previously widow *Bental.*

PILGRIM, John. (58); (1599–*c.* 1652); son of George and Sarah; married Cicely; made a will on 5 December 1650, to which a codicil was added two days later.

PINDAR, John. (?); (?–?); styled Mr; had child christened in EC on 12 June 1678 with wife Mary; otherwise nothing known.

POLLY, John. (?); (1613–?); son of Adam and Joan; married Jane.

POTTER, Edmund. (?); (?–1668); oatmeal-maker and maltmaker; married Anne Sachre in 1628; householder with three hearths in 1662; left a will in which he was 'aged and frail'.

POTTER, EDWARD. (38); (1585–1668); son of Edmund and Margaret; yeoman; married Susan and then in *c.* 1634 to Mary Hull; householder with two hearths in 1662 and 1666; left a will and signed, as witness, an inventory; his inventory total was £8. 16*s.* 11*d.*; he was frequently cited to the ecclesiastical courts between 1609 and 1635 for various offences including incontinency, throwing stones through the church windows and, at the Q/S, for poaching and disturbing the peace.

POTTER, GEORGE. (47); (1649–72); son of Edward and Mary; yeoman; never married; made a will.

POTTER, MARY. (20); (1638–?); daughter of *Robert* and Margaret; servant to RJ; married *John Penhacke* in 1658.

POTTER, ROBERT. (39); (?–*c.* 1675); son of William; yeoman; married Margaret who died in 1651 and then Judith Tanner in 1653; two hearths in 1662–6; previously of Aldham in 1637; with reference to RJ's comment, Potter's daughter Elizabeth married Edward Johnson, widower, on 7 August 1667 and his daughter Judith married John Newton on 23 June 1674.

PRYOR, THOMAS. (dead when mentioned); (1577–1645); son of Albery and Mary; husbandman and yeoman; married Anne Greenwood and Mary Baker in 1618; marked various wills; the reversion of all his land was to Edward Elliston, gentleman.

READ, JOHN. (41); (1615–?); son of John and Anne; married Ellen; in 1649 he was noted in the Harlakenden Fine Book as 'out of the kingdom'.

REEVE, GRACE. (?); (?–1658); married to John Reeve in *c.* 1612 who died in 1624, thus a widow for thirty-four years.

REYNER, THOMAS. (?); (?–1656); married Priscilla *c.* 1639; only one child is noted as christened in EC, in 1641, although nine are alluded to by RJ; a tenant of Sir John Jacob.

RUGGLES, EDITH. (15); (?–1667); daughter of Thomas Smith; married Thomas, a baker, who was buried in 1643 as a householder; she had a four-hearth house in 1666.

RUSHBROOKE, JOHN. (55); (1611–89); son of John and Mary; fishmonger; married Mary Harvie in 1636; one hearth from 1662 to 1671.

SCOT, JOHN. (?); (?–1699); carpenter; married Bridget, buried in 1659, and then Mary, buried in 1679; three hearths in 1662, three hearths (empty) in 1666; two hearths in 1671; one hearth (discharged) in 1673; when buried he was termed 'old'.

SEWELL, ALSE. (dead when mentioned); (?–1633); servant to *Edward Potter*; in 1634 John Sewell of Boreham had her goods at Feering and in September he alleged at the ecclesiastical court that they were not worth above £5.

SILLITO, CALVIN. (?); (1615–72); son of Albon; married Anne; one hearth in 1671; had children christened from 1652.

SPOONER, EDWARD. (71); (?–1658); yeoman; married Anne who died in 1662; made a will (PROB. 11/294/403) in 1652; churchwarden in 1630.

SPRINGAT, SUSANNAH. (26); (?–?); the only reference to her is that she was a tenant of 'Swinesty' in 1640.

STEVENS, EDWARD. (59); (?–1684); married Mary, buried in 1658, then Hellen, buried in 1664 and then, three months later, Mary Bowles; two hearths in 1671, one hearth (discharged) in 1673 and one and three hearths (both discharged) in 1675.

TALBOT, THOMAS. (40); (?–1665); recently moved to EC, according to RJ.

TAYLOR, EDWARD. (54); (1589–1659); son of Moses and Alice; (carpenter); married in 1614 to Agnes Polly, in 1624 to Joan Bosely, in 1641 to Susan Andrews, and then in 1653 to Mary Pilgrim, widow; marked, as witness, a will; a frequent non-attender at church 1625–37.

TIBBALL, ROBERT. (1); (?–1662); (farmer); remarried in 1655 to Sarah Brown, widow; five-hearth house in 1662.

TOLLER, GEORGE. (?); (?–1712); gentleman; married Elizabeth Abbott daughter of *Henry II*; his will included landholdings in Stanway, Copford, Fordham, White Colne, and Earls Colne; signed the 1696 Roll.

TURNER, CLEMENT. (4); (1562–*c.* 1644); son of Clement and Helen; labourer, weaver; married in 1592 to Cicely Mortimer who was buried in 1641; his daughter Alice married *Abraham Markham*; his daughter Elizabeth's son, John Prentice, left four rooms to him in 'the house where Markham lives' in 1640.

WADE, ROBERT. (?); (?–*c.* 1671); his first wife died of the plague and was buried on 28 April 1666 and he re-married Margaret; a five hearth house in 1662–6; he was cited to the ecclesiastical court for absence from church in 1663 and 1665 and was probably a Quaker; his son Robert was a Quaker and emigrated to New England in 1675; left goods inventoried at £13. 1*s.* 4*d.*

WADE, THOMAS. (57); (?–1685); married Sarah; one hearth in 1671–3; possibly a Quaker as he was noted at his burial as 'buried in a field'.

WALLER, AMBROSE. (28); (?–1653); married Susannah who was buried on 12 August 1658; householder; a churchwarden who left his signature.

WILLOWS, AN. (?); (?–1658); in 1606 cited for incontinency and in 1608 cited for not receiving communion, both at ecclesiastical court.

WISEMAN, HENRY. (3); (?–1688); married Priscilla and then Anne Smith, in 1647; one hearth (discharged) from 1671 to 1675; the children referred to by RJ were probably Ann, born 8 September 1649 and Henry, born 15 September 1653.

WRIGHT, ROBERT. (71); (?–1679); yeoman, 'Mr'; married Katherine; householder with two hearths in 1666 and five in 1671–5; a will with land in Linsey, Suffolk; inventory worth £379. 13*s.* 6*d.*; buried in the 'Quaker ground'.

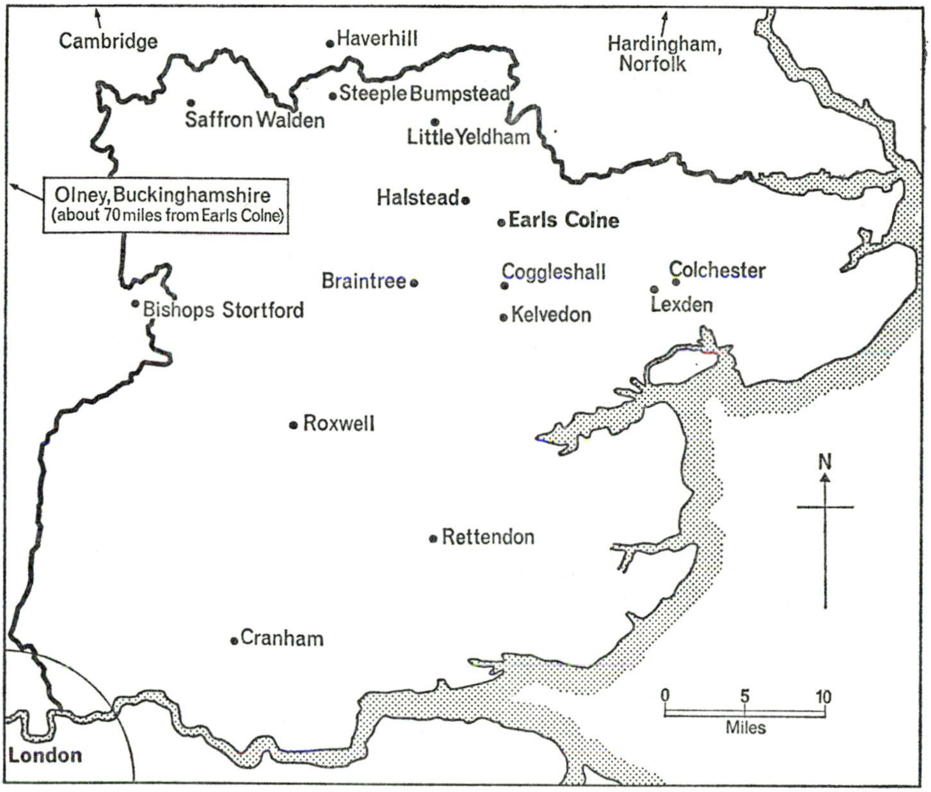

MAP I. The County of Essex, showing the location of Earls Colne and of other places mentioned in Josselin's Diary

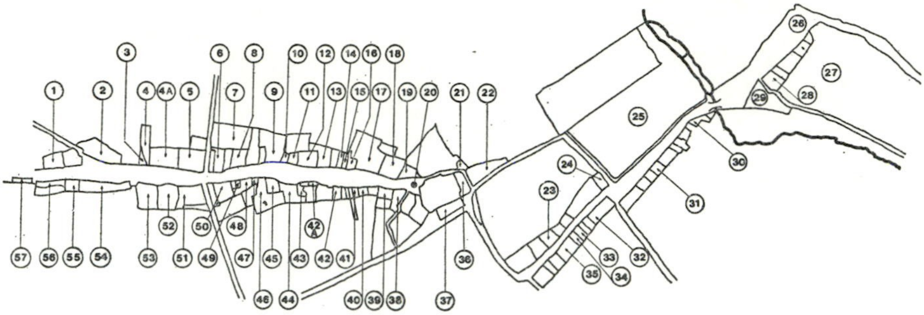

Map II. The main street of Earls Colne; residence of people mentioned in Josselin's Diary

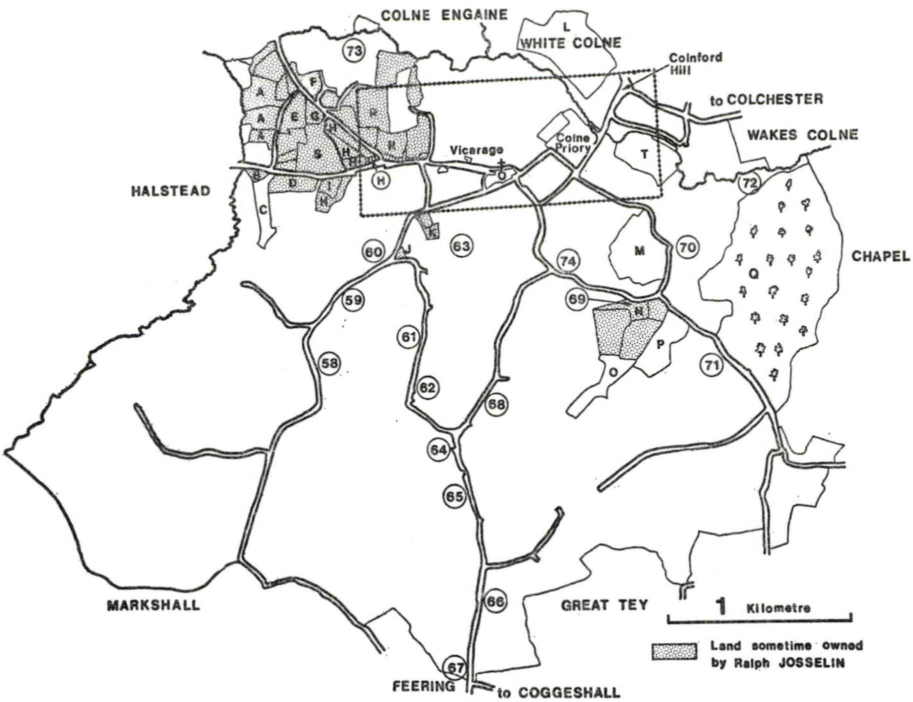

Map III. The parish of Earls Colne; also land owned by Josselin

Maps drawn by Mr. D. Rowan of the Audio Visual Aid Unit, Cambridge

1. Robert and Sarah Tibball (Clarks).
2. Richard Nevill (Collyn's Farm).
3. Henry Wiseman (Sewells).
4. Clement Turner and Abraham Markham (Hitchcocks).
4a. John Church I and John Church II (Sonnells).
5. William Fossett (Sebrights).
6. Toby and Theodosia Harris (The Lyon).
7. Quaker Meeting House built by John Garrad, 1674.
8. John Fletcher (Boomes).
9. John Garrad (Mallories).
10. Walter Pease until 1654, then John Iserson (Carters).
11. Philip Mole (Garlands).
12. Sam Burton I and his wife Anne; Sam Burton II and Susan Burton (The Bell).
13. Vicarage.
14. Sam Burton I and wife Anne about 1659 (Waites).
15. Edith Ruggles (Tottes).
16. Robert Abbott I then Edward Abbott.
17. William Cosin (Mathews Acre).
18. William Hatch II and John Ludgater (Tredgolds).
19. Robert Davey I and wife, Katherine (The Blew Bore).
20. John Penhacke and wife, Mary (The Taverne).
21. John Owers (Prills).
22. Christopher and Bridget Mathews, then from 1666 Robert and Mary Finch (Ruffles).
23. Henry Hutton I (Boxteds).
24. Richard Hatch (Sextens).
25. Richard Harlakenden and family (Colne Priory).
26. Susannah Springat, then Robert Davy II (Swinesty).
27. James Day (Shawes).
28. Ambrose Waller until 1658, later William Allen (Morses).
29. Richard and Mary Caplin and their son, James (White Hart).
30. James Niccols (Drewes).
31. Adam Brewer (Francis).
32. Robert Crow (The George).
33. Henry Hutton II (Middle House).
34. Robert Lea.
35. Edward Cressener until 1649, then George Cressener (Chandlers).
36. Henry and Dorothy Hatch and their daughter, Sarah (Trasers).
37. Mary Peake.
38. Edward Potter (Skinners and Gentries).
39. Robert Potter (Sonningwells).
40. William Harlakenden, then Thomas Talbot (Newhouse).
41. John Read (Littmans).
42. Rose Church and her daughter, Mary (Squires).
42a. Anthony Garrad, then John and Hannah Finch (Francis).
43. John Clark and his wife, Elizabeth (Goolds).
44. William Adam.
45. Robert Harris (Wallers).
46. Bridget Aylward (Mordens).
47. Henry and Elizabeth Dow, then from 1669 George Potter (Mordens).
48. Bartholomew Clarke, then John Alston (Jouldens).
49. William Peartree.
50. John Foster (Cloviers).
51. John Amies (Firmantylers).
52. John Holden (Spicers).
53. Edward Browne (Wards).
54. Edward Taylor, then Robert Pain alias Allen (Lophams).
55. John Rushbrooke (Filbricks).
56. William Fossett I (Cawches).
57. John Bowles, then Thomas Wade from 1659 (Gillots).
58. John Pilgrim (Gouldsgate).
59. Edward Stevens.
60. Henry Abbott I and wife, Dorothy; Henry Abbott II and daughter, Rose (Hayhouse).
61. Edward Elliston and wife, Mabel I and daughter, Mabel II (Curds).
62. Robert Carter II (Stacies and Wastlins).
63. (exact site uncertain) Edward Clarke, then John Coleman (Pound Farm).
64. John Bullocke (Rushpit).
65. Robert Mighill (Garretts).
66. William and Elizabeth Death (Procknuts).
67. Robert Carter I (Cowland or Colneland).
68. Thomas Osborne (Blakes).
69. John Kent, Ann Bental, Henry Denham, Sam Brewer and wife, Mary (Mallories).
70. Cornelius and Martha Brownson (Humphreys).
71. Edward Spooner, later Robert Wright (Mills Farm).
72. John Chrismas, later John Burton (Chalkney Mill).
73. (uncertain) John Mullins.
74. William Brand, then Sam Newton (Tilekiln).

A. Hobstevens
B. Stonebridge Croft
C. Dagnal Hill
D. Brockhole
E. Loveland
F. Sonnels
G. Little Bridgemans
H. Clarks (farm on the green)
I. Sawyers
J. Vicaridge Close
K. Sprigs Marsh
L. Ten Acres
M. Chiffin
N. Mallories
O. Aldercar, Oxenfen
P. Mills Fenn
Q. Chalkney Wood
R. Coes
S. Pitchers
T. Hall Meadow

INDEX OF PLACES

Note

Places italicized in this index are within the parish of Earls Colne; their location is shown on the map of the parish, page 696 above.

Josselin's spelling of place names has been preserved. Where modern spelling is very different, the present version has been given in brackets.

All references are to the marginal date under which the place is mentioned in the Diary, even if this marginal date is slightly different from the date within the text. The dates have been contracted; thus 23/4/50 stands for 23 April 1650. Josselin's conventions concerning dates between January 1 and March 24 have been followed (see the note on dating in Abbreviations and Conventions above, p. xvii).

Some places are mentioned in the miscellaneous jottings printed at the end of the text. These are referred to by the page numbers of this edition on which they appear rather than by date since at this point there are no marginal dates in the Diary.

Aldercar, Oxenfen, 23/4/50
Aldham, 10/1/46/7
Algiers, 6/2/80/1
Alnewicke, 11/8/51
Alsace, 656
Alsford, 29/3/44
America, 13/3/50/1
Ardleigh, 9/7/50, 17/3/50/1, 23/12/53, 30/4/54, 10/11/55, 21/4/56
Arras, 22/8/54, 651
Ashby, 17/9/45, 18/9/45
Asia, 13/3/50/1
Ason (Assington) Suffolk, 24/5/52
Austins Church, London, 6/12/52
Austria, 10/8/64, 648, 653
Aynstone, Oxfordshire, 27/3/59, 31/3/59

Badew, Little, 5/10/69
Barbados, 9/6/51, 20/2/55/6, 651
Barbican, 10/11/68
Barcelona, Catalonia, 24/1/51/2, 24/1/52/3
Barwicke, 649
Basing, 16/10/45
Bavaria, 649
Beaconsfield, 1/4/59
Bedford, 8/8/47
Bedfordshire, 25/9/58
Bently Hall, 5/12/57
Benyfield Lawn, 19/5/51
Berne, 652
Bilboa, Spain, 24/1/51/2
Bilsden, Leicestershire, 16/9/45
Birch, 25/3/52
Birch, Great, 8/4/53
Bishop Stortford, Herts., 1618, 22/4/48, 30/4/48, 23/5/48, 11/10/48, 18/6/49, 29/11/59
Bishops Stortford School, 17/2/44/5
Blackepoint, New England, Ligonia, 25/3/58
Bocking, 27/5/66
Bollinhatch, 30/4/47, 10:11/7/49, 27/3/49/50, 29/3/51, 21/3/51/2, 9/4/59, 28/10/73
Borborg-Flanders, 653
Bourdeaux, 22/1/53/4, 651
Brabant, 656
Braintree, 4/3/44/5, 11/12/46, 4/6/48, 11/6/48, 8/10/65, 1/7/66, 15/7/66, 29/7/66, 5/8/66, 23/9/66, 20/9/67, 17/6/73, 25:26/5/75
Brandenberg, 653
Brazil, 25/1/57/8
Bredali, 4/8/67
Breme, 24/8/56, 652
Bremeland, 25/1/57/8, 653
Brest, 22/1/53/4
Bridgemans, Little, 17/9/50
Bridgemans, 10/2/51/2, 4/11/56, 3/2/59/60
Bristol, 1643, 13/9/45
Brockhole, 24/9/56, 22/9/60, 25/9/60, 7/12/60, 11/4/75
Bromly, 30/9/77, 17/9/80, 28/12/80
Brooke Street, 23/1/44/5
Buckinghamshire, 2/5/48

Buers (Bewers), 24/11/45, 24/5/55, 26/12/55, 21/5/56, 24/12/56, 7/5/57, 23/12/57, 14/4/58, 9/9/58, 16/11/76
Bulmere, 21/5/56
Bumpstead, Essex, 1632, 1636, 26/9/44, 18/7/54, 7/8/55
Burleigh House, 13/9/45
Burntwood, 15/3/59/60
Bury, 16/5/48, 2/8/56, 22/4/74, 14/5/74, 27/5/74, 27/9/74

Cadiz, 654
Callendar House, 26/7/51
Cambridge, 24/10/44, 20/11/44, 27/8/45, 9/9/45, 22/9/45, 30/11/46, 18/6/49, 9/1/49/50, 26/9/50, 29/9/50, 2/10/50, 19/5/51, 28/9/52, 10/11/56, 27/10/65, 1/7/66, 12/12/69
Canaryes (Canaries), 6/3/44/5, 7/5/57
Candia, 24/1/50/1, 10/5/54, 649, 654
Canea, 649
Carickfergus (Ireland), 29/7/49
Carisbrook Castle, 11/9/56
Carlingford, 29/7/49
Carlisle, 6/6/51, 16/8/51
Casal in Montferrat, 24/1/52/3
Catalonia, 22/1/53/4, 25/1/57/8, 651
Chalk-end, 1616
Chalkney Wood, 6/8/60, 6/8/73, 9/8/78
Chappell (Chappel), 15/9/46, 10/3/54/5, 19/11/55, 22/1/56/7, 31/8/58, 20/2/67/8
Chatham, 9/6/67, 654
Chelmsford, 7/2/44/5, 11/2/44/5, 12/2/44/5, 27/9/45, 21/10/45, 8/1/45/6, 4/8/46, 28/9/46, 8/10/46, 11/12/46, 2/6/48, 10/7/49, 18/12/49, 22/2/49/50, 17/3/49/50, 17/8/50, 4/12/50, 7/1/52/3, 13/1/52/3, 5/10/55, 20/8/56, 28/12/58, 13/3/69/70, 16/3/69/70
Cheshire, 6/10/44, 21/8/51, 23/8/59
Chester, 14/11/45, 16/11/45, 25/2/45/6, 5/3/45/6, 17/9/47
Chesterford, Great, 27/8/45
Chiffin, Upper, 2/8/57
Clare, 26/9/44, 23/8/53, 2/9/53, 2/6/59
Clare Hall, 12/11/79
Clarks, 23/1/57/8
Coes Pond, 2/8/76
Coggeshall, 19/8/44, 30/12/44, 23/1/44/5, 8/6/45, 8/2/45/6, 31/3/46, 16/7/46, 20/7/46, 22/7/46, 3/6/47, 21/6/47, 29/7/47, 5/8/47, 11/11/47, 6/4/48, 3/6/48, 12/6/48, 26/4/49, 23/7/49, 6/1/49/50, 6/6/50, 15/12/50, 3/8/51, 12/10/51, 12:13/12/51, 18/3/51/2, 1/6/54, 10/3/54/5, 15/7/55, 9/4/56, 13/4/56, 8/6/56, 2/4/57, 30/4/57, 29/10/57, 24/4/58, 12/6/58, 21/8/58, 12/11/58, 13/11/58, 10/2/58/9, 20/7/62, 9/11/62, 17/7/64, 24/4/65, 21/5/65, 8/10/65, 26/8/66, 16/9/66, 30/12/66, 5/8/70, 3/10/78, 22/10/78, 29/1/79/80
Colchester, 1642, 5/8/44, 26/8/44, 1/9/44, 14/9/44, 3/10/44, 17/3/44/5, 20/8/45, 6/10/45, 14/10/45, 8/5/46, 8/7/46, 22/7/46, 7/10/46, 9/6/47, 31/3/48, 1/5/48, 3/6/48, 4/6/48, 11/6/48, 13/6/48, 24/8/48, 25/8/48, 27/8/48, 28/8/48, 30/8/48, 5/9/48, 9/6/49, 7/7/49, 9/1/49/50, 5/3/49/50, 16/4/50, 13/7/50, 21/7/50, 2/8/50, 2/9/50, 29/3/50/1, 22/8/51, 1/9/51, 26/2/51/2, 2/3/51/2, 20/11/52, 11/6/53, 23/3/53/4, 11/11/54, 7/3/54/5, 11/8/55, 27/8/55, 21/3/55/6, 5/4/56, 15/4/56, 6/5/56, 10/5/56, 16/6/56, 3/7/56, 5/7/56, 18/9/56, 20/9/56, 5/1/56/7, 23/1/56/7, 27/3/57, 17/4/58, 4/8/58, 1/3/59/60, 29/9/60, 17/2/61/2, 12/11/62, 18/12/62, 25/6/65, 13/8/65, 16/8/65, 20/8/65, 27/8/65, 3/9/65, 16/9/65, 23/9/65, 1/10/65, 4/10/65, 8/10/65, 15/10/65, 22/10/65, 29/10/65, 5/11/65, 12/11/65, 19/11/65, 26/11/65, 3/12/65, 6/12/65, 9/12/65, 17/12/65, 24/12/65, 3/1/65/6, 7/1/65/6, 14/1/65/6, 21/1/65/6, 28/1/65/6, 4/2/65/6, 11/2/65/6, 18/2/65/6, 25/2/65/6, 4/3/65/6, 11/3/65/6, 18/3/65/6, 25/3/66, 1/4/66, 8/4/66, 15/4/66, 22/4/66, 29/4/66, 2/5/66, 6/5/66, 13/5/66, 20/5/66, 27/5/66, 3/6/66, 10/6/66, 17/6/66, 24/6/66, 1/7/66, 15/7/66, 22/7/66, 29/7/66, 5/8/66, 12/8/66, 26/8/66, 2/9/66, 9/9/66, 16/9/66, 23/9/66, 30/9/66, 6/10/66, 14/10/66, 28/10/66, 4/11/66, 11/11/66, 18/11/66, 25/11/66, 26/9/68, 27/3/75, 29/1/79/80, 10/6/80, 15/7/83
Colne, 1641, 29/10/43, 28/9/45, 16/2/45/6, 19/5/46
Colne, Earls, Essex, 1640
Colne, Gaines
(Colne Engaine), 5/4/45, 18/1/46/7, 26/2/47/8, 8/3/47/8, 17/1/52/3, 24/1/52/3, 30/1/52/3, 31/1/52/3, 6/2/52/3, 9/2/52/3, 13/2/52/3, 4/7/54, 3/10/54, 6/2/54/5, 3/7/55, 1/6/56, 28/6/56, 8/2/56/7, 5/7/57, 23/7/57, 9/11/62, 20/11/64, 26/5/67, 26/4/68, 17/1/74/5, 22/7/77
Colne, Priory, 1640, 24/9/44, 22/4/45, 5/3/45/6, 2/5/46, 12/5/46, 3/8/46, 13/8/46, 31/12/46, 17/9/47, 22/2/47/8, 30/4/49, 18/5/49, 1/8/49, 29/8/49, 22/10/49, 1/11/49, 8/4/50, 22/5/50, 16/7/50, 10/11/50, 23/2/50/1, 13/3/50/1, 2/4/51, 1/7/51, 24/9/51, 10/2/51/2, 30/6/52, 29/10/52, 29/1/52/3, 6/9/53, 3/1/53/4, 10/5/54, 9/6/54, 13/12/54,

13/2/54/5, 6/3/54/5, 25/5/55, 13/3/55/6, 1/4/56, 7/7/56, 18/7/56, 25/7/56, 17/9/56, 27/9/56, 15/10/56, 15/11/56, 8/3/56/7, 18/3/56/7, 6/4/57, 29/5/57, 2/6/57, 29/6/57, 9/11/57, 15/12/57, 13/3/57/8, 14/3/57/8, 16/6/58, 22/9/58, 19/1/58/9, 31/1/58/9, 10/4/59, 28/7/59, 25/9/59, 10/11/59, 25/1/59/60, 15/7/60, 17/10/60, 23/10/60, 28/9/61, 27/10/61, 28/1/61/2, 17/2/61/2, 23/3/61/2, 26/6/64, 26/7/64, 24/11/64, 27/3/65, 6/3/73/4, 13/5/74, 30/9/74, 27/11/74, 15/10/76, 4/11/76, 9/9/77, 31/10/77, 26/1/77/8, 28/3/78, 3/10/78, 17/1/78/9, 5/3/81/2, 3/3/82/3

Colne, Wakes, 23/6/49, 29/9/52, 7/10/52, 28/10/52, 4/1/52/3, 13/1/52/3, 27/1/52/3, 3/2/52/3, 24/2/52/3, 10/3/52/3, 23/6/53, 30/6/53, 7/7/53, 27/10/53, 5/1/53/4, 13/4/54, 10/5/54, 22/6/54, 28/8/54, 4/1/54/5, 20/9/55, 18/10/55, 2/1/55/6, 24/3/55/6, 17/4/56, 15/5/56, 4/9/56, 6/9/56, 11/9/56, 4/11/56, 11/12/56, 22/1/56/7, 5/2/56/7, 12/2/56/7, 26/2/56/7, 19/3/56/7, 12/4/57, 25/6/57, 31/12/57, 7/1/57/8, 6/5/58, 9/9/58, 3/3/58/9, 5/5/59, 27/10/59, 4/1/59/60, 18/1/59/60, 26/1/59/60, 19/4/60

Colne, White, 24/3/53/4, 5/9/56, 16/9/56, 6/8/65, 27/8/65, 2/2/67/8, 28/3/75

Colne Ford hill (Colnford Hill), 1/10/65, 15/10/65, 22/10/65

Cologne (Germany), 12/10/51

Colen, 27/9/63

Connaught, Ireland, 6/7/51, 650

Copenhagen, 13/3/58/9, 20/3/58/9

Copford (Coptford), 6/10/45, 21/8/57, 27/5/58, 1/10/71, 15/10/71, 19/11/71

Cornards Mill, Suffolk, 16/4/58

Cornet Castle, 3/1/51/2

Cracow, 653, 654

Cranham, Essex, 1640, 29/3/44, 31/8/46, 1/2/46/7, 3/2/46/7, 9/3/46/7, 11/3/46/7, 25/5/48, 2/4/50, 5/5/51, 3/10/51, 22/11/51, 14/6/52, 24/3/53/4, 15/6/57

Crete, 31/3/67

Cronenburg, 653

Culmore Castle, 14/7/49

Curland, 653

Dagnal, 3/5/51, 24/6/51, 9/12/51, 1/1/51/2, 30/3/52, 7/4/52, 21/5/52, 15:16:17/3/52/3, 24/3/52/3, 28/3/53, 12/7/53, 7:8/3/53/4

Dagnal further Hill, 24/3/51/2

Dagnal, Further, 24/1/52/3

Dagnall Hill, 6/3/51/2

Dalmatia, 649

Deane, Beds., 1636, 1637, 1639, 1641, 12/7/54, 29/10/79

Dedham, 17/3/44/5, 19/8/45, 18/1/59/60, 6/2/59/60, 22/2/59/60, 1/3/59/60, 8/4/66, 7/4/76, 21/4/76/7

Dendermond, 4/8/67

Denmark, 24/1/52/3, 25/1/57/8, 23/12/60, 2/2/61/2, 24/1/63/4, 649, 651, 653

Derby House, 650

Derry, 14/7/49

Domingo, 25/1/55/6

Dorsetshire, 23/8/51

Douglas 7:8/3/78/9

Dover, 26/6/70, 655

Dublin, 1/7/49, 29/7/49, 1/8/49, 14/8/49, 31/1/51/2, 650

Dumfries, 11/8/51, 21/9/51

Dunbar, 650

Dundalke, 29/7/49

Dundee, 30/8/51, 21/9/51

Dunkirk, 12/9/52, 24/1/52/3, 22/1/53/4, 649, 653, 654

Dunmow, Great, 27/11/46, 23/12/46

Dunmow, 21/10/53, 11/1/56/7, 19/12/57, 21/12/57

Dunstable, 21/8/51

Easthorp, 12/9/78

Edgehill, 1642, 23/10/53

Edinburgh Castle, 31/12/50, 650

Elizabeth Castle, 3/1/51/2

Eltham, Kent, 11/5/60

Ely, 20/10/78

England, 648

Essex, 1637, 9/12/46, 4/6/48, 12/6/48, 30/8/48, 4/9/70

Etna–Sicily, 654

Europe, 13/3/50/1, 10/8/51, 25/3/58, 13/6/60, 7/5/76

Evora, 28/6/63

Exeter, 16/4/46, 19/4/46

Fambridge Creek, 26/5/56

Farm on the Green (*Clarks*), 30/6/56, 25/11/57, 4:5/1/58/9, 25/11/62, 26/1/62/3, 22/3/67/8

Feering Bury, 8/10/46, 31/10/46, 27/11/46, 23/12/46, 6/6/49, 18/3/50/1, 10/8/56, 8/10/65

Felsted, 1640, 5/9/47

Fife, 26/7/51

Flanders, 24/1/50/1, 21/3/56/7, 25/1/57/8, 15/3/57/8, 4/8/67, 12/8/77, 1/3/77/8, 654, 656

Fordham, 1643

Fordham Street, 16/9/47

Fordmead, 13/6/74

France, 13/11/50, 9/2/50/1, 30/3/51,

20/4/51, 9/6/51, 12/10/51, 2/11/51, 23/11/51, 29/11/51, 6/1/51/2, 15/1/51/2, 24/1/51/2, 12/9/52, 14/11/52, 21/11/52, 24/1/52/3, 28/3/53, 9/1/53/4, 10/3/53/4, 25/1/55/6, 26/1/56/7, 25/1/57/8, 25/1/59/60, 8/1/61/2, 24/1/63/4, 2/7/65, 23/12/66, 4/8/67, 26/4/68, 26/6/70, 26/1/77/8, 23/6/78, 18/8/78, 16/2/78/9, 26/1/79/80, 648, 649, 651, 652, 653, 654, 655, 656
Frankford, 653
Friuli, 649

Gallicia sud, 652
Gaunt (Ghent), 1/3/77/8, 10/3/77/8, 656
Geddington, Northants., 24/1/50/1
Germany, 3/6/49, 24/1/51/2, 24/1/52/3, 2/2/61/2, 20/9/63, 24/1/63/4, 17/2/77/8, 1/3/77/8, 648, 650, 656
Geton Pastures, 29/3/44
Glamorganshire, 25/2/45/6
Glensford, 29/7/49
Godmanchester, 1636
Gosfield Gate, 1/10/44
Gottenburgh, 653
Grantham, 9/9/45, 11/9/45, 20/9/54
Gravelin, 24/1/52/3
Gravesend, 9/6/67, 654
Greenwich, 11/5/60
Grove Hall, 16/2/57/8
Guernsey, 3/1/51/2, 24/1/51/2, 23/12/60
Guinee, 2/10/64
Gynnee, 654

Hackney, 17/5/77
Hackney School, London, 2/6/75
Hadham Berry, 10/1/44/5, 18/4/45
Hague, 656
Hall Meadow, 15/5/49, 5/7/50, 1/7/51
Halsted, 6/9/44, 20/9/44, 9/10/44, 30/12/44, 18/4/45, 10/6/45, 13/8/45, 1/4/46, 31/5/46, 27/9/46, 16/10/46, 6/11/46, 28/12/46, 6/3/46/7, 8/3/47, 11/6/48, 20/5/49, 5/8/49, 2/9/49, 21/10/49, 28/10/49, 23/12/49, 15/1/49/50, 18/1/49/50, 27/1/49/50, 3/3/49/50, 4/3/49/50, 5/3/49/50, 10/3/49/50, 14/4/50, 9/5/50, 12/5/50, 27/6/50, 18/8/50, 27/10/50, 5/3/50/1, 25/3/51, 30/4/51, 6/6/51, 19/6/51, 4/7/51, 3/8/51, 10/8/51, 30/9/51, 19/11/51, 22/12/51, 15/1/51/2, 1/2/51/2, 26/2/51/2, 2/4/52, 30/4/52, 8/9/52, 15/10/52, 22/10/52, 11/3/52/3, 27/5/53, 30/5/53, 9/5/54, 10/5/54, 1/6/54, 28/7/54, 29/9/54, 18/5/55, 14/9/55, 20/12/55, 29/2/55/6, 9/5/56, 17/5/56, 17/6/56, 20/6/56, 24/10/56, 30/1/56/7, 3/4/57, 17/4/57, 17/7/57, 8/1/57/8, 9/4/58, 30/7/58, 5/10/60, 10/8/63, 31/1/63/4, 18/8/64, 3/9/65, 8/10/65, 29/10/65, 17/12/65, 23/7/66, 11/10/69, 10/10/70, 4/11/70, 16/6/79
Hamburg, 7/4/53
Hampton Court, 14/11/47, 15/1/47/8, 25/7/70
Hardingham, 22/8/49, 24/8/49, 2/6/55
Harwich, 8/10/65, 12/11/65, 9/6/67, 7:8/3/78/9
Harwich Point, 17/3/44/5
Hasselt, 1/3/77/8
Hassia, 649
Hatfield, 3/8/59, 6/10/59, 12/9/78
Hatfield Peverel, 17/7/58
Haverhill (Haverill), 23/10/49, 24/10/49, 19/5/51, 10/3/53/4, 3/5/54, 7/8/55, 6/5/58, 27/5/58, 20/9/67, 17/8/68, 9/9/74
Havingfield, 31/8/46
Hedingham, Sible, 30/10/53
Heney, Little, 21/5/56
Hereford, 23/12/45
Hicks Hall, 22/7/83
Higham (Hingham), Suffolk, 21/8/49, 2/6/55, 17/6/56
Hinningham (Hedingham), 1/9/44, 26/3/47, 24/7/56, 19/10/58, 21/1/58/9, 25/1/58/9, 31/1/58/9, 17/5/59, 25/10/59, 16/4/76
Hinningham, Castle (Castle Hedingham; Pannels Ash, Castle Hedingham), 9/5/48, 27/9/55, 21/8/58, 19/8/62, 6/3/62/3
Hispaniola, 3/8/55, 652
Hisson (Hysson), 1/9/58, 5/9/58
Hobstevens, 3/2/59/60, 12/10/69, 10/9/74, 3/10/80
Holland, 30/12/46, 20/4/51, 9/6/51, 6/7/51, 22/10/51, 15/1/51/2, 24/1/51/2, 20/6/52, 19/9/52, 13/10/52, 24/1/52/3, 7/8/53, 10/3/53/4, 8/1/61/2, 17/2/61/2, 29/11/63, 24/1/63/4, 31/7/64, 19/8/66, 9/6/72, 23/6/72, 30/6/72, 23/6/78, 18/8/78, 7:8/3/78/9, 26/1/79/80, 651, 654, 655, 656
Holstein, 653
Homeby (Holmeby), 21/2/46/7, 13/7/51
Hornechurch, 1640
Horsely, Little, 21/4/65
Houghton, 16/9/45
Hull, 1643
Hungary, 31/7/64, 654, 655
Huntington, 1636, 24/8/45, 10/9/45, 22/9/45
Huntington Bridge, 1636, 1640

Ibstocke, 17/9/45, 18/9/45
Ilford, 16/6/52

Ingerstone, 22:24/3/63/4
Inspruch–Germany, 652
Ipres, 656
Ipswich, 19/8/49, 8/10/65, 27/2/75
Ireland, 14/11/45, 2/5/46, 16/8/46, 6/12/46, 9/5/47, 15/5/49, 1/6/49, 8/7/49, 14/7/49, 18/7/49, 29/7/49, 1/8/49, 9/8/49, 19/8/49, 16/9/49, 28/10/49, 4/11/49, 25/11/49, 13/1/49/50, 29:30/7/50, 23/12/50, 31/12/50, 13/1/50/1, 9/2/50/1, 20/4/51, 9/6/51, 28/7/51, 30/10/51, 19/11/51, 7/12/51, 3/1/51/2, 24/1/51/2, 3/3/52/3, 29/9/58, 11/8/60, 29/3/63/4, 9/7/65, 27/10/67, 22/2/73/4, 7:8/3/78/9, 648, 650
Istria, 649
Italy, 3/6/49, 15/1/51/2, 24/1/51/2, 22/1/53/4, 10/5/54, 24/8/56, 26/1/56/7, 25/1/57/8, 23/12/60, 24/1/63/4, 16/6/72, 655

Jamaica, 27/1/55/6, 29/2/55/6, 652
Jersey Island, 30/10/51, 2/11/51, 3/1/51/2, 24/1/51/2
Jesus College, Cambridge, 1632, 1636, 1649, 18/6/49
Juitland, 25/1/57/8

Kelvedon, 14/10/45, 30/8/48, 9/7/50, 6/4/51, 20/5/52, 8/5/56, 8/10/65, 8/9/69, 2/1/71/2
Kemsey, 30/3/59
Kendal, 16/8/51
Kent, 651
Kimbold, 30/8/68
Kimbolton, 1640
Kimbolton Castle, 1637

Lamersh, 20/12/70
Lancashire, 8/7/49, 13/8/51, 30/8/51
Lancaster, 16/8/51
Langer Fort, 2/7/67, 654
Langford, 5/2/54/5, 17/4/55, 26/9/55, 7/10/56
Layham, 8/10/75
Leadenhall Street, 9/9/66
Lees, Much, (Great Leighs), 31/8/47
Leez, 2/7/74, 5/7/74
Leicester, 1/6/45, 2/6/45, 18/6/45, 17/9/45, 19/9/45, 21/6/46
Leinster, 650
Leopol, 656
Levant, 12/11/65
Lexden, 26/8/44, 13/6/48, 21/11/54, 18/6/57, 27/11/72, 28/2/74/5, 28/9/75, 5/6/77, 16/3/78/9, 7/9/79, 2/10/81, 25/6/82, 24/9/82
Lichfield, 18/9/45, 22/8/51
Liefland, 652
Limbricke, Ireland, 10/8/51, 2/11/51, 12:13/12/51
Lincoln, 9/9/45
Lincolnshire, 1/11/44, 13/3/54/5
Lisbon, 13/1/50/1, 28/6/63
Lisle, 4/8/67
Livonia, 25/1/57/8
London, 1640, 1642, 29/11/45, 20/4/46, 2/5/46, 26/11/46, 27/11/46, 11/12/46, 21/12/46, 3/1/46/7, 2/2/46/7, 22/2/46/7, 27/2/46/7, 11/3/46/7, 29/7/47, 5/8/47, 8/8/47, 17/10/47, 23/1/47/8, 24/4/48, 1/5/48, 2/5/48, 25/5/48, 25/9/48, 11/10/48, 30/11/48, 14/7/49, 29/7/49, 7/9/49, 13/1/49/50, 17/3/49/50, 2/4/50, 9/5/50, 29:31/7/50, 13/1/50/1, 14/2/50/1, 4/5/51, 5/5/51, 15/7/51, 24/8/51, 27/8/51, 13/9/51, 20/9/51, 5/10/51, 22/10/51, 18/11/51, 29/11/51, 6/12/51, 21/5/52, 7/6/52, 13/6/52, 2/10/52, 20/11/52, 6/12/52, 30/12/52, 6/3/52/3, 27/3/53, 9/5/53, 6/11/53, 10/11/53, 19/11/53, 26/11/53, 9/12/53, 19/2/53/4, 24/3/53/4, 23/4/54, 13/9/54, 3/10/54, 25/1/54/5, 13/2/54/5, 18/2/54/5, 10/5/55, 24/6/55, 2/10/55, 13/10/55, 28/3/56, 9/5/56, 18/6/56, 26/6/56, 5/7/56, 10/8/56, 5/12/56, 30/1/56/7, 28/3/57, 15/5/57, 12/6/57, 15/6/57, 17/6/57, 4/7/57, 2/11/57, 17/11/57, 22/11/57, 27/11/57, 30/11/57, 9/1/57/8, 1/2/57/8, 2/5/58, 19/5/58, 6/6/58, 31/10/58, 18/11/58, 3/12/58, 29/1/58/9, 25/2/58/9, 25/3/59, 30/3/59, 10/4/59, 30/4/59, 22/5/59, 24/5/59, 25/5/59, 10/6/59, 11/6/59, 16/6/59, 10/10/59, 5/11/59, 8/11/59, 10/11/59, 20/11/59, 26/11/59, 11/12/59, 6/1/59/60, 15/1/59/60, 12/2/59/60, 18/2/59/60, 15/3/59/60, 11/5/60, 22/8/60, 29/9/60, 13/11/60, 13/1/60/1, 19/1/60/1, 21/1/60/1, 27/3/61, 1/4/61, 22:23/4/61, 26/4/61, 3/5/61, 5/5/61, 7/5/61, 13/7/61, 2/8/61, 29/9/61, 15/3/61/2, 8/6/62, 2/11/62, 24/2/62/3, 28/2/62/3, 23/3/62/3, 14/3/63, 27/9/63, 5/10/63, 16/10/63, 30/1/63/4, 6/3/63/4, 22:24/3/63/4, 3/4/64, 8/7/64, 1:2/8/64, 19/8/64, 27/3/65, 28/4/65, 28/5/65, 9/7/65, 16/7/65, 28/7/65, 2/8/65, 20/8/65, 10/9/65, 1/10/65, 8/10/65, 15/10/65, 22/10/65, 27/10/65, 5/11/65, 12/11/65, 19/11/65, 26/11/65, 3/12/65, 24/12/65, 31/12/65, 7/1/65/6, 14/1/65/6, 21/1/65/6, 28/1/65/6, 31/1/65/6, 25/2/65/6, 7/3/65/6, 11/3/65/6, 18/3/65/6, 25/3/66, 1/4/66, 8/4/66, 15/4/66, 22/4/66, 29/4/66, 6/5/66, 13/5/66, 20/5/66, 27/5/66, 1/6/66,

3/6/66, 17/6/66, 24/6/66, 1/7/66, 8/7/66, 15/7/66, 22/7/66, 29/7/66, 5/8/66, 12/8/66, 19/8/66, 26/8/66, 2/9/66, 9/9/66, 12/9/66, 23/9/66, 10/10/66, 14/10/66, 27/10/66, 28/10/66, 4/11/66, 11/11/66, 18/11/66, 19/11/66, 25/11/66, 2/12/66, 9/1/66/7, 12/5/67, 28/7/67, 10/5/68, 21/6/68, 12/7/68, 26/9/68, 11/10/68, 14/10/68, 25/10/68, 7/2/68/9, 6/5/69, 16/5/69, 23/5/69, 27/5/69, 18/7/69, 24/7/69, 1/8/69, 29/8/69, 5/9/69, 8/9/69, 12/9/69, 24/10/69, 25/10/69, 27/2/69/70, 16/4/70, 8/5/70, 15/7/70, 6/10/70, 25/12/70, 19/1/70/1, 6/5/71, 8/5/72, 17/6/73, 31/7/73, 4/9/74, 19/9/74, 23/10/74, 2/6/75, 7/11/75, 16/4/76, 9/7/76, 19/12/76, 29/12/76, 17/5/77, 5/6/77, 16/6/77, 8/7/77, 13/7/77, 15/7/77, 22/7/77, 29/7/77, 2/9/77, 5/9/77, 8/9/77, 30/9/77, 28/10/77, 28/3/78, 5/5/78, 16/5/78, 6/10/78, 23/10/78, 12/11/78, 17/11/78, 1/12/78, 27/1/78/9, 16/3/78/9, 16/6/79, 9/7/79, 1/8/79, 14/9/79, 28/9/79, 23/11/79, 14/12/79, 24/10/80, 27/3/81, 3/4/81, 18/9/81, 25/9/81, 23/10/81, 11/11/81, 17/11/81, 5/3/81/2, 12/3/81/2, 26/3/82, 16/5/82, 15/8/82, 3/9/82, 19/9/82, 24/9/82, 8/10/82, 10/12/82, 17/12/82, 24/12/82, Jan/82/3, 21/1/82/3, 30/1/82/3, 11/2/82/3, 18/2/82/3, 3/3/82/3, 8/4/83, 11/4/83, 15/4/83, 2/5/83, 20/5/83, 22/6/83, 1/7/83, 7/7/83, 29/7/83, 653, 655, 656, 657

City of London, 1643, 29/7/47, 5/8/47, 8/8/47, 30/8/48, 5/10/51, 24/4/78, 2/1/80/1, 16/5/82

Longacre, 16/6/79

Lorrain, 655

Loveland, 24/7/78, 28/8/80

Maestricht, 655

Malaga, 24/8/56

Maldon, 26/9/55, 1/10/55

Mallories, 23/9/46, 28/3/47, 27/3/49/50, 27/4/50, 25/3/51, 29/3/51, 9/4/51, 21/4/51, 30/4/51, 22/10/51, 21/3/51/2

Man, Isle of, 2/11/51, 24/1/51/2

Mantua, 24/1/52/3

Maplested (Maplestead), 27/2/44/5, 12/5/45, 13/6/49, 23/12/49, 8/3/49/50

Mardike–Flanders, 653

Markshall, 14/10/44, 16/10/44, 17/6/45, 6/7/45, 23/11/45, 27/11/46, 23/12/46, 18/6/48, 3/9/48, 21/1/48/9, 1/1/49/50, 30/3/51, 5/9/51, 19/9/51, 13/2/54/5, 15/7/55, 30/4/57, 23/8/57, 28/8/57, 16/10/57, 7/11/58, 16/4/65, 1/6/66, 21/4/67, 24/7/69, 27/3/70, 20/9/70, 27/12/72, 11/5/73, 7/11/75, 4/9/76, 5/2/76/7, 1/7/77, 14/10/77, 20/11/81

Marlborough, 28/8/53

Melford, 29/7/49

Messing, 25/6/50, 1/1/50/1, 5/1/51/2, 25/3/53, 25/4/54, 12/4/55, 21/9/55, 26/9/55, 9/4/56, 23/6/56, 25/3/57

Midleton, 28/8/46

Mills Fenn, 23/4/50

Moregate, 9/9/66

Moscow, 651, 652, 655

Munster, 24/1/51/2

Namur, 1/3/77/8

Nancy, in Lorraine, 1/3/77/8

Naples, 13/1/50/1, 8/12/54, 649

Naseby Field, 27/6/45

Nayland, 17/10/75

Needham, 1/7/66

Netherlands, 17/12/65, 17/2/77/8

Newarke, 29/3/44, 1/6/45, 10/10/45

Newark House, 26/7/51

Newbery, 20/9/1643

Newcastle, 6/2/46/7

New England, 6/3/44/5, 27/4/45, 11/3/45/6, 18/1/47/8, 6/9/48, 16/4/50, 13/3/50/1, 18/3/50/1, 18/11/51, 11/1/51/2, 8/4/52, 19/12/52, 9/1/52/3, 24/1/52/3, 19/3/52/3, 18/4/53, 13/2/53/4, 22/2/57/8, 25/3/58

Newgate, 11/1/62/3

Newhal, 16/4/76

Newhouse, Earls Colne, 21/5/65

Newhouse Lands, Colne, 3/10/76

Newmarket, 16/4/76, 12/3/81/2

Newport, 28/8/72

Newport Pannell, Northants., 29/3/44

Newsol, 27/9/63

Norfolk, 1636, 1637, 1639, 1640, 3/12/50, 4/12/50, 7/7/53, 31/5/55, 24/6/55, 28/10/55, 7/3/55/6, 16/8/59

Northampton, 26/9/75

Northamptonshire, 23/4/60

Norway, 653

Norwich, 1/5/48, 11/5/56

Nottingham, 13/3/54/5

Olivenca, 24/5/57, 652

Olivers, 28/3/78, 10/4/78, 1/7/78, 17/9/78, 24/11/78, 29/11/78, 10/12/78, 28/12/80

Olny, Bucks., 1639, 1640, 1641, 1642, 20/9/43, 11/11/44, 6/2/44/5, 19/5/46, 26/11/46, 21/5/48, 3/10/48, 19/5/51, 23/7/51, 20/9/56, 15/6/57, 12/1/60/1

Omsted, 11/4/47

Orkney Islands, 12/12/50

Oundle, 1/7/66

Oxford, 30/9/44, 2/5/46, 11/9/49, 22/10/65, 29/10/65

Paris, 13/1/50/1, 650, 656
Pateswicke, 2/11/77
Pauls (Cathedral), 13/9/51, 5/10/51
Pebmarsh (Pedmarsh), 12/5/45, 28/10/47, 9/4/48, 31/3/50, 25/8/52, 15/9/52, 19/5/57, 8/4/59
Peterborough, 15/6/57
Peterburg, 1639
Picardy, 4/8/67
Pickstones, 23/12/50
Pitchers, 16/9/75, 25/9/75, 9/7/81, 9/4/82
Pitchers Pond, 18/12/69
Plymouth, 17/2/44/5, 21/3/55/6
Podolia, 654
Poland, 30/3/51, 24/1/51/2, 2/9/55, 25/1/55/6, 26/1/56/7, 25/1/57/8, 25/4/58, 1/5/58, 31/7/64, 31/3/67, 649, 651, 652, 653, 655, 656
Pomerania, 653
Pomfrett, 25/2/48/9
Portsmouth, 20/5/62
Portugal, 9/6/51, 29/11/51, 24/1/52/3, 24/2/55/6, 24/5/57, 25/1/57/8, 7/11/58, 24/2/60/1, 28/6/63, 24/1/63/4, 648, 652
Potton, 1636
Prussia, 25/1/57/8, 653
Pudding Lane, 9/9/66, 11/11/66

Rapperschwill, 652
Rattesden, Suffolk, 1/5/74
Readings, (Farther), 25/9/75, 5/10/78, 1/11/80
Redgewell, 23/9/44, 3/7/51, 15/7/52, 2/6/59
Redhouse, Scotland, 3/9/50
Rhine, 655
Riga, 652
Ripon, 16/8/51
Rochell, 648
Rockingham Forest, 19/5/51
Rome, 31/12/50, 13/1/50/1, 30/3/51, 3/1/51/2, 15/1/51/2, 14/1/52, 28/3/53
Romford, 2/4/59
Rottenden, 26/5/56
Rounston, Derbyshire, 18/9/45, 19/9/45
Roxwell, 1618, 18/11/47
Royden, 8/10/75, 7/4/76, 21/4/76/7
Royston, 31/8/45, 27/10/65
Runhall, 2/6/55
Rutlandshire, 16/9/45

St Albans, 22/3/48/9
St James, 656
St Johnstons, 11/8/51
St Martins, London, 10/4/83, 17/6/83
St Mary Overies, London, 25/10/69
St Marys Stamford, 12/9/45
Salisbury, 2/7/65
Savoy, 26/1/56/7, 652
Sawyers, 11/4/50, 16/6/54, 22/6/54, 4/11/54, 3/2/59/60, 25/9/75
Scarborough, 23/2/44/5
Schodraw, 655
Schonen, 12/8/77
Scily Isles, 9/6/51, 24/1/51/2
Scotland, 1641, 12/9/45, 22/10/48, 7/7/50, 16/7/50, 21/8/50, 8/10/50, 13/11/50, 15/12/50, 17/12/50, 27/12/50, 31/12/50, 2/1/50/1, 13/1/50/1, 30/1/50/1, 9/2/50/1, 2/3/50/1, 25/3/51, 20/4/51, 9/6/51, 6/7/51, 26/7/51, 2/8/51, 10/8/51, 30/8/51, 21/9/51, 7/10/51, 12/10/51, 19/11/51, 3/1/51/2, 24/1/51/2, 31/1/51/2, 20/2/51/2, 3/3/52/3, 17/2/61/2, 2/12/66, 8/2/79/80, 648, 649, 650, 651, 657
Sealand, 653
Severn (River), 29/3/59, 15/3/59/60
Sextins, 17/5/51
Seyne, Paris, 24/1/50/1
Shemington, 20/9/45
Shropshire, 13/3/54/5
Sicily, 3/6/49
Siena, 651
Silesia, 30/3/51
Sligo, 2/8/51
Some, Camb., 9/11/44
Southwark, 8/8/47, 26/5/76, 17/5/77
Spain, 3/6/49, 2/1/50/1, 20/4/51, 9/6/51, 6/1/51/2, 24/1/52/3, 28/3/53, 10/3/53/4, 30/9/55, 25/1/55/6, 4/9/56, 26/1/56/7, 24/5/57, 25/1/57/8, 25/1/59/60, 8/1/61/2, 24/1/63/4, 31/7/64, 20/5/66, 26/4/68, 30/1/69/70, 17/2/77/8, 23/6/78, 19/1/78/9 649, 651, 652, 653, 656
Spalditch, 1636
Spanish Netherlands, 656
Sprigs Marsh, 9/4/59, 28/6/59, 23/1/59/60, 18/2/59/60, 28/11/60, 6/9/63
Stamford, 10/9/45, 11/9/45, 13/9/45, 14/9/45, 20/9/45, 21/9/45
Stamford Rivers, 3/10/51
Stangate Hole, 10/9/45
Stanly Hall, 26/6/63
Stansted Hall, 18/11/46
Stanway, 29/10/43, 2/6/45, 3/11/45, 30/3/52, 29/12/57, 29/9/64, 9/9/74, 10/12/78
Stanway Hall, 5/10/64
Stebbing, 24/1/52/3
Sterling, Scotland, 23/3/50/1
Stilton, 10/9/45
Stirling Castle, 30/8/51
Stisted (Stistead), 7/10/44, 9/10/44, 24/12/46, 31/8/77

Stonebridge, 17/7/55
Stonebridge Meadow, 648
Stow, 15/3/59/60
Stowton, Woodhall, 28/3/59
Sturbridge (Stourbridge), 9/9/57, 8/9/58, 9/9/79
Sudbury, 17/9/44
Suffolk, 8/8/47, 30/8/48, 30/1/56/7, 2/7/67
Sunderland, 5/8/44, 14/9/44
Sussex, 25/7/70, 4/8/70, 5/6/71
Sutton, Beds., 1636
Swannels (Sonnels), 24/9/56, 3/2/59/60
Sweden, 24/1/52/3, 29/11/57, 2/2/61/2, 24/1/63/4, 648, 649, 652, 653, 656
Swinford, Old, Staffs., 16/12/77
Switzerland, 26/1/56/7, 652
Sydney College, Cambridge, 9/9/45

Taine (Gt. Tey; Gt. Taine), 6/2/44/5, 29/4/52, 28/5/55, 10/8/56, 5/10/56, 3/5/76
Tangiers, 12/11/65
Taunton, 12/10/45
Tay, Much, 29/10/60
Temple Bar, 9/9/66
Ten Acres, 30/6/56
Tenariffe, 652
Tenedos, 25/1/57/8
Texell, 14/6/53
Thames, 31/7/47, 7/4/67, 25/7/70
Thaxted, 1643, 31/10/45, 6/11/45
Tilbury, Essex, 31/7/47
Toleshunt Bush (Tolleshunt), 1/1/50/1
Topsfield (Toppesfield), 3/8/59, 3/8/60
Torbay, 652
Torrington, 25/2/45/6, 5/3/45/6
Transilvania, 652, 653
Tredagh, 14/7/49, 29/7/49, 1/11/49
Trim, Ireland, 29/7/49
Tuam, Conaught, 29/7/60
Tunbridge Wells, 11/7/75, 12/7/75
Turkey, 24/1/52/3, 649, 650, 653, 656

Ulster, 648, 650
Upminster, 1640, 9/3/46/7
Utrech, 655
Uxbridge, 26/3/59

Valenchienne, 17/7/56, 652
Venice, 3/6/49, 649, 650
Vicaridge, 28/3/47, 25/11/62
Vicaridge Close, 9/7/50
Vienna, 2/2/61/2, 651
Vivarets, 655

Wainsford Bridge, 10/9/45
Walden, (Saffron), 1/9/44, 10/6/45, 10/7/45, 5/4/47
Waldenses (Vaudois), 652
Wales, 14/11/45, 14/5/48, 13/3/54/5, 12/6/57
Wales, South, 25/2/45/6
Waltam, 6/7/79
Wapping, 26/11/82
Warnham, Sussex, 4/9/70
Warsaw, 24/8/56, 652
Warwick, 30/8/51
Wenden, 10/6/45
West Indies, 7/8/55, 20/9/55, 25/1/55/6
Westminster, 651
Westminster Hall, 652
Wethersfield, 26/9/44, 1/10/44, 1/7/45, 27/11/46, 23/12/46, 28/8/54, 22/2/57/8, 24/3/58/9, 29/12/59
Wexford, 1/11/49
Whitehall, 650, 656
Wight, Isle of, 14/11/47, 15/9/50, 11/9/56, 649
Wilborough Hill, Great, 9/7/45
Wilton, 2/7/65
Wiltshire, 13/3/54/5
Windsor, 19/4/79
Wittam (Witham), 12/2/44/5, 27/11/46, 23/12/46, 18/12/49, 13/7/52, 29/3/58, 17/7/58, 2/11/58, 21/6/59, 10/9/59, 15/3/59/60, 20/8/62, 20/9/69, 11/11/74, 12/9/78
Woodham Waters, 11/8/46
Worcester, 22/8/51, 27/8/51, 29/8/51, 30/8/51, 2/9/51, 7/9/51, 21/9/51, 24/10/51, 24/1/51/2, 3/5/54, 15/3/57/8, 3/4/58, 25/3/59, 29/3/59, 10/4/59, 15/3/59/60, 651
Wormingford, 1/9/44, 16/2/45/6, 28/8/46, 8/9/46, 25/3/47
Wormington, Northants., 1639

Yarmouth, 4/12/64, 28/5/65, 4/3/65/6, 12/3/81/2
Yeldham, 5/10/46
Yeldham, Nether, 24/8/45
Yeldham, Upper, 24/8/45
Yorkshire, 21/2/59/60

Zurich, 652

INDEX OF PERSONS

Note:

Persons italicized in this index are inhabitants of Earls Colne. Those for whom further information could be found are described in the short biographies in Appendix 2 and their residences shown on the maps of the main street and parish of Earls Colne, page 696.

Josselin's spelling or abbreviated form for all personal names has been retained. Where possible, missing surnames and forenames have been added in brackets. Some places have also been added. Where Josselin gives alternative spellings of surnames, all references are under the first spelling; the chronologically later variant is in brackets.

All references are to the marginal date under which the person is mentioned in the Diary, even if this marginal date is slightly different from the date within the text. The dates have been contracted; thus 8/8/47 stands for 8 August 1647. Josselin's conventions concerning dates between January 1 and March 24 have been followed (see the note on dating in Abbreviations and Conventions above, p. xvii).

Some persons are mentioned in the miscellaneous jottings printed at the end of the text. They are referred to by the page numbers of this edition rather than by date since at this point there are no marginal dates in the Diary.

References to Josselin's wife have not been indexed since they occur throughout. General references to the 'King', where no name is given, have not been included.

Where Josselin refers to his uncles or cousins, these have been cross-referenced and placed under 'Josselin' where appropriate.

Josselin frequently refers to the same man by a number of different terms. For example, in an extreme case, he termed Richard Harlakenden his patron as follows: Mr H., Mr R. H., Mr Harlakenden, Brother Harlakenden, Captain Harlakenden, Colonel Harlakenden, Mr High Sheriff, and Mr Richard Harlakenden. It has been decided to keep the references separate under each term. It is often difficult to be absolutely sure that the same person is being referred to and it seems preferable not to prejudge the issue. Furthermore, those using the index may wish to look up other references to 'Mr. H' or 'Goodman Abbott' and if all instances were standardized, this would be impossible. For ease of reference, however, other names have been supplied (in brackets) where the entry is deficient. It should be noted that in order to be certain that all references to a particular person have been located in the index, it is necessary to look through all the surnames starting with that letter.

When no surname can be discovered, for example when only the forename of a maid servant is given, the name is indexed as a surname.

? denotes the fact that Josselin gives no surname/forename, as appropriate.

R.A. (Robert ABBOTT senior), 8/8/47, 14/4/56, 16/4/57
R.A. (Robert ABBOTT junior), 21/1/57/8
? ABBOTT (Richard) of London, 3/2/46/7
? *ABBOTT*, 26/11/54, 25/12/74, 17/10/75, 25/9/76
Edward ABBOTT, 12/11/76
Goodman ABBOTT (Henry senior), 28/10/44, 2/9/50, 28/10/50
Goodwife ABBOTT (Dorothy), 11/8/55
Henry ABBOTT, (senior), 20/10/44, 8/12/46
ABBOTT, Old H(enry), 7/8/55
Henry ABBOTT, (*junior*), 14/3/54/5, 7/4/56
Henry ABBOTT, 2/1/56/7, 13/6/74, 20/7/74, 20/2/75/6, 19/9/77, 9/8/78, 13/8/78
wife of Henry ABBOTT, (Joan), 20/8/45
Mrs ABBOTT, 22/2/57/8
Mother ABBOTT, 24/12/45
Robert ABBOTT, (junior), 31/12/56, 2/1/56/7, 26/1/56/7, 2/11/57, 9/1/57/8, 3/2/57/8
Robert ABBOTT, senior, 31/8/56, 'old'– 28/1/57/8, 30/12/77, 1/1/77/8
Rose ABBOTT, 25:26/5/75
ABBUTT family, 5/3/81/2
Cousin Abraham? (see JOSSELIN)
William ADAM, 1/4/51, 29/4/52
St ALBANS, 5/9/69
?*Alice, maid*, 22/8/60
? ALLEN, butcher (Matthew) of Colne Engaine, 17/7/55
? *ALLEN* (William), 25/1/79/80
ALLINGTON, L., 27/6/80
ALLISTON (ELLISTON) (kinsman to Mr HARRINGTON), 8/3/49/50, 2/4/50, 8/4/50
? ALLURED, 26/12/59
? *ALSTON*, (John), 13/5/66
Mr ALSTONE of Stisted, 14/10/44, 24/12/46
Daniel ALSTONE, of Stisted, 24/12/46
? *AMES*, (Henry), 20/10/46
? *AMIES*, (John), 25/12/75
Mr ANDROWS (Daniel), 8/5/72, 20/3/77/8, 1/4/78, 25/2/78/9, 10/10/79, 26/1/81/2
Mr ANDROWS senior (Daniel) of London, 24/10/80
Mrs ANDROWS, mother of Daniel, 17/2/77/8
Mrs ANDROWS, 15/3/77/8, 24/3/77/8, 17/9/80, 5/3/81/2
ANDROWS, Dol, 7/4/76
Mrs ANDROWS, Mary, 11/11/74
Anjou, 654
Sister Anne? (see HODSON)
Apaffi, 24/1/63/4
? *APPLETON*, 6/11/48, 15/1/50/1, 1/4/78
Father APPLETON (Richard), 28/1/55/6
Richard APPLETON, (neighbour), 15/11/44, 23/7/51
APPLETON, wife of Richard (Grace?), 23/3/47/8
Mr ARCHER, 7/10/44, 23/7/45, 21/10/45, 13/3/45/6, 23/5/48, 20/8/56
? ARLINGTON, 22/2/73/4, 27/9/74
Sir Jacob ASHLEY, 25/3/46, 16/4/46
? ATTHAYES, at Messing, 25/6/50
Mrs AYLETT of Stisted, 31/8/77
? AYLOFFE, 27/8/55
Bridget AYLWARD, 14/2/51/2, 30/10/55
'*poor Bridget* ?' (AYLWARD), 9/9/47, 18/12/59

Mr B., 8/2/54/5
S.B. (Samuel BURTON), 19/10/54
Judge BACON (Sir Francis), 5/8/46
Mr BACON (Nathaniel), Master of Requests, 21/3/55/6
? BALLS of Markshall, 13/11/76
? BARFOOT, 19/11/71
? BARKSTEAD, 16/3/61/2, 27/5/62, 646
Mr BARNARDISTON at Colchester, 29/3/51, 8/3/54/5, 27/8/55
Mr BARRADALE. (BORRADALE) (John), of Steeple Bumpstead, 1632, 1636
? *BARRET* (John), 22/7/66
Mrs BARRHAM, 23/12/50
Mr BARRINGTON, Gob(art), 20/8/56
Duke of Bavaria, 12/10/51
? BAXTER, 19/9/58, 25/4/60
Wife of (Robert) BECKWITH (Mary), 25/3/49
John BEEREMAN (BEARMAN), 26/7/49, 16/8/49, 25/7/50
BELL, Edward, 1636
Widow BENTAL (Ann), 18/7/46, 20/7/46, 21/7/46, 22/7/46, 1/10/46
Mr BENTON, 1/9/44
Cousin BENTON (Jeremy), 1/9/44, 6/3/44/5, 24/8/45, 6/11/46, 12/5/47, 24/3/53/4, 6/10/61, 8/6/79
Uncle BENTON (John) of Norfolk, 1636
Mrs BENYON at Markshall, 1/7/77
Aunt BERRILL of Olney, 21/5/48
BERRY, 646
BESSE, John, 27/4/45
? BET, 10/4/83
Mrs Bettee (HARLAKENDEN), 30/11/50
Sister Betty (WORRALL?), 19/5/51

BIFORD, J. (John), 30/8/56
Cousin BIRD, 20/10/72
? BLAKE, (Admiral), 8/12/54, 7/5/57, 652
Cousin BLONDELL (BLUNDEL), 11/4/58, 17/7/58
Queen of Bohemia, 655
Philip, son of Queen of Bohemia, 2/1/50/1
Frederick, King of Bohemia, 649
Mr BOROUGHS, 7/10/44, 9/10/44
Major BOWES (Thomas) at Bromley, 28/12/80
Mr BOWES (Thomas), 25/4/74, 15/10/76, 26/11/76, 21/4/77, 4/9/77, 20/3/77/8, 28/3/78
Squire BOWES (Thomas) of Great Bromley, 3/4/64
Mr BOWES (Richard) of Great Bromley, 30/9/77
BOWES Esq., Thomas, 23/10/74
Sir Thomas BOWES, 20/8/56
? *BOWLES* (John), 16/1/49/50, 10/2/51/2
John BOWLES, 16/7/52
? BOX, 10/9/82
W. BR. (William BRAND), 26/3/53
Mr BRACLYE (BRACKLEYE or BRACKLY) (Thomas) of Colne Engaine, 1/10/46, 25/11/47, 16/1/52/3, 17/1/52/3, 6/3/56/7
Mrs BRACKLY, 31/1/52/3
? BRADSHAW, 31/1/48/9
Captain BRAG (Nicholas), 2/6/75, 16/6/75, 12/7/75
BRAGANZA Duke of, 648
Mrs BRAGES (Mary), 18/10/76, 19/6/77, 1/3/77/8, 24/3/77/8
BRAMSTON, Sir Mundeford, 5/10/69
Goodman BRAND (William), 12/10/58
William BRAND, 21/4/51, 15/7/51, 29/11/51, 9/1/51/2, 14/2/59/60, 11/4/62
BRETHETON, Sir William of Cheshire, 6/10/44, 13/10/44, 14/10/44, 26/3/45
? BRETT (John) of White Colne, 16/9/1656
? *BREWER* (Samuel), 24/7/46, 9/10/46, 27/4/47
Goodman BREWER (Samuel), 27/6/46
Goodwife BREWER (Mary), 29/6/49
Mr BREWER (Edmund) of Castle Hedingham, 4/5/48, 21/8/58, 23/8/58
Widow BREWER (Mary), 16/10/46
Adam BREWER, 28/7/59
Samuel BREWER, 25/8/46, 27/8/46
? BRIDGE at Messing, 25/6/50, 31/12/52
? BRIDGE of White Colne, 28/8/54
BRIDGE'S daughter (Mary) of Wakes Colne, 11/12/56
Goodman BRIDGES (Richard) of Wakes Colne, 7/10/44, 17/10/44
Goodman BRIDGE (Richard) of Wakes Colne, 29/9/52, 28/10/54
Goodwife BRIDGE (Mary) of Wakes Colne, 7/10/44
Old BRIDGE, 24/7/69
Roydon BRIDGE, of Messing, 5/8/56
BRIDGE, (junior) of Messing, 1/5/72
Sister BRIDGE (Mary) (of Wakes Colne), 15/9/60, 18/9/60
Poor Bridget ? (AYLWARD), 9/9/47, 18/12/59
? *BROCKE*, (Frances), 26/5/65
Lady BROOKS (Elizabeth), 9/10/58
Mr BROOKS, 7/11/58, 12/11/58
? *BROWNE* (Edward), 2/3/50/1
Brother BROWNE (Robert), 28/12/52
Sister BROWN, 20/9/55, 19/8/56
Widow BROWN, 14/5/51, 8/3/51/2, 4/11/54
Goodwife BROWNE (Mary), 1/7/51
Mr BROWN, 29/4/70
Major BROWN, 29/3/44
Edward BROWN, 30/3/55
Sarah BROWNE, 1641
Sarah? (*BROWN*), 20/10/45, 26/10/45
? *BROWNSON* (Martha), 26/5/65
Brother BROWNSON (Cornelius), 30/3/53, 25/5/55
BROWNSON, Cornelius, 14/9/51, 30/7/56, 18/3/56/7
Goodman BRUCE of White Colne, 24/2/44/5
Mr BUCKLEY, 15/9/52
Mr BUCKLEY, 23/6/53, 24/11/64
Mr BUGGIN at Globe in Barbican, 10/11/68
Mrs BULKLEY at Stanway, 29/9/64, 5/10/64
? BULL of White Colne, 28/1/65/6, 2/11/73
George BULL, of White Colne, 5/9/56
Grace BULL, of White Colne, 30/6/47
Mathye BULL, 22/12/50
? *BULLOCKE* (John), 25/8/77
? *BUNNER* (Richard), 18/4/69
? BURROUGHS, 31/12/52
Mr BURROUGHES (Thomas) of Pebmarsh, 28/10/47, 23/1/47/8, 31/3/50, 25/8/52, 15/9/52
Mrs BURROUGHS, 15/5/54, 19/5/57
Goodman BURTON (Samuel senior), 11/10/44, 17/10/44, 11/5/45, 16/2/46/7, 11/3/47/8, 20/9/49, 2/9/50, 5/11/52, 27/7/54, 19/8/55, 4/9/55
BURTON (Samuel junior), 3/1/66/7
Goodwife BURTON (Ann), 29/3/49, 3/6/49, 6/12/51
Neighbour BURTON (Samuel senior), 11/1/48/9, 25/1/54/5, 12/1/57/8

Old Neighbour BURTON (Ann), 17/7/81
Wife of Neighbour BURTON (Ann), 29/11/45
John BURTON, 27/6/49, 8/7/49, 29/7/49, 24/11/82
BURTON (Samuel junior), 27/12/74
Samuel BURTON, (senior), 27/9/48, 22/12/61
Samuel son of Samuel BURTON, 17/8/56
Susan BURTON, 28/10/51
Mr BUTCHER (Matthew) of Castle Hedingham, 3/6/56, 4/7/56, 5/7/56, 23/12/56, 26/3/57, 2/4/57, 23/12/58, 31/1/58/9, 12/3/58/9, 17/5/59, 6/3/62/3
Young BUTCHER (Matthew) of Castle Hedingham, 3/5/55, 10/5/55
BUTLER, 646
Lame BYAT (Francis), 17/8/56

E.C., 8/9/44
H.C., (Humphrey CRESSENER), 14/6/68
L.C. Gr (CROMWELL), 29/4/49
M.C. (Mr George CRESSENER), 21/12/51
Mr C. (CRESSENER?), 3/2/52/3, 30/8/56
Mrs C. (Rose CHURCH), 29/1/44/5, 27/2/53/4
? CALANY (Edmund CALAMY), 25/4/60, 11/1/62/3
Archbishop of Canterbury, 26/6/70
? *CAPLIN* (Richard), 29/11/51, 12:13/12/51, 27/10/53, 21/5/65
? *CAPLIN'S son* (James), 21/5/65
Mrs CAPLIN (Mary), 31/7/71
Mr CAPLYN (Richard), 24/10/51
? CAREW, 17/10/60
Mr CARLTON, 14/4/56
? CARR, 12/12/50, 27/12/50, 31/12/50
Mr CARR(E) (Gamaliel) of Markshall, 16/10/44, 26/9/46
Mary CAR at Markshall, 27/3/70
CARTER, Robert (senior), 15/11/44, 29/10/52
CARTER, Robert (junior), 24/4/79
? *CATT* (Paul), 29/4/52
Mr CAVAL, 26/9/55
Mr CHANDLER (Francis) of Woodham Ferrers, 23/6/53
King Charles I, 1641, 1642, 30/9/44, 1/6/45, 24/8/45, 27/8/45, 14/11/45, 2/5/46, 8/5/46, 30/12/46, 6/2/46/7, 21/2/46/7, 26/7/47, 14/11/47, 9/1/47/8, 15/1/47/8, 4/1/48/9, 31/1/48/9, 4/2/48/9, 19/2/48/9, 2/4/54, 28/3/55/6, 11/9/56, 11/5/60, 3/6/60, 6/6/60, 3/5/61, 29/5/61, 26/1/77/8, 648, 650
Scots King, 24/1/50/1, 16/8/51, 16/10/51, 24/1/51/2, 1/6/54, 11/6/54, 4/9/56
Charles Stuart, 23/11/51, 23/1/51/2, 13/2/54/5, 25/1/59/60
Prince (Charles), 22/10/51, 2/3/54/5, 8/3/54/5, 16/8/59, 648
King (Charles II), 4/12/50, 2/1/50/1, 13/1/50/1, 13/7/51, 29/8/51, 30/10/51, 2/11/51, 3/1/51/2, 20/6/52, 10/6/60, 17/8/60, 29/8/60, 15/9/60, 17/10/60, 27/10/60, 30/1/60/1, 24/2/60/1, 19/5/61, 19/5/62, 29/5/62, 13/7/62, 16/10/63, 29/5/64, 5/6/64, 10/7/64, 18/8/64, 2/7/65, 21/10/66, 18/11/66, 10/10/67, 27/10/67, 9/2/67/8, 21/3/68/9, 2/2/69/70, 26/6/70, 13/3/71/2, 11/1/73/4, 10/2/73/4, 22/2/73/4, 23/10/74, 13/6/75, 28/12/75, 18/1/75/6, 16/4/76, 17/2/77/8, 24/2/77/8, 28/3/78, 24/4/78, 5/5/78, 19/5/78, 26/5/78, 23/6/78, 8/12/78, 29/12/78, 21/1/78/9, 9/2/78/9, 16/2/78/9, 18/4/79, 19/4/79, 27/4/79, 4/5/79, 31/8/79, 26/1/79/80, 17/5/80, 30/5/80, 12/3/80/1, 30/1/82/3, 651, 653, 654, 655, 657
Lady Elizabeth, daughter of King Charles, 15/9/50
Mary, daughter of Charles I, 650
'King's only sister', 26/6/70
Colonel CHESTER, 5/9/48
Captain CHIPBURNE (Hanamell) of Messing, 1/9/44
John CHRISMAS, 17/3/56/7
Mrs CHURCH (Rose), 24/9/44, 16/6/46, 8/12/46, 10/12/46, 31/12/46, 16/4/47, 20/4/47, 22/2/47/8, 30/5/48, 13/6/48, 20/8/48, 27/12/48, 15/1/48/9, 5/5/49, 6/2/49/50, 19/4/50, 6/6/50, 27/7/50, 16/11/50, 13/3/50/1, 31/12/51, 1/4/52, 2/5/52, 6/5/52, 9/5/52, 16/5/52, 29/5/54, 21/8/55, 30/6/56, 31/7/56, 23/1/57/8, 12/12/58, 19/12/58, 20/12/58, 21/12/58, 24/12/58, 29/1/58/9
John CHURCH, (senior), 19/11/54
John CHURCH, (junior), 23/2/58/9
Mrs CHURCH, Mary, 23/10/45, 20/4/46, 26/4/46, 24/5/46, 17/7/46, 31/8/46, 8/9/46, 25/10/46, 29/10/46, 2/12/46, 8/12/46, 15/12/46, 16/12/46, 20/12/46, 8/1/46/7, 19/1/46/7, 4/2/46/7, 26/3/47, 21/6/47, 6/9/47, 11/2/47/8, 15/2/47/8, 17/2/47/8, 22/2/47/8, 7/3/47/8, 9/3/47/8, 19/3/47/8, 29/8/48, 23/1/48/9, 29/3/49, 5/5/49, 7/7/49, 30/9/49, 10/10/49, 13/10/49, 14/10/49, 7/1/49/50, 17/2/49/50, 3/3/49/50, 19/4/50, 22/4/50, 24/4/50, 28/4/50, 5/5/50, 7/5/50, 17/5/50, 28/5/50, 1/6/50, 2/6/50, 4/6/50, 6/6/50, 9/6/50, 19/6/50, 9/7/50,

23:24/7/50, 27/7/50, 23/12/50, 19/1/50/1, 29/3/51, 21/3/51/2, 26/3/53, 24/3/63/4, 30/3/55, 28/3/56, 26/3/57, 26/3/58, 11/12/60
Earl of CLARINGDON, 10/10/67
Goodman CLARKE (Edward), 15/9/44, 18/10/44, 3/12/44, 19/4/51
Mrs CLARKE (daughter of Mrs KING), 4/4/49
Widow CLARKE (Elizabeth), 20/4/47
Widow CLARKE (of Maldon), 26/8/58
CLARKE (Bartholomew), 21/6/47, 4/1/51/2, 6/1/51/2, 10/5/54, 4/4/58
Brother CLARKE (Bartholomew), 2/5/52, 25/7/52
Edward CLARKE, 26/8/44, 20/10/46, 26/8/51
John CLARKE, 1/1/44/5, 19/7/46
Mr CLARKE (John) of Colne Engaine, 15/5/56, 22/2/56/7, 4/7/57, 23/7/57
CLEMENT, Gregory, 17/10/60
Mrs CLENCH (Jane), of Halstead, 30/7/51, 27/5/53
Mrs CLENCH, Jane, 28/5/50, 29/5/53
Mrs Jane (CLENCH), 9/1/56/7, 3/4/58, 12/8/60
Jonathon CLERKE, of White Colne, 8/12/67
Major CLETHEROE, 23/9/44
? CLOGHER, 26/7/50
Mr CLOPTON, (William) of Markshall, 18/6/48, 3/9/48, 7/3/48/9, 10/4/49, 7/9/49, 6/1/49/50, 18/1/49/50, 25/1/49/50 2/2/49/50, 29/1/50/1, 15/12/52, 7/1/52/3, 24/1/52/3, 18/10/53, 21/10/53, 3/12/54, 31/12/54
COB (Daniel), 27/8/82
COBBS, John, 22/11/68
? *COLEMAN* (John), 5/5/57
? COLEMAN, 27/1/78/9
Elector of Cohen, 653
Dr COLIER (Abel) of London, 18/1/61/2, 28/1/61/2, 1:2/8/64, 8/8/64, 19/8/64, 29/4/70, 15/7/70
Mrs COLIER (Mary), 14/4/63, 6/3/63/4, 8/7/64, 14/8/64, 19/8/64, 17/12/65, 12/5/67, 10/11/68, 29/5/70, 12/6/70, 8/5/72, 13/5/74, 4/9/74, 31/3/75, 2/6/75, 16/6/75, 27/6/75, 12/7/75
? *COLLIER*, 8/5/79
Mr COLLINS, 27/10/50
Mr Commissary General (HARLAKENDEN), 18/10/44
Sir William COMPTON, 5/9/48
Prince of Condé, 12/10/51, 23/11/51, 11/4/52, 24/1/52/3, 22/1/53/4
Conde, 651
? CONSTABLE, father-in-law (Thomas), 1641, 1643
'My mother' (CONSTABLE) (Anne), 19/5/51
Mother-in-law CONSTABLE (Anne), 1642, 5/8/44, 1/10/44, 14/10/55
Sister Betty CONSTABLE wife of Jeremy?, 19/5/51
Elizabeth CONSTABLE, wife's sister, of Olny (WORRALL), 26/11/46
Jane CONSTABLE, 1639, 1640
Brother Jeremy CONSTABLE, 4/9/44, 13/12/44, 20/12/44, 17/3/44/5, 26/11/46, 19/5/51, 22/7/51, 20/8/54, 26/9/57, 1/10/57
? COOK, 1/1/67/8
Colonel COOKE (Thomas) of Pebmarsh, 21/10/45, 24/12/45, 8/2/45/6, 28/10/47, 26/1/47/8, 2/6/48, 26/3/50, 31/3/50, 2/4/50, 13/6/50, 15/5/54, 8/8/54, 15/8/54, 11/10/69
Wife of Colonel COOKE, 31/1/45/6
Mr John COOK of Pebmarsh, 8/4/59
Jo: COOKE (John), 17/10/60
Mrs COOKE at Colchester, 9/1/49/50, 27/8/51, 2/9/51
Mrs COOK, 4/1/69/70
Brother COOPER of Sible Hedingham, 30/10/53, 28/11/55
'Poor' COOPER of Sible Hedingham, 21/1/58/9
? CORBET, 16/3/61/2, 27/4/62
Mr COSIN (William), 12/5/47, 4/5/48, 647
Mrs COSINS at Ipswich, 19/8/49
Sir Jo: COTTON (John) of Connington, Hunts., 23/10/63
Mrs COUSINS, 1641
Brother COWEL (William) of White Colne, 17/11/52, 27/3/53, 12/7/56
Thomas COWELL, 11/1/46/7, 27/5/47, 1/5/48, 2/5/48
William COWELL of White Colne, 21/9/47, 23/2/50/1, 9/7/51, 23/12/51, 17/2/51/2
? COXE of Coggeshall, 23/7/46
Mr COX, 7/10/56
Dr COX, 15/4/83, 4/5/83, 8/5/83
Mr CRANE, lieutenant-colonel, 1642, 1/11/44, 28/1/44/5, 10/11/45, 19/3/52/3, 27/8/55
Mrs CRANE, 7/9/49
? CREAKE of Coggeshall, 12/6/58
? *CREFFEILD*, 11/11/81
Mr CRESSENER (Edward), 1641, 20/11/44, 2/2/46/7, 3/3/46/7, 12/7/47, 13/2/48/9, 17/2/48/9
Mr CRESSENER (*George*), 23/3/50/1, 1/5/51, 24/7/51, 31/10/51, 4/3/51/2, 16/7/52, 2/1/52/3, 17/5/53, 25/10/53, 10/12/53, 18/3/55/6, 21/9/56, 8/10/56,

31/10/57, 3:4/11/57, 3/12/57, 13/12/57, 10/5/58, 16/6/58, 23/4/59, 16/5/59, 8/3/59/60, 14/10/60, 16/8/65, 9/10/70, 10/9/74, 13/9/76, 4/7/77, 6/1/77/8, 26/1/77/8
John CRESSENER, 10/11/53
Mr John CRESSENER of London, 21/2/56/7, 13/11/58, 18/11/58, 3/12/58, 23/4/59, 25/5/59, 26/6/59
Mr CRESSENER's son, 7/6/68
Mr CRESSENER's son, 4/10/68
Mrs CRESSENER, 25/9/48, 11/10/48, 12/4/49, 24/7/49, 26/7/49, 25/11/51, 3/4/56, 25/2/58/9
Edward (CRESSENER) child, 3/4/56; Ned-, 24/10/56, 27/10/56
Mrs Hester CRESSENER, 9/7/79
Humphrey CRESSENER, 16/1/55/6
Rose CRESSENER, 20/4/79
Sibilla CRESSENER, 10/5/58
Mr Toby CRESSENER, 8/9/46
CROMWELL, 7/9/48, 8/7/49, 14/7/49, 29/7/49, 28/10/49, 30/6/50, 29:31/7/50, 27/12/50, 31/12/50, 17/1/50/1, 22/3/50/1, 23/3/50/1, 25/3/51, 2/4/51, 6/4/51, 6/6/51, 28/7/51, 11/8/51, 30/8/51, 2/9/51, 28/12/51, 5/5/53, 25/5/53, 22/1/53/4, 31/1/53/4, 2/4/54-protector, 28/7/54, 31/8/54, 1/9/54, 22/11/54, 25/1/54/5-protector 13/2/54/5, 6/3/54/5, 8/3/54/5, 22/3/54/5, 7/7/55, 27/7/55, 23/11/55, 650, 651
Protector CROMWELL, 30/5/55, 3/7/55, 15/7/55, 20/2/55/6, 24/2/55/6, 4/9/56, 7/9/56, 19/9/56, 30/1/56/7, 20/2/56/7, 27/2/56/7, 19/3/56/7, 17/4/57, 19/4/57, 25/4/57, 17/7/57, 12/12/57, 25/1/57/8, 3/2/57/8, 14/2/57/8, 3/9/58, 19/9/58, 23/1/58/9, 16/3/61/2, 651, 652
New Protector, 12/9/58, 23/4/59, 27/4/59, 30/4/59
CROMWELL's daughter, 14/11/47
CROMWELL's family, 8/5/59, 25/1/59/60
Secretary to the Protector, 23/11/55
Henry CROMWELL, 25/11/55, 29/9/58
Mr CROSMAN (Samuel) of Sudbury & Little Henny, 2/11/62
? *CROW* (John), 28/10/57, 3/2/59/60
An CROW of Colne Engaine, 23/7/57
Giles CROW of Colne Engaine, 5/7/56, 30/9/56, 21/10/78
John CROWE, 19/5/51, 13/3/55/6, 9/4/59, 29/9/59
Nurse CROW, 12/10/58
Robert CROWE (senior), 1/6/50, 22/7/51, 2/8/51, 20/1/59/60
Robert CROWE (junior), 30/11/50
Mr CROXON, 22/10/78
Colonel CULPEPPER, 5/9/48

Treasurer DANBY, 19/4/79
Daniel ? (LEAPER), 1/5/56
Thomas DANIEL, 20/7/60, 25/9/60
? DAVY, 1/1/67/8
Goodwife DAVYE, 5/10/46, 16/10/46, 6/11/46
? *DAVIE's daughter*, 22/1/56/7
Mother DAVY (Katherine), 2/3/56/7
Robert DAVY, 28/1/44/5
? DAWKIN, 28/6/50
? DAY, of Halstead, 5/3/50/1, 25/3/51, 21/4/51, 30/4/51
? *DAY* (Ann), 28/10/57
? DAY's daughter, 16/6/51
Goodman DAY (Edmund), 22/10/51
Goodwife DAY (Ann), 9/4/51, 10/6/51, 31/12/51
Mr DAY senior, 29/10/82, 11/4/83
Mr Edward DAY junior, 29/10/82, 24/12/82, 30/1/82/3, 3/3/82/3, 10/4/83, 11/4/83
James DAY, 5/1/51/2, 6/1/56/7, 10/10/62
James DAY's wife (Grace), 25/10/53
Major General DEANE, 12/10/51
Goodman DEATH (William), 24/9/46, 19/4/51, 27/1/52/3
William DEATH, 28/1/52/3
W. DEATH (Widow Elizabeth), 31/7/59
Widow DEATH (Elizabeth), 3/8/54, 28/7/59
Widow DEATH (Susannah) of Great Tey, 20/4/70
? *DENHAM* (Henry), 9/10/46
Mr DENHAM, 28/7/51
King of Denmark, 23/11/51
? DENNIES, 29/11/59, 7/12/59
Lady DENNIE, 1641, 18/1/47/8, 22/1/47/8, 22/4/48
Mr DENNY, 15/8/48
Sir Edward DENNY, 15/8/48
? DERBY, 22/7/51, 30/8/51
Major DESBOROUGH, 5/4/47, 646
Earl of DEVONSHIRE, 17/9/45
Mr DILLINGHAM of Deane, 25/3/37, 29/10/79
Mrs Dorothy DILLINGHAM, 12/11/79
Mr DIXON, 18/1/46/7
? DOD's wife, 1/11/53
Dorothy ? (sister-see HUMPHRY)
Mrs DOUGHTIE, 17/9/78
Goodman DOWE (Henry), 16/6/51
Mr DOW (Zachary) of Wakes Colne, 21/10/58
Sister DOW (Elizabeth), 28/9/56
Mr DOWNING (Joseph) of Layer Marney, 1/4/47
Sir George DOWNING, 16/3/61/2

Dr DRAKE, 16/10/51
Old DRANE (Richard) of Colne Engaine, 5/9/60
John DUNCALF of Staffs., 16/12/77
Dutchesse, 656

L.E. (Lord ESSEX), 5/4/47
Mrs M.E. (Mabel ELLISTON), 27/7/55
Mr EARLE (Christopher) of Toppesfield, 20/4/46, 21/12/46, 3/1/46/7
Edward (CRESSENER), 3/4/56
? EDEN (John) of Ballingdon, 20/8/49, 27/8/55
Lady EDEN (Mary) of Ballingdon, 20/9/43
Dame EDGECOMBE, 15/8/48
Edw./Ned., Mr R.H.'s man, 3/11/57, 30/3/59
Edward III, 21/1/65/6
Justice ELDRED (John), 19/6/63
Little ELDRED (John), 18/12/64
Mr ELDRED (John) of Stanway, 19/12/53, 28/1/53/4, 16/12/54, 9/10/57, 16/4/58, 27/5/58, 26/3/59, 22/4/59, 12/9/59, 21/10/60, 28/1/61/2, 31/9/63, 31/10/64, 5/11/64, 24/11/64, 25/12/64, 9/2/64/5, 12/3/64/5, 27/3/65, 28/4/65, 3/5/65, 10/5/65, 5/11/65, 22/8/69, 9/10/70, 19/11/71, 11/4/72, 27/3/73, 17/10/73, 15/12/74, 3/10/76, 4/9/77, 17/2/77/8, 20/3/77/8, 28/3/78, 1/4/78, 30/9/78, 3/10/78, 10/12/78
Mr ELDRED's little daughter (Margaret), 5/11/65
Mrs ELDRED (Margaret), 27/12/57, 22/2/57/8, 26/9/58, 7/11/66, 5/5/70, 10/12/78
Mrs ELDRED (Anne) senior of Stanway, 10/4/78
Elizabeth ELDRED, 22:23/4/61
John ELDRED, 23/6/57
John ELDRED of Stanway, 15/12/57
Mary ELDRED, 15/12/71
William ELDRED's wife (Mary) of Stanway, 19/11/71
Mr ELDRED (William) of Stanway, 7/1/76/7
John ELIOT, 13/3/50/1
Elizabeth ? (WORRALL), 26/11/46
Elizabeth ?, (maid), 15/12/46
Mrs Ellin (JOSSELIN) of Much Lees, 31/8/47, 14/10/47
Mr ELLIS, 14/9/44
For ELLISTON see also ALLISTON
Mr ELLISTON (Edward), 31/5/46, 18/6/46, 19/9/47, 24/9/48, 7/11/48, 8/11/48, 21/12/48, 25/12/48, 13/2/48/9, 10/10/49, 20:21/12/49, 19/4/50, 1/6/50, 30/7/51, 9/1/51/2, 24/2/53/4, 6/4/54, 30/3/55, 9/1/56/7, 2/4/57, 3/4/57, 6/4/57, 27/5/57, 8/10/57, 26/3/59
Mr ELLISTON, 10/8/51, 21/8/58, 24/7/69
Mrs ELLISTON (Mabel), 25/11/49, 23/1/63/4
Mrs ELLISTON, 9/4/82
Mrs ELLISTON's daughter (Mabel), 25/2/48/9
Mr Edward ELLISTON, 1/6/54, 26/3/59, 12/4/63, 13/4/63, 14/4/63, 20/4/63, 8/5/63
Mrs Mabel ELLISTON, 7/7/49, 3/11/49, 28/5/50, 9/1/51/2, 9/5/52, 6/3/52/3, 26/11/54, 25/3/55, 14/9/56, 15/9/56, 29/3/57, 1/4/57, 4/4/57, 6/4/57
Mr ELMES (Thomas) of Wormington, Northants., 1639
William ELMES at Deane, 12/7/54
Emperor, 24/6/51, 31/7/58, 14/5/76, 19/1/78/9, 649, 654, 655
Duke d'Enguyen, 24/1/63/4, 649
Earl of ESSEX, 1643, 9/9/45, 20/9/46, 30/8/48
Sir Richard EVERED, 20/8/56
? EYRES, 13/2/54/5

Mr F. (FARRINGDON), 1/11/44, 11/11/44, 12/11/44, 28/12/44
Sir J. FAGGE, 13/6/75
? FAIRFAX, 30/6/50, 650
Lord FAIRFAX, 21/2/59/60
Sir Thomas FAIRFAX, 1643, 6/3/44/5, 27/6/45, 6/3/46/7, 26/3/47, 649
Mr FARRINGDON, 20/10/44, 23/10/44, 28/10/44
Mr FAULKNER (Daniel) of Aldham, 2/1/46/7, 10/1/46/7, 11/1/46/7, 16/9/47, 28/10/47
Christopher FEAK(E), 25/2/54/5
Mr FEARFUL, 13/7/57
Ferdinand IV., King of Romans, 22/1/53/4, 29/7/54, 651
Emperor Ferdinand III, 652
? FINCH at Halstead, 13/8/45
? FINCH, 7:8/3/53/4
? FINCH of Halstead, 23/7/66
Brother-in-law FINCH (Robert), 20/2/77/8
Chancellor FINCH, 10/2/76/7
Sister FINCH of Halstead, 30/4/52
John FINCH's wife (Hannah), 9/2/74/5
? FISHER, 9/11/57
? FLEETWOOD, 7/10/47, 15/4/56, 646
? *FLETCHER* (John), 24/7/78
Mr FOOKES, 16/10/46
? *FOSSETT* (William senior), 7/1/46/7

William FOSSET (junior), 23/11/62
? *FOSTER* (John), 9/4/82, 23/4/82
Alderman FOWK, 7/5/61
Queen Mother of France, 21/1/65/6, 649
King of France, 651, 654
Mr FULLER (John) of Stebbing, 4/1/52/3, 24/1/52/3, 30/1/52/3
? FULMER, 10/3/72/3

? *GAME* (James), 22/4/58
? GARDEN (GAUDEN), 25/4/60
Captain GARRAD, 26/1/57/8
Mrs GARRAD, 11/9/44
Anthony GARRAD, 17/8/51
John GARRAD, 25/12/74
John GARRAD's wife (Ann), 25/12/74
Thomas GARRAD, 15/3/56/7
Sir Barnaby GASCOINE, 28/8/48
Cousin GATTON, 28/12/79
B. GATTON, 24/12/82
Goodman GAUNT (John) of Cranham, 1/7/46
Goodman GAYNES of Olny, 1639
Emperor of Germany, 25/1/57/8, 649
Empress of Germany, 649
Cardinal Ghisi, 651
Martha GIBSON, 6/4/58
Mr GIFFORD (Richard) of Olny, Bucks., 1639, 1640, 22/5/57
Mrs GIFFORD, 22/5/57
Mrs GLADDIN, 10/2/58/9
Dr GLISSON (Francis), 8/4/49
Duke of GLOCESTER, 15/9/60, 653, 655
Mr GLOVER (Hugh) of Debden, 9/2/52/3
GOFFE, 646
Bettie GOODMAN at Halstead, 16/6/79
? GORING, 4/6/48, 30/8/48, 19/1/50/1, 15/6/57
(Grandfather-see JOSSELIN)
Mary GRANT, 27/4/45
? GRAY (Ann) of Coggeshall, 23/7/46
Mr GRESHAM, 21/6/68
? GREY, 13/2/54/5
? GREY, 1/7/83
Mr GREY (Robert), 17/6/45
Lieutenant Colonel GRIMES, 24/10/45, 19/4/46
M. GRIMES, 25/6/74
Mr GRIMSTON (Harbotle), 21/10/45, 8/10/46, 11/10/46
Sir Harbotle GRIMSTON, 20/8/56
? GROVES, 29/12/78
Nel GUIN, 3/8/79
Mr GUOYON (Robert) of White Colne, 5/4/46, 6/3/56/7, 7/3/56/7
Richard GUOYON, 4/12/64
Joi GURDONS (John), 24/5/52

M.H., 14/6/68
Susan HADLEY, 8/12/58
? HAINES, 7/8/55
Captain HAYNES (Hezekiah) of Foxearth, Major of the foot, 18/12/44, 28/1/44/5, 9/7/45, 9/9/45, 10/9/45, 11/9/45, 15/9/45, 18/10/45, 9/11/45, 4/1/45/6, 6/1/45/6, 8/1/45/6, 10/1/45/6, 24/10/46, 22/2/46/7, 27/3/47, 31/8/48, 22/10/48, 30/4/49, 28/6/49, 7/7/49, 16/7/49, 20/8/49, 27/3/50, 2/4/50, 16/4/50, 22/5/50, 15/9/50, 24/11/50, 12/12/50, 25/1/50/1, 9/2/50/1, 22/3/50/1, 7/10/51, 9/12/51, 11/1/51/2, 21/2/51/2, 21/5/52, 4/7/52, 24/7/52, 22/9/52, 28/9/52, 5/10/52, 18/4/53, 15/7/53, 25/7/53, 26/7/53, 17/8/53, 25/8/53, 2/10/53, 2/7/54, 13/2/54/5, 7/3/54/5, 8/3/54/5, 30/3/55, 7/7/55, 15/7/55, 3/8/55, 1/11/55, 17/11/55, 6/3/55/6, 9/3/55/6, 30/3/56, 31/3/56, 8/7/56, 25/7/56, 2/8/56, 20/8/56, 17/9/56, 11/1/56/7, 30/1/56/7, 24/5/57, 2/6/57, 23/8/57, 28/8/57, 31/8/57, 11/9/57, 27/9/57, 14/10/57, 16/10/57, 27/11/57, 16/2/57/8, 14/3/57/8, 1/9/58, 19/5/59, 28/7/59, 12/9/59, 23/11/61, 10/7/64, 3/4/70
Mr HAINES, 8/4/52, 3/12/54, 21/12/57
Mr HAINES, 28/1/59/60
Mr HAINES in New England, 18/1/47/8
Mr HAINES to New England, 8/2/47/8
Mrs HAINES (Anne) of Foxearth, 4/3/54/5, 1/11/55, 17/11/55, 18/7/56, 8/9/58
James HAYNES, 10/7/64
Mr Jo: HAYNES (John), of New England, 18/3/50/1
Robert HAINES of Copford, 21/8/57, 19/5/59
? HAMILTON, 30/8/48, 650
Colonel HAMMOND, 14/11/47
Hannah ? (see Anne HODSON)
Thomasin HARDING, 17/4/51, 4/1/51/2, sister-27/1/51/2, 2/5/52, poor-21/10/58
Mr H., (Richard HARLAKENDEN), 1/11/44, 4/11/44, 9/11/44, 10/11/44, 20/11/44, 3/12/44, 13/12/44, 20/12/44, 1/2/44/5, 17/2/44/5, 23/2/44/5, 25/4/45, 14/11/45, 28/1/45/6, 31/5/47, 21/6/47, 21/9/47, 22/1/47/8, 18/2/47/8, 30/4/48, 30/5/48, 4/6/48, 11/10/48, 21/12/48, 25/12/48, 18/6/49, 23/7/49, 17/8/50, 28/8/51, 28/10/51, 9/12/51, 2/6/52, 16/6/52, 1/7/52, 29/6/53, 6/11/53, 10/11/53, 19/11/53, 9/12/53, 5/11/54, 25/5/55, 14/4/56, 26/6/56, 5/7/56, 31/8/56, 7/9/56, 17/9/56, 26/2/56/7,

22/3/56/7, 10/6/57, 9/9/57, 15/12/57, 28/1/57/8, 13/3/57/8, 14/3/57/8, 18/3/57/8, 16/4/58, 7/11/58, 29/1/58/9, 25/3/59, 30/3/59, 4/1/59/60, 25/1/59/60, 13/7/60, 12/3/60/1, 24/3/60/1, 2:3/4/61, 13/4/61, 21/4/61, 7/5/61, 26/7/64

Mr R.H. (Richard HARLAKENDEN), 27/10/45, 12/1/57/8

Mr R.H., little boy (Richard HARLAKENDEN), 25/10/55, 18/11/55, 19/11/55

Mr W.H. (see William HARLAKENDEN)

Mr HARLAKENDEN (Richard), 17/9/44, 18/10/44, 24/10/44, 18/12/44, 21/1/44/5, 28/1/44/5, 22/4/45, 6/8/45, 17/8/45, 27/9/45, 10/11/45, 23/11/45, 29/11/45, 5/3/45/6, 2/5/46, 20/7/46, 23/7/46, 15/9/46, 1/10/46, 20/10/46, 23/10/46, 21/11/46, 27/11/46, 21/12/46, 31/12/46, 2/1/46/7, 10/1/46/7, 11/1/46/7, 27/4/47, 27/5/47, 16/9/47, 9/10/47, 14/10/47, 28/10/47, 22/2/47/8, 10/4/48, 22/4/48, 12/9/48, 30/11/48, 17/12/48, 27/12/48, 17/1/48/9, 19:20/1/48/9, 29/3/49, 18/5/49, 22/5/49, 18/6/49, 28/6/49, 22/7/49, 24/7/49, 29/8/49, 10/9/49, 1/11/49, 20:21/12/49, 9/1/49/50, 20/4/50, 23/4/50, 9/5/50, 1/6/50, 19/6/50, 23/10/50, 11/11/50, 24/11/50, 4/12/50, 18/12/50, 23/12/50, 30/1/50/1, 14/2/50/1, 23/2/50/1, 17/3/50/1, 21/4/51, 3/5/51, 24/6/51, 8/7/51, 15/7/51, 22/7/51, 30/9/51, 16/11/51, 22/11/51, 1/1/51/2, 24/1/52/3, 3/5/55, 17/9/55, 18/3/55/6, 3/6/56, 14/7/56, 14/8/56, 30/1/56/7, 13/3/56/7, 9/4/57, 12/6/57, 17/6/57, 22/11/57, 29/12/57, 27/3/58, 8/5/58, 15/1/58/9, 31/1/58/9, 26/3/59, 29/3/59, 9/4/59, 10/4/59, 22/4/59, 12/5/59, 29/11/59, 7/12/59, 29/8/60, 26/4/61, 5/5/61, 7/5/61, 12/5/61, 10/11/61, 9/4/62, 24/2/62/3, 8/5/63, 22:24/3/63/4, 13/7/64, 19/1/64/5, 26/3/76, 5/8/77, 4/9/77, 5/3/81/2

Brother HARLAKENDEN (Richard), 5/8/55

Captain HARLAKENDEN (Richard), 9/4/57, 27/12/59

Colonel HARLAKENDEN (Richard), 7/6/45, 10/6/45, 18/6/45, 10/7/45, 27/8/45, 6/10/45

'High Sheriff', Mr (Richard HARLAKENDEN), 23/12/45, 20/4/46, 31/5/46, 4/8/46, 8/8/46, 9/12/46, 11/12/46, 16/4/50

Dear Friend HARLAKENDEN (Richard), 11/5/60, 3/7/60, 12/7/60, 27/11/60, 8/3/60/1, 10/3/60/1

Justice HARLAKENDEN (see William HARLAKENDEN)

Mrs H. (Mary HARLAKENDEN senior), 2/11/44, 20/8/48, 11/10/48, 7/1/56/7, 18/3/56/7, 29/5/57, 9/4/59, 3/4/64

Mrs H. (Mary junior), 14/10/55, 10/6/57, 5/5/59, 14/5/59, 18/1/59/60, 29/1/59/60, 5/2/59/60, 6/2/59/60, 29/4/60, 1/9/60, 23/9/60, 18/1/61/2

Mrs HARLAKENDEN (Mary senior), 27/12/48, 29/3/49, 30/11/50, 9/12/53, 5/10/67, 30/9/74, 23/12/76, 28/3/78, 1/4/78, 1/7/78, 17/9/78, 24/11/78, 29/11/78, 10/12/78

Mrs HARLAKENDEN (Alicia, wife of Thomas junior), 1/10/52

Mrs HARLAKENDEN (Sarah, wife of Thomas senior), 24/2/47/8, 26/2/47/8, 1/3/47/8, 2/3/47/8

Mrs HARLAKENDEN (Mary junior), 2/10/55, 7/7/56, 5/4/57, 10/6/57, 12/6/57, 25/7/57, 5/1/57/8, 12/1/57/8, 14/1/57/8, 26/1/57/8, 14/10/58, 11/12/58, 19/1/58/9, 25/3/59, 26/3/59, 2/4/59, 17/4/59, 23/4/59, 6/5/59, 22/5/59, 25/5/59, 27/6/59, 21/9/59, 12/12/59, 2/2/59/60, 22/2/59/60, 1/3/59/60, 14/3/59/60, 15/3/59/60, 22/4/60, 26/5/60, 3/6/60, 9/6/60, 20/6/60, 12/7/60, 23/9/60, 13/11/60, 19/1/60/1, 28/1/61/2,

Mrs HARLAKENDEN (Mary), daughter of Mrs Mary, 8/7/64

Mrs B. HARLAKENDEN (Betty), 22/4/59

Betty HARLAKENDEN, 10/6/57

Mrs Elizabeth HARLAKENDEN, 22/8/58, 31/5/59, 12/3/60/1

Mrs Elizabeth HARLAKENDEN elder, 18/6/57

Mrs Elizabeth HARLAKENDEN, 16/4/57, 18/6/57, 19/4/58, 22/4/58

Mrs Margaret HARLAKENDEN, 9/10/57, 17/11/57, 15/12/57

Mary HARLAKENDEN, 26/11/53, 2/4/59, 6/5/59, 8/6/64, 21/11/69

Mrs Peg HARLAKENDEN, 28/5/50, 8/9/56

Mr Richard HARLAKENDEN, 1640, 1641, 1642, 7/4/45, 18/4/45, 6/1/46/7, 17/1/46/7, 24/1/46/7, 23/5/47, 11/7/47, 15/1/47/8, 23/5/48, 20/8/48, 12/9/48, 27/9/48, 22/2/48/9, 18/3/48/9, 29/3/49, 2/4/49, 3/4/49, 20/6/49, 9/1/49/50, 26/7/50, 26/9/50, 2/1/50/1, 1/3/50/1, 17/4/51, 8/6/51, 16/11/51, 22/11/51, 6/12/51, 1/1/51/2, 4/3/51/2, 7/6/52, 6/12/52, 31/1/52/3, 26/11/53, 13/9/54, 14/6/55, 25/10/55, 19/11/55, 13/12/55, 16/2/55/6, 15/4/56, 4/7/56, 7/7/56,

27/10/56, 6/1/56/7, 9/1/56/7, 4/4/57, 25/6/57, 4/7/57, 2/8/57, 3:4/11/57, 17/11/57, 30/11/57, 12/1/57/8, 1/2/57/8, 3/4/58, 18/11/58, 3/12/58, 3/3/58/9, 2/5/59, 4/6/59, 14/10/59, 31/12/59, 24/7/60, 22/8/60, 24/2/60/1, 25/2/60/1, 31/3/61, 3/4/64, 17/9/77, 19/9/77, 26/1/77/8, 15/3/77/8, 5/3/81/2

Mr Richard HARLAKENDEN junior, 18/6/49, 9/1/49/50, 26/9/50, 29/9/50, 2/10/50, 23/10/50, 22/11/51, 6/12/52, 18/12/52, 18/4/53, 19/9/53, 19/2/53/4, 22/2/53/4, 3/5/54, 27/10/55, 13/4/56, 18/6/56, 7/7/56, 14/7/56, 18/7/56, 9/1/56/7, 20/2/56/7, 21/2/56/7, 25/7/57, 9/11/57, 19/12/57, 3/1/57/8, 5/1/57/8, 26/1/57/8, 15/3/57/8, 3/4/58, 22/9/58, 29/9/58, 19/1/58/9, 25/3/59, 28/3/59, 30/3/59, 5/4/59, 9/4/59, 15/3/77/8

Young Richard HARLAKENDEN, 31/12/58, 1/1/58/9, 3/1/58/9

Tutor to Richard HARLAKENDEN junior, 23/10/50

Mr Richard HARLAKENDEN from Ireland (brother of William), 20/9/63

R. HARLAKENDEN in New England (Roger), 13/2/53/4

Mrs Smythee HARLAKENDEN, 28/6/51

Mr Thomas HARLAKENDEN (senior) of Great Bromley, 1640, 29/12/43, 14/6/46, 8/1/46/7, 27/1/46/7, 5/9/47, 10/11/47, 24/3/47/8, 27/3/48

Mr Thomas HARLAKENDEN (junior) of Great Bromley, 27/3/48, 29/5/48, 22/5/49, 2/5/50, 28/9/52

Mr William HARLAKENDEN, 4/9/44, 28/11/44, 24/2/45/6, 5/4/46, 19/11/46, 9/12/46, 11/12/46, 6/1/46/7, 9/10/47, 20/10/47, 10/11/47, 7/2/47/8, 30/4/48, 18/3/48/9, 22/3/48/9, 11/9/49, 18/9/49, 15/10/49, 17/3/49/50, 17/1/50/1, 13/9/51, 16/11/51, 9/1/51/2, 8/3/51/2, 21/5/52, 7/6/52, 28/9/52, 5/11/52, 3/1/52/3, 13/1/52/3, 22/1/52/3, 26/3/53, 5/2/54/5, 30/3/55, 24/10/55, 28/11/55, 23/9/56, 18/3/56/7, 21/3/56/7, 1/4/57, 27/4/59, 28/1/59/60, 4/2/74/5, 7/3/74/5, 18/3/74/5, 19/3/74/5

Mrs William HARLAKENDEN (Smithee), 15/2/47/8, 17/3/49/50, 17/1/50/1, 12/5/51, 18/5/51, 19/5/51, 23/6/51, 26/6/51, 16/11/51, 7/11/52

Justice HARLAKENDEN (William), 27/3/49, 29/10/52, 21/11/54, 10/5/55, 17/6/56, 17/8/56, 2/1/56/7, 10/3/56/7, 15/3/56/7, 27/3/57, 9/4/57, 18/4/57, 25/4/57, 26/4/57, 30/4/57, 3/5/57, 5/5/57, 28/8/57, 22/2/57/8, 10/4/59, 20/9/63

Haro, 653

? HARRINGTON (Daniel) of White Colne, 24/3/53/4

Mr HARRINGTON (William) of Maplestead, 24/10/46, 27/11/46, 23/12/49, 8/3/49/50, 27/3/50, 2/4/50, 23/4/50, 27/4/50, 9/5/50, 13/5/50, 21/5/50, 28/6/50, 29/8/50, 7/10/50

Mr HARRINGTON (James), 2/10/48, 19/10/48, 13/1/48/9, 12/7/49, 14/8/49, 10/1/49/50, 2/2/49/50, 8/2/49/50, 10/2/49/50, 21/2/49/50

? HARRIS at Coggeshall, 6/6/50

Ned HARRIS 12/6/74

Robin HARRIS, 16/6/79

Wife of Toby HARRIS (Theodesia), 21/1/59/60, 22/1/59/60

? HARRISON, 26/7/51, 16/8/51, 13/2/54/5, 25/2/54/5, 17/10/60

Mr HARRISON, 29/1/79/80

? HARVY, 8/12/74

? HARVY, 25/2/78/9

Thomas HARVY, 31/8/56

Baron HASTIVILE, 22/9/44

? *HATCH*, 17/9/50, 30/10/76

? *HATCH*'s children, 10/8/51

? *HATCH*'s family, 19/12/75

? *HATCH*'s apprentice, 11/1/62/3

Widow HATCH (Ann), 5/3/59/60

Bartholomew HATCH, 16/10/59

Henry HATCH, 10/6/66

Henry HATCH's son (Richard), 22/1/56/7

Henry HATCH's wife (Dorothy), 6/7/51

Richard HATCH, 24/11/56, 15/6/80

Sarah HATCH, 23/5/68

William HATCH, 9/9/47

William HATCH son-in-law (Richard ELLIS), 27/3/75

Mr HAUKESBYE at Colchester, 5/3/49/50, 27/3/50

Richard HAUKESBEE of Colchester, 9/11/57

Sarah HAUKESBEE, 26/7/49, 16/8/49

Mr William HAUKESBEE of Bulphan, 10/10/49, 24/3/49/50, 11/4/50, 23:24/7/50, 9/11/57

Mr HAUKS, 5/7/56

Mr HAWKER, 15/9/52

? HEDGE at Ardleigh, 28/6/50, 9/7/50, 18/10/53, 30/12/53, 6/11/55, 5/4/56, 3/7/56, 16/9/56

? HECKFORD (HICKFORD) (William) of Halstead, 9/7/50

Mr HECKFORD of Halstead (William HICKFORD), 15/1/49/50, 8/9/52

William HICKFORD (HECKFORD), 19/10/51, 14/2/51/2, 22/10/52

Queen Henrietta Maria, 1641, 23/1/51/2

M. HEY, 21/3/68/9
? HIDE, 27/10/60
HIDE'S daughter, 27/10/60
High Sheriff (see HARLAKENDEN)
High Sherrif, (not Richard HARLAKENDEN), 16/4/50
? HODSON (Thomas), 1636
Sister HODSON, 14/9/73
Anna HODSON (née JOSSELIN), 1636, 17/1/46/7, 9/10/47, 'Hannah'-26/8/44, 17/1/46/7, 9/10/47
Sister Anne HODSON of Haverill, 28/6/49, 21/7/49, 10/8/49, 13/10/49, 20/10/49, 23/10/49, 19/5/50, 21/5/50, 9/3/50/1, 1/10/52, 4/10/52, 10/3/53/4, 19/11/54?, 5/4/55, 12/6/56
Sister Anne ? (HODSON), 6/5/58, 23/8/58, 12/11/58, 23/1/59/60, 13/10/61, 25/9/73, 25/12/73
Isaac HODSON, 5/10/67
Brother Thomas? (HODSON), 13/12/44
Thomas HODSON, 9/10/47
Tom HODSON, cousin, 7/11/57
Thomas HODSON, son of Anne, 8/4/57
? HOLBORNE, 29/3/45
? *HOLDEN* (John), 25/3/49, 1/3/50/1, 29/4/70, 658
Sir Robert HOLMES, 13/3/71/2
Lady HONYWOOD (Hester) of Markshall, 29/3/44, 11/10/44, 10/12/44, 28/5/45, 14/6/45, 1/4/46, 17/4/46, 19/4/46, 22/4/46, 8/5/46, 21/5/46, 16/6/46, 14/7/46, 4/9/46, 12/5/47, 3/6/48, 12/6/48, 13/6/48, 13/8/48, 18/8/48, 19/8/48, 20/8/48, 22/8/48, 27/8/48, 29/8/48, 3/9/48, 12/9/48, 19/10/48, 11/1/48/9, 2/3/48/9, 7/3/48/9, 24/4/49, 15/5/49, 18/5/49, 22/5/49, 3/8/49, 25/8/49, 27/8/49, 31/8/49, 7/9/49, 18/9/49, 20:21/12/49, 30/12/49, 7/1/49/50, 16/4/50, 2/5/50, 7/5/50, 9/6/50, 16/8/50, 17/8/50, 23/10/50, 14/12/50, 10/6/51, 28/8/51, 30/8/51, 3/9/51, 15/9/51, 19/3/51/2, 18/10/52, 30/12/52, 9/5/53, 19/9/53, 9/1/53/4, 16/4/54, 22/8/54, 13/5/55, 15/7/55, 2/1/55/6, 22/6/56, 9/6/57, 10/6/57, 11/9/57, 14/10/57, 17/4/58, 9/10/58, 7/11/58, 12/11/58, 23/11/61, 3/11/67, 9/1/67/8, 20/9/70, 3/9/72, 27/1/72/3, 10/3/72/3, 25/12/73, 2/7/74, 8/12/74, 7/11/75, 13/11/76, 19/10/81, 26/10/81
Mr HONYWOOD, 18/8/48, 10/11/56, 23/12/58, 29/12/58, 31/12/58, 19/10/81
Mrs HONYWOOD (Elizabeth), 9/8/57, 7/11/58, 12/11/58
Mrs Elizabeth HONYWOOD, 18/5/49, 23/10/63
John HONYWOOD, 9/6/57
Mr John Lamott (HONYWOOD), 16:17/8/48
Martha HONYWOOD, 22/4/46
Mathew HONYWOOD, 24/3/45/6
Mr Thomas HONYWOOD, 24/4/49, 22/5/49, 17/6/56
Thomas HONYWOOD Esquire, 14/11/72
Sir Thomas HONYWOOD of Markshall, 29/3/44, 6/9/44, 14/9/44, 23/12/45, 24/3/45/6, 11/5/46, 21/5/46, 27/11/46, 11/1/46/7, 29/12/47, 2/6/48, 3/6/48, 5/1/48/9, 10/4/49, 1/1/49/50, 8/4/50, 11/6/50, 15/9/51, 26/7/53, 31/8/54, 17/6/56, 28/6/56, 20/8/56, 30/8/56, 28/1/65/6, 1/6/66
? HOPTON, 29/3/44
? HOVENER, 29/4/70
Mr HUBBARD of London, 15/5/57
Uncle HUDSON (Daniel), 14/10/46, 12/11/46, 11/3/46/7
John HUDSON, cousin, 20/6/53
? HUGGINS, 28/6/50
Mr HUMPHRY, 20/10/78
Sister Dorothy HUMPHRY, 13/1/44/5, 28/2/45/6, 23/12/46, 20/10/47, 5/1/49/50, 4/10/52, 5/10/52, 7/10/56, 9/10/56, 11/10/56, 21/7/58, 24/7/58, 1/11/60, 10/9/76, 3/10/76
Sister Dorothy's boy (Thomas HUMPHREY), 5/1/49/50
John HUMPHRY 'my brother', 19/12/52, 10/11/53, 16/4/57, 9/12/57
Thomas HUMPHRY, 2/10/50, 16/3/50/1, 1/10/52, 15/10/52, 22/8/53, 28/8/53, 18/9/53, 19/9/53, 17/7/55, 29/3/57, 5/4/57, 8/4/57
William HUMPHRY, 8/1/70/1, 27/7/73, 25/9/73
King of Hungary, 25/1/57/8
Sister HUNT of Taine, 29/4/52, 2/5/52, 10/12/53
? HUNT's wife, 31/7/59
? *HUNWICKE*, 1/11/53
? HUNWICK of Braintree, 26/6/78
Mr HURRELL (Nicholas) of Sible Hedingham, 18/1/47/8
Cousin HURREL, 12/7/63, 24/1/63/4, 30/1/63/4, 22:24/3/63/4, 15/5/64, 7/3/64/5
Nicholas HURREL, 31/10/51, 12:13/12/51, 20/2/52/3, 15/4/53, 9/11/57
Mr HUSON of Halstead, 28/12/46
Old HUTTON (Henry senior), 19/1/64/5
Guy HUTTON, 19/1/64/5
Henry HUTTON, 29/11/54
Henry HUTTON (junior), 19/1/64/5

Inchiqueene, 641
? IRELAND, 29/12/78
? IRETON, 12:13/12/51, 28/12/51, 15/2/51/2
? *ISERSON* (John), 27/7/51, 7/8/53, 30/9/56
ISERSON's prentice, 27/7/51
Manasseh Ben Israel, 13/3/50/1, 20/12/51, 22/12/51
Mrs IVE (Ann), 12/7/56

E.J. (Edward JOHNSON) of Witham, 26/3/53
Mr JACOB, 10/11/47, 12/9/48, 11/9/49, 28/10/50, 2/12/57
Mr JACOB's bailiff, 24/3/50/1
Mrs JACOB, 9/9/49, 7/2/49/50
Sir John JACOB senior, 27/6/80
Sir John JACOB junior, 27/6/80
Sir John JACOBS of Halstead, 28/11/44, 13/1/44/5, 17/1/44/5, 18/11/46, 10/11/47, 28/7/56, 6/9/56, 12/8/58, 11/11/60, 5/10/63, 18/8/64
King James I, 1/10/44, 2/5/46, 3/5/61, 648
Jane ?, maid, 29/2/55/6
Jeremy, brother (CONSTABLE), 4/9/44, 13/12/44, 20/12/44, 17/3/44/5, 19/5/51, 22/7/51, 20/8/54
Colonel JERMAINE, Major of Foot, 28/1/44/5
Mr JESSOP (Thomas) of Coggeshall, 9/11/62, 4/9/76, 22/10/78, 29/1/79/80
Joan ?, maid, 22/4/45, 28/4/45
? JOHNSON, 22/7/51
Cousin JOHNSON (Edward) of Witham, 14/9/51, 29/3/58, 17/7/58, 24/11/70
Goodman JOHNSON, 17/3/46/7, 1/5/48, 25/9/48
Edward JOHNSON of Wittam, 20/9/69
Robert JOHNSON, 1/6/50, 17/3/50/1
Jo: JONES (John), 17/10/60, 650
? JOSSELIN (John) father, 1616, 1618, 1631, 1632, 1636
Aunt JOSSELIN (Grace) of Cranham, wife of Ralph, 1/7/46
'Cousin' JOSSELIN (John) steward to Mr Richard HARLAKENDEN, 22/7/46, 13/8/46, 7/9/46, 2/2/46/7, 1/6/47, 9/6/47, 31/8/47, 14/10/47
Grandfather (Ralph JOSSELIN), 1631
Minister JOSSELIN (Hezekiah) of Copford, 28/4/71
Mr JOSSELIN, uncle, of Norfolk, 1639
Mr JOSSELIN of Chelmsford, 10/6/45
Mother, (Anne JOSSELIN), 1616, 1618
Stepmother, (Helen JOSSELIN), 1631, 1632, 1636, 5/8/44, 16/2/67/8
'My sister' (?), 16/5/68, 28/10/68, 1/11/68, 5/8/70, 28/7/72, 28/1/73/4, 27/6/79
Uncle JOSSELIN (Ralph) of Cranham, 30/4/49, 10:11/7/49, 22/10/51
Uncle JOSSELIN, 28/12/56
Uncle (JOSSELIN) of Epping, 22/2/46/7
Uncle (JOSSELIN) of Hingham, 21/8/49, 7/7/53, 30/7/53, 15/6/56
Uncle JOSSELIN'S only son, 27/6/59
'My Uncle and his daughter', 19/9/47, 21/9/47
Cousin Abraham (JOSSELIN), 1/9/44, 27/4/45
Cousin Abraham JOSSELIN, of New England, 6/3/44/5, 22/2/57/8, 25/3/58
Anne JOSSELIN (sister), 1632
Ann JOSSELIN (daughter), 12/7/54, 19/7/54, 6/8/54, 8/8/54, 13/8/54, 17/8/54, 20/8/54, 1/9/54, 8/10/54, 15/4/55, 20/5/55, 8/10/55, 14/10/55, 21/10/55, 28/10/55, 16/3/55/6, 11/4/56, 18/5/56, 15/6/56, 8/7/56, 27/7/56, 24/8/56, 6/1/56/7, 11/1/56/7, 10/5/57, 22/2/57/8, 19/4/58, 24/7/58, 25/7/58, 27/10/58, 22/4/59, 7/8/59, 10/8/59, 14/8/59, 21/8/59, 4/9/59, 22/9/59, 12/2/59/60, 9/12/60, 14/6/68, 21/6/68, 12/7/68, 23/8/68, 26/9/68, 4/10/68, 10/11/68, 13/6/69, 20/6/69, 27/6/69, 18/7/69, 15/8/69, 22/8/69, 22/1/69/70, 20/2/69/70, 10/7/70, 5/8/70, 4/9/70, 23/10/70, 17/6/73, 20/7/73, 23/7/73, 27/7/73, 31/7/73, 25/12/73, 659
Cousin Betty JOSSELIN, 29/6/57
Elizabeth JOSSELIN at Feering, 18/3/50/1
Elizabeth JOSSELIN (daughter), 20/6/60, 24/6/60, 21/10/60, 3/2/60/1, 10/2/60/1, 24/2/60/1, 17/3/60/1, 24/3/60/1, 14/4/61, 9/6/61, 11/8/61, 27/10/61, 2/11/62, 3/1/66/7, 17/10/73, 2/6/75, 29/12/75, 13/5/77, 5/6/77, 659
Grace JOSSELIN, 7/10/56, 25/3/58
Cousin Henry JOSSELIN in New England, 25/3/58
Jane JOSSELIN (daughter), 24/11/45, 21/12/45, 26/4/46, 25/5/46, 15/11/46, 20/12/46, 16/4/47, 9/5/47, 23/5/47, 30/5/47, 13/6/47, 20/6/47, 29/8/47, 30/10/47, 20/2/47/8, 29/8/48, 11/2/48/9, 13:14:15/6/49, 1/11/49, 4/11/49, 17/3/49/50, 28/4/50, 19/5/50, 28/5/50, 1/9/50, 29/9/50, 19/1/50/1, 2/3/50/1, 15/6/51, 19/10/51, 29/11/51, 30/11/51, 6/6/52, 20/6/52, 27/6/52, 4/7/52, 2/1/52/3, 4/1/52/3, 16/1/52/3, 23/1/52/3, 24/1/52/3, 30/1/52/3, 6/2/52/3, 13/2/52/3,

26/2/52/3, 30/7/53, 30/6/54, 8/8/54, 13/8/54, 20/8/54, 1/9/54, 29/2/55/6, 9/3/55/6, 16/3/55/6, 21/3/55/6, 21/4/56, 10/5/56, 16/6/56, 27/7/56, 3/8/56, 20/9/56, 5/1/56/7, 22/2/57/8, 19/3/57/8, 13/4/58, 17/4/58, 4/8/58, 6/3/58/9, 15/5/59, 23/1/59/60, 12/2/59/60, 1/3/59/60, 11/3/59/60, 28/10/60, 13/10/61, 27/10/61, 10/11/61, 15/12/61, 14/8/64, 20/10/64, 26/3/65, 4/2/65/6, 18/2/65/6, 5/9/67, 5/10/67, 8/11/68, 24/10/69, 21/1/69/70, 16/3/69/70, 29/4/70, 30/8/70, 659

'Cousin' John JOSSELIN, 29/5/48, 6/6/49, 3/8/49, 9/8/49, 1/6/50, 12/4/55, 5/7/56, 14/7/56, 25/11/57, 2/1/71/2

John JOSSELIN, 2/1/71/2

John JOSSELIN (son), 19/9/51, 21/9/51, 28/9/51, 14/11/51, 16/11/51, 23/11/51, 18/2/51/2, 22/2/51/2, 14/3/51/2, 21/3/51/2, 18/4/52, 25/4/52, 26/9/52, 21/11/52, 13/3/52/3, 3/4/53, 17/7/53, 30/7/53, 27/11/53, 29/11/53, 4/12/53, 11/12/53, 26/2/53/4, 12/3/53/4, 19/3/53/4, 8/8/54, 13/8/54, 17/8/54, 1/9/54, 10/12/54, 21/1/54/5, 29/7/55, 24/3/55/6, 20/9/56, 3/10/57, 22/2/57/8, 19/3/57/8, 11/7/58, 16/7/58, 31/7/58, 4/8/58, 14/4/63, 21/2/63/4, 8/8/64, 14/8/64, 9/1/66/7, 27/1/66/7, 28/1/66/7, 30/1/66/7, 17/2/66/7, 28/2/66/7, 14/10/67, 8/12/67, 2/2/67/8, 11/10/68, 14/10/68, 10/11/68, 22/11/68, 14/3/68/9, 18/4/69, 25/4/69, 16/5/69, 2/1/69/70, 4/1/69/70, 16/1/69/70, 20/2/69/70, 21/5/70, 29/5/70, 12/6/70, 19/6/70, 3/7/70, 15/7/70, 2/10/70, 9/10/70, 27/11/70, 4/12/70, 19/1/70/1, 22/1/70/1, 4/2/70/1, 12/2/70/1, 19/2/70/1, 19/3/70/1, 2/4/70/1, 4/6/71, 5/6/71, 9/7/71, 29/10/71, 5/11/71, 26/11/71, 11/8/72, 16/8/72, 8/9/72, 15/9/72, 6/10/72, 27/7/73, 3/8/73, 5/10/73, 28/10/73, 2/12/73, 25/1/73/4, 26/1/73/4, 15/2/73/4, 22/3/73/4, 12/4/74, 10/5/74, 31/5/74, 7/6/74, 14/6/74, 20/6/74, 27/9/74, 30/9/74, 23/10/74, 15/12/74, 10/1/74/5, 24/1/74/5, 30/5/75, 6/6/75, 1/7/75, 25/11/75, 23/3/75/6, 23/4/76, 5/8/76, 15/10/76, 16/11/76, 26/11/76, 3/12/76, 19/12/76, 28/2/76/7, 15/7/77, 7/10/77, 26/1/77/8, 26/1/78/9, 23/11/79, 1/11/80, 7/8/81, 16/10/81, 14/5/82, 648, 659

Wife of John JOSSELIN (Martha), 24/9/82

Joseph JOSSELIN of Cranham, Uncle, 5/8/46, 13/8/46, 31/8/46, 7/9/46, 8/10/46, 12/11/46, 29/1/46/7, 30/4/47

Mary JOSSELIN (sister), 5/8/44, 1/9/44, 11/10/44, 22/4/45, 17/1/46/7, 9/10/47, 20/10/47, 28/6/49, 1/1/51/2, 23/1/51/2, 15/8/53, 25/8/53, 24/11/53, 28/1/54/5, 30/10/55, 8/3/56/7, 13/10/61

Mary JOSSELIN (daughter), 1642, 26/8/44, 20/9/44, 7/10/44, 11/11/44, 25/5/45, 28/5/45, 1/6/45, 14/12/45, 1/4/46, 14/6/46, 18/6/46, 15/11/46, 31/1/46/7, 14/2/46/7, 21/2/46/7, 28/2/46/7, 7/3/46/7, 13/3/46/7, 13/6/48, 1/11/49, 1/12/49, 25/12/49, 13/1/49/50, 1/3/49/50, 3/3/49/50, 24/3/49/50, 11/4/50, 28/4/50, 12/5/50, 15/5/50, 19/5/50, 21/5/50, 22/5/50, 23/5/50, 24/5/50, 25/5/50, 26/5/50, 27/5/50, 28/5/50, 16/6/50, 4/7/50, 19/1/50/1, 30/6/54, 8/12/54, 31/7/73, 17/10/73, 659

Mary JOSSELIN (daughter), 14/1/57/8, 4/8/58, 11/12/58, 7/8/59, 26/6/60, 22/8/60, 2/9/60, 9/12/60, 23/11/61, 19/1/61/2, 26/1/61/2, 9/2/61/2, 2/11/62, 2/2/67/8, Jan. 68/9, 2/12/73, 14/5/74, 2/6/75, 2/9/76, 25/9/76, 3/10/76, 16/11/76, 17/5/77, 22/7/77, 5/9/77, 16/9/77, 11/11/77, 6/10/78, 12/1/78/9, 24/4/79, 1/5/79, 26/8/79, 28/9/79, 23/11/79, 28/12/79, 1/2/79/80, 22/2/79/80, 18/4/80, 16/5/80, 27/3/81, 2/6/81, 2/10/81, 3/9/82, 29/10/82, 3/3/82/3, 10/4/83, 659

Nathaniel JOSSELIN son of 'Cousin', 9/6/47

Nathaniel JOSSELIN, Uncle, 31/5/49, 22:23/8/49, 14/6/52, 3/2/52/3, 26/10/54, 15/6/56, 21/9/58, 27/6/59, 25/7/63, 2/6/67, 24/9/68

Uncle N. JOSSELIN'S daughter, 21/5/64

Cousin R. JOSSELIN of Colchester, 9/6/49

Ralph JOSSELIN of Cranham, uncle, 1640, 1/7/46, 31/8/46, 28/12/46, 11/3/46/7, 1/1/47/8, 29/3/48, 8/5/53, 7/7/53, 30/7/53, 16/11/56, 28/3/57, 3/4/57

Uncle Ralph JOSSELIN'S children, 18/3/49/50, 23/6/56

Ralph JOSSELIN (son), 18/2/47/8, 19/2/47/8, 20/2/47/8, 21/2/47/8

Ralph JOSSELIN (son), 5/5/49, 13/5/49, 9/9/49, 25/11/49, 1/12/49, 13/1/49/50, 27/1/49/50, 5/2/49/50, 18/2/49/50, 1/3/49/50, 14/4/50, 28/4/50, 5/5/50, 7/5/50, 12/5/50, 15/5/50, 19/5/50, 24/5/50, 25/5/50, 26/5/50, 2/6/50, 4/6/50, 19/1/50/1, 30/6/54, 31/7/73, 659

Rebecca JOSSELIN (daughter), 13/12/63, 14/1/63/4, 27/3/64, 16/5/64, 23/5/64, 24/11/67, 17/10/68, 30/7/69, 3/1/70/1, 27/9/72, 11/1/73/4, 17/5/77, 8/9/77, 24/7/78, 26/8/79, 31/8/79, 7/9/79, 28/9/79, 27/5/80, 19/9/80, 12/3/81/2, 19/9/82, 8/5/83, 659
Richard JOSSELIN, uncle, 12/11/44, 13/11/44, 8/12/44, 13/12/44, 12/11/46, 11/3/46/7, 28/6/49
Simon JOSSELIN of Chelmsford, uncle, 23/9/46, 8/10/46, 14/10/46, 11/3/46/7, 30/4/47, 22/2/49/50, 24/3/53/4, 26/5/56
Uncle Simon JOSSELIN'S children, 26/5/56, 3/1/57/8
Thomas JOSSELIN (son), 29/12/43, 14/3/43/4, 9/10/44, 6/12/44, 30/1/44/5, 7/2/44/5, 24/3/45/6, 17/7/46, 3/8/46, 9/8/46, 24/8/46, 28/8/46, 30/8/46, 31/8/46, 27/11/46, 10/1/46/7, 16/4/47, 20/2/47/8, 14/1/48/9, 12/7/49, 18/7/49, 1/11/49, 25/11/49, 1/12/49, 3/2/49/50, 1/3/49/50, 5/3/49/50, 28/4/50, 18/7/50, 23:24/7/50, 11/8/50, 22/9/50, 9/1/50/1, 10/1/50/1, 11/1/50/1, 13/1/50/1, 15/1/50/1, 17/1/50/1, 9/2/50/1, 16/2/50/1, 6/7/51, 2/11/51, 9/11/51, 16/11/51, 1/12/51, 28/3/52, 4/4/52, 4/7/52, 22/7/52, 30/7/52, 1/8/52, 8/12/54, 17/12/54, 3/2/54/5, 15/11/57, 9/12/57, 26/3/58, 6/6/58, 13/11/58, 8/12/58, 9/4/59, 22/5/59, 24/5/59, 25/5/59, 10/6/59, 11/6/59, 12/6/59, 14/6/59, 15/6/59, 16/6/59, 19/6/59, 26/6/59, 27/6/59, 10/7/59, 17/7/59, 3/11/59, 8/11/59, 20/11/59, 26/11/59, 4/12/59, 11/12/59, 12/12/59, 28/1/59/60, 12/2/59/60, 14/4/60, 30/12/60, 13/7/61, 2/8/61, 8/1/61/2, 11/1/61/2, 18/1/61/2, 9/3/61/2, 20/4/62, 19/7/63, 25/7/63, 2/8/63, 19/3/63/4, 27/3/64, 16/7/64, 4/6/65, 30/1/65/6, 12/9/66, 27/10/66, 4/11/66, 5/11/66, 19/11/66, 25/11/66, 31/3/67, 2/6/67, 13/10/67, 2/10/70, 4/10/70, 6/10/70, 23/10/70, 25/12/70, 6/4/71, 9/7/71, 2/6/72, 8/9/72, 27/10/72, 22/3/72/3, 15/6/73, 17/6/73, 17/10/73, 647, 659
? JOYCE, 13/7/51
Archbishop JUXON, 7/6/63

KELSY, 646
Mrs KEAM, 7/5/57
Mr KEMPE of Sutton, Beds., 1636
? *KENDALL*, son in law of Robert DAVY, 28/1/44/5
? *KENDAL*, 1/4/51, 8/11/59, 28/1/59/60
William KENDALL, 27/1/46/7, 31/1/46/7, 10/11/47
? *KENT* (John), 23/4/50
John KENT, (father of Widow BENTAL), 20/7/46, 21/7/46, 22/7/46
Mr KEQUICKE, 11/3/46/7
KIMBOLTON, 649
Mrs KING, Oct. 1641, 19/3/46/7, 22/2/47/8, 24/4/48, 4/4/49, 24/1/50/1, 25/1/50/1, 9/6/52, 30/8/57, 31/8/57
Mrs KING's daughter, 27/1/46/7
Mrs Elizabeth KING, 11/3/46/7, 21/2/49/50, 12/1/50/1, 25/1/50/1, 4/5/51
Mrs KITELY of Ilford, 16/6/52
? KNIGHT of Hinningham, 1/9/44

Mrs E.L. (Elizabeth LITTLE), 12/5/47
Mr J.L. (LITTLE), 21/3/51/2, 26/3/53
'My Lady', (See Lady HONYWOOD)
Mr LAGDEN (Giles), 8/11/48, 15/1/48/9
? LAMBERT (Major General), 7/9/48, 26/7/51, 14/10/59, 6/1/59/60, 23/4/60, 646
Mr John Lamott (HONYWOOD), 16: 17/8/48
Mr LAMOTT (John), 15/5/49, 15/7/55, 2/1/55/6
Mr LAMPKIN (William LAMPLUGH) of Hatfield Peverel, 12/9/78
Mr Thomas LANE, 1632
Mrs LANEY, 13/5/58
Archbishop LAUD, 9/9/44, 10/1/44/5
Captain LAURENCE, 6/4/47
Widow LAURENCE (Ann), 26/8/73
? LAWSON, 2/7/65
? *LAYER*, 4/12/50, 2/11/57, 30/7/69
Dorothy LAYER, 8/9/58
John LAYES, 30/9/44
Mr LAYFIELD (Edward) of Wakes Colne, 20/3/47/8, 23/6/53, 14/4/56, 15/1/56/7, 17/5/63
Mrs LAYFIELD, 26/8/56, 6/3/56/7
Old LEA (Robert), 20/5/66
Daniel LEAPER, 8/10/55
Mr LEIGH (Thomas) of Bishop Stortford, 1618
LESLY, 649
Mr LEWIS of London, 24/2/47/8
Lewis 13 of France, 649
Princess de Ligne, 24/2/60/1
Lieutenant Colonel LILBURNE, 22/3/48/9
Jo: LILBURNE (John), 27/1/51/2
Sir George LILE, 28/3/48
Mr LINCH, 17/3/49/50
Earl of LINCOLNE, 26/9/69
James LINNET of Colne Engaine, 26/7/53

Mrs LITTELL, 18/3/58/9
Mr LITTLE of Halstead, 6/3/45/6, 24/8/46, 19/10/46, 18/11/46, 5/9/48, 5/2/49/50, 30/4/51, 1/6/51, 10/6/51, 8/7/51, 9/7/51, 26/8/51, 1/1/51/2, 1/2/51/2, 18/2/51/2, 21/3/51/2, 24/1/52/3, 9/2/52/3, 24/10/54, 17/7/55, 17/8/55, 17/5/56, 16/8/59, 3/2/59/60, 19/4/60
Mr LITTLE (Jeffrey) of Little Heney, 21/5/56
Mr LITTLE'S sisters, 16/10/46
Mrs Elizabeth LITTLE, 29/10/46, 12/5/47
Mr Jeffrey LITTLE of Halstead, 23/9/46, 30/9/51, 21/3/51/2, 26/3/53, 15/8/53, 7/8/55
Mr John LITTLE of Halstead, 1642, 27/3/50, 17/4/50, 29/3/51, 25/7/51, 30/9/51, 28/4/53, 30/11/58, 23/10/60
Mr LIVERMORE (John) of Markshall, 13/11/76, 4/5/83, 20/5/83, 10/6/83, 1/7/83
? LODDINGTON, 20/8/56
Bishop of London, 1640, 8/10/46, 14/9/64, 7/10/75, 12/9/78, 3/10/78
Lord Mayor of London, 20/9/51, 5/10/51
Mr Roger LONDON of Colne Engaine, 1/3/47/8, 2/3/47/8
Wife of Roger LONDON of Colne Engaine, 26/2/47/8
Sarah LONDON of Colne Engaine, 12/1/71/2
Bishop of Londonderry, 22/7/60
Mr LORKYN (John) of Markshall, 6/7/45, 23/11/45, 26/9/46
Duke of Lorraine, 27/4/51, 11/5/51, 30/10/51, 7/12/51, 20/6/52, 656
Louis, King of France, 8/2/50/1, 30/3/51, 17/2/77/8, 1/3/77/8, 4/2/78/9
Mr LOVE (Christopher), 13/7/51, 15/7/51
Dr LOVEDYN, 17/9/45
Mr LOWRY (Thomas), 17/7/46
Sir Charles LUCAS, 28/8/48
Lord LUCAS, 26/3/71, 31/7/71
Mr LUCKIN, (Capell) of Messing, 24/6/56
Mr LUDGATER (John) of Great Birch, 7/7/45, 25/3/46, 1/10/46, 27/5/47
Mr LUDGATER (John), 3/5/76, 3/12/77, 1/4/83
? LUDLOW, 12:13/12/51
Luther, 14/9/44

Captain MAIDSTONE (John), 3/6/48, 26/2/51/2
Major, (See HAINES)
Mr MAN of Dunmow?, 21/10/53
Lord MANCHESTER, 18/10/44, 28/11/44, 3/12/44
Lord MANDEVILLE of Kimbolton Castle, 1637, 1640
Mr MANWOOD, 29/1/58/9
Margaret ? (maid), 15/12/45, 14/12/46
Margaret ? (maid), 7/4/52
Mrs Margaret (ELDRED), 27/5/58
? *MARKHAM* (Abraham), 4/11/44
Col. MARKHAM, 28/1/59/60
Goodwife MARKHAM, 17/3/49/50
Mr MARRYON of Braintree, 25:26/5/75
Mr MARSHAL (Stephen) of Finchingfield, 25/11/55
? MARTIN, 22/3/48/9
Mrs MARTIN, 20/2/67/8
Mr MARTIN (William) of Wakes Colne, 2/12/73
Mary ? (maid), 26/11/54
Lady Mary (later Queen), 28/10/77, 648
Sister Mary (FINCH), 13/10/61
? MASSEY, 29/7/47
Goodman MATHEWS (Christopher), 29/10/45, 29/11/46, 16/5/48, 9/8/49, 7/2/49/50, 9/1/50/1, 16/1/50/1, 17/4/51, 3/6/51, 12/6/51, 9/7/51, 25/11/51, 3/4/53, 4/3/55/6, 27/4/58, 29/9/58
Goodwife MATHEWS (Bridget), 13/10/49, 6/2/49/50, 24/6/50, 27/12/51, 5/1/51/2, 9/1/51/2, 15/1/51/2, 23/1/51/2
Neighbour MATHEWS (Christopher) 30/5/48, 24/1/50/1, 3/5/63
Sister MATHEWS (Bridget), 22/7/52
Wife of MATHEWS (Bridget), 10/4/59
W. MATHEWS (Widow Bridget), 28/7/72
C. MATHEWS (Christopher), 10/5/63
Christopher MATHEWS, 20/10/46
Goodman MAYERS, 21/8/44
Mayor of Colchester, 9/1/49/50, 6/6/60, 29/8/60
Mr Mayor (John LANGLEY), 7/10/46
Mazarin, 9/2/50/1, 12/10/51, 651, 653
? MEDCALFE of Messing, 25/6/50, 25/3/53
Mr MEDE, 17/9/56
Mr MEREDITH (Christopher) of London, 22/11/51, 6/12/51, 9/6/52, 8/9/52, 12/9/52, 18/9/52, 2/10/52, 10/11/52, 20/11/52, 6/12/52, 31/12/52, 13/1/52/3, 24/1/52/3, 20/5/53
Mr MEREDITH'S daughter (Mary), 8/9/52, 20/11/52
Mrs MEREDITH of London, 30/7/52, 8/9/52, 6/12/52, 21/6/56
Mary MEREDITH of London, 6/12/52
Mr MERITON (John) of Pebmarsh, 26/9/69

Mr MERRILL of Kimbolton, Hunts., 1637
Mr MICHEL (William) of Chickney, 10/9/44
'Poor' MIGHILL (Robert), 3/8/51
? MILDMAY, 25/2/78/9
Lady MILDMAY, (Amy), 3/1/70/1
Colonel MILDMAY (Henry), 3/8/79
Mrs MILDMAY, 3/6/47, 3/1/70/1
Mr Carey MILDMAY, 20/8/56
Mrs Frances MILDMAY of Chelmsford, 8/1/45/6
Mr H. MILDMAY (Henry), 20/8/56
Colonel Henry MILDMAY'S son (Henry), 5/10/71
Mrs Mary MILDMAY, 1642
Aunt MILES (Elizabeth), 7/4/50
Uncle MILES (Thomas), 1636, 7/4/45, 8/4/45
Edward MILES, 10/1/44/5, 7/4/45
Thomas MILES (uncle) of Hadham Berry, 15/4/45, 18/4/45
? MILLS of Buers, 16/11/76
Modena's daughter, 5/11/73, 10/2/73/4
? *MOALE* (*MOLE*) (Francis), 13/7/47, 24/1/49/50, 23/2/50/1 30/9/56, 10/2/56/7
Goodman MOLE (Francis), 9/1/50/1
Goodwife MOLE (Rose), 12/6/51
? *MOLE'S wife*, 25/3/72
? *MOLE* (Philip), 5/10/63, 11/3/69/70, 25/3/72
? *MOLINS* (John), 5/4/45
Old MOLINS (Henry?) of Colne Engaine, 5/4/45
MONK, 653
General MONKE, 15/1/59/60, 14/2/59/60, 26/8/60, 7/1/65/6, 9/1/69/70
MONK'S Dutchess, 2/2/69/70
MONMOUTH, 14/9/79
? MONTAGUE, 24/2/55/6
Montery, 3/12/71
Mr MONTJOY, 1/2/44/5, 7/4/45, 14/8/56
MONTROS, 649
MONTROSE, 16/9/45, 18/9/45
? MORLEY (John) of Chapel, 3/12/58, 12/3/58/9, 17/5/59, 25/4/74
Mr MORLEY (John) of Chapel, 24/9/56, 11/5/63, 19/12/63
H. MORLY (Henry), 28/4/67
John MORLY of Chapel, 22/1/56/7
Mother (See JOSSELIN)
'My Mother' (CONSTABLE), 19/5/51
Mother in Law (CONSTABLE), 1642, 5/8/44, 11/10/44, 14/10/55
Bishop of Munster, 22/10/65, 26/4/66
? MULLINS children at Colne Engaine, 6/2/54/5
? MUNT, 26/2/56/7

R.N. (Robert NICHOLS) of Colne Engaine, 4/7/57
? NAILOR, (James), 26/1/56/7
Nan ? (maid), 18/1/52/3
Duke of Navailes, 654
Mr NEALE of Deane, Beds., 1636
Mr NEGUZ, 2/10/47
Mr NETTLES (Stephen) of Lexden, 26/8/44
NEVILL family of Chapel, 6/8/45, 19/11/55, 3/6/56, 14/7/56, 4:5/1/58/9, 11/5/63
NEVIL sisters of Chapel, 17/12/58
Mr NEVILL (Richard), 15/9/46, 14/5/51, 8/3/51/2, 9/1/53/4
Orphan of the NEVILLS, 24/9/46
Mrs Bridget NEVILL of Chapel, 31/8/58
Mrs Mary NEVILL of Chapel, 15/9/46
Peg NEVIL (Margaret), of Chapel, 10/5/55
Mr NEWBOLD, 14/10/44
Mr NEWCOMEN (Mathew), 22/10/45, 31/3/48, 8/4/48
Goodman NEWMAN of Clare, 23/8/53
? NEWTON, 30/10/76, 1/4/78
(Samuel) *NEWTON's daughter* (Elizabeth), 20/9/74, 23/9/74
Mr NEWTON, 10/6/80
Grace NEWTON, 5/10/60
John NEWTON, 28/7/59
? NICCOLS (Captain) of Chapel, 12/10/69
Mr NICOLS, 8/9/56
James NICCOLS, 15/11/44
Robert NIC(OLS), of Colne Engaine, 9/2/51/2
Nicholas? (HURREL), 31/10/51, 10/11/52, 31/12/52, 1/1/52/3
Nic. (HURREL) servant to Mr HARLAKENDEN, 26/3/59
Mr NICHOLSON (Francis) of Marks Tey, 18/1/46/7, 11/6/48, 27/3/49
Neighbour Mr NICHOLSON, 23/9/49
Mr NOEL, 8/7/56

? OATES (Samuel), 29/6/46
? OKEY, 26/12/59, 16/3/61/2, 27/4/62
ONEALE, 25/11/49, 650
Prince of Orange, 17/11/50, 28/10/77, 5/5/78, 648, 650, 655, 656
Orleans, 24/1/52/3, 651
ORMAND, 6/12/46, 14/8/49, 29/8/49, 25/11/49, 28/11/69, 650
ORRERY, 28/11/69
? *OSBORNE* (Thomas), 23/4/50, 29/10/57
John OUTING, 15/6/74

Widow OVERAL of Stisted, 23/12/50
? OVERELL of Stisted, 28/6/50
Mr OWEN (John), 31/3/46, 27/3/47, 1/7/47, 24/10/47, 31/3/48, 25/5/48, 10/4/49, 22/7/49, 23/7/49, 16/9/49, 2/5/50, 24/11/50, 15/12/50, 9/2/50/1, 23/3/50/1, 18/3/51/2, 19/3/51/2
Dr. OWEN (John), 6/3/55/6, 8/7/56, 19/9/56
? *OWERS* (John), 21/4/77
OXFORD, (See VEER)

Mr P. (POTTER), 21/3/51/2, 26/3/53
Wife of R.P. (Robert POTTER'S wife, Margaret), 6/9/47
? PAFLIN, 22/12/45, 24/12/45
? *PAIN* (Alias ALLEN), (Robert), 5/11/75, 18/4/80
Goodman PAIN, 28/3/50
Ann PAIN, 20/10/64
John PAIN, 15/12/78
? PARKER, (Mr ELDRED's Aunt), 17/2/77/8
? PARNEL (James), 15/4/56, 9/4/57
James PARNEL, 11/4/56
Mr PAUL (Obadiah) of Easthorp, 12/9/78
Brother PEACOCKE, 20/9/44
Mary PEACOCKE, 23/8/50
Mary PEAKE, 23/11/52, 12/12/52, 24/6/55, 8/7/55
? *PEAKE's son*, 19/2/59/60
M. PEARTREE, 25/12/56
William PEARTREE, 23/1/73/4
William PEARTREE's daughter (Anne), 24/2/63/4
? *PEASE* (Walter), 29/4/52
Mr PECK, 21/3/57/8
Mr PELHAM (Herbert) of Buers, 29/10/51, 1/11/53, 8/9/56, 6/12/60, 8/9/68, 29/6/74
Mr PELHAM's son, 29/10/51
? PELHAM, (Henry), 29/7/47
Justice PELHAM (Herbert), 11/12/56
Mrs PELHAM of Buers, 12/10/58
PEN, 651
Wife of ? PENHACKE (Ann), 1/10/46
Guy PENHACKE, 3/9/44, 24/8/46, 17/7/55
Jo: PENHACKE (John), 14/10/58
Sarah PENHACKE, 5/10/69
Mr PERKINS (Thomas) of Colne Engaine, 20/12/74, 8/5/83, 1/6/83, 22/6/83
Mr PERKIN's son, 9/8/79
? PERRY, 3/10/57, 17/8/73
Nathan PERRY, 22/10/51, 30/4/55
Peter ? (Servant), 11/10/69, 27/10/70, 4/2/70/1
Bishop of Peterburg, 1639
Hugh PETERS, 17/10/60
? PICKERING, 29/12/78
? PIGG (Bridget MATHEW's brother), 8/6/62
Mrs PIGGOT, 21/3/55/6, 21/4/56, 13/4/58, 1/3/59/60
? *PILGRIM*, (John), 9/10/50
Mr PILGRIM (Thomas) of Wormingford, 1/9/44, 16/2/45/6
Mrs PILGRIM of Wormingford, 25/3/47
Mr PINDAR, 15/9/52
Mr PINDAR (John), 19/4/78
Mr PLUMBE (Samuel) of Great Yeldham and Maldon, 28/8/56
Polish King, 24/1/63/4, 649, 654, 656
? *POLLY* (John), 27/6/50, 19/9/52
Pope, 3/6/49, 27/12/50; Innocent: 2/1/50/1, 24/6/51, 22/11/54; Innocent X: 651; Alexander VII: 25/1/55/6, 12/12/57, 27/12/63, 24/1/63/4, 651; Clement IX: 2/7/67; Urbane, 649
? *POTTER* (Edward), 12/4/46, 14/7/59
? *POTTER*, 1/10/65, 11/3/76/7
Goodman POTTER (Edmund), 6/3/45/6
Goodman POTTER (Robert), 24/11/45
Goodwife POTTER (Margaret), 29/1/46/7, 29/3/49, 18/5/51, 19/5/51
Mr POTTER, 12/11/79
Mr POTTER, 21/2/49/50, 24/2/49/50, 12/1/50/1, 4/5/51
Neighbour POTTER (Robert), 4/1/48/9, 28/5/50
Edward POTTER, 14/12/45, 22/12/45 24/12/45, 13/2/45/6, 23/6/51
G. POTTER (George), 14/11/72
George POTTER of White Colne?, 14/10/45
Margaret POTTER, 19/12/49, 22/12/50
Mary POTTER, 24/11/53, 26/11/54, 5/2/56/7, 14/10/58
Robert POTTER, 13/8/46, 18/1/46/7, 6/3/46/7, 24/3/53/4, 27/7/54
Goodman PRENTICE (Thomas) of White Colne, 17/1/47/8
Thomas PRENTICE of White Colne, 6/12/44, 30/6/47, 8/7/47, 30/5/48, 6/9/48
Servant of Thomas PRENTICE, 6/9/48
Protector and New Protector (See CROMWELL)
? *PRYOR* (Thomas), 8/11/48
Lord of Oxford's Chaplain, Dr PULLEIN, 3:4/11/57
Dr PULLEIN (Samuel), 9/11/57, 26/11/57, 27/11/57, 3/12/57, 5/12/57, 22/2/57/8, 9/7/58, 11/7/58, 12/7/58, 16/7/58, 19/10/58, 24/11/59, 22/7/60, 29/7/60, 26/8/60

Archbishop of Tuam, Dr PULLEIN, 12/8/60
Mrs PULLEIN, 27/4/58
? PURCHAS, 6/11/46
Mr PYOTT (John) of Low Leyton, 21/12/46

Sir Robert QUARLES, 10/1/46/7
Queen, 20/5/62, 23/10/63, 25/10/63, 25/2/65/6, 27/5/69, 24/11/78, 1/12/78
Queen Mother, 5/9/69
Queen Mother of France, 649
Old Queen, 2/7/65

Colonel RAINSBROUGH, 4/11/48
? RAVENS (John) of White Colne, 1/4/78
Mr Ol(iver) RAYMOND of Belchamp Walter, 20/8/56
Jone RAYNER, 10/5/51
Paul RAYNHAM of Chapel, 22/10/56, 20/2/67/8
Mrs READ, 29/10/66
John READ, 15/11/44, 17/8/45, 21/7/46, 8/11/48
John READ's maid, 2/10/48
Sister Rebekah ?, 10/9/71
Widow REEVE (Grace) 7/4/54
Robert REEVE, 19/4/51
Lady RENULA (RANELAGH) (Katherine), 2/7/74
? REYNER, (Widow Priscilla), 5/10/63
Old REYNER (Thomas), 16/7/56
W. REYNER (Widow Priscilla), 2/12/57
Mr RHEA (Ambrose) of Wakes Colne, 2/6/81, 8/5/83, 17/6/83
? RICH, 13/2/54/5, 6/3/54/5
Mr Charles RICH, 28/12/58
Mr Richard (HARLAKENDEN jun.), 18/1/46/7
Uncle Richard (See JOSSELIN)
Mr RICHARDSON, 2/10/67
Duke of RICHMOND, 2/5/46
Joan RICHMOND, 9/4/59, 10/4/59
Rob. ? (servant), 10/8/69
Goodman ROBJOHN (John) of Cranham, 1640/1
? ROGERS (Daniel), 2/1/56/7
? ROGERS, 22/10/78
(Daniel) ROGER's wife (Elizabeth), 2/1/56/7
Cousin ROGERS, 4/8/46, 12/7/74
Mr ROGERS (Daniel) of Wethersfield, 1/4/47, 12/2/47/8, 12/11/48, 1/12/49, 9/5/50
Mr ROGERS (Nehemiah) of Doddinghurst, 14/1/56/7
Mr ROGERS of Great Tey, 15/1/48/9
Mr Daniel ROGERS of Wethersfield, 10/11/48, 15/9/52
Mr ROLLS (Richard), 19/10/48
Colonel ROSSITER (Edward), 16/9/45, 17/9/45, 20/9/45
? *RUGGLES*, 17/10/75
Widow RUGLES (Edith), 27/5/47, 14/4/51
Prince Rupert, 29/3/44, 2/1/50/1, 9/10/64
Jo: RUSHBROCKE (John), 11/9/49
Lord RUSSEL, 1/7/83, 22/7/83
? RUST, 8/5/46
? Ruyter, 7/1/65/6, 654

Mr S., 30/6/59
Sabbatai, 26/4/66
Mr SADLER (John) Master of Requests, 27/7/55
Lady SALTONSTALL, 17/2/61/2
Mr SAMMES, 11/8/46
Mr SAMS (John) of Kelveden, 18/3/51/2, 8/6/54, 30/3/55, 12/4/55, 5/10/55, 23/10/55, 4/11/55, 26/5/56, 5/7/56, 26/2/56/7
Sarah ? (BROWN), 20/10/45, 26/10/45
Mr SARJANT (John) of Chapel, 31/8/58, 7/2/58/9, 8/10/71, 7/7/83
Mr SAVIL, 4/12/64
Elias SAVILL, 10/11/47
Mr SAWYER of Colchester, 30/12/44, 14/10/45, 3/6/48
Mr SAYER, 21/10/45, 31/10/46
? *SCOT* (John), 9/7/59
Thomas SCOT, 17/10/60
Adrian SCROOPE, 17/10/60
? SEAVER, 3/5/51
Mr SEDGWICKE, (Obadiah) of Coggeshall, 17/6/45
Mr William SEDGWICKE, 11/4/47
? SELLS, 7/11/75
Alce SEWELL, 24/12/45, 13/2/45/6
Mr SEYMER (Samuel) of Colchester, 2/5/46, 8/11/48
Mrs SEYMOUR, 10/6/80
Earl of SHAFTESBURY, 27/11/81, 656
? SHAWE, 25/6/50, 15/10/52, 4/11/55, 24/6/56, 5/8/56
Aunt SHEPHEARD of Olny, 29/12/43, 29/9/44, 19/5/46, 3/11/48, 23/8/53, 26/9/57, 2/6/59
Goodwife SHEPHEARD of Olny, 1639
Mr SHEPHEARD (Edward) of Maplested, 12/5/45
Mr SHEPHEARD (Thomas) in New England, 11/3/45/6
Uncle SHEPHEARD (Lawrence) of Olny, 26/9/44, 20/8/60, 31/3/61
Sir Abraham SHIPMAN, 5/9/48
Mr SHIRLY (James) of Braintree, 9/2/64/5, 2/2/67/8, 9/7/76

James SHIRLEY, 25/9/76, 3/10/76, 23/11/77
Mrs SIBLEY (Mary) of London, 28/6/77
Call. SILLITO (Calvin), 17/8/53
Mr Richard SIMONS, 9/5/47, 16/5/47
Mr SIMPSON (John) of Mount Buers, 1/6/56
? SKIPPEN, 9/5/47, 29/7/47
Joseph SLIE, 23/1/73/4
? *SMITH*, 24/6/50, 25/6/50, 6/9/50, 30/7/51, 27/12/51, 8/10/70, 29/1/70/1
? SMITH at Messing, 25/3/53
? SMITH of Colchester, 27/8/55
? *SMITH's daughter*, 25/3/72
Brother SMITH, 20/9/44
Mr SMITH (John), 19:20/1/48/9
Mr SMITH, 14/9/64
Mr SMITH, 2/9/76, 8/10/76
Mr SMITH (Gilbert) of London, 23/12/76 26/12/76, 26/2/76/7, 28/2/76/7, 13/5/77
Daughter Elizabeth SMITH, 16/6/77, 8/9/77, 20/2/77/8, 28/7/78, 23/10/78, 27/10/78, 3/11/78, 9/11/78, 12/11/78, 17/11/78, 24/11/78, 16/6/79, 1/8/79, 11:12/6/81, 24/7/81, 2/10/81, 26/2/81/2, 5/3/81/2, 18/6/82, 15/8/82, 3/3/82/3
Mr Gilbert SMITH, 5/6/77, 11/11/77, 3/3/82/3
Son SMITH (Gilbert), 3/4/81, 12/2/81/2, 3/3/82/3, 8/4/83, 11/4/83, 8/5/83
Jo: SMITH (John), 12:13/12/51
Mr SMYTHEE, 15/9/52
Sobienski, 656
King of Spain (Philip), 8/10/65, 21/1/65/6, 648
Queen of Spain, 25/1/57/8
Mr SP. (SPARROW) (William) of Halstead, 28/11/52, 15/9/54, 12/2/56/7
? SPARROW, 10/6/83
Colonel SPARROW (John) of Havering Park, 4/12/64
Goodman SPARROW, 23/1/51/2
Mr SPARROW (William) of Halstead, 1/6/50, 7/3/51/2, 28/11/52, 4/1/52/3, 3/2/52/3, 11/3/52/3, 23/6/53, 28/7/53, 15/9/54, 20/12/55, 20/2/55/6, 9/5/56, 11/5/56, 17/5/56, 17/6/56, 12/4/57, 27/11/57, 30/11/58, 1/6/60, 24/11/64, 9/2/64/5
Mrs SPARROW of Halstead, 28/6/57, 18/8/62
William SPARROW of Halstead, 11/3/52/3
Mr SPICER (Stewart), 24/12/82, 8/4/83, 11/4/83, 8/5/83, 20/5/83
Mrs SPICER, 20/5/83
? *SPOONER* (Edward), 5/10/56
? *SPOONER's wife* (Anne), 29/11/53
Goodman SPOONER (Edward), 23/6/49
Goodwife SPOONER (Anne), 14/3/61/2
Old SPOONER (Edward) 24/7/46, 14/2/48/9, 17/2/48/9, 15/1/49/50, 12/6/58
? *SPRINGAT's daughter*, 11/10/46
Mr STANBRIDGE (William), 9/12/51, 24/7/52, 22/9/52, 28/9/52, 5/10/52, 6/12/52
Captain STEBBEN at Great Tey, 9/2/52/3, 9/11/72
Mr STEBBIN, 24/1/52/3
Mrs STEBBINGS of Coggeshall, 7/4/55, 6/8/57
Mr STEPHENS (William), 19:20/1/48/9
? *STEVENS* (Edward), 2/6/55, 14/6/55
Edward STEVENS, 20/7/62
Mr STOCKDALE (Owen STOCKTON) Lecturer at Colchester, 29/8/60, 24/11/64, 9/2/64/5
Mr STRONG (William) at Westminster, 10/7/54
Charles STUART, 23/11/51, 25/1/59/60
Esme STUART, Duke of LENNOX, 15/9/60
? SUNDERCOMB, 20/2/56/7
Major SWALLOW, 15/1/47/8
Christian, Queen of Sweden, 652
Mr SYMKINS, 16/10/44
Mr SYMONDS (Samuel) of Colne Engaine, 9/11/62
Mr SYMONS, 1632

Mr T. (TOMPSON), 12/5/47
? TABOR, 17/5/75
Captain TAILOUR, 7/10/47
Dr TALBER, 7/6/75
Mr TALBOT (Thomas), 21/5/65
? TALLER of Great Tey, 10/8/56, 12/2/57/8
Goodman TALLER (George) of Aldham, 10/1/46/7, 11/1/46/7, 16/9/47
Goodman TAVENER (John) of Cranham, 1640
Mrs TAYLOR of Huntingdon, 10/9/45
Old TAYLOR (Edward), 15/1/50/1
Mr TEMPLAR (Dudley), 20/8/56, 28/8/56, 29/12/59
Dudley TEMPLAR, 25/12/59
Mr TEMPLER, 7/10/44
? THACKER, 27/6/80
Brother Thomas ? (HODSON), 13/12/44
Poor Thomasin and Sister Thomasin (See Thomasin HARDING)
? THOMPSON, 1/6/52
Mr TOMPSON (THOMPSON) (Robert) of Copford, 13/10/45, 16/10/46, 19/10/46, 29/10/46, 8/12/46, 12/5/47, 29/7/47, 18/2/47/8, 8/4/48, 25/3/52,

8/4/53, 4/5/53, 25/7/53, 15/8/53, 17/4/55, 26/9/55, 24/3/55/6, 2/8/56, 5/2/56/7, 25/3/57, 12/4/57, 31/12/57, 22/2/57/8, 18/3/57/8, 13/4/58, 21/4/65
Mrs THOMPSON, 10/5/65
Mr THORNBECKE, 1636
Mr THRALE (Thomas) of London, 4/5/57, 15/5/57
Mrs THRALE, 7/11/58
Mr THURGOOD of Cranham, 28/12/46
? THURLOE (THIRLOE) (John), 4/1/54/5, 23/4/59
? THURSTON, 19/11/71
Mr Edward THURSTON, 10/1/74/5
? *TIBBALL* (TIBBALD) (Robert), 19/11/55, 2/6/56, 24/9/56, 7/11/57, 9/4/59, 3/2/59/60, 29/9/60, 7/1/60/1, 14/5/61, 15/9/62
(Robert) *TIBBALL's wife* (Sarah), 3/8/59
Widow TIBBALL (Sarah), 28/7/65, 8/10/65
Mr TIFFIN (William) of Wakes Colne, 19:20/1/48/9
Mrs TIFFIN (Elizabeth) of Wakes Colne, 19/12/45, 15/10/48, 8/11/48, 17/12/48
? TILL (Robert) of Colne Engaine?, 23/4/50
? TILLAM (Thomas), 6/5/56, 23/1/56/7
Mr TIMS, 8/9/77, 11/11/77
Lieutenant Colonel TINDALL, 13/8/45
Mr TINDALL, 3/6/48
? *TOLLER* (George), 23/3/75/6
? TOMKINS, 10/10/67
Mr TOOKY, 12/12/59
Prince of Transilvania, 25/1/57/8, 652, 653
TROMP, 651
Van Trump, 17/8/53
Lady TRYON's husband, 24/9/68
Sir Samuel TRYON of Halstead, 4/12/64
Turenne, 22/8/54
? TURNER's daughter, 9/4/56
Colonel TURNER, 30/1/63/4
Mr TURNER (Thomas) of Wormingford, 28/8/46, 8/9/46
Mr TURNER (Edward), 20/8/56, 28/12/58
Mrs TURNER, 11/9/47
Old TURNER (Clement), 4/11/44
Sergeant TURNER (Arthur) of Parndon, 5/8/46, 2/2/46/7, 11/3/46/7
Roger TURNER, 17/8/53

Uncle (See JOSSELIN)

S. H. VANE (Sir Henry), 11/9/56
Countess of OXFORD (VEER), 3/11/58
Lady VEERE (Mary) of Castle Hedingham, 26/3/47, 10/8/63, 26/9/69, 7/1/71/2
Lord of OXFORD (VEER), 10/4/48, 3/12/57, 5/12/57, 8/5/58
Lord Mayor VINER of London, 23/10/74
Vizier, 654

? *WADE*, 16/3/44/5
? *WADE* (Robert), 16/2/55/6, 31/3/67
? *WADE's wife*, 23/9/65
? *WADE's wife* (Robert's), 28/4/66
Mr WADE (John) of Halstead, 15/1/49/50, 2/4/52
Sir C. WAKEMAN, 20/7/79
Justice WAKERING, 28/11/56
Mr WAKERING (Dionisius) of Kelveden, 3/8/49, 6/4/51, 15/8/54, 28/8/54, 20/8/56, 24/11/56
Lady WALDGRAVE (Jemima) of Wormingford, 16/2/45/6
? WALLER, 1643, 29/3/45
? *WALLER* (Suzanne), 4/8/57
Goodwife WALLER (Suzanne), 23/5/48
Sister WALLER (Suzanne), 12/8/58
Ambros WALLER, 10/10/49
Sir William WALLER, 29/3/44
Susan WALLIS, 1/9/58
Mr WALWYN of Olny, 23/7/51
Widow WARD, 14/12/45, 22/12/45
Captain WARNER, 10/9/45
Mr WARREN, 5/9/48
John WARREN of Olny, 12/1/60/1
Countess of WARWICK, 4/9/76
Dowager Countess of WARWICK, 2/7/74, 5/7/74
Earl of WARWICK, 23/10/45
Mr WATSON (Robert) of Cranham, 1/7/46, 28/12/46, 22/11/51
Wife of Mr WATSON, 3/2/46/7
Mr WEALES (Henry), 3/6/56, 4/7/56, 5/7/56, 7/7/56, 26/3/57
(William) WEB's wife (Elizabeth) of Colne Engaine, 19/3/53/4
Sister WEBB (Jane) of Colne Engaine, 7/10/52
Elizabeth WEB of Colne Engaine, 11/12/60
William WEBB of Colne Engaine, 26/11/51, 17/8/53, 24/3/53/4, 6/4/54, 30/3/55, 28/6/56, 23/7/57
Mr WESTLY (John) of Stanway, 16/7/46, 1/4/47, 29/4/47, 8/4/53, 15/8/53
? WESTNEY (Edward) of Halstead, 27/6/50
Lydia WESTON, 5/8/44, 31/8/46
? WHALEY, 15/1/47/8
WHALLEY, 646
Mr WHARTON (Samuel) of Felsted, 1640, 20/9/43
Mr WHEELER, 29/1/79/80

Mr WHEELY (John) of Chelmsford, 26/8/58
Colonel WHITE, 13/12/57
Mr WHITING (John) of Easthorpe, 26/8/47
Mr WHITING (John) of Lexden, 18/6/57
Michael Wiesniewiski, 654, 656
? WILDMAN, 13/2/54/5
Mr WILLIAMS, 28/12/79
Secretary WILLIAMSON, 24/11/78
An WILLOWS, 2/3/57/8
Mrs WILSBY, 19/7/46
Mrs WILSON, 28/7/59
? *WISEMAN* (Henry), 19/5/57
Sir William WISEMAN, 10/1/74/5
Mrs WITHERS, 22/8/60
De Witt, 651
Mr WOLPH, 11/9/45
Mr WOODCOCKE, 18/8/50, 5/1/50/1
Daughter Jane WOODTHORPE, 4/9/70, 19/1/70/1, 26/2/70/1, 17/11/71, 29/4/72, 4/8/72, 11/8/72, 16/8/72, 3/9/72, 8/9/72, 27/11/72, 15/6/73, 23/7/73, 21/9/73, 12/10/73, 21/10/73, 2/12/73, 5/7/74, 18/3/74/5, 28/3/75, 13/8/76, 24/8/76, 20/11/76, 7/7/77, 1/1/77/8, 1/7/78, 6/10/78, 25/10/78, 7/9/79, 16/5/80, 26/3/82, 9/7/82, 2/5/83
Jane WOODTHORPE (grandchild), 21/10/73, 2/12/73, 1/11/74, 28/11/74, 1/1/81/2, 3/3/82/3
Jonathan WOODTHORPE, 21/1/69/70, 16/3/69/70, 30/8/70, 18/12/70, 31/7/71, 17/11/71, 15/12/71, 30/4/76, 10/6/80, 17/12/82, 3/3/82/3, 15/7/83
John WOODTHORPE (grandchild), 2/6/72
Mary WOODTHORP (grandchild), 4/6/76
Mrs WOODTHROP of Lamersh, 18/12/70, 20/12/70
Mr WOOLHOUSE, 5/10/63, 24/9/68
Brother WORRALL, 2/5/48, 1/7/68, 13/9/76
Sister WORRALL (Elizabeth) in Ireland, 9/7/65
Elizabeth ? (WORRALL), 26/11/46
Dr WRIGHT (Laurence), 25/5/48, 2/4/50, 23/4/50, 24/5/50, 13/6/50, 11/11/50, 5/5/51, 14/2/51/2, 10/6/52, 17/1/56/7, 25/1/56/7, 30/1/56/7, 31/1/56/7, 1/2/56/7, 23/7/57, 15/8/57, 8/10/57, 11/10/57, 25/1/57/8, 26/3/58
Dr WRIGHT's son, 9/8/57
Mr WRIGHT, 22/4/46
Mr WRIGHT (Robert), 16/3/69/70

Duke of YORK, 27/10/60, 7/5/61, 21/3/68/9, 10/2/73/4, 21/2/78/9, 7:8/3/78/9, 12/3/81/2, 656, 657
? YOUNG of Halstead, 19/11/51, 12:13/12/51, 22/12/51, 26/3/53
Dr YOUNG's son, 29/12/50
G. Y. (YOUNG), 21/3/51/2